Fodor's 97

Great Britain

"When it comes to information on regional history, what to see and do, and shopping, these guides are exhaustive."

—*USAir Magazine*

"Usable, sophisticated restaurant coverage, with an emphasis on good value."

—Andy Birsh, *Gourmet Magazine* columnist

"Valuable because of their comprehensiveness."

—*Minneapolis Star-Tribune*

"Fodor's always delivers high quality...thoughtfully presented...thorough."

—*Houston Post*

"An excellent choice for those who want everything under one cover."

—*Washington Post*

Fodor's Travel Publications, Inc.
New York • Toronto • London • Sydney • Auckland
http://www.fodors.com/

Fodor's Great Britain

Editor: Robert I.C. Fisher

Contributors: Robert Andrews, Robert Blake, Jules Brown, David Low, Caroline Merz, Tracy Patruno, Kate Sekules, Gilbert Summers, Roger Thomas, Greg Ward, Brandy Whittingham, Daniel Williams

Creative Director: Fabrizio La Rocca

Cartographers: David Lindroth; Maryland Cartographics

Cover Photograph: Bob Krist

Text Design: Between the Covers

Copyright

Copyright © 1996 by Fodor's Travel Publications, Inc.

Fodor's is a registered trademark of Fodor's Travel Publications, Inc.

All rights reserved under International and Pan-American Copyright Conventions. Published in the United States by Fodor's Travel Publications, Inc., a subsidiary of Random House, Inc., New York, and simultaneously in Canada by Random House of Canada Limited, Toronto. Distributed by Random House, Inc., New York.

No maps, illustrations, or other portions of this book may be reproduced in any form without written permission from the publisher.

ISBN 0-679-03226-6

Special Sales

Fodor's Travel Publications are available at special discounts for bulk purchases for sales promotions or premiums. Special editions, including personalized covers, excerpts of existing guides, and corporate imprints, can be created in large quantities for special needs. For more information, contact your local bookseller or write to Special Markets, Fodor's Travel Publications, 201 East 50th Street, New York, NY 10022. Inquiries from Canada should be directed to your local Canadian bookseller or sent to Random House of Canada, Ltd., Marketing Department, 1265 Aerowood Drive, Mississauga, Ontario L4W 1B9. Inquiries from the United Kingdom should be sent to Fodor's Travel Publications, 20 Vauxhall Bridge Road, London SW1V 2SA.

PRINTED IN THE UNITED STATES OF AMERICA

10 9 8 7 6 5 4 3 2 1

Dedication

For Richard Moore

In fond appreciation of your 20 years of contributions to Fodor's guides, your grace in the face of deadlines, and your abundant good humor.

CONTENTS

ON THE ROAD WITH FODOR'S

WE'RE ALWAYS THRILLED to get letters from readers, especially one like this:

It took us an hour to decide what book to buy and we now know we picked the best one. Your book was wonderful, easy to follow, very accurate, and good on pointing out eating places, informal as well as formal. When we saw other people using your book, we would look at each other and smile.

Our editors and writers are deeply committed to making every Fodor's guide "the best one"—not only accurate but always charming, brimming with sound recommendations and solid ideas, right on the mark in describing restaurants and hotels, and full of fascinating facts that make you view what you've traveled to see in a rich new light.

About Our Writers

Our success in achieving our goals—and in helping to make your trip the best of all possible vacations—is a credit to the hard work of our extraordinary writers and editors.

Since **Kate Sekules** lives with a foot on either side of the Atlantic, her mission is getting the best of both worlds—and Fodor's is much the winner. Author of Fodor's guidebook to London, she has also updated the chapter on that amazing metropolis for this edition. Thanks for her knack for coming up with the mots—both *bon* and *juste*—her wit is much in demand: *Vogue, W, The New Yorker, BBC Holidays,* and the *Time Out Guide to Eating and Drinking* are just some of the publications she writes for. Like a homing pigeon, she often returns to England. Her idea of a smashing Saturday in old London town? The latest avant-garde art show at the Serpentine Gallery, dinner at Wódka, then a Baroque-period concert at Kenwood House.

Robert Andrews lives in Bristol, England, from which he emerges periodically to make forays into the West Country, the Mendip Hills, and the Cotswolds. He revised our chapters on the Southeast, the South, the Southwest, the Channel Islands, the Thames Valley, the Heart of England, and the Welsh Borders. Combining life as an anthologist of quotations with that of a dauntless travel writer, he roams near and far, as often as not lugging a suitcase of books behind him.

Always hoping to entertain—and surprise—his readers, **Roger Thomas** spends most every minute tracking down the latest and the best of Wales. He has to: He's editor of *A View of Wales* magazine. In its pages, he has such noted contributors as Sir Anthony Hopkins and Sir Roy Strong uncover all the delights of "Britain's best-kept secret." A long time writer and editor for Fodor's, he happens to possess one of the most eloquent and lilting voices around: even a bus schedule sounds positively Shakespearian when he fills us in. Roger has written many books on Wales and is an acknowledged Welsh expert.

Now based in Yorkshire, **Jules Brown** updated our chapters on the Lake District, Yorkshire, and Lancashire and the Peaks. His writing career has taken him from Spanish mountains to Norwegian fjords; across the Far East from Thailand to China; deep into the Utah desert; and to the Bahamas. But for real kicks, he pulls on a pair of walking boots and strides across his home country, along Cornish, Yorkshire, and Northumberland coasts, and up and down the Lake District—real, on-the-ground experience that turns up some of the best of Britain for his readers.

Born and raised in the north of England, **Caroline Merz** now lives in East Anglia—just the person to update our East Anglia chapter. Lecturer in cinema studies and arts administrator, she enjoys touring the region by bicycle and loves to vacation in the warmer climes of Australia and the Mediterranean. On the whole, she believes it's better to travel hopefully than to arrive.

Greg Ward, who revised the Northeast chapter, is a London-based writer and editor whose travels have taken him across India, China, and the United States. He enjoys spending leisurely weekends exploring the English heartlands.

If he's not in the National Gallery of Scotland looking at his favorite Titian, you'll probably find **Daniel Williams**—updater of our chapter on Edinburgh and the Borders—at an orchestral concert in the Usher Hall or organizing a concert or exhibition at one of Edinbrugh's many smaller venues. If it's late in the evening, chances are this Edinburgh native and graduate of Oxford University will be at Whistle Binkies, listening to the glorious drums and fife of Scottish folk music.

New York native **Brandy Whittingham** flung a tartan scarf around her neck and set off on a voyage of discovery to the Inverness area and Royal Deeside to help us update our chapter on northern Scotland. A lifelong fan of castles, she found plenty to fire her passion in Queen Victoria's beloved Royal Deeside. She gained much assistance from the pages of Fodor's guide to Scotland, written with wit and wisdom by Gilbert Summers, Fodor's much treasured Scotland area editor (he's taken a sabbatical this year from this edition).

Though the sun may have set on the British Empire, there will always be an England—especially in the hearts of all Anglophiles, as **Robert I.C. Fisher,** the editor of *Great Britain '97*, can attest. He often dreams of Vita Sackville-West's famous garden (in his heart, at least, he's part-owner) and of waking up one day with Jeremy Irons's accent. Recently, he was reduced to a Little Lord Fauntleroy—all moon-sized eyes and gaping mouth—when he met Lady Juliet de Chair to write a magazine piece on her 18th-century ancestral home, Wentworth Woodhouse—thanks to its 365 bedrooms, the largest house in Great Britain.

New This Year

This year we've reformatted our guides to make them easier to use. Each chapter of *Great Britain '97* begins with brand-new **recommended itineraries** to help you decide what to see in the time you have; a section called When to Tour points out the optimal time of day, day of the week, and season for your journey. You may also notice our **fresh graphics,** new in 1996. More readable and more helpful than ever? We think so—and we hope you do, too.

Like an intricate painting, London takes careful study to fully appreciate its myriad wonders. To help you do that, we've more than **doubled our London coverage** to uncover the city in a new way—from its broad, rough strokes down to the tiniest details that will capture the most demanding traveler's interest. We first let you in on the big picture, then follow with separate neighborhood sections that suggest—in A Good Walk—a wonderful way to discover each, then list all the neighborhood's sights alphabetically. To allow you the delights of free-form touring, this helps you to design your own personalized itinerary and, also, allows you to find your list of must-sees in a snap.

On the Web

Also, check out Fodor's Web site (http://www.fodors.com/), where you'll find travel information on major destinations around the world and an ever-changing array of travel-savvy interactive features.

How to Use This Book

Organization

Up front is the **Gold Guide.** Its first section, Important Contacts A to Z, gives addresses and telephone numbers of organizations and companies that offer destination-related services and detailed information and publications. Smart Travel Tips A to Z, the Gold Guide's second section, gives specific information on how to accomplish what you need to in Great Britain as well as tips on savvy traveling. Both sections are in alphabetical order by topic.

Chapters in *Great Britain '97* are arranged geographically. The guidebook begins with a chapter on London and proceeds to southern, central, and western England, pausing to stop in Wales. The book then moves up England's west coast to the Lake District, continues on to eastern England, and finally heads north to Scotland. Each chapter covers exploring, then highlights regional topics such as shopping, sports and the outdoors, dining and lodging, and nightlife and the arts.

The London chapter is subdivided by neighborhood; each subsection recommends a walking tour and lists sights in alphabetical order. **Each regional chapter** is divided by geographical area; within each area, towns are covered in logical geographical order, and attractive stretches of road and minor points of interest between them are indicated by the designation *En Route*. Throughout, Off the Beaten Path sights appear after the places from which they are most easily accessible. And within town sections, all restaurants and lodgings are grouped together.

To help you decide what to visit in the time you have, all chapters begin with **recommended itineraries;** you can mix and match those from several chapters to create a complete vacation. The **A to Z section** that ends all chapters covers getting there, getting around, and helpful contacts and resources.

At the end of the book you'll find **Portraits**—a historical chronology, a list of kings and queens, and a fascinating essay about architecture in Great Britain—followed by suggestions for pretrip reading, both fiction and nonfiction, and movies on tape with Great Britain as a backdrop.

Icons and Symbols

★ Our special recommendations
✕ Restaurant
Lodging establishment
Lodging establishment whose restaurant warrants a detour
Rubber duckie (good for kids)
☞ Sends you to another section of the guide for more info
✉ Address
☎ Telephone number
⏲ Opening and closing times
Admission prices (those we give apply only to adults; substantially reduced fees are almost always available for children, students, and senior citizens)

Numbers in white and black circles—② and ❷, for example—that appear on the maps, in the margins, and within the tours correspond to one another.

Dining and Lodging

The restaurants and lodgings we list are the cream of the crop in each price range. Price charts for each region appear in the Pleasures and Pastimes section that follows each chapter introduction.

Hotel Facilities

We always list the facilities that are available—but we don't specify whether they cost extra: When pricing accommodations, always ask what's included.

Assume that hotels operate on the **European Plan** (EP, with no meals) unless we note that they use the **Full American Plan** (FAP, with all meals), the **Modified American Plan** (MAP, with breakfast and dinner daily), the **Continental Plan** (CP, with a Continental breakfast daily), or are **all-inclusive** (all meals and most activities).

Restaurant Reservations and Dress Codes

Reservations are always a good idea; the more expensive the place is, the more essential they are. It never hurts to book as far ahead as you can, and reconfirm when you get to town. Unless otherwise noted, the restaurants listed are open daily for lunch and dinner. We mention dress only when men are required to wear a jacket or a jacket and tie. Look for an overview of local habits under Dining in Smart Travel Tips A to Z and in the Pleasures and Pastimes section that follows each chapter introduction.

Credit Cards

The following abbreviations are used: **AE,** American Express; **DC,** Diners Club; **MC,** MasterCard; and **V,** Visa.

Please Write to Us

You can use this book in the confidence that all prices and opening times are based on information supplied to us at press time; Fodor's cannot accept responsibility for any errors. Time inevitably brings changes, so always confirm information when it matters—especially if you're making a detour to visit a specific place. In addition, when making reservations be sure to mention if you have a disability or are traveling with children, if you prefer a private bath or a certain type of bed, or if you have specific dietary needs or any other concerns.

Were the restaurants we recommended as described? Did our hotel picks exceed your expectations? Did you find a museum we recommended a waste of time? If you have complaints, we'll look into them and revise our entries when the facts warrant it. If you've discovered a special place that we haven't included, we'll pass the information along to our correspondents and have them check it out. So send your feedback, positive *and* negative, to the Great Britain Editor at 201 East 50th Street, New York, New York 10022—and have a wonderful trip!

Karen Cure
Editorial Director

Great Britain

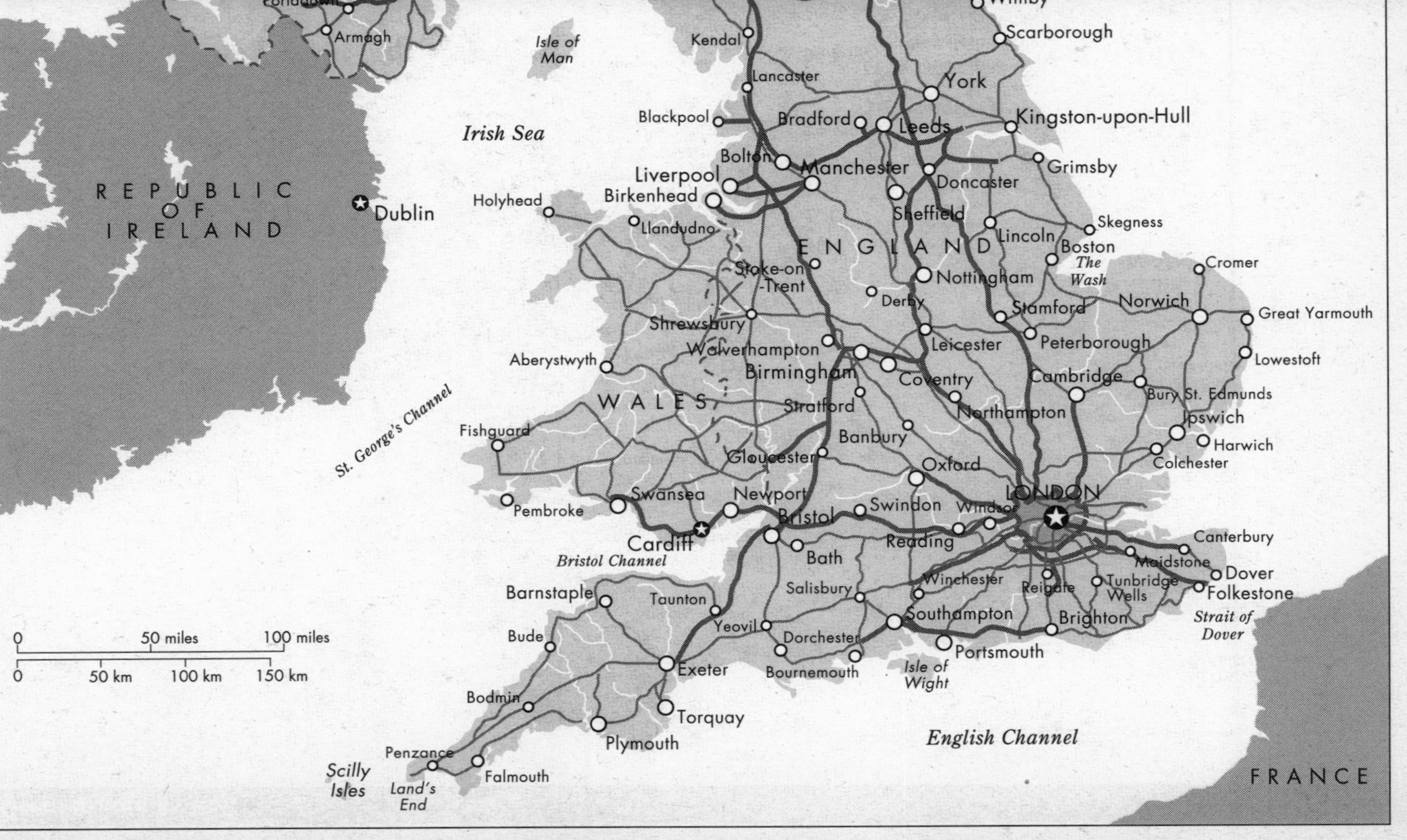
Armagh
Isle of Man
Kendal
Scarborough
Lancaster
York
Blackpool
Bradford
Leeds
Kingston-upon-Hull
Irish Sea
Bolton
Manchester
Grimsby
Liverpool
Doncaster
REPUBLIC OF IRELAND
Dublin
Holyhead
Birkenhead
Sheffield
Llandudno
Lincoln
Skegness
ENGLAND
Boston
The Wash
Cromer
Stoke-on-Trent
Nottingham
Derby
Stamford
Norwich
Great Yarmouth
Shrewsbury
Leicester
Peterborough
Wolverhampton
Lowestoft
Aberystwyth
Birmingham
Coventry
Cambridge
Bury St. Edmunds
WALES
Stratford
Northampton
St. George's Channel
Ipswich
Fishguard
Banbury
Harwich
Gloucester
Colchester
Oxford
LONDON
Pembroke
Swansea
Newport
Swindon
Windsor
Bristol
Canterbury
Cardiff
Reading
Bath
Maidstone
Bristol Channel
Dover
Winchester
Tunbridge Wells
Barnstaple
Salisbury
Reigate
Folkestone
Taunton
Strait of Dover
Yeovil
Southampton
Brighton
0
50 miles
100 miles
Bude
Dorchester
Portsmouth
0
50 km
100 km
150 km
Exeter
Bournemouth
Isle of Wight
Bodmin
Torquay
English Channel
Plymouth
Penzance
Scilly Isles
Falmouth
FRANCE
Land's End

Great Britain By Rail

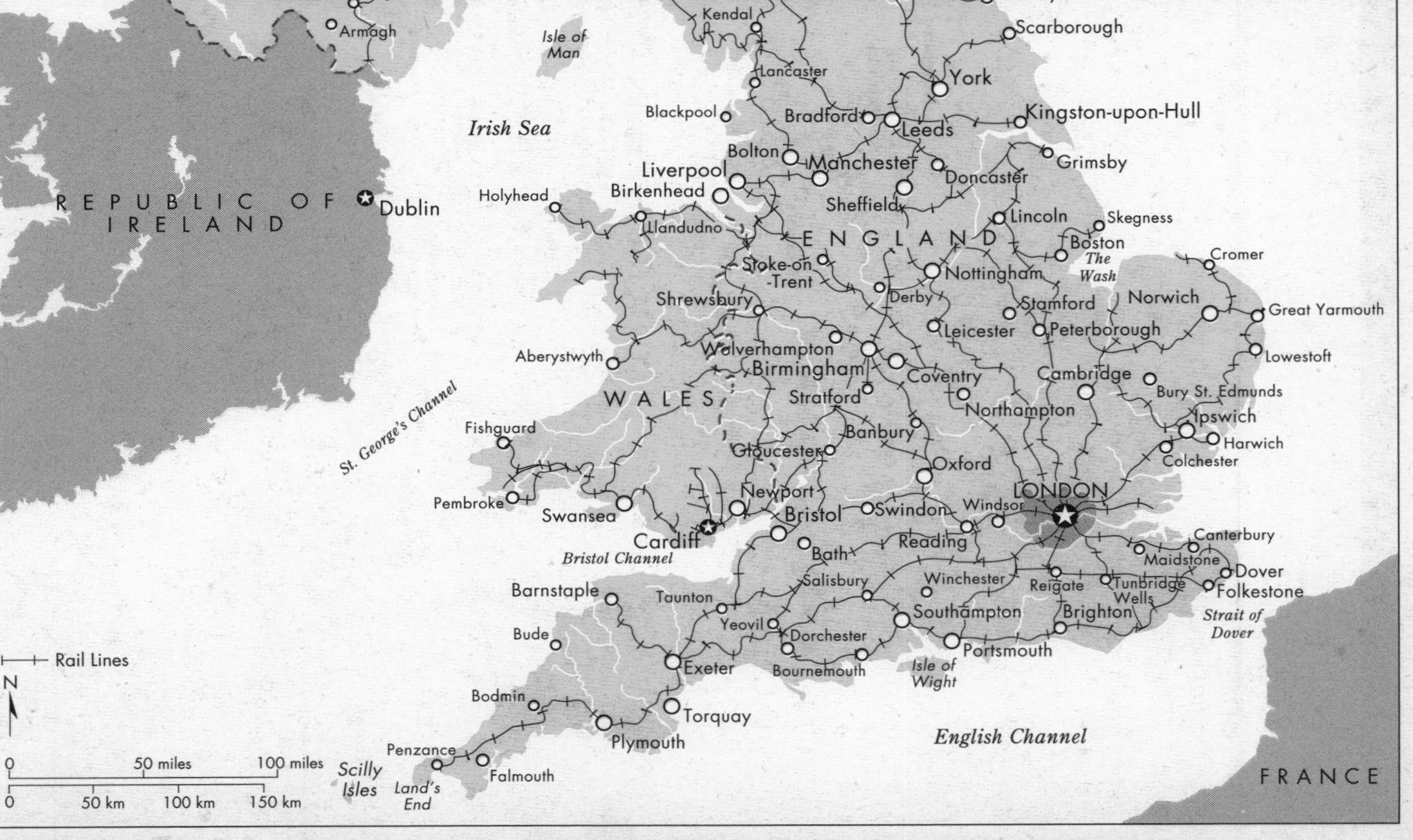
Armagh
Kendal
Scarborough
Isle of Man
Lancaster
York
Blackpool
Bradford
Leeds
Kingston-upon-Hull
Irish Sea
Bolton
Manchester
Grimsby
Liverpool
Doncaster
Birkenhead
Sheffield
Holyhead
REPUBLIC OF IRELAND
Dublin
Llandudno
ENGLAND
Lincoln
Skegness
Boston
The Wash
Cromer
Stoke-on-Trent
Nottingham
Derby
Shrewsbury
Stamford
Norwich
Great Yarmouth
Leicester
Peterborough
Wolverhampton
Lowestoft
Aberystwyth
Birmingham
Coventry
Cambridge
Bury St. Edmunds
WALES
Stratford
Northampton
Ipswich
St. George's Channel
Harwich
Fishguard
Banbury
Colchester
Gloucester
Oxford
LONDON
Newport
Pembroke
Swindon
Windsor
Swansea
Bristol
Cardiff
Reading
Canterbury
Bath
Maidstone
Bristol Channel
Dover
Salisbury
Winchester
Barnstaple
Reigate
Tunbridge Wells
Folkestone
Taunton
Southampton
Brighton
Strait of Dover
Yeovil
Dorchester
Bude
Portsmouth
Rail Lines
Exeter
Bournemouth
Isle of Wight
N
Bodmin
Torquay
Plymouth
English Channel
Penzance
0
50 miles
100 miles
Scilly Isles
Falmouth
FRANCE
0
50 km
100 km
150 km
Land's End

Europe

Reykjavík
ICELAND
NORWAY
Bergen
SCOTLAND
NORTHERN IRELAND
Edinburgh
North Sea
Skagerrak
Belfast
IRELAND
Irish Sea
Dublin
UNITED KINGDOM
DENMARK
WALES
Hamburg
ENGLAND
NETHERLANDS
Cardiff
Amsterdam
The Hague
London
Rotterdam
ATLANTIC OCEAN
English Channel
GERM
Brussels
Bonn
BELGIUM
Frankfurt
Paris
LUXEMBOURG
FRANCE
Zürich
Munich
Bern
SWITZERLAND
Lyon
LIECHTENSTEIN
Milan
Venice
Monte Carlo
Nice
MONACO
Marseille
PORTUGAL
ANDORRA
Florence
Madrid
Lisbon
Barcelona
Corsica
SPAIN
Sardinia
Seville
Granada
Balearic Islands
Tyrrhenian
Gibraltar
Mediterranean Sea
MOROCCO
ALGERIA
0
400 miles
TUNISIA
0
600 km

FINLAND
Gulf of Bothnia
Oslo
SWEDEN
Helsinki
Gulf of Finland
St. Petersburg
Tallinn
Stockholm
ESTONIA
Kattegat
Göteborg
Riga
LATVIA
Moscow
Copenhagen
LITHUANIA
Kaunas
Baltic Sea
RUSSIA
Vilnius
RUSSIA
Kaliningrad
Minsk
Berlin
POLAND
BELARUS
MANY
Warsaw
Kraków
Kiev
Prague
CZECH REPUBLIC
UKRAINE
SLOVAKIA
ich
Vienna
Bratislava
Salzburg
MOLDOVA
Budapest
AUSTRIA
Chişinău
HUNGARY
EIN
SLOVENIA
Ljubljana
Zagreb
ROMANIA
nice
CROATIA
Novi Sad
Bucharest
BOSNIA AND HERZEGOVINA
Belgrade
Black Sea
SERBIA
Adriatic Sea
Sarajevo
BULGARIA
MONTENEGRO
Priština
Rome
Sofia
Skopje
Podgorica
F.Y.R. of MACEDONIA
ITALY
Istanbul
Tiranë
Ankara
Naples
ALBANIA
TURKEY
nian Sea
GREECE
Aegean Sea
Ionian Sea
Athens
Sicily
CYPRUS
MALTA
Crete
Mediterranean Sea

IMPORTANT CONTACTS A TO Z

An Alphabetical Listing of Publications, Organizations, & Companies That Will Help You Before, During, & After Your Trip

A

AIR TRAVEL

The major gateways to Great Britain are London's **Heathrow** (☎ 011–44–181/759–4321) and **Gatwick** (☎ 011–44–1293/535–353) airports.

FLYING TIME

Flying time is 6½ hours from New York, 7½ hours from Chicago, and 10 hours from Los Angeles.

CARRIERS

Carriers that serve both London gateways from the United States include **American Airlines** (☎ 800/433–7300), **British Airways** (☎ 800/247–9297), **Continental** (☎ 800/525–0280), **Delta** (☎ 800/221–2121), **Northwest Airlines** (☎ 800/447–4747), **TWA** (☎ 800/892–4141), **United** (☎ 800/241–6522), **USAir** (☎ 800/428–4322), and **Virgin Atlantic** (☎ 800/862–8621).

British Airways (0181/897–4000; outside London, 0345/222–111); from Stansted **Air UK** (☎ 0345/666–777) flies to Scotland, Newcastle, and the Channel Islands; from Heathrow **British Midland** (☎ 0181/754–7321 or 0345/554–554) serves Belfast, Scotland, and the Midlands.

COMPLAINTS

To register complaints about charter and scheduled airlines, contact the U.S. Department of Transportation's **Aviation Consumer Protection Division** (✉ C-75, Washington, DC 20590, ☎ 202/366–2220). Complaints about lost baggage or ticketing problems and safety concerns may also be logged with the **Federal Aviation Administration (FAA) Consumer Hotline** (☎ 800/322–7873).

CONSOLIDATORS

For services that will help you find the lowest airfares, *see* Discounts & Deals, *below.*

PUBLICATIONS

For general information about charter carriers, ask for the Department of Transportation's free brochure **"Plane Talk: Public Charter Flights"** (✉ Aviation Consumer Protection Division, C-75, Washington, DC 20590, ☎ 202/366–2220). The Department of Transportation also publishes a 58-page booklet, **"Fly Rights,"** available from the Consumer Information Center (✉ Supt. of Documents, Dept. 136C, Pueblo, CO 81009; $1.75).

For other tips and hints, consult the Consumers Union's monthly **"Consumer Reports Travel Letter"** (✉ Box 53629, Boulder, CO 80322, ☎ 800/234–1970; $39 1st year) and the newsletter **"Travel Smart"** (✉ 40 Beechdale Rd., Dobbs Ferry, NY 10522, ☎ 800/327–3633; $37 per year).

Some worthwhile publications on the subject are ***The Official Frequent Flyer Guidebook,*** by Randy Petersen (✉ Airpress, 4715-C Town Center Dr., Colorado Springs, CO 80916, ☎ 719/597–8899 or 800/487–8893; $14.99 plus $3 shipping); ***Airfare Secrets Exposed,*** by Sharon Tyler and Matthew Wunder (✉ Studio 4 Productions, Box 280400, Northridge, CA 91328, ☎ 818/700–2522 or 800/408–7369; $16.95 plus $2.50 shipping); ***202 Tips Even the Best Business Travelers May Not Know,*** by Christopher McGinnis (✉ Irwin Professional Publishing, 1333 Burr Ridge Pkwy., Burr Ridge, IL 60521, ☎ 800/634–3966; $11 plus $3.25 shipping); and ***Travel Rights,*** by Charles Leocha (✉ World Leisure Corporation, 177 Paris St., Boston, MA 02128, ☎ 800/444–2524; $7.95 plus $3.95 shipping).

For information on how to avoid jet lag, two publications are ***Jet Lag, A Pocket Guide to Modern Treatment*** by

Peter Casano M.D. (✉ MedEd Publications, Box 12415, Columbus, OH 43212, ☎ 614/488–9457; $5.95) and ***How to Beat Jet Lag*** (✉ Henry Holt, 115 W. 18th St., New York, NY 10011, ☎ 800/288–2131; $14.95).

Travelers who experience motion sickness or ear problems in flight should get the brochures **"Ears, Altitude, and Airplane Travel"** and **"What You Can Do for Dizziness & Motion Sickness"** from the American Academy of Otolaryngology (✉ 1 Prince St., Alexandria, VA 22314, ☎ 703/836–4444, FAX 703/683–5100, TTY 703/519–1585).

WITHIN GREAT BRITAIN

British Airways operates shuttle services between London Heathrow and Edinburgh, Glasgow, Belfast, and Manchester. Passengers can simply turn up and get a flight (usually hourly) without booking. There are also shuttle services from Gatwick. **British Midland** operates from Heathrow to Teesside, Belfast, Glasgow, Liverpool, and the Isle of Man. The Scottish islands are served by **Loganair** from Glasgow and Edinburgh. For services to the Channel Islands, *see* Chapter 7.

B

BARGE TRAVEL

See the British Tourist Authority's booklet *U.K. Waterway Holidays*, and contact the **Inland Waterways Association** (✉ 114 Regents Park Rd., London NW1 8UQ, ☎ 0171/586–2510), the **British Waterways Board** (✉ Willow Grange, Church Rd., Watford WD1 3QA, ☎ 01923/226422), or **U.K. Waterway Holidays** (✉ 1 Port Hill, Hertford SG14 1PJ, ☎ 01992/550616).

BETTER BUSINESS BUREAU

For local contacts in the hometown of a tour operator you may be considering, consult the **Council of Better Business Bureaus** (✉ 4200 Wilson Blvd., Suite 800, Arlington, VA 22203, ☎ 703/276–0100, FAX 703/525–8277).

BUS TRAVEL

For details on coach service throughout Britain, contact **Victoria Coach Station** (✉ Buckingham Palace Rd., London SW1W 9TP, ☎ 0990/808080) and **Scottish Citylink** (☎ 0990/505050) in Glasgow.

BUS PASSES

National Express's **Tourist Trail Pass** costs £49 for three consecutive days of travel, £79 for five days of travel out of 10 consecutive days, £119 for eight days out of 16, and £179 for 15 days out of 30. A **National Express Coach Card** for students and under-25s, which costs £7, qualifies you for 30% discounts on those prices. A Tourist Trail Pass can be bought with U.S. dollars from **British Travel Associates** (Box 299, Elkton, VA 22827, ☎ 703/298–2232 or 800/327–6097).

C

CAR RENTAL

The major car-rental companies represented in Great Britain are **Alamo** (☎ 800/327–9633; in the U.K., 0800/272–2000), **Avis** (☎ 800/331–1084; in Canada, 800/879–2847), **Budget** (☎ 800/527–0700; in the U.K., 0800/181181), **Dollar** (☎ 800/800–4000; in the U.K., 0990/565656, where it is known as Eurodollar), **Hertz** (☎ 800/654–3001; in Canada, 800/263–0600; in the U.K., 0345/555888), and **National InterRent** (sometimes known as Europcar InterRent outside North America; ☎ 800/227–3876; in the U.K., 01345/222–525). Rates in the U.K. begin at $25 a day and $103 a week for an economy car with unlimited mileage, VAT, Collision Damage Waiver and insurance. This does not include tax on car rentals, which is 17.5%.

RENTAL WHOLESALERS

Contact **Auto Europe** (☎ 207/828–2525 or 800/223–5555), **Europe by Car** (☎ 800/223–1516; in CA, 800/252–9401), or the **Kemwel Group** (☎ 914/835–5555 or 800/678–0678).

THE CHANNEL TUNNEL

For information, contact **Le Shuttle** (in the U.S., ☎ 800/388–3876; in the U.K., 0990/353535), which transports cars, or **Eurostar** (in the U.S., ☎ 800/942–4866; in the U.K.,

0345/881881), the high-speed train service between London (Waterloo) and Paris (Gare du Nord). Eurostar tickets are available in the United Kingdom through **InterCity Europe,** the international wing of BritRail (☒ Victoria Station, London, ☎ 0171/834–2345 or 0171/828–0892 for credit-card bookings), and in the United States through **Rail Europe** (☎ 800/942–4866) and **BritRail Travel** (☎ 800/677–8585).

CHILDREN & TRAVEL

BABY-SITTING

In London, try **Nanny Service** (☒ 9 Paddington St., London WIM 3LA, ☎ 0171/935–3515) and **Universal Aunts** (☒ 19 The Chase, London SW4 0NP ☎ 0171/738–8937).

FLYING

Look into **"Flying with Baby"** (☒ Third Street Press, Box 261250, Littleton, CO 80163, ☎ 303/595–5959; $4.95 includes shipping), cowritten by a flight attendant. **"Kids and Teens in Flight,"** free from the U.S. Department of Transportation's Aviation Consumer Protection Division (☒ C-75, Washington, DC 20590, ☎ 202/366–2220), offers tips on children flying alone. Every two years the February issue of ***Family Travel Times*** details children's services on three dozen airlines. **"Flying Alone, Handy Advice for Kids Traveling Solo"** is available free from the American Automobile Association (AAA) (send SASE: ☒ Flying Alone, Mail Stop 800, 1000 AAA Dr., Heathrow, FL 32746).

LOCAL INFORMATION

For information and advice when in London, call **Kidsline** (☎ 0171/222–8070).

LODGING

Hotels that are noticeably family- and child-friendly include **Basil Street Hotel** (☒ Basil St., Knightsbridge, London SW3 1AH, ☎ 0171/581–3311), **Edward Lear** (☒ 28 Seymour St., London W1H 5WD, ☎ 0171/402–5401), **Forte Hotels** (various London locations), and **Novotel** (☎ 800/221–4542 in the U.S.).

CUSTOMS

IN THE U.S.

The **U.S. Customs Service** (☒ Box 7407, Washington, DC 20044, ☎ 202/927–6724) can answer questions on duty-free limits and publishes a helpful brochure, "Know Before You Go." For information on registering foreign-made articles, call 202/927–0540.

COMPLAINTS➢ Note the inspector's badge number and write to the commissioner's office (☒ 1301 Constitution Ave. NW, Washington, DC 20229).

CANADIANS

Contact **Revenue Canada** (☒ 2265 St. Laurent Blvd. S, Ottawa, Ontario K1G 4K3, ☎ 613/993–0534) for a copy of the free brochure **"I Declare/Je Déclare"** and for details on duty-free limits. For recorded information (within Canada only), call 800/461–9999.

D

DISABILITIES & ACCESSIBILITY

COMPLAINTS

To register complaints under the provisions of the Americans with Disabilities Act, contact the U.S. Department of Justice's **Disability Rights Section** (☒ Box 66738, Washington, DC 20035, ☎ 202/514–0301 or 800/514–0301, FAX 202/307–1198, TTY 202/514–0383 or 800/514–0383). For airline-related problems, contact the U.S. Department of Transportation's **Aviation Consumer Protection Division** (☞ Air Travel, *above*). For complaints about surface transportation, contact the Department of Transportation's **Civil Rights Office** (☎ 202/366–4648).

ORGANIZATIONS

TRAVELERS WITH HEARING IMPAIRMENTS➢ The **American Academy of Otolaryngology** (☒ 1 Prince St., Alexandria, VA 22314, ☎ 703/836–4444, FAX 703/683–5100, TTY 703/519–1585) publishes a brochure, "Travel Tips for Hearing Impaired People."

TRAVELERS WITH MOBILITY PROBLEMS➢ Contact **Mobility International USA** (☒ Box 10767, Eugene, OR 97440, ☎ and TTY 541/343–1284, FAX 541/343–6812), the U.S. branch of a Belgium-based organization (☞ *below*) with affiliates in 30 countries; and the **Society for the Advancement of Travel for the Handicapped** (✉ 347 5th Ave., Suite 610, New York, NY 10016, ☎ 212/447–7284, FAX 212/725–8253; membership $45).

TRAVELERS WITH VISION IMPAIRMENTS➢ Contact the **American Council of the Blind** (✉ 1155 15th St. NW, Suite 720, Washington, DC 20005, ☎ 202/467–5081, FAX 202/467–5085) for a list of travelers' resources or the **American Foundation for the Blind** (✉ 11 Penn Plaza, Suite 300, New York, NY 10001, ☎ 212/502–7600 or 800/232–5463, TTY 212/502–7662), which provides general advice and publishes "Access to Art" ($19.95), a directory of museums that accommodate travelers with vision impairments.

IN THE U.K.

Holiday Care Service (✉ Imperial Buildings, 2nd floor, Victoria Rd., Horley, Surrey, RH6 7PZ, ☎ 01293/774535) is Britain's central source of holiday and travel information for people with disabilities.

Contact the **Royal Association for Disability and Rehabilitation** (✉ RADAR, 12 City Forum, 250 City Rd., London EC1V 8AF, ☎ 0171/250–3222) or **Mobility International** (✉ rue de Manchester 25, B-1080 Brussels, Belgium, ☎ 00–322–410–6297, FAX 00–322–410–6874), an international travel-information clearing-house for people with disabilities.

PUBLICATIONS

The 500-page ***Travelin' Talk Directory*** (✉ Box 3534, Clarksville, TN 37043, ☎ 615/552–6670, FAX 615/552–1182; $35) lists people and organizations who help travelers with disabilities. For travel agents worldwide, consult the ***Directory of Travel Agencies for the Disabled*** (✉ Twin Peaks Press, Box 129, Vancouver, WA 98666, ☎ 360/694–2462 or 800/637–2256, FAX 360/696–3210; $19.95 plus $3 shipping).

TRAVEL AGENCIES, TOUR OPERATORS

The Americans with Disabilities Act requires that all travel firms serve the needs of all travelers. That said, you should note that some agencies and operators specialize in making travel arrangements for individuals and groups with disabilities, among them **Access Adventures** (✉ 206 Chestnut Ridge Rd., Rochester, NY 14624, ☎ 716/889–9096), run by a former physical-rehab counselor.

TRAVELERS WITH MOBILITY PROBLEMS➢ Contact **Accessible Journeys** (✉ 35 W. Sellers Ave., Ridley Park, PA 19078, ☎ 610/521–0339 or 800/846–4537, FAX 610/521–6959), a registered nursing service that arranges vacations; **Hinsdale Travel Service** (✉ 201 E. Ogden Ave., Suite 100, Hinsdale, IL 60521, ☎ 708/325–1335), a travel agency that benefits from the advice of wheelchair traveler Janice Perkins; and **Wheelchair Journeys** (✉ 16979 Redmond Way, Redmond, WA 98052, ☎ 206/885–2210 or 800/313–4751), which can handle arrangements worldwide.

DISCOUNTS & DEALS

AIRFARES

For the lowest airfares to Great Britain, call 800/FLY–4–LESS.

CLUBS

Contact **Entertainment Travel Editions** (✉ Box 1068, Trumbull, CT 06611, ☎ 800/445–4137; $28–$53, depending on destination), **Great American Traveler** (✉ Box 27965, Salt Lake City, UT 84127, ☎ 800/548–2812; $49.95 per year), **Moment's Notice Discount Travel Club** (✉ 7301 New Utrecht Ave., Brooklyn, New York, NY 11204, ☎ 718/234–6295; $25 per year, single or family), **Privilege Card** (✉ 3391 Peachtree Rd. NE, Suite 110, Atlanta, GA 30326, ☎ 404/262–0222 or 800/236–9732; $74.95 per year), **Travelers Advantage** (✉ CUC Travel Service, 49 Music Sq. W, Nashville, TN 37203, ☎ 800/548–1116 or 800/648–4037; $49 per year, single or family), or **Worldwide Discount Travel Club** (✉ 1674 Meridian Ave., Miami Beach, FL 33139, ☎ 305/534–2082; $50 per year for family, $40 single).

HOTEL ROOMS

For hotel room rates guaranteed in U.S. dollars, call **Steigenberger Reservation Service** (☎ 800/223–5652).

PASSES

☞ Bus Travel, *above, and* Train Travel, *below.*

PUBLICATIONS

Consult ***The Frugal Globetrotter,*** by Bruce Northam (✉ Fulcrum Publishing, 350 Indiana St., Suite 350, Golden, CO 80401, ☎ 800/ 992–2908; $15.95). For publications that tell how to find the lowest prices on plane tickets, *see* Air Travel, *above.*

Also check out Fodor's ***Affordable Great Britain*** (available in bookstores, or ☎ 800/533–6478; $17).

STUDENTS

Members of Hostelling International–American Youth Hostels (☞ Students, *below*) are eligible for discounts on car rentals, admissions to attractions, and other selected travel expenses.

DRIVING

AUTO CLUBS

The **Automobile Association** (✉ Fanum House, Basing View, Basingstoke, Hampshire, RQ21 2 EA, ☎ 01256/20123) and the **Royal Automobile Club** (✉ RAC House, Bartlett St., Box 10, Croydon, Surrey CR2 6XW, ☎ 0181/ 686–2525) offer associate membership for overseas visitors and a wealth of detailed information about motoring in Britain.

MAPS

Good planning maps are available from the **AA** and the **RAC** (☞ *above*).

G

GAY & LESBIAN TRAVEL

ORGANIZATIONS

The **International Gay Travel Association** (✉ Box 4974, Key West, FL 33041, ☎ 800/448–8550, FAX 305/296–6633), a consortium of more than 1,000 travel companies, can supply names of gay-friendly travel agents, tour operators, and accommodations.

TOUR OPERATORS

Hanns Ebensten Travel (✉ 513 Fleming St., Key West, FL 33040, ☎ 305/294–8174), one of the nation's oldest operators in the gay market, and **Toto Tours** (✉ 1326 W. Albion Ave., Suite 3W, Chicago, IL 60626, ☎ 312/274–8686 or 800/565–1241, FAX 312/274–8695) offer group tours to worldwide destinations.

TRAVEL AGENCIES

The largest agencies serving gay travelers are **Advance Travel** (✉ 10700 Northwest Fwy., Suite 160, Houston, TX 77092, ☎ 713/682–2002 or 800/292–0500), **Islanders/ Kennedy Travel** (✉ 183 W. 10th St., New York, NY 10014, ☎ 212/ 242–3222 or 800/988–1181), **Now Voyager** (✉ 4406 18th St., San Francisco, CA 94114, ☎ 415/626–1169 or 800/255–6951), and **Yellowbrick Road** (✉ 1500 W. Balmoral Ave., Chicago, IL 60640, ☎ 312/561–1800 or 800/642–2488). **Skylink Women's Travel** (✉ 2460 W. 3rd St., Suite 215, Santa Rosa, CA 95401, ☎ 707/ 570–0105 or 800/225–5759) serves lesbian travelers.

H

HEALTH ISSUES

MEDICAL ASSISTANCE COMPANIES

The following companies are concerned primarily with emergency medical assistance, although they may provide some insurance as part of their coverage. For a list of full-service travel insurance companies, *see* Insurance, *below.*

Contact **International SOS Assistance** (✉ Box 11568, Philadelphia, PA 19116, ☎ 215/ 244–1500 or 800/ 523–8930; ✉ Box 466, Pl. Bonaventure, Montréal, Québec H5A 1C1, ☎ 514/874–7674 or 800/363–0263; ✉ 7 Old Lodge Pl., St. Margarets, Twickenham TW1 1RQ, England, ☎ 0181/744–0033), **Medex Assistance Corporation** (✉ Box 5375, Timonium, MD 21094-5375, ☎ 410/453–6300 or 800/537–2029), **Traveler's Emergency Network** (✉ 3100 Tower Blvd., Suite 3100A, Durham, NC 27702, ☎ 919/490–6065 or 800/275–4836, FAX 919/493–8262), **TravMed** (✉ Box 5375, Timonium, MD 21094, ☎ 410/453–6380 or 800/732–5309), or **Worldwide Assistance Services** (✉ 1133 15th St. NW, Suite 400, Washington, DC 20005, ☎ 202/331–1609 or 800/821–2828, FAX 202/ 828–5896).

I
INSURANCE

IN CANADA

Contact **Mutual of Omaha** (✉ Travel Division, 500 University Ave., Toronto, Ontario M5G 1V8, ☎ 800/465–0267 in Canada or 416/598–4083).

IN THE U.S.

Travel insurance covering baggage, health, and trip cancellation or interruptions is available from **Access America** (✉ 6600 W. Broad St., Richmond, VA 23230, ☎ 804/285–3300 or 800/334–7525), **Carefree Travel Insurance** (✉ Box 9366, 100 Garden City Plaza, Garden City, NY 11530, ☎ 516/294–0220 or 800/323–3149), **Near Travel Services** (✉ Box 1339, Calumet City, IL 60409, ☎ 708/868–6700 or 800/654–6700), **Tele-Trip** (✉ Mutual of Omaha Plaza, Box 31716, Omaha, NE 68131, ☎ 800/228–9792), **Travel Guard International** (✉ 1145 Clark St., Stevens Point, WI 54481, ☎ 715/345–0505 or 800/826–1300), **Travel Insured International** (✉ Box 280568, East Hartford, CT 06128, ☎ 203/528–7663 or 800/243–3174), and **Wallach & Company** (✉ 107 W. Federal St., Box 480, Middleburg, VA 22117, ☎ 540/687–3166 or 800/237–6615).

L
LODGING

APARTMENT & VILLA RENTAL

Among the companies to contact are **At Home Abroad** (✉ 405 E. 56th St., Suite 6H, New York, NY 10022, ☎ 212/421–9165, FAX 212/752–1591), **Europa-Let** (✉ 92 N. Main St., Ashland, OR 97520, ☎ 541/482–5806 or 800/462–4486, FAX 541/482–0660), **Property Rentals International** (✉ 1008 Mansfield Crossing Rd., Richmond, VA 23236, ☎ 804/378–6054 or 800/220–3332, FAX 804/379–2073), **Rental Directories International** (✉ 2044 Rittenhouse Sq., Philadelphia, PA 19103, ☎ 215/985–4001, FAX 215/985–0323), **Rent-a-Home International** (✉ 7200 34th Ave. NW, Seattle, WA 98117, ☎ 206/789–9377 or 800/488–7368, FAX 206/789–9379), **Villas and Apartments Abroad** (✉ 420 Madison Ave., Suite 1003, New York, NY 10017, ☎ 212/759–1025 or 800/433–3020, FAX 212/755–8316), and **Villas International** (✉ 605 Market St., Suite 510, San Francisco, CA 94105, ☎ 415/281–0910 or 800/221–2260, FAX 415/281–0919).

BED-AND-BREAKFASTS

The famous ***Cottages, B&Bs and Country Inns of England and Wales,*** by Elizabeth H. Gundrey, covers the waterfront and has given its author's name to the language, as in "Let's go Gundreying."

COTTAGES

For lists of properties, consult the British Tourist Authority and the *Good Holiday Cottage Guide* (✉ Swallow Press, ☎ 01438/869489; £3.50).

FARMHOUSES

Ask for the BTA booklet *Farmhouse Vacations.* Also contact the **Farm Holiday Bureau** (✉ National Agricultural Centre, Stoneleigh, Kenilworth, Warwickshire CV8 2LZ, ☎ 01203/696909).

HISTORIC BUILDINGS

For lodgings with a past, try the **Landmark Trust** (✉ Shottesbrooke, Maidenhead, Berkshire SL6 3SW, ☎ 01628/825925), the **National Trust** (✉ Box 101, Western Way, Melksham, Wiltshire SN12 8EA, ☎ 01225/705676), **Portmeirion Cottages** (✉ Portmeirion, Gwynedd, Wales LL48 6ET, ☎ 01766/770228), and the rather upscale **Rural Retreats** (✉ Retreat House, Station Rd., Blockley, Moreton-in-Marsh, Gloucestershire GL56 9DZ, ☎ 01386/701177).

HOME EXCHANGE

Some of the principal clearinghouses are **HomeLink International/Vacation Exchange Club** (✉ Box 650, Key West, FL 33041, ☎ 305/294–1448 or 800/638–3841, FAX 305/294–1148; $70 per year), which sends members three annual directories, with a listing in one, plus updates; and **Intervac International** (✉ Box 590504, San Francisco, CA 94159, ☎ 415/435–3497, FAX 415/435–7440; $65 per year), which publishes four annual directories.

UNIVERSITIES

Contact the **British Universities Accommodation Consortium** (✉ Box 1328, University Park, Nottingham NG7 2RD, ☎ 0115/9504571).

M

MONEY MATTERS

ATMS

For specific foreign **Cirrus** locations, call 800/424–7787; for foreign **Plus** locations, consult the Plus directory at your local bank.

CURRENCY EXCHANGE

If your bank doesn't exchange currency, contact **Thomas Cook Currency Services** (☎ 800/287–7362 for locations). **Ruesch International** (☎ 800/424–2923 for locations) can also provide you with foreign banknotes before you leave home and publishes a number of useful brochures, including a "Foreign Currency Guide" and "Foreign Exchange Tips."

WIRING FUNDS

Funds can be wired via **MoneyGram℠** (for locations and information in the U.S. and Canada, ☎ 800/926–9400) or **Western Union** (for agent locations or to send money using MasterCard or Visa, ☎ 800/325–6000; in Canada, 800/321–2923; in the U.K., 0800/833833; or visit the Western Union office at the nearest major post office).

P

PACKING

For strategies on packing light, get a copy of ***The Packing Book,*** by Judith Gilford (✉ Ten Speed Press, Box 7123, Berkeley, CA 94707, ☎ 510/559–1600 or 800/841–2665, FAX 510/524–4588; $7.95).

PASSPORTS & VISAS

IN THE U.S.

For fees, documentation requirements, and other information, call the State Department's **Office of Passport Services** information line (☎ 202/647–0518).

CANADIANS

For fees, documentation requirements, and other information, call the Ministry of Foreign Affairs and International Trade's **Passport Office** (☎ 819/994–3500 or 800/567–6868).

PHOTO HELP

The **Kodak Information Center** (☎ 800/242–2424) answers consumer questions about film and photography. The ***Kodak Guide to Shooting Great Travel Pictures*** (available in bookstores; or contact Fodor's Travel Publications, ☎ 800/533–6478; $16.50) explains how to take expert travel photographs.

S

SAFETY

"Trouble-Free Travel," from the AAA, is a booklet of tips for protecting yourself and your belongings when away from home. Send a stamped, self-addressed, legal-size envelope to Trouble-Free Travel (✉ Mail Stop 75, 1000 AAA Dr., Heathrow, FL 32746).

SENIOR CITIZENS

EDUCATIONAL TRAVEL

The nonprofit **Elderhostel** (✉ 75 Federal St., 3rd floor, Boston, MA 02110, ☎ 617/426–7788), for people 60 and older, has offered inexpensive study programs since 1975. Courses cover everything from marine science to Greek mythology and cowboy poetry. Costs for two- to three-week international trips—including room, board, and transportation from the United States—range from $1,800 to $4,500.

For people 50 and over and their children and grandchildren, **Interhostel** (✉ University of New Hampshire, 6 Garrison Ave., Durham, NH 03824, ☎ 603/862–1147 or 800/733–9753) runs 10-day summer programs that feature lectures, field trips, and sightseeing. Most last two weeks and cost $2,125–$3,100, including airfare.

ORGANIZATIONS

Contact the **American Association of Retired Persons** (✉ AARP, 601 E St. NW, Washington, DC 20049, ☎ 202/434–2277; annual dues $8 per person or couple). Its Purchase Privilege Program secures discounts for members on lodging, car rentals, and sightseeing.

Additional sources for discounts on lodgings, car rentals, and other travel expenses, as well as helpful magazines and newsletters, are the **National Council of**

Senior Citizens (✉ 1331 F St. NW, Washington, DC 20004, ☎ 202/347–8800; annual membership $12) and Sears's **Mature Outlook** (✉ Box 10448, Des Moines, IA 50306, ☎ 800/336–6330; annual membership $9.95).

SHIP TRAVEL

Cunard Line (✉ 555 5th Ave., New York, NY 10017, ☎ 800/221–4770) operates four ships that make transatlantic crossings. The ***Queen Elizabeth 2*** (*QE2*) makes regular crossings April–December, between Southampton, England, and Baltimore, Boston, and New York City. Arrangements for the *QE2* can include one-way airfare. Cunard Line also offers fly/cruise packages and pre- and post-land packages. Check the travel pages of your Sunday newspaper for other cruise ships that sail to Britain.

SPORTS

BICYCLING

The national body promoting cycle touring is the **Cyclists' Touring Club** (£25 a year, £12.50 for students and those under 18, £16.50 for those over 65, and £42 for a family of more than three; ✉ 69 Meadrow, Godalming, Surrey GU7 3HS, ☎ 01483/417217). Members get free advice and route information, a bed-and-breakfast handbook, and a magazine.

BOATING

For boat-rental operators along Britain's several hundred miles of historic canals and waterways, contact the **Association of Pleasure Craft Operators** (✉ 35a High St., Newport, Shropshire TF10 7AT, ☎ 01952/813572).

CAMPING

Contact the British Tourist Authority in the U.S. or the **Camping and Caravanning Club** (✉ Greenfields House, Westwood Way, Coventry, West Midlands CV4 8JH, ☎ 01203/694995) for details on Britain's many and varied campsites.

GOLF

If you plan to play often on the Britain's hundreds of fine courses, consult ***The Golf Guide*** (FHG Publications, ✉ Abbey Mill Business Centre, Seed Hill, Paisley, PA1 1TJ Scotland, ☎ 0141/887–0428; £8.99).

WALKING

The Ramblers Association (✉ 1–5 Wandsworth Rd., London SW8 2XX, ☎ 0171/582–6878), publishes a bimonthly magazine and a yearbook full of resources, and a list of B&Bs within 2 miles of selected long-distance footpaths.

Other organizations include the **Byways and Bridleways Trust** (✉ The Granary, Charlcutt, Calne, Wiltshire SN11 9HL); **Long Distance Walkers Association** (✉ c/o The Membership Secretary, 117 Higher La., Rainford, St. Helens, Merseyside, WA11 8BQ); and the **Farm Holiday Bureau,** (✉ National Agricultural Centre, Stoneleigh, Kenilworth, Warwickshire CV8 2LZ, ☎ 01203/696909).

STUDENTS

GROUPS

The major tour operators specializing in student travel are **Contiki Holidays** (✉ 300 Plaza Alicante, Suite 900, Garden Grove, CA 92640, ☎ 714/740–0808 or 800/266–8454) and **AESU Travel** (✉ 2 Hamill Rd., Suite 248, Baltimore, MD 21210-1807, ☎ 410/323–4416 or 800/638–7640).

HOSTELING

In the United States, contact **Hostelling International–American Youth Hostels** (✉ 733 15th St. NW, Suite 840, Washington, DC 20005, ☎ 202/783–6161 or 800/444–6111 for reservations at selected hostels, FAX 202/783–6171); in Canada, **Hostelling International–Canada** (✉ 205 Catherine St., Suite 400, Ottawa, Ontario K2P 1C3, ☎ 613/237–7884); and in the United Kingdom, the **Youth Hostel Association of England and Wales** (✉ Trevelyan House, 8 St. Stephen's Hill, St. Albans, Hertfordshire AL1 2DY, ☎ 01727/855215 or 01727/845047). Membership (in the U.S., $25; in Canada, C$26.75; in the U.K., £9.30) gives you access to 5,000 hostels in 77 countries that charge $5–$30 per person per night.

I.D. CARDS

To be eligible for discounts on transportation and admissions, get either the **International Student**

Identity Card, if you're a bona fide student, or the **GO 25: International Youth Travel Card,** if you're not a student but under age 26. Each includes basic travel-accident and illness coverage, plus a toll-free travel hot line. In the United States, either card costs $18; apply through the Council on International Educational Exchange (☞ Organizations, *below*). In Canada, cards are available for $15 each ($16 by mail) from Travel Cuts (☞ Organizations, *below*), and in the United Kingdom for £5 each at student unions and student travel companies.

ORGANIZATIONS

A major contact is the **Council on International Educational Exchange** (mail orders only: ☒ CIEE, 205 E. 42nd St., 16th floor, New York, NY 10017, ☎ 212/822–2600). The **Educational Travel Centre** (☒ 438 N. Frances St., Madison, WI 53703, ☎ 608/256–5551 or 800/747–5551, FAX 608/256–2042) offers rail passes and low-cost airline tickets, mostly for flights that depart from Chicago.

PUBLICATIONS

Check out the ***Berkeley Guide to Great Britain and Ireland*** (available in bookstores; or contact Fodor's Travel Publications, ☎ 800/533–6478; $17.50).

T

TELEPHONE MATTERS

The country code for the United Kingdom is 44, and for the Republic of Ireland, 353. For local access numbers abroad, contact **AT&T** USADirect (☎ 800/874–4000), **MCI** Call USA (☎ 800/444–4444), or **Sprint** Express (☎ 800/793–1153).

TOUR OPERATORS

Among the companies that sell tours and packages to Great Britain, the following are nationally known, have a proven reputation, and offer plenty of options.

GROUP TOURS

SUPER-DELUXE➢ **Abercrombie & Kent** (☒ 1520 Kensington Rd., Oak Brook, IL 60521-2141, ☎ 708/954–2944 or 800/323–7308, FAX 708/954–3324) and **Travcoa** (☒ Box 2630, 2350 S.E. Bristol St., Newport Beach, CA 92660, ☎ 714/476–2800 or 800/992–2003, FAX 714/476–2538).

DELUXE➢ **Globus** (5301 S. Federal Circle, Littleton, CO 80123-2980, ☎ 303/797–2800 or 800/221–0090, FAX 303/795–0962), **Maupintour** (☒ Box 807, 1515 St. Andrews Dr., Lawrence, KS 66047, ☎ 913/843–1211 or 800/255–4266, FAX 913/843–8351), and **Tauck Tours** (☒ Box 5027, 276 Post Rd. W, Westport, CT 06881, ☎ 203/226–6911 or 800/468–2825, FAX 203/221–6828).

FIRST CLASS➢ **Brendan Tours** (☒ 15137 Califa St., Van Nuys, CA 91411, ☎ 818/785–9696 or 800/421–8446, FAX 818/902–9876), **British Airways Holidays** (☎ 800/247–9297), **Caravan Tours** (☒ 401 N. Michigan Ave., Chicago, IL 60611, ☎ 312/321–9800 or 800/227–2826), **CIE Tours** (☒ Box 501, 100 Hanover Ave., Cedar Knolls, NJ 07927-0501, ☎ 201/292–3899 or 800/243–8687), **Collette Tours** (☒ 162 Middle St., Pawtucket, RI 02860, ☎ 401/728–3805 or 800/832–4656, FAX 401/728–1380), **Gadabout Tours** (☒ 700 E. Tahquitz Canyon Way, Palm Springs, CA 92262, ☎ 619/325–5556 or 800/952–5068), **Insight International Tours** (☒ 745 Atlantic Ave., #720, Boston, MA 02111, ☎ 617/482–2000 or 800/582–8380, FAX 617/482–2884 or 800/622–5015), and **Trafalgar Tours** (☒ 11 E. 26th St., New York, NY 10010, ☎ 212/689–8977 or 800/854–0103, FAX 800/457–6644).

BUDGET➢ **Cosmos** (☞ Globus, *above*) and **Trafalgar Tours** (☞ *above*).

PACKAGES

Just about every airline that flies to Great Britain sells packages that include round-trip airfare and hotel accommodations. Carriers to contact are **Adventure Vacations** (☒ 10612 Beaver Dam Rd., Hunt Valley, MD 21030-2205, ☎ 410/785–3500 or 800/638–9040, FAX 410/584–2771), **American Airlines Fly AAway Vacations** (☎ 800/321–2121), **British Airways Holidays** (☞ *above*), **Continental Vacations** (☎ 800/634–5555), **Delta Dream Vacations** (☎ 800/872–7786), and **United Vacations** (☎ 800/328–6877).

For independent self-drive itineraries, contact **Budget WorldClass Drive** (☎ 800/527–0700; in the U.K., 0800/181181).

FROM THE U.K.

Contact **Highlife** (✉ Box 139, Leeds LS2 7TE, ☎ 0800/700–400) for hotel and country-house packages and for theater and entertainment; **Wallace Arnold Tours** (✉ Gelderd Rd., Leeds LS12 6DH, ☎ 0181/686–4962) arranges coach tours with hotel accommodations, and **Hoseasons Holidays** (✉ Sunway House, Lowestoft NR32 2LW, ☎ 01502/500–500) arranges holidays in lodges, cottages, and chalets.

THEME TRIPS

Travel Contacts (✉ Box 173, Camberley, GU15 1YE, England, ☎ 011/44/1/27667–7217, FAX 011/44/1/2766–3477), which represents 150 tour operators, can satisfy virtually any special interest in Great Britain. **Great British Vacations** (✉ 4800 S.W. Griffith Dr., #125, Beaverton, OR 97005, ☎ 503/643–8080 or 800/452–8434) creates custom-designed itineraries that include walking and visiting gardens and stately homes.

ADVENTURE➢ **Himalayan Travel** (✉ 112 Prospect St., Stamford, CT 06901, ☎ 203/359–3711 or 800/225–2380, FAX 203/359–3669) operates a range of adventure tours. **Francine Atkins' Scotland Ireland** (✉ 2 Ross Court, Trophy Club, TX 76262, ☎ 817/491–1105 or 800/742–0355, FAX 817/491–2025) arranges fishing, golfing, shooting, and hunting trips.

ANTIQUES➢ **Travel Keys Tours** (✉ Box 162266, Sacramento, CA 95816-2266, ☎ 916/452–5200) specializes in customized tours to the antique fairs and flea markets of England and France.

ARCHAEOLOGY➢ **Far Horizons Archaeological & Cultural Trips** (✉ Box 91900, Albuquerque, NM 87199-1900, ☎ 505/343–9400 or 800/552–4575, FAX 505/343–8076) explores England's prehistoric stone ruins and medieval castles.

BARGE/RIVER CRUISES➢ For barge cruising through the canals of England, contact **Abercrombie & Kent** (☞ Group Tours, *above*), **Alden Yacht Charters** (✉ 1909 Alden Landing, Portsmouth, RI 02871, ☎ 401/683–1782 or 800/662–2628, FAX 401/683–3668), **European Waterways** (✉ 140 E. 56th St., #4C, New York, NY 10022, ☎ 212/688–9489 or 800/217–4447, FAX 212/688–3778 or 800/296–4554), **Kemwel's Premier Selections** (✉ 106 Calvert St., Harrison, NY 10528, ☎ 914/835–5555 or 800/234–4000, FAX 914/835–5449), and **Le Boat** (☎ 201/342–1838 or 800/922–0291).

BEER➢ **MIR Corporation** (✉ 85 S. Washington St., #210, Seattle, WA 98104, ☎ 206/624–7289 or 800/424–7289, FAX 206/624–7360) has packages for beer lovers.

BICYCLING➢ Bike tours are available from **Backroads** (✉ 1516 5th St., Berkeley, CA 94710-1740, ☎ 510/577–1555 or 800/462–2848, FAX 510/527–1444), **Butterfield & Robinson** (✉ 70 Bond St., Toronto, Ontario, Canada M5B 1X3, ☎ 416/864–1354 or 800/678–1147, FAX 416/864–0541), and **Uniquely Europe** (✉ 2819 1st Ave., #280, Seattle, WA 98121-1113, ☎ 206/441–8682 or 800/426–3615, FAX 206/441–8862).

COOKING➢ **Cuisine International** (✉ Box 25228, Dallas, TX 75225, ☎ 214/373–1161 or FAX 214/373–1162) has weeklong cooking programs taught by famous chefs in Oxford.

FISHING➢ Try **Rod & Reel Adventures** (✉ 3507 Tully Rd., #B6, Modesto, CA 95356-1052, ☎ 209/524–7775 or 800/356–6982, FAX 209/524–1220).

GOLF➢ **Francine Atkins' Scotland Ireland** (☞ Adventure, *above*), **Golf International** (✉ 275 Madison Ave., New York, NY 10016, ☎ 212/986–9176 or 800/833–1389, FAX 212/986–3720), **ITC Golf Tours** (✉ 4134 Atlantic Ave., #205, Long Beach, CA 90807, ☎ 310/595–6905 or 800/257–4981), and **Stine's Golftrips** (✉ Box 2314, Winter Haven, FL 33883-2314, ☎ 813/324–1300 or 800/428–1940, FAX 941/325–0384) offer several itineraries in

England and arrange customized itineraries.

HOMES AND GARDENS➢ **Coopersmith's England** (✉ Box 900, Inverness, CA 94937, ☎ 415/669–1914, FAX 415/669–1942) wines and dines you with gourmet meals and books your accommodations in castles, historic country inns, and manor houses. **Expo Garden Tours** (✉ 101 Sunrise Hill Rd., Norwalk, CT 06851, ☎ 203/840–1441 or 800/448–2685, FAX 203/840–1224) visits the annual Chelsea Flower Show.

HORSEBACK RIDING➢ **FITS Equestrian** (✉ 685 Lateen Rd., Solvang, CA 93463, ☎ 805/688–9494 or 800/666–3487, FAX 805/688–2943) is a top horseback-riding operator with year-round departures and tours for every level of rider.

LEARNING➢ **Earthwatch** (✉ Box 403, 680 Mount Auburn St., Watertown, MA 02272, ☎ 617/926–8200 or 800/776–0188, FAX 617/926–8532) recruits volunteers to serve in its EarthCorps as short-term assistants to scientists on research expeditions. **National Audobon Society** (✉ 700 Broadway, New York, NY 10003, ☎ 212/979–3066, FAX 212/353–0190) has a train tour on board the *Royal Scotsman.* **Smithsonian Study Tours and Seminars** (✉ 1100 Jefferson Dr. SW, Room 3045, MRC 702, Washington, DC 20560, ☎ 202/357–4700, FAX 202/633–9250) has tours that showcase Great Britain's natural history and culture.

NATURAL HISTORY➢ **Esplanade Tours** (✉ 581 Boylston St., Boston, MA 02116, ☎ 617/266–7465 or 800/426–5492, FAX 617/262–9829) sells natural-history cruises.

NORTHERN ENGLAND➢ **Saranjan Tours** (✉ 12865 N.E. 85th St., Ste. 102, Kirkland, WA 98033, ☎ 206/869–8586, FAX 206/869–8586) offers private escorted tours from York to Bamburgh and Grasmere, with stops at Castle Howard and many other attractions, including the Ryedale Music Festival.

SPAS➢ **Spa-Finders** (✉ 91 5th Ave., #301, New York, NY 10003-3039, ☎ 212/924–6800 or 800/255–7727) represents several spas in England.

TENNIS➢ **Championship Tennis Tours** (✉ 7350 E. Stetson Dr., #106, Scottsdale, AZ 85251, ☎ 602/990–8760 or 800/468–3664, FAX 602/990–8744), **Sportstours** (✉ 2301 Collins Ave., #A1540, Miami Beach, FL 33139, ☎ 800/879–8647, FAX 305/535–0008), and **Steve Furgal's International Tennis Tours** (✉ 11828 Rancho Bernardo Rd., #123-305, San Diego, CA 92128, ☎ 619/487–7777 or 800/258–3664) have packages to Wimbledon, held each summer in London.

VILLA RENTALS➢ Contact **Villas International** (✉ 605 Market St., San Francisco, CA 94105, ☎ 415/281–0910 or 800/221–2260, FAX 415/281–0919).

WALKING➢ **Above the Clouds Trekking** (✉ Box 398, Worcester, MA 01602, ☎ 508/799–4499 or 800/233–4499, FAX 508/797–4779) has walking-hiking tours through the Cotswolds and Cornwall. Cotswolds walking tours also are available from **Abercrombie & Kent** (☞ Group Tours, *above*), **Backroads** (☞ *above*), **Euro-Bike Tours** (✉ Box 990, De Kalb, IL 60115, ☎ 800/321–6060, FAX 815/758–8851), and **Uniquely Europe** (☞ Bicycling, *above*). Cotswolds, Lake District, and Cornwall coast tours are run by and **Country Walkers** (✉ Box 180, Waterbury, VT 05676-0180, ☎ 802/244–1387 or 800/464–9255, FAX 802/244–5661). **English Adventures** (✉ 803 Front Range Rd., Littleton, CO 80120, ☎ FAX 303/797–2365 or 800/253–3485) and **English Lakeland Ramblers** (✉ 18 Stuyvesant Oval, #1A, New York, NY 10009, ☎ 212/505–1020 or 800/724–8801, FAX 212/979–5342) hike and walk the English Lake District with visits to castles and the homes of Wordsworth and Beatrix Potter. **Mountain Travel-Sobek** (✉ 6420 Fairmount Ave., El Cerrito, CA 94530, ☎ 510/527–8100 or 800/227–2384, FAX 510/525–7710) roams northern England and Wales. **Wilderness Travel** (✉ 801 Allston Way, Berkeley, CA 94710, ☎ 510/548–0420 or 800/368–2794, FAX

510/548–0347) operates coast-to-coast and Cotswolds walking and hiking trips.

PUBLICATIONS

Contact the USTOA (☞ Organizations, *above*) for its **"Smart Traveler's Planning Kit."** Pamphlets in the kit include the "Worldwide Tour and Vacation Package Finder," "How to Select a Tour or Vacation Package," and information on the organization's consumer protection plan. Also get copy of the Better Business Bureau's **"Tips on Travel Packages"** (✉ Publication 24-195, 4200 Wilson Blvd., Arlington, VA 22203; $2).

TRAIN TRAVEL

DISCOUNT PASSES

BritRail Passes are available from most travel agents or from **BritRail Travel International** (✉ 1500 Broadway, New York, NY 10036, ☏ 212/575–2667 or 800/677–8585; ✉ 94 Cumberland St., Toronto, Ontario M5R 1A3, ☏ 416/482–1777). In London, contact the **British Rail Travel Centre** (✉ Euston Station, London NW1 1DF, ☏ 0171/387–7070).

TRAVEL AGENCIES

For names of reputable agencies in your area, contact the **American Society of Travel Agents** (✉ ASTA, 1101 King St., Suite 200, Alexandria, VA 22314, ☏ 703/739–2782), the **Association of Canadian Travel Agents** (✉ Suite 201, 1729 Bank St., Ottawa, Ontario K1V 7Z5, ☏ 613/521–0474, FAX 613/521–0805) or the **Association of British Travel Agents** (✉ 55-57 Newman St., London W1P 4AH, ☏ 0171/637–2444, FAX 0171/637–0713).

V

VISITOR INFORMATION

Contact the **British Tourist Authority** (BTA).

In the United States: ✉ 551 5th Ave., Suite 701, New York, NY 10176, ☏ 212/986–2200; outside 212 and 718 area codes, 800/462–2748; FAX 212/986–1188.

In Canada: ✉ 111 Avenue Rd., Suite 450, Toronto, Ontario M5R 3J8, ☏ 416/925–6326.

In the United Kingdom: ✉ Thames Tower, Black's Rd., London W6 9EL, ☏ 0181/846–9000.

In London go in person to the **London Tourist Information Centre** at Victoria Station Forecourt for general information Monday–Saturday 8–7 and Sunday 8–5, or to the **British Travel Centre** (✉ 12 Regent St., SW1Y 4PQ) for travel, hotel, and entertainment information weekdays 9–6:30, weekends 10–4. The **London Travel Service** (✉ High Road, Broxbourne, Hertfordshire EN10 7DT, ☏ 01992/456–177) offers travel, hotel, and tour reservations. The office is open weekdays 9–5:30, Saturday 9–5.

The London Tourist Board's **Visitorcall** (☏ 0839/123456) phone guide to London gives information about events, theater, museums, transport, shopping, and restaurants. A three-month events calendar (☏ 0839/401279) and an annual version (☏ 0839/401278) are available by fax (set fax machine to polling mode, or press start/receive after the tone). Visitorcall charges a rate of 39p–49p per minute, depending on the time of the call.

W

WEATHER

For current conditions and forecasts, plus the local time and helpful travel tips, call the **Weather Channel Connection** (☏ 900/932–8437; 95¢ per minute) from a Touch-Tone phone.

The ***International Traveler's Weather Guide*** (✉ Weather Press, Box 660606, Sacramento, CA 95866, ☏ 916/974–0201 or 800/972–0201; $10.95 includes shipping), written by two meteorologists, provides month-by-month information on temperature, humidity, and precipitation in more than 175 cities worldwide.

SMART TRAVEL TIPS A TO Z

Basic Information on Traveling in Great Britain & Savvy Tips to Make Your Trip a Breeze

A

AIR TRAVEL

If time is an issue, **always look for nonstop flights,** which require no change of plane. If possible, **avoid connecting flights,** which stop at least once and can involve a change of plane, even though the flight number remains the same; if the first leg is late, the second waits.

For better service, **fly smaller or regional carriers,** which often have higher passenger satisfaction ratings. Sometimes they have such in-flight amenities as leather seats or greater legroom and they often have better food.

CUTTING COSTS

The Sunday travel section of most newspapers is a good place to look for deals.

MAJOR AIRLINES➢ The least-expensive airfares from the major airlines are priced for round-trip travel and are subject to restrictions. Usually, you must **book in advance and buy the ticket within 24 hours** to get cheaper fares, and you may have to **stay over a Saturday night.** The lowest fare is subject to availability, and only a small percentage of the plane's total seats is sold at that price. It's smart to **call a number of airlines, and when you are quoted a good price, book it on the spot**—the same fare may not be available on the same flight the next day. Airlines generally allow you to change your return date for a $25 to $50 fee. If you don't use your ticket, you can apply the cost toward the purchase of a new ticket, again for a small charge. However, most low-fare tickets are nonrefundable. To get the lowest airfare, **check different routings.** If your destination has more than one gateway, **compare prices to different airports.**

FROM THE U.K.➢ To save money on flights, **look into an APEX or Super-Pex ticket.** APEX tickets must be booked in advance and have certain restrictions. Super-PEX tickets can be purchased right at the airport.

CONSOLIDATORS➢ Consolidators buy tickets for scheduled flights at reduced rates from the airlines, then sell them at prices below the lowest available from the airlines directly—usually without advance restrictions. Sometimes you can even get your money back if you need to return the ticket. Carefully read the fine print detailing penalties for changes and cancellations. If you doubt the reliability of a consolidator, **confirm your reservation with the airline.**

ALOFT

AIRLINE FOOD➢ If you hate airline food, **ask for special meals when booking.** These can be vegetarian, low-cholesterol, or kosher, for example; commonly prepared to order in smaller quantities than standard fare, they can be tastier.

JET LAG➢ To avoid this syndrome, which occurs when travel disrupts your body's natural cycles, try to maintain a normal routine. At night, **get some sleep.** By day, move about the cabin to **stretch your legs, eat light meals, and drink water—not alcohol.**

SMOKING➢ Smoking is not allowed on flights of six hours or less within the continental United States. Smoking is also prohibited on flights within Canada. For U.S. flights longer than six hours or international flights, **contact your carrier regarding their smoking policy.** Some carriers have prohibited smoking throughout their system; others allow smoking only on certain routes or even certain departures of that route.

WITHIN GREAT BRITAIN

Because Britain is such a small country, internal air travel is much less important there than in the United States. Broadly speaking, for trips of less than 200 miles, the train is quicker given the time required to get to and from city centers and airports, compared with the centrally based rail stations. Flying tends to cost more, and many internal U.K. flights exist primarily as feeders from provincial airports into Heathrow and Gatwick for international flights. For trips of more than 200 miles—for example, between London and Glasgow or Edinburgh—or where a sea crossing is involved, to places such as the Isle of Man, Belfast, the Channel Islands, or the Scottish islands, air travel has a considerable time advantage.

B

BICYCLING

Bikes are banned from motorways and most dual carriageways or main trunk roads, but on side roads and country lanes, the bike is one of the best ways to explore Britain. You will find the Ordnance Survey 1:50,000 maps invaluable. Some parts of Britain have bicycle routes in towns and through parts of the countryside; for example, in the Peak District National Parks, bikes can be hired by the day for use on special traffic-free trails. Cyclists can legally use public bridleways—green, unsurfaced tracks reserved for horses, walkers, and cyclists.

BUS TRAVEL

Britain has a comprehensive bus (short-haul) and coach (long-distance) network, which offers an inexpensive way of seeing the country. Coaches are much cheaper than trains, usually about half the price or even less, but are generally slower, although some motorway services with the modern Rapide coaches reduce the margin considerably. Seats on these supercoaches are comfortable, with meal and rest stops usually arranged on longer trips. (Some coaches have toilet facilities on board.)

The British equivalent to Greyhound is **National Express,** which with its Scottish associate, **Caledonian Express,** is by far the largest British operator. Victoria Coach Station in London is the hub of the National Express network, serving around 1,500 destinations. Information is available from any of the company's 2,500 agents nationwide. There are also National Express sales offices at London's Heathrow and Gatwick airport coach stations.

The classic British double-decker buses still operate on many of the routes of Britain's extensive network of local bus services. It's difficult to plan a journey by country bus, because privatization of lines has led to the development of many small companies and schedules are constantly changing. But the local bus station wherever you're staying, and maybe the local tourist information center, will have precise information. Most companies offer day or week "Explorer" or "Rover" unlimited-travel tickets, and those in popular tourist areas invariably operate special scenic tours in summer. The top deck of a stately double-decker bus is a great place from which to view the surrounding countryside.

BUSINESS HOURS

BANKS

Most banks are open weekdays 9:30–4:30. Some have Thursday evening hours, and a few are open Saturday morning.

SHOPS

Usual business hours are Monday–Saturday 9–5:30; on Sunday, small shops stay open all day if they wish to, and larger stores now can too, since the Sunday trading laws were relaxed in late 1994. Outside the main centers, most shops close at 1 PM once a week, often Wednesday or Thursday. In small villages, many also close for lunch. In large cities—especially London—department stores stay open late (usually until 7:30 or 8) one day a week.

PUBS

Pubs are generally open Monday–Saturday 11 AM–11 PM, Sunday 11 AM–10:30 PM.

NATIONAL HOLIDAYS

ENGLAND AND WALES➢ January 1; March 28 (Good Friday); March 31 (Easter Monday); May 1 (May Day); May 6, 27 (Spring Bank Holidays); August 26 (Summer Bank Holiday); December 25–26.

SCOTLAND➢ January 1–2; March 28, 31; May 27 (Spring Bank Holiday); August 26; December 25–26.

C

CAMERAS, CAMCORDERS, & COMPUTERS

IN TRANSIT

Always **keep your film, tape, or disks out of the sun;** never put these on the dashboard of a car. Carry an extra supply of batteries, and **be prepared to turn on your camera, camcorder, or laptop computer for security personnel** to prove that it's real.

X-RAYS

Always **ask for hand inspection at security.** Such requests are virtually always honored at U.S. airports and are usually accommodated abroad. Photographic film becomes clouded after successive exposure to airport x-ray machines. Videotape and computer disks are not by X-rays, but **keep your tapes and disks away from metal detectors.**

CUSTOMS

Before departing, **register your foreign-made camera or laptop with U.S. Customs.** If your equipment is U.S.-made, call the consulate of the country you'll be visiting to find out whether it should be registered with local customs upon arrival.

VIDEO

Prerecorded videotape sold in Great Britain is based on the SECAM standard, which will not play back in the United States. Blank tapes bought in Great Britain can be used for camcorder taping, but they are pricey. Some U.S. audiovisual shops convert foreign tapes to U.S. standards; contact an electronics dealer to find the nearest.

CAR RENTAL

CUTTING COSTS

To get the best deal, **book through a travel agent who is willing to shop around.** Ask your agent to **look for fly-drive packages,** which also save you money, and **ask if local taxes are included** in the rental or fly-drive price. These can be as high as 20% in some destinations. Don't forget to find out about required deposits, cancellation penalties, drop-off charges, and the cost of any required insurance coverage.

Also **ask your travel agent about a company's customer-service record.** How has it responded to late plane arrivals and vehicle mishaps? Are there often lines at the rental counter, and—if you're traveling during a holiday period—does a confirmed reservation guarantee you a car?

Always **find out what equipment is standard** at your destination before specifying what you want; automatic transmission and air-conditioning are usually optional—and very expensive. You may, however, consider paying extra for an automatic if you are unfamiliar with manual transmissions. Driving on the "wrong" side of the road will probably be enough to worry about.

Be sure to **look into wholesalers**—companies that do not own their own fleets but rent in bulk from those that do and often offer better rates than traditional car-rental operations. Prices are best during off-peak periods; rentals booked through wholesalers must be paid for before you leave the United States.

INSURANCE

When driving a rented car, you are generally responsible for any damage to or loss of the rental vehicle. Before you rent, **see what coverage you already have** under the terms of your personal auto insurance policy and credit cards.

If you do not have auto insurance or an umbrella insurance policy that covers damage to third parties, purchasing CDW or LDW is highly recommended.

LICENSE REQUIREMENTS

In Great Britain your own driver's license is acceptable. An International Driver's Permit is available from the American or Canadian automobile associations, or, in the United Kingdom, from the AA or RAC.

SURCHARGES

Before you pick up a car in one city and leave it in another, **ask about drop-off charges or one-way service fees,** which can be substantial. Note, too, that some rental agencies charge extra if you return the car before the time specified on your contract. To avoid a hefty refueling fee, **fill the**

tank just before you turn in the car—but be aware that gas stations near the rental outlet may overcharge.

THE CHANNEL TUNNEL

The Channel Tunnel provides the fastest route across the Channel—35 minutes from Folkestone to Calais, 60 minutes from motorway to motorway, or 3 hours from Waterloo, London, to Paris, Gare du Nord. It consists of two large 50-kilometer (31-mile) long tunnels for trains, one in each direction, linked by a smaller service tunnel running between them.

Le Shuttle, a special car, bus, and truck train, operates a continuous loop, with trains departing every 15 minutes at peak times and at least once every 75 minutes through the night. No reservations are necessary, although tickets may be purchased in advance from travel agents. Most passengers travel in their own car, staying with the vehicle throughout the "crossing," with progress updates via radio and display screens. Motorcyclists park their bikes in a separate section with its own passenger compartment, while foot passengers must book passage by coach. At press time, prices for a one-day round-trip ticket began at £49–£99 for a car and its occupants. Prices for a five-day round-trip ticket began at £75 (for a pre-6 AM start and £115 for departures anytime after 6 AM).

Eurostar operates high-speed passenger-only trains, which whisk riders between new stations in Paris (Gare du Nord) and London (Waterloo) in three hours and between London and Brussels (Midi) in 3¼ hours. At press time, fares were one-way first class to either Paris or Brussels for £110 and one-way economy at £77.50.

The Tunnel is reached from exit 11a of the M20 and exit 12 of the A20. Tickets for either tunnel service can be purchased in advance (☞ Important Contacts A to Z, *above*).

CHILDREN & TRAVEL

When traveling with children, **plan ahead** and **involve your youngsters** as you outline your trip. When packing, **include a supply of things to keep them busy** en route. On sightseeing days, try to **schedule activities of special interest to your children,** like a trip to a zoo or a playground. If you **plan your itinerary around seasonal festivals,** you'll never lack for things to do. In addition, **check local newspapers for special events** mounted by public libraries, museums, and parks.

BABY-SITTING

For recommended local sitters, **check with your hotel desk.**

DRIVING

If you are renting a car, don't forget to **arrange for a car seat when you reserve.** Sometimes they're free.

FLYING

Always **ask about discounted children's fares.** On international flights, infants under 2 not occupying a seat generally travel free or for 10% of the accompanying adult's fare; the fare for children ages 2–11 is usually half to two-thirds of the adult fare. On domestic flights, children under 2 not occupying a seat travel free, and older children are charged at the lowest applicable adult rate.

BAGGAGE➢ In general, the adult baggage allowance applies to children paying half or more of the adult fare. If you are traveling with an infant, **ask about carry-on allowances** before departure. In general, for infants charged 10% of the adult fare you are allowed one carry-on bag and a collapsible stroller; you may be limited to less if the flight is full.

SAFETY SEATS➢ According to the FAA, it's a good idea to **use safety seats aloft** for children weighing less than 40 pounds.

FACILITIES➢ When making your reservation, **request for children's meals or freestanding bassinets** if you need them; the latter are available only to those seated at the bulkhead, where there's enough legroom. If you don't need a bassinet, **think twice before requesting bulkhead seats**—the only storage space for in-flight necessities is in inconveniently distant overhead bins.

GAMES

In local toy stores, look for travel versions of popular games such as Trouble, Sorry, and Monopoly ($5–$8).

LODGING

Most hotels allow children under a certain age to stay in their parents' room at no extra charge; others charge them as extra adults. Be sure to **ask about the cutoff age.**

CUSTOMS & DUTIES

To speed your clearance through customs, **keep receipts for all your purchases abroad.** If you feel that you've been incorrectly or unfairly charged a duty, you can **appeal assessments in dispute.** First ask to see a supervisor. If you are still unsatisfied, **write to the port director** your point of entry, sending your customs receipt and any other appropriate documentation. The address will be listed on your receipt. If you still don't get satisfaction, you can take your case to customs headquarters in Washington.

IN GREAT BRITAIN

There are two levels of duty-free allowance for travelers entering Great Britain: one for goods bought outside the EU, the other for goods bought in the EU (Belgium, Greece, the Netherlands, Denmark, Italy, Portugal, France, the Irish Republic, Spain, Germany, or Luxembourg).

Of goods purchased outside the EU, you may import duty-free: 200 cigarettes or 100 cigarillos or 50 cigars or 250 grams of tobacco; two liters of table wine and, in addition, (a) one liter of alcohol over 22% by volume (most spirits), (b) two liters of alcohol under 22% by volume (fortified or sparkling wine), or (c) two more liters of table wine; 60 milliliters of perfume; ¼ liter of toilet water; and other goods up to a value of £136, but not more than 50 liters of beer or 25 cigarette lighters.

If you are entering the United Kingdom from another EU country, you no longer need to pass through customs. If you plan to bring large quantities of alcohol or tobacco, check in advance on EU limits with Customs and Excise, ☎ 0181/910–3600.

No animals or pets of any kind can be brought into the United Kingdom without a lengthy quarantine. The penalties are severe and strictly enforced. Similarly, fresh meats, plants and vegetables, illegal drugs, and firearms and ammunition may not be brought into Great Britain.

You will face no customs formalities if you enter Scotland or Wales from any other part of the United Kingdom, though anyone coming from Northern Ireland should expect a security check.

IN THE U.S.

You may bring home $400 worth of foreign goods duty-free if you've been out of the country for at least 48 hours and haven't already used the $400 allowance, or any part of it, in the past 30 days.

Travelers 21 or older may bring back 1 liter of alcohol duty-free, provided the beverage laws of the state through which they reenter the United States allow it. In addition, regardless of their age, they are allowed 100 non-Cuban cigars and 200 cigarettes. Antiques and works of art more than 100 years old are duty-free.

Duty-free, travelers may mail packages valued at up to $200 to themselves and up to $100 to others, with a limit of one parcel per addressee per day (and no alcohol or tobacco products or perfume valued at more than $5); on the outside, the package should be labeled as being either for personal use or an unsolicited gift, and a list of its contents and their retail value should be attached. Mailed items do not affect your duty-free allowance on your return.

IN CANADA

If you've been out of Canada for at least seven days, you may bring in C$500 worth of goods duty-free. If you've been away for fewer than seven days but for more than 48 hours, the duty-free allowance drops to C$200; if your trip lasts between 24 and 48 hours, the allowance is C$50. You cannot pool allowances with family members. Goods claimed under the C$500 exemption may follow you by mail; those claimed under the lesser exemptions must accompany you.

Alcohol and tobacco products may be included in the seven-day and 48-hour exemptions but not in the 24-hour exemption. If you meet the age requirements of the province or territory through which you reenter Canada, you may bring in, duty-free, 1.14 liters (40 imperial ounces) of wine or liquor *or* 24 12-ounce cans or bottles of beer or ale. If you are 16 or older, you may bring in, duty-free, 200 cigarettes, 50 cigars or cigarillos, and 400 tobacco sticks or 400 grams of manufactured tobacco. Alcohol and tobacco must accompany you on your return.

An unlimited number of gifts with a value of up to C$60 each may be mailed to Canada duty-free. These do not affect your duty-free allowance on your return. Label the package "Unsolicited Gift—Value Under $60." Alcohol and tobacco are excluded.

D

DINING

Restaurants in Britain can be outrageously expensive for what they offer. Be very sure to **check the menu posted outside** almost all establishments before venturing inside. As a general rule of thumb, wine bars and bistros offer reasonably priced meals in interesting surroundings, and you will find excellent budget food at lunchtime in good pubs and inns. **Be careful of the prices of drinks** in a restaurant. Many restaurants will charge you as much for a glass of mineral water as a whole 2-liter bottle would cost you in a supermarket.

MEALTIMES

Breakfast is generally served between 7:30 and 9 and lunch between noon and 2. Tea—often a meal in itself—is taken between 4 and 5:30, dinner or supper between 7:30 and 9:30, sometimes earlier, seldom later except in large cities. High tea, at about 6, replaces dinner in some areas.

DISABILITIES & ACCESSIBILITY

When discussing accessibility with an operator or reservationist, **ask hard questions.** Are there any stairs, inside *or* out? Are there grab bars next to the toilet *and* in the shower/tub? How wide is the doorway to the room? To the bathroom? For the most extensive facilities, meeting the latest legal specifications, **opt for newer accommodations,** which more often have been designed with access in mind. Older properties or ships must usually be retrofitted and may offer more limited facilities as a result. Be sure to **discuss your needs before booking.**

DISCOUNTS & DEALS

You shouldn't have to pay for a discount. In fact, you may already be eligible for all kinds of savings. Here are some time-honored strategies for getting the best deal.

LOOK IN YOUR WALLET

When you **use your credit card to make travel purchases,** you may get free travel-accident insurance, collision damage insurance, medical or legal assistance, depending on the card and bank that issued it. Visa and MasterCard provide one or more of these services, so **get a copy of your card's travel benefits.** If you are a member of the AAA or an oil-company-sponsored road-assistance plan, always **ask hotel or car-rental reservationists for auto-club discounts.** Some clubs offer additional discounts on tours, cruises, or admission to attractions. And don't forget that auto-club membership entitles you to free maps and trip-planning services.

SENIORS CITIZENS & STUDENTS

As a senior-citizen traveler, you may be eligible for special rates, but you should **mention your senior-citizen status up front.** If you're a students or under 26 can also get discounts, especially if you have an official ID card (☞ Senior-Citizen Discounts *and* Students on the Road, *below*).

DIAL FOR DOLLARS

To save money, **look into "1-800" discount reservations services,** which often have lower rates. These services use their buying power to get a better price on hotels, airline tickets, and sometimes even car rentals. When booking a room, always **call the hotel's local toll-free number** (if one is available) rather than the central reservations number—you'll often get a better price. Ask the reservationist about special packages or corporate rates, which are usually available even if you're not traveling on business.

JOIN A CLUB?

Discount clubs can be a legitimate source of savings, but you must use the participating hotels and visit the participating attractions in order to realize any benefits. Remember, too, that you have to pay a fee to join, so **determine if you'll save enough to warrant your membership fee.** Before booking with a club, **make sure the hotel or other supplier isn't offering a better deal.**

GET A GUARANTEE

When shopping for the best deal on hotels and car rentals, **look for guaranteed exchange rates,** which protect you against a falling dollar. With your rate locked in, you won't pay more even if the price goes up in the local currency.

DRIVING

With well over 55 million inhabitants in a country about the size of California, Britain has some of the most crowded roads in the world. But away from the towns and cities, you can find miles of little-used roads and lanes where driving can be a real pleasure—and adventure.

MOTORAIL

One way to combine the convenience of the car with the speed of the train, useful for travel between Britain and the rest of Europe, is Motorail. The car is put on a specially designed rail car while passengers relax in comfortable coaches or, in some cases, overnight sleeping compartments. Check for the latest services available. Book in advance through British Rail agencies.

RULES OF THE ROAD

Drive on the left in Britain; this takes a bit of getting used to, and it's much easier if you're driving a British car where the steering and mirrors are designed for U.K. conditions. Study your map before leaving the airport, and be sure to give yourself plenty of time to adjust. The use of seat belts is obligatory in the front seat and in the back seat where they exist.

Speed limits are complicated, and traffic police can be hard on speeders, especially in urban areas. In those areas, the limit (shown on circular red signs) is generally 30 mph, but 40 mph on some main roads. In rural areas the limit is 60 mph on ordinary roads and 70 mph on motorways (☞ *below*). At traffic circles ("roundabouts"), circulation is clockwise, and entering motorists must give way to cars coming from their right.

TYPES OF ROADS

There's a very good network of superhighways (motorways) and divided highways (dual carriageways) throughout most of Britain, though in remoter parts, especially Wales and Scotland, travel is noticeably slower. Motorways (with the prefix *M*), shown in blue on most maps and road signs, are mainly two or three lanes in each direction, without any right-hand turns. Dual carriageways with the prefix *A*, shown on maps as thick red lines, have both traffic lights and traffic circles, and right turns are sometimes permitted. Turnoffs are often marked by highway numbers, rather than place names, so it's a good idea to always take note of connecting road numbers.

The vast network of lesser roads, for the most part old coach and turnpike roads, might make your trip take twice the time and show you twice as much. Minor roads drawn in yellow or white, unlettered and unnumbered, are the ancient lanes and byways, a superb way of discovering the real Britain. Some of these are potholed switchbacks, littered with blind corners and cowpats, and barely wide enough for one car, let alone for two to pass. Be prepared to reverse into a passing place if you meet an oncoming car or truck.

Service stations on motorways are located at regular intervals and are usually open 24 hours a day; elsewhere they usually close overnight, and by 6 PM and all day Sunday in country areas.

I

INSURANCE

Travel insurance can protect your monetary investment, replace your luggage and its contents, or provide for medical coverage should you fall ill during your trip. Most tour operators, travel agents, and insurance agents sell specialized health-and-accident, flight, trip-cancellation, and luggage insurance as well as comprehensive policies with some or all of these coverages. Comprehensive policies may also reimburse you for delays due to weather—an important consideration if you're traveling during the winter months. Some health-insurance policies do not cover preexisting conditions, but waivers may be available in specific cases. Coverage is sold by the companies listed in Important Contacts A to Z; these companies act as the policy's administrators. The actual insurance is usually underwritten by a well-known name, such as The Travelers or Continental Insurance.

Before you make any purchase, **review your existing health and homeowner's policies** to find out whether they cover expenses incurred while traveling.

BAGGAGE

Airline liability for baggage is limited to $1,250 per person on domestic flights. On international flights, it amounts to $9.07 per pound or $20 per kilogram for checked baggage (roughly $640 per 70-pound bag) and $400 per passenger for unchecked baggage. Insurance for losses exceeding the terms of your airline ticket can be bought directly from the airline at check-in for about $10 per $1,000 of coverage; note that it excludes a rather extensive list of items, shown on your airline ticket.

COMPREHENSIVE

Comprehensive insurance policies include all the coverages described above plus some that may not be available in more specific policies. If you have purchased an expensive vacation, especially one that involves travel abroad, comprehensive insurance is a must; **look for policies that include trip delay insurance,** which will protect you in the event that weather problems cause you to miss your flight, tour, or cruise. A few insurers will also sell you a waiver for preexisting medical conditions. Some of the companies that offer both these features are Access America, Carefree Travel, Travel Insured International, and TravelGuard (☞ Insurance *in* Important Contacts A to Z).

FLIGHT

You should **think twice before buying flight insurance.** Often purchased as a last-minute impulse at the airport, it pays a lump sum when a plane crashes, either to a beneficiary if the insured dies or sometimes to a surviving passenger who loses his or her eyesight or a limb. Supplementing the airlines' coverage described in the limits-of-liability paragraphs on your ticket, it's expensive and basically unnecessary. Charging an airline ticket to a major credit card often automatically provides you with coverage that may also extend to travel by bus, train, and ship.

HEALTH

Medicare generally does not cover health care costs outside the United States; nor do many privately issued policies. If your own health insurance policy does not cover you outside the United States, **consider buying supplemental medical coverage.** It can reimburse you for $1,000–$150,000 worth of medical and/or dental expenses incurred as a result of an accident or illness during a trip.

TRIP

Without insurance, you will lose all or most of your money if you cancel your trip regardless of the reason. Especially if your airline ticket, cruise, or package tour is nonrefundable and cannot be changed, it's essential that you **buy trip-cancellation-and-interruption insurance.** When considering how much coverage you need, look for a policy that will cover the cost of your trip plus the nondiscounted price of a one-way airline ticket should you need to return home early. Read the fine print carefully, especially sections that define "family member" and "preexisting medical conditions." Also **consider default or bankruptcy insurance,** which protects you against a supplier's failure to deliver. Be aware, however, that if you buy such a policy from a travel agency, tour operator, airline, or cruise line, it may not cover default by the firm in question.

L

LODGING

APARTMENT & VILLA RENTAL

If you want a home base that's roomy enough for a family and comes with cooking facilities, **consider taking a furnished rental.** This can also save you money, but not always—some rentals are luxury properties (economical only when your party is large). Home-exchange directories list rentals—often second homes owned by prospective house swappers—and some services search for a house or apartment for you (even a castle if that's your fancy) and handle the paperwork. Some send an illustrated catalog; others send photographs only of specific properties, sometimes at a charge; up-front registration fees may apply.

BED-AND-BREAKFASTS

These are a special British tradition, and the backbone of budget travel. They are usually in a family home, few have private bathrooms, and most offer only breakfast. Guest houses are a slightly larger, somewhat more luxurious version. The first of a new breed of upscale B&Bs, more along the line of American B&Bs, have been spotted in the capital. All provide a glimpse of everyday British life.

COTTAGES

Furnished apartments, houses, cottages, and trailers are available for weekly rental in all areas of the country. These vary from quaint, cleverly converted farmhouses to brand-new buildings set in scenic surroundings. For families and large groups, they offer the best value-for-money accommodations, but as they are often in isolated locations, a car is vital. Lists of rental properties are available free of charge from the British Tourist Authority. Discounts of up to 50% apply during the off-season (October–March).

FARMHOUSES

These have become increasingly popular in recent years; their special appeal is the rustic, rural experience. Consider this option only if you are touring by car. Prices are generally very reasonable.

HISTORIC BUILDINGS

Want to spend your vacation in a Gothic banqueting house, an old lighthouse, or maybe in a gatehouse that sheltered Mary, Queen of Scots in 1586? Several organizations, such as the Landmark Trust and the National Trust, have specially adapted historic buildings to rent. Most of them are self-catering, so for a short while you can pretend you live there.

HOME EXCHANGE

If you would like to find a house, an apartment, or some other type of vacation property to exchange for your own while on holiday, **become a member of a home-exchange organization,** which will send you its updated listings of available exchanges for a year, and will include your own listing in at least one of them. Arrangements for the actual exchange are made by the two parties involved, not by the organization.

HOTELS

Most hotels have rooms with private bathrooms, although some older ones may have only washbasins; in this case, showers and bathtubs (and toilets) are usually just down the hall. Generally, hotel prices include breakfast, but it's often only a Continental breakfast. Prices in London are significantly higher than in the rest of the country, they usually do *not* include breakfast, and often the quality and service are not as good. TICs will reserve rooms for you, usually for a small fee. A great many hotels offer special weekend and off-season bargain packages.

UNIVERSITY HOUSING

In larger cities and in some towns, certain universities offer their residence halls to paying vacationers out of term time. The facilities available are usually compact single sleeping units, and they can be rented on a nightly basis.

YOUTH HOSTELS

There are more than 350 youth hostels throughout Britain, ranging from very basic to almost luxurious. Many are in remote and beautiful areas; others on the outskirts of large cities. Despite the name, there is no age restriction. They are inexpensive, generally reliable, and usually contain cooking facilities.

M

MAIL

Airmail letters to the United States and Canada cost 41p for 10 grams; postcards 35p; aerogrammes 36p. Letters and postcards to Europe not over 20 grams, 30p (25p to EU member countries). Letters within the United Kingdom, first class 25p, second class and postcards 19p. These rates may have increased by early 1996.

RECEIVING MAIL

If you're uncertain where you'll be staying, **arrange to have your mail sent to American Express.** The service is free to cardholders and travelers check holders; all others pay a small fee. You can also **collect letters at London's main post office** Monday–Saturday 8–8. Ask to have them sent to Poste Restante, Main Post Office, London. You'll need your passport or another official form of identification.

MONEY & EXPENSES

The unit of currency in Britain is the pound sterling, divided into 100 pence (p). The bills are 50, 20, 10, and 5 pounds (Scotland and the Channel Islands have their own £1 bills). Coins are £1, 50, 20, 10, 5, 2, and 1p. At press time (spring 1995), the exchange rate was about U.S. $1.47 and Canadian $2.01 to the pound sterling.

ATMS

CASH ADVANCES➢ Before leaving home, **make sure that your credit cards have been programmed for ATM use** in Great Britain. Note that Discover is accepted mostly in the United States. Local bank cards often do not work overseas either; **ask your bank about a Global Access debit card,** which works like a bank card but can be used at any ATM displaying a Visa logo.

TRANSACTION FEES➢ On credit-card cash advances you are charged interest from the day you receive the money, whether from a teller or an ATM. Although fees charged for ATM transactions may be higher abroad than at home, Cirrus and Plus exchange rates are excellent, because they are based on wholesale rates offered only by major banks.

EXCHANGING CURRENCY

For the most favorable rates, **change money at banks.** You won't do as well at exchange booths in airports or rail and bus stations, in hotels, in restaurants, or in stores, although you may find their hours more convenient. To avoid lines at airport exchange booths, **get a small amount of the local currency before you leave home.**

SAMPLE COSTS

A local paper will cost you about 35p and a national daily 50p (up to £1 on Sunday). A pint of beer is about £1.80, and a gin and tonic £2 (mixers are pricey in pubs, and remember that British measures for spirits are on the mean side). A cup of coffee will run from 60p to £2, depending on where you drink it; a ham sandwich £1.75–£3.50; lunch in a pub, £2 and up (plus your drink).

A theater seat will cost from £7.50 to £40 or more in London, less elsewhere, while an evening of opera or ballet at Covent Garden could set you back around £120 each for the best seats, although you can get returns or "the gods" (seats high up) for a small fraction of that. Movie theater prices vary widely—from £2.50 in the daytime in the provinces (more in the evening) to anything up to £8 in central London. Nightclubs operate under no known system—even the membership fees are variable.

Gasoline costs about £2.60 a gallon (57p a liter), and up to 10p a gallon higher in remote locations for unleaded petrol, and roughly £2.79 a gallon (61.9p a liter) for normal leaded gasoline.

TAXES

The British sales tax (VAT, Value Added Tax) is 17½%. The tax is almost always included in quoted prices in shops, hotels, and restaurants.

AIRPORT➢ An airport departure tax of £10 (£5 to EU countries) per person is payable.

VAT REFUNDS➢ You can **get a VAT refund** by either the Over the Counter or the Direct Export method. Most larger stores provide these services, but only if you request them, and will handle the paperwork. For the Over the Counter method, you must spend more than £75 in one store. Ask the store for Form VAT 407 (you must have identification—passports are best), to be given to customs when you leave the country. (Lines at major airports are usually long, so allow plenty of time.) The refund will be forwarded to you in about eight weeks, minus a small service charge, either in the form of a British check or as a credit to your charge card, but American banks will charge a fee to cash the check, so it's better to use your credit card. The Direct Export method, where the goods go directly to your home, is more cumbersome. VAT Form 407 must be certified by Customs, police, or a notary public when you get home and then sent back to the store, which will refund your money.

TRAVELER'S CHECKS

Whether or not to buy traveler's checks depends on where you are headed; **take cash to rural areas and small towns, traveler's checks to cities.** The most widely recognized checks are issued by American Express, Citicorp, Thomas Cook, and Visa. These are sold by major commercial banks for 1%–3% of the checks' face value—it pays to **shop around.** Both American Express and Thomas Cook issue checks that can be countersigned and used by either you or your traveling companion, and they both provide checks, at no extra charge, valued in pounds. So you won't be left with excess foreign currency, **buy a few checks in small denominations** to cash toward the end of your trip. Before leaving home, **contact your issuer for information on where to cash your checks** without a incurring a transaction fee. Record the numbers of all your checks, and keep this listing in a separate place, crossing off the numbers of checks you have cashed.

WIRING MONEY

For a fee of 3%–10%, depending on the amount of the transaction, you can have money sent to you from home through MoneyGram[SM] or Western Union (☞ Money Matters *in* Important Contacts A to Z). The transferred funds and the service fee can be charged to a MasterCard or Visa account.

P

PACKING FOR GREAT BRITAIN

Britain can be cool, damp, and overcast, even in summer. You'll want a heavy coat for winter and a lightweight coat or warm jacket for summer. There's no time of year when a raincoat or umbrella won't come in handy. For the cities, **pack as you would for an American city:** coats and ties for expensive restaurants and night spots, casual clothes elsewhere. Jeans are popular in Britain and are perfectly acceptable for sightseeing and informal dining. Tweeds and sports jackets are popular here with men. For women, ordinary street dress is acceptable everywhere.

If you plan to stay in budget hotels, take your own soap. Many do not provide soap and some give guests only one tiny bar per room. Bring an extra pair of eyeglasses or contact lenses in your carry-on luggage, and if you have a health problem, **pack enough medication** to last the trip or have your doctor write you a prescription using the drug's generic name, because brand names vary from country to country (you'll then need a duplicate prescription from a local doctor). It's important that you **don't put prescription drugs or valuables in luggage to be checked,** for it could go astray. To avoid problems with customs officials, carry medications in the original packaging. Also, don't forget the addresses of offices that handle refunds of lost traveler's checks.

ELECTRICITY

To use your U.S.-purchased electric-powered equipment, **bring a converter and an adapter.** The electrical current in Great Britain is 220 volts, 50 cycles alternating current (AC); wall outlets take plugs with two round oversized prongs. If your appliances are dual-voltage, you'll need only an adapter. Hotels sometimes have 110-volt outlets for low-wattage appliances near the sink, marked FOR SHAVERS ONLY; don't use them for high-wattage appliances like blow-dryers. If your laptop computer is older, carry a converter; new laptops operate equally well on 110 and 220 volts, so you need only an adapter.

LUGGAGE

If you are flying between two foreign destinations, note that baggage allowances may be determined not by piece but by weight—generally 88 pounds (40 kilograms) in first class, 66 pounds (30 kilograms) in business class, and 44 pounds (20 kilograms) in economy. If your flight between two cities abroad *connects* with your transatlantic or transpacific flight, the piece method still applies.

SAFEGUARDING YOUR LUGGAGE➢ Before leaving home, **itemize your bags' contents** and their worth, and label them with your name, address, and phone number. (If you use your home address, cover it so that potential thieves can't see it readily.) Inside each bag, **pack a copy of your itinerary.** At check-in, **make sure that each bag is correctly tagged** with the destination airport's three-letter code. If your bags arrive damaged—or fail to arrive at all—file a written report with the airline before leaving the airport.

PASSPORTS & VISAS

If you don't already have one, **get a passport.** It is advisable that you **leave one photocopy of your passport's data page** with someone at home and keep another with you, separated from your passport, while traveling. If you lose your passport, promptly call the nearest embassy or consulate and the local police; having the data page information can speed replacement.

IN THE U.S.

All U.S. citizens, even infants, need only a valid passport to enter Great Britain for stays of up to 90 days. Application forms for both first-time and renewal passports are available at any of the 13 U.S. Passport Agency offices and at some post offices and courthouses. Passports are usually mailed within four weeks; allow five weeks or more in spring and summer.

CANADIANS

You need only a valid passport to enter Great Britain for stays of up to 90 days. Passport application forms are available at 28 regional passport offices, as well as post offices and travel agencies. Whether for a first or a renewal passport, you must apply in person. Children under 16 may be included on a parent's passport but must have their own to travel alone. Passports are valid for five years and are usually mailed within two to three weeks of application.

S

SENIOR-CITIZEN DISCOUNTS

To qualify for age-related discounts, **mention your senior-citizen status up front** when booking hotel reservations, not when checking out, and before you're seated in restaurants, not when paying the bill. Note that discounts may be limited to certain menus, days, or hours. When renting a car, **ask about promotional car-rental discounts**—they can net even lower costs than your senior-citizen discount.

STUDENTS ON THE ROAD

To save money, **look into deals available through student-oriented travel agencies.** To qualify, you'll need to have a bona fide student ID card. Members of international student groups are also eligible (☞ Students *in* Important Contacts A to Z).

T

TELEPHONES

There are two area codes in London: 0171 for inner London, 0181 for outer London. You do not need to dial either if calling from inside the same zone. Drop the zero from the prefix and dial only 171 or 181 when calling London from overseas.

To call the operator, dial 100; directory inquiries (information) 192; international directory inquiries, 153.

LONG-DISTANCE

For long-distance calls within Britain, dial the area code (which usually begins with a 01), followed by the number. For direct overseas dialing, dial 010, then the country code, area code, and number. For the international operator, credit card, or collect calls, dial 155. Bear in mind that hotels usually levy a hefty (up to 300%) surcharge on calls; it's better to use the pay phones located in most hotel foyers or a U.S. calling card.

The long-distance services of AT&T, MCI, and Sprint make calling home relatively convenient, but in many hotels you may find it impossible to dial the access number. The hotel operator may also refuse to make the connection. Instead, the hotel will charge you a premium rate—as much as 400% more than a calling card—for calls placed from your hotel room. To avoid such price gouging, **travel with more than one company's long-distance calling card**—a hotel may block Sprint but not MCI. If the hotel operator claims that you cannot use any phone card, ask to be connected to an international operator, who will help you to access your phone card. You can also dial the international operator yourself. If none of this works, try calling your phone company collect in the United States. If collect calls are also blocked, call from a pay phone in the hotel lobby. Before you go, **find out the local access codes** for your destinations.

PAY PHONES

There are three types of public pay phones: those that accept only coins, those that accept only phonecards, and those that take phonecards and credit cards. For coin-only phones, insert coins *before* dialing (minimum charge is 10p). Sometimes phones have a "press on answer" (POA) button, which you press when the caller answers.

For phonecard telephones, buy BT (British Telecom) cards from shops, post offices, or newsstands. They are ideal for longer calls, are composed of units of 10p, and come in values of £2, £4, £10 and more. An indicator panel on the phone shows the number of units you've used; at the end of your call the card is returned.

TIPPING

Some restaurants and most hotels add a service charge of 10%–15% to the bill. In this case, you are not obliged to tip extra. If no service charge is indicated, add 10%–15% to your total bill. Taxi drivers should also get 10%–15%. You are not expected to tip theater or cinema ushers, elevator operators, or bartenders in pubs. Hairdressers and barbers should receive 10%–15%.

TOUR OPERATORS

A package or tour to Great Britain can make your vacation less expensive and more hassle-free. Firms that sell tours and packages reserve airline seats, hotel rooms, and rental cars in bulk and pass some of the savings on to you. In addition, the best operators have local representatives available to help you at your destination.

A GOOD DEAL?

The more your package or tour includes, the better you can predict the ultimate cost of your vacation. Make sure you know exactly what is covered, and **beware of hidden costs.** Are taxes, tips, and service charges included? Transfers and baggage handling? Entertainment and excursions? These can add up.

Most packages and tours are rated deluxe, first-class superior, first class, tourist, or budget. The key difference is usually accommodations. If the package or tour you are considering is priced lower than in your wildest dreams, **be skeptical.** Also,

make sure your travel agent knows the accommodations and other services. Ask about the hotel's location, room size, beds, and whether it has a pool, room service, or programs for children, if you care about these. Has your agent been there in person or sent others you can contact?

BUYER BEWARE

Each year a number of consumers are stranded or lose their money when operators—even very large ones with excellent reputations—go out of business. To avoid becoming one of them, take the time to **check out the operator**—find out how long the company has been in business and ask several agents about its reputation. Next, **don't book unless the firm has a consumer-protection program.** Members of the USTOA and the NTA are required to set aside funds for the sole purpose of covering your payments and travel arrangements in case of default. Nonmember operators may instead carry insurance; look for the details in the operator's brochure—and for the name of an underwriter with a solid reputation. Note: When it comes to tour operators, **don't trust escrow accounts.** Although there are laws governing those of charter-flight operators, no governmental body prevents tour operators from raiding the till.

Next, **contact your local Better Business Bureau and the attorney general's offices** in both your own state and the operator's; have any complaints been filed? Finally, **pay with a major credit card.** Then you can cancel payment, provided that you can document your complaint. Always **consider trip-cancellation insurance** (☞ Insurance, *above*).

USING AN AGENT

Travel agents are excellent resources. In fact, large operators accept bookings made only through travel agents. But it's good to **collect brochures from several agencies** because some agents' suggestions may be skewed by promotional relationships with tour and package firms that reward them for volume sales. If you have a special interest, **find an agent with expertise in that area**; ASTA can provide leads in the United States. (Don't rely solely on your agent, though; agents may be unaware of small-niche operators, and some special-interest travel companies only sell direct.)

TRAIN TRAVEL

The long-awaited privatization of the British rail system raises many questions about the future. Although changes are happening far more slowly than was originally projected, by the time you read this, rail service could be substantially different.

The semiannual *British Rail Passenger Timetable* (about £7.50) covers all BritRail services, including private, narrow-gauge, and steam lines, as well as special services and rail-based tourist facilities. You can also find detailed timetables of most rail services in Britain and some ferry services in the *Thomas Cook European Timetable,* issued monthly and available at travel agents and some general bookstores in the United States.

BRITRAIL PASSES

If you plan to travel by train in Great Britain, **consider purchasing a BritRail Pass,** which gives unlimited travel over the entire British Rail Network and will save you money. You must **buy your BritRail Pass before you leave home.** They are available from most travel agents or from BritRail Travel International (☞ Train Travel *in* Important Contacts A to Z). Note that EurailPasses are not honored in Britain.

The cost of a BritRail adult pass for 8 days is $235 standard and $325 first-class; for 15 days, $365 standard and $525 first-class; for 22 days, $465 and $665; and for a month, $545 and $765. The BritRail Youth Pass, for those ages 16–25, provides unlimited second-class travel and costs $189 for 8 days, $289 for 15 days, $369 for 22 days, and $435 for one month. The BritRail Senior Citizen Pass, for passengers over 60, is first-class only and costs $275 for 8 days, $445 for 15 days, $565 for 22 days, and $650 for one month. (These are U.S.

dollar figures; Canadian prices will be a bit higher.) There are also Flexipasses, which allow four, eight, or 15 days' travel in one month.

If you want the flexibility of a car combined with the speed and comfort of the train, try BritRail/Drive (from about $285 for one adult, with a $148 supplement for additional adults and $72.50 for children 5–15); this gives you a three-day BritRail Flexipass and three vouchers valid for Hertz car rental from more than 100 locations throughout Great Britain. A six-day rail pass with seven days of car rental is also available (from $490 car and driver, with $210 adult supplement, $105 children, with a current "free child per adult" deal for children under 5 traveling gratis). Larger cars, automatic transmission, and first-class rail seats will cost you more. If you call your travel agency or Hertz's international desk (☞ Car Rental *in* Important Contacts A to Z), the car of your choice will be waiting for you at the station as you alight from your train.

There is also a BritRail + Eurostar Flexipass that includes a round-trip rail journey through the Channel Tunnel to Paris; prices range from $383 (for a four-day round trip) to $445 (for an eight-day round trip).

Many travelers assume that rail passes guarantee them seats on the trains they wish to ride. Not so. You need to **book seats ahead even if you are using a rail pass**; seat reservations are required on some European trains, particularly high-speed trains, and are a good idea on trains that may be crowded—particularly in summer on popular routes. You will also need a reservation if you purchase sleeping accommodations.

OTHER DISCOUNTS

If you want to explore a specific part of Britain in greater detail, the series of Regional Rail Rover unlimited travel tickets offers excellent value; there are also All Line tickets, covering the whole of Britain. Contact the British Rail Travel Centre (☞ Train Travel *in* Important Contacts A to Z) for details.

The Freedom of Scotland Travelpass allows unlimited standard-class travel: $159 for 8 days, $220 for 15 days, and $289 for 22 days. A Scotland Flexipass allows 8 days of travel over a 15-day period for $185.

TRAVEL GEAR

Travel catalogs specialize in useful items that can **save space when packing** and make life on the road more convenient. Compact alarm clocks, travel irons, travel wallets, and personal-care kits are among the most common items you'll find. They also carry dual-voltage appliances, currency converters and foreign-language phrase books. Some catalogs even carry miniature coffeemakers and water purifiers.

W

WHEN TO GO

The British tourist season is year-round—with short lulls. It peaks from mid-April to mid-October, with another burst at Christmas (although most historic houses are closed from October to Easter). Spring is the time to see the countryside at its freshest and greenest, while in fall the northern moorlands and Scottish Highlands are at their most colorful. June is a good month to visit Wales and the Lake District. During July and August, when most of the British take their vacations, accommodations in the most popular resorts and areas are in high demand and at their most expensive. The winter season in London is lively with the opera, ballet, and West End theater among the prime attractions.

CLIMATE

In the main, the climate is mild, although the weather has been extremely volatile in recent years. Summer temperatures can reach the 90s and the atmosphere can be humid. In winter there can be heavy frost, snow, thick fog, and, of course, rain.

What follows are the average daily maximum and minimum temperatures for three major cities in Britain—but note that they are based on long-term averages and do not necessarily reflect the climatic swings of the last few years:

Climate in Great Britain

ABERYSTWYTH (WALES)

Jan.	44F	7C	May	58F	15C	Sept.	62F	16C
	36	2		45	7		51	11
Feb.	44F	7C	June	62F	16C	Oct.	56F	13C
	35	2		50	10		46	8
Mar.	49F	9C	July	64F	18C	Nov.	50F	10C
	38	4		54	12		41	5
Apr.	52F	11C	Aug.	65F	18C	Dec.	47F	8C
	41	5		54	12		38	4

EDINBURGH (SCOTLAND)

Jan.	42F	5C	May	56F	14C	Sept.	60F	18C
	34	1		43	6		49	9
Feb.	43F	6C	June	62F	17C	Oct.	54F	12C
	34	1		49	9		44	7
Mar.	46F	8C	July	65F	18C	Nov.	48F	9C
	36	2		52	11		39	4
Apr.	51F	11C	Aug.	64F	18C	Dec.	44F	7C
	39	4		52	11		36	2

LONDON

Jan.	43F	6C	May	62F	17C	Sept.	65F	19C
	36	2		47	8		52	11
Feb.	44F	7C	June	69F	20C	Oct.	58F	14C
	36	2		53	12		46	8
Mar.	50F	10C	July	71F	22C	Nov.	50F	10C
	38	3		56	14		42	5
Apr.	56F	13C	Aug.	71F	21C	Dec.	45F	7C
	42	6		56	13		38	4

1 Destination: Great Britain

RULE BRITANNIA!

THE BRITISH ARE DIFFERENT, and proud of it. They still have odd customs, like driving on the left and playing cricket. Only reluctantly have they decimalized, turning their cherished pints into liters (except when ordering beer) and inches into centimeters. Until 1971 they still had a bizarre, three-tier, nondecimal coinage, whereby a meal check might add up, say, to four pounds six shillings and sevenpence halfpenny (today that would translate as £4.33). And although the rest of Europe counts distances in kilometers, the British still cling to their miles—though they now buy fabric in meters, not yards. Logic is not a prominent feature of the British character.

These are symptoms of a certain psychological gulf still existing between Britain and the rest of Europe, a gulf not greatly narrowed by its membership in the European Union since 1973. The English Channel, a mere 22 miles of water between Dover and Calais, has played a crucial role in British history, acting as a kind of moat to protect the "island fortress" from invaders (witness 1940), and preserving a separate mentality. Many Britons want to keep that moat, hence their wariness—more emotional than economic—of the Channel Tunnel. It is difficult to estimate just how the opening of the tunnel will eventually affect the British psyche. They have resisted integration into Europe for so many centuries that the reality of a link open for 24 hours a day, whatever the weather, may well be traumatic. Even today, that oft-quoted old newspaper headline, "Fog in Channel, Continent isolated," retains some validity. But this proud and insular nation is not unwelcoming to visitors. On its own terms, it is glad to show them the delights and virtues of what it believes to be one of the most genuinely civilized societies in the world.

There is still some truth in the popular foreign perception that the British are reserved. They are given to understatement—"It's not bad" is the nearest a Briton may get to showing enthusiasm—and may look a little solemn and stiff-upper-lipped, because they don't easily show their emotions. But they are not on the whole unhappy, even in today's anxious times. (In fact, an international Gallup survey showed that far more people in Britain than in neighboring countries thought of themselves as leading happy lives.) The British are easygoing, accepting of nonconformity and eccentricity, and their strong sense of humor and love of the absurd keeps them on an even keel. They have a strange habit of poking good-humored fun at what they love without meaning disrespect, not least at royalty and religion, although the recent undignified capers of the royal family have honed an edge to the good humor. This kind of humor often disconcerts foreigners.

It is a densely populated land. Scotland and Wales have wide open spaces but in England people are crammed 940 to the square mile, more thickly than in any European country save Holland. But it is also a green and fertile land, and because the countryside is a limited commodity, the English tend it with special loving care. Everywhere are trim hedgerows, tidy flower beds, and lawns mown smooth as billiard tables—one Oxford don, asked by an American visitor how the college lawn came to be so perfect, said casually, "Oh, it's been mown every Tuesday for the past 500 years." The English love gardens but are also at ease in untamed surroundings. They relish hiking over moors where the westerly gales blow, or splashing rubber-booted through streams, or bird-watching in a quiet copse. A few people, in their black or scarlet coats and riding caps, still go fox hunting with hounds—"the unspeakable in full pursuit of the uneatable," as Oscar Wilde put it. Others are violent in their condemnation of this blood sport.

This smallish island contains great scenic variety. The Midlands and much of eastern England tend to be flat and dull. But the watery fenlands, between Cambridge and the sea, the low horizons broken by rows of poplars or by a distant windmill or tall church spire have a misty, poetic quality, and the sunsets and swirling clouds evoke Turner skyscapes. Kent, southeast of London, with its cherry and apple orchards, is known as the garden of England; west of here are the wooded hills of Surrey, and to the southwest the bold, bare ridge of the South Downs, beloved of Kipling. While the east coast of Britain is mainly smooth, with long sandy beaches and an occasional chalky cliff, the west coast is far more rugged: Here the Atlantic gales set the seas lashing against the rocky headlands of Cornwall and south Wales.

The spine of northern England is a line of high hills, the Pennines, where sheep graze on lonely moors, and just to the west is the beautiful, mountainous Lake District, where Wordsworth lived. Scotland is even more lonely and mountainous. Beyond the urban belt of the lowlands around Edinburgh, you enter the romantic realm of the Highlands, a thinly populated region where heather and gorse cover the hillsides above silent fjordlike lochs and verdant glens. Roads here are few, but they all seem to lead westward to the Isles, blue-gray jewels in a silver Atlantic sea, with their strange Celtic names: Barra, Eigg, Benbecula, Skye.

Western Britain is washed by the warm waters of the Gulf Stream, and therefore its climate is mild and damp. Indeed, Britain's weather is something of a stock joke, and some foreigners imagine the whole country permanently shrouded in fog. This has not been true for years, since the use of smokeless fuel has cleared polluted mists from urban skies. Yet the weather *is* very changeable, by south European standards, with shower and shine often following each other in swift succession. At least it provides the thrill of the unexpected.

THE PEOPLE ARE AS VARIED as the landscape, coming as they do from a variety of origins: Celtic, Viking, Saxon, Norman, not to mention later immigrations. Modern mobility and the drift toward cities and to the warmer and wealthier South has tended to mix them up in the urban centers. But the countryside populations have remained much the same. The gap between the two has widened enormously, so that now those in the country simply cannot understand the problems that bedevil the cities. Regional differences remain distinct, and local loyalties are fierce, even parochial. A London politician newly settled in north Yorkshire was warned by his constituents, "Take no notice o' folk t'oother side o' water!" He feared, as well he might, that this was some anti-EU or anti-American hostility—but discovered they were referring to the people just 10 miles away across the river Tees, in County Durham.

The millions of foreigners who have come to live in Britain during the last few decades have widened the horizons of an insular—in every sense of the word—people, even in such matters as cuisine. Until the '50s almost all restaurants served dull British fare, but today in even the smallest provincial town you will find Indians, Chinese, Greeks, Italians, French and others all serving their national dishes—and they are very popular indeed.

The same can't always be said of the immigrants themselves, especially those from what is euphemistically dubbed the "New Commonwealth"—meaning the Asians and Afro-Caribbeans brought into Britain in the '50s and '60s to provide essential services and fill a chronic labor shortage. Most middle-class British people will profess themselves broadminded, of course, but their day-to-day attitudes still suggest that their commitment to a truly racially egalitarian society is only skin deep (if that). The debate over assimilation—to what extent the immigrant communities should be asked to surrender their own identities—still rages. Should schools in Bradford, where a majority of pupils are Muslims, base their moral precepts on the Koran rather than the Bible? Should the history of the Caribbean islands or of Africa be taught to young blacks in south London as part of their culture?

The British are clearly torn between their traditions of tolerance and their belief that even a somewhat anachronistic law must be upheld. Never has this situation been more clear-cut than in the confrontation over Rushdie's *Satanic Verses,* when British Muslims saw themselves discriminated against under Britain's ancient blasphemy laws, which applied only to the God of the Christians. Until a clear line is drawn—either rigorous assimilation, or multiculturalism that implies a new respect for alien cultures taking root in their towns and cities—the British will be constantly wrongfooted, embarrassed, and occasionally very frightened by the newcomers erupting in their midst.

Britain is a land where the arts flourish. It is true that the artist, writer, or philosopher is not held in the same public esteem as, say, in France. The average Briton affects a certain philistinism, and "intellectual" and "arty" are common terms of reproach. Yet sales of books and of theater and concert tickets are amazingly high. Helped by the worldwide spread of the English language, the British publishing industry produces around 50,000 new titles a year—too many for profitability. A passion for classical music developed during the last war and has continued ever since, so that even the smallest town has its choral society performing Bach or Handel. London theater is regarded by many as the best in the world. In the provinces, hundreds of theaters, some of them small fringe groups in makeshift premises, attract ready audiences.

CULTURE THRIVES ALSO in a classical mode—for example, through the Royal Shakespeare Company with its base in the bard's hometown of Stratford-upon-Avon. Like Shakespeare, many leading British writers and other creative artists are closely associated with some particular place, in a land where literature and the other arts have always been nourished by strong local roots, by some *genius loci.* A tour around Britain can thus become a series of cultural pilgrimages: to the Dorset that inspired the novels of Thomas Hardy, to the wild Yorkshire moors where the Brontë sisters lived and wrote, to Wordsworth's beloved Lake District, to the Scottish Border landscapes that pervade the novels of Walter Scott, to Laugharne on the south Wales coast that Dylan Thomas's *Under Milk Wood* has immortalized, to Dickensian London, to the Constable country on the Suffolk/Essex border, or to nearby Aldeburgh where composer Benjamin Britten lived.

These personalities are significant parts of a long national history that lies buried deep in the British psyche. The history began centuries before Christ, when huge stone circles were raised at Stonehenge and Avebury, on the Wiltshire downs. Then came the Romans, who left their imprint across the land up to Hadrian's Wall in the north. Great feudal castles survive as reminders of the dark days when barons and kings were in constant conflict, and peaceful fields the length and breadth of the land became nightmarish landscapes of blood and death. Stately redbrick Elizabethan manors bear witness to the more settled and civilized age of Good Queen Bess.

Britain is rich in old towns and villages whose streets are lined with buildings dating back for centuries, with old half-timber houses where black beams crisscross the white plasterwork, or with carefully proportioned facades that bring a measured classical elegance to the townscape. In many areas, buildings are of local stone—most strikingly in the mellow golden-brown Cotswold villages—and often a simple cottage is topped with a neat thatch roof. Above all, British architecture is famed for its cathedrals dating mostly from the Middle Ages, with Wells, Ely, and Durham among the finest. Local churches, too, are often of great beauty, especially in East Anglia where the wealth of the 15th-century wool trade led to the building of majestic churches on the edge of quite modest villages. Church builders of the past were profligate in their service to God, and modern Britain is deeply in their debt. Unfortunately, the Church is just as deeply in debt, because it has these mammoth edifices to maintain with dwindling congregations to help with its finances.

Despite constant social upheavals, the British maintain many of their special traditions. On a village green in summer, you may see a cricket match in progress between two white-clad teams. It is a slow and stately game that will seem boring to the uninitiated, yet is full of its own skills and subtleties. In village pubs people frequently play darts, or perhaps backgammon, checkers, or chess.

British society, although troubled by doubts and uncertainties, and constantly challenged to resolve key social problems, is certainly not in terminal decline, or even slowly fading away. But it is deeply troubled and seriously questioning many of its traditional, long-accepted institutions. As an American observer remarked during the Falklands War, "The British can be relied upon to fall at every hurdle—except the last." When the chips are down, the British come up trumps. This can't be explained rationally. What was it that sank the Spanish Armada or defeated Goering's Luftwaffe? It certainly wasn't superior economic resources or disciplined social organization. Maybe there is more in the souls of a free people united in a common purpose than generations of economists and sociologists could ever hope to understand. The British are such a people; and their quirkiness, their social "distance," and their habit of driving on the left are inseparable parts of a greater whole. Without Britain, even a changed Britain, the world would be a poorer place.

WHAT'S WHERE

London

If London contained only its famous landmarks—the Tower of London, St. Paul's, Big Ben, Parliament, Buckingham Palace—and its fabulous museums—the Victoria & Albert, the Tate and National Galleries, and the British Museum—it would still rank as one of the world's top tourist destinations. But London is more—much, much more. It is a bevy of British Bobbies, an ocean of black umbrellas, an unconquered continuance of more than 2,000 years of history. It's really a case of East End, West End, All Around the Town. The trick to taming Europe's largest city is to regard it as a number of villages. There is the heraldic splendor of Westminster, the chic of artistic Chelsea, the glamour of Kensington, the cosmopolitan charms of Soho, the ancient core of The City, and the East End, home of the irrepressible Cockney. No matter which district you adopt as your home-away-from-home, London's contrasts can best be savored by strolling from one neighborhood to another, wandering thoroughfares of stately houses that lie next to a melange of mean streets. With some of the best restaurants, hotels, shops, theater, dance, and opera around, London is simply the most interesting city in Europe.

The Southeast

The densely populated Southeast has seaside resorts, historic towns once ruled by Romans and Saxons, and lovely countryside dotted with small farms, quaint villages, and round brick oasthouses. Because of the area's close proximity to London, visitors with limited time can make easy excursions to Canterbury, with its grand Norman cathedral and medieval walls; Dover, a busy gateway port to Europe, with its famous white cliffs and spectacular medieval castle; Brighton, a popular seaside haven renowned for its extravagant Royal Pavilion; and Tunbridge Wells, home to many London commuters and close to a remarkable number of historical residences, castles, and other monuments.

The South

Central to England's history for more than four centuries, the varied landscape of the South encompasses the tranquil gardens of the home counties, the harsh Salisbury Plain terrain, the Isle of Wight's peaceful shores, the New Forest's wild scenery, and the heaths and rugged coastline of Dorset, immortalized by Thomas Hardy. Visitors to the region can explore the lovely cathedral cities of Winchester and Salisbury, bustling ports such as Southhampton and Portsmouth, attractive market villages, and numerous prehistoric remains, most notably Avebury and Stonehenge.

The Southwest

This region—the peninsula known as the West Country—juxtaposes rugged moorlands, unspoiled woods, towering sea cliffs, lush river valleys, popular coastal resorts, and ancient market towns. The counties of Somerset, Devon, and Cornwall make up this area, which is strongly associated with the legend of King Arthur. Quiet Somerset has long stretches of hilly countryside, while Devon is renowned for its wild moorland, strange rock formations, small villages with thatched cottages, and large coastal towns once frequented by Sir Francis Drake and other Elizabethan seafarers. Popular with walkers, Cornwall has England's mildest climate, a jagged northern shore, and a south coast full of pleasant beaches and coves.

The Channel Islands

Off the coast of France, the Channel Islands became part of Britain in 1066, but they maintain their own ruling system. Jersey is the most visited island because of its mild climate, fabulous beaches, and efficiently managed hotels and restaurants. Also popular is Guernsey, with a relaxed pace, luxurious homes, and some 2,000 hours of sunshine per year. These islands have excellent walking trails along majestic cliffs with fantastic ocean views.

The Thames Valley

Easily accessible to London, the Thames Valley area takes in Windsor, famous home to the British royal family; Henley, a charming riverside town renowned for its summer regatta; Oxford, a bustling modern town with one of England's most distinguished universities; and the section of the Thames River, from Caversham to Mapledurham, immortalized in the children's classic *The Wind in the Willows*.

The Heart of England

This west-central region includes some of Britain's most popular attractions. Stratford-upon-Avon, the birthplace of Shakespeare, is a living shrine to the playwright, a charming market town with historic buildings and a superb theater devoted to the dramatist's works. Nearby is Warwick Castle, the finest medieval castle in the country. Walkers adore the Cotwolds area, full of well-kept villages of golden stone houses. South of this region is Bath, founded in the 1st century by the Romans. Bath became a fashionable spa in the 18th century, which encouraged the construction of beautiful terraces, crescents, and villas still on view today.

The Welsh Borders

Along England's border with the principality of Wales lies some of England's loveliest and most peaceful countryside. The border stretches from the town of Chepstow on the Severn estuary in the south to the city of Chester in the north. Herefordshire, in the south, has rich, rolling countryside and river valleys, gradually opening out to Shropshire's high hills and plateaus. In the north, the gentler Cheshire plain is dairy country, dotted with small villages and market towns, full of 13th- and 14th-century black-and-white, half-timber buildings typical of northwestern England. Built to repel invaders, a string of medieval castles in this region bears witness to the sometimes strained relationship that once existed between England and Wales. Gateway to the region from the British heartland is the bustling city of Birmingham, now undergoing an urban renaissance.

Wales

On the western border of England, Wales is a country of outstanding natural beauty, with unspoiled mountain scenery in its interior and long stretches of magnificent coastline. Visitors have many riches to choose from: numerous medieval castles, the slate caverns at Blaenau Ffestiniog, charming seaside resorts, restored 19th-century mining villages, the glorious Bodnant Garden, the Victorian spa of Llandrindod Wells, and steam train rides through the mountains of Snowdonia and central Wales.

Lancashire and the Peaks

The center for England's Industrial Revolution beginning in the 18th-century, this northwest area claims the bustling cities of Manchester and Liverpool, renowned for their championship soccer teams and their influential music groups, most notably, the Beatles. The Lancashire coast has a number of popular seaside resorts, the largest being Blackpool, with miles of beaches, a huge amusement park, and acres of gardens. Hikers and ramblers won't want to miss the Peak District, a grand, unspoiled national park of rocky outcrops and meadowland at the southern end of the Pennines mountain range.

The Lake District

Bordered by Scotland and the waters of Solway Firth, Morecambe Bay, and the Irish Sea, this heavily visited northern region of England is a gorgeous national park with steep, craggy mountains, lush green valleys, quiet farms and villages, waterfalls, and of course, more than 100 stunning blue lakes—from tiny mountain pools to England's largest lake, 11-mile-long Lake Windemere. The Lake District is world-renowned for the literary figures who have lived here, among them William Wordsworth, Samuel Taylor Coleridge, John Ruskin, Matthew Arnold, and Beatrix Potter.

East Anglia

Most of this region of southeastern England is not well-known to tourists, but it is easily reached from London. Enchanted Cambridge is the most visited place in the area, with its stately university buildings, towering trees, and medieval streets and passages enhanced by gardens and riverbanks. Bypassed by the Industrial Revolution, East Anglia's cities and villages have preserved their medieval architecture, and Norwich and Lincoln both have majestic cathedrals. In Norfolk and Suffolk, the canals and lakes of the reed-bordered Broads give the locals endless opportunities for peaceful boating.

Yorkshire

A wilder, grander part of England in the north, the heather-covered Yorkshire Moors—full of open spaces, wide horizons, and hills that appear to rear violently out of the plain—were inspiration for the Brontë sisters' novels, *Jane Eyre* and *Wuthering Heights*. The Moors are linked to the contrasting landscape of the Yorkshire Dales, with luxuriant green valleys, burgeoning rivers, waterfalls, and some of England's most tranquil villages. The Yorkshire region also has the friendly city of York, with the largest Gothic church in the country and a well-preserved medieval wall; the quaint seaside resort of Scarborough; and the grand Castle Howard, one of England's most famous houses.

The Northeast

England's northeast corner includes among its attractions the English side of the Scottish Border area, renowned in ballads and romantic literature for feuds, raids, and battles. The region has Hadrian's Wall, which once marked the northern limit of the Roman Empire; Kielder Forest, Europe's largest planted forest; and parts of Northumberland National Park. In the western side lie the hills known as the Pennines, with some of England's wildest and least populated countryside. On the eastern side are 100 miles of largely undeveloped coastline, with quiet stone-built villages, vast empty beaches, and several outstanding castles. For 1,000 years, the great cathedral of Durham was the seat of bishops who had their own armies and ruled the turbulent northern diocese as prince-bishops with quasi-royal authority.

Scotland: Edinburgh and the Borders

In southeast Scotland, Edinburgh is a thoroughly delightful city built, like Rome, on seven hills, with its own brooding castle affording spectacular views; the Old Town district, with all the evidence of its colorful medieval history; a large number of elegant, 18th-century classical buildings; and Arthur's Seat, a green and yellow-furze backdrop jutting up 800 feet behind the spires of the Old Town. Edinburgh also has some fine art museums, atmospheric pubs, a lovely botanical garden, and an annual theater festival. The Borders area—immortalized in the tales of Sir Walter Scott—takes in the rolling hills, moors, and farmland that stretch south from Lothian, the region crowned by Edinburgh, to England. An excursion to St. Andrews is a pilgrimage for golf aficionados; many a traveler hopes to return home with the tale of a Road Hole birdie on the Old Course of the Royal & Ancient.

Scotland: Royal Deeside to Inverness

After exploring Edinburgh, all feet march in the direction of mythical Brigadoon—toward those splendid heath-clad mountain slopes, shimmering lochs, and the great castles of baronial pride standing hard among the hills. To enjoy the Highlands at their picture-postcard best, head for Royal Deeside, the burg that Queen Victoria made her own. Her Majesty's Balmoral—and numerous other castles—polka-dot this picturesque region of northeast Scotland. Northward lies Inverness and Loch Ness; perhaps you'll be the lucky person to sight Nessie—everyone's favorite monster and a founding member of the local chamber of commerce.

PLEASURES AND PASTIMES

Stately Homes

Curiosity as to how the other half lives is undoubtedly one of the most deep-seated traits of human nature, and it's extremely pleasing to know you can satisfy your healthy desire to snoop through Great Britain's stately homes for the payment of a very small amount of conscience money. The fact that you will see some of the greatest of the world's treasures at the same time is a happy bonus. But even the most highly developed sense of curiosity isn't enough to explain the fact that millions of people have surged on to the Stately Home trail. They have been urged to move by a great deal of exposure—the houses touched by the royal family upheavals, such as Althorp, the ancestral home of Princess Diana, and the Mountbatten home, Broadlands; the numerous television serials, which have brought new fame to such spectacular houses as Castle Howard and Blenheim Palace; the new spate of historical movies shot on location, such as Franco Zefferelli's *Jane Eyre* (filmed at that beau ideal of the English country house, Haddon Hall), *The Madness of King George* (the spectacular interiors of Wilton House dazzled here), *Sense and Sensibility* (partly shot at Saltram), or the over-the-top style of Charles II on view in *Restoration*. Today, thousands follow in the footsteps of Elizabeth Bennet and the Gardiners who paid a call on Mr. Darcy's regal Pemberely, one of the more fetching episodes of Jane Austen's *Pride and Prejudice*.

The reason for the pressing need for the owners of stately homes to throw them open is simply that they need the ready money. Spiritually rewarding as it must be to own vast tracts of countryside, paintings by Rembrandt and Gainsborough, a house designed by one of the Adam Brothers and furnished by Chippendale, tapestries by the mile and porcelain by the ton—it is all a dead loss as far as cash flow (and death duties) are concerned.

What you get for your entrance fee differs enormously from one house to another. In some houses you are left completely free to wander at will, soaking up the atmosphere. In some you are organized into groups that then process through the house like bands of prisoners behind enemy lines. Occasionally you may find that your mentor is a member of the family, who will gleefully relate stories of uncles, aunts, and cousins back to the Crusades. Those are often the best.

Three facts should be kept in mind. Many houses are unreachable except by car. Hours are always subject to change, so it's always best to ring up the day before and inquire: At times, people arrive standing on the doorstep staring at a bolted door. Also, most houses are only open in the warm-weather seasons, from April to October. However, some of these have celebrated parks—Blenheim Palace and Chatsworth come to mind—that are utter delights in themselves and are open through much of the year. Everyone has his or her own top ten list—Knole, Longleat, Woburn, etc.—but don't forget lesser known Neoclassical abodes and those wonderful mock-medieval Victorian piles, such as Castle Drogo in Devon, designed for Sir Julius Drewe, the founder of a chain of grocery stores. There is something keenly appropriate about the fact that the last great castle built in Britain was created for a shopkeeper. Napoléon would have approved.

The Performing Arts

One of the main reasons so many people want to visit Britain is its enviable reputation in the performing arts. The country is exactly what Shakespeare described, an "isle full of noises, sounds and sweet airs that give delight and hurt not." In music and drama, opera and ballet, there are endless opportunities for visitors to enjoy themselves to the hilt. Although the political dogmas of Thatcherism and the restraints of the recession hit the bank accounts of arts organizations badly, thanks to private sponsorship, the performing arts scene is still surprisingly healthy.

BALLET➤ Ballet is a surprising art to flourish in Britain, and it must be admitted that it only does so with a struggle. The premier company is located at the Royal Opera House, Covent Garden, sharing it with the Royal Opera company. The Royal Ballet is going through a rather bad patch, suffering as it does from artistic arteriosclerosis. It is no longer adventuresome enough in its choice of repertoire, having to dance endless performances of favorite three-act classics just to make ends meet. But on a good night, as with the Royal Opera, a ballet performance in that lovely theater can be memorable.

The sibling Birmingham Royal Ballet is just the reverse. Young, zesty, with an adventuresome director in Peter Wright, it is yet another excellent reason for visiting Birmingham. The Festival Ballet, which renamed itself the English National Ballet with very little cause, is Britain's only major dance company without a permanent home. It regularly tours its repertoire of classics countrywide. There are several other smaller companies that tour the country, but that have suffered serious cutbacks from the financial restrictions of recent years.

FESTIVALS➤ Britain is a land of festivals, mostly, though not exclusively, in the summer. Whatever the size of the town, it'll have a festival some time. Some are of international scope, while others are small local wingdings. Leading the parade is the Edinburgh Festival (mid-August–early September), born in the dark days after World War II, when people needed cheering up. Today it is still going strong, with opera, drama, recitals, and ballet by artists from all over the world. The festival now has the added attraction of the Fringe, a concurrent event, with as many as 800 performances crammed into three weeks: small-scale productions from the classic to the bizarre, held in everything from telephone kiosks to church halls.

Smaller than Edinburgh's event, but still notable, are the dozens of festivals up and down the country. In Bath, the International Festival (late May–mid-June) is noted for its music especially. In Aldeburgh, a windswept East Anglian seaside town, the Festival of Music and the Arts (mid–late June) is dedicated to the memory of Benjamin Britten, and again is mainly a music festival. In Cheltenham there are two festivals, one musical (July), the other (early–mid-October) dedicated to literature, with readings, seminars, and lectures. York has both an early-music festival (summer), and a Viking one (February). Llandridnod Wells, in Wales, goes Victorian and dresses up (late August). Worcester, Hereford, and Gloucester take turns mounting the annual Three Choirs Festival (mid-August), the oldest in the world, which has seen premieres of some notable music. Truro stages a Three Spires Festival (June) in imitation. Wales has an annual feast of song and poetry (late July–early August) called the Royal National Eisteddfod. At Chichester in Sussex there is a summer drama festival that has been so popular that the town has managed to build a theater specially for it. At Ludlow, Shakespeare is performed during the summer in the open air, with the dramatic castle as backdrop. All these festivals have the advantage of focussing a visit to a town and helping you to meet the locals, but be sure to book well in advance, as they are extremely popular.

MUSIC➤ Music performance, too, has seen a tremendous surge in popularity in the last 50 years. Recently, this popularity has been made concrete, as it were, with the opening of two major new concert halls, both with notable acoustics. Symphony Hall in Birmingham is the new home of the Birmingham Symphony, under its phenomenal young conductor, Simon Rattle. Apart from Birmingham, other cities have fine resident orchestras, including Liverpool, Manchester, and even the seaside town of Bournemouth.

In London, the three concert halls on the South Bank, together with the Barbican, the Albert Hall, and the Wigmore Hall, all provide the capital with venues for a rich and varied musical fare. For example, every night for six weeks in the summer, sponsored by the BBC, the Albert Hall hosts the "Proms"—the biggest series of concerts in the world, involving 10 or more orchestras and dozens of other artists.

Musical life around the country flourishes even outside the festival season. One particularly interesting aspect is the increasing number of empty churches that are being turned into community concert halls, and excellent ones they make, too. The prime example is London's lovely Baroque church of St. John's, Smith Square.

OPERA➤ Apart from the two major companies in London, the English National Opera, and the Royal Opera at Covent Garden, there are two other national companies, the Welsh National at Cardiff, and the Scottish National in Glasgow. They both have adventuresome artistic policies, attacking such blockbusters as Wagner's *Ring* and *The Trojans* of Berlioz. They also tour, the Welsh National especially, appearing in small towns around the principality, even performing in movie houses when no other stage is available. There is also a northern England company, originally a spin-off from the English National, called Opera North, which is based in Leeds, and is as venturesome as its begetter.

Opera has always been an extravagant art form, and the recession has hit it severely. But one company has managed to build itself a new home. Glyndebourne, in deepest Sussex, relies entirely on sponsors and its ticket sales, having no state subsidy. It opened a new theater in 1994, ending 50 years of its "let's-do-an-opera-in-the-barn" image. A visit there will cost you an arm and a leg, but you'll feel like a guest at a very superior house party.

The two London companies are poles apart. The Royal Opera at Covent Garden is socially the most prestigious. It is housed in an atmospheric, plush-and-gilt, 1812 theater. But it suffers from the problems that bedevil all companies that rely largely on international stars—not enough rehearsal time, a wobbly artistic policy, and stratospherically expensive seat prices. The English National Opera (ENO) was originally a *Volksoper,* based at the small Sadler's Wells Theater in north London. It moved to the Coliseum, beside Trafalgar Square, some 30 years ago. It is still a peoples' opera, though now housed in a huge theater. For the last decade it has had a brilliantly innovative directorial team that has settled its reputation as the leader of opera fashion. Seat prices here are half those at Covent Garden, and the productions are excitingly inventive. The company is a team, mostly of British singers, who act as well as they sing. The one drawback is that the auditorium sometimes dwarfs the voices.

THEATER➢ An evening taking in a play is a vital element of any visitor's trip to Britain. And not just in London's West End. There are provincial theaters in most of the cities and large towns up and down the land. Several of the most interesting were built soon after World War II, and are often impressive pieces of civic architecture. The Birmingham Rep's modern building, with its great glass wall, dominated the city center for years before it was joined by the new Symphony Hall. The theaters in Sheffield, Derby, Nottingham, and Leicester all dramatically expressed the role that the arts were expected to play in their cities' postwar lives. In Coventry it was as important to build a new theater as a new cathedral.

But not all theaters are in recent buildings. The Bristol Old Vic has modern theatrical quarters that surround a delightful Georgian auditorium, lovingly preserved. In Manchester, the Royal Exchange Theatre is a space-capsule theater-in-the-round constructed inside an 1840s Victorian stock exchange, like a giant metal spider trapped in an ornate teapot. The productions here are some of the most exciting in the country.

Many of the provincial theaters have developed their own national and international reputations. The Haymarket in Leicester is renowned for musicals, many of which have transferred to London. Theatre Clwyd in Mold, North Wales, is almost a national theater for Wales, with brilliantly cast revivals of the classics, which travel far afield. In Scarborough, a seaside town in Yorkshire, the dramatist-director Alan Ayckbourn has run for many years the Stephen Joseph Theatre, where he tries out his own plays, most of which are regularly transferred to London, appearing as often as not at the National Theatre.

But the delight of British regional theaters lies in their great diversity and local panache. In the little town of Richmond, in Yorkshire, is a charming little Georgian theater, seating about 200 in rows and balconies that still reflect the 18th-century class divisions. In Bagnor, near Newbury, Berkshire, a water mill has been converted into a lovely little theater overlooking a lake. Porthcurno, near Penzance, Cornwall, has the Minack Theatre, which is situated on a cliff top, overlooking the sea. The lovely 1819 Theatre Royal in Bury St. Edmunds is owned and run by the National Trust and is still fully functioning. There are woodland theaters, theaters in barns, and several in grand old country houses.

Of course, the pinnacle of the dramatic scene consists of two great national companies, the Royal National Theatre and the Royal Shakespeare Company (RSC). They do have separate identities, though it is not always easy to pin down the way in which they differ. The RSC (as it is always known) is the more prolific, performing in five auditoriums, including two at the Barbican in London—one a large house built to its own specifications, the other called The Pit, a small studio space. RSC has three stages at Stratford-upon-Avon—the large Memorial Theatre, the Swan, and The Other Place. Thanks to the financial help of an American philanthropist, the Swan was constructed inside the only part left of a Victorian theater, which burnt down in 1936. Constructed on the lines of Shakespeare's Globe, it is one of the most exciting acting spaces anywhere in the country. The Other Place is a newer venue used for experimental staging. The RSC has also been keen on touring, but unfortunately, the Company has announced that it had to cancel its tours, yet another victim of the recession.

The National Theatre plays in the three auditoriums in its concrete fortress on the South Bank—the Olivier, the Lyttleton, and the Cottesloe, in descending order of size, the Olivier being huge and the Cottesloe studio-sized. Of the two companies, the RSC is the more cohesive, with a very impressive volume of work and a steadily developing style, though it also suffers from serious lapses of taste and concentration in its productions. The great majority of its offerings are works of Shakespeare and the English classics, with occasional ventures into musicals. The National, on the other hand, ransacks world drama, and has had notable successes with Greek classics and French tragedy, as well as mounting some of the best stagings of American musicals anywhere outside Broadway. It also attracts star performers more than the RSC, which relies largely on teamwork, and creates stars from its own ranks. Both companies suffer from serious financial problems, even though some of their best productions are transferred to the commercial sector, and often develop into considerable hits.

Pubs

The venerable English pub is endlessly diverse. With some exceptions, pubs in towns tend to be dull, and many have been modernized in dubious taste, with too much chrome, plush, and plastic. But the country pub can be a real joy. It will often be called by the name of the local landed family—*The Bath Arms,* or *Lord Crewe's Arms,* "arms" meaning the family coat of heraldic arms on the inn sign—and very possibly it will have old beams and inglenooks, and a blazing log fire in winter. If you sit at a table in the corner, you can have privacy of a sort; but between those who prop up the bar, conversation is general, no introductions are needed, and new acquaintances are quickly made.

Shopping

Throughout Britain, souvenir and gift shops abound, and museum and gallery shops offer high-quality posters, books, art prints, and crafts. Both Wales and Scotland are famous for woolen products, and retail outlets sell sweaters, tartans, tweeds, scarves, skirts, and hats at reasonable prices. Traditional Celtic jewelry is also popular. The Midlands offers world-renowned china and pottery, including Wedgwood, Royal Doulton, and Royal Worcester. The factory outlet shops, where you can buy seconds, are well worth a detour. The Southwest, especially Devon and Cornwall, is known for its edibles—"scrumpy" (strong local cider), homemade toffees, rich fudge, and heavenly clotted cream. At factory shops that sell directly to the public, you can save as much as 50% on the normal store price.

Sports and the Outdoors

BOATING➢ Canals crisscross Britain, a legacy of pre-railway days that now enriches the weekend of many a Briton. In major tourist centers such as York, Bristol, Bath, and Stratford-upon-Avon you'll find many short river and canal cruises in season. The Broads in Norfolk and Suffolk, East Anglia, is one of the most popular areas in England for boating on canals and lakes. The Lake District has numerous opportunities for sailing, canoeing, rowing, and other boating excursions.

GOLF➢ There are hundreds of fine courses all over Great Britain, especially in Scotland, the birthplace of the sport, and visiting golfers are welcome at many private clubs.

TENNIS➢ Tennis is a favorite recreation in Britain, and most towns have municipal courts where you can play for a small fee. Country hotels, too, often have courts. The hotel service information in each chapter lists tennis availability. In addition, there's the Wimbledon Fortnight, held in late June and early July.

WALKING➢ The whole country is crisscrossed by meandering trails—there are more than 100,000 miles of footpaths in England and Wales. Some are tiny and local, some very long and of historic significance, such as Peddar's Way in East Anglia and the Pennine Way in Yorkshire.

WATER SPORTS➢ Britain brims with rivers and lakes, and it is possible to swim and fish on many of them. One drawback is that waters are often polluted; the other problem is that the water can be icy cold! Most local authorities operate indoor pools, and a few have outdoor ones; entrance fees are minimal. Nearly all large hotels now have pools, as indicated in the hotel entries.

In some areas, like Cornwall and the coast of Wales, there are excellent sandy beaches with good swimming, but generally, the sea around Britain is very cold most of the year and much of the coast is fringed with pebbled beaches. Many seaside towns have windsurfing boards available. Some beaches are awarded a European Blue Flag, granted to beaches with a high standard of water quality (they should be cleaned daily during high season), and good facilities. Britain wins very few each year, usually only a couple of dozen, mostly in Wales and the Southwest. To counter the disturbing picture created by winning so few European Blue Flags, Britain has instituted its own awards, the Seaside Awards—which, coincidentally, are also blue! Always ask if a beach has been given either a Flag or a Seaside Award before deciding to use it.

FODOR'S CHOICE

No two people agree on what makes a perfect vacation, but it's fun and helpful to know what others think. Here's a compendium drawn from the must-see lists of hundreds of Britain-based tourists. For detailed information about these memories-in-the-making, refer to the appropriate sections in this book.

Stately Homes

★**Blenheim Palace, Thames Valley.** England's only rival to Versailles, this is Britain's largest stately home and the birthplace of Winston Churchill. Home to the Dukes of Marlborough, the early 18th-century Italianate mansion in Woodstock stands majestically in 2,000 acres of parkland and exquisite gardens landscaped by Capability Brown.

★**Castle Howard, Yorkshire.** Built over 60 years (1699–1759), this famous home (the setting for TV's "Brideshead Revisited") is without equal in Northern England; a magnificent central hall spanned by a handpainted ceiling leads to staterooms and galleries overflowing with precious furniture and works of fine art. Outside is a magnificent park, dotted with beautiful marble temples and follies.

★**Haddon Hall, Lancashire and the Peaks.** Set within the Wye Valley—"the most beautiful vale in England"—Haddon Hall seems to be a medieval book illumination come to life: a 15th-century castellated manor bristling with slate roofs and towers, it appears like a miniature town from the surrounding hills (a fabulous photo op) and remains, in the words of historian Hugo Massingbird-Montgomery, "the beau ideal of an English country house." It's just a few miles away from its more famous neighbor, Chatsworth House.

★**Chatsworth House, Lancashire and the Peaks.** This Palladian palace in the Peak District—surrounded by glorious parkland, gardens, cascading water, and terraces—is the ancestral home of the dukes of Devonshire; its 175 are adorned with portraits by Van Dyck and Rembrandt, sculptures, tapestries, and some of the finest Old Master drawings in Europe.

★**Holkham Hall, East Anglia.** Set amid a huge expanse of sandy beaches, dunes, and salt marsh backed by pine woods, this neoclassical Italian-style mansion in Holkham has the most spectacular room in Britain: a great hall modeled after ancient Rome's Baths of Diocletian, adorned with gold and alabaster and 12 stately brocade-lined rooms filled with paintings by Gainsborough, Rubens, Raphael, Van Dyck, and other European old masters.

★**Ightham Mote, Southeast.** Everyone's dream of a moated medieval manor house, this enchanting 14th-century abode has several additions reflecting different periods—a medieval Great Hall, a Tudor chapel, handpainted Chinese wallpaper, and an 18th-century Palladian window.

Restaurants

★**Bibendum, London.** Once London's leading scene-arena, this chic-and-be-seen spot is housed in the marvelous Michelin House, with its art deco decorations and brilliant stained glass. The kitchen serves simple dishes prepared perfectly by Michael Harris—steak au poivre, boeuf bourgignon, tripe as it ought to be cooked, and Christmas pudding ice-cream not to be missed. ££££

★**Carved Angel, Dartmouth, Southwest.** Situated on the quay with views of the harbor, this eatery has long been considered one of Britain's best, serving Provençal cuisine and fresh local products, such as Dart River salmon and samphire, a seashore plant used in fish dishes. £££–££££

★**Landgate Bistro, Rye, Southeast.** All the local fish is excellent at this lively, bustling establishment popular with locals. Be sure to sample the walnut and treacle tart. £–££

★**Le Caprice, London.** This may command the deepest loyalty of any London restaurant because it gets everything right: the glamorous, glossy black interior, the perfect pitch of the service, and the food, halfway between Euro-peasant and fashion plate. It also features some of the best people-watching in town. ££££

★**Le Gavroche, London.** *Tres formidable!* Many consider this to be London's finest. The basement dining room is comfortable and serious, hung with oil paintings, with dark racing-green walls. Michel Roux offers capital-C-classical dishes that are among the most expensive in town—so try this place for its relatively affordable lunch. ££££

★**Le Manoir aux Quat' Saisons, Great Milton, Thames Valley.** This 15th/16th-century manor house with sumptuous rooms has held its position as one of Britain's leading restaurants for years, where owner-chef Raymond Blanc exercises his award-winning French culinary skills. The set menus at lunch time make it almost reasonable. ££££

★**Miller Howe, Windermere, Lake District.** At this small, white Edwardian hotel with an international reputation for comfort and fine cuisine, every attention has been given to the interior decor, which includes fine antiques and paintings. It's beautifully situated, with views across Windermere to the Langdale Pikes. ££££

★**The People's Palace, London.** Thank goodness—thanks to this palace, you can finally have a civilized meal during your South Bank arts encounter. With menus by trendy chef Gary Rhodes, this has remarkably low prices considering it has the greatest river view in town. Here, the more British the dish, the more reliable it is. ££

★**Rules, London.** An institution—an Edwardian restaurant that was a great favorite of Lily Langtry's, among others—this spot features veddy-veddy period atmosphere. This makes it more than a little touristy, but that's because it's so quaint. £££

★**Thornbury Castle, Thornbury, Heart of England.** People come from all over England to dine on traditional British food at this genuine 16th-century castle with huge fireplaces, antiques, paintings, and mullioned windows, to say nothing of an extensive garden. £££–££££

★**Ye Olde Cheshire Cheese, London.** Yes, it is a tourist trap, but this most historic of all London pubs (it dates from 1667) deserves a visit because of its authentic heritage-rich decor—London at its Time Machine best. And this regular of Dr. Johnson and Dickens offers up the quintessential steak-and-kidney pie.

Hotels

★**Balmoral Hotel, Edinburgh, Scotland.** The attention to detail in the elegant rooms, the plush and stylish Grill Room restaurant, and the sheer élan that has recreated the Edwardian splendor of this former grand railroad hotel all make staying at the Balmoral very special. ££££

★**Black Hostelry, Ely, East Anglia.** You'll have lots of privacy at this highly popular bed-and-breakfast with enormous rooms and old-fashioned English furnishings—it's right on the city's cathedral grounds, in one of the finest medieval domestic buildings still in use. £

★**Dukes, London.** This small, exclusive, Edwardian-style hotel is possibly London's quietest hotel, secreted in its cul-de-sac in the heart of St. James's. Decorated in patrician, antiques-splattered style, it's filled with squashy sofas and portraits of assorted dukes, and it offers the best in personal service. £££

★**Ettington Park, Stratford-upon-Avon, Heart of England.** To avoid the crowds in Stratford, stay at this marvelously restored, huge Victorian house that stands in its own grounds and looks across tranquil river meadows haunted by herons. £££–££££

★**Hazlitt's, London.** Located in Soho, this hotel is in three connected early 18th-century houses, one the former home of famed essayist William Hazlitt. Disarmingly friendly, full of personality, devoid of room service, the hotel is loved for its

Victorian charm. Book way ahead—this place is the London address of literary types and antique dealers everywhere. £££

★ **Middlethorpe Hall, York, Yorkshire.** This handsome, superbly restored 18th-century mansion on the edge of the city has an award-winning French restaurant and rooms filled with antiques, paintings, and fresh flowers; the extensive grounds boast a lake, a 17th-century dovecote, and "ha-ha's"—drops in the garden level that create cunning views. ££££

★ **Old Parsonage, Oxford, Thames Valley.** It's rare to find an attractive, restored, 17th-century country-house hotel with stone gables and mullioned windows in the middle of a city. Open fires, fascinating pictures, comfortable rooms, and immaculate service make this a hotel to remember.

★ **Rising Sun, Lynmouth, Southwest.** A recent conversion from a 14th-century inn and a row of thatched cottages created this intriguing hotel with great views over Lynmouth fishing village, especially from the terraced garden out back. Legend has it that the poet Shelley spent his honeymoon on this site. ££

★ **Queensberry Hotel, Bath, Heart of England.** This intimate, elegant hotel on a quiet residential street near The Circus is in three 1772 town houses built for the marquis of Queensberry. Renovations have preserved the Regency stucco ceilings and cornices and original marble tiling on the fireplaces. £££

★ **The Savoy, London.** This historic, grand, late-Victorian hotel, beloved by the international influential, has spacious, tasteful, bright, and comfortable rooms, furnished with antiques and serviced by valets. A room facing the Thames costs an arm and a leg, but there are few better views in London. ££££

Cathedrals and Churches

★ **Canterbury Cathedral, Southeast.** The focal point of the city of Canterbury, this cathedral is a living textbook of medieval architecture, combining Gothic and Norman styles. The church is well known as the site of archbishop Thomas á Becket's murder in 1170, and a series of 13th-century stained glass windows illustrates Becket's miracles.

★ **King's College Chapel, East Anglia.** One of the most beautiful buildings in England, this late-Gothic, English-style church has great fan-vaulting supported by soaring side columns. Its huge interior is filled with ever-changing light from the vast stained-glass windows. Every Christmas Eve, a festival of carols sung by the chapel's famous choir is broadcast around the world.

★ **Salisbury Cathedral, South.** Built in a short span of only 38 years (1220–58), the towering cathedral has a spire that is a miraculous feat of medieval engineering, and an interior with remarkable lancet windows and sculpted tombs of crusaders and other medieval heroes.

★ **Westminster Abbey, London.** Britain's monarchs have been crowned at this most ancient of great churches since 1066. The present abbey, a largely 13th- and 14th-century rebuilding of an 11th-century church, has many memorials to royalty, writers, and statemen, and the famous Tomb of the Unknown Warrior; its Henry VII Chapel is an exquisite example of the rich late-Gothic style.

★ **York Minster, Yorkshire.** The city of York has the largest Gothic church in England. Contributing to its singular beauty and magnificence are its soaring columns; the ornamentation of its 14th-century nave; the great east window, one of the world's finest examples of medieval glazing; and the splendid Rose Window commemorating the marriage of Henry VII and Elizabeth of York.

Museums and Galleries

★ **British Museum, London.** In a monumental Greek edifice built in the first half of the 19th century, the vast collection of treasures here includes Egyptian, Greek, and Roman antiquities; Renaissance jewelry, pottery, coins, glass; and drawings from virtually every European school since the 15th century.

★ **Fitzwilliam Museum, Cambridge, East Anglia.** In a classical building with an opulent interior, you'll discover an outstanding collection of art (including paintings by John Constable, Gainsborough, and the French Impressionists) and antiquities, including a notable Egyptian section, a large display of English Staffordshire and other pottery, and a fascinating room full of armor and muskets.

★**Museum of the Moving Image, London.** In the South Bank Arts Complex, MOMI joyfully celebrates every aspect of the moving image, from Chinese shadow plays of 2,500 BC to the latest fiber optics and satellite images; cinema and television take center stage.

★**National Gallery of Scotland, Edinburgh, Scotland.** The attractively decorated spacious rooms display a wide-ranging selection of paintings, from Renaissance times to Postimpressionism, with works by Velásquez, El Greco, Rembrandt, Turner, Degas, Monet, and van Gogh, among many others, as well as a fine collection of Scottish art.

NEW AND NOTEWORTHY

Why are the streets in London deserted around 7 PM on a Saturday night? Where is everyone? Well, nearly all Londoners are in front of their telly watching the winning numbers for the day's drawing of the **National Lottery.** Whatever may be the moral implications of so much money being printed, the city is a better place for it. Among the capital's beneficiaries of Lottery money are megaliths of the arts, like the **South Bank Centre,** due to be canopied in undulating glass by Sir Richard Rogers (architect of the Paris Pompidou Centre and the Lloyd's building here), and the **Tate Gallery,** which will split in two by the new century. Underway now is the conversion of the former Bankside Power Station, opposite St. Paul's Cathedral, into the **Tate Gallery of Modern Art.**

Another vast chunk of cash—almost £80 million—is going to the **Royal Opera House,** which needs some spit and polish, having had its last major renovation over 90 years ago. The work will bring the existing Opera House up to snuff and also improve the nearby Covent Garden Piazza, but the biggest sum of money goes toward building a brand new home for the **Royal Ballet.**

Much else has been happening in the cultural centers of London. The **Victoria & Albert** pioneered a move that will surely spread to all the major museums, with its Wednesday night **Late View.** One of the first innovations of new Director, Alan Borg, this isn't merely extended opening hours, but a tiny party, with wine bars, gallery talks, and high-profile lecture series. **Kensington Palace** has reopened with its state rooms refurbished to appear just as they did when young Princess Victoria was growing up. Miles away in the City, the **Museum of London** has added the Roman London Gallery, complete with Roman street, and several Roman interiors, both patrician and working class. Less edifying, but more attractive to the kids, is Windsor Castle's new neighbor, the **Legoland Theme Park,** with gadzillions of Lego and Duplo bricks formed into a "Miniland" version of Europe, a fairy-tale boat ride, a pirate treasure trail and—believe it or not—a children's driving school.

Finally, we must pay homage to the continuing rise of the restaurant as all things to all people in this increasingly Continental city. Everyone's a foodie, and—although a national newspaper propounded the theory that it is in fact the same 900 people who are keeping every one of London's restaurants going—everyone eats out. Among the bigger, newer places we do and don't list are **Coast, The Avenue, Mezzo, L'Odeon, Vong, The Astral, The Criterion, The People's Palace,** and . . . Well, sorry, but the crystal ball's a little cloudy; come and see for yourself.

The reconstruction of **Shakespeare's Globe**—Britain's most eagerly anticipated four-star, must-see attraction—has put off its official opening date once again, now scheduled for the summer of 1997 (until then, visitors can tour the site under construction for a fascinating behind-the-scenes look). Throughout Britain, however, new attractions are up and running, including the **Royal Armouries Museum** in Leeds (housing some of the great collections formerly at the Tower of London), the **Shrewsbury Quest**—a recreation of a medieval monastery relating to the literary sleuth Brother Cadfael—which opened across from Shrewsbury's Abbey Church, and the new gallery now open at **Hereford Cathedral,** displaying the cathedral's extraordinary Mappa Mundi medieval map. For stately-house buffs, **Uppark,** near Harting, is due to reopen its doors soon—

after a devastating fire—thanks to a superlative National Trust reconstruction.

East Anglia will host the national **Year of Opera and Musical Theatre,** which takes place throughout 1997. As well as major international productions in the ancient cultural centers of Cambridge, Norwich, Lincoln, and Colchester—with their historic theaters and celebrated heritage sites—there will be a year-round feast of smaller-scale and local productions. Edinburgh's world-famous annual **Edinburgh Festival** will take place August 10–30, with the concurrent **Edinburgh Tattoo** scheduled for August 2–24, 1997.

The privatization of **BritRail** continues apace. In the past, train travel throughout Britain was maintained by one government agency; today, British Rail is organizing itself into 25 separate companies. Reports that this has led to chaos at the ticket counters have been greatly exaggerated. The government has largely come through on its promises to retain through-ticketing and an integrated timetable. Travelers who avail themselves in advance of BritRail's special package deals and passes can bypass any confusion. The latest package is the BritRail Pass + Eurostar combination, which allows transport via the Channel Tunnel plus a four- or eight-day Flexipass—valid for a three-month period—in Britain. In addition, you can now avail yourself of Eurostar service from many new points within the BritRail system. In the past, you could only train at London for Europe; now, you can embark at Plymouth, Bristol, and many other cities, and pull into Paris, Brussels, or Amsterdam.

If you are intending to fly to Scotland from London, take advantage of the current **fare wars** on the route between London's three airports and Edinburgh or Glasgow. At press time, Ryanair leads the field for lowest fares between London Stansted (with its excellent rail links from London's Liverpool St. Station) and Glasgow Prestwick.

Aberdeen is still talking about 1991's **Tall Ships Race,** which returns in 1997, from July 12 through 15. The gathering of the world's finest and largest sailing vessels is visually spectacular, especially as they parade offshore before beginning their race to Trondheim in Norway across the North Sea. Since the road between Edinburgh and Aberdeen is all divided highway, Scotland's most northerly city is only a couple of hours above the central belt of Scotland by car.

GREAT ITINERARIES

Writers at Home: Southwest England

All of Britain contains a wealth of fictional and real literary figures and places; there are several literary walking tours of London alone. For those who like to venture out on their own and explore more than just isolated plaques commemorating who slept (or was born or died) where, the following excursion takes in some lovely settings as well as enough artistic associations to keep any literature buff happy. For a free copy of the new pamphlet "Literary Britain," send a SASE (business size, 52¢) to any office of the British Tourist Authority (☞ Visitor Information *in* Important Contacts A to Z).

DURATION➢ Four days

GETTING AROUND➢ **By Car:** It is 220 miles round-trip from London (southwest). **By Public Transportation:** Trains and buses depart regularly from London to Dorchester and Bath. Local services are available within the region, but plan carefully.

TWO DAYS➢ **Hardy's Wessex**

The environs of Dorchester are Hardy country. The early years of his life were spent in **Higher Brockhampton** (2 mi west of Dorchester on A31), part of the parish of Stinsford, or "Mellstock." Leave at least a day to visit Sherborne, Cranborne, and Bridport, and to travel to Lullworth Cove, to get a true sense of the countryside that inspired so much of his work. All the sights are within 25 miles of Dorchester. You can also include Salisbury and Stonehenge, which figure prominently in *Jude the Obscure* and *Tess of the D'Urbervilles,* respectively, by going northwest 30 miles on A31/A350/A30.

TWO DAYS➢ **The Homes of Jane Austen**

From rural delights we head for the civilized society of Jane Austen's world and novels. *Persuasion* and *Northanger Abbey* are especially associated with the city of **Bath** (105 miles west of London on A4). She visited Bath frequently in her youth, and lived here between the ages of 26 and 31 (1801–1806). In 1809, Austen moved with her mother and sister Cassandra to **Chawton,** 50 miles south and 30 miles east of Bath on A36/A31. You will pass through Southampton, where she lived for three years, although all records of precisely where have been lost. She lived in Chawton until 1817, and her home there is now a museum. In the last year of her life she moved to lodgings in **Winchester,** 10 miles south on A31. She lived here at 8 College Street, and she is buried at Winchester Cathedral.

Aristocratic Houses of West Yorkshire and Derbyshire

Set between the industrial cities of England's east Midlands and Yorkshire are some of the finest mansions and grounds in the country. Many are within easy reach of one another, making a few days' manor-house spotting easy as well as fun. These two outings start from York and Nottingham, but you can just as easily start out from a base in Derby, Leeds, or Sheffield.

DURATION➢ Four–five days

GETTING AROUND➢ **By Car:** It is 60 miles round-trip from York; 80 miles round-trip from Nottingham.

TWO DAYS➢ **Stately Houses in West Yorkshire**

There are three houses to visit on this itinerary, which traces an ellipse southeast of York. The first stop is **Harewood House,** home of the earl and countess of Harewood and designed in 1759 with grounds landscaped by Capability Brown. It is on A64/A659, 25 miles west of York. **Oakwell Hall,** 12 miles south through Leeds, is an Elizabethan manor house complete with moat. **Lotherton Hall,** east on M62 and north on A642, is a country-house museum, with an Edwardian garden, bird garden, and deer park.

TWO–THREE DAYS➢ **Stately Houses in Derbyshire**

From Nottingham, follow A453/B587 to Melbourne, and **Melbourne Hall.** Ten miles northwest via the road to Derby and A52 brings you to **Kedleston Hall,** a magnificent mansion designed by the Adam brothers. Head due north for 20 miles to reach **Haddon Hall,** and 3 miles farther, **Chatsworth.** The first is medieval; the second dates from the 17th century. Finally, turning back toward Nottingham for 10 miles on A617, you will come to **Hardwick Hall,** built in 1597.

Castles and Strongholds

This itinerary, based in northeastern Kent, offers a quick history of castle architecture and the opportunity to visit some of the best examples Britain has to offer.

DURATION➢ Two–three days

GETTING AROUND➢ **By Car:** It is 150 miles round-trip from London. **By Public Transportation:** Check with British Rail information centers and National Express or other bus companies.

ONE–TWO DAYS➢ **Down to Dover**

Heading southeast from London on A2/A257 for Sandwich brings you to **Richborough Castle,** a 4th-century Saxon fort. From here take A258 to Deal, where you will find both **Deal Castle,** dating from 1540, and **Walmer Castle,** another Renaissance fortification, converted in the 18th century. Next comes **Dover Castle,** one of England's most impressive castles, which was still in military use as late as World War II.

ONE DAY➢ **The Coast and Leeds**

South down the coast is the town of Hythe and **Lympne Castle,** a 14th- to 15th-century building with a 13th-century Norman east tower. Leaving the best for last, M20 northwest will take you to **Leeds Castle,** a magnificent Norman fortress with 19th-century additions, set on two islands in a lake, surrounded by landscaped parkland.

FESTIVALS AND SEASONAL EVENTS

Tickets for popular sporting events must be obtained months in advance—check first to see if your travel agent can get them. There is a complete list of ticket agencies in *Britain Events*, free from the British Tourist Authority.

WINTER

1ST 2 WKS JAN.➢ **London International Boat Show** is the largest boat show in Europe. ✉ *Earls Court Exhibition Centre, Warwick Rd., London SW5 9TA,* ☎ *01784/473377.*

FEB.–MAR.➢ **London Arts Season** showcases the city's extensive arts scene, with bargain-priced tickets and special events. ✉ *British Travel Centre, 12 Regent St., SW1Y 4PQ,* ☎ *0171/839–6181 (Arts season only).*

SPRING

APR.–JAN.➢ **Shakespeare Season** is held by the world-renowned Royal Shakespeare Company. ✉ *Stratford-upon-Avon, Warwickshire CV37 6BB,* ☎ *01789/295623 for box office.*

MID-APR.➢ **London Marathon.** *Information:* ✉ *Box 262, Richmond, Surrey TW10 5JB,* ☎ *0181/948–7935.*

LATE MAY➢ **Chelsea Flower Show** is Britain's major flower show, covering 22 acres. ✉ *Royal Hospital, Chelsea, London SW3,* ☎ *0171/834–4333.*

LATE MAY–EARLY JUNE➢ **Glyndebourne Opera** opens its third season in its brand new auditorium. ✉ *Glyndebourne Festival Opera, Glyndebourne, Lewes, East Sussex BN8 5UU,* ☎ *01273/812321.*

SUMMER

EARLY JUNE➢ **Derby Day** is the world-renowned horse-racing event, at Epsom Racecourse, Epsom, Surrey. *Information:* ✉ *United Racecourses Ltd., Racecourse Paddock, Epsom, Surrey KT18 5NJ,* ☎ *01372/463072.*

MID-JUNE➢ **Trooping the Colour** is Queen Elizabeth's colorful official birthday show at Horse Guards Parade, Whitehall, London. (Her actual birthdate is in April.) *Write for tickets early in the year:* ✉ *The Brigade Major, H.Q. Household Division, Chelsea Barracks, London SW1 8RF.*

LATE JUNE–EARLY JULY➢ The **Wimbledon Lawn Tennis Championships** are bigger every year. Applications for the ticket lottery are available Oct.–Dec. ✉ *All-England Lawn Tennis and Croquet Club, Church Rd., Wimbledon, London SW19 5AE,* ☎ *0181/946–2244.*

EARLY–MID-JULY➢ **Llangollen International Musical Eisteddfod** sees the little Welsh town of Llangollen overflow with music, costumes, and color. ✉ *Musical Eisteddfod Office, Llangollen, Clwyd LL20 8NG,* ☎ *01978/860236.*

MID-JULY➢ **Royal Tournament** features military displays and pageantry by the Royal Navy, Royal Marines, Army, and Royal Air Force. ✉ *Earls Court Exhibition Centre, Warwick Rd., London SW5 9TA,* ☎ *0171/373–8141.*

MID-JULY➢ **British Open Championship** is played at a different course each year. It will be held in St. Andrews in 1995, July 20–23. ✉ *Royal & Ancient Golf Club, St. Andrews, Fife KY16 9JD,* ☎ *01334/72112.*

MID-JULY–MID-SEPT.➢ **Henry Wood Promenade Concerts** is a celebrated series of concerts, founded in 1895. ✉ *Royal Albert Hall, Kensington Gore, London SW7 2AP,* ☎ *0171/589–8212.*

MID-AUG.➢ **Three Choirs Festival** is an ancient choral and orchestral music festival, to be held in Hereford in 1997. ✉ *John Harris, The Gable, South St., Leominster, Hereford HR6 8JN,* ☎ *01568/615223.*

MID-AUG.–EARLY SEPT.➢ **Edinburgh International Festival,** the world's largest festival of the arts, includes the nighttime Edinburgh Military Tattoo. ✉ *Edinburgh Festival Society, 21 Market St., Edinburgh EH1 1BW,* ☎ *0131/226-4001.*

AUTUMN

EARLY NOV.➤ **Lord Mayor's Procession and Show** coincides with the Lord Mayor's inauguration, with a procession from the Guildhall to the Royal Courts of Justice. No tickets. *The City of London,* ☎ *0171/606-3030.*

2 London

If London contained only its famous landmarks—the Tower of London, Big Ben, Parliament, Buckingham Palace—it would still rank as one of the world's top destinations. But London is much more. It is a bevy of British Bobbies, an ocean of black umbrellas, and an unconquered continuance of more than 2,000 years of history. A city that loves to be explored, it beckons with great museums, green parks, and history-steeped houses. Then discover London's ever-changing dining scene, its chic boutiques—not for nothing is Princess Di a world-class shopper—and the best theater in the world.

Updated by Kate Sekules

LONDON IS AN ANCIENT CITY and its history greets you at every corner. To gain a sense of its continuity, stand on Waterloo Bridge at sunset. To the east, the great globe of St. Paul's Cathedral glows golden in the dying sunlight as it has since the 17th century: still majestic amid the towers of glass and steel that hem it in. To the west stand the mock-medieval ramparts of Westminster, home to the "Mother of Parliaments," which has met here or hereabouts since the 1250s. And past them both snakes the swift, dark Thames, as it flowed past the first Roman settlement nearly 2,000 years ago.

For much of its history, innumerable epigrams and observations have been coined about London by her enthusiasts and detractors. The great 18th-century author and wit, Samuel Johnson, said that a man who is tired of London is tired of life. Oliver Wendell Holmes said, "No person can be said to know London. The most that anyone can claim is that he knows something of it." In all likelihood a more appropriate tribute paid to London would state that the capital of Great Britain is—simply stated—one of the most interesting places on earth. There is no other place like it in its agglomeration of architectural sins and sudden intervention of almost rural sights, in its medley of styles, in its mixture of the green loveliness of parks and the modern gleam of neon. Thankfully, the old London of Queen Anne and Georgian architecture can still be discovered, as in a palimpsest parchment, under the hasty routine of later architecture.

Discovering it takes a bit of work, however. Modern-day London still largely reflects its medieval layout, a willfully difficult tangle of streets. This swirl of spaghetti will be totally confusing to anyone brought up on the rigidity of a grid system. Even Londoners get lost in their own city, and all own at least one dog-eared copy of the indispensable A–Z streetfinder (they come under different names). But London's bewildering street pattern will be a plus for the visitor who wants to experience its indefinable historic atmosphere. London is a walking city and will repay every moment you spend exploring on foot. The visitor to London who wants to penetrate beyond the crust of popular knowledge about London is well advised not only to pay visits to St. Paul's Cathedral and to the Tower, but also to set aside some of his or her limited time for wandering. Walk in the city's back streets and mews, around Park Lane and Kensington. Pass up Buckingham Palace for the more truly authentic Kensington Palace (Princess Di's abode). Take in the National Gallery, but don't forget London's "Time Machine" museums, such as the 19th-century homes of Linley Sambourne and Sir John Soane. Abandon the city's identikit shopping streets to discover unique shopping emporia, such as that Victorian-era wonderland, Pollock's Toys. In such ways can you best visualize the shape or, rather, the various shapes of Old London, a curious city that engulfed its own past for the sake of modernity but still lives and breathes the breath of history.

Don't let the tag of "typical tourist" stop you from enjoying the pageantry of the British Royal Family, one of the greatest free shows in the world. Line up for the Changing of the Guard and poke into the Royal Mews for a look at the Coronation Coach. Pomp reaches its zenith in mid-June when the Queen celebrates her official birthday with a parade called Trooping the Color. Royalty watching is by no means restricted to fascinated foreigners. You only have to open the tabloid newspapers to read reports of lurid rumors and family spats. Why not strike up a friendship with a native by discussing the latest installment of "Dallas at the Palace"?

Any vibrant metropolis changes, and crowded, noisy, frequently dirty London is no exception. New skyscrapers now puncture the city's skyline, gleaming and modern in a way that is difficult to accept in this stronghold of conservatism. The black taxi is being supplanted by a sleeker model and by versions of the old one in red, white, gold, and other colors. But all is not under threat. The British bobby is alive and well. The tall, red, double-decker buses still lumber from stop to stop, though their aesthetic match at street level, the glossy red telephone booths, are slowly disappearing. And, of course, teatime is till a hallowed part of the day, with, if you search hard enough, toasted crumpets in winter still honeycombed with sweet butter.

The London you'll discover will surely include some of our enthusiastic recommendations, but be prepared to be taken by surprise. The best that a great city has to offer often comes to you in unexpected ways. Armed with energy and curiosity, and all the practical information and helpful hints in the following pages, one thing remains certain: To quote Dr. Johnson again, you can find "in London all that life can afford."

Pleasures and Pastimes

Dining

London now ranks—and longtime absentees must suspend disbelief here—among the world's top dining scenes. A new generation of chefs has precipitated a fresh approach to food preparation, which you could call "London-style" though most refer to it as "Modern British." Everyone seems to have an opinion about it, and newspapers and magazines now devote columns if not pages to food and restaurant reviews. Everyone reads them and everyone dines out to the point where London has become a significant foodies' town. This healthy scene rests on a solid foundation of ethnic cuisines. Thousands of (mostly northern) Indian restaurants have long ensured that Londoners view a tasty tandoori as a birthright. Chinese—Cantonese, primarily—outposts in London's tiny Chinatown have been around a long time, as have Greek tavernas; now, Thai eateries are proliferating. Places serving Malaysian, Spanish, Russian, Korean, and a trace of Japanese (with more on the way?) are adding to the density of dining choices. After all this, traditional British food, lately revived from its deathbed, appears as one more exotic cuisine in the pantheon.

As for cost, the democratization of restaurants means lighter checks than during the '80s, partly due to the popularity of prix-fixe menus; still, London is not an inexpensive city for dining. Damage-control methods include having lunch as your main meal—many top places feature good-value lunch menus, halving the price of evening à la carte—and ordering a pair of appetizers instead of an entrée, to which few places object. Seek out prix-fixe menus, but watch for hidden extras added to the check, including a "cover," bread and vegetables charged separately, and a service tariff. Many restaurants exclude service charges from the printed menu (which the law obliges them to display outside), then add 10%–15% to the check, or else stamp SERVICE NOT INCLUDED along the bottom, in which case you should add the 10%–15% yourself. Just don't pay twice for service—unscrupulous restaurateurs have been known to add service, but leave off the total on the credit card slip blank. A final caveat: Beware of Sundays. Many restaurants are closed on this day, especially for dinner; likewise, on public holidays. Over the Christmas period, the London restaurant community all but shuts down—only hotels will be prepared to feed you. When in doubt, call ahead.

The Pub

Londoners could no more live without their "local" than they could forgo dinner. The pub—or public house, to give it its full title—is ingrained in the British psyche as social center, bolt-hole, second home. Pub culture—revolving around pints, pool, darts, and sports—is still male-dominated; however, as a result of the gentrification trend that was started in the late '80s by the major breweries (which own most pubs), transforming many ancient smoke- and spittle-stained dives into fantasy Edwardian drawing rooms, women have been entering their welcoming doors in increasing numbers. This decade, the trend has been toward The Bar, superficially identified by its cocktail list, creative paintwork, bare floorboards, and chrome fittings, but the social consequences are the same: These are English pubs, but not as we formerly knew them. When doing a London pub crawl, you must remember one thing: Arcane licensing laws forbid the serving of alcohol after 11 PM (10:30 on Sunday; there are different rules for restaurants)—a circumstance you see in action at 10 minutes to 11, when the "last orders" bell signals a stampede to the bar.

The Arts

There isn't *a* London "arts scene"—there is an infinite variety of them. As long as there are audiences for Feydeau revivals, drag queens, obscure teenage rock bands, hit musicals, body-painted Parisian dancers, and improvised stand-up comedy, someone will figure out how to stage them. Admission prices are not always bargain-basement, but when you consider the cost of a London hotel room, the city's arts and entertainment are easily affordable.

To find out what's showing during your stay, the weekly magazine *Time Out* (it comes out every Wednesday; Tuesday in central London) is an invaluable resource. The *Evening Standard*—especially the Friday edition—also carries listings, as do the "quality" Sunday papers and the Friday and Saturday *Independent, Guardian,* and *Times.* You'll find racks overflowing with leaflets and flyers in most cinema and theater foyers, and you can pick up the free fortnightly "London Theatre Guide" leaflet from most hotels as well as tourist information centers.

THEATER

From Shakespeare to the umpteenth year of *Les Misérables* (or "The Glums," as it's affectionately known), London's West End has the cream of the city's theater offerings. But there's much more to see in London than the offerings of Theaterland and the national companies: Of the 100 or so legitimate theaters operating in the capital, only about half are officially "West End," while the remainder fall under the blanket title of "Fringe." Much like New York's Off- and Off-Off-Broadway, Fringe Theater encompasses everything from off-the-wall "physical theater" pieces to premiers of new plays and revivals of old ones. If you're a theater junkie and want to put together a West End package, the *Complete Guide to London's West End Theatres* has seating plans and booking information for all of the houses. It costs £9.95 from the Society of London Theatres.

MUSIC

London is home to four world-class orchestras. The London Symphony Orchestra is in residence at the Barbican Centre, while the London Philharmonic lives at the Royal Festival Hall—one of the finest concert halls in Europe. Between the Barbican and South Bank, there are concert performances almost every night of the year. The Barbican also presents chamber-music concerts in partnership with such celebrated orchestras as the City of London Sinfonia. The Royal Albert Hall during the Promenade Concert season—July to September—is an unmissable pleasure. Also look for the lunchtime concerts held throughout the city in either smaller concert halls, arts-center foyers, or churches; they usually cost under £5 or are free. St. John's, Smith Square, and St. Martin-in-the-Fields are the major venues and also present evening concerts.

Walking

London's a great walking city, since so many of its treasures are discovered as untouted details—tiny alleyways barely visible on the map, garden squares, churchyards, shop windows, sudden vistas of skyline or park. However, it is big, *very big*. And often rather damp. With the obvious precautions of comfortable, weatherproof shoes and an umbrella, this least expensive of tourist activities might well become your favorite pastime.

EXPLORING LONDON

London grew from a wooden bridge built over the Thames in the year AD 43 to its current 600 square miles and 7 million souls in haphazard fashion, meandering from its two official centers: Westminster, seat of government and royalty, and the City, site of finance and commerce. However, London's *un*official centers multiply and mutate year after year, and it would be a shame to stop only at the postcard views. Life is not lived in monuments, as the patrician patrons of the great Georgian architects understood when they commissioned the city's elegant squares and town houses. Close by, Westminster Abbey's original vegetable patch (or convent garden), which became the site of London's first square, Covent Garden, is now an unmissable stop on any agenda.

If the great, green parks are, as in Lord Chatham's phrase, "the lungs of London," then the river Thames is its backbone. The South Bank section absorbs the Southwark stews of Shakespeare's day and the current reconstruction of his original Globe Theatre, the concert hall from the '50s Festival of Britain, the arts complex from the '70s, and—farther downstream—the gorgeous 17th- and 18th-century symmetry of Greenwich, where the world's time is measured.

Great Itineraries

Numbers in the text correspond to numbers in the margin and on the London map.

IF YOU HAVE 1 DAY

Doing the biggest city in Europe in the space of one day should be an impossible task, but it's actually possible to pull off "London 101" in the space of one sunrise to sunset. Start out at postcard London come to life—the **Houses of Parliament** ⑩, admired best from Westminster Bridge. If you're lucky enough, you'll hear the chiming of **Big Ben**—its sound is nothing less than a mystic link with the heart and soul of the entire commonwealth. Move on to centuries-old **Westminster Abbey** ⑪—if Prince Charles does become king, this is where he'll have his coronation—then walk up Whitehall to **Trafalgar Square** (pigeons are everywhere, and also many photographers, equipped with birdseed to entice the semi-tame birds to settle on snap-happy tourists). Visit the square's leading attraction, the **National Gallery** ②—it ranks right up there with the Louvre and the Uffizi—then, if you can do it flip-book fast, the adjacent **National Portrait Gallery** ③. Take in Trafalgar Square's other sights, including **St. Martin-in-the-Fields** ④—perhaps London's most beloved church—and **Nelson's Column,** then walk through Admiralty Arch down the **Mall** to what there is every reason to believe—though there is no proof, of course—is the most photographed building in the world, **Buckingham Palace** ⑥. During summer weeks, its pomp and circumstance can be viewed when its state rooms are open to the public.

IF YOU HAVE 3 DAYS

Your first—literally—breathtaking day in London has been outlined above. On your second day, you can slow down a bit. Begin where you finished yesterday, **Buckingham Palace** ⑥, so that you can catch that ultimate photo op, the Changing of the Guard, usually held April through July daily at 11:30, August through March on alternate days. Before this ceremony, take in the amazing treasures on view at the adjacent **Queen's Gallery** ⑦—Her Majesty's greatest paintings are here—and don't feel bad if you miss out on the palace state rooms that can be seen on the palace's official tour—they're rather cold and forlorn. Nearby, check out the **Royal Mews** ⑧. Walk to the river and visit the **Tate Gallery** ⑯ and take in its incomparable collection of artworks by J. M. W. Turner, the Romantic-period artist who painted the most beautiful sunsets in 19th-century art. Get the tube to **Bond Street** for shopping, or (if you have enough time and energy left) visit the **Wallace Collection** (67) for a glance at London's most elegant museum. Your third day can begin at the fabulous **Tower of London** ㊴: From April to October, you can actually arrive at the tower by a boat taken from Charing Cross Pier. Once you've taken in the Crown Jewels, the ravens, and the Beefeaters, skip the centuries and head for the South Bank Arts Centre to visit the **Museum of the Moving Image** (52). Cross the Charing Cross pedestrian bridge and head over to Eliza Doolittle's old haunt at **Covent Garden** ⑰ for some serious retail therapy, then catch the fascinating Theatre Museum on Russell Street. Along the way, be sure to get off the main byways and savor London's neighborhoods. Seek out winding lanes and narrow courts and take a little time to smell the roses in all those lovely well-kept squares.

IF YOU HAVE 7 DAYS

Every part of London provides its own clues to the city's past and, so far, you've been gradually piecing together the story of this great, crowded, endless city. Your first three days' itinerary has been outlined above—now you're ready for some totally different sides of the city's charm. Day four starts at the South Kensington museums: the **Victoria & Albert** (57) or the **Natural History Museum** (58) and the **Science Museum** (59). Art lovers will adore the first, while budding Einsteins will want to explore the latter two. Be careful, these cultural palaces can easily devour your entire day. Make your way slowly through Hyde Park to **Kensington Gardens** with the famous **Peter Pan statue**—this might be the most beloved sight in all of England—and, startlingly close to throngs of people, **Kensington Palace** (62), still home to 14 members of the royal family. Its address—Palace Green—is London's most fashionable and parts of the palace are even open for viewing. For modern art buffs, the **Serpentine Gallery** will be the next stop. Nearby, discover the endless cavalcade of glitzy emporiums of **Sloane Street** and **Sloane Square**—not for nothing is Princess Diana a world-class shopper. Day five dawns at the **British Museum** ㉑ —a single visit will only scratch the surface of Mankind's Attic, but you'll obviously want to see the Elgin Marbles, the Rosetta Stone, and the Egyptian mummies. This could take a few hours—the special tour is quite good—or most of the day. Then take off for **Bloomsbury,** its leafy 17th- and 18th-century square, its Bloomsbury Group landmarks, and that regal time machine, **Sir John Soane's Museum** ㉖. Cross High Holborn into Legal London and explore the **Inns of Court** ㉔–㉕. On your sixth day, head out of the city for a break and discover pleasures up and down the Thames at **Greenwich** and the storied palace and gardens of **Hampton Court.** Your last day will begin with a tour of **the City**—most of London's banking and insurance companies are here, as well as the highlight of the day, magnificent **St. Paul's Cathedral** ㉛, a case of the money changers encompassing the temple. Until the 17th century, this *was* London, and its sights still offer color in heraldic proportions. Take in the **Barbican** ㉝, then visit the **Museum of London** ㉜—now that you've seen much of the city, you can really understand the exhibits here—passing the **Temple of Mithras** ㊲ en route to the **Monument** ㊳. For your grand finale, cross the Southwick Bridge to the reconstruction of **Shakespeare's Globe** theatre ㊾. If you can't catch a gala and glittering performance there, don't fret: by now, you've learned that London is the most wonderful free show in the world.

Westminster and Royal London

Westminster and Royal London could be called "London for Beginners." If you went no farther than these few acres, you would have seen many of the famous sights, from the Houses of Parliament, Big Ben, Westminster Abbey, and Buckingham Palace, to two of the world's greatest art collections, the National and Tate galleries. You can truly call this area Royal London, since it is neatly bounded by the triangle of streets that make up the route that the queen usually takes when journeying from Buckingham Palace to Westminster Abbey or to the Houses of Parliament on state occasions. The three points on this royal triangle are Trafalgar Square, Westminster, and Buckingham Palace. Naturally, in an area that regularly sees the pomp and pageantry of royal occasions, the streets are wide and the vistas long. With beautifully kept St. James's Park at the heart of the triangle, there is a feeling here of timeless dignity—flower beds bursting with color, long avenues of ancient trees framing classically proportioned buildings, constant glimpses of pinnacles and towers over the treetops, the distant throb of military bands on the march, the deep tones of Big Ben counting off the hours. This is concentrated sightseeing, so pace yourself. Remember that for a large part of the year, a lot of Royal London is floodlit at night, adding to the theatricality of the experience.

A Good Walk

Trafalgar Square is the obvious place to start for several reasons. It is the actual center of London, by dint of a plaque on the corner of the Strand and Charing Cross Road from which distances on U.K. signposts are measured. It is home to many political demonstrations, a raucous New Year's party, and the highest concentration of bus stops and pigeons in the capital. After taking in the instantly identifiable **Nelson's Column** ① in the middle of the square (read about the area on a plaque marking its 150th anniversary), head for the **National Gallery** ②—Britain's greatest trove of masterpieces (everybody's favorite here is Jan van Eyck's *Arnolfini Marriage*)—on the north side of the square. Detour around the corner to see the **National Portrait Gallery** ③—a veritable parade of the famous, often in unexpected guise—that can be very rewarding to anyone interested in what makes the British tick. East of the National Gallery, still on Trafalgar Square, see the much-loved church of **St. Martin-in-the-Fields** ④, then, stepping through grand Admiralty Arch down on the southwest corner, enter the royal pink road, the Mall, with St. James's Park running along the south side. On your right is the Institute of Contemporary Arts, known as the ICA, housed in the great Regency architect John Nash's **Carlton House Terrace** ⑤. At the foot of the Mall is one of London's most famous sights, **Buckingham Palace** ⑥, home, of course, to the monarch of the land, with the nearby **Queen's Gallery** ⑦—a trove of her magnificent Old Master paintings—and the **Royal Mews** ⑧ nearby. Turning left and left again, almost doubling back on yourself, follow the southern perimeter of St. James's Park around Birdcage Walk, passing the headquarters of the Queen's Guard, the **Wellington Barracks** ⑨, on your right. Cross Horse Guard's Road at the eastern edge of the park, walk down Great George Street, and across Parliament Square, and you come to another of the great sights of London, the incomparably august **Houses of Parliament** ⑩—a mock-medieval extravaganza designed by two celebrated Victorian-era architects, down to the last detail (Gothic umbrella stands)—built along the Thames and including the famous Clock Tower, usually (erroneously) known as Big Ben. Try to stick around for the sonorous chiming of the bell: For millions of citizens of the British empire, the sound of Big Ben's chimes is a mystic link with the heart and soul of the commonwealth. A clockwise turn around the square brings you to yet another major landmark, breathtaking **Westminster Abbey** ⑪. Complete the circuit and head north up Whitehall, where you'll see a simple monolith in the middle of the street—the Cenotaph, designed by Edwin Lutyens in 1920 in commemoration of the 1918 Armistice. The gated alley there on your left is **Downing Street** ⑫, where England's modest "White House" stands at Number 10. Soon after that you pass **Horseguards Parade** ⑬, setting for the queen's birthday celebration, Trooping the Colour, with the perfect classical Inigo Jones **Banqueting House** ⑭, scene of Charles I's execution, opposite.

TIMING

You could achieve this walk of roughly 3 miles in just over an hour, but you could easily spend a week's vacation on this route alone. Allow as much time as you can for the two great museums—the National Gallery requires at least two hours; the National Portrait Gallery can be whizzed round in less than one. Westminster Abbey can take half a day—especially in summer, when lines are long, both to get in and to get around. In summer, you can get inside Buckingham Palace, too, which might be a half day's operation increased to a whole day if you see the Royal Mews, the Queen's Gallery, and/or the Guards' Museum. If the Changing of the Guard is a priority, make sure you time this walk right.

Sights to See

⓮ **Banqueting House.** Commissioned by James I, Inigo Jones (1573–1652), one of England's great architects, created this banqueting hall out of an old remnant of the Tudor Palace of Whitehall in 1652. Influenced by Andrea Palladio's work when he saw it during a sojourn in Italy, Jones remade the palace with Palladian sophistication and purity. James I's son, Charles I, enhanced the interior by employing the Flemish painter Peter Paul Rubens to glorify his father all over the ceiling. As it turned out, these allegorical paintings, depicting a wise monarch being received into heaven, were the last thing Charles saw before he was beheaded on a scaffold outside in 1649. ✉ *Whitehall,* ☎ *0171/930–4179.* 💷 *£3.* ⏲ *Mon.–Sat. 10–5; closed Good Fri., Dec. 24–26, Jan. 1, and at short notice for banquets, so call first. Tube: Westminster.*

❻ **Buckingham Palace.** Supreme among the symbols of London, indeed of Britain generally, and of the Royal Family, Buckingham Palace tops the must-see lists—although the building itself is no masterpiece and has housed the monarch only since Victoria moved here from Kensington Palace on her accession in 1837. Its great gray bulk sums up the imperious splendor of so much of the city: stately, magnificent,

London

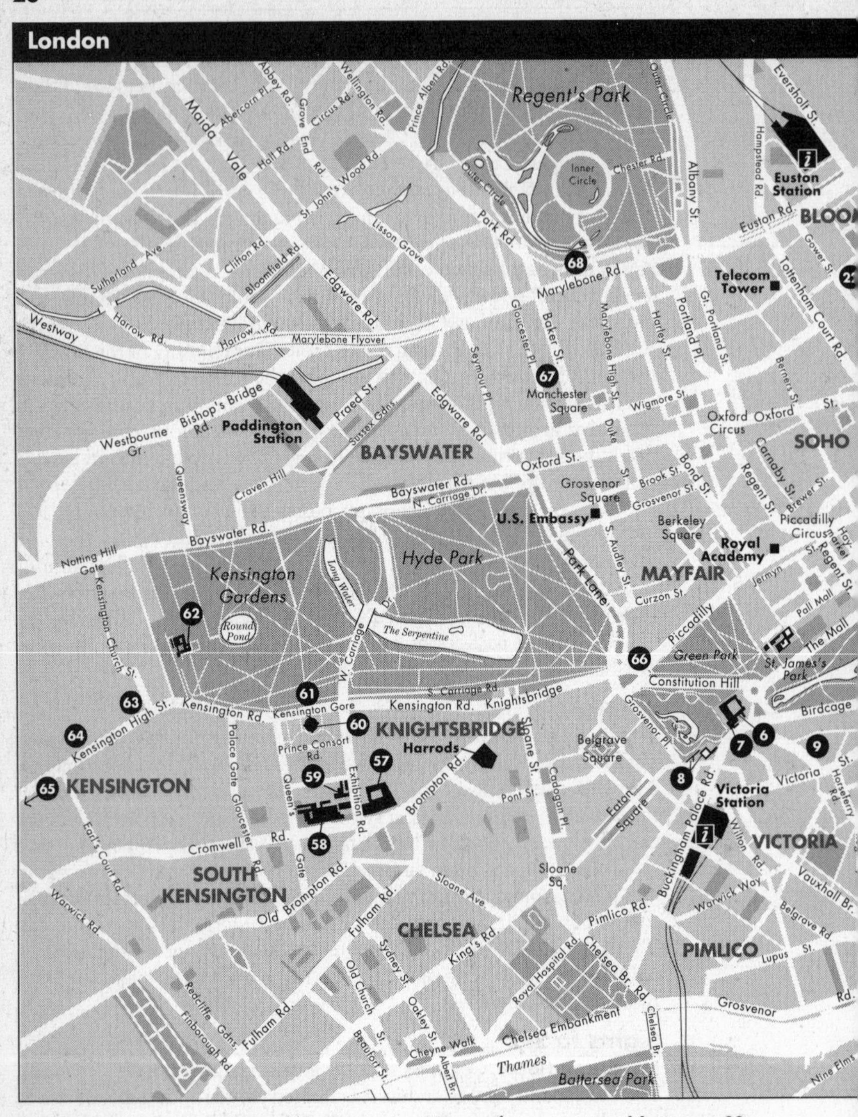

Adelphi, **20**
Albert Memorial, **61**
Bank of England, **36**
Banqueting House, **14**
Barbican Centre, **33**
British Museum, **21**
Buckingham Palace, **6**
Butler's Wharf, **41**
Cabinet War Rooms, **15**
Carlton House Terrace, **5**
The Clink, **48**
Courtauld Institute Galleries, **19**
Covent Garden, **17**
Design Museum, **42**
Dickens House Museum, **23**
Dr. Johnson's House, **28**
Florence Nightingale Museum, **54**
Gray's Inn, **24**
Guildhall, **34**
H.M.S. *Belfast*, **43**
Hay's Galleria, **44**
Horse Guards Parade, **13**
Houses of Parliament, **10**
Imperial War Museum, **56**
Kensington Palace, **62**
Kensington Palace Gardens, **63**
Lambeth Palace, **55**
Leighton House, **65**
Lincoln's Inn, **25**
Linley Sambourne House, **64**
London Dungeon, **45**
Madame Tussaud's Waxworks, **68**
Monument, **38**
Museum of London, **32**
Museum of the Moving Image (MOMI), **52**
National Gallery, **2**
National Portrait Gallery, **3**
Natural History Museum, **58**
Nelson's Column, **1**
Old Bailey, **30**
Old St. Thomas's Operating Theatre, **46**

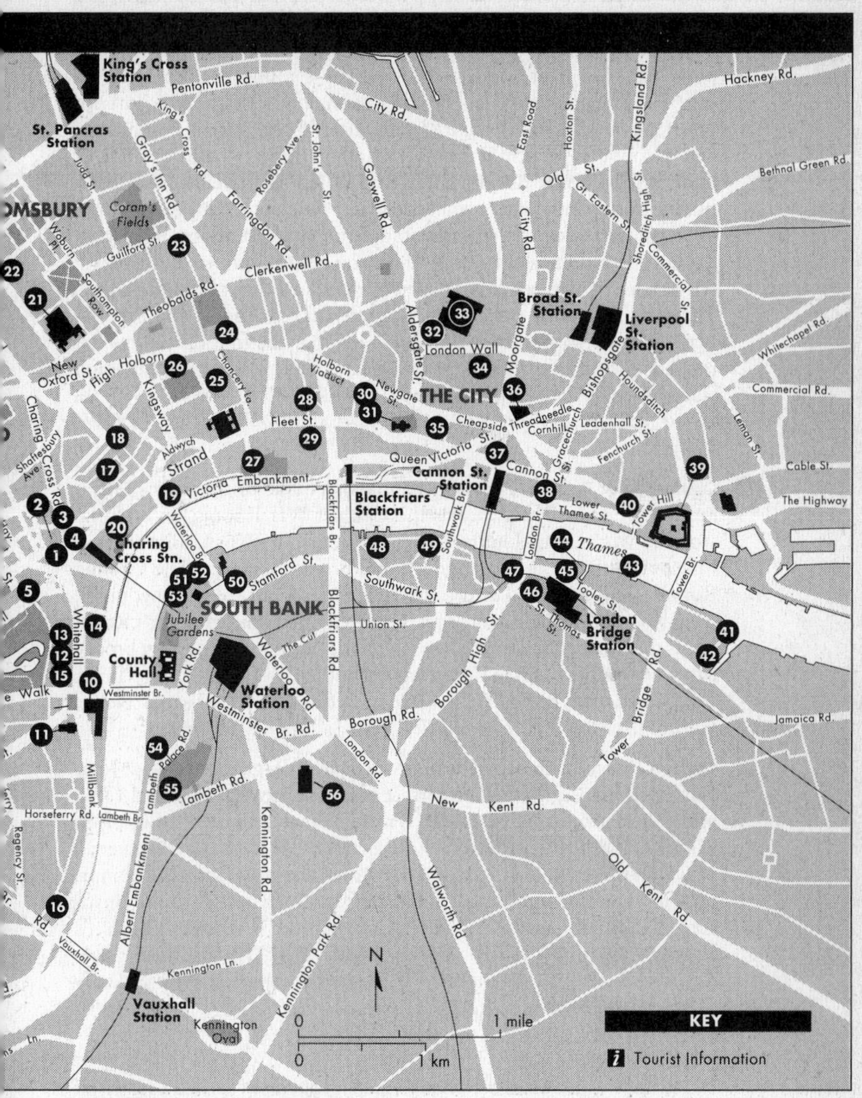

Queen's Gallery, **7**
Royal Albert Hall, **60**
Royal Festival Hall, **53**
Royal National Theatre, **51**
Royal Mews, **8**
Royal Opera House, **18**
Science Museum, **59**
Shakespeare's Globe, **49**
Sir John Soane's Museum, **26**
South Bank Centre, **50**
Southwark Cathedral, **47**
St. Bride's Church, **29**
St. Mary-le-Bow, **35**
St. Martin-in-the-Fields, **4**
St. Paul's Cathedral, **31**
Tate Gallery, **16**
10 Downing St., **12**
Temple, **27**
Temple of Mithras, **37**
Tower Hill Pageant, **40**
Tower of London, **39**
University of London, **22**
Victoria & Albert Museum, **57**
Wallace Collection, **67**
Wellington Barracks, **9**
Wellington Museum (Apsley House), **66**
Westminster Abbey, **11**

and ponderous. In 1824 the palace was substantially rebuilt by John Nash, that tireless architect, for George IV, that tireless spendthrift. Compared to other great London residences, it is a johnny-come-lately affair: The Portland stone facade dates from only 1913, and the interior was renovated and redecorated only after World War II bomb damage. It contains some 600 rooms, including the State Ballroom and, of course, the Throne Room. You'll find pomp and circumstance here, but little else. These state rooms are where much of the business of royalty is played out—investitures, state banquets, receptions, lunch parties for the famous, and so on. The royal apartments are in the north wing; when the queen is in, the royal standard flies at the masthead. The state rooms are on show for eight weeks in August and September, when the royal family is away. Note that the finest artworks her majesty owns are on view at the ☞ **Queen's Gallery,** located at the south side of the palace. ✉ *Buckingham Palace Rd.,* ☎ *0171/839–1377.* 🎫 *£8.50.* ⏲ *Aug. 8–Sept. 30, daily 9:30–4:30. Tube: St. James's Park, Victoria.*

15 **Cabinet War Rooms.** Between the massive bulks of the Home Office and the Foreign Office nestles the Cabinet War Rooms, an essential stop for World War II buffs. During air raids, the War Cabinet met in this warren of 17 underground bomb-proof chambers. The Cabinet Room is still arranged as if a meeting were about to convene; in the Map Room, the Allied campaign is charted; the Prime Minister's Room holds the desk from which Churchill made his morale-boosting broadcasts; and the Telephone Room has his hot line to FDR. ✉ *Clive Steps, King Charles St.,* ☎ *0171/930–6961.* 🎫 *£4.* ⏲ *Daily 10–5:15; closed Good Fri., May Day, Dec. 24–26, Jan. 1. Tube: Westminster.*

5 **Carlton House Terrace.** A glorious example of Regency architect John Nash's genius, Carlton House Terrace was built between 1812 and 1830, under the patronage of George IV (Prince Regent until George III's death in 1820). Nash was responsible for a series of West End developments, of which these white-stucco facades and massive Corinthian columns may be the most imposing. Today, the structure houses the ☞ **Institute of Contemporary Arts,** better known as the ICA, one of Britain's leading modern-art centers. ✉ *The Mall,* ☎ *0171/930–3647.* 🎫 *1-day membership £1.50; additional charge for specific events.* ⏲ *Daily noon–9:30, later for some events; closed Dec. 24–27, Jan. 1. Tube: Charing Cross.*

NEED A BREAK?

The **ICAfé** is windowless but brightly spotlit, with a self-service counter offering good hot dishes, salads, quiches, and desserts. The bar upstairs, which serves baguette sandwiches, has a picture window overlooking the Mall.

13 **Horse Guards Parade.** Facing Horse Guards Road—opposite St. James's Park at one end and Whitehall on the other—Horse Guards Parade is now notable mainly for the annual Trooping the Colour ceremony, in which the queen takes the Royal Salute, her official birthday gift, on the second Saturday in June. (Like Paddington Bear, the queen has two birthdays; her real one is on April 21.) There is pageantry galore, with marching bands and the occasional guardsman fainting clean away in his busby (those curious, furry hats). It's practically impossible to get tickets for the parade, but it's always televised and also broadcast on Radio 4. You can also see it from the Mall, but you have to get there very early in the morning for any kind of decent view. You can also attend the queenless rehearsals on the preceding two Saturdays. At the Whitehall facade of Horse Guards, two mounted sentries known as the Queen's Life Guard provide what may be London's most fre-

quently exploited photo opportunity. They change, quietly, at 11 AM Monday–Saturday, 10 on Sunday.

★ ⑩ **Houses of Parliament.** Postcard London come to life, the Houses of Parliament are, arguably, the city's most famous and photogenic sight. Facing them you see, from left to right: Big Ben—keeping watch on the corner, the Houses of Parliament themselves, Westminster Hall (the oldest part of the complex), and the Victoria Tower. The most romantic view of the complex is from the opposite, south side of the river, a vista especially dramatic at night when the spires, pinnacles, and towers of the great building are floodlit green and gold. After a catastrophic fire in 1834, these buildings arose, designed in a delightful mock-medieval style by two Victorian-era architects: Sir Charles Barry and Augustus Pugin. The Palace of Westminster, as the complex is still properly called, was established by Edward the Confessor in the 11th century, when he moved his court from the City, and has been the seat of English administrative power ever since.

Now virtually the symbol of London, the 1858 **Clock Tower** designed by Pugin contains the bell that chimes the hour (and the quarter) known as Big Ben; weighing a mighty 13 tons, the bell takes its name from Sir Benjamin Hall, First Commissioner of Works when it was installed. There are two Houses, the Lords and the Commons. The Visitors' Galleries of the House of Commons affords a view of the best free show in London staged in the world's most renowned ego chamber (if you want to take it in during its liveliest hour, Prime Minister's Question Time, you'll need to book tickets in advance). ✉ *St. Stephen's Entrance, St. Margaret St., SW1,* ☎ *0171/219–3000.* 🎫 *Free.* ⏲ *Commons Mon.–Thurs. 2:30–10, Fri. 9:30–3; Lords Mon.–Thurs. 2:30–10. Closed Easter wk, May bank holiday, July–Oct., 3 wks at Christmas. Tube: Westminster.*

★ ❷ **National Gallery.** Jan van Eyck's *Arnolfini Marriage,* Leonardo da Vinci's *Virgin and Child,* Velázquez's *Rokeby Venus,* Constable's *Hay Wain* . . . you get the picture. There are approximately 2,200 other paintings in this museum—many of them instantly recognizable and among the most treasured works of art anywhere. The museum's low, gray, colonnaded neoclassical facade fills the north side of Trafalgar Square. The collection ranges from painters of the Italian Renaissance and earlier—housed in the 1991 Sainsbury Wing, designed by the American architect Robert Venturi—through the Flemish and Dutch masters, the Spanish school, and of course the English tradition, including Hogarth, Gainsborough, Stubbs, and Constable.

The collection is really too overwhelming to absorb in a single viewing. The **Micro Gallery,** a computer information center in the Sainsbury Wing, might be the place to start. You can access in-depth information on any work here, choose your favorites, and print out a free personal tour map that marks the paintings you most want to see. Rounding out the top 10 list (the first four lead off above) are Uccello's *Battle of San Romano* (children love its knights on horseback), Bellini's *Doge Leonardo Loredan* (notice the snail-shell buttons), Botticelli's *Venus and Mars,* Caravaggio's *Supper at Emmaus* (almost cinematically lit), Turner's *Fighting Téméeaire* (one of the artist's greatest sunsets), and Seurat's *Bathers at Asnières.* Note that free admission encourages repeat visits: While you can try to just see the top of the top, the National Gallery, like so many first-rate collections, reveals more gems the more one explores. ✉ *Trafalgar Sq.,* ☎ *0171/839–3321, 0171/839–3526 (recorded general information), 0171/389–1773 (recorded exhibition information).* 🎫 *Free; admission charge for special exhibitions.* ⏲ *Mon.–Sat. 10–6, Sun. 2–6; June–Aug., also Wed. until 8; free 1-hr* *guided tours start at the Sainsbury Wing weekdays at 11:30 and 2:30, Sat. at 2 and 3:30; closed Good Fri., May Day, Dec. 24–26, Jan. 1. Tube: Charing Cross.*

NEED A BREAK? The **Brasserie** in the Sainsbury Wing of the National Gallery offers a fashionable lunch—mussels, gravlax, charcuterie, salads, a hot dish—in a sophisticated, spacious room on the second floor. In the basement of the main gallery, get sandwiches, cakes, ice cream, coffee, and fresh juices from the excellent London chain Pret-à-Manger.

❸ **National Portrait Gallery.** Just around the corner from the National Gallery, this is a much more idiosyncratic collection that presents a potted history of Britain through its residents, past and present. As an art collection it is eccentric, since the subject, not the artist, is the point. Highlights range from Holbein to Hockney. ✉ *St. Martin's Pl.,* ☎ *0171/306–0055.* 🎫 *Free.* 🕑 *Weekdays 10–5, Sat. 10–6, Sun. 2–6. Closed public holidays. Tube: Charing Cross, Leicester Square.*

❶ **Nelson's Column.** Centerpiece of Trafalgar Square, this famed landmark is topped with E. H. Baily's 1843 statue of Admiral Lord Horatio Nelson, keeping watch from his 145-foot granite perch. The bas reliefs depicting scenes of his life, installed around the base, were cast from cannons he captured. The four majestic lions, designed by the Victorian painter Sir Edwin Landseer, were added in 1867. The calling cards of generations of picturesque pigeons have been a corrosive problem for the statue, which may have been finally solved by the statue's new gel coating.

❼ **Queen's Gallery.** Housed in a former chapel at the south side of **Buckingham Palace,** this showcase offers a rotating sample of what is generally regarded as the finest private art collection in the world. There are spectacular paintings here, including Vermeer's *The Music Lesson* and works by Rubens, Rembrandt, Canaletto . . . and Queen Victoria. If you're lucky, you'll find some of Her Majesty's Leonardo da Vinci drawings on view—she owns them by the dozen. ✉ *Buckingham Palace Rd.,* ☎ *0171/799–2331.* 🎫 *£3.50; combined ticket for Queen's Gallery and Royal Mews £6.* 🕑 *Tues.–Sat. 10–5, Sun. 2–5; closed Dec. 24–Mar. 4, Good Fri. Tube: St. James's Park, Victoria.*

❽ **Royal Mews.** Designed by celebrated Regency-era architect John Nash, the Royal Mews stands nearly next door to the Queen's Gallery, close to Buckingham Palace. Mews were originally falcons' quarters (the name comes from their "mewing," or feather shedding), but horses gradually eclipsed birds of prey. Now some of the magnificent royal beasts live here alongside the fabulous bejeweled, glass, and golden coaches they draw on state occasions. The place is unmissable children's entertainment. ✉ *Buckingham Palace Rd.,* ☎ *0171/799–2331.* 🎫 *£3.50; combined ticket for Queen's Gallery and Royal Mews £6.* 🕑 *Oct.–Mar., Wed. noon–4; Apr.–Oct., Tues.–Thurs. noon–4; closed Mar. 25–29, Oct. 1–5, Dec. 23–Jan. 5. Tube: St. James's Park, Victoria.*

St. James's Park. London's smallest, most ornamental park is also the oldest of its royal ones. Its present shape more or less reflects what John Nash designed under George IV, turning the canal into a graceful lake (which was cemented in at a depth of 4 feet in 1855, so don't even think of swimming) and generally naturalizing the gardens. More than 30 species of birds—including swans that belong to the queen—congregate on Duck Island at the east end of the lake. Later on summer days the deck chairs (which you must pay to use) are crammed with office lunchers being serenaded by music from the bandstands. The best time to stroll the leafy walkways, though, is after dark, with Westminster

Abbey and the Houses of Parliament rising above the floodlit lake, and peace reigning.

4 **St. Martin-in-the-Fields.** One of Britain's best-loved churches, St. Martin's was completed in 1726; ever since, James Gibbs's classical-temple-with-spire design has become familiar as the pattern for churches in Colonial America. The church is also a haven for music lovers, since the internationally known Academy of St. Martin-in-the-Fields was founded here, and a popular program of lunchtime (free) and evening concerts continues today. The church's fusty interior has a wonderful atmosphere for music making—but the wooden benches can make it hard to give your undivided attention to the music. The **London Brass-Rubbing Centre,** where you can make your own souvenir knight from replica tomb brasses, with metallic waxes, paper, and instructions provided, is in the crypt. ✉ *Trafalgar Sq.,* ☎ *0171/930–0089. Credit card bookings for evening concerts,* ☎ *0171/839–8362.* 🎫 *Brass rubbings from £1.* ⏲ *Church daily 8–8, crypt Mon.–Sat. 10–8, Sun. noon–6. Tube: Charing Cross, Leicester Square.*

NEED A BREAK? St. Martin's **Café-in-the-Crypt** serves full meals, sandwiches, snacks, and even a glass of wine, Monday–Saturday 10–8; noon–6 on Sunday.

16 **Tate Gallery.** The Tate—everyone drops the word "gallery"—overlooks the Thames, about 20 minutes' walk from the Houses of Parliament, and is widely known as Britain's leading collection of modern art. "Modern" is slightly misleading, since one of the three collections here consists of British art from 1545 to the present, including works by Hogarth, Gainsborough, Reynolds, and Stubbs from the 18th century, and by Constable, Blake, and the Pre-Raphaelite painters from the 19th. Also from the 19th century is the J.W.M. Turner Bequest, now housed magnificently in the James Stirling–designed **Clore Gallery,** the largest collection of works by the leading British Romantic artist. The Tate has an innovative policy of rehanging the whole gallery every nine months, which means that a favorite work may not be on view. Usually, however, your tour can deal you multiple shocks of recognition (Rodin's *The Kiss,* Lichtenstein's *Whaam!*). ✉ *Millbank,* ☎ *0171/821–1313 or 0171/821–7128 (recorded information).* 🎫 *Free; admission charged for special exhibitions.* ⏲ *Mon.–Sat. 10–5:50, Sun. 2–5:50; closed Good Fri., May Day, Dec. 24–26, Jan. 1.*

12 **Ten Downing Street.** South of the Banqueting House (☞ *above*), you'll find the British version of the White House, occupying three unassuming 18th-century houses. No. 10 has been the official residence of the prime minister since 1732. The cabinet office, hub of the British system of government, is on the ground floor; the prime minister's private apartment is on the top floor. The chancellor of the exchequer occupies No. 11. Downing Street is cordoned off, but you should be able to catch a glimpse of it from Whitehall. *Tube: Westminster.*

Trafalgar Square. A commanding open space—originally built to reflect the width and breadth of an empire that once reached to the farthest corners of the globe—Trafalgar Square remains the focus of modern London. It contain a bevy of must-see attractions, including the ☞ **National Gallery.** Today, street performers enhance the square's intermittent atmosphere of celebration, which is strongest in December, first when the lights on the gigantic Christmas tree are turned on, and then—less festively—when thousands see in the New Year.

9 **Wellington Barracks.** This is the august headquarters of the Guards Division, the queen's five regiments of elite foot guards who protect the sovereign and patrol her palace dressed in tunics of gold-purled scar-

let and tall busbies of Canadian brown bearskin. If you want to learn more about the guards, you can visit the **Guards Museum;** the entrance is next to the Guards Chapel. ✉ *Wellington Barracks, Birdcage Walk,* ☎ *0171/930–4466, ext. 3430.* 💰 *£2.* ⏲ *Sat.–Thurs. 10–4; closed national holidays. Tube: St. James's Park.*

★ 11 **Westminster Abbey.** Nearly all of Britain's monarchs have been crowned here since the coronation of William the Conqueror on Christmas Day 1066—and most are buried here, too. As the most ancient of London's great churches, the place is crammed with spectacular medieval architecture and pomp and circumstance. Other than the mysterious gloom of the vast interior, the first thing to strike most people is the fantastic proliferation of statues, tombs, and commemorative tablets: In parts, the building seems more like a stonemason's yard than a place of worship. But it is in its latter capacity that this landmark truly comes into its own: While attending a service is not something to undertake purely for sightseeing reasons, it provides a glimpse of the abbey in its full majesty, accompanied by music from the Westminster choristers and the organ that Henry Purcell once played.

The present abbey is a largely 13th- and 14th-century rebuilding of the 11th-century church founded by Edward the Confessor, with one notable addition being the 18th-century twin towers over the west entrance, completed by Sir Christopher Wren. The nave is your first sight on entering; you need to look up to gain a perspective on the awe-inspiring scale of the church, since the eye-level view is obscured by the choir screen, past which point admission is charged. Before paying, look at the poignant **Tomb of the Unknown Warrior,** an anonymous World War I martyr who lies buried here in memory of the soldiers fallen in both world wars. Passing through the Choir, with its mid–19th-century choir stalls, into the North Transept, look up to your right to see the painted-glass Rose Window, the largest of its kind. You then proceed into the **Henry VII Chapel,** passing the huge white marble tomb of Elizabeth I, buried with her half sister, "Bloody" Mary I. All around are magnificent sculptures of saints, philosophers, and kings, with wild mermaids and monsters carved on the choir stall misericords (undersides), and exquisite fan vaulting above (binoculars will help you spot the statues high on the walls)—the last riot of medieval design in England and one of the miracles of Western architecture.

Next you enter the **Chapel of Edward the Confessor,** where beside the royal saint's shrine stands the **Coronation Chair,** which has been briefly graced by nearly every royal posterior. In 1400, Geoffrey Chaucer became the first poet to be buried in **Poets' Corner,** which also has memorials devoted to William Shakespeare, William Blake, and Charles Dickens. Exit the abbey by a door from the South Transept. Outside the west front is an archway into the quiet, green **Dean's Yard** and the entrance to the **Cloisters** and the **Brass-Rubbing Centre** (☎ 0171/222–2085). ✉ *Broad Sanctuary,* ☎ *0171/222–5152.* 💰 *Nave free, Royal Chapels and Poets' Corner £4.* ⏲ *Mon.–Tues. and Thurs.–Fri. 9–4, Wed. 9–7:45, Sat. 9–2 and 3:45–5, Sun. all day for services only; closed weekdays to visitors during services. Tube: Westminster. Undercroft, Pyx Chamber, Chapter House, and Treasury,* ☎ *0171/222–5152.* 💰 *Joint ticket £2.50.* ⏲ *Daily 10:30–4; closed Good Fri., Dec. 24–26. Tube: Westminster.*

Soho and Covent Garden

A quadrilateral described by Regent Street, Coventry/Cranbourn streets, Charing Cross Road, and the eastern half of Oxford Street encloses Soho, the most fun part of the West End. This appellation, unlike the

New York neighborhood's similar one, is not an abbreviation of anything, but a blast from the past—derived (as far as we know) from the shouts of "So-ho!" that royal huntsmen in Whitehall Palace's parklands were once heard to cry. One of Charles II's illegitimate sons, the Duke of Monmouth, was an early resident, his dubious pedigree setting the tone for the future: For many years Soho was London's strip show/peep show/clip joint/sex shop/brothel center. The mid-'80s brought legislation that granted expensive licenses to a few such establishments and closed down the rest. Today, Soho remains the address for many wonderful ethnic restaurants, including those of London's Chinatown.

Best known as Eliza Doolittle's stomping grounds in Shaw's *Pygmalion* and Lerner and Loewe's *My Fair Lady,* the former Covent Garden Market became the Piazza in 1980, and it still functions as the center of a neighborhood—one that has always been alluded to as "colorful." It was originally the "convent garden" belonging to the Abbey of St. Peter at Westminster (later Westminster Abbey). Centuries of magnificence and misery, vice and mayhem, and more recent periods of art-literary bohemia followed, until it became the vegetable supplier of London when its market building went up in the 1830s, followed by the Flower Market in 1870. When the produce moved out to the bigger, better Nine Elms Market in Vauxhall in 1974, the (now sadly defunct) Greater London Council stepped in with a rehabilitation scheme, and a new neighborhood was born.

A Good Walk

Soho, being small, is easy to explore, though it's also easy to mistake one narrow, crowded street for another, and even Londoners get lost here. Enter from the northwest corner, Oxford Circus, and head south about 200 yards down Regent Street, turn left onto Great Marlborough Street, and head to the top of Carnaby Street. Turn right off Broadwick Street onto Berwick (pronounced "Berrick") Street, famed as central London's best fruit and vegetable market. Then step through tiny Walker's Court (ignoring the notorious hookers' bulletin board), cross Brewer Street and you'll have arrived at Soho's hip hangout, Old Compton Street. From here, Wardour, Dean, Frith, and Greek streets lead north, all of them bursting with restaurants and clubs. Either of the latter two lead north to Soho Square, but head one block south instead, to Shaftesbury Avenue, heart of theaterland, across which you'll find Chinatown's main drag, Gerrard Street. Below Gerrard Street is Leicester Square, and running along its west side is Charing Cross Road, the bibliophile's dream. You'll find some of the best of the specialist bookshops in little Cecil Court, running east just before Trafalgar Square.

The easiest way to find the **Covent Garden** ⑰ market building and the Piazza is to walk down Cranbourn Street, next to Leicester Square tube, then down Long Acre, and turn right at James Street. Here, and around here, are St. Paul's—the actors' church—and the **Theatre Museum,** as well as plenty of shops and cafés. (If your aim is to shop, Neal Street, Floral Street, the streets around Seven Dials, and the Thomas Neale's mall all repay exploration.) From Seven Dials, veer 45 degrees south onto Mercer Street, turning right on Long Acre, then left onto Garrick Street, left onto Rose Street, and right onto Floral Street. At the other end you'll emerge onto Bow Street, right next to the **Royal Opera House** ⑱. Continuing on—passing the Manet-stocked **Courtauld Institute Galleries** ⑲—and turning left onto Russell Street, you reach Drury Lane, and the Theatre Royal. At the end of Drury Lane, turn right at the Aldwych, follow the ¾-mile-long Strand to the southern end, and take Villiers Street down to the Thames. See the York Watergate and Cleopatra's

Needle by Victoria Embankment Gardens, cross the gardens northwest to the **Adelphi** ⑳, circumnavigating the Strand by sticking to the embankment walk, and you'll soon reach Waterloo Bridge, where (weather permitting) you can catch some of London's most glamorous views, toward both the City and Westminster around the Thames bend.

TIMING

The distance covered here is around 5 miles, if you include the lengthy walk down the Strand and riverside stroll back. Skip that, and it's barely a couple of miles, but you will almost certainly get lost, since the streets in both Covent Garden and Soho are winding and chaotic, and not logically laid out. Although getting lost is half the fun, it does make it hard to predict how long this walk will take. You can whiz round both neighborhoods in an hour, but if the area appeals at all, you'll want all day—for shopping, lunch, the Theatre and Transport museums, and the Courtauld Galleries. One way to do it is to start at Leicester Square at 2 PM, when the Half Price Theatre Booth opens, pick up tickets for later, and walk, shop, and eat in between.

Sights to See

20 **Adelphi.** Near the triangular-handkerchief Victoria Embankment Gardens, this regal riverfront row of houses was the work of all four of the brothers Adam (John, Robert, James, and William: hence the name, from the Greek *adelphoi,* meaning "brothers"), London's Scottish architects. 7 Adam Street is the best mansion.

19 **Courtauld Institute Galleries.** Several years ago, this collection was moved to a setting worthy of its fame: a grand 18th-century classical mansion, Somerset House. Founded in 1931 by the textile maven Samuel Courtauld, this is London's finest Impressionist and post-Impressionist collection, with bonus post-Renaissance works thrown in. Botticelli, Breughel, Tiepolo, and Rubens are represented, but the younger French painters are the stars—here, for example, is Manet's famed *Bar at the Folies-Bergère.* ✉ *The Strand,* ☎ *0171/873–2526.* *£3; White Card accepted.* ⏲ *Mon.–Sat. 10–6, Sun. 2–6; closed public holidays. Tube: Temple, Embankment.*

17 **Covent Garden (The Piazza).** The original "convent garden" produced fruits and vegetables for the 13th-century Abbey of St. Peter at Westminster. In 1630, the Duke of Bedford, having become owner, commissioned Inigo Jones to lay out a square, with St. Paul's Church at one end. The fruit, flower, and vegetable market established in the 1700s flourished until 1974, when its traffic grew to be too much for the narrow streets, and it was moved south of the Thames. Since then, the area has been transformed into the Piazza, a mostly higher-class shopping mall, which features a couple of cafés and some knickknack stores that are good for gifts. Open-air entertainers perform under the portico of St. Paul's Church, where George Bernard Shaw set the first scene of *Pygmalion* (reshaped as the musical *My Fair Lady*).

Leicester Square. This is the big magnet for nightlife lovers. Looking at the neon of the major movie houses, the fast-food outlets, and the disco entrances, you'd never guess the square—it's pronounced "lester"—was laid out around 1630. The Odeon, on the east side, is the venue for all the Royal Film Performances, and the movie theme is continued by a jaunty little statue of Charlie Chaplin in the opposite corner. Shakespeare sulks in the middle, chin on hand, clearly wishing he were somewhere else. One landmark certainly worth visiting is the **Society of London Theatre ticket kiosk,** on the southwest corner, which sells half-price tickets for many of that evening's performances (☞ Nightlife and the Arts, *below*).

18 **Royal Opera House.** Here, the Royal Ballet and Britain's finest opera company put on their grandest spectacles; here, Joan Sutherland once brought down the house as Lucia di Lammermoor and Rudolf Nureyev and Margot Fonteyn became the greatest ballet duo of all time. For such delights, seats can be top dollar—nearly £150—or just a 10th of that lordly amount. Whatever the price, it will be worth it if you love red-and-gold Victorian decor (designed in 1858), which gives a very special feel to that hush that precedes the start of a performance. The bars, especially the Crush Bar, add opulence to the pastime of people-watching during an intermission. For information on tickets and hours, *see* Nightlife and the Arts, *below.* ✉ *Bow St. (Box Office, 48 Floral St.),* ☎ *0171/240–1911. Tube: Covent Garden.*

NEED A BREAK? Take any excuse you can think of to visit either of Soho's wonderful rival patisseries: **Maison Bertaux** (✉ 8 Greek St.) or **Pâtisserie Valerie** (✉ 44 Old Compton St.). Both serve divine gâteaux, milles-feuilles, croissants, and éclairs.

The **Theatre Museum** aims to re-create the excitement of theater itself. There are usually programs in progress allowing children to get in a mess with make-up or have a giant dressing-up session. Permanent exhibits attempt a history of the English stage from the 16th century to Mick Jagger's jumpsuit, with tens of thousands of theater playbills and sections on such topics as Hamlet-through-the-ages and pantomime. ✉ *7 Russell St.,* ☎ *0171/836–7891.* *£3.* *Tues.–Sun. 11–7; closed Good Fri., Dec. 24–26, Jan. 1. Tube: Covent Garden.*

Bloomsbury and Legal London

Bloomsbury is best known for its famous flowering of literary-arty bohemia during this century's first three decades, the Bloomsbury Group—think Virginia Woolf, E. M. Forster, Vanessa Bell, and Lytton Strachey—and for the British Museum and the University of London, which dominate it now. Ghosts of their literary salons lead into the time-warp territory of interlocking alleys, gardens and cobbled courts, town houses and halls where London's legal profession grew up. The Great Fire of 1666 razed most of the city but spared the buildings of legal London, and the whole neighborhood—known as the City—oozes history. Leading landmarks here are the Inns of Court, where the country's top solicitors and barristers have had their chambers for centuries.

A Good Walk

From Russell Square tube station, walk south down Southampton Row, and west on Great Russell Street, passing Bloomsbury Square on the left, en route to London's biggest and most important collection of antiquities, the **British Museum** ㉑. Leaving this via the back exit leads you to Montague Place, which you should cross to Malet Street, straight ahead, to reach the **University of London** ㉒. On the left after you pass the university buildings is the back of the Royal Academy of Dramatic Art, or RADA (its entrance is on Gower Street), where at least half of the most stellar British thespians got their training. Circumvent University College at the top of Malet Place and head south down Gordon Street to reach Gordon Square, continuing south down busy Woburn Place, and veering left down Guilford Street to reach Coram's Fields, then turn left south of there on Guilford Place, then right to Doughty Street and the **Dickens House Museum** ㉓. Two streets west, parallel to Doughty Street, is pretty Lamb's Conduit Street (whose pretty pub, the Lamb, Dickens inevitably frequented), with Great Ormond Street, off it, where lies the Hospital for Sick Children.

At the bottom of Lamb's Conduit Street you reach Theobald's Road, where you enter the first of the Inns of Court, **Gray's Inn** ㉔, emerging from here onto High Holborn ("Hoe-bun"), heavy with traffic, since it (with the Strand) is the main route from the City to the West End and Westminster. Hatton Garden, running north from Holborn Circus and still the center of London's diamond and jewelry trade, is a reminder of when it *was* the west end. Pass another ghost of former trading, Staple Inn, and turn left down tiny Great Turnstile Row to reach **Lincoln's Inn** ㉕, where you pass its famous hall and continue around the west side of New Square to Carey Street, which leads you round into Portugal Street. Here you'll find **The Old Curiosity Shop,** probably one of the rare places in London Dickens did *not* frequent. Recross to the north side of Lincoln's Inn Fields to **Sir John Soane's Museum** ㉖. Cross the Strand to Temple Bar of the **Temple** ㉗, and pass through the elaborate stone arch to Middle Temple Lane, which you follow to the Thames.

TIMING

This is a substantial walk of 3 to 4 miles, and it has two distinct halves. The first half, around Bloomsbury, is not so interesting on the surface, but features a major highlight of London, the British Museum, where you could easily add a mile to your total, and certainly at least two hours. The Dickens House is also worth a stop. The second, legal London, half is a real walker's walk, with most of the highlights in the architecture and atmosphere of the buildings and streets. The exception is Sir John Soane's Museum, which will absorb an extra hour. The walk alone can be done comfortably in two hours and is best on a sunny day.

Sights to See

㉑ **British Museum.** With a facade like a great temple, this celebrated treasure house—filled with plunder of incalculable value and beauty from around the globe—is housed in a ponderously dignified Greco–Victorian building that makes a suitably grand impression. This is only appropriate, for inside you'll find some of the greatest relics of humankind: the Elgin Marbles, the Rosetta Stone, the Magna Carta, the Ur Treasure—everything, it seems, but the Ark of the Covenant. The place is vast, so arm yourself with a free floor plan directly as you go in or they'll have to send out search parties to rescue you.

The collection began in 1753 and grew quickly thanks to enthusiastic kleptomaniacs during the Napoleonic Wars—most notoriously the seventh Earl of Elgin, who lifted marbles from the Parthenon and Erechtheum while on a Greek vacation between 1801 and 1804. Here follows a highly edited résumé (in order of encounter) of the BM's greatest hits:

Close to the entrance hall, in the south end of Room 25, is the **Rosetta Stone,** found in 1799, and carved in 196 BC with a decree of Ptolemy V in Egyptian hieroglyphics, demotic, and Greek. It was this multilingual inscription that provided the French Egyptologist Jean-François Champollion with the key to deciphering hieroglyphics. Maybe the **Elgin Marbles** ought to be back in Greece, but since they are here—and they are, after all, among the most graceful and heartbreakingly beautiful sculptures on earth—make a beeline for them in Room 8, west of the entrance. The best part is what remains of the Parthenon frieze that girdled the cella of Athena's temple on the Acropolis, carved around 440 BC. Also in the West Wing is one of the Seven Wonders of the Ancient World—in fragment form, unfortunately—in Room 12: the **Mausoleum of Halicarnassus.** Close to the main entrance are originals of King John's 1215 charter, the Magna Carta, as well as the spectacularly illuminated 7th-century Lindisfarne Gospels.

Upstairs are some of the most perennially popular galleries, especially beloved by children: Rooms 60 and 61, where the **Egyptian mummies** live. Nearby are the glittering 4th-century Mildenhall Treasure and the equally splendid Sutton Hoo Treasure. A more prosaic exhibit is Pete Marsh, so named by the archaeologists who unearthed the Lindow Man from a Cheshire peat marsh; poor Pete was ritually slain, probably as a human sacrifice. ✉ *Great Russell St.,* ☎ *0171/636–1555 or 0171/580–1788 (recorded information).* *Free; 1½-hr guided tours £6.* *Mon.–Sat. 10–5, Sun. 2:30–6; tours twice a day in winter, 4 times daily in summer (phone for times); closed Good Fri., May Day, Dec. 23–26, Jan. 1. Tube: Tottenham Court Road, Holborn, Russell Square.*

23 **Dickens House Museum.** This is the only one of the many London houses Dickens inhabited that's still standing, and would have had a real claim to his fame in any case, since he wrote *Oliver Twist* and *Nicholas Nickleby* and finished *Pickwick Papers* here between 1837 and 1839. The house looks exactly as it would have in Dickens's day, complete with first editions, letters, and desk, plus a treat for Lionel Bart fans—his score of *Oliver!* ✉ *48 Doughty St.,* ☎ *0171/405–2127.* *£3.* *Mon.–Sat. 10–5; closed national holidays, Dec. 24–Jan. 1. Tube: Russell Square.*

24 **Gray's Inn.** The least architecturally interesting of the four Inns of Court, it still has its romantic associations. In 1594, Shakespeare's *Comedy of Errors* was performed for the first time in its hall—which was lovingly restored after a World War II bombing. You must make advance arrangements to view Gray's Inn's hall, but you can stroll around the secluded and spacious gardens, first planted by Francis Bacon in 1606. ✉ *Holborn,* ☎ *0171/405–8164. Visits only by advance written application to the librarian.* *Chapel weekdays 10–4; closed national holidays. Tube: Holborn, Temple.*

25 **Lincoln's Inn.** One of the oldest, best preserved, and most comely of the Inns of Court, Lincoln's Inn offers plenty to see—from the Chancery Lane Tudor brick gatehouse to the wide-open, tree-lined, atmospheric Lincoln's Inn Fields and the 15th-century Chapel remodeled by Inigo Jones in 1620. The wisteria-clad New Square is London's only complete 17th-century square. ✉ *Chancery La.,* ☎ *0171/405–1393.* *Gardens and chapel weekdays 12:30–2:30; guided tours available; closed national holidays. Tube: Chancery Lane.*

Pollock's Toy Museum. Historians tell us that the Victorians invented the concept of childhood and no better proof can be offered than this magical place, a treasure trove of a small museum in a 19th-century town house. Most of the objects are dolls, dolls' houses, teddy bears, folk toys—and those bedazzling mementoes of Victorian childhood, Pollock's famed cardboard cut-out toy theaters, all red velvet, gold trim, with moveable scenery and figurines. Happily, Pollock's still sells these toy theaters—a souvenir that will drive both children and connoisseurs mad with joy. ✉ *1 Scala St.,* ☎ *0171/636–3452.* *£2.* *Mon.–Sat. 10–5. Tube: Goodge St.*

26 **Sir John Soane's Museum.** Guaranteed to raise a smile from the most blasé and footsore tourist, this beloved collection hardly deserves the burden of its dry name. Sir John, architect of the Bank of England, who lived here from 1790 to 1831, created one of London's most idiosyncratic and fascinating houses. Everywhere mirrors and colors play tricks with light and space, and split-level floors worthy of a fairground fun house disorient you. In a basement chamber sits the vast 1300 BC sarcophagus of Seti I, lit by a domed skylight two stories up.

✉ *13 Lincoln's Inn Fields,* ☎ *0171/405–2107.* 🎫 *Free.* ⏲ *Tues.–Sat. 10–5; closed national holidays. Tube: Holburn, Temple.*

27 **Temple.** This is the collective name for **Inner Temple** and **Middle Temple,** and its entrance—the exact point of entry into the City—is marked by a young (1880) bronze griffin, the **Temple Bar Memorial.** In the buildings opposite is an elaborate stone arch through which you pass into Middle Temple Lane, past a row of 17th-century timber-frame houses, and on into Fountain Court. If the Elizabethan **Middle Temple Hall** is open, don't miss its hammer-beam roof—among the finest in the land. ☎ *0171/353–4355.* ⏲ *Weekdays 10–noon and (when not in use) 3–4. Tube: Temple.*

22 **University of London.** A relatively youthful institution that grew out of the need for a nondenominational center for higher education, the University of London was founded by Dissenters in 1826, with its first examinations held 12 years later. Jews and Roman Catholics were not the only people admitted for the first time to an English university—women were, too, though they had to wait 50 years (until 1878) to sit for a degree.

The City

The City is London's most ancient part—an autonomous district, separately governed since William the Conqueror started building the Tower of London, and despite its compact size (it's known as the Square Mile), the financial engine of Britain and one of the world's leading centers of trade. It was after Edward the Confessor moved his court to Westminster in 1060 that the City gathered momentum. As Westminster took over the administrative role, the City was free to develop the commercial heart that still beats strong. The Romans had already found Londinium's position handy for trade, but it was the establishment of craft guilds in the Middle Ages, followed in Tudor and Stuart times by the proliferation of great trading companies (the Honourable East India Company, founded in 1600, was the star), that really started the cash flowing.

Twice, the City has nearly been wiped off the face of the earth. The Great Fire of 1666 necessitated a total reconstruction, in which Sir Christopher Wren had a big hand, contributing not only his masterpiece, St. Paul's Cathedral, but 49 additional parish churches. The second wave of destruction was dealt by the German bombers of World War II. The ruins were rebuilt, but slowly, and with no overall plan, leaving the City a patchwork of the old and the new, the interesting and the flagrantly awful. Since a mere 8,000 or so people call it home, the financial center of Britain is deserted outside the working week, with restaurants shuttered and streets forlorn and windswept.

A Good Walk

Begin at the gateway to the City, the Temple Bar of the **Temple** district, a bronze griffin on the Strand opposite the Royal Courts of Justice. Walk east to Fleet Street and turn left on Bolt Court to Gough Square, and **Dr. Johnson's House** ㉘, passing Ye Olde Cheshire Cheese on Wine Office Court en route back to Fleet Street and the journalists' church, **St. Bride's** ㉙. At the end of Fleet Street, cross Ludgate Circus to Ludgate Hill to reach **Old Bailey** ㉚, and the Central Criminal Courts. Continuing along Ludgate Hill, you reach **St. Paul's Cathedral** ㉛, Wren's masterpiece. The spirits of those who used to feed the pigeons on its steps—remember the old lady from *Mary Poppins*?—seem to hover nearby.

Retrace your steps to Newgate Street to reach London's meat market, Smithfield—in centuries gone by, living livestock used to be sold here by dealers who liked to stampede their herds around the district's houses "like a bull in a china shop," which is where that phrase comes from. Cross Aldersgate Street and take the right fork to London Wall, named for the Roman rampart that stood along it, with a remaining section of 2nd- to 4th-century wall at St. Alphege Garden. There's another bit outside the **Museum of London** ㉜, behind which is the important arts mecca of gray concrete, the **Barbican Centre** ㉝. Back on London Wall, turn south onto Coleman Street, then right onto Masons Avenue to reach Basinghall Street and the **Guildhall** ㉞, then follow Milk Street south to Cheapside. Here is another symbolic center of London, the **church of St. Mary-le-Bow** ㉟.

Walk to the east end of Cheapside, where seven roads meet, and you will be facing the **Bank of England** ㊱. Turn your back on the bank and there's the Lord Mayor's abode, Mansion House, with Wren's St. Stephen Walbrook church—considered his finest effort by architectural historians—behind it, and the Royal Exchange in between Threadneedle Street and Cornhill. Now head down Queen Victoria Street, where you'll pass the remains of the Roman **Temple of Mithras** ㊲, then, after a sharp left turn onto Cannon Street, you'll come upon the **Monument** ㊳, Wren's memorial to the Great Fire of London. Just south of there is London Bridge. Turn left onto Lower Thames Street, and it's just under a mile's walk—passing Billingsgate, London's principal fish market for 900 years, until 1982, and the Custom House, built early in the last century—to the **Tower of London** ㊴, which may be the single most unmissable of London's sights. Children will want to head for the **Tower Hill Pageant** ㊵ and children of all ages will be enchanted by that Thames icon, the **Tower Bridge.**

TIMING

This is a marathon. Unless you want to be walking all day, without a chance to do justice to London's most famous sights, the Tower of London and St. Paul's Cathedral—not to mention the Museum of London, Tower Bridge, and the Barbican Centre—you should consider splitting the walk into sections. Conversely, if you're not planning to go inside, this walk is a great day out, with lots of surprising vistas, river views, and history. The City is a wasteland on weekends and after dark, so choose your time. There's a certain romantic charm to the streets when they're deserted, but it's hard to find lunch.

Sights to See

㊱ **Bank of England.** Known familiarly for the past couple of centuries as "The Old Lady of Threadneedle Street," the bank has been central to the British economy since 1694. Sir John Soane designed the neoclassical hulk in 1788, wrapping it in windowless walls (which are all that survive of his building) to suggest a stability that the ailing economy of the post-Thatcher years tends to belie. ✉ *Bartholomew La.,* ☎ *0171/601–5545.* 🎟 *Free.* ⏲ *Easter–Sept., weekdays 10–5, Sun. and public holidays 11–5; Oct.–Easter, weekdays 10–6; closed public holidays Oct.–Easter. Tube: Bank, Monument.*

㉝ **The Barbican Centre.** An enormous concrete maze Londoners love to hate, the Barbican is home to the Royal Shakespeare Company and its two theaters, the London Symphony Orchestra and its auditorium, the Guildhall School of Music and Drama, a major gallery for touring exhibitions, two cinemas, and a convention center. Londoners have come to accept the place, if not exactly love it, because of its contents. ✉ *Silk St.,* ☎ *0171/638–4141 or 0171/628–3351 (for RSC backstage tours).* 🎟 *Free.* ⏲ *Mon.–Sat. 9 AM–11 PM, Sun. noon–11 PM; gallery*

Mon.–Sat. 10–7:30, Sun. and national holidays noon–7:30; conservatory weekends noon–5:30 when not in use for private functions (always call first). 🎫 *Gallery £4.50, conservatory 80p; White Card accepted.* ⏲ *Guided tours,* ☎ *0171/628–0183,* 🎫 *£3.50. Tube: Moorgate, Barbican.*

NEED A BREAK? The Barbican Centre's **Waterside Café** has salads, sandwiches, and pastries; they're unremarkable but are served in a tranquil enclosed concrete (naturally) waterside terrace. Sometimes customers are serenaded by practice sessions of the Guildhall School of Music and Drama's orchestra next door.

28 **Dr. Johnson's House.** Samuel Johnson lived here between 1746 and 1759, in the worst of health, compiling his famous dictionary in the attic. Like Dickens, he lived all over town, but, like Dickens's House, this is the only one of his abodes remaining today. It is a shrine to the man possibly more attached to London than anyone else, ever, and includes a first edition of his dictionary among the Johnson-and-Boswell mementos. ✉ *17 Gough Sq.,* ☎ *0171/353–3745.* 🎫 *£3.* ⏲ *May–Sept., Mon.–Sat. 11–5:30; Oct.–Apr., Mon.–Sat. 11–5; closed national holidays. Tube: Chancery Lane, Temple.*

34 **Guildhall.** The symbolic nerve center of the City, the Guildhall houses the Corporation of London, which ceremonially elects and installs the Lord Mayor here as it has done for 800 years. The Guildhall was built in 1411, and though it failed to escape either the 1666 or 1940 flames, its core survived. The fabulous hall is a psychedelic patchwork of coats of arms and banners of the City Livery Companies. ✉ *Gresham St.,* ☎ *0171/606–3030.* 🎫 *Free.* ⏲ *Mon.–Sat. 10–5 (library closed Sat.); closed national holidays. Tube: St. Paul's, Moorgate, Bank, Mansion House.*

Lloyd's of London. Richard Rogers's (of Paris's Pompidou Centre fame) fantastical steel-and-glass medium-rise of six towers around a vast atrium, with his trademark inside-out ventilation shafts, stairwells, and gantries, may be the most exciting recent structure London can claim. The building housing the famous insurance agency is best seen at night, when cobalt and lime spotlights make it leap out of the deeply boring gray skyline like Carmen Miranda at a funeral. Since the firm nearly went bankrupt recently, the atrium gallery, once open to public view, has been closed. ✉ *1 Lime St.,* ☎ *0171/623–7100.*

38 **Monument.** Built to commemorate the "dreadful visitation" of the Great Fire of 1666, this is the world's tallest isolated stone column—the work of Wren. There is a viewing gallery (311 steps up—better than any StairMaster). ✉ *Monument St.,* ☎ *0171/626–2717.* 🎫 *£1.* ⏲ *Apr.–Sept., weekdays 9–5:30, weekends 2–5:30; Oct.–Mar., Mon.–Sat. 9–3:30. Tube: Monument.*

32 **Museum of London.** Anyone with the least interest in how this city evolved will adore this museum, especially its reconstructions and dioramas—of the Great Fire (flickering flames! sound effects!), a 1940s air-raid shelter, a Georgian prison cell, and a Victorian street complete with fully stocked shops. ✉ *London Wall,* ☎ *0171/600–3699.* 🎫 *£3.50; free 4:30–6; all tickets allow unlimited return visits for three months; White Card accepted.* ⏲ *Tues.–Sat. 10–6, Sun. noon–6; closed Good Fri., Dec. 24–25.*

30 **Old Bailey.** The present-day Central Criminal Court is where legendary Newgate Prison stood from the 12th century right until the beginning of this one. Dickens visited Newgate several times (in between pubs)—

Fagin ended up in the Condemned Hold here in *Oliver Twist.* Ask the doorman which current trial is likely to prove juicy, if you're that kind of ghoul—you may catch the conviction of the next Crippen or Christie (England's most notorious wife-murderers, both tried here). ✉ *Old Bailey at Newgate St.,* ☎ *0171/248–3277.* ⏲ *Public Gallery weekdays 10–1 and 2–4; queue at the Newgate St. entrance. No cameras allowed. Tube: Blackfriars.*

29 **St. Bride's.** One of the first of Wren's city churches, St. Bride's was also one of the bomb-damaged ones, reconsecrated only in 1960 after a 17-year restoration. As St. Paul's is the actor's church, so St. Bride's belongs to journalists, many of whom have been buried here. Even before the press moved in, it was a popular place to take the final rest. By 1664 the crypts were so crowded that Samuel Pepys had to bribe the grave digger to "justle together" some bodies to make room for his deceased brother. ✉ *Fleet St.,* ☎ *0171/353–1301.* *Free.* ⏲ *Mon.–Sat. 9–5, Sun. between services at 11 and 6:30. Tube: Chancery Lane.*

35 **St. Mary-le-Bow.** This Wren church, dating from 1673, has one of the most famous sets of bells around—a Londoner must be born within the sound of Bow bells to be a true cockney. The origin of that idea was probably the curfew rung on the bow Bells during the 14th century, even though "cockney" only came to mean Londoner three centuries later, and then it was an insult.

NEED A BREAK? **The Place Below** is literally below, in St. Mary-le-Bow's crypt, and gets packed weekday lunchtimes, since the soup and quiche are particularly good. It's also open for breakfast, and Thursday and Friday evenings feature a posh vegetarian dinner.

31 **St. Paul's Cathedral.** The dome—the world's third largest—will already be familiar, since you see it peeping through on the skyline from many an angle. The cathedral is, of course, Sir Christopher Wren's masterpiece, completed in 1710 after 35 years of building, then, much later, miraculously (mostly) spared by World War II bombs. Wren's first plan, known as the New Model, did not make it past the drawing board, while the second, known as the Great Model, got as far as the 20-foot oak rendering you can see here today before being rejected, too, whereupon Wren is said to have burst into tears. The third, however, was accepted, with the fortunate coda that the architect be allowed to make changes as he saw fit. Without that, there would be no dome, since the approved design had featured a steeple.

When you enter and see the dome from the inside, you may find that it seems smaller than you expected. You aren't imagining things; it *is* smaller, and 60 feet lower, than the lead-covered outer dome. Beneath the lantern is Wren's famous memorial, which his son composed and had set into the pavement, and which reads succinctly: *Lector, si monumentum requiris, circumspice*—"Reader, if you seek his monument, look around you." Up 259 spiral steps is the **Whispering Gallery,** an acoustic phenomenon; you whisper something to the wall on one side, and a second later it transmits clearly to the other side, 107 feet away. Ascend farther to the Stone Gallery, which encircles the outside of the dome and affords a spectacular panorama of London.

The poet John Donne, who had been Dean of St. Paul's for his final 10 years (he died in 1631), lies in the south choir aisle. The vivacious choir stall carvings nearby are the work of Grinling Gibbons, as is the organ, which Wren designed and Handel played. Behind the high altar, you'll find the **American Memorial Chapel,** dedicated in 1958 to the 28,000 GIs stationed here who lost their lives in World War II. ✉ *St.*

Paul's Churchyard, ☏ *0171/248–2705.* 🎫 *Cathedral, ambulatory (American Chapel), crypt, and treasury £3, galleries £2.50, combined ticket £5.* ⏲ *Cathedral Mon.–Sat. 8:30–4:30 (closed occasionally for special services); ambulatory, crypt, and galleries Mon.–Sat. 9:30–4:15. Tube: St. Paul's.*

37 **Temple of Mithras.** Unearthed on a building site in 1954 and taken, at first, for an early Christian church, this was a minor place of pilgrimage in the Roman City. In fact, worshipers here favored Christ's chief rival during the 3rd and 4th centuries, Mithras, the Persian god of light.

Tower Bridge. Despite its venerable, nay medieval, appearance, this is a Victorian youngster that celebrated its centenary in June 1994. Constructed of steel, then clothed in Portland stone, it was deliberately styled in the Gothic persuasion to complement the Tower next door and is famous for its enormous bascules—the "arms," which open to allow large ships through, which is a rare occurrence these days.

The bridge's 100th-birthday gift was a new exhibition, one of London's most imaginative and fun. You are conducted in the company of "Harry Stoner," an animatronic bridge construction worker worthy of Disneyland, back in time to witness the birth of the Thames's last downstream bridge. Be sure to hang on to your ticket and follow the signs to the Engine Rooms for part two, where the original steam-driven hydraulic engines gleam, and a cute rococo theater is the setting for an Edwardian music-hall production of the bridge's story. ☏ *0171/403–3761.* 🎫 *£5.* ⏲ *Apr.–Oct., daily 10–6:30; Nov.–Mar., daily 10–5:15 (last entry 1¼ hrs before closing); closed Good Fri., Dec. 24–25, Jan. 1. Tube: Tower Hill.*

40 **Tower Hill Pageant.** London's first "dark-ride" museum features automated cars that take you past mock-ups of scenes from most periods of London's past, complete with "people," sound effects, and even smells. There's also an archaeological museum with finds from the Thames, set up by the Museum of London. ✉ *Tower Hill Terrace,* ☏ *0171/709–0081.* 🎫 *£5.95.* ⏲ *Apr.–Oct., daily 9:30–5:30; Nov.–Mar., daily 9:30–4:30; closed Dec. 25. Tube: Tower Hill.*

39 **Tower of London.** This remains top billing on every tourist itinerary for good reason. Nowhere else does London's history come to life so vividly as in this mini-city of melodramatic towers stuffed to bursting with heraldry and treasure, the intimate details of lords and dukes and princes and sovereigns etched in the walls (literally in some places, as you'll see), and quite a few pints of royal blue blood spilled on the stones. Be warned that visitor traffic at the sight of sights is copious, meaning not only lines for the best bits, but a certain dilution of atmosphere, which can be disappointing if you've been fantasizing scenes from *Elizabeth and Essex*. At least you need no longer spend all day in line for the prize exhibit, the Crown Jewels, since they have been transplanted to a new home where moving walkways hasten progress at the busiest times. The reason the Tower holds the royal gems is that it is still one of the royal palaces, although no monarch since Henry VIII has called it home. Its most renowned and titillating function has been, of course, as a jail and place of torture and execution.

A person was mighty privileged to be beheaded in the peace and seclusion of **Tower Green** instead of before the mob at Tower Hill. In fact, only seven people were ever important enough—among them Anne Boleyn and Catherine Howard, wives two and five of Henry VIII's six; Elizabeth I's friend Robert Devereux, Earl of Essex; and the nine-days' queen, Lady Jane Grey, age 17. You can see the executioner's block, with its charming forehead-sized dent, and his axe—along with the equally famous rack plus other assorted thumbscrews, iron maidens, etc.—in the **Martin Tower,** which stands in the northeast corner.

Free tours depart every half hour or so from the Middle Tower. They are conducted by the 42 Yeoman Warders, better known as "Beefeaters"—ex-servicemen dressed in resplendent navy-and-red (scarlet-and-gold on special occasions) Tudor outfits. Beefeaters have been guarding the Tower since Henry VII appointed them in 1485. One of them, the Yeoman Ravenmaster, is responsible for making life comfortable for the eight ravens who live in the Tower—an important duty, since if they were to desert the Tower (goes the legend), the kingdom would fall.

In prime position stands the oldest part of the Tower and the most conspicuous of its buildings, the **White Tower.** Henry III (1207–72) had it whitewashed, which is where the name comes from. The spiral staircase is the only way up, and here you'll find the **Royal Armouries,** Britain's national museum of arms and armor, with about 40,000 pieces on display. Most of the interior of the White Tower has been much altered over the centuries, but the **Chapel of St. John,** downstairs from the armouries, is unadulterated 11th-century Norman—very rare, very simple, and very beautiful. Across the moat, the **Traitors' Gate** lies to the right. Immediately opposite Traitors' Gate is the former Garden Tower, better known since about 1570 as the **Bloody Tower.** Its name comes from one of the most famous unsolved murders in history, the saga of the "little princes in the Tower." In 1483 the boy king, Edward V, and his brother Richard were left here by their uncle, Richard of Gloucester, after the death of their father, Edward I. They were never seen again, Gloucester was crowned Richard III, and in 1674 two little skeletons were found under the stairs to St. John's Chapel. The obvious conclusions have always been drawn—and were, in fact, even before the skeletons were discovered.

The shiniest, the most expensive, and absolutely the most famous exhibits here are, of course, the **Crown Jewels,** now housed in the Duke of Wellington's Barracks. In their new setting you get so close that you could lick the gems (if it weren't for the wafers of bulletproof glass). Before you meet them in person, you are given a high-definition-film preview along with a few scenes from Elizabeth's 1953 coronation. Security is as fiendish as you'd expect, since the jewels—even though they would be literally impossible for thieves to sell—are *so* priceless that they're not insured. A brief résumé of the top jewels: Finest of all is the Royal Sceptre, containing the earth's largest cut diamond, the 530-carat Star of Africa. This is also known as Cullinan I, having been cut from the South African Cullinan, which weighed 20 ounces when dug up from a De Beers mine at the beginning of the century. Another chip off the block, Cullinan II, lives on the Imperial Crown of State that Prince Charles is due to wear at his coronation—the same one that Elizabeth II wore in her coronation procession; it had been made for Victoria's in 1838. The other most famous gem is the Koh-i-noor, or "Mountain of Light," which adorns the Queen Mother's crown. When Victoria was presented with this gift horse in 1850, she looked it in the mouth, found it lacking in glitteriness, and had it chopped down to almost half its weight.

The little chapel of **St. Peter ad Vincula** can be visited only as part of a Yeoman Warder tour. The third church on the site, it conceals the remains of some 2,000 people executed at the Tower, Anne Boleyn and Catherine Howard among them. Don't forget to stroll along the battlements before you leave; from them, you get a wonderful overview of the whole Tower of London.

✉ H. M. Tower of London, ☎ 0171/709–0765. £8.30. ⊙ Mar.–Oct., Mon.–Sat. 9:30–6:30, Sun. 2–6; Nov.–Feb., Mon.–Sat. 9:30–5; closed Good Fri., Dec. 24–26, Jan. 1. Yeoman Warder guided tours leave daily (subject to weather and availability) from Middle Tower, at no charge (but a tip is always appreciated), about every 30 min until 3:30 in summer, 2:30 in winter. For tickets to Ceremony of the Keys (the locking of the main gates, nightly at 10), write well in advance: ✉ The Resident Governor and Keeper of the Jewel House, Queen's House, H. M. Tower of London, EC3. Give your name, the dates you wish to attend (including alternate dates), and number of people (up to 7), and enclose a SASE. Tube: Tower Hill.

The South Bank

London's oldest "suburb," Southwark, though just across the river from London Bridge, was conveniently outside the City walls and laws, and therefore was the ideal location for the taverns and cock-fighting arenas that served as after-hours entertainment in the Middle Ages. By Shakespeare's time it had become a veritable den of iniquity, famous above all for the "Southwark stews," or brothels, and for being very rough. The Globe Theatre, in which Shakespeare acted and held shares, was one of several established here after theaters were banished from the City in 1574 for encouraging truancy in young apprentices. The Globe was as likely to stage a few bouts of bearbaiting as the latest Shakespeare play.

Southwark was heavily bombed during World War II, then neglected for a few decades. This circumstance began to change when theater returned to the Bankside environs (Bankside being the street along the South Bank from Southwark to Blackfriars Bridges) in the form of the national arts complex that opened downstream in 1976, but it took another decade or so for developers and local authorities to catch on to the potential farther east. Now the pockets of the new and the renovated—Gabriel's Wharf, London Bridge City, Hay's Galleria, Butler's Wharf—have practically connected to form a South Bank that even Londoners, who have an attitude problem about crossing the river, have been known to admire and even frequent.

A Good Walk

Start scenically at the south end of **Tower Bridge,** finding the steps on the east (left) side, which descend to the start of a pedestrians-only street, Shad Thames. Now turn your back on the bridge and follow this quaint path between cliffs of the good-as-new warehouses, which are now **Butler's Wharf** ㊶, but were once the seedy, dingy, dangerous shadowlands where Dickens killed off evil Bill Sikes in *Oliver Twist.* See the foodies' center, the Gastrodrome, and the **Design Museum** ㊷, then just before you get back to Tower Bridge, turn away from the river, along Horsleydown Lane, follow Tooley Street, take the right turn at Morgan Lane to **HMS *Belfast*** ㊸, or continue to **Hay's Galleria** ㊹ with **London Bridge** and the **London Dungeon** ㊺ beyond. Next, turn left onto Joiner Street underneath the arches of London's first (1836) railway, then right onto St. Thomas Street, where you'll find the **Old St. Thomas's Operating Theatre and Herb Garret** ㊻, with **Southwark Cathedral** ㊼, just across Borough High Street, and another of the South Bank's recent office developments, St. Mary Overie Dock down Cathedral Street. See the west wall, with rose window outline, of Winchester House, palace of the Bishops of Winchester until 1626, built into it, and **the Clink** ㊽ next door. Continue to the end of Clink Street onto Bankside, detouring left up Rose Alley, where in 1989 the remains of a famous Jacobean theater, the Rose Theatre, were unearthed, though the office development surrounding the preserved foundations means there's not much to see. The next little alley is New Globe Walk, where there is much to see: the reconstruction of that most famous of Jacobean theaters, **Shakespeare's Globe** ㊾. Next along Bankside is the 17th-century Cardinal's Wharf, where, as a plaque explains, Wren lived while St. Paul's Cathedral was being built, then Bankside Power Station, which is to become the new Tate Gallery by the year 2000.

Now you reach your fourth bridge on this walk, **Blackfriars Bridge,** which you pass beneath to join the street called Upper Ground, passing the Coin Street Community Builders' embryo neighborhood, including Gabriel's Wharf, a small shopping mall. Farther along Upper Ground, you reach the **South Bank Centre** ㊿, with the **Royal National Theatre** 51 first, followed by the **National Film Theatre, MOMI** (Museum of the Moving Image) 52 and the **Royal Festival Hall** 53. You'll find distractions all over here, especially in summer—secondhand bookstalls, entertainers, and a series of plaques annotating the buildings opposite. Look to the opposite bank for the quintessential postcard vista of the Houses of Parliament—it's good from Jubilee Gardens, past the County Hall and Westminster Bridge to St. Thomas's Hospital and its **Florence Nightingale Museum** 54. Farther along the river **Lambeth Palace** 55—for 800 years the London base of the Archbishop of Canterbury, top man in the Church of England—stands by Lambeth Bridge. Now if you take a detour to the right off Lambeth Road, you could be "doing the Lambeth Walk" down the street of the same name. A cockney tradition ever since the 17th century, when there was a spa here, the Sunday stroll was immortalized in a song from the 1937 musical *Me and My Gal.* A little farther east along Lambeth Road you reach the **Imperial War Museum** 56.

TIMING

On a fine day, this 2- to 3-mile walk makes a very scenic wander, since you're following the south bank of the great Thames nearly all the way. Fabulous views across to the north bank take you past St. Paul's and the Houses of Parliament, and you pass—under, over, or around—no fewer than seven bridges. It's bound to take far longer than a couple of hours, since the sightseeing is heavy. The Imperial War Museum, MOMI, Shakespeare's Globe, the Hayward Gallery, and the Design Museum are major events, needing at least an hour apiece (depending on your interests), while the London Dungeon doesn't take long, unless you have kids in tow—which is why you'd go in at all. The other museums on this route—the Clink, Garden History, Old Operating Theatre, Florence Nightingale, the South Bank Centre foyers, and the Bankside Gallery—are compact enough to squeeze together en route to your main event. And that's the nicest thing to do with this walk; have tickets waiting at the end. The National Theatres, the NFT, or Shakespeare's Globe can all oblige, but remember the theaters are dark on Sunday. Dinner or a riverside drink at the Gastrodrome restaurants or the People's Palace are another idea for a big finish. Public transportation is thin on the ground around this way, so pick a day when you're feeling energetic, since there are no short cuts once you're underway.

Sights to See

41 **Butler's Wharf.** An '80s development that is maturing gracefully, Butler's Wharf has many empty apartments in its deluxe loft-style warehouse conversions and swanky new blocks, but there *is* life here, thanks partly to London's saint of the stomach, Sir Terence Conran (also responsible for high-profile central London restaurants Bibendum, Mezzo,

and Quaglino's). He gave it his "Gastrodrome" of four restaurants, a vintner's, a deli, a bakery, and who knows what else by now.

48 **The Clink.** The prison attached to Winchester House, palace of the Bishops of Winchester until 1626, its name still serves as a general term for jail. This was one of the first prisons to detain women, most of whom were "Winchester Geese"—a euphemism meaning prostitutes. The oldest profession was endemic in Southwark and now there is, of all things, a museum tracing the history of prostitution here, showing what the Clink was like during its 16th-century scandalous heyday. ⊠ *1 Clink St.,* ☎ *0171/403–6515.* *£2.50.* *Daily 10–6; closed Dec. 25–26. Tube: London Bridge.*

42 **Design Museum.** Opened in 1989, this was the first museum in the world to elevate the everyday design we take for granted to the status of exhibit, slotting it into its social and cultural context. The top floor traces the evolution of mass-produced goods. Check out the very good Blueprint Café with its own river terrace. ⊠ *Butler's Wharf,* ☎ *0171/403–6933.* *£4.50.* *Daily 10:30–5:30; closed Dec. 24–26, Jan. 1. Tube: Tower Hill, then walk across river.*

54 **Florence Nightingale Museum.** Here you can learn all about the that most famous of nursing reformers, "The Lady with the Lamp." On view are fascinating reconstructions of the barracks ward at Scutari (Turkey), where she tended soldiers during the Crimean War (1854–56) and earned her nickname, and a Victorian East End slum cottage, to show what she did to improve living conditions among the poor. The museum is in **St. Thomas's Hospital.** ⊠ *2 Lambeth Palace Rd.,* ☎ *0171/620–0374.* *£2.50.* *Tues.–Sun. and public holidays 10–4; closed Good Fri., Easter, Dec. 25–26, Jan. 1. Tube: Waterloo, or Westminster and walk over the bridge.*

44 **Hay's Galleria.** Once known as "London's larder" on account of the edibles sold here, it was reborn in 1987 as a Covent Garden–esque parade of bars and restaurants, offices, and shops, all weatherproofed by an arched glass atrium roof supported by tall iron columns. Inevitably, jugglers, string quartets, and crafts stalls abound.

Hayward Gallery. One of the city's major art-exhibition spaces, the Hayward Gallery is fixed firmly in this century due to its stark modern architecture. This stained and windowless bunker tucked behind the South Bank Centre concert halls has come in for the most flak of all the Thames-side buildings, enduring constant threats to flatten it and start again, but it's still here, topped by its multicolored neon tube sculpture, the most familiar feature on the South Bank skyline. ⊠ *South Bank Complex,* ☎ *0171/928–3144.* *Admission varies according to exhibition.* *Daily 10–6, Tues. and Wed. until 8; closed Good Fri., May Day, Dec. 25–26, Jan. 1. Tube: Waterloo.*

43 **HMS *Belfast*.** At 656 feet, this is one of the largest and most powerful cruisers the Royal Navy ever had. It played a role in the D-Day landings off Normandy. On board there's an outpost of the Imperial War Museum. ⊠ *Morgan's La., Tooley St.,* ☎ *0171/407–6434.* *£4.* *Mid-Mar.–Oct., daily 10–5:30; Nov.–mid-Mar., daily 10–4; closed Dec. 24–26, Jan. 1. Tube: London Bridge.*

56 **Imperial War Museum.** Housed in an elegantly colonnaded 19th-century building once the home of the infamous insane asylum called Bedlam, this museum of 20th-century warfare does not glorify bloodshed but attempts to evoke what it was like to live through the two world wars. Of course, there is hardware—a Battle of Britain Spitfire, a German V2 rocket—but there is an equal amount of war art (John Singer

Sargent to Henry Moore). One very affecting exhibit is *The Blitz Experience,* which is what it sounds like—a 10-minute taste of an air raid in a street of acrid smoke with sirens blaring and searchlights glaring. ✉ *Lambeth Rd.,* ☎ *0171/416–5000.* 🎫 *£4.10.* ⏲ *Daily 10–6; closed Dec. 24–26, Jan. 1. Tube: Lambeth North.*

55 **Lambeth Palace.** The London residence of the Archbishop of Canterbury—the senior archbishop of the Church of England—since the 13th century is rarely open to the public, but you can admire the fine Tudor gatehouse.

45 **The London Dungeon.** Clearly, the most gory, grisly, gruesome museum in town. Here realistic waxwork people are subjected in graphic detail to all the historical horrors the Tower of London merely suggests. Tableaus depict famous bloody moments—like Anne Boleyn's decapitation, or the martyrdom of St. George—alongside the torture, murder, and ritual slaughter of more anonymous victims, all to a soundtrack of screaming, wailing, and agonized moaning. London's times of deepest terror—the Great Fire and the Great Plague—are brought to life, too. And did you ever wonder what a disembowelment actually looks like? See it here. Children seem to adore this place, which is among London's top tourist attractions and usually has long lines. ✉ *28–34 Tooley St.,* ☎ *0171/403–0606.* 🎫 *£7.50.* ⏲ *Apr.–Sept., daily 10–5:30; Oct.–Mar., daily 10–4:30; closed Dec. 24–26. Tube: London Bridge.*

52 **Museum of the Moving Image (MOMI).** Attached to the National Film Theatre (or NFT) underneath Waterloo Bridge—whose two movie theaters offer easily the best repertory programming in London—MOMI may be the most fun of all London's museums. The main feature is a history of cinema from 4,000-year-old Javanese shadow puppets to Spielbergian special effects, but the supporting program is even better, and it stars *you.* Actors dressed as John Wayne or Mae West, or usherettes, or chorus girls pluck you out of obscurity to read the TV news or audition for the chorus line or fly like Superman over the Thames. Needless to say, this is always a big hit with kids. ✉ *South Bank Centre,* ☎ *0171/401–2636.* 🎫 *£5.95; White Card accepted.* ⏲ *Daily 10–6 (last admission at 5); closed Dec. 24–26. Tube: Waterloo.*

NEED A BREAK? The NFT restaurant and cafeteria—especially the big wooden tables outside—are popular for lunch or supper.

46 **Old St. Thomas's Operating Theatre.** One of England's oldest hospitals stood here from the 12th century until the railway forced it to move in 1862. Today, its operating theater has been restored into an exhibition of early 19th-century medical practices: the operating table onto which the gagged and blindfolded patients were roped; the box of sawdust underneath for catching their blood; the knives, pliers, and handsaws the surgeons wielded; and—this was a theater in the round—the spectators' seats. ✉ *9A St. Thomas St.,* ☎ *0171/955–4791.* 🎫 *£2.* ⏲ *Tues.–Sun. 10–4; closed Dec. 15–Jan. 5. Tube: London Bridge.*

53 **Royal Festival Hall.** The largest auditorium of the South Bank Centre, this hall features superb acoustics and a 3,000-plus capacity. It is the oldest of the riverside blocks, raised as the centerpiece of the 1951 Festival of Britain, a postwar morale-boosting exercise. The London Philharmonic resides here; symphony orchestras from the world over like to visit; and choral works, ballet, serious jazz and pop, and even film with live accompaniment are also staged. There is a good, independently run restaurant, the People's Palace, and a very good bookstore. The next building you come to also contains two concert halls, the **Queen**

Elizabeth Hall and the **Purcell Room.** ⊠ *South Bank Centre at South Bank,* ☎ *0171/928–8800.*

51 **Royal National Theatre.** Londoners generally felt the same way about Sir Denys Lasdun's Brutalist-style function-dictates-form building when it opened in 1976, as they would a decade later about the far nastier Barbican. But whatever its merits or demerits as a landscape feature, the Royal National Theatre—still abbreviated colloquially to the pre-royal warrant "NT"—has wonderful insides. Three auditoriums—the Olivier, named after Sir Laurence, first artistic director of the National Theatre Company; the Lyttleton; and the Cottesloe—host an ever-changing array of presentations. The NT does not rest on its laurels. It attracts many of the nation's top actors (Anthony Hopkins, for one, does time here) in addition to launching future stars. ⊠ *South Bank,* ☎ *0171/928–2252 (box office) or 0171/633–0880 (backstage tours).* 🎟 *Tours £3.50.* ⏲ *Foyers Mon.–Sat. 10* AM*–11* PM*; hr-long backstage tours Mon.–Sat. at 10:15, 12:30, and 5:30; closed Dec. 24–25. Tube: Waterloo.*

49 **Shakespeare's Globe.** Largely the fruit of the late American actor and film director Sam Wanamaker, this new complex, due to open officially in 1997, will be Britain's leading center for the study and worship of the Bard of Bards. In addition to an exact replica of Shakespeare's open-roof Globe Playhouse (built in 1599; incinerated in 1613)—using authentic Elizabethan materials and craft techniques and the first thatched roof in London since the Great Fire—there is a second, indoor theater, built to a design of the 17th-century architect Inigo Jones. The whole thing stands 100 yards from the original Globe. The Globe is a celebration of the great bard's life and work, an actual rebirth of his "wooden O" (see *Henry V*), where his plays are presented in natural light (and sometimes rain), to 1,000 people on wooden benches in the "bays," plus 500 "groundlings," standing on a carpet of filbert shells and clinker, just as they did nearly four centuries ago. For any theater buff, this stunning project is a must. ⊠ *New Globe Walk, Bankside,* ☎ *0171/928–6406.* 🎟 *Exhibition £4.* ⏲ *Daily 10–5; call for performance schedule; closed Dec. 24–25. Tube: Mansion House, then walk across Southwark Bridge.*

50 **South Bank Centre.** On either side of Waterloo Bridge is London's chief arts center. Along Upper Ground, you'll first reach the ☞ **Royal National Theatre**—three auditoriums that are home to some of the finest theater in Britain. Underneath Waterloo Bridge is the **National Film Theatre**—the best repertory cinema house in London—and its most intriguing attraction, the ☞ **Museum of the Moving Image.** Also here are the ☞ **Royal Festival Hall,** the **Queen Elizabeth Hall** and the **Purcell Room**—three of London's finest venues for classical music. Finally, tucked away behind the concert halls is the ☞ **Hayward Gallery.** Along the wide paths of the complex you'll find distractions of every sort—secondhand bookstalls, entertainers, and arrogant pigeons. ⊠ *South Bank Centre,* ☎ *0171/401–2636. Tube: Waterloo.*

47 **Southwark Cathedral.** This cathedral, pronounced "suth-uck," is the second-oldest Gothic church in London, next to Westminster Abbey, with parts dating from the 12th century. Although it houses some remarkable memorials, not to mention a program of lunchtime concerts, it is little visited. Look for the gaudily renovated 1408 tomb of the poet John Gower, friend of Chaucer, and for the Harvard Chapel, named after John Harvard, founder of the American college, who was baptized here in 1608. Another notable buried here is Edmund Shakespeare, brother of William.

Kensington, Knightsbridge, and Hyde Park

Salubrious Knightsbridge, east of Belgravia and north of Chelsea, offers approximately equal doses of elite residential streets and ultra-shopping opportunities. To *its* east is one of the highest concentrations of important artifacts anywhere, the "museum mile" of South Kensington, with the rest of Kensington offering peaceful strolls, a noisy main street, and another palace. Kensington first became the *Royal* Borough of Kensington (and Chelsea) when William III, who suffered terribly from the Thames mists over Whitehall, decided in 1689 to buy Nottingham House in the rural village of Kensington so that he could breathe more easily. Courtiers and functionaries and society folk soon followed where the crowns led, and by the time Queen Anne was on the throne (1702–14), Kensington was overflowing. In a way, it still is, since most of its grand houses have been divided into apartments, or else are serving as foreign embassies.

Now visitors enter Kensington Gardens to see Kensington Palace—home to Princess Diana—and to explore the parks themselves. Hyde Park and Kensington Gardens together form by far the biggest of central London's royal parks. It's probably been centuries since any major royal had a casual stroll here, but the parks remain the property of the Crown, and it was the Crown that saved them from being devoured by the city's late 18th-century growth spurt.

A Good Walk

When you surface from the Knightsbridge tube station—one of London's deepest—you are immediately engulfed by the angry drivers, professional shoppers, and ladies-who-lunch who comprise the local population. Walk west down Brompton Road, past Harrods, to the junction of Cromwell Road and the pale, Italianate Brompton Oratory, which marks the beginning of museum territory. The **Victoria & Albert** ⑰ or V&A, is first, at the start of Cromwell Road, followed by the **Natural History Museum** ⑱ and the **Science Museum** ⑲ behind it. Turn left to continue north up Exhibition Road, a kind of unfinished cultural main drag that was Prince Albert's conception, toward the road after which British moviemakers named their fake blood, Kensington Gore, to reach the giant round Wedgwood china box of the **Royal Albert Hall** ⑳ and the scaffolding-shrouded **Albert Memorial** (61) opposite.

Enter **Kensington Gardens** across the road, and walk west until you reach **Kensington Palace** (62). From here you can either head west to check out some of London's current homes of the rich and famous at **Kensington Palace Gardens** (63) or take an extra leg of the journey to visit two historic residences, the **Linley Sambourne House** (64) and **Leighton House** (65). If opulent 19th-century interiors are not your cup of tea, head east instead to explore Kensington Gardens itself. You'll encounter the Round Pond, the statues of **Peter Pan** and the horse and rider called Physical Energy, then the formal garden at the end of the Long Water, The Fountains, and finally the **Serpentine Gallery,** beside the lake of the same name. When you pass its bridge, you leave Kensington Gardens and enter **Hyde Park.** Walk to the southern perimeter and along the sand track called Rotten Row. It was Henry VIII's royal path to the hunt—hence the name, a corruption of *route du roi.* It's still used by the Household Cavalry (the brigade that mounts the guard at the palace), who live at the Knightsbridge Barracks to the left. Then head toward the Hyde Park Corner exit of the park and discover the **Wellington Museum** (66). For a jaunt off the well-trodden path, head northward to discover the sights around Regents's Park: London's most elegant museum, the **Wallace Collection** 67, **Madame Tussaud's Waxworks** 68, and the **Zoo.**

TIMING

This walk is at least 4 miles long, and is almost impossible to achieve without going inside somewhere. The best way to approach these neighborhoods is to treat Knightsbridge shopping and the South Kensington museums as separate days out—though you may find all three of the museums too much to take in at once. The parks are best in the growing seasons—from the crocuses and daffodils of early spring through the tulips to the roses—and during fall, when the foliage show easily rivals New England's. Sunday, the Hyde Park and Kensington Gardens railings all along the Bayswater Road are hung with very bad art, which may slow your progress; also this is prime perambulation day for locals. Whatever your priorities, this is a long walk if you explore every corner, with the perimeter of the two parks alone covering a good 4 miles, and about half as far again around the remainder of the route. You could cut out a lot of park without missing out on essential sights, and walk the whole thing in a brisk three hours. Remember that the parks close their gates at sundown.

Sights to See

61 **Albert Memorial.** Permanently shrouded in the world's tallest free-standing piece of scaffolding, the intricate structure housing the 14-foot bronze statue of Albert is undergoing a £14-million renovation and is not due to be finished until the year 2000. Albert's grieving widow, Queen Victoria, had this elaborate confection erected on the spot where his Great Exhibition had stood a mere decade before his early death from typhoid in 1861.

Harrods. Just in case you didn't notice it, Harrods has its domed terra-cotta Edwardian bulk outlined in thousands of white lights by night. The 15-acre Egyptian-owned store's sales weeks are world-class, and the place is as frenetic as a stock market floor. Don't miss the extravagant **Food Hall,** with its stunning Art Nouveau tiling in the neighborhood of meat and poultry. This is the department to acquire your green-and-gold souvenir Harrods bag in, since food prices are surprisingly competitive. ✉ *87 Brompton Rd.,* ☎ *0171/730–1234.*

NEED A BREAK? **Patisserie Valerie** (✉ 215 Brompton Rd., ☎ 0171/832–9971), just down the road from Harrods, offers light meals and a gorgeous array of pastries. It's perfect for breakfast, lunch, or tea.

Hyde Park. Along with the smaller St. James's and Green parks to the east, Hyde Park started as Henry VIII's hunting grounds. Along its south side runs **Rotten Row,** still used by the Household Cavalry, who live at the **Knightsbridge Barracks**—a high-rise and a long, low, ugly red block to the left. This is the brigade that mounts the guard at the palace, and you can see them leave to perform this duty, in full regalia, at about 10:30, or see the exhausted calvary return about noon.

Kensington Gardens. More formal than neighboring Hyde Park, Kensington Gardens was first laid out as palace grounds. The paved Italian garden at the top of the Long Water, **The Fountains** is a reminder of this, though, of course **Kensington Palace** itself is the main clue to its royal status, with its early 19th-century Sunken Garden north of it. Nearby is George Frampton's beloved 1912 ***Peter Pan,*** a bronze of the boy who lived on an island in the Serpentine and never grew up, and whose creator, J. M. Barrie, lived at 100 Bayswater Road, not 500 yards from here. The **Round Pond,** is a magnet for model-boat enthusiasts and duck feeders.

62 **Kensington Palace.** Near the western edge of Kensington Gardens, this abode is the erstwhile address of Prince Charles and Princess Di. Royals have lived here since William and Mary—and some have died here, too. In 1760, poor George II burst a blood vessel while on the toilet (the official line was, presumably, that he was on the throne). The state rooms where Victoria had her ultra-strict upbringing have recently been completely renovated, and depict the life of the royal family through the past century. Because of the ongoing refurbishment program, the palace will be open only from May through September during 1996, 1997, and 1998. The public is admitted only by guided tour. ✉ *Kensington Gdns.,* ☎ *0171/937–9561.* *£4.50.* *May 1–Sept. 28, daily 9:30–3:30. Tube: High Street Kensington.*

63 **Kensington Palace Gardens.** Immediately behind Kensington Palace is Kensington Palace Gardens (called Palace Green at the south end), a wide, leafy avenue of mid-19th-century mansions that has always comprised one of the most elegant addresses in London. This is one of the few private roads in London with uniformed guards at each end; there are several foreign embassies here, including that of Russia. Other mansions are homes to Britain's rich and famous, including the residence of the Marquesses of Cholmondeley. *Tube: High Street Kensington.*

65 **Leighton House.** The exotic richness of late 19th-century aesthetic tastes is captured in this fascinating home, once the abode of Lord Leighton, the Victorian painter par excellence. The Arab Hall is lavishly lined with Persian tiles and pieced woodwork. Thanks to the generosity of John Paul Getty II, the somewhat neglected property has undergone a full renovation. Its neighborhood was one of the principal artists' colonies of Victorian London. If you are interested in domestic architecture of the 19th century, wander through the surrounding streets. ✉ *14 Holland Park Rd.,* ☎ *0171/602–3316.* *Free.* *Mon.–Sat. 11–5. Tube: Holland Park.*

64 **Linley Sambourne House.** On the eastern side of the Commonwealth Institute discover this delightful Victorian residence, built and furnished in the 1870s by Mr. Sambourne, for more than 30 years the political cartoonist for the satirical magazine *Punch*. Full of pictures, furniture, and ornaments, it provides a marvelous insight into the day-to-day life of a prosperous, cultured family in late Victorian times. Some of the scenes from the movie *A Room with a View* were shot here. ✉ *18 Stafford Terr.,* ☎ *0181/944–1019.* *£3.* *Mar.–Oct., Wed. 10–4, Sun. 2–5. Tube: High Street Kensington.*

68 **Madame Tussaud's.** This is nothing more, nothing less, than the world's premier exhibition of lifelike waxwork models of celebrities. Madame T. learned her craft while making death masks of French Revolution victims and in 1835 set up her first show of the famous ones near this spot. You can see everyone from Shakespeare to Benny Hill here, but top billing still goes to the murderers in the Chamber of Horrors, who stare glassy-eyed at you—this one from the electric chair, that one next to the tin bath where he dissolved several wives in quicklime. ✉ *Marylebone Rd.,* ☎ *0171/935–6861.* *£8.75, joint ticket with planetarium (*☞ below*) £10.95.* *Sept.–June, weekdays 10–5:30, weekends 9:30–5:30; July–Aug., daily 9:30–5:30; closed Dec. 25. Tube: Baker Street.*

58 **Natural History Museum.** Along this museum's outrageously ornate French-Romanesque–style terra-cotta facade, architect Alfred Waterhouse had relief panels installed depicting living creatures to the left of the entrance, extinct ones to the right. Inside, that categoriza-

tion is sort of continued in reverse, with Dinosaurs on the left and the Ecology Gallery on the right. Both these newly renovated exhibits (the former with life-size moving dinosaurs, the latter complete with moonlit "rain forest") make essential viewing in a museum that realized it was getting crusty and has consequently invested millions overhauling itself in recent years. Don't miss the Creepy Crawlies Gallery, which features a nightmarish superenlarged scorpion, yet ends up making tarantulas cute. Understandably, this place usually resembles grade-school recess. ⊠ *Cromwell Rd.,* ☎ *0171/938–9123.* *£5.50; free weekdays 4:30–5:50, weekends 5–5:50; White Card accepted.* *Mon.–Sat. 10–5:50, Sun. 11–5:50; closed Dec. 24–26, Jan. 1. Tube: South Kensington.*

60 **Royal Albert Hall.** This famous theater was made possible by the Victorian public, who donated funds for the domed, circular 8,000-seat auditorium. More money was raised, however, by selling 1,300 future seats at £100 apiece—not for the first night, but for every night for 999 years. (Some descendants of purchasers still use the seats.) The Albert Hall is best known and best loved for its annual July–September Henry Wood Promenade Concerts (the "Proms"), with bargain standing (or promenading, or sitting-on-the-floor) tickets sold on the night of the world-class classical concerts. ⊠ *Kensington Gore,* ☎ *0171/589–3203.* *Admission varies according to event. Tube: South Kensington.*

59 **Science Museum.** Standing behind the Natural History Museum, this features loads of hands-on exhibits. Highlights include the Launch Pad gallery, the Computing Then and Now show, ***Puffing Billy,*** the oldest train in the world; and the actual ***Apollo 10*** capsule. ⊠ *Exhibition Rd.,* ☎ *0171/938–8000.* *£5; White Card accepted.* *Mon.–Sat. 10–6, Sun. 11–6; closed Dec. 24–26, Jan. 1. Tube: South Kensington.*

Serpentine Gallery. Princess Diana is the current royal benefactress of this gallery, which remains influential on the trendy artist circuit. Several exhibitions of modern work a year are held here, often very avant-garde indeed. It overlooks the west bank of the **Serpentine,** a beloved lake, much frequented in summer, when the south shore Lido resembles a beach and the water is dotted with hired rowboats. ⊠ *Kensington Gardens,* ☎ *0171/402–6075.* *Free.* *Daily 10–6; closed Christmas wk. Tube: Lancaster Gate.*

57 **Victoria & Albert Museum.** Recognizable by the copy of Victoria's Imperial Crown it wears on the lantern above the central cupola, this museum is always referred to as the V&A. It is a huge museum, showcasing the applied arts of all disciplines, all periods, all nationalities, and all tastes, and is a wonderful, generous place to get lost in. The collections are *so* all-encompassing that confusion is a hazard—one minute you're gazing on the Jacobean oak 12-foot-square four-poster Great Bed of Ware (one of the V&A's most prized possessions, given that Shakespeare immortalized it in *Twelfth Night*); the next, you're in the 20th-century end of the equally celebrated Dress Collection, coveting a Jean Muir frock you could actually buy at nearby Harrods. Prince Albert, Victoria's adored consort, was responsible for the genesis of this permanent version of the 1851 Great Exhibition, and his queen laid its foundation stone in her final public London appearance in 1899. Be sure to check out young designer Danny Lane's breathtaking glass balustrade in the Glass Gallery. The special events program here is one of the most exciting in the world—unique lectures, dinners, and concerts have changed a once-stuffy museum into a very happening place, luring the young and trendy. ⊠ *Cromwell Rd.,* ☎ *0171/938–8500.* *Suggested contribution £4.50; White Card accepted.* *Mon.*

noon–5:50, Tues.–Sun. 10–5:50; closed Good Fri., May Day, Dec. 24–26, Jan. 1. Tube: South Kensington.

NEED A BREAK? Rest your overstimulated eyes in the brick-walled **V&A café,** where full meals and small snacks are available, and the Sunday Jazz Brunch (11–5) is fast becoming a London institution.

67 **Wallace Collection.** Assembled by four generations of marquesses of Hertford, the Wallace Collection is important, exciting, undervisited—and free. As at the Frick Collection in New York, the setting here, Hertford House, is part of the show—a fine late-18th-century mansion. It was the eccentric fourth marquess who really built the collection, snapping up Bouchers, Fragonards, Watteaus, and Lancrets for a song (the French Revolution having rendered them dangerously unfashionable). The highlight is Fragonard's *The Swing,* which conjures up the 18th century's let-them-eat-cake *frivolité* better than any other painting around. Don't forget to say hello to Frans Hals's *Laughing Cavalier* in the Big Gallery. ✉ *Hertford House, Manchester Sq.,* ☎ *0171/935–0687.* 🎟 *Free.* 🕓 *Mon.–Sat. 10–5, Sun. 2–5; closed Good Fri., May Day, Dec. 24–26, Jan. 1.*

66 **Wellington Museum (Apsley House).** Once known, quite simply, as Number 1, London, this was celebrated as the best address in town. Built by Robert Adam in the 1770s and reopened in 1995 after a complete renovation, this mansion was home to the celebrated conqueror of Napoléon, the Duke of Wellington, who lived here from the 1820s until his death in 1852. The great yellow-brocaded gallery—scene of legendary dinners—is one of the most spectacular rooms in England. Not to be missed, in every sense, is the gigantic Canova statue of a nude (but fig-leafed) Bonaparte in the entry stairwell. ✉ *149 Piccadilly,* ☎ *0171/499–5676.* 🎟 *£3.* 🕓 *Tues.–Sun. 11–5.*

London Zoo. The zoo has been open for more than 150 years and peaked in popularity during the 1950s, but recently faced the prospect of closing its gates forever. The problems started when animal-crazy Brits, apparently anxious about the morality of caging wild beasts, simply stopped visiting. But the zoo fought back, pulling heartstrings with a "Save Our Zoo" campaign and tragic predictions of mass euthanasia for homeless polar bears, and, at the 11th hour, found commercial sponsorship that was generous enough not only to keep the wolves from the door (or the wolves indoors) but also to fund a great big modernization program. Highlights include the Elephant and Rhino Pavilion and the graceful Snowdon Aviary. ✉ *Regent's Park,* ☎ *0171/722–3333.* 🎟 *£7.* 🕓 *Summer, daily 9–6; winter, daily 10–4; closed Dec. 25. Penguin feed at 2:30; aquarium feed 2:30; reptile feed 2:30 Fri. only; elephant bath 3:45. Tube: Camden Town, and Bus 74.*

Up and Down the Thames

About 8 miles downstream—which means seaward, to the east—from central London lies a neighborhood you'd think had been designed to provide the perfect day out. Greenwich is another of London's self-contained "villages," only one with unique and splendid sights surrounding the residential portion. Sir Christopher Wren's Royal Naval College and Inigo Jones's Queen's House reach architectural heights; the Old Royal Observatory measures time for our entire planet; and the Greenwich Meridian divides the world in two—you can stand astride it with one foot in either hemisphere. The National Maritime Museum and the proud clipper ship *Cutty Sark* are thrilling to seafaring types, and landlubbers can stroll the green acres of parkland that surround the buildings, the quaint 19th-century houses, and the weekend crafts and antiques markets. Meanwhile, upstream, the royal palaces and grand houses that dot the area were built not as town houses but as country residences with easy access to London by river, and Hampton Court Palace is the best and biggest of all.

A Good Walk

There's no way to combine up- and downstream visits in a single day, so this walk concentrates on Greenwich, a place tailor-made to explore on foot. First of all, do bear in mind that the journey to Greenwich is fun in itself, especially if you approach by river, arriving to the best possible vista of the Royal Naval College, with the Queen's House behind. On the way, the boat glides past famous sights on the London skyline. You could also take the Docklands Light Railway (DLR) from Bank to Island Gardens, where you should enter the squat little circular brick building with its glass-domed roof. This is the entrance to the Greenwich Foot Tunnel, where an ancient elevator takes you down to a walkway under the Thames that brings you up very close to the *Cutty Sark.*

By continuing along King William Walk, you come to the wrought-iron gates of the **Royal Naval College,** from the south end of which you approach the building that Wren's majestic quadrangles frame, the **Queen's House,** followed by the **National Maritime Museum.** Now head up the hill in Greenwich Park overlooking the Naval College and Maritime Museum to the **Old Royal Observatory.** Walking back through the park toward the river, you'll enter the pretty streets of Greenwich Village to the west. There are plenty of bookstores and antiques shops for browsing, and, at the foot of Crooms Hill, the modern Greenwich Theatre—a West End theater, despite its location, which mounts well-regarded, often star-spangled productions. Finish up at the excellent Greenwich Antique Market (on Burney Street near the museum and theater), and the Victorian Covered Crafts Market by the *Cutty Sark,* on College Approach.

TIMING

First of all, the boat trip takes about an hour from Westminster Pier (next to Big Ben), or 25 minutes from the Tower of London, so figure in enough time for the round-trip, unless the weather's really awful or it's winter and the boats have stopped. Aim for an early start. Although the distance covered in this walk is barely a mile, Greenwich can't be "done" in a day. There are such riches here, especially if the maritime theme is your thing, that whatever time you allow will seem halved. If the weather's good, you'll be tempted to stroll aimlessly around the quaint un-citylike streets, too, and maybe take a turn in the park. If you want to take in the markets, you'll need to come on a weekend. The antiques market is open 8–4; the crafts market 9–5.

Sights to See

GREENWICH

Cutty Sark. This romantic tea clipper was built in 1869, one of fleets and fleets of similar wooden tall-masted clippers, which during the 19th century plied the seven seas trading in exotic commodities—tea, in this case. The *Cutty Sark,* the last to survive, was also the fastest, sailing the China–London route in 1871 in only 107 days. Now the photogenic vessel lies in dry dock, a museum of one kind of seafaring life—and not a comfortable kind for the 28-strong crew, as you'll see. The collection of figureheads is amusing, too. The famous *Gipsy Moth IV* (☞ *below*) is docked right next door. ✉ *King William Walk,* ☎ *0181/858–3445.* 🎫 *£3.25.* ⏲ *Apr.–Sept., Mon.–Sat. 10–6, Sun. and public holidays noon–6; Oct.–Mar., Mon.–Sat. 10–5, Sun. and* *public holidays noon–5. Last admission 30 min before closing. Closed Dec. 24–26.*

Gipsy Moth IV. The boat in which Sir Francis Chichester achieved the first single-handed circumnavigation of the globe in 1966 is dry-docked beside the *Cutty Sark*. Inside you'll see the tiny space the sailor endured for 226 days, and the ingenious way everything he needed was installed. The queen knighted him on board here, using the same sword with which the previous Elizabeth had knighted that other seagoing Francis, Sir Francis Drake, three centuries before. ✉ *King William Walk,* ☎ *0181/858–3445.* *50p.* *Apr.–Oct., Mon.–Sat. 10–6, Sun. noon–6; closed Nov.–Mar.*

National Maritime Museum. Greenwich's star attraction contains everything to do with the British at sea, in the form of paintings, models, maps, globes, sextants, uniforms (including the one Nelson died in at Trafalgar, complete with bloodstained bullet hole), and—best of all—actual boats, including a collection of ornate, gilded royal barges. ✉ *Romney Rd.,* ☎ *0181/858–4422.* *£5.50, including the Queen's House and Old Royal Observatory.* *Mon.–Sat. 10–6, Sun. noon–6; closed Good Fri., May Day, Dec. 24–27, Jan. 1.*

NEED A BREAK? The **Dolphin Coffee Shop** on the National Maritime Museum grounds is a good place to recuperate after the rigors of the museum; non-museum visitors are also welcome.

Old Royal Observatory. Founded in 1675 by Charles II, this observatory was designed the same year by Christopher Wren for John Flamsteed, the first Astronomer Royal. The red ball you see on its roof has been there only since 1833. It drops every day at 1 PM, and you can set your watch by it, as the sailors on the Thames always have. In fact, nearly everyone sets their watch by it, since this "Greenwich Timeball," along with the Gate Clock inside the observatory, are the most visible manifestations of Greenwich Mean Time, since 1884 the ultimate standard for time around the world. Also here is the **Prime Meridian,** a brass line laid on the cobblestones at zero degrees longitude, one side being the eastern, one the western hemisphere. ✉ *Greenwich Park,* ☎ *0181/858–4422.* *Joint admission with National Maritime Museum (*☞ below*).* *Mon.–Sat. 10–6, Sun. noon–6; closed Good Fri., May Day, Dec. 24–27, Jan. 1.*

★ **Queen's House.** The queen whom Inigo Jones began designing it for in 1616 was James I's Anne of Denmark, but she died three years later, and it was Charles I's French wife, Henrietta Maria, who inherited the building when it was completed in 1635. It is no less than Britain's first Classical building—the first, that is, to use the lessons of Italian Renaissance architecture—and is therefore of enormous importance in the history of English architecture. The Great Hall is a perfect cube, exactly 40 feet in all three directions, and decorated with paintings of the Muses, the Virtues, and the Liberal Arts. *£5.50, including National Maritime Museum and Old Royal Observatory; White Card accepted.* *Mon.–Sat. 10–6, Sun. noon–6; closed Good Fri., May Day, Dec. 24–27, Jan. 1.*

Royal Naval College. Begun by Christopher Wren in 1694 as a home for ancient mariners, it became a school for young ones in 1873. You'll notice how the blocks part to reveal the **Queen's House** across the central lawns—one of England's most famous architectural set-pieces. Wren, with the help of his assistant, Hawksmoor, was at pains to preserve the river vista from the house, and there are few more majestic views in London than the awe-inspiring symmetry he achieved. The

Painted Hall and the College Chapel are the two outstanding interiors on view here. ✉ *Royal Naval College, King William Walk,* ☎ *0181/858–2154.* 🎟 *Free.* ⏲ *Daily except Fri.–Wed. 2:30–4:45.*

HAMPTON COURT PALACE

Some 20 miles from central London, on a loop of the Thames upstream from Richmond, lies **Hampton Court,** one of London's oldest royal palaces, more like a small town in size, and requiring a day of your time to do it justice. The magnificent Tudor brick house was begun in 1514 by Cardinal Wolsey, the ambitious and worldly lord chancellor (roughly, prime minister) of England and archbishop of York. He wanted it to be the absolute best palace in the land, and in this he succeeded so effectively that Henry VIII grew deeply envious, whereupon Wolsey felt obliged to give Hampton Court to the king. Henry moved in in 1525, adding a great hall and chapel, and proceeded to live much of his astonishing life here. Later, during the reign of William and Mary, the palace was much expanded by Sir Christopher Wren.

The site beside the slow-moving Thames is perfect. The palace itself, steeped in history, hung with priceless paintings, full of echoing cobbled courtyards and cavernous Tudor kitchens, complete with deer pies and cooking pots—not to mention the ghost of Catherine Howard, who is still abroad, screaming her innocence (of adultery) to an unheeding Henry VIII—is set in a fantastic array of ornamental gardens, lakes, and ponds, which must be seen on a sunny day. ✉ *East Molesey,* ☎ *0181/977–8441.* 🎟 *Apartments and maze £7.50, maze only £1.75, grounds free.* ⏲ *State apartments Apr.–Oct., Tues.–Sun. 9:30–6, Mon. 10:15–6; Nov.–Mar., Tues.–Sun. 9:30–4:30, Mon. 10:15–4:30. Grounds daily 8–dusk. Closed Good Fri., Dec. 24–25, Jan. 1.*

KEW

The **Royal Botanic Gardens** at Kew are the headquarters of the country's leading botanical institute as well as a public garden of 300 acres and more than 60,000 species of plants. Two 18th-century royal ladies, Queen Caroline and Princess Augusta, were responsible for its founding. The highlights here are the 19th-century greenhouses and the ultramodern Princess of Wales Conservatory, opened in 1987. Kew Palace, on the grounds, was home to George III for much of his life. Its formal garden has been redeveloped on a 17th-century pattern. *Gardens,* ☎ *0181/940–1171; Kew Palace 0181/940–3321.* 🎟 *Gardens £4, palace £1.20.* ⏲ *Gardens daily 9:30–6:30, greenhouses 10–6:30 (Sun. and national holidays until 8); in winter, closing times depend on the light. Kew Palace Apr.–Sept., daily 11–5:30.*

DINING

Be prepared for a shock: London is a great city for dining. Nearly everyone eats out regularly these days, and an increasingly knowledgeable and, therefore, demanding public has had its effect on the quality, value, and variety of the capital's restaurants. You can eat your way around the world (India, Thailand, and the Mediterranean are particularly easy to find), or hit the zenith of food fashion. Few places these days mind if you order a second appetizer instead of an entrée, and you will often find set-price menus at lunchtime, bringing even the very finest and fanciest establishments within reach. Prix-fixe dinners are beginning to proliferate, too. Note that many places are closed on Sunday or late at night, and virtually everywhere closes down for the Christmas holiday period.

The law obliges all British restaurants to display their prices, including VAT (sales tax) outside, but watch for hidden extras such as bread and vegetables charged separately, and service. Most restaurants add 10%–15% automatically to the check, or stamp "Service Not Included" along the bottom, and/or leave the total on the credit-card slip blank. Beware of paying twice for service, especially if it was less than satisfactory.

CATEGORY	COST*
££££	over £50
£££	£30–£50
££	£20–£30
£	under £20

**per person, including first course, main course, dessert, and VAT; excluding drinks and service*

St. James's

££££ ✕ **The Ritz.** Constantly accused of being London's prettiest dining room, this Belle Époque palace of marble, gilt, and trompe l'oeil would moisten even Marie Antoinette's eye; add the view over Green Park and the Ritz's secret sunken garden, and it seems obsolete to eat. But David Nicholls's British/French cuisine stands up to the visual onslaught with costly morsels (foie gras, lobster, truffles, caviar, etc.), super-rich, all served with a flourish. Englishness is wrested from Louis XVI by a daily roast "from the trolley," and a "British speciality" like Irish stew or braised oxtail. A three-course prix-fixe lunch at £28 and a dinner at £33 make the check more bearable, but the wine list is pricey. A Friday and Saturday dinner dance sweetly maintains a dying tradition. ✉ *Piccadilly, W1,* ☎ *0171/493–8181. Reservations essential. Jacket and tie. AE, DC, MC, V. Tube: Green Park.*

£££ ★ ✕ **Le Caprice.** Secreted on a small street behind the Ritz, Caprice may command the deepest loyalty of any London restaurant, because it gets everything right: the glamorous, glossy black Eva Jiricna interior, the perfect pitch of the informal but respectful service, the food, halfway between Euro-peasant and fashion-plate. This food—crispy duck and watercress salad; seared scallops with bacon and sorrel; risotto nero; Lincolnshire sausage with bubble-and-squeak (potato-and-cabbage hash); grilled rabbit with black olive polenta; and divine desserts, too—it has no business being so good, because the other reason everyone comes here is that everyone else does, which leads to the best people-watching in town. (Also try its sister restaurant, the Ivy; ☞ Covent Garden, *below.*) ✉ *Arlington House, Arlington St., SW1,* ☎ *0171/629–2239. AE, DC, MC, V. No lunch Sat. Tube: Green Park.*

£££ ✕ **Green's Restaurant and Oyster Bar.** The oyster side of things and the comfy-wood-panel-restaurant angle are in equal balance at this reliable purveyor of the British dining experience, complete with the whiff of public (meaning private and exclusive) school, and its former inmates. Oysters, of course, are served in two varieties, "small" or "large," but there are comforting English unfishy dishes, like shepherd's pie, too, and—the proper ending to a nanny-sanctioned meal—warm and fattening "nursery puddings," like steamed sponge with custard, and treacle tart. ✉ *36 Duke St., SW1,* ☎ *0171/930–4566. Jacket and tie. AE, DC, MC, V. No dinner Sun. Closed national holidays. Tube: Green Park.*

£££ ✕ **Quaglino's.** Sir Terence Conran—of Bibendum, Mezzo, and Pont de la Tour fame—lavished £2.5 million doing up this famous pre–World War II haunt of the rich, bored, and well-connected. Now past its fifth birthday, "Quags" is *the* out-of-towners' post-theater or celebration destination, while Londoners like its late hours. The gigantic sunken restaurant boasts a glamorous staircase, "Crustacea Altar," large bar,

London Dining

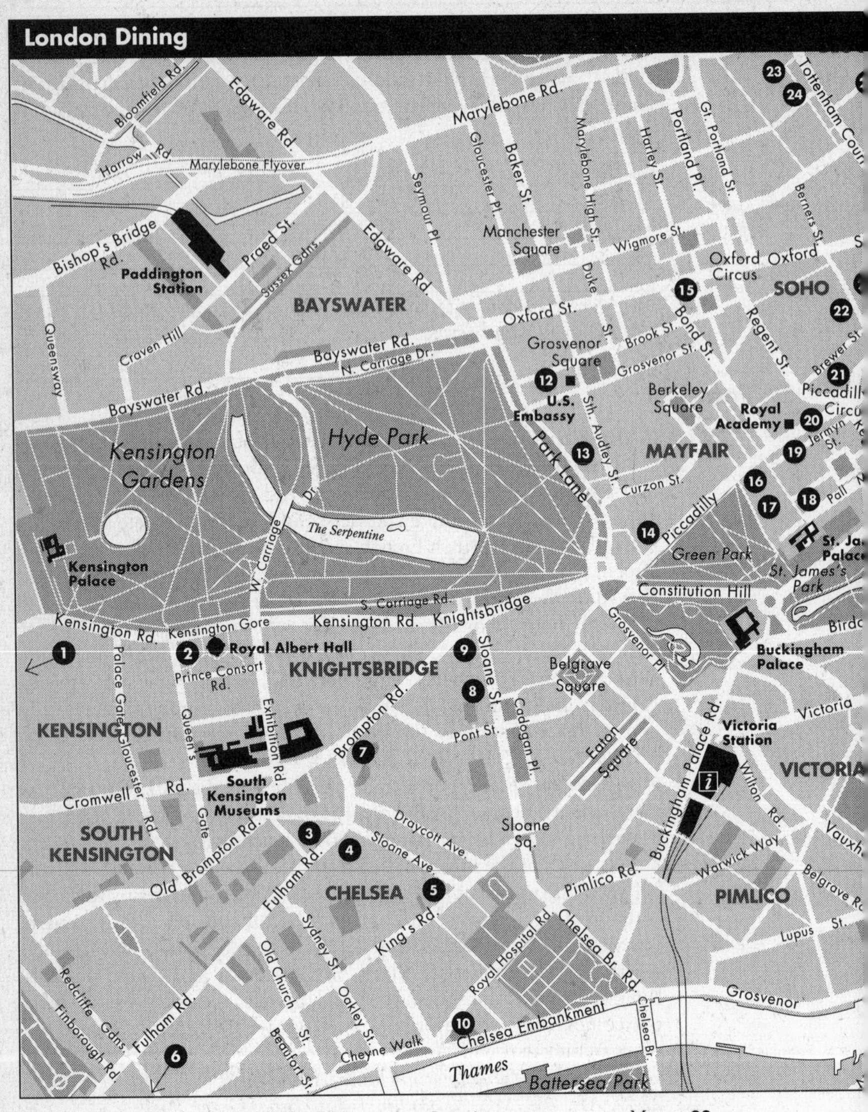

Alastair Little, **27**
Belgo Centraal, **32**
Bertorelli's, **35**
Bibendum, **4**
Bistrot 190, **2**
Bulloch's, **14**
The Capital, **9**
Chelsea Kitchen, **5**
Chez Nico at Ninety Park Lane, **13**
Chez Gerard, **24**
Chicago Pizza Pie Factory, **15**
Chutney Mary, **6**
Criterion, **21**
dell'Ugo, **26**
Elena's L'Etoile, **23**
Fatboy's Diner, **38**
Food for Thought, **34**
The Fountain, **19**
Green's Restaurant and Oyster Bar, **18**
The Ivy, **31**
Joe Allen, **39**
La Tante Claire, **10**
Le Caprice, **17**
Le Gavroche, **12**
Le Pont de la Tour, **41**
Maxwell's, **33**
Mezzo, **22**
Museum Street Café, **30**
The North Sea Fish Restaurant, **25**
Orso, **37**
People's Palace, **11**
PJ's, **3**
Quaglino's, **20**
The Ritz, **16**

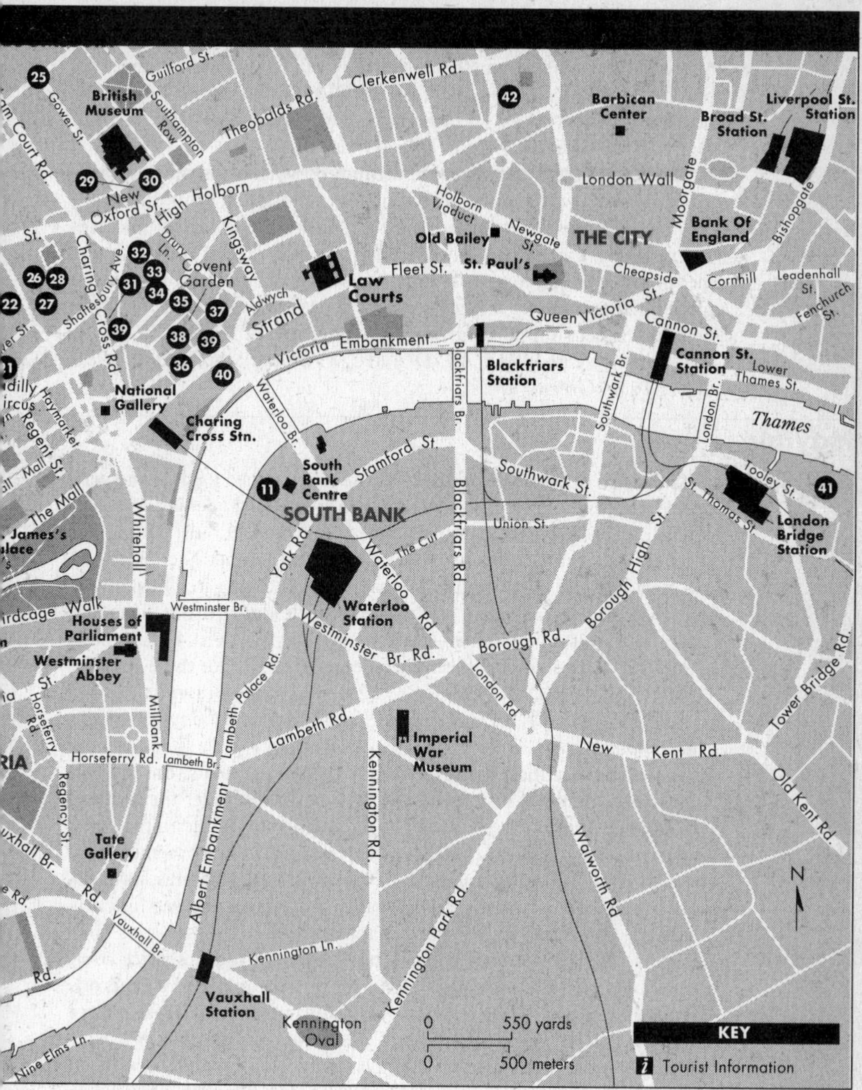

Rules, **36**
St. John, **42**
St. Quentin, **7**
Savoy Grill, **40**
Soho Soho, **28**
Stockpot, **8**
Wagamama, **29**
Wòdka, **1**

and live jazz music. The food is fashionably pan-European with some Oriental trimmings. Desserts come from somewhere between the Paris bistro and the English nursery (raspberry sablé, parkin pudding with butterscotch sauce), and wine from the Old World and the New, some bottles at modest prices. ✉ *16 Bury St., SW1,* ☎ *0171/930–6767. AE, DC, MC, V. Closed Dec. 25. Tube: Green Park.*

£ ★ ✕ **The Fountain.** At the back of Fortnum & Mason's is this old-fashioned restaurant, frumpy and popular as a boarding school matron, serving delicious light meals, toasted snacks, sandwiches, and ice-cream sodas. During the day, go for the Welsh rarebit or cold game pie; in the evening, a no-frills fillet steak is a typical option. Just the place for afternoon tea and ice-cream sundaes after the Royal Academy or Bond Street shopping, or for pre-theater meals. ✉ *181 Piccadilly, W1,* ☎ *0171/734–4938. AE, DC, MC, V. Closed Sun., national holidays. Tube: Green Park.*

Mayfair

££££ ✕ **Chez Nico at Ninety Park Lane.** Those with refined palates and very deep pockets would be well advised not to miss Nico Ladenis's exquisite cuisine, served in this suitably hushed and plush Louis XV dining room next to the Grosvenor House Hotel. Autodidact Nico is one of the world's great chefs, and he's famous for knowing it. The menu is in French and untranslated; vegetarians and children are not welcome. There is no salt on the table—ask for some at your peril. It's all more affordable in daylight, proffering set menus from £29 for three courses. ✉ *90 Park La., W1,* ☎ *0171/409–1290. Reservations essential. Jacket and tie. AE, DC, MC, V. Closed weekends, public holidays, 3 wks in Aug. Tube: Marble Arch.*

££££ ★ ✕ **Le Gavroche.** Albert Roux has handed the toque to his son, Michel, who retains many of his capital-C Classical dishes under the heading "*Hommage à mon père,*" as well as adding his own style to the place that many still consider London's finest restaurant. The basement dining room is comfortable and serious, hung with oil paintings, its darkness intensified by racing-green walls. Yet again, the set lunch is relatively affordable at £37 (for canapés and three courses, plus mineral water, a half-bottle of wine, coffee, and petit fours, service *compris*). In fact, it's the only way to eat here if you don't have a generous expense account at your disposal—as most patrons do. ✉ *43 Upper Brook St., W1,* ☎ *0171/408–0881. Reservations essential at least 1 wk in advance. Jacket and tie. AE, DC, MC, V. Closed weekends, 10 days at Christmas, national holidays. Tube: Marble Arch.*

£££ ✕ **Criterion.** This palatial neo-Byzantine mirrored marble hall, which first opened in 1874, is firmly back on the map, with the arrival of a new regime led by the somewhat self-promoting but super-talented Marco Pierre White. The glamour of the soaring golden ceiling, peacock-blue theater-size drapes, oil paintings, and attentive Gallic service adds up to an elegant night out. ✉ *Piccadilly Circus, W1,* ☎ *0171/930–2626. Reservations essential. AE, DC, MC, V. Closed Dec. 25. Tube: Piccadilly Circus.*

££ ✕ **Bullochs.** The recently refreshed Atheneum Hotel is the least stuffy of the Piccadilly grands, so it's no shock that its restaurant is laid back, too. Surrounded by a weird Jerusalem stone, trompe-l'oeil bookcase, and mirror decor, try London's most generously anchovied and Parmesaned Caesar salad, then something Mediterranean (tuna steak with ratatouille), Italian (osso bucco), French-ish (turbot with champagne and lemon sauce), or even British (calves' liver, bacon, and onions), all good, unpretentious food, and, conveniently, all at one price. ✉ *116 Piccadilly, W1,* ☎ *0171/499–3464. AE, DC, MC, V. Tube: Green Park.*

£ ✕ **The Chicago Pizza Pie Factory.** Enormous deep-dish pies with the usual toppings are served in a wood-floor basement, loud with the sounds of WJMK, the Windy City's oldies station. The rest rooms are labeled "Elton John" and "Olivia Newton John." ✉ *17 Hanover Sq., W1,* ☎ *0171/629–2669. AE, MC, V. Closed Dec. 25–26. Tube: Oxford Circus.*

Soho

£££ ✕ **Alastair Little.** Little is one of London's most original—and most imitated—chefs, drawing inspiration from practically everywhere—Thailand, Japan, Scandinavia, France—and bringing it off brilliantly. His restaurant is starkly modern, so all attention focuses on the menu, which changes not once but twice daily in order to take advantage of the best ingredients. Look out also for his newer, smaller, cheaper version just by Ladbroke Grove tube station. ✉ *49 Frith St., W1,* ☎ *0171/734–5183. No credit cards. Closed weekends, national holidays, 2 wks at Christmas, 3 wks in Aug. Tube: Leicester Square.*

£–£££ ✕ **Mezzo.** This is what Sir Terence Conran did after Quaglino's. The 700-seat Mezzo isn't just the biggest restaurant in London—it's the most gigantic in all Europe. Downstairs is the restaurant proper, with its huge glass-walled show kitchen, its Allen Jones murals, its grand piano and dance floor, and its typically Conran-French menu of things such as seafood, rabbit stew, steak-frites, fig tart. Upstairs, the bar overlooks a canteen-style operation called Mezzonine. A late-night café/patisserie/newsstand has a separate entrance next door. The place was a London landmark from day one, with a chic-and-be-seen bustle, despite its low celebrity count. ✉ *100 Wardour St., W1.* ☎ *0171/314–4000. AE, DC, MC, V. Closed Dec. 25, Jan. 1. Tube: Leicester Square.*

££ ✕ **Soho Soho.** The ground floor is a lively café-bar with a (no reservations) rotisserie, while upstairs is a more formal and expensive restaurant. Inspiration comes from Provence, both in the olive-oil cooking style and the decor, with its murals, primary colors, and pale ocher terra-cotta floor tiles. The rotisserie serves omelets, salads, charcuterie, and cheeses, plus a handful of such bistro dishes as Toulouse sausages with fries; herbed, grilled poussin; and tarte tatin. Or you can stay in the café-bar and have just a kir or a beer. ✉ *11–13 Frith St., W1,* ☎ *0171/494–3491. Reservations essential upstairs. AE, DC, MC, V. No lunch Sat (upstairs). Closed Sun., Dec. 25–26, Jan. 1. Tube: Leicester Square.*

££ ✕ **dell'Ugo.** From the stable of Anthony Worrall-Thompson (☞ Bistro 190 *in* South Kensington, *below*), this three-floor Mediterranean café-restaurant remains popular. You can choose light fare—bruschetta loaded with marinated vegetables, mozzarella, Parmesan, etc., Tuscan soups, and country bread—or feast on wintry, warming one-pot ensembles and large platefuls of such sunny dishes as spicy sausages and white bean casserole with onion confit. The place gets overrun with hormone-swapping youth some weekends, but trendiness, on the whole, doesn't mar pleasure. ✉ *56 Frith St., W1,* ☎ *0171/734–8300. AE, MC, V. Closed Sun., Dec. 25. Tube: Leicester Square.*

Covent Garden

££££ ✕ **Savoy Grill.** The grill continues in the first rank of power dining locations. Politicians, newspaper barons, and tycoons like the comforting food and impeccably discreet and attentive service in the low-key, yew-panel salon. On the menu, an omelet Arnold Bennett (with cheese and smoked fish) is perennial, as is beef Wellington on Tuesday and roast Norfolk duck on Friday. Playgoers can split their theater menu, eating part of their meal before the show, the rest after. ✉ *Strand, WC2,*

☎ *0171/836–4343. Reservations essential for lunch and Thurs.–Sat. dinner. Jacket and tie. AE, DC, MC, V. No lunch Sat. Closed Sun. Tube: Aldwych.*

£££ ★ ✕ **The Ivy.** This seems to be everybody's favorite restaurant—everybody who works in the media or the arts, that is. In a Deco dining room with blinding white tablecloths, and Hodgkins and Paolozzis on the walls, the celebrated and the wannabes eat Caesar salad, roast grouse, shrimp gumbo, braised oxtail, and rice pudding with Armagnac prunes or sticky toffee pudding. ✉ *1 West St., WC2,* ☎ *0171/836–4751. AE, DC, MC, V. Closed Dec. 25. Tube: Covent Garden.*

£££ ✕ **Orso.** The Italian brother of Joe Allen (☞ *below*), this basement restaurant has the same snappy staff and a glitzy clientele of showbiz types and hacks. The Tuscan-style menu changes every day, but always includes excellent pizza and pasta dishes. Food here is never boring, much like the place itself. ✉ *27 Wellington St., WC2,* ☎ *0171/240–5269. No credit cards. Closed Dec. 25–26. Tube: Covent Garden.*

£££ ✕ **Rules.** A London institution—an Edwardian restaurant that was a great favorite of Lily Langtry's, among others. After decades the restaurant remains interesting for its splendid period atmosphere, but annoying for its slow service. For a main dish, try the seasonal entrées on the list of daily specials, which will, in season, include game from Rules's own Scottish estate (venison is disconcertingly called "deer"). It is more than a little touristy, but that's because it's so quaint. ✉ *35 Maiden La., WC2,* ☎ *0171/836–5314. Reservations essential at least 1 day in advance. AE, DC, MC, V. Closed Dec. 25. Tube: Covent Garden.*

££ ★ ✕ **Joe Allen.** Long hours (thespians flock after the curtain falls in theaterland) and a welcoming, if loud, brick-wall interior mean New York Joe's London branch is still swinging after nearly two decades. The fun, California-inflected menu helps: Roast, stuffed poblano chili, or black bean soup are typical starters; entrées feature barbecue ribs with black-eyed peas and London's best (and only?) available corn muffins, or roast monkfish with sun-dried-tomato salsa. It can get chaotic, with long waits for the cute waiters, but at least there'll be famous faces to ogle in the meantime. ✉ *13 Exeter St., WC2,* ☎ *0171/836–0651. No credit cards. Closed Easter, Dec. 25–26. Tube: Covent Garden.*

££ ✕ **Bertorelli's.** Right across from the stage door of the Royal Opera House, Bertorelli's is quietly chic, the food tempting, if not innovative: Poached cotechino sausage with lentils or monkfish ragout with fennel, tomato, and olives are typical dishes. Downstairs is a very relaxed inexpensive wine bar serving a simpler menu of pizza, pasta, salads, and daily specials. ✉ *44A Floral St., WC2,* ☎ *0171/836–3969. AE, DC, MC, V. Closed Dec. 25. Tube: Covent Garden.*

£–££ ✕ **Belgo Centraal.** The wackiest dining concept in town started in Camden (☞ *below*), and was so adored, it was cloned uptown in a big basement space you have to enter by elevator. Have mussels and fries in vast quantity, served with 100 Belgian beers (fruit-flavored, Trappist-brewed, white, or light) by people dressed as monks in a hall like a refectory in a Martian monastery. The luxury index may be low, but so is the check. ✉ *50 Earlham St., WC2.* ☎ *0171/813–2233. AE, DC, MC, V. Closed Dec. 25, Jan. 1. Tube: Covent Garden.*

£ ✕ **Fatboy's Diner.** One for the kids, this is a 1941 chrome trailer transplanted from the banks of the Susquehanna in Pennsylvania and now secreted, unexpectedly, in a backstreet, complete with Astroturf "garden." A '50s jukebox accompanies the dogs, burgers, and fries. ✉ *21 Maiden La., WC2,* ☎ *0171/240–1902. Reservations not accepted. No credit cards. Closed Dec. 25. Tube: Covent Garden.*

£ ★ ✕ **Food for Thought.** This simple basement restaurant (no liquor license) seats only 50 and is extremely popular, so you'll almost always find a line of people down the stairs. The menu—stir-fries, casseroles, salads, and desserts—changes every day, and each dish is freshly made; there's no microwave. ✉ *31 Neal St., WC2,* ☎ *0171/836–0239. Reservations not accepted. No credit cards. Closed after 8 PM, 2 wks at Christmas, national holidays. Tube: Covent Garden.*

£ ✕ **Maxwell's.** London's first-ever burger joint, 21 in '93, cloned itself and then grew up. Here's the result, a happy place under the Opera House serving the kind of food you're homesick for: quesadillas and nachos, Buffalo chicken wings, barbecue ribs, Cajun chicken, chef's salad, a real NYC Reuben, and a burger to die for. ✉ *8–9 James St., WC2,* ☎ *0171/836–0303. AE, DC, V. Closed Dec. 25. Tube: Covent Garden.*

Bloomsbury

££–£££ ★ ✕ **Elena's L'Etoile.** Elena Salvoni presided for years and years over L'Escargot in Soho, where she made so many friends among happy customers, she was rewarded with her name in lights—at 75 years old. This understated and long-established place is one of London's few remaining untouched-by-renovation French bistro restaurants. There's duck braised with red cabbage in an individual casserole, *poulet rôti* (roast chicken), terrines, tarte au citron, and a warm smile from Elena—whether you're one of the politician/journalist/actor regulars, or just you. Upstairs is a communal table—useful for single travelers. ✉ *30 Charlotte St., W1,* ☎ *0171/636–7189. Reservations essential. AE, DC, MC, V. No lunch weekends, dinner Sun. Closed Dec. 25, Jan. 1. Tube: Goodge Street.*

££ ✕ **Chez Gerard.** One of a small chain of steak-frites restaurants, this one has expanded its utterly Gallic menu to include more for non–red meat eaters. Steak, served with shoestring fries and béarnaise sauce, remains the reason to visit. ✉ *8 Charlotte St., W1,* ☎ *0171/636–4975. AE, DC, MC, V. Closed Dec. 25. Tube: Goodge Street.*

££ ✕ **The Museum Street Café.** This useful and reliable restaurant near the British Museum serves a limited selection of impeccably fresh dishes, intelligently and plainly cooked by the two young owners, and charged prix fixe. The evening menu might feature char-grilled, maize-fed chicken with pesto, followed by a rich chocolate cake; at lunchtime you might choose a sandwich of Stilton on walnut bread and a big bowl of soup. Repeat customers, prepare for a shock—the place has doubled in size, and you no longer have to bring your own wine, but there's still an atypical (for London) ban on smoking. ✉ *47 Museum St., WC1,* ☎ *0171/405–3211. MC, V. Closed weekends, public holidays. Tube: Tottenham Court Road.*

£ ✕ **The North Sea Fish Restaurant.** This is the place for the British national dish of fish-and-chips—battered and deep-fried whitefish with thick fries shaken with salt and vinegar. It's a bit tricky to find—three blocks south of St. Pancras station, down Judd Street. Only freshly caught fish is served, and you can order it grilled—though that would defeat the purpose. You can take your meals out in true grab-and-gulp fashion or eat in. ✉ *7–8 Leigh St., WC1,* ☎ *0171/387–5892. AE, DC, MC, V. Closed Sun., national holidays, Dec. 25. Tube: Russell Square.*

£ ★ ✕ **Wagamama.** London's gone wild for Japanese noodles in this big basement. It's high-tech (your order is taken on a hand-held computer), high-volume—there are always crowds, with which you share wooden refectory tables—and high-turnover, with a fast-moving line always at the door. You can choose ramen in or out of soup, topped with sliced meats or tempura; or "raw energy" dishes—rice, curries, tofu, and so on—all at give-away prices and doggy-bag sizes. Many of them alternate this Wagamama experience with the newer one at 10a Lexington Street (☎ 0171/292–0990), near Oxford Circus. ✉ *4 Streatham St.,*

WC1, ☎ 0171/323–9223. Reservations not accepted. No credit cards. Closed Dec. 25. Tube: Tottenham Court Road.

Knightsbridge

££££ ✕ **The Capital.** This elegant, clublike dining room has chandeliers and greige rag-rolled walls, a grown-up atmosphere, and formal service. Chef Philip Britten keeps his star bright with perhaps a subtle baked mousse of haddock and ginger, an emincé of chicken with olives, or pot-roasted pigeon with Armagnac, then a perfect caramel soufflé with butterscotch sauce. Set-price menus both at lunch (£25) and in the evening (£40—for *six* courses) make it somewhat more affordable, although the best dishes are found à la carte. ✉ *22–24 Basil St., SW3, ☎ 0171/589–5171. Reservations essential. Jacket and tie. AE, DC, MC, V. Tube: Knightsbridge.*

££ ✕ **St. Quentin.** A very popular slice of Paris, frequented by French expatriates and locals alike. Every inch of the Gallic menu is explored—quiche, escargots, cassoulet, lemon tart—in the bourgeois provincial comfort so many London chains (the Dômes, the Cafés Rouges) try hard to attain yet fail to achieve. ✉ *243 Brompton Rd., SW3, ☎ 0171/589–8005. AE, DC, MC, V. Tube: South Kensington.*

£ ✕ **Stockpot.** You'll find speedy service in this large, jolly restaurant, packed with young people and shoppers. The food is filling and wholesome, in a Lancashire-hot-pot, spaghetti-Bolognese, apple-crumble way. ✉ *6 Basil St., SW3, ☎ 0171/589–8627. No credit cards. Closed Dec. 25, national holidays. Tube: Knightsbridge. Other branches: ✉ 40 Panton St., off Leicester Sq., ☎ 0171/839–5142; ✉ 18 Old Compton St., Soho, ☎ 0171/287–1066; and ✉ 273 King's Rd., Chelsea, ☎ 0171/823–3175.*

South Kensington

££££ ★ ✕ **Bibendum.** In the swinging '80s, this was one of London's hottest scene-arenas. It's cooled down now, but everyone still loves its reconditioned Michelin House setting, with its Art Deco decorations and brilliant stained glass, Conran Shop, and Oyster Bar. New chef Matthew Harris aspires to simple but perfect dishes—herrings with sour cream, a risotto, or leeks vinaigrette followed by steak au poivre, or you might try brains or tripe as they ought to be cooked. The £27 set-price menu at lunchtime is money well spent. ✉ *Michelin House, 81 Fulham Rd., SW3, ☎ 0171/581–5817. Reservations essential. MC, V. Closed Sun. Tube: South Kensington.*

££ ✕ **Bistro 190.** Chef-restaurateur and popular guy Antony Worrall-Thompson dominates this town's medium-price eating scene with his happy, hearty food from southern Europe and around the Mediterranean rim. The identifiable feature of an AWT menu is its lists of about a hundred loosely related ingredients (pork chop with rhubarb compote, cheese, and mustard mash, for instance), which when read all at once force you to salivate. This place, all hardwood and modern art, was Worrall-Thompson's first, and is handy for Albert Hall evenings. ✉ *190 Queen's Gate, SW7, ☎ 0171/581–5666. Reservations not accepted. AE, DC, MC, V. No lunch Sat. Closed Sun., Dec. 25–26, Jan. 1. Tube: Gloucester Road.*

££ ✕ **Wódka.** This smart, modern Polish restaurant serves the smartest, most modern Polish food around. It is popular with elegant locals plus a sprinkling of celebs and often has the atmosphere of a dinner party. With your smoked salmon, herring, caviar, eggplant *blinis,* or venison sausages, order a carafe of the purest vodka in town (and watch the check inflate); it's encased in a block of ice and hand-flavored with rowanberries. ✉ *12 St. Albans Grove, ☎ 0171/937–6513. AE, DC,*

MC, V. No lunch weekends. Closed public holidays. Tube: High Street Kensington.

Chelsea

££££ ★ ✕ **La Tante Claire.** Justly famous, cripplingly expensive, this restaurant has a light and sophisticated decor, impeccable service, an impressive French wine list—but the food remains the point. From the *carte,* you might choose hot pâté de foie gras on shredded potatoes with a sweet wine and shallot sauce, roast spiced pigeon, or Pierre Koffmann's famous signature dish of pig's feet stuffed with mousse of white meat with sweetbreads and wild mushrooms. As every gourmet expense-accounter knows, the set lunch menu (£26) is a genuine bargain. ✉ *68 Royal Hospital Rd., SW3,* ☎ *0171/352–6045. Reservations essential 3–4 wks in advance for dinner, 2–3 days for lunch. Jacket and tie. AE, DC, MC, V. Closed weekends, 2 wks at Christmas, Jan. 1, 10 days at Easter, 3 wks in Aug.–Sept. Tube: Sloane Square.*

£££ ✕ **Chutney Mary.** London's first-and-only Anglo-Indian restaurant provides a fantasy version of the British Raj, all giant wicker armchairs and palms. Dishes like Masala roast lamb (practically a whole leg, marinated and spiced) and "Country Captain" (braised chicken with almonds, raisins, chilies, and spices) alternate with the more familiar North Indian dishes such as roghan josh (lamb curry). The best choices are certainly the dishes re-created from the kitchens of Indian chefs cooking for English palates back in the old Raj days. ✉ *535 King's Rd., SW10,* ☎ *0171/351–3113. AE, DC, MC, V. Closed Dec. 25 dinner, Dec. 26. Tube: Fulham Broadway.*

££ ✕ **PJ's.** The decor here evokes the Bulldog Drummond lifestyle, with wooden floors and stained glass, a vast, slowly revolving propeller from a 1940s Curtis flying boat, and polo memorabilia. A menu of all-American staples should please all but vegetarians. This place is more remarkable for ambience than for food—it's open late, it's relaxed, friendly, and efficient, and it has bartenders who can mix anything. The sister PJ's in Covent Garden (✉ 30 Wellington St., ☎ 0171/240–7529) is worth remembering for its excellent weekend "Fun Club" for kids. ✉ *52 Fulham Rd., SW3,* ☎ *0171/581–0025. AE, DC, MC, V. Closed Dec. 25–26, Jan. 1. Tube: South Kensington.*

£ ✕ **Chelsea Kitchen.** This café has been crowded since the '60s with hungry people after hot, filling, and inexpensive food. Expect nothing more fancy than pasta, omelets, salads, stews, and casseroles. The menu changes every day. ✉ *98 King's Rd., SW3,* ☎ *0171/589–1330. Reservations not accepted. No credit cards. Closed Dec. 25. Tube: Sloane Square.*

City and South Bank

£££ ✕ **Le Pont de la Tour.** Sir Terence Conran's place across the river, overlooking the bridge that gives it its name, comes into its own in summer, when the outside tables are heaven. Inside this "Gastrodrome" (his word) there's a vintner, baker, deli, seafood bar, brasserie, and this '30s diner-style restaurant, smart as the captain's table. Fish and seafood (lobster salad; Baltic herrings in crème fraîche; roast halibut with aioli), meat and game (venison fillet, port and blueberry sauce; roast veal, caramelized endive) feature heavily—vegetarians are out of luck. Prune and Armagnac tart or chocolate terrine could finish a glamorous—and expensive—meal. By contrast, an impeccable salade niçoise in the brasserie is about £9. ✉ *36D Shad Thames, Butler's Wharf, SE1,* ☎ *0171/403–8403. Reservations essential for lunch and weekend dinner. MC, V. Closed Dec. 25. Tube: Tower Hill.*

££ ✕ **The People's Palace.** Thank goodness—thanks to this place, you can finally have a civilized meal during your South Bank arts encounter. With menus by trendy chef Gary Rhodes, this has remarkably low prices considering it has the greatest river view in town. As the baying critics noted around opening time, there are occasional mistakes here, but the more British the dish, the more reliable it proves—suckling pig sandwich on granary bread, marmalade sponge, sticky toffee pudding. ✉ *Royal Festival Hall, Level 3, South Bank, SE1,* ☎ *0171/928–9999. AE, DC, MC, V. Tube: Waterloo.*

££ ★ ✕ **St. John.** This former smokehouse (ham, not cigars), converted by erstwhile architect owner-chef, Fergus Henderson, wowed the town when it opened, with its soaring white walls, schoolroom lamps, stone floors, iron railings, plain wooden chairs, and its uncompromising menu. Entrées (roast lamb and parsnip; smoked haddock and fennel; deviled crab) are hearty and unadorned, but usually taste great. Service is efficiently matey. ✉ *26 St. John St., EC1,* ☎ *0171/251–0848. AE, MC, V. No dinner Sun. Closed Dec. 25. Tube: Farringdon.*

Pubs

An integral part of the British way of life, public houses dispense beer "on tap," and usually a basic, inexpensive menu of sandwiches, quiche, and salads, and other snacks at lunchtime.

✕ **Black Friar.** A step from Blackfriars tube, this pub has an arts-and-crafts interior that is entertainingly, satirically ecclesiastical, with inlaid mother-of-pearl, wood carvings, stained glass, and marble pillars all over the place, and reliefs of monks and friars poised above finely lettered temperance tracts, regardless of which there are six beers on tap. ✉ *174 Queen Victoria St., EC4,* ☎ *0171/236–5650.*

✕ **The Cow.** Oh not *another* Conran. Yes, this place belongs to Tom, son of Sir Terence, though it's at the opposite end of the scale from Quag's and Mezzo. A faux-Dublin back room bar serves oysters, crab salad, and pasta with the wine and Guinness to hordes of the local ab-fab people, with a proper restaurant upstairs. ✉ *89 Westbourne Park Rd., W2,* ☎ *0171/221–0021.*

✕ **Dove Inn.** Read the list of famous ex-regulars, from Charles II and Nell Gwynn (mere rumor, but a likely one) to Ernest Hemingway, as you queue ages for a beer at this very popular, very comely 16th-century riverside pub by Hammersmith Bridge. If it's *too* full, stroll upstream to the Old Ship or the Blue Anchor. ✉ *19 Upper Mall, W6,* ☎ *0181/748–5405.*

✕ **George Inn.** Sitting in a courtyard where Shakespeare's plays were once performed, the present building dates from the late 17th century and is central London's last remaining galleried inn. Dickens was a regular—the inn is featured in *Little Dorrit.* ✉ *77 Borough High St., SE1,* ☎ *0171/407–2056.*

✕ **Lamb and Flag.** This 17th-century pub was once known as "The Bucket of Blood," because the upstairs room was used as a ring for bare-knuckle boxing. Now, it's a trendy, friendly, and entirely bloodless pub, serving food (at lunchtime only) and real ale. It's on the edge of Covent Garden, off Garrick Street. ✉ *33 Rose St., WC2,* ☎ *0171/836–4108.*

✕ **Mayflower.** An atmospheric 17th-century riverside inn, with exposed beams and a terrace, this is practically the very place from which the Pilgrims set sail for Plymouth Rock. The inn is licensed to sell American postage stamps. ✉ *117 Rotherhithe St., SE16,* ☎ *0171/237–4088.*

✕ **Museum Tavern.** Across the street from the British Museum, this gloriously Victorian pub makes an ideal resting place after the rigors of the culture trail. With lots of fancy glass—etched mirrors and stained glass panels—gilded pillars, and carvings, the heavily restored hostelry once helped Karl Marx to unwind after a hard day in the Library. He could have spent his kapital on any one of six beers available on tap. ✉ *49 Great Russell St., WC1,* ☎ *0171/242–8987.*

✕ **Sherlock Holmes.** This pub used to be known as the Northumberland Arms, and Arthur Conan Doyle popped in regularly for a pint. It figures in *The Hound of the Baskervilles,* and you can see the hound's head and plaster casts of its huge paws among other Holmes memorabilia in the bar. ✉ *10 Northumberland St., WC2,* ☎ *0171/930–2644.*

✕ **Ye Olde Cheshire Cheese.** Yes, it is a tourist trap, but this most historic of all London pubs (it dates from 1667) deserves a visit anyway, for its sawdust-covered floors, low wood-beam ceilings, the 14th-century crypt of a Whitefriars' monastery under the cellar bar, and the set of 17th-century pornographic tiles upstairs. This was the most regular of Dr. Johnson's and Dickens's *many* locals. ✉ *145 Fleet St., EC4,* ☎ *0171/353–6170.*

Afternoon Tea

✕ **Brown's Hotel.** Famous for its teas, this hotel lounge does rest on its laurels somewhat, with a packaged aura and nobody around but fellow tourists. For £14.95 you get sandwiches, a scone with cream and jam (jelly), and two cream cakes. ✉ *33 Albermarle St., W1,* ☎ *0171/493–6020. Tea served daily 3–6.*

✕ **Claridges.** The real McCoy, complete with liveried footmen proffering sandwiches, a scone, and superior pastries (£15.50) in the palatial yet genteel Foyer, all to the tune of the resident "Hungarian orchestra" (actually a string quartet). ✉ *Brook St., W1,* ☎ *0171/629–8860. Tea served daily 3–5.*

✕ **Fortnum & Mason's.** Upstairs at the Queen's grocer's, three set teas are ceremoniously offered: standard Afternoon Tea (sandwiches, scone, cakes, £10.50), old-fashioned High Tea (the traditional nursery meal, adding something more robust and savory, £12.25), and Champagne Tea (£15.75). ✉ *St. James's Restaurant, 4th floor, 181 Piccadilly, W1,* ☎ *0171/734–8040. Tea served Mon.–Sat. 3–5:20.*

✕ **Harrods.** One for sweet-toothed and greedy people, the Georgian Room at the ridiculously well-known department store has a serve-it-yourself afternoon tea *buffet* that'll give you a sugar rush for a week. ✉ *Brompton Rd., SW3,* ☎ *0171/730–1234. Tea served Mon.–Sat. 3–5:30.*

✕ **The Ritz.** The Ritz's new owners have put the once-peerless Palm Court tea back on the map, with proper tiered cake stands and silver pots, a harpist, and Louis XVI chaises, plus a leisurely four-hour time slot. A good excuse for a glass of champagne. Reservations are taken only to 50% capacity. ✉ *Piccadilly, W1,* ☎ *0171/493–8181. Tea served daily 2–6.*

✕ **Savoy.** The glamorous Thames-side hotel does one of the pleasantest teas, its triple-tiered cake stands packed with goodies, its tailcoated waiters thrillingly polite. ✉ *The Strand, WC2,* ☎ *0171/836–4343. Tea served daily 3–5:30.*

LODGING

London hotels are among Europe's—indeed the world's!—most expensive. We are aware that readers feel some London hotels do not merit their inflated prices, especially when compared with their courteous Continental counterparts. Therefore, although we list hotels by price (which does not always indicate quality), we have attempted to select the ones whose caliber is tried and proven. We quote the average room cost as of spring 1996; in some establishments, especially those in the ££££ category, you could pay considerably more—well past the £200 mark in some cases. In any event, you should confirm *exactly* what your room costs before checking in. British hotels are obliged by law to display a price chart at the reception desk; study it carefully. In January and February you'll often find reduced rates, and large hotels with a business clientele have frequent weekend packages.

The custom these days in all but the cheaper hotels is for quoted prices to cover room alone; breakfast, whether Continental or "Full English," comes as extra. VAT (Value Added Tax—sales tax) is usually included, and service, too, in nearly all cases. Be sure to reserve, as special events can fill hotel rooms for sudden, brief periods.

If you arrive in London without a room, the following organizations can help: **The British Travel Centre** (✉ 12 Regent St., Piccadilly Circus, SW1Y 4PQ, stop by in person only); **Central London Accommodations** (✉ 83 Addison Gardens, W14 ODT, ☎ 0171/602–9668), specializing in B&Bs; **Hotel Reservation Centre** (✉ Near Platform 8 at Victoria Station, ☎ 0171/828–1849); and **The London Tourist Board Information Centres** (Heathrow, Liverpool Street Station, and Victoria Station forecourt, no phone reservations). Credit card bookings can be made with Visa or MasterCard on the LTB Accommodation Line (☎ 0171/824–8844). **Uptown Reservations** (✉ 50 Christchurch St., SW3 4AR, ☎ 0171/351–3445, FAX 0171/351–9383) lists 50 host homes in fashionable areas of central London that have rooms for rent (with bath and Continental breakfast) for about £62.50 double, £35 single. Visitors to London should be aware that certain accommodations agencies (though not the above) charge outrageous booking fees, so contact hotels directly wherever possible.

CATEGORY	COST*
££££	over £180
£££	£120–£180
££	£70–£120
£	under £70

**All prices are for a double room; VAT included.*

Mayfair and St James's

££££ **Brown's.** Founded in 1837 by Lord Byron's "gentleman's gentleman," James Brown, this Victorian country house in central Mayfair occupies 11 Georgian houses and is frequented by many Anglophile Americans—a habit that was established by the two Roosevelts (Teddy while on honeymoon). Bedrooms feature thick carpets, soft armchairs, sweeping drapes, brass chandeliers, and moiré or brocade wallpapers, as well as, in the newly refitted ones, air-conditioning; the public rooms retain their cozy oak-panel, chintz-laden, grandfather-clock-ticking-in-the-parlor ambience. ✉ *34 Albemarle St., W1A 4SW,* ☎ *0171/493–6020,* FAX *0171/493–9381. 132 rooms. Restaurant, bar, lounge. AE, DC, MC, V. Tube: Green Park.*

££££ ★ **Claridges.** A hotel legend, with one of the world's classiest guest lists. The liveried staff are friendly and not in the least condescending, and the rooms are never less than luxurious. It was founded in 1812, but present decor is either 1930s Art Deco or country-house traditional. Have a drink in the Foyer lounge with its Hungarian mini-orchestra, or retreat to the reading room for perfect quiet, interrupted only by the sound of pages turning. The bedrooms are spacious, as are the bathrooms. Beds are handmade and supremely comfortable—the King of Morocco once brought his own, couldn't sleep, and ended up ordering 30 from Claridges to take home. ✉ *Brook St., W1A 2JQ,* ☎ *0171/629–8860 or 800/223–6800,* FAX *0171/499–2210. 200 rooms. 2 restaurants, lounge, beauty salon, parking. AE, DC, MC, V. Tube: Bond Street.*

££££ ★ **The Dorchester.** A London institution, the Dorchester appears on every "World's Best" list. The glamour level is off the scale: 1,500 square meters of gold leaf, 1,100 of marble, and 2,300 of hand-tufted carpet gild this lily, and bedrooms feature Irish linen sheets on canopied beds, brocades and velvets, Italian marble and etched glass bathrooms with Floris goodies, individual climate control, dual voltage outlets, and cable TV. Afternoon tea, drinking, lounging, and posing are all accomplished in the catwalk-shape Promenade lounge, where you may spot one of the film-star types who will stay nowhere else. Probably no other hotel this opulent manages to be this charming. ✉ *Park La., W1A 2HJ,* ☎ *0171/629–8888,* FAX *0171/409–0114. 197 rooms, 55 suites. 3 restaurants, bar, lounge, air-conditioning, health club (no pool), nightclub, business services, meeting rooms. AE, DC, MC, V. Tube: Marble Arch.*

££££ **Grosvenor House.** "The old lady of Park Lane" had settled happily back into top-dowager position, having thrown off her creeping frumpiness during a complete overhaul. It's not the kind of place that encourages hushed whispers or that frowns on jeans, despite the marble floors and wood-panel "library," open fires, oils, and fine antiques, all inspired by the Earl of Grosvenor's residence, which occupied the site during the 18th century. The hotel health club is just about the best around, especially since the gym part was completely redone in 1995; the pool didn't need any help. Bedrooms are spacious, and most of the freshly glamorized big marble bathrooms have natural light. ✉ *Park La., W1A 3AA,* ☎ *0171/499–6363,* FAX *0171/493–3341. 360 rooms, 70 suites. 3 restaurants, bar, lounge, indoor pool, health club. AE, DC, MC, V. Tube: Marble Arch.*

£££ **Dukes.** This small, exclusive, Edwardian-style hotel is possibly London's quietest hotel, secreted in its cul-de-sac in the heart of St. James's. It's filled with squashy sofas, oils of assorted dukes, and muted, rich colors, and offers guest rooms newly decorated in patrician, antiques-spattered style, plus the best in personal service (they greet you by name every time). ✉ *35 St. James's Pl., SW1A 1NY,* ☎ *0171/491–4840,* FAX *0171/493–1264. 62 rooms. Restaurant, dining room. AE, DC, MC, V. Tube: Green Park.*

£ **Edward Lear.** Once the house of Edward Lear (of "The Owl and the Pussycat" fame), this good-value, homey hotel has spotless, styleless rooms of varying size—triple and family rooms are huge; number 14 is a closet—with peace and quiet at the back. In the brick-wall breakfast room you're served sausages and bacon from the Queen's butcher. ✉ *28–30 Seymour St., W1H 5WD,* ☎ *0171/402–5401,* FAX *0171/706–3766. 31 rooms, 15 with shower, 4 with full bath. Breakfast room, lounge. MC, V. Tube: Marble Arch.*

Marylebone

£££ **Dorset Square Hotel.** This pair of Regency town houses in Sherlock Holmes territory belongs to the welcome new breed of small, luxurious, privately run hotels. The creation of architect–interior designer husband-and-wife team, Tim and Kit Kemp, this is *House Beautiful* come to life, from marble and mahogany bathrooms to antique lace counterpanes, and the staff bends over backward to accommodate your wishes. For on-the-town jaunts, there's even a vintage Bentley available. ✉ *39–40 Dorset Sq., NW1 6QN,* ☎ *0171/723–7874,*

Abbey Court, **2**
Beaufort, **11**
Berkeley, **15**
Blakes, **9**
Brown's, **23**
Capital, **12**
Claridge's, **22**
Columbia, **5**
Commodore, **3**
The Dorchester, **19**
Dorset Square, **13**
Duke's, **29**
Durrants, **21**
Edward Lear, **14**
Fielding, **26**
The Gore, **6**
Grosvenor House, **20**
The Halkin, **17**
Hazlitt's, **24**
Hotel 167, **7**
Kingsley, **25**
The Lanesborough, **16**
London Elizabeth, **4**
Morgan, **27**
The Pelham, **10**
Periquito Queensgate, **8**
The Savoy, **28**
The Sloane, **18**
Vicarage, **1**

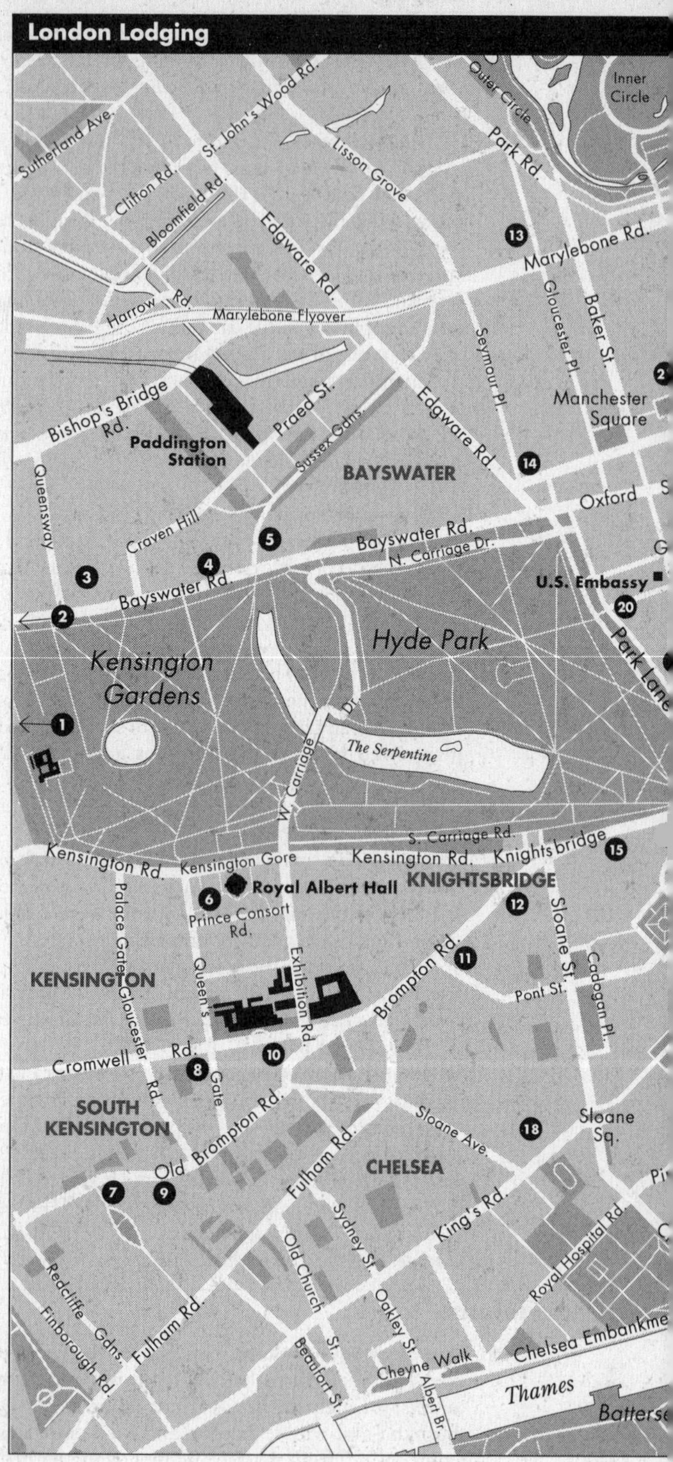

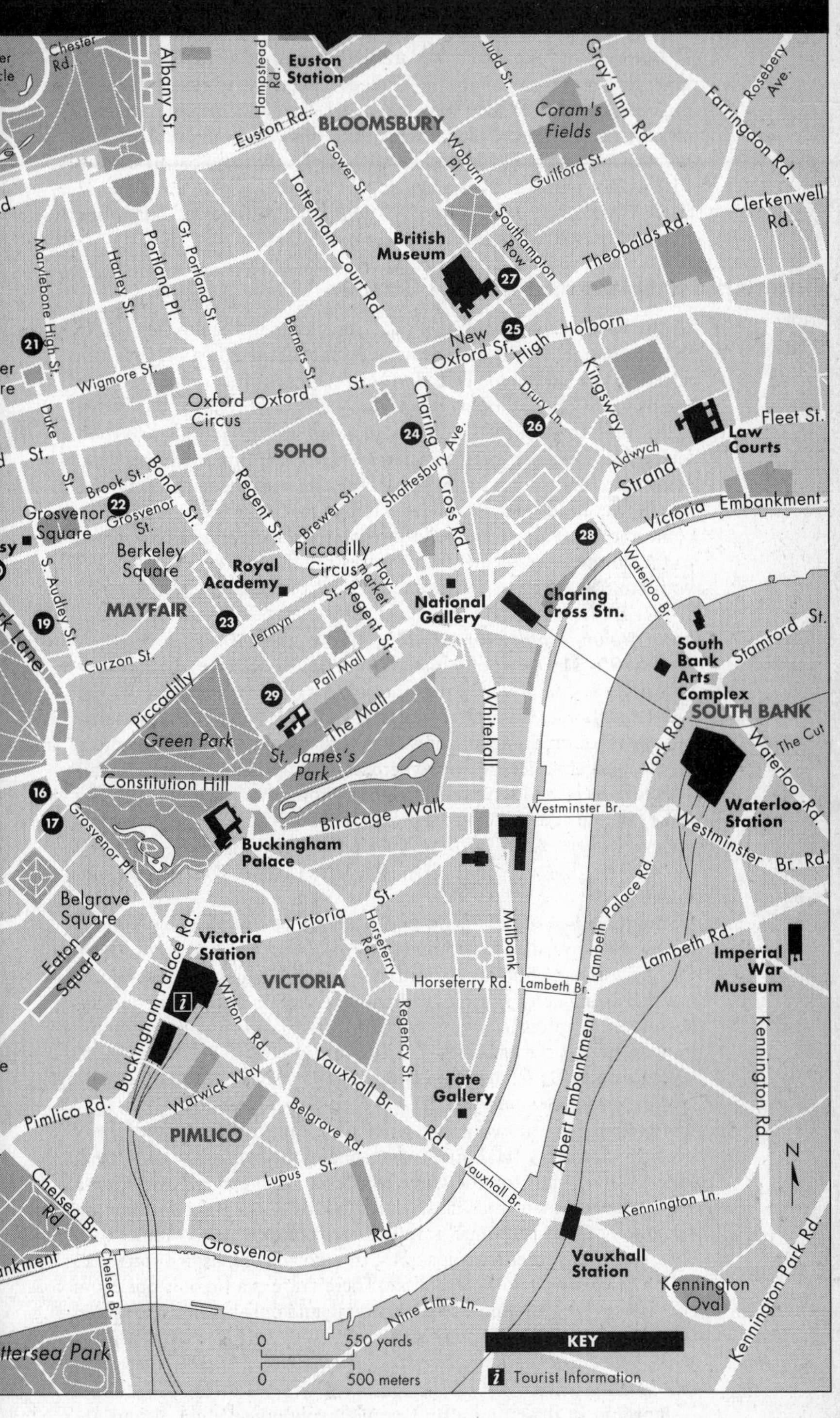
Euston Station
BLOOMSBURY
Coram's Fields
British Museum
SOHO
MAYFAIR
Royal Academy
National Gallery
Charing Cross Stn.
Law Courts
South Bank Arts Complex
SOUTH BANK
Waterloo Station
Buckingham Palace
Victoria Station
VICTORIA
Tate Gallery
PIMLICO
Imperial War Museum
Vauxhall Station
Kennington Oval
Green Park
St. James's Park
Oxford Circus
Piccadilly Circus
Grosvenor Square
Berkeley Square
Belgrave Square
Eaton Square
Euston Rd.
Tottenham Court Rd.
Gower St.
Woburn Pl.
Southampton Row
Guilford St.
Gray's Inn Rd.
Farringdon Rd.
Clerkenwell Rd.
Theobalds Rd.
Rosebery Ave.
Judd St.
Hampstead Rd.
Albany St.
Chester Rd.
Marylebone High St.
Harley St.
Portland Pl.
Gt. Portland St.
Berners St.
New Oxford St.
High Holborn
Kingsway
Drury Ln.
Fleet St.
Aldwych
Strand
Victoria Embankment
Wigmore St.
Oxford St.
Charing Cross Rd.
Shaftesbury Ave.
Regent St.
Brewer St.
Bond St.
Brook St.
Grosvenor St.
Duke St.
S. Audley St.
Park Lane
Curzon St.
Jermyn St.
Haymarket
Pall Mall
The Mall
Piccadilly
Constitution Hill
Birdcage Walk
Whitehall
Waterloo Br.
Stamford St.
York Rd.
Waterloo Rd.
The Cut
Westminster Br.
Westminster Br. Rd.
Lambeth Palace Rd.
Lambeth Rd.
Grosvenor Pl.
Victoria St.
Horseferry Rd.
Millbank
Lambeth Br.
Buckingham Palace Rd.
Wilton Rd.
Regency St.
Vauxhall Br. Rd.
Warwick Way
Belgrave Rd.
Pimlico Rd.
Lupus St.
Albert Embankment
Kennington Rd.
Kennington Ln.
Kennington Park Rd.
Vauxhall Br.
Chelsea Br. Rd.
Chelsea Br.
Grosvenor Rd.
Nine Elms Ln.
Battersea Park
N
0
550 yards
0
500 meters
KEY
Tourist Information
16
17
19
21
22
23
24
25
26
27
28
29

FAX *0171/724–3328. 37 rooms. Restaurant, bar. AE, MC, V. Tube: Baker Street.*

££ **Durrants.** A hotel since the late 18th century, Durrants occupies a quiet corner almost next to the Wallace Collection. It's good value for the area, and if you like ye wood-panel, leather-armchair, dark-red-pattern-carpet style of olde Englishness, this will suit you. Bedrooms are wan and motel-like but adequate—the few with no bathrooms are £10 a night cheaper. ✉ *George St., W1H 6BH,* ☎ *0171/935–8131,* FAX *0171/487–3510. 96 rooms, 85 with bath. Restaurant, bar, dining rooms, lounges. AE, MC, V. Tube: Bond Street.*

Bloomsbury, Soho, and Covent Garden

££££ ★ **The Savoy.** This historic, grand, late Victorian hotel is beloved by the international influential, now as ever. Like the other Savoy Group hotels, it has handmade beds and staff who are often graduates of its exclusive training school. The spacious, elegant, bright, and comfortable rooms are furnished with antiques and serviced by valets. A room facing the Thames costs an arm and a leg, but there are few better views in London. Bathrooms have original fittings, with the same sunflower-size shower heads as at Claridges. Though the Savoy is as grand as they come, the air is tinged with a certain theatrical naughtiness (due in part to the on-premises theater, recently restored), which goes down well with Hollywood types. ✉ *Strand, WC2R 0EU,* ☎ *0171/836–4343,* FAX *0171/240–6040. 202 rooms. 3 restaurants, 2 bars, indoor pool, beauty salon, health club. AE, DC, MC, V. Tube: Aldwych.*

£££ ★ **Hazlitt's.** The solo Soho hotel is in three connected early 18th-century houses, one of which was the essayist William Hazlitt's (1778–1830) last home. It's a disarmingly friendly place, full of personality, but devoid of such hotel features as elevators, room service, and porterage. Robust antiques are everywhere, assorted prints crowd every wall, a Victorian claw-foot tub sits in all bathrooms. Book way ahead—this is the London address of media people, literary types, and antiques dealers everywhere. ✉ *6 Frith St., W1V 5TZ,* ☎ *0171/434–1771,* FAX *0171/439–1524. 23 rooms. AE, DC, MC, V. Tube: Tottenham Court Road.*

££–£££ **The Kingsley.** On the main street, steps from the British Museum, this is one Edwardian-style hotel that really does feel sweetly old-fashioned, avoiding shabbiness or stuffiness. English country–housey decor has the strong color schemes currently favored in hotel land, and has been recently refreshed, with tea- and coffeemakers and free in-house movies among the facilities. ✉ *Bloomsbury Way, WC1A 2SD,* ☎ *0171/242–5881,* FAX *0171/831–0225. 145 rooms. Restaurant, bar, lounge, meeting rooms. AE, DC, MC, V. Tube: Holborn.*

££ **Fielding.** Tucked away in a quiet alley, this very small and pretty hotel is adored for the homey atmosphere, the continuity of a loyal, friendly staff, and for the convenience of having the Royal Opera House, the theater district, and half of London's restaurants within spitting distance. The bedrooms are all different, shabby-homey rather than chic, and cozy rather than spacious, though you can have a suite here for the price of a chain-hotel double. There's no elevator; only one room comes with bathtub (most have showers); and only breakfast is served in the restaurant. ✉ *4 Broad Ct., Bow St., WC2B 5QZ,* ☎ *0171/836–8305,* FAX *0171/497–0064. 26 rooms, 1 with bath, 23 with shower. Bar, breakfast room. AE, DC, MC, V. Tube: Covent Garden.*

£ ★ **Morgan.** In this family-run Georgian row-house hotel, rooms are small and functionally furnished, yet friendly and cheerful overall, with phones and TVs. The five newish apartments are particularly pleasing: three times the size of normal rooms (and an extra £15/night, placing them in the ££ category), complete with eat-in kitchens and private phone lines. ✉ *24 Bloomsbury St., WC1B 3QJ,* ☎ *0171/636–3735. 15 rooms with bath or shower, 5 apartments. Breakfast room. No credit cards. Tube: Russell Square.*

Kensington

££££ ★ **Blakes.** This has got to be the most exotic hotel in town, the work of Lady Weinberg, a.k.a. Anouska Hempel, '70s style goddess. A sober, dark green Victorian exterior belies the arty mix of Biedermeier, bamboo, four-poster beds, and Oriental screens inside, with rooms bedecked in anything from black moiré silk to dove gray or top-to-toe blush pink. Guests tend to be music or movie mavens. Look for her new hotel, The Hempel, too. ✉ *33 Roland Gardens, SW7 3PF,* ☎ *0171/370–6701,* FAX *0171/373–0442. 52 rooms with bath. Restaurant. AE, DC, MC, V. Tube: Gloucester Road.*

£££ ★ **The Gore.** Just down the road from the Albert Hall, this small, very friendly hotel, run by the same people who run Hazlitt's (☞ Soho, *above*), features a similarly eclectic selection of prints, etchings, and antiques. Here, though, are spectacular folly-like rooms—Room 101 is a Tudor fantasy with a minstrel gallery, stained glass, and four-poster bed. Despite all that, the Gore manages to remain most elegant. ✉ *189 Queen's Gate, SW7 5EX,* ☎ *0171/584–6601,* FAX *0171/589–8127. 54 rooms with bath. Restaurant, lobby lounge. AE, DC, MC, V.*

££ **Hotel 167.** This friendly little bed-and-breakfast is a two-minute walk from the V&A, in a grand white-stucco Victorian corner house. The lobby is immediately cheering, with its round marble tables, wrought-iron chairs, palms, and modern paintings; it also does duty as lounge and breakfast room. Bedrooms have a hybrid antiquey/Ikea style. ✉ *167 Old Brompton Rd., SW5 0AN,* ☎ *0171/373–0672,* FAX *0171/373–3360. 19 rooms with bath or shower. Breakfast room. AE, DC, MC, V. Tube: Gloucester Road.*

££ **Kensington Close.** This large, utilitarian hotel feels like a smaller one and offers extras you wouldn't expect for the reasonable rate and convenient location (in a quiet lane off Kensington High Street). The main attraction is the health club, with an 18-meter pool, two squash courts, a steam room, and a beauty salon. Standard rooms are on the small side, with plain chain-hotel built-in furniture. ✉ *Wrights La., W8 5SP,* ☎ *0171/937–8170,* FAX *0171/937–8289. 530 rooms. 2 restaurants, 2 bars, lounge, indoor pool, health club, baby-sitting. AE, DC, MC, V. Tube: High Street Kensington.*

£ **Periquito Queensgate.** When a hotel calls its own rooms "compact," you should imagine a double bed, then add a foot all round, and, yes, that is about the measure of a room here. However, like a cruise ship state room, all you need (closet, mirror, satellite TV, tea/coffeemaker, hairdryer) is creatively secreted. Rooms are double-glazed against noisy Cromwell Road, though color schemes are LOUD. Kids share free or get their own room at half price—and the Natural History Museum is just across the street. ✉ *68–69 Queensgate, London SW7 5JT,* ☎ *0171/370–6111,* FAX *0171/370–0932. 61 rooms. Bar, lounge. AE, MC, V. Tube: Gloucester Road.*

£ ★ **Vicarage.** A family concern for nearly 30 years, the Vicarage feels like a private house. It's beautifully decorated, and quiet, overlooking a garden square near Kensington's shopping streets. ✉ *10 Vicarage Gate, W8 4AG,* ☎ *0171/229–4030. 19 rooms without bath. No credit cards.*

Knightsbridge, Chelsea, and Belgravia

££££ 🏨 **Berkeley.** A remarkable mixture of the old and new, the Berkeley stars a splendid penthouse swimming pool that opens to the sky when the weather's good. The bedrooms are decorated by various designers, but tend to be serious and opulent, some with swags of William Morris prints, others plain and masculine with little balconies overlooking the street. All have sitting areas and big, tiled bathrooms with bidets. Its restaurant is Vong, the Thai/French hybrid cloned from New York. ✉ *Wilton Pl., SW1X 7RL,* ☎ *0171/235–6000,* FAX *0171/235–4330. 160 rooms. 2 restaurants, indoor and outdoor pools, beauty salon, health club, cinema. AE, DC, MC, V. Tube: Knightsbridge.*

££££ 🏨 **Capital.** This grand hotel decanted into a private house is the work of David and Margaret Levin, who also run The People's Palace (☞ Dining, *above*), and it exudes their irreproachable taste, with French floral fabrics, fine-grained woods, sober prints, and shelves of books. The 10 rooms of the Edwardian Wing, with its carved wooden staircase, enjoyed the attentions of superstar designer Nina Campbell, and were already the height of fashion in the 1920s, when this was the Squires Hotel. ✉ *22–24 Basil St., SW3 1AT,* ☎ *0171/589–5171,* FAX *0171/225–0011. 48 rooms. Bar, lounge, air-conditioning. AE, DC, MC, V. Tube: Knightsbridge.*

££££ ★ 🏨 **The Halkin.** This luxurious little place is so contemporary you worry it will be outdated in a couple of years and they'll have to redo the whole thing. Milanese designers were responsible for the clean-cut white marble lobby, and the gray-on-gray bedrooms that light up when you insert your electronic key and contain every high-tech toy you never knew you needed. It might be like living in the Design Museum, except that this place employs some of the friendliest people around—and they look pretty good in their white Armani uniforms, too. ✉ *Halkin St., SW1X 7DJ,* ☎ *0171/333–1000,* FAX *0171/333–1100. 41 rooms. Restaurant. AE, DC, MC, V. Tube: Hyde Park Corner.*

££££ 🏨 **The Lanesborough.** London's swankiest grand hotel acts for all the world as though the Prince Regent (or is it Liberace?) took a ride through time and is about to resume residence. Everything coruscates with richness—gaudy brocades and Regency stripes, moiré silks and fleurs-de-lys, multiple antiques and oil paintings, handwoven £250-per-square-yard carpet. If you yearn for a bygone age, demand that room service includes a personal butler, and are very rich, this is for you. ✉ *1 Lanesborough Pl., SW1X 7TA,* ☎ *0171/259–5599,* FAX *0171/259–5606. 95 rooms. 2 restaurants, bar. AE, DC, MC, V. Tube: Hyde Park Corner.*

£££ ★ 🏨 **Beaufort.** You can practically hear the jingle of Harrods's cash registers from a room at the Beaufort. Actually, "hotel" is a misnomer for this elegant pair of Victorian houses. There's a sitting room instead of Reception; guests have a front door key and the run of the drinks cabinet, and even their own phone number, with the customary astronomical hotel surcharges waived. The high-ceiling, generously proportioned rooms are decorated in muted, sophisticated shades to suit the muted, sophisticated atmosphere—but don't worry, you're encouraged by the incredibly sweet staff to feel at home. ✉ *33 Beaufort Gardens, SW3 1PP,* ☎ *0171/584–5252,* FAX *0171/589–2834. 29 rooms. Air-conditioning. AE, DC, MC, V. Tube: Knightsbridge.*

£££ 🏨 **The Pelham.** The second of Tim and Kit Kemp's gorgeous hotels opened in 1989 and is run along exactly the same lines as the Dorset Square, except that this one looks less town than country. There's 18th-century pine paneling in the drawing room, flowers galore, quite a bit of glazed chintz, and the odd four-poster and bedroom fireplace. The Pelham stands opposite the South Kensington tube stop, by the big museums, and close to the shops of Knightsbridge, with Kemps supplying an on-site trendy menu. Lauren Bacall deserted the Athenaeum for this hotel. ✉ *15 Cromwell Pl., SW7 2LA,* ☎ *0171/589–8288,* FAX *0171/584–8444. 37 rooms. Restaurant, air-conditioning, pool. AE, MC, V. Tube: South Kensington.*

££–£££ **The Sloane.** The tiny Sloane is the only hotel we know in which you can lie in your canopy bed, pick up the phone, and buy the bed—and the phone, too, and the tasty antiques all around you. Nothing so tacky as a price tag besmirches the gorgeous decor; instead, the sweet, young Euro staff harbors a book of price lists at the desk. There's an aerie of a secret roof terrace, with upholstered garden furniture and a panorama over Chelsea, where meals are served to guests. ✉ *29 Draycott Pl., SW3 2SH,* ☎ *0171/581–5757,* FAX *0171/584–1348. 12 rooms. Restaurant. AE, DC, MC, V. Tube: Sloane Square.*

Bayswater and Notting Hill Gate

£££ **Abbey Court.** You enter this 1850 building through a stately, double-front portico to find yourself in a luxury bed-and-breakfast filled with Empire furniture, oil portraits, and the odd four-poster bed. Kensington Gardens is close by, or you could save the walk and relax in the pretty conservatory. ✉ *20 Pembridge Gardens, W2 4DU,* ☎ *0171/221–7518,* FAX *0171/792–0858. 22 rooms. AE, DC, MC, V. Tube: Notting Hill.*

££ **London Elizabeth.** This family-owned gem steps from Hyde Park has a foyer and lounge crammed with chintz drapery, lace antimacassars, and little chandeliers—a country sensibility that's carried through to the bedrooms. With their palest blue–striped walls, wooden picture rails and Welsh wool bedspreads, or pink cabbage rose prints and mahogany furniture, they do vary in size, and some lack a full-length mirror, but they all have TV, direct-dial phone, and hairdryer, and they're serviced by an exceptionally charming Anglo-Irish staff. ✉ *Lancaster Terrace, W2 3PF,* ☎ *0171/402–6641,* FAX *0171/224–8900. 55 rooms. Restaurant, bar, lounge. AE, DC, MC, V. Tube: Lancaster Gate.*

£ **Columbia.** The public rooms in these five joined-up Victorians are as big as museum halls. Late at night they contain the most hip band du jour drinking alcohol; in the morning, there are sightseers sipping coffee—a unique paradox among London's bargain hotels. Rooms are clean and ceilings high, TV, hairdryer, tea- coffeemaker, direct-dial phone, and safe are provided, and some are very large (especially those with three or four beds), with park views and balconies. The teak veneer, khaki-beige-brown color schemes, and avocado bathroom suites are not pretty. ✉ *95–99 Lancaster Gate, W2 3NS,* ☎ *0171/402–0021,* FAX *0171/706–4691. 103 rooms. Restaurant, bar, lounge, meeting rooms. AE, MC, V. Tube: Lancaster Gate.*

£ ★ **Commodore.** This peaceful hotel of three converted Victorians has some amazing rooms for the price—as superior to the regular ones (which usually go to package tour groups) as Harrods is to Woolworths. Twenty are mini-duplexes, with sleeping gallery (which cost more than the ££ category); all have the full deck of tea- coffeemakers, hairdryer, and TV with pay movies. No. 11 is a real duplex, entered through a secret mirrored door. *50 Lancaster Gate, W2 3NA,* ☎ *0171/402–5291,* FAX *0171/262–1088. 90 rooms. Bar, lounge, business services. AE, MC, V. Tube: Lancaster Gate.*

NIGHTLIFE AND THE ARTS

Nightlife

Bars

The Atlantic. This vast, glamorous, wood-floor basement was the first central London bar to be granted a late, late alcohol license. The restaurant is more dominant these days, and reserving a table is the only way to get in late on weekends. ✉ *20 Glasshouse St., W1,* ☎ *0171/734–4888.* ⏲ *Mon.–Sat. noon–3 AM, Sun. noon–11 PM. AE, MC, V.*

Beach Blanket Babylon. In Notting Hill, close to Portobello market, this always-packed singles bar is distinguishable by its fanciful decor—like a fairy tale grotto, or a medieval dungeon, visited by the gargoyles of Notre Dame. ✉ *45 Ledbury Rd., W11,* ☎ *0171/229–2907.* ⏲ *Daily noon–11 PM. AE, MC, V.*

The Library. The comfortable, self-consciously "period" bar at the swanky Lanesborough Hotel harbors a collection of ancient cognacs, made in years when something important happened. Don't ask for brandy Alexander. ✉ *Hyde Park Corner, SW1,* ☎ *0171/259–5599.* ⏲ *Mon.–Sat. 11–11, Sun. noon–2:30 and 7–10:30. AE, DC, MC, V.*

Clubs

Camden Palace. It would be difficult to find a facial wrinkle, even if you could see through the laser lights and find your way around the three floors of bars at this rejuvenated and hip-once-more megaclub. ✉ *1A Camden High St., NW1,* ☎ *0171/387–0428.* 🎟 *£3–£9.* ⏲ *Tues.–Sat. 9 PM–3 AM. No credit cards.*

Heaven. London's premier (mainly) gay club is the best place for dancing wildly for hours. A state-of-the-art laser show and a large, throbbing dance floor complement a labyrinth of quieter bars and lounges. ✉ *Under the Arches, Villiers St., WC2,* ☎ *0171/839–2520.* 🎟 *£4–£8 depending on night.* ⏲ *Call for opening times (Tues.–Sat. approx. 10 PM–3:30 AM). AE, DC, MC, V.*

Stringfellows. Peter Stringfellow's first London nightclub is not at all hip, but is very glitzy, with mirrored walls, light show, and an expensive art deco–style restaurant. Suburbanites and middle-age swingers frequent it. ✉ *16–19 Upper St. Martin's La., WC2,* ☎ *0171/240–5534.* 🎟 *Mon.–Wed. £8; Thurs. £10; Fri.–Sat. before 10 PM £10, after 10 PM £15.* ⏲ *Mon.–Sat. 8 PM–3:30 AM. AE, DC, MC, V.*

Cabaret

Comedy Store. The improv factory where the United Kingdom's funniest standups cut their teeth, relocated to a bigger and better place. ✉ *Haymarket House, Oxendon St., SW1,* ☎ *0171/344–4444 or 01426/914433 for information.* 🎟 *£8–£9.* ⏲ *Shows Tues.–Thurs., Sun. at 8, Fri.–Sat. at 8 and midnight. AE, MC, V.*

Madame Jo Jo's. By no means devoid of straight spectators, this place has long been one of the most fun drag cabarets in town—civilized of atmosphere, with barechested bar boys. Many nights are club nights, so call ahead. ✉ *8 Brewer St.,* ☎ *0171/287–1414.* 🎟 *Mon.–Thurs. £6, Fri.–Sat. £8.* ⏲ *Doors open at 10 PM; shows at 12:15 and 1:15.*

Jazz

Jazz Café. This palace of high-tech cool in a converted bank in bohemian Camden is the essential hangout for mainstream jazz, world beat, and younger crossover performers. It's steps from Camden Town tube station. ✉ *5–7 Pkwy., NW1,* ☎ *0171/916–6000.* 🎟 *£7–£12, depend-*

ing on band. ⏲ Mon.–Sat. 7 PM–late (time varies). Reservations advised for balcony restaurant. AE, DC, MC, V.

Ronnie Scott's. The legendary Soho jazz club that, since its opening in the early '60s, has been attracting all the big names. It's usually packed and hot, but the atmosphere can't be beat, and it's probably still London's best. ✉ *47 Frith St., W1,* ☎ *0171/439–0747. Admission £10–£12 nonmembers.* ⏲ *Mon.–Sat. 8:30 PM–3 AM, Sun. 8–11:30 PM. Reservations advised; essential some nights. AE, DC, MC, V.*

Rock

The Astoria. Very central, quite hip, this place hosts bands that there's a buzz about, plus late club nights. ✉ *157 Charing Cross Rd., W1,* ☎ *0171/434–0403.* 🎫 *About £8–£12.* ⏲ *Check listings for opening times. No credit cards.*

The Forum. This ex-ballroom with balcony and dance floor packs in the customers and consistently attracts the best medium-to-big-name performers, too. Get the tube to Kentish Town, then follow the hordes. ✉ *9–17 Highgate Rd., NW5,* ☎ *0171/284–2200.* 🎫 *About £8–£12.* ⏲ *Most nights 7–11. AE, MC, V.*

Casinos

Any person wishing to gamble *must* make a declaration of intent to gamble at the gaming house in question and *must* apply for membership in person at least 48 hours in advance. In many cases, clubs prefer for the applicant's membership to be proposed by an existing member. Personal guests of existing members are, however, allowed to participate.

Crockford's. A civilized, 150-year-old club, which has attracted a large international clientele since its move from St. James's to Mayfair, for American roulette, Punto Banco, and blackjack. ✉ *30 Curzon St., W1,* ☎ *0171/493–7771.* 🎫 *Membership £150 a year.* ⏲ *Daily 2 PM–4 AM. Jacket and tie.*

The Golden Nugget. This large casino just off Piccadilly has blackjack, roulette, and Punto Banco. ✉ *22 Shaftesbury Ave., W1,* ☎ *0171/439–0099.* 🎫 *Membership £3.50 for life.* ⏲ *Daily 2 PM–4 AM. Jacket required.*

Sportsman Club. This has a dice table as well as Punto Banco, American roulette, and blackjack. ✉ *3 Tottenham Court Rd., W1,* ☎ *0171/637–5464.* 🎫 *Membership £3.45 a year.* ⏲ *Daily 2 PM–4 AM. Jacket and tie.*

The Arts

Theater

London is well known for its excellent theater scene, consisting, broadly, of the state-subsidized companies, the Royal National Theatre and the Royal Shakespeare Company; the commercial West End, equivalent to Broadway; and the Fringe—small, experimental companies. Another category could be added, known in the weekly listings magazine *Time Out* (the best reference guide to what's on), as Off-West End, shows staged at the longer-established fringe theaters. Other sources of arts information are the *Evening Standard,* the major Sunday papers, the daily *Independent* and *Guardian,* and Friday's *Times.*

Most theaters have a matinee twice a week (Wednesday or Thursday and Saturday) and nightly performances at 7:30 or 8, except Sunday. Prices vary; expect to pay from £6 for an upper balcony seat to at least £20 for the stalls (orchestra) or dress circle. Reserve tickets at the box office, over the phone by credit card (numbers in the phone book or newspaper marked "cc" are for credit card reservations), or (for a couple of pounds) through ticket agents such as First Call (☎ 0171/240–7941 or 0171/497–9977). To reserve before your trip use Ticketmaster's U.S. booking line (☎ 800/775–2525), or reserve once in London (☎ 0171/413–3321). Half-price, same-day tickets are sold for cash only (subject to availability) from a booth on the southwest corner of Leicester Square, open Monday–Saturday noon–2 for matinees, 2:30–6:30 for evening shows. There is always a long line. Larger hotels have reservation services, but add hefty service charges.

Concerts

Ticket prices for symphony concerts range £5–£15. International guest appearances usually mean higher prices; you should reserve well in advance for such performances. Those without reservations might go to the hall half an hour before the performance for a chance at returns.

The London Symphony Orchestra is in residence at the **Barbican Arts Centre** (☎ 0171/638–8891); the Philharmonia and the Royal Philharmonic also perform here. The **South Bank Arts Complex** (☎ 0171/928–3002), which includes the Royal Festival Hall, Queen Elizabeth Hall, and the small Purcell Room, forms another major venue. Between the Barbican and South Bank, there are concert performances every night of the year. The Barbican also features chamber music concerts with such smaller orchestras as the City of London Sinfonia.

To experience a great British institution, try for the **Royal Albert Hall** during "The Proms" (July–Sept., ☎ 0171/589–8212). Special "promenade" (standing) tickets cost about £3 and are usually available at the hall on the night of the performance. If you're in town during the summer, don't miss the outdoor concerts by the lake at Kenwood (Hampstead Heath) or Holland Park.

Numerous lunchtime concerts take place across London in smaller concert halls and churches. They feature string quartets, vocalists, jazz ensembles, and gospel choirs. **St. Martin-in-the-Fields** (☎ 0171/839–1930) is a particularly popular location. Performances usually begin about 1 PM and last an hour. Some are free.

Opera

The main venue for opera in London is the **Royal Opera House** (✉ Covent Garden, WC2E 9DD, ☎ 0171/240–1066), which ranks with the Metropolitan Opera House in New York—in cost as well as stature. Prices range from £5 in the upper slips to well over £100. Performances are sold individually or divided into booking periods, and tickets often sell out early.

English-language productions are staged at the **Coliseum** (✉ St. Martin's La., WC2N 4ES, ☎ 0171/836–3161), home of the English National Opera Company. Prices here are generally lower than at the Royal Opera House, ranging from £4 for standing room to about £50 for the best seats, and productions are often innovative and exciting.

Ballet

The Royal Opera House (☞ Opera, *above*) is also the home of the world-famous **Royal Ballet.** Prices are slightly lower for the ballet than for opera, but tickets go faster; reserve ahead. The English National Ballet and visiting international companies perform at the Coliseum and the Royal Festival Hall from time to time. The **London City Ballet** is based at Sadler's Wells Theatre (✉ Rosebery Ave., EC1R 4TN, ☎ 0171/713–6000), which also hosts various other ballet companies and regional and international modern dance troupes. **The Place** (✉ 17 Duke's Rd., WC1, ☎ 0171/387–0031) is indeed the place for contemporary dance, physical theater, and the avant garde. Prices at these are much cheaper than at Covent Garden.

Movies

Despite the video invasion, West End movies still thrive. The largest major first-run houses (**Odeon, MGM,** etc.) are found in the Leicester Square/Piccadilly Circus area, where tickets average £7. Monday and matinees are usually half price; lines are also shorter. The best revival house is the **National Film Theatre,** part of the South Bank Arts Complex (☞ The South Bank *in* Exploring London, *above*), which screens big past hits, plus work neglected by the more ticket-sales-dependent houses, since it comes under the auspices of the British Film Institute. The main events of the annual London Film Festival take place here in the fall. Daily membership costs 40p. The **Institute of Contemporary Art** (ICA; ☞ Carlton House Terrace *in* Westminster and Royal London, *above*) presents a repertory program and various museums and galleries also have occasional screenings. Check listings for screenings at the principal repertory houses: the Everyman, Prince Charles, Rio, Ritzy, and Riverside.

OUTDOOR ACTIVITIES AND SPORTS

For information on London's sports clubs and facilities, call **Sportsline,** weekdays 10–6, ☎ 0171/222–8000.

Spectator Sports

Cricket

Lord's (✉ St. John's Wood, NW8, ☎ 0171/289–1611) has been hallowed turf for worshipers of England's summer game since 1811. The World Series of cricket, the Tests, are played here, but tickets are hard to procure. One-day internationals and top-class county matches can usually be seen by lining up on the day of the match.

Running

The London Marathon starts at 9 AM on the third Sunday in April, with some 25,000 athletes running from Blackheath or Greenwich to Westminster Bridge or the Mall. Entry forms for the following year are available starting in May (☎ 01891/234234).

Soccer

Three British football (soccer) clubs competing in the **Premier League** are particular popular: Arsenal (✉ Avenell Rd., Highbury, N5, ☎ 0171/359–0131), Chelsea (✉ Stamford Bridge, Fulham Rd., SW6, ☎ 0171/385–5545), and Tottenham Hotspur (✉ White Hart Lane, 748 High Rd., N17, ☎ 0181/808–3030). More than likely you won't see a hint of the infamous hooliganism but will be quite carried away by the electric atmosphere only a vast football crowd can generate.

Tennis

The Wimbledon Lawn Tennis Championships is, of course, one of the top four Grand Slam events of the tennis year. There's a lottery system for advance purchase of tickets. To apply, send a self-addressed, stamped envelope between October and December (✉ All England Lawn Tennis & Croquet Club, Box 98, Church Rd., Wimbledon SW19 5AE, ☎ 0181/946–2244), then fill in the application form, and hope. Alternatively, during the last-week-of-June, first-week-of-July tournament, tickets collected from departed spectators are resold (profits go to charity). These can provide grandstand seats with plenty to see—play continues till dusk. Call the LTB **Wimbledon Information Line** (☎ 01839/123417; 49p/min, 39p cheap rate) from the beginning of June.

Participant Sports

Biking

London is reasonably cycle-friendly for a big city, with special lanes marked for bicycles on some major roads, but it is never safe to ride without a helmet. **Bikepark** (✉ 14 Stukeley St., WC2, ☎ 0171/430–0083. Tube: Covent Garden) rents mountain, hybrid, or road bikes from £10/day, £30/weekend, or £30/week, plus a deposit (MC, V). All machines are new and issued with locks. Reserve ahead in summer.

Fitness Centers

Jubilee Hall (✉ 30 The Piazza, Covent Garden, WC2, ☎ 0171/379–0008. Tube: Covent Garden). Many are addicted to Jamie Addicoat's "Fatbuster" classes, but there are plenty more, from body sculpting and step to pilates and jazz dance. **The Peak** (✉ Hyatt Carlton Tower Hotel, 2 Cadogan Pl., SW1, ☎ 0171/235–1234. Tube: Sloane Square). This hotel club has top equipment, great ninth-floor views over Knightsbridge, beauty spa, and sauna—with TV. About £30/day for non-guests.

Golf

Regent's Park Golf and Tennis School (✉ Outer Circle, Regent's Park, NW1, ☎ 0171/724–0643. Tube: Regent's Park). These driving ranges and putting greens are just by the zoo. The instructors have a good reputation. **Richmond Park** (✉ Roehampton Gate, SW15, ☎ 0181/876–1795. Tube: Richmond). There are two well-kept but very busy 18-hole courses here. You can hire half or full sets of clubs, plus buggies and trollies.

Running

Green Park and **St. James's Park** are convenient to the Piccadilly hotels. It's about 2 miles around both. **Hyde Park** and **Kensington Gardens** together supply a 4-mile perimeter route, or you can do a 2½-mile run in Hyde Park alone if you start at Hyde Park Corner or Marble Arch and encircle the Serpentine. Near the Park Lane hotels, **Regent's Park** has the Outer Circle loop measuring about 2½ miles. **London Hash House Harriers** (☎ 0181/995–7879) organize noncompetitive hour-long runs (£1) round interesting bits of town, with loops and checkpoints built in.

Swimming

Ironmonger Row (✉ Ironmonger Row, EC1, ☎ 0171/253–4011. Tube: Old Street). This 33- by 12-yard City pool is in a '30s complex that includes a Turkish bath. **Oasis** (✉ 32 Endell St., WC2, ☎ 0171/831–1804. Tube: Covent Garden) is just that, with a heated pool (⏲ May–Sept.) right in Covent Garden, and a 30- by 10-yard one indoors. **Seymour Leisure Centre** (✉ Seymour Pl., W2, ☎ 0171/402–5795. Tube: Marylebone) has a very central 44- by 20-yard pool.

SHOPPING

Chelsea

Chelsea centers on the King's Road, once synonymous with ultra-fashion; it still harbors some designer boutiques, plus antiques and home furnishings stores.

Covent Garden

This something-for-everyone neighborhood has chain clothing stores and top designers, stalls selling crafts, and shops selling gifts of every type—bikes, kites, tea, herbs, beads, hats, you name it.

Kensington

Kensington's main drag, Kensington High Street, is a smaller, classier version of Oxford Street, with some larger stores at the eastern end. Try Kensington Church Street for expensive antiques, plus a little fashion.

Knightsbridge

Neighboring Knightsbridge has Harrods, of course, but also Harvey Nichols, the top clothes stop, and many expensive designers' boutiques along Sloane Street, Walton Street, and Beauchamp Place.

Mayfair

In Mayfair are the two Bond streets, Old and New, with desirable dress designers, jewelers, and fine art. South Molton Street has high-price high-style fashion—especially at Browns—and the tailors of Savile Row are of worldwide repute.

Regent Street

At right angles to Oxford Street is Regent Street, with possibly London's pleasantest department store, Liberty's, plus Hamley's, the capital's toy mecca. Shops around once-famous Carnaby Street stock designer youth paraphernalia and 57 varieties of T-shirt.

St. James's

Here the English gentleman buys everything but the suit (which is from Savile Row): handmade hats, shirts, and shoes, silver shaving kits and hip flasks; you'll also find the world's best cheese shop, Paxton & Whitfield. Nothing in this neighborhood is cheap, in any sense.

Specialty Stores

London is full of wonderful and also offbeat merchandise. We have space to include only a few stores in each category.

Antiques

Antiquarius (☒ 131–141 King's Rd., SW3, ☎ 0171/351–5353), at the Sloane Square end of the King's Road, is an indoor antiques market with more than 200 stalls offering a wide variety of collectibles, including things that won't bust your baggage allowance: Art Deco brooches, meerschaum pipes, silver salt cellars . . . **Gray's Antique Market** (☒ 58 Davies St., W1, ☎ 0171/629–7034) is conveniently central. It assembles dealers specializing in everything from Sheffield plate to Chippendale furniture. Bargains are not impossible, and proper pedigrees are guaranteed.

Books

Charing Cross Road is London's booksville, with a couple of dozen antiquarian booksellers, and many new bookshops, too.

Books for Cooks (☒ 4 Blenheim Cres., W11, ☎ 0171/221–1992) is a unique one-stop resource, complete with the aroma of daily dishes cooked by the staff from its pages. It's worth the trip west for foodies. **Cecil Court.** Just off the Charing Cross Road is this pedestrians-only lane where

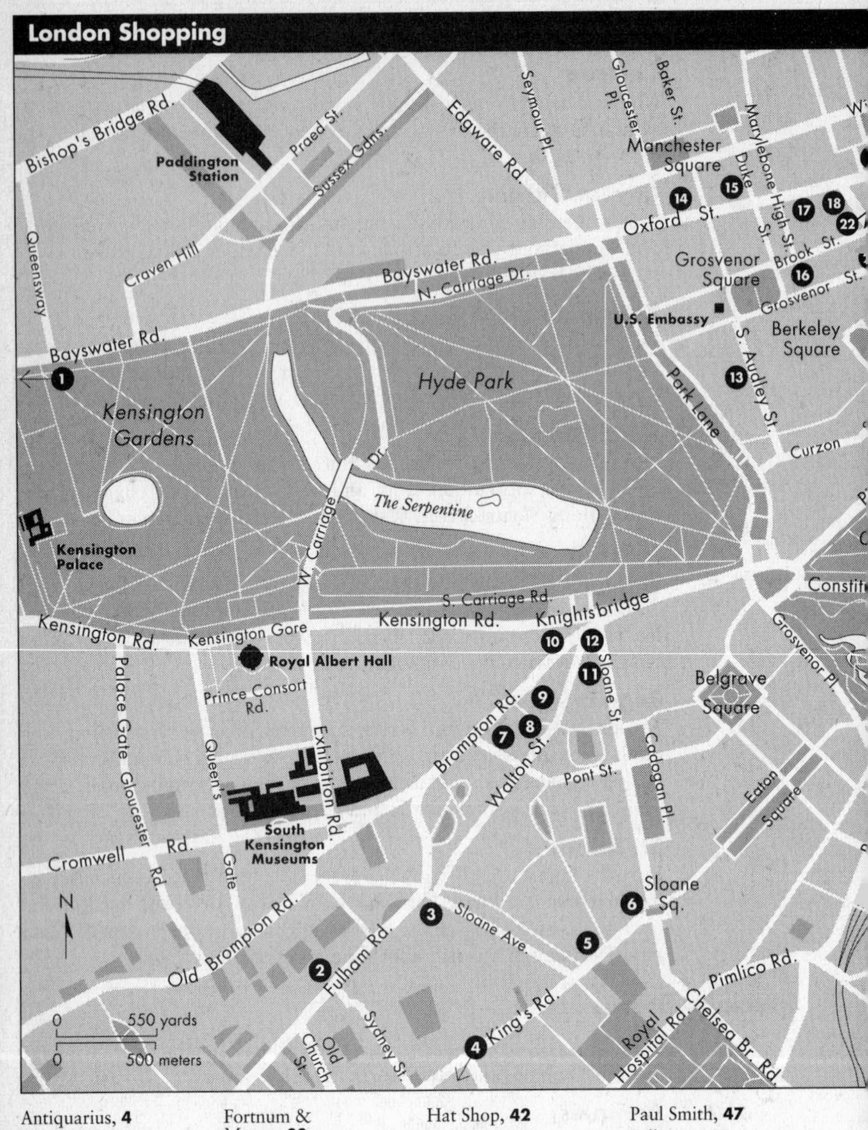

Antiquarius, **4**
Aquascutum, **32**
Asprey's, **20**
Books for Cooks, **1**
Browns, **11, 18**
Burberrys, **27, 37**
Butler and Wilson, **2, 17**
Cecil Court, **49**
Contemporary Applied Arts, **46**
Contemporary Ceramics, **30**
Favourbrook, **34**
Forbidden Planet, **41**
Fortnum & Mason, **33**
Foyle's, **39**
Gabriel's Wharf, **52**
Garrard, **31**
General Trading Co., **6**
Gray's Antique Market/Gray's Mews, **16**
Grosvenor Prints, **48**
Halcyon Days, **21**
Hamleys, **26**
Harrods, **9**
Harvey Nichols, **12**
Hat Shop, **42**
Hatchards, **35**
Herbert Johnson, **28**
Janet Reger, **7**
John Lewis, **19**
Laura Ashley, **5, 24**
Liberty's, **25**
London Silver Vault, **51**
Map House, **8**
Marks & Spencer, **14, 29**
Miss Selfridge, **23**
The Outlaws Club, **43**
Paul Smith, **47**
Pellicano, **22**
Penhaligon's, **50**
Scotch House, **3**
Selfridges, **15**
Stanfords, **45**
The Tea House, **44**
Thomas Goode, **13**
Turnbull & Asser, **36**
Warehouse, **10**
Waterstone's, **38**
Zwemmer, **40**

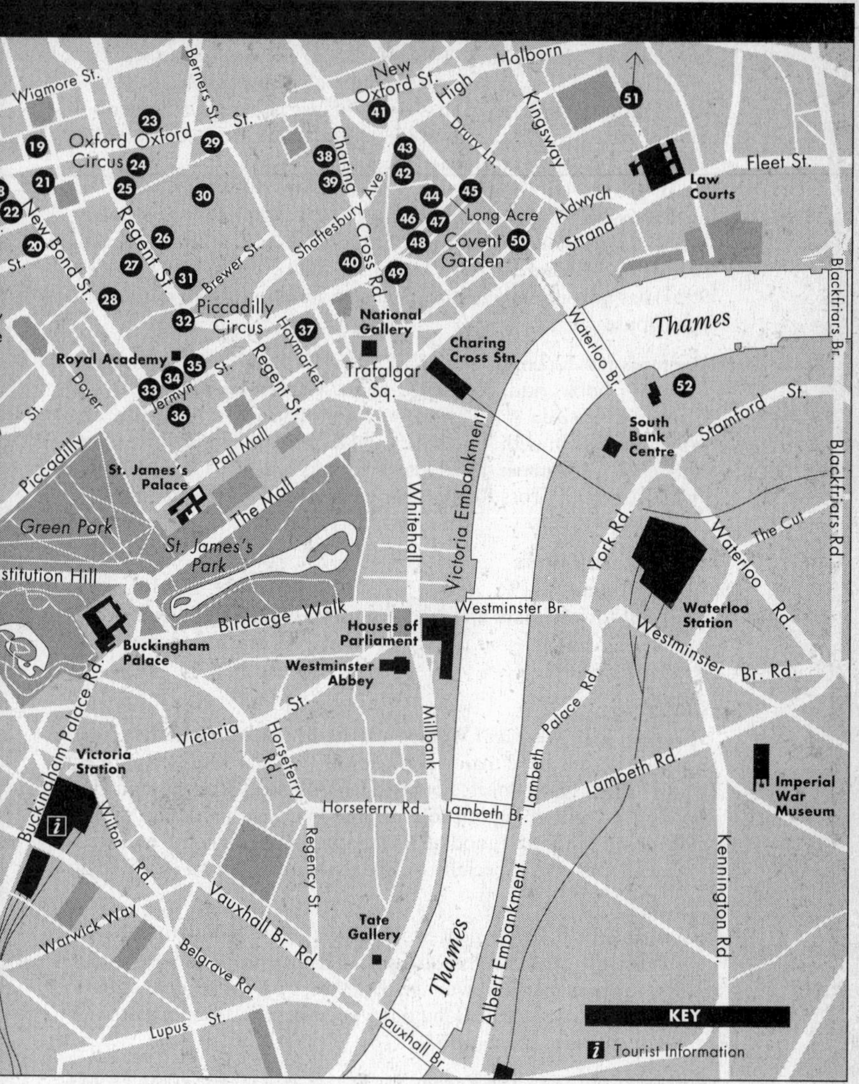

Wigmore St.
Berners St.
New Oxford St.
High Holborn
Kingsway
Drury Ln.
Oxford St.
Oxford Circus
Charing Cross Rd.
Shaftesbury Ave.
Long Acre
Aldwych
Strand
Fleet St.
Law Courts
Covent Garden
New Bond St.
Regent St.
Brewer St.
Piccadilly Circus
Haymarket
National Gallery
Charing Cross Stn.
Thames
Waterloo Br.
Blackfriars Br.
Royal Academy
Dover St.
Jermyn St.
Regent St.
Trafalgar Sq.
South Bank Centre
Stamford St.
Piccadilly
Pall Mall
St. James's Palace
The Mall
Green Park
St. James's Park
Whitehall
Victoria Embankment
York Rd.
Waterloo Rd.
The Cut
Blackfriars Rd.
stitution Hill
Birdcage Walk
Westminster Br.
Waterloo Station
Buckingham Palace
Houses of Parliament
Westminster Abbey
Westminster Br. Rd.
Buckingham Palace Rd.
Victoria St.
Horseferry Rd.
Millbank
Palace Rd.
Lambeth
Victoria Station
Lambeth Rd.
Imperial War Museum
Horseferry Rd.
Lambeth Br.
Wilton Rd.
Regency St.
Albert Embankment
Kennington Rd.
Vauxhall Br. Rd.
Warwick Way
Belgrave Rd.
Tate Gallery
Thames
Lupus St.
Vauxhall Br.
KEY
Tourist Information

every shop is a specialty bookstore. **Bell, Book and Radmell** (✉ No. 4, ☎ 0171/240–2161) has quality antiquarian volumes and modern first editions; **Marchpane** (✉ No. 16, ☎ 0171/836–8661) stocks covetable rare and antique illustrated children's books; **Dance Books** (✉ No. 9, ☎ 0171/836–2314) has—yes—dance books; and **Pleasures of Times Past** (✉ No. 11, ☎ 0171/836–1142) indulges the collective nostalgia for Victoriana. **Forbidden Planet** (✉ 71 New Oxford St., WC1, ☎ 0171/836–4179) is the place for sci-fi, fantasy, horror, and comic books. **Foyles** (✉ 119 Charing Cross Rd. ☎ 0171/437–5660) is especially large, though it has to be the most chaotic and confusing shop in London. **Hatchards** (✉ 187–188 Piccadilly, WC2, ☎ 0171/439–9921) has not only a huge stock; but also a well-informed staff to help you choose.

Stanfords (✉ 12 Long Acre, WC2, ☎ 0171/836–1321) is the place for travel books and, especially, maps. **Waterstone's** (✉ 121–125 Charing Cross Rd., ☎ 0171/434–4291) is part of an admirable, and expanding, chain with long hours and a program of author readings and signings. **Zwemmer** (✉ 24 Litchfield St., WC2, ☎ 0171/240–4158), just off Charing Cross Road, is for art books, with various specialist offshoots.

China and Glass

Thomas Goode (✉ 19 S. Audley St., W1, ☎ 0171/499–2823) has vast ranges of formal china and leaded crystal—including English Wedgwood and Minton—and is not only London's finest, but one of the world's top shops.

Clothing

See also Men's Wear *and* Women's Wear, *below.* Many leading international houses have major branches in London. Most department stores have fashion floors, notably Harrods and Selfridges, and Harvey Nichols is nothing but top fashion. Simpson and Liberty's provide more traditional, good quality clothes. London is still renowned for men's clothing, especially for the exquisite tailoring of the Savile Row masters.

Aquascutum (✉ 100 Regent St., W1, ☎ 0171/734–6090) is known for its classic raincoats, but also stocks the garments to wear underneath, for both men and women. Style keeps up with the times but is firmly on the safe side, making this a good bet for solvent professionals with an antifashion attitude.

Burberrys (✉ 161–165 Regent St., W1, ☎ 0171/734–4060; ✉ 18–22 The Haymarket, SW1, ☎ 0171/930–3343) tries to evoke an English Heritage ambience, with mahogany closets and stacks of neatly folded neckerchiefs alongside the trademark "Burberry Check" tartan, which adorns—in addition to those famous raincoat linings—scarves, umbrellas, and even shortbread tins in the provisions line. **Marks & Spencer** (✉ 458 Oxford St., W1, ☎ 0171/935–7954, and branches) is a major chain of stores that's an integral part of the British way of life—sturdy practical clothes, good materials and workmanship, and basic accessories, all at moderate, though not bargain basement, prices. M&S has never been renowned for its high style, though that is changing as it continues to bring in (anonymously) big-name designers to spice up its ranges. What it *is* renowned for is underwear. All of England buys theirs here. **The Scotch House** (✉ 2 Brompton Rd., SW3, ☎ 0171/581–2151), as you'd guess is the place to buy your kilts, tartan scarves, and Argyll socks without going to Edinburgh. It's also well stocked with cashmere and accessories.

Crafts

Contemporary Ceramics (✉ 7 Marshall St., W1, ☎ 0171/437–7605) has been formed by some of the best British potters as a cooperative venture to market their wares. For thoroughly practical pitchers, plates, and bowls to ceramic sculptures, the prices range from the reasonable to way up. **Contemporary Applied Arts** (✉ 43 Earlham St., WC2, ☎ 0171/836–6993) has a mixed bag of designers and craftspeople displaying their wares over two floors. Anything from glassware and jewelry to furniture and lighting can be found here. **Gabriel's Wharf** (✉ Upper Ground, SE1, ☎ 0171/620–0544) consists of a collection of craftspeople who have set up a cute, brightly painted village near the South Bank Centre, selling porcelain, jewelry, mirrors, clothes, toys, papier-mâché wares and more. In August 1996, the nearby OXO tower gave about 30 further designers workshop and selling space—and London a fabulous river-view restaurant.

Gifts

Fortnum & Mason (✉ 181 Piccadilly, W1, ☎ 0171/734–8040), the queen's grocer, is, paradoxically, the most egalitarian of gift stores, with plenty of irresistibly packaged luxury foods, stamped with the gold "by appointment" crest, for under £5. Try the teas, preserves, blocks of chocolate, tins of pâté, or turtle soup. **General Trading Co.** (✉ 144 Sloane St., SW1, ☎ 0171/730–0411) "does" just about every upper-class wedding gift list, but caters also to slimmer pockets with its merchandise shipped from far shores (as the name suggests) but moored securely to English taste. **Halcyon Days** (✉ 14 Brook St., W1, ☎ 0171/629–8811) specializes in enamelware. It's best known for its precious little pillboxes: These can be adorned with pastoral scenes or Regency dandies or even plain colors, and personalized with initials or messages. **Hamleys** (✉ 188–196 Regent St., W1, ☎ 0171/734–3161) has six floors of toys and games for both children and adults. **Penhaligon's** (✉ 41 Wellington St., WC2, ☎ 0171/836–2150) was established by William Penhaligon, court barber to Queen Victoria. He blended perfumes, soaps, talcs, bath oils, and toilet waters in the back of his shop, using essential oils and natural, often exotic ingredients, and you can buy the very same formulations today. **The Tea House** (✉ 15A Neal St., WC2, ☎ 0171/240–7539) purveys everything to do with the British national drink; you can dispatch your entire gift list here and delight in what the terms "teaphernalia," i.e., strainers, trivets, infusers, and such.

Jewelry

Asprey's (✉ 165–169 New Bond St., W1, ☎ 0171/493–6767) has been described as the "classiest and most luxurious shop in the world." It offers a range of exquisite jewelry and gifts, both antique and modern. **Butler and Wilson** (✉ 20 South Molton St., W1, ☎ 0171/409–2955) has irresistible costume jewelry displayed against dramatic black. Especially strong on diamanté, jet, and French gilt. **Garrard** (✉ 112 Regent St., W1, ☎ 0171/734–7020) has connections with the royal family going back to 1722 and is still in charge of the upkeep of the Crown Jewels. But they are also family jewelers, and offer an enormous range of items, from antique to modern. **London Silver Vaults** (✉ Chancery Lane, ☎ 0171/242–5506) has 36 dealers specializing in antique silver and jewelry in a building that used to be a safety deposit during Queen Victoria's reign. **The Outlaws Club** (✉ 49 Endell St., WC2, ☎ 0171/379–6940) stocks the work of about 100 designers, with prices ranging from a few pounds up to £200. It's pretty avant-garde, and has been a favorite with fashion writers for a decade.

Men's Wear

Favourbrook (✉ 19-21 Piccadilly Arcade, W1, ☎ 0171/491–2337) tailors exquisite, handmade vests and jackets, ties and cummerbunds. There's a range made up for both men and women, or order your own *Four Weddings and a Funeral* outfit. **Herbert Johnson** (✉ 30 New Bond St., W1, ☎ 0171/408–1174) is one of a handful of gentleman's hatters who still know how to construct deerstalkers, bowlers, flat caps, and panamas—all the classic headgear, and Ascot hats for women, too. **Paul Smith** (✉ 41 Floral St., WC2, ☎ 0171/379–7133) is your man if you don't want to look outlandish but you're bored with plain pants and sober jackets. **Turnbull & Asser** (✉ 70 Jermyn St., W1, ☎ 0171/930–0502) is *the* custom shirtmaker. Unfortunately for those of average means, the first order must be for a minimum of six shirts, from about £100 each. But there's a range of less expensive, still exquisitely made ready-to-wear shirts, too.

Prints

Grosvenor Prints (✉ 28–32 Shelton St., WC2, ☎ 0171/836–1979) sells antiquarian prints, with an emphasis on views and architecture of London—and dogs! **The Map House** (✉ 54 Beauchamp Pl., SW3, ☎ 0171/589–4325) has antique maps from a few pounds to several thousand, but the shop also has excellent reproductions of maps and prints, especially of botanical subjects and cityscapes.

Women's Wear

Browns (✉ 23–27 South Molton St., W1, ☎ 0171/491–7833; ✉ 6C Sloane St., SW1, ☎ 0171/493–4232) was the first notable store to populate the South Molton Street pedestrian mall, and seems to sprout more offshoots every time you see it. Well-established, collectible designers (Donna Karan, Romeo Gigli, Jasper Conran, Jil Sander, Yohji Yamamoto) rub shoulder pads here with younger, funkier names (Dries Van Noten, Jean Paul Gaultier, Hussein Chalayan). Its July and January sales are famed. **The Hat Shop** (✉ 58 Neal St., WC2, ☎ 0171/836–6718) is keeping the art of millinery alive and bringing it within reach of the average pocket. The stock here ranges from classic trilbies, toppers, panamas, and matador hats to frivolous tulle-and-feather constructions, with scores of inexpensive, fun toppers in between. **Janet Reger** (✉ 2 Beauchamp Pl., SW3, ☎ 0171/584–9360) is still queen of the silk teddy, having become synonymous with the ultimate in luxurious negligees and lingerie many years ago. **Laura Ashley** (✉ 256–258 Regent St., W1, ☎ 0171/437–9760, and other branches) offers design from the firm founded by the late high priestess of English traditional. The romantic look has received a recent update. **Pellicano** (✉ 63 South Molton St., W1, ☎ 0171/629–2205) stocks only cutting-edge designers, like Brit phenoms Alexander McQueen, Bella Freud, and Sonnentag Mulligan, and the *Vogue*-ier of the internationals (Prada). **Warehouse** (19 Argyll St., W1, ☎ 0171/437–7101, and other branches) stocks practical, directional, reasonably priced separates in easy fabrics and lots of fun colors.

Department Stores

Harrods (✉ 87 Brompton Rd., ☎ 0171/730–1234), one of the world's most famous department stores, can be forgiven its immodest motto, *Omnia, omnibus, ubique* ("everything, for everyone, everywhere"), since it has more than 230 well-stocked departments. Although it's now perhaps less exclusive than its former self, it is still a British institution. The food halls are stunning—so are the crowds! **Harvey Nichols** (✉ 109 Knightsbridge, ☎ 0171/235–5000) is famed for five floors of ultimate fashion—every label you covet is here. (No wonder Edina Monsoon and Patsy Stone in the hit TV comedy *Absolutely Fabulous* regard it as their second home.) It's also known for its restaurant, Fifth Floor. **John Lewis** (✉ 278 Oxford St., ☎ 0171/629–7711) claims as its motto, "Never knowingly undersold." This is a traditional English department store, with a good selection of dress fabrics and curtain and upholstery materials. **Liberty's** (✉ 200 Regent St., ☎ 0171/734–1234), full of nooks and crannies, is like a dream of an eastern bazaar realized as a western store. Famous principally for its fabrics, it also carries Oriental goods, menswear, womenswear, fragrances, soaps, and accessories. **Selfridges** (✉ 400 Oxford St., ☎ 0171/629–1234), London's mammoth upscale version of Macy's, includes a food hall, a branch of the London Tourist Board, a theater ticket counter, and a Thomas Cook travel agency. **Miss Selfridge** (also on Oxford Street, east of Oxford Circus, and other branches) is its outpost for trendy, affordable young women's clothes.

Street Markets

Bermondsey (✉ Tower Bridge Rd., SE1, Fri. 4 AM–2 PM). This is one of London's largest markets, and the one the dealers frequent, which gives you an idea of its scope. The real bargains start going at 4 AM, but there'll be a few left if you arrive later. Take Bus 15 or 25 to Aldgate, then Bus 42 over Tower Bridge to Bermondsey Square; or take the tube to London Bridge and walk.

Camden Passage (✉ Islington, N1, Wed. 7–4 and Sat. 8–5). Hugged by curio stores, the passage drips with jewelry, silverware, and myriad other antiques. Saturday and Wednesday are when the stalls go up; the rest of the week, only the stores are open. Bus 19 or 38 or the tube to the Angel stop will get you there.

Portobello Market (✉ Portobello Rd., W11: fruit and vegetables Mon.–Wed., Fri.–Sat. 8–5, Thurs. 8–1; antiques Sat. 6 AM–5 PM). There are 1,500 antiques dealers trading here, so bargains are still possible. Nearer Notting Hill Gate, prices and quality are highest, with bric-à-brac appearing as you walk toward Ladbroke Grove and the flea market under the Westway and beyond. Take Bus 52 or the tube to Ladbroke Grove or Notting Hill Gate.

LONDON A TO Z

Arriving and Departing

By Bus

National Express buses (☎ 0990/808080)—or coaches, as long-distance services are known—operate from Victoria Coach Station to more than 1,000 major towns and cities. Buses are about half as expensive as the train but trips can take twice as long. **Green Line** buses (☎ 0181/668–7261) cover an area within a 30- to 40-mile radius from London, ideal for excursions. The **Golden Rover** ticket allows unlimited travel for one day (£6).

By Car

The major approach roads to London are motorways (six-lane highways; look for an "M" followed by a number) or "A" roads; the latter may be "dual carriageways" (divided highways), or two-lane highways. Motorways are usually the faster option for getting in and out of town, although rush-hour traffic is horrendous. Stay tuned to local radio stations for regular traffic updates.

By Plane

London is admirably served by two major airports—**Gatwick,** 28 miles to the south, and **Heathrow,** 15 miles to the west—and three smaller ones: Luton, 35 miles northwest; Stansted, 34 miles northeast; and London City, in the Docklands.

U.S. airlines flying to London include **Delta** (☎ 800/241–4141); **TWA** (☎ 800/892–4141); **United Airlines** (☎ 800/241–6522); **USAir** (☎ 800/428–4322); **American Airlines** (☎ 800/433–7300), which also serves Manchester; and **Northwest Airlines** (☎ 800/447–4747), which also serves Glasgow. U.K. airlines with offices in the United States include **British Airways** (☎ 800/247–9297) and **Virgin Atlantic** (☎ 800/862–8621). Flying time is about 6½ hours from New York, 7½ hours from Chicago, and 10 hours from Los Angeles.

BETWEEN THE AIRPORTS AND DOWNTOWN

Heathrow: The quickest and least expensive route into London is via the **Piccadilly Line** of the **Underground** (London's subway system). Trains run every four to eight minutes from all terminals; the 40-minute trip costs £3.10 one-way.

London Transport (☎ 0171/222–1234) runs two bus services from the airport; each costs £6 one-way and £10 round-trip and travel time each direction is about one hour. The A1 leaves for Victoria Station, with stops along Cromwell Road, at Earls Court, and at Hyde Park Corner, every 30 minutes 5:40 AM–8:30 PM. The A2 leaves for Russell Square, with stops at Marble Arch, every 30 minutes 6 AM–9:30 PM.

Gatwick: Fast, nonstop **Gatwick Express** trains leave for Victoria Station every 15 minutes 5:30 AM–9:45 PM; hourly 10 PM–5 AM. The 40-minute trip costs £8.90 one-way. An hourly local train also runs all night.

Speedlink's Flightline 777 bus leaves for Victoria Coach Station every 30 minutes; travel time is about 70 minutes and the cost is £7.50 one-way. A round-trip ticket valid for three months costs £11.

Stansted: London's newest airport, opened in 1991, serves mainly European destinations. The **Stansted Express** to Liverpool Street Station runs every half hour and costs £10 one-way.

By Train

London has 15 major train stations, each serving a different area of the country, all accessible by Underground or bus. Since April 1994, **Railtrack** has been operating all these stations, as well as the tracks countrywide, while **British Rail** still controls all train services (British Rail inquiries, ☎ 0171/387–7070; British Rail Credit Card Bookings, ☎ 0800/450450), until they are sold off as franchises. These major changes in the structure of Britain's railways should not affect the traveler unduly, although nobody can predict exactly what will happen to the fares.

Getting Around

By Bus

In central London, buses are traditionally bright red double- and single-deckers, though there are now many privately owned buses of different colors. Not all buses run the full length of their route at all times; check with the driver or conductor. On some buses you pay the conductor after finding a seat, on others you pay the driver upon boarding. Bus stops are clearly indicated; the main stops have a red LT symbol on a plain white background. When the word "Request" is written across the sign, you must flag the bus down. Buses are a good way of seeing the town, but don't take one if you are in a hurry. Fares start at 90p for short distances.

London is divided into six concentric zones for both bus and tube fares: The more zones you cross, the higher the fare. Regular single-journey or round-trip **One Day Travelcards** (£2.80–£3.80) allow unrestricted travel on bus and tube after 9:30 AM and all day on weekends and national holidays. **LT Cards** (£3.90–£6.50) do not have any restricted times of travel. **Visitor Travelcards** (£3.70) are the same as the One Day Travelcards, but with the bonus of a booklet of money-off vouchers to major attractions (these are also available in the United States, for three, four, and seven days, from BritRail Travel International, 1500 Broadway, New York, NY 10036, ☏ 212/382–3737).

Traveling without a valid ticket makes you liable for an on-the-spot fine (£10 at press time), so always pay your fare before you travel. For more information, stop at an LT Travel Information Centre at the following tube stations: Heathrow, Oxford Circus, Piccadilly Circus, St. James's Park, and Victoria, or call 0171/222–1234.

By Car

The simple advice about driving in London is: don't. Because the city grew as a series of villages, there was never a central street plan, and the result is a chaotic winding mass, made no easier by the one-way street systems. If you must drive in London, remember to drive on the left, and stick to the speed limit.

By Taxi

Hotels and main tourist areas have taxi ranks; you can also flag taxis down on the street. If the yellow "for hire" sign is lit on top, the taxi is available. But drivers often cruise at night with their signs unlit to avoid unsavory characters, so if you see an unlit cab, keep your hand up and you might be lucky. Fares are £1 for the first 582 yards, increasing by units of 20p per 291 yards or 60 seconds. Surcharges are added after 8 PM and on weekends and public holidays. Fares generally increase annually.

By Underground

Known colloquially as "the tube," London's extensive Underground system is by far the most widely used form of city transport. (In Britain, the word "subway" means "pedestrian underpass.") Trains run both beneath and above ground out into the suburbs, and are all one class. There are 10 basic lines—all named—plus the Docklands Light Railway and the East London line, which runs from Shoreditch and Whitechapel across the Thames and south to New Cross. From Monday to Saturday, trains start just after 5 AM and run until midnight or 12:30. On Sunday trains start two hours later and finish about an hour earlier. The maximum wait should be no more than about 10 minutes in central areas. A pocket map is available free from most ticket counters, and there are large maps on the platforms.

Guided Tours

Orientation

BY BUS

Guided sightseeing tours offer passengers a good introduction to the city from double-decker buses, which are open-topped in summer. Tours run daily and depart from Haymarket, Baker Street, Grosvenor Gardens, Marble Arch, and Victoria. You may board or alight at any of about 21 stops to view the sights, and then get back on the next bus. Tickets (£10) may be bought from the driver. Agencies include **Evan Evans** (☏ 0171/930–2377), **Frames Rickards** (☏ 0171/837–3111), **The**

London Underground
UNDERGROUND
Travel Information 071-222-1234
Travelcheck 071-222-1200
Interchange stations
Connections with British Rail
Connections within walking distance
Closed Sundays
Closed Saturdays and Sundays
Served by Piccadilly line early mornings and late evenings Monday to Saturday and all day Sundays
For opening times see poster journey planners
Certain stations are closed during public holidays
Diary 2D 9/90
Key to lines
Bakerloo
Central
Circle
District
East London
Hammersmith & City
Jubilee
Metropolitan
Northern
Piccadilly
Victoria
Docklands Light Railway
Network SouthEast
© Copyright London Regional Transport
River Thames
West Ruislip
Uxbridge
Amersham
Harrow & Wealdstone
Stanmore
Edgware
High Barnet
Mill Hill East
Cockfosters
Walthamstow Central
Ongar
Epping
Hainault
Fairlop
Barkingside
Newbury Park
Ruislip Gardens
South Ruislip
Northolt
Greenford
Perivale
Hanger Lane
Ealing Broadway
Ealing Common
Acton Town
South Ealing
Northfields
Boston Manor
Osterley
Hounslow East
Hounslow Central
Hounslow West
Hatton Cross
Heathrow Terminals 1, 2, 3
Heathrow Terminal 4
Rayners Lane
South Harrow
Sudbury Hill
Sudbury Town
Alperton
Park Royal
North Ealing
West Harrow
Harrow-on-the-Hill
North Acton
West Acton
East Acton
Acton Central
South Acton
Chiswick Park
Turnham Green
Stamford Brook
Ravenscourt Park
Gunnersbury
Kew Gardens
Richmond
Hammersmith
Barons Court
West Kensington
Goldhawk Road
Shepherd's Bush
White City
Latimer Road
Ladbroke Grove
Westbourne Park
Royal Oak
Warwick Avenue
Maida Vale
Kilburn Park
Queen's Park
Kensal Green
Kensal Rise
Willesden Junction
Harlesden
Stonebridge Park
Wembley Central
North Wembley
South Kenton
Wembley Park
Neasden
Dollis Hill
Willesden Green
Kilburn
Brondesbury
Brondesbury Park
West Hampstead
Finchley Road
Finchley Road & Frognal
Swiss Cottage
St. John's Wood
Hampstead Heath
Gospel Oak
Kentish Town West
Belsize Park
Chalk Farm
Camden Town
Camden Road
Kentish Town
Caledonian Road
Holloway Road
Arsenal
Finsbury Park
Drayton Park
Highbury & Islington
Canonbury
Caledonian Road & Barnsbury
Tottenham Hale
Seven Sisters
Blackhorse Road
Dalston Kingsland
Hackney Central
Hackney Wick
Homerton
Stratford
Leyton
Leytonstone
Snaresbrook
South Woodford
Wanstead
Redbridge
Gants Hill
West Ham
Plaistow
Upton Park
East Ham
Barking
Upney
Becontree
Dagenham Heathway
Dagenham East
Elm Park
Hornchurch
Upminster Bridge
Upminster
Bromley-by-Bow
Bow Church
Bow Road
Devons Road
All Saints
Poplar
Mile End
Stepney Green
Whitechapel
Bethnal Green
Shoreditch
Aldgate East
Aldgate
Tower Hill
Tower Gateway
Shadwell
Limehouse
Westferry
Wapping
Rotherhithe
Surrey Quays
New Cross Gate
New Cross
West India Quay
Canary Wharf
Heron Quays
South Quay
Crossharbour
Mudchute
Island Gardens
Greenwich via Foot Tunnel
Blackwall
Brunswick Wharf
Canning Town
Royal Victoria
Custom House
Prince Regent
Royal Albert
Beckton Park
Cyprus
Gallions Reach
Beckton
Silvertown & London City Airport
North Woolwich
Under construction
Paddington
Edgware Road
Marylebone
Baker Street
Great Portland Street
Regent's Park
Warren Street
Euston
Euston Square
Mornington Crescent
King's Cross St. Pancras
Angel
Farringdon
Barbican
Moorgate
Old Street
Liverpool Street
Essex Road
Bank
Monument
Fenchurch Street
Mansion House
Cannon Street
St. Paul's
Chancery Lane
Russell Square
Goodge Street
Holborn
Aldwych
Blackfriars
Temple
Covent Garden
Leicester Square
Tottenham Court Road
Oxford Circus
Bond Street
Marble Arch
Lancaster Gate
Queensway
Bayswater
Notting Hill Gate
Holland Park
Kensington (Olympia)
High Street Kensington
Gloucester Road
South Kensington
Knightsbridge
Hyde Park Corner
Green Park
Piccadilly Circus
Charing Cross
Embankment
Westminster
St. James's Park
Victoria
Sloane Square
Earl's Court
West Brompton
Fulham Broadway
Parsons Green
Putney Bridge
East Putney
Southfields
Wimbledon Park
Wimbledon
Pimlico
Vauxhall
Waterloo
Lambeth North
Elephant & Castle
London Bridge
Borough
Kennington
Oval
Stockwell
Brixton
Clapham North
Clapham Common
Clapham South
Balham
Morden
Thameslink
North London
Waterloo & City

Original London Sightseeing Tour (☎ 0181/877–1722), and **The Big Bus Company** (☎ 0181/944–7810). These tours include stops at places such as St. Paul's Cathedral and Westminster Abbey. Prices and pickup points vary according to the sights visited, but many pickup points are at major hotels.

BY CANAL

During summer, narrow boats and barges cruise London's two canals, the Grand Union and Regent's Canal. Companies include **Jason's Trip** (☎ 0171/286–3428), **London Waterbus Co.** (☎ 0171/482–2550), and **Canal Cruises** (☎ 0171/485–4433). London Waterbus Co. also features weekend cruises throughout the winter from Camden Lock to Little Venice (45 minutes), £3.30 one-way, £4.40 round-trip.

BY RIVER

Boats also cruise the Thames throughout the year. Most leave from Westminster Pier (☎ 0171/930–4097), Charing Cross Pier (☎ 0171/839–3572), and Tower Pier (☎ 0171/488–0344). Downstream routes go to the Tower of London, Greenwich, and the Thames Barrier; upstream destinations include Kew, Richmond, and Hampton Court. Depending upon destination, river trips may last from one to four hours.

Walking Tours

One of the best ways to get to know London is on foot, and there are many guided walking tours from which to choose. **Original London Walks** (☎ 0171/624–3978) has a very wide selection and takes great pride in the infectious enthusiasm of its guides. Other firms include **City Walks** (☎ 0171/700–6931), **Streets of London** (☎ 0181/346–9255), and **Citisights** (☎ 0181/806–4325).

Excursions

London Regional Transport, **Evan Evans,** and **Frames Rickards** all offer day excursions by bus to places within easy reach of London, such as Hampton Court, Oxford, Stratford, and Bath.

Contacts and Resources

Embassies

American Embassy (✉ 24 Grosvenor Sq., W1A 1AE, ☎ 0171/499–9000). **Canadian High Commission** (✉ McDonald House, 1 Grosvenor Sq., W1, ☎ 0171/258–6600).

Emergencies

For police, fire department, or ambulance, dial 999.

The following hospitals have 24-hour emergency sections: **Charing Cross,** ☎ 0181/846–1234; **Royal Free,** Pond St., Hampstead, ☎ 0171/794–0500; **St. Thomas's,** Lambeth Palace Rd., ☎ 0171/928–9292.

Pharmacies

Bliss Chemist (✉ 5 Marble Arch, ☎ 0171/723–6116; ✉ 50 Willesden La., ☎ 0171/624–8000) is open daily 9 AM–midnight.

Travel Agencies

American Express: ✉ 6 Haymarket, ☎ 0171/930–4411; ✉ 89 Mount St., ☎ 0171/499–4436. **Thomas Cook:** ✉ Oxford St., ☎ 0171/493–4537; ✉ 4 Henrietta St., WC2, ☎ 0171/240–4872; ✉ 1 Marble Arch, W1, ☎ 0171/706–4188; and other branches.

Visitor Information

The main **London Tourist Information Centre** at Victoria Station also provides information on the rest of Britain and is open weekdays and Saturday 8–6, Sunday 9–4. There are other TICs in Selfridges (✉ Oxford St., open store hours only) and at Heathrow Airport (Terminals

1, 2, and 3). The **British Travel Centre** (✉ 12 Regent St.), open weekdays 9–6:30 and Saturday 10–4, provides details about travel, accommodations, and entertainment for the whole of Britain. You need to visit the Centre in person to get information. **Visitorcall** is the London Tourist Board's phone service—it's a premium-rate (49p per minute; 39p off-peak) recorded information line, with different numbers for theater, events, museums, sports, getting around, etc. To access the list of options, call 0839/123456, or see the display advertisement in the city phone book. A faxed events calendar is also available (FAX 0839/401278).

3 The Southeast

Canterbury, Dover, Brighton, Tunbridge Wells

Everyone wins in the Southeast. Here you'll find Kent—the "Garden of England"—major English icons, such as Canterbury Cathedral, the white cliffs of Dover, and the Royal Pavilion at Brighton, and everywhere there are villages that have grown drowsy with age. Here, too, is that triumph of civilization, the stately country house in all its splendor. Knole, Hever Castle, Penshurst Place, Sissinghurst—when viewed from afar, they seem to look like old master paintings set on easels.

Updated by Robert Andrews

IN AN ERA WHEN IT HAS BECOME FASHIONABLE to have everything as small as possible—from transistor radios to cameras—the Southeast will inevitably have great appeal to overseas visitors. People from vast countries, visiting England for the first time, journey through this region and take away an impression of rural perfection in miniature. For the portrait, once its grosser elements, the industrial blemishes, have been struck out, shows a land of little features and particular hills; from the air, the tiny fields, neatly hedged, look like a patchwork quilt. On the ground, once away from the fast motorways and commuter tract housing, the Southeast—Surrey, Kent, and Sussex, East and West—reveals some of England's loveliest countryside, punctuated with hundreds of small farms, with gentle, rolling hills and woodlands, and with cathedral towns to be explored and sleepy villages to be discovered.

Though it is one of the most densely populated areas of Britain—the inevitable result of its close proximity to London—the Southeast is, happily, home to Kent, the famous "Garden of England." Here, fields of hops and acre upon acre of orchards that burst into a mass of pink and white blossom in the spring stretch away into the distance. Here, too, are ancient Canterbury, site of the mother cathedral of England, and Dover, whose chalky white cliffs and brooding castle have become veritable symbols of Britain.

A series of famous seaside towns and resorts is ranged along the coasts of Sussex and Kent, the most famous being that picturesque marriage of carnival and culture, Brighton, site of that 19th-century English Xanadu, the Royal Pavilion. "South for Sunshine" has been the slogan of south of England holiday resorts since the early 20th century. And, except for the unaccountable moods that mark English weather the country wide, this area lives up to its watchword. In addition, the coast is home to the busy ports of Newhaven, Folkestone, Dover, and Ramsgate, which have served for centuries as gateways to Continental Europe. Fittingly, the Channel Tunnel now runs from near Folkestone.

Indeed, a great deal of British history has been forged in the Southeast because the English Channel is at its narrowest here. The Romans landed in this area and stayed to rule Britain for four centuries. So did the Saxons (Sussex means "the land of the South Saxons"). William of Normandy defeated the Saxons at a battle near Hastings in 1066. Canterbury has been the seat of the Primate of All England—the archbishop of Canterbury—since Pope Gregory the Great dispatched St. Augustine to convert the heathen hordes of Britain in 597. And long before any of these invaders, the ancient Britons blazed trails that formed the routes for today's modern highways.

Pleasures and Pastimes

Stately Homes

While Britain has a rich heritage of stately homes scattered all over the nation, there is one of the greatest concentrations of ancestral houses in this region. To select just the superlatives: Chartwell was home and is permanent memorial to Sir Winston Churchill; Hever Castle was the abode of Henry VIII's second wife, Anne Boleyn, and was restored in this century by William Waldorf Astor; Ightham Mote is perhaps the most enchanting medieval house in all Europe, a small 14th-century structure surrounded by a moat and, usually, a flock of beautiful swans preening themselves; Knole is one of the largest houses in Europe—more a town than a residence, it's built around seven romantic courtyards; Leeds Castle, pretty as a picture, stands in the middle of a lake; Penshurst Place, dating from 1340, was once home to poet Sir Philip Sidney, whose direct ancestors still live there; and Sissinghurst Castle Garden was made world-famous through the efforts of renowned author Vita Sackville-West.

Dining

Around the coast, seafood—much of it locally caught—is a specialty. If you are in a seaside town, make sure you look for fish and chips. Perhaps "look" isn't the word—just follow your nose! You'll also discover local dishes such as Sussex smokies and some of the most succulent oysters in Britain. In the larger towns, trendy restaurants tend to spring up for a time and then disappear. This is an area in which to experiment.

CATEGORY	COST*
££££	over £50
£££	£30–£50
££	£20–£30
£	under £20

**per person, including first course, main course, dessert, and VAT; excluding drinks*

Lodging

All around this coast, resort towns stretch along beaches, their hotels cheek by jowl. Only a few of the smaller hotels and guest houses remain open throughout the year, as most of them do seasonal business only from Easter to September. Note that some hotels feature all-inclusive rates for a week's stay, which works out cheaper than taking room and meals by the day. Of course, prices rise in July and August, and during the height of the season the seaside resorts can get booked up, especially Brighton and Eastbourne, which are also popular as conference centers.

CATEGORY	COST*
££££	over £150
£££	£80–£150
££	£60–£80
£	under £60

**All prices are for two people sharing a double room, including service, breakfast, and VAT.*

Walking

Ardent walkers can explore both the **North Downs Way** (141 miles) and the **South Downs Way** (106 miles), following ancient paths along the tops of the downs. They both offer wide views over the countryside. The North Downs Way follows in part the ancient Pilgrims' Way to Canterbury. The South Downs Way crosses the chalk landscape of beautiful Sussex Downs, with parts of the route going through deep woodland. You can easily do short sections of both trails. Along the way, there are frequent towns and villages, mostly just off the main trail, all with handy old inns. The two routes are joined (north/south) by the 30-mile **Downs Link.** One way of seeing the Kent coast is to follow the **Saxon Shore Way,** 143 miles from Gravesend to Rye, passing through many historical sites, including four Roman forts. Section-by-section guides are available from the Southeast England Tourist Board.

Exploring the Southeast

Divided into four sections, this chapter begins in the heart of Kent, in the cathedral town of Canterbury, and works its way south to Dover, England's "Continental gateway." It then heads west along the Sussex coast to Brighton, taking in the historic seaside towns along the way. The third itinerary travels west to Chichester, then swings north into Surrey, stopping in Guildford before leading to Tunbridge Wells, where our last excursion begins a final circuit through western Kent and its numerous historic landmarks.

Many of the towns described can easily be reached by public transportation from London for a day trip. Local buses, trains, and sometimes even steam trains provide regular service to most major tourist sites. But if you're especially interested in stately homes or quiet villages, it might be wiser to rent a car and strike out on your own.

Great Itineraries

Though the Southeast is a relatively small and compact region, it is a dense one, packed with interest. Most of the essential sights are contained in and around the towns, while the rustic attractions—castles, country homes, and gardens—invite a more leisurely appreciation. Note that your own transport is essential for some. Since the area lacks many fast roads (unless you're traveling to or from London), and the public transport system is similarly limited, you will need to reckon on a considerable portion of your time spent on the road, though this need not be any kind of hardship if you plan your route to pass through some of the places outlined here. It is most advisable to take aboard a good road map to minimize the amount of time spent in charming but miles-off-the-beaten-track hamlets that baffle your navigation skills.

Numbers in the text correspond to numbers in the margin and on the maps.

IF YOU HAVE 3 DAYS

With three days at your disposal, you should confine your travels to one or two specific areas of the Southeast region. Most tourists would opt for the glories of historic **Canterbury** ① as their first choice. Stay one night here, making the cathedral your priority stop, and spend any extra time meandering through the old streets, taking in the city's secondary sights. For your next two nights, pencil in **Brighton** ㉚, whose Royal Pavilion is a must on any itinerary. Keeping Brighton as your base, you could spend a third day exploring **Lewes** ㉙, with its castle in a commanding position over the town and an impressive collection of Tudor timber-frame buildings scattered along its steep lanes.

IF YOU HAVE 7 DAYS

Seven days or so will allow you to absorb the region's more inaccessible spots and give you the opportunity to unearth some of the Southeast's better-kept secrets. Either on your way to or from **Canterbury** ①, for example, spend half a day at the superbly situated **Leeds Castle** ㊺, whose lovely grounds vie for your attention with the treasures within. Leeds Castle lies a short distance outside **Maidstone** ㊹; not far north of the town, the dockyards at Chatham and the castle and cathedral at neighboring Rochester are equally fascinating and should be a great hit with children of all ages. South of Maidstone, the gardens of **Sissinghurst Castle** ㊼ attract the green-fingered brigade from all over the world, and will convert even those who have never lifted a trowel. To the west, stay for at least an overnight visit to **Royal Tunbridge Wells** ㊽, center of an area rich with magnificent country houses, most notably the medieval manor house **Penshurst Place** ㊾; **Hever Castle** ㊿, indelibly associated with two famous families, the Boleyns of the Tudor era and the Astors of our own; beautiful **Ightham Mote** (53); and **Chartwell** (51), home of Sir Winston Churchill for more than 40 years. One famous structure lies over the Sussex border, the moated **Bodiam Castle** (58), though here the dominant note is abandonment and ruin. A short distance to the southwest, you can visit **Bateman's,** the home of Rudyard Kipling in the historical hamlet of **Burwash** (59), and proceed on to the site of the Battle of Hastings—at **Battle** ㉖, where one of the most momentous events in English history is marked by the atmospheric remains of an abbey founded by William the Conqueror. **Hastings** ㉕ itself is a typical south-coast town where you might consider spending a night. If not, move on to Rye and Winchelsea to the east, or **Pevensey** ㉗ to the west, containing another evocative ruin. From here, drive or take a train to **Brighton** ㉚. Spend one or two nights ambling around the promenades of this sparky seaside town and shopping in the Lanes. Take care not to miss the pretty town of **Lewes** ㉙, just eight miles inland. Westward along the coast, find a hotel in **Arundel** ㊴ or **Chichester** ㊷ in order to explore the area more conveniently: Arundel is dominated by the memorable silhouette of Arundel Castle, while Chichester has a Norman cathedral at the center of town and an impressive Roman villa outside. If you are heading back to London from here, you might pass through **Guildford** ㊹, a commuter town in the county of Surrey with some good 18th-century remnants. Just east of here, **West Clandon** ㊺ features a graceful Italianate palace, and there is more elegant artistry, furniture, and *objets* at the Regency mansion, **Polesden Lacy,** in the nearby village of **Great Bookham** ㊻. From here, it is only 25 miles or so to central London.

When to Tour the Southeast

Because the counties of Kent, Surrey, and Sussex offer some of the most scenic landscape in southern England, lovers of the open air will want to get the most of the outdoor attractions here. And because most of the privately owned castles and mansions are open only between April and September (a few have restricted winter openings), it's best to tour the Southwest in the spring, summer, or early fall. The great parks surrounding the stately houses are often open all year, however. In Canterbury and the seaside towns, you would do well to avoid August, Sundays, and national holidays if you prefer to avoid the hordes, though Sunday at the seaside is the best time to view a great national institution.

CANTERBURY TO DOVER

The ancient city of Canterbury—worldwide seat of the Church of England, shrine of Thomas à Becket, and immortalized in Geoffrey Chaucer's *Canterbury Tales*—is indeed a historic center. Even in prehistoric times, this part of England was relatively well settled. Saxon settlers, Norman conquerors, and the folk who lived here in more settled late medieval times all left their mark—most notably in the city's magnificent cathedral, the Mother Church of England. There are endless excursions to be made through the varied countryside surrounding Canterbury on the road to Dover. Here, the Kentish landscape ravishes the eye with apple blossoms in the spring, the woodlands are colored with primroses and wood anemones and, later, are covered with a mist of bluebells. It is a county of orchards, market gardens, and the typical round, red-roofed oasthouses, used for drying hops.

Canterbury

❶ *56 mi southeast from London.*

The city of Canterbury, cradled in the rolling Kent countryside on the river Stour, is the undisputed star of the Southeast region. Iron Age capital of the kingdom of Kent, headquarters of the Anglican Church, and center of international pilgrimage, Canterbury offers a wealth of historic treasures. It also maintains a lively atmosphere, a fact that has impressed visitors since 1388, when poet Geoffrey Chaucer wrote *The Canterbury Tales,* chronicling the journey from London to the shrine

The Southeast

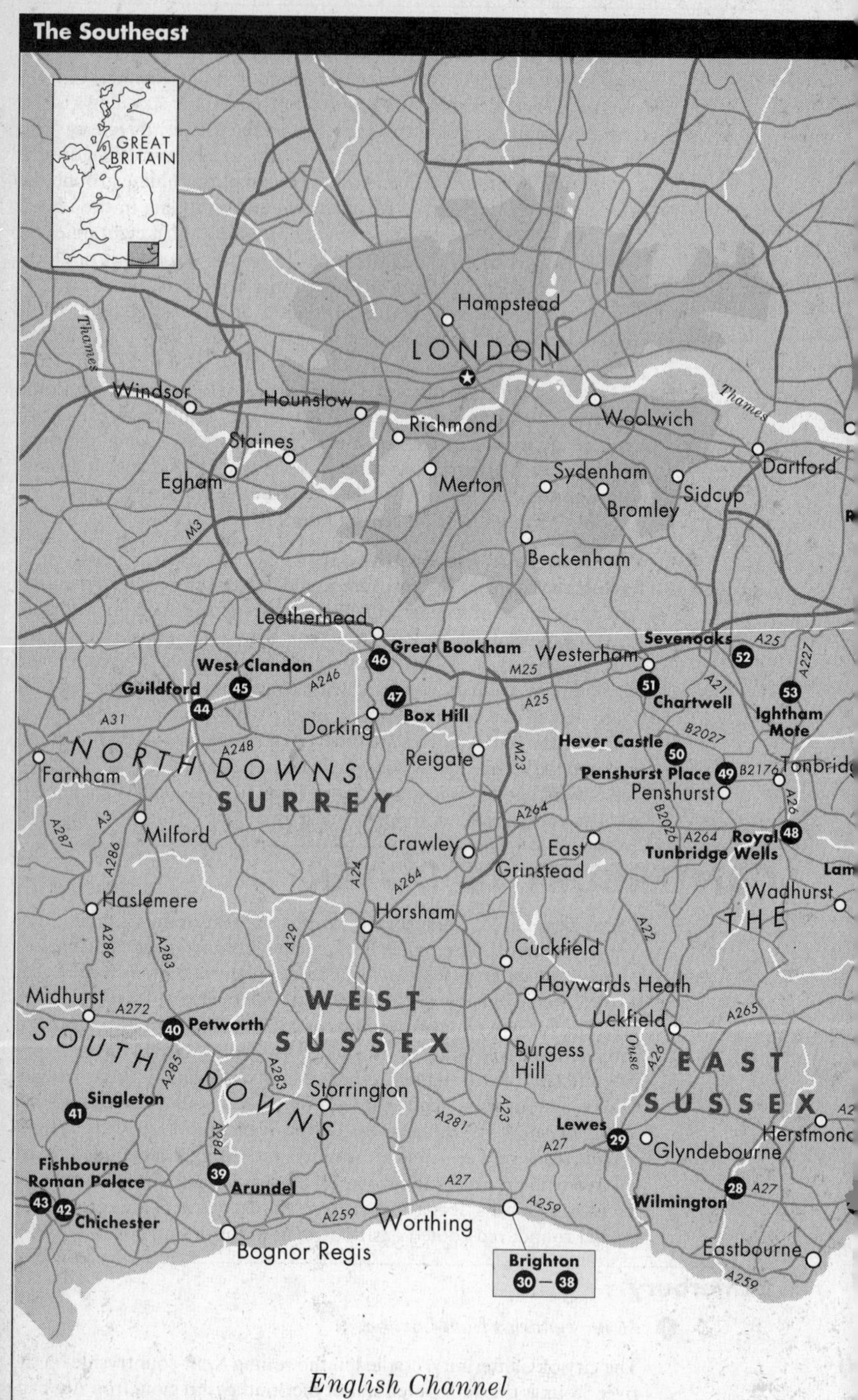

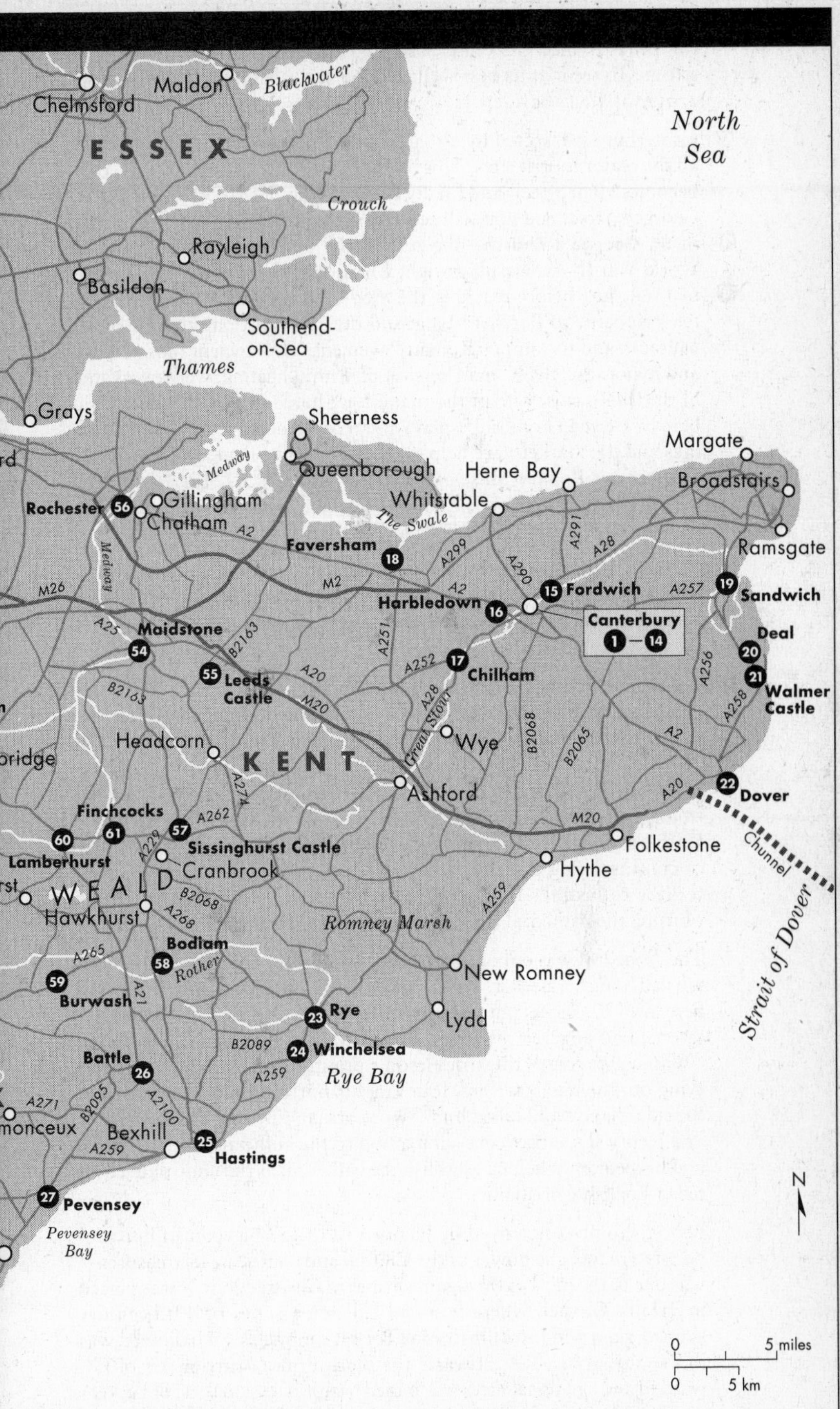
Chelmsford
Maldon
Blackwater
ESSEX
North Sea
Crouch
Rayleigh
Basildon
Southend-on-Sea
Thames
Grays
Sheerness
Margate
Medway
Queenborough
Herne Bay
Broadstairs
Rochester 56
Gillingham
Chatham
Whitstable
The Swale
Ramsgate
Faversham 18
15 Fordwich
19 Sandwich
Harbledown 16
Canterbury 1–14
Maidstone 54
Deal 20
55 Leeds Castle
17 Chilham
21 Walmer Castle
Headcorn
Wye
KENT
Great Stour
Ashford
22 Dover
Finchcocks 61
60
57 Sissinghurst Castle
Folkestone
Lamberhurst
Cranbrook
Hythe
Chunnel
WEALD
Hawkhurst
Romney Marsh
Bodiam 58
Rother
New Romney
Strait of Dover
59 Burwash
23 Rye
Lydd
24 Winchelsea
Battle 26
Rye Bay
Bexhill
25 Hastings
27 Pevensey
Pevensey Bay
0 5 miles
0 5 km
N

of St. Thomas à Becket. Canterbury was one of the first cities in Britain to "pedestrianize" its center, bringing a measure of tranquility to its streets. To see it at its best walk around early, before the tourist buses arrive, or after they depart.

Canterbury is bisected by a road running northwest, beside which lie
all the major tourist sites. This road begins as St. George's Street, then
becomes High Street, and finally turns into St. Peter's Street. At the St.
George's Street end you will see a lone church tower marking the site
❷ of **St. George's Church**—the rest of the building was destroyed in
World War II—where playwright Christopher Marlowe was baptized
❸ in 1564. Just before reaching the modern **Longmarket** shopping center, you come to Butchery Lane and the colorful Canterbury Roman Museum and its famous Roman Pavement. This ancient mosaic floor and hypocaust, the Roman version of central heating, were excavated in the 1940s, just one of the many long-hidden relics that were laid bare by German bombs. Displays and reconstructions of Roman buildings and the marketplace help to re-create the ancient atmosphere. ✉ *Canterbury Roman Museum, Butchery La.,* ☎ *01227/785575.* 🎟 *£1.75; Passport ticket £3.* ⏲ *June–Oct., Mon.–Sat. 10–5, Sun. 1:30–5; Nov.–May, Mon.–Sat. 10–5; last entry at 4.*

Mercery Lane, with its medieval-style cottages and massive, overhanging timber roofs, runs right off High Street and ends in the tiny
❹ ❺ **Buttermarket.** The immense **Christchurch Gate,** built in 1517, leads into
the cathedral close.

★ ❻ **Christchurch Cathedral,** focal point of the city, is the first of England's great Norman cathedrals. Nucleus of worldwide Anglicanism, it is a living textbook of medieval architecture. The building was begun in 1070, demolished, begun anew in 1096, and then systematically expanded over the next three centuries. When the original choir burned to the ground in 1174, it was replaced by a new one, designed in the Gothic style, with tall, pointed arches. Don't be surprised to find a play or concert taking place in the nave; in recent years the dean and chapter (the cathedral's ruling body) have revived the medieval tradition of using the cathedral for occasional secular performances.

The cathedral was only a century old, and still relatively small in size, when Thomas à Becket, the archbishop of Canterbury, was murdered here in 1170. Becket, an uncompromising defender of ecclesiastical interests, had angered his friend Henry II, who was heard to exclaim, "Who will rid me of this troublesome priest?" Thinking they were carrying out the king's wishes, four knights burst in on Becket in one of the side chapels and killed him. Two years later Becket was canonized, and Henry II's subsequent submission to the authority of the Church and his penitence helped establish the cathedral as the undisputed center of English Christianity.

Becket's tomb—destroyed by Henry VIII in 1538 as part of his campaign to reduce the power of the Church and confiscate its treasures—was one of the most extravagant shrines in Christendom. It was placed in **Trinity Chapel**, where you can still see a series of 13th-century stained-glass windows illustrating Becket's miracles. So hallowed was this spot that in 1376, Edward, the Black Prince, warrior son of Edward III and a national hero, was buried near it. The actual site of Becket's murder is down a flight of steps just to the left of the nave. In the corner, a second flight of steps leads down to the enormous Norman undercroft, or vaulted cellarage, built in the early 12th century. Its roof is supported by a row of squat pillars whose capitals dance with fantastic animals and strange monsters.

Buttermarket, **4**
The Canterbury Tales Exhibition, **7**
Christchurch Cathedral, **6**
Christchurch Gate, **5**
Dane John Mound, **14**
Eastbridge Hospital, **9**
Longmarket and Roman Pavement, **3**
Medieval City Walls, **12**
Poor Priests' Hospital/ Canter-bury Heritage Museum, **10**
St. Augustine's Abbey, **13**
St. George's Church, **2**
Weavers' Houses, **8**
Westgate Museum, **11**

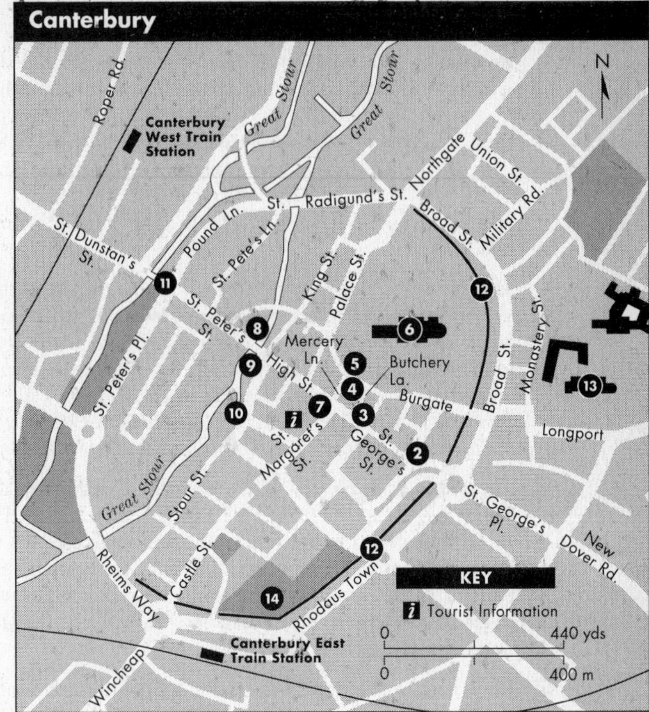

If time permits, be sure to explore the **Cloisters** and other small monastic buildings to the north of the cathedral. The 12th-century octagonal water tower is still part of the cathedral's water supply. As you pass through the great gatehouse back into the city, look up at the sculpted heads of two young figures: Prince Arthur, elder brother of Henry VIII, and the young Catherine of Aragon, to whom he was betrothed. After Arthur's death, Catherine married Henry. Her failure to produce a male heir led to Henry's decision to divorce her after 25 years of marriage, creating an irrevocable breach with the Catholic Church that altered the course of English history.

The cathedral has undergone massive renovation in recent years. In 1993, the paving in most of the interior was relaid. ✉ *Cathedral Precincts,* ☎ *01227/762862.* 🎫 *£2.* ⏲ *Mon.–Sat. 9–5, Sun. 4–5* PM *(open all day Sun. for worship).*

To help bring Canterbury's rich history alive, head to St. Margaret's Street, near the great cathedral, down High Street. Here, in a disused 7 church, you will find a unique and vivid exhibition called **The Canterbury Tales,** which is a dramatization also of 14th-century English life. First you will "meet" Chaucer's pilgrims at the Tabard Inn near London; next you will come to a series of tableaus illustrating five of the tales. Then, passing through a reconstruction of the city gate, you may enter the marketplace. Don't be surprised if one of the figures comes to life: An actor dressed in period costume often forms part of the scene. ✉ *St. Margaret's St.,* ☎ *01227/454888.* 🎫 *£4.50.* ⏲ *Mar.–Oct., daily 9:30–5:30; Nov.–Feb., Sun.–Fri. 10–4:30, Sat. 9:30–5:30.*

NEED A BREAK? If you are hungry on your pilgrimage, try **Il Vaticano** (✉ 35 St. Margaret's St.) for fresh pasta with a wide selection of delicious sauces.

Just past where High Street crosses the little river Stour, you will see
8 a distinctive group of half-timber cottages known as the **Weavers' Houses,** built in the 16th century. These were occupied by Huguenot weavers who settled in Canterbury after escaping religious persecution in France. Before you cross the bridge over the river, stop in at
9 the 12th-century **Eastbridge Hospital.** The hospital (which we would now call a hostel) lodged poor pilgrims who came to pray at the tomb of Thomas à Becket. The infirmary hall, the chapel, and the crypt are open to the public. ✉ *25 High St.* 🎫 *Free.* ⏲ *Mon.–Sat. 10–5, Sun. 11–5.*

The medieval Poor Priests' Hospital is now the site of the comprehen-
10 sive and popular **Canterbury Heritage Museum,** whose exhibits provide an excellent overview of the city's history and architecture. Visit early in the day to avoid the crowds. The hospital building can be found on a street leading off High Street, an extension of St. Peter's Street. ✉ *20 Stour St.,* ☎ *01227/452747.* 🎫 *£1.70.* ⏲ *June–Oct., Mon.–Sat. 10:30–5, Sun. 1:30–5; Nov.–May, Mon.–Sat. 10:30–5; last entry at 4.*

11 The only surviving city gatehouse now contains the **Westgate Museum,** at one end of St. Peter's Street (an extension of High Street). Inside are medieval bric-a-brac and armaments used by the city guard as well as more contemporary weaponry. Climb to the roof to catch a panoramic view of the city spires before walking along the landscaped riverside gardens. ☎ *01227/452747.* 🎫 *70p.* ⏲ *Oct.–Mar., Mon.–Sat. 2–4; Apr.–Sept., Mon.–Sat. 2–5.*

12 For a panoramic view of the town, follow the circuit of the **medieval city walls,** built on the line of the original Roman walls. Those to the south survived intact, towering some 20 feet high. Follow the walkway along the top clockwise, along Broad Street, passing the ruins of
13 **St. Augustine's Abbey.** This is the burial place of Augustine, England's first Christian missionary. The abbey was later seized by Henry VIII, who destroyed some of the buildings and converted others into a royal manor for his fourth wife, Anne of Cleves. Just opposite the Canter-
14 bury East train station, you will see the **Dane John Mound,** originally part of the city defenses.

The Arts

FESTIVALS AND THEATER

Canterbury has a three-week arts festival every October (☎ 01227/452853). The town features two theaters. The **Gulbenkian Theatre** (✉ Giles La., ☎ 01227/769075), part of the University of Kent, mounts a full range of plays, particularly experimental works. The **Marlowe** (✉ St. Margaret's St., ☎ 01227/787787) is named after the Elizabethan playwright, atheist, and spy, who was born in Canterbury.

Dining and Lodging

£ ✕ **Alberry's Wine Bar.** This popular bistro makes a good place to sit and recharge your batteries. Easy to find (on the same street as the tourist office), Alberry's offers a wide, daily-changing selection of inexpensive and hearty soups, salads, and pies. All dishes are conscientiously prepared, using fresh ingredients. Sample the venison casserole, if it's offered, or the turkey and ham pie. Gammon steak is a regular. ✉ *38 St. Margaret St.,* ☎ *01227/452378. AE, MC, V. Closed Sun.*

£££ ✕🏨 **County.** This traditional English hotel was first licensed in the year of the Spanish Armada, 1588, and it still maintains certain links with the past—ask for a room with a four-poster bed. The bar is pleasantly traditional, and the formal **Sully's Restaurant** has a reputation as a gourmet's choice. The hotel offers special weekend rates. ✉ *High St.,*

CT1 2RX, ☎ 01227/766266, FAX 01227/451512. 73 rooms with bath. Restaurant (reservations essential, jacket and tie), bar, coffee shop. AE, DC, MC, V.

££ **Pointers.** This friendly hotel in a Georgian building is within easy walking distance of the cathedral and city center (straight out beyond Westgate). ✉ *1 London Rd., CT2 8LR, ☎ 01227/456846, FAX 01227/831131. 13 rooms, 11 with bath or shower. Restaurant, bar, parking. AE, DC, MC, V. Closed Dec. 24–mid-Jan.*

£ **Zan Stel Lodge.** Canterbury offers plenty of choices when it comes to B&Bs; this is one of the best values. Right next to the Kent county cricket ground and backed by a walled garden, it's a tranquil place to stay. The house itself is spick-and-span and has some lovely examples of stained glass. The only drawback might be the 15-minute walk into town. ✉ *140 Old Dover Rd., CT1 3NX, ☎ 01227/453654. 4 rooms, 2 with bath or shower. No credit cards.*

Shopping

National Trust Shop (✉ 24 The Burgate, ☎ 01227/457120) stocks the National Trust line of household items—ideal for gifts.

Fordwich

15 *1½ mi east of Canterbury.*

Before beginning your wide, counterclockwise tour of the region around Canterbury, drive to the village of Fordwich. This was originally the river port for Canterbury, where the Caen stone quarried in Normandy and shipped across the Channel to be used in the construction of the cathedral was brought ashore.

Harbledown

16 *1 mi west of Canterbury.*

Along the Roman road to London (now A2), lies the village of Harbledown with its cluster of almshouses. Built in the 11th century to house the poor, they provide a scenic backdrop for this peaceful hamlet. Harbledown was customarily the spot from which pilgrims caught their first glimpse of Canterbury Cathedral.

Chilham

17 *5 mi southwest of Canterbury.*

The hilltop village of Chilham lies midway between Canterbury and Ashford on the A252 (off the A28). Energetic visitors will find this a good place from which to walk the last few miles of the traditional Pilgrim's Way back to Canterbury. The Chilham village square is filled with textbook examples of English rural architecture. The 14th-century church contains an old school desk covered with carved initials from the early 18th century onward. Nearby, **Chilham Castle** has 25 acres of gardens landscaped by "Capability" Brown with formal terraces and superlative views. On public holidays in the summer, the **Chilham Castle Gardens** are the setting for medieval jousting and demonstrations of falconry. *☎ 01227/730319. £2.50. Apr.–mid-Oct., daily 11–5.*

NEED A BREAK? The **White Horse,** a 16th-century inn nestled in the shadow of Chilham's church, offers a pleasant beer garden and wholesome afternoon and evening meals; there's a log fire in winter.

Faversham

18 *9 mi west of Canterbury, 11 mi northwest of Chilham.*

In Roman times, Faversham was a thriving seaport. Today the port is hidden from sight, and you could pass through the town without knowing it was there, but the town is a must for those in search of a picture-postcard English village: The town center with its Tudor houses grouped around the market hall looks like a perfect stage set.

NEED A BREAK? The **Sun Inn** on West Street is the flagship of the Shepherde Neame Brewery chain, established in Faversham in the 17th century. The pub dates back to the 16th century. The inn follows the local tradition of hanging up hops in September; they are not only decorative, but add a distinctive fragrance.

Dining and Lodging

£££ ✕ **Read's.** Just outside Faversham, this restaurant is quite a find. The food, mainly modern British in character, is magnificent, the work of chef-proprietor David Pitchford. In elegant surroundings he presents cuisine to challenge the serious eater. The regularly changing menu features a selection of prix-fixe meals, with four courses at lunch, six at dinner, all prepared with great assurance and sensitivity—for instance, sautéed herring roes with parsley butter, medallions of venison fillet on a poivrade sauce with kumquats and braised chestnuts, or noisettes of Romney Marsh lamb. The wine list contains some unusual bottles. This is an excellent spot for lunch, when there's a set menu from £16.50. ✉ *Painters Forstal (2¼ mi southwest of Faversham off A2),* ☏ *01795/535344. AE, DC, MC, V. Closed Sun.–Mon. and last 2 wks in Aug.*

£ ★ ✕🏨 **White Horse Inn.** Just outside Faversham on the old London-to-Dover road (now A2), this 15th-century coaching inn retains much of its traditional character, although it has been fully and comfortably modernized. There's a friendly bar and an excellent restaurant with daily specials supplementing an à la carte menu. The back rooms are the quietest. ✉ *The Street, Boughton ME13 9AX,* ☏ *01227/751343,* FAX *01227/751090. 12 rooms with bath or shower. Restaurant (reservations essential), bar. MC, V.*

En Route From Faversham you can either take A299 north to the seaside towns of **Whitstable, Herne Bay, Margate, Broadstairs,** and **Ramsgate**—long the playground of vacationing Londoners. Charles Dickens wrote glowingly of the bracing freshness of Broadstairs, where he spent many summers (1837–51). A number of houses record the fact that he lived in them. Bleak House is not the setting for the novel of that title, but is open to the public in the summer, and each year in June a Dickens Festival is organized in this town, with local people donning Dickensian dress. Instead of exploring such seaside resorts, you may wish to take A2 through Canterbury to pick up A257 for the ancient **Cinque Ports** (pronounced "sink" ports) lining the eastern and southern coast. These offer much in the way of history and atmosphere and are generally much less crowded than the resort towns. The ports, originally five in number (hence *cinque,* from the Norman French), were Sandwich, Dover, Hythe, Romney, and Hastings. They were granted considerable privileges and powers of self-government in the Middle Ages in return for providing armed patrols—the legendary "Wooden Walls"—of the English Channel against the threat of French or Spanish invasion.

Sandwich

19 *12 mi east of Canterbury, 8 mi south of Ramsgate.*

Sandwich still preserves its Tudor air. The 16th-century barbican (gatehouse) beside the toll bridge is one of the town's oldest surviving buildings. The 16th-century **Guildhall** has its small museum of local history, open to visitors when the court is not in session.

Deal

20 *8 mi northeast of Dover, 7 mi south of Sandwich.*

The large seaside town of Deal is famous in history books as the place where Caesar's legions landed in 55 BC, and from here William Penn set sail in 1682 on his first journey to America. **Deal Castle,** erected in 1540 and built in an intricate design of concentric circles, is the largest of the coastal defenses built by Henry VIII. Cannons perched on the battlements overlook the gaping moat. The castle museum offers a range of exhibits of prehistoric, Roman, and Saxon Britain. ✉ *Victoria Rd.,* ☎ *01304/372762.* 🎟 *£2.80.* ⏲ *Apr.–Oct., daily 10–6 or dusk; Nov.–Mar., Wed.–Sun. 10–4.*

Walmer Castle

21 *7 mi northeast of Dover, 1 mi south of Deal.*

Walmer Castle, one of Henry VIII's fortifications, was converted in 1730 into the official residence of the lord warden of the Cinque Ports, and now has the atmosphere of a cozy country house. Among the famous lord wardens once in residence were the Duke of Wellington, hero of the Battle of Waterloo, who lived here from 1829 until his death here in 1852 (there's a small museum of Wellington memorabilia), and Sir Winston Churchill. The present lord warden is the Queen Mother, though she rarely stays here. After you have seen the castle chambers, take a stroll in the gardens. The moat has been converted to a grassy walk flanked by flower beds. ☎ *01304/364288.* 🎟 *£3.80.* ⏲ *Apr.–Oct., daily 10–6 or dusk; Nov.–Mar., Wed.–Sun. 10–4.*

Dover

22 *78 mi east of London, 7 mi south of Walmer Castle on A258.*

Dover has been for centuries Britain's historic gateway to Europe. Many visitors find the town disappointing; the savage bombardments of World War II and the shortsightedness of postwar developers have ★ left their scars on the city center. But **Dover Castle,** towering high above the chalk ramparts of the famous White Cliffs, is a spectacular sight and well worth a visit. It was one of the mightiest medieval castles in Western Europe. Most of the castle dates back to Norman times. It was begun by Henry II in 1181 but incorporates additions from almost every succeeding century, and was still in use as a defense during World War II. A museum offers an interesting range of exhibits, one of them a large-scale model of the Battle of Waterloo. ✉ *Castle Rd.,* ☎ *01304/211067.* 🎟 *£6.* ⏲ *Apr.–Oct., daily 10–6 or dusk; Nov.–Mar., Wed.–Sun. 10–4.*

Before you leave Dover, visit the 14th-century **Maison Dieu Hall,** in the town hall. It was founded in 1221 as a hostel for pilgrims traveling to Canterbury. A museum houses a varied collection of flags and armor, while the stained-glass windows tell the story of Dover through the ages. ✉ *Biggin St.,* ☎ *01304/201200.* 🎟 *Free.* ⏲ *Mon.–Sat. 10–4:30, Sun. 2–4:30; closed Mon.–Tues. in winter.*

Lodging

£ **Number One.** This popular guest house is a great bargain. A corner terrace home built at the beginning of the 19th century, it's cozy and friendly, decorated with mural wallpapers and porcelain collections. The walled garden offers a view of the castle, and the owners are happy to give advice on local sightseeing. ✉ *1 Castle St., CT16 1QH,* ☎ *01304/202007. 6 rooms with bath or shower. Parking. No credit cards.*

ALONG THE SOUTH COAST: FOLKESTONE TO LEWES

From Dover, the coast road winds through Folkestone, genteel resort and small port, across Romney Marsh—reclaimed from the sea and famous for its sheep and, at one time, its ruthless smugglers—to the town of Rye. The region—noted for Lamb House, the pretty town of Winchelsea, and the history-rich sites of Hastings and Lewes—is partly serviced by one of the three steam railroads in the Southeast, the Romney, Hythe, and Dymchurch Railway, a main-line service in miniature with locomotives one-third normal size. In addition to delighting tourists, some lucky children use it regularly to travel to school.

Rye

★ 23 *68 mi southeast of London, 34 mi southwest of Dover.*

With cobbled streets and timbered dwellings, Rye remains an artist's dream, dotted with such historic buildings as the Mermaid Inn, a collector's piece with its oak paneling, beamed ceilings, huge fireplaces, curious staircases, and secret places that made it a smuggler's strategic retreat. In fact, the former port of Rye now lies nearly 2 miles inland. Its steep hill provides dramatic views of the surrounding countryside. The medieval **Landgate,** one of three city gates, and the 13th-century **Ypres Tower**—part of the original 13th-century fortifications—remain intact. The tower, also known as Rye Castle, contains the town's museum, which has a collection of local prints, drawings, and pottery, as well as one of the oldest fire engines in the world. The tower is scheduled to undergo restoration work throughout 1996, but should be open in 1997. ✉ *Gungarden,* ☎ *01797/226728.* 🎫 *£1.50.* ⏲ *Apr.–Oct., daily 10:30–5:30; Nov.–Mar., weekends 11:30–3:30.*

Sharing the Rye Heritage Centre with the tourist information office, the **Rye Town Model** is a huge scale model of the town incorporating an imaginative and historic *son et lumière* show. The building is at the bottom of Mermaid Street on the site of the ancient port. ✉ *Strand Quay,* ☎ *01797/226696.* 🎫 *£2.* ⏲ *Apr.–Oct., daily 10–5:30; Nov.–Mar., weekdays 10–3, weekends 10–4 (shows on the ½ hr).*

Lamb House, an early Georgian structure, has been home to several well-known writers. The most famous was the American Henry James, who lived here from 1898 to 1916; a later resident was E.F. Benson, author of the "Lucia" novels. The ground-floor rooms contain some of James's furniture and personal belongings. There is also a pretty walled garden. ✉ *West St.,* ☎ *01892/890651.* 🎫 *£2.20.* ⏲ *Apr.–Oct., Wed. and Sat. 2–6, last admission 5:30.*

Dining and Lodging

£–££ ★ ✕ **Landgate Bistro.** Although definitely a bistro, with all its liveliness and bustle, the Landgate is serious about its food. It has won awards—and deserved them. Try the scallops and brill in an orange and vermouth sauce—all the local fish is excellent—or the walnut and treacle tart. In an old, small building, in keeping with Rye's atmosphere, the restaurant attracts a steady local clientele. A fixed-price menu is available Tuesday through Thursday. ✉ *5–6 Landgate,* ☏ *01797/222829. AE, DC, MC, V. No lunch. Closed Sun.–Mon.*

£££ ✕🏨 **The Mermaid.** This classic old inn has served this ancient town for nearly six centuries; it was once the headquarters of one of the notorious smuggling gangs that ruled Romney Marsh. Its age can be seen in every nook and cranny, with sloping, creaky floors, oak beams and low ceilings, a huge open hearth in the bar, and five four-poster beds. Every detail in this inn will make the seeker of atmosphere very happy. But be warned, the Mermaid is *very* popular with tourists. ✉ *Mermaid St., TN31 7EU,* ☏ *01797/223065,* FAX *01797/225069. 28 rooms, 25 with bath. Restaurant. AE, DC, MC, V.*

£ 🏨 **Jeake's House.** The cozy bedrooms in this lovely old house (1689), on the same cobblestone street as the Mermaid, are furnished with antiques, and many have views over the town. Breakfast is served in a former chapel. ✉ *Mermaid St., TN31 7ET,* ☏ *01797/222828,* FAX *01797/222623. 12 rooms, 10 with bath or shower. MC, V.*

Winchelsea

24 *71 mi southeast of London, 2 mi southwest of Rye.*

Like Rye, perched atop its own small hill amid farmland and tiny villages, Winchelsea is one of the prettiest villages in the region. Like Canterbury, it has a splendid church built with stone from Normandy. The town was built on a grid system devised in 1283, after the sea destroyed an earlier settlement at the foot of the hill, then receded, leaving the town high and dry. Some of the original town gates still stand.

NEED A BREAK? The 18th-century **New Inn** in Winchelsea is an excellent place to stop for a pub lunch. It also has six inexpensive bedrooms (☏ 01797/226252).

Hastings

25 *68 mi southeast of London, 9 mi southwest of Winchelsea.*

Hastings, famous for the Norman invasion of 1066, is now a large, slightly run-down seaside resort. A visit to the old town provides an interesting overview of 900 years of English maritime history. Along the beach, the tall wooden **Net Shops**, unique to the town, are used for drying local fishermen's nets. And in the town hall you'll find the 250-foot **Hastings Embroidery**, made in 1966 to mark the 900th anniversary of the battle. It depicts legends and great moments from British history. ✉ *Queen's Rd.,* ☏ *01424/781066.* 🎟 *£1.50.* ⏲ *Oct.–Apr., weekdays 11:30–3 (last admission); May–Sept., weekdays 10–4:30 (last admission).*

All that remains of **Hastings Castle**, built by William the Conqueror in 1069, are fragments of the fortifications, some ancient walls, and a number of gloomy dungeons. Nevertheless, it is worth a visit—especially for the excellent view it provides of the chalky cliffs, the coast, and the town below. ✉ *West Hill,* ☏ *01424/717963.* 🎟 *£2.60.* ⏲ *Apr.–Sept., daily 10–5; Feb.–Mar., daily 11–4.*

Dining and Lodging

££ ✕ **Rösers.** This restaurant takes food very seriously. It stands on the seafront and has dark walls with booths for dining. Chef-proprietor Röser is German, though his cuisine is mainly French. Try the game sausages with wild boar bacon, or the chicken breasts with wild mushrooms. The desserts are scrumptious, especially the Belgian chocolate mousse. There are reasonably priced set menus and an extensive wine list. ✉ *64 Eversfield Pl., St. Leonards,* ☎ *01424/712218. AE, DC, MC, V. No lunch Sat. Closed Sun.–Mon.*

£ **Eagle House.** This guest house, in a large detached Victorian building, is surrounded by its own attractive garden. In St. Leonards, the western section of Hastings, the lodging is within easy reach of the town center. The rooms are spacious and comfortable, and the dining room uses fresh produce from local farms. ✉ *12 Pevensy Rd., St. Leonards TN38 0JZ,* ☎ *01424/430535,* FAX *01424/437771. 19 rooms with bath. Restaurant. AE, DC, MC, V.*

Battle

26 *61 mi southeast of London, 7 mi northwest of Hastings.*

Battle is the actual site of the crucial Battle of Hastings. The ruins of **Battle Abbey,** the great Benedictine abbey William erected after his victory, are worth the trip. The high altar stood on the spot where the last Saxon king, Harold II, was killed. Though the abbey was destroyed in 1539 during Henry VIII's destructive binge, you can wander across the battlefield and see the remains of many of the domestic buildings. The **Abbot's House** (closed to the public) is now a girls' school. ✉ *High St.,* ☎ *01424/773792.* *£3.50.* *Apr.–Sept., daily 10–6; Oct.–Mar., daily 10–4.*

Dining and Lodging

££ ✕ **Orangery Restaurant.** In the Powder Mills Hotel, a Georgian country house just behind the abbey, the airy conservatory-style dining room makes a pleasant stop for lunch during a day of sightseeing. The food, especially the seafood, is surprisingly good; try the fish panache or the crab ravioli, with a homemade sorbet to follow. Set three-course menus are priced at £14.50 for lunch, £19.95 for dinner. Bar snacks are also available. ✉ *Powdermill La.,* ☎ *01424/772035. AE, DC, MC, V.*

£££ **Netherfield Place.** This is a spacious, quiet hotel, set in 30 acres of park and gardens. The large bedrooms are comfortably furnished, with plenty of cozy armchairs, and have well-equipped bathrooms (towels are especially thick). The paneled restaurant looks out at the gardens and features sensible fixed-price menus, as well as extensive table d'hôte ones. Try the salmon and sole terrine, the Sussex lamb, local venison, and the home-grown vegetables. ✉ *Netherfield, TN33 9PP,* ☎ *01424/774455,* FAX *01424/774024. 14 rooms with bath. Restaurant, tennis, croquet. AE, DC, MC, V.*

Pevensey

27 *61 mi southeast of London, 11 mi southwest of Battle.*

Off the A259, Pevensey was an important Roman settlement (called Anderida) and was where William the Conqueror landed. The town is dominated by the extensive remains of **Pevensey Castle,** once an important Norman stronghold. Its massive outer walls, built by the Romans, enclose a smaller castle built in the early 1100s by Count Robert de Mortain, William's half brother. Inside, you will notice 20th-century machine-gun emplacements added in 1940 against a possible German invasion. ☎ *01323/762604.* *£2.* *Apr.–Oct., daily 10–6 or dusk; Oct.–Mar., Wed.–Sun. 10–4.*

Drusilla's Park has a miniature railroad and adventure playground. ✉ *Alfriston, East Sussex,* ☎ *01323/870656.* 🎟 *£5.50.* ⏲ *Daily summer 10–6, winter 10–4.*

Dining

£££–£££ ★ ✕ **The Sundial.** In the village of Herstmonceaux—site of one of England's most impressive castles (government property and closed to the public, unfortunately)—this old Sussex farmhouse, skillfully enlarged, is the setting for a popular restaurant, which chef Giuseppe Bertoli and his French wife, Laurette, have run since 1966. The menu is extensive, with some imaginative combinations. The fish dishes are particularly successful and the vegetables fresh and expertly cooked. The Dover sole flavored with thyme is recommended. ✉ *Gardner St., Herstmonceaux (6 mi north of Pevensey),* ☎ *01323/832217. AE, DC, MC, V. No dinner Sun. Closed Mon.*

Wilmington

28 *7 mi west of Pevensey on A27.*

While passing through the pretty village of Wilmington, you will have no trouble identifying its most famous landmark. High on the downs above the village a giant white figure, 226 feet tall, known as the **Long Man of Wilmington,** is carved into the chalk; he has a club in either hand. His age is a subject of great debate, but because Roman coins bearing a similar figure have been found in the neighborhood, he might originate from Roman times.

Lewes

★ 29 *54 mi south of London, 18 mi west of Pevensey, 8 mi northeast of Brighton.*

Lewes is a town so rich in architectural history that the Council for British Archaeology has named it one of the 50 most important English cities. Today Lewes is a place to walk in rather than drive in, not least so that the period architecture can be appreciated and the secret lanes behind the castle with their huge beeches can be enjoyed. Here and there, along the picturesque winding streets, you'll find exceptional antiques shops and secondhand-book dealers. **High Street** is lined with old buildings of all descriptions, dating from the late Middle Ages onward, including a timber-frame house once occupied by Thomas Paine, author of *Common Sense.*

High above the valley of the river Ouse, and towering over the town so that, originally, the Normans could keep a more efficient eye on the conquered English, stand the majestic ruins of **Lewes Castle,** an early Norman edifice, begun in 1100. For a panoramic view of the surrounding region, climb the keep and look out from the top. The **Living History Centre** has been moved inside the castle; at Barbican House you can see the Town Model. ✉ *169 High St.,* ☎ *01273/486290.* 🎟 *£2.40.* ⏲ *Mon.–Sat. 10–5, Sun. 11–5; closed Dec. 25.*

Lewes is one of the few towns left in England that still celebrates in high style Guy Fawkes Night (Nov. 5), the anniversary of Guy Fawkes's attempt to blow up the Houses of Parliament in 1605. It is rather like an autumnal Mardi Gras, with costumed processions and flaming tar barrels rolled down the steep High Street.

Dining and Lodging

£ ✕ **Léonies.** This friendly restaurant-cum-bistro is in a big converted shop by the war memorial on High Street. It has greenery, polished wood floors, and bentwood chairs. The food is hearty—try the boeuf bourguignon or the rabbit-and-prune stew. ✉ *197 High St.,* ☎ *01273/487766. AE, MC, V. No dinner Tues. Closed Sun.–Mon.*

£££ ✗ 🏨 **Horsted Place.** Just a few minutes' drive from Glyndebourne, and ★ 6 miles north of Lewes, this very special hotel once belonged to Prince Philip's treasurer, and it frequently accommodated the queen and other members of the royal family. It is still beautifully furnished and has such interesting features as a magnificent Victorian staircase and a Gothic library with a secret door that leads to a hidden courtyard. The dining room—Gothic like the library—offers superb haute cuisine (try the roasted guinea fowl). ✉ *Little Horsted (2½ mi from Uckfield, 6 mi north of Lewes), TN22 5TS,* ☎ *01825/750581,* FAX *01825/750459. 17 rooms with bath. Restaurant, indoor pool, tennis, golf. AE, DC, MC, V.*

£££ 🏨 **Shelleys.** An elegant 17th-century building in this town of attractive architecture, the hotel is on the hilly main road and is a traditional overnight stop for visitors to the opera at Glyndebourne. Many antiques are scattered about, the wisteria on the facade is splendid in season, and the garden is a constant joy. The hotel maintains a reputation for old-fashioned, friendly service. Have lunch in either the bar or the more formal dining room. ✉ *High St., BN7 1XS,* ☎ *01273/472361,* FAX *01273/483152. 19 rooms with bath. Restaurant, bar. AE, DC, MC, V.*

The Arts

Glyndebourne Opera House (✉ Glyndebourne, near Lewes, East Sussex, ☎ 01273/812321) is one of the world's leading opera houses. Nestled beneath the downs and surrounded by superb gardens, Glyndebourne combines excellent productions with its lovely setting. Seats are *very* expensive but worth every cent to the aficionado. The rebuilt auditorium, opened in 1994, seats a slightly larger audience than the original house and is equipped with the latest in stage gadgetry and backstage facilities. Tickets are even more difficult to get than before.

To head for the nearest city on leaving Lewes, continue west on A27 for 8 miles until you reach Brighton.

BRIGHTON TO DORKING

The self-proclaimed belle of the coast, Brighton is a friendly, garish old-new sprawl. It started as a tiny fishing village called Brighthelmstone, with no claim to fame until a certain Dr. Russell sent his patients there for its dry, bracing, crystal-clear air. The Prince Regent, later George IV, went, discovered sea-bathing, and for nearly 200 years, the place prospered—deservedly so, for few British resorts have ever catered so well as Brighton to its appreciative patronage from London and the world over. Today, the city is an odd mixture of carnival and culture, but it contains one of the must-sees of Britain—the gorgeous and fantastic palace known as the Royal Pavilion. Built mainly by John Nash in a mock Oriental manner with domes and pinnacles abounding, the Royal Pavilion has never failed to shock and delight in equal measure. After taking in that Regency-era wonder—and after the children have had their fill of Brighton's funfairs—the road ahead beckons with other great residences, including Arundel Castle, Petworth House, and Polesden Lacey. Along the way, you'll discover the largest Roman villa in Britain, the bustling city of Guildford, and Chichester, whose cathedral, a poem in stone, should captivate anyone.

Numbers in the margin correspond to points of interest on the Southeast and Brighton maps.

Brighton

30 *54 mi south of London, 9 mi southwest of Lewes.*

An article in Britain's *Independent* newspaper summed up the attractions of Brighton this way: "Pleasing decay is a very English taste. It is best indulged in at the seaside, especially off-season, when wind and rain enhance the melancholy romance of cracked stucco, rusting ironwork, and boarded-up shops. Brighton is a supreme example, with its faded glamour combined with raucous vulgarity." Unfortunately, with the ongoing recession, Brighton's decay has accelerated and become a lot less pleasing.

Brighton was mentioned in the *Domesday Book* as Brighthelmstone in 1086, when it paid the annual rent of 4,000 herrings to the lord of the manor; it changed its name in the 18th century. The town owes its modern fame and fortune to the supposed medicinal virtues of seawater. In 1750, physician Richard Russell published a book recommending seawater treatment for glandular diseases. The fashionable world flocked to Brighton to take Dr. Russell's "cure," and sea-bathing became a popular pastime.

The next windfall for the town was the arrival of the Prince of Wales (later George IV), who acted as prince regent during the madness of his father, George III. "Prinny," as he was called, created the Royal Pavilion, an extraordinary pleasure palace that attracted London society. The influx of visitors triggered a wave of villa building. Fortunately this was one of the greatest periods in English architecture. The elegant terraces of Regency houses are today among the town's greatest attractions.

The coming of the railroad set the seal on Brighton's popularity: One of the most luxurious trains in the country, the Pullman *Brighton Belle,* brought Londoners to the coast within an hour. They expected to find the same comforts and recreations they had in London and, as they were prepared to pay for them, Brighton obliged. This helps to explain the town's remarkable range of restaurants, hotels, and pubs. Horse racing was—and still is—another strong attraction.

Although fast rail service to London has made Brighton an important base for commuters, the town has unashamedly set itself out to be a pleasure resort. In the 1840s it featured the very first example of that peculiarly British institution, the amusement pier. Although that first
31 pier is now a rusting wreck, the restored **Palace Pier** follows the great tradition. The original mechanical amusements, including the celebrated flipcard device, "What the Butler Saw," are now exhibits in the town museum, but you can still admire the pier's handsome ironwork.

32 The heart of Brighton is the **Steine** (pronounced "steen"), the large open area close to the seafront. This was a river mouth until the Prince of Wales had it drained in 1793. One of the houses here was the home of Mrs. Maria Fitzherbert, later the prince's wife. The most remarkable building on the Steine, perhaps in all Britain, is unques-
★ 33 tionably the **Royal Pavilion,** the Prince of Wales's extravagant fairytale palace. First planned as a simple seaside villa and built in the fashionable classical style of 1787, the Pavilion was rebuilt between 1815 and 1822 for the prince regent, who favored an exotic, eastern design with Chinese interiors. When Queen Victoria came to the throne in 1837, she so disapproved of the palace that she stripped it of its furniture and planned to demolish it. Fortunately, the Brighton city council bought it from her, and it is now lovingly preserved and recognized as unique in Europe. After a lengthy process of restoration, the Pavilion looks much as it did in its Regency heyday. The in-

Brighton Museum and Art Gallery, **34**
The Lanes, **35**
Marina, **37**
Palace Pier, **31**
Preston Manor, **38**
Royal Pavilion, **33**
Steine, **32**
Volk's Electric Railway, **36**

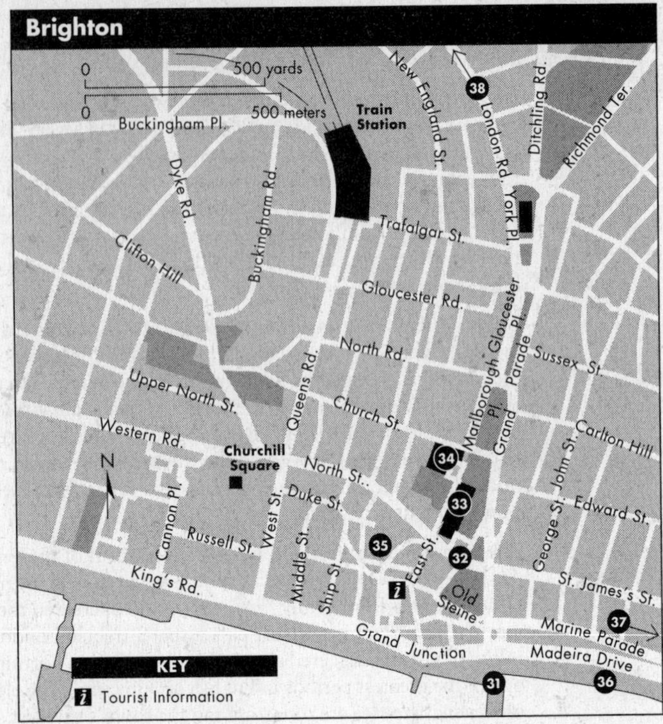

terior is once more filled with quantities of period furniture and ornaments, some given or lent by the present royal family. The two great set pieces are the **Music Room**, styled in the form of an Oriental pavilion, and the **Banqueting Room**, with its enormous flying-dragon "gasolier," or gaslight chandelier, a revolutionary new invention in the early 19th century. Also remarkable are the kitchens, whose ceilings are supported by extraordinary palm-tree columns. The upstairs rooms (once used as bedrooms) contain a selection of cruel caricatures of the prince regent, most produced during his lifetime, and illustrations of the Pavilion at various stages of its construction. Following the decade-long renovation of the palace, attention has now turned to the gardens, which are being restored. ✉ *Old Steine,* ☎ *01273/603005.* 🎫 *£3.95.* ⏲ *Oct.–May, daily 10–5 (last admission); June–Sept., daily 10–6 (last admission).*

NEED A BREAK? One of the elegant upstairs bedrooms in the Pavilion is now a **tearoom,** offering a variety of snacks and light meals.

34 The grounds of Brighton Pavilion contain the **Brighton Museum and Art Gallery,** whose buildings were designed as a stable block for the prince's horses. The museum has especially interesting Art Nouveau and Art Deco collections. ✉ *Church St.,* ☎ *01273/603005.* 🎫 *Free.* ⏲ *Mon.–Tues. and Thurs.–Sat. 10–5, Sun. 2–5.*

35 Just west of the Old Steine lies the **Lanes,** a maze of alleys and passageways that was once home to legions of fishermen and their families. It is said that the name "Lanes" refers to their fishing lines. Today the Lanes is filled with restaurants, boutiques, and, especially, antiques shops. Vehicular traffic is barred from the area, and visitors may wander at will. The heart of the Lanes is Market Street and Square, lined with fish and seafood restaurants.

36 37 If you feel an urge to escape Brighton's summer crowds, take **Volk's Electric Railway** along the Marine Parade to the **Marina.** Built by inventor Magnus Volk in 1883, this was the first public electric railroad in Britain.

38 North of the Brighton town center, on the main London road, is **Preston Manor.** This beautifully preserved gentleman's residence, with its collection of paintings, silver, porcelain, and furniture, evokes the opulence of Edwardian times. The present house was built in 1738, with additions in 1903. You can also wander through the extensive grounds. ✉ *Preston Park,* ☎ *01273/603005, ext. 59.* *£2.85.* ⊙ *Mon. 1–5, Tues.–Sat. 10–5, Sun. 2–5.*

Dining and Lodging

££ ✕ **Donatello.** This popular Italian restaurant in the Lanes has a brick wall and pine decor, bright with plants and checked cloths. The food is standard Italian, with an emphasis on pizzas. Donatello is a brother eatery to Pinocchio's, close to the Theatre Royal. ✉ *3 Brighton Pl.,* ☎ *01273/775477. AE, DC, MC, V.*

£ ★ ✕ **English's Oyster Bar.** Buried in the Lanes, this is one of the few old-fashioned seafood havens left in England. It's been a restaurant for more than 200 years and a family business for more than 50. You can either eat succulent oysters and other seafood dishes at the counter or have a table in the restaurant section. It's keenly priced and ideal for lunch after antiques hunting. ✉ *29–31 East St.,* ☎ *01273/327980. AE, DC, MC, V.*

££££ ✕ **Brighton Thistle Hotel.** This hotel, a little east of the Grand, is built around a huge atrium, with sea views, and is very popular with conference delegates. It's smoothly designed, with an excellent color sense and ultramodern bedrooms, but on the pricey side for what it offers. The restaurant, **La Noblesse,** has delicious food, with not-too-expensive fixed menus. ✉ *King's Rd., BN1 2GS,* ☎ *01273/206700,* FAX *01273/820692. 204 rooms with bath. Restaurant, indoor pool, sauna, exercise room. AE, DC, MC, V.*

££ ✕ **Granville Hotel.** On hotel row, to the west of the Grand, the hotel has been converted from three former grand residences facing the sea. It is moderate in size, so service can be attentive. The bedrooms are all very comfortable; several are quite large, six have four-poster beds, three include Jacuzzis, and one has a waterbed. The restaurant caters especially to vegetarians. ✉ *124 King's Rd., BN1 2FA,* ☎ *01273/326302,* FAX *01273/728294. 23 rooms with bath. Restaurant, bar, coffee shop. AE, DC, MC, V.*

££ ★ ✕ **Topps.** Two Regency houses have been turned into this delightful hotel, run by the owners Paul and Pauline Collins. All the rooms are attractive and well equipped, with lush bathrooms. The atmosphere is relaxed and friendly. The basement restaurant (no dinner Sun. and Mon.), with an interesting fixed-price menu prepared by Pauline Collins, is worth a visit even if you're not staying at the hotel. Fish soup is a regular on the menu. ✉ *17 Regency Sq., BN1 2FG,* ☎ *01273/729334,* FAX *01273/203679. 15 rooms with bath. Restaurant (no lunch, closed Jan.). AE, DC, MC, V.*

££££ **Grand Hotel.** This classic old hotel, on the seafront site of a bomb attack on Prime Minister Margaret Thatcher, has recently been refurbished for the second time in a decade. The decor, especially in the public rooms, is of the spectacular chandelier-and-marble variety, but the bedrooms are traditionally comfortable. The restaurant's formerly good reputation has declined in recent years. ✉ *King's Rd., BN1 2FW,*

☎ *01273/321188,* FAX *01273/202694. 200 rooms with bath. Restaurant, indoor pool, sauna, exercise room, parking. AE, DC, MC, V.*

££ **The Dove.** An alternative if Topps is full, The Dove, next door, is another well-converted Regency house where you will receive a warm welcome from its husband-and-wife owners. There is one large room with a balcony facing the sea, and four of the rooms have a sideways sea view from their bow windows. There is no restaurant, but there is an à la carte breakfast. ✉ *18 Regency Sq., BN1 2FG,* ☎ *01273/779222,* FAX *01273/746912. 10 rooms with bath. AE, DC, MC, V.*

The Arts

The **Brighton Festival** (☎ 01273/676926), an international event held every May, covers drama, music from classical to rock, dance, visual arts, and literature at various venues throughout the city.

Brighton has several theaters. **The Dome** (☎ 01273/674357), beside the Pavilion, was converted into an auditorium from the prince regent's stables in the 1930s. It stages classical and pop concerts. The **Theatre Royal** (✉ New Rd., ☎ 01273/328488), close to the Pavilion, is a very attractive Regency building with a period gem of an auditorium. It is a favorite venue for shows either on their way to or fresh from London's West End. The **Gardner Centre for the Arts** (☎ 01273/685861), on the campus of Sussex University, a few miles northeast of town at Falmer, presents plays, concerts, and cabaret.

Shopping

The main shopping area to head for is **The Lanes,** especially for antiques or jewelry. It also has clothing boutiques, coffee shops, and pubs. Across North Street from the Lanes lie the North Lanes, a network of narrow streets full of interesting little stores, less glossy than those in the Lanes, but sometimes more interesting. **The Pavilion Shop** (✉ 4–5 Pavilion Bldgs., ☎ 01273/603005) next door to the Royal Pavilion not only carries well-designed souvenirs of Regency Brighton, but has high-quality fabrics, wallpapers, and ceramics based on material in the Pavilion itself. **Holleyman and Treacher** (✉ 21A Duke St., at the western edge of the Lanes, ☎ 01273/328007) is a book collector's dream, with a wealth of books on all subjects and a large stock of antique prints at all prices. **Pecksniff's Bespoke Perfumery** (45–46 Meeting House La., ☎ 01273/328904) has an original approach to the art of fragrance. In a room full of wooden drawers and brown glass bottles, an assistant will mix and match ingredients to suit your wishes.

Arundel

39 *60 mi south of London, 23 mi west of Brighton.*

The tiny hilltop town of Arundel is dominated by the great 11th-century castle, much-restored home of the dukes of Norfolk for more than 700 years, and an imposing **Roman Catholic cathedral**—the duke is Britain's leading Catholic peer.

The ceremonial entrance to **Arundel Castle** is at the top of High Street, but visitors can enter at the bottom, close to the parking lot. The keep, rising from its conical mound, is as old as the original castle, while the barbican (gatehouse) and the Barons' Hall date from the 13th century. The interior of the castle was reconstructed in the then-fashionable Gothic style of the 19th century. Among the treasures on view are the rosary beads and prayer book used by Mary, Queen of Scots, at her execution. As is so often the case with a British historic property still in private hands, Arundel Castle has a shabby-genteel air about it. The spacious grounds are open to the public and there is a restaurant. ☎ *01903/883136.* 🎫 *£5.* ⏲ *Apr.–Oct., Sun.–Fri. noon–5 (gates close at 4).*

NEED A BREAK?

The Black Rabbit, an 18th-century pub, is a find (and you must persevere along Mill Road in order *to* find it). Its location by the river, with views of the castle and the bird sanctuary, makes it ideal for a summer lunch. The bar food is good and reasonably priced, and there's a proper seafood restaurant if you want something more substantial.

The Arts

The **Arundel Festival** (☎ 01903/883690) features drama productions and music on the castle grounds for a week in August or September.

Lodging

£££ **Norfolk Arms Hotel.** Like the cathedral and the castle in Arundel, this 18th-century coaching inn was also built by the dukes of Norfolk. The main body of the hotel is traditional in appearance, with lots of narrow passages and cozy little rooms. There is an annex with modern rooms in the courtyard block. ✉ *22 High St., BN18 9AD,* ☎ *01903/882101,* FAX *01903/884275. 34 rooms with bath. Restaurant. AE, DC, MC, V.*

£££ **Stakis Arundel.** Formerly the Avisford Park Hotel, this converted Georgian house is set on 62 acres of parkland, just 3 miles west of Arundel off the A27 on B2132. It began as the home of an admiral and was a private school before its conversion into a hotel in 1974. The rooms have been carefully refurbished, with close attention to detail. The hotel is very popular for conferences. ✉ *Yapton La., Walberton BN18 0LS,* ☎ *01243/551215,* FAX *01243/552458. 127 rooms with bath. Restaurant, indoor and outdoor pools, sauna, 18-hole golf course, squash court, tennis courts, exercise room, croquet, helipad. AE, DC, MC, V.*

Petworth

40 *54 mi south of London, 12 mi northwest of Arundel.*

★ **Petworth House,** one of the National Trust's treasures, stands in a particularly picturesque stretch of Sussex. A near-perfect picture-postcard village, Wisborough Green, leads to the house, built between 1688 and 1696. A 700-acre deer park was added later by the celebrated landscape architect Lancelot "Capability" Brown. The house holds a fine collection of English paintings, including works by Thomas Gainsborough, Sir Joshua Reynolds, Sir Anthony Van Dyck, and J.M.W. Turner, the great proponent of Romanticism, who immortalized Petworth's sumptuous interiors in some of his most evocative watercolors. Other treasures include Greek and Roman sculpture and Grinling Gibbons wood carvings. Restoration work in the old kitchens was completed in 1995, when they were opened to view for the first time since the 1940s. Don't forget to explore the town of Petworth itself, a jewel studded with old, narrow streets and timbered houses. Enjoy a light lunch in the Servants' Block. ☎ *01798/342207.* 🎫 *£4.20.* ⏲ *Apr.–Oct., Tues.–Thurs. and weekends 1–5:30; last admission 4:30.*

Dining

£££ ★ ✕ **Fleur de Sel.** Twelve miles northwest of Petworth, in the town of Haslemere, this restaurant remains one of the top dining spots of the region. Happily, a recent change of ownership has not diminished the high culinary standards of its previous chef, Jean-Yves Morel. The focus here continues to be on provincial French dishes, the creations of Michel Perraud, who is also co-proprietor with his wife, Bernardette. In an interesting, varied dining space, the intimate ambience retains its cool white and blue decor. Regularly changing specialties have included fish terrine, Gressingham duck, and lamb fillet, with the accent on fish. Reasonably priced set menus are available. ✉ *23 Lower St., Haslemere,* ☎ *01428/651462. AE, DC, MC, V. No lunch Sat., no dinner Sun. Closed Mon. and 3 wks in Sept.*

Singleton

41 *59 mi south of London, 12 mi southwest of Petworth.*

Outside the secluded village of Singleton, the **Weald and Downland Open Air Museum** gives sanctuary to endangered historical buildings. Among the "rescued" structures are a cluster of medieval houses, a working water mill, a Tudor market hall, and an ancient blacksmith's shop. The architectural styles on display span more than 400 years. ✉ *Singleton,* ☎ *01243/811348.* 🎫 *£4.50.* ⏲ *Mar.–Oct., daily 10:30–5; Nov.–Feb., Wed. and weekends 10:30–4.*

Chichester

42 *66 mi southwest of London, 7 mi south of Singleton.*

On the low-lying plains between the wooded south downs and the sea, the capital city of West Sussex, Chichester, was founded by the Romans. Though it features its own giant cathedral and has all the trappings of a large, commercial city, Chichester is not much bigger than many of the provincial towns around it. The city walls and major streets follow the original Roman plan; the intersection of the four principal streets is marked by a 15th-century cross. The Norman **cathedral,** near the corner of West and South streets, also stands on Roman foundations. Inside, a glass panel reveals a group of Roman mosaics uncovered during recent restoration efforts. Other treasures include two of the most important Norman sculptures in Britain: *The Raising of Lazarus* and *Christ Arriving in Bethany,* both in the choir aisle.

Pallant House was built in 1712 as a wine merchant's mansion for the cost of £3,000 (a huge sum in those days). It was state of the art for architecture then, with the latest in complicated brick work and superb wood carving. The rooms have been faithfully restored and furnished with appropriate antiques and porcelain. The building also showcases a small collection of British art, as well as regularly changing exhibitions. ✉ *9 North Pallant,* ☎ *01243/774557.* 🎫 *£2.50.* ⏲ *Tues.–Sat. 10–5:15; last admission 4:45.*

Dining and Lodging

££ ✕ **Comme Ça.** This attractively converted pub is about a five-minute walk across the park from the Festival Theatre, making it a very good spot for a meal before a performance. Plenty of dried hops, suspended from the ceiling, and antique children's toys decorate the dining room. The Norman owner, Michel Navet, also the chef, cooks authentic French dishes, and simpler fare is served in the bar at much lower prices. ✉ *67 Broyle Rd.,* ☎ *01243/788724. AE, MC, V. No dinner Sun. Closed Mon.*

££ ✕ **Droveway.** Formerly named Thompsons, this restaurant has been given a new name and a face-lift—softening the rather spartan surroundings. There is now, for instance, a cozy reception area on the spacious second floor. But the cuisine is still inventive; try the calves' liver with shredded celeriac and balsamic vinegar, or the honeyed magret of duck with burnt orange. ✉ *30A Southgate,* ☎ *01243/528832. AE, MC, V. Closed Sun.–Mon.*

££ 🏨 **Ship Hotel.** Staying in this hotel is something of an architectural experience. Built in 1790, it was originally the home of Admiral Sir George Murray (one of Admiral Nelson's right-hand men). Outstanding features are the classic Adam staircase and colonnade. The hotel, which has recently changed hands, is gradually being restored to its 18th-century elegance. It is close to the Festival Theatre. ✉ *North St., PO19 1NH,* ☎ *01243/778000,* FAX *01243/788000. 36 rooms with bath. Restaurant. AE, DC, MC, V.*

The Arts

The Festival Theatre, Chichester (☎ 01243/784437), presents middle-of-the-road productions of classics and modern plays from May to September. Like Glyndebourne, it has an international reputation and can be the evening focus for a relaxed day out of London.

Fishbourne Roman Palace

43 *66 mi southwest of London, ½ mile west of Chichester.*

Fishbourne Roman Palace, about half a mile outside Chichester, is the largest Roman villa in Britain. Probably built as a residence for Roman emperor Tiberius, the villa contains a remarkable range of mosaics. Sophisticated bathing and heating systems remain, and the gardens have been laid out much as they were in the 1st century AD. ✉ *Salthill Rd., Fishbourne,* ☎ *01243/785859.* 🎫 *£3.60.* ⏲ *Mar.–July and Sept.–Oct., daily 10–5; Aug., daily 10–6; Nov.–mid-Dec. and late Feb., daily 10–4; mid-Dec.–mid-Feb., Sun. 10–4.*

To continue on the northward circuit into Surrey, return to Chichester and take A286/A287/A3 to Guildford.

Guildford

44 *28 mi southwest of London, 35 mi north of Chichester.*

Guildford, the largest town in Surrey and the county's capital, is an important commuter town—and it is growing at an alarming rate—but Guildford has managed to retain a faint 18th-century air. No other English town can claim such a brilliant succession of royal visits, from Alfred the Great down to the present queen. Aldermen still appear in royal scarlet, a privilege granted them by James II. The steep **High Street** is lined with gabled merchants' houses and preserves a pleasant, provincial appearance. **Guildford Grammar School**, at the top end of Guildford's High Street, contains one of Britain's three surviving medieval chained libraries (books were so precious during the Middle Ages, they were literally chained to prevent theft). The school was founded in 1507. ✉ *Upper High St.,* ☎ *01483/502424.* ⏲ *By appointment only.*

On High Street, you'll find the **Hospital of the Blessed Trinity,** with its massive Tudor facade. It was founded in 1619 as an almshouse by George Abbot, archbishop of Canterbury. Abbot, one of the translators of the King James Bible, was born in Guildford. The hospital is now an old people's home; the male residents wear Tudor hats and coats bearing Abbot's emblem. ✉ *High St.,* ☎ *01483/562670.* ⏲ *Chapel and common room by appointment.*

NEED A BREAK? **Rats Castle** (✉ 80 Sydenham Rd.), near the center of town, presents a wide range of food in a pub decorated with Edwardian tiles. There's a summer garden, a setting for barbecues.

For centuries, the **Guildhall** served as the center for Guildford's government. A 17th-century facade conceals an exquisite 16th-century structure within; be sure to visit the **courtroom**, with its original paneling and stained-glass windows. The impressive **Guildhall Clock**, glittering with gold, reaches out over the street like a giant outstretched arm. ✉ *High St.,* ☎ *01483/444035.* 🎫 *Free.* ⏲ *Tues., Thurs. 2–5.*

All that remains of the entrance of the old castle, **Castle Arch**, still displays a slot for a portcullis. The building now contains the **Guildford Museum,** with interesting exhibits on local history, along with memorabilia of Charles Dodgson, better known, of course, as Lewis Carroll, the immortal author of *Alice in Wonderland.* Dodgson spent the last years of his life in a house on nearby Castle Hill, dying there with his two sisters at his side; he was buried in The Mount Cemetery, up the hill on High Street. Beyond the arch lie the remains of the castle itself. ✉ *Quarry St.,* ☏ *01483/444750.* 🎟 *Free.* ⏲ *Mon.–Sat. 11–5.*

Guildford Cathedral, looming on its hilltop across the river Wey, is only the second Anglican cathedral to be built on a new site since Henry VIII's Reformation of the 1500s. It was consecrated in 1961. The red-brick exterior is severely simple, while the interior, with its stone and plaster, looks bright and cool. The Refectory Restaurant is open for light refreshments from 9:30 to 4:30. ✉ *Stag Hill,* ☏ *01483/560421.* 🎟 *Donation requested.*

The Arts

In Guildford, the **Yvonne Arnaud Theatre** (✉ Milbrook, ☏ 01483/60191) is an unusual horseshoe-shaped building on an island in the river Wey. It frequently previews West End productions and also has a restaurant.

Dining and Lodging

£ ★ ✕ **Rumwong.** The elegant waitresses at this Thai restaurant wear their traditional long-skirted costumes, so at busy times the dining room looks like a swirling flower garden. On the incredibly long menu, the Thai name of each dish is given with a clear English description. Try the fisherman's soup, a mass of delicious saltwater fish in a clear broth, or *yam pla muek,* a hot salad with squid. ✉ *16–18 London Rd.,* ☏ *01483/36092. MC, V. Closed Mon.*

£££ ★ 🏨 **The Angel.** The Angel is the last of the old coaching inns for which Guildford was famous. The courtyard, into which coaches and horses rattled, is still open to the sky, and light lunches are served here in summer. The hotel is at least 400 years old and is even said to have a ghost. Guest rooms have attractive fabrics, reproduction antiques, and marble-lined bathrooms. There's an excellent restaurant in the medieval stone cellar and an informal coffee shop for light refreshments. A modern annex containing 10 rooms was opened in 1995. ✉ *91 High St., GU1 3DP,* ☏ *01483/564555,* FAX *01483/33770. 21 rooms with bath. Restaurant, coffee shop. AE, DC, MC, V.*

West Clandon

45 *29 mi southwest of London, 3 mi east of Guildford.*

Just east of Guildford at West Clandon, you'll want to visit **Clandon Park,** which started out as an Elizabethan manor house but was transformed in the 1730s by Venetian architect Giacomo Leoni into the graceful Palladian-style residence you see today. The real glory of the house, now a National Trust property, is its interior, especially the two-story Marble Hall, one of the most imposing rooms created in the 18th century. There's a fine collection of furniture, needlework, and porcelain and, in the basement, an interesting regimental museum, full of weapons and medals. The extensive parkland (not open to the public) was another of Capability Brown's landscaping achievements. ☏ *01483/222482.* 🎟 *£4.* ⏲ *Apr.–Oct., Sun.–Wed. 1:30–5:30, Sat. noon–4; national holidays 11–5:30; last admission 30 min before closing; gardens also open Sun. in Mar. noon–5:30.*

Great Bookham

46 *25 mi southwest of London, 8 mi northeast of Guildford, 3 mi southwest of Leatherhead.*

Great Bookham has some fine old buildings, including a 12th-century church, one of the most complete medieval buildings in Surrey. The main reason to be here, however, is to visit **Polesden Lacey.** This handsome Regency house, built on the site of one owned by 18th-century playwright Richard Brinsley Sheridan, was from 1906 to 1942 the home of society hostess Mrs. Ronald Greville. Her many famous guests included Edward VII. Elizabeth, now the Queen Mother, and her husband, the Duke of York (later George VI), stayed here on their honeymoon. Today owned and maintained by the National Trust, Polesden Lacey contains beautiful collections of furniture, paintings, porcelain, and tapestries. In the summer, open-air theatrical performances are given on the grounds. Coffee, lunches, and teas are available in the courtyard restaurant. ☎ *01372/458203.* 🎫 *House £3, grounds £3; may vary with time of yr.* ⏲ *House Apr.–Oct., Wed.–Sun. 1:30–5:30; Mar., weekends 1:30–4:30; national holidays 11–5:30; grounds daily 11–6 or sunset.*

En Route 47 As you start making your way southeast to Royal Tunbridge Wells via Dorking (about 28 miles), you'll pass under the shadow of **Box Hill,** named after the box trees that grow in such profusion here. It is a favorite spot for walking excursions. At Dorking, take any of the major roads and follow the signs to Royal Turnbrige Wells.

Dorking

6 mi southeast of Great Bookham, 29 mi south of London

The southeasterly route to Royal Tunbridge Wells leads to the busy market town of Dorking, a pleasant neighborhood that has inspired the pens of so many writers. Its wide High Street houses The White Horse Inn, or "The Marquis o' Granby," as Dickens dubbed it for his *Pickwick Papers.* At Burford Bridge Hotel, Keats wrote the last chapters of *Endymion* (and Nelson stayed there when traveling down to Portsmouth, and on to fame and death at Trafalgar).

Dining and Lodging

££ ✕ **Partners West Street.** Behind the genuine 16th-century, half-timber facade is a grand, well-established restaurant, at least downstairs, where expensive fabrics are in plentiful use. Upstairs is more relaxed. There is a very reasonable three-course set-price menu at lunch. Try the ragout of monkfish in a red wine sauce, piccatas of turkey on a vegetable risotto, roast and braised pheasant, or the loin of pork with goat's cheese. ✉ *2–4 West St.,* ☎ *01306/882826. Reservations essential. Jacket and tie. AE, DC, MC, V. No lunch Sat., no dinner Sun.*

££–£££ 🏨 **White Horse.** For a taste of both ancient and modern, stay at this inn. The foundations of the hotel probably go back to the 13th century, while the interior is mostly 18th century and has been attractively—but carefully—brought up-to-date. All the rooms are cheerfully furnished and offer high standards of comfort. There is an adequate if unremarkable restaurant. ✉ *High St., RH4 1BE,* ☎ *01306/881138,* FAX *01306/887241. 68 rooms with bath. Restaurant. AE, DC, MC, V.*

MASTERPIECES AND MOATS: FROM TUNBRIDGE WELLS TO FINCHCOCKS

One of England's greatest attractions is its many magnificent stately homes and castles. For those who love great treasure houses, there are almost endless opportunities in Great Britain, but for those with limited vacation time, the dismaying fact is that the greatness is thinly spread, with many houses scattered far and wide across the country. Within a 15-mile radius of Tunbridge Wells, however, lies a remarkable array of historic homes, castles, and other monuments: Penshurst Place, Hever Castle, Chartwell, Knole, Ightham Mote, Leeds Castle, Sissinghurst Castle Gardens, Bodiam Castle, Rudyard Kipling's Batemans, and Finchcocks.

Royal Tunbridge Wells

48 *39 mi southeast of London, 36 mi east of Great Bookham.*

Butt of humorists who have always made it out to be unbelievably strait-laced, this city is officially known as Royal Tunbridge Wells, but locals ignore the prefix "royal" (it was added only in 1909, during the reign of Edward VII). Tunbridge Wells owes its prosperity to the 17th and 18th centuries' passion for spas and mineral baths, initially as medicinal treatments and later as social gathering places. In 1606, a spring of chalybeate (mineral) water was discovered here, drawing legions of royal visitors from the court of King James I. It is still possible to drink the waters when a "dipper" (the traditional water dispenser) is in attendance, from Easter to September. Tunbridge Wells reached its zenith in the mid-18th century, when Richard "Beau" Nash presided over its social life. Today it is a pleasant town and home to many London commuters.

Start your tour at the **Pantiles,** a promenade near the spring on the other side of town, which derives its odd name from the Dutch "pan tiles" that originally paved the area. Now bordered on two sides by busy main roads, the Pantiles remains a tranquil oasis. Across the road from the Pantiles, the **Church of King Charles the Martyr** dates from 1678 when it was dedicated to Charles I, who was executed by Parliament in 1649 following the English Civil War. Its plain exterior belies its splendid interior; take special note of the beautifully plastered ceiling. A network of alleyways behind the church leads north back to High Street.

NEED A BREAK? **The Hogshead and Compasses** (✉ Little Mount Sion), a spacious, well-kept Victorian-style pub on a tiny, steep lane off High Street, offers tasty homemade food and, in the winter, cozy open fires.

The buildings at the lower end of High Street are mostly 18th century, but as the street climbs the hill north, changing its name to Mount Pleasant Road, the buildings become more modern. Here you'll find the **Tunbridge Wells Museum and Art Gallery,** which houses a fascinating jumble of local artifacts, prehistoric relics, and Victorian toys, as well as a permanent exhibition of interesting Tunbridge Ware pieces: small, wood-carved items inlaid with different-color wooden fragments. ✉ *Mount Pleasant Rd.,* ☎ *01892/526121, ext. 317.* *Free.* *Mon.–Sat. 9:30–5.*

Dining and Lodging

£££ ✕ **Thackeray's House.** Gourmets flock to this mid-17th-century house, once the home of Victorian novelist William Makepeace Thackeray. Its owner, Bruce Wass, is also the chef and tolerates none but the freshest ingredients. Everything is cooked with great flair and imagination.

Specialties include warm scallop and skate salad with ginger vinaigrette and chocolate Armagnac loaf with coffee sauce. Below the main restaurant, there is a friendly little bistro, Downstairs at Thackeray's, with food every bit as good as upstairs, but less expensive (entrance in the courtyard). ✉ *85 London Rd.,* ☎ *01892/511921. MC, V. No dinner Sun. Closed Mon.*

£–££ ✕ **Sankey's.** This double eatery features a basement wine bar and a lively upstairs restaurant. The wine bar has inexpensive food—try the Moroccan lamb—while the restaurant specializes in wonderfully fresh fish. The *soupe de poissons* is excellent, and there's a good selection of British cheeses. ✉ *39 Mount Ephraim,* ☎ *01892/511422. AE, DC, MC, V.*

££–£££ **Spa Hotel.** Carefully chosen furnishings and details help give this Georgian mansion the atmosphere of a country house, though guest rooms are equipped with many thoughtful modern extras. This hotel is run by the Goring family, who also own the Goring Hotel in London. The extensive grounds give superb views across the town and into the Weald of Kent. The Chandelier Restaurant is very popular with locals. ✉ *Mount Ephraim, TN4 8XJ,* ☎ *01892/520331,* FAX *01892/510575. 76 rooms with bath. Restaurant, indoor pool, beauty salon, sauna, tennis, jogging. AE, DC, MC, V.*

£ **Old Parsonage.** This very comfortable and friendly guest house, 2 miles south of Tunbridge Wells via the A267, stands beside the village church. Built in 1820, the place has a country-house feel to it, with lovely old furniture, including two four-posters, and a big conservatory for afternoon tea. The lodging stands amid 3 acres of grounds. ✉ *Church La., Frant TN3 9DX,* ☎ FAX *01892/750773. 3 rooms with bath. MC, V.*

Outdoor Activities and Sports

GOLF

The golf course at Langton Rd., Tunbridge Wells, ☎ 01892/523034, welcomes visitors.

Penshurst

49 *35 mi southeast of London, 7 mi northwest of Tunbridge Wells.*

At the center of the hamlet of Penshurst (from Tunbridge Wells follow A26 and B2176), one of England's finest medieval manor houses, ★ **Penshurst Place,** lies hidden behind tall trees and a walled garden. While retaining its Baron's Hall dating from the 14th century, the house is mainly Elizabethan, having been in the Sidney family for centuries. It still is. The most famous Sidney is the Elizabethan poet, Sir Philip, author of *Arcadia.* This family continuity brings a particular richness to the Place. The **Baron's Hall**, topped in 1341 with a timber roof, is one of the grandest interiors to survive from the early middle ages. The house stands in a splendid garden, itself in parkland; there is a convenient tearoom. ☎ *01892/870307.* *House and grounds £5.50; grounds only £4.* ⏲ *House Apr.–Sept. daily noon–5:30; Mar. and Oct., weekends noon–5:30; grounds 11–6.*

NEED A BREAK? **The Spotted Dog,** on Smarts Hill, which first opened its doors in 1520, today tempts visitors with an inglenook fireplace, heavy beams, imaginative food, and a splendid view of Penshurst Place.

Lodging

££ **Rose and Crown.** Originally a 16th-century inn, this hotel on the main street in Tonbridge (5 miles east of Penshurst, 5 miles north of Tunbridge Wells) features a distinctive portico, added later. Inside, low-beam ceilings and Jacobean woodwork make both the bars and the restaurant snug and inviting. Guest rooms in the main building are traditionally furnished, while in the new annex they are more modern in style; all are attractive and cozy. ✉ *125 High St., Tonbridge TN9 1DD,* ☎ *01732/357966,* FAX *01732/357194. 48 rooms with bath. Restaurant, bars. AE, DC, MC, V.*

Hever Castle

50 *30 mi southeast of London, 10 mi northwest of Tunbridge Wells, 3 mi west of Penshurst.*

For some, 13th-century Hever fits the stereotype of what a castle should look like, all turrets and battlements, the whole encircled by a waterlily-bound moat; for others, it's a bit too squat in structure and perhaps too renovated. Its main attraction is its past association with the ill-fated Anne Boleyn. It was here that she was courted and won by Henry VIII. He later gave Hever to his fourth wife, Anne of Cleves. The castle was acquired in 1903 by American millionaire William Waldorf Astor, who built an entire Tudor village to house his staff and had the gardens laid out in Italianate style, with a large topiary maze. ✉ *Near Edenbridge,* ☎ *01732/865224.* 🎫 *Castle and grounds £6; grounds only £4.40.* ⏲ *Castle Mar.–Nov., daily noon–5; grounds 11–6.*

Chartwell

51 *28 mi southeast of London, 12 mi northwest of Tunbridge Wells, 9 mi north of Hever Castle.*

Chartwell was Sir Winston Churchill's home from 1922 until his death in 1965. The Victorian house was acquired by the National Trust and has been decorated to appear as it did in Churchill's lifetime—even down to a half-smoked cigar in an ashtray. In the garden you can see a wall he built himself. To arrive here from Hever, take the minor roads B2027 and B2026 north. ✉ *Near Westerham,* ☎ *01732/866368.* 🎫 *House and garden £4.50; garden only £2; house only (Mar. and Nov.) £2.50.* ⏲ *Apr.–Oct., Tues.–Thurs. and weekends 11–5:30; Mar. and Nov., Wed. and weekends 11–4:30; last admission 1 hr before closing.*

Sevenoaks

52 *27 mi southeast of London, 11 mi north of Tunbridge Wells, 8 mi east of Chartwell.*

Sevenoaks in Kent lies in London's commuter belt, a world away from ★ the baronial air of its premier attraction, **Knole,** the home of the Sackville family since 1603. Begun in the 15th century, Knole, with its vast complex of courtyards and buildings, resembles a small town. You'll need most of an afternoon to explore it thoroughly. The house is famous for its collection of tapestries, embroidered furnishings, and the most famous set of 17th-century silver furniture to survive. Paintings on display include a series of portraits by 18th-century artists Thomas Gainsborough and Sir Joshua Reynolds. The floridly decorated staircase was a novelty in its Elizabethan heyday. Set in a 1,000-acre deer park, the house lies in the center of Sevenoaks; to get there from Chartwell, drive north to Westerham, then pick up A25 and head east for 8 miles. ☎ *01732/450608.* 🎫 *£4.50; grounds free.* ⏲ *Apr.–Oct., Wed. and Fri.–Sun. 11–5, Thurs. 2–5; last admission at 4; gardens May–Sept., 1st Wed. of each month.*

Ightham Mote

★ 53 *31 mi southeast of London, 10 mi north of Tunbridge Wells, 7 mi east of Sevenoaks.*

Finding Ightham Mote requires careful navigation, but it is worth the effort, for it is a vision out of the middle ages. An outstanding example of a small manor house, it's surrounded by a moat accessorized with two swans preening themselves in the sun—the absolute quintessence of medieval romanticism. This moat, however, does not relate to the "mote" in the name, which refers to the role of the house as a meeting place, or "moot." Ightham (pronounced "Item") Mote's exterior has changed little since it was built in the 14th century, but within you'll find it does encompass styles of several different periods, Tudor to Palladian. The Great Hall is an antiquarian's delight—both comfy and grand. To reach the house from Sevenoaks, follow A25 east to A227 (8 miles) and follow the signs. ✉ *Ightham,* ☎ *01732/810378.* 🎫 *£4.* ⏲ *Apr.–Oct., Mon. and Wed.–Fri. noon–5:30, Sun. and national holidays 11–5:30.*

Maidstone

54 *40 mi southeast of London, 18 mi east of Sevenoaks, 19 mi northwest of Tunbridge Wells, 12 mi east of Ightham.*

The bubbling river Medway runs right through Maidstone, Kent's county seat, with its backdrop of chalky downs. Only 5 miles east on A20 stands
★ 55 **Leeds Castle,** a fairy-tale stronghold commanding two small islands on a peaceful lake. Since the 10th century this site has held a castle, and some of the present structure is 13th-century Tudor. Leeds (not to be confused with Leeds in the North) was a favorite home of many English queens, and Henry VIII liked the place so much he had it converted from a fortress into a grand palace. The house offers a fine collection of paintings and furniture, plus an unusual dog-collar museum. To get to Maidstone from Ightham, go east along the A20 then the A25. ☎ *01622/765400.* 🎫 *Castle and grounds £8, grounds only £6.* ⏲ *Mar.–Oct., daily 10–5; Nov.–Feb., daily 10–3. Castle closed June 24, July 1, Nov. 4, Dec. 25.*

Outdoor Activities and Sports

GOLF

A scenically beautiful and challenging course is located near **Leeds Castle,** Maidstone, ☎ 01627/880467.

Rochester

56 *28 mi southeast of London.*

Kent is Charles Dickens country and all Dickens aficionados will want to detour north to head to Rochester, the place most closely associated with the great author. Just outside of town, he lived for many years at Gad's Hill Place. In town, look for High Street— once "full of gables with old beams and timbers" and its noted gabled Tudor building, legendary abode of Uncle Pumblechook in *Great Expectations.* Opposite the Pumblechook house is the **Charles Dickens Centre,** which underwent a major refurbishment in 1996, with new state-of-the-art displays added. It features life-size models of scenes from the author's books that can amuse and horrify you at the same time (parents be warned). ✉ *Eastgate House, High St.,* ☎ *01634/844176.* 🎫 *£2.90.* ⏲ *Daily 10–5:30; last admission 4:30.*

Rochester Castle is one of the finest surviving examples of Norman military architecture. The keep, built in the 1100s, partly based on the Roman city wall, is the tallest in England. ✉ *Boley Hill,* ☎ *01634/*

402276. 🎫 *£2.60.* ⏲ *Apr.–Sept, daily 10–6; Oct., daily 10–4; Nov.–Mar., daily 10–4.*

Just across from Rochester Castle, **Rochester Cathedral** is England's second-oldest cathedral, where the first English bishop was ordained by Augustine of Canterbury. With a Norman front graced by an elaborate recessed doorway, it was built in the 11th, 12th, and 14th centuries on a site consecrated in AD 604. ✉ *Boley Hill,* ☎ *01634/843366.* 🎫 *Donation requested.*

The Arts

There is a **Dickens festival** held in Rochester in May, at which thousands of people in period dress attend enactments of scenes from the author's novels. Call ☎ 01634/843666 for details. In another town associated with the writer, **Broadstairs** (40 miles east), another festival takes place usually in June, including performances, music, and a garden party, suitable for all ages (☎ 01843/863453).

Sissinghurst Castle

57 *53 mi southeast of London, 12 mi east of Tunbridge Wells, 15 mi south of Maidstone.*

What's left of Sissinghurst Castle is nestled deep in the Kentish countryside. The gardens, laid out in the 1930s around the remains of this moated Tudor castle, were the creation of the writer Vita Sackville-West (one of the Sackvilles of Knole) and her husband, the diplomat Harold Nicolson. The grounds are at their best in June and July, when the roses are in bloom. From Leeds Castle, make your way south on B2163 and A274 through Headcorn, then follow signs. ✉ *Cranbrook,* ☎ *01580/712850.* 🎫 *£5.* ⏲ *Apr.–mid-Oct., Tues.–Fri. 1–6:30, weekends and Good Fri. 10–5:30. Admission often restricted since space is limited.*

NEED A BREAK? **Claris's Tea Shop** (✉ 3 High St., Biddenden), near Sissinghurst Castle, serves traditional English teas in a 15th-century setting and displays attractive English craft items. There's a pretty garden for summer teas.

Dining and Lodging

£££ ★ ✗🏨 **Kennel Holt Hotel.** This is a quiet hotel in a redbrick Elizabethan manor house, surrounded by beautiful, well-kept gardens. Visitors are treated like guests in a private house. The library, for example, is well stocked with books for a rainy day. The restaurant offers three- and four-course set-price menus, which include such dishes as salmon with cream, tomato, herb, and cucumber sauce, or guinea fowl with wild mushroom sauce. Antiques and flowers grace the restaurant as well as the rest of the hotel. The hotel is 3 miles from Goudhurst, off the A262. ✉ *Goudhurst Rd., Cranbrook TN17 2PT,* ☎ *01580/712032,* FAX *01580/715495. 10 rooms with bath or shower. Restaurant (reservations essential), croquet. AE, DC, MC, V.*

En Route As you leave Sissinghurst, continue south along A229 through Hawkhurst, a little village that was once the headquarters of a notorious and ruthless gang of smugglers. Turn at the Curlew pub to arrive in the tiny Sussex village of Bodiam.

Bodiam

58 *57 mi southeast of London, 15 mi southeast of Tunbridge Wells, 9 mi south of Cranbrook, 14 mi north of Hastings.*

Immortalized in 1,001 travel posters, Bodiam Castle is Britain's most picturesque medieval stronghold. Unfortunately, it's now a virtual shell. Built in 1385 to withstand a threatened French invasion, it was "slighted" (partly demolished) during the English Civil War of 1642–45 and has been uninhabited ever since. Nevertheless, you can climb some of the towers and enjoy the illusion of manning the battlements against an enemy. Surrounded by a lovely moat, this photogenic castle is just about designed for the view-finders of today's video cameras. ☎ *01580/830436.* 🎫 *£2.70.* ⏲ *Mid-Feb.–Oct., daily 10–6 or sunset; Nov.–Dec., Tues.–Sun. 10–sunset; last admission 1 hr before closing; closed Dec. 25–28 and Jan.*

Burwash

59 *58 mi southeast of London, 14 mi south of Tunbridge Wells, 10 mi west of Bodiam.*

Half a mile south of the village of Burwash, the writer Rudyard Kipling lived from 1902 to 1936 at **Bateman's,** a beautiful 17th-century house just off the main road. It was built for a prominent ironmaster when Sussex was the center of England's iron industry. Kipling's study looks exactly as it did when he lived here. The garden contains a water mill that still grinds flour; it is thought to be one of the oldest working water turbines. Close by, between Burwash Common and the river, is the setting for *Puck of Pook's Hill,* one of Kipling's well-known children's books. To get to Burwash, turn west from Hawkhurst onto A265. ☎ *01435/882302.* 🎫 *£4.* ⏲ *Apr.–Oct., Sat.–Wed. 11–5:30.*

Lamberhurst

60 *46 mi southeast of London, 7 mi east of Tunbridge Wells, 11 mi north of Burwash.*

One of England's most famous vineyards lies (signposted) outside the village of Lamberhurst. Thirty years ago, grape-growing in England was a rich man's hobby. Today it is an important rural industry, and the wines produced here are world-renowned. ✉ *Ridge Farm,* ☎ *01892/890844.* 🎫 *Free; guided tours £3.95.* ⏲ *Daily 9–5:30.*

Outdoor Activities and Sports

Bewl Water Activity Centre (✉ Lamberhurst, ☎ 01892/890661) takes advantage of its location at one of England's largest reservoirs (just east of Wadhurst, 6 mi southeast of Tunbridge Wells by A267 and B2099), providing a wide range of aquatic sports. There's also an adventure playground.

Finchcocks

61 *48 mi southeast of London, 10 mi east of Tunbridge Wells, 2 mi east of Lamberhurst.*

A visit to Finchcocks, an elegant Georgian mansion located between Lamberhurst and Goudhurst, is a must for music lovers. It contains a magnificent collection of historic keyboard instruments (**Finchcocks Living Museum of Music**), which are played whenever the house is open. (Demonstration recitals are included in the admission fee.) Concerts are held here during the spring and fall. ✉ *Goudhurst,* ☎ *01580/211702.* 🎫 *£5.* ⏲ *Easter–July, Sept., Sun. and national holidays 2–6; Aug., Wed.–Sun. 2–6. Private visits by arrangement.*

Lodging

£ 🏨 **Star and Eagle.** This traditional village inn has been serving pints and offering hospitality since 1600. The place swims with atmosphere, with exposed beams, open brick fireplaces, and some rooms overlooking the village graveyard. Rooms come in all sizes: One of them (No. 5) has a huge four-poster, though others have better views. Snacks and full meals are available in the popular bar downstairs. ✉ *High St., Goudhurst TN17 1AL,* ☎ *01580/211512,* FAX *01580/211416. 11 rooms with bath or shower. Restaurant, bar. AE, MC, V.*

SOUTHEAST A TO Z

Arriving and Departing

By Bus

National Express (☎ 0990/808080) serves the region from London's Victoria Coach Station. Trips to Brighton and Canterbury take under two hours; to Chichester, about 3½ hours.

By Car

Major routes radiating outward from London to the Southeast are, from west to east: A23/M23 to Brighton (52 miles); A21, passing by Tunbridge Wells to Hastings (65 miles); A20/M20 to Folkestone; and A2/M2 via Canterbury (56 miles) to Dover (71 miles).

By Plane

Gatwick Airport (☎ 01293/531229) has direct flights from many U.S. cities and is more convenient for this region than Heathrow. The terminal for the British Rail line is in the airport buildings, and the train system fans out from there to feed all the major coastal towns.

By Train

British Rail serves the area from London's Victoria and Charing Cross (for eastern areas) and Waterloo (for the west). From London, the trip to Brighton takes about one hour by the fast train; and to Dover, about two hours.

Getting Around

By Bus

Private companies operating within the region are linked by county coordinating offices: **East Sussex** (☎ 01273/474747), **West Sussex** (☎ 01243/777556), **Surrey** (☎ 01737/223000), and **Kent** (☎ 0800/696996). Maps and timetables are available at bus depots, train stations, local libraries, and TICs.

By Car

A good link route for traveling through the region, from Hampshire across the border into Sussex and Kent, is A272 (which becomes A265). It runs through the Weald (uplands), which separates the north downs from the more inviting south downs. Though smaller, less busy roads forge deeper into the downs, even the main roads take you through lovely countryside and villages. The main route east from the downs to the Channel ports and resorts of Kent is A27. To get to Romney Marsh (just across the Sussex border in Kent), take A259 from Rye. The principal roads in the Southeast are constantly being enlarged and upgraded to handle the ever-increasing flow of traffic to the Channel ports. Be warned that more traffic tickets are issued per traffic warden in Brighton than anywhere else in the country!

By Train

The line running west from Dover passes through Ashford, where you can change trains for Hastings and Eastbourne. There are connections from Eastbourne for Lewes, and from Brighton for Chichester. A "Network" card, valid throughout the southern and southeastern regions for a year, entitles you to one-third off particular fares. For local information, call British Rail in Sevenoaks (☎ 01732/770111) or Brighton (☎ 01273/206755).

Guided Tours

The Southeast England Tourist Board (☎ 01892/540766) can arrange private tours with qualified Blue Badge guides.

The Guild of Guides (☎ 01227/459779 or 01227/462017) provides guides who have a specialized knowledge of Canterbury.

Guide Friday (head office ☎ 01789/294466) has a go-as-you-please bus tour of Brighton lasting at least an hour. It operates between April and September, costing £6.

Contacts and Resources

Car-Rental Agencies

Brighton: Avis, ✉ 6A Brighton Marina, ☎ 01273/673738; **Hertz,** Mercury Enterprises, ✉ 47 Trafalgar St., ☎ 01273/738227.

Canterbury: Avis, ✉ 130 Sturry Rd., ☎ 01227/768339.

Dover: Avis, ✉ Eastern Docks, ☎ 01304/206265; **Hertz,** ✉ 173–177 Snargate St., ☎ 01304/207303.

Travel Agencies

American Express: ✉ 66 Churchill Sq., Brighton, ☎ 01273/321242; ✕ 29 High St., Canterbury, ☎ 01227/784865.

Thomas Cook: ✉ 58 North St., Brighton, ☎ 01273/325711; ✉ 109 Mount Pleasant Rd., Tunbridge Wells, ☎ 01892/532372. There are other offices in Dover, Eastbourne, and Hove.

Visitor Information

The **Southeast England Tourist Board** will send you a free illustrated booklet and also arrange tours and excursions. ✉ *The Old Brewhouse, 1 Warwick Park, Tunbridge Wells, Kent TN2 5TA,* ☎ *01892/540766,* FAX *01892/511008.* ⏲ *Mon.–Thurs. 9–5:30, Fri. 9–5.*

Local tourist information centers (TICs) are normally open Monday–Saturday 9:30–5:30, but vary seasonally. **Arundel:** ✉ 61 High St., ☎ 01903/882268. **Brighton:** ✉ 10 Bartholomew Sq., ☎ 01273/323755. **Canterbury:** ✉ 34 St. Margaret's St., ☎ 01227/766567. **Chichester:** ✉ 29A South St., ☎ 01243/775888. **Dover:** ✉ Townwall St., ☎ 01304/205108. **Eastbourne:** ✉ 3 Cornfield Rd., ☎ 01323/411400. **Gatwick Airport:** ✉ International Arrivals Concourse, South Terminal, ☎ 01293/535353. **Guildford:** ✉ 14 Tunsgate, ☎ 01483/444007. **Hastings:** ✉ 4 Robertson Terr., ☎ 01424/781111 and 0800/181066. **Lewes:** ✉ 187 High St., ☎ 01273/483448. **Maidstone:** ✉ The Gatehouse, Palace Gardens, Mill St., ☎ 01622/673581. **Rye:** ✉ The Heritage Centre, Strand Quay, ☎ 01797/226696. **Tunbridge Wells:** ✉ The Old Fish Market, The Pantiles, ☎ 01892/515675.

4 The South

Winchester, Salisbury, Stonehenge

The South is for time travelers. In just a few days (or even a long weekend) you can go from prehistoric Stonehenge to Victorian Salisbury. History has highlights by the hundreds here—Winchester Cathedral, Wilton House, Longleat, Beaulieu Abbey are just a few of the superlatives. And like a library, the South is tailormade for browsing, thanks to its many literary landmarks. Make a pilgrimage to Jane Austen's home or travel to Dorset—immortalized by Thomas Hardy as his part-fact, part-fiction county of Wessex—to get far from the madding crowd.

Updated by Robert Andrews

THE SOUTH, MADE UP OF HAMPSHIRE (Hants), Dorset, and Wiltshire, offers a wide range of attractions and quiet pleasures. Two important cathedrals, Winchester and Salisbury (pronounced "Sawlsbry"), are here; stately homes—Longleat, Stourhead, and Wilton House, among them—attractive market towns, and literally hundreds of prehistoric remains, two of which, Avebury and Stonehenge, should not be missed.

Hampshire has been called the Cinderella County because it is just a county to be crossed in the feverish holiday migration from London to the familiar cliffs and coves of Devon and Cornwall, much as weekend London-to-Brighton-goers feel about the Thames, or as travelers to Winchester, when it was the capital, used to regard the counties between. To many others, Hampshire means the last sight of England from departing steamers, or a first solid acquaintance with her on stepping ashore at Southampton. For this seems but the gateway to England, through which to pass hurriedly. Nothing could be further from the truth, for the sandwich shire is a seventh heaven for the perceptive visitor.

Here history has highlights by the hundred, beginning when Alfred the Great, teaching religion and letters, made Winchester the capital of 9th-century England and helped to lay plans for Britain's first navy, sowing the seeds of its Commonwealth. King Alfred was crowned in the town's huge cathedral, an imposing edifice dotted with the Gothic tombs of 15th-century bishops, who lie peacefully behind grillwork, their marble hands crossed for eternity. The town is a good center from which to visit Hampshire's quiet villages where so many of England's great lived or died. Florence Nightingale lies under a simple stone in East Wellow churchyard in Romsey, near her house at Embley Park. Thanks to a new bevy of filmed versions of her classic novels, Jane Austen's home at Chawton—restored several decades ago by the Duke of Wellington—has become a favored pilgrimage spot. But everywhere, the unscheming hand of time has scattered pretty villages over Hampshire. Many are centered around cottages grouped about the green—as one feels they should be in every English village.

Moving beyond the gentle, garden-like features of Hampshire, visitors can explore the harsher terrain of Salisbury Plain. Two monuments, millennia apart, stand sentinel over the plain. One is the 404-foot stone spire of Salisbury Cathedral, immortalized in paint by John Constable, which dominates the entire Salisbury valley. Not far away is the most imposing and dramatic prehistoric structure in Europe. Stonehenge is now believed to have been constructed by Greek, not British, builders—hardly a surprise given that the locals were then wandering around in animal skins and living in the crudest of shelters. Just why ancient masons from Mycenae should have languished in Britain putting up this great monument is harder to say.

There are numerous other districts to explore: This area of England is like a library—created for browsing. The literary metaphor is apt if you turn your sights to the Dorset heathlands, the countryside explored in the novels of Thomas Hardy. This district is spanned by rolling grass-covered chalk hills—the Downs—wooded valleys and meadows through which flow deep rivers. Along the coast line you'll find Lyme Regis, where the tides and currents strike fear into the hearts of sailors, and Cowes on the Isle of Wight—Queen Victoria's favorite getaway place—which welcomes high-flyers who enter their yachts in the famous regattas.

The south has been quietly central to England's history for well over 4,000 years, occupied successively by prehistoric man, the Celts, the Romans, and the Saxons, and the modern British. History has continued to be made here, right up to the modern era. Forces sailed from ports along this coast for Normandy on D-Day and to recover the Falklands nearly 40 years later.

Pleasures and Pastimes

Thomas Hardy Country

Among this region's proudest claims is its connection with Thomas Hardy (1840–1928), one of England's most celebrated novelists. If you have a chance to read some of Hardy's novels before visiting Dorset—immortalized by Hardy as his part-fact, part-fiction county of Wessex—you'll already have a feeling for it, and indeed, you'll recognize some places immediately from his descriptions. The quiet, tranquil countryside surrounding Dorchester, in particular, is lovingly described in *Far From the Madding Crowd,* and Casterbridge, in *The Mayor of Casterbridge,* stands for Dorchester itself. Aficionados can actually walk the farm track where Tess of the d'Urbervilles's pony fell or share the timeless vista of the Blackmore Vale that the tragic heroine so loved. Any pilgrimage to Hardy's Wessex begins at the author's birthplace in Higher Bockhampton, 3 miles east of Dorchester. Here, in a lovely thatched cottage, Hardy penned the story of Bathsheba Everdene. Salisbury makes an appearance as "Melchester" in *Jude the Obscure;* Walk in the footsteps of Jude Fawley by climbing Shaftesbury ("Shaston") and its steeply picturesque Gold Hill. Today, many of these sights seem frozen in time and Hardy's spirit is everpresent.

Dining

Fertile soil, well-stocked rivers, and a long coastline ensure excellent farm produce and a plentiful stock of fish throughout the South. Try fresh-grilled river trout or sea bass poached in brine, or dine like a king on the New Forest's famous venison.

CATEGORY	COST*
££££	over £50
£££	£30–£50
££	£20–£30
£	under £20

**per person including first course, main course, dessert, and VAT; excluding drinks*

Lodging

Modern hotel chains are well represented, and in rural areas there are elegant country-house hotels, traditional coaching inns, and modest guest houses. Note that some seaside hotels won't accept one-night bookings in the busy season.

CATEGORY	COST*
££££	over £150
£££	£80–£150
££	£60–£80
£	under £60

**All prices are for two people sharing a double room, including service, breakfast, and VAT.*

Markets

Open-air markets are almost daily events—for a complete list, inquire at the Southern Tourist Board. Among the best are Salisbury's traditional city market (Tues. and Sat.), Kingsland Market in Southampton for bric-a-brac (Thurs.), and a general country market (Wed.) at Ringwood, near Bournemouth.

Exploring the South

The South of England ranges from the broad plains of Wiltshire, including the Marlborough Downs, the Vale of Pewsey, and the great Salisbury Plain, to the gaudy bucket-and-spade resorts of the coast, and the sedate retirement homes of the Isle of Wight. The wide-open, windblown feel of the inland county of Wiltshire offers a sharp contrast both to the tame, sequestered villages of Hampshire and Dorset, and the self-important bustle of Southampton and Portsmouth. On the whole, you will not want to spend much time in these two ports, which are best visited *en passant,* in favor of spending your nights in the more compelling cities of Salisbury and Winchester.

Great Itineraries

Each of our tours listed below constitutes a self-contained entity, with its own distinctive character. The cathedral city of Winchester makes a useful base for visiting a handful of villages within easy reach, before you move on to the historic ports of Southampton and Portsmouth, each of which has its appeal—though most of their historic architecture was blown away in World War II. The tour finishes on the Isle of Wight, an easy and accessible destination to cover. Next, we concentrate on the city of Salisbury, comparable in many aspects to Winchester, though wholly different in feel. The obvious draw outside town is Stonehenge, one of Britain's most popular tourist attractions, and within reach of another, less well-known but equally interesting prehistoric monument, Avebury. From there, the tour swings south to the cultivated woodlands of the New Forest. Finally, we explore the southern coast of Dorset, taking in a couple of popular holiday resorts, Bournemouth and Weymouth, and a string of ancient sites that have a very different allure: Corfe Castle, Maiden Castle, and Cerne Abbas. We end in Lyme Regis, on the Devon border, and at the center of the wide arc of Lyme Bay, another favorite holiday destination.

Numbers in the text correspond to numbers in the margin and on the maps.

IF YOU HAVE 3 DAYS

With three days at your disposal, you will want to combine the most sights with the least amount of traveling. If you are coming from London or southeast England, **Winchester** ①–⑨ will be your first stop, a quiet, solid town, conducive to walking about, with its great cathedral at its heart. Other historic sights here include the Great Hall and Winchester College, one of the country's great "public" schools. Spend a night in the city, then move across to the other cathedral city described in this chapter, **Salisbury** ㉓–㉚, worth two nights' stay to take in the sights of the city itself, and, most important, **Stonehenge** ㊳, an easy ride out of town. Even closer to Salisbury is magnificent **Wilton House** ㉛ and its gardens, which you could see on your way to visiting the village of **Shaftesbury** ㉜ and two more country estates, **Stourhead** ㉝ and **Longleat House** ㉞: The former features—many believe—the most beautiful garden in England, the latter marries an African game-park with a great Elizabethan house.

IF YOU HAVE 5 DAYS

A longer stay in the South will give you greater freedom to explore some of the region's lower-key but no less enjoyable sights. After a day touring **Winchester** ① and nearby **Chawton** ⑪, indelibly associated with Jane Austen, return to overnight in the cathedral city. The next morn-

The South

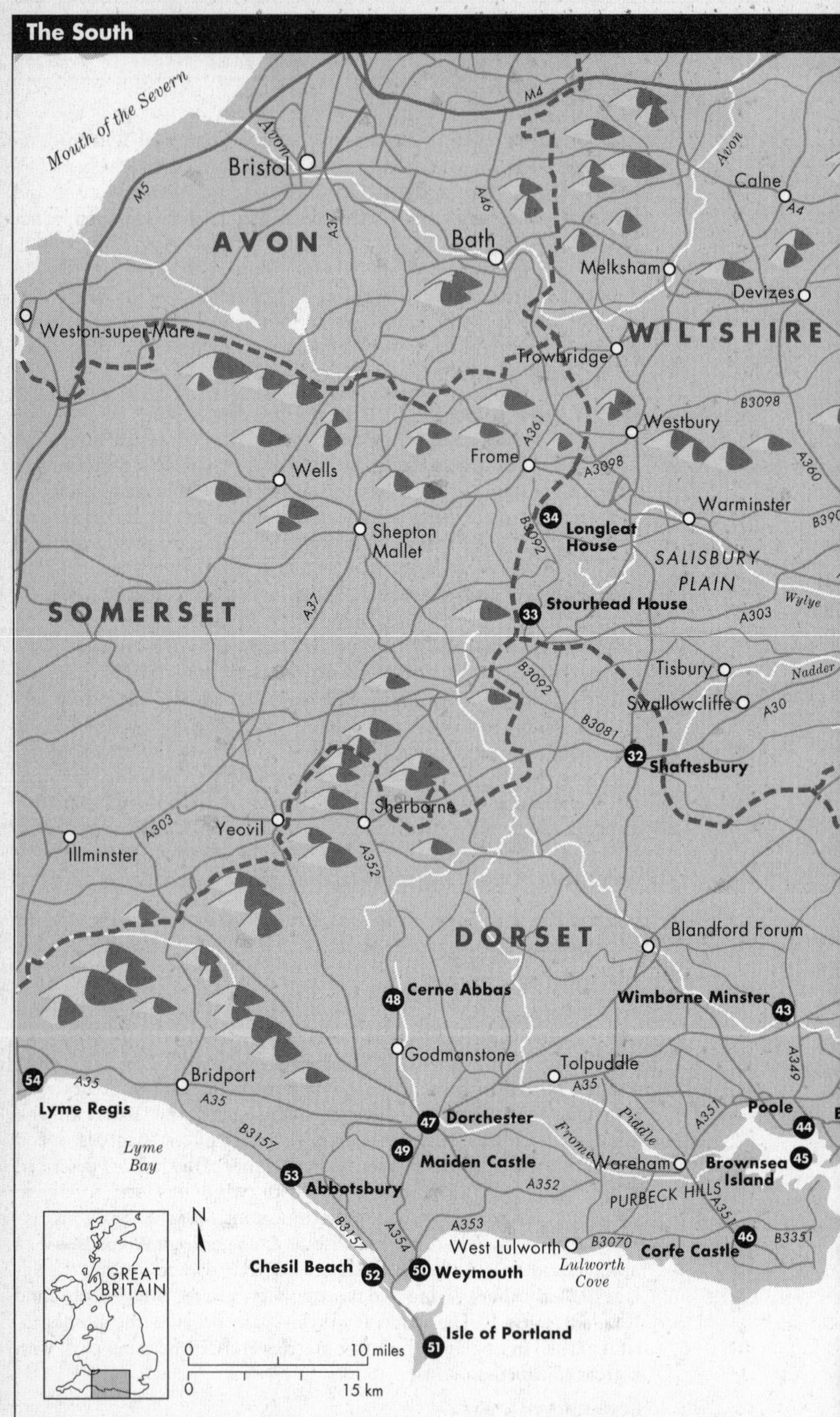
Mouth of the Severn
M4
M5
Avon
Bristol
A37
A46
AVON
Bath
Calne
A4
Melksham
Devizes
WILTSHIRE
Weston-super-Mare
Trowbridge
B3098
A361
Westbury
A360
Wells
Frome
A3098
Warminster
34 Longleat House
B3092
Shepton Mallet
SALISBURY PLAIN
Wylye
SOMERSET
A37
33 Stourhead House
A303
Tisbury
Nadder
B3092
Swallowcliffe
A30
B3081
32 Shaftesbury
Sherborne
Yeovil
A303
Illminster
A352
DORSET
Blandford Forum
48 Cerne Abbas
Wimborne Minster 43
A349
Godmanstone
Tolpuddle
A35
54 Lyme Regis
A35
Bridport
A35
Piddle
A351
Poole 44
47 Dorchester
Frome
B3157
49 Maiden Castle
Wareham
Brownsea Island 45
Lyme Bay
53 Abbotsbury
A352
PURBECK HILLS
A351
B3157
A354
A353
West Lulworth
B3070
Corfe Castle 46
B3351
Chesil Beach 52
50 Weymouth
Lulworth Cove
GREAT BRITAIN
N
Isle of Portland 51
0
10 miles
0
15 km

BERKSHIRE
Reading
TO LONDON
M4
MARLBOROUGH DOWNS
Avebury
35
Marlborough
37
A4
Newbury
A4
36 Silbury Hill
A361
A345
VALE OF PEWSEY
Basingstoke
B3400
Andover
A303
A343
B390
38
Stonehenge
Amesbury
Bourne
A36
A360
Stockbridge
A30
A30
A272
Test
B3046
M3
B3046
Old Alresford
10
Chawton
11
Alton
A31
B3006
Salisbury
23—30
31
Wilton
Ebble
A3057
Ovington
Winchester
1—9
A272
A32
A325
Petersfield
12
A338
A36
HAMPSHIRE
Broadlands
15
Romsey
A3
Meon
Southampton
14
A3025
Southampton Water
Hamble
A27
M27
A333
A3
A31
Avon
Lyndhurst
39
Ringwood
A35
B3056
B3055
NEW FOREST
Beaulieu
40
Exbury
41
Buckler's Hard
Portsmouth
13
Southsea
Hayling Island
New Milton
A337
Lymington
The Solent
Cowes
16
A3021
A3054
Ryde
17
A341
42
Bournemouth
A3020
Wootton Common
Newport
Yarmouth
Carisbrooke
22
Alum Bay
21
The Needles
Freshwater
B3401
Arreton
19
18
Brading
A3055
A3056
Sandown
Shanklin
ISLE OF WIGHT
A3055
Blackgang
Bonchurch
20
Ventnor
English Channel

ing, head for the south coast and **Portsmouth** ⑬, which possesses England's richest collection of maritime memorabilia including the Royal Navy Museum and some well-preserved warships from the 18th century and beyond. Spend the next two nights in **Salisbury** ㉓ to discover the city and the marvels surrounding it, including **Stonehenge** ㊳ and **Wilton House** ㉛. Head south again to **Wimborne Minster** ㊸, a town dwarfed by the twin towers of its great church. If you have time, carry on farther to see **Corfe Castle** ㊻, whose jagged ruins cast an eerie spell over the village at its foot. Spend your last two days in the area around **Dorchester** ㊼, a must for fans of Thomas Hardy, though even without this literary connection it would be a captivating town, with the excavations of a Roman villa and an amphitheater just outside. Farther afield lies the grassy site of **Maiden Castle** ㊾, a bare but still powerfully evocative spot that is one of the South's chief prehistoric settlements. North of town, the chalk giant at **Cerne Abbas** ㊽ provides more links with the distant past.

IF YOU HAVE 7 DAYS

More time will enable you to tread farther off the beaten track and pursue a more adventurous itinerary. Spend your first day and night in **Winchester,** then head down to Portsmouth to take a ferry across to the **Isle of Wight,** a favorite haven for both Queen Victoria and Charles Dickens. The former vacationed at **Osborne House,** an Italianate villa just east of **Cowes** ⑯ while one of her forebears, Charles I, was the unwilling guest of the Parliamentary army during his incarceration in **Carisbrooke Castle** ㉒ in the center of the island. Overnight in nearby **Ryde** ⑰. Leave the Isle of Wight from Cowes, disembarking at **Southampton** ⑭, not a particularly noteworthy place, but home to a couple of absorbing museums as well as the Pilgrim Fathers' Memorial. North of town, the village of **Romsey** is an attractive spot, with the lovely 18th-century mansion of **Broadlands** ⑮ lying just outside. From here, you are well-placed to spend two nights in **Salisbury** ㉓ to take in the city and the attractions around it, as far north as the stone circles of **Avebury** ㉟ and the nearby town of **Marlborough** ㊲, said to be the burial place of Merlin. If you have already toured this area, you might swoop down instead to the leafy glades of the **New Forest,** an excellent place to take a breather and some exercise. It is a favorite area for riding, and there are numerous stables where you can take a day's jaunt on horseback. Heading westward, stop in at **Bournemouth** ㊷, containing the house of Percy Bysshe Shelley and the grave of his wife Mary, creator of Frankenstein. If the seaside frivolity doesn't grab you, carry on as far as **Poole** ㊹, from which you can take a brief ferry-ride to **Brownsea Island** ㊺, a refuge for wildlife and some more splendid woods and beaches. **Corfe Castle** ㊻ is a brief drive from here, and farther west is the genteel resort of **Weymouth** ㊿, where you can eat fish by the harborside. South of Weymouth lies the **Isle of Portland** (51), which together with **Chesil Beach** (52) will provide both beach fun and interest to anyone intrigued by geological phenomena. **Dorchester** ㊼ and **Maiden Castle** ㊾ lie just north of here, while a few miles west, **Abbotsbury** (53) contains a famous 600-year-old swannery. Farther along Lyme Bay, the small port of **Lyme Regis** (54) will appeal to fans of both John Fowles and Meryl Streep: It was where the *French Lieutenant's Woman* was set and filmed.

When to Tour the South

Make sure you don't see the great cathedrals of Salisbury and Winchester on a Sunday, when your visit will be restricted (and—during services—not greatly appreciated). Places such as Stonehenge and Longleat House attract plenty of visitors at all times, so try to minimize the congestion factor by bypassing such sights on weekends or public holidays.

In summer, the coastal resorts of Bournemouth and Weymouth are magnets for day-trippers and longer-stay tourists, so that movement can be hampered by the crowds, not to mention the difficulty of finding suitable accommodation. The Isle of Wight, too, gets its fair share of visitors, and you may have to wait longer for the ferries. Some of the smaller, less frequented stops on our tours should always be reasonably free of the crush, however, and you should choose these lower-profile attractions when the going gets tough. Otherwise, this is one area of the country when you are relatively free to choose your own time of year. Fall in the New Forest is spectacular, though you should take waterproof boots for the puddles!

FROM WINCHESTER TO THE ISLE OF WIGHT

We begin our tour in the lovely cathedral city of Winchester, 70 miles southwest of London. From there we meander southward to the coast, stopping at the bustling ports of Southampton and Portsmouth before striking out for the restful shores of the Isle of Wight, vacation home to Queen Victoria. The island is keenly aware of tourism, and it is always worthwhile asking about the latest package tours.

Numbers in the margin correspond to points of interest on the South and Winchester maps.

Winchester

❶ *70 mi southwest of London, 14 mi north of Southampton.*

Winchester is among the most historic of English cities, and as you walk its graceful, unspoiled streets, a sense of the past envelops you. Though it is now merely the county seat of Hampshire, for more than four centuries Winchester served as England's capital. Here, in AD 827, Egbert was crowned first king of England, and his successor, Alfred the Great, held court until his death in 899. After the Norman Conquest in 1066, William I ("the Conqueror") had himself crowned in London, but took the precaution of repeating the ceremony in Winchester. The city remained the center of ecclesiastical, commercial, and political power until the 13th century.

★ ❷ Start your tour at the **Cathedral,** the city's greatest monument, begun in 1079 and consecrated in 1093. In the cathedral's tower, transepts, and crypt, as in the core of the great nave, you can see some of the world's best surviving examples of Norman architecture. Other features, such as the arcades, the clerestory (the wall dividing the aisles from the nave), and the windows, are Gothic alterations carried out during the 12th and 13th centuries. The remodeling of the nave in the Perpendicular style was not completed until the 15th century. Little of the original stained glass has survived, thanks to Cromwell's Puritan troops, who ransacked the cathedral in the 17th century, during the English Civil War.

Among the well-known people buried in the cathedral are William the Conqueror's son, William II (Rufus), mysteriously murdered in the New Forest in 1100; Izaak Walton, author of *The Compleat Angler,* whose memorial window in Silkestede's Chapel was paid for by "the fishermen of England and America"; and Jane Austen, whose memorial window can be seen in the north aisle of the nave. ✉ *Cathedral Precincts.*

❸ Behind the cathedral is the **Close,** an area containing the Deanery, Dome Alley, and Cheyney Court. On the right, as you enter Cheyney Court,

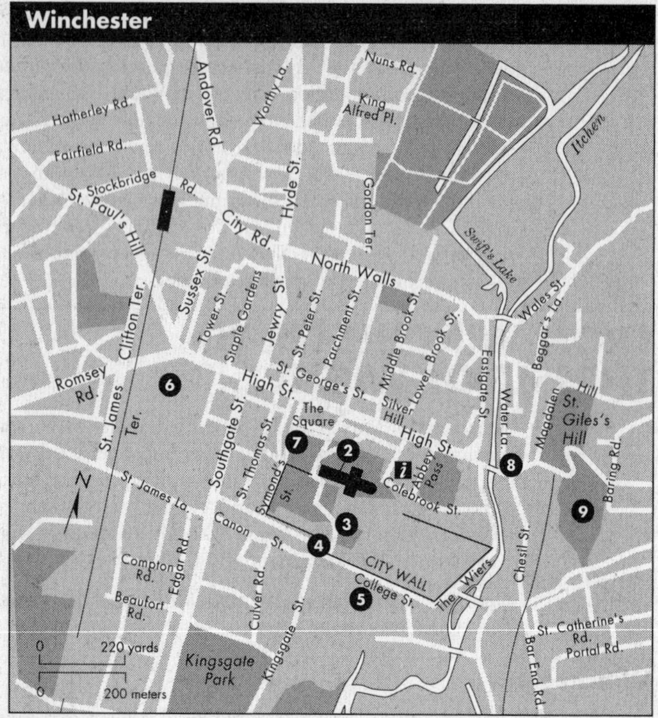

❹ on St. Swithun Street, you will see the **King's Gate,** built in the 13th century, one of two gates remaining from the original city wall. **St. Swithun's Church** is built over the King's Gate. Turn left onto College Street and proceed to No. 8, the house where Jane Austen died on July 18, 1817, three days after writing a comic poem (copies are usually available in the cathedral) about the legend of St. Swithun's Day.

❺ Founded in 1382, **Winchester College** is one of England's oldest "public" schools. Among the original buildings still in use is Chamber Court, center of college life for six centuries. Look out for "scholars"—students holding academic scholarships—clad in their traditional gowns. ✉ *College St.,* ☎ *01962/868778.* 🎫 *£2.50.* ⏲ *1-hr guided tours (must be booked in advance) Apr.–Sept., Mon.–Sat. 10–1 and 2–5, Sun. 2–5.*

NEED A BREAK?

Try a half-pint of draft bitter or dry cider at **The Royal Oak** (✉ Royal Oak Passage, off High St.), a traditional pub that claims to have Britain's oldest bar (it has a Saxon wall). Unusually, it has a no-smoking cellar bar.

❻ A few blocks west of the cathedral is the medieval **Great Hall,** which is all that remains of the city's castle. The English Parliament met here for the first time in 1246; Sir Walter Raleigh was tried for conspiracy against King James I and condemned to death here in 1603 (though he wasn't beheaded until 1618); and Dame Alice Lisle was sentenced here by the infamous Judge Jeffreys to be burned at the stake for sheltering a fugitive, following Monmouth's Rebellion in 1685. (King James II, in a rare act of mercy, commuted her sentence to beheading.) On the west wall of the hall hangs what is said to be King Arthur's Round Table, with places for 24 knights, and a portrait of Arthur, which bears a remarkable resemblance to King Henry VII. In fact, the table is a Tudor forgery; the real Arthur was probably a Celtic cavalry general who held off the invading Saxons following the fall of the Roman Empire. Henry VII revived the Arthurian legend for political purposes. ✉ *Castle Hill,* ☎ *01962/846476.* 🎟 *Free.* ⏲ *Apr.–Oct., daily 10–5; Nov.–Mar., daily 10–4.*

7 Across from the cathedral, the **City Museum** displays Winchester's past through Celtic pottery, Roman mosaics, and Saxon coins. ✉ *The Square,* ☎ *01962/848269.* 🎟 *Free.* ⏲ *Weekdays 10–5, Sat. 10–1 and 2–5, Sun. 2–5 (closed Mon. Oct.–Mar.).*

8 For a change of scenery and era, visit the **City Mill,** an 18th-century water
9 mill at the foot of **St. Giles's Hill,** at the east end of High Street. There are a National Trust gift shop and a café at the mill (open year-round), part of the building being used as a youth hostel. Then climb the hill for a panoramic view of the city. ✉ *Bridge St.,* ☎ *01962/870057.* 🎟 *£1.* ⏲ *Apr.–Oct., daily 11–4:45.*

Dining and Lodging

£–££ ✕ **Nine the Square.** Until recently, this restaurant and wine bar was known as Brann's. Overhauled and modernized, it continues to attract discerning diners. Soups, pastas, and vegetarian dishes are among the items offered at the wine bar; the restaurant menu regularly features imaginatively prepared dishes of poultry and game. While you're eating, you can feast your eyes on the cathedral that towers outside. ✉ *9 Great Minster St., The Square,* ☎ *01962/864004. AE, DC, MC, V. Closed Sun.*

££ ✕🏨 **Royal.** At this classy hotel, you'll find an attractive walled garden and some very comfortable bedrooms. It's within easy reach of the cathedral, but lies on a quiet side street. You can have an excellent lunch in the bar, or a fuller meal in the moderately priced restaurant. This is a Best Western hotel, and one of the swankier links in the chain. Some of the rooms are in a recent extension, but the older rooms have more atmosphere. ✉ *St. Peter St., S022 8BS,* ☎ *01962/840840,* FAX *01962/841582. 75 rooms with bath. Restaurant. AE, DC, MC, V.*

££ ✕🏨 **Wykeham Arms.** This old inn is centrally located, close to the cathedral and the college. The bars, warmed by log fires in winter, are happily cluttered with everything from old sports equipment to pewter mugs, and the seven handsomely furnished bedrooms also reflect the proprietor's eclectic tastes. The award-winning restaurant, whose French and English dishes are set off by a good wine list, is very popular with locals, so call ahead. ✉ *75 Kingsgate St., SO23 9PE,* ☎ *01962/853834,* FAX *01962/854411. 7 rooms with bath. Restaurant, sauna. AE, MC, V.*

£££ 🏨 **Lainston House.** Dating from 1668, this elegant country-house hotel has wood paneling and other restored 17th-century features. All rooms are attractively decorated and comfortably furnished, but do try for the ground-floor Garden or Chapel Suites, which have access to the gardens. There are more rooms in an attractively converted stable wing, some with four-posters and Jacuzzis. ✉ *Sparsholt (2½ mi northwest of Winchester) SO21 2LT,* ☎ *01962/863588,* FAX *01962/776672. 38 rooms with bath. Tennis, croquet, putting green, 63 acres of parkland, helipad. AE, DC, MC, V.*

Shopping

The **Antiques Market** (✉ King's Walk, ☎ 01962/862277) sells crafts and gift items, as well as antiques. A complete list of local antiques stores is available from Winchester Tourist Information Center (☎ 01962/840500). **H. M. Gilbert** (✉ 19 The Square, ☎ 01962/226420), an antiquarian bookseller, is housed in five medieval cottages, set amid a network of ancient streets.

Old Alresford

10 *8 mi northeast of Winchester, by A31 and B3046.*

Old Alresford (pronounced "Awlsford") has a pleasant village green crossed by a stream. The village is now the starting point of the **Watercress Line,** a 10-mile railroad reserved for steam locomotives. Originally named for its special deliveries of local watercress, the line takes visitors on a nostalgic tour through reminders of 19th-century England. ☎ *01962/733810.* ⏲ *Timetable varies throughout yr, with daily departures July and Aug.; call for details.*

NEED A BREAK? About halfway between Winchester and Old Alresford, turn north off A31 for Ovington. Here you will find **The Bush Inn,** an unspoiled pub with open log fires and a quiet riverside garden.

Chawton

11 *8 mi east of Old Alresford along A31.*

Jane Austen lived the last eight years of her life in the village of Chawton (she moved to Winchester only during her final illness). Here, in an unassuming, redbrick house, she revised *Sense and Sensibility,* created *Pride and Prejudice,* and worked on *Emma, Persuasion,* and *Mansfield Park.* The rooms of the house retain the atmosphere of restricted gentility suitable to the unmarried daughter of a clergyman. In the left-hand parlor, Jane would play her piano every morning, then repair to her mahogany writing desk in the family sitting room—leaving her sister Cassandra the household chores ("I find composition impossible with my head full of joints of mutton and doses of rhubarb," Jane wrote). In the 18th century, the house was much closer to a bustling thoroughfare, and one traveler reported that a window view proved that the Misses Austen were "looking very comfortable at breakfast." Jane was famous for working unperturbed by any and all interruptions, but one protection against the outside world was the famous door that creaked, whose hinges she asked might remain unattended to because they gave her warning that someone was coming. ☎ *01420/83262.* 🎫 *£2.* ⏲ *Mar.–Dec., daily 11–4:30; Jan.–Feb. weekends 11–4:30.*

Petersfield

12 *10 mi south of Chawton.*

The Georgian market town of Petersfield is set in a wide valley between wooded hills and open downs. From Chawton, follow B3006, then A325 for Petersfield. Four miles south of the town on A3 will lead you to **Queen Elizabeth Country Park,** which has 1,400 acres of chalk hills and shady beechwood with scenic hiking trails. You can climb to the top of Butser Hill (888 feet), to take in a splendid view of the coast. ☎ *01705/595040.* 🎫 *Free.*

Portsmouth

13 *15 mi south of Petersfield along A3, 77 mi southwest of London.*

The city of Portsmouth has been England's naval capital and principal port of departure for centuries. The harbor covers about 7 square miles, incorporating the world's first dry dock (built in 1495) and extensive defenses. These include **Portchester Castle,** founded more than 1,600 years ago, which has the most complete set of Roman walls in northern Europe. The keep's central tower affords a sweeping view of the harbor and coastline. ✉ *Near Fareham,* ☎ *01705/378291.* *£2.50.* ⏲ *Apr.–Oct., daily 10–6 or dusk; Nov.–Mar., daily 10–4.*

Portsmouth Naval Base has an unrivaled collection of ships: HMS *Victory,* the *Mary Rose,* HMS *Warrior,* and the Royal Naval Museum, all run by the Portsmouth Heritage Trust (☎ 01705/839766). Nelson's flagship, ★ **HMS *Victory,*** has been painstakingly restored to appear as she did at the battle at Trafalgar (1805). You can inspect the cramped gun-decks, visit the cabin where Nelson entertained his officers, and stand on the spot where he was mortally wounded by a French sniper. ★ The ***Mary Rose,*** former flagship of the Tudor navy, which capsized and sank in the harbor in 1545, was raised in 1982 in a much-publicized exercise in marine archaeology. Described at the time as "the flower of all the ships that ever sailed," the *Mary Rose* is now housed in a fascinating, specially constructed enclosure, where her timbers are continuously sprayed with water to prevent them from drying out and breaking up. The **Royal Navy Museum** has a fine collection of painted figureheads, relics of Nelson's family, and galleries of paintings and mementos recalling different periods of naval history. *Each ship £5.15; HMS* Victory *includes museum.* ⏲ *Mar.–Oct., daily 10–6; Nov.–Feb., daily 10–5.*

NEED A BREAK? After you've visited the *Victory* and the *Mary Rose,* stop in at the refurbished **Sally Port** (✉ High St.) for a tasty pub lunch.

In the popular **D-Day Museum,** near the corner of Southsea Common, exhibits vividly reconstruct the many stages of planning, the communications, and logistics involved, as well as the actual invasion. The centerpiece of the museum is the Overlord Embroidery ("Overlord" was the code name for the invasion), a 272-foot tapestry with 34 panels illustrating the history of World War II, from the Battle of Britain in 1940 to D-Day (June 6, 1944) and the first days of the liberation. ✉ *Clarence Esplanade, Southsea,* ☎ *01705/827261.* *£4.* ⏲ *Daily 10–5:30.*

Dining and Lodging

££ ✕ **Bistro Montparnasse.** Candles, prints, and pink tablecloths help foster the intimate atmosphere of a traditional French restaurant. Among the dishes featured are turbot with a basil and champagne sauce, and a refreshingly sharp lemon soufflé. ✉ *103 Palmerston Rd., Southsea,* ☎ *01705/816754. AE, MC, V. No lunch. Closed Sun.–Mon. and 3 wks around Christmas.*

£ ★ **Westfield Hall.** Portsmouth is well supplied with Hiltons, Fortes, and Holiday Inns, but here's a pleasant smaller establishment with personal service and character. Westfield Hall is in a converted turn-of-the-century house with big bay windows, close to the water in Southsea, the quieter, southern part of Portsmouth. It has satellite TV and a video channel in all rooms, five of which are on the ground floor. Dinner is available. ✉ *65 Festing Rd., PO4 0NQ,* ☎ *01705/826971,* FAX *01705/870200. 20 rooms with bath. Dining room. AE, MC, V.*

Southampton

14 *21 mi northwest of Portsmouth, 25 mi southwest of Salisbury, 79 mi southwest of London.*

The maritime history of Southampton is commercial, rather than military. It boasts the best natural deepwater harbor in the country. Though the city was badly damaged during World War II, considerable parts of its castellated walls remain. They incorporate a variety of old buildings, including **God's House Tower,** originally a gunpowder factory, and now the archaeology museum. ✉ *Town Quay,* ☎ *01703/635904.* 🎫 *Free.* ⏲ *Tues.–Sat. 10–noon, 1–5, Sun. 2–5.*

Mayflower Park and the **Pilgrim Fathers' Memorial** on Western Esplanade commemorate the sailing of the *Mayflower* from Southampton to the New World on August 15, 1620. (The ship was forced to stop in Plymouth for repairs.) John Alden, the hero of Longfellow's poem *The Courtship of Miles Standish,* was a native of Southampton.

Southampton's attractions include a good art gallery, extensive parks, and the superb **Tudor House Museum** and garden. ✉ *St. Michael's Sq.,* ☎ *01703/635904.* 🎫 *Free.* ⏲ *Tues.–Sat. 10–noon and 1–5, Sun. 2–5.*

NEED A BREAK? A good place to stop for lunch is **The Red Lion** (✉ 55 High St.). While modern on the outside, its ancient inside, with a huge half-timbered bar and minstrels' gallery, creates an intriguing Tudor ambience.

Paulton's Park is a large leisure park with a Gypsy Museum, Rio Grande Train, Magic Forest, and more than 40 other attractions. There's enough to occupy a full day, and refreshments are also available. ✉ *Just off exit 2 of M27, near Southampton,* ☎ *01703/814442.* 🎫 *£7.50.* ⏲ *Mid-Mar.–Oct., daily 10–6:30 (last admission 4:30); Nov.–Dec., weekends only 10–dusk; 3rd week in Dec., daily 10–dusk.*

The Arts

THEATERS

The refurbished **Mayflower Theatre** (✉ Commercial Rd., ☎ 01703/711811) in Southampton, among the larger theaters outside London, has a full program of popular plays and concerts. The **Nuffield Theatre** (☎ 01703/671771), on Southampton University campus, has its own repertory company and also hosts national touring groups, which perform some of the leading West End productions.

Dining and Lodging

£ ✕ **La Brasserie.** This is a busy spot at lunchtime, popular with the business community, though it quiets down in the evening. The decor is straightforward and ungimmicky, while the atmosphere is as traditionally French as the menu. ✉ *33–34 Oxford St.,* ☎ *01703/635043. AE, DC, MC, V. No lunch Sat. Closed Sun.*

£££ 🏨 **Dolphin Hotel.** Originally a Georgian coaching inn—though there's been an inn of some sort on this site for seven centuries—the Dolphin offers stylish accommodations in large, comfortable rooms. The service is excellent—discreet but attentive. ✉ *35 High St., SO19 2DS,* ☎ *01703/339955,* FAX *01703/333650. 73 rooms with bath. Restaurant. AE, DC, MC, V.*

Romsey

10 mi northwest of Southampton.

This small town on the river Test has an authentic Norman abbey church and, in the market place, an iron bracket said to have been used to hang two of Cromwell's soldiers. The flint and stone house nearby, known as King John's Hunting Box, dates from the 13th century.

15 Outside Romsey, just off A3057, **Broadlands** was home of the late Lord Mountbatten, uncle of Queen Elizabeth II. This beautiful 18th-century Palladian mansion, with gardens laid out by Capability Brown and wide lawns sweeping down to the banks of the river Test, is un-

doubtedly the grandest house in Hampshire. It abounds with ornate plaster moldings and paintings of British and Continental royalty, as well as personal mementos of Lord Mountbatten's distinguished career in the navy and in India. In 1947, the Queen and the Duke of Edinburgh spent their honeymoon here, and the Prince and Princess of Wales spent a few days of theirs here in 1981. ✉ *Romsey,* ☎ *01794/516878.* 🎫 *£5.* ⏲ *July–Aug., daily noon–5:30; last admission 4:05.*

Dining and Lodging

£££ ✕ **Old Manor House.** This is one of those restaurants that is inseparable from its owner-chef, in this case Mauro Bregoli. The decor is typical of the area, with oak beams and huge fireplaces, and the Italian-influenced food is rich and flavorsome. Specialties include quenelle of pike, duck breast with apples, hare, suckling pig, and venison. The wine list is exceptionally good. There are worthwhile set menus, especially at lunch. ✉ *21 Palmerston St.,* ☎ *01794/517353. AE, MC, V. No dinner Sun. Closed Mon., Dec. 25.*

£££ ★ 🏨 **Potters Heron Hotel.** An ideal place to stay if you're visiting Broadlands, this hotel has been renovated, adding a modern extension to the original thatched building. Choose an old or new room to suit your taste; many have balconies. Dine in the English restaurant with its table d'hôte and à la carte menus. ✉ *Ampfield (3 mi east of Romsey) SO51 9ZF,* ☎ *01703/266611,* FAX *01703/251359. 54 rooms with bath. Sauna. AE, DC, MC, V. Closed Dec. 25.*

Outdoor Activities and Sports

GOLF

Dunwood Manor Country Club (✉ Shootash Hill, near Romsey, ☎ 01794/40549).

Isle of Wight

Ferries, hovercraft, and hydrofoils connect the Isle of Wight with Southampton, Portsmouth, Southsea, and Lymington. Since the 19th century, when Queen Victoria chose it for her vacation home, the small, diamond-shape island has been an important resort. It has no highways or large housing complexes and is only 23 miles long. It presents a peaceful picture of steep chalk cliffs, curving bays, sandy beaches, and quiet villages, with the occasional elegant country house.

Cowes

16 *11 mi northwest of Ryde.*

If you embark from Southampton, your ferry will cross the Solent and dock at Cowes (pronounced "cows"), a magic name in the sailing world and internationally known for the "Cowes Week" annual yachting festival, held in July or August. Fifty years ago, Cowes Regatta was a supreme event, attended by Imperial Majesties and Serene Highnesses from all over the world; wealthy americans raced against the Czar of Russia and the fantastically green lawns of the Royal Yacht Squadron were crowded with the world's most famous figures, eating strawberries and cream as they strolled about with parasols and swishing dresses, or in blazers, white trousers, and yachting caps. Although elegance is a thing of the past, the Cowes Regatta is still an important event in yachting circles and is occasionally attended by that latest royal seaman, the Duke of Edinburgh. At the north end of High Street, on the **Parade,** a tablet commemorates the sailing from Cowes in 1633 of two ships carrying the founders of the state of Maryland.

Just to the east of Cowes, Queen Victoria built **Osborne House** (designed by Prince Albert after an Italian villa) and spent much time here during her last years. Though the queen was happy here, there is an underlying sadness to the place. Here one sees the engineer manqué of Prince Albert and his clever innovations—even central heating—and the desperate attempt of Victoria to give her children a normal but disciplined upbringing. For anyone drawn to the domestic side of history, Osborne is enormously interesting. The state rooms have scarcely been altered since her death here in 1901. ☎ *01983/200022.* *House and grounds £6; grounds only £3.50.* ⊙ *Apr.–Sept., daily 10–6 (last admission 4:30); Oct., daily 10–6 or dusk.*

Ryde

17 *11 mi southeast of Cowes.*

The town of Ryde has long been one of the Isle of Wight's most popular summer resorts offering a variety of family attractions. Following the construction of **Ryde Pier** in 1814, elegant (and occasionally ostentatious) town houses sprang up along the seafront and on the slopes behind, commanding fine views of the harbor. In addition to its long, sandy beach, Ryde has a large boating lake (rowboats and pedalboats can be rented) and children's playgrounds. To get here from Cowes, leave on A3021, then follow the signs on A3054.

NEED A BREAK? A 10-minute walk along the seafront brings you to **The Solent Inn** (✉ The Esplanade), which serves lunches (weather permitting) in its pleasant garden. For a snack with panoramic views, stop in at the **Balcony Café** (✉ The Esplanade).

At the waterfowl reserve of **Flamingo Park,** 2½ miles east of Ryde, many of the birds will eat from your hand. ✉ *Springvale, Seaview,* ☎ *01983/612153.* *£3.95.* ⊙ *Easter–Sept., daily 10–5 (last admission at 4); Oct., daily 10:30–4 (last admission at 3).*

Dining and Lodging

££ ✕ **Seaview Hotel.** Set in the heart of a harbor village just outside Ryde, this smart hotel offers a strong maritime flavor and comfortable, well-equipped bedrooms. The main attraction, however, is the restaurant, which specializes in fresh island produce. Try the hot crab ramekin (baked with cream and tarragon with a cheese topping) to start, and lobster or grilled plaice (subject to availability) for an entrée. The desserts are a revelation. ✉ *High St., Seaview PO34 5EX,* ☎ *01983/612711,* FAX *01983/613729. 16 rooms with bath. Restaurant (no dinner Sun.), 2 bars. AE, DC, MC, V.*

£ **Biskra House.** Guests at this spacious Victorian hotel can expect a genuine welcome from its Italian proprietor. The building is located off the Esplanade, so the noise level is low. You can enjoy the excellent views over the Solent from the tastefully furnished back bedrooms as well as from the restaurant, which lays on sumptuous Italian cuisine. ✉ *17 St. Thomas' St., Ryde, PO33 2DL,* ☎ *01983/567913,* FAX *01983/616976. 10 rooms with bath. Restaurant, bar. AE, MC, V.*

Brading

18 *3 mi south of Ryde on A3055.*

The village of Brading contains St. Mary's Church, dating from Norman times, and a 16th-century house said to be the oldest on the island. It now contains a **Wax Museum** with thrills and horrors enhanced by sound and light wizardry. ✉ *High St.,* ☎ *01983/407286.* 🎟 *£4.50.* ⏲ *May–Sept., daily 10–10; Oct.–Apr., daily 10–5; last admission 1 hr before closing.*

A mile or so south of the village of Brading lie the remains of the substantial, 3rd-century **Brading Roman Villa,** whose splendid mosaic floors and heating system have been preserved. ☎ *01983/406223.* 🎟 *£2.* ⏲ *Apr.–Oct., Mon.–Sat. 10–5, Sun. 10:30–5:30.*

Arreton

19 *6 mi southwest of Ryde, 5 mi west of Brady.*

In the medieval village of Arreton, a group of old farm buildings that were once part of the local manor have been restored as a **Country Crafts Village.** More than a dozen local craftspeople have studios in the village, working in wood, wool, clay, metal, and other materials. You can browse and buy items direct from the makers or have a snack at the handy cafeteria or a drink at the bar. ☎ *01983/528353.* 🎟 *Free.* ⏲ *Daily 9:30–5.*

Ventnor

20 *7 mi southeast of Arreton, 11 mi south of Ryde.*

The south coast resorts are the sunniest and most sheltered on the Isle of Wight. Ventnor itself rises from such a steep slope that the ground floors of some of its houses are level with the roofs of those across the road. The **Botanic Gardens** here, laid out over 22 acres, contain more than 3,500 species of trees, plants, and shrubs; there's also an excellent restaurant, the Gardens. ✉ *Undercliff Dr.* 🎟 *Free.* ⏲ *Year-round.*

Lodging

£££ 🏨 **Winterbourne Hotel.** This manor house was one of Charles Dickens's many homes; bedrooms are named after characters in *David Copperfield,* part of which he wrote here. The furnishings are, of course, Victorian, and the gardens, with waterfalls, are beautifully kept. ✉ *Bonchurch, near Ventnor, PO38 1RQ,* ☎ *01983/852535,* FAX *01983/853056. 15 rooms with bath. Restaurant, pool. AE, DC, MC, V. Closed Nov.–Feb.*

Outdoor Activities and Sports

GOLF

Shanklin and Sandown (✉ The Fairway, Sandown, Isle of Wight, ☎ 01983/403170).

En Route The southwestern coast is the least developed part of the shoreline but contains one famous natural sight, the **Needles,** a long line of jagged chalk stacks jutting out of the sea like monstrous teeth, which can be found west of Blackgang. Another attraction is a fantasy theme park, **Blackgang Chine,** built in a deep chine (cleft in the cliffs) overlooking a former smugglers' landing place. It features Dinosaur-Land, Smugglers-Land, Jungle-Land, and other attractions for ages 3–12. ✉ *Ventnor, Isle of Wight,* ☎ *01983/730330.* 🎟 *£4.99.* ⏲ *Apr.–May and Oct., daily 10–5:30; June–Sept., daily 10–10.*

Alum Bay

21 *19 mi northwest of Ventnor, 18 mi southwest of Cowes.*

Take the chairlift to the beach at Alum Bay, where you can catch a good view of the multicolored sands in the cliff strata. The **Alum Bay Glass Company** welcomes visitors interested in buying souvenirs or just watching glassblowing and jewelry crafting. ☎ *01983/753473.* 🎟

60p. ⏲ Daily 9–5, with regular tours, talks, and demonstrations in summer; no glassmaking on weekends.

Lodging

££ **Farringford Hotel.** Once the splendid home of the Victorian poet laureate Alfred, Lord Tennyson, this is now an unpretentious hotel. The 18th-century house is set on 33 acres of grounds; outbuildings contain 24 self-catering suites and cottages, as well as normal bedrooms. *✉ Bedbury La., Freshwater PO40 9PE, near Alum Bay, ☎ 01983/752500, FAX 01983/756515. 68 rooms with bath. Restaurant, pool, 9-hole golf course, tennis. AE, DC, MC, V.*

Outdoor Activities and Sports

GOLF

Freshwater Bay Golf Club (✉ Freshwater Bay, Isle of Wight, ☎ 01983/752955).

Carisbrooke

22 *14 mi east of Alum Bay, 1¼ mi southwest of Newport, 5 mi south of Cowes.*

A short distance outside the Isle of Wight's modern-day capital, Newport, lies the former capital, Carisbrooke), now a village. Above it stands ★ **Carisbrooke Castle,** built by the Normans but enlarged in Elizabethan times. King Charles I was imprisoned here during the English Civil War. You can see the small window in the north curtain wall through which he tried to escape and stroll along the battlements to watch the donkey-wheel, where a team of donkeys draws water from a deep well. *☎ 01983/523660. £3.80. ⏲ Apr.–Oct., 10–6 or dusk; Nov.–Mar., daily 10–4.*

Take the ferry back to Southampton and follow A36 north to Salisbury, about 25 miles away.

SALISBURY, STONEHENGE, AND THE NEW FOREST

This tour kicks off in Salisbury, renowned for its glorious cathedral, then loops west around Salisbury Plain, up to Avebury, and back to Stonehenge, in Wiltshire. From Stonehenge we dip south to the wild, scenic expanse of the New Forest, ancient hunting preserve of William the Conqueror. Your own transport is essential to see anything beyond Salisbury, though there are also plenty of opportunities en route to stretch your legs.

Numbers in the margin correspond to points of interest on the South and Salisbury maps.

Salisbury

23 *25 mi northeast of Southampton, 55 mi southeast of Bristol, 90 mi southwest of London.*

Although Salisbury is a historic city, and its old stone shops and houses grew up in the shadow of the great church, the city did not become important until the diocese of Old Sarum (the original settlement 2 miles to the north) was transferred here in the 13th century. The cathedral
★ 24 at Old Sarum was razed (today only ruins remain), **Salisbury Cathedral** was built, and the city of Salisbury was born. In the 19th century, novelist Anthony Trollope based his tales of ecclesiastical life, notably

Barchester Towers, on life here, although his fictional city of Barchester is really an amalgam of Salisbury and Winchester.

Salisbury continues to be dominated by its towering cathedral, a soaring hymn in stone. It is unique in that it was conceived and built as a whole, in the amazingly short span of only 38 years (1220–58). The spire, added in 1320, is a miraculous feat of medieval engineering—even though the point, 404 feet above the ground, is 2½ feet off vertical. For a fictional, keenly imaginative reconstruction of the human drama underlying such an achievement, read William Golding's novel *The Spire.*

The interior of the cathedral is remarkable for its lancet windows and sculpted tombs of crusaders and other medieval heroes. The clock in the north aisle—probably the oldest working mechanism in Europe, if not the world—was made in 1386. The spacious **cloisters** are the largest in England, and the octagonal **Chapter House** contains a marvelous 13th-century frieze showing scenes from the Old Testament. Here you can also see one of the four original copies of the **Magna Carta,** the charter of rights the English barons forced King John to accept in 1215; it was sent here for safekeeping in the 13th century. ✉ *Cathedral Close.*

The **Cathedral Close** (grounds) appears much as it did when it was first
laid out. Its wide lawns are flanked by historic houses, some of which
are open to the public. On the north side of Cathedral Close, the im-
25 pressive **Mompesson House** boasts some fine original paneling and plasterwork, as well as a fascinating collection of 18th-century drinking
glasses, and an attractive walled garden. ✉ *The Close.* ☎ *01722/335659.*
🎫 *£3.10.* ⏲ *Apr.–Oct., Sat.–Wed. noon–5:30.*

26 On the north side of the Cathedral Close you'll find **High Street Gate,**
one of the four castellated stone gateways built to separate the close
from the rest of the city. Passing through it, you enter into the heart
of the modern town. One of Salisbury's best-known landmarks, the
27 hexagonal **Poultry Cross,** on Silver Street, is the last remaining of the
four original market crosses, and dealers still set up their stalls beside
28 it. A narrow side street links Poultry Cross to **Market Square,** site of
one of southern England's most popular markets, held on Tuesday and
Saturday. Permission to hold an annual fair here was granted in 1221,
and that right is exercised for three days every October.

NEED A BREAK?

Here's a historic place for lunch: The **Haunch of Venison** (✉ 1 Minster St., opposite the Poultry Cross, ☎ 01722/322024) has been going strong for more than six centuries, and is brimful with period details (like the mummified arm of an 18th-century card player still clutching his cards that was found in 1903 by workmen). The dining room has heavy beams, an open fire, and antique, leather-covered settles.

West of High Street lies Mill Road, which leads you across Queen Eliz-
29 abeth Gardens to **Long Bridge.** Cross the bridge and continue on the
town path; the view from here inspired that 19th-century icon, John
Constable's *Salisbury Cathedral,* now hung in the Constable Room of
London's National Gallery. A 20-minute walk southwest of the town
30 center along the town path, the **Old Mill,** dating from the 12th century,
makes a pleasant destination. It is now a restaurant and coffee shop
under the same management as the Old Mill Hotel next door. ✉ *Town
Path, West Harnham.*

Dining and Lodging

£ ✕ **Harper's.** This is a spacious, airy, second-floor restaurant overlooking the marketplace. Its cuisine mingles English and French dishes, and its specialties include boeuf bourguignon and fillet of salmon.

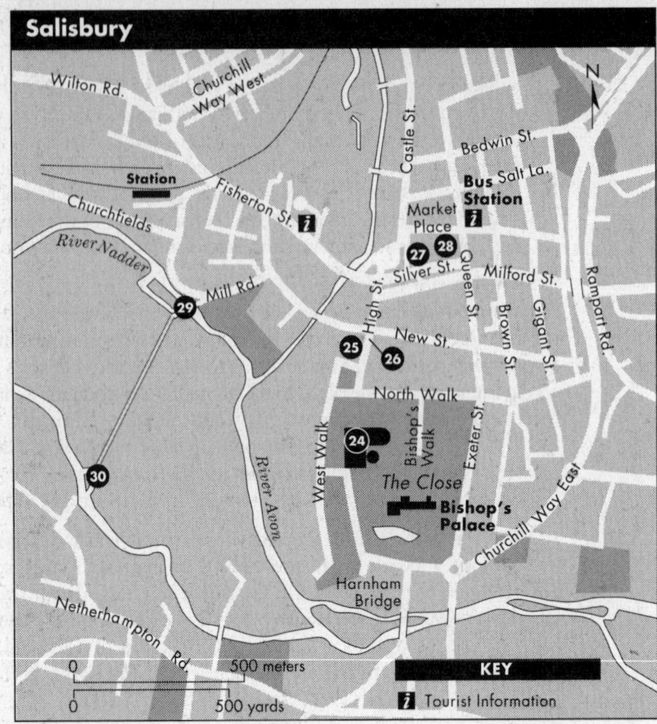

There is a good-value Shopper's Special lunch. Friendly service makes dining here a pleasure. ✉ *7 Ox Row, Market Pl.,* ☎ *01722/333118. AE, DC, MC, V. Closed Sun. in winter.*

£ ✕ **Pinocchio.** This small Italian trattoria has been making customers smile since 1988. There are six varieties of veal on offer, and there is also fish on the menu, which finds its way into a homemade fish minestrone. Pizzas are also available, and, for dessert, the tiramisù is sublime. The restaurant is conveniently located near the train station. ✉ *139 Fisherton St.,* ☎ *01722/413069. MC, V. No lunch Sun.*

£££ ✕🏨 **Red Lion Hotel.** A former coaching inn—parts of the building date from 1220—this hotel is now in the Best Western consortium. There's a choice of comfortable rooms in either modern or antique style. It's centrally located and an ideal base for exploring the city. ✉ *Milford St., SP1 2AN,* ☎ *01722/323334,* FAX *01722/325756. 54 rooms with bath. Restaurant. AE, DC, MC, V.*

££ ✕🏨 **Grasmere House.** A large late-Victorian edifice (1896), this red-brick lodging covered with creeper has fine views over the river to the cathedral. The comfortable bedrooms are named after local worthies (a saint, a canon, and so on); some are in the new extension. The restaurant, located in a conservatory, also provides peaceful country views. Its menu features fresh local ingredients. ✉ *70 Harnham Rd., SP2 8JN,* ☎ *01722/338388,* FAX *01722/333710. 20 rooms with bath. Restaurant. MC, V.*

£ ★ ✕🏨 **Byways House.** Friendly service, good value, and a quiet location are some of the reasons why this double-fronted Victorian house is popular with visitors. It was recently redecorated, and the ground-floor accommodation refurbished, with some rooms adapted for use by guests with disabilities. The hotel offers large vegetarian or traditional English breakfasts. Ask for a room with a view of the cathedral. ✉ *31*

Fowlers Rd., SP1 2QP, ☏ 01722/328364, FAX 01722/322146. 23 rooms, 19 with bath. MC, V.

The Arts

FESTIVALS

The **Salisbury Festival** (☏ 01722/323883), in May, features excellent classical concerts, recitals, and plays.

THEATERS

The **Salisbury Playhouse** (✉ Malthouse La., ☏ 01722/320117) presents high-caliber drama all year and is the focus for the Salisbury Festival.

Shopping

Watsons (✉ 8–9 Queen St., ☏ 01722/320311) is worth visiting for its circa-1306 building, which has some original windows, a carved oak mantelpiece, and other period features. The company specializes in Aynsley and Wedgwood bone china, Waterford and Dartington glass, Royal Doulton, and a wide range of fine ornaments.

Outdoor Activities and Sports

BICYCLING

You can rent a range of bikes at **Hayball's Cycle Shop** (✉ 26–30 Winchester St., Salisbury, ☏ 01722/411378); £7.50 per day, £65 per week, £25 deposit.

Wilton

31 *4 mi west of Salisbury along A30.*

Five rivers—the Avon, the Bourne, the Nadder, the Wylye, and the Ebble—wind slowly from Salisbury into the rich heart of Wiltshire. Following the valley of the Nadder will lead you to the ancient town of Wilton, from which the county takes its name. A traditional market is ★ held here every Thursday, but the main attraction is **Wilton House and Gardens,** home of the 17th Earl of Pembroke. The original Tudor house burned down in 1647; the present mansion replacing it was designed by Inigo Jones, Ben Jonson's stage designer and the architect of London's Banqueting House. In fine weather, the lordly expanse of sweeping lawns that surrounds the house, bisected by the river Avon and dotted with towering oaks and a gracious Palladian bridge, makes up one of the most quintessentially English of scenes. Even if your taste in stately homes is limited or suffering from overexposure, tour the house, for it contains one of the most extravagantly beautiful rooms in the history of interior decoration, the aptly named Double Cube Room. The curious name refers to its simple proportions, evidence of Jones's classically inspired belief that beauty in architecture derives from the harmony and balance of its proportions. The room's headliner is the spectacular, Cinerama-size Van Dyck portrait of the Pembroke family. Adorned with gilded William Kent furniture and swimming in plush reds and gold, the Double Cube was where Eisenhower prepared some of his plans for the Normandy invasion. Other delights include an exhibition of 7,000 toy soldiers and some great Old Master paintings by Rubens and Brueghel. *☏ 01722/743115. House and grounds £6.20; grounds only £2.50. ⏲ Easter–Oct., daily 11–6 (last admission at 5).*

Shaftesbury

32 *18 mi west of Wilton on A30, 22 mi west of Salisbury.*

The charming village of Shaftesbury—the model for the town of Shaston in Thomas Hardy's *Jude the Obscure*—lies just inside the Dorset county border. When you reach the village, head for **Gold Hill,** a steep, relentlessly picturesque street lined with cottages. From the top you can catch a sweeping view of the surrounding countryside. Though Gold Hill itself is something of a tourist cliché (it has even appeared in TV commercials), it is still well worth visiting.

Stourton

9 mi northwest of Shaftesbury (follow B3081 to B3092), 30 mi west of Salisbury.

Close to the village of Stourton lies one of Wiltshire's most idyllic sights, ★ 33 **Stourhead,** a country-house-and-garden combination that has few parallels. Most of Stourhead was built between 1721 and 1725 by a wealthy banker named Henry Hoare. The pavilions (containing the library and picture gallery) were added by his grandson about 70 years later. Many of the rooms contain Chinese and French porcelain and other objets d'art. The house must take second place to its garden, the most celebrated example of the English 18th-century taste for "natural" landscaping. Temples, grottoes, and bridges have been skillfully placed among colorful shrubs, trees, and flowers to make the grounds look like a three-dimensional Old Master painting. A walk around the lake (1½ mi) reveals a series of ever-changing vistas. The best time to visit is early summer, when the massive banks of rhododendrons are in full bloom, but it is beautiful at any time of year. The Spread Eagle Inn and a small restaurant on the grounds provide food and refreshments. ⊠ *Stourton, near Mere,* ☎ *01747/840348.* *House £4.20; gardens £4.20 (Mar.–Oct.), £3.20 (Nov.–Feb.); house and gardens £7.50.* ⏲ *House Apr.–Oct., Sat.–Wed. noon–5:30 or dusk; gardens daily 9–7 or sunset.*

Longleat House

★ 34 *6 mi north of Stourhead on B3092, 19 mi south of Bath, 27 mi northwest of Salisbury.*

Longleat House, home of the marquess of Bath, is one of southern England's most famous private estates. The glorious Italian Renaissance building was completed in 1580 (for just over £8,000, an astronomical sum at the time), and contains outstanding tapestries, paintings, porcelain, and furniture, as well as notable period features of its own, such as the Victorian kitchens, the Elizabethan minstrels' gallery, and the great hall, with its massive wooden beams. Giant antlers of the extinct Irish elk decorate the walls. In 1966, the grounds of Longleat became Britain's first safari park, with giraffes, zebras, camels, rhinos, and lions all on view. Longleat also has dollhouses, a butterfly garden, a private railroad, the world's largest hedge maze, and an adventure castle, all of which make it extremely popular, particularly in summer and during school vacations—don't expect to have the place to yourself! ⊠ *Near Warminster,* ☎ *01985/844400 for house, 01985/844328 for safari park.* *Inclusive ticket £11, house only £4.80, safari park £5.50.* ⏲ *House Easter–Sept., 10–6; Oct.–Easter, 10–4; closed Dec. 25. Safari park Easter–Oct., daily 10–6.*

Dining and Lodging

£££ ★ **Bishopstrow House.** It's not often that you'll find a Georgian house converted into a luxurious hotel that combines Jacuzzis with antiques and fine carpets. There's an airy conservatory, attractive public areas, and peaceful rooms overlooking the grounds (25 acres) or an interior courtyard. The restaurant offers imaginatively prepared meals, appealing views of the gardens, and a menu that is regularly changed. Bishopstrow House is 1½ miles out of town. ⊠ *Boreham Rd., Warminster BA12 9HH,* ☎ *01985/212312,* FAX *01985/216769. 32 rooms with* *bath. Restaurant, indoor and outdoor pools, exercise room, sauna, beauty salon, golf, tennis, fishing, helipad. AE, DC, MC, V.*

En Route As you approach Avebury, on your left you will pass **Cherhill Down,** with a vivid white horse carved into its slope. This is the first in a series of hillside carvings in Wiltshire, but, unlike the others, this one isn't an ancient symbol—it was put there in 1780 to indicate the highest point of the downs between London and Bath. (The best view of the horse is from A4, on the approach from Calne.)

Avebury

35 *25 mi northwest of Longleat, 27 mi east of Bath, 34 mi north of Salisbury.*

★ The **Avebury monument** is one of England's most evocative prehistoric monuments—not so famous as Stonehenge, but all the more powerful for its lack of commercial exploitation. The main site consists of a wide, circular ditch and bank, about 1,400 feet across and well over half a mile around. The perimeter is broken by entrances at roughly the four points of the compass, and inside stand the remains of three stone circles. The largest one originally had 98 stones, though only 27 remain. Many of the stones on the site were destroyed centuries ago, especially in the 17th century, when they were the target of religious fanaticism. To reach Avebury from Longleat, go north on B3092 to Frome, then take A361 to Trowbridge. Follow it through Devizes and follow the signs.

The first stones at Avebury predate those at Stonehenge by at least 200 years, but here they are much more domesticated—literally so, for many were pillaged to build the thatched cottages you see flanking the fields. Finds from the Avebury area are displayed in the **Alexander Kieller Museum,** run by English Heritage. ☎ *01672/539250.* 🎫 *£1.50.* ⏲ *Apr.–Oct., daily 10–6 or dusk; Nov.–Mar., daily 10–4.*

The Avebury monument lies at the end of the **Kennett Stone Avenue,** a sort of prehistoric processional way leading to Avebury. The stones of the avenue were spaced 80 feet apart, but only the half-mile nearest the main monument survives intact. The lost ones are marked with concrete. The entire Avebury area is crowded with relics of the prehistoric age. Be sure to stop off at the **West Kennett Long Barrow,** a chambered tomb dating from about 3250 BC, a mile east of Avebury on A4.

NEED A BREAK? **The Waggon and Horses** (✉ Beckhampton), just beside the traffic circle linking A4 and A361, serves an excellent sandwich lunch (it has won prizes for them) beside a blazing fire. The thatch-roofed pub is built of stones taken from the Avebury site.

36 As you turn right at the traffic circle onto A4, **Silbury Hill** rises up on your right. This man-made mound, 130 feet high, dates from about 2500 BC. Excavations over 200 years have provided no clue as to its original purpose, but the generally accepted notion is that it was a massive burial chamber.

Marlborough

37 *7 mi east of Avebury on A4, 28 mi north of Salisbury.*

The attractive town of Marlborough developed as an important staging post on the old London–Bath stagecoach route. Today it is better known for its unusually wide main street, its elegant Georgian houses—these replace the medieval town center, which was destroyed in a great fire in 1653—and its celebrated public school. The grounds of the school, on the west side of town, enclose a small, man-made hill called Castle Mound, or Maerl's Barrow, which gave the town its name. This was said to be the grave of Merlin, King Arthur's court wizard, but it is clearly much older than the period when the historic Arthur may have lived. A Tourist Information Center (Mon.–Sat. year-round) is housed in the car park on George Lane (☎ 01672/513989).

Lodging

££ **Ivy House.** This Georgian house right on the attractive, colonnaded High Street makes an excellent touring base. The bedrooms are comfortably furnished, with small modern bathrooms attached. There is a courtyard bistro for relaxed meals. ✉ *43 High St., SN8 1HJ,* ☎ *01672/515333,* FAX *01672/515338. 34 rooms with bath. Restaurant. AE, MC, V.*

Outdoor Activities and Sports

GOLF

Marlborough Golf Club (✉ The Common, Marlborough, ☎ 01672/512147).

OFF THE BEATEN PATH **THE WHITE HORSE** – From east to west between Salisbury Plain and the Marlborough Downs lies the beautiful Vale of Pewsey. It is especially famous for its splendid (though relatively modern) White Horse cut into the hillside.

Stonehenge

★ 38 *21 mi south of Marlborough, 8 mi north of Salisbury.*

One of England's most visited and most puzzling monuments, Stonehenge is dwarfed by its lonely isolation on the wide sweep of Salisbury Plain. Sadly, the great circle of stones has been enclosed by barriers to keep back both the relentless throngs of tourists and, during the summer solstice, crowds of New-Age druids who embark on an annual struggle with the police to celebrate, in the monument's imposing shadow, an obscure pagan festival. But if you visit in the early morning, when the crowds have not yet arrived, or in the evening, when the sky is heavy with scudding clouds, you can experience Stonehenge as it once was: a magical, mystical, awe-inspiring place.

Stonehenge was begun about 2800 BC, enlarged between 2100 and 1900 BC, and altered yet again by 150 BC. It has been excavated and rearranged several times over the centuries. The medieval phrase "Stonehenge" means "hanging stones." Many of the huge stones that ringed the center were brought here from great distances. The original 80 bluestones (dolerite), which made up the two internal circles, were transported from the Preseli mountains, near Fishguard on the Atlantic coast of Wales, presumably by raft on sea and river. Next they were dragged on rollers across country—a total journey of 130 miles as the crow flies, but closer to 240 by the easiest route. Later, great blocks of sarsen stone were quarried in north Wiltshire, dressed, and fitted together with primitive joints. The labor involved in quarrying, transporting, and carving these stones is astonishing, all the more so when you remember that it was accomplished before the major pyramids of Egypt were built.

If some of the mysteries concerning the site have been solved (for a good account, see one of the latest of books on the subject, *Stonehenge,* by Julian Richards), we still do not know why Stonehenge was undertaken in the first place. It is fairly certain that it was a religious site, and that worship here involved the cycles of the sun; the alignment of the stones to point to sunrise at midsummer and sunset in midwinter makes this clear. One thing is certain: The Druids had nothing to do with the construction. The monument had already been in existence for nearly 2,000 years by the time they appeared. A new theory that has received a good deal of controversy is that the builders were Greek rather than British and may have come from Mycenae. Evidence of the link between Greece is provided by the purpose of Stonehenge. Most historians feel that Stonehenge may have been a kind of neolithic computer, with a sophisticated astronomical purpose—an observatory of sorts. At all events, it's known that at much the same time that Stonehenge was built, the Greeks were discovering astronomy and devising for themselves a whole new set of heavenly deities to replace their original earth gods.

You can't get very close to the monoliths, and then only along one section of the site, so it's a good idea to take a pair of binoculars along to make out the details more clearly. The visitors' amenities at Stonehenge are rather squalid, but there are plans to improve them. Visitors from Marlborough should join the A345 south for Stonehenge, turning west onto A303 at Amesbury. The monument stands near the junction with A344. ✉ *Near Amesbury,* ☎ *01980/623108.* 🎫 *£3.50.* ⏲ *June–Aug., daily 9–7; mid-Mar.–May and Sept.–mid-Oct., daily 9:30–6; mid-Oct.–mid-Mar., daily 9:30–4.*

Lyndhurst

39 *28 mi south of Stonehenge, 22 mi southeast of Salisbury, 9 mi west of Southampton.*

Lyndhurst is famous as the capital of the **New Forest.** To explore the depths of this natural wonder, take A35 out of Lyndhurst (the road continues southwest to Bournemouth). The New Forest consists of 145 square miles of mainly open, unfenced countryside interspersed with dense woodland, a natural haven for herds of free-roaming deer, cattle, and hardy New Forest ponies. The forest was "new" in 1079, when William the Conqueror cleared the area of farms and villages and turned it into his private hunting forest. Three centuries ago, large numbers of oaks were cut down to build houses and ships, but otherwise the landscape has not changed much over the last 1,000 years. Although some favorite spots can get crowded in summer, there are ample parking lots, picnic grounds, and campgrounds. Miles of walking trails crisscross the region and the best way to explore is on foot.

Lewis Carroll fans should note that Alice Hargreaves (*née* Liddell), Lewis Carroll's Alice, is buried in the churchyard at Lyndhurst. To get here from Stonehenge, head south along A360 to Salisbury, then follow A36, B3079, and continue along A337 another 15 miles or so.

Outdoor Activities and Sports

GOLF

New Forest Golf Course (✉ Southampton Rd., Lyndhurst, ☎ 01703/282262).

HORSEBACK RIDING

The New Forest was custom-built for riding and there's no better way to enjoy it than on horseback. **The New Park Manor Stables** (✉ New Park, Brockenhurst, ☎ 01590/623467) gives full instruction. Try also **Forest Park Stables** (✉ Rhinefields Rd., Brockenhurst, ☎ 01590/623429).

WALKING

The **New Forest** is more domesticated than, for example, the Forest of Dean, and the walks it provides are not much more than easy strolls. For one such walk (about 4 miles), start from Lyndhurst, and head for

Brockenhurst, a commuter village. You will pass through woods, pastureland, and leafy river valleys—you may even see some New Forest ponies. For information, contact the New Forest Museum and Visitors Centre, Main Car Park, Lyndhurst, Hampshire S043 7NY, ☎ 01703/282269.

Beaulieu

40 *7 mi southwest of Lyndhurst.*

The unspoiled village of Beaulieu (pronounced "Bewley") offers three major attractions. **Beaulieu Abbey** was established by King John in 1204 for the Cistercian monks, who gave their new home its name, which means "beautiful place" in French. It was badly damaged during the reign of Henry VIII, leaving only the cloister, the doorway, the gatehouse, and two buildings, one of which today contains a well-planned exhibition re-creating daily life in the monastery. The gatehouse has been incorporated into **Palace House,** home of the Montagu family since 1538. In this stately home you can see drawing rooms, dining halls, and a number of very fine family portraits. The present Lord Montagu is noted for his work in establishing the **National Motor Museum,** which traces the development of motor transport from 1895 to the present, with more than 200 classic cars, buses, and motorcycles. Museum attractions include a monorail, audiovisual presentations, and a trip in a 1912 London bus. ☎ *01590/612345.* *Palace House, Abbey, and Motor Museum £7.75.* *Easter–Sept., daily 10–6; Oct.–Easter, 10–5. Closed Dec. 25.*

Buckler's Hard

41 *2 mi south of Beaulieu.*

Among local places of interest around Beaulieu is Buckler's Hard, an almost perfectly restored 18th-century hamlet of 24 brick cottages, leading down to an old shipyard on the river Beaulieu. Nelson's favorite ship, HMS *Agamemnon,* was built here of New Forest oak, as recalled in the fascinating **Maritime Museum.** ☎ *01590/616203.* *2.90.* *Mar.–May, daily 10–6; June–mid-Sept., daily 10–9; mid-Sept.–Feb., daily 10–4:30. Closed Dec. 25.*

En Route From Beaulieu, take any of the minor roads leading west through Lymington and pick up A337 for the popular seaside resort of Bournemouth, a journey of about 18 miles.

FAR FROM THE MADDING CROWD: BOURNEMOUTH TO LYME REGIS

"I am convinced that it is better for a writer to know a little bit of the world remarkably well than to know a great part of the world remarkably little," wrote Thomas Hardy, the immortal author of *Far From the Madding Crowd* and other classic Victorian-era novels. His "little bit" was the county of Dorset, the setting for most of his books and, today, a green and hilly county that is very largely unspoiled. Our tour of one of the last remaining corners of old, rural England follows the Dorset coastline, immortalized by Hardy and John Fowles. Places of historic interest such as Maiden Castle and the chalk-cut giant of Cerne Abbas are interspersed with the seaside leisure resorts of Bournemouth and Weymouth, though you may find the quieter towns of Lyme Regis and the smaller picturesque villages scattered along the route closer to your ideal of rural England. Chief glory of the tour is the county town of Dorchester, an ancient agricultural center with a host of historical and lterary associations, and worth a prolonged visit.

Bournemouth

42 *30 mi southwest of Southampton, 30 mi south of Salisbury, 30 mi east of Dorchester.*

Bournemouth was founded in 1810 by Lewis Tregonwell, an ex-army officer who had taken a liking to the area when stationed there some years before. He settled near what is now **The Square** and planted the first pine trees in the steep little valleys—or chines—cutting through the cliffs to the famous Bournemouth sands. The scent of fir trees was said to be good for "consumption" (tuberculosis) sufferers, and the town grew steadily as more and more people came for prolonged rest cures. The Square and the beach are linked by gardens laid out with flowering trees and lawns. This is an excellent spot to relax and listen to stirring music wafting from the Pine Walk bandstand. Regular musical programs take place at the Pavilion and at the Winter Gardens (home of the Bournemouth Symphony Orchestra) nearby. Concerts and shows take place at the Bournemouth International Centre on Exeter Road (☎ 01202/297297), which includes a selection of restaurants, bars, and a swimming pool.

NEED A BREAK? For an old-fashioned tea, try the **Cumberland Hotel** (✉ East Overcliffe Drive), which serves out of doors in summer.

On the corner of Hilton Road stands **St. Peter's** parish church, easily recognizable by its 200-foot-high tower and spire. Lewis Tregonwell is buried in the churchyard. Here, too, you will notice the elaborate tombstone of Mary Shelley, author of *Frankenstein* and wife of the great Romantic poet Percy Bysshe Shelley, whose heart is buried with her. Admirers of Shelley will want to visit the **Casa Magni Shelley Museum** in **Boscombe** (on the west side of Bournemouth), with its touching collection of Shelley memorabilia. ✉ *Boscombe Manor, Beechwood Ave.,* ☎ *01202/303571.* 🎫 *Free.* ⏲ *Tues.–Sun. 2–5.*

In the center of Bournemouth you will find the interesting **Russell-Cotes Art Gallery and Museum.** This late Victorian mansion, perched on top of East Cliff, overflows with Victorian paintings and miniatures, cases of butterflies, and treasures from the Far East, including an exquisite suit of Japanese armor. ✉ *East Cliff,* ☎ *01202/451800.* 🎫 *Free.* ⏲ *Tues.–Sun. 10–5.*

Dining and Lodging

££ ✕ **Sophisticats.** As the name suggests, there's a lot of felinity in the decor here. This useful restaurant, hidden in a shopping mall, just outside the center of town, is especially adept with seafood, though there's Javanese fillet steak on the menu, too. It's quite small (seating just 34), so a reservation's a good idea. ✉ *43 Charminster Rd.,* ☎ *01202/291019. No credit cards. No lunch. Closed 2 wks Feb. and Nov., 1 wk July.*

££££ ★ ✕🏨 **Chewton Glen.** Once the home of Captain Frederick Marryat, author of *The Children of the New Forest* and many naval adventure novels, this 18th-century country house is now a deluxe hotel, among the most expensive in Britain, set on extensive grounds 12 miles east of Bournemouth. All the rooms are sumptuously furnished with an eye to the minutest detail. Gourmets consider its restaurant, the Marryat Room, and the cooking of its chef, Pierre Chevillard, worthy of a pilgrimage. With a genuinely helpful and friendly staff, Chewton Glen deserves its fine reputation. ✉ *Christchurch Rd., New Milton BH25*

6QS, ☎ 01425/275341, FAX 01425/272310. 53 rooms with bath. Restaurant (reservations essential, jacket and tie), indoor pool, tennis, golf course, helipad. AE, DC, MC, V.

££ **Langtry Manor Hotel.** Edward VII built this house for his mistress Lillie Langtry in 1877, and it still preserves its Edwardian atmosphere. Individually named rooms continue the theme, and in the restaurant, lacy tablecloths, real silver cutlery, and other details set off the dishes, which are mainly British with French trimmings, and include Lillie's Special—meringue in the shape of a swan. There's an Edwardian banquet every Saturday. ✉ *26 Derby Rd., East Cliff,* ☎ *01202/553887,* FAX *01202/290115. 27 rooms. Restaurant (reservations essential, jacket and tie). AE, DC, MC, V.*

££££ **Swallow-Highcliff Hotel.** This large Victorian hotel has some of its rooms in converted coast-guard cottages. The bedrooms are full of period atmosphere, with mahogany wardrobes. There is a funicular that takes you down to the promenade. ✉ *105 St. Michael's Rd., West Cliff BH2 5DU,* ☎ *01202/557702,* FAX *01202/292734. 157 rooms with bath. 2 restaurants, 2 bars, pool, sauna, tennis court, recreation rooms. AE, DC, MC, V.*

£ **San Remo.** This well-built Victorian hotel is near the sea and the town center. The whole lodging has been refurbished, with cheerful flower-pattern wallpapers in the bedrooms, all of which have TVs. Dinner is available at 6 PM (bring your own wine). ✉ *7 Durley Rd., BH2 5JQ,* ☎ *01202/290558. 18 rooms, 14 with bath or shower. No credit cards. Closed Oct.–Easter.*

The Arts

FESTIVALS

Bournemouth holds a **Music Festival** (☎ 01202/451718) June–July, with choirs, brass bands, and orchestras, some from overseas.

Wimborne Minster

43 *7 mi northwest of Bournemouth.*

The impressive twin-towered minster of the quiet market town of Wimborne Minster makes it seem like a miniature cathedral city. To get here from Bournemouth, follow the signs northwest on A341. **The Priest's House Museum,** in a Tudor building with a garden, features Roman and Iron-Age exhibits, including a cryptic, three-face Celtic stone head. ✉ *23 High St.,* ☎ *01202/882533.* *£1.95.* *Apr.–Oct., Mon.–Sat. 10:30–5 (June–Sept., also Sun. 2–5); closed July 17.*

NEED A BREAK? At 26 Westborough you'll find **Quinneys,** a bakery and eating house run by the Skidmore family for nearly 30 years. They sell delicious pastries and cakes and have a daily-changing blackboard selection of such lunch specialties as grilled trout.

Blandford Forum

11 mi northeast of Wimbourne Minster.

Endowed with perhaps the handsomest Georgian town center in the southwest, this market town on the river Stour was Thomas Hardy's "Shottesford Forum." The church, with an imposing cupola and dating from 1739, is worth a detour on its own.

Dining and Lodging

££ **La Belle Alliance.** With constantly changing set menus (bistro and gourmet), this attractive, small, country restaurant offers relaxed decor and friendly owners. Try the noisettes of lamb. This is one of the increasing number of British restaurants that ban smoking. There are also six bedrooms with canopied beds. *Portnam Lodge, Whitecliffe Mill St., 01258/452842, FAX 01258/453727. 5 rooms. Restaurant. V. No lunch. Closed Sun.–Mon.*

Poole

44 *6 mi south of Wimborne Minster, 5 mi west of Bournemouth, 31 mi south of Salisbury.*

The fast-growing modern town of Poole is built around a huge natural harbor, with more than 90 miles of serrated coastline and myriad
45 bays, inlets, and islands. Ferries make regular trips to **Brownsea Island,** which belongs to the National Trust; visitors enjoy roaming the woods, relaxing on the beach, and observing rare waterfowl. *01202/666226. Round-trip from Poole Quay £3.60, from Sandbanks £2.20; landing charge £2.20 (available only Apr.–June and Sept.). Boats from Poole Quay and Sandbanks run Apr.–Sept., daily 10–8 or dusk, leaving about every 30 min; check times for last boat.*

Lodging

£ **Antelope Hotel.** Near the quay, this historic coaching inn—partly 15th-century, partly 18th-century—has been well modernized. The bedrooms at the back are the quietest, but those in front have more character. *8 Old High St., BH15 1BP, 01202/672029, FAX 01202/678286. 20 rooms with bath or shower. Restaurant. AE, DC, MC, V.*

£ **Sheldon Lodge.** Set in the Branksome Park area of Poole, this guest house is surrounded by trees and features many amenities, including billiards, a bar, and a solarium. The sunny bedrooms, all with private bathrooms, have TVs and appliances for making tea and coffee. *22 Forest Rd., Branksome Park, BH13 6DH, 01202/761186, FAX 01202/769891. 14 rooms with bath or shower. MC, V.*

Shopping

Poole Pottery (The Quay, 01202/666200) has a shop where you can buy the popular creamy ware as well as watch demonstrations of potting and decorating.

Corfe Castle

★ 46 *15 mi south of Poole, 6 mi south of Wareham.*

The spectacular ruins of Corfe Castle overlook the pretty village of Corfe. The castle site guards a gap in the surrounding range of hills and has been fortified from very early times. The present ruins are of the castle built between 1105, when the great central keep was erected, and the 1270s, when the outer walls and towers were built. It owes its ramshackle state to Cromwell's soldiers, who blew it up in 1646 during the Civil War. This is one of the most impressive ruins in Britain and will stir the imagination of all history buffs. *01929/481294. £3. Mar., daily 10–4:30; Apr.–Oct., daily 10–5:30; Nov.–early Mar., daily 11–3:30.*

NEED A BREAK? **The Fox** in Corfe (West St.) is an age-old pub with a fine view of the castle from its flowery garden and an ancient well in the lounge bar.

Lodging

£ **Castle Inn.** This charming, thatched hotel, 10 miles west of Corfe and just five minutes' walk from the sea, has a flagstone bar and other 15th-century features. There's a good restaurant with an à la carte menu for evening meals and Sunday lunch, as well as an extensive bar menu. The bedrooms are plain but comfortable, and there is a lovely rose garden to sit in and satisfying walks to take nearby. ✉ *Main St., West Lulworth, BH20 5RN,* ☎ *01929/400311,* FAX *01929/400415. 14 rooms, 10 with bath. Restaurant, bar. AE, DC, MC, V.*

Dorchester

47 *21 mi west of Corfe on A351 and A352, 30 mi west of Bournemouth, 43 mi southwest of Salisbury.*

In many ways Dorchester is a traditional southern country town. To appreciate its character, visit the local Wednesday market in the **Market Square,** where you can find Dorset delicacies, such as Blue Vinney cheese (which some connoisseurs prefer to Blue Stilton), and various handcrafted items.

Dorchester owes much of its fame to its connection with Thomas Hardy, whose bronze statue looks westward from a bank on Colliton Walk. Born in a cottage (now preserved by the National Trust) in the hamlet of Higher Brockhampton, about 3 miles northeast of Dorchester, Hardy attended school in the town and was apprentice to an architect here. Later he had a house, Max Gate (not open to the public), built to his own design on the edge of Dorchester. Hardy's study there has been reconstructed in the **Dorset County Museum,** which houses a diverse and fascinating collection. Exhibits range from ancient Celtic and Roman remains to a vicious 19th-century mantrap used to snare poachers. It was this very trap that Hardy had in mind when writing the mantrap episode in *The Woodlanders.* ✉ *High West St.,* ☎ *01305/262735.* 💷 *£2.35.* ⏲ *Daily 10–5 (except Sun., Sept.–June).*

Roman history and artifacts abound in Dorchester. The town was laid out by the Romans about AD 70, and if you walk along Bowling Alley Walk, West Walk, and Colliton Walk, you will have followed the approximate line of the original Roman town walls. On the north side of Colliton Park lies an excavated **Roman villa** with a marvelously preserved mosaic floor. The **Maumbury Rings** are one of Dorchester's most interesting sights, the remains of a Roman amphitheater on the edge of town. The site was later used as a place of execution. (Hardy's *Mayor of Casterbridge* contains a vivid evocation of the Rings.) As late as 1706, a girl was burned at the stake here. Dorchester is also associated with Monmouth's Rebellion of 1685, when Charles II's illegitimate son, the duke of Monmouth, led a rising against his unpopular uncle, James II. The rising was ruthlessly put down, and the chief justice, Lord Jeffreys, conducted the Bloody Assizes to try rebels and sympathizers. A swearing, bullying drunkard, Jeffreys was the prototypical hanging judge, and memories of his mass executions lingered for centuries throughout the South. His courtroom in Dorchester was located in what is now the Antelope Hotel on South Street.

NEED A BREAK? Try **The Potter Inn** (✉ 19 Durngate St.) for deliciously fattening cakes and pastries. It is on two floors of an attractive little 17th-century house, where local crafts are also sold.

Dorchester's popular **Dinosaur Museum** has life-size models and interactive displays. ✉ *Icen Way, off High East St.,* ☎ *01305/269880.* *£3.50.* *Apr.–Sept., daily 9:30–5:30, Oct.–Mar., daily 10–4:30.*

Dining and Lodging

£ ★ **Casterbridge Hotel.** This Georgian building (1790) reflects its age, with period furniture and Old World elegance—it's small (with no restaurant) but full of character. ✉ *49 High East St., DT1 1HU,* ☎ *01305/264043,* FAX *01305/260884. 16 rooms with bath. Bar, conservatory. AE, DC, MC, V. Closed Dec. 25–26.*

£ **Lamperts Cottage.** Here's an idyllic little B&B about 6 miles from Dorchester. It has a thatched roof and a stream in front and back so you have to cross a little bridge to reach it; in summer, it is covered with roses. The house, dating from the 16th century, is very comfortable though small; the interior has exposed beams and fireplaces. ✉ *Dorchester Rd., Sydling St. Nicholas, Cerne Abbas, DT2 9NU,* ☎ *01300/341659,* FAX *01300/341699. 3 rooms share 2 baths. No credit cards.*

££ ★ **Yalbury Cottage.** A thatch roof and inglenook fireplaces enhance the traditional ambience here, just 2½ miles east of Dorchester, close to Hardy's cottage. The three-course fixed-price menu, changed daily and featuring English and Continental dishes, might include rack of lamb (with cassis and caramelized shallot sauce), or medallions of venison with a red-currant and gin sauce. There are also eight comfortable bedrooms available in a discreet extension overlooking gardens or adjacent fields. ✉ *Lower Bockhampton,* ☎ *01305/262382,* FAX *01305/266412. MC, V. Closed 2 wks mid-winter.*

Outdoor Activities and Sports

WALKING

A 15-mile walk through Hardy country, the **Tess of the D'Urbervilles Tour** (Tour 2 from the Thomas Hardy Society, ✉ Box 1438, Dorchester, Dorset DT1 1YH, ☎ 01305/251501) follows in the sad steps of Hardy's heroine on her Sunday mission to her father-in-law, Parson Clare of Beauminster, in an attempt to rescue her failed marriage.

Cerne Abbas

48 *6 mi north of Dorchester on A352.*

The village of Cerne Abbas is worth a short exploration on foot. Some appealing Tudor houses line the road beside the church. Nearby you can also see the original village stocks. If you pass through the graveyard, you will arrive at a shallow pool known as **St. Augustine's Well.** Legend holds that the saint created it by striking the ground with his staff, thereby ensuring a regular supply of baptismal water. Tenth-century **Cerne Abbey** is now a ruin, with little left to see except its old gateway, though the nearby Abbey House is still in use. Cerne Abbas's main claim to fame is the colossal **figure of a giant,** cut in chalk on a hillside overlooking the village. The 180-foot-long giant with a huge club bears a striking resemblance to Hercules, although he probably originated as a tribal fertility symbol long before the Romans. His outlines are formed by 2-foot-wide trenches. The present giant is thought to have been carved in the chalk about AD 1200, but he could well be based on a very much older figure.

Maiden Castle

★ 49 *2 mi southwest of Dorchester, on A354.*

After Stonehenge, Maiden Castle is the most extraordinary pre-Roman archaeological site in England. It is not a castle at all, but an enormous, complex hill fort of stone and earth, built by England's mysterious prehistoric inhabitants. Many centuries later it was a Celtic stronghold. In AD 43, the invading Romans, under the general (later emperor) Vespasian, stormed it. One of the grimmest exhibits now on display in the Dorset County Museum in Dorchester was excavated here: the skeleton of a Celtic warrior transfixed by a Roman arrow. To experience an uncanny silence and sense of mystery, climb Maiden Castle early in the day (access to it is unrestricted), when other tourists are unlikely to be stirring.

Any road leading south from Dorchester will bring you to the characteristic quiet bays, shingle beaches, and low chalk cliffs of the Dorset coast. The well-marked **Dorset Coast Path** enables you to walk along some or all of the shoreline, or you can drive the narrow, country lanes hugging the coast.

Weymouth

50 *8 mi south of Dorchester on A354.*

Dorset's main coastal resort, Weymouth, is known both for its wide, safe, sandy beaches and its royal connections. King George III took up sea bathing here for his health in 1789, setting a trend among the wealthy and fashionable people of his day. They left Weymouth with many fine period buildings, including the Georgian row houses lining the esplanade. Historical details clamor for your attention. A wall on Maiden Street, for example, still holds a cannonball that was embedded in it during the Civil War. Near Maiden Street, a column commemorates the launching of the American forces from Weymouth on D-Day, June 6, 1944.

NEED A BREAK? Try the **Old Rooms** (✉ Trinity Rd.) for a fisherman's pub full of character and low beams—it has great views over the harbor.

Dining and Lodging

££ ✕ **Perry's.** A fairly basic restaurant, right by the harbor, with simple dishes of the best local seafood. Try the lemon sole and moules marinière. The meat dishes such as medallions of venison are tasty, too. ✉ *The Harbourside, 4 Trinity Rd.,* ☎ *01305/785799. MC, V. No lunch Mon., Sat.; no dinner Sun. in winter.*

££ ★ ✕🏨 **Streamside Hotel.** Quiet and cozy, this hotel/restaurant on the outskirts of town always graces its tables with fresh flowers and candles. The cuisine is English, with specialties such as smoked salmon with melon, and steak in cream and brandy sauce. There are 15 comfortable rooms available, and the hotel, with award-winning gardens, is only 200 yards from the beach. ✉ *29 Preston Rd., Overcombe DT3 6PX,* ☎ *01305/833121,* FAX *01305/832043. AE, DC, MC, V.*

Isle of Portland

51 *4 mi south of Weymouth.*

A 5-mile-long peninsula jutting south from Weymouth leads to the Isle of Portland, the eastern end of the unique geological curiosity
52 known as **Chesil Beach**—a 200-yard-wide, 30-foot-high bank of pebbles that decrease in size from east to west. The beach extends for 18 miles. A powerful undertow makes swimming dangerous, and tombstones in local churchyards attest to the many shipwrecks the beach has caused.

Abbotsbury

53 *10 mi west of Weymouth.*

At the western end of Chesil Beach lies the village of Abbotsbury. A lagoon here is a famous breeding place for swans, first introduced by Benedictine monks as a source of meat in winter. The swans have remained for centuries, building new nests every year in the soft, moist pampas grass. *Abbotsbury Swannery,* ✉ *New Barn Rd.,* ☎ *01305/871684.* 💴 *£4.50.* ⏲ *Apr.–Oct., daily 10–6 (last admission at 5).*

On the hills above Abbotsbury stands **Hardy's Monument**—dedicated not to the novelist, as many suppose, but to Sir Thomas Masterman Hardy, Nelson's flag captain at Trafalgar, to whom Nelson's dying words, "Kiss me, Hardy" (or was it, "Kismet, Hardy"?) were addressed. The monument itself is without much charm, but the surrounding view more than makes up for it. In clear weather you can scan the whole coastline between the Isle of Wight and Start Point in Devon.

NEED A BREAK? The rambling, thatched **Ilchester Arms,** near the Swannery, is an ideal spot for a good hot lunch in a conservatory.

Dining and Lodging

££ ✕🏨 **Manor Hotel.** This comfortable hotel/restaurant's pedigree goes back more than 700 years—note its flagstone floors, oak paneling, and beamed ceilings. Among the English and French dishes in which the Manor specializes are seafood and game. It also has 13 pine-furnished bedrooms. ✉ *Beach Rd., West Bexington DT2 9DF (3 mi west of Abbotsbury),* ☎ *01308/897785,* FAX *01308/897035. 13 rooms with bath or shower. Restaurant, fishing, playground. AE, DC, MC, V.*

Lyme Regis

54 *19 mi west of Abbotsbury.*

Southwest Dorset has two more places of interest: the ancient town of Lyme Regis and the so-called Fossil Coast. The cliffs in this area are especially fossil-rich. In 1810, a local child named Mary Anning dug out a complete ichthyosaurus here (it is on display in London's Natural History Museum). You may prefer to browse in the Fossil Shop in Lyme Regis. Lyme Regis is famous for its curving stone breakwater, **The Cobb,** built by King Edward I in the 13th century to improve the harbor. It was here that the duke of Monmouth landed in 1685 in his ill-fated attempt to overthrow his uncle, James II. The Cobb figures prominently in the movie *The French Lieutenant's Woman,* based on John Fowles's novel. Fowles himself is currently Lyme's most famous resident.

Outdoor Activities and Sports

WALKING

The **Dorset Coast Path** runs from Lyme Regis to Poole, bypassing Weymouth, 72 miles in all. Some highlights along the way are Golden Cap, the highest point on the South Coast; the Swannery at Abbotsbury; Lulworth Cove (between Corfe Castle and Weymouth); and Chesil Bank. As with most walks in Britain, the route is dotted with villages and isolated pubs for meals; there are also a lot of rural B&Bs, and many isolated farmhouses take guests.

THE SOUTH A TO Z

Arriving and Departing

By Bus

National Express (☎ 0990/808080) buses from London's Victoria Coach Station depart every two hours for Southampton (2½ hrs), Portsmouth (3 hrs, 20 min), Winchester (2 hrs), and Bournemouth (2½ hrs). There are two or three buses daily to Salisbury (2¾ hrs).

By Car

The South is linked to London and other major cities by a well-developed road network, which includes M3 to Winchester (59 mi) and Southampton (77 mi); A3 to Portsmouth (70 mi), and M27 along the coast, from the New Forest and Southampton to Portsmouth. For Salisbury, take the M3 to A303, then A30. A31 and A35 connect Bournemouth to Dorchester and the rest of Dorset.

By Train

British Rail serves the South from London's Waterloo Station (☎ 0171/928–5100). Travel times average an hour to Winchester; 1¼ hours to Southampton; two hours to Bournemouth; and 2½ hours to Weymouth. Salisbury takes an hour and 40 minutes, and Portsmouth about two hours (usually with a change at Winchester). There is at least one fast train every hour on all these routes.

Getting Around

By Bus

Hampshire Bus (☎ 01256/464501) has a comprehensive service in the Southampton, Eastleigh, Winchester, Andover, and Basingstoke areas. **Southern Vectis** (☎ 01983/522456) covers the Isle of Wight; ask about its "Rover" tickets. **Wilts (Wiltshire) & Dorset Bus Co.** (☎ 01722/336855) offers both one-day "Explorer" and seven-day "Busabout" tickets; it also conducts "Explorer Special" tours around Bournemouth.

By Car

The area covered in this chapter involves very easy driving. In northeast Hampshire and in many parts of neighboring Wiltshire there are lanes overhung by trees and lined with thatched cottages and Georgian houses. Often the network of such lanes starts immediately as you leave a main highway. Salisbury Plain has long, straight roads surrounded by endless vistas, and the problem here is to keep to the speed limit!

By Ferry

Wightlink (☎ 01705/827744) operates a car-ferry service between the mainland and the Isle of Wight. The crossing takes about 35 minutes from Lymington to Yarmouth; 40 minutes from Portsmouth to Fishbourne. **Red Funnel Ferries** (☎ 01703/330333) runs a car-ferry and hydrofoil service between Southampton and Cowes. **Hovertravel** (☎ 01983/811000) has a hovercraft shuttle between Southsea and Ryde.

By Plane

There is a small airport (☎ 01703/629600) at Southampton, useful for flights to the Channel Islands (☞ Chapter 6).

By Train

A "Network" card, valid throughout the South and Southeast for a year, entitles you to one-third off particular fares. For local information, call British Rail at Bournemouth, ☎ 01202/292474, or, for Salisbury, Southampton, or Winchester, ☎ 01703/229393 or 01256/464966.

Guided Tours

The **Southern Tourist Board** (☎ 01703/620555) and **Wessexplore** (☎ 01722/326304) can reserve qualified Blue Badge guides who will arrange to meet you anywhere in the region for private tours of different lengths and themes.

Guide Friday (☎ 01789/294466) has a daily Stonehenge tour from Salisbury, May to September, and weekends in April and October to mid-November, costing £12, but check for availability.

Contacts and Resources

Car-Rental Agencies

Bournemouth: Avis, ✉ 400 Poole Rd., Branksome, Bournemouth, ☎ 01202/751974; **Hertz,** Palace Parking, ✉ Hinton Rd., ☎ 01202/291231.

Ryde: Avis, St. John's Railway Station, ✉ St. John's Rd., ☎ 01983/615522; **Esplanade,** ✉ 9–11 George St., ☎ 01983/562322.

Salisbury: Budget Rent-a-Car, ✉ Brunel Rd., Churchfields Industrial Estate, ☎ 01722/336444; **Europcar Ltd.,** ✉ Fisherton Yard, Fisherton St., ☎ 01722/335625.

Travel Agencies

American Express: ✉ 99 Above Bar, Southampton, Hants SO14 7SG, ☎ 01703/634722.

Thomas Cook: ✉ 7 Richmond Hill, Bournemouth, Dorset BH2 6HF, ☎ 01202/292541; 47 High St., Newport, Isle of Wight PO30 1SX, ☎ 01983/521111; ✉ 18 Queen St., Salisbury, Wilts SP1 1EY, ☎ 01722/412787; and ✉ 30 High St., Winchester, Hants SO23 9BL, ☎ 01962/841661.

Visitor Information

The Southern Tourist Board (✉ 40 Chamberlayne Rd., Eastleigh, Hants S050 5JH, ☎ 01703/620006, FAX 01703/620010) is open Monday–Thursday 8:30–5, Friday 8:30–4:30. Local TICs are normally open Monday–Saturday 9:30–5:30.

Bournemouth: ✉ Westover Rd. (overlooking the bandstand), ☎ 01202/451700). **Dorchester:** ✉ 1 Acland Rd., ☎ 01305/267992. **Portsmouth:** ✉ The Hard, ☎ 01705/826722; ✉ Clarence Esplanade, Southsea [Easter–Oct.], ☎ 01705/832464. **Ryde:** ✉ 14 The Esplanade, ☎ 01983/562905. **Salisbury:** ✉ Fish Row, just off Market Sq., ☎ 01722/334956. **Winchester:** ✉ The Guildhall, The Broadway, ☎ 01962/840500.

5 The Southwest

Somerset, Devon, Cornwall

Half the fun of exploring the peninsula known as the West Country is getting lost. On your way down to Land's End, every zig and zag of the road reveals rugged moorlands—this is where The Hound of the Baskervilles *was set—lush river valleys, and festive coastal resorts. Explore the mist-wreathed sights of King Arthur Country, then head for Clovelly, jewel of the British Riviera. Along the way, take in the region's beaches for that bracing wind-in-your-face feeling. Whatever your itinerary, be sure to stray from the main roads—it would be a great pity not to.*

Updated by Robert Andrews

IF YOU HAVE TIME TO LEAVE LONDON for more than a few days, the southwest of England can be one of the most relaxing places to visit. The three counties that make up the long southern peninsula known as the West Country are Somerset, Devon, and Cornwall, and each has a distinct flavor. In the peninsula you'll be surprised to discover a regionalism that amounts almost to patriotism. Somerset is noted for its rolling green countryside; Devon's wild and dramatic moors contract with the restfulness of its many sandy beaches and coves. And Cornwall has managed to retain something of its old insularity, despite the annual invasion of thousands of holidaymakers who flock here for vacations by the sea or English Channel. Natives don't mind the water's very doubtful temperature, but foreigners, pampered by the warm waves of the Mediterranean, are not so eager to brave the elements. The sea—even in Cornwall, where it seems to be warmer than anywhere else in the British Isles—is not to be enjoyed in a sensuous way: It is a bracing experience that sometimes leaves you rather breathless and shivering.

Many travelers first head for King Arthur Country. Although King Arthur's name is linked with more than 150 places in Britain, no area can claim stronger ties than the West Country. According to tradition, Arthur was born at Tintagel Castle in Cornwall and later lived at Camelot, in the kingdom of Avalon (said to be Glastonbury, in Somerset).

Somerset, the region's tranquil northernmost county, is characterized by miles and miles of rolling green countryside—best seen in a cloak of summer heat when its orchards give ample shade, its bees are singing their humming song, and its old stone houses and inns welcome you with a breath of coolness. Along the north coast stand the Quantock and Mendip hills, and at their feet the stark, heather-covered expanse of Exmoor, setting for R. D. Blackmore's historical romance, *Lorna Doone.*

Devon, farther west, is famed for its wild moorland—especially Dartmoor, fictional home of the "hound of the Baskervilles," and actual home to wild ponies and an assortment of strange "tors," rock outcrops eroded into weird shapes. Devon's large coastal towns are as interesting for their cultural and historical appeal—many were smugglers' havens—as for their scenic beauty. Some propagandists of south Devon speak of the "red cliffs of Devon" in contrast to the allegedly "white cliffs of Dover." This reddish soil is perhaps one of the reasons why the coast of Devon is sometimes referred to as the British Riviera; you meet the same hue in southern France. The best time to visit Devon is late summer and early fall, during the end-of-summer festivals, especially in the small towns of eastern Dartmoor.

Cornwall, England's southernmost county, has a mild climate, and nowhere are you more than 20 miles from the sea. Until relatively recently, the county regarded itself as separate from the rest of Britain. Its Atlantic coast is punctuated with high jagged cliffs that look dangerous and dramatic and are a menace to passing ships, while the south coast relaxes with sunny beaches, delightful coves, and popular resorts.

Pleasures and Pastimes

Dining

Somerset is the home of Britain's most famous cheese, the ubiquitous Cheddar, from the Mendip Hills village. If you are lucky enough to taste real farmhouse Cheddar, made in the traditional "truckle," you may find it hard to return to processed cheese. The calorie-conscious should beware of Devon's cream teas, which traditionally consist of a pot of tea, homemade scones, and lots of thickened "clotted" cream and strawberry jam. Cornwall's specialty is the "pasty," a pastry shell filled with chopped meat, onions, and potatoes. The pasty was originally devised as a handy way for miners to carry their dinner to work. "Scrumpy," a homemade dry cider, is refreshing but carries a kick. English wine, which is similar to German wine, is made in Somerset, while in Cornwall you can get mead made from local honey.

CATEGORY	COST*
££££	over £50
£££	£30–£50
££	£20–£30
£	under £20

**per person, including first course, main course, dessert, and VAT; excluding drinks*

Horseback Riding

The Southwest is ideal for cross-country pony riding, and it is often possible to ride the Dartmoor and Exmoor breeds of ponies.

Lodging

Accommodations in the Southwest range from national hotel chains that extend as far west as Plymouth, to bed-and-breakfast places. With the growth of the tourist industry, many farmhouses in rural areas have begun renting out rooms.

CATEGORY	COST*
££££	over £150
£££	£80–£150
££	£60–£80
£	under £60

**All prices are for two people sharing a double room, including service, breakfast, and VAT.*

Walking

A wonderful 10-mile walk is a clifftop hike along the coast from Hartland Quay down to Lower Sharpnose Point, just above Bude. The coast below Bude is also ideal for walking, especially the section around Tintagel. Experienced hikers may find many Dartmoor walks of great interest. The areas around Widgery Cross, Becky Falls, and the Bovey Valley, and—for the really energetic and adventuresome—Highest Dartmoor, south of Okehampton, are all worth considering. A much shorter walk, but no less spectacular, is along the Lydford Gorge. Long walks on Dartmoor, which is a lonely region, are only for the most experienced walkers. For complete information, contact the National Parks Authority.

For those interested in "theme" walks, there is the Saints Way, a 25-mile Cornish walk between Padstow and the Camel Estuary on the north coast to Fowey on the south coast. The path follows a Bronze Age trading route, later used by Celtic saints to reach scattered farms and moor communities, and several relics of such times can be seen along the way. Contact the Cornwall Tourist Board.

Water Sports

Looe, on the south coast of Cornwall, is known for shark fishing, and boats can be rented for mackerel fishing from most harbors on the south coast. This is also a good sailing area, with plenty of safe harbors, new marinas, and deepwater channels, mainly at Falmouth, Plymouth

Sound, and Torbay. Its beaches have long made the Southwest one of Britain's main family vacation areas. Be aware of the tides if you want to explore around an adjoining headland; otherwise you may find yourself cut off. At many of the major resorts, flags show the limits of safe swimming, as there can be strong undertows, especially on the northern coast.

Exploring the Southwest

There is plenty of contrast to be found within this peninsula, though the farther west you travel, the more the sea becomes an overwhelming presence. On the whole, the northern coast is more rugged, the cliffs dropping dramatically to tiny coves and beaches, while the south coast shelters many more resorts and much wider expanses of sand. In general, this is where the crowds will be, but there are also plenty of secluded inlets and estuaries along this southern littoral, and you do not need to go far to find a degree of tranquillity.

Great Itineraries

Our circular tour of the Southwest covers a lot of territory, from the gentle hills of Somerset, two hours outside London, to the remote and rocky headlands of Devon and Cornwall. Unless you confine yourself to a few choice towns—for example Exeter, Penzance, and Plymouth—you will be at a huge disadvantage without your own transport. The main arteries of the region are the M5 motorway, ending at Exeter, the A30, which burrows through the center of Devon and Cornwall all the way to Land's End, and the A38, which loops south of Dartmoor to take in Plymouth. Beyond Plymouth, there are few main roads, which means lots of traffic congestion in the summer months. Take minor roads whenever possible, if only to see the real West Country, which should be appreciated at a leisurely pace with frequent stops. Rail travelers can make use of a fast service connecting Exeter, Plymouth, and Penzance, and there is also a good network of coach services.

Numbers in the text correspond to numbers in the margin and on the maps.

IF YOU HAVE 3 DAYS

Three days will provide a sadly limited view of what the Southwest has to offer, and you should concentrate on only one area in order to avoid unnecessary traveling at the expense of exploring. Pass through the tiny cathedral city of **Wells** ①, stopping long enough to whirl round the great church, on your way down to **Glastonbury** ②, a small town awash with layers of Arthurian and early Christian myth. Move on to spend your first night in 🏨 **Exeter** ㊻. The cathedral here is of a very different order to that of Wells, but equally grand, and the city itself has plenty more to offer, not least the quayside, home to the Maritime Museum. After a day in Exeter, follow the A30 back east, which will take you to 🏨 **Honiton** ㊾, a handsome Georgian town renowned for its lace industry, for your second overnight. For your third day, head out to some of the Southwest's most magical sights, including **Montecute House** ⑥⓪ and **Cadbury Castle** ⑥②.

IF YOU HAVE 5 DAYS

As above, your first day will take in **Wells** ① and **Glastonbury** ②, driving on to spend your first night in 🏨 **Exeter** ㊻. Explore the city on your second day and then drive west to 🏨 **Plymouth** ㊳ for your second night. For all its unprepossessing appearance, Plymouth offers a wide gamut of attractions. Arguably the most impressive of these is Plymouth Hoe itself, a spectacular platform overlooking Plymouth Sound, where you can look down on a timeless scene of craft of all

The Southwest

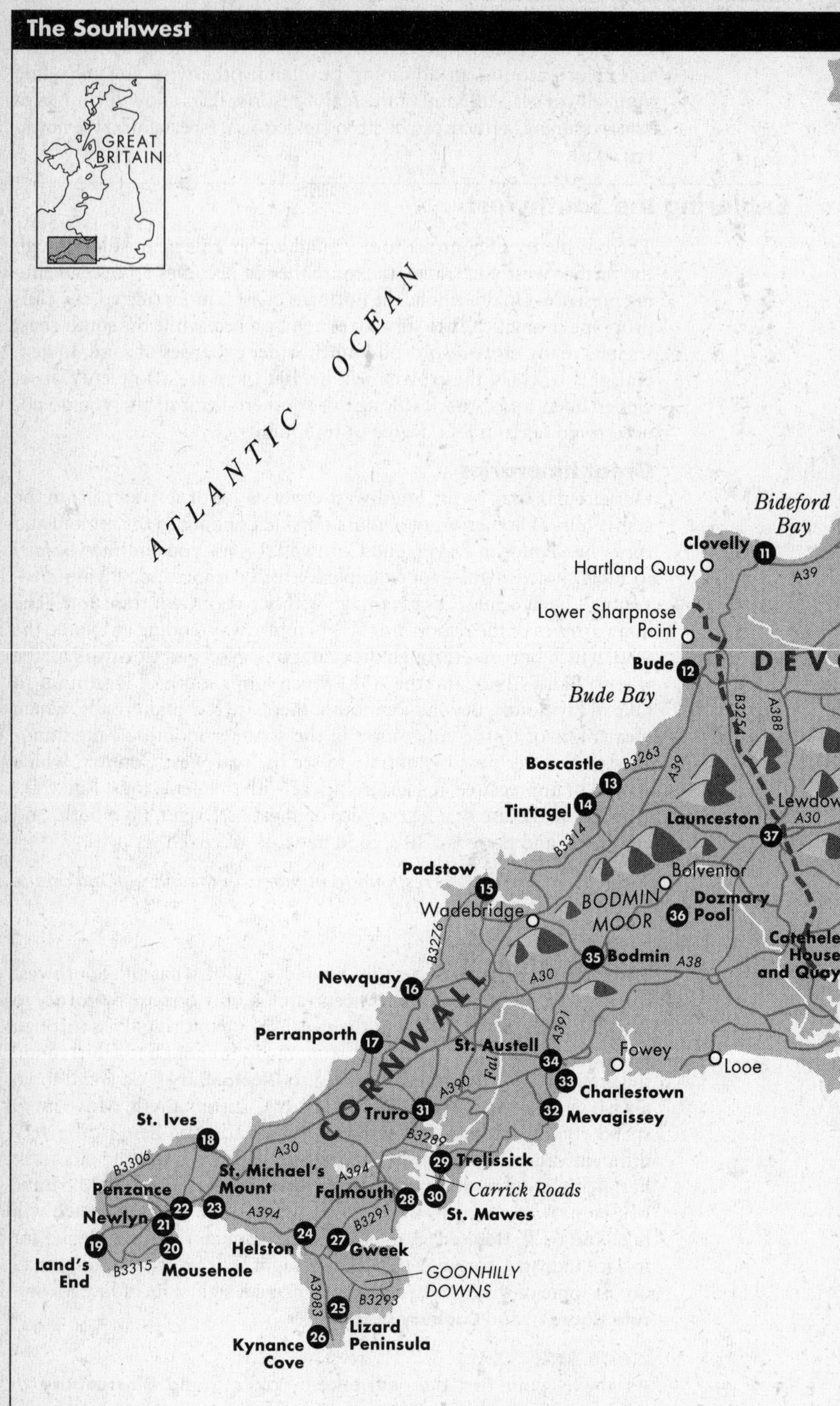

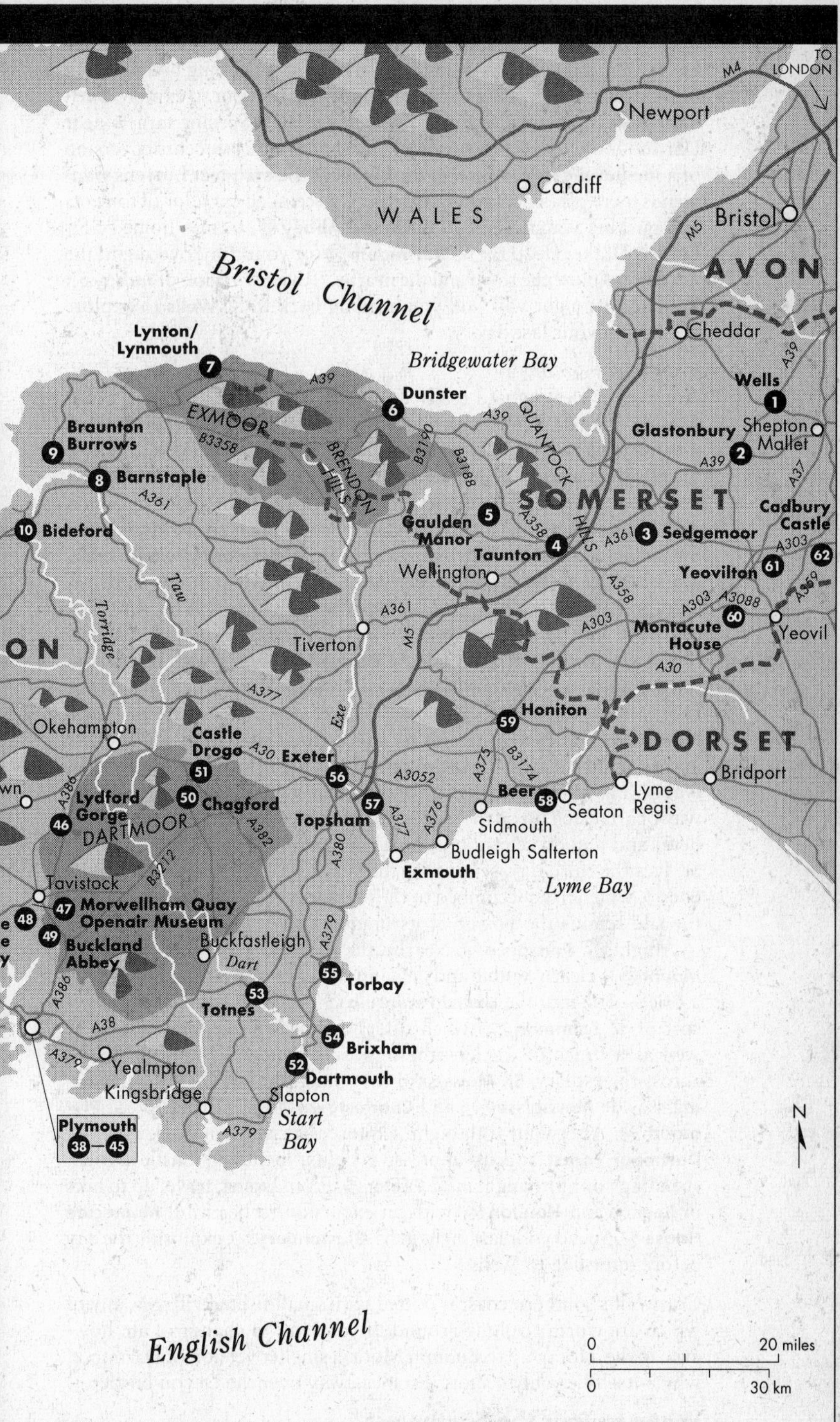
TO LONDON
M4
Newport
Cardiff
WALES
Bristol
M5
AVON
Bristol Channel
Cheddar
Lynton/ Lynmouth
7
Bridgewater Bay
A39
Wells
1
Dunster
6
A39
QUANTOCK HILLS
EXMOOR
Glastonbury
Shepton Mallet
2
Braunton Burrows
9
B3358
BRENDON HILLS
B3190
B3188
A39
A37
8
Barnstaple
A361
SOMERSET
Cadbury Castle
10
Bideford
Gaulden Manor
5
A358
4
Taunton
A361
3
Sedgemoor
A303
62
Yeovilton
61
Wellington
Taw
Torridge
A358
A3088
A303
60
Yeovil
A361
Montacute House
ON
Tiverton
M5
A303
A30
A377
Exe
Honiton
59
Okehampton
Castle Drogo
51
A30
Exeter
56
DORSET
A386
A375
B3174
Lyme Regis
Bridport
A3052
Lydford Gorge
50
Chagford
57
Beer
58
Seaton
46
DARTMOOR
A382
Topsham
A377
A376
Sidmouth
Budleigh Salterton
A380
Exmouth
Tavistock
B3212
Lyme Bay
47
Morwellham Quay Openair Museum
48
49
Buckland Abbey
Buckfastleigh
A379
Dart
55
Torbay
A386
53
Totnes
A38
54
Brixham
A379
Yealmpton
52
Dartmouth
Kingsbridge
Slapton
Start Bay
A379
Plymouth
38—45
N
English Channel
0
20 miles
0
30 km

shapes against the mighty backdrop of the Atlantic. Don't miss the Mayfair Steps, point of embarkation of the Pilgrim Fathers, or the old Barbican area, a nucleus of shops, restaurants, and bobbing boats, which repays an aimless wander. The third morning pull out to explore **Dartmoor Forest,** one of England's last wildernesses. Specific targets near Dartmoor include **Castle Drogo** (51), an impressive 20th-century version of a medieval castle, which in the hands of the architect Lutyens transcends mere pastiche, **Lydford Gorge** ㊻, a secluded corridor of torrents and gushing waterfalls, and **Buckland Abbey** ㊾, former home of Sir Francis Drake. Head for **Dartmouth** (52) for your third overnight; the next day explore the town and the nearby "Riviera" region of **Torbay** (55). Your fourth night will find you heading back to **Wells** to explore the city on your last day.

IF YOU HAVE 8 DAYS

Not even a week would really do justice to this dense region, but it would certainly give you a chance to push on into Cornwall, and get a better idea of what the Southwest has to offer. First up is a tour of the northern coast of Somerset and Devon, making stops at **Dunster** ⑥, site of a turreted and battlemented castle, or the twin towns of **Lynton** and **Lynmouth** ⑦, in a narrow cleft once likened to a fragment of Switzerland, but thankfully outliving the hype. **Bideford** ⑩ would make a good place to break for lunch, while Bideford Bay holds the postcard-pretty clifftop village of **Clovelly** ⑪, which will be your first overnight stay. The second day explore this relentlessly picturesque harbor town, then press on to take in **Tintagel** ⑭, which with or without the Arthurian associations presents a dramatic sight perched on its black rock above the swirling waves. Make stops in **Padstow** ⑮ and **Newquay** ⑯ only if you want to sample the fish'n'chips atmosphere and generous beaches of these typical seaside resorts. Pull into **St. Ives** ⑱ for your second night; the town has a great deal to offer in the way of art (catch up on the local scene displayed in the new Tate Gallery here) and a good selection of hotels and restaurants. After taking in St. Ives the third day, set out for the very tip of the peninsula, **Land's End** ⑲, which has succumbed to the pressures of mass tourism, though the site retains the power of its unique locale. Head for your next overnight, **Penzance** ㉒. Nearby, the island fortress of **St. Michael's Mount** ㉓ is clearly visible and demands a closer inspection. Now make a brief sortie into the **Lizard Peninsula** ㉕ and base yourself in the resort of **Falmouth** ㉘, which offers a range of accommodation as well as a brace of castles—the imposing Pendennis and its sibling across the estuary, **St. Mawes** ㉚. On your fifth day, begin by exploring seaside **Mevagissey** ㉜ and **Charlestown** ㉝, then head for **Plymouth** ㊳. After your fifth night, explore the city, then track down to **Dartmoor Forest** and its impressive sights, including Castle Drogo, spending your fifth night in **Exeter** (56). From Exeter, travel up to take in **Beer** (58) and **Honiton** (59), with an excursion to beautiful **Montecute House** (60). Spend your last night in **Glastonbury** ②, exploring the city before returning to Wells.

Cornwall's southern coast is dotted with small fishing villages, any of which are worth strolling around. If you fancy a change of air, however, make a foray up to Bodmin Moor, a smaller version of Dartmoor, which itself lies only a short distance away over the Devon border.

When to Tour the Southwest

Come July and August and the roads leading into the Southwest are choked with endless streams of traffic. Somehow, the region seems able to absorb all the "grockles," or tourists, though the chances of finding a remote oasis of peace and quiet are severely curtailed at this time of year. The beaches, in particular, heave with hopeful sun-seekers, and the resort towns are either bubbling with zest or unbearably tacky depending on your point of view. If you can't avoid visiting in the holiday season, you will need to work harder to find your own space, and your best option would be to hole up in a secluded hotel and make brief excursions from there. Otherwise, try to time your visit to coincide with the beginning or end of the summer. The West Country gets more hours of sunshine than most other parts of Britain, so you can afford to take your chances with the weather. That said, the winter has its own special appeal, when the Atlantic waves crash dramatically against the coast, and austere Cornish cliffs come into their own.

KING ARTHUR COUNTRY: FROM WELLS TO TINTAGEL

Exloring King Arthur Country means wending your way between documented history and the world of myth. Start in the cathedral city of Wells and continue on via Glastonbury, possibly the Avalon of Arthurian legend. From there head south to Taunton, the capital of cider country, and also at the center of some monumental tussles in the English Civil War. Proceed west along the Somerset coast into Devon, skirting Exmoor, tracing the northern coast via Clovelly and Bude, and end at the cliff-top ruins of Tintagel Castle in Cornwall, legendary birthplace of Arthur.

Numbers in the margin correspond to points of interest on the Southwest map.

Wells

❶ *22 mi south of Bristol, 20 mi southwest of Bath, 132 mi west of London.*

Wells, England's smallest cathedral city, lies at the foot of the Mendip Hills. While it feels more like a quiet country town than a city, Wells is home to one of the great masterpieces of Gothic architecture. The city's name refers to the underground streams that bubble up into St. Andrew's Well within the grounds of the Bishop's Palace. Spring water has run through the High Street since the 15th century. The ancient Market Place in the city center is surrounded by 17th-century buildings. William Penn was arrested here in 1695 for preaching without a license at the Crown Hotel (☞ Dining and Lodging, *below*). Though the elaborate fountain at the entrance to the square is only 200 years old, it's on the same spot as the lead conduit that brought fresh spring water to the market in medieval times. Wells has a Market Day on Wednesday and Saturday.

★ The great west towers of the famous **Cathedral Church of St. Andrew** are visible for miles. To appreciate the elaborate west front facade, approach the building on foot from the cathedral green, accessible from Market Place through a great medieval gate called "penniless porch" (named after the beggars who once waited here to collect alms from worshipers). The cathedral's west front is twice as wide as it is high and is adorned with some 300 statues. This is the oldest surviving English Gothic church, begun in the 12th century. Vast inverted arches were added in 1338 to stop the central tower from sinking to one side. Present erosion is causing a great deal of anxiety, and a restoration program is under way. The cathedral also has a rare, medieval clock, consisting of the seated figure of a man called Jack Blandiver, who strikes a bell on the quarter hour while mounted knights circle in mock battle. Near the clock you will find the entrance to the chapter house—a small, wooden door opening onto a great sweep of stairs worn down on one side by the tread of pilgrims over the centuries.

NEED A BREAK? The **Cathedral Cloisters Café,** inside the cathedral, serves scones, cake, sandwiches, soup, and a hot dish at lunchtime.

The second great gate leading from Market Place, the Bishop's Eye, takes you to the **Bishop's Palace.** Most of its original 12th- and 13th-century residences remain, and you can also see the ruins of a late 13th-century great hall, which lost its roof in the 16th century because Edward VI needed the lead! The palace is surrounded by a moat that's home to a variety of waterfowl, including swans. ✉ *Market Pl.,* ☎ *01749/678691.* 🎫 *£2.50.* ⏲ *Easter–Oct., Tues.–Thurs. 10–6, Sun. 2–6; Aug. and national holidays, daily 10–6.*

North of the cathedral, **Vicar's Close,** Europe's oldest street, has terraces of handsome 14th-century houses with strange, tall chimneys, and a tiny medieval chapel that's still in use.

Dining and Lodging

£ ✕ **Ancient Gate House.** Traditional Italian dishes made largely from local produce are the specialty here. There is also an English menu. ✉ *20 Sadler St.,* ☎ *01749/672029. AE, DC, MC, V.*

£ ✕ **Ritcher's.** Choose between eating downstairs or in the plant-filled loft upstairs in this bistro, where you can get good-value two- or three-course fixed-price meals. Among the dishes on offer are steak and mushroom pie, pork with Stilton, and guinea fowl en croûte. ✉ *5 Sadler St.,* ☎ *01749/679085. AE, DC, MC, V.*

£££ ✕🏨 **Swan Hotel.** Built in the 15th century, this former coaching inn faces the cathedral. Nine of the rooms have four-poster beds, and on cold days you can relax in front of a log fire in one of the lounges. The restaurant displays costumes owned by the great Victorian actor, Sir Henry Irving. Its menus change daily. ✉ *11 Sadler St., BA5 2RX,* ☎ *01749/678877,* FAX *01749/677647. 38 rooms with bath. Restaurant. AE, DC, MC, V.*

£ ✕🏨 **The Crown.** This hotel has been a landmark in Wells since the Middle Ages; William Penn was arrested here in 1695 for illegal preaching. There is a period atmosphere to the place, enhanced by the fact that four of the rooms have four-poster beds. There's also a particularly helpful staff. The Penn Bar and Eating House serves salads and such hot dishes as steak-and-kidney pie. ✉ *Market Pl., BA5 2RP,* ☎ *01749/673457,* FAX *01749/679792. 15 rooms with bath. Restaurant, bar. AE, DC, MC, V.*

OFF THE BEATEN PATH **WOOKEY HOLE –** Signs in Wells town center will direct you 2 miles north to Wookey Hole, a fascinating complex of limestone caves in the Mendip Hills that may have been the home of Iron Age people. In addition to a museum, there is an underground lake and several newly opened chambers to explore, plus a working paper mill and a display of Madame Tussaud's early waxwork collection dating from the 1830s. ☎ *01749/672243.* 🎫 *£6.* ⏲ *Mar.–Oct., daily 9:30–5:30; Nov.–Feb., daily 10:30–4:30. Closed Dec. 25.*

Six miles farther north by A371 lie the **Cheddar Caves.** This beautiful, subterranean world of stalactites, stalagmites, and naturally colored stone is enhanced by holograms and stunning man-made optical effects. ✉ *Cheddar,* ☎ *01934/742343.* 🎫 *£6.50.* ⏲ *Summer, daily 10–5; winter, daily 10:30–4:30.*

At **Chewton Cheese Dairy** north of Cheddar Gorge, you can see how Cheddar cheese is made in the traditional truckles, and watch butter being churned by hand. ✉ *Priory Farm, Chewton Mendip (north of Wells),* ☎ *01761/241666.* 🎟 *£2.50.* ⏲ *Shop and restaurant Mon.–Sat. 9–5, Sun. 10–4:30; cheesemaking Mon.–Wed. and Fri.–Sat., best viewing noon–2:30.*

Glastonbury

❷ *5 mi southwest of Wells, just off A39, 27 mi south of Bristol, 27 mi southwest of Bath.*

★ At the foot of **Glastonbury Tor,** a grassy hill rising 520 feet, the town of Glastonbury is steeped in history, myth, and legend. In legend, Glastonbury is identified with Avalon, the paradise into which King Arthur was born after his death. It is also said to be the burial place of Arthur and Guinevere, his queen. And according to Christian tradition, it was to Glastonbury, the first Christian settlement in England, that Joseph of Arimathea brought the Holy Grail, the chalice used by Christ at the Last Supper. At the foot of the tor is **Chalice Well,** the legendary burial place of the Grail. It's a stiff climb up the tor, but you'll be rewarded by the view across the Vale of Avalon. At the top stands a ruined tower, all that's left of **St. Michael's Church,** which collapsed after a landslide in 1271.

The ruins of the great **Abbey of Glastonbury** lie in the center of town. According to legend, this is the site where Joseph of Arimathea built a church in the 1st century; a monastery had certainly been erected here by the 9th century. The ruins are those of the abbey completed in 1524 and destroyed in 1539, during Henry VIII's dissolution of the monasteries. ☎ *01458/832267.* 🎟 *£2.50.* ⏲ *June–Aug., daily 9–6; Sept.–May, daily 9:30–dusk.*

While you are in Glastonbury, visit the Abbey Barn, which now houses the **Somerset Rural Life Museum.** This 14th-century tithe barn stored the one-tenth portion of the town's produce due the church, and it is more than 90 feet long. ✉ *Chilkwell St.,* ☎ *01458/831197.* 🎟 *£1.80.* ⏲ *Apr.–Oct., Tues.–Fri. 10–5, weekends 2–6; Nov.–Mar., Tues.–Fri. 10–5, Sat. 11–4.*

Lodging

££ 🏨 **George and Pilgrims Hotel.** Pilgrims en route to Glastonbury Abbey stayed here in the 15th century. Today, all the modern comforts are here, but you can enjoy them in rooms with flagstone floors, wooden beams, and antique furniture; ask for one of the three rooms with a four-poster bed. ✉ *1 High St., BA6 9DP,* ☎ *01458/831146,* FAX *01458/832252. 13 rooms with bath or shower. Restaurant, bar. AE, DC, MC, V.*

££ 🏨 **No. 3.** This Georgian house next to the abbey ruins offers log fires in the winter and a terrace for summer evenings. Bedrooms are attractive and well-equipped and the ambience is elegant yet relaxed. ✉ *3 Magdalene St., BA6 9EW,* ☎ *01458/832129. 5 rooms with bath. Beauty salon. MC, V.*

Shopping

Morlands Factory Shop (✉ 2 mi southwest of Glastonbury on A39, ☎ 01458/835042) is one of several good outlets for sheepskin products in Somerset sheep country, selling coats, slippers, and rugs. Glastonbury's market day is Tuesday.

En Route West of Glastonbury, the A39 and A361 toward Taunton cross the Somerset Levels, marshes that have been drained by open ditches (known

3 as rhines), where peat is dug. **Sedgemoor** is where, in 1685, the duke of Monmouth's troops were routed by those of his uncle James II in the last battle fought on English soil. R. D. Blackmore's novel, *Lorna Doone,* is set during Monmouth's Rebellion.

Taunton

4 *22 mi southwest of Glastonbury, 50 mi southwest of Bristol, 18 mi northeast of Exeter.*

Somerset's principal town lies in the heart of the cider-making country. In these parts, cider rather than beer is the traditional beverage. Fermented and alcoholic, it can be a lot more potent than English beer. In the fall, some cider mills open their doors to visitors. If you're interested, visit **Sheppys,** a local farm, shop, and cider museum. ✉ *Three Bridges, Bradford-on-Tone (on A38 west of Taunton),* ☎ *01823/461233.* 🎫 *£1.75; guided tour (2½ hrs), £3.50.* ⏲ *Mon.–Sat. 8:30–6; Easter–Dec. 25, also Sun. noon–2.*

NEED A BREAK? **Porters Wine Bar** (✉ 49 E. Reach) in Taunton serves both light lunches and more substantial meals at very reasonable prices.

Dining and Lodging

£££ ★ ✕🏨 **The Castle.** The battlements and towers of this 300-year-old building will leave you in no doubt as to why this hotel, reputed to be among England's finest, has the name it does. The facade is covered by a huge, 350-year-old wisteria, magnificent when in flower. Bedrooms are individually decorated, and garden suites have separate dressing rooms. In the hotel's restaurant, with its daily-changing, fixed-price menus, the *haute cuisine* ranges from braised shoulder of lamb with thyme and garlic to elaborate desserts such as baked egg custard tart with nutmeg ice cream. The cheese selection includes many English cheeses and is served with homemade bacon-and-onion bread. ✉ *Castle Green, TA1 1NF,* ☎ *01823/272671,* FAX *01823/336066. 36 rooms with bath. Restaurant (reservations essential, jacket and tie). AE, DC, MC, V.*

OFF THE BEATEN PATH **COLDHARBOUR MILL** – The wool trade was the mainstay of Devon's wealth for centuries, and at Uffculme, 6 miles east of Tiverton by A373, Coldharbour Mill has been restored as a working museum where you can see the stages in the transformation of fleece into cloth. The Mill now displays a New World Tapestry, depicting the story of colonization between 1583 and 1642. ✉ *Uffculme, Cullompton,* ☎ *01884/840960.* 🎫 *£4.* ⏲ *Easter–Oct., daily 11–5; Nov.–Easter, weekdays: check for times.*

En Route North of Taunton you will see the outlines of the **Quantock** and **Brendon hills.** The eastern Quantocks are covered with beech trees and are home to herds of handsome red deer. Climb to the top of the hills for a spectacular view of the Vale of Taunton Deane and to the north the Bristol Channel.

Tolland

9 mi northwest of Taunton.

5 In a quiet valley between the Quantock and Brendon hills, **Gaulden Manor** is a small 12th-century estate, whose house is built of red sandstone. Its elegant grounds include an Elizabethan herb garden. It was the home of the Turberville family, a name familiar to readers of *Tess of the d'Urbervilles,* by Thomas Hardy. ✉ *Tolland,* ☎ *01984/667213.*

£3.50; garden only, £1.50 1st Sun. in May–1st Sun. in Sept., Sun. and Thurs. and national holidays 2–5:30.

Dunster

6 *12 mi northwest of Tolland, 43 mi north of Exeter.*

Lying between the Somerset coast and the edge of Exmoor National Park, Dunster is a picture-book village with a broad main street. Look for the eight-sided yarn-market building dating from 1589. The village is dominated by its 13th-century fortress, **Dunster Castle,** a National Trust property boasting fine plaster ceilings and a magnificent 17th-century staircase. Note that there is a steep climb up to the castle from the parking lot. To reach Dunster from Tolland, follow B3188, B3190, and A39. *01643/821314. £5, gardens only £2.70. Apr.–Sept., Sat.–Wed. 11–5; Oct., Sat.–Wed. 11–4. Gardens Jan.–mid-Dec., daily 11–4 (11–5 Apr.–Sept.).*

En Route Heading west, the coast road A39 mounts **Porlock Hill,** an incline so steep that signs are posted to encourage drivers to "Keep Going." The views across Exmoor and north to the Bristol Channel and Wales are worth it.

Lynton and Lynmouth

7 *19 mi west of Dunster, 60 mi northwest of Exeter.*

This pretty pair of Devonshire villages is separated by a hugely steep hill. Lynmouth, a fishing village, is at the bottom, crouching below 1,000-foot cliffs at the mouths of the rivers East and West Lynne.

Lodging

££ ★ **Rising Sun.** A recent conversion from a 14th-century inn and a row of thatched cottages has created this intriguing hotel. It has great views over Lynmouth, especially from the terraced garden out back. The whole effect is comfortable and welcoming, the rooms furnished either in pine or older pieces: Nos. 4 and 5 are especially recommended, as is the detached cottage in the garden (also available for weekly rental). This is one of two places in Lynmouth claiming to be where the poet Shelley spent his honeymoon. *Harbourside, Lynmouth EX35 6EQ, 01598/753223, FAX 01598/753480. 16 rooms with bath. Restaurant, fishing. AE, DC, MC, V.*

Barnstaple

8 *21 mi southwest of Lynton on A39, 42 mi northwest of Exeter.*

Barnstaple, on the banks of the river Taw, is northern Devon's largest city. It's a bustling market town surrounded by modern developments, though the center retains its traditional look. Try to visit on Friday, market day, to see the colorful scene in Butchers' Row and Pannier Market. West of Barnstaple, along the Taw estuary, lie desolate stretches of sand dunes offering long vistas of marram grass and sea.

Dining and Lodging

££ **Royal and Fortescue Hotel.** Edward VII, who stayed here when he was Prince of Wales, gave this Victorian hotel the royal part of its name. It's in the center of town and has recently been refurbished. All rooms are furnished to a high standard, and there's a choice of à la carte or table d'hôte menu in the restaurant. *Boutport St., EX31 1HG, 01271/42289, FAX 01271/42289. 62 rooms with bath or shower. Restaurant. AE, DC, MC, V.*

Braunton Burrows

9 *10 mi west of Lynton.*

Braunton Burrows, on the north side of the Taw estuary, is a National Nature Reserve, with miles of trails running through the dunes. This is a first-class bird-watching spot, especially in winter.

Bideford

10 *8 mi west of Barnstaple by A39, 49 mi northwest of Exeter.*

Broad Bideford Bay is fed by the confluence of the Taw and Torridge rivers. Bideford lies on the Torridge, which you can cross either by the 14th-century, 24-arch bridge or by the more modern structure to reach the scenic hillside sheltering the town's elegant houses. At one time they were all painted white, and Bideford is still sometimes called the "little white town." The area was a mainstay of 16th-century shipbuilding; the trusty vessels of Sir Francis Drake among others were built here.

Clovelly

11 *12 mi west of Bideford, 60 mi northwest of Exeter.*

Clovelly always seems to have the sun shining on its stepped and cobbled streets. A village of quaint atmosphere and picturesqueness, it can be compared with villages in the south of France, such as St. Tropez (it can also be as overrun with day-trippers as that Provence pleasure spot). Perched precariously among cliffs, a steep, cobbled road (tumbling down at such an angle that it has to be closed to cars) leads to the toy-like harbor. The climb back has been compared to the Bataan Death March, but, happily, a Land Rover service (in summer) will take you to and from the parking lot at the top.

Lodging

££ **Red Lion Hotel.** One of only two hotels in this picturesque coastal village, the Red Lion is an 18th-century inn right on the harbor. All rooms enjoy sea views and are well-equipped, though you have to put up with uneven floors, tiny windows, and restricted space. The climb up through Clovelly is perilously steep, but hotel guests can bring cars via a back road to and from the Red Lion. ✉ *The Quay, EX39 5TF,* ☎ *01237/431237,* FAX *01237/431044. 12 rooms with bath. Restaurant, bar. MC, V.*

Bude

12 *15 mi south of Clovelly.*

Just across the Cornish border, the popular Victorian seaside town of Bude is known for its long sandy beaches. But beware: In summer, the town and beaches are overrun with tourists.

Boscastle

13 *15 mi southwest of Bude.*

In tranquil Boscastle, some of the stone and slate cottages at the foot of the steep valley date from the 1300s. The town is centered around a quaint little harbor, set snug within towering cliffs. Nearby, 2 miles up the valley of the Valency is the "Endelstow" referred to in Thomas Hardy's *A Pair of Blue Eyes*—the famed author had worked on the restoration of this church.

Tintagel

★ 14 *5 mi southwest of Boscastle.*

Occupying a rocky spur off the Cornish coast, the ruined clifftop **castle of Tintagel** is said to have been the birthplace of King Arthur. Archaeological evidence, however, suggests that the castle dates from much later, about 1150, when it was the stronghold of the earls of Cornwall, and the site may have been occupied by the Romans. The earliest identified remains at the castle are of Celtic (5th-century) origin, and these may have some connection with the legendary Arthur. But legends aside, nothing can detract from the stunning castle ruins, dramatically set on the wild, windswept Cornish coast, part on the mainland, part on an island connected by a narrow isthmus. (There are also traces of a Celtic monastery on the island.) You can still see the ruins of the great hall, some walls, and the outlines of various buildings. Paths lead down to the pebble beach, to a cavern known as **Merlin's Cave.** Exploring Tintagel Castle involves some arduous climbing up and down steep steps. ☎ *01840/770328.* £2.50. *Apr.–Oct., daily 10–6 or dusk; Nov.–Mar., daily 10–4.*

In the town of Tintagel, which has more than its share of tourist junk—including Excaliburgers!—stop in at the **Old Post Office,** in a 15th-century stone manor house with smoke-blackened beams. ☎ *01840/770024.* £2. *Apr.–Sept., daily 11–5:30; Oct., daily 11–5.*

THE CORNWALL COAST—FROM TINTAGEL TO PLYMOUTH

This excursion covers the whole of Cornwall, first traveling southwest from Tintagel along the north Cornish coast to Land's End, the westernmost tip of Britain, known for its savage land- and seascapes and panoramic views. From Land's End we turn northeast, stopping in the popular seaside resort of Penzance, the harbor city of Falmouth, and a string of pretty Cornish fishing villages. Next we set off across the boggy, heath-covered expanse of Bodmin Moor, and then turn south to Plymouth, Devon's largest city, whose present-day dockyards recall a rich centuries-old naval tradition.

Padstow

15 *15 mi southwest of Tintagel on A39 and A389, 16 mi northwest of Bodmin.*

Padstow used to be an important port until a treacherous sandbar formed here. According to legend, this "Doom Bar" appeared when a fisherman shot at a mermaid; in retaliation she flung sand across the estuary mouth. Though modern development has crowded the town's Tudor and medieval buildings—a few survive, such as the Elizabethan facade of Prideaux Place—the sand dunes remain unspoiled and are popular bird-watching points.

The Arts

At **St. Endellion,** near Wadebridge in Cornwall (8 miles farther up the Camel estuary), a music festival is regularly held at Easter.

Newquay

16 *14 mi southwest of Padstow by B3276.*

The principal resort on the north Cornwall coast, Newquay, is a largish town established in 1439. It was once the center of the trade in pilchards (a small herring-like fish), and on the headland you can still see a little white hut where a lookout known as a "huer" watched for pilchard schools and directed the boats to the fishing grounds. In recent years, Newquay has become the country's surfing capital, and the wide beaches can be uncomfortably packed in summer.

Perranporth

17 *8 mi south of Newquay, 13 mi northwest of Truro.*

Past the sandy shores of Perran Bay, Perranporth, one of Cornwall's most popular seaside spots, is extremely crowded in high season. The swell off this 3-mile stretch of beach attracts swarms of surfers, too. The best times to visit are the beginning and end of the summer. There are enchanting coastal walks along the dunes and cliffs.

St. Ives

18 *20 mi southwest of Perranporth on A30, 10 mi north of Penzance.*

The fishing village of St. Ives is named after St. Ia, a 5th-century female Irish missionary said to have arrived on a floating leaf. The town has attracted artists and tourists for more than 100 years and is now a well-established artists' colony. Dame Barbara Hepworth, who pioneered abstract sculpture in England, lived here for 26 years. Her house and garden, now the **Barbara Hepworth Museum and Sculpture Garden,** is run by London's prominent Tate Gallery and is fascinating to anyone interested in sculpture. It is best to park outside the town. *Trewyn Studio,* ✉ *Barnoon Hill,* ☎ *01736/796226.* 🎫 *£2.50; combined ticket with Tate Gallery St. Ives* (☞ below) *£3.50.* ⏲ *Apr.–Oct., Mon.–Sat. 11–7, Sun. and national holidays 11–5; Nov.–Mar., Tues.–Sun. 11–5.*

Fittingly, in a town home to many artists, the spectacular **Tate Gallery St. Ives** is now the leading attraction. The lavish modernist building—a fantasia on seaside Deco-period architecture—opened in spring 1993 and has drawn critical raves from all. The four-story gallery, stunningly set at the base of a cliff fronted by Porthmeor Beach, houses the work of artists who lived and worked in St. Ives, mostly from 1925 to 1975, drawn from the rich collection of the Tate Gallery in London. This is the latest move in the Tate's plan to spread its artistic wealth outside the capital. It may be the only art gallery in the world with a special storage space for visitors' surfboards. ✉ *Porthmeor Beach,* ☎ *01736/796226.* 🎫 *£3;* (☞ *Hepworth Museum,* above, *for combined ticket).* ⏲ *Apr.–Sept., Mon.–Sat. 11–7, Sun. and national holidays 11–5; Oct.–Mar., Tues.–Sun. 11–5. Closed 10 days at end of Oct.*

Examples of current artists' work can be found for sale at the St. Ives Society of Artists in the **Old Mariner's Church.** ✉ *Norway Sq.,* ☎ *01736/795582.* 🎫 *25p.* ⏲ *Apr.–Nov., Mon.–Sat. 10–12:30, 2–4:30.*

NEED A BREAK? Built in 1312, the **Sloop Inn** beside St. Ives harbor is one of England's oldest pubs. Pub lunches are available in the wood-beam rooms.

Dining and Lodging

££ ✕ **Pig 'n' Fish.** Concentrate on the "fish" here, because it's a great spot for seafood. This simple, small restaurant has worthwhile pictures on display—after all this is St. Ives. Try the oysters (less pricey than elsewhere), or the salmon with fennel and basil vinegar. The desserts are scrumptious. ✉ *Norway La.,* ☎ *01736/794204. MC, V. Closed Sun.–Mon. and Nov.–mid-Mar.*

£££ ★ ✕🏨 **Garrack Hotel.** A family-run, ivy-clad hotel on a height overlooking the beach, the Garrack offers a relaxed, undemanding atmosphere. The staff is courteous and personable, helpful with local information. The restaurant, open to nonresidents, is worth going out of your way for. ✉ *Burthallan La., TR26 3AA,* ☎ *01736/796199,* FAX *01736/798955. 18 rooms with bath. Restaurant, indoor pool, sauna. AE, DC, MC, V.*

En Route The B3306 coastal road southwest from St. Ives is a winding route passing through some of Cornwall's most beautiful countryside. Stark hills crisscrossed by low stone walls drop abruptly to rocky cliffs and wide bays. Evidence of the ancient tin-mining industry—the remains of smokestacks and pumping houses—is everywhere. In some places the workings extended beneath the sea, forcing miners to toil away with the noise of waves crashing over their heads. Be careful if you decide to explore: Many of the old shafts are open and unprotected.

Land's End

★ 19 *10 mi southeast of St. Ives, 10 mi west of Penzance.*

B3306 ends at the western tip of Britain at what is, quite literally, Land's End. Although the point draws tourists from all over the world, and a multimillion-dollar glitzy theme park has been added, its savage grandeur remains undiminished. The sea crashes against its rocks and lashes ships battling their way around it. Approach it from one of the coastal footpaths for the best panoramic view. Over the years, sightseers have caused some erosion of the paths, but new ones have recently been built, and Cornish "hedges" (granite walls covered with turf) have been planted to prevent future erosion.

Mousehole

20 *3 mi south of Penzance, 7 mi east of Land's End.*

If you're taking the B3315 minor road between Land's End and Penzance, it's worth stopping in at Mousehole (pronounced "Mowzel"), an archetypal Cornish fishing village of tiny stone cottages. It was the home of Dolly Pentreath, supposedly the last native Cornish speaker, who died in 1777.

Newlyn

21 *2 mi north of Mousehole.*

Newlyn has long been the county's most important fishing port and became the magnet for a popular artists' colony at the end of the 19th century. A few of the appealing fishermen's cottages that first attracted artists here remain. The **Penzance and District Museum and Art Gallery** in Penzance exhibits paintings by members of the so-called Newlyn School. ✉ *Penlee Park,* ☎ *01736/63625.* 🎫 *£2.* ⏲ *Mon.–Sat. 10:30–4:30, Sun. 1–3.*

Penzance

22 *1½ mi north of Newlyn, 10 mi south of St. Ives.*

The popular seaside resort of Penzance enjoys spectacular views over Mount's Bay. Because of the town's isolated position, it has always been open to attack from the sea. During the 16th century, Spanish raiders destroyed most of the original town, and the majority of old buildings you see date from as late as the 18th century. The main street is called Market Jew Street, a folk mistranslation of the Cornish expression

"Marghas Yow," which actually means "Thursday Market." Look for **Market House,** constructed in 1837, an impressive, domed granite building that is now a bank. One of the prettiest streets in Penzance is **Chapel Street,** formerly the main street. It winds down from Market House to the harbor, its predominantly Georgian and Regency houses suddenly giving way to the extraordinary **Egyptian House,** on Chapel Street, whose facade is an evocation of ancient Egypt. Built around 1830 as a geological museum, today it houses a National Trust shop. Across Chapel Street from the Egyptian House is the 17th-century **Union Hotel,** where in 1805 the death of Lord Nelson and the victory of Trafalgar were first announced from the minstrels' gallery in the assembly rooms. Near the Union Hotel on Chapel Street is one of the few remnants of old Penzance, the **Turk's Head,** an inn said to date from the 13th century.

NEED A BREAK? One of the most famous inns in Penzance, the 15th-century **Admiral Benbow** (✉ Chapel St.), was once a smugglers' pub and is full of seafaring memorabilia, a brass cannon, model ships, ropes, and figureheads. Opt for the steak and Guinness pie.

The town's **Maritime Museum** simulates the lower decks of a four-deck man-of-war, and exhibits items salvaged from shipwrecks off the Cornish coast. ✉ *19 Chapel St.,* ☎ *01736/68890.* 🎫 *£2.* ⏲ *Easter–Oct., Mon.–Sat. 10:30–4:30.*

The Arts

THEATERS

At the open-air **Minack Theatre** (☎ 01736/810181) in Porthcurno, near Penzance, begun in the early 1930s, the natural slope of the cliff forms an amphitheater, with terraces and bench seats and the sea as a backdrop. Plays are performed here throughout the summer, ranging from classical dramas to modern comedies.

Dining and Lodging

£££ ✕ **Harris's.** Tucked away off Market Jew Street, Harris's fills a void of quality cuisine in Penzance. Two small rooms, one upstairs and one down, provide an elegant refuge for the travel-weary, even if the decor might be a shade overpowering. Try the corn-fed chicken breast in pastry with apple and Calvados sauce, or crab Florentine, grilled on a bed of spinach with cheese sauce. ✉ *46 New St.,* ☎ *01736/64408. AE, MC, V. No lunch Mon. Closed Sun., Mon. in winter, 2 wks in Nov., 1 wk in Feb.*

£££ ★ 🏨 **Abbey Hotel.** Owned by former model Jean Shrimpton and her husband, this small, 17th-century hotel has a marvelous homey feel; the drawing room is filled with books and many of the rooms are furnished with antiques. The attractive restaurant has a short but intriguing menu, with seafood gratin, rack of lamb, and homemade ice cream. Dining privileges are normally reserved for residents, but you may be able to get a table. ✉ *Abbey St., TR18 4AR,* ☎ *01736/66906,* FAX *01736/51163. 7 rooms with bath. AE, DC, MC, V. Closed Dec. 25.*

£ 🏨 **Camilla House.** The comfortably furnished Camilla stands on a parallel road to the Promenade, close to the harbor; the front rooms have sea views. The owners are agents for the ferry line and can help with trips to the Scilly Isles. The restaurant specializes in fresh fish from Newlyn harbor. ✉ *Regent Terr., TR18 4DW,* ☎ *01736/63771. 8 rooms, 4 with bath. MC, V.*

St. Michael's Mount

★ 23 *3 mi east of Penzance on A394.*

Rising out of Mount's Bay just off the coast, the spectacular granite and slate island of St. Michael's Mount is one of Cornwall's greatest natural attractions. A 14th-century castle perched at the highest point, 200 feet above the sea, was built on the site of a Benedictine chapel founded by Edward the Confessor. In its time, it has been a church, a fortress, and a private residence. The buildings around the base of the rock range from medieval to Victorian, but appear harmonious. The Mount is surrounded by fascinating gardens, where a great variety of plants flourish in micro-climates—snow can lie briefly on one part, while it can be 70° in another. To get there, follow the causeway or, when the tide is in the summer, take the ferry. If you have to wait for the ferry, there is a handy restaurant at the harbor. ✉ *Marazion,* ☎ *01736/710507.* 🎫 *£3.70.* ⏲ *Apr.–Oct., weekdays 10:30–5:30 (last admission at 4:45); July–Aug., also most weekends 10:30–5:30; Nov.–Mar., Mon., Wed., Fri. (phone for hrs).*

Helston

24 *13 mi east of Marazion, 14 mi east of Penzance, 18 mi southeast of Truro.*

The attractive Georgian town of Helston is most famous for its annual "Furry Dance," which takes place on Floral Day, May 8 (unless the date is a Sunday or Monday, when it takes place on the nearest Saturday). The whole town is decked with flowers for the occasion, while dancers weave their way in and out of the houses following a 3-mile route.

Flambards Theme Park has an aircraft collection, a re-creation of a wartime street during the Blitz, and a reconstructed Victorian village. ✉ *Near Helston,* ☎ *01326/574549 or 01326/573404.* 🎫 *£4.99 Apr.–mid-July and Sept.–Oct.; £6.99 mid-July–Aug.* ⏲ *Apr.–Oct., daily 10–5.*

Dining and Lodging

£££ **Nansloe Manor.** Although near Helston's center, this peaceful manor house gives the impression of being deep in the country, with its attractive half-mile driveway and 5 acres of grounds. Accommodation rates drop sharply in winter. The à la carte menu in the dining room has a wide choice and changes daily. Fish is top choice, for example baked monkfish Provençale. ✉ *Meneage Rd., TR13 0SB,* ☎ *01326/574691,* FAX *01326/564680. 7 rooms with bath. MC, V.*

Lizard Peninsula

★ 25 *10 mi south of Helston.*

The Lizard Peninsula is the southernmost point on mainland Britain and is an officially designated Area of Outstanding Natural Beauty. The huge, eerily rotating dish antennae of the **Goonhilly Satellite Communications Earth Station** are visible from the road as it crosses Goonhilly Downs, the backbone of the peninsula. One path, close to the tip,
26 plunges down 200-foot cliffs to tiny **Kynance Cove,** with its handful of pint-size islands. The sands here are reachable only in the 2½ hours before and after low tide. The Lizard's cliffs are made of greenish, serpentine rock, interspersed with granite; local souvenirs are carved out of the stone.

Gweek

27 *2 mi east of Helston.*

At the head of the Helford River, the fishing village of Gweek is known for its **Seal Sanctuary,** which shelters sick and injured seals brought in from all over the country. Try to be there for feeding time, usually at 10:30, 11:30, 2:30, and 3:30, also 12:30 and 4:30 in summer. ☎ *01326/221361.* *£4.95.* *Summer, daily 9–6; winter 10–5.*

Falmouth

28 *7 mi northeast of Gweek on B3291, 12 mi south of Truro.*

Falmouth has one of the finest natural harbors in the country. The bustling confusion of this busy resort town's fishing harbor, yachting center, and commercial port only adds to its charm. In the 18th century, Falmouth was a mailboat port, and in Flushing, a village across the inlet, are the slate-covered houses built by prosperous mailboat captains. A ferry service now links the two towns. On Falmouth's quay, near the Customs House, is the King's Pipe, an oven in which seized contraband was burned. At the end of the Peninsula stands formidable **Pendennis Castle,** built by Henry VIII in the 1540s and later improved by his daughter Elizabeth I. From here there are sweeping views over the English Channel and across the water known as Carrick Roads, to St. Mawes Castle (☞ *below*) on the Roseland Peninsula, designed as a companion fortress to guard the roads. ✉ *Pendennis Head,* ☎ *01326/316594.* *£2.50.* *Apr.–Oct., daily 10–6 or dusk; Nov.–Mar., daily 10–4.*

Dining and Lodging

££ ✕ **Pandora Inn.** Four miles north of Falmouth, this thatched pub, with both a patio and a moored pontoon for summer dining, is a great discovery. The ambience derives from maritime memorabilia and fresh flowers, and you can eat either in the bars or in the candlelit restaurant. The backbone of the menu is fresh seafood—try the seafood stroganoff or crab thermidor. The menu depends on the catch of the day. ✉ *Restronguet Creek, Mylor Bridge,* ☎ *01326/372678. Dinner only in restaurant. AE, MC, V.*

££ ★ ✕ **Seafood Bar.** The window of this restaurant on the quay is a fish tank, and beyond it is the very best seafood. Try the thick crab soup; the turbot cooked with cider, apples, and cream; or the locally caught lemon sole. ✉ *Lower Quay Hill,* ☎ *01326/315129. MC, V. No lunch. Closed Sun.–Mon.*

£££ **Royal Duchy.** This late-Victorian, cliff-top hotel is in an imposing position with wide sea views. The comfortable rooms are furnished with Regency-style pieces and have functional bathrooms. ✉ *Cliff Rd., TR11 4NX,* ☎ *01326/313042,* FAX *01326/319420. 47 rooms with bath. Restaurant, indoor pool, wading pool, sauna. AE, DC, MC, V.*

£££ **St. Michael's Hotel.** At this seaside hotel in a long, low white building overlooking Falmouth Bay, there are beautiful gardens sweeping down to the sea. St. Michael's is constantly being updated—the bedrooms have all recently had a face-lift. With a special baby-sitting service, this place is recommended especially for families. ✉ *Stracey Rd., TR11 4NB,* ☎ *01326/312707,* FAX *01326/211772. 66 rooms with bath. Indoor pool, hot tub, sauna, billiards. AE, DC, MC, V.*

£ **Gyllyngvase House Hotel.** This hotel is centrally located, near the seafront. The bedrooms are a bit small but pleasantly furnished. There is a garden at the back. Evening meals are available on request. ✉ *Gyl-*

lyngvase Rd., TR11 4DJ, ☎ 01326/312956. 15 rooms, 12 with bath or shower. No credit cards. Closed Nov.–Mar.

Trelissick

❷❾ *6 mi north of Falmouth on B3289.*

At Trelissick, the **King Harry Ferry,** a chain-drawn car ferry, runs to the Roseland Peninsula at regular intervals daily, except Sundays during the winter. From its decks you can see all the way up and down the Fal, a deep, narrow river with steep, wooded banks. The river's great depth provides ideal mooring for old ships waiting to be sold; these mammoth shapes lend a surreal touch to the riverscape.

St. Mawes

❸⓿ *16 mi north and south of Falmouth (by road), 1½ mi by sea, 11 mi south of Truro.*

At the tip of the Roseland Peninsula, outside the village of St. Mawes, stands the Tudor-era **St. Mawes Castle.** Its cloverleaf shape makes it seemingly impregnable, yet during the Civil War, its royalist commander surrendered without firing a shot. (In contrast, Pendennis Castle held out at the time for 23 weeks before submitting to the siege.) ✉ *St. Mawes,* ☎ *01326/270526.* 🎫 *£2.* ⏲ *Apr.–Oct., daily 10–6 or dusk; Nov.–Mar., Wed.–Sun., 10–1 and 2–4.*

En Route The shortest route from St. Mawes to Truro is via the ferry. The longer way swings in a circle on A3078 for 19 miles through attractive countryside, where subtropical shrubs and flowers thrive in the gardens along the way, past the town of Portloe (and its cozy hotel) and the 123-foot church tower in the village of Probus, flaunting its gargoyles and pierced stonework.

Truro

❸❶ *12 mi north of Falmouth, 14 mi southeast of St. Austell.*

Truro is a compact, elegant Georgian city, nestled in a crook at the head of the river Truro. Though Bodmin is the county seat of Cornwall, Truro is Cornwall's only real city. The **Cathedral Church of St. Mary**—the first cathedral built in England since the completion of St. Paul's in London in the early 1700s—dominates the city; although comparatively modern (built 1880–1910), it evokes the feeling of a medieval church, with an impressive exterior in early English Gothic style. The inside is not so interesting, apart from a side chapel, all that remains of the original 16th-century parish church. In front of the west porch there is an open, cobbled area called High Cross, and the city's main shopping streets fan out from here.

For an overview of Truro's Georgian housefronts, take a stroll down Lemon Street. The 18th-century facades along this steep, broad street are of mellow-colored stone, unusual for Cornwall, where granite is predominant. Like Lemon Street, Walsingham Place is a typical Georgian street, a curving, flower-lined, pedestrian oasis. Near Walsingham Place, the **Royal Cornwall Museum** offers a sampling of Cornish art, archaeology, an extensive collection of minerals, and a new café and shop. ✉ *River St.,* ☎ *01872/72205.* 🎫 *£2.* ⏲ *Mon.–Sat. 10–5; closed national holidays.*

Dining and Lodging

£££ ✕🏨 **Alverton Manor.** This was once a bishop's house, then a convent, and is now an up-to-date hotel/restaurant, both efficient and atmo-

spheric. The former chapel is used as an unusual conference room. The rooms are large, with French cherrywood furniture. Quiet elegance is the keynote of the public rooms, and in the Terrace restaurant, standards are kept high with the use of the best local produce. ✉ *Tregolls Rd., TR1 1XQ,* ☎ *01872/76633,* FAX *01872/222989. 34 rooms with bath or shower. Restaurant (reservations essential, jacket and tie). AE, DC, MC, V.*

££££ **The Lugger.** This small hotel on the edge of a tiny cove a short drive from Truro is made up of several 17th-century cottages. Many of the snug cottage bedrooms look out to sea, while in the beamed bar the world of the smugglers doesn't seem so far away. It's definitely worth the drive through the narrow, banked roads 12 miles southeast from Truro to get here. ✉ *Portloe, TR2 5RD,* ☎ *01872/501322,* FAX *01872/501691. 19 rooms with bath. Restaurant, sauna. AE, DC, MC, V. Closed Dec.–Jan.*

The Arts

The **Three Spires Festival** (☎ 01872/70220), based in Truro Cathedral, takes place in June.

Mevagissey

32 *15 mi east of Truro, 5 mi south of St. Austell.*

The busy fishing town of Mevagissey has attracted a sizable influx of tourism in recent years that sometimes threatens to overwhelm its fragile charm. Like most Cornish coastal villages, it is not suitable for cars, so if you stop to visit, use the large parking lot on the outskirts. From Truro, continue eastward on A390, turn right at Sticker, and follow signs.

Charlestown

33 *4 mi north of Mevagissey, 1 mi south of St. Austell.*

Charlestown, a harbor town built in 1791, is still active in china-clay export, which explains the strange white dust coating the 18th-century houses along the port. It was also one of the ports from which 19th-century emigrants left for America. Its period look has made it a popular film location.

St. Austell

34 *1 mi north of Charlestown, 14 mi northeast of Truro, 13 mi south of Bodmin.*

The center of the china-clay industry is St. Austell, just inland from Charlestown. The hinterland here, with its brilliantly white heaps of clay waste visible for miles around is known as the White Alps of Cornwall.

China clay has been St. Austell's main industry for 200 years. **Wheal Martyn,** an old mine located in Carthewm, 2 miles north of St. Austell on A391, offers an audio-visual presentation on the history and processes of the china-clay industry, a history trail through the mine, and several other exhibits, including two waterwheels. ☎ *01726/850362.* *£4.25,* ⏲ *Apr.–Oct., daily 10–6.*

Bodmin

35 *13 mi north of St. Austell on A391.*

Bodmin was the only Cornish town recorded in the 11th-century *Domesday Book*, William the Conqueror's census of English towns and holdings. During World War I, both the *Domesday Book* and the Crown Jewels were sent to Bodmin Prison for safekeeping. From the Gilbert Memorial on Beacon Hill you can see both of Cornwall's coasts.

Dozmary Pool

36 *10 mi northeast of Bodmin.*

For another taste of Arthurian legend, follow A30 northeast out of Bodmin across the boggy, heather-clad granite plateau of Bodmin Moor, and turn right at Bolventor to get to Dozmary Pool. A considerable lake rather than a pool, it was here that King Arthur's magic sword Excalibur was supposedly returned to the Lady of the Lake after Arthur's last battle.

NEED A BREAK? At Bolventor, in the center of Bodmin Moor, just off A30, look for **Jamaica Inn,** made famous by Daphne du Maurier's novel of the same name. Originally a farmstead, it is now Cornwall's best-known pub and a good spot to try a Cornish pasty.

Launceston

37 *25 mi northwest of Plymouth.*

Cornwall's ancient capital, Launceston (pronounced "Lanston"), on the eastern side of Bodmin Moor, retains parts of its medieval walls, including the South Gate. For a full view of the surrounding countryside, climb up to the ruins of 14th-century **Launceston Castle.** ☎ *01566/772365.* *£1.50.* ⏲ *Apr.–Oct., daily 10–6 or dusk.*

Dining and Lodging

£££ ✕ **Lewtrenchard Manor.** This spacious 1620 manor house, on the northwestern edge of Dartmoor (off old A30), is full of paneled rooms, stone fireplaces, and ornate leaded windows. Some bedrooms have antique four-posters. The restaurant, with its big log fire and family portraits, serves good fresh fish, caught an hour away. ✉ *Lewdown, between Launceston and Okehampton, EX20 4PN,* ☎ *01566/783256,* FAX *01566/783332. 8 rooms with bath. Restaurant (jacket and tie), fishing, helipad. AE, DC, MC, V.*

Plymouth

38 *48 mi southwest of Exeter, 124 mi southwest of Bristol, 240 mi southwest of London.*

Numbers in the margin correspond to points of interest on the Plymouth map.

Devon's largest city has long been linked with England's commercial
39 and maritime history. From the **Hoe,** a wide, grassy esplanade with crisscrossing walkways high above the city you can get a magnificent view of the many inlets, bays, and harbors that make up Plymouth Sound.
40 The best vista is provided atop **Smeaton's Tower,** found along the
41 Hoe. At the end of the Hoe stands the huge **Royal Citadel,** built by Charles II in 1666. A new visitors center displays exhibits on both old and new Plymouth.

42 The **Barbican,** which lies east of the Royal Citadel, is the oldest surviving section of Plymouth (much of the city center was destroyed by air raids in World War II). Here, Tudor houses and warehouses rise from a maze of narrow streets leading down to the fishing docks

Barbican, **42**
The Hoe, **39**
Mayflower Stone, **43**
Merchant's House, **44**
Royal Citadel, **41**
Royal Naval Dockyard, **45**
Smeaton's Tower, **40**

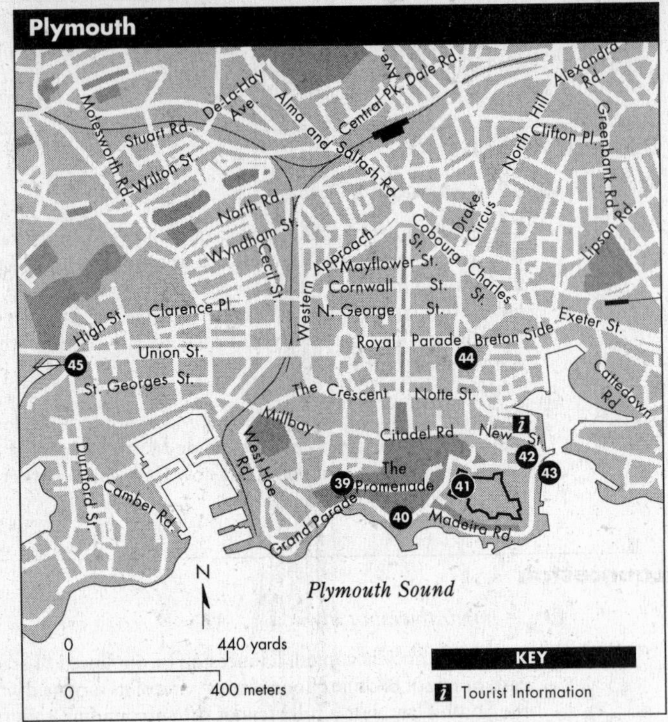

and harbor. Many of these buildings have become antiques shops, art shops, and bookstores. By the harbor you can visit the
★ **Mayflower Steps,** where the Pilgrims embarked in 1620; the
43 **Mayflower Stone** marks the exact spot. Near the Barbican, just off
44 the Royal Parade, the largely 18th-century **Merchant's House** has a museum of local history. ✉ *33 St. Andrew's St.,* ☎ *01752/264878.* *Small admission charge.* ⏲ *Apr.–Oct., weekdays 10–1 and 2–5:30, Sat. 10–1 and 2–5.*

45 The **Royal Naval Dockyard,** on the west side of town, was begun in the late 17th century by William III. It is still a navy base and much is hidden behind the high dock walls, but parts of the 2-mile-long frontage can be seen from pleasure boats that travel up the river Tamar. ✉ *Plymouth Boat Cruises Ltd., Millpoolhead, Millbrook, Torpoint, Cornwall,* ☎ *01752/822797; also* ✉ *Tamar Cruising, Penhellis, Maker La., Millbrook, Torpoint, Cornwall,* ☎ *01752/822105.* ⏲ *Both companies run 1-hr boat trips around the sound and the dockyard, leaving every 40 min from Phoenix Wharf and the Mayflower Steps, Easter–Oct., daily 10–4.* *£3.*

Dining and Lodging

£££ ★ ✕ **Chez Nous.** This French—*very* French—restaurant is worth searching for among the rows of stores in the shopping precinct. Fresh local fish is served, and the atmosphere is pleasant and relaxed. Chez Nous is at the top of the £££ range, but there are good-value set-price menus. ✉ *13 Frankfort Gate,* ☎ *01752/266793. AE, DC, MC, V. Closed Sun., Mon., national holidays, and 1st 3 wks in Feb. and Sept.*

££ ✕ **Piermaster's.** Fresh fish landed at nearby piers is served here. Located in the Barbican, Piermaster's has "basic seafront" decor, with a tiled floor and wooden tables. ✉ *33 Southside St., Barbican,* ☎ *01752/229345. AE, DC, MC, V. Closed Sun.*

££–£££ **Copthorne Hotel.** Situated downtown, this large, efficient, modern hotel offers the expected comforts. Its Burlington Restaurant has been given an Edwardian look, and there is also a brasserie. *Armada Centre, Armada Way, PL1 1AR, 01752/224161, FAX 01752/670688. 135 rooms with bath. Restaurant, bar, pool, sauna. AE, DC, MC, V.*

£ **Bowling Green Hotel.** This refurbished Victorian house overlooks Sir Francis Drake's bowling green on Plymouth Hoe. It's in a central location for shopping and sightseeing. *9–10 Osborne Pl., Lockyer St., PL1 2PU, 01752/667485, FAX 01752/255150. 12 rooms with bath or shower. AE, DC, MC, V.*

The Arts

THEATERS

Plymouth's **Theatre Royal** (01752/267222) often shows plays by some of the best London companies.

Saltram House

3½ mi east of Plymouth city center.

One of Plymouth's most outstanding attractions requires a short excursion from the center: Saltram House, a lovely 18th-century house built around the remains of a late Tudor mansion. It has one of the finest rooms designed by the great Neoclassical designer Robert Adam, adorned with paintings by Sir Joshua Reynolds, first president of the Royal Academy of Arts, who was born nearby in 1723. The house is set in a beautiful garden, with rare trees and shrubs (recently used for the 1995 film of *Sense and Sensibility*). There is a restaurant in the house and a cafeteria in the Coach House. *Plympton, 01752/336546. £5.20; garden only, £2.40. Apr.–Oct., Sun.–Thurs. 12:30–5:30; garden only, same as house, but open from 10:30.*

En Route From Plymouth, you have a choice of routes northeast to Exeter. If rugged, desolate, moorland scenery appeals to you, take A386 and B3212 northeast across Dartmoor Forest.

FROM PLYMOUTH TO WELLS

For the final stretch from Plymouth back to Wells, you have a choice of heading north to explore the vast, boggy reaches of Dartmoor Forest (setting for the Sherlock Holmes classic *The Hound of the Baskervilles*), or continuing east along Start Bay to Torbay, known as the English Riviera. Both routes end in the ancient Roman capital of Exeter, Devon's county seat. From Exeter we meander south to Exmouth, then turn northeast to Yeovil in Somerset, re-entering King Arthur country at Cadbury Castle, the legendary Camelot.

Numbers in the margin correspond to points of interest on the Southwest map.

Dartmoor Forest

Between Plymouth and Exeter.

Even on a summer's day, the scarred and brooding hills of this sprawling national park appear a likely haunt for such monsters as the Hound of the Baskervilles. Sir Arthur Conan Doyle set his Sherlock Holmes thriller in this landscape. Sometimes the wet, peaty wasteland vanishes in rain and mist, while in very clear weather you can see as far north as Exmoor. Much of northern Dartmoor consists of open heath and moorland, uninvaded by roads—wonderful walking territory, but an easy place to lose your bearings. Dartmoor's earliest inhabitants left behind stone monuments, burial mounds, and hut circles, which make it easy to imagine prehistoric man roaming the bogs and pastures here.

Horseback Riding

Stables offering trekking facilities on Dartmoor include **Lydford House Riding Stables** (✉ Lydford House Hotel, Lydford, ☎ 01822/820347) and **Skaigh Stables Farm** (✉ Skaigh La., near Okehampton, ☎ 01837/840429).

Lydford Gorge

★ 46 *9 mi east of Launceston, 7 mi north of Tavistock, 24 mi north of Plymouth.*

The river Lyd has carved a spectacular chasm through the rock at Lydford Gorge. Two paths follow the gorge past gurgling whirlpools and waterfalls with names such as the Devil's Cauldron and the White Lady. Stout footwear is recommended. The walk can be quite arduous, though it can still get congested during busy periods. To drive here from Launceston, continue east along A30, following the signs. ✉ *Lydford,* ☎ *01822/820441 or 01822/820320.* *£3.* *Apr.–Oct., daily 10–5:30; Nov.–Mar., daily 10:30–3 (walk restricted to main waterfall).*

Morwellham Quay Openair Museum

47 *12 mi south of Lydford Gorge, 5 mi southwest of Tavistock, 18 mi north of Plymouth.*

Morwellham Quay was England's main copper-exporting port in the 19th century, and it has been restored as a working museum, with quay workers and coachmen in costume, and a copper mine open to visitors. From Lydford, head east and pick up A386 south via Tavistock, then A390. The museum is off the Gunnislake to Tavistock road. ☎ *01822/832766 or 01822/833808 (recorded information).* *£7.50.* *Apr.–Oct., daily 10–5:30 (last admission at 4); Nov.–Mar., daily 10–4:30 (last admission at 2:30).*

Dining and Lodging

££ ★ **Horn of Plenty.** A "restaurant with rooms" is the way this establishment describes itself. From the restaurant in a Georgian house there are magnificent views across the wooded, rhododendron-filled Tamar Valley. The set menu is changed monthly, and the cooking is mainly classic French with some imaginative seafood recipes (try the sea bass with star anise, saffron, and fried basil leaves). A converted barn next to the house offers six modern guest rooms. ✉ *Gulworthy (3 mi west of Tavistock on A390), PL19 8JD,* ☎ FAX *01822/832528. 7 rooms with bath. Restaurant. AE, MC, V. No lunch Mon. Closed Dec. 25.*

Cotehele House and Quay

48 *2 mi west of Morwellham Quay.*

Formerly a busy port, Cotehele now offers a late medieval manor house complete with original furniture, armor, and needlework; gardens; a restored mill; and a quay museum, the whole complex now run by the National Trust. You can find Cotehele House turning left off A390 at Albaston. ✉ *St. Dominick (north of Saltash),* ☎ *01579/351346.* *£5.60, gardens and mill only £2.80.* *Apr.–Oct., Sat.–Thurs., 11–5:30; gardens daily year-round 11–dusk.*

Buckland Abbey

★ 49 *8 mi north of Plymouth.*

This 13th-century Cistercian monastery became the home of Sir Francis Drake in 1581. Today it is full of mementos of Drake and the Spanish Armada. The abbey has a licensed restaurant. From Tavistock, take A386 south to Crapstone, then west. ✉ *Yelverton,* ☎ *01822/853607.* 🎫 *£4.20.* ⏲ *Apr.–Oct., Fri.–Wed. 10:30–5:30; Nov.–Mar., weekends 2–5.*

One mile northwest of Buckland Abbey in Buckland Monachorum is **The Garden House,** an incredibly rich garden that should not to be missed by horticulturists. Terraced around the remains of a 16th-century vicarage and incorporating its walled garden, this superb spot is vivid with wisterias rioting over ancient brick walls, along with azaleas, roses, and innumerable other flowering plants, many of them rare. ✉ *Buckland Monachorum, near Yelverton,* ☎ *01822/854769.* 🎫 *£3.* ⏲ *Mar.–Oct., daily 10:30–5.*

Chagford

50 *3½ mi northwest of Moretonhampstead, 30 mi northeast of Plymouth, 20 mi west of Exeter.*

Chagford was once a tin-weighing station and an area of fierce fighting between the Roundheads and the Cavaliers in the Civil War. A Roundhead was hanged in front of one of the pubs on the village square.

51 An intriguing house near Chagford is **Castle Drogo,** at Drewsteignton across A382. Though designed by Sir Edwin Lutyens and built between 1910 and 1930, it is an extraordinary interpretation of a medieval castle, complete with battlements. Unfortunately, the rich grocer who commissioned it ran out of cash, so only half of the planned castle was built. ☎ *01647/433306.* 🎫 *£4.80; grounds only, £2.20.* ⏲ *Apr.–Oct., daily 11–5:30.*

Kingsbridge

21 mi east of Plymouth.

Kingsbridge is the capital of the South Hams area of Devon. Six miles east lies **Slapton Ley,** a lake and a haven for wildfowl, separated from Start Bay by the A379. Here, a Sherman tank remains as a memorial to 700 U.S. soldiers killed here during a rehearsal for the D-Day landings—a disaster kept secret until very recently.

Dartmouth

52 *14 mi northeast of Kingsbridge, 35 mi south of Exeter.*

Dartmouth was an important port in the Middle Ages and is today a favorite haunt of yacht owners. Traces of its past include the old houses in **Bayard's Cove** near Lower Ferry, the 16th-century covered Butterwalk, and the two castles guarding the entrance to the river Dart. The town is dominated by the **Royal Naval College,** built in 1905.

Dart Valley Steam Railway runs through 7 wooded miles of the Dart valley to Kingswear, across from Dartmouth. ✉ *Buckfastleigh,* ☎ *01364/642338.* ⏲ *Easter and mid-May–early Oct., daily; check for other times.*

Dining and Lodging

£££–££££ ★ ✕ **Carved Angel.** On the quay with views of the harbor, its offerings include Provençal cuisine and fresh local products, such as Dart River salmon and samphire, a seashore plant used in fish dishes. The restaurant enjoys a longstanding reputation as one of Britain's finest eateries. ✉ *2 S. Embankment,* ☎ *01803/832465. No credit cards. No dinner Sun. Closed Mon., Jan., 2 wks in Feb.*

££ ✕ **Billy Budd's.** This is a rather stylish, though friendly, bistro, elegantly candlelit for evening dinners. The seafood dishes take the prize here; the fish pie is especially good. You might also try the noisettes of lamb. To finish your meal indulge in one of the scrumptious desserts such as sticky toffee pudding, lemon icicle, or the locally made ice creams. ✉ *7 Foss St.,* ☎ *01803/834842. MC, V. Closed Sun.–Mon., 1 wk in Nov., 3 wks in Feb. and Mar.*

£££ **Royal Castle Hotel.** Here's a hotel that really earned the name "Royal"—several monarchs have slept here. Part of Dartmouth's historic waterfront, it was built in the 17th century, reputedly of timber from wrecks of the Spanish Armada. There are traditional fireplaces and beamed ceilings, and five rooms have four-poster beds. ✉ *11 The Quay, TQ6 9PS,* ☎ *01803/833033,* FAX *01803/835445. 25 rooms with bath or shower. Restaurant, bar, nightclub. MC, V.*

En Route Two **ferries** cross the river at Dartmouth; in summer, to avoid long waiting lines, you may want to try the inland route via A3122 and A381 to Totnes.

Totnes

53 *9 mi northwest of Dartmouth, 28 mi southwest of Exeter.*

This busy market town preserves an atmosphere of the past, particularly on summer Tuesdays and Saturdays, when most of the shopkeepers dress in Elizabethan costume. If you climb up to the ruins of Totnes's **Norman castle,** you can get a wonderful view of the town and the river. ☎ *01803/864406.* *£2.20.* *Apr.–Oct., daily 10–6 or dusk; Nov.–Mar., Wed.–Sun. 10–4.*

Buckfast Butterfly Farm and Dartmoor Otter Sanctuary's colorful inhabitants come from around the world. The farm is on A38, halfway between Exeter and Plymouth, 6 miles northwest of Totnes. ✉ *Buckfastleigh,* ☎ *01364/642916.* *£4.25.* *Otters Mar.–Nov., daily 10–5:30 or dusk; butterflies Apr.–Oct., daily 10–5:30 or dusk.*

Lodging

£ **The Cott.** The exterior of this inn has remained almost completely unchanged since 1320. It is a long, low, thatched building with flagstone floors, thick ceiling beams, and open fireplaces. Bar snacks and more elaborate meals are available from the restaurant. ✉ *Shinner's Bridge, Dartington (2 mi west of Totnes on A385) TQ9 6HE,* ☎ *01803/863777,* FAX *01803/866629. 6 rooms with bath or shower. Restaurant. AE, MC, V.*

Shopping

Near Dartington Hall (2 mi north of Totnes) is a collection of stores selling world-famous Dartington lead crystal as well as shoes, woolens, farm foods, kitchenware, pottery, and many other Devon wares. **Dartington Trading Centre** (✉ Shinners Bridge, 2 mi west of Totnes, ☎ 01803/864171), a collection of shops and two restaurants, housed inside the old Dartington Cider Press, sells handmade crafts from Devon, including clothes, glassware, and kitchenware.

Brixham

54 *10 mi from Totnes by A385 and A3022.*

Brixham, at the southern point of Tor Bay, has kept much of its original charm, partly because it is still an active fishing village.

Torbay

55 *5 mi north of Brixham via A3022, 23 mi south of Exeter.*

Torbay describes itself as the center of the "English Riviera." Since 1968, the towns of Paignton and Torquay (pronounced "Torkee") have been amalgamated from the Southwest's most important resort. Torquay is the supposed site of the hotel in the popular British television show *Fawlty Towers.*

Dining and Lodging

££ ★ ✕ **Capers.** A spot for anyone who likes enthusiasm along with the food, this small, select restaurant goes in for serious cooking. Local fish ranks high on the menu, with vegetables and herbs grown by the chef. Try the turbot with lime and ginger and the crispy duck salad, or the monkfish with green peppercorns. ✉ *7 Lisburne Sq.,* ☎ *01803/291177. MC, V. No lunch. Closed Sun.*

£–££ ✕ **Remy's.** Come here for delightful, straightforward French country cooking. Lamb with basil and tomato, sweetbreads with a Calvados sauce, and above all fish freshly caught by local boats are among the specialties. The wine list has a selection of good Alsatian vintages. ✉ *3 Croft Rd.,* ☎ *01803/292359. AE, MC, V. No lunch. Closed Sun.–Mon.*

££££ ★ **The Imperial.** This is arguably Devon's most luxurious hotel, perched high above the sea, overlooking Torbay. The gardens surrounding the hotel are magnificent, and the interior is . . . well, imperial, with chandeliers, marble floors, and the general air of a bygone world. Most bedrooms are large and very comfortable, some with seaward balconies. The staff is attentive. ✉ *Park Hill Rd., TQ1 2DG,* ☎ *01803/294301,* FAX *01803/298293. 166 rooms with bath. Restaurant, indoor and outdoor pools, beauty parlor, health club, sauna, tennis, squash. AE, DC, MC, V.*

£ **Fairmount House Hotel.** Near the village of Cockington, on the edge of Torquay, this Victorian hotel has a pretty garden and a restaurant that favors fresh homegrown and local produce. The Victorian Conservatory Bar gives onto the garden. ✉ *Herbert Rd., Chelston, TQ2 6RW,* ☎ FAX *01803/605446. 8 rooms with bath or shower. Restaurant. AE, MC, V. Closed Nov.–Feb.*

Exeter

56 *23 mi north of Torbay, 48 mi northeast of Plymouth, 85 mi southwest of Bristol, 205 mi southwest of London.*

Devon's county seat, Exeter, has been the capital of the region since the Romans established a fortress here 2,000 years ago. Little evidence of the Roman occupation exists, apart from the great city walls. Despite being badly bombed in 1942, Exeter retains much of its medieval character, as well as the gracious architecture of the 18th and 19th centuries.

At the heart of Exeter is the great Gothic **Cathedral of St. Peter,** begun in 1275 and completed almost a century later. The twin towers are even older survivors of an earlier Norman cathedral. The 300-foot stretch of unbroken Gothic vaulting, rising from a forest of ribbed columns, is the longest in the world. Myriad statues, tombs, and memorial plaques adorn the interior. In the minstrels' gallery, high up on the left of the nave, stands a group of carved figures singing and playing musical instruments, including bagpipes. The cathedral is surrounded by a charming **Close,** a pleasant green space for relaxing on a sunny day. Don't miss the 400-year-old door to No. 10, the bishop of Crediton's house, which is ornately carved with angels' and lions' heads.

In one corner of the Close is **Mol's Coffee House** (now a store), with its black-and-white, half-timber facade bearing the coat of arms of Elizabeth I. It is said that Sir Francis Drake met his admirals here to plan strategy against the Spanish Armada in 1588. Opposite Exeter Cathedral stands the **Royal Clarence Hotel** (☞ Dining and Lodging, *below*). Built in 1769, it was the first inn in England to be described as a "hotel"— a designation applied by an enterprising French manager. It is named after the duchess of Clarence, who stayed here in 1827 on her way to visit her husband, the future William IV.

NEED A BREAK? While you're exploring the Close, stop in at **Hansons,** ideal for lunch, coffee, snacks, or one of Devon's famous cream teas (served with jam, scones, and cream).

On High Street, just behind the Close, stands the **Guildhall,** the oldest municipal building in the country. The present hall dates from 1330, although a guildhall has been on this site since at least 1160. Its timber-braced roof is one of the earliest in England, dating from about 1460. ☎ *01392/265500.* 🎫 *Free.* ⏲ *Weekdays 10:30–1 and 2–4, Sat. 10:30–1, unless in use for a civic function; closed national holidays.*

Behind the Guildhall lie Exeter's main shopping areas, Harlequins Arcade and the Guildhall Shopping Centre. In their midst stands the tiny, 11th-century Norman **Church of St. Pancras,** a survivor not only of the 1942 Blitz, but of the dramatic urban-renewal efforts of the 1950s and '60s.

Off Queen Street, behind the museum, is **Rougemont Gardens,** which was first laid out at the end of the 18th century. The land was once part of the defensive ditch of Rougemont Castle, built in 1068 by decree of William the Conqueror. Here you will find the original Norman gatehouse and the remains of the Roman city wall, the latter forming part of the ancient castle's outer wall; nothing else is left. The spot offers a panoramic view of the countryside and the Haldon Hills rising up in the west.

Exeter's historic waterfront on the banks of the river Exe was once the center of Exeter's medieval wool industry. The **Customs House,** built in 1682 on The Quay, is the earliest surviving brick building in the city; it is flanked by Victorian warehouses. There is a Heritage Centre in **Quay House** (a stone warehouse contemporary with the Customs House) that documents the maritime history of the city and offers an audiovisual display. ✉ *The Quay,* ☎ *01392/265213.* 🎫 *Free.* ⏲ *Daily 10–5.*

Close to the Customs House, in the canal basin, the **Exeter Maritime Museum** comprises the largest collection of historic, working ships in the country. The more than 140 vessels on exhibit include a dhow (used for pearl diving in the Persian Gulf), a Chinese junk, a Danish steam tug, and a swan-shaped rowboat. This is a hands-on museum; you can board nearly all the boats, as well as try your hand at winding a winch or turning a capstan. ✉ *Haven Banks,* ☎ *01392/58075.* 🎫 *£4.25.* ⏲

Apr.–Sept., daily 10–5; Oct.–Mar., daily 10–4; closed Dec. 25–26 and national holidays.

The Arts

Among the best known of the West Country's festivals is the **Exeter Festival** (☎ 01392/265200), a mixture of musical and theater events held in July. At the **Northcott Theatre** (☎ 01392/493493 in Exeter, you can often see plays by some of the best London companies.

Dining and Lodging

££ ✕ **Golsworthy's.** Part of St. Olaves Court Hotel, set in a Georgian house with a walled garden, this restaurant offers both set and à la carte menus. Try the steamed medallions of monkfish, or for dessert the hot chestnut dumplings with madeira and chocolate sauce. ✉ *Mary Arches St.,* ☎ *01392/217736. AE, DC, MC, V. No lunch weekends.*

£££ **Rougemont Hotel.** Large, rambling, and Victorian—complete with chandeliers, molded ceilings, and pillars—this hotel is ideal for those who want comfortable accommodations downtown. All rooms have recently been refurbished. ✉ *Queen St., EX4 3SP,* ☎ *01392/54982,* FAX *01392/420928. 90 rooms with bath. Restaurant. AE, DC, MC, V.*

£££ **Royal Clarence Hotel.** This historic hotel is located within the cathedral Close. It boasts a good restaurant and has been made a great deal more attractive by recent redecoration. The most expensive rooms are those with a view of the cathedral. Many rooms feature oak paneling. ✉ *Cathedral Yard, EX1 1HD,* ☎ *01392/58464,* FAX *01392/439423. 56 rooms with bath. Restaurant, 2 bars. AE, DC, MC, V.*

££ **White Hart.** It is said that Oliver Cromwell stabled his horses here; in any event, guests have been welcomed since the 15th century. The main building has all the trappings of a period inn—beams, stone walls, a central courtyard, and warm hospitality—but there are also fully modern bedrooms in a new wing. ✉ *65 South St., EX1 1EE,* ☎ *01392/79897,* FAX *01392/50159. 59 rooms with bath or shower. Restaurant, bar. AE, DC, MC, V.*

Shopping

Until 1882 Exeter was the silver-assay office for the entire West Country, and it is still possible to find **Exeter silver,** particularly spoons, in some antiques and silverware stores. The earliest example of Exeter silver dates from 1218 (a museum piece), but Victorian pieces are still sold—the Exeter assay mark is three castles. **William Bruford** (✉ 1 Bedford St., ☎ 01392/54901) sells interesting antique jewelry and silver. Exeter has a daily market on Sidwell Street.

Topsham

57 *4 mi south of Exeter on B3182.*

The town of Topsham is full of narrow streets and hidden courtyards. Once a bustling port, it is rich in 18th-century houses and inns. **Topsham Museum** occupies a 17th-century Dutch-style merchant's house, which has recently been refurbished, beside the river. ✉ *25 the Strand,* ☎ *01392/873244.* *£1.* *Mar.–Oct., Mon., Wed., Sat. 2–5; also May–Sept., Sun. 2–5.*

Near Lympstone, 5 miles south of Topsham off the A376 is A la Ronde, one of the most unusual houses in England. A 16-sided, nearly circular house, now run by the National Trust, it was built in 1798 and inspired by the Church of San Vitale in Ravenna, Italy. Among the 18th- and 19th-century curiosities here is an elaborate display of feathers and shells. ✉ *Summer La., on A376 near Exmouth,* ☎ *01395/265514.* *£3.10.* *Apr.–Oct., Sun.–Thurs. 11–5:30.*

En Route The Devon coast from Exmouth to the Dorset border 26 miles to the east has been designated an Area of Outstanding Natural Beauty. The reddish, grass-topped cliffs of the region are punctuated by quiet, seaside resorts such as Budleigh Salterton, Sidmouth, and Seaton.

Beer

58 *26 mi east of Exeter, 33 mi south of Taunton.*

Beer, just outside Seaton, was once a favorite smugglers' haunt. It was also the source of the white stone used to build Exeter Cathedral. Some of the old quarries can still be visited. *Beer Quarry Caves,* ✉ *Quarry La.,* ☎ *01297/680282.* *£3.* *Apr.–Oct., daily 10–5; Oct., daily 11–4.*

Honiton

59 *10 mi northwest of Beer on A3052/A375, 19 mi south of Taunton.*

Honiton's long High Street is lined with handsome Georgian houses. Modern storefronts have intruded, but the original facades have been preserved at second-floor level. For three centuries the town was known for lacemaking, and the Honiton lace industry was revived when Queen Victoria selected the fabric for her wedding veil in 1840. The town has a **lace museum,** as well as stores where both old and new lace are sold. ✉ *All Hallows Museum, High St.,* ☎ *01404/44966.* *£1.* *Apr.–Oct., Mon.–Sat. 10–5.*

NEED A BREAK? For a satisfying lunch, try **Dominoes** winebar (✉ 178 High St.), where you can get everything from crispy Szechuan duck to steak-and-oyster pie.

Lodging

£££ **Combe House Hotel.** Rolling parkland, 3,000 acres in all, surrounds this Elizabethan manor house. From the imposing entrance hall with its huge, open fireplace, to the individually decorated bedrooms—all of them large and two with four-posters—the emphasis is on style and comfort. ✉ *Gittisham, near Honiton, EX14 0AD,* ☎ *01404/42756,* FAX *01404/46004. 15 rooms with bath. Restaurant, fishing. AE, DC, MC, V. Closed Jan.–mid-Feb.*

£ **New Dolphin Hotel.** The age of this former coaching inn shows in the sloping floors, but every room has modern comforts. It's in the town center. ✉ *High St., EX14 8LS,* ☎ *01404/42377. 15 rooms, 13 with bath. Restaurant, bar. AE, DC, MC, V.*

Montacute House

★ 60 *30 mi northeast of Honiton on A30 and A303, 30 mi east of Taunton, 44 mi south of Bristol, 21 mi northwest of Dorchester.*

This part of Somerset is famous for its golden limestone, used in the construction of local villages and mansions. A fine example is in Yeovil, **Montacute House** (on A3088—turn right off A303 at Stoke sub Hamdon), built in the late 16th century. This Renaissance house has a 189-foot gallery brimming with Elizabethan and Jacobean portraits, most on loan from the National Portrait Gallery. ✉ *Montacute,* ☎ *01935/823289.* *£5; garden and park only, £2.80 (Mar.–Oct.), £1.50 (Nov.–Apr.).* *House Apr.–Oct., Wed.–Mon. noon–5:30; garden and park Wed.–Mon. 11:30–5:30 or dusk.*

Dining and Lodging

££ ★ **King's Arms.** Built of the same warm, golden stone as nearby Montacute House, this 16th-century inn features charming interior decor;

one room has a four-poster bed. Meals available range from bar snacks to a full à la carte menu in the Abbey Room restaurant. ✉ *Bishopston, Montacute TA15 6UU,* ☎ *01935/822513,* FAX *01935/826549. 13 rooms with bath. Restaurant. AE, DC, MC, V.*

Yeovilton

61 *7 mi north of Yeovil.*

The 20th century reasserts itself in the village of Yeovilton, with the **Fleet Air Arm Museum.** Here, more than 50 historic aircraft are on show, including the Concorde 002. The spectacular "Carrier" display, opened in 1994, includes a simulated helicopter ride over the ocean to an aircraft carrier; a unique re-creation of the flight deck of a working carrier, complete with 12 real planes from the 1960s and 1970s; and an "experience" chamber simulation of the launch and recovery of the carrier's aircraft. ✉ *Royal Naval Air Station,* ☎ *01935/840565.* *£6.* *Apr.–Oct., daily 10–5:30; Nov.–Mar., daily 10–4:30.*

Cadbury Castle

62 *7 mi northeast of Yeovilton, off A303, 17 mi south of Wells.*

Cadbury Castle is said to be the site of Camelot—one among several contenders for the honor. Glastonbury Tor, rising dramatically in the distance across the plain, adds to the atmosphere of Arthurian romance. There is even a legend that every seven years the hillside opens and Arthur and his followers ride forth to water their horses at close-by Sutton Montis. Cadbury Castle is, in fact, an Iron Age fort (circa 650 BC), with grass-covered, earthen ramparts forming a green wall 300 feet above the surrounding fields. From here it's about 17 miles to Wells, our original starting point. Or the A303/M3 will take you back to London.

SOUTHWEST A TO Z

Arriving and Departing

By Bus

National Express (☎ 0990/808080) buses leave London's Victoria Coach Station for Bristol (2½ hrs), Exeter (3¾ hrs), Plymouth (4½ hrs), and Penzance (about 8 hrs).

By Car

The fastest way from London to the Southwest is via the M4 and M5 motorways, bypassing Bristol (115 mi) and heading south to Exeter, in Devon (172 mi).

By Plane

Plymouth has a small airport (☎ 01752/705151 or 03452/222111) 3 miles from town.

By Train

British Rail serves the region from London's Paddington Station (☎ 0171/262–6767). Average travel time to Exeter, 2½ hours; to Plymouth, 3½ hours; and to Penzance, about 5½ hours.

Getting Around

By Bus

Western National Ltd. (☎ 01752/222666) operates a regular service in Plymouth and throughout Cornwall, and also offers one-day Explorer and seven-day **Key West** tickets.

By Car

Driving can be tricky, especially in the western parts. Most of the small roads are twisting country lanes flanked by high stone walls and thick hedges, which severely restrict visibility. The main roads heading west are A30, which leads all the way to Land's End, at the tip of Cornwall, A39 (to the north) and A38 (to the south).

By Train

Regional **Rail Rover** tickets are available for seven days' unlimited travel throughout the Southwest, and there are localized Rovers covering Devon or Cornwall.

Guided Tours

The **West Country Tourist Board** (☎ 01392/425426) and local TICs have lists of qualified guides. **Designer Touring** (✉ 28 Peasland Rd., Torquay TQ2 8PA, ☎ 01803/326832) offers guided tours by bus or car.

Contacts and Resources

Car-Rental Agencies

Exeter: Avis, ✉ 29 Marsh Green Rd., Marsh Barton Trading Estate, ☎ 01392/59713. **Plymouth: Avis,** Airport, ☎ 01752/221550; **Europcar Ltd.,** Grevan Cars Ltd., ✉ 19 Union St., ☎ 01752/669859; **Hertz,** Scot Hire, ✉ Walkham Business Park, ☎ 01752/705819. **Truro: Avis,** ✉ Tregolls Rd., ☎ 01872/262226.

Travel Agencies

American Express: ✉ 139 Armada Way, Plymouth, ☎ 01752/228708. **Thomas Cook:** ✉ 177 Sidwell St., Exeter, ☎ 01392/54971; ✉ 9 Old Town St., Plymouth, ☎ 01752/667245.

Visitor Information

The West Country Tourist Board: ✉ 60 St. David's Hill, Exeter, Devon EX4 4SY, ☎ 01392/425426, FAX 01703/420891, ⏲ Weekdays 9:30–5. **The Cornwall Tourist Board:** ✉ Lander Buildings, Daniel Rd., Truro, Cornwall TR1 2DA, ☎ 01872/74057, FAX 01872/40423. **Devon Tourism:** Exeter Services, ✉ Sandygate (M5), Exeter, Devon EX2 7NJ, ☎ 01392/437581. **Somerset Tourism:** ✉ County Hall, Taunton, Somerset TA1 4DY, ☎ 01823/255036, FAX 01823/255572. **National Tourist Board:** ✉ Parke, Haytor Rd., Bovey Tracey, Newton Abbot, Devon TQ13 9JQ, ☎ 0162/832093.

Local TICs are usually open Monday–Saturday 9:30–5:30. **Exeter:** ✉ Civic Centre, Paris St., ☎ 01392/265700. **Penzance:** ✉ Station Rd., ☎ 01736/62207. **Plymouth:** ✉ Island House, 9 The Barbican, ☎ 01752/264849. **St. Ives:** ✉ The Guildhall, Street-an-Pol, ☎ 01736/796297. **Truro:** ✉ City Hall, Boscawen St., ☎ 01872/74555. **Wells:** ✉ Town Hall, Market Pl., ☎ 01749/672552.

6 The Channel Islands

Guernsey, Jersey

With more than 2,000 hours of sunshine every year, the Channel Isles remain a favorite forgetaway for Britishers and tourists alike. This is England with a French accent; Jersey and Guernsey lie just off the coast of Brittany. Pleasures await—pretty fishing harbors, princely villas (don't miss Victor Hugo's historic house in St. Peter Port), and sublime crab Creole. But everyone winds up on the white-sand beaches; after all, the sun is yours for the basking.

Updated by Robert Andrews

THE CHANNEL ISLANDS became part of the British Isles when their ruler, Duke William of Normandy, or William the Conqueror, seized the English throne in 1066. The connection with the British royal house has lasted ever since, with only very few breaks, but the Channel Islands claim no allegiance to the Parliament in Westminster—just to the monarch. They are self-ruling, with a Common Law based on the Norman code of law, which differs from the legal system followed in the rest of Britain. The islands do not impose VAT (which means that shopping is 17.5% cheaper), and they issue their own currency and stamps.

The islands served as the background for struggles between Royalists and Roundheads in the 17th-century Civil War. In 1781, the French made an unsuccessful attempt to invade, but since 1066, the islands have only been seriously invaded once. The Germans occupied them from 1940 to 1945, incorporating them into their great Western defense system, the "Atlantic Wall." All over the islands there is still evidence of the German fortifications, which were built by thousands of slaves who used 613,000 cubic meters of reinforced concrete. The coasts bristled with gun emplacements, and the rocky landscape was honeycombed with tunnels to provide hospitals and ammunition magazines. In fact, the islands became total fortresses. When the Allies overran Europe in 1944, they circumvented the islands, leaving their elaborate defenses untouched.

The most popular island is Jersey (44½ sq mi), because of its mild climate, magnificent beaches, and well-run hotels and restaurants, all promoted by a strong department of tourism. Second to Jersey, both in size and popularity, is Guernsey (24½ sq mi), which has 2,000 hours of sunshine a year and runs at a more relaxed pace. The islands are bordered by magnificent cliffs that provide superb walking trails—very tough on the leg muscles—with great views both seaward and inland. The landscapes of both Jersey and Guernsey are crowded with prosperous, neat houses, all threaded together by an interminable network of winding lanes. For this reason the islands are very difficult to explore by car, even for a visitor who is extremely adept at map reading. But both islands have excellent bus services, which provide a cheap, worry-free means of sightseeing.

Pleasures and Pastimes

Dining

The specialty of the Channel Islands is seafood in all its delectable glory. Crab and lobster dishes are on many menus, but don't overlook the daily catch from the tiny harbors or the mollusk called Jersey Ormer or sea ear (appropriately named). When you tire of seafood, the locally bred lamb is superb, and thick cream slathers the desserts.

CATEGORY	COST*
££££	over £50
£££	£30–£50
££	£20–£30
£	under £20

**per person, including first course, main course, and dessert; excluding drinks*

Lodging

Jersey is chockablock with hotels, guest houses, and bed-and-breakfasts, all organized and well regulated by the Jersey Hotel and Guest

The Channel Islands

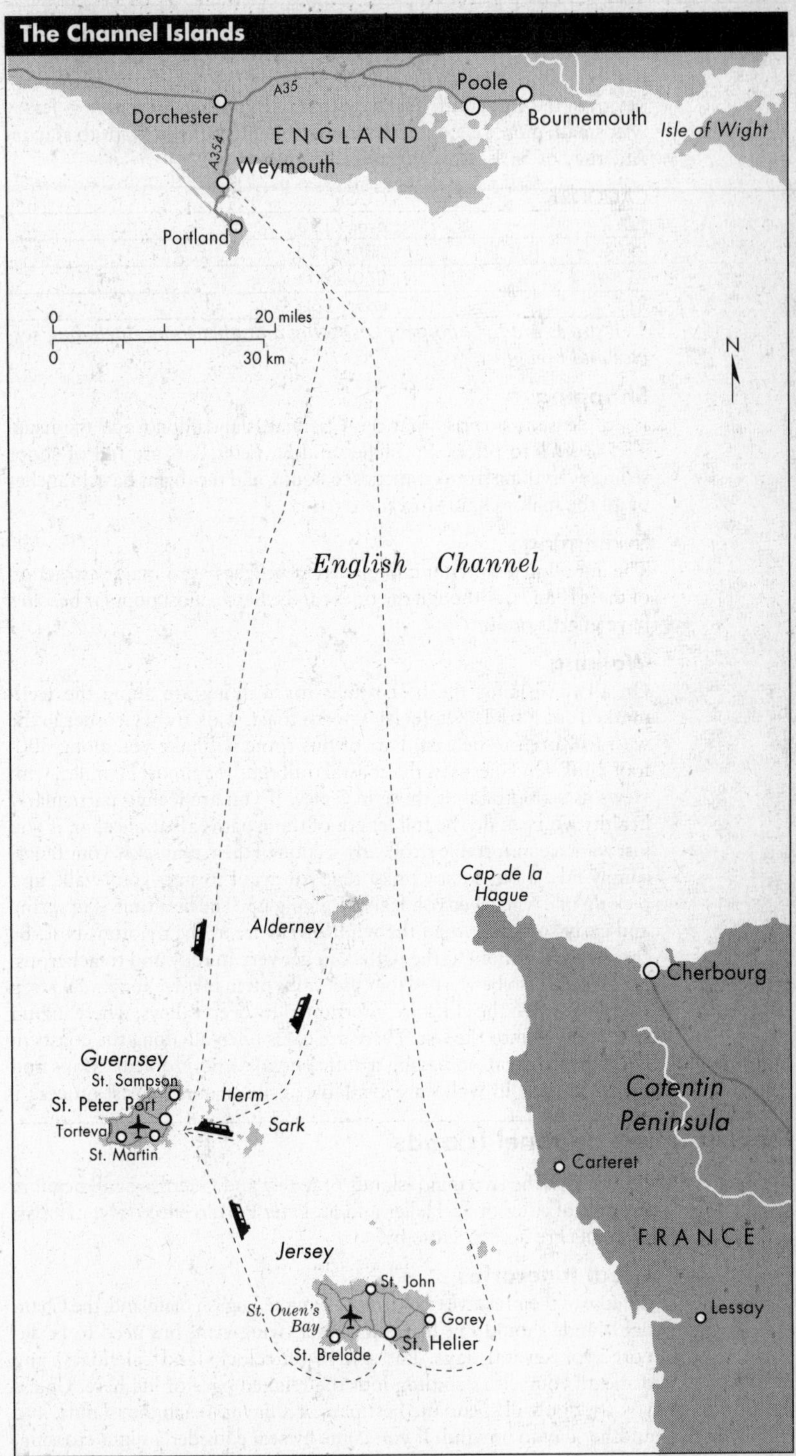

House Association. You can also get a comprehensive listing from the Jersey tourist board or the Guernsey tourist board. Many places offer half-board (MAP), at a savings. Outlying parts of Jersey are more low-key than the comparative razzmatazz of St. Helier. Guernsey is Jersey writ small, more relaxed, with hotels to match. If you want to stay on Alderney or Sark, plan well ahead.

CATEGORY	COST*
££££	over £150
£££	£80–£150
££	£60–£80
£	under £60

**All prices are for two people sharing a double room, including service and breakfast.*

Shopping

It's a pleasant surprise that the Channel Islands don't add the usual 17.5% VAT to prices. St. Helier and St. Peter Port are full of shops selling everything from cosmetics to liquor, and the towns have branches of all the major chain stores.

Swimming

The unpolluted water and magnificent beaches are a major attraction of these islands. Although the tides can be fierce, most popular beaches have guards on duty.

Walking

On all the islands the best routes for walking are along the well-marked coast trails. On Jersey's north coast, walk from Grosnez in the west to Rozel in the east. Part of this route will take you along 300-foot-cliffs. On Guernsey, the coastal trail runs for almost 30 miles, with views as sensational as those in Jersey. If you are feeling particularly healthy, you can do the full length of these paths all at once, or, if you just want a comfortable stroll, any section of them that takes your fancy; simply take a bus to any point that you want to start your walk, and pick up one whenever you feel like giving up. The best time is in spring and early summer, when the wildflowers are at their riotous best. Be careful in fall, though; the paths can get very muddy and treacherous. You should also be warned that the walks often involve some very steep climbing, when the cliffs are interrupted by deep valleys, where inland streams flow into the sea. There are cafés open all along the coasts in the tourist season, so having a coffee break is no problem. Maps and guides to the cliff walks are available at the islands' tourist offices.

Exploring the Channel Islands

Any visit to the two main islands of Jersey and Guernsey will begin in the capital cities of St. Helier and St. Peter Port, respectively; most attractions are here or close by.

Great Itineraries

Because of their relative remoteness from the English mainland, the Channel Islands should not be visited on a flying visit, but need to be savored for several days. Put away your clocks and calendars, and dedicate yourself to settling into the relaxed pace of life here. Unless you fly, you will spend the best part of a day to reach the islands, and another day to unwind. If you come by sea, consider a night crossing, to make the most of your time. You might disembark at one of the main islands, returning from the other. Each of the two main islands is certainly worth seeing, but with limited time at your disposal, confine yourself to one. You will appreciate the opportunity to stop traveling—and start relaxing.

Numbers in the text correspond to numbers in the margin and on the maps.

IF YOU HAVE 3 DAYS

Spend two days in **St. Helier**, main town of **Jersey.** Get your bearings by climbing up to **Fort Regent** ① and the rest of the morning will be taken up by strolling through the town's streets and along the seafront, perhaps walking out to **Elizabeth Castle** ⑥, the 16th-century stronghold lying on an island in St Aubin's Bay. Spend an afternoon at the absorbing **Jersey Museum** ④. On your second day, you can see something more of the island: A morning would be enough to visit the world-famous **Jersey Wildlife Trust,** while the afternoon could be spent seeing **Gorey Castle,** on the island's eastern side. End the day with a meal in the village of Gorey. Your last day should be devoted to a day trip to **Guernsey.** Arrive mid-morning for a walk around **St. Peter Port,** taking in **Castle Cornet** ⑨ and the elegant **Hauteville House** ⑩, where Victor Hugo lived. In the afternoon, you should rent a car or bicycle to see some of the rest of Guernsey, especially **Sausmarez Manor** ⑫ and one of the relics of the German occupation, for example the **German Military Underground Hospital** ⑬. Take the ferry (or plane) back from Guernsey.

IF YOU HAVE 5 DAYS

A couple of days on Jersey will allow you to take in the pleasures of **St. Helier,** including the attractions mentioned above and the newly completed **Occupation Tapestry** and **The Island Fortress–Occupation Museum** ⑤, both of which vividly recapture the experience of living under the German jackboot. A little farther out, the "Glass Church" at Millbrook makes an easy excursion, perhaps en route to the **Battle of Flowers Museum,** outside St. Ouen. The theme of flowers is a prominent one on Jersey, which can be pursued further at the **Eric Young Orchid Foundation.** Nearby, the **Jersey Wildlife Trust** shouldn't be missed. Spend the next two days on **Guernsey,** where **Castle Cornet** ⑨ and **Hauteville House** ⑩ are must-sees in **St. Peter Port.** Outside town, **Sausmarez Manor** ⑫ and the meticulous reconstructions of the **German Military Underground Hospital** ⑬ provide plenty of interest. From Guernsey, there are regular ferries to the tiny isle of **Sark,** 45 minutes from Guernsey. Sark can be toured on foot, by bicycle, or on a horse and cart. A day would be enough to absorb its pace, though you'll find it hard to leave—just don't expect bright lights or ready-made entertainment.

When to Tour the Channel Islands

The Channel Islands show their best face under a blue sky. Since they boast more sunshine than any other part of the British Isles, they're a good bet at any time of year outside the depths of winter, when fierce storms can put a damper on your trip, particularly if your ferry ride there or back is delayed because of rough seas. The season from April to September is best if you want to approach the beaches, and note, too, that many of the best attractions close after October.

Numbers in the margin correspond to points of interest on the St. Helier map.

Jersey

Begin your island tour in St. Helier, Jersey's capital. It is a lovely vacation center, full of hotels, good bathing places, and quaint streets. Nearby are secluded coves, difficult of access but a delight to achieve, rugged rocks, and Nikon-worthy scenery. You'll soon appreciate the reason why the French call Jersey "La Reine de la Manche"—Queen of the Channel. But not only are the climate soothing and the surroundings lush—there's an atmosphere of Continental know-how that appeals to all visitors, an atmosphere flavored with a touch of France.

1 In St. Helier, start out at **Fort Regent**—the panoramic view will give you an idea of the town's layout. The fort was built between 1806 and 1811, high on a rock, as a defense against Napoleon's army (although the measure was never tested). During World War II, German anti-aircraft guns were sited in the fort. In 1958, the British government sold the fortification to the State of Jersey, which in 1967 turned it into a vast leisure complex, with a terraced swimming pool, concert hall, squash courts, World of the Sea Aquarium, a good-size amusement park, restaurants, bars, and cafés. ☎ *01534/500228.* 🎟 *£3.60; after 4* PM *£1.50; extra fees for amusements.*

2 Now shaded by chestnut trees, **Royal Square** (behind Hill Street in the center of town) used to be the site of executions and the town pillory. Witchcraft and its punishment were constant elements in Jersey life for most of the 16th and 17th centuries, with endless trials all over the island. At present, the States offices, the **Royal Court,** and the **States Chamber** (Jersey's parliament) surround the square. On the west side of Royal
3 Square is the **parish church** of St. Helier, or "Town Church," the latest in the 900-year-old series of churches that have stood here.

Next to the bus station off Liberation Square, the newly refurbished
4 **Jersey Museum** has won awards for its design and user-friendliness, boasting facilities geared toward persons with disabilities, mothers and tots, and foreign-language visitors. Housed in a lovely building completed in 1817 for the merchant and shipbuilder Philippe Nicolle, the museum contains some fascinating collections that shed light on Jersey's past: works by local artists; re-creations of Victorian rooms; and memorabilia of Lillie Langtry, the beautiful mistress of Edward VII. "The Jersey Lily" was born on the island and is buried in St. Saviour's churchyard. ⊠ *The Weighbridge,* ☎ *01534/30511.* 🎟 *£2.90. "Passport" combined tickets (£8.50) for 6 of Jersey's principal museums (including Elizabeth Castle and Gorey Castle).* ⏲ *Summer, Mon.–Sat. 10–5, Sun. 1–5; winter, Mon.–Sat. 10–4, Sun. 1–4.*

A few steps away from Liberation Square, the busy center of St. He-
5 lier's harbor life, **The Island Fortress–Occupation Museum** has an extensive display of World War II propaganda relating to Germany's presence on the island. Videos describing the event are screened. ⊠ *9 Esplanade,* ☎ *01534/34306.* 🎟 *£2.50.* ⏲ *Mar.–Nov., daily 9* AM*–10:30* PM*; Nov.–Mar., daily 10–4.*

A Victorian warehouse adjacent to Liberation Square was newly converted in 1996 to display the **Occupation Tapestry,** a huge collective undertaking to commemorate the 50th anniversary of the islands' liberation from Nazi occupation. The tapestry consists of 12 panels, each embroidered by the people of one of Jersey's parishes, and each focusing on one of the themes of the experience of occupation and liberation. ⊠ *New North Quay,* ☎ *01534/30511.* 🎟 *£1.50.* ⏲ *Summer, daily 10–5; winter, daily 10–4.*

West along the Esplanade, yachts from all over the world berth at the Albert Harbour Marina. You can take short or long cruises from here, including an evening cocktail trip down the coast or a weekend jaunt
6 to Brittany. Across the main harbor is **Elizabeth Castle,** on an island joined to the Esplanade by a causeway that begins opposite the Grand
7 Hotel, by **People's Park.** You can cross the causeway between high tides but keep an ear open for the bell that is rung from the castle's gatehouse half an hour before the sea covers the stones; the water can get

Elizabeth Castle, **6**
Fort Regent, **1**
Jersey Museum, **4**
The Island Fortress-Occupation Museum, **5**
Parish Church, **3**
People's Park, **7**
Royal Square, **2**

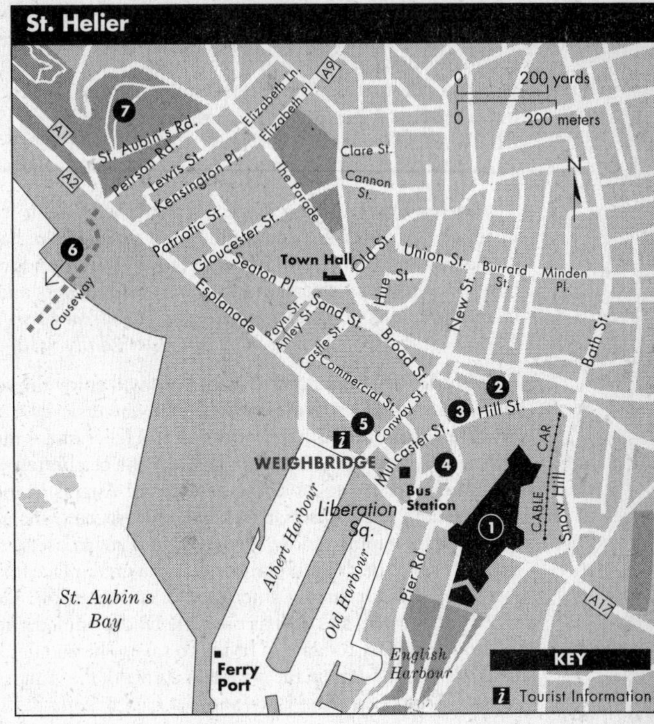

up to 15 feet deep. When the causeway is not usable, an amphibious craft takes visitors across.

The little island was a holy isle beginning in the 6th century with the arrival of Helier, the missionary son of a Belgian aristocrat. Legend places his cell on the headland beyond the castle, still called Hermitage Rock. Close to the castle's entrance is a military museum, in former barracks, housing an exhibition that tells the building's story. In the granite-built Governor's House in the heart of the complex, there are waxwork tableaus of events in the castle's long history, notably the meeting of Sir Philippe de Carteret and Charles II, who took refuge here in 1646. ✉ *St. Aubin's Bay,* ☏ *01534/23971.* 🎫 *£2.90.* ⏲ *Apr.–Oct., daily 9:30–5:30.*

The following Jersey highlights are arranged clockwise, starting just west of the capital. About 1½ miles from Elizabeth Castle is St. ★ Matthew's Church, the **"Glass Church"** in Millbrook, a Victorian chapel restored in 1934 as a memorial to Sir Jesse Boot, a millionaire pharmacist known throughout Britain for his drugstore chain, Boots. The fashionable Parisian glass sculptor, René Lalique (1860–1945), transformed the interior with glass. Inside, the church is embellished with fluid Art Deco glass forms—the front seems to be supported by a cluster of icicles; the glass cross, pillars, and altar rail all glitter with refracted light. ✉ *Millbrook, St. Aubin's Rd., St. Lawrence,* ☏ *01534/615905.* 🎫 *Free.* ⏲ *Weekdays 9–6 (or dusk), Sat. 9–1, Sun. for worship only.*

Reached from St Aubin's Bay via A12 (Grand Route de St. Ouen), in the northwest corner of the island, 5 miles northwest of St. Helier and 1 mile west of St. Ouen, the **Battle of Flowers Museum** is devoted to the parade of flowers, usually taking place in August, which has been held annually (except during wartime) since 1902. Originally, the decorated floats were torn to pieces for ammunition in the battle, but now they survive longer, some to become exhibits in this museum (with materials like dyed hare's tail and marram grass instead of flowers). There is a lakeside tearoom beside the museum that's open from May to September. ✉ *La Robeline, Mont des Corvées, St. Ouen,* ☎ *01534/482408; parade information, 01534/30178.* 🎫 *£2.* ⏲ *Mar.–Oct., daily 10–5.*

The **Jersey Flower Centre** in the north of the island (off B23), 3 miles northwest of St. Helier and 2 miles east of St. Ouen, has magnificent displays of carnations grown under glass on the grounds of an old farmhouse. Visitors can also wander among wild flowers and exotic birds, including a flock of Greater Flamingos. ✉ *Retreat Farm, St. Lawrence,* ☎ *01534/865665.* 🎫 *£3.25.* ⏲ *Apr.–Oct., daily 9:30–5:30.*

★ Even those who hold no brief with zoos will enjoy the country setting and educational programs that are an intrinsic part of the **Jersey Wildlife Trust,** based 3 miles north of St. Helier and 4 miles east of St. Ouen. The trust was started in 1963 by the celebrated wildlife writer Gerald Durrell, who chose the 25 acres of Augres Manor as a center for breeding and conserving endangered species, including gorillas, orangutans, lemurs, snow leopards, and marmosets, together with many kinds of birds and reptiles. This is a great place for a family outing, as well as for anyone interested in conservation. There are talks, videos and displays as well as the Café Dodo, named after a bird Durrell was a century too late in trying to save. The zoo lies half a mile inland from Bouley Bay, in the northeast corner of the island. ✉ *Les Augres Manor, Trinity,* ☎ *01534/864666.* 🎫 *£5.* ⏲ *Daily 9:30–6 (or dusk).*

★ One of the world's finest collections of orchids can be seen at the **Eric Young Orchid Foundation,** 2 miles north of St. Helier and 1 mile south of the Jersey Wildlife Trust. Five big greenhouses re-create the particular environments needed for certain orchids. ✉ *Victoria Village, Trinity,* ☎ *01534/861963.* 🎫 *£2.50.* ⏲ *Thurs.–Sat. 10–4.*

★ **Gorey Castle,** otherwise named **Mont Orgeuil** (Mount Pride), rises square-cut on its granite rock above the busy harbor, 4 miles northeast of St. Helier and 3 miles east of Victoria Village. For centuries Jersey's chief fortress, it was built mainly in the 14th century as a series of concentric defenses, pierced by five gateways. There are also waxwork tableaus of historic events. ☎ *01534/853292.* 🎫 *£2.90;* see *Jersey Museum,* above, *for details on combined tickets.* ⏲ *Apr.–Oct., daily 9:30–5, Nov.–Mar., Sat.–Mon. 10–dusk.*

La Hougue Bie

2 mi northwest of St. Helier, 1½ mi west of Mont Orgueil.

At La Hougue Bie, one of the finest neolithic tombs in Western Europe lies in a mound topped by two medieval chapels. It was excavated in 1924, and the site now has a museum with archaeological, farming, and old Jersey Railway exhibits. There is also a German bunker with an extensive occupation display. ✉ *Grouville,* ☎ *01534/853823.* 🎫 *£2.90;* see *Jersey Museum,* above, *for details on combined tickets.* ⏲ *Apr.–Oct., daily 10–5.*

The Arts

Jersey has an international **Jazz Festival** (☎ 01534/873767) in April in St. Helier. The **Battle of Flowers** (☞ Exploring, *above*) is held in August, and a **World Music Festival** is held in September, in St. Helier.

Films, theater, and celebrity concerts are presented all year in Fort Regent in St. Helier (☞ Exploring, *above*). During the summer months there are concerts by visiting bands in the Howard Davis Park, St. Helier. The **Jersey Arts Centre** (✉ Phillips St., St. Helier, ☏ 01534/873767) has regular exhibitions of art as well as drama, films, and music.

Dining and Lodging

££ ✕ **Apple Cottage.** Set in an attractive little cottage, tucked away beside Rozel Bay, this is a place where you can choose between an extravagant blow-out or a more modest repast—either way, you dine well. If you need a change from the island's prevalent fishy cuisine, you can order dishes such as grilled lamb cutlets or calves' liver. Seafood, however, is the specialty and comes in all forms, ranging from scallops and skate to lobster thermidor. ✉ *Rozel Bay, St. Martin,* ☏ *01534/861002. MC, V. No dinner Sun. Closed Mon. and 5 wks Dec.–Feb.*

££ ✕ **Jersey Pottery.** This restaurant is part of the Jersey Pottery complex and claims that Queen Elizabeth lunched here when visiting her dukedom. The restaurant, in an attractive conservatory, offers great seafood, but as it's very popular and often full, the cafeteria is an alternative. ✉ *Gorey Village, Grouville,* ☏ *01534/851119. AE, DC, MC, V. No dinner. Closed weekends (except Sat. in summer).*

££ ✕ **Victoria's.** The Grand Hotel's restaurant is *the* place to go for dinner and dancing. The decor is firmly Victorian. There's a long menu, but the critics' choice is the lemon sole or the medallions of pork. ✉ *Grand Hotel, Pierson Rd., St. Helier,* ☏ *01534/22301. Jacket and tie. AE, DC, MC, V. No dinner Sun.*

££££ ✕🏨 **Hotel l'Horizon.** L'Horizon is one of Jersey's luxury hotels, with wonderful views over St. Brelade's Bay. Though the hotel is big, it manages to maintain a bright, upbeat feeling, with large, comfortable bedrooms and plenty of places to relax in comfort. There are two restaurants—the **Crystal Room** and the **Star Grill.** The food is the same in both, but the atmosphere differs; the Crystal Room is traditionally elegant, while the Grill is more relaxed. Try the quail salad, roast saddle of lamb, or any of the wonderful seafood dishes, especially the scampi in mouthwatering ginger, honey, and lemon sauce. If you want to drop by for a special tea, try one of the sumptuous lounges. ✉ *St. Brelade's Bay, St. Brelade, JE3 8EF,* ☏ *01534/43101,* FAX *01534/46269. 107 rooms with bath. 3 restaurants (reservations essential, jacket and tie), pool, sauna, spa, steam room. AE, DC, MC, V.*

££££ ★ ✕🏨 **Longueville Manor.** The Manor is one of Britain's few members of the Relais and Châteaux group. It's set on lovely grounds and has the look of polished age, elegance, and comfort, derived from long-established, caring proprietors. Antiques abound, the bedrooms are supremely comfortable, and the bathrooms luxurious. The food in the paneled dining room is essentially traditional English, but venison pâté with onion marmalade, grilled salmon with béarnaise sauce, liver with sausage, and black pudding are all standouts. Try the Eton Mess, an unbelievable creation with crushed meringue and strawberries, with Jersey cream topping it off. ✉ *Longueville, St. Saviour, JE2 7WF,* ☏ *01534/25501,* FAX *01534/31613. 32 rooms with bath. Restaurant (reservations essential, jacket and tie), pool. AE, DC, MC, V.*

£££ ✕🏨 **Château la Chaire.** This dignified mansion is hidden on a cul-de-sac just above Rozel Harbour. The building is large but offers only 14 bedrooms, though all are luxurious and sunny; some of the bathrooms have Jacuzzis. The property is opulent, and the restaurant is no exception. This is the place to try Jersey's excellent fresh fish in a variety of elegant preparations. ✉ *Rozel Valley, St. Martin, JE3 6AJ,* ☏ *01534/863354,* FAX *01534/865137. 14 rooms with bath. Restaurant (reservations essential, jacket and tie). AE, DC, MC, V.*

££–£££ ✕ 🅃 **Old Court House Inn.** This is an ancient inn—the core of the building is about 500 years old—with a few rooms, two atmospheric lunchtime bars, and a fine restaurant. Grilled oysters, crab Creole, Jersey plaice—all feature on the big menu. The busy inn overlooks the harbor; the best view, though, is from the penthouse. ✉ *The Bulwarks, St. Aubin's Harbour, JE3 8AB,* ☎ *01534/46433,* FAX *01534/45103. 9 rooms with bath. Restaurant, 2 bars. AE, DC, MC, V.*

££ ✕ 🅃 **Moorings Hotel.** Although this seaside hotel is not one of Jersey's fanciest, it does offer attractively decorated, very cozy bedrooms (nine with harbor views), and friendly, helpful service. The restaurant, too, is on the simple side, but the lamb carved from the trolley and the superbly fresh seafood dishes are well above average. ✉ *Gorey Pier, St. Martin, JE3 6EW,* ☎ *01534/853633,* FAX *01534/857618. 16 rooms with bath. Restaurant. AE, MC, V.*

Outdoor Activities and Sports

BICYCLING

While in St. Helier, Jersey, rent from **Doubleday Garage** (✉ 19 Stopford Rd., ☎ 01534/31505), **Lawrence de Gruchy** (✉ 46 Don St., ☎ 01534/872002), and **Hireride** (✉ 1 St. John's Rd., ☎ 01534/31995).

DIVING

To dive in Jersey, contact **Watersports** (✉ First Tower, St. Helier, ☎ 01534/32813) or the **Diving Centre** (✉ Bouley Bay, ☎ 01534/861817).

GOLF

Jersey has two 18-hole courses, both of which can be used by any visitor who is affiliated with a golf club back home. These are **La Moye** (✉ St. Brelade, ☎ 01534/43401) and **Royal Jersey Golf Club** (✉ Grouville, ☎ 01534/854416).

SAIL-BOARDING AND SURFING

At St. Ouen Bay, in Jersey, there's great surfing. Windsurfing is popular at St. Aubin and St. Brelade's Bay. Rent equipment from **Atlantic Waves** (✉ Le Port, St. Ouen's Bay, ☎ 01534/865492) or the **Gorey Watersports Centre** (✉ Grouville Bay, ☎ 01534/853250).

SWIMMING

On Jersey, **St. Clement's Bay** and **Royal Bay** of Grouville have excellent sand and safe water.

Shopping

In St. Helier pedestrian malls on **Queen Street** and **King Street** have classic shops selling international brands, while smaller boutiques line roads like **Bath Street, New Street,** and **Halkett Place.** Two major markets are the **Central Market** and **Indoor Market,** also in this area. The **Jersey Pottery Shop,** (✉ 1 Bond St., St. Helier, ☎ 01534/25115) has a selection of wonderful pottery, which can also be bought directly from the source at **The Jersey Pottery** (✉ Gorey Village, Grouville, ☎ 01534/851119), where there's a good restaurant and brasserie. **Jersey Pearl** (✉ La Route des Issues, St. John, ☎ 01534/862137) exhibits the largest collection of pearl jewelry on the island, and you can watch pearlworkers crafting new pieces; Jersey Pearl also has two retail outlets (✉ 11 Halkett St. and 2 Broad St., St. Helier).

Guernsey

About 16,000 people, just over one third of the population of Guernsey, live in **St. Peter Port,** which has prospered over the centuries from the harbor around which it climbs. Guernsey is well placed for trade—legal or illegal—between France and England. In the 18th and 19th centuries, St. Peter Port was a haven for privateers who preyed on merchantmen.

Victor Hugo furnished his house, Hauteville (☞ *below*), with some of the looted pieces flooding the Guernsey market. In a modern version of its privateering past, St. Peter Port is now home to many tax exiles, who have luxurious houses on the town's outskirts.

Numbers in the margin correspond to points of interest on the St. Peter Port map.

The heart of the old town, around the harbor, is usually jammed with
8 traffic. The **parish church of St. Peter,** right beside The Quay, dates back at least to the days of William the Conqueror, though the oldest part of the present building is from the 12th century. Events through the centuries have played havoc with it, not least an air raid in 1944. Walking along the quaint streets in the old quarter will provide at least a morning's entertainment. You might start at Trinity Church Square and continue on Mansell Street.

The southern arm of St. Peter Port's harbor, Castle Emplacement,
★ 9 leads out to **Castle Cornet,** where you can get a bird's-eye view of St. Peter Port and an 8-miles-away glimpse of France. The castle was built early in the 13th century and contains several small museums, including the **Royal Guernsey Militia Museum,** the **Armoury,** and the **Main Guard Museum,** whose collection ranges from model ships to relics from the German occupation to island art. There's a cafeteria. ☎ *01481/721657.* *£3.50.* *Apr.–Oct., daily 10:30–5:30.*

You will have to climb up from Castle Pier to Hauteville (High
★ 10 Town) in order to reach **Hauteville House,** once the home of writer Victor Hugo (1802–85). For 18 years he was a political exile on Guernsey; in 1856 he bought this house. It is now owned by the City of Paris and is a completely French enclave, filled with lovely old furniture and tapestries. From the top floor he could see across to his beloved France and also into the house of his mistress, Juliette Drouet, who lived close by. ✉ *38 Rue de Hauteville, St. Peter Port,* ☎ *01481/721911.* *£3.* *Apr.–Sept., Mon.–Sat. 10–11:30 (last tour) and 2–4:30 (last tour). Guided tours only, limited to 15 people; early arrival recommended.*

Just north of St. Peter Port's town center, inland from the North Beach
11 Marina, is the **Beau Sejour Centre,** a multipurpose sports and entertainment complex. Equipped with an indoor heated pool, squash, badminton, and tennis courts, a "trim trail," a cinema/theater, a cafeteria, and a bar, this is the perfect place to come on a rainy day. ✉ *Amherst,* ☎ *01481/727211.* *Holiday membership £2.50.* *Daily 9 AM–11 PM, but check for pool schedule and other activities.*

Hidden beneath the rocks south of the center of St. Peter Port lies one of the underground networks of tunnels built on Guernsey by the German occupying forces and their slave labor. Now **La Valette Military Museum,** the complex focuses on Guernsey's military history dating back to the Victorian island militia and holds various World War II exhibits including the German truck used in the film *Indiana Jones and the Last Crusade.* ✉ *La Valette,* ☎ *01481/722300.* *£2.50.* *Daily 10–5, closed Tues.–Wed. in winter.*

★ 12 **Sausmarez Manor** (not to be confused with Saumarez Park, northwest of St. Peter Port), is 2 miles south of St. Peter Port and Guernsey's only stately home open to the public. Although there was a Norman house on the site, the present building, a solid, plain structure, dates to the 18th century and has been called the country's finest example of the Queen Anne colonial style of architecture. It is set among lovely gardens, the most important of which is the Woodland Garden, full of trop-

Beau Sejour Centre, **11**
Castle Cornet, **9**
German Military Underground Hospital, **13**
Hauteville House, **10**
Parish Church of St. Peter, **8**
Sausmarez Manor, **12**

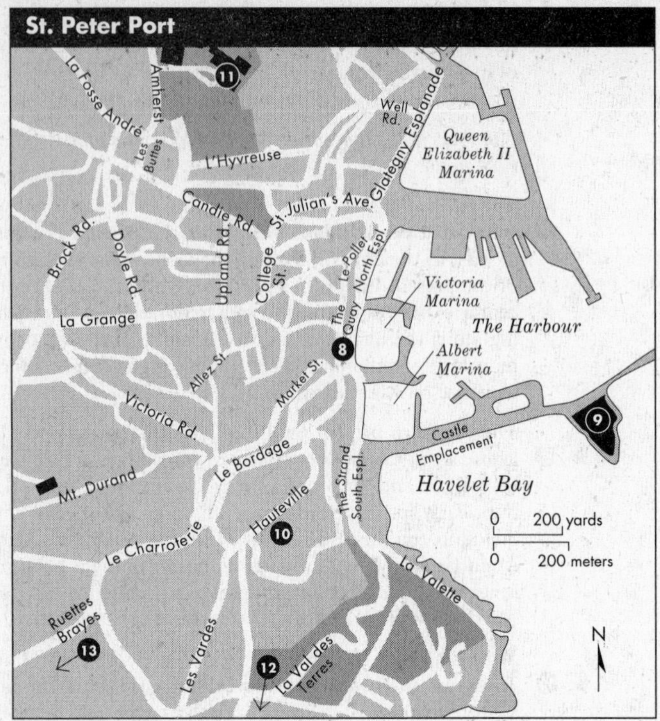

ical plants. Inside, tapestries, family portraits, and James II's wedding attire are on display. The manor has a notable collection of dollhouses, as well as two model railways (extra admission fees charged). ☎ *01481/35571.* 🎫 *£4.* 🕑 *Apr.–Oct., Mon.–Thurs. for guided tours only at 10:30 and 11:30.*

13 Three miles southwest of St. Peter Port, the **German Military Underground Hospital** is one of the main relics attesting to the German occupation on Guernsey. These grim catacombs were built by slave labor, and many of the workers died on the job and are entombed in the concrete. ✉ *La Vassalerie Rd., St. Andrew's,* ☎ *01481/39100.* 🎫 *£2.* 🕑 *Nov. and Mar., Sun. and Thurs. 2–3; Apr. and Oct., daily 2–4; May–Sept., daily 10–noon and 2–4 (4:30 in July and Aug.).*

The Nazi presence on Guernsey is remembered at the **German Occupation Museum,** 4 miles southwest of St. Peter Port, featuring a reconstruction of a street during the occupation, as well as numerous tableaus, videos, and access to old fortifications. ✉ *Forest (near the airport),* ☎ *01481/38205.* 🎫 *£2.50.* 🕑 *Apr.–Oct., daily 1:30–5:30; Nov.–Mar., Sun. 1:30–5:30.*

The Arts

FESTIVALS

Guernsey has an **Eisteddfod** during February, a **Square Dance Festival** at the end of June, and a **Battle of Flowers** at the end of August. Contact the tourist board for the latest dates.

Dining and Lodging

££ ✕ **The Absolute End.** This quietly elegant little restaurant in a neat, white building facing the sea is about a mile north along the coast from the center of St. Peter Port. The emphasis here is, of course, on seafood dishes, with home-smoked fish and shellfish as a very tasty starter. Try the salmon coubiliac. There is a good-value set menu at lunch for £11. The Absolute End won the best island restaurant award in 1993. ✉ *Longstore, St. George's Esplanade, St. Peter Port,* ☎ *01481/723822. AE, DC, MC, V. Closed Sun. and Jan.*

££ ★ ✕ **Café du Moulin.** This restaurant is in a converted watermill in a peaceful valley on the east of the island, close to the Longfree nature reserve. Try the crêpinette of seafood, or loin of lamb roasted with pistu (garlic, basil, and Parmesan) crust. It's all ultrafresh and tasty, with a touch of East Asia in many of the dishes. ✉ *Rue du Quanteraine, St. Peters,* ☎ *01481/65944. MC, V. No dinner Sun. Closed Mon.*

££ ✕ **La Nautique.** As with all the best restaurants in the Channel Islands, fish is the order of the day here. In this old-established eatery it comes with every sauce imaginable—lobster flambéed with whisky, monkfish *duglère,* turbot *hollandaise.* The cooking is French, and the service stylish, which is not the case with many Guernsey restaurants. ✉ *The Quay Steps, St. Peter Port,* ☎ *01481/721714. AE, DC, MC, V. Closed Sun., 2 wks after Christmas.*

£££ ✕ **La Frégate.** This small 17th-century manor house has been carefully converted into a hotel. Its setting in colorful gardens on a quiet hillside that overlooks the harbor makes it an excellent choice for a restful vacation. The bedrooms are all comfortable and sizable, some have balconies, and the staff is attentive. The restaurant, with big windows overlooking the town, serves topnotch cuisine, especially seafood dishes. ✉ *Les Côtils, St. Peter Port,GY1 1UT,* ☎ *01481/724624,* FAX *01481/720443. 13 rooms with bath. Restaurant (jacket and tie). AE, DC, MC, V.*

£–££ **Imperial Hotel.** Here is a simple hotel that's very popular for family vacations. The bedrooms, decorated with sturdy furnishings, are uncluttered, and some offer views of the sandy beaches of Rocquaine Bay. There are two bars reserved for residents, and another, the Portlet Bar, is the haunt of locals. ✉ *Torteval, GY8 0PS,* ☎ *01481/64044,* FAX *01481/66139. 16 rooms, 14 with bath. MC, V. Closed Nov.–Mar.*

Outdoor Activities and Sports

BICYCLING

On Guernsey, you can rent bikes from **The Cycle Centre** (✉ The Bridge, St. Sampson's, ☎ 01481/49311), **Quay Cycle Hire** (✉ White Rock, St. Peter Port, ☎ 01481/714146), and **West Coast Cycles** (✉ Les Tamaris, Portinfer Coast Rd., Vale, ☎ 01481/53654).

DIVING

To dive in Guernsey contact the **Blue Dolphin Sun Aqua Club** (✉ Boniface, Rocque Es Rousse, L'Ancresse, ☎ 01481/47665).

GOLF

The 18-hole **Royal Guernsey** (✉ L'Ancresse, Vale, ☎ 01481/47022) has wonderful views of the beach and sea. To play here visitors must produce handicap certificates, and they can't play on Sunday, or Thursday and Saturday afternoons.

SAIL-BOARDING AND SURFING

In Guernsey try the surf at Vazon Bay. For rentals and classes, contact **Nauti-Fun** (✉ L'Islet Crossroads, St Sampson's, ☎ 01481/46690), **West Coast Surfing** (✉ c/o Nyallo, Rue des Rocquettes, Vazon, Castel, ☎ 01481/55318), or **Sail or Surf** (✉ Pembroke Bay Hotel, Vale, ☎ 01481/44338). The island's windsurfing authority is **Windsurfing International** (✉ Cobô, ☎ 01481/53313).

SWIMMING

Guernsey's beaches are one of its chief attractions. Try **Vazon Bay,** which has one section reserved for surfers; **Petit Pot Bay,** especially for sunbathing; and **L'Ancresse Bay,** where the water is shallow.

Shopping

The main shopping district in St. Peter Port, not as glitzy as St. Helier, begins in **Le Pollet,** near Queen Elizabeth Marina. The mostly pedestrian area is a network of lanes with specialty shops—particularly jewelers. This is a great place to buy a watch. For antiques and women's fashions head for the old quarter and **Mill Street, Mansell Square,** and **Trinity Square. Moulin Houet Pottery** (✉ Moulin Houet Bay, ☎ 01481/37201) is a good source for sturdy, attractive pottery; it's located at the head of a lush valley running down to the sea. **Guernsey Toys** (✉ 25–27 Victoria Rd., St. Peter Port, ☎ 01481/723871) produces cuddly soft toys, and children can see how they are made. For crafts, visit the **Oatlands Craft Centre** (✉ St. Sampson's, ☎ 01481/49478), where silversmiths and potters demonstrate and sell their works.

Sark

Sark, the odd-man-out of the Channel Islands, has turned its back on the 20th century and banned the automobile, allowing only horse- or tractor-drawn carriages. Even planes are prohibited from flying overhead unless special permission has been granted. The tranquil island is in two sections, the smaller part, Little Sark, joined to the main island by a narrow neck of land whose vertiginous drop is 260 feet.

Dining and Lodging

£–££ ✕🏨 **Stock's Island Hotel.** For a relaxed lunch—and what else would you expect on Sark?—try the restaurant here. Lunchtime fare in the Courtyard Bistro (£) might be quiche or the local lobster and crab. The fillet of sea-bass is memorable. If you feel like staying over, there are 24 bedrooms. The Cider Press Restaurant also serves more formal meals, while there is a bistro for light snacks, where Stock's cakes and pastries rank high on the menu. ✉ *Sark GY9 0SD,* ☎ *01481/832001,* FAX *01481/832130. 24 rooms, 20 with bath or shower. 2 restaurants. AE, DC, MC, V. Closed Oct.–Easter.*

Outdoor Activities and Sports

BICYCLING

On Sark, **Avenue Cycle Hire** (✉ The Avenue, ☎ 01481/832102) and **Isle of Sark Carriage and Cycle Hire** (☎ 01481/832262) rent bikes.

CHANNEL ISLANDS A TO Z

Arriving and Departing

By Boat

You can sail to Jersey or Guernsey from Weymouth. **Condor Ltd.** (☎ 01305/761551) has daily ferry sailings (five a week in winter) and, in summer, a much faster catamaran service from Weymouth. Most boats stop at Guernsey first. The average time from Weymouth by the night ferry is 9–12 hours to Guernsey, 2¼ hours more to Jersey. In summer, catamarans make the crossing in about four hours. An average fare runs from £55 for a four-day Saver round-trip for a foot passenger to £250 and up for a car with two passengers.

By Plane

Jersey is well served by flights from both mainland Britain and the Continent. There are direct flights from Heathrow (British Airways),

Gatwick (BA, Jersey European), Bristol (BA), Exeter (Jersey European), Plymouth (BA), Southampton (Air UK, Channel Island Travel Service), Birmingham (British Midland, Jersey European), Manchester (BA, Jersey European), Edinburgh (BA), and Glasgow (British Midland, Channel Island Travel Service). Flying time from London is one hour, from Manchester 90 minutes, from Plymouth 70 minutes. The London/Jersey round-trip fare is about £75 (£97 in summer).

Guernsey Airport is served by Air UK, Aurigny Air Services, British Airways, British Midland, and Jersey European.

For further flight information contact: British Airways (☏ 0345/222111); Jersey European (☏ 0345/676676); Channel Island Travel Service (☏ 01534/46181); Aurigny Air Services (☏ 01481/822886); Air UK (☏ 0345/666777); British Midland (☏ 0345/554554).

Getting Around

By Bus

Jersey and Guernsey have excellent services, including regular buses to and from both airports, and all over both islands. The services are **Jersey Motor Transport Co.** (✉ Central Bus Station, Weighbridge, St. Helier, ☏ 01534/21201) and **Guernseybus** (✉ Picquet House, St. Peter Port, ☏ 01481/724677). They both have reasonably priced Rover tickets, which provide unlimited travel over a short period of time. Jersey also offers the chance to ride in the **Heritage Bus,** a restored Bedford Country Bus from 1937, which tours between the major attractions on the island, departing from the Jersey Museum in St. Helier four times daily between Easter and October. Ticket-holders can use it as often as they wish during one day, embarking and disembarking at will. Departure times are 10:30, 12:30, 2:30, and 4:30, finally returning to the Jersey Museum. Tickets cost £3.50 adults, £1.75 children under 10, and can be bought from the museum.

By Car

You can ship your car by ferry from mainland Britain at fairly low rates or rent a car (☞ Contacts and Resources, *below*), but the islands are small and can easily be explored by local bus. The traffic, especially on Jersey, can be regularly snarled up, particularly in high season. Driving is on the left, and the speed limit is 40 mph on Jersey; 35 on Guernsey and Alderney; cars are not permitted on Sark.

Between the Islands

Island hopping by sea or air will add fun to your archipelago vacation. There are regular daily flights all summer between Jersey and Guernsey, fewer flights in winter. You can also fly to the islands from France for a quick visit.

Larger ferries travel between Jersey and Guernsey; those from the British mainland stop at both islands going and returning. Fast hydrofoils skim around all the islands. Sark can be reached from Guernsey in about 45 minutes by **Sark Shipping** (☏ 01481/724059) and in the same time from Jersey by **Trident** (☏ 01534/66566); Herm can be reached from Guernsey in 15 minutes by **Herm Seaways** (☏ 01481/724677), **Trident Charter Co.** (☏ 01481/721379), and **Munson Herm Ferry** (☏ 01481/722613); and **Condor** (☏ 01481/726121) has a twice-weekly service from both Jersey and Guernsey to Alderney in summer and hydrofoil service to St. Malo.

Currency

Although the islands use pounds and pence, both of the bailiwicks have their own version of them, with specially printed bills. This currency is *not* legal tender elsewhere in the United Kingdom, though you will be able to use U.K. currency on the islands. Financial wheeling and dealing is big business here, and you'll find bureaus de change at banks, travel agencies, the main post offices, airports, and the main harbors. Note that only local stamps may be used to post letters.

Contacts and Resources

Car-Rental Agencies

JERSEY

Avis, ✉ Rue Cappelain, St. Peter, ☎ 01534/499499; **Budget Rent-a-Car,** ✉ Grande Route de St. Pierre, St. Peter, ☎ 0800/614270; **Europcar,** ✉ Arrivals Hall, Jersey Airport, St. Peter, ☎ 01534/47770; **Hertz,** ✉ Arrivals Hall, Jersey Airport, ☎ 01534/45621.

GUERNSEY

Avis, ✉ Les Caches, St. Martin, ☎ 01481/35266; **Budget Rent-a-Car,** ✉ Landes du Marche Garage, Vale, ☎ 01481/51744; **Hertz,** ✉ Jackson's Garage, Airport Forecourt, ☎ 01481/37638; **Harlequin Hire Cars,** ✉ Les Caches, St. Martin, ☎ 01481/39511.

Lodging

For information on Channel Islands hotels, contact the **Jersey Hotel and Guest House Association** (✉ 60 Stopford Rd., St. Helier, Jersey JE2 4LB, ☎ 01534/21421, FAX 01534/22496).

Travel Agencies

Bellingham Travel, ✉ 33 Queen St., St. Helier, Jersey, ☎ 01534/27575; ✉ 41 Commercial Arcade, St. Peter Port, Guernsey, ☎ 01481/726333. **Channel Islands Travel Service,** ✉ Old Mill, St. Martin, Guernsey, ☎ 01481/35551. **Marshall's Travel,** ✉ 1 Quennevais Precinct, St. Brelade, Jersey, ☎ 01534/41278. **Thomas Cook,** ✉ 14 Charing Cross, St. Helier, Jersey, ☎ 01534/506900; ✉ 22 Le Pollet, St. Peter Port, Guernsey, ☎ 01481/724111.

Visitor Information

In London, **Jersey Tourism Office,** ✉ 38 Dover St., London W1X 3RB, ☎ 0171/493–5278. On the islands, there are various tourist offices. **Jersey Tourism Department:** ✉ Liberation Sq., St. Helier JE1 1BB, ☎ 01534/500777, 01534/500888 for accommodations, FAX 01534/500808. **Guernsey Tourist Board:** ✉ North Esplanade, St. Peter Port, ☎ 01481/723552, FAX 01481/721246. **Sark Tourism Committee:** ✉ Information Centre, ☎ 01481/832345.

7 The Thames Valley

Windsor, Henley-on-Thames, Oxford

The crack of a polo ball echoes across Windsor Great Park as Prince Charles scores another point. He loves to escape to his family castle here, and many Londoners follow, heading for tranquil Thames-side villages, each more charming than the last. In June and July, all head for the Henley Royal Regatta to toast rowing's best with Pimm's "champers" and Kent strawberries. The top magnet here is the great city of Oxford—seat of Britain's oldest university—but be sure to catch the power, pomp, and solid magnificence of Blenheim Palace nearby.

THE THAMES EXERCISES A SPELL. Like many another great river, the Thames creates the illusion that it flows not only through the prosperous countryside of Berkshire and Oxfordshire, but through long centuries of history, too. The magic of past times seems to rise from its swiftly moving waters like an intangible mist. In London, where it is a broad, oily stream, it speeds almost silently past great buildings, menacingly impressive. Higher upstream it is a busy part of the living landscape, flooding meadows in spring and fall and rippling past places of significance not just to England but to the world. Runnymede is one of these. Here, on a riverside greensward, the Magna Carta was signed, that first crucial step in the Western world's progress toward democracy.

Updated by Robert Andrews

Nearby rises the medieval bulk of Windsor Castle, home to eight successive royal houses. Anyone who wants to understand the mystique of the British monarchy should visit Windsor, where a fraction of the present queen's vast wealth is on display in surroundings of pomp, power, and solid magnificence. Farther upstream lies Oxford, where generations of the ruling elite have been educated. In the bustling modern city, with industrial development on its outskirts, the colleges maintain their scholarly calm amid the traffic's clamorous rush. The less one is guided in a place like Oxford, the better. The main thing is to explore at your own pace, hoping that the combined forces of history, of the luster of college lawns, of the grace of the quadrangles, spires, and bridges, will overwhelm you.

Along the Thames River, scattered throughout the spreading landscape of trees, meadows, and rolling hills, are endless small villages and larger towns, some totally spoiled by ill-considered modern building, some still sleepily preserving their ancient charm. Superhighways carrying heavy traffic between London, the West Country, and the Midlands and the railroad have made much of this area into commuter territory, but you can easily leave these beaten tracks, and head down leafy lanes to discover timeless villages in a landscape kept green by the river and its wandering tributaries. The stretches of the Thames near Marlow, Henley, Bray, and Sonning-on-Thames are a holidaymakers's paradise. There are rowing clubs and piers all over that part of the river, excellent lawns, and well-built cottages and villas. This is the Thames's shop window, and any visitor who comes to London in summer and has a little time to spare would be well advised to spend his or her weekend on the river.

Pleasures and Pastimes

Henley Royal Regatta

During the cusp of June and July Henley hosts rowing's most elegant race, the Henley Royal Regatta. Its riverbanks become one gigantic, opulent lawn party as 500,000 visitors descend en masse during the week. Dozens of Jaguars and Rolls-Royces disgorge favored guests at the invitation-only Stewards' Enclosure, while everywhere, English oarsmen appear in short-brimmed school caps, straw boaters, and those eye-catching rowing jackets, color-coded in piping to signify the college or club that aided their rowing careers. Members of the royal family invariably attend—most notably Prince Michael of Kent, who once pulled oars at Sandhurst. Each day, the racing pauses twice—at noon for luncheon and at 4 PM for tea (or rather a bottle of Pimm's "champers" and some Kent strawberries with fresh Henley cream). If you're lucky enough to get a spot near the finish line, you'll swear you were back in Edwardian England: Winning crews cheer for the losers with three "hip, hip, hoorays"!

Dining

Simple pub food, as well as classic French cuisine, can be enjoyed in waterside settings at many restaurants beside the Thames. Even in towns away from the river, well-heeled commuters and Oxford professors support top-flight establishments. At weekends it is advisable to make reservations.

CATEGORY	COST*
££££	over £50
£££	£30–£50
££	£20–£30
£	under £20

**per person, including first course, main course, dessert, and VAT; excluding drinks*

Hiking and Walking

For long-distance walkers, the **Oxfordshire Way** runs 65 miles from Henley-on-Thames to Bourton-on-the-Water, on the eastern edge of the Cotswolds. A 13-mile ramble starts in Henley, runs north through the **Hambleden Valley,** takes in Stonor Park, and returns to Henley via the Assendons, Lower and Middle. For a less arduous walk, try the trails through the beechwoods at **Burnham Beeches.**

All the Thames Valley walks include busy traffic areas. One that is almost completely free of traffic is the **Thames Path,** a 180-mile route following the river from the London flood barrier to its source near Cirencester. The path is scheduled to be officially inaugurated in the fall of 1996, though most of it, following towpaths from the outskirts of London, through Windsor, to Oxford and Lechlade, has been open to the public for years. The stretch from Lechlade to the source of the river is new. The Thames Valley is a good area for gentle walking, not too hilly, with handy eateries, especially pubs—many of them beside the river—and plenty of easily accessible, civilized lodgings. There is also good public transportation in the region, so you can easily start and stop anywhere along the route you fancy.

Lodging

Many hotels in the area started out centuries ago as coaching inns. Others have been converted more recently from country mansions. Both types usually have plenty of character, with antiques and attractive decor—and often, well-kept gardens.

CATEGORY	COST*
££££	over £150
£££	£80–£150
££	£60–£80
£	under £60

**All prices are for two people sharing a double room, including service, breakfast, and VAT.*

Exploring the Thames Valley

We begin exploring the Thames Valley in the lively tourist town of Windsor, favorite home-away-from-home of Britain's royal family. From there we follow the river to Henley, site of the famous regatta, and then follow a counterclockwise sweep west to Wallingford—the countryside immortalized by *The Wind in the Willows.* Finally we go to Oxford, and end with a visit to some of the region's stately homes and palaces. Of course, these are the Thames Valley's superlatives. The area also abounds with tiny villages hidden from the major highways. While you are driving along the main roads, it's worth turning off from time to time to see if that tiny hamlet, deep in the trees, is as attractive as its name sounds.

Great Itineraries

With your own transport, you could see all the places outlined below on day trips from London, but to get the most out of the region, it's worth winkling out that perfect riverside inn or High-Street hotel and settling in for the night. Evenings in Windsor or Oxford will allow you to take in some world-class theater, and to make the most out of the mornings for touring the surrounding countryside. The area offers the greatest pleasure to those willing to leave the main roads and explore the smaller centers, while the Thames itself is best appreciated by locking up the car and setting off on foot along the towpath that runs alongside much of the river. It won't take long to shrug off those big city blues and absorb some of the most beautiful tracts of the English countryside.

Numbers in the text correspond to numbers in the margin and on the maps.

IF YOU HAVE 3 DAYS

It would require a bulky volume—and a month-long tour—to describe the Thames Valley in all its aspects, for the Thames, like the Seine, the Rhine, and the Danube, is a river flowing with history. However, if you only have three days, begin at **Windsor** ①, where royalty is the predominant flavor, and spend a morning visiting the castle, leaving part of the day for **Eton College** and **Windsor Great Park.** The next day, follow the river upstream, taking in the grandeur of the great Astor estate at **Cliveden** ④ and the smart village of **Marlow** ⑤, where the beamed pubs offer decent snacks for lunch. Head toward **Henley** ⑥, where the Thames forms a harmonious dialogue with the medieval buildings alongside, and easy and tranquil walks beckon upstream or down. Reserve the last day for **Oxford** ⑪–㉗, whose scholastic air does not dampen the aesthetic and gastronomic pleasures on tap.

IF YOU HAVE 5 DAYS

A longer sojourn will allow you to unearth the rustic charms of the region, including all the hamlets strung along the Thames. Making your base at **Windsor** ① for a couple of nights, from which you can make excursions to **Runnymede,** site of King John's signing of the Magna Carta, and, to the west, **Cliveden** ④ and the much lower-key charm of **Cookham,** a small village harboring an absorbing art gallery. For your third night, consider staying in **Henley** ⑥, from which it is an easy trip to two aristocratic mansions—**Stonor Park** ⑧ and **Mapledurham House** ⑦, and a cluster of picturesque Thameside villages, such as **Ewelme** ⑨, **Sonning, Dorchester-on-Thames** ㉛, and **Wallingford** ⑩. Reserve two days for **Oxford** ⑪, which will allow you to see more of the colleges as well as make an outing to **Woodstock** ㉘, site of the grand **Blenheim Palace,** birthplace of Winston Churchill and probably the most spectacular house in Britain. A small detour could take in the village of **Bladon** ㉙, Churchill's burial-place.

When to Tour the Thames Valley

Although the countryside around the Thames can be alluring at any time of year, the depths of winter may not be the most conducive time to appreciate its special beauty—nor is rain and cold wind the best accompaniment to soaking up the charms of such places as Windsor or Oxford. Moreover, many of the aristocratic country houses close between October and Easter. On the other hand, high summer can see droves of tourists in these places; while the main centers see little let-up in the year-long procession of visitors, avoid the months of August and September if you can, if only to escape the queues. Spring and autumn reveal the countryside at its best, and you can usually venture outdoors and onto the river at these times without too much discomfort. Remember that Eton College and the Oxford Colleges are much more restricted during term-time, and avoid any driving in the London area during the rush-hour, which starts an hour or two earlier on Friday evenings.

Numbers in the margin correspond to points of interest on the Thames Valley map.

ROYAL BERKSHIRE: WINDSOR AND ENVIRONS

Windsor

★ ❶ *21 mi west of London.*

Easily accessible from London, the town of Windsor makes a rewarding day trip. The principal attraction is **Windsor Castle,** rising majestically on its bluff above the Thames, visible for miles around. The city itself, with its narrow streets brimming with shops and ancient buildings, is well worth a visit, but the royal residence—the largest inhabited castle in the world—remains the prime attraction. From William the Conqueror to Queen Victoria, the kings and rulers of England have constantly added towers and wings to the brooding structure. Yet despite the multiplicity of hands that have gone into its making, the palace has managed to retain a unity of style and a very marked character of its own.

It is from the North Terrace that entry is gained into the State Apartments, which can be visited by the public when the Queen is not in residence. The queen, in fact, uses the castle far more than any of her predecessors. It has become over the last decade a sort of country weekend residence, which allows the royal family a few days of relaxation and informality away, as much as possible, from the public eye. Nevertheless, it still possible to catch Prince Charles joining a polo team for a match in Windsor Great Park.

The most impressive view of Windsor Castle is from the A332 road, on the southern approach to the town. Although there have been settlements here from time immemorial, including a Roman villa, the present castle was begun by William the Conqueror in the 11th century, and modified and extended by Edward III in the mid-1300s. One of his largest contributions was the enormous and distinctive round tower. Finally, between 1824 and 1837, George IV transformed what was essentially still a medieval castle into the fortified royal palace you see today. In all, work on the castle was spread over more than eight centuries, with most of the kings and queens of England demonstrating their undying attachment to it. In fact, Windsor is the only royal residence that has been in continuous use by the royal family since the Middle Ages.

As you enter the castle, **Henry VIII's gateway** leads uphill into the wide castle precincts, where visitors are free to wander. Directly opposite the entrance is **St. George's Chapel.** Comparable in its beauty only to that of King's College in Cambridge, this is the chapel where the queen invests new knights at the colorful Order of the Garter ceremonies in June. Here lie some of the most famous kings of England, beginning with Henry VI, and including Charles I, Henry VIII (Jane Seymour is

The Thames Valley
OXFORDSHIRE
Chipping Norton
Bourton-on-the-Water
A424
A44
Weston-on-the-Green
Woodstock 28
29 Bladon
A4260
A34
4095
Oxford 11–27
Burford
A40
Witney
A40
Stanton Harcourt Manor 34
Cumnor
Isis
A361
B4449
Thames
Kelmscott Manor 33
A420
30 Abingdon
A4074
4095
Faringdon
VALE OF WHITE HORSE
31 Dorchester-on-Thames
A38
B4508
Wallingford 10
A420
32 Uffington
A417
Wantage
A329
Swindon
LAMBOURN DOWNS
Thames
M4
A34(T)
Pangbourne
M4
BERKSHIRE
Hungerford Newtown
Marlborough
Hungerford
Newbury
A4
A4
N
WILTSHIRE
GREAT BRITAIN
0
10 miles
0
15 km
HAMPSHIRE

Dunstable
Aylesbury
A41(T)
BUCKINGHAMSHIRE
Cherwell
Amersham
Great Milton
A40
M40
CHILTERN HILLS
Watford
Rickmansworth
High Wycombe
Beaconsfield
Ewelme 9
Stonor Park 8
A4130
Nuffield
B480
Marlow 5
A4155
Cookham
Cliveden 4
Burnam Beeches
Burnham
B416
Henley 6
A423
Hurley
A404
A4094
Maidenhead
Slough
Sonning Common
A4074
B481
A4155
Thames
Mapledurham House 7
Eton 2
M4
A4
Windsor 1
Heathrow Airport
Caversham
Sonning-on-Thames
M4
A329
Runnymede 3
Staines
Reading
A308
A332
Windsor Great Park
Thames
Wokingham
Shinfield
M3
Silchester
Riseley
A30
Camberley
SURREY
M3
Frimley
Basingstoke
NORTH DOWNS

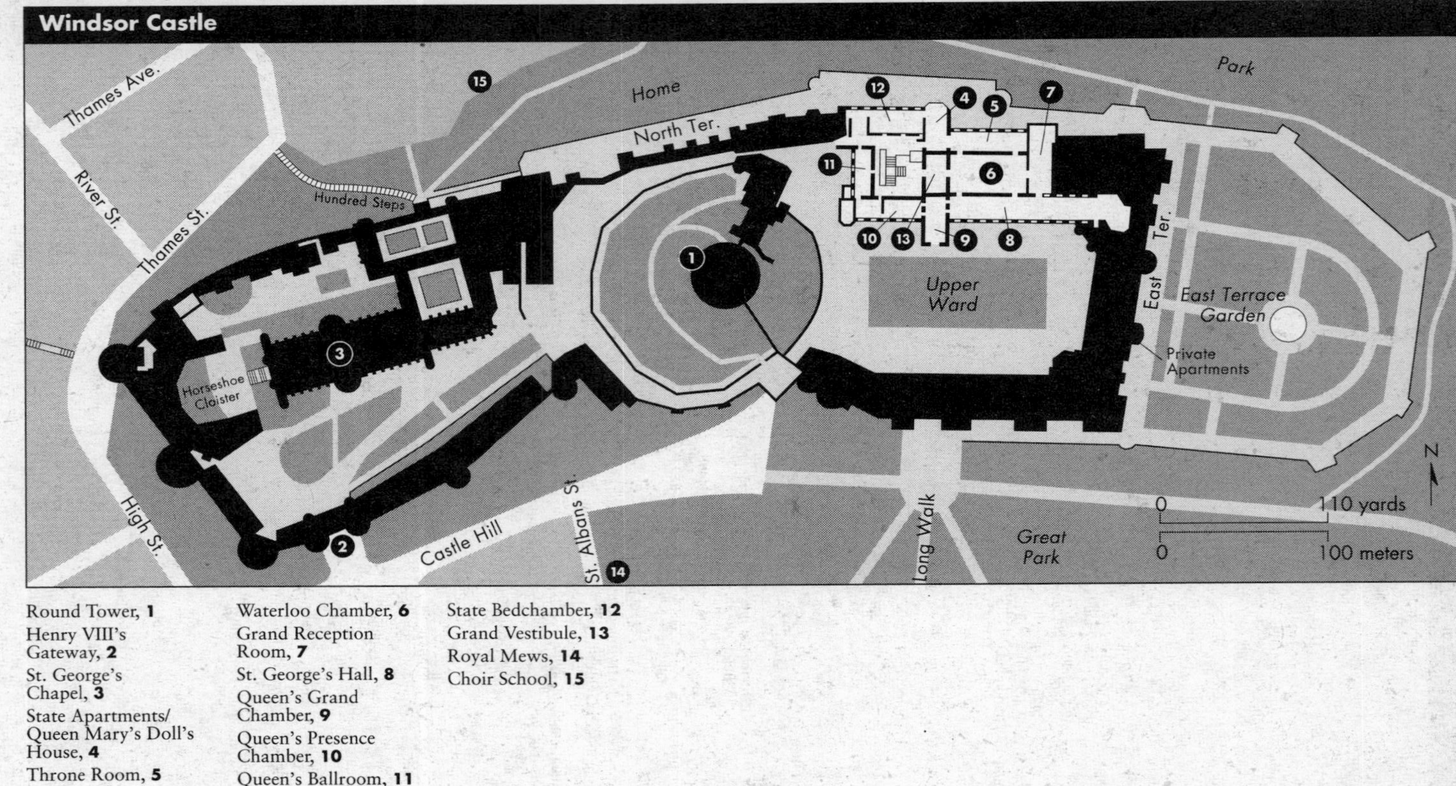

Round Tower, **1**
Henry VIII's Gateway, **2**
St. George's Chapel, **3**
State Apartments/ Queen Mary's Doll's House, **4**
Throne Room, **5**
Waterloo Chamber, **6**
Grand Reception Room, **7**
St. George's Hall, **8**
Queen's Grand Chamber, **9**
Queen's Presence Chamber, **10**
Queen's Ballroom, **11**
State Bedchamber, **12**
Grand Vestibule, **13**
Royal Mews, **14**
Choir School, **15**

the only one of his eight wives buried here), and many others. One of the noblest buildings in England, the chapel was built in the 15th- and 16th-century Perpendicular style and features elegant stained-glass windows, a high, vaulted ceiling, and intricately carved choir stalls. The heraldic banners of the Knights of the Garter hang in the choir, giving it a richly medieval look. The ceremony in which the knights are installed as members of the order has been held here with much pageantry for more than five centuries. Note that St. George's Chapel is closed to the public on Sunday.

The **North Terrace** provides especially good views across the Thames to Eton College (☞ *below*), perhaps the most famous of Britain's exclusive "public" boys' schools. From the terrace, you enter the **State Apartments,** a series of splendid rooms containing priceless furniture, including a magnificent Louis XVI bed; Gobelin tapestries and paintings by Canaletto, Rubens, Van Dyck, Holbein, Dürer, and del Sarto. The high points of the tour are the **Throne Room** and the **Waterloo Chamber,** where Sir Thomas Lawrence's portraits of Napoléon's victorious foes line the walls. You can also see a collection of arms and armor, much of it exotic, and an exhibition of items from the **Queen's Collection of Master Drawings**: works by Leonardo da Vinci, plus 87 Holbein portraits, and many others. All these rooms may not be open to the public at any one time.

The terrible fire of November 1992, which started in the Queen's private chapel, totally gutted some of the State Apartments. A swift rescue effort meant that, miraculously, hardly any works of art were lost. Repairs are scheduled to last until 1997, but all except the Great Hall and two of the state rooms previously visitable were open again at press time, as well as all the other public areas.

Queen Mary's Doll's House, on display to the left of the entrance to the State Apartments, is a perfect palace-within-a-palace, with functioning lights, running water, and even a library of Lilliputian-size books especially written by famous authors of the 1920s. Just outside the castle, on St. Albans Street, is the **Royal Mews,** where the royal horses are kept, with carriages, coaches, and splendid red and gold harnesses. The highlight is the Scottish State Coach. ☎ *01753/868286.* *£8.50 for the Precincts, the State Apartments, the Gallery, St. George's Chapel, and the Albert Memorial Chapel; Doll's House additional £1, or separately (including entry to the Precincts) £3.50; tickets are £1–£2 less on Sun., when St. George's Chapel is closed.* *Mar.–Oct., daily 10–5:30 (last admission at 4); Nov.–Feb., daily 10–4 (last admission at 3).*

Only a small part of old Windsor—the settlement that grew up around the castle in the Middle Ages—has survived. Windsor Town is not what it used to be in the time of Sir John Falstaff and the *Merry Wives of Windsor* when it was famous for its inns, of which, in 1650, it boasted about 70. Today, there are only a handful of them, and beer is not so strong, wit not so boisterous. But seekers of romantic history will enjoy tiny Church Lane and Queen Charlotte Street, both narrow and cobbled, opposite the castle entrance. The old buildings now house antiques shops or restaurants.

NEED A BREAK?

The **Slug and Lettuce** (✉ 5 Thames St.) is a relaxed and roomy café/restaurant for soups, salads, puddings, or just a cup of tea or coffee.

Windsor Great Park is the remains of an ancient royal hunting forest, stretching for some 8 miles (about 5,000 acres) south of Windsor Castle. Much of it is open to the public and can be explored by car or on foot. Focal points include the romantic and spectacular 3-mile **Long Walk**—designed by Charles II to join castle and park—the **Royal Mausoleum at Frogmore,** where Queen Victoria and her husband, Prince Albert, are buried (open only two days a year, in May); **Virginia Water,** a 2-mile-long lake; and the **Savill Garden,** which offers a huge variety of trees and shrubs. ✉ *Wick La., Englefield Green, Egham,* ☎ *01753/860222.* 🎟 *Garden £3.50.* ⏲ *Mar.–Oct., daily 10–6; Nov.–Feb., daily 10–4.*

The Arts

The **Windsor Festival** is usually held in early fall, September or October, with occasional events taking place in the castle itself.

Windsor's **Theatre Royal** (✉ Thames St., ☎ 01753/853888), where productions have been staged for nearly 200 years, is one of Britain's leading provincial theaters. It puts on a range of plays and musicals throughout the year, including pantomime for six weeks after Christmas.

Dining and Lodging

££££ ✕🏨 **Oakley Court.** This ornate hotel stands on large grounds beside the river, 3 miles west of Windsor. It was originally a Victorian mansion, but half the rooms are in a modern annex. There is an excellent restaurant, the **Boulestin,** which serves essentially English fare, such as fillet of beef with Stilton mousse, and has a good wine list. ✉ *Windsor Rd., Water Oakley, SL4 5UR,* ☎ *01753/609988,* FAX *01628/37011. 92 rooms with bath. Restaurant (reservations essential, jacket and tie), sauna, putting green, croquet, exercise room, fishing, billiards, helipad. AE, DC, MC, V.*

£££ ✕🏨 **Sir Christopher Wren's House Hotel.** This was a private mansion built by the famous architect in 1676, but modern additions have converted it into a hotel, now under the same ownership as the Great House at Sonning (☞ Sonning-on-Thames, *below*). Restoration of antique features complements the fine design, though the Baroque frills and flounces can be wearing. The restaurant overlooks the river, and cream teas are served on the terrace. ✉ *Thames St., SL4 1PX,* ☎ *01753/861354,* FAX *01753/860172. 42 rooms with bath. AE, DC, MC, V.*

Outdoor Activities and Sports

BICYCLING

Bikes can be rented in Windsor at **Windsor Cycle Hire** (✉ 50 The Arches, Alma Rd., ☎ 01753/830220).

Shopping

Many Windsor stores are open on Sunday, particularly those selling antiques. Try Peascod Street, High Street, and King Edward Court, a new precinct. The **Edinburgh Woollen Mill** (✉ 10 Castle Hill, ☎ 01753/855151) has a large range of Scottish knitwear, tartans and tweeds, particularly for women. **Best of British** (✉ 44 King Edward Ct., ☎ 01753/859929) has handmade items that are good for gifts.

Eton

❷ *23 mi west of London, linked by a footbridge across the Thames to Windsor.*

Some people may find it symbolic that almost opposite Windsor Castle, which embodies the continuity of the royal tradition, a school was established that for centuries was responsible for the upbringing of future leaders of the country. This, of course, is Eton. With its single main street leading from the river to the famous school, the town itself is a much quieter place than Windsor, retaining an old-fashioned charm. ★ The splendid redbrick, Tudor-style buildings of **Eton College,** founded in 1440 by King Henry VI, border the north end of High Street; drivers are warned of "Boys Crossing." During the college semesters, the schoolboys are a distinctive sight, dressed in their pinstripe trousers, swallow-tailed coats, top hats, and white collars. The oldest buildings, grouped around a quadrangle called School Yard, include the **Lower School,** which is one of the oldest schoolrooms in use in Britain. The Gothic **Chapel** rivals St. George's at Windsor in both size and magnificence and is impressively austere and intimate at one and the same time. Beyond the cloisters are the school's famous playing fields where, according to the duke of Wellington, the Battle of Waterloo was won, since so many of his officers had learned discipline in their schooldays there. The **Museum of Eton Life** has displays on the school's history, and there are guided tours of the Lower School and chapel. ⊠ *Brewhouse Yard,* ☏ *01753/671177.* 🎫 *£2.50; with tour, £3.50.* ⏲ *During term, daily 2–4:30; out-of-term, daily 10:30–4:30; guided tours Apr.–Sept., daily at 2:15 and 3:30.*

Dining

£££–£££ ✕ **The Cockpit.** Cockfighting once took place in the courtyard of this 500-year-old inn with oak beams. Now a restaurant with a strong Italian flavor, its specialties include calves' liver and fresh fish. ⊠ *47–49 High St.,* ☏ *01753/860944. AE, DC, MC, V. No dinner Sun., no lunch Mon.*

Shopping

Eton has a reputation for excellent, if pricey, antiques shops, most of them along the High Street. **Turk's Head Antiques** (⊠ 98 High St., ☏ 01753/863939) has jewelry, silver, and Victoriana.

Runnymede

★ ❸ *5 mi southeast of Windsor on the A308.*

A giant step in the history of democracy was taken at Runnymede, outside Egham. On this tiny island in the middle of the Thames, King John, under his barons' compulsion, signed the Magna Carta in 1215, affirming the individual's right to justice and liberty. On the wooded hillside, in a meadow given to the United States by Queen Elizabeth in 1965, stands a **memorial to President John F. Kennedy.** Nearby is another memorial, in the style of a classical temple, erected by the American Bar Association to commemorate the 750th anniversary of the signing.

Cliveden

❹ *26 mi west of London, 8 mi northwest of Windsor.*

In woods high above the river Thames, north of Windsor, this magnificent country mansion was made famous by the Astors, who had it rebuilt in the 1860s. For 250 years, Cliveden was one of the most important houses in England. Set in glorious rural river scenery, yet easily accessible from London, it attracted generations of eminent politicians and writers as house guests. In the 1920s and '30s it was the setting for the Cliveden Set, the strongly political *salon* presided over by Nancy Astor, who was the first woman to sit in Parliament, though she was an American, born in Danville, Virginia, in 1879. The house now belongs to the National Trust, which has leased it for use as a *very* exclusive hotel (☞ *below*) . The public can visit the spectacular grounds and formal gardens that run down to bluffs overlooking the Thames, as well as three rooms in the west wing of the house. There is a convenient restaurant in the Orangery for lunch, or you can eat more formally in the hotel (☞ Dining and Lodging, *below*). ☏ *01628/605069.* 🎫 *Grounds £4;*

house £1 extra. ⊗ Grounds Mar.–Oct., daily 11–6; Nov.–Dec., daily 11–4; house Apr.–Oct., Thurs. and Sun. 3–6; restaurant in the Orangery Apr.–Oct., Wed.–Sun. 11–5; Nov.–mid-Dec., weekends noon–2.

Dining and Lodging

££££ ★ ✕🅷 **Cliveden.** Cliveden has to be one of the grandest hotels in Britain—and one of the most expensive. This is sophisticated luxury at its very best and a chance to actually experience the "Stately Houses" lifestyle in all its grandeur. There are 376 acres of magnificently tended gardens and parkland with wonderful river views. The interior is opulent in the extreme, featuring: the Orkney Tapestries in the Great Hall; suits of armor; a library; a richly paneled staircase; endless paintings, mostly fine historic portraits; and room after room with beautifully molded plaster ceilings. The ultracomfortable bedrooms are named after the famous people who once stayed here—including the one used by Lady Astor herself (which costs £850 a night); a basic double costs £245 a night. There is every kind of activity available; you can venture onto the Thames on an Edwardian boat or tour the area in the hotel's Bentley. There are two main restaurants: the **Terrace Dining Room,** recently refurbished, which has fine garden views, and **Waldo's,** paneled and with more atmosphere. ✉ *Taplow, near Maidenhead SL6 0JF,* ☎ *01628/668561,* FAX *01628/661837. 37 rooms with bath. 2 restaurants, indoor and outdoor pools, tennis courts, health club, horseback riding, squash, boating. AE, DC, MC, V.*

BOATING ON THE THAMES: TO AND FROM HENLEY

"Nothing—absolutely nothing—half so much worth doing as simply messing about in boats. Simply messing," he went on dreamily: "messing–about–in–boats; messing–" . . . and you'll probably agree with Water Rat's opinion, voiced in Kenneth Grahame's immortal classic *The Wind in the Willows,* if you tour this stretch of the Thames Valley, from Marlow to Wallingford. Boat-borne or by foot, you'll find some of the most delightfully wooded scenery gracing the valley here. On each bank there are fine wooded hills, with spacious houses, greenhouses, flower beds, and clean lawns that stretch down to the water's edge. It was to Pangbourne, along this stretch of the river, that Grahame retired to write his beloved book. E.H. Shepard used the lock at Mapledurham as the model for some of his delightful illustrations for the book. Most travelers enjoy a stay Thameside here because of the famed Henley Royal Regatta.

Marlow

❺ *30 mi west of London, 15 mi northwest of Windsor.*

Just inside the Buckinghamshire border, Marlow is a smaller version of Henley, overflowing with Thameside charm and often overwhelmed by tourism on summer weekends. Take particular note of its unusual suspension bridge, which William Tierney Clark built in the 1830s. (He also built the bridge over the Danube linking Buda with Pest.) Marlow has a number of striking old buildings, particularly the stylish, privately owned Georgian houses along Peter and West streets. In 1817, the Romantic poet Percy Bysshe Shelley stayed with friends at 67 West Street and then bought **Albion House** on the same street. His second wife, Mary, completed her Gothic novel *Frankenstein* here. Marlow Place, on Station Road, dates from 1721, and has been lived in by several princes of Wales.

NEED A BREAK? One of the town's fine old pubs is the 400-year-old **Ship Inn** (✉ West St.), whose beams were once ship timbers.

Henley

 *7 mi southwest of Marlow on A4155, 8 mi north of Reading, and 36 mi west of central London.*

Mention Henley to Britons, and even those who have scarcely seen a boat will conjure up idyllic scenes of summer rowing. Indeed, Henley Royal Regatta, held in early July each year on a long, straight stretch of the river Thames, has made the charming little riverside town—set in a broad valley between gentle hillsides just off A423—famous throughout the world. Competition in this event is between the best oarsmen from all over the world, and many an over-enthusiastic supporter who has forgotten he is standing in a rowing boat has found himself unwittingly in the water while cheering a favorite on. Henley during Regatta Week is one of the high points of the social summer, rating with Ascot and Wimbledon as a sports event and a fashionable outing all in one.

Townspeople launched the Henley Regatta in 1839, initiating the Grand Challenge Cup, the most famous of its many trophies. After 1851, when Prince Albert, Queen Victoria's consort, became its patron, it was known as the Royal Regatta. Oarsmen compete in crews of eight, four, or two, or as single scullers. For many of the spectators, however, the social side of the event is far more important. Elderly oarsmen wear brightly colored blazers and tiny caps; businesspeople entertain wealthy clients, and everyone admires the ladies' fashions. For more on the Henley Regatta and its festivities, *see* Outdoor Activities and Sports, *below.*

Another traditional event in the third week of July is **Swan-Upping,** which dates back 800 years. Most of the swans on the Thames are owned by the Queen. Swan markers in Thames skiffs start from Sunbury-on-Thames, catching the new cygnets and marking their beaks in order to establish ownership. The Queen's Swan Keeper, dressed in scarlet livery, presides over this colorful ceremony, complete with festive banners.

Henley's many historic buildings, including one of Britain's oldest theaters, are all within a few minutes' walk. Half-timber Georgian cottages and inns abound. The mellow brick **Red Lion Hotel,** beside the bridge (☞ Dining and Lodging, *below*), has been the town's focal point for nearly 500 years. Kings, dukes, and writers have stayed here, including Charles I and James Boswell. The duke of Marlborough used the hotel as a base during the building of Blenheim Palace.

NEED A BREAK? You are never far from a pub in Henley, a town where beer has been brewed for more than 200 years. One of the most popular inns is the **Three Tuns** (✉ 5 Market Pl.), which has a buttery with massive beams and a small summer terrace. The bar food is reasonable and filling—cottage pie, savory pancakes, sandwiches—and should be washed down with good local beer.

The 16th-century "checkerboard" tower of **St. Mary's Church** overlooks Henley's bridge on Hart Street. The building is made of alternating squares of local flint and white stone. If the church's rector is about, you can ask permission to climb to the top for the superb views up and down the river. The **Chantry House,** connected to the church by a gallery, was built as a school for poor boys in 1420. It is an unspoiled example of the rare timber-frame design, with upper floors jutting out. ✉ *Hart St.,* ☎ *01491/577062.* 🎫 *Free.* ⏲ *Church services or by appointment.*

The Arts

Henley Festival takes place during the week following the regatta each year. All kinds of open-air concerts and events are staged at this popular summer occasion. ✉ *Henley Festival, Festival Yard, 42 Bell St., Henley, RG9 2BG,* ☎ *01491/411353.*

Dining and Lodging

££ ✕ **Little Angel Inn.** Housed in a quaint building more than 500 years old, this is an associate of the French Routier chain of restaurants, which are known for their good value and no-nonsense food. Specialties include fish and duck. Less expensive meals are served in the bistro/bar, which is open even when the restaurant is closed. ✉ *Remenham (¼ mi from Henley on A423),* ☎ *01491/574165. AE, DC, MC, V. No dinner Sun. Closed Mon.*

££ ✕ **Stonor Arms.** Four miles north of Henley lies this 18th-century restaurant, once a pub. There is a simple brasserie in two conservatories and a more formal dining room. The food is as good to eat as it is to look at—local game, duck confit, fried mussels and scallops—and there's a comprehensive wine list. ✉ *Stonor,* ☎ *01491/638345,* FAX *01491/638863. MC, V.*

£££ ✕🏨 **Red Lion.** This historic hotel overlooks the river and the town bridge. During its 400-year history, guests have included King Charles I and Dr. Samuel Johnson, the 18th-century critic, poet, and lexicographer. The hotel has recently been refurbished. ✉ *Hart St., RG9 2AR,* ☎ *01491/572161,* FAX *01491/410039. 26 rooms, 21 with bath. Restaurant, garage. AE, MC, V.*

££ ✕🏨 **Flohr's.** Just a short walk from the town center, this small, elegant Georgian hotel has an expensive *cordon bleu* restaurant supervised by the owner, Gerd Flohr. ✉ *15 Northfield End, RG9 2JG,* ☎ *01491/573412,* FAX *01491/579721. 9 rooms, 3 with bath. MC, V.*

Outdoor Activities and Sports

GOLF

At **Badgemore Park,** Henley-on-Thames (☎ 01491/573667), a parkland 18-hole course, visitors are welcome on weekdays, and on weekends by arrangement.

HENLEY ROYAL REGATTA

Henley Royal Regatta (☎ 01491/572153), one of the highlights of Britain's sporting and social calendar, takes place over four days at the beginning of July each year. A vast community of large tents goes up, especially along both sides of the unique stretch of straight river here (1 mile, 550 yards), and every surrounding field becomes a parking lot. The most prestigious place for spectators is the Stewards' Enclosure, but admission is by invitation only and, however hot, men must wear jackets and ties—ladies in trousers are refused entry. Fortunately, there is plenty of space on the public towpath to see the early stages of the races.

En Route Across the river, on the eastern side, follow the towpath north along the pleasant, shady banks to **Temple Island,** a tiny, privately owned island with trailing willows and a solitary house. This is where the regatta races start. On the south side of the town bridge, a riverside promenade passes **Mill Meadows,** where there are gardens and a pleasant picnic area. Along both stretches, the river is alive with boats of every shape and size, from luxury "gin palace" cabin cruisers to tiny rowboats.

Edged by the gently sloping Chiltern Hills and in a wide horseshoe-shaped valley, the Thames meanders from Henley through a cluster of small country towns and villages. Main roads follow the river on both sides, but it is along the narrow lanes that the villages and wooded countryside—generally prettiest north of the river—are best explored. For more serious sightseers, the region offers a wide range of earthworks, churches, and stately homes.

Sonning-on-Thames

5 mi south of Henley, 4 mi northeast of Reading

If put to the vote, many natives would choose Sonning-on-Thames as the quintessential Thames Valley village. There is nothing of outstanding historic note here. However, its old bridge charmingly spans the Thames with eleven arches, and the Georgian-fronted houses, the ancient mill that is mentioned in the *Domesday Book,* and the black, white, and yellow cottages make it all too perfect a Thameside village.

Dining and Lodging

££££ ★ ✕ **L'Ortolan.** Worth the excursion from Sonning-on-Thames, this elegant country restaurant lies just over 4 miles south of Reading, on A327. It's most attractive, with an airy, light feel to the dining room. The nouvelle dishes are every bit as interesting as the setting. Try the *suprême de canard sauvage* (wild duck breast roasted and flamed in Armagnac). ✉ *The Old Vicarage, Church La., Shinfield,* ☎ *01734/883783. AE, DC, MC, V. No dinner Sun. Closed Mon., last 2 wks in Feb. and Aug.*

£££ **The Great House.** A former 16th-century inn, this hotel commands superb views over the river and has extensive gardens—the roses are lovely—leading to a half-mile of moorings. Diners can pick between two restaurants, while overnight guests have a choice of period or modern rooms. The best rooms lie in the original Great House, a redbrick building standing apart from the main hotel, sumptuously furnished and wood-paneled. Readers have written to say the worse rooms are just that—either housed over an adjacent Thai restaurant or cramped quarters with dismal views and downwind from a large dairy farm. Book the best—or none at all. ✉ *Thames St., RG4 0UT,* ☎ *01734/692277,* FAX *01734/441296. 36 rooms with bath or shower. 2 restaurants, bar, moorings. AE, DC, MC, V.*

Mapledurham House

❼ *5 mi southwest of Henley.*

A redbrick Elizabethan mansion with tall chimneys, mullioned windows, and battlements, Mapledurham is still the home of the Eyston family, and so has kept a warm, friendly atmosphere along with pictures, family portraits, magnificent oak staircases, and Tudor plasterwork ceilings. Here you can see a 15th-century water mill—the last working grain mill on the Thames. The house can also be reached by boat from Caversham Promenade in Reading. (The boat leaves at 1:45 PM, and travel time is about 40 minutes.) ✉ *Mapledurham, near Reading,* ☎ *01734/723350. House and mill £4; house only £3; grounds and mill £2.50. Easter–Sept., weekends only 2:30–5. House also has 11 self-catering cottages (some more than 300 years old) available for rent, for £155–£475 a week.*

This section of the river, from Caversham to Mapledurham, inspired Kenneth Grahame's classic children's book, *The Wind in the Willows,* which began as a bedtime story for Grahame's son Alastair while the Grahames were living at Pangbourne. Some of E. F. Shepherd's charming illustrations are of specific sites along the river. If children have read (or been read) *The Wind in the Willows,* they'll like a boat trip on the Thames from Caversham to Mapledurham. They'll also enjoy exploring the extensive grounds of Mapledurham House.

Stonor Park

❽ *5 mi northwest of Henley on A4130/B480.*

Home to the Catholic Stonor family for more than 800 years, this ancestral estate is lost in the network of leafy country lanes on the fringes of the Chiltern Hills. A medieval mansion with a Georgian facade, it stands in a wooded deer park. Mass has been celebrated in its tiny chapel since the Middle Ages, and there is an exhibition of the life and work of the Jesuit Edmund Campion, who took shelter here in 1581 before his martyrdom. ⊠ *Stonor,* ☎ *01491/638587.* *£4; gardens and chapel only £2.* ⏲ *Hrs are very restricted and changeable, so check locally.*

Ewelme

★ ❾ *10 mi northwest of Henley off A4130, 6 mi west of Stonor Park.*

One of England's prettiest and most unspoiled villages lies near the town of Benson, in Oxfordshire. Its picturebook almshouses, church, and school—one of the oldest in Britain—huddle close together, all built more than 500 years ago. The church shelters the carved alabaster tomb of Alice, duchess of Suffolk, the granddaughter of England's greatest medieval poet, Geoffrey Chaucer. Jerome K. Jerome, author of the humorous book *Three Men in a Boat,* describing a 19th-century Thameside vacation, is also buried here.

Wallingford

❿ *13 mi southeast of Oxford on A4074, 2 mi west of Ewelme.*

The busy marketplace of this typical riverside market town is bordered by a town hall, built in 1670, and an Italianate corn exchange, now a theater and cinema. Market day is Friday.

OXFORD AND SURROUNDINGS

The river Thames takes on a new graciousness as it flows along the borders of Oxfordshire for 71 miles, and with each mile it increases in size and importance. Four tributaries swell the river as it passes through the country: the Windrush, the Evenlode, the Cherwell, and the Thame. Although the Thames is so important to the county, Oxfordshire is not all meadows, willow trees, locks, and boats. It is also the site of one of the greatest founts of culture and science ever created by man: the University of Oxford. With the Parisian Sorbonne heading the list of the oldest universities in Europe, Oxford comes second in that venerable procession of seniority. But Oxford is not only an ancient institution, it is also a mental atmosphere, an intellectual and moral climate, and through its age-long tradition, well-established rules and customs, other-world atmosphere, and exacting standards, it became a training ground for the nation's élite. To help accomplish this, the university's founding fathers realized that young minds mature much quicker in tranquil repose rather than in the bustle of towns—so they created a group of colleges, many built around beautiful cloisters, whose very tenor appeared monastic—small wonder that not until 1858 did the reform of the university statute admit married dons.

Oxford

11 *60 mi northwest of London.*

Whatever preconceived notions you may have about Oxford, your first sight of the city will doubtlessly confirm them all. Stop on one of the low hills that surround it, to look at the skyline. If you are fortunate, and the sun is shining, the towers, spires, turrets and pinnacles will look like a scene from a medieval fairy story. Here stretched out in front of you is Oxford, the home of erudition and scholarship, of Oxford England and—of Oxford marmalade. From here, time appears to have passed the city by and it almost looks like it did 200 years or even longer ago. First appearances are deceptive, however. The last 50 years have seen changes in Oxford that have revolutionized not only the town, but the very basis of university life itself. It is, in fact, one of the fastest growing manufacturing towns in England. Today, the rarefied air of academia and the bustle of modern life compete with one another. In addition to its historic university, Oxford is home to two major industrial complexes: the Rover car factory and the Pressed Steel works. In the city center, "town and gown" merge, as modern stores sit side by side with centuries-old colleges and their peaceful quadrangles.

The most picturesque approach is from the east, over Magdalen (pronounced "Maudlin") Bridge. Among the ancient honey-colored buildings and elegant spires, you will see the 15th-century tower of Magdalen College, famous for its May Day carol service. Magdalen Bridge leads you directly into the broad, gently curving High Street, flanked by ancient colleges.

Newcomers are surprised to learn that the University of Oxford is not one unified campus, but a collection of many colleges and buildings, new as well as old, scattered across the city. All together there are 40 different colleges where undergraduates live and study. Most of the college grounds are open to tourists, including the magnificent dining halls and chapels, though the opening times (displayed at the entrance lodges) vary greatly. Some colleges are open only in the afternoons during university semesters, when the undergraduates are in residence.

Numbers in the margin correspond to points of interest on the Oxford map.

Although the earliest colleges were founded in the 11th century, succeeding ages enhanced Oxford's splendor by a good deal of reconstruction, often sacrificing medieval almshouses and friaries for magnificent buildings of later eras, such as the Sheldonian Theatre and the Radcliffe Camera. In fact, there is such a bewildering display of architectural styles in Oxford that the less good often takes the atten-
★ 12 tion away from the best. **Magdalen College** is one of the richest and most impressive of Oxford's colleges, founded in 1458, with an impressive main quadrangle and a supremely monastic air. A walk around the Deer Park and along Addison's Walk will lead you to envy the members of the college for the experience of living here. They have included such diverse people as Cardinal Wolsey, Gibbon, and Oscar Wilde. £2. *Daily 2–6.*

At the foot of **Magdalen Bridge** you can rent (for £7–£10 an hour, plus a £25 refundable deposit) a punt, a shallow-bottomed boat that is poled slowly up the river. You may wish, like many an Oxford student, to spend a summer afternoon punting—while dangling your champagne bottle in the water to cool. The bridge is famous for the May Day celebrations after an evening of May Balls; at dawn, undergraduates

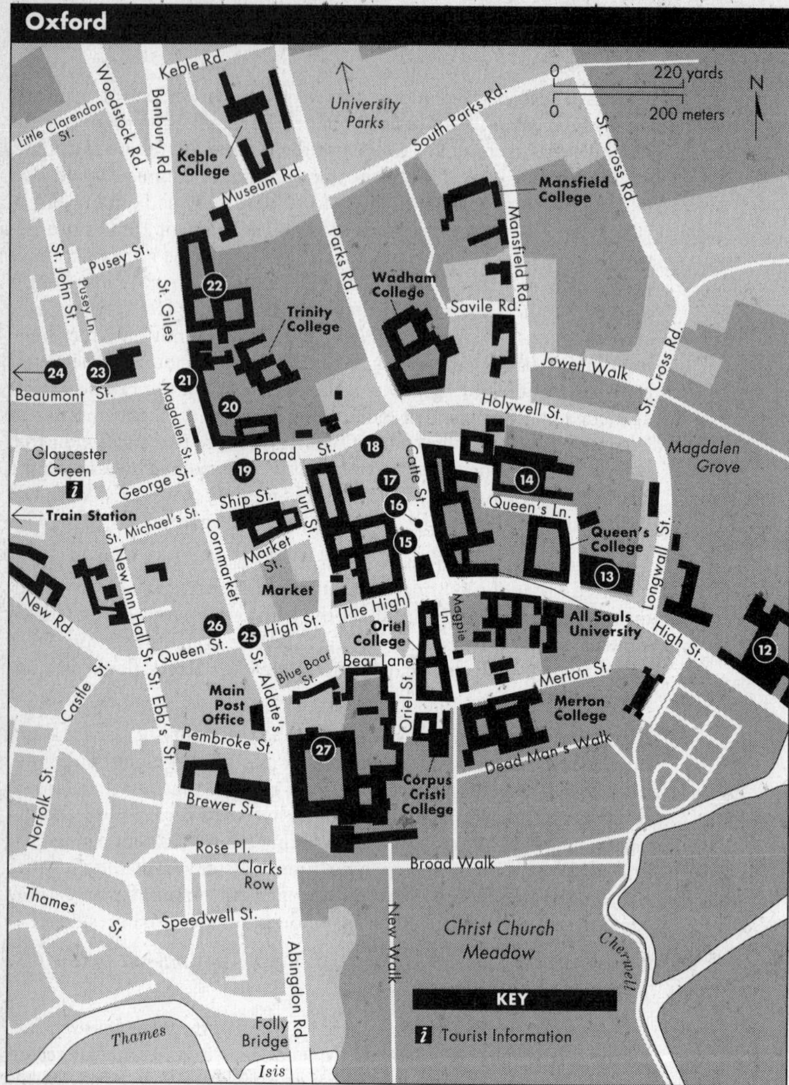

Ashmolean, **23**
Balliol College, **20**
Bodleian Library, **17**
Carfax, **25**
Christ Church College, **27**
Magdalen College, **12**
Martyrs' Memorial, **21**
New College, **14**
Oxford Story Exhibition, **19**
Radcliffe Camera, **16**
St. Edmund Hall, **13**
St. John's College, **22**
St. Martin's Church, **26**
Sheldonian Theatre, **18**
University Church, **15**
Worcester College, **24**

gather in punts under the bridge to hear choristers singing the May Day anthem from the Carfax Tower. ⊠ *High St.*

13 **St. Edmund Hall** is one of the smallest and oldest colleges (founded circa 1220). Its tiny quadrangle, entered through a narrow archway off Queen's Lane, has an ancient well in the center. On up Queen's Lane
14 you come to **New College** (founded in 1379), with its extensive gardens overlooking part of the medieval city wall. This was the home of the celebrated Dr. Spooner, father of "spoonerisms"—sentences where transposed opening sounds of words create comic new meanings, as in his reputed comment to a wayward student, "You have hissed your mystery lectures and tasted a whole worm." ⊠ *High St.*

15 Halfway up High Street, the 14th-century tower of the **University Church** (St. Mary the Virgin) provides a splendid panoramic view of the city's famous skyline—the pinnacles, towers, domes, and spires spanning every architectural style since the 11th century. The interior is crowded with 700 years' worth of funeral monuments, including one belonging to Amy Robsart, the wife of Dudley, Elizabeth I's favorite. ⊠ *High St.,* ☎ *01865/243806.* 🎟 *Tower £1.40.* 🕒 *Tower daily 9–7 (until 4:30 in winter).*

16 One of the largest domes in Britain, that of the **Radcliffe Camera,** rises in the middle of a large open space behind the church of St. Mary the
17 Virgin. This building contains part of the **Bodleian Library's** collection, which was begun in 1602 and has grown to more than 2 million volumes. Part of the library can be visited on a tour: weekdays at 10:30, 11:30, 2, and 3; Sat. at 10:30 and 11:30; Nov.–mid-Mar. not weekday mornings; tickets £3; closed for degree ceremonies; children under 14 not admitted—for more information call 01865/277165. Otherwise, the general public can visit only the former Divinity School, a superbly vaulted room with constantly changing exhibitions of manuscripts and rare books.

18 The university's ornate **Sheldonian Theatre** is where the impressive graduation ceremonies are held, conducted entirely in Latin. Built in 1663, it was the first building designed by Sir Christopher Wren. Semicircular like a Roman theater, it has pillars, balconies, and an elaborately painted ceiling. Outside, beige stone pillars are topped by the massive stone heads of 18 Roman emperors, sculpted in the 1970s to replace the originals that had been rendered faceless by air pollution. ⊠ *Broad St.,* ☎ *01865/277299.* 🎟 *£1.* 🕒 *Mon.–Sat. 10–12:30 and 2–4:30; mid-Nov.–Feb., closes 3:30; closed for 10 days at Christmas and Easter.*

Broad Street, known to undergraduates as "the Broad," is a wide, straight thoroughfare lined with colleges and bow-fronted, half-timber shops. Among them is **Blackwell's,** a family-run bookstore offering one of the largest selections of books in the world. It has been in business since 1879.

19 Stop in at the **Oxford Story Exhibition,** in a converted warehouse. The imaginative presentation makes 800 years of Oxford life come alive with models, sounds, and smells. Visitors ride through the exhibition in small cars shaped like medieval students' desks. ⊠ *6 Broad St.,* ☎ *01865/790055.* 🎟 *£4.50.* 🕒 *Daily 10–4:30, with seasonal variations.*

Broad Street leads westward to **St. Giles,** reputed to be the widest street in Europe. At the corner of St. Giles and the Broad is prestigious
20 **Balliol College** (1263), open daily 2–4, admission £1. The wooden doors between Balliol's inner and outer quadrangles still bear scorch marks from 1555 and 1556, during the reign of Mary I ("Bloody Mary"), when Bishops Latimer and Ridley and Archbishop Cranmer were

burned on huge pyres in Broad Street for their Protestant beliefs. A small
cross on the roadway marks the actual spot. The three men are also
21 commemorated by the tall **Martyrs' Memorial** in St. Giles. For a quiet
22 pause, step inside **St. John's College** (1555), whose huge gardens are
among the city's loveliest. ⊠ *St. Giles.* ⏲ *1–5 or dusk in winter.*

NEED A BREAK? Stop in for lunch at the **Eagle and Child** pub (⊠ St. Giles), with its narrow interior leading to a conservatory and small terrace. This was the meeting place of J. R. R. Tolkien and his friends, the "Inklings." It gets crowded on weekends.

23 The **Ashmolean,** Britain's oldest public museum, stands on the corner of St. Giles and Beaumont streets. Among its priceless collections (all university owned) are many Egyptian, Greek, and Roman artifacts uncovered during archaeological expeditions conducted by the university. Michelangelo drawings, antique silver, and a wealth of important paintings are also on display. ⊠ *Beaumont St.,* ☎ *01865/278000.* 🎟 *Free.* ⏲ *Tues.–Sat. 10–4, Sun. 2–4.*

24 The wide lawns, colorful cottage garden, and large lake of **Worcester College** (1714) lie at the bottom of Beaumont Street. It was built on the site of a former college, founded in 1283. ⊠ *Worcester St.*

A side trip into the southern part of town should begin in **Cornmar-**
25 **ket,** Oxford's main shopping street. As you pass through **Carfax,**
26 where four roads meet, you will see the tower of **St. Martin's Church,**
where Shakespeare once stood as godfather for William Davenant, who
27 himself became a playwright. **Christ Church College** (1546), referred to
by its members as "The House," is the site of Oxford's largest quadrangle, "Tom Quad," named after the huge bell (6¼ tons) that hangs in the gate tower. The vaulted, 800-year-old chapel in one corner has been Oxford's cathedral since the time of Henry VIII. The college's medieval dining hall contains portraits of many famous alumni, including John Wesley, William Penn, and 14 of Britain's prime ministers. Lewis Carroll was a teacher of mathematics here for many years; a shop opposite the meadows in St. Aldate's was the inspiration for the shop in *Through the Looking Glass.* ⊠ *St. Aldate's,* 🎟 *£3.* ⏲ *Mon.–Sat. 9:30–4:30, Sun. 2–4:30.*

Christ Church's **Canterbury Quadrangle** offers a fine picture gallery exhibiting works by Leonardo, Michelangelo, Rubens, Dürer, and other old masters. ⊠ *Deanery Gardens,* ☎ *01865/276172.* 🎟 *£1.* ⏲ *Mon.–Sat. 10:30–1 and 2–4:30, Sun. 2–4:30 (later in summer).*

NEED A BREAK? Close to the river just outside town, the thatched **Perch** (⊠ Binsey, ☎ 01865/240386) attracts connoisseurs at lunchtime who come to enjoy its wide lawn, unusual sandwiches, and cooing doves. It makes a pleasant place to arrive on foot from Walton Street. The creeper-covered **Trout** (⊠ Godstow, ☎ 01865/54485) is an excellent Thameside pub on the northern edge of Oxford. Come in the evening for a meal or a drink and to watch its peacocks strutting back and forth beside the weir.

Punting on the river Cherwell, a favorite pastime at Oxford, will appeal to most children.

Dining and Lodging

£££ ✕ **Restaurant Elizabeth.** These small, elegant dining rooms in a 16th-century bishop's palace have wonderful views overlooking Christ Church College. Salmon rolls, roast lamb, duck à l'orange, and crème brûlée are among the Spanish chef's specialties. ⊠ *84 St. Aldate's,* ☎ *01865/242230. AE, DC, MC, V. Closed Mon.*

££ ★ ✕ **Gee's.** This brasserie in a conservatory, formerly a florist's shop, is just north of the town center. The menu features French and English dishes, including venison and prawns, and the place is popular with both town and gown. ✉ *61 Banbury Rd.,* ☎ *01865/53540. AE, MC, V.*

£–££ ✕ **Cherwell Boathouse.** About a mile north of town, this is an ideal spot for a meal in a riverside setting. The menus change weekly, but may include mussels in white wine and cream; loin of lamb with red wine, lime, and garlic; or hare with a vinegar and pepper sauce. It's a very friendly spot so be prepared to linger. There is a good set menu available. ✉ *Bardwell Rd. (off Banbury Rd.),* ☎ *01865/52746. AE, DC, MC, V. No lunch Mon. and Tues., no dinner Sun.*

£ ✕ **Browns.** So popular is this restaurant with both undergraduates and local people that you may have to wait for a table. The wide choice of informal dishes includes steak-mushroom-and-Guinness pie and hot chicken salad. Potted palms and mirrors give the otherwise plain rooms a cheery atmosphere. ✉ *5–11 Woodstock Rd.,* ☎ *01865/511995. Reservations not accepted. MC, V.*

££££ ★ **Old Parsonage.** This is a discovery. It's rare to find an attractive country-house hotel, with stone gables and mullioned windows, in the middle of a city. The Old Parsonage was established in 1660, but completely restored and refurbished in 1991. Open fires, fascinating pictures, comfortable rooms, and immaculate service make this a hotel to remember—and return to. The Parsonage Bar serves excellent simple food. ✉ *1 Banbury Rd., OX2 6NN,* ☎ *01865/310210,* FAX *01865/311262. 30 rooms with bath. Restaurant. AE, DC, MC, V.*

££££ **The Randolph.** Oxford's only large, central hotel is very much part of the local landscape. Built in neo-Gothic style, it is just across from the Ashmolean, and is a regular place for undergraduates to be entertained for tea or drinks in the Fellows Bar by their visiting families. One of its four-poster suites overlooks the Martyr's Memorial, and there is a spaciously handsome restaurant, Spires. Scenes from PBS's Inspector Morse *Mystery* series and the film *Shadowlands* were shot here. ✉ *Beaumont St., OX1 2LN,* ☎ *01865/247481,* FAX *01865/791678. 109 rooms with bath. Restaurant, bar, parking. AE, DC, MC, V.*

£ **Cotswold House.** This small, modern guest house, about 2 miles north, on the Banbury Road (A4260), is pleasantly furnished with modern pieces. The bedrooms are comfortable and of a good size, all with TV and fridges. The owners are ever ready to help with sightseeing problems. ✉ *363 Banbury Rd., OX2 7PL,* ☎ FAX *01865/310558. 7 rooms with shower. No credit cards.*

The Arts

FESTIVALS AND MUSIC

Music at Oxford is a highly acclaimed series of weekend classical concerts performed from mid-September to June in such illustrious surroundings as Christ Church Cathedral and Sir Christopher Wren's Sheldonian Theatre. The music is performed by musicians and orchestras from all over the world, as well as from both Oxford and Cambridge. Information and tickets are available from the Oxford Playhouse (✉ Beaumont St., ☎ 01865/798600). **Oxford Coffee Concerts** is a program of chamber concerts performed on Sunday at the Holywell Music Room, Holywell Street, Oxford. String quartets, piano trios, and soloists present a variety of Baroque and classical pieces in this venerable old hall, dating from 1748. Tickets are very reasonably priced, available from Blackwell's Music Shop, Holywell Street (☎ 01865/261384). **Music & Fireworks** combines classical concerts, opera, and jazz with fireworks displays in a series of weekend events throughout July, staged in such venues as Blenheim Palace, Mentmore Towers

(Bedfordshire), and Oxford colleges. Ticket prices range from £18 to £25 (☎ 01865/864466).

THEATERS

The Apollo (✉ George St., ☎ 01865/244544) is Oxford's main theater. It stages a varied program of plays, opera, ballet, pantomime, and concerts, and is the recognized second home of the Welsh National Opera and the Glyndebourne Touring Opera. **The Oxford Playhouse** (✉ Beaumont St., ☎ 01865/798600) is an altogether more serious theater, presenting classical and modern drama productions appropriate for a university city. During university terms, many undergraduate productions are held in the colleges or local halls. In the summer, there are usually some outdoor performances in ancient quadrangles or college gardens. Look for announcement posters.

Shopping

Oxford now has several malls within easy walking distance of Carfax. Cornmarket and Queen streets are lined with small shops, while the Clarendon and Westgate centers, which lead off them, have branches of several nationally known stores. **Shepherd & Woodward** (✉ 109 High St., ☎ 01865/249491) is a traditional tailor and specialist in Scottish woolens and tweeds. The **Oxford Gallery** (✉ 23 High St., ☎ 01865/242731) carries prints in limited editions, as well as a wide stock of crafts. Specialty stores are gathered around Golden Cross, a cobbled courtyard with pretty window boxes, between Cornmarket and the excellent covered food market. The **Oxford Collection** (✉ Golden Cross, ☎ 01865/247414) sells stylish glassware and table mats. The **Tea House** (✉ Golden Cross, ☎ 01865/728838) specializes in teapots and tea. **Blackwell's** (✉ Broad St., ☎ 01865/792792) is one of the world's great bookstores.

Outdoor Activities and Sports

BICYCLING

Bikes can be rented in Oxford at **Denton's** (✉ 294 Banbury Rd., ☎ 01865/53859) and **Pennyfarthing** (✉ 5 George St., ☎ 01865/249368).

GOLF

Southfield (✉ Hill Top Rd., ☎ 01865/244258) is a parkland 18-hole course close to Oxford, where visiting players are welcome on weekdays (call first). Rented equipment is available.

SPECTATOR SPORTS

Oxford's Eights Week is held at the end of May. From mid-afternoon to early evening, Wednesday to Saturday, men and women from the university's colleges compete to be "Head of the River." Because the river is too narrow and twisting for eights to race side-by-side, they set off, 13 at a time, one behind another. Each boat tries to catch and bump the one in front. Spectators can watch all the way.

Oxford University Cricket Club competes against leading county teams and also has a game each summer against the major foreign team visiting Britain. The massive trees surrounding the club's grounds in the University Parks make it one of the loveliest in England.

Numbers in the margin correspond to points of interest on the Thames Valley map.

Woodstock

28 *8 mi north of Oxford on A44.*

Woodstock is the perfect little English town, its trim streets lined with handsome 17th- and 18th-century houses. Moreover, it stands almost on the grounds of England's grandest and most imposing country ★ house, **Blenheim Palace,** ancestral home of the dukes of Marlborough and the birthplace of Winston Churchill. During the summer you can catch an open-top bus from the Oxford train station, although it hardly needs saying that this is not the best season to visit, for Woodstock's ancient streets are clogged with tour buses and the lofty halls of Blenheim ring to the sounds of voices from all parts of the world.

The first thing to be said about Blenheim Palace is that it isn't actually a palace at all, at least not in the sense that royalty live in it. But so far as splendor, scale, and opulence are concerned, the building and surrounding parkland—all 2,700 acres of it—are the equal of just about any real palace anywhere in the world, Versailles (perhaps) excepted. Built by Sir John Vanbrugh in the early 1700s, Blenheim was given by Queen Anne and the nation to General John Churchill, first duke of Marlborough. The exterior is mind-boggling, comprised of gigantic columns, enormous pediments, upturned obelisks, all designed in the most spectacular English Baroque manner. Inside, the house is imposing and lavish—more a monument than a real abode. Huge family portraits—including incomparable sittings of the 4th and 9th dukes and their families painted by Sir Joshua Reynolds and John Singer Sargent—look down at sumptuous furniture and immense pieces of silver. For some, the most memorable room is the small, low-ceiling chamber where Winston Churchill (his father was the younger brother of the then-duke), was born in 1874.

Sir Winston once wrote that the unique beauty of Blenheim lay in its perfect adaptation of an English parkland to an Italian palace. Indeed, the grounds, the work of Capability Brown, 18th-century England's foremost landscape gardener, are arguably the best example of the "cunningly natural" park in the country. Brown declared that his object at Blenheim was to "make the Thames look like a small stream compared with the winding Danube." At points, he almost succeeds—the scale of these grounds must be seen to be believed. Tucked away here is the little summerhouse where Winston Churchill proposed to his future wife, Clementine. A short detour away to the neighboring hamlet of Bladon (☞ *below*) will lead you to the grave site of the great man. ✉ *Woodstock,* ☎ *01993/811091.* 🎫 *Palace £7.30; park free.* ⏲ *Palace mid-Mar.–Oct., daily 10:30–4:45; park daily 9–4:45; full schedule of special events, fairs, and concerts throughout yr. Palace has restaurant and cafeteria.*

Dining and Lodging

££££ ★ ✕🏨 **The Feathers.** The hotel here is small but very comfortable and expertly staffed. It's a 17th-century building that has been thoughtfully restored. In the restaurant's luxurious, wood-paneled rooms, you can choose from the à la carte or a two- or three-course set-price menu. Among the specialties are tartare of tuna with vinaigrette, marinated scallops with shallot and chili dressing, roasted breast and confit leg of Norfolk duckling, and a selection of rich desserts. ✉ *Market St., OX20 1SX,* ☎ *01993/812291,* FAX *01993/813158. 15 rooms with bath. Restaurant. AE, DC, MC, V.*

£££ 🏨 **Weston Manor Hotel.** Nine miles east of Woodstock, this hotel is one for the history buffs. Once a monastery, it's set on 13 acres of grounds. The oak-paneled restaurant has a minstrels' gallery, and one of the bedrooms claims a ghost. ✉ *Weston-on-the-Green, OX6 8QL,* ☎ *01869/350621,* FAX *01869/350901. 36 rooms with bath. Pool, croquet, squash, fishing. AE, DC, MC, V.*

Bladon

29 *2 mi south of Woodstock on A4095; 6 mi north of Oxford.*

A small, tree-lined churchyard holds the burial-place of Sir Winston Churchill, his grave all the more impressive for its total simplicity.

Great Milton

7 mi east of Oxford.

With attractive thatched cottages built of local stone and a single street about a mile long with wide grass verges, this is another stop on the literary pilgrim's route, for the poet John Milton, author of *Paradise Lost* (1667), was married in the church here. The church also has an unusual collection of old musical instruments.

Dining and Lodging

££££ ★ ✕ **Le Manoir aux Quat' Saisons.** Although this 15th- to 16th-century manor house is also a hotel—with sumptuously luxurious rooms—it has held its position as one of Britain's leading restaurants for years. The owner-chef, Raymond Blanc, exercises his award-winning French culinary skills in a captivating setting. Aux Quat' Saisons is both very popular and *very* expensive (well above our normal range), though the set menus (£29.50 at lunchtime, not Sun.) can make it almost reasonable. ✉ *Church Rd., OX44 7PD,* ☎ *01844/278881; from the U.S., 800/845–4274;* FAX *01844/278847. 19 rooms with bath. Restaurant (reservations essential, jacket and tie), heated pool, tennis. AE, DC, MC, V.*

Abingdon

30 *8 mi south of Oxford on A34.*

The origins of this market town can be traced to AD 675, when its **abbey** was founded. St. Ethelwold, the 10th-century abbot, diverted water from the Thames to create a millstream here. Today the Upper Reaches Hotel stands on the tiny island that Ethelwold's millstream formed. ✉ *Abbey Buildings, Thames St.,* ☎ *01235/553701.* *Small charge.* *May–Sept., daily 10–4.*

Lodging

£££ **Upper Reaches.** This Forte hotel has a spectacular setting overlooking the Thames. Surrounded by a millstream, it was once a grain mill and has been cleverly converted, complete with a river mooring handy for river travelers. ✉ *Thames St., OX14 3TA,* ☎ *01235/522311,* FAX *01235/555182. 25 rooms with bath, 6 in annex. Restaurant. AE, DC, MC, V.*

Dorchester-on-Thames

31 *9 mi south of Oxford, 7 mi southeast of Abingdon.*

An important center in Saxon times, when it was the seat of a bishopric, Dorchester deserves a visit chiefly for its ancient abbey. In addition to secluded cloisters and gardens, this one has a spacious church (1170), with traceried medieval windows. The east window was restored in 1966 by the American Friends of the Abbey in memory of Sir Winston Churchill. ☎ *01865/340056.* *Free.* *Easter–May, Sat. 10:30–12:30 and 2–6, Sun. 2–6; May–Sept., Tues.–Sat. 10:30–12:30 and 2–6, Sun. 2–6.*

Dorchester, founded by the Romans, is a charming village with timber houses, thatched cottages, and ancient inns. Crossing the Thames at Day's Lock and turning left at Little Wittenham takes you on a pleasant walk past the intriguing remains of the village's Iron Age settlements.

Lodging

££ **George Hotel.** Overlooking Dorchester Abbey, this 500-year-old hotel was built as a coaching inn—there's still an old coach parked outside—and it retains whitewashed walls, exposed beams, and log fires. Each room has an individual style and two have four-poster beds. ✉ *25 High St., OX10 7HH,* ☎ *01865/340404,* FAX *01865/341620. 17 rooms with bath. Restaurant. AE, DC, MC, V.*

Uffington and the Vale of the White Horse

32 *18 mi southwest of Oxford, 9 mi northeast of Swindon.*

Stretching up into the foothills of the Berkshire Downs between Swindon and Oxford is a wide, fertile plain known as the Vale of the White Horse. To reach it from Oxford, follow A420, then B4508 to the village of Uffington. Here, cut into the chalk hillside, is the huge figure of a white horse. Until recently, some historians believed that it may have been carved to commemorate King Alfred's victory over the Danes in 871, while others dated it back to the Iron Age, around 750 BC. New research suggests that it is at least 1,000 years older, created at the beginning of the second millennium BC. **Dragon Hill,** below, is equally mysterious. An unlikely legend suggests that St. George slew his dragon there. Uffington was the home of Tom Brown, fictional hero of the Victorian classic *Tom Brown's Schooldays.* The novel's author, Thomas Hughes, was born in Uffington in 1822.

Kelmscott Manor

33 *20 mi west of Oxford, 7 mi north of Uffington.*

Oxford has been a major focus for Britain's writers and artists for centuries, so the area's estates and country villages are alive with literary associations. Kelmscott Manor was the home of the Victorian artist, writer, and socialist William Morris (1834–96). It was at this handsome, 400-year-old gabled stone house that Morris and Dante Gabriel Rossetti established the revolutionary Arts and Crafts movement more than a century ago. Even the most perfunctory look at the surrounding countryside will reveal the principal sources of Morris's inspiration: Some of the clusters of the trees look as if they have stepped straight from one of his textile designs. The house is now owned by Oxford University and is a unique monument to the "Brotherhood." Morris died at Kelmscott and is buried in the local churchyard. ☎ *01367/252486.* 🎫 *£6.* ⏲ *Apr.–Sept., Wed. 11–1 and 2–5, 3rd Sat. of each month 2–6; Thurs. and Fri. prebooked guided tours.*

Stanton Harcourt Manor

34 *9 mi west of Oxford.*

Reached along through twisting lanes, Stanton Harcourt Manor lies nestled among streams, small lakes, and woods. It was here, in 1718, that Alexander Pope translated Homer's *Iliad.* But the manor—stuffed with silver, pictures, and antique furniture—is worth a visit apart from this association; it has 12 acres of gardens. ✉ *Stanton Harcourt,* ☎ *01865/881928.* 🎫 *House and garden £4; garden only £2.50.* ⏲ *Easter–Sept., certain Sun., Mon., and Thurs. 2–6; check locally.*

Dining

£ ★ ✕ **Bear and Ragged Staff.** Found in Cumnor, 3 miles east of Stanton Harcourt and 4½miles southwest of Oxford via A420, this excellent spot is a 17th-century inn—the name comes from the medieval insignia of the Warwick family—and has long been a popular haunt of Oxford town and gown. The food is traditional British, with such fare as roast duck and venison with a wine sauce. ✉ *28 Appleton Rd., Cumnor,* ☎ *01865/862329. AE, DC, MC, V.*

THAMES VALLEY A TO Z

Arriving and Departing

By Bus

City Link (☎ 0181/668–7261 or 01865/711312) runs a regular London–Oxford service (1 hr, 40 min), with departures every 15–30 minutes from London's Victoria Coach Station. **London Link** (☎ 01734/581358) has a regular London–Reading shuttle, and service from Heathrow and Gatwick airports to Oxford. The Reading-based **Bee Line** (☎ 01734/581358) serves the smaller towns of Berkshire.

By Car

The M4 and M40 radiate west from London, bringing Oxford (57 mi) and Reading (42 mi) within an hour's drive except in rush hour.

By Train

British Rail serves the region from London's Paddington Station (☎ 0171/262–6767) with fast trains to the main towns and a reliable commuter service. There's also hourly service to Oxford (travel time is one hour).

Getting Around

By Bus

The **Oxford Bus Company** (☎ 01865/711312) offers a one-day "Compass" ticket and a seven-day "Freedom" ticket, for unlimited bus travel within Oxford. The Oxford Bus Company and other local bus services such as **Thames Transit** (☎ 01865/727000) link the towns between Oxford and Henley.

By Car

Although the roads are good, this wealthy section of the commuter belt has surprisingly heavy traffic, even on the smaller roads. Parking in towns can be a problem, too, so allow plenty of time.

By Train

For local timetables, phone 01865/722333 (Oxford area), 01734/595911 (Reading area), or 01753/538621 (Windsor area).

Guided Tours

Orientation

Guide Friday (Windsor ☎ 01753/855755, Oxford ☎ 01865/790522) runs guided tours by open-top bus of Windsor (mid-Mar.–Nov., £6) and Oxford (£7).

Aficionados of the British television detective Inspector Morse can join one of the "Morse Tours of Oxford" arranged by **Spires and Shires** (✉ 40 Kendal Crescent, Oxford OX2 8NG, ☎ 01865/251785), visiting various Morse locations. Spires and Shires has a range of other tours round the city, all student-led, which give a real insight into university life, and it also has tours to the Cotswolds, Blenheim Palace, Bath, Stratford, and Stonehenge.

Themed walking tours, including "Oxford Detectives" and "Ghosts and Gargoyles," leave several times daily from outside **Oxford's tourist office** in Gloucester Green (£4). Call for details (☎ 01865/726871).

River Tours

The best way to see the Thames region is from the water; summertime trips range from 30 minutes to all day. **Hobbs and Sons** (☎ 01491/572035) covers the Henley Reach and also rents boats from Station Road, Henley-on-Thames. **Salter Brothers** (✉ Folly Bridge, Oxford, ☎ 01865/243421) runs daily steamer cruises, mid-May to mid-September from Windsor, Oxford, Abingdon, Henley, Marlow, and Reading. **Thames River Cruises** (☎ 01734/481088) conducts outings from Caversham Bridge, Reading, Easter–September. **French Brothers** (☎ 01753/851900) operates 35-minute and two-hour river trips from The Promenade, Windsor, and from Runnymede.

Contacts and Resources

Car-Rental Agencies

Oxford: Europcar Interrent, ✉ Hartford Motors, Seacourt Tower, Botley, ☎ 01865/246373; **Hertz,** ✉ City Motors Ltd., The Roundabout, Woodstock Rd., ☎ 01865/57291.

Windsor: Windsorian, ✉ A. A. Clark, 72–74 Arthur Rd., ☎ 01753/856419.

Hiking and Walking

The **Countryside Commission** (✉ John Dower House, Crescent Pl., Cheltenham, Gloucestershire GL50 3RA, ☎ 01242/521381) has been working for years on the Thames paths and offers publications about them. Write the Countryside Commission Postal Sales, ✉ Box 124, Walgrave, Northampton NN6 9TL, or call the number above. The **Rambler's Association** also publishes an excellent book on the subject, *The Thames Walk,* by David Sharp (£3.95 from the Rambler's Association, ✉ 1 Wandsworth Rd., London SW8 2XX, ☎ 0171/582–6878), a guide to the whole length of the river, from Greenwich to Gloucestershire, with detailed maps.

Travel Agencies

Thomas Cook, ✉ 5 Queen St., Oxford, ☎ 01865/240441. **Windsor Travel House,** ✉ 1 Bolton Rd., Windsor, ☎ 01753/857117.

Visitor Information

Henley: ✉ Town Hall, ☎ 01491/578034. **Marlow:** (summer only) ✉ c/o Court Garden Leisure Complex, Pound La., ☎ 01628/483597. **Oxford:** ✉ The Old School, Gloucester Green, ☎ 01865/726871. **Windsor:** ✉ 24 High St., ☎ 01753/852010. **Woodstock:** ✉ Hensington Rd., ☎ 01993/811038.

8 The Heart of England

Stratford-upon-Avon, the Cotswolds, the Forest of Dean, Bath, Bristol

Even if England's heartland wasn't home to Stratford-upon-Avon, it would still lure countless visitors every year. Heaping doses of history await: Warwick Castle, the Regency-era mansions of Cheltenham, the enchanting villages of the Cotswolds—the absolute quintessence of English rural life—and the Georgian elegance of 18th-century Bath. Birthplace of Shakespeare, Stratford remains at the top of the list. As you stroll down the country road to Anne Hathaway's cottage, you'll wonder if the Bard composed one of his immortal sonnets along this very way.

Updated by Robert Andrews

THE HEART OF ENGLAND is a name we have borrowed from the tourist powers-that-be—and by which is meant the heart of *tourist* England, so immensely popular are its attractions. Here it means the three counties of west-central England, Warwickshire (pronounced "Worrick"), Gloucestershire (pronounced "Gloster"), and Avon. Together they make up a sweep of land stretching from Shakespeare Country in the north down through Bath to the Bristol Channel in the south.

Stratford is the key town for the visitor. It is a small market town, like dozens of others across the land, but set apart from them by being the birthplace of Shakespeare. It is that rare thing, a living shrine—living because it contains, apart from the houses connected with Shakespeare, a theater that performs his works, and, for the most part, performs them to the highest international standard. The town can be vulgar—it is full to overflowing with souvenir shops—but it also has a lot of quiet charm. To wander along the riverbank from the theater to the parish church on a spring day can be a gently fulfilling experience. Only a few miles away, Warwick, with its magnificent castle and picturesque houses, provides yet another "Heart of England" thrill.

Near the spires and shires of Shakespeare Country, however, is another region that conjures up "olde Englande" at its most blissfully rural: the Cotswolds. If you've come in search of picture-postcard English countryside, with soft rolling hills and mellow stone-built villages, this is your destination. It can hardly claim to be undiscovered, but its timeless appeal has a way of surviving the tour groups and other visitors who descend on its rural tranquillity. One has to go to this region to taste fully the old glory of the English village with its thatched roofs, low-ceiling rooms, and gardens meticulously built on a gentle slope. Its Old World atmosphere is as thick there as honey, and as pleasant and sweet.

To the south of this region is the city of Bath—like Stratford, one of the tourist meccas of Britain. Although it was originally founded by the Romans when they discovered here the only true hot springs in England, the town's popularity during the 17th and 18th centuries ensured its immortality. Bath's fashionable period luckily coincided with one of Britain's most elegant architectural eras, producing quite a remarkable urban phenomenon—money available to create virtually a whole town of stylish buildings. Today's city fathers have been wise enough to make sure that Bath is kept spruce and welcoming; its present prosperity keeps the streets overflowing with flowers in the summer and is channeled into cleaning and painting the city center, making it a joy to explore. Gainsborough, Lord Nelson, and Queen Victoria traveled here to sip the waters, which Dickens described as tasting like "warm flat irons," but most travelers today opt for tea and clotted-cream-and-strawberries in one of the town's elegant eateries.

Pleasures and Pastimes

Dining

Even in the old days when critics would joke about British *cuisine* ("if you can call it that"), few people carped about the abundance of fresh regional produce available to restaurants. Not even the worst English cook was able, so they said, to spoil a dish cooked with some of the best raw material in the world. Here, in the heart of England, chefs have never had a problem with a supply of excellent produce—salmon from the rivers Severn and Wye, local lamb, and venison from the Forest of Dean, and pheasant, partridge, quail, and grouse in season. Now more than ever, this region is dotted with good restaurants, thanks to a steady flow of fine chefs seeking to cater to the waves of tourists.

CATEGORY	COST*
££££	over £50
£££	£30–£50
££	£20–£30
£	under £20

**per person, including first course, main course, dessert, and VAT; excluding drinks*

Lodging

As one of the most popular, and wealthiest, areas of Britain, this one sports plenty of excellent hotels—ranging from bed-and-breakfasts in village homes and farmhouses to ultimate luxury in country-house hotels. But, because it *is* so popular, you really must be sure to book ahead whenever possible. You should also brace yourself for some very fancy prices. Most hotels offer two- and three-day packages.

CATEGORY	COST*
££££	over £150
£££	£80–£150
££	£60–£80
£	under £60

**All prices are for two people sharing a double room, including service, breakfast, and VAT.*

Shopping

Once the happiest of all hunting-grounds for antiques lovers, the Cotswolds now offer few of those "anything in this tray for £5" dealers. Marketing antiques has reached the level of a major industry there, to accommodate the droves of visitors. But go ahead—splurge on an 18th-century silver saltspoon! For more general and affordable markets, head for **Moreton-in-Marsh** on Tuesday and **Chipping Norton** on Wednesday. Ask about others.

Walking

This part of England offers glorious, gentle countryside, with many short walks in the areas around the historic towns of the region. The local Tourist Information Centers often have route maps for themed walks available. If you want to branch out on your own and not get lost, one way is to track the rivers on which most of these towns are built. They usually have towpaths running alongside them that are easy to follow and scenically very attractive. The only thing is that they wind a lot, and you may find yourself walking for much longer than you had intended! The **Forest of Dean** is quite special for walking. It is densely wooded, with interesting villages and monastic ruins to view. Many of its public footpaths are way-marked, as are most of the Forestry Commission trails. You'll find easy walks out of Newland, around New Fancy (great view) and Mallards Pike Lake, and a slightly longer one (three hours), which takes in Wench Ford, Danby Lodge, and Blackpool Bridge. There are picnic grounds, good car parking, and hidden old pubs where you can wet your thirst.

Exploring the Heartland of England

The four tours in this chapter have been organized around the region's major points of interest for visitors: Stratford-upon-Avon, the Cotswold Hills, the Gloucester/Cheltenham axis, and the elegant city of Bath and its environs.

Stratford is well suited as an exploring base for a limited area containing tiny villages, several with legends connected with Shakespeare (dubious for the most part), some beautiful architecture dating from his time, and one magnificent castle, Warwick. The Cotswold Hills cover some of southern England's most beautiful terrain, with which the characteristic stone cottages sprinkled generously throughout the area form a perfect harmony. Some villages have become overrun by coach parties and twee antiques shops, but at least they have for the most part retained their historical appearance and can be fun. To the west of the Cotswolds lie Gloucester and Cheltenham, almost twin towns, and beyond them, between the Severn River and the border of Wales, the mysterious Forest of Dean. The road from Gloucester to Bath takes you by the evocative castle at Berkeley. Bath, which can also be easily visited on a day out from London, makes an elegant center from which to travel westward to Bristol, the Severn Estuary, and prehistoric sites, this time in the Chew Valley.

Great Itineraries

Stratford-upon-Avon will be the lead destination for most travelers—as a small city, it's ideal for either day visits or as a convenient base from which to explore Shakespeare Country and the nearby Cotswolds. Once outside Stratford, you'll discover that the Heart of England should be relished on a slow schedule, to allow you leisure to absorb the rustic attractions without hurry. Note that the Cotswolds area covers a large amount of ground, for which your own transport is essential, though both here and in the Forest of Dean you should be prepared to abandon your vehicle in order to enjoy the countryside at walking pace. In the towns that fringe this area however—Gloucester, Cheltenham, Bristol, and Bath—a car is a positive encumbrance. Park it up or leave it at your hotel, and forego the stress-factor involved in finding parking-slots and negotiating one-way systems.

Ten days would just about do justice to the different areas contained in this chapter, though with careful planning you could see plenty in less time. With just three days or less, confine your roamings to one or two centers, and ignore the rest.

Numbers in the text correspond to numbers in the margin and on the maps.

IF YOU HAVE 3 DAYS

Stratford-upon-Avon ① deserves at least a full day and drama-packed night—that is, if you wish to catch a performance of the Bard's works at the Royal Shakespeare Theatre on the banks of the Avon. Among the attractions, pride of place goes to the five properties administered by the Shakespeare Birthplace Trust: Three are in town—**Shakespeare's Henley Street birthplace** ②, the **New Place/Nash's House** property ④, and **Hall's Croft** ⑥—while the others, **Anne Hathaway's Cottage** ⑫ and **Mary Arden's House** ⑬, are 1 and 3 miles respectively out of town. Depending on exactly how tight your schedule is, opt for taking one of the popular open-top double-decker bus tours, which allow you to get on and off at the Shakespeare properties. If you want to spend two days in Stratford and wish to enjoy these attractions (and many other sights) more leisurely, follow the self-guiding Town Heritage Trail or the black and gold signposts that direct you to the historic landmarks. After your Stratford sojourn, some sedation therapy may be in order, so spend the next day driving through the Cotswold Hills, taking a peek at **Stow-on-the-Wold** ㉑ and **Bourton-on-the-Water** ⑳, but not forgetting smaller places such as **Upper** and **Lower Slaughter** and **Moreton-in-Marsh** ㉒. Spend your second night in one of these towns or that Cotswold showpiece, **Chipping**

Campden ㉓, then head west toward **Cheltenham** ㉜, whose Regency architecture and fashionable shops will occupy a pleasant afternoon's amble. The town offers a good choice of accommodations and places to eat (and could justify an overnight stop). If you don't have a car at your disposal, pass up the Cotswolds and Cheltenham and head directly to **Bath** ㊶ (south from Stratford, down the M5, then east on the M4). This is one of the country's most popular tourist destinations, and deservedly so, for it contains a handful of must-see museums and a generous helping of panoramic crescents backed by some of the most harmonious Georgian architecture you'll ever see. Choose to spend your last night here, and sup at one of the town's amiable restaurants.

IF YOU HAVE 5 DAYS

You will be most tempted to spend any extra time you can spare in the Heart of England cruising the Cotswolds. However, even confining your stay there to a couple of days will allow you to spend—in addition to the day in **Stratford-upon-Avon** ① exploring the attractions listed above—another day touring Shakespeare Country, including the lovely manse of **Baddesley Clinton** ⑯, **Warwick Castle** ⑱—the crowning glory of England's medieval castles—and **Charlecote Park** ⑲, the magnificent manor house where legend has it that Shakespeare was once caught poaching deer. After these august abodes, some charming Cotswold cottages will be just the ticket, so after your two-night stay in Stratford, head for **Broadway** ㉕, mecca for antique-hunters, and the less visited but no less charming village of **Chipping Campden** ㉓. The fascinating stately house pile that is **Snowshill Manor** ㉖ awaits, while horticultural enthusiasts will love the famous **Hidcote Manor Garden** ㉔, in the north of this area. For your fourth day, check out **Cheltenham** ㉜, which, though it is better-known for its gentrified Regency architecture, touts itself as the gateway to the Cotswolds, or head instead to that treasure chest of Georgian elegance, **Bath** ㊶.

IF YOU HAVE 7 DAYS

After two days spent touring **Stratford-upon-Avon** ① and the surrounding attractions of Shakespeare Country, as outlined above, spend two days unearthing those lesser-known corners of the Cotswolds, for example the majestic grounds of **Sudeley Castle** ㉗ and the Roman villa at **Chedworth** ㉘, in addition to its more famous towns, mentioned in the itineraries above. From your ovenight base at **Chipping Campden** ㉓, proceed to two more irresistible Cotswold villages, **Northleach** ㉙ and **Bibury** ㉚, then drive south to **Dyrham Park** ㊵ and overnight in Georgian **Bath** ㊶. The latter has a wealth of accommodations and deserves a full day of sightseeing. The next day opt to head east to **Castle Combe** ㊿, "the prettiest village in England," or go west to take in either **Bristol** ㊾ and the **S.S. *Great Britain*** or continue directly up on the M4 and M5 motorways, making stops at the stern **Berkeley Castle** ㊴ and the bird sanctuary at **Slimbridge** ㊳. From here, it's a short hop to **Gloucester** ㉝, whose restored docks hold the National Waterways Museum, an interactive permanent exhibition that is absorbing for all ages. Spend a night in Gloucester, then cross the Severn and head southwest toward the **Forest of Dean** area, to which you should devote your last day. The **Dean Heritage Centre** ㉞ at Soudley makes a good introduction to this ancient woodland, but you will need to put on your walking shoes to get the best of the panoramic country on offer here. If you have children along, the underground caves at **Clearwell** ㊲ can be special fun. From here, either proceed into Wales, or trace the borderlands north, or head back to Gloucester and its near neighbor Cheltenham, a useful re-entry point for the Cotswolds.

When to Tour the Heart of England

This chapter contains some of the most popular tourist destinations in the country, and you would do well to avoid weekends in the busier areas of the Cotswold Hills. During the week, you will hardly see a soul. Bath, too, is one of the key spots on any tourist itinerary, and you will find it particularly congested in summer, when students flock to the language schools here. On the other hand, the cities of Bristol, Gloucester, and Cheltenham are workaday places that can effortlessly absorb the visiting coach tours and can be seen comfortably at any time. Note that the private properties of Hidcote Manor, Snowshill Manor, and Sudeley Castle close during the winter months. Hidcote Manor Garden is at its best in the spring and fall.

STRATFORD-UPON-AVON AND SHAKESPEARE COUNTRY

Numbers in the margin correspond to points of interest on the Stratford-upon-Avon and Shakespeare Country map and on the Stratford-upon-Avon map.

"Famous people do seem to have made a habit of being born in pretty places—Mozart in Salzburg, Wordsworth in the Lake District, Hardy in Dorset, the Brontës in Yorkshire," begins the text to Susan Hill's 1987 book, *Shakespeare Country*—one of the most perceptive travel books ever written. "It all helps to establish them as focuses for visitors, but those visitors would still come, simply to enjoy the charms of the locality. And Stratford's charms are very evident." Under the swarming bus loads of visitors from every part of the globe, Stratford, in fact, has, hung on to its original character as a charming English market town on the banks of the slow-flowing river Avon.

Still, it is Shakespeare who counts. You can see his birthplace on Henley Street; his burial place (and baptismal record) in Holy Trinity Church; Anne Hathaway's cottage (she was his wife); his mother's home at Wilmcote; New Place, where Shakespeare died, and the neighboring Nash's House, home of Shakespeare's granddaughter; and Hall's Croft, home of the Stratford physician who married the Bard's daughter. Whether or not their connections to Shakespeare are historically valid, these sites reveal Elizabethan England at its most lovely.

Then, of course, there is the theater, a sturdy brick-built structure opened in 1932 and home of the Royal Shakespeare Company. Like the true church, Britain's theater is founded on a rock: Shakespeare. There can hardly have been a day since the one on which the Bard breathed his last, when one of his plays, in some shape or form, was not being performed. They have survived being turned into musicals (from Purcell to Rock), they have made the reputations of generations of famous actors (and broken not a few), they have seen women playing Hamlet and men playing Rosalind. However his plays are twisted and reshaped by directors and actors, they always seem to reveal a new facet of some eternal truth about Man. Make the Royal Shakespeare Theatre the real reason for visiting Stratford: Productions here are unrivaled. Anyone who thinks that attending a Shakespeare play is something of a duty, an experience to be endured rather than enjoyed, will be delightfully proved wrong. Believers will need no persuading.

Basing yourself in Stratford itself, you will be best placed to take in evening theater performances and also take full advantage of those hours at the beginning and end of each day when the coach-parties are absent. Most

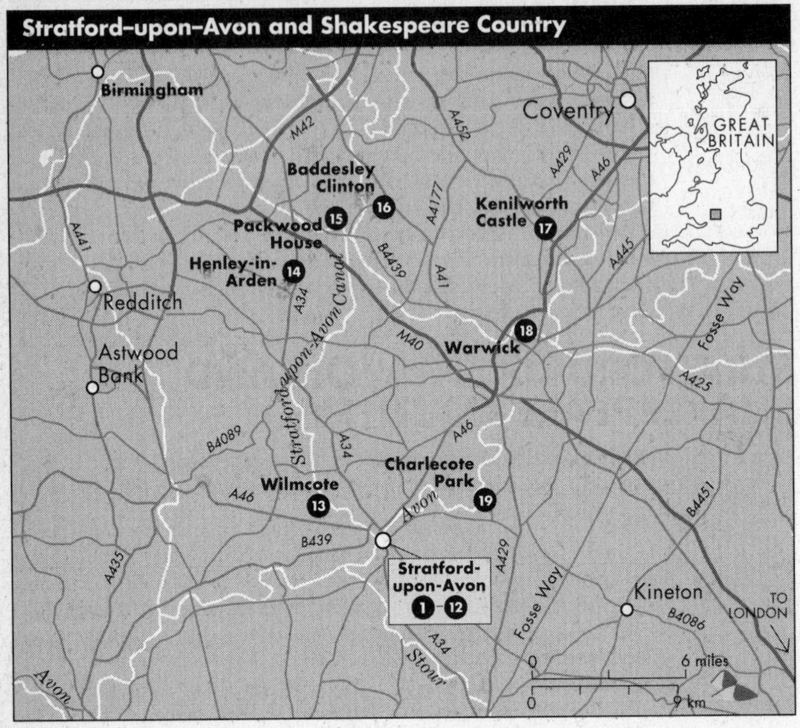

of the peripheral attractions can be seen by public transport, so this is one area of Britain where you definitely don't need a car.

Stratford-upon-Avon

❶ *37 mi southeast of Birmingham, 102 mi northwest of London.*

By Elizabethan times (16th century), Stratford-upon-Avon was a prosperous market town with thriving guilds and industries. Its characteristic half-timber houses from this era have been preserved over the centuries, and they are set off by the charm of later architecture, such as the elegant Georgian storefronts on Bridge Street, with their 18th-century porticoes and arched doorways. Yet Stratford is far from being a museum piece; it has adapted itself well to the rising tide of visitors. Though the town is full of souvenir shops—every back lane seems to have been converted into a shopping mall, with boutiques selling everything from sweaters to china models of Anne Hathaway's Cottage—Stratford isn't particularly strident in its search for the quick buck.

The main places of Shakespearean interest are run by the **Shakespeare Birthplace Trust.** They all have similar opening times, and you can buy a combination ticket to the five properties or pay separate entry fees if you want to visit only one or two. *Joint ticket £9. Mid-Mar.–mid-Oct., Mon.–Sat. 9:30–5:30, Sun. 10–5:30; mid-Oct.–mid-Mar., Mon.–Sat. 10–4, Sun. 10:30–4; last entry 30 min before closing; closed Dec. 24–26, open at 1:30 Jan. 1 and Good Fri.*

❷ All tours of the town should start at the **Shakespeare Centre** on Henley Street, home of the Shakespeare Birthplace Trust. This modern building was erected in 1964 as a 400th-anniversary tribute to the playwright; it contains a small BBC Television **Shakespeare Costume Exhibition.** Next door, and reached from the center, is **Shakespeare's Birthplace,**

Anne Hathaway's Cottage, **12**
Guildhall/ Grammar School, **5**
Hall's Croft, **6**
Harvard House, **3**
Holy Trinity Church, **7**
Nash's House and New Place, **4**
The Other Place, **8**
Royal Shakespeare Theatre, **9**
Shakespeare Centre and Birthplace, **2**
Swan Theatre, **10**
World of Shakespeare, **11**

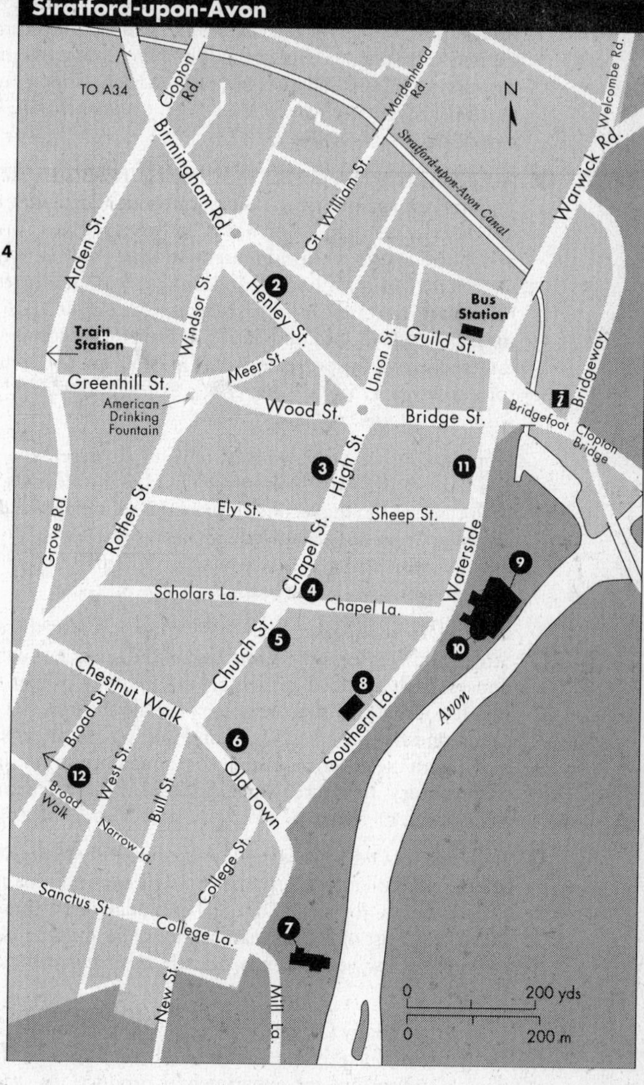

a half-timber house typical of its time, although much altered and restored since Shakespeare lived here. In bloom, its garden is a vision of enchantment, which helps disguise the fact that the structure is surrounding by bustling shops and motorways. Half the house has been furnished to reflect Elizabethan domestic life, the other half contains an exhibition illustrating Shakespeare's professional life and work. ✉ *Henley St.,* ☎ *01789/204016.* 🎫 *Shakespeare's Birthplace only £3.30; Town Heritage Trail ticket (includes 3 town properties) £6; Shakespeare Trust joint ticket,* ☞ above.

NEED A BREAK?

The Brasserie on Henley Street (✉ 59–60 Henley St.) serves meals and snacks throughout the day. Look for its jigsaw tree sculpture as you climb the stairs.

The town's **tourist office** is found if you go down Henley Street, then at the bottom Bridge Street toward the river, at Bridgefoot. From

3 Bridgefoot, return to High Street and make a left turn to find **Harvard House,** next to the Garrick Inn, a half-timber, 16th-century home of Catherine Rogers, mother of the John Harvard who founded Harvard University in 1636. There is little to see here, as the house is virtually unfurnished. ⊠ *High St.* ⏲ *May–Sept. Contact the Shakespeare Centre for hrs.*

4 Across the street from Harvard House is **Nash's House,** home of the Thomas Nash who married Shakespeare's granddaughter, Elizabeth Hall. The heavily restored house has been furnished in 17th-century style, and it also contains a local museum. In the gardens (where there's an intricately laid-out Elizabethan knot garden), are the foundations of **New Place,** the house in which Shakespeare died in 1616. Built in 1483 for a Lord Mayor of London, it was Stratford's grandest piece of real estate when Shakespeare bought it in 1597 for £60; but, sadly, it was torn down in 1759. ⊠ *Chapel St.,* ☎ *01789/292325.* 🎟 *£2; Shakespeare Trust joint ticket,* ☞ above.

Opposite the site of New Place, on Church Street, you'll find timber-
and-daub poorhouses built by the Guild of the Holy Cross in the early
5 15th century. On the second floor of the adjoining **Guildhall** is the picturesque **Grammar School,** which Shakespeare probably attended as a
boy and which is still used as a school. ☎ *01789/293351.* ⏲ *Easter
and summer school vacations, daily 10–6.*

On Old Town, a street reached by turning left at the end of Church
6 Street, you will see **Hall's Croft,** one of the finest surviving Tudor town
houses, with a walled garden behind that is a delight to visit. Tradition has it that this was the home of Shakespeare's elder daughter Susanna and her husband, Dr. John Hall, whose dispensary is on view
along with the other rooms, all containing heavy oak Jacobean (early
17th-century) furniture. ☎ *01789/292107.* 🎟 *£2; Shakespeare Trust
joint ticket,* ☞ above.

7 At the end of Old Town is the 13th-century **Holy Trinity Church,** in which are buried William Shakespeare; his wife, Anne; his daughter Susanna; his son-in-law John Hall; and his granddaughter's husband, Thomas Nash. The bust of Shakespeare is thought to be an authentic likeness, executed a few years after his death. ⊠ *Trinity St.* 🎟 *Small fee for chancel.*

From Holy Trinity Church, walk north along Southern Lane or through
8 the gardens along the river Avon, and you'll pass by **The Other Place,**
a new auditorium for experimental productions, and come to the
9 **Royal Shakespeare Theatre,** where the Royal Shakespeare Company
(RSC) stages plays from late March to late January (☞ The Arts,
10 *below*). At the rear is the **Swan Theatre,** created in the only part of the
Victorian theater to survive a fire in the 1930s. The theater follows the
lines of Shakespeare's original Globe and is one of the most exciting
acting spaces in Britain. Beside the Swan is an art gallery, where you
can see portraits and depictions of scenes from the plays, try on some
of the RSC's costumes, and book tours of the theater, preferably well
in advance. ⊠ *Southern La.,* ☎ *01789/296655, for tours 01789/412602.*
🎟 *Tours £4, exhibition £1.50.* ⏲ *Tours weekdays (except matinee days)
at 1:30 and 5:30; matinee days 5:30 and after show; 4 tours Sun. Exhibition Mon.–Sat. 9:15–8, Sun. noon–4:30.*

NEED A BREAK?

The **Black Swan** (⊠ Southern La.), locally called the Dirty Duck, has a little veranda overlooking the theaters and the river. It serves draft beer and bar meals.

Across the small park in front of the Royal Shakespeare Theatre is the
11 Heritage Theatre's **World of Shakespeare,** a glorified waxworks show, using recorded dialogue and dramatic lighting to re-create the "royal progress" of Queen Elizabeth I from London to Kenilworth, where she was lavishly entertained by her favorite, the earl of Leicester (pronounced "Lester"), in 1575. Some will consider it a mite pricey for just under half an hour's show. ✉ *13 Waterside,* ☎ *01789/269190.* 🎟 *£4.* ⏲ *Daily 9:30–5:30 (until 9:30 in summer); performances every ½ hr. Closed Dec. 25.*

★ 12 The most picturesque of the **Shakespeare Trust properties** is **Anne Hathaway's Cottage,** family home of the woman Shakespeare married in 1582, in what was evidently a shotgun wedding. The Hathaway "cottage," actually a beautiful and substantial farmhouse, with a thatch roof and large garden, is in the village of Shottery, now a western suburb of Stratford. Although there is regular bus service from Stratford, the best way to get there is to walk, especially in late spring when the hawthorns and apple trees are in blossom; you'll be taking the same route Shakespeare used when he went a-courting Mistress Hathaway. ☎ *01789/292100.* 🎟 *£2.40. Shakespeare Trust joint ticket,* ☞ above.

Dining and Lodging

£££ ★ ✕ **Box Tree Restaurant.** This attractive dining spot in the Royal Shakespeare Theatre overlooks the river Avon and has some of the best food in town. It's worth eating here, either before or after a play. Specialties include roast rack of lamb, and grilled fillet of Scottish beef. ✉ *Waterside,* ☎ *01789/293226. AE, MC, V. Closed when theater is closed.*

£ ✕ **River Terrace.** At this informal cafeteria in the theater, the meals and snacks are crowd-pleasers. They include lasagna, shepherd's pie, salads, sandwiches, and cakes, with wine and beer available. ✉ *Royal Shakespeare Theatre, Waterside,* ☎ *01789/293226. Reservations not accepted. No credit cards. Closed when theater is closed.*

£ ✕ **The Slug and Lettuce.** Don't let the name put you off—this pine-panel pub serves excellent meals. Long-standing favorites are chicken breast baked in avocado and garlic, and poached cushion of salmon. ✉ *38 Guild St.,* ☎ *01789/299700. MC, V.*

£ ✕ **Vintner Wine Bar.** Just up the hill from the theater, this bar/restaurant serves imaginative food from a menu that changes daily. If it's available, go for the chicken breast stuffed with Parma ham with apricot sauce (delicious). You order from the counter and the food is delivered to your table, so be sure to stake your table first, especially if you are dining before curtain time when the restaurant gets crowded with out-of-town visitors. ✉ *5 Sheep St.,* ☎ *01789/297259. AE, MC, V.*

££££ 🏨 **Alveston Manor.** Across the river from the Royal Shakespeare Theatre, this redbrick Elizabethan manor house has a modern extension. In the old manor house, rooms have individual, Old World style. Decor is modern in the extension, but all rooms have up-to-date bathrooms. ✉ *Clopton Bridge, CV37 7HP,* ☎ *01789/204581,* FAX *01789/414095. 106 rooms with bath. Restaurant. AE, DC, MC, V.*

£££–££££ 🏨 **Ettington Park Hotel.** This marvelously restored, huge Victorian house makes an ideal spot to stay if you want to see the plays at Stratford but don't want to cope with the crowds. It stands on its own grounds—which contain a ruined church—and looks across tranquil river meadows haunted by herons. Individually furnished bedrooms are complemented by elegant, harmonious decor. The restaurant has extremely good food, imaginatively cooked. The hotel is southeast from Stratford, 6 miles on A34. ✉ *Alderminster, CV37 8BS,* ☎ *01789/450123,* FAX *01789/450472. 48 rooms with bath. Restaurant,* *indoor heated pool, spa, sauna, tennis courts, health club, fishing. AE, DC, MC, V.*

££ **Charlecote Pheasant.** Farm buildings have been converted into a pleasant, country-house hotel across from Charlecote Park (follow B4086 northeast out of Stratford for about 5 miles). The fine, 17th-century redbrick has been matched in the new wing, and the bedrooms—some with four-poster beds—in both the old and the new buildings are prettily decorated and have ceiling beams. ✉ *CV35 9EW,* ☎ *01789/279954,* FAX *01789/470222. 67 rooms with bath. Restaurant, bar, pool, tennis court, Turkish baths, sauna, exercise room, billiards. AE, DC, MC, V.*

£££ **Shakespeare Hotel.** Minutes from the theater and right in the heart of Stratford, this half-timber Elizabethan town house is also close to most of the Shakespeare Trust properties. Inside, it has been comfortably modernized. ✉ *Chapel St., CV37 6ER,* ☎ *01789/294771,* FAX *01789/415111. 63 rooms with bath. Restaurant. AE, DC, MC, V.*

££ ★ **Caterham House.** Built in 1830, this comfortable old building is in the center of town, within an easy walk of the theater. You may spot an actor or two among the guests. Its bedrooms are individually decorated in early 19th-century style, featuring brass beds and antique furniture, and the public rooms, too, show a discriminating taste at work. ✉ *58 Rother St., CV37 6LT,* ☎ *01789/267309,* FAX *01789/414836. 10 rooms with bath or shower. Bar, parking. MC, V.*

£ **Penryn House.** The convenient location of this lodging—halfway between the city center and Anne Hathaway's Cottage, and within an easy walk of both—makes it a useful, if somewhat uninspiring, budget choice. Comfortably furnished rooms have TVs, hair dryers and tea/coffeemaking facilities. ✉ *126 Alcester Rd., CV37 9DP,* ☎ *01789/293718. 8 rooms, 6 with bath or shower. AE, DC, MC, V.*

The Arts

FESTIVALS

The **Stratford-upon-Avon Shakespeare Birthday Celebrations** take place on the weekend nearest to April 23, with colorful receptions, processions, a special performance of one of the plays, and other events. ✉ *Shakespeare Centre, Henley St., Stratford-upon-Avon CV37 6QW,* ☎ *01789/204016.*

THEATER

The **Royal Shakespeare Theatre** (✉ Stratford-upon-Avon CV37 6BB, ☎ 01789/295623) usually puts on five of Shakespeare's plays in a season lasting from March to January each year. In the **Swan Theatre** at the rear, plays by Shakespeare contemporaries such as Christopher Marlowe and Ben Jonson are staged. In **The Other Place**, some of the RSC's most advanced work is performed. Seats go fast, but "day of performance" and returned tickets are often available.

Shopping

Stratford-upon-Avon has a bustling shopping district, and there's an open market every Friday in the Market Square. **Waterstone** (✉ 18 High St., ☎ 01789/414418) is a prime bookstore. **Antique Arcade** (✉ 10–11 Sheep St., ☎ 01789/294659) has 14 dealers selling china, jewelry, and art deco. The **Antique Market** (✉ Ely St.) features 50 stalls of jewelry, silver, linens, porcelain, and memorabilia. **Robert Vaughan** (✉ 20 Chapel St., ☎ 01789/205312) is the best of Stratford's many secondhand bookshops. **Once a Tree** (✉ 8 Bard's Walk, ☎ 01789/297790) is thoroughly "green," selling items crafted from sustainable wood sources—animals, bowls, and dozens of imaginative articles. **B&W Thornton** (✉ 23 Henley St., ☎ 01789/269405), just above Shakespeare's birthplace, has an extensive range of exclusive Moorcroft ware.

Wilmcote

13 *3 mi northwest of Stratford, off A3400.*

The hamlet of Wilmcote holds the fifth Shakespeare Birthplace Trust Property, **Mary Arden's House,** a Tudor farmhouse, the family home of Shakespeare's mother. Combined with the adjoining glebe (church-owned farm) it forms the Shakespeare Countryside Museum, with crafts exhibits, falconry demonstrations, a café, and a garden of trees mentioned in the plays. Don't forget to note the magical 16th-century dovecote: Susan Hill describes it as one of those places where "the centuries seem to touch, with no time in between." You can get to Wilmcote on a regular bus from Stratford, organized by Guide Friday Tours. ☎ *01789/293455.* 🎫 *£3.30; Shakespeare Trust joint ticket,* ☞ above.

En Route From Wilmcote, continue north on A3400, passing under the Strat-
14 ford-upon-Avon Canal aqueduct and through **Henley-in-Arden,** whose wide main street is an architectural pageant, presenting attractive buildings of various periods. You are now in the area of what was once the Forest of Arden, where Shakespeare set one of his greatest comedies, *As You Like It.*

Packwood House

15 *12 mi north of Stratford-upon-Avon, 5 mi north of Henley-in-Arden.*

Packwood House combines red brick and half-timbering, while its tall chimneys are another distinctive Tudor characteristic. The grounds include a formal 17th-century garden, as well as a remarkable topiary garden of that period, in which yew trees depict Christ's Sermon on the Mount. To get here from Henley-in-Arden, follow A3400 north another 4 or 5 miles, turn right, just before Hockley Heath, onto B4439, and follow the signs for 2 miles farther on a back road. ✉ *Near Hockley Heath,* ☎ *01564/782024.* 🎫 *£3.80.* ⏲ *Apr.–Sept., Wed.–Sun. and national holiday Mon. 2–6; Oct., Wed.–Sun. 12:30–4:30; closed Good Fri.*

Baddesley Clinton

16 *2 mi east of Packwood House, off A4141, 15 mi north of Stratford-upon-Avon.*

The architectural historian Sir Nikolaus Pevsner once called Baddesley Clinton "the perfect late medieval manor house." Off a winding back road, the moated manor still retains its great fireplaces, 17th-century paneling, and priest holes (secret chambers for Roman Catholic priests, who were persecuted at various times throughout the 16th and 17th centuries). ✉ *Near Chadwick End, 6 mi northwest of Warwick,* ☎ *01564/783294.* 🎫 *£4.50.* ⏲ *Mar.–Sept., Wed.–Sun. and national holiday Mon. 2–6; Oct., Wed.–Sun. 12:30–4:30; closed Good Fri.; restaurant, National Trust store, and grounds open at 12:30.*

Kenilworth Castle

17 *5 mi east of Baddesley Clinton direct, 10 mi by road, 5 mi north of Warwick.*

The great, red ruins of Kenilworth Castle loom over the rather nondescript village of Kenilworth. Founded in 1120, this castle remained one of the most formidable fortresses in England until it was finally dismantled by Oliver Cromwell after the Civil War in the mid-17th century. Still intact are its keep (central tower), with 20-foot-thick walls; its great hall; and its curtain walls (low outer walls forming the castle's first line of defense). Here the earl of Leicester, one of Queen Elizabeth I's favorites, entertained her four times, most notably in 1575 with 19 days of sumptuous feasting and revelry. From Baddesley Clinton village, turn right onto A4141; then left, northeast, onto A4177; and finally right again, onto A452. ✉ *Kenilworth,* ☎ *01926/52078.* 🎫 *£2.50.* ⏲ *Daily 10–6 or dusk; closed Dec. 24–26.*

NEED A BREAK? Have a substantial bar meal in the **Clarendon Arms** (✉ Castle Green, Kenilworth), a cozy, flagstone-floored pub.

Dining

££ ✕ **Restaurant Bosquet.** This attractive, small restaurant serves set menus cooked by the French *patron,* with regularly changing à la carte selections. Try the veal or venison with wild mushrooms, The desserts are mouth-watering. It is mainly a dinner spot, though lunch is available on request. ✉ *97A Warwick Rd.,* ☎ *01926/852463. AE, MC, V. No dinner Mon. Closed Sun.*

Warwick

18 *4 mi south of Kenilworth on A46, 9 mi northeast of Stratford-upon-Avon.*

Warwick, the county seat of Warwickshire, is an interesting architectural mixture of Georgian red brick and Elizabethan half-timbering. Much of the town center has been spoiled by unattractive postwar development, but look for the 15th-century **Lord Leycester Hospital,** which has been a home for old soldiers since the earl of Leicester dedicated it to that purpose in 1571. ✉ *High St.,* ☎ *01926/491422.* 🎫 *£2.50.* ⏲ *Apr.–Sept., Tues.–Sun. 10–5; Oct.–Mar., Tues.–Sun. 10–4; closed Good Fri. and Dec. 25.*

Visitors to Warwick will find the **Collegiate Church of St. Mary** well worth visiting, especially for the florid Beauchamp (pronounced Beecham) Chapel, burial chapel of the earls of Warwick. Its gilded, carved, and painted tombs are the very essence of late medieval and Tudor chivalry. ✉ *Church St.*

★ The city's chief attraction is **Warwick Castle,** the finest medieval castle in England, which is built on a cliff overlooking the Avon. Its most powerful commander was the 15th-century earl of Warwick, known during the Wars of the Roses as "the Kingmaker." He was killed in battle near London in 1471 by Edward IV, whom he had just deposed in favor of Henry VI. Warwick Castle's monumental walls now enclose one of the best collections of medieval armor and weapons in Europe, as well as historic furnishings and paintings by Rubens, Van Dyck, and other old masters. Twelve rooms are devoted to an imaginative Madame Tussaud's wax exhibition, "A Royal Weekend Party—1898." A new exhibit, opened in 1994, displays the sights and sounds of a great medieval household as it prepares for an important battle. The year chosen is 1471, when the earl of Warwick was killed by Edward IV at the Battle of Barnet. Below the castle, along the Avon, strutting peacocks patrol 60 acres of grounds landscaped by Capability Brown in the 18th century. There is a restaurant in the cellars, for lunch during your visit. ☎ *01926/495421.* 🎫 *£8.75.* ⏲ *Apr.–mid-Oct., daily 10–6 (until 7 on national holiday Mon. in Aug.); mid-Oct.–Mar., daily 10–5; closed Dec. 25.*

In Warwick, **St. John's House** (☎ 01926/412021, ⏲ daily 12-4.) exhibits a Victorian schoolroom, costumes, and scenes of domestic life. The **Warwickshire Doll Museum** (✉ Oken's House, Castle St., ☎ 01926/495546, ⏲ Easter–Sept.) houses a large collection of dolls, toys, and games.

Dining and Lodging

£–££ ✕ **Fanshawe's.** Centrally located on the market square in Warwick, this friendly restaurant features cheerful prints and vases of flowers. The menu is wide-ranging—you can have simple open sandwiches if you just want a light lunch, or try the saddle of lamb with tomato or the cod with chervil butter. Game is also served in season. ✉ *22 Market Pl.,* ☎ *01926/410590. AE, MC, V. No lunch Mon. Closed Sun.*

£ ✕🏨 **Tudor House Inn.** Here is a simple hotel and restaurant of genuine character. The Tudor House dates from 1472, having survived the great Warwick fire of 1694 by being situated on the road to Stratford, beyond the West Gate, outside the devastated medieval town center. The rooms are beamed and basic, and the floors creak satisfactorily. The great hall, with its cavernous fireplace and gallery, acts as the bar and restaurant, and the inexpensive food served here is hearty and plentiful. This inn is a must for collectors of historic atmosphere. ✉ *90–92 West St., CV34 6AW,* ☎ *01926/495447,* FAX *01926/492948. 11 rooms, 6 with bath. Restaurant, bar. AE, DC, MC, V.*

Charlecote Park

⓳ *6 mi south of Warwick, 3 mi east of Stratford-upon-Avon.*

Queen Elizabeth I is known to have stayed at Charlecote Park, the Tudor manor house of the Lucy family, which was extensively renovated in neo-Elizabethan style in the 19th century. According to tradition, soon after his marriage Shakespeare was caught poaching deer here and was forced to flee to London. Years later he is supposed to have retaliated by portraying Charlecote's owner, Sir Thomas Lucy, in *Henry IV Part 2* as the foolish Justice Shallow. From Warwick, take A429 south 4 or 5 miles, and then turn right onto B4088. ✉ *Charlecote,* ☎ *01789/470277.* 🎫 *£4.40.* ⏲ *Apr.–Oct., Fri.–Tues. and national holiday Mon. 11–1 and 2–6; closed Good Fri.*

OFF THE BEATEN PATH

COVENTRY – From Warwick, take A46 north about 10 miles to Coventry to visit the **cathedral.** As a testament to history, the 1,000-year-old building, destroyed by air raids in 1940 and 1941, has been left as a bombed-out shell next to the magnificent new cathedral. The new one contains the best of modern religious art in Britain of the time (1954–62), including an engraved glass screen by John Hutton; a tapestry by Graham Sutherland; stained-glass windows by John Piper; and various pieces by Sir Jacob Epstein, the New York–born sculptor. The visitors center beneath the cathedral uses audio, video, and holograms to show the history of Coventry and its cathedrals. About the rest of the city, which contains some of the worst postwar rebuilding to be seen in Britain, the less said the better. From Stratford, take A46 north about 20 miles to reach Coventry. ✉ *Priory Row,* ☎ *01203/227597.* 🎫 *Suggested donation £2, tower £1, visitors center £1.25.* ⏲ *Daily 9–6; closed during services.*

THE COTSWOLDS

A great deal has been written about the pretty towns of the Cotswolds, which age has mellowed rather than withered, and perhaps, when one considers the matter deeply, one realizes that there is very little difference in the architecture of the individual villages from other regions of England. Rather it is in the character of their surroundings. The valleys are deep and sheltered and one finds cozy hamlets that appear to drip in foliage from high church tower to garden gate. Beyond the village limits, you'll often find the "high wild hills and rough uneven ways" that Shakespeare talked about.

There is an evasive spirit about the Cotswolds. Its secret seems shared by two things—sheep and stone. And if such a combination sounds strange, perhaps some further explanation is necessary. Time was when the Cotswold Hills were the great sheep rearing areas of England, and Cotswold wool was in demand the world over. All this prosperity meant that the Cotswold merchants were thriving rich, but many were men of magnanimous disposition. They gave back to the Cotswolds something to replace that taken away, and for wool they gave stone—restoring old churches or building rows of almshouses, built of granite now seasoned to a glorious golden-gray.

Our circular swing around this area, using Bourton-on-the-Water as a base, goes to Chipping Campden; the oversold village of Broadway, which has many rivals for beauty hereabouts; Winchcombe and Sudeley Castle; Northleach; Burford; and back to Bourton. This is definitely a region where it pays to wander off the beaten track to take a look at that village hidden in the trees.

Numbers in the margin correspond to points of interest on the Cotswold Hills map.

Bourton-on-the-Water

20 *4 mi northeast of Stow-on-the-Wold, 12 mi east of Cheltenham.*

Taking either the M40 southeast from Birmingham, or the A34 southeast from Stratford, turn south on A429, the Fosse Way, to reach the Cotswolds. Bourton-on-the-Water, off A429 on the eastern edge of the Cotswold Hills, is deservedly famous as a classic Cotswold village. The little river Windrush runs through Bourton, crossed by low stone bridges. This village makes a good touring base, but in summer, like Stratford and Broadway, it's overcrowded with tourists.

A stroll through Bourton takes you past Cotswold cottages, many now converted to little stores and coffee shops. Follow the rushing stream and its ducks to the end of the village and the old mill, now the **Cotswold Motor Museum and Exhibition of Village Life.** In addition to 30 vintage motor vehicles and a collection of old advertising signs, this museum offers an Edwardian store, a blacksmith's forge, a wheelwright's shop, a country kitchen, and a huge trove of children's toys. ✉ *The Old Mill,* ☎ *01451/821255.* *£1.40.* *Feb.–Nov., daily 10–6.*

In Bourton-on-the-Water the **Model Railway Exhibition** (✉ Box Bush, High St., ☎ 01451/820686) is in itself interesting and it has some toys on sale. **The Model Village** (✉ The Old New Inn, ☎ 01451/820467) is an outdoor working replica of Bourton village, built in 1937 to a scale of one-ninth.

Lodging

£ **Coombe House.** At this neat guest house you'll find an attractive garden with some unusual and interesting plants. The comfortable bedrooms have TVs and appliances for making tea or coffee, and the lounge has a patio. This is a no-smoking establishment. There's ample parking. ✉ *Rissington Rd., GL54 2DT,* ☎ *01451/821966,* FAX *01451/810477. 7 rooms with bath. AE, MC, V.*

Shopping

The **Cotswold Perfumery** (✉ Victoria St., ☎ 01451/820698) has a wide range of perfumes, which are manufactured here. While deciding what to buy, visit the **Exhibition of Perfumery** and the **Perfumed Garden** (

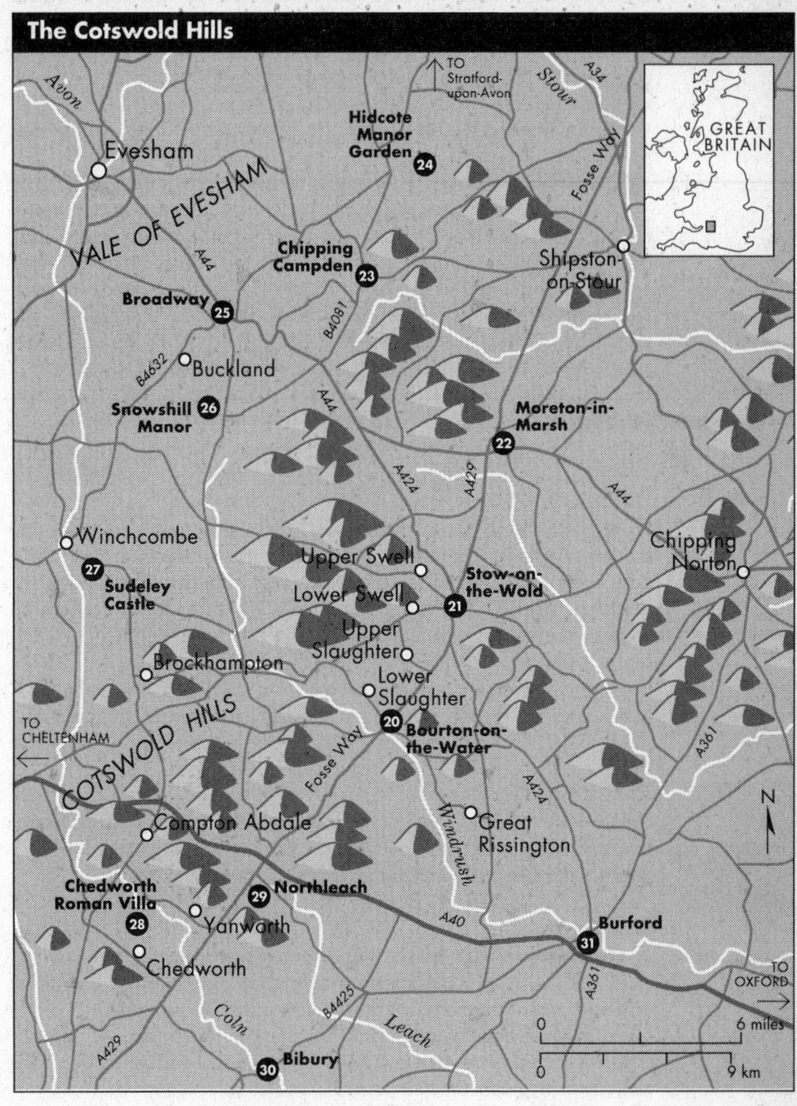

Exhibition £1.50). Perfume bottles, jewelry, and porcelain dolls are also on sale.

Upper and Lower Slaughter

2 mi north of Bourton-on-the-Water, 21 mi south of Stratford-upon-Avon, 15 mi east of Cheltenham.

Rather than follow the beaten path to such tourist centers as Broadway and Bourton-on-the-Water, you will find a quieter, more typical Cotswolds atmosphere in nearby villages with such evocative names as **Upper Slaughter** and **Lower Slaughter** (the names have nothing to do with mass murder, but come from the Saxon word *sloh,* which means "a marshy place") or Upper and Lower Swell.

Dining and Lodging

£££ ✕🏨 **Lords of the Manor Hotel.** A characteristic 16th-century Cotswolds manor house, "the Lords" also has its own fishing stream. It offers comfort and a warm welcome, and its location, Upper Slaughter, is a quintessential Cotswolds village. Extensive refurbishment has meant additional bedrooms available in converted outbuildings, now more modern than those in the main house. ✉ *Upper Slaughter, GL54 2JD,* ☎ *01451/820243,* FAX *01451/820696. 27 rooms with bath. Restaurant, fishing. AE, DC, MC, V.*

£££ ✕ **Washbourne Court.** This fine 17th-century building stands amid 4 acres of grounds beside the river Eye. The interior has stone-flagged floors, beams, and open fires. The bedrooms in the main building have a deliberately country feel to them, while rooms are more modern in the converted barn and cottages. The food in the award-winning restaurant is appropriately traditional English. ✉ *Lower Slaughter, GL54 2HS,* ☎ *01451/822143,* FAX *01451/821045. 21 rooms and suites, all with bath or shower. Restaurant, tennis court. AE, DC, MC, V.*

Stow-on-the-Wold

21 *3 mi north of Bourton-on-the-Water, 21 mi south of Stratford-upon-Avon, 15 mi east of Cheltenham.*

Stow-on-the-Wold is an exemplary Cotswolds town, its imposing golden stone houses built around a wide square. Many of these have now been discreetly converted into quality antiques stores. Look for the Kings Arms Old Posting House, its wide entrance still seeming to wait for the stagecoaches that once stopped here on their way to Cheltenham. At 800 feet elevation, Stow is the highest, as well as the largest, town in the Cotswolds—"Stow-on-the-Wold, where the wind blows cold" is the age-old saying. It's also an antiques hunter's paradise, and a convenient base: Eight main Cotswolds roads intersect here but they all—happily—bypass the town center.

NEED A BREAK? The **Queen's Head** (✉ The Square) is an excellent stopping-off spot for a pub lunch. In summer, the courtyard out back or the bench in front, under a climbing rose, makes for relaxed outdoor drinking.

Lodging

£££ **Fosse Manor.** This lovely manor-house hotel, just out of town (1 mile south on A429), has a long-standing reputation for solid comfort and service. Family-run for years, it was just refurbished in 1994–95. There are golf and riding available nearby. ✉ *Fosse Way, GL54 1JX,* ☎ *01451/830354,* FAX *01451/832486. 20 rooms, 18 with bath. Restaurant, putting green, croquet. AE, DC, MC, V.*

££ **Stow Lodge Hotel.** Set well back from the main square of Stow-on-the-Wold in its own quiet gardens, the lodge is a typical Cotswold manor house; its large, open fireplaces provide added warmth in the winter. Smoking is permitted only in the bar/lounge. ✉ *The Square, GL54 1AB,* ☎ *01451/830485. 22 rooms, 20 with bath. Restaurant. AE, DC, MC, V. Closed Dec. 25–Jan. 31.*

Moreton-in-Marsh

22 *5 mi north of Stow-on-the-Wold on A429, 18 mi northeast of Cheltenham, 17 mi south of Stratford-upon-Avon.*

In Moreton-in-Marsh, the houses have been built not around a central square but along a street wide enough to accommodate a market every Tuesday. The village enjoys fine views across the hills. A landmark of the town is St. David's Church, which has a lovely tower of honey-gold ashlar. The town also possesses one of the last remaining curfew towers, dated 1633; Curfew dates back to the time of the Norman Conquest, when a bell was rung to "cover-fire" for the night against any invaders.

Chipping Campden

23 *6 mi northwest (10 mi by road) of Moreton-in-Marsh, off A44, 18 mi northeast of Cheltenham, 10 mi south of Stratford-upon-Avon.*

Undoubtedly one of the most beautiful towns in the heart of England, Chipping Campden is the Cotswolds in a microcosm—it has St. James, the most impressive church of the region, frozen-in-time streets, a timbered Woolstaplers Hall, and charming (and un-touristy) shops. It also features one of the most seductive settings of the area, which will unfold before you as you travel on the B4081 through sublimely lovely English countryside to happen upon the town tucked in a slight valley. Near St. James, on Church Street, is an important row of almshouses dating from King James I's reign. The broad High Street follows a picturesque curve and is lined with attractive houses and shops. In the center, on Market Street, is the **Market Hall**, a gabled Jacobean structure built by Sir Baptiste Hycks in 1627 "for the sale of local produce." One of the oldest buildings in Chipping Campden, built in the 14th century, is **Woolstaplers Hall.** It houses the museum, a 1920s movie theater, and collections of medical equipment. ✉ *High St.,* ☎ *01386/840289.* £2. ⏲ *Apr.–Oct., daily 10–5; Nov.–Dec., weekends 10–5.*

NEED A BREAK? **Greenstocks** (✉ Cotswold House Hotel, The Square) is just the place for a delicious lunch or a coffee break.

Dining and Lodging

£££ ✕🏨 **Charingworth Manor.** Views of the Cotswolds countryside are limitless from this 14th-century manor-house hotel. A new section in light golden stone was added in 1988. Each room is named after previous owners or local villages and is individually done in English floral fabrics, with antique and period furniture. Rooms in the old manor have the best views and original oak beams. ✉ *Charingworth, 3 mi east of Chipping Campden, GL55 6NS,* ☎ *01386/593555,* FAX *01386/593353. 26 rooms with bath, 3 suites. Restaurant, indoor pool, sauna, steam room, tennis court, billiards. AE, DC, MC, V.*

£££ ✕🏨 **Cotswold House Hotel.** Though it is in the center of a small country town, the Cotswold House has an acre of stone-walled garden at the back and a flair for dramatic design inside. The bedrooms here are small masterpieces of theme decor. There's an Indian room, a French room, and, for homesick travelers, a Colonial room. The restaurant is also striking, with windows onto the garden. The game and fish dishes are always interestingly presented. ✉ *The Square, GL55 6AN,* ☎ *01386/840330,* FAX *01386/840310. 15 rooms with bath. Restaurant (jacket and tie, no lunch except Sun.), brasserie. AE, MC, V.*

££ 🏨 **Noel Arms Hotel.** In the heart of Chipping Campden, this inn was built for foreign wool traders in the 14th century and is the oldest inn in the town. It retains its period atmosphere with exposed beams and stonework, even though it has been recently enlarged. Its individually decorated bedrooms—some with four-posters—offer every modern comfort. ✉ *High St., GL55 6AT,* ☎ *01386/840317,* FAX *01386/841136. 26 rooms with bath. Restaurant. AE, MC, V.*

Hidcote Manor Garden

★ 24 *4 mi northeast of Chipping Camden, 9 mi south of Stratford-upon-Avon.*

Laid out around a Cotswold manor house, Hidcote Manor Garden is arguably the most interesting and attractive large garden in Britain—it can also be terribly overcrowded at the height of the season. It was created in 1907 by an American horticulturalist, Major Lawrence Johnstone. Johnstone was not just an imaginative gardener, but a widely traveled plantsman as well, who brought back specimens from all over the world. The formal part of the garden is arranged in "rooms" without roofs, separated by hedges, often with fine topiary work and walls. The White Garden was probably the forerunner of the popular white gardens at Sissinghurst and Glyndebourne. During summer, Shakespearean plays are performed on the Theater Lawn; Those who have caught *A Midsummer's Night Dream* on a July evening here say it is one of the more unforgettable treats England has to offer. ✉ *Hidcote Bartrim,* ☎ *01386/438333.* 🎟 *£5.20.* ⏲ *Apr.–Oct., Mon., Wed., Thurs., and weekends 11–7 (11–6 in Oct.), also Tues. June–July 11–7; last admission at 6 or 1 hr before sunset.*

Broadway

25 *4 mi southwest of Hidcote Manor, 15 mi northeast of Cheltenham, 15 mi southwest of Stratford-upon-Avon.*

From Hidcote Manor, take B4081 and then A44 west to reach Broadway, on the way glimpsing the distant Malvern Hills to the west in Worcestershire. William Morris discovered the delights of this village, J.M. Barrie, Vaughan Williams, and Elgar followed, and soon Broadway became a mecca for day-trippers; Today, sophisticated travelers tend to avoid Broadway in the summer, when it is clogged with cars and buses. Named for its wide main street, Broadway offers many shops and a renowned hotel, the Lygon Arms (☞ Dining and Lodging, *below*). Its striking facade dates from 1620, but the restored building has several modern extensions. On the outskirts of Broadway, off A44, is **Broadway Tower Country Park**. From the top of the tower, an 18th-century "folly" built by the sixth earl of Coventry, you can see over 12 counties in a breathtakingly beautiful vista. Nature trails, picnic grounds with barbecue grills, an adventure playground, and rare animals and birds are surrounded by peaceful countryside. ☎ *01386/852390.* 🎟 *£2.95.* ⏲ *Apr.–Oct., daily 10–6.*

Dining and Lodging

£££ ★ ✕🏨 **Buckland Manor.** As an alternative to the razzmatazz of Broadway, try this exceptional hotel 2 miles away, just off B4632. Parts of the building date back to Jacobean times and there are pleasant old pictures and fine antiques everywhere. The garden is lovely, and the place is so peaceful you can hear a swan's feather drop. ✉ *Near Broadway, WR12 7LY,* ☎ *01386/852626,* FAX *01386/853557. 13 rooms with bath. Restaurant, pool, tennis court, croquet, horseback riding. AE, MC, V.*

££££ ✕🏨 **Lygon Arms.** Here you'll find luxury combined with Old World charm—the Lygon has been in business since 1532 and is now part of the Savoy Hotels group. Although on the main street, it has 3 acres of formal gardens for guests to enjoy. ✉ *High St., WR12 7DU,* ☎ *01386/852255,* FAX *01386/858611. 65 rooms with bath. Restaurant, indoor pool, sauna, spa, golf course, tennis court, billiards, helipad. AE, DC, MC, V.*

£££ ★ ✕🏨 **Dormy House Hotel.** Guest rooms here overlook the Vale of Evesham from high on the Cotswolds ridge. This luxurious country-house hotel has been converted from a 17th-century Cotswolds farmhouse. Bedrooms are individually and beautifully furnished, some with four-poster beds. ✉ *Willersey Hill (2 mi north from Broadway), WR12 7LF,* ☎ *01386/852711,* FAX *01386/858636. 49 rooms with bath. Restaurant. AE, DC, MC, V. Closed Christmas period.*

Snowshill Manor

26 *2 mi south of Broadway, 13 mi northeast of Cheltenham, 17 mi southwest of Stratford-upon-Avon.*

The 17th-century facade of Snowshill Manor hides its Tudor origins. Inside you will find a delightful clutter of musical instruments, clocks, toys, bicycles, weavers' and spinners' tools, Japanese Samurai armor, and more. Children love it. ✉ *Snowshill,* ☎ *01386/852410.* 🎫 *£5.20.* ⏲ *May–Sept., Wed.–Mon. 1–6; Apr. and Oct., Wed.–Mon. 1–5; grounds open at noon; closed Good Fri.*

Sudeley Castle

★ 27 *4 mi southwest of Snowshill Manor, 9 mi northeast of Cheltenham, 21 mi southwest of Stratford-upon-Avon.*

A mile southeast of the village of Winchcombe, on the B4632, stands Sudeley Castle, the home and burial place of Catherine Parr (1512–48), Henry VIII's sixth and last wife, who outlived him by one year. Today the castle's peaceful air belies its turbulent history; its magnificent grounds are the setting for outdoor theater, concerts, and other events in summer. ✉ *Winchcombe,* ☎ *01242/602308.* 🎫 *£5.40.* ⏲ *Grounds Apr.–Oct., daily 10:30–5:30; castle 11–5.*

Chedworth Roman Villa

★ 28 *10 mi southeast of Cheltenham.*

Surrounded by woodland and overlooking the Cotswold Hills, Chedworth Roman Villa is the best-preserved Roman villa in England. Thirty-two rooms, including two complete bath suites, have been identified. The visitor center and museum give a picture of Roman life in Britain. From Winchcombe, head west, but soon turn left (south) and follow the back roads, many of which are single-track, passing through Brockhampton and across A40 to Compton Abdale and on to Yanworth and Chedworth, where you will pick up the signs. The villa is also signposted from the A40 and A429. ✉ *Yanworth,* ☎ *01242/890256.* 🎫 *£3.* ⏲ *Mar.–Oct., Tues.–Sun. and national holidays 10–5; Nov., Tues.–Sun. 10–4; closed Good Fri.*

Northleach

29 *14 mi southeast of Cheltenham.*

From the Roman Villa follow the signs east to Northleach for a look at the magnificent church of St. Peter and St. Paul, dating from the 15th century. It is one of Cotswold's most notable "wool" churches and within can be seen a unique collection of memorial brasses, all bearing the likenesses of leading medieval woolmen. Here, too, in a renovated 18th-century prison is the Lloyd-Baker agricultural-skills antiques collection.

Bibury

30 *6 mi northeast of Cirencester, 15 mi north of Swindon.*

The tiny town of Bibury, on the B4425, occupies an idyllic setting beside the little river Coln—this was William Morris's choice for Britain's most beautiful village. Fine old cottages, a river-meadow, the church of St. Mary's, and Arlington Row—a picturesque stone group of 17th-century weavers' cottages—are some of the delights here. Just outside, on a site recorded in the *Domesday Book,* stands the huge, 17th-century **Arlington Mill,** a working corn mill containing examples of agricultural implements and machinery from the Victorian era, as well as country exhibits. ☎ *01285/740368.* *£1.80.* *Daily 10–6.*

Burford

31 *10 mi northeast of Bibury, 18 mi north of Swindon, 18 mi west of Oxford.*

Burford's broad main street leads steeply down to a narrow bridge across the river Windrush. The village boasts many historic inns, having been a stagecoach stop for centuries. From Bibury, take B4425/A40 east to reach here.

NEED A BREAK? At **The Golden Pheasant Hotel** (✉ High St., Burford), have afternoon tea in the lounge while relaxing in a deep, velvet armchair. In winter you can sit by a log fire, but afternoon tea is served only on weekends.

Dining and Lodging

£££ **Bay Tree.** Quietly located away from Burford's bustle, the atmospheric Bay Tree is in a 16th-century stone house, visited in its prime by both Elizabeth I and James I. Try for a room in the main house. The restaurant, looking out into the garden, serves a three-course set menu of mainly English dishes, stressing healthy eating. ✉ *Sheep St., OX18 4LW,* ☎ *01993/822791,* FAX *01993/823008. 22 rooms with bath. Restaurant. AE, DC, MC, V.*

CHELTENHAM, GLOUCESTER, AND THE FOREST OF DEAN

West of the Cotswolds there's a rather urbanized axis connecting Gloucester with Cheltenham. Despite their proximity, on either side of the M5 motorway, the towns have a very different feel, the former built around docks connected to the Severn River, the latter a gentrified spa town of Regency architecture and notorious for its high-falutin' airs. To the southeast, the low-lying Forest of Dean, once a private hunting ground of kings, is now a recreation area for the general public, with some of the most extensive and beautiful woodlands in the country. Rich with conifers and broad-leaved trees, it makes an ideal spot for either a quiet stroll or a more serious hike.

Numbers in the margin correspond to points of interest on the Forest of Dean and Bath Environs map.

Cheltenham

32 *13 mi east of Gloucester, 50 mi south of Birmingham, 99 mi west of London.*

Cheltenham has managed to acquire an undeserved reputation for Victorian stuffiness. Its renown for architectural distinction, however, is well deserved, for it rivals Bath in its Georgian elegance, with wide, tree-lined streets and graceful secluded villas. If you visit this historic health resort in the spring or summer, you'll see its stunning architecture enhanced by a profusion of flower gardens. The flowers cover even traffic circles, while the elegantly laid-out avenues, crescents, and terraces, with their characteristic row houses, balconies, and iron railings, make Cheltenham an outstanding example of the Regency style.

Like Bath, the town owes part of its fame to mineral springs. By 1740, Cheltenham's first spa was built, and the town became the vogue with a visit from George III and Queen Charlotte in 1788. During the Regency period Cheltenham's status was ensured by the visits of the Duke of Wellington, the national hero of Waterloo. The **Rotunda** building at the top of Montpellier Walk—now a bank—contains the spa's original "pump room," i.e., the room in which the mineral waters were on draft; such rooms, as in Bath, often evolved into public drawing rooms of polite society. More than 30 statues, like the caryatids on the Acropolis in Athens, adorn the storefronts of **Montpellier Walk.** Wander past **Imperial Square,** with its intricate ironwork balconies, past the ornate Neptune's Fountain and along the elegant Promenade.

A 20-minute walk from the town center brings you to the **Pittville Pump Room,** built in the late 1820s, where the mineral waters can still be tasted. The pump room now houses the **Gallery of Fashion,** which tells the history of the town through an extensive costume collection. ✉ *Pittville,* ☎ *01242/523852.* 🎫 *£1.50.* ⏲ *May–Sept., Wed.–Mon. 10–4:30; Oct.–Apr., Wed.–Mon. 11–4.*

NEED A BREAK? The **Old Swan** (✉ 37 High St.), a large, comfortable old pub, serves homemade lunches and has tea and coffee on tap.

Dining and Lodging

£££ ✗ **Epicurean.** Recently relocated to an Edwardian house on Cheltenham's elegant Promenade, this restaurant is now just one of three dining possibilities on the premises. If you want to snack on tapas and beer, head for the basement; the ground floor is a bistro with hot food and a strong contemporary mood; the formal restaurant upstairs is the place to appreciate more gourmet creations. Dishes include poached pheasant in foie gras cream, lobster, and some memorable desserts. Set-price menus at lunch and dinner help to keep the cost down. ✉ *81 The Promenade,* ☎ *01242/222466. AE, DC, MC, V. Closed Sun.*

£££ ✗ **Le Champignon Sauvage.** Everything is made on the premises here, including bread and vinegar! Perk up your palate with dishes such as roasted rump of Cinderford lamb with ratatouille, and such award-winning desserts as hot pistachio tart with roasted strawberries. There is an excellent "Tasting Menu" until 8:30 PM, consisting of seven or eight courses, but give notice for this. ✉ *24 Suffolk Rd.,* ☎ *01242/573449. AE, DC, MC, V. No lunch Sat. Closed Sun.*

££ ✗ **Staithes Restaurant.** This is a busy, colorful, but still elegant bistro, run with ebullience by the owner-chef, Paul Lucas. British Impressionist paintings adorn the walls, and service is calm and personable. Favorite dishes include cured Scottish salmon, medallions of venison, or the baked Alaska. There is no smoking in the dining room. ✉ *12 Suffolk Rd.,* ☎ *01242/260666. AE, DC, MC, V. Closed Sun., 2 wks June, 1 wk Christmas.*

£££ 🏨 **Queen's Hotel.** Overlooking Imperial Gardens from the center of The Promenade, this classic Regency building has welcomed visitors to Cheltenham since 1838. The hotel's decor is very British, and every

The Forest of Dean and Bath Environs

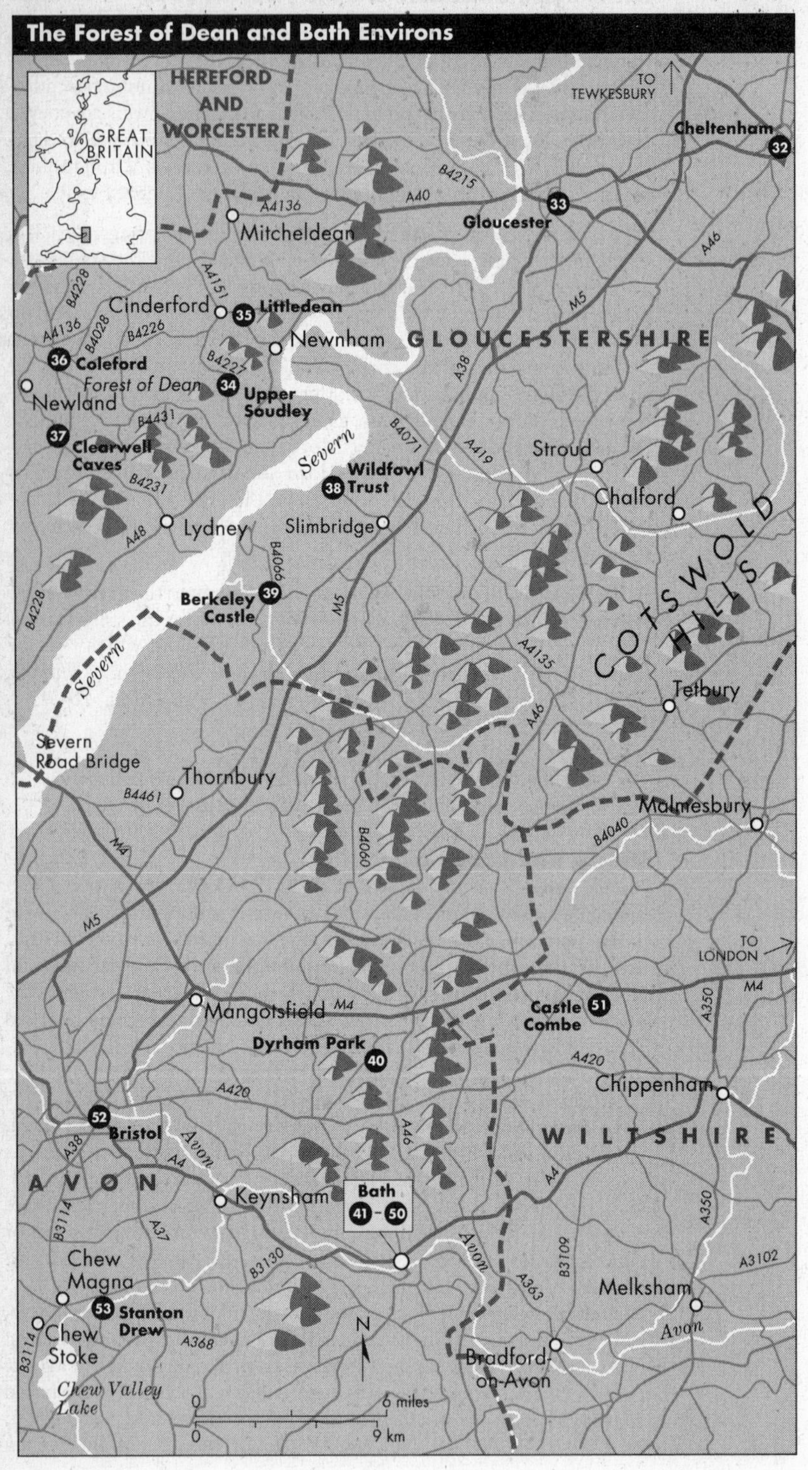

bedroom is individually designed. It has a garden. ✉ *The Promenade, GL50 1NN,* ☎ *01242/514724,* FAX *01242/224145. 74 rooms with bath. Restaurant. AE, DC, MC, V.*

££ ★ **Lypiatt House.** This splendid Victorian house is an award-winning bed-and-breakfast—only a short walk from central Cheltenham. The bedrooms are a comfortable size, with modern bathrooms. There's a small dining room and attentive service from the husband-and-wife team that took over the property in 1992. Young children are not accommodated. ✉ *Lypiatt Rd., GL50 2QW,* ☎ *01242/224994,* FAX *01242/224996. 10 rooms with bath or shower. MC, V.*

££ **Stretton Lodge Guest House.** Bedrooms here are decorated with color-coordinated curtains and quilt covers, and comfortably furnished. Although set in a quiet Regency street, the lodge is only 10 minutes' walk from Cheltenham's busy center. ✉ *Western Rd., GL50 3RN,* ☎ *01242/528724,* FAX *01242/570771. 5 rooms with bath. AE, MC, V.*

£ ★ **Regency House.** This attractive guest house is quite exceptional—it's beautifully furnished with antiques and period-style wallpaper. The front rooms have views of trees in the square, and the back ones look out at a garden. All rooms have TVs, tea- and coffeemaking appliances, and hair dryers. ✉ *50 Clarence Sq., Pittville, GL50 4JR,* ☎ *01242/582718,* FAX *01242/262697. 8 rooms with bath. AE, MC, V.*

The Arts

Cheltenham's annual **International Festival of Music** (July) highlights new compositions, often conducted by the composers, together with classical repertory pieces. The town's **Festival of Literature** (October) brings together world-renowned authors, actors, and critics. ✉ *Festival Office, Town Hall, Imperial Sq., Cheltenham GL50 1QA,* ☎ *01242/227979.*

Shopping

A walk along elegant Montpellier Walk and then along the flower-bedecked Promenade will take you past boutiques like Liberty and Hoopers. Both Martin and Scott Cooper on the Promenade are worth visiting for jewelry and silver. Behind the Promenade is the Regent Arcade, a modern shopping area with a wide variety of stores. A market is held every Sunday at the racecourse, a produce market every Thursday morning on Market Street, and an indoor antiques market Monday through Saturday at 54 Suffolk Road.

Outdoor Activities and Sports

HORSE RACING

Important steeplechase races take place at **Cheltenham** (☎ 01242/513014); the National Hunt Festival in mid-March is crowned by the Gold Cup awards on the last day.

Gloucester

33 *13 mi west of Cheltenham, 56 mi south of Birmingham, 105 mi west of London.*

Much of the ancient heritage of this county seat has been lost to nondescript modern stores and offices, but the **Gloucester Folk Museum** is housed in a row of fine Tudor and Jacobean half-timber houses. ✉ 99–*103 Westgate St.,* ☎ *01452/526467.* *Free.* *Oct.–June, Mon.–Sat. 10–5; July–Sept., Mon.–Sat. 10–5, Sun. 10–4.*

★ Across Westgate Street is the magnificent **Gloucester Cathedral,** originally a Norman abbey church, consecrated in 1100. The exterior soars in elegant lines, and the interior has largely been spared the sterilizing attentions of modern architects who like to strip cathedrals down to their original bare bones. The place is a mishmash of periods, and the clutter of centuries mirrors perfectly the slow growth of ecclesiastical taste, good, bad, and indifferent. The interior is almost completely Norman, with the massive pillars of the nave left untouched since their completion. The fan-vaulted roof of the cloisters is the finest in Europe. The cloisters enclose a peaceful garden, where one can easily imagine medieval monks at prayer. ✉ *Westgate St.,* ☎ *01452/528095.* 🎫 *Requested donation £3.* ⏲ *Daily 8–6, except during services and special events.*

NEED A BREAK? The **Dick Whittington** (✉ 100 Westgate St.), a large, wooden-floor pub serving beer and wine from the barrel, commemorates a famous native son, who was three times Lord Mayor of London in the Middle Ages.

A short walk from the cathedral, at the end of Westgate Street, along the canal, are the historic **Gloucester Docks.** The docks still function, though now on a much reduced scale. The vast Victorian warehouses are being restored, and new shops and cafés added to bring the area back to life. One of the warehouses circling Gloucester Docks is now the Antique Centre (☞ Shopping, *below*). Another holds **The National Waterways Museum,** with examples of canal houseboats and barges. Tours, starting at the National Waterways Museum are conducted every Sunday in August at 2:30. ✉ *Llanthony Warehouse, Gloucester Docks,* ☎ *01452/318054.* 🎫 *£4.25.* ⏲ *Apr.–Sept., daily 10–6; Oct.–Mar., daily 10–5.*

Dining and Lodging

£ ✕ **College Green.** With a keen notion of the right meal in the right place, this upstairs restaurant, with views out over the cathedral, serves classic English cooking—pork and cider casserole, fresh salmon—and provides a respectable wine list. ✉ *7 College St.,* ☎ *01452/520739. AE, MC, V.*

£££ 🏨 **Hatherley Manor.** Standing on 37 acres of grounds 2 miles north of Gloucester, this renovated 17th-century house is fairly quiet unless a conference is going on—which happens frequently. There's a four-poster honeymoon suite. ✉ *Down Hatherley La., GL2 9QA,* ☎ *01452/730217,* FAX *01452/731032. 56 rooms with bath. Restaurant, exercise room, croquet, helipad. AE, DC, MC, V.*

£££ 🏨 **Royal Hop Pole.** One of the most famous old English inns, this is now a part of the Trusthouse Forte chain. The rooms at the rear have wood beams and views of the pretty gardens running down to the river. One of the front rooms has a four-poster. ✉ *Church St., GL20 5RT,* ☎ *01684/293236,* FAX *01684/296680. 29 rooms with bath. Restaurant. AE, DC, MC, V.*

£££ 🏨 **Tewkesbury Park Hotel, Golf and Country Club.** Just outside town (1¼ miles south on A38), this former 18th-century mansion is the ideal stopover point for the athletically inclined. There's almost every sports facility anyone could want, plus the wonderful countryside. The Park also caters to a flourishing conference trade. ✉ *Lincoln Green La., GL20 7DN,* ☎ *01684/295405,* FAX *01684/292386. 78 rooms with bath. Restaurant, coffee shop, indoor pool, sauna, golf privileges, tennis court, squash. AE, DC, MC, V.*

Shopping

The locals say it's best to look in Cheltenham and buy in Gloucester, where prices are lower. Gloucester offers neither the variety nor the sophistication of Cheltenham stores, but you might find a bargain or two. The **Antique Centre** (☎ 01452/529716) offers some good buys, in a restored Victorian warehouse at Gloucester Docks. The **Beatrix Potter Gift Shop** (✉ College Ct., ☎ 01452/422856), next to the Cathedral Gate, is the house of the tailor featured in Potter's story *The Tailor of Gloucester.*

Outdoor Activities and Sports

BICYCLING

The Gloucester Tourist office (☎ 01452/421188) has a full range of "go as you please" cycle touring route packs (£2).

BOATING

This is an area crisscrossed with rivers and canals. From the pier outside the National Waterways Museum, you can take a brief tour of the Gloucester Docks, lasting 45 minutes, or longer all-day cruises north as far as Tewkesbury or south to the Severn Estuary at Sharpness. Contact the Waterways Museum for dates and prices. ✉ *Llanthony Warehouse, Gloucester Docks,* ☎ *01452/318054.*

GOLF

The **Tewkesbury Park Hotel** (☞ Dining and Lodging, *above*) has an 18-hole course, and visitors are welcome with a handicap certificate.

OFF THE BEATEN PATH

CIRENCESTER – From Gloucester head southeast on A417, which follows the Roman Ermin Way for 11 miles and should get you in the mood for the Roman experience you are about to have. Cirencester (sometimes pronounced "Cīcester") has been the hub of the Cotswolds since Roman times when it was called Corinium and lay at the intersection of the Fosse Way and the Ermin Way. Cirencester is a lovely old market town, full of mellow stone buildings—take a stroll down Dollar Street to see the bow-fronted stores—and with a magnificent parish church, St. John the Baptist. The **Corinium Museum** has an excellent collection of Roman artifacts, as well as full-scale reconstructions of local Roman interiors. ✉ *Park St.,* ☎ *01285/655611.* 🎫 *£1.60.* ⏲ *Mon.–Sat. 10–5, Sun. 2–5; Nov.–Mar. closed Mon.*

Upper Soudley

34 *11 mi south of Ross-on-Wye, 15 mi west of Gloucester.*

★ The mysterious **Forest of Dean** covers much of the valley between the rivers Severn and Wye. Although the primordial forest has long since been cut down and replanted, the landscape here remains one of strange beauty, hiding in its folds and under its hills deposits of iron, silver, and coal that have been mined for thousands of years.

Your first stop should be Upper Soudley, where you'll find the **Dean Heritage Centre.** Based in a restored mill building in a wooded valley, the center tells the history of the forest, with reconstructions of a mine and a miner's cottage, a water wheel, and a "beam engine" (a primitive steam engine used to pump water from flooded coal mines). Outside the center is a tiny farm with a pig and poultry, as well as natural-history exhibitions. Watch craftspeople at work in the outbuildings. ✉ *Soudley, Cinderford (on B4227),* ☎ *01594/822170.* 🎫 *£2.75.* ⏲ *Feb.–Mar., daily 10–5; Apr.–Oct., daily 10–6; Nov.–Jan., weekends only 10–4.*

Littledean

35 *1 mi east of Cinderford, 15 mi west Gloucester.*

From Littledean, "Scenic Drive" signs direct you through the best of the forest. Of the original royal forest established in 1016 by King Canute, 27,000 acres are preserved by the Forestry Commission. It's still an important source of timber, but parking lots and picnic grounds have been created and eight nature trails marked. One trail links sculptures, commissioned by the Forestry Commission, around **Speech House,** the medieval verderer's court in the forest's center. The verderer was responsible for the enforcement of the forest laws. It was usually a capital offense to kill game or cut wood without authorization. To get to Littledean from Soudley, backtrack north on B4227, turn east on A4151.

Coleford

36 *10 mi south of Ross-on-Wye, 6 mi east of Monmouth.*

The TIC (☎ 01594/836307) at Coleford (drive west on A4151, and then west again on B4226 and B4028) has details of picnic grounds, nature trails, and tours of the forest. The area is a maze of weathered and moss-covered rocks, huge ferns, and ancient yew trees—a shady haven on a summer's day. An insight into the region's mining for iron and coal, which had gone on continuously from Roman times to 1945, can be had
37 through a visit to the **Clearwell Caves.** ✉ *Clearwell Caves, near Coleford, (off B4228),* ☎ *01594/832535.* *£3.* *Mar.–Oct. daily 10–5; Dec., Christmas workshops (£3) weekdays 2–6, weekends 10–5.*

Dining and Lodging

££ ★ ✕ **Wyndham Arms.** Located in the Forest of Dean, this may be a modest, Old World village inn, but its restaurant offers sophisticated cuisine. Try the local wild salmon, guinea-fowl, or one of the excellent steaks, followed by *zuppa inglese*—a mouth-watering chocolate, rum, and meringue concoction. ✉ *Near Coleford,* ☎ *01594/833666. AE, DC, MC, V.*

£–££ **Tudor Farmhouse.** Despite the name, parts of this converted farmhouse actually date back to the 13th century. Polished oak staircases, mullioned windows, and a huge stone fireplace in the lounge help to imbue the place with a sense of antique calm. There are four-poster beds in two of the bedrooms, and the restaurant serves four-course meals. ✉ *Clearwell (near Coleford), GL16 8JS,* ☎ *01594/833046,* FAX *01594/837093. 8 rooms with bath or shower. Restaurant. AE, MC, V.*

Slimbridge

12 mi southwest of Gloucester, 20 mi northeast of Bristol, 8 mi southwest of Stroud.

Outside the village of Slimbridge (head west and across the little swing
38 bridge over the Sharpness Canal), **Wildfowl Trust** occupies a site on the banks of the Severn. Its 73 acres of rich marshland harbor Britain's largest collection of wildfowl. Thousands of swans, ducks, and geese come to winter here; in spring and early summer, you will be delighted by cygnets, ducklings, and goslings. To get to Slimbridge from Gloucester, take the M5 motorway southwest, leave at exit 13, and follow the A38 south. ☎ *01453/890065.* *£4.70.* *Mar.–Oct. daily 9:30–5; Nov.–Feb. daily 9:30–4; closed Dec. 25.*

Berkeley

★ 39 *4 mi south of Slimbridge, 17 mi south of Gloucester, 21 mi north of Bristol.*

Berkeley Castle in the sleepy little village of Berkeley (pronounced "Barkley"), is perfectly preserved, everyone's ideal castle. It was the setting for the gruesome murder of King Edward II in 1327—the cell can still be seen. He was deposed by his French consort, Queen Isabella, and her paramour, the earl of Mortimer. They then connived at his imprisonment and subsequent death. The castle was begun in 1153 by Roger De Berkeley, a Norman knight, and has remained in the family ever since. The state apartments here are full of magnificent furniture, tapestries, and pictures. The surrounding meadows, now the setting for pleasant Elizabethan gardens, were once flooded to make a formidable moat. ✉ *Berkeley,* ☎ *01453/810332.* 🎟 *£4.50.* ⏲ *Apr., Tues.–Sun. 2–5; May.–June and Sept., Tues.–Sat. 11–5, Sun. 2–5; July–Aug., Mon.–Sat. 11–5, Sun. 2–5; Oct., Sun. only 2–4:30; national holidays 11–5.*

Dining and Lodging

£££–££££ ★ ✕🏨 **Thornbury Castle.** Cricket fans may know the town of Thornbury as the home of the celebrated batsman, W.G. Grace (1848–1915). Others will appreciate the buttressed tower of the 16th-century church, built at about the same time as the castle that dominates the village. Still others cherish its impressive castle hotel. Here are the kind of baronial surroundings where you might expect to see Douglas Fairbanks come sliding down a velvet drape. Thornbury has everything a genuine 16th-century castle needs: huge fireplaces, antiques, paintings, and mullioned windows, to say nothing of an extensive garden. The standards of comfort and luxury are famous, and people come from all over to eat in the restaurant. Note that children under 12 are not accommodated, and there is no elevator. ✉ *Thornbury (12 mi north of Bristol, off A38), Castle St., BS12 1HH,* ☎ *01454/281182,* FAX *01454/416188. 18 rooms with bath. Restaurant (reservations essential, jacket and tie). AE, DC, MC, V. Closed 1st wk of Jan.*

£ ✕🏨 **Greenacres Farm.** Inglenook fireplaces and pretty bedrooms with sweeping views are some of the features of this 300-year-old farmhouse; it is located on a sheep farm. The dining room offers three-course dinners with home-grown produce. ✉ *A38 north from Bristol, then B4509. Breadstone, near Berkeley, GL13 9HF,* ☎ *01453/810348,* FAX *01453/511217. 4 rooms with bath or shower. MC.*

En Route From Berkeley you can take A38 or M5 southeast to Bristol (21 miles) or cross back over the M5 and head southeast toward Bath (30 miles via A4135 and A46), both on the river Avon.

Dyrham Park

40 *8 mi north of Bath.*

Occupying a high, scenic ridge to the north of Bath, Dyrham Park takes its name from an ancient deer park covering 263 acres, the abode of a herd of fallow deer. At its center stands a late 17th-century country house with paneled interiors, the setting for occasional open-air concerts in the summer. ✉ *Dyrham,* ☎ *0117/937–2501.* 🎟 *£5; deer park only £1.60; garden only £1.* ⏲ *House and garden Apr.–Oct., Fri.–Tues. noon–5:30; park daily noon–5:30 or dusk; closed Dec. 25.*

BATH AND BEYOND

Anyone who listens to the local speech of Bath and Bristol will note the inflections that herald the beginning of England's West Country. Yet both places retain an inescapable element of the Heart of England: Bath itself is right at the bottom edge of the Cotswold Hills, while the Georgian architecture and mellow stone so prominent in both cities are reminders of the stone mansions and cottages of the Cotswolds. In the hinterland of the county of Avon, the mellow countryside harbors hidden country pubs and the gentle green landscape around the Chew Valley.

Bath

★ 41 *13 mi southeast of Bristol, 115 mi west of London.*

"I really believe I shall always be talking of Bath....I do like it so very much. Oh! who can ever be tired of Bath," wrote Jane Austen in *Northanger Abbey* and, today, thousands of visitors heartily agree with the great 19th-century author. One of the delights of staying in Bath is being surrounded by the magnificent 18th-century architecture, a lasting reminder of the elegant world described by Austen. Bath suffered slightly from World War II bombing and even more from urban renewal, but the damage was halted before it could ruin the Georgian elegance of the city. This doesn't mean that Bath is a museum. It is lively and interesting, offering dining and entertainment, excellent art galleries, and theater, music, and other performances throughout the year. The Romans first put Bath on the map in the 1st century, when they built a temple here in honor of the goddess Minerva, and a sophisticated network of baths to make full use of the mineral springs, which gush from the earth at a constant temperature of 116°F. Much later, 18th-century People of Quality took the city to its heart, and Bath became the most fashionable spa in Britain. The architect John Wood (1704–54) created a harmonious city, building beautiful terraces, crescents, and Palladian villas of the same local stone used by the Romans.

Numbers in the margin correspond to points of interest on the Bath map.

42 The **Pump Room** is Bath's primary "watering hole." People still gather here to drink the mineral waters—which taste revolting—and to socialize. The baths as such are no longer in use, and this magnificent Georgian building now houses a tourist information desk, a souvenir store, and a restaurant. Almost the entire Roman bath complex has been excavated. ✉ *Abbey Churchyard,* ☎ *01225/477785.* 🎟 *Pump Room free; Roman baths £5.60; combined ticket with Costume Museum £7.50.* 🕘 *Apr.–Sept. daily 9–6 (and Aug. 8 PM–10 PM), Oct.–Mar., Mon.–Sat. 9:30–5, Sun. 10:30–5.*

NEED A BREAK? The **Pump Room** (✉ Abbey Churchyard) serves morning coffee and afternoon tea, often to music by a string trio. Near the abbey, **Sally Lunn's** (✉ North Parade Passage), the oldest house in Bath, still serves the famous Sally Lunn bun invented here.

43 Next to the Pump Room is the **Abbey,** dating from the 15th century. It was built in the Perpendicular (English Gothic) style on the site of a Saxon abbey, and has superb, fan-vaulted ceilings in the nave. ✉ *Abbey Churchyard.* 🎟 *Donation requested.* 🕘 *Visitors are asked not to enter during services.*

Off Abbey Churchyard, where buskers (strolling musicians) of all kinds perform, are tiny alleys leading to little squares of stores, galleries, and eating places. Walk up Stall and Union streets toward Milsom Street, and you'll find numerous alleyways with fascinating small stores (☞ Shopping, *below*). Work your way east to Bridge Street and
44 one of the most famous landmarks of the city, **Pulteney Bridge,** an 18th-century span. Inspired by Florence's Ponte Vecchio, it is the only work of Robert Adam in the city and is unique in all Britain because it's lined
45 with shops. Head along Upper Borough Walls to find the **Theatre Royal,** on Saw Close, which opened in 1805 and was restored in 1982. Next door to the Theatre Royal, the former home of Richard "Beau" Nash—the dictator of fashion for mid-18th-century society in Bath—and his mistress Juliana Popjoy, is now a restaurant called Popjoy's (☞ Dining and Lodging, *below*).

North of Saw Close you can admire the Georgian houses along Queen
46 Square, Gay Street, and **The Circus,** where three perfectly proportioned
Georgian terraces outline the round garden in the center. A few steps
47 from the Circus stand the **Assembly Rooms,** a classical-style building
that figures in Jane Austen's novel *Persuasion.* Once a social center like
the Pump Room, it now houses the entertaining **Museum of Costume,**
displaying costumes from Beau Nash's day up to the present, in lavish settings. ⊠ *Bennett St.,* ☎ *01225/477000, ext. 2785.* 🎟 *£3.50.* ⏲ *Mon.–Sat. 10–5, Sun. 11–5.*

West of the Circus is the Royal Crescent, the crowning glory of architecture in Bath, and much used as a location for period films. A house
at the center is now Bath's most elegant hotel, the Royal Crescent (☞
Dining and Lodging, *below*). On the corner of Brock St. and the Royal
48 Crescent, **Number 1, Royal Crescent,** has been turned into a museum
and furnished as it might have been at the turn of the 19th century.
The museum crystallizes a view of the English class system: Upstairs all is gentility and elegance; downstairs is a fascinating kitchen museum. ☎ *01225/428126.* 🎟 *£3.50.* ⏲ *Mid-Feb..–Oct., Tues.–Sun. 10:30–5; Nov., Tues.–Sun. 10:30–4.*

49 Across the Avon, in an elegant 18th-century building, is the **Holburne Museum and Crafts Study Centre,** which houses a small but superb collection of 17th- and 18th-century fine and decorative arts. There are also some 20th-century crafts. ⊠ *Great Pulteney St.,* ☎ *01225/466669.* 🎟 *£3.50.* ⏲ *Easter–mid-Dec., Mon.–Sat. 11–5, Sun. 2:30–5:30; mid-Feb.–Easter, Tues.–Sat. 11–5, Sun. 2:30–5:30; closed mid-Dec.–mid-Feb.*

High above the city—2½ miles southeast on the Warminster road,
50 A36—is **Claverton Manor,** a Greek Revival (19th-century) mansion
housing the first museum of Americana to be established outside the United States. The fine parkland includes a replica of George Washington's garden. ⊠ *Claverton Down,* ☎ *01225/460503.* 🎟 *£5.* ⏲ *Easter–Oct., Tues.–Sun. 2–5, national holidays and preceding Sun. 11–5; closed Mon.*

Readers warn prospective travelers to Bath about parking regulations in the city. Except for notices posted on the outskirts of the city, restricted parking signs are few and far between in the city and cars—especially rental cars—seem to have been targeted for ticketing, according to readers' letters. If your car is towed away, hundreds of dollars in fees may have to be paid to retrieve it; To quote one reader, "Having 'taken a Bath' financially in that fair city, I must advise potential visitors to perhaps stay home instead—and duplicate the experience by taking a cold shower."

Dining and Lodging

££ ★ ✕ **Popjoy's Restaurant.** Named for the mistress of Beau Nash, the restaurant provides an elegant setting for a fine, English-style, after-theater dinner. Coffee and petits fours are served upstairs in a lovely Georgian drawing room. ⊠ *Beau Nash House, Sawclose,* ☎ *01225/460494. AE, MC, V. Closed Mon.*

££ ✕ **Rascals.** This is a good spot, close to the abbey, for a meal on a sightseeing day. In a network of small and snug cellar rooms, you can choose chef Nick Anderson's set menu or the daily specials. The dishes change regularly—try the sushi starter or the poached veal with lentils and capers—and then there's the chocolate truffle cake. There's a very good wine list. ⊠ *8 Pierrepont Pl.,* ☎ *01225/330201. MC, V. No lunch Sun.*

£ ✕ **Number Five.** Just over the Pulteney Bridge from the center of town, this airy bistro, with its plants, framed posters, and cane-backed chairs,

Abbey, **43**
Assembly Rooms, **47**
The Circus, **46**
Claverton Manor, **50**
Holburne Museum and Crafts Study Centre, **49**
Number 1, Royal Crescent, **48**
Pulteney Bridge, **44**
Pump Room, **42**
Theatre Royal, **45**

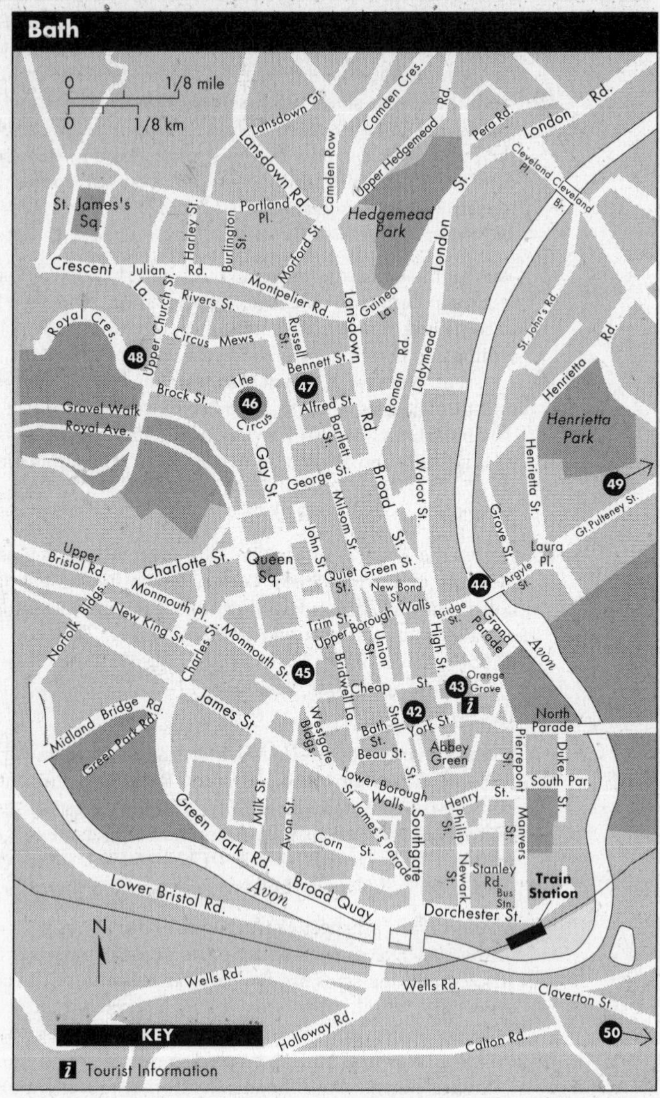

is an ideal spot for a light lunch. The regularly changing menu includes tasty homemade soups, and such dishes as seafood terrine. You can bring your own bottle of wine on Monday and Tuesday. ✉ *5 Argyle St.,* ☏ *01225/444499. AE, DC, MC, V. No lunch Mon. Closed Sun.*

££££ ★ **Royal Crescent Hotel.** This lavishly converted house, part of the Royal Crescent, is an architectural treasure. The decor has been carefully designed to preserve the building's period elegance, and if some of the bedrooms are on the small side, there are ample luxuries to compensate. The hotel's formal **Dower House** restaurant has won consistent praise, and a Palladian villa in the garden provides extra rooms. ✉ *16 Royal Crescent, BA1 2LS,* ☏ *01225/739955,* FAX *01225/339401. 46 rooms with bath, including 17 suites. Restaurant, parking. AE, DC, MC, V.*

£££ **Priory Hotel.** Out beyond the Royal Crescent, the Priory is an early 19th-century Gothic building, standing in attractive grounds. Guest rooms are spacious and comfortable, the public areas elegant with fine old furniture, and big windows look out on the 2 acres of gardens. Three dining rooms offer classic French cuisine. ✉ *Weston Rd., BA1 2XT,* ☎ *01225/331922,* FAX *01225/448276. 29 rooms with bath. Restaurant, indoor-outdoor pool, sauna, gym. AE, DC, MC, V.*

£££ ★ **Queensberry Hotel.** This intimate, elegant hotel, in a quiet residential street near the Circus, is in three 1772 town houses built by the architect John Wood for the Marquis of Queensberry. Renovations have preserved the Regency stucco ceilings and cornices and original marble tiling on the fireplaces. Each room is uniquely decorated in pastels and flower prints. Below stairs, the Olive Tree restaurant serves English and Mediterranean dishes. ✉ *Russell St., BA1 2QF,* ☎ *01225/447928,* FAX *01225/446065. 22 rooms with bath. Restaurant, bar. MC, V. Closed Dec. 24–30.*

££ **Paradise House.** Don't be put off by the 10-minute uphill walk from the center of Bath—you'll be rewarded by a wonderful prospect of the city from the upper stories of this Georgian guest house. Cheerfully decorated in cool green and white, it features open fires in winter and a lush, secluded garden for the spring and summer. ✉ *88 Holloway, BA2 4PX,* ☎ *01225/317723,* FAX *01225/482005. 9 rooms, 7 with bath or shower. AE, MC, V.*

£ **Cranleigh.** Standing on the hill high above the city, Cranleigh offers wonderful views over Bath from some of the back rooms. All the comfortable bedrooms have TVs, and one has a four-poster. Excellent breakfasts are served in the dining room, which looks out on the garden, but there are no evening meals. Smoking is not permitted. ✉ *159 Newbridge Hill, BA1 3PX,* ☎ *01225/310197,* FAX *01225/423143. 5 rooms with bath or shower. MC, V.*

The Arts

FESTIVALS

The **Bath International Festival** is 47 years old in 1996 (two weeks in May/June). Concerts, dance, and exhibitions will be held in and around Bath. Some take place in the Assembly Rooms and the Abbey, and opening night festivities are held in Royal Victoria Park, near the Royal Crescent. ✉ *Bath Festival Office, Linley House, 1 Pierrepont Pl., Bath BA1 1JY,* ☎ *01225/462231.*

THEATER

The **Theatre Royal** in Bath, a superb example of a Regency playhouse, restored in 1982, has a year-round program that often includes pre- or post-London tours. You have to reserve the best seats well in advance, but you can line up for same-day standby seats or standing room. Check the location of your seats—sightlines can be poor. ✉ *Box Office, Sawclose, Bath BA1 1ET,* ☎ *01225/448844.*

Shopping

Bath's excellent shopping district centers on Stall and Union streets (modern stores) and Milsom Street (traditional stores). Leading off these main streets are fascinating alleyways and passages lined with galleries and a wealth of antiques shops. The **Bath Antiques Market** (✉ Guinea La., ⏲ Wed. 6:30 AM–2:30 PM) is a wonderful place to browse; ninety dealers have stalls here, and there's also a restaurant. **Great Western Antique Centre** (✉ Bartlett St.) delights antiques lovers with more than 100 stalls selling every kind of antique imaginable, including clothing, linens, and furniture. **Beaux Arts Ceramics** (✉ York St., ☎ 01225/464850) carries the work of prominent potters, and holds eight solo exhibitions a year. **Margaret's Buildings** (✉ Halfway between the Circus and Royal Crescent) is a lane with several secondhand and antiquarian bookshops.

Castle Combe

51 *10 mi northeast of Bath, 5 mi northwest of Chippenham.*

This Wiltshire village had lived a sleepy existence until one Sunday morning in 1962 when its villagers woke up to find that national newspapers carried photographs of the hamlet on front pages: Castle Combe had been voted the Prettiest Village in England—without any of its inhabitants knowing that it had even been a contender. By lunchtime, the locals remember, the main narrow street had become an enormous traffic jam. The village's magic is that it is so toy-like, so delightfully all-of-a-piece: You can almost see the whole town at one glance from any one position. It consists of little more than a brook, a pack bridge, a street—which is called The Street—of simple stone cottages, a market cross from the 13th-century, and the Perpendicular-style church of St. Andrew. For centuries, the town was occupied by weavers and legend has it that the Blanket brothers, susceptible to the rising damp from the Bybrook, had their workmen weave a new cover for their bed, which they named—the blanket. The most famous house in the village is the Upper Manor House, built in the 15th century by Sir John Fastolf and chosen to be Dr. Doolittle's house in the 1967 Rex Harrison film. Most visitors will have to admit that Castle Coombe makes a perfect stand-in for Puddleby-on-the-Marsh.

Dining and Lodging

£££–££££ ✕🏨 **Castle Combe Manor House.** This lodging is partly 14th-century, though as a manor it dates back to the Normans. Just 10 miles northeast of Bath, it stands in a large park, which is ideal for exploring, and on the edge of a pretty village. The bedrooms are very comfortably furnished, with lavish bathrooms attached; some are in separate cottages. There are log fires in the public rooms and antiques everywhere. The restaurant serves imaginative cuisine—try the fish casserole with water chestnuts, or the French-inspired soufflé specialties. ✉ *Castle Combe SN14 7HR,* ☎ *01249/782206,* FAX *01249/782159. 36 rooms with bath. Restaurant (jacket and tie), pool, tennis, helipad. AE, DC, MC, V.*

Numbers in the margin correspond to points of interest on the Forest of Dean and Bath Environs map.

Bristol

52 *13 mi northwest of Bath, 46 mi south of Birmingham, 120 mi west of London.*

Bristol, which has been a major city since medieval times, was in the 17th and 18th centuries an important port for the North American trade. Now that the city's industries no longer rely on the docks, the historic harbor along the Avon River has been largely given over to pleasure craft. The quayside offers an arts center, movie theaters, museums, stores, pubs, and restaurants; carnivals, speedboat races, and regattas are held regularly.

On view in the harbor is the **S.S. *Great Britain,*** the first iron ship to cross the Atlantic. Built by the great English engineer Isambard Kingdom Brunel in 1843, it remained in service until the end of the century, first on the North American route and then on the Australian. ✉ *Great Western Dock, off Cumberland Rd.,* ☎ *0117/926–0680.* 🎫 *£3.70.* ⏲ *Apr.–Sept., daily 10–5:30; Oct.–Mar., 10–4:30; closed Dec. 24–25.*

NEED A BREAK? The **Watershed Media Centre** (✉ St. Augustine's Reach) holds a pleasant café and snack bar overlooking the Floating Harbour.

Bristol is the home of the **Church of St. Mary Redcliffe,** called "the fairest in England" by Queen Elizabeth I. It features rib-vaulting and dates from the 1300s, built by Bristol merchants who wanted a place in which to pray for the safe (and profitable) voyages of their ships. ✉ *Redcliffe Way, a 5-min walk from Temple Meads train station toward the docks.*

Among the Dissenters from the Church of England who found a home in Bristol was John Wesley, who built the first Methodist church here in 1739, the **New Room.** Its austerity contrasts sharply with the Anglican churches. ✉ *Broadmead,* ☎ *0117/926–4740.* 🎫 *£2.* ⏲ *Mon.–Sat. 10–1 and 2–4; closed Wed. in winter and national holidays.*

In the Georgian suburb of Clifton—a sort of Bath in miniature—take in that monument to Victorian engineering, the Clifton Suspension Bridge, built in 1828 by Brunel. Crossing the Avon Gorge, you will reach the **Bristol Zoo,** where more than 1,000 species of animals live on 12 acres of landscaped gardens. ✉ *Clifton,* ☎ *0117/973–8951.* 🎫 *£4.20.* ⏲ *Apr.–Sept., daily 9–5:30; Oct.–Mar., daily 9–5; closed Dec. 25.*

Dining and Lodging

££ ✕ **Bell's Diner.** Though it's a Bristol institution, this bistro is rather hidden—take the A38 (Stokes Croft) north, then turn right into Picton Street, which will lead you to York Road. Bell's is in a converted corner shop, with Bristol prints on its pale gray walls, polished wooden floors, and open fires. The inventive menu changes regularly, with light dishes and toothsome desserts. ✉ *1 York Rd., Montpelier,* ☎ *0117/924–0357. MC, V. No lunch Sat. Closed Sun. (except for lunch Oct.–Apr.), Mon., and 1st wk in Sept.*

££ ✕ **Markwicks.** This restaurant, in busy downtown Bristol, is in a basement that was once a safety deposit. Black-and-white marble floors and iron grille doors retain the vault-like atmosphere, but the food is excellent. Try the fish soup, or the local turbot and sea bass. The daily changing set menus are good value. ✉ *43 Corn St.,* ☎ *0117/926–2658. AE, MC, V. No lunch Sat. Closed Sun. and 2 wks in Aug.*

££ ✕ **Michael's.** Informal elegance is the predominant tone in this restaurant across Bristol's Floating Harbour from the S.S. *Great Britain.* Apéritifs and post-dinner drinks are taken in a comfortable lounge area, where a log fire provides the centerpiece; while next door, meals are served by an attentive and friendly staff. The imaginative dishes are the creations of proprietor Michael MacGowan and might include pigeon breasts in a Madeira jus with red currants, or vegetable strudel with blue cheese sauce. The desserts are a high point. ✉ *129 Hotwell Road, BS8 4RU,* ☎ *0117/927–6190. MC, V. No lunch Mon.–Sat., no dinner Sun. Closed 1 wk in Aug.*

£££–££££ 🏨 **Bristol Marriott.** If you'd like the amenities of an international chain hotel, try the Bristol Marriott near the city center, where its front rooms overlook Castle Park. A Continental and traditional English menu is offered in Le Chateau restaurant, and there's also a less formal brasserie. ✉ *Lower Castle St., Old Market, BS1 3AD,* ☎ *0117/929–4281,* FAX *0117/922–5838. 289 rooms with bath. 2 restaurants, bar, pool, health club. AE, DC, MC, V.*

£££ 🏨 **Redwood Lodge Hotel.** This is a handy stopover for anyone touring by car—it's just off A4 close to the Clifton Suspension Bridge. Modern and attractively furnished, it has a number of amenities, including 16 acres of pleasant woodland surroundings. ✉ *Beggar Bush La., Failand, BS8 3TG,* ☎ *01275/393901,* FAX *01275/392104. 108 rooms with bath. Restaurant, coffee shop, indoor-outdoor pool, tennis court, exercise room, squash. AE, DC, MC, V.*

Outdoor Activities and Sports

SHOW JUMPING

The Badminton Horse Trials are held annually in May at the duke of Beaufort's magnificent estate in **Badminton,** 12 miles northeast of Bristol (☎ 01454/218272).

En Route The area south of Bristol is notable for its scenery and walks, its photogenic villages, and the ancient stone circles. Take A38 (follow signs for airport), then B3130 and B3114 to the villages of Chew Magna and Chew Stoke and on to Chew Valley Lake, a reservoir in a drowned valley surrounded by woods, which shelters 240 species of birds. At Chew Magna note the gargoyles on the ancient church.

Stanton Drew

53 *6 mi south of Bristol, 10 mi west of Bath.*

Just east of the village of Stanton Drew, are the neolithic **Stanton Drew Circles,** where three rings, two avenues of standing stones, and a burial chamber make up one of the grandest and most mysterious monuments in the country. The site lies in a field reached through a farmyard—you'll need suitable shoes to visit it. The stones stand on private land, but are supervised by English Heritage. To get here from Chew Magna, turn east on B3130. *Small fee. Any reasonable time (not Sun.).*

HEART OF ENGLAND A TO Z

Getting Around

By Bus

National Express (☎ 0990/808080) serves the region from London's Victoria Coach Station. **Flights Coach Travel Ltd. of Birmingham** (☎ 0121/322–2222) operates "Flightlink" services from London's Heathrow and Gatwick airports to Coventry and Warwick. **Midland Red (South) Ltd.** and **Stratford Blue** (☎ 01788/535555) serve the Stratford-upon-Avon, Birmingham, and Coventry areas. Various private companies serve Gloucestershire and the Cotswolds region. Call 01452/425543 for specific information.

By Car

M4 is the principal route west from London to Gloucestershire and Avon. From exit 18, take A46 south to Bath. From exit 20, take M5 north to Gloucester (25 mi), Cheltenham, and Tewkesbury; and from exit 15 take A419 to A429 north to the Cotswolds. From London take M40 for Stratford-upon-Avon (97 mi).

By Train

British Rail serves the western part of the region from London's Paddington Station (☎ 0171/262–6767). Travel time from London's Euston Station (☎ 0171/387–7070) to Bath, 90 minutes; to Stratford-upon-Avon, 2¼ hours (with bus connections from Leamington Spa or Warwick on winter Sundays, when the Stratford station is closed). A seven-day "Heart of England Rover" ticket is valid for unlimited travel within the region.

Guided Tours

The Heart of England Tourist Board (☎ 01905/763436) and the **West Country Tourist Board** (☎ 01392/425426) can arrange a variety of tours. **Gloucester Civic Trust** organizes tours of the city and docks by appointment. Contact Gloucester's tourist office for details (☎ 01452/421188). **Guide Friday** (☎ 01789/294466 in Stratford or 01225/464446 in Bath) runs guided tours of Stratford and Bath in open-top single- and double-decker buses (Stratford £7; Bath £6).

Contacts and Resources

Car-Rental Agencies

Bath: Avis, ✉ Unit 4B, Bath Riverside Business Park, Riverside Rd., ☎ 01225/446680. **Cheltenham: Budget Rent-a-Car,** ✉ Haines & Strange Ltd., 53 Albion St., ☎ 01242/235222; **Hertz,** ✉ Pike House Service Station, Tewkesbury Rd., ☎ 01242/242547. **Gloucester: Avis,** ✉ Cotswold Service Station, 122 London Rd., ☎ 01452/380356. **Stratford-upon-Avon: Hertz,** ✉ Rail Station, ☎ 01789/298827.

Hiking and Walking

For information on hiking in the Forest of Dean, contact the **Forestry Commission** (✉ 231 Corstophine Rd., Edinburgh EH12 7AT, ☎ 0131/334–0303).

Travel Agencies

American Express, ✉ 5 Bridge St., Bath, ☎ 01225/444747. **Thomas Cook,** ✉ 20 New Bond St., Bath, ☎ 01225/463191; ✉ 24 Upper Precinct, Coventry, ☎ 01203/229233; ✉ 24 Eastgate St., Gloucester, ☎ 01452/529511.

Visitor Information

The Heart of England Tourist Board: ✉ Woodside, Larkhill, Worcester WR5 2EF, ☎ 01905/425426, FAX 01905/763450, ⏲ Mon.–Thurs. 9–5:30, Fri. 9–5. **The West Country Tourist Board:** ✉ 60 St. David's Hill, Exeter, Devon EX4 4SY, ☎ 01392/76351, FAX 01392/420891; information on Bath/Avon.

Local tourist information centers are normally open Monday–Saturday 9:30–5:30, but times vary according to season.

Bath: ✉ Abbey Chambers, Abbey Church Yard, ☎ 01225/462831. **Bristol:** ✉ St. Nicholas Church, St. Nicholas St., ☎ 0117/926–0767. **Cheltenham:** ✉ 77 Promenade, ☎ 01242/522878. **Gloucester:** ✉ St. Michael's Tower, The Cross, ☎ 01452/421188. **Stow-on-the-Wold:** ✉ Hollis House, The Square, ☎ 01451/831082. **Stratford-upon-Avon:** ✉ Bridgefoot, ☎ 01789/293127.

9 The Welsh Borders

Birmingham, Worcester, Hereford, Shrewsbury, Chester

Along England's border with the principality of Wales lies some of England's loveliest and most peaceful countryside. Herefordshire, in the south, has rich, rolling landscape and river valleys, gradually opening out to Shropshire's high hills and plateaus. In the north, the gentler Cheshire plain is dairy country, dotted with small villages and market towns, full of 13th- and 14th-century black-and-white, half-timber buildings typical of northwestern England. A string of medieval castles in this region bears witness to the sometimes strained relationship that once existed between England and Wales.

Updated by Robert Andrews

ENGLAND'S BORDER with the principality of Wales stretches from the town of Chepstow on the Severn estuary in the south to the city of Chester in the north. Along this border, in the counties of Herefordshire, Shropshire, and southern Cheshire, lies some of England's loveliest countryside, remote and tranquil. But today's rural peace belies a turbulent past. Relations between the English and the Welsh have seldom been easy, and from the earliest times the English have felt it necessary to keep the "troublesome" Welsh firmly on the other side of the border. A string of medieval castles bears witness to this history. Many are romantic ruins; some are dark and brooding fortresses. Built to control the countryside and repel invaders, they still radiate a sense of mystery and menace.

For the last 500 years or so, the people of this border country have enjoyed more peaceful lives, with little to disturb the traditional patterns of country life. In the 18th century, however, one small corner of Shropshire heralded the birth of the Industrial Revolution, for here, in a wooded stretch of the Severn Gorge, the first coke blast furnace was invented and the first iron bridge was erected (1774).

The ramifications of that technological leap forward led to the growth of Britain's second-largest city, Birmingham, the capital of the Midlands. While Birmingham continues to rise above its reputation as one of the ugliest cities in Britain, its active artistic life is drawing people who have now begun to appreciate its historic civic architecture, some of the most fascinating to be found anywhere.

Herefordshire, in the south, is a county of rich, rolling countryside and river valleys, gradually opening out in the high hills and plateaus of Shropshire. North of the Shropshire hills, the gentler Cheshire plain stretches toward the great industrial cities of Liverpool and Manchester (☞ Chapter 11). This is dairy country, dotted with small villages and market towns, many rich in the 13th- and 14th-century black-and-white, half-timber buildings so typical of northwestern England. These are the legacy of a forested countryside, where wood was easier to come by than stone. In the market towns of Chester and Shrewsbury, the more elaborately decorated half-timber buildings are monuments to wealth, dating mostly from the early Jacobean period at the beginning of the 17th century.

Pleasures and Pastimes

Dining

Formal restaurants are few and far between in this rural area, and those that exist are mostly small. Many concentrate on English country fare and use local produce whenever possible.

CATEGORY	COST*
££££	over £50
£££	£30–£50
££	£20–£30
£	under £20

**per person, including first course, main course, dessert, and VAT; excluding drinks*

Lodging

You won't find many large, international-style hotels in the Welsh borders. Our selection aims to present a mix of larger hotels, often with considerable local historical significance, and smaller, family-owned establishments that form the bulk of the accommodations available. The latter are homier, friendlier, and invariably cheaper. In Birmingham, all the best moderately priced lodging is well out of the city center, but there are fairly good suburban bus and train services.

CATEGORY	COST*
££££	over £150
£££	£80–£150
££	£60–£80
£	under £60

**All prices are for two people sharing a double room, including service, breakfast, and VAT.*

Walking

The Malvern Hills make for climbs and walks of varying length and difficulty. The best places to start are Great Malvern and Ledbury. The route designated the "Elgar Way" extends for 45 miles, but you don't need to do the whole thing. Views across the countryside from the top of the hills are spectacular—the isolated hills rise up from the fairly flat plain rather like Ayers Rock does in Australia, providing vistas for many miles around. The area around Ross-on-Wye offers ideal walks with scenic river views.

One of Britain's major long-distance hikes lies mostly within this area: the Offa's Dyke Path, named after the earthwork built by an 8th-century king to mark the boundary with Wales. The whole route is 168 miles, but only about 60 miles is along the actual dike. The Offa's Dyke Association promotes the conservation and understanding of the Welsh border region, including the Dyke itself; it publishes guides, along with other materials. This is an area of lush woods and swift rivers, with hidden villages and spectacular views; you'll find it very rewarding walking country. Lodging and dining are easily found. Local TICs and bookstores have details, books, and maps.

Exploring the Welsh Borders

The main gateway to the region is bustling Birmingham, now one of the best places in England for the performing arts and rapidly redeeming itself from its reputation as a badly built city. Using this as a starting point, we move on to the city of Worcester, renowned for its proud cathedral and fine bone china. From there we work our way south and west, along the lovely Malvern Hills, taking in the peaceful spa town of Great Malvern and others before stopping in the prosperous agricultural city of Hereford. Then we head north to Bewdley, terminus of the Severn Valley Railway, and continue into the West Midlands—birthplace of modern British industry.

The second excursion begins in the handsome medieval city of Shrewsbury, moves on to the wooded banks of the river Severn to visit the cluster of Ironbridge museums, explores Ludlow, an architectural jewel of a town, and takes in an extra leg with a trip northward to the ancient city of Chester.

Great Itineraries

Although it is the main towns of the Welsh Borders region—Worcester, Hereford, Shrewsbury, and Chester—that distill the essence of the surrounding countryside, there lies much in between that should not be neglected. It would be easy to base yourself in one of these towns and launch expeditions from there, but you would do well to lodge in some of the smaller centers or the remoter country inns to absorb the full flavor of the borderlands. There are some tracts of fast road connecting the main towns, but generally don't count on speeding through

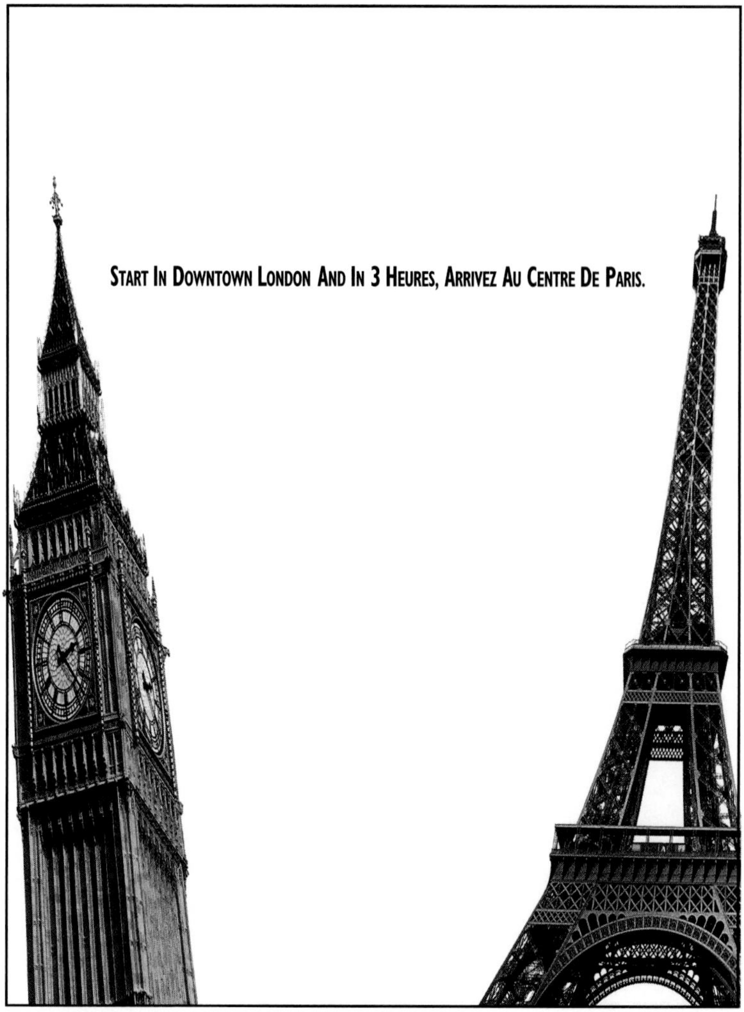

Start In Downtown London And In 3 Heures, Arrivez Au Centre De Paris.

Rail Europe

Imagine traveling directly between London and Paris with no connections to run for, no busses to board, no taxis to hail. In fact, the only thing you have to change is the tongue you speak upon arrival.

That's exactly what you'll experience aboard the high-speed Eurostar passenger train.

Board the Eurostar at the center of one city, travel through the new Channel Tunnel, and arrive directly in the center of the other. Simple as that. And at speeds of up to 200 miles per hour, the entire trip lasts just three short hours. We can also get you between London and Brussels in three and a quarter.

For more information, contact your travel agent or Rail Europe at 1-800-EUROSTAR.

If a quick, comfortable trip between London and Paris is on your itinerary, you'll find we speak your language perfectly.

EUROSTAR. DIRECT. **CALL 1-800-EUROSTAR**

Eurostar is a service provided together by the railways of Belgium, Britain and France

We think about your holiday as much as you do.

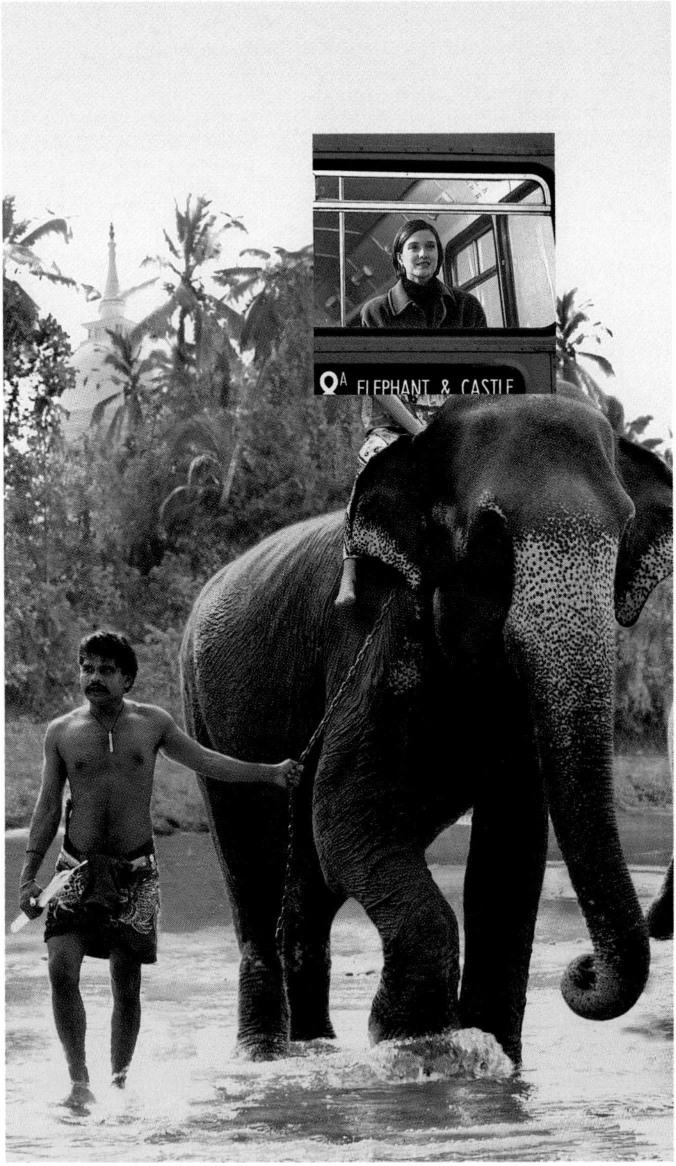

The moment you choose a British Airways Holiday, you can start anticipating a well-deserved break. Our expertise and experience mean we can offer you the best value in the widest range of worldwide destinations. For more information and a free brochure, call your travel agent or 1-800-AIRWAYS.

the area. Leaving aside the necessary delays that the minor roads entail, there is every reason to dawdle in some of the more enticing backwaters with which the Borders are richly furnished: The area is not unduly frequented by tourists, and you will be sorely tempted to probe at leisure. In particular, there are plenty of bracing walks that can be enjoyed, and travelers should take every opportunity to roam the hilly hinterland. With less time, you will have to make some difficult choices. Seven days will give you the luxury of a pretty thorough acquaintance with the region, but you can still count on taking home some warm memories from much briefer incursions.

Numbers in the text correspond to numbers in the margin and on the maps.

IF YOU HAVE 3 DAYS

The city of **Worcester** ⑪ makes a convenient entry to the Welsh Borders. Spend your first night here, making sure you see the aged and majestic cathedral and the Commandery, the country's only museum devoted exclusively to the 17th-century tussle between Cavaliers and Roundheads. Take a whirl round the famous Royal Worcester Porcelain Factory, where you can pick up some authentic souvenirs after admiring the rare porcelain in the attached museum. On your second day, take the A443 northwest, making a stop at **Great Witley** ㉒ for the evocative ruins of Witley Court, a good place for a picnic; alternatively opt for a pub meal in the nearby village. Keep on the same road as far as **Ludlow** ㊶, stopping long enough to view its magnificent castle as well as the crowd of listed Tudor, Jacobean, and Georgian buildings that give the small town its unique aspect. On your final stretch, head for **Hereford** ㉑, to the south, boasting another stout cathedral—Norman this time—and numerous reminders of the city's importance as a market town for the surrounding area. You can see most of the interesting sites here in a morning, leaving the afternoon free to explore **Ross-on-Wye** ⑰ and the nearby attractions of **Goodrich** ⑱, dramatically poised over the river Wye, and the famous beauty-spot of **Symond's Yat** ⑲.

IF YOU HAVE 7 DAYS

Devote at least a day to **Birmingham** ①, in particular rooting out the Barber Institute of Fine Arts, beloved by cognoscenti everywhere. After an overnight stay, head south to Worcester and the Malverns, dropping in on your way at **Hellen's** ⑯, a manor house dating from the 13th century. You could take a lunch-break at the generously timbered village of **Ledbury** ⑭, before continuing on toward the Wye Valley, where the nearby ruins of the castle at **Goodrich** ⑱ and **Symond's Yat** ⑲ provide good excuses to stop traveling for a while and stretch your legs. A night in **Hereford** ㉑ will allow you to absorb the flavor of this old market town, before heading up to Ludlow for a couple of hours' ramble around the castle and its surrounding streets. A few miles north of here, you could once more abandon your car for a hike on Wenlock Edge, with its inspiring views. A little farther on is the village of **Much Wenlock** ㊵, where Wenlock Priory is a must-see. Spend the next two nights in **Worcester** ⑪, taking in the Malverns and, to the north, the quiet riverside town of **Bewdley** ㉓, with its fine array of Georgian architecture. From here you could take a trip on the Severn Valley Railway, whose old-style steam train affords marvelous opportunities to stroll around the banks of the Severn from the remote stations on the route. One of the larger stops is **Bridgnorth** ㊴, occupying a sandstone ridge high above the Severn, and within a short distance of the **Ironbridge Gorge Museum** ㊳, a fascinating collection of sites that formed the crucible of the Industrial Revolution—probably the best industrial heritage site in the country. You could stay here, or

The Welsh Borders

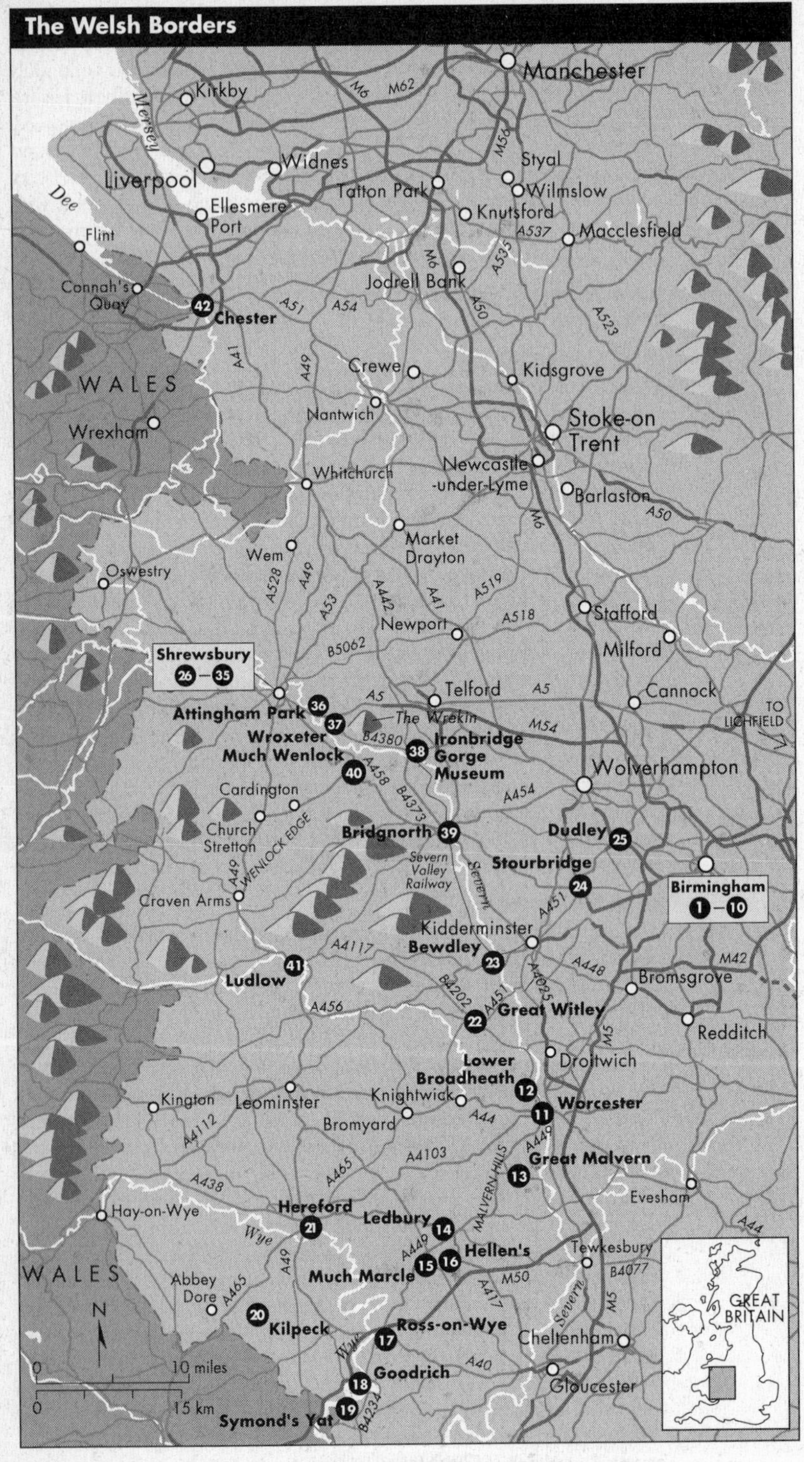

else visit it on a day's excursion from **Shrewsbury** ㉖. Other sights outside this historic town are **Wroxeter** ㊲—the old Roman garrison-town of Viroconium—and **Attingham Park** ㊱, a mansion dating from 1785 with a deer park designed by Humphrey Repton. Your last overnight—entailing a sizeable journey northward, however—could be spent in **Chester** ㊷, famous for its black-and-white "magpie" buildings and worthy of a full day's sightseeing along and within its famous city walls.

When to Tour the Welsh Borders

Most of the rural sights have limited opening hours in winter, so travelers at this time of year should set off early to make the most of daylight hours. Even in the towns, the majority of the attractions close at 5, which leaves several hours of dark and often chilly winter evenings to fill. Photographers, in particular, will want to be on the road early to catch the best light. In the winter's favor are the creeping mists shrouding the valleys, and the warm hearths to toast your toes next to in inns and hotels. Otherwise, try to be here in the warmer weather between April and September. Culture vultures will want to catch the official and fringe festivals at Malvern at the end of May, the open-air performances at Ludlow Castle at the end of June, and the Shrewsbury Festival in June and July, while the Three Choirs Festival, rotating between Hereford, Gloucester, and Worcester, takes place in mid-August, for which you need to book as early as you can to guarantee the best seats.

Numbers in the margin correspond to points of interest on the Welsh Borders map.

FROM BIRMINGHAM TO SHREWSBURY

Birmingham

❶ *25 mi north from Stratford, 120 mi northwest of London.*

England's second-largest city was grossly disfigured by injudicious planning and building in the post–World War II period. The center of Britain's "second city" had undergone so many structural alterations that, as an official guide book once put it, "there is more of the future to be seen coming into being than there is of the past left to contemplate." Indeed, Birmingham was well on the way to becoming a monument to the late 20th century. Whether you agreed that it was a *fitting* monument depended on your feelings toward the 20th century. Mercifully, the city fathers have adopted a new policy in the last few years of humanizing the areas and buildings which their immediate predecessors did so much to ruin.

The city first flourished in the boom years of the 19th century's Industrial Revolution. Birmingham's inventive, hard-working citizens accumulated great wealth, and at one time the city had some of the finest Victorian buildings in the country. But 20th-century civic "planning" managed to destroy many of them. There are still architectural treasures to be found, but it means a dedicated search, carefully negotiating the city's impossible road network. While most communities manage to keep their manic motorways on the edge of town, Birmingham's inner ring road twists right through the city center. But this is all changing: City planners are making Birmingham pedestrian-friendly by replacing the ring road with a network of local access roads and by turning the downtown shopping area into pedestrian arcades and buses-only streets.

Birmingham, believe it or not, has more canals than Venice. It is at the center of a system of restored waterways built during the Industrial Revolution to connect inland factories to rivers and seaports—by 1840 the canals extended more than 4,000 miles throughout the British Isles. Contact the Convention and Visitors Bureau for maps of walks along the towpaths and for details on canal barge cruises.

Numbers in the margin correspond to points of interest on the Birmingham map.

2 Start your visit in the heart of the city at the **International Convention Centre,** which was opened in June 1991 by the queen. Inside there is a good tourist desk to help you with further information. The main atrium of this high-tech building is dominated by a network of blue struts and gleaming air ducts, somewhat softened by banks of indoor plants. ✉ *Broad St.*

★ 3 Connected to the Convention Centre is the **Symphony Hall**—a significant addition to English musical life. This auditorium has been hailed as an acoustical triumph: Hearing a concert in it is a good reason to visit Birmingham. The internationally recognized City of Birmingham Symphony Orchestra, which has won awards for its recordings under its former young conductor Simon Rattle, has found a very welcome home here (☞ The Arts, *below*). ✉ *Broad St.*

4 Once outside the Convention Centre, you are in **Centenary Square,** a sort of miniature complex for the performing arts. It is paved with a pattern of bricks of various shades, like a Persian carpet, designed by
5 artist Tess Jaray. To one side of Centenary Square stands the **Birmingham Repertory Theatre,** which houses one of England's oldest and most esteemed theater companies (☞ The Arts, *below*).

NEED A BREAK? The **Birmingham Rep.** (✉ Centenary Sq.)—as it's always called—has an excellent cafeteria/restaurant in its foyer, behind sweeping windows that allow for a great view over the square.

6 Across the square from the Convention Centre you will find the **Hall of Memory,** an octagonal war memorial built in the 1920s in remembrance of those who fell during World War I. Inside, there is a book containing their names: The pages are turned regularly. ✉ *Centenary Sq.* 🎫 *Free.* ⏲ *Mon.–Sat. 10–4.*

7 Prince Charles said the **Central Library** "looks like a place where books are incinerated." It used to be bare, brutal concrete, but now sports boxes of flowers and plants in an attempt to soften its facade. In the Shakespeare Memorial Room, on the sixth floor of the library, there are about 50,000 books in the Shakespeare collection and thousands of illustrations. ✉ *Chamberlain Sq.* ⏲ *Library weekdays 9–8, Sat. 9–5.*

8 Across Chamberlain Square from the library is the **City Museum and Art Gallery,** a huge place containing a magnificent collection of Victorian art, featuring works by the Pre-Raphaelites. All the big names are here—Ford Madox Brown, Holman Hunt, Edward Burne-Jones (who was born in Birmingham), Dante Gabriel Rossetti, and many more. One room houses the Arthurian *Holy Grail* tapestries, designed by Burne-Jones and executed by the William Morris Arts Workers' Guild. The collection reflects the enormous wealth of 19th-century Birmingham and the taste of its industrialists. ✉ *Chamberlain Sq.,* ☎ *0121/235–2834.* 🎫 *Free.* ⏲ *Mon.–Sat. 10–5, Sun. 12:30–5:30.*

9 Near the City Museum and Art Gallery is the **Town Hall,** surrounded by classical columns. It is a copy of the Temple of Castor and Pollux

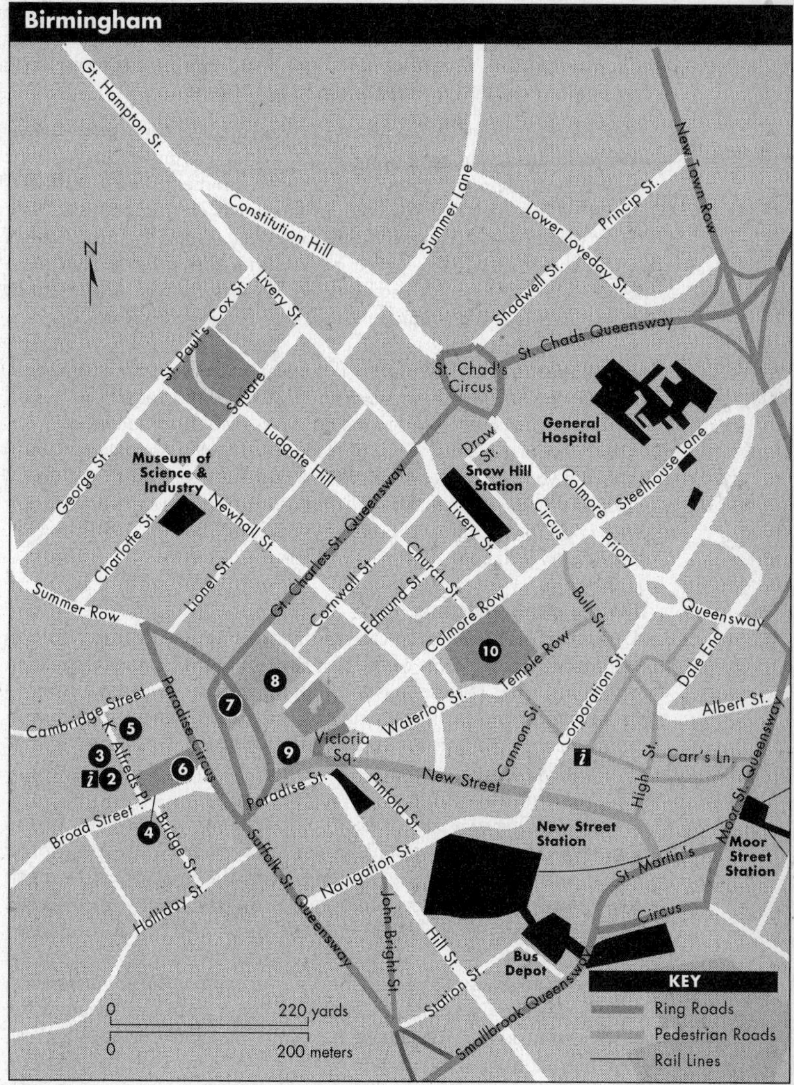

Birmingham Cathedral (St. Philip's), **10**

Birmingham Repertory Theatre, **5**

Centenary Square, **4**

Central Library, **7**

City Museum and Art Gallery, **8**

Hall of Memory, **6**

International Convention Centre, **2**

Symphony Hall, **3**

Town Hall, **9**

in Rome and took two decades to build. It used to be the home of the symphony orchestra—it heard the first performances of Mendelssohn's *Elijah* and Elgar's *Dream of Gerontius*—and now is host to concerts and exhibitions. ✉ *Victoria Sq.,* ☎ *0121/235–3942.*

10 A few blocks from newly renovated Victoria Square is **Birmingham Cathedral** (St. Philip's). The early 18th-century building is undergoing a major restoration and preservation program at the moment, so it is shrouded in scaffolding. The gilded Georgian interior is elegant and has some lovely plasterwork. You will immediately be struck by the windows behind the altar, which seem to glow with a garnet light. They were designed by Burne-Jones and made by William Morris. At the end of the south aisle is a vivid modern tapestry. ✉ *Colmore Row.*

OFF THE BEATEN PATH

BARBER INSTITUTE OF FINE ARTS – This jewel-like collection, belonging to University of Birmingham, is looked on by art lovers as paradise. There's a small but choice selection, including works by Bellini, Canaletto, Guardi, Poussin, Murillo, Gainsborough, Turner, Whistler, Renoir, Gauguin, and van Gogh. ✉ *Off Edgbaston Park Rd. near East Gate (take Cross City Line train from New St. Station south to University Station, or Bus 61, 62, or 63 from city center),* ☎ *0121/472–0962.* 🎫 *Free.* ⏲ *Mon.–Sat. 10–5, Sun. 2–5.*

Dining and Lodging

££–£££ ★ ✕ **Sloans.** This restaurant in the southeast shopping district comes as a pleasant surprise (most of the best things in Birmingham are hidden in the outskirts). The menu is fairly large, with an interesting range—try the veal and mushrooms with a leek and truffle sauce, or lamb with soubise sauce, and finish with a mouth-watering lime soufflé. ✉ *27–29 Chad Sq., Hawthorne Rd.,* ☎ *0121/455–6697. AE, DC, MC, V. No lunch Sat. Closed Sun.*

££ ✕ **Henry's.** One of a pair of Cantonese restaurants, this is located in the jewelry district, so it is a haven for lunch during a shopping spree. The other one, Henry Wong, is 2 miles from the city center. The menu offers more than 100 dishes, and vegetarians have plenty of choice. ✉ *27 St. Paul's Sq.,* ☎ *0121/200–1136. AE, DC, MC, V. Closed Sun.*

££££ ✕🏨 **Hyatt Regency.** The Hyatt Regency occupies a sheer glass tower, right beside the Convention Centre, adding a futuristic touch to the Birmingham skyline. The inside is as smooth as the outside—a glass-roof, marble-floor atrium is filled with the obligatory plants and trees; floor-to-ceiling windows in the luxury bedrooms give stunning views over the city. The restaurant serves up excellent seafood selections. ✉ *2 Bridge St., B1 2JZ,* ☎ *0121/643–1234,* FAX *0121/616–2323. 319 rooms. Restaurant, exercise room. AE, DC, MC, V.*

£££ ★ ✕🏨 **New Hall.** A lush tree-lined drive leads through 26 acres of gardens and open land to this moated 12th-century manor house–turned–country hotel. The guest rooms, decorated in English country style with marble-tile baths, all have expansive views overlooking the grounds. The public rooms feature 16th-century oak-panel walls and Flemish glass, 18th-century chandeliers, and a stone fireplace from the 17th century. The formal restaurant is an elegant setting in which to indulge in chef Valentine Rodriguez's award-winning cuisine. ✉ *Walmley Rd., Sutton Coldfield, Birmingham B76 1QX,* ☎ *0121/378–2442,* FAX *0121/378–4637. 60 rooms with bath. Restaurant (reservations essential, jacket and tie), 9-hole golf course, tennis court, croquet, meeting rooms. AE, MC, V.*

£££ ✕🏨 **Swallow Hotel.** Once a group of offices, this very elegant turn-of-the-century building is now a luxuriously renovated hotel. The building has an interior rich with dark wood and chandeliers; the spacious bedrooms offer air-conditioning and all the latest comforts. The Sir Edward Elgar formal restaurant (reservations essential, jacket and tie) has a fixed-price menu that changes daily, and Langtry's Restaurant (££) serves traditional British dishes in a more casual surrounding. ✉ *12 Hagley Rd., Five Ways, B16 8SJ,* ☎ *0121/452–1144,* FAX *0121/456–3442. 98 rooms with bath. 2 restaurants, indoor pool, health club. AE, DC, MC, V.*

£ ✕▣ **Copperfield House Hotel.** In a quiet location with secluded lawns, this Victorian family-run hotel is nevertheless convenient for the hustle and bustle of the center. The restaurant serves good English cooking, including delicious homemade puddings, and you can eat outside in summer. ✉ *60 Upland Rd., Selly Park, Birmingham, B29 7JS,* ☎ *0121/472–8344,* FAX *0121/415–5655. 17 rooms with bath. Restaurant. AE, MC, V.*

The Arts

BALLET

The second company of the Royal Ballet, which used to be based at Sadler's Wells in London, has become the **Birmingham Royal Ballet.** It is based at the Hippodrome Theatre, which also hosts visiting companies like the Welsh National Opera. ✉ *Hurst St.,* ☎ *0121/622–7468.*

CONCERTS

The **City of Birmingham Symphony Orchestra** performs regularly in Symphony Hall, also the venue for visiting artists. ✉ *International Convention Centre,* ☎ *0121/212–3333.*

THEATER

The **Birmingham Repertory Theatre** (✉ Centenary Sq., Broad St., ☎ 0121/236–4455), founded in 1913, is equally at home in modern or classical work. There is a restaurant on the ground floor. The Alexandra Theatre in Birmingham welcomes touring companies on their way to or from London's West End. It is also home to the **D'Oyly Carte Opera Company** (✉ Station St., ☎ 0121/643–3168), world-renowned for Gilbert and Sullivan operas.

Shopping

Ten minutes' walk northward from the city center is the **Jewelery Quarter,** with more than 200 manufacturing jewelers and 50 silversmiths. Work with precious metals was first recorded here in 1460, and there are still more than 100 shops that sell and repair gold and silver handcrafted jewelry, clocks, and watches. The city has its own Assay Office with an anchor as its silver mark. The history of the neighborhood and the craft of the jeweler are explained at the Discovery Centre. ✉ *77–79 Vyse St.,* ☎ *0121/554–3598.* 🎫 *£2.* ⏲ *Weekdays 10–4, Sat. 11–5.*

Worcester

⓫ *118 mi northwest of London, 27 mi southwest of Birmingham, 63 mi north of London.*

Worcester (pronounced as in Wooster, Ohio) sits on the Severn River in the center of Worcestershire. It is an ancient city proud of its history, and in particular, its nickname, "The Faithful City," bestowed on it for its steadfast allegiance to the crown during the English Civil War. In this conflict between king and Parliament two major battles were waged here. The second one, the decisive Battle of Worcester in 1651, resulted in the exile of the future Charles II. More recently the town's name has become synonymous with the fine bone china produced here. Despite "modernization" during the 1960s, some of medieval

Worcester remains. This ancient section forms a convenient and pleasant walking route around the great cathedral.

★ There are few more quintessentially English sights than that of **Worcester Cathedral,** its towers overlooking the green expanse of the county cricket ground, its majestic image reflected in the swift-flowing—and frequently flooding—waters of the river Severn. There has been a cathedral here since the year 680, and much of what remains dates from the 13th and 14th centuries. Notable exceptions are the Norman crypt (built in the 1080s), the largest in England, and the ambulatory, a cloister built around the east end. The most important tomb in the cathedral is that of King John (1167–1216), one of the country's least admired monarchs, who alienated his barons and subjects through bad administration and heavy taxation and in 1215 was forced to sign the Magna Carta, the great charter of liberty. The cathedral's most beautiful decoration is in the vaulted **chantry chapel of Prince Arthur,** Henry VII's elder son, whose body was brought to Worcester after his death at Ludlow in 1502. (Chantry chapels were endowed by the wealthy to enable priests to celebrate masses there for the souls of the deceased.) ☏ *01905/611002.* ⏲ *Daily 7:30–6.*

At the **Royal Worcester Porcelain Factory,** you can browse in the showrooms or rummage in the "seconds" stores; especially good bargains can be had in the January and July sales. Tours of the factory take you through the process of making porcelain. The **Dyson Perrins Museum,** in another part of the factory, houses a comprehensive collection of rare Worcester porcelain, from the start of manufacturing in 1751 to the present. The factory lies south of Worcester Cathedral (follow Severn St.). ✉ *Severn St.,* ☏ *01905/23221.* 🎫 *£1.50; prebooked ¾-hr tours of factory, £3.50; prebooked 2-hr Connoisseur Tours, £11.* ⏲ *Mon.–Sat. 9:30–5:30; tours Mon.–Sat. 10:30–3:30. Children under 11 not admitted on tours.*

The Commandery occupies a cluster of 15th-century half-timber buildings that were originally built as a poorhouse and later became the headquarters of the Royalist troops during the Battle of Worcester. Now a museum, it presents a colorful audiovisual presentation about the Civil War in the magnificent, oak-beam Great Hall. The museum is across the road from the porcelain factory, minutes from the cathedral. The Commandery has a tearoom terrace. ✉ *Sidbury,* ☏ *01905/355071.* 🎫 *£3.15.* ⏲ *Mon.–Sat. 10–5, Sun. 1:30–5:30.*

Between the Commandery and the cathedral lies medieval Friar Street. As you walk toward the Cornmarket there are several buildings of particular interest, among them the timber-frame **Museum of Local Life,** which focuses on Worcester's domestic and social history. You can see reconstructions of Victorian and Edwardian shops and homes, and an exhibition of life in the city during World War II. ✉ *Friar St.,* ☏ *01905/722349.* 🎫 *£1.50.* ⏲ *Mon.–Wed. and Fri.–Sat. 10:30–5.*

On New Street you'll find **King Charles's House,** now the King Charles II Restaurant (☞ Dining and Lodging, *below*), where the beleaguered Charles II hid before his escape from the city.

Worcester's mainly pedestrianized High Street runs through the center of town from the cathedral to Foregate Street train station. On your left, with the cathedral behind you, you will see the **Guildhall** set back behind ornate iron railings (also the location of the tourist information office). The hall's 18th-century facade features gilded statues of Queen Anne, Charles I, and Charles II, and a carving of Cromwell's head pinned up by the ears, a savage addition by the royalist citizens of Worcester. Inside, the walls of the Assembly Room are hung with an impressive collection of patrician portraits, which you can admire over tea and buns under the painted ceiling. ✉ *High St.,* ☎ *01905/723471.* 🎟 *Free.* ⏲ *Mon.–Sat. 9–5.*

Facing the cathedral at the bottom of High Street stands a **statue of Sir Edward Elgar** (1857–1934), one of Britain's best-known composers, who spent his early childhood in his parents' music store just a few yards from the cathedral. If you walk down Deansway, you can turn left into the riverside gardens and work your way back along the river below the cathedral and porcelain factory.

Dining and Lodging

£££ ★ ✕ **Brown's.** A former grain mill houses this light and airy riverside restaurant. The fixed-price menu and daily specialties include warm salad with breast of duck and croutons, and crayfish-and-bacon kebabs. ✉ *24 Quay St.,* ☎ *01905/26263. AE, MC, V. No lunch Sat., no dinner Sun. Closed Mon.*

££ ✕ **King Charles II Restaurant.** Here you can enjoy dining in the black-and-white, half-timber house in which Charles II hid after the Battle of Worcester. It is now an oak-panel, silver-service restaurant with a very friendly atmosphere. Cuisine is mainly French and Italian, but there are also traditional English selections, such as beef Wellington, and such fresh fish dishes as Dover sole meunière. ✉ *29 New St.,* ☎ *01905/22449. AE, DC, MC, V. Closed Sun.*

££ ✕ **King's Restaurant.** The deluxe Fownes Hotel, a converted Victorian glove factory, now houses this classic English restaurant, where meals are served on Royal Worcester porcelain. The old-fashioned tone is countered by a good selection of modern and exotic dishes, such as strips of pork with sesame and ginger. ✉ *Fownes Hotel, City Walls Rd.,* ☎ *01905/613151. AE, DC, MC, V.*

£ 🏨 **Burgage House.** In a cobbled lane right next to the cathedral, this traditional Georgian B&B offers a hearty welcome. Breakfast in the spacious dining room includes free-range hens' eggs and homemade marmalade. ✉ *4 College Precincts, WR1 2LG,* ☎ *01905/25396. 3 rooms with bath or shower. No credit cards.*

£ 🏨 **40 Britannia Square.** This attractive guest house in a quiet, elegant, Georgian square is half a mile from downtown. ✉ *40 Britannia Sq., WR1 3DN,* ☎ *01905/611920,* FAX *01905/27152. 3 rooms with bath or shower. No credit cards. Closed Dec. 25–Jan. 1.*

£ 🏨 **Ye Old Talbot Hotel.** The Old Talbot was originally a courtroom belonging to the cathedral, which stands close by. The hotel has been refurbished, and there are modern extensions to the 16th-century core of the building. ✉ *Friar St., WR1 2NA,* ☎ *01905/23573,* FAX *01905/612760. 29 rooms with bath. Restaurant. AE, DC, MC, V.*

Shopping

All shoppers will first head for the emporium at the **Royal Worcester Porcelain** factory (☞ *above*), where, among other items, you can buy "seconds." **Bygones** (✉ 32 College St., ☎ 01905/25388; ✉ 55 Sidbury, ☎ 01905/23132) sells antiques, items of fine craftsmanship, and a selection of small gifts in silver, glass, and porcelain.

Outdoor Activities and Sports

BICYCLING

Bikes can be rented from **Peddlers** (✉ 46 Barbourne Rd., Worcester, ☎ 01905/24238).

BOATING

There are plenty of opportunities in the Worcester area to rent boats or take short cruises on the Severn. **Bickerline River Trips** (✉ South Quay, near the cathedral, ☎ 01531/670679) has 45-minute excursions on a small passenger boat leaving several times daily.

Lower Broadheath

⓬ *2 mi west of Worcester on B4204.*

Southwest of Worcester lie the Malvern Hills, their long, low, purple profile rising starkly from the surrounding plain. These were the hills that inspired much of Elgar's oh-so-English music, as well as his remark that "there is music in the air, music all around us." Stop in the village of Lower Broadheath to visit the **Elgar Birthplace Museum** before exploring the hills. Set in a peaceful little garden, the tiny brick cottage in which the composer was born now exhibits photographs, musical scores, letters, and such. ✉ *Crown East La., Lower Broadheath,* ☎ *01905/333224.* *£3.* *Mid-Feb.–Apr. and Oct.–mid-Jan., Thurs.–Tues. 1:30–4:30; May–Sept., Thurs.–Tues. 10:30–6.*

Great Malvern

⓭ *7 mi south of Worcester off A449.*

The Malverns shelter a string of communities whose main town is Great Malvern, a Victorian spa town in which the architecture has changed little since the mid-1800s. Exceptionally pure spring water is still bottled here and exported all over the world—the Queen never travels without a supply. Great Malvern is known today both as an educational center and as a great place for old folks' homes. The town also has a Winter Gardens complex with a theater, movie theater, and gardens, but it is the **Priory** that dominates the steep streets downtown. This is an early Norman Benedictine abbey in Perpendicular style, decorated with vertical lines of airy tracery and fine 15th-century glass. *Entrance opposite the church.* *Free.* *8 AM–dusk.*

Dining and Lodging

£££ ★ ✕ **Croque en Bouche.** In this traditional French restaurant, the food is the very best bourgeois cuisine, with superb handling of excellent local ingredients. The chef-proprietor, Marion Jones, has earned a considerable reputation. Specialties include skate with pesto sauce, ragout of venison, sushi, and roast guinea fowl with coriander. ✉ *221 Wells Rd., Malvern Wells,* ☎ *01684/565612. MC, V. No lunch Wed.–Sat.*

£££ ✕ **Cottage in the Wood.** This hotel sits on its shady grounds high up the side of the Malvern Hills with splendid views of the countryside. The furnishings are country-house comfortable; the rooms vary in size, and the ones with a view are equipped with binoculars! The restaurant has the best of the panorama through its tall windows. ✉ *Holywell Rd., WR14 4LG,* ☎ *01684/575859,* FAX *01684/560662. 20 rooms with bath. Restaurant (reservations essential, jacket and tie). AE, MC, V.*

£££ ✕ **Welland Court.** A Georgian gem of a house, Welland Court is a red-brick, white-sash-window 18th-century manor, transformed into a B&B by the Archers, a delightful couple. Inside, the decor is comfortable with Jane Austen-period touches and antiques. The Penthouse accommodation upstairs is more rustic in appeal, with a rough-hewed beamed roof; two other guest suites are available. Downstairs, the dining room offers tailormade menus at night (only breakfast is included in the room price). Based at the foot of the Malvern Hills, the grounds offer pleasant walks and a 2-acre lake, heavily stocked with trout. ✉ *Welland Court Lane, Upton-Upon-Severn (4 miles southeast of Great Malvern),* ☎ *01684/594426. 3 rooms with bath. Fishing. MC, V.*

£ ✕🏨 **Sidney House.** In addition to its stunning views, this dignified Georgian hotel, run by a friendly husband-and-wife team, is also near the town center. The adequately sized bedrooms with television make this lodging a good bet for people traveling on a budget. On a clear afternoon you can gaze out over the Vale of Evesham to the Cotswolds. ✉ *40 Worcester Rd., WR14 4AA,* ☎ *01684/574994. 8 rooms, 5 with bath or shower. AE, MC, V.*

The Arts

Malvern has historical connections with Sir Edward Elgar as well as with George Bernard Shaw, who premiered many of his plays here. The **Malvern Festival** was originally devoted to their works, although now it also offers a wide variety of new music and new drama. The **Malvern Fringe Festival** has an exceptional program of alternative events. Both festivals run for two or three weeks from the end of May to early June. *Details from Malvern TIC:* ✉ *Winter Garden Complex, Grange Rd., Hereford & Worcestershire WR14 3HB,* ☎ *01684/892289.*

Ledbury

14 *10 mi southwest of Great Malvern on A449.*

Among the black-and-white half-timber buildings that make up the market town of Ledbury, take special note of two late-16th-century ones: the Feathers Hotel and the Talbot Inn. At the 17th-century **market house,** perched on 16 oak columns, you can still buy produce on Saturday. Look for the cheesemaker, and be sure to sample his very rare Single Gloucester, less rich and oily than the traditional orange-red Double Gloucester.

Almost hidden behind the market house is a cobbled lane leading to the church, crowded with medieval, half-timber buildings. The **Old Grammar School** is now a Heritage Center tracing the history of some local industries, and some displays on two literary celebrities linked to the area, John Masefield and Elizabeth Barrett Browning. ✉ *Church La.,* ☎ *01531/635680.* 🎟 *Free.* ⏲ *May–Sept., daily 10:30–4:30; Easter–May, also weekends 10:30–4:30 (hrs may vary; call ahead).*

Dining and Lodging

£££ ★ ✕🏨 **Hope End Country House Hotel.** An 18th-century house well off the beaten track (2 miles north on B4214), with Oriental embellishments and period decorations, this hotel is surrounded by 40 acres of wooded parkland. It was the childhood home of the poet Elizabeth Barrett Browning and is set amid an extensive garden laid out in 1809 for her father. Much of the house burned in 1910, but what's left is architecturally interesting. The restaurant, which uses vegetables and herbs from its own kitchen garden, has won awards. ✉ *Hope End, HR8 1JQ,* ☎ *01531/633613,* FAX *01531/636366. 8 rooms with bath. Restaurant. MC, V. Closed Dec. 25–Jan.*

Much Marcle

15 *4 mi southwest of Ledbury on A449, 6 mi northeast of Ross-on-Wye.*

Much Marcle is one English village that still holds an ancient annual ceremony. On Twelfth Night, January 6, the villagers go "wassailing," beating the apple trees to make them fruitful in the coming year. If you have a detailed map and plenty of time to spare, this is an area to wander around and discover tiny villages down sleepy lanes overhung by high hedges.

Just outside the village of Much Marcle lies the beautiful mansion of
16 **Hellen's,** in singularly authentic and pristine condition (part of it from the 13th century). The gloom and dust are part of the atmosphere; the house is still lit by candles, and central heating has been scorned. ☎ *01531/660668.* *£3.* *Easter–Sept., Wed., weekends, and national holidays 2–6; tours on the hr (last tour at 5).*

Ross-on-Wye

17 *6 mi southwest of Much Marcle on A449.*

Perched high above the river Wye, Ross-on-Wye seems oblivious to 20th-century intrusions and remains at heart a small market town. Its steep streets come alive on Thursday and Saturday—market days—but they are always a happy hunting ground for antiques.

Lodging

£££ **Chase Hotel.** This well-renovated Georgian-style country-house hotel is set on 11 acres. Rooms are simply and comfortably furnished in the main house, and more modern in the newer wing. ✉ *Gloucester Rd., HR9 5LH,* ☎ *01989/763161,* FAX *01989/768330. 39 rooms with bath. Restaurant. AE, DC, MC, V.*

Goodrich

18 *3 mi north of Symond's Yat on B4229, 3 mi south of Ross-on-Wye on B4234.*

The village of Goodrich is dominated by the ruins of **Goodrich Castle,** the English equivalent of a Rhine castle. Looming dramatically over the Wye River crossing at Kerne Bridge, the castle from the south looks picturesque in its setting of green fields, but you quickly see its grimmer face standing on its battlements on the north side. Dating from the late 12th century, the castle is surrounded by a deep moat carved out of solid rock, from which its walls appear to soar upward. Built to repel Welsh raiders, Goodrich was destroyed in the 17th century during the Civil War. ☎ *01600/890538.* *£2.20.* *Apr.–Oct., daily 10–6 or dusk; Nov.–Mar., daily 10–1 and 2–4.*

Symond's Yat

19 *15 mi north of Coleford on A4136 and A40, 6 mi south of Ross-on-Wye.*

Outside the village of Symond's Yat ("gate"), the 473-foot-high Yat Rock commands superb views of the river Wye as it winds through a narrow gorge and swings around in a great 5-mile loop.

Kilpeck

20 *15 mi northwest of Goodrich, 7 mi southwest of Hereford on A465.*

Tucked away on a minor road off the A465, the tiny hamlet Kilpeck is blessed with one of the best-preserved Norman churches in Britain. It is lavishly decorated inside and out, with exceptional carving for a country church. The carvings depict all manner of subjects, from rabbits to scenes so lewd that they were removed by high-minded Victorians. (One or two ribald ones remain, however, so look carefully.) Don't miss the gargoyle rainwater spouts, either.

Hereford

21 *7 mi northeast of Kilpeck, 56 mi southwest of Birmingham, 31 mi northwest of Gloucester, 54 mi northeast of Cardiff.*

Hereford is a busy country town, the center of a wealthy agricultural area known for its cider, fruit, and cattle—the white-faced Hereford breed has spread across the world. It is also an important cathedral city, its massive Norman cathedral towering proudly over the river Wye. Before 1066, Hereford was the capital of the Anglo-Saxon kingdom of Mercia and, earlier still, the site of Roman, Celtic, and Iron Age settlements. Today, tourists come primarily to see the cathedral, but quickly discover the charms of a town that has changed slowly but fairly unobtrusively with the passing centuries.

★ **Hereford Cathedral,** built of local red sandstone with a massive central tower, has some fine 11th-century Norman carvings but suffered considerable "restoration" in the 19th century. Inside, the greatest glories include the 14th-century bishop's throne; some fine misericords (the elaborately carved undersides of choristers' seats); and the extraordinary **Mappa Mundi,** Hereford's own picture of the medieval world. This great map shows the Earth as flat, with Jerusalem at its center. It is now thought that the Mappa Mundi was the center section of an altarpiece, dating from 1290. The dean of the cathedral caused a furor in 1988 when he began negotiations with Sotheby's to put the piece on the market, to raise funds for the cathedral. Britain suddenly realized that the rich heritage of art treasures held mostly in cathedrals might be under threat. The map was withdrawn from sale and is now on view in a purpose-built exhibition center—funded by philanthropist millionaire John Paul Getty, Jr.—completed in spring 1996, and accessible from the 15th-century southwest cloister.

The new building also contains Hereford's other great attraction, the **chained library,** containing some 1,500 chained books. Among the most valuable volumes is an 8th-century copy of the Four Gospels. Chained libraries are extremely rare: They date from medieval times, when books were as precious as gold. ✉ *Cathedral Close,* ☎ *01432/359880.* 🎫 *Cathedral free.* ⏲ *Mon.–Sat. 7:30–6:30, Sun. 8–4:30.* 🎫 *Mappa Mundi and Chained Library £4.* ⏲ *Mon.–Sat. 10–4:15, Sun. noon–4.*

NEED A BREAK? After leaving the cathedral by its north door, walk down Church Street to find the town's more unusual stores—jewelers, bookstores, and antiques shops—and the **Lichfield Vaults** (✉ Church St.), an attractive half-timber pub on a pedestrians-only street near the cathedral. There's good bar food and space for outdoor eating and drinking.

From Church Street, cross East Street and follow the passageway to High Town, a large pedestrian square, and **The Old House,** a fine example of domestic Jacobean architecture, furnished in 17th-century style on three floors. ☎ *01432/354598,* 🎫 *£1.* ⏲ *Apr.–Sept., Mon. 10–1, Tues.–Sat. 10–1 and 2–5:30, Sun. 10–4; Oct.–Mar., Mon. and Sat. 10–1, Tues.–Fri. 10–1 and 2–5:30.*

On the west side of High Town is the 13th-century **All Saints Church,** which contains an additional 300 chained books, as well as canopied stalls and fine misericords. From All Saints, walk down the pedestrian Eign Gate, through the pedestrian underpass, and down Eign Street, which continues as Whitecross Road. At the traffic lights turn left onto Grimmer Road and bear right for the **Cider Museum.** A farm cider-house and a cooper's workshop have been re-created here, and you can tour ancient cider cellars, complete with huge oak vats. Cider brandy (applejack) has recently been made here for the first time in hundreds of years, and the museum has its own brand for sale. ✉ *Pomona Pl., off Whitecross Rd.,* ☎ *01432/354207.* 🎫 *£2.* ⏲ *Apr.–Oct., daily 10–5:30; Nov.–Mar., Mon.–Sat. 1–5.*

The Arts

The **Three Choirs' Festival** has been held on a three-year rotation between the cathedral cities of Gloucester, Worcester, and Hereford since about 1717. In 1997 it will be held in Hereford (August 17–24). The festival celebrates the English choral tradition, often with specially commissioned works. The program is published in March. *Details from the festival Secretary, ✉ Three Choirs' Festival, Community House, College Green, Gloucester GL1 2LZ, ☎ 01452/529819.*

Dining and Lodging

£ ★ ✕ **Orange Tree.** This is a refurbished, wood-paneled pub conveniently located on King Street where it joins Bridge Street, near the cathedral. It is a comfortable stopping place on a sightseeing day, with good, solid bar food at lunchtime. *✉ 16 King St., ☎ 01432/267698. No credit cards.*

££ 🏨 **Castle Pool.** All that's left of Hereford Castle is the moat, home to a family of ducks. Next to the moat, this 1850 building, dubbed Castle Pool, now features blandly furnished but comfortable and quiet bedrooms. *✉ Castle St., HR1 2NR, ☎ 01432/356321. 27 rooms with bath. Restaurant. AE, DC, MC, V.*

£ 🏨 **Hopbine Hotel.** The Hopbine is a mile from the center of town in the direction of Leominster, but it's worth the jaunt. This Victorian guest house stands amid 2 acres of grounds. The very comfortable, quiet rooms come equipped with a television and appliances for making tea and coffee. Evening meals are available. You'll appreciate the friendliness of this simple place. *✉ Roman Rd., HR1 1LE, ☎ 01432/268722, FAX 01432/268722. 20 rooms with bath. No credit cards.*

Shopping

The Hereford Book Shop (✉ Church St., ☎ 01432/357617) has new and secondhand books, guidebooks, maps, and greeting cards. **Capuchin Yard** (✉ Off 29 Church St.) has a wide variety of crafts for sale, including handmade shoes and knitwear; other outlets here sell books, posters, and watercolors. Hereford has a different market each day—food, clothing, livestock—on New Market Street.

Great Witley

㉒ *27 mi northeast of Hereford, 10 mi northwest of Worcester.*

Just under a mile outside the village of Great Witley (off the A443), the shell of Witley Court will conjure up a haunting vision of the heyday of this imposing stately home, before it was ravaged by fire in 1937. In contrast to this ruin, the tiny Baroque parish church is perfectly preserved. Note its balustraded parapet, a small golden dome over its cupola, and, inside, a painted ceiling by Bellucci, 10 colored windows, and the ornate case of an organ once used by Handel. *✉ Witley Ct., ☎ 01299/896636. 🎫 £2.50. ⏲ Apr.–Oct., daily 10–6 or dusk; Nov.–Mar., Wed.–Sun. 10–1 and 2–4.*

Dining and Lodging

££££ ✕🏨 **Elms Hotel.** This traditional country-house hotel, in an ivy-clad Queen Anne building surrounded by formal gardens, is 16 miles northeast of Worcester and near Great Witley. All the rooms are individually and comfortably decorated in this former mansion. The restaurant, with its imaginative cooking and pleasant, family-dining-room ambience, is worth a visit on its own. *✉ Stockton Rd., Abberley WR6 6AT, ☎ 01299/896666, FAX 01299/896804. 16 rooms with bath. Restaurant (reservations essential), tennis court, helipad. AE, DC, MC, V.*

Bewdley

23 *8 mi north of Great Witley, 14 mi north of Worcester, 3 mi west of Kidderminster.*

Bewdley is an exceptionally attractive Severn Valley town, with many tall, narrow-fronted Georgian buildings clustered around the river bridge. In what was the 18th-century butchers' market, the **Shambles,** there is now a museum of local crafts. Workshops occupy either side of the old cobbled yard, and there are exhibitions and practical demonstrations of rope making, charcoal burning, clay pipe making, and wood carving; there is also a working brass foundry. ✉ *Load St.,* ☎ *01299/403573.* 🎫 *£2.* ⏲ *Mid-Apr.–Oct., Mon.–Sun. 11–5.*

Bewdley is the southern terminus of the **Severn Valley Railway,** a restored steam railroad running 16 miles north along the river to Bridgnorth. It stops at a handful of sleepy stations where time has apparently stood still since the age of steam. You can get off at any of these little stations, enjoy a picnic by the river, and walk to the next station to get a train back. ✉ *Railway Station, Bewdley, Worcestershire DY12 1BG,* ☎ *01299/403816.* ⏲ *May–Sept., trains run daily; check for irregular winter hrs (weekends mostly).*

Stourbridge

24 *8 mi northeast of Bewdley via A451, 11 mi west of Birmingham.*

In Stourbridge, home of Britain's **crystal-glass industry,** you can find bargains at "factory seconds" stores and tour the factories, too. There is a shop at **Stuart Crystal** (✉ Redhouse Glassworks, Vine St., Wordsley, ☎ 01384/828282), and shops as well as tours at **Royal Brierley Crystal** (✉ North St., Brierley Hill, ☎ 01384/70161) and **Royal Doulton Crystal** (✉ Webb-Corbett Glassworks, High St., Amblecote, ☎ 01384/552900); call for tour schedules and prices.

Outdoor Activities and Sports

BOATING

Between Easter and September, you can join a passenger cruise for short river trips on Sunday and national holidays, and for longer journeys as far as Worcester on Wednesday. Contact the **Severn Steamboat Company** (✉ Riverside Walk, Stourbridge, DY13 8UY, ☎ 01299/871177).

Dudley

25 *6 mi northeast of Stourbridge, 8 mi west of central Birmingham.*

★ On the edge of Birmingham, Dudley is home to the **Black Country Museum,** established to ensure that the area's industrial heritage is not forgotten. An entire industrial village has been constructed with disused buildings from around the region. There is a chain-maker's house and workshop, with demonstrations of chain making; a druggist and general store, where costumed women describe life in a poor industrial community in the last century; a Methodist chapel; the Bottle & Glass pub, serving local ales and cheese rolls; Stables restaurant, offering such traditional delicacies as faggots and peas (a fried pork liver dish); and a coal mine and wharf. You can also ride on a canal houseboat through a tunnel, where an audiovisual show portrays canal travel of yesteryear. ✉ *Tipton Rd.,* ☎ *0121/557–9643.* 🎫 *£5.95.* ⏲ *Mar.–Oct., daily 10–5; Nov.–Feb., Wed.–Sun. 10–4.*

SKIRTING THE "BLACK COUNTRY"—FROM SHREWSBURY TO CHESTER

The "peak" of this region—in more ways than one—used to be the Wrekin, a hill geologists claim to be the oldest in the land. That may mean little to the average visitor. Far better to record that A.W. Housman and others have invested it with some of their poetic charm. To stand on its isolated summit and look around is to see what makes up so much of the Midland scene. During the last few years, however, the Wrekin has taken on a new tourist significance because of the enormous popularity of Ironbridge, several miles from the hill. Ironbridge has two identities—as a place as well as a thing. The thing is the first bridge made of iron, erected between 1777 and 1779. Now taken over by the Ironbridge Gorge Museum Trust, it is the centerpiece of a vast Industrial Revolution museum complex. The place is the 6-mile stretch of the Ironbridge Gorge, once an awesome scene of mining, charcoal burning, reeking with smoke and the stench of sulphur, has been now completely transformed into a scene of idyllic beauty, scars grassed over, woodland filling the gaps left by tree-felling. Within easy reach of this complex, rural Shropshire spreads invitingly, offering lovely towns long famed as beauty spots, such as Bridgnorth and Ludlow.

We bookend this itinerary with two important cities of the Welsh Border region: Shrewsbury and Chester, both famous for their medieval heritage and their wealth of half-timber buildings and black-and-white "magpie" architecture.

Shrewsbury

26 *47 mi northwest of Dudley, 55 mi north of Hereford, 46 mi south of Chester, 48 mi northwest of Birmingham, 150 mi northwest of London.*

Shrewsbury (usually pronounced "Shrose-bury"), the county seat of Shropshire, is within a great horseshoe loop of the Severn. One of England's most important medieval towns, it has a wealth of 16th-century half-timber buildings and elegant ones from later periods. The market square forms the natural center of the town; leading off it are narrow alleys overhung with timbered gables. These alleys, called "shuts," were designed to be closed off at night to afford their residents greater protection. The town is especially proud of its flower displays, for which it has won many national awards. In the summer, window boxes and hanging baskets are a vivid contrast to the stark black-and-white buildings.

Numbers in the margin correspond to points of interest on the Shrewsbury map.

Shrewsbury is an ideal town to see on foot, and indeed, traffic has been banned on some of the most historic streets. A good starting point for a walking tour is the small square between Fish Street and Butcher Row. These streets are little changed since medieval times, when some of them took their names from the principal trades carried on there, but Peacock Alley, Gullet Passage, and Grope Lane clearly got their names from
27 somewhere else. In the center, off Castle Street, the stone spire of **St. Mary's church,** built around 1200, is one of the three tallest in England and merits a visit for its iron-framed stained glass (an indication of the proximity of the Ironbridge Gorge).

28 Near St. Mary's church, off Fish Street, **St. Alkmund's** (⊠ St. Alkmund's Pl.) is another prominent feature of the Shrewsbury skyline and also worth seeing for its stained glass. It was built in 1795 on the site of a

Castle/ Shropshire Regimental Museum, **33**
Clive House, **31**
Ireland's Mansion, **29**
Quarry Park, **32**
Rowley's House Museum, **30**
St. Alkmund's, **28**
St. Mary's, **27**
Shrewsbury Abbey Church, **34**
Shrewsbury Quest, **35**

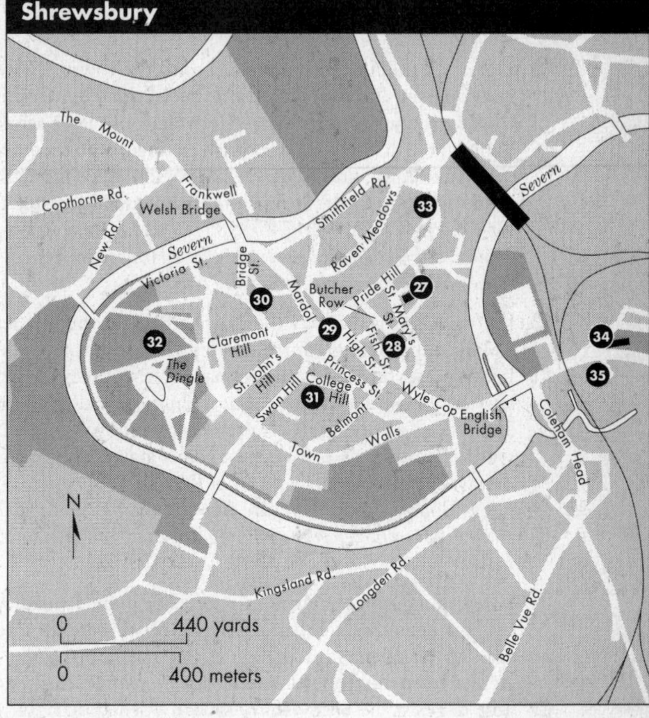

much earlier church. Bear Steps is a cluster of restored half-timber buildings that link Fish Street with Market Square. Here the most notable
29 building is **Ireland's Mansion,** a massive house with elaborate Jacobean timbering, richly decorated with quatrefoils.

A magnificent 16th-century timber-frame warehouse and adjoining brick and stone mansion built in 1618 together form an eye-catching ensemble
30 in the center of Shrewsbury. Today they house **Rowley's House Museum,** containing clothing, Shropshire pottery and ceramics, Roman finds from Wroxeter, a reconstructed 17th-century bedroom with lovely oak, holly, and walnut paneling and a four-poster bed, and other items of local history. ⊠ *Barker St.,* ☎ *01743/361196.* *£2; joint ticket for Rowley's House, Clive House, Shropshire Regimental Museum, and castle £3.* *Tues.–Sat. 10–5, national holidays and summer Sun. 10–4.*

31 **Clive House** was the home of Sir Robert Clive when he was Shrewsbury's member of Parliament in the mid-18th century. Better known as "Clive of India," this soldier-statesman was especially famous for winning the Battle of Plassey in 1757, thereby avenging the atrocity of the Black Hole of Calcutta. The house contains rooms furnished in Clive's period, and striking displays of fragile Staffordshire wares, particularly pieces from the Caughley and Coalport factories. ⊠ *College Hill,* ☎ *01743/354811.* *£1; joint ticket with Rowley's House and castle (☞ Rowley's House,* above*) £3.* *Tues.–Sat., national holidays, and summer Sun. 10–4.*

32 Below Swan Hill you will see the manicured lawn of **Quarry Park** sloping down to the river. In a sheltered corner is the Dingle, a colorful garden offering changing floral displays throughout the year. To get here from Clive House, turn left, then left again. St. John's Hill in the Mardol, another of Shrewsbury's strangely named streets, will take you

back into town, or you can head for Welsh Bridge and stroll along the riverbank.

33 Guarding the northern approaches to the town, Shrewsbury's **castle** rises up over the river at the bottom of Pride Hill. Originally Norman, it was dismantled during the Civil War and later rebuilt by Thomas Telford, the distinguished Scottish engineer who designed a host of notable buildings and bridges at the beginning of the 19th century. The castle now houses the **Shropshire Regimental Museum.** ✉ *Shrewsbury Castle, Pride Hill,* ☎ *01743/358516.* 🎫 *£2; joint ticket with Rowley's House and Clive House (☞ Rowley's House,* above*) £3.* ⏲ *Mon.–Sat., national holidays, summer Sun. 10–5.*

34 If you cross the river by the English Bridge, you'll reach **Shrewsbury Abbey,** unbecomingly surrounded by busy roads. Founded in 1083 and later a powerful Benedictine monastery, the Abbey Church has survived various vicissitudes throughout its history, including the Dissolution, and retains a good 14th-century west window above a Norman doorway. The Abbey Restoration Project has developed intriguing medieval walking tours. *Details from Restoration Project Office,* ✉ *1 Holy Cross Houses, Abbey Foregate, Shrewsbury SY2 6BS,* ☎ *01743/232723. Abbey Church,* ✉ *Abbey Foregate,* ☎ *01743/232723.* 🎫 *Free.* ⏲ *Easter–Oct., 9:30–5:30, Nov.–Easter, 10:30–3.*

Shrewsbury Abbey figures in a series of popular medieval whodunits by Ellis Peters, which feature the detective Brother Cadfael and provide an excellent idea of life in this area during the Middle Ages. Across from the Abbey Church, devotees of Brother Cadfael won't be
35 able to resist the **Shrewsbury Quest,** opened in 1994, which encompasses the scanty remains of the original monastery, and illustrates monastic life in the Middle Ages with the help of a reconstructed scriptorium, library, cloisters, and even a trail of clues to help solve a medieval mystery. Children will be particularly interested, even without a knowledge of the sandaled sleuth. ✉ *Abbey Foregate,* ☎ *01743/243324.* 🎫 *£3.75.* ⏲ *Daily 10–5 or dusk.*

Dining and Lodging

£££ ✕ **Country Friends.** An attractive, imitation black-and-white building, 5 miles south of Shrewsbury by the A49, houses this light and airy restaurant overlooking a garden and pool. Specialties include halibut with wild mushrooms and smoked oysters, venison with black currant sauce, and lamb noisettes roasted in mustard crust with mint hollandaise. There are also three simple bedrooms available. ✉ *Dorrington,* ☎ *01743/718707. AE, MC, V. Closed Sun.–Mon. (except last Sun. of month), 2 wks mid-July, mid-wk in Oct.*

£ ✕ **Traitor's Gate.** Installed in a series of 13th-century, vaulted, brick cellars, this atmospheric restaurant serves freshly prepared, reasonably priced meals. Close to the local castle, the Traitor's Gate gets its name from an incident in the Civil War, when a young Roundhead lieutenant ransacked the Cavalier-held fortress. He was later executed as a traitor. ✉ *St. Mary's Water La.,* ☎ *01743/249152. AE, MC, V. Closed Sun. and Mon., Tues. evening in winter.*

££–£££ 🏨 **Prince Rupert Hotel.** This black-and-white, half-timber inn in the historic city center was the headquarters of Prince Rupert, the most famous Royalist general (he was also the nephew of Charles I) during the Civil War. It is now furnished in modern style, although two rooms have four-poster beds. ✉ *Butcher Row, SY1 1UQ,* ☎ *01743/499955,* FAX *01743/357306. 65 rooms with bath. Restaurant, recreation room. AE, DC, MC, V.*

£ **Sandford House.** This late-Georgian B&B, close to the river and the town center, is run by the hospitable Richards family. The bedrooms are clean and functional, but well furnished. There is an attractive rear garden. ☒ *St. Julian Friars, SY1 1XL,* ☎ *01743/343829. 10 rooms, 8 with bath or shower. MC, V.*

The Arts

FESTIVALS

During the **Shrewsbury International Music Festival,** in June and July, the town vibrates to traditional and not-so-traditional music by groups from America, western Europe, and sometimes eastern Europe. In 1997, the festival will take place June 27–July 4. ☒ *Shrewsbury Festival Office, 98 King St., Knutsford, Cheshire WA16 6EP,* ☎ *01565/652667.*

Shopping

The Parade, just behind St. Mary's Church, is a shopping mall created from the former Royal Infirmary, built in 1830. It's one of the most appealing malls England has to offer, with attractive boutiques, posh apartments upstairs, a restaurant, and a terrace overlooking the river and the abbey. **Manser & Son** (☒ 53–54 Wyle Cop [extension of High St.], ☎ 01743/351120), close to the English Bridge, displays quality antiques. **St. Julian's Crafts Centre** (☒ Wyle Cop, ☎ 01743/353516) is worth visiting (closed Thurs., Sun.) for gifts of pottery, wood, or jewelry. Housed in a deconsecrated church, it is quite unlike any craft center you have seen before. In Shrewsbury, there is an indoor market on Tuesday, Wednesday, Friday, and Saturday.

Numbers in the margin correspond to points of interest on the Welsh Borders map.

Attingham Park

36 *4 mi southeast of Shrewsbury, just off A5.*

Built in 1785 by George Steuart, who designed the round church of St. Chad's in Shrewsbury, this elegant mansion has an impressive three-story portico, with a pediment carried on four tall columns. The building overlooks a wide sweep of parkland, including a deer park landscaped by Humphrey Repton. Inside are painted ceilings, delicate plasterwork, and a collection of 19th-century Neapolitan furniture. ☎ *01743/709203.* 🎟 *£3.50, park and grounds only £1.40.* ⏲ *Apr.–Sept., Sat.–Wed. 1:30–5, national holiday Mon. 11–5; Oct., weekends 1:30–5; park and grounds daily until dusk.*

Wroxeter

37 *1 mi east of Attingham Park, 5 mi southeast of Shrewsbury.*

Wroxeter, originally Viroconium, flourished around AD 150 and was the fourth-largest city in Roman Britain. Excavations beginning in 1863 revealed the foundations of the shattered pillars of the forum and fragments of the town walls. A complex of buildings around the forum has now been unearthed, providing a clear impression of the original town plan. The small museum houses the Roman artifacts found in the last 100 years. ☎ *01743/761330.* 🎟 *£2.50.* ⏲ *Apr.–Sept., daily 10–6; Oct., daily 10–4; Nov.–Mar., Wed.–Sun. 10–4.*

Ironbridge Gorge

★ 38 *15 mi east of Shrewsbury, 28 mi northwest of Birmingham.*

Continuing southeast on B4380, you will see, rising on the left, the **Wrekin,** a strange, conical extinct volcano. A few miles farther on you enter the wooded gorge of the Severn River. Here you can see the world's earliest iron bridge (1779), a monument to the discovery of how to smelt iron ore using coke (a coal residue), rather than charcoal.

The Shropshire coalfields were of enormous importance to the development of the coke smelting process which, in turn, helped usher in the Industrial Revolution. This fascinating history is preserved and recounted at the **Ironbridge Gorge Museum.** Spread over 6 square miles, it has six component sections. A good half-day will let you take in the major sites and stroll around the famous bridge, perhaps hunting for Coalport china in the stores clustered near it. The best starting point is the **Severn Warehouse,** which has a good selection of literature and an audiovisual show on the gorge's history. From here you can drive (or in summer, take the museum's "park and ride" service) to Coalbrookdale and the **Museum of Iron,** which explains the production of iron and steel. You can see the original blast furnace built by Abraham Darby, who developed the original coke process. Retrace your steps along the river until the arches of the **Iron Bridge** come into view; it was designed by T. F. Pritchard, smelted by Darby, and erected between 1777 and 1779. An infinitely graceful arch spanning the river, it can best be seen—and photographed or painted—from the tow path, a charming riverside walk edged with wild flowers and dense shrubs. The tollhouse on the far side houses an exhibition on the bridge's history and restoration.

A mile farther along the river is the old factory and the **Coalport China Museum** (the china is now made in Stoke-on-Trent). There are exhibits of some of the factory's most beautiful wares, and craftsmen give demonstrations. Above Coalport is **Blists Hill Open-Air Museum,** where you can see old mines, furnaces, and a wrought-iron works. But the main draw is the re-creation of a Victorian town, with the doctor's office, the sweet-smelling bakery, the candlemaker's, the sawmill, the printing shop, and the candy store. ✉ *Ironbridge Gorge Museum Trust, Ironbridge, Telford, Shropshire TF8 7AW,* ☎ *01952/433522.* 🎫 *Ticket to all sites £8.* ⏲ *Daily 10–5 (July and Aug. until 6).*

NEED A BREAK? **The New Inn** (✉ Blists Hill Museum), a Victorian building, was moved to Blists Hill from Walsall, 22 miles away, so that it could be part of the open-air museum. It is a fully functioning pub, with gas lamps, sawdust on the floor, and traditional ales served from the cask. For an inexpensive meal, you can try a ploughman's lunch, a pasty from the antique-style bakery, or a pork pie from the butcher's store next door.

Lodging

£ **Library House.** Nestled into the hillside near the Ironbridge museums, and only a few steps away from the bridge itself, this small hotel has kept its attractive Victorian style. ✉ *11 Severn Bank, TF8 7AN,* ☎ *01952/432299,* FAX *01952/433967. 4 rooms with bath. No credit cards.*

Bridgnorth

39 *9 mi south of Ironbridge, 22 mi southeast of Shrewsbury, 25 mi west of Birmingham.*

Perching perilously on a high sandstone ridge on the banks of the Severn, the pretty market town of Bridgnorth has two distinct parts, High Town and Low Town, connected by a winding road, flights of steep steps, and—best of all—a cliff railroad. Even the tower of the Norman castle seems to suffer from vertigo, having a 17-degree list (three times the angle of the Leaning Tower of Pisa). The Severn Valley Railway terminates here.

Much Wenlock

40 *8 mi northwest of Bridgnorth off A458, 12 mi southeast of Shrewsbury.*

The small town of Much Wenlock is peppered with half-timber buildings, including a 16th-century guildhall on Wilmore Street. The prime attraction here is the romantic ruins of the Norman **Wenlock Priory,** set in an attractive garden full of topiary. ✉ *The Bull Ring,* ☏ *01952/727466.* *£2.* *Apr.–Oct., daily 10–6 or dusk; Nov.–Mar., Wed.–Sun. 10–1 and 2–4.*

En Route Running southwest from Much Wenlock is the high scarp of **Wenlock Edge,** which provides a splendid view. This is hiking country, and if a healthy walk sounds inviting, turn off the Edge down through Cardington, and drive through Church Stretton into Cardingmill Valley, or to the wide, heather uplands on top of Long Mynd. In one of these inviting places, leave your car and set off on foot.

Ludlow

★ 41 *29 mi south of Shrewsbury, 24 mi north of Hereford.*

Ludlow has often been described as the most beautiful small town in England, with medieval, Georgian, and Victorian buildings and a finer display of black-and-white buildings than even Shrewsbury itself. The center is dominated by the great **Church of St. Lawrence** on College Street, its extravagant size a testimony to the town's prosperous wool-trade. Look for the **Feathers Hotel** on the street called The Bull Ring, to admire its extravagantly decorated half-timber facade. Cross the river and climb **Whitcliff** for the most spectacular view. The town is dwarfed by the massive, ruined, red sandstone **castle,** which dates from 1085 and was a vital stronghold for centuries. It was the seat of the Marcher Lords who ruled "the Marches," the local name for the border region. It was in this castle that John Milton wrote his verse drama *Comus,* and it is still privately owned by the earl of Powys. Follow the terraced walk around the castle for a lovely view. ✉ *Castle Sq.,* ☏ *01584/873355.* *£2.50.* *Feb.–Apr. and Oct.–Dec., daily 10:30–4; May–Sept., daily 10:30–5.*

The Arts

In Shropshire, the **Ludlow Festival,** starting at the end of June, sums up all that is English: Shakespeare is performed in the open air against the romantic backdrop of the ruined castle to an audience armed with cushions, raincoats, lap robes, and picnic baskets—as well as hip flasks. Reservations are accepted starting in early May. *Details from the Festival Box Office,* ✉ *Castle Sq., Ludlow, Shropshire SY8 1AY,* ☏ *01584/872150.*

Dining and Lodging

£££ **Dinham Hall.** Near Ludlow Castle, this property is a converted merchant's town house dating from 1792. The new owners have managed to combine the original historic elements in the house with modern comforts. The dining room serves imaginative dishes such as salmon with wild mushrooms and chicken with honey and ginger sauce. This is a good base for exploring the region. ✉ *Off Market Sq., SY8 1EJ,* ☏ *01584/876464,* FAX *01584/876019. 11 rooms with bath. Restaurant (reservations essential, jacket and tie, ££), sauna. AE, DC, MC, V.*

CHESTER

Cheshire is mainly a land of well-kept farms, supporting their herds of equally well-kept cattle, but there are numerous places here steeped in history. Villages contain many fine examples of the black-and-white "magpie" type of architecture more often associated with the Midlands (and every bit as attractive as anything to be found there). The thriving center of the region is **Chester,** located 46 miles north of Shrewsbury.

Chester is in some ways similar to Shrewsbury, though it has many more black-and-white half-timber buildings, and its medieval walls are still standing. Chester has been a prominent city since the late 1st century AD, when the Roman Empire expanded northward to the banks of the river Dee. The original Roman town plan is still evident: The principal streets, Eastgate, Northgate, Watergate, and Bridge Street, lead out from the Cross—the site of the central area of the Roman fortress—to the four city gates.

Since Roman times, seagoing vessels have sailed up the estuary of the Dee and anchored under the walls of Chester. The port enjoyed its most prosperous period during the 12th and 13th centuries. This was also ★ the time when Chester's unique **Rows** originated. Essentially, they are double rows of stores, one at street level, and the other on the second floor with galleries overlooking the street. The Rows line the junction of the four streets in the old town. They have medieval crypts below them, and some reveal Roman foundations. History seems more tangible in Chester than in many other ancient cities. So much medieval architecture remains that the town center is quite compact, and modern buildings have not been allowed to intrude. A negative result of this perfection is that Chester has become a favorite bus-tour destination, with gift shops and casual restaurants, noise, and crowds.

Chester's city **walls** are accessible from various points and provide splendid views of the city and its surroundings. The whole circuit is 2 miles, but if your time is short, climb the steps at Newgate and walk along toward Eastgate to see the great ornamental clock, erected to commemorate Queen Victoria's Diamond Jubilee in 1897. Lots of small shops by this part of the walls sell old books, old postcards, antiques, and jewelry. Where the **Bridge of Sighs**—named after the enclosed bridge in Venice it closely resembles—crosses the canal, descend to street level and walk up Northgate Street into Market Square.

The **cathedral** is just off Market Square. Tradition has it that a church of some sort stood on this site in Roman times, but the earliest records indicate construction around AD 900. The earliest work traceable today, mainly in the north transept, is that of the 11th-century Benedictine abbey. After Henry VIII dissolved the monasteries in the 16th century, the abbey church became the cathedral church of the new diocese of Chester. ✉ *St. Werburgh St.,* ☎ *01244/324756.* *Free.* ⏲ *Daily 7–6:30.*

On Eastgate Street you will see the impressive frontage of the Grosvenor Hotel (☞ Dining and Lodging, *below*), surrounded by the best of the city's boutiques. Over the Cross in Watergate Street, the stores specialize in antiques and arts and crafts.

NEED A BREAK? The **Falcon** (✉ Lower Bridge St.) is a typical old pub that serves a wide range of lunch food. **Roberts & Co.** (✉ Godstall La.), near the cathedral, serves a range of fine coffees as well as rolls and salads.

Overlooking the river Dee, Chester's **castle** lost its moats and battlements at the end of the 18th century to make way for the classical-style civil and criminal courts, jail, and barracks. The castle now houses the **Cheshire Military Museum**, exhibiting uniforms, memorabilia, and some fine silver. ✉ *Castle St.,* ☎ *01244/327617.* *Small admission fee.* ⏲ *Daily 9–5.*

From the castle you can follow the riverbank past the old bridge to the site of the **Roman amphitheater** beside Newgate, now a simple, grassy spot with an information board. ✉ *St. John St.*

Dining and Lodging

££ ✕ **Abbey Green and Garden House.** This two-section restaurant in downtown Chester serves award-winning vegetarian cuisine in one part, and meat and fish in the other. Specialties include wild boar sautéed with wild mushrooms in a red wine sauce, and a vegetarian lasagna gâteau. There is a garden and patio for eating out in summer. ✉ *1 Rufus Ct., off Northgate St.,* ☎ *01244/313251. AE, DC, MC, V. Closed Sun.*

££££ ✕▣ **Chester Grosvenor Hotel.** This is a traditional deluxe hotel in a Tudor-style, downtown building; it's remarkable to find such quiet luxury and sumptuous comfort in a small country town. The Arkle Restaurant is just as splendid as the rest of the hotel, with marble and stone walls, solid mahogany tables, candlelight, and gleaming silver. The style here is *cuisine légère,* using little cream or butter, only natural ingredients, and sauces made by reduction rather than thickening. ✉ *Eastgate St., CH1 1LT,* ☎ *01244/324024,* FAX *01244/313246. 86 rooms with bath. Restaurant (reservations essential, jacket and tie), brasserie, sauna, exercise room. AE, DC, MC, V.*

£££ ★ ✕▣ **Crabwall Manor.** This dramatic, castellated, part-Tudor, part-neo-Gothic mansion is set on 11 acres of farm and parkland (2¼ miles northwest on A540). It has elegant, subtle furnishings in floral chintzes, a wonderful stone staircase, and extremely comfortable bedrooms. The spacious restaurant offers *cordon bleu* cooking and is worth visiting—say, for lunch, while exploring the neighborhood. ✉ *Parkgate Rd., Mollington CH1 6NE,* ☎ *01244/851666,* FAX *01244/851400. 48 rooms with bath. Restaurant. AE, DC, MC, V.*

£ ✕▣ **Green Bough Hotel.** The Green Bough is in a large, late Victorian house, with a variety of antiques and bric-a-brac. Both the main building and the refurbished and restored annex contain roomy, comfortable bedrooms, one with a four-poster. The dining room offers an imaginative and reasonably priced table d'hôte menu that changes daily. ✉ *60 Hoole Rd., CH2 3NL,* ☎ *01244/326241,* FAX *01244/326265. 20 rooms with bath or shower. Dining room. AE, MC, V.*

Shopping

Melodies Galleries (✉ 32 City Rd., ☎ 01244/328968), with 16 dealers on two floors of an old Georgian building, offers a wide mix of fine furniture and bric-a-brac. **Bookland** (✉ 12 Bridge St., ☎ 01244/347323), in an ancient building with a converted 14th-century crypt, has a wealth of travel and general-interest books. Chester has an indoor market in the Forum, near the Town Hall, every day except Wednesday afternoon and Sunday.

WELSH BORDERS A TO Z

Arriving and Departing

By Bus

National Express (☎ 0990/808080) serves the region from London's Victoria Coach Station. Average travel time to Chester is five hours; to Hereford and Shrewsbury, four hours; and to Worcester, 3½ hours.

By Car

From London take M40 and keep on it for M42 and Birmingham (120 mi). M4/M5 from London takes you to Worcester in just under three hours. The prettier, more direct route (120 mi) on M40 via Oxford to A40 across the Cotswolds is actually slower because it is only partly motorway. For Shrewsbury (150 mi) and Chester (180 mi), take M1/M6.

By Train

British Rail serves the region from London's Paddington (☎ 0171/262–6767) and Euston (☎ 0171/387–7070) stations. Average travel times are: Paddington to Hereford, three hours; to Worcester, 2½ hours; to Birmingham, 1 hour 45 minutes from London's Euston Station (☎ 0171/387–7070); Euston to Shrewsbury and Chester, with a change at Wolverhampton or Birmingham, three hours.

Getting Around

By Bus

For information about local services and Rover tickets, contact **Crosville Bus Station** in Chester (☎ 01244/381515) and **Midland Red (West) Travel** in Worcester (☎ 01905/763888). **Flights Coach Travel Ltd. of Birmingham** (☎ 0121/322–2222) operates "Flightlink" services from London's Heathrow and Gatwick airports to Coventry and Warwick. **Midland Red (South) Ltd.** and **Stratford Blue** (☎ 01788/535555) serve the Stratford-upon-Avon, Birmingham, and Coventry areas.

By Car

Driving can be difficult in the western reaches of this region—especially in the hills and valleys west of Hereford, where steep, twisting roads often narrow into mere trackways. Winter travel here can be particularly grueling.

By Train

A direct local service links Hereford and Shrewsbury, with a change at Oswestry or Wrexham for Chester. **Midland Day Ranger** tickets and seven-day **Heart of England Regional Rover** tickets allow unlimited travel.

Guided Tours

Local tourist offices can recommend day or half-day tours of the region and will have the names of registered Blue Badge guides. **Yeomans Travel** (✉ Coach Station, Baker's La., Hereford, ☎ 01432/356201) conducts tours of the Wye Valley, the Black and White Villages, and the Bulmers Cider factory.

Contacts and Resources

Car-Rental Agencies

Birmingham: Avis, ✉ 7–9 Park St., ☎ 0121/632–4361; **EuroDollar Rent-a-Car,** ✉ Snow Hill Service Station, St. Chads, ☎ 0121/200–3010. **Chester: Avis,** ✉ 128 Brook St., ☎ 01244/311463; **Hertz,** Auto Travel Agency, ✉ Abley House, Trafford St., ☎ 01244/374705. **Hereford: Practical Car and Van Rental, Puremass Ltd.,** ✉ Coningsby St., ☎ 01432/278989. **Worcester: Kenning,** ✉ Hylton Rd., ☎ 01905/748403; **Hertz,** Brandrick Holdings Ltd., ✉ 14 Carden St., ☎ 01905/24844.

Hiking and Walking

For information on hiking the Malvern Hills, contact **Malvern Tourist Office** (✉ Winter Gardens Complex, Grange Rd., Worcestershire WR14 3HB, ☎ 01684/892289) or **Ross-on-Wye Tourist Office** (✉ The Swan, Edde Cross St., Herefordshire HR9 7BZ, ☎ 01989/562768).

For information on the Offa Dyke Path, contact the **Offa Dyke Centre** (⊠ West St., Knighton, Powys LD7 1EW, ☎ 01547/528753).

Travel Agencies

Thomas Cook: ⊠ 10 Bridge St., Chester, ☎ 01244/323045; ⊠ 4 St. Peter's St., Hereford, ☎ 01432/356461; ⊠ 36–37 Pride Hill, Shrewsbury, ☎ 01743/231144; and ⊠ 26 High St., Worcester, ☎ 01905/28228.

American Express: ⊠ 27 Claremont St., Shrewsbury, ☎ 01743/236387; ⊠ 23 St. Werburgh St., Chester, ☎ 01244/311145.

Visitor Information

The Heart of England Tourist Board: ⊠ Woodside, Larkhill, Worcester WR5 2EF, ☎ 01905/763436, FAX 01905/763450, ⊙ Mon.–Thurs. 9–5:30, Fri. 9–5.

Local tourist information centers are normally open Monday–Saturday 9:30–5:30. **Birmingham:** ⊠ Convention and Visitor Bureau, 2 City Arcade, ☎ 0121/643–2514. **Chester:** ⊠ Town Hall, Northgate St., CH1 2HJ, ☎ 01244/318356. **Hereford:** ⊠ 1 King St., HR4 9BW, ☎ 01432/268430. **Ludlow:** ⊠ Castle St., SY8 1AF, ☎ 01584/875053. **Ross-on-Wye:** ⊠ The Swan, Edde Cross St., HR9 7BZ, ☎ 01989/562768. **Shrewsbury:** ⊠ The Music Hall, The Square, SY1 1LM, ☎ 01743/350761. **Worcester:** ⊠ The Guildhall, High St., WR1 2EY, ☎ 01905/726311.

10 Wales

"The Land of Castles," Wales is an ancient stronghold that is one of Britain's best kept secrets. Many visitors still perceive it in terms of the How Green Was My Valley *film of half a century ago—but today Wales is evergreen and unspoiled. As conclusive proof of its scenic grandeur, it's home to three national parks, with Snowdonia the monarch of all it surveys. Beyond nature's bounty, there are other treasures: the stately houses of Powis and Erddig, steam train rides thorugh tree-clad chasms, the capital of Cardiff, and the glory of the Welsh language.*

Updated by Roger Thomas

WALES, APART FROM BEING CALLED the Land of Song, is also a land of mountain and flood, where wild peaks challenge the sky and waterfalls thunder down steep, tree-clad chasms. It is a land of gray-stone medieval castles, ruined abbeys, little steam trains chugging through dramatic scenery, male-voice choirs, and a handful of cities. Small pockets of the south and northeast have been heavily industrialized—largely with mining and steelmaking—since the 19th century, but long stretches of the coast and the mountainous interior remain areas of unmarred beauty. As conclusive proof of its scenic grandeur, small, self-contained Wales has three national parks (Snowdonia, the Brecon Beacons, and the Pembrokeshire Coast) and five "Areas of Outstanding Natural Beauty" (the Wye Valley, Gower Peninsula, Llŷn Peninsula, Isle of Anglesey, and Clwydian Range), as well as large tracts of unspoiled moor and mountain in mid-Wales, the least traveled part of the country. Dotted over the entire country are riches of other sort: numerous medieval castles, charming seaside resorts, restored 19th-century mining villages, the glorious Bodnant Garden, the Victorian spa of Llandrindod Wells, the great stately houses of Powis and Erddig, steam train rides through the mountains of Snowdonia and central Wales, and the cosmopolitan capital of Cardiff.

Wales suffers more than most destinations from the curse of the stereotype. Many visitors still perceive the country in terms of the *How Green Was My Valley* film of half a century ago, in which Wales was depicted as an industrial cauldron filled with coal mines. The picture was not accurate then; it is certainly not accurate now—Wales has only one fully operational mine today. In any case, industrial activity has always been concentrated in a relatively small corner of southeast Wales, leaving the vast majority of the landscape untouched by modern development. In fact, one of the great glories of Wales is the way in which you can drive uninterrupted from south to north through beautiful countryside without having to pass through any large towns. The same applies to the country's 750-mile coast, which consists mainly of sandy beaches, grassy headlands, cliffs and estuaries. Stretches of the coast and the mountainous interior remain areas of unmarred beauty.

Wales's distinctive personality comes in part from its history. Wales was finally united with England in 1536, under the Tudor King Henry VIII (the Tudors came originally from the Isle of Anglesey off the Welsh coast), but it has nonetheless retained an identity and character quite separate from that of the rest of Britain; the Welsh will not thank you if you confuse their country with England.

The Welsh are a Celtic race. When, toward the middle of the first millennium AD, the Anglo-Saxons spread through Britain, they pushed the indigenous Celts farther back into their Welsh mountain strongholds. (In fact, "Wales" comes from the Saxon word "Weallas," which means "strangers," the impertinent name given by the new arrivals to the natives. The Welsh, however, have always called themselves "Y Cymry," "the companions.") It was not until the fearsome English king Edward I (1272–1307) waged a brutal and determined campaign to conquer Wales that English supremacy was established. Welsh hopes were finally crushed with the death in battle of Llywelyn ap Gruffudd, last native prince of Wales, in 1282.

In the 15th and 16th centuries, the Tudor kings Henry VII and Henry VIII continued England's ruthless domination of the Welsh, principally by attempting to abolish their language. Ironically it was another

Tudor monarch, Elizabeth I, who ensured its survival by authorizing a Welsh translation of the Bible in 1588. Today, many people still say they owe their knowledge of Welsh to the Bible. The language is spoken by only a fifth of the population, but it still flourishes. Terms that crop up frequently are *bach* or *fach* (small), *craig* or *graig* (rock), *cwm* (valley), *dyffryn* (valley), *eglwys* (church), *glyn* (glen), *llyn* (lake), *mawr* or *fawr* (great, big), *mynydd* or *fynydd* (mountain, moorland), *pentre* (village, homestead), *plas* (hall, mansion), and *pont* or *bont* (bridge). Signs are bilingual, but don't worry; everyone speaks English, too.

The language is just one key to Wales's distinctiveness. English-speaking Welsh—the vast majority of the country's 2.75 million inhabitants—regard themselves as being just as Welsh as anyone else, which sometimes leads to differences of opinion, mainly about cultural affairs. But everyone feels a deep-rooted attachment to the country, and there's a strong sense of Welsh identity, as well as a genuine friendliness.

Pleasures and Pastimes

Castles

History addicts love Wales because it's well known as a "Land of Castles." With more than 100 fortresses worth a visit, there's an inexhaustible supply of inspiration in these ancient strongholds that dot the landscape from south to north—ranging from romantic ruins to well-preserved fortresses still standing to their original imperious height. The great North Wales castles, such as Caernarfon, are nearly intact and particularly famous. But for many visitors, the lasting memory of Wales is the sight of weather-beaten ruins crowning hilltops or guarding mountain passes deep in the lush countryside.

Dining

Twenty-five years ago, Wales was regarded as a gastronomic desert. How times change: You can now eat exceedingly well here, and even country pubs are more interested in offering meals than serving pints of beer. Talented chefs have moved in, making the best use of Wales's bountiful natural resources. Succulent Welsh lamb is regarded as the best in the world, there is a plentiful supply of seafood, and there has been a revival in Welsh cheesemaking to such an extent that the suppliers have difficulty in coping with the demand. For traditionalists, there is the old favorite of Welsh lamb served with vegetables. Another traditional feast is *cawl,* a nourishing broth with vegetables and meat. The most unusual traditional delicacy is laverbread, made from seaweed and cooked to resemble a black puréed substance. Don't be put off by its appearance: It has a taste all its own and is usually eaten with bacon. For more cosmopolitan palates, there's everything from French to Far Eastern, especially in Cardiff. For a special treat, have dinner at one of Wales's leading country house hotels—you don't have to be a overnight guest to enjoy the experience.

CATEGORY	COST*
££££	over £40
£££	£25–£40
££	£15–£25
£	under £15

**per person, including first course, main course, dessert, and VAT; excluding drinks*

Lodging

Wales's accommodations are wide-ranging. Cardiff and Swansea have their large international hotels, while at the other end of the spectrum you can stay on a working farm deep in the hills. For luxury and top-class service, there's a good choice of country house hotels. An added attraction is that prices are generally lower than equivalent properties in the Cotswolds, Scotland, or southeast England. For informality and warmth, stay at a country pub, inn, or historic hotel where stagecoaches used to stop. These places are full of character, with low-beam ceilings, wood paneling, and cozy fireplaces. Farmhouse accommodation has grown in leaps and bounds in the last 10 or 15 years: It's friendly, it's fun, and it's the best way to experience the rural way of life firsthand.

CATEGORY	COST*
££££	over £110
£££	£60–£110
££	£50–£60
£	under £50

**All prices are for two people sharing a double room, including service, breakfast, and VAT.*

Walking

Wales is a wonderful country for walking. There are long-distance paths to follow, such as the Pembrokeshire Coast Path (which runs all the way along the spectacular shores of southwest Wales) and the south–north Offa's Dyke Path, based on the ancient border between England and Wales established by King Offa in the 8th century. In Wales's forested areas you will find waymarked footpaths and nature trails that are short and easy to follow. Enthusiasts might prefer the more challenging wide, open spaces of the Brecon Beacons National Park or the rugged mountains of Snowdonia.

Exploring Wales

Wales has three main regions—south, mid, and north. The south is the most varied, for its boundaries include everything from Wales's capital city to unspoiled coastline, grassy mountains to wooded valleys. Mid-Wales is pure countryside, fringed on its western shores by the great arc of Cardigan Bay. North Wales is a mixture of high, rocky mountains, popular sandy beaches, and coastal hideaways.

Great Itineraries

Do not be misled by Wales's relatively small size. Although less than 200 miles from south to north, the country is packed with scenic variety and a daunting range of places to visit. Many visitors make the mistake of thinking that they can see Wales in a day or so. In that time, you will only have the opportunity to scratch the surface of this fascinating little country.

You can easily spend a day or two—or three—wandering around the capital city of Cardiff, or exploring country towns and their surroundings, or relaxing in a small resort, or walking a coast path, or riding scenic narrow-gauge railways, or following historic trails to the great Welsh castles, or pony trekking in the hills. The message is clear: A few days in Wales are not really enough, though we have included a short itinerary if you're in a rush. Wales is endlessly fascinating, so take your time.

Numbers in the text correspond to numbers in the margin and on the maps.

IF YOU HAVE 3 DAYS

Start off in **Cardiff** ㉘, Wales's capital city. You will want to spend at least a half day here before driving through the Brecon Beacons National Park to 🏨 **Llandrindod Wells** ⑰, a Victorian town conveniently

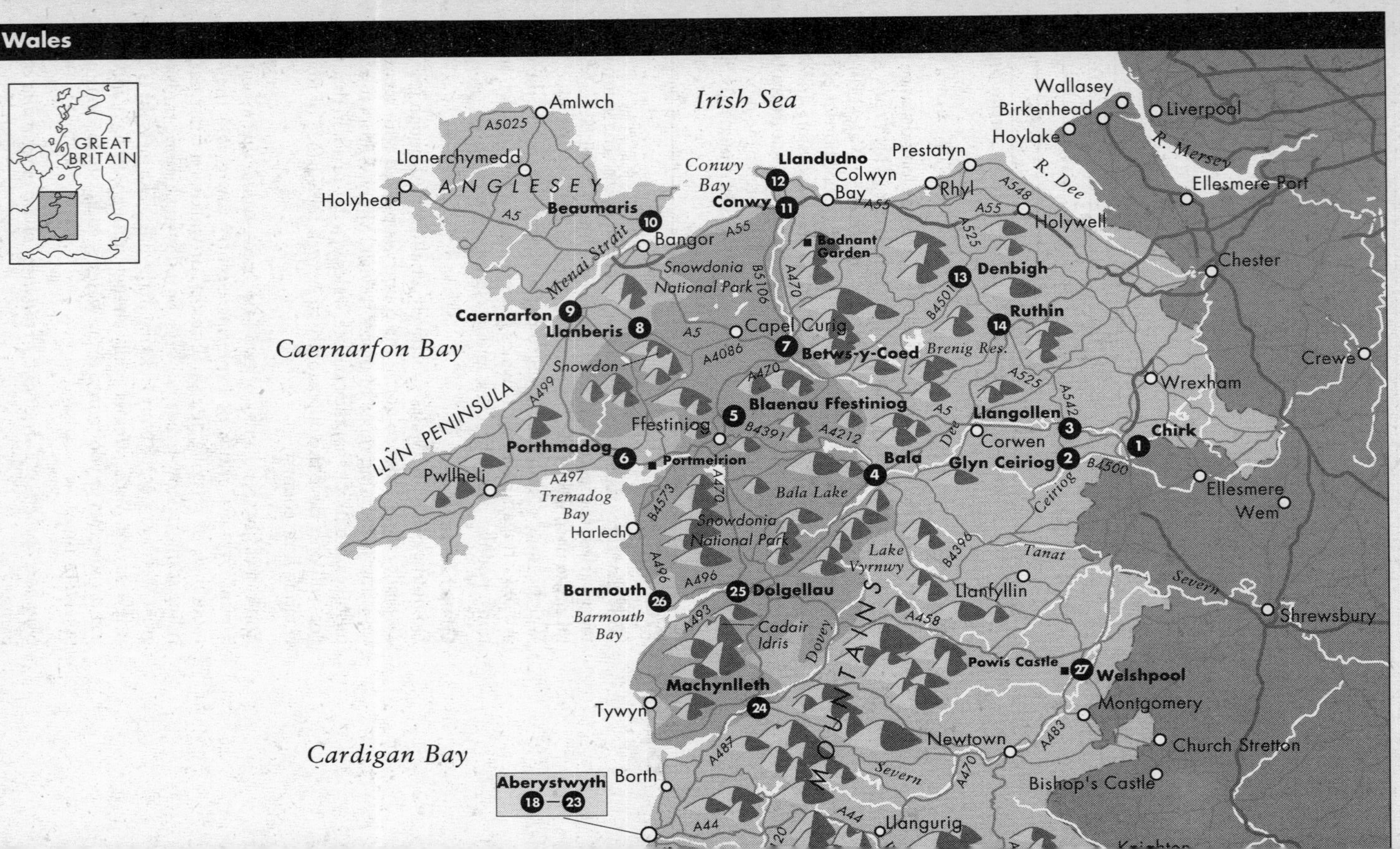
Wales
GREAT BRITAIN
Irish Sea
Caernarfon Bay
Cardigan Bay
ANGLESEY
LLŶN PENINSULA
MOUNTAINS
Amlwch
Llanerchymedd
Holyhead
Beaumaris 10
Bangor
Menai Strait
Caernarfon 9
Llanberis 8
Snowdon
Snowdonia National Park
Conwy Bay
Llandudno 12
Conwy 11
Colwyn Bay
Prestatyn
Rhyl
Holywell
Bodnant Garden
Denbigh 13
Ruthin 14
Capel Curig
Betws-y-Coed 7
Brenig Res.
Blaenau Ffestiniog 5
Ffestiniog
Porthmadog 6
Portmeirion
Pwllheli
Tremadog Bay
Harlech
Llangollen 3
Corwen
Bala 4
Bala Lake
Glyn Ceiriog 2
Ceiriog
Chirk 1
Wrexham
Chester
Crewe
Wallasey
Birkenhead
Hoylake
Liverpool
R. Mersey
R. Dee
Dee
Ellesmere Port
Ellesmere
Wem
Lake Vyrnwy
Tanat
Llanfyllin
Severn
Shrewsbury
Barmouth 26
Barmouth Bay
Dolgellau 25
Cadair Idris
Dovey
Powis Castle
Welshpool 27
Montgomery
Church Stretton
Bishop's Castle
Newtown
Machynlleth 24
Tywyn
Borth
Aberystwyth 18—23
Llangurig
A5025
A5
A55
A548
A525
B4501
B5106
A470
A4086
A499
A497
B4391
A4212
A542
B4500
B4573
A496
A493
B4396
A458
A483
A487
A44

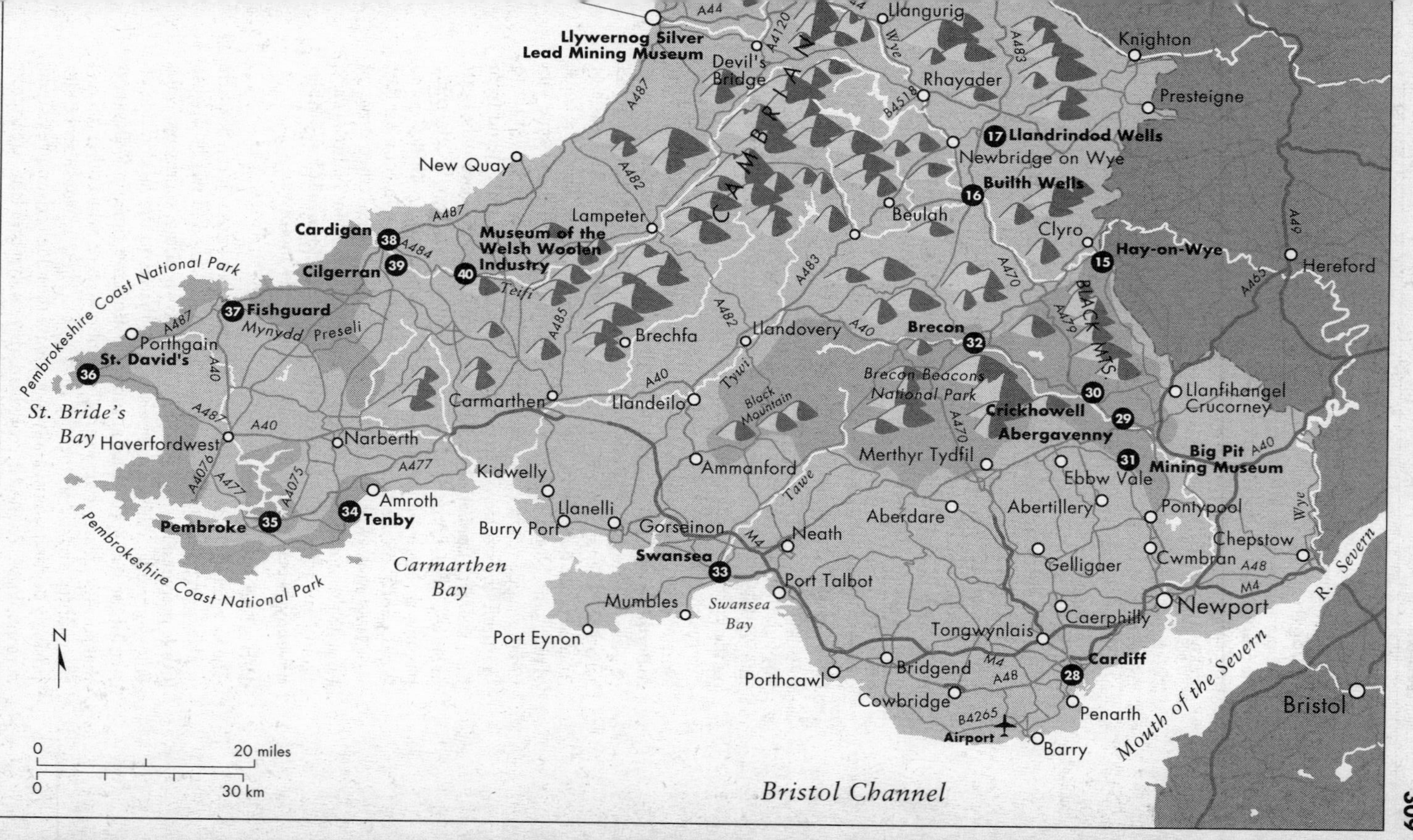

Llywernog Silver Lead Mining Museum
A44
A4120
Devil's Bridge
Llangurig
Wye
Rhayader
B4518
A483
Knighton
Presteigne
17 Llandrindod Wells
Newbridge on Wye
16 Builth Wells
Beulah
Clyro
15 Hay-on-Wye
A49
Hereford
A465
CAMBRIAN
New Quay
A487
A482
Lampeter
Cardigan 38
A484
Cilgerran 39
40 Museum of the Welsh Woolen Industry
Teifi
A485
Brechfa
A483
A470
A479
BLACK MTS.
Pembrokeshire Coast National Park
37 Fishguard
Mynydd Preseli
Porthgain
36 St. David's
A40
Llandovery
Brecon 32
Brecon Beacons National Park
Tywi
Black Mountain
30 Crickhowell
29 Abergavenny
Llanfihangel Crucorney
31 Big Pit Mining Museum
St. Bride's Bay
Haverfordwest
A4076
A477
A4075
Narberth
Carmarthen
Llandeilo
Ammanford
Tawe
Merthyr Tydfil
Ebbw Vale
Abertillery
Pontypool
Wye
Chepstow
Cwmbran
A48
M4
Kidwelly
Amroth
34 Tenby
35 Pembroke
Llanelli
Burry Port
Gorseinon
Neath
Aberdare
Gelligaer
Swansea 33
Port Talbot
Carmarthen Bay
Mumbles
Swansea Bay
Port Eynon
Caerphilly
Newport
R. Severn
Tongwynlais
Cardiff 28
Bridgend
Porthcawl
Cowbridge
B4265
Airport
Penarth
Barry
Mouth of the Severn
Bristol
N
0 20 miles
0 30 km
Bristol Channel

situated between the border and the mountains. On day two, drive via Rhayader and the Elan Valley—Wales's "Lake District"—to **Aberystwyth** ⑱, then along the north coast of Cardigan Bay to **Porthmadog** ⑥ (handy accommodations are in nearby Harlech and Portmeirion). For your final day, drive via **Blaenau Ffestiniog** ⑤ through the Snowdonia National Park to **Betws-y-Coed** ⑦, and if you have the time call into medieval **Conwy** ⑪ before leaving Wales via the A55 "Expressway" route to England.

IF YOU HAVE 9 DAYS

Travel to **Cardiff** ㉘ for a full day's visit and overnight stop, making sure that you have time to call at the Museum of Welsh Life at St. Fagans on the eastern outskirts of the city. On day two, drive via **Swansea** ㉝ to **Tenby** ㉞, a resort at the southern gateway to the Pembrokeshire Coast National Park. Day three is taken up by a tour of this wild and beautiful stretch of seashore. Drive to **St. David's** ㊱ in the far west to visit the cathedral built on a religious site founded by Wales's patron saint in the 6th century. If you have time, walk a stretch of the coast path before continuing on to **Fishguard** ㊲. Day four is taken up by more beautiful coastline on the way to **Cardigan** ㊳, then a tour along the lovely Vale of Teifi through **Cilgerran** ㊴ to Drefach Felindre to explore the **Museum of the Welsh Woolen Industry** ㊵. From here, continue on to **Aberystwyth** ⑱. From Aberystwyth, drive along the Cardigan Bay coast via **Machynlleth** ㉔ to **Dolgellau** ㉕, then head inland through the southern section of the Snowdonia National Park to lakeside **Bala** ④. There is more dramatic mountain scenery on day six on the way from Bala to **Blaenau Ffestiniog** ⑤, where you can visit the caverns that gave this town its past reputation as the "slate capital of North Wales." From here, follow the wooded Vale of Ffestiniog west to **Porthmadog** ⑥ then continue northward to **Caernarfon** ⑨, home of one of Wales's most famous medieval castles. Day seven takes you across the Menai Strait by the road bridge near Bangor to the Isle of Anglesey and **Beaumaris** ⑩ for a brief visit, then back along the coast of mainland North Wales via medieval **Conwy** ⑪ to the handsome Victorian seaside resort of **Llandudno** ⑫ (on this leg, you may want to substitute the trip across to Anglesey with a short detour inland from Caernarfon to **Llanberis** ⑧ and the spectacular Llanberis Pass in the heart of Snowdonia). Borderland Wales is the theme of the next day, the route passing through **Denbigh** ⑬, **Ruthin** ⑭, **Llangollen** ③, **Chirk** ①, and **Welshpool** ㉗ on the way to **Llandrindod Wells** ⑰. On your last day, visit **Hay-on-Wye** ⑮, the borderland "town of books," then drive on through the mountains to **Brecon** ㉜ in the Brecon Beacons National Park. From here, follow the Vale of Usk through **Crickhowell** ㉚ and **Abergavenny** ㉙ before leaving Wales along the M4 motorway.

When to Tour Wales

The weather in Wales, as in the rest of Britain, is a lottery. It can be warm in the spring and cool in the summer, dry in May and wet in August. Come prepared for rain or shine. Generally speaking, southwest Wales enjoys a milder climate than elsewhere, thanks to the moderating effects of the sea. Spring and autumn are attractive times in Wales (note that spring can arrive very early in Pembrokeshire, while other parts of the country are still in the grip of winter). These seasons can be surprisingly dry and sunny, and you will have the added advantage of quiet surroundings. That noted, crowds are very rarely a problem—apart from the main tourist centers—for many parts of Wales remain peaceful even in the height of summer.

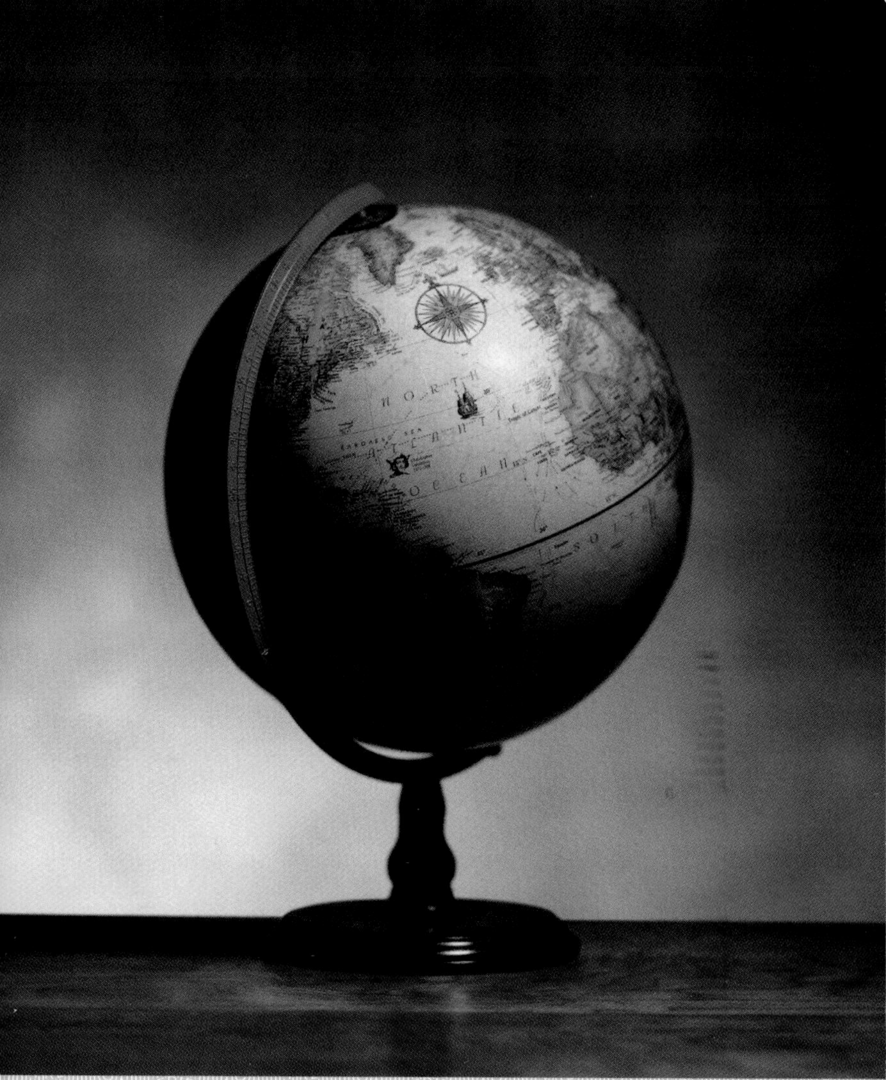

In case you want to see the world.

At American Express, we're here to make your journey a smooth one. So we have over 1,700 travel service locations in over 120 countries ready to help. What else would you expect from the world's largest travel agency?

do more

http://www.americanexpress.com/travel

Travel

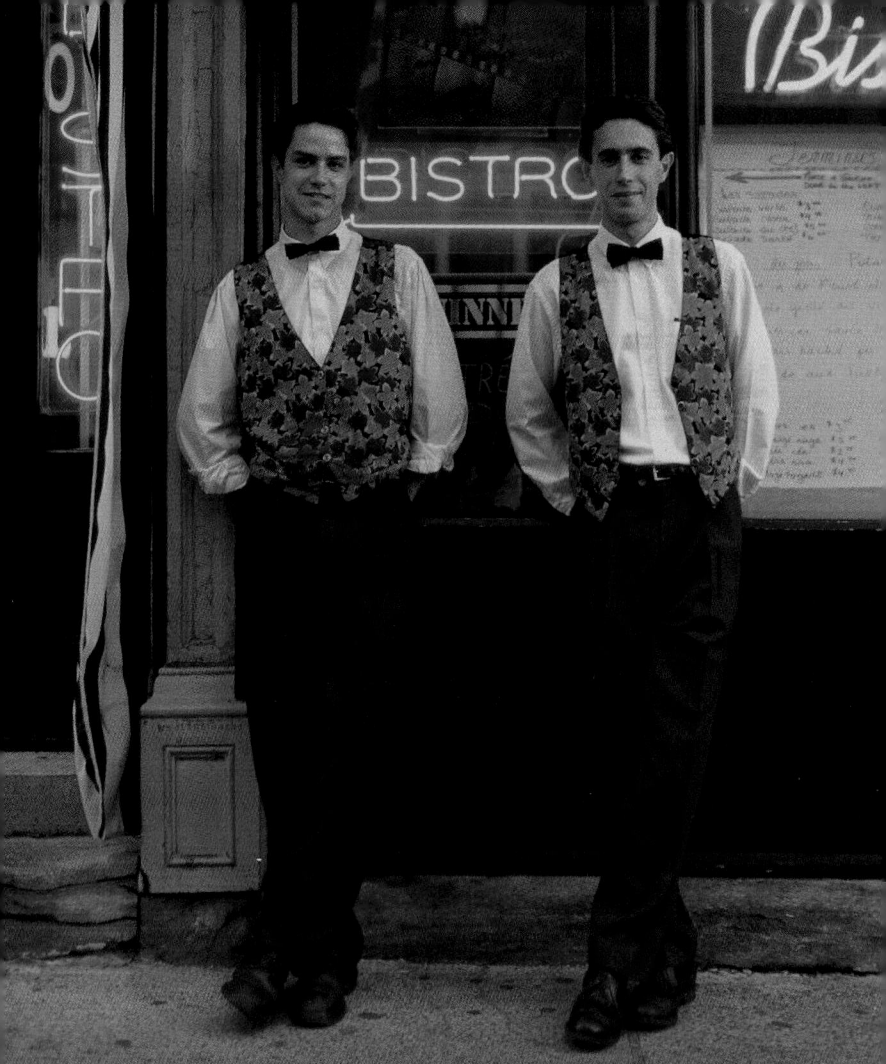

In case you want to be welcomed there.

We're here to see that you're always welcomed at establishments everywhere. That's why millions of people carry the American Express® Card – for peace of mind, confidence, and security, around the world or just around the corner.

do more.

Cards

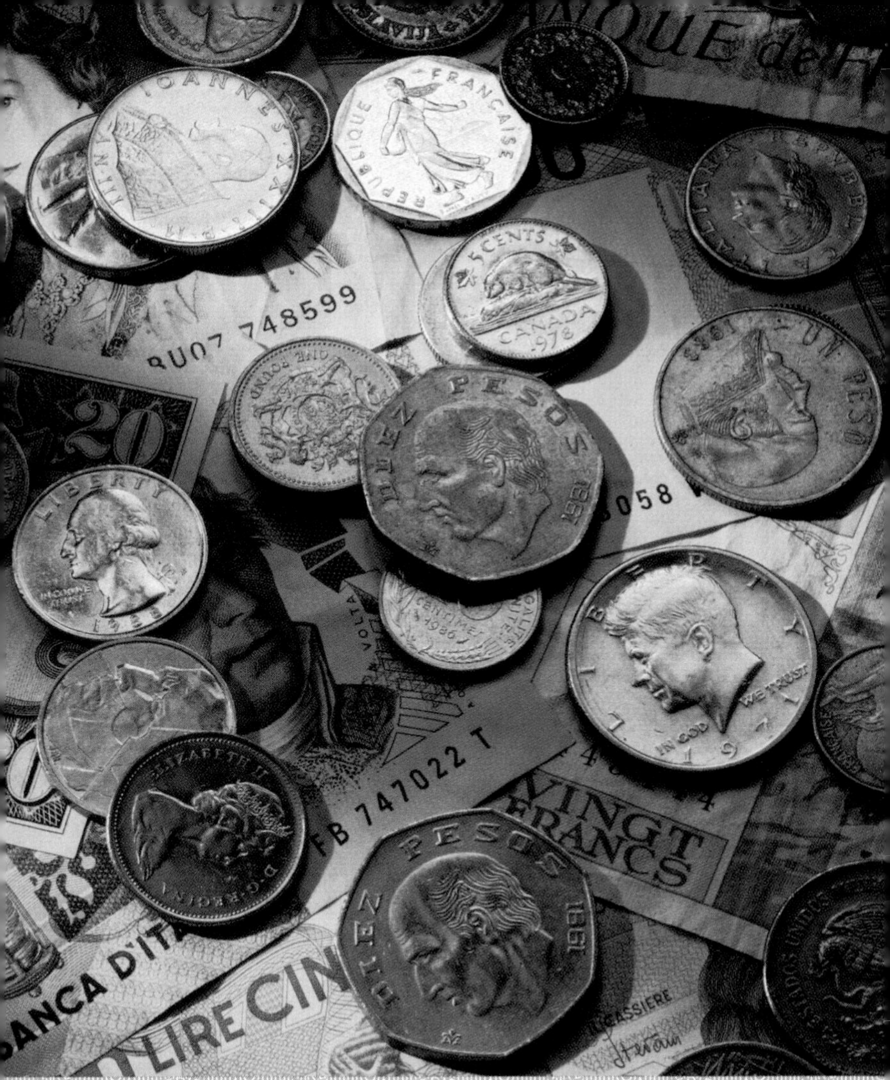

In case you're running low.

We're here to help with more than 118,000 Express Cash locations around the world. In order to enroll, just call American Express before you start your vacation.

do more

Express Cash

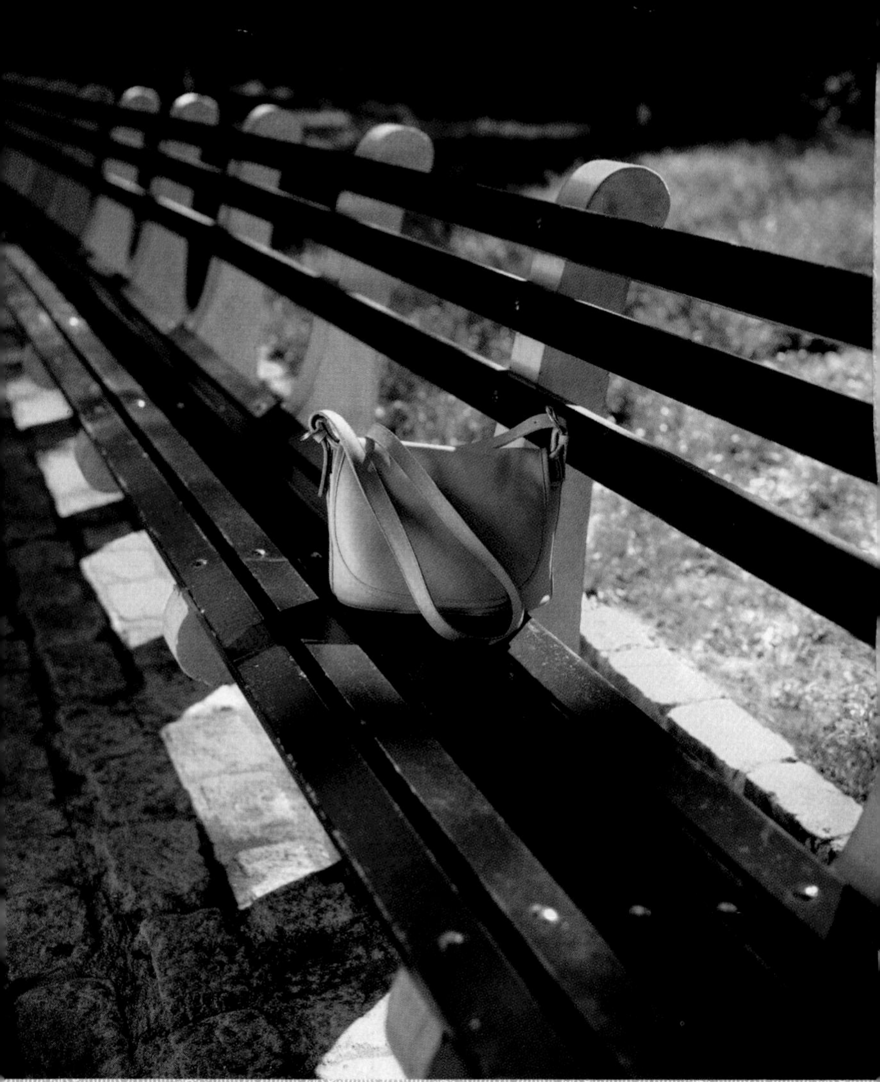

And just in case.

We're here with American Express® Travelers Cheques and Cheques *for Two*.® They're the safest way to carry money on your vacation and the surest way to get a refund, practically anywhere, anytime.

Another way we help you...

do more®

Travelers Cheques

©1996 American Express Travel Related Services Company, Inc.

NORTH WALES: IN THE REALM OF SNOWDONIA

The north was the first region in Wales to experience the arrival of visitors on a large scale, and it's easy to see why. This is the region where Wales masses all its savage splendor, its fierce beauty. Dominating its southwestern corner is Snowdon, at 3,560 feet the highest mountain in England and Wales. It is impossible to describe the magnificence of the view on a clear day—to the northwest the Straits of Menai, Anglesey, and beyond to the Irish Sea, to the south the mountains of Merioneth, Harlech Castle, and Cader Idris, and all around great towering masses of wild and barren rock. If you ascend the peak by the Llanberis railway, telephone from the terminus to ascertain whether Snowdon is free from mist, for you will lose much if you arrive when clouds, as often happens, encircle the monster's brow.

The peak gives its name to the Snowdonia National Park, which extends southward all the way to Machynlleth in mid-Wales. The park consists of 840 square miles of rocky mountains, valleys clothed in oakwoods, moorlands, lakes and rivers, all with one thing in common—natural beauty; and, to a lesser extent, solitude. Increasingly, however, the park has become a popular climbing center and there are fears that Snowdon itself is becoming worn away by the boots of too many walkers. East of Snowdonia, the high landscape subsides into rolling green hills and vales around the Wales/England border. Along the sandy, north-facing coast, a string of seaside resorts has also been attracting visitors for well over a century. Llandudno, the dignified "Queen of the North Wales coast," was built in Victorian times as a seaside watering hole. For those who prefer away-from-it-all seashore, there are two official "Areas of Outstanding Beauty"—the Isle of Anglesey (connected by bridge to mainland Wales) and the Llŷn Peninsula—dotted with quieter small resorts and coastal villages.

Numbers in the margins correspond to points of interest on the Wales map.

Chirk and the Ceiriog Valley

❶ *22 mi southwest of Chester.*

A favored first stop in Wales for travelers coming from England is Chirk, poised on the very border between the two entities. It's a handy gateway to the Ceiriog Valley, an area described by the Wales Tourist Board as one of outstanding beauty—although a few tourists say them nay. Chirk is the site of an imposing medieval **castle,** which has over the centuries evolved into a grand home. Standing amid beautiful formal gardens and grounds, it is now owned by the National Trust. ☎ *01691/777701.* 🎫 *£4; garden only £2.* ⏲ *Apr.–June and Sept., Tues.–Fri. and Sun.; July–Aug., Sun.–Fri.; Oct., weekends only. Castle noon–5, garden 11–6.*

From Chirk head to the Vale of Ceiriog, nicknamed—and somewhat hyped as—Little Switzerland. Take B4500 west 6 miles through the pic-
❷ turesque valley to the village of **Glyn Ceiriog,** where the **Chwarel Wynne slate mine** gives a fascinating glimpse into Britain's industrial past. ☎ *01691/718343.* 🎫 *£2.50.* ⏲ *Easter–Oct., daily 10–5 (last admission 4:30).*

Continue on B4500 southwest from Glyn Ceiriog, and then its unnumbered continuation, to reach Llanrhaeadr ym Mochnant, in the peaceful Tanat Valley. Here, in 1588, the Bible was translated into Welsh, thus ensuring the survival of the language. Turn northwest and go 4 miles up the road to Pistyll Rhaeadr, the highest waterfall in Wales, with its peat-brown water thundering down a 290-foot double cascade.

NEED A BREAK? **Tanypistyll,** at the foot of the waterfall, specializes in steak pies, scones, and *bara brith* (Welsh currant bread).

Dining and Lodging

££–£££ ✕🏨 **Golden Pheasant.** Jenny Gibourg searched the country to furnish the 200-year-old hotel with antiques and Victorian-style fabrics, and the result is chinoiserie in the bar, horse prints and aspidistras in the lounge, draped curtains and parlor palms in the dining room, and no two bedrooms alike. Specialties include Ceiriog trout, pheasant, and game pie. ✉ *Glyn Ceiriog, near Chirk LL20 7BB,* ☎ *01691/718281. 18 rooms with bath. Restaurant, horseback riding. AE, DC, MC, V.*

£ 🏨 **Bron Heulog.** This guest house at Llanrhaeadr ym Mochnant, a former Victorian doctor's surgery, has been lovingly restored and has antique furniture and paintings. It serves excellent dinners for about £10. ✉ *Waterfall Rd., near Oswestry, Shropshire SY10 0JX,* ☎ *01691/780521. 3 rooms with bath. No credit cards.*

Llangollen

❸ *5 mi northwest of Chirk, 23 mi southwest of Chester.*

Llangollen, set in a deep valley carved by the river Dee, is the birthplace of the International Musical Eisteddfod. The tradition of the *eisteddfod,* held throughout Wales, goes back to the 12th century. Originally gatherings of bards, the *eisteddfodau* of today are more like competitions or festivals. The Llangollen event was started as a gesture of friendship after World War II by a newspaperman who wanted, in effect, to have a concert and invite the whole world to join in. Amazingly, it worked, and now choirs and dancers from all over the world make for an unusual arts festival. The six-day event takes place each year in early July. The evening concerts are of international standard. ☎ *01978/860236.*

While you are in Llangollen, visit **Plas Newydd** (not to be confused with the grand estate on the Isle of Anglesey with the same name), home from 1778 to 1828 of the eccentric Ladies of Llangollen, who set up a scandalous single-sex household, collected curios and magnificent wood carvings, and made it into a tourist attraction even during their lifetimes, entertaining celebrated guests, among them William Wordsworth, Sir Walter Scott, and the Duke of Wellington. The Ladies had a servant with the unforgettable name of "Mollie the Basher." ✉ *Hill St.,* ☎ *01978/861314.* 🎫 *£1.80.* ⏲ *Apr.–end Oct., daily 10–5.*

From the **canal wharf** take a horse-drawn boat along the Shropshire Union Canal to the largest navigable aqueduct in the world at Pontcysyllte. ☎ *01978/860702.*

Llangollen's bridge, over the river Dee, a 14th-century stone structure, is named in a traditional Welsh folk song as one of the "Seven Wonders of Wales." Near the bridge is the terminus of the **Llangollen Railway,** a restored standard-gauge, steam-powered line. It runs for a few miles along the scenic Dee Valley. ☎ *01978/860979 or 01978/860951 (24-hr recorded information).* 🎫 *Round-trip £6.* ⏲ *Mar.–Nov., daily 10–5.*

There are easy walks along the banks of the river Dee or along part of **Offa's Dyke Path.** The 167-mile-long dyke, a defensive wall whose earthen foundations still stand, was built along the border with En-

LL48 6ET, ☎ 01766/770228, FAX 01766/771331. 14 rooms with bath in main hotel, 20 rooms with bath in village. Restaurant, pool, tennis court. AE, DC, MC, V.

££ **Castle Cottage.** Close to Harlech's mighty castle, this cozy, friendly hotel is a charming "restaurant with rooms." The emphasis here is on the exceptional cuisine served by chef-proprietor Glyn Roberts, who makes the best possible use of fresh ingredients to create imaginative, beautifully presented dishes. The rooms, though small, are attractively appointed and decorated. Guests should find this lodging a wonderful little find, not to say an excellent all-round value. ✉ *Harlech LL46 2YL, ☎ 01766/780479. 6 rooms, 4 with bath. AE, MC, V.*

Betws-y-Coed

7 *25 mi northeast of Porthmadog, 19 mi south of Llandudno.*

On the western approach to this mountain resort are the **Swallow Falls** (small admission charge), a famous North Wales beauty spot where the river Llugwy tumbles down through a wooded chasm. The rivers Llugwy and Conwy meet at Betws-y-Coed, a popular tourist village set amongst wooded hills affording excellent views of Snowdonia, busy in summer, with a good selection of hotels and crafts shops. The chief landmark here is the ornate iron bridge (1815) over the Conwy, designed by Telford, while the magnificent Bodnant Garden in the town of Conwy (☞ *below*) is a delightful excursion away.

Dining

£–££ **Ty Gwyn.** After a browse through the small antiques shop next door, stop for a bite at the restaurant, which is under the same management. Inside the 17th-century building it's all prints and chintz, old beams and copper pans, and there's a nice view of the nearby Waterloo bridge. Homemade pâté is a specialty. ✉ *Betws-y-Coed, ☎ 01690/710383. MC, V.*

Llanberis

8 *17 mi west of Betws-y-Coed, 7 mi southeast of Caernarfon.*

Llanberis, like Betws-y-Coed, is a focal point for visitors to the Snowdonia National Park. It stands beside twin lakes at the foot of the rocky **Llanberis Pass,** which cuts through the highest mountains in the park and is lined with fearsome slabs popular with rock climbers. There are hiking trails from the top of the pass, but the going can be rough for the inexperienced; ask local advice before starting on even the briefest ramble. At the Pen-y-Gwryd Hotel just beyond the summit of the pass, Lord Hunt and his team planned their successful ascent of Everest in 1953.

★ Llanberis has many attractions, but its most famous is the rack-and-pinion **Snowdon Mountain Railway**—some of its track at a gradient of 1 in 5—which terminates within 70 feet of the 3,560-foot summit. Snowdon, *Yr Wyddfa* in Welsh, is the highest peak south of Scotland and is set on more than 800 square miles of national park. From the summit on a clear day you can see as far as the Irish Wicklow Mountains, about 90 miles away. *☎ 01286/870223. Maximum round-trip fare £13.50. ⏲ Mar.–Oct., daily from 9 AM; weather permitting, trains go all the way to summit May–Sept.*

Across the lake in the Padarn Country Park, the workshops of the old Dinorwig slate quarry now contain the **Welsh Slate Museum.** ✉ *Dinorwig Quarry, Llanberis, ☎ 01286/870630. £2. ⏲ Easter–Sept., daily 9:30–5:30; Oct., weekdays 10–4.*

Beauty is not only skin deep in Llanberis, as you'll discover by going on one of the **underground tours** of the awesome tunnels carved into Snowdon (part of a huge—but largely invisible—scheme to create hydro-electricity by pumping the waters of the lake up to a mountain reservoir). There is also a gentler alternative to the Snowdon Mountain Railway in the form of the **Llanberis Lake Railway** (☎ 01286/870549), which once transported slate along a scenic lakeside route.

Caernarfon

❾ *7 mi northwest of Llanberis, 26 mi southwest of Llandudno.*

★ Standing like a warning finger, the grim majestic mass of **Caernarfon Castle**—"that most magnificent badge of our subjection," wrote Pennant—looms over the now peaceful waters of the Seiont River. Numerous bloody encounters were witnessed by these sullen walls, erected by Edward I in the 13th century as a symbol of his determination to reduce the Welsh to complete subjugation. Begun in 1283, its towers, unlike those of Edward I's other castles, are polygonal and patterned with bands of different colored stone. In 1284, the crafty monarch thought of an amazing scheme to steal the Welsh throne. Knowing that the proud Welsh chieftains would accept no foreign prince, he promised to designate a ruler who could speak no word of English. He sent his queen, Eleanor of Castile, who was expecting a child, posthaste to Caernarfon that she might be delivered there, and in this cold stone fortress the queen gave birth to a son. Triumphantly, Edward presented the infant to the assembled chieftains as their prince "who spoke no English, had been born on Welsh soil, and whose first words would be spoken in Welsh." The ruse worked, and on that historic day was created the first prince of Wales of English lineage. This tradition still holds: In July 1969, Elizabeth II presented Prince Charles to the people of Wales as their prince from this castle. In the Queen's Tower, an intriguing museum charts the history of the local regiment, The Royal Welch Fusiliers. *☎ 01286/677617. Castle £3.80. Late Mar.–late Oct., daily 9:30–6:30; late Oct.–late Mar., Mon.–Sat. 9:30–4, Sun. 11–4.*

The town of Caernarfon, which has an historic pedigree as a walled medieval settlement, has nothing to rival the splendor of its castle and, in fact, is now overrun with tourist buses. But don't miss the garrison church of St. Mary, built into the city walls. Outside Caernarfon is the extensive excavation site of the **Roman Fortress of Segontium,** a branch of the National Museums and Galleries of Wales. It contains material found on the site, one of Britain's most famous Roman forts. *☎ 01286/675625. £1. Mar.–Oct., Mon.–Sat. 9:30–6 (closes at 5:30 Mar.–Apr., Oct.), Sun. 2–6 (closes at 5 Mar.–Apr., Oct.); Nov.–Feb., Mon.–Sat. 9:30–4, Sun. 2–4.*

NEED A BREAK? **Y Gegin Fach,** on Pool Hill about a five-minute walk from the castle, is a friendly café and tea shop serving delicious freshly baked scones, traditional *bara brith* currant bread, and snacks. It is open until about 4 PM.

Caernarfon Airport (at the end of Dinas Dinlle beach road) operates **Pleasure Flights** in light aircraft (including a vintage Rapide) over Snowdon, Anglesey, and Caernarfon. The airport also contains the **Caernarfon Air World** museum. *☎ 01286/830800. From £17–£30 per seat. Flights daily, year-round.*

Lodging

£££ ★ **Ty'n Rhos.** This is an immaculate farmhouse with a difference: It offers the highest standard of accommodation. It has a beautifully furnished lounge and dining room, with views across the fields to the Isle of Anglesey. The cooking is exceptional, and there are homemade cheeses and yogurt. The bedrooms are comfortable and nicely decorated. This is an ideal touring base, because it stands between Snowdonia and the sea close to Caernarfon and Anglesey. ⊠ *Llanddeiniolen, near Caernarfon LL55 3AE,* ☎ *01248/670489,* FAX *01248/670079. 11 rooms with bath. MC, V.*

Beaumaris

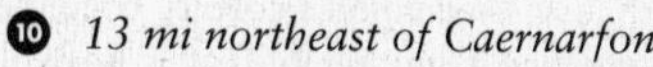

10 *13 mi northeast of Caernarfon.*

Handsome Beaumaris is on the Isle of Anglesey, the largest island directly off the shore of either Wales or England. It's linked to the mainland by the Britannia road and rail bridge and by Thomas Telford's remarkable chain suspension bridge, built in 1826 over the dividing Menai Strait. Though its name means "beautiful marsh," Beaumaris today is an elegant town of simple cottages, Georgian terraces, and bright shops. The nearest mainline train station is in Bangor, 10 minutes away on the mainland; a regular bus service operates between it and Beaumaris. The town dates from 1295, when Edward I commenced work on the **castle,** the last and largest link in an "iron ring" of fortifications around north Wales built to contain the Welsh. Guarding the western approach to the Menai Strait, the castle is solid and symmetrical, with arrow slits and a moat: a fine example of medieval defensive planning. ☎ *01248/810361.* 🎫 *£1.70.* ⏲ *Late Mar.–late Oct., daily 9:30–6:30; late Oct.–late Mar., Mon.–Sat. 9:30–4, Sun. 11–4.*

Opposite the castle is the **courthouse** (☎ 01286/679090; call for details), built in 1614. A plaque depicts one view of the legal profession: Two farmers pull a cow, one by the horns, one by the tail, while a lawyer sits in the middle milking. Beyond the courthouse is the **Museum and Memorabilia of Childhood,** an Aladdin's cave of music boxes, magic lanterns, trains, cars, toy soldiers, rocking horses, and mechanical savings banks. ⊠ *1 Castle St.,* ☎ *01248/712498.* 🎫 *£2.50.* ⏲ *Mar.–Oct., Mon.–Sat. 10–5:30, Sun. noon–5.*

On Castle Street, look for **The Tudor Rose,** a house dating back to 1400 that's an excellent example of Tudor timberwork.

NEED A BREAK? At the other end of Castle Street from the castle, the **Liverpool Arms** pub, with its nautical bar, specializes in inexpensive seafood—try the crab sandwiches.

Head for Steeple Lane to find the old **gaol,** built in 1829 by Joseph Hansom, who was also the designer of the Hansom cab. It was considered a model prison, the best in Britain at the time, but an exhibition shows what life there was really like. You can wander the corridors, be locked in the soundproof punishment cell or the condemned cell, and see the country's only working treadwheel, where prisoners trudged hopelessly around like hamsters in a cage. ☎ *01286/679090; call for details.*

Opposite the gaol is the 14th-century **parish church.** In 1862 an innocent man was hanged on the gibbet outside the prison wall—to give the crowd a good view—and he cursed the clock on the church tower. Locals say that from that day the clock never kept good time until it was overhauled in 1980.

The Arts

The **Beaumaris Festival** (☎ 01248/713177) is held annually late May–early June. The whole town is used as a site, from the 14th-century parish church to the concert hall, with special concerts, dance performances, and plays performed.

OFF THE BEATEN PATH

PLAS NEWYDD – While off the main tourist routes, the celebrated mansion of Plas Newydd is well worth a special detour, for historians rate it the finest house in Wales. Built in the 18th century for the marquesses of Anglesey, it stands on the Menai Strait close to the Menai Bridge about 7 miles southwest of Beaumaris (don't confuse it with the Plas Newydd at Llangollen). In 1936–40 the society artist Rex Whistler painted the mural in the dining room here, his largest work and a great favorite for stately-home buffs. A military museum commemorates the Battle of Waterloo, where the first marquess, Wellington's cavalry commander, lost his leg. The interior has some fine 18th-century Gothic Revival decorations, and the gardens have been restored to their original design. There are magnificent views across the strait from here. ✉ *Llanfairpwll, Anglesey,* ☎ *01248/714795.* 🎟 *£4.* ⏲ *Apr.–Sept., Sun.–Fri. noon–5; Oct., Fri. and Sun. noon–5; last admission ½ hr before closing.*

Dining and Lodging

£££ ✕🏨 **Ye Olde Bull's Head.** Originally a coaching inn built in 1472, this place is small and charming. The oak-beamed dining room, dating from 1617, serves French specialties, including warm salad of pigeon breast with hazelnut oil, as well as local widgeon (wild duck), and is also noted for its seafood. ✉ *Beaumaris, Castle St., Anglesey LL58 8AP,* ☎ *01248/810329,* FAX *01248/811294. 15 rooms with bath. Restaurant (££). MC, V.*

££ ★ 🏨 **Llwydiarth Fawr.** It's worth seeking out this outstanding place at Llanerchymedd in the north central part of Anglesey. Llwydiarth Fawr offers exceptional farmhouse accommodation as well as being a convenient touring base for the island. It's a spacious, elegant Georgian house on an 850-acre cattle and sheep farm, whose deluxe rooms are superior to those in many hotels. Owner Margaret Hughes welcomes guests warmly, serves good country cooking, and, in a nutshell, offers country living in style. ✉ *Llanerchymedd, Anglesey LL71 8DF,* ☎ *01248/470321. 3 rooms with bath. No credit cards.*

Conwy

★ ⓫ *23 mi east of Beaumaris, 48 mi northwest of Chester.*

This still-authentic medieval town grew up around its **castle** on the west bank of the river Conwy. Conwy's mighty, many-turreted stronghold, built by Edward I, the English invader, can be approached on foot by a dramatic suspension bridge designed by 19th-century engineer Thomas Telford to blend in with the fortress's presence. Of all of Edward's castles, Conwy preserves most convincingly the spirit of medieval times. The strong sense of period atmosphere is aided and abetted by a ring of ancient but extremely well-preserved walls that enclose the old town. Visitors can walk along sections of the wall, which have breathtaking views across the huddled rooftops of the town to the castle and its estuary setting. ☎ *01492/592358.* 🎟 *£3.* ⏲ *Mid-Mar.–mid-Oct., daily 9:30–6:30; mid-Oct.–mid-Mar., Mon.–Sat. 9:30–4, Sun. 11–4.*

On the quay is what is said to be the smallest house in Britain, furnished in mid-Victorian Welsh style—it can hold only a few people at a time.

★ About 5 miles south of Conwy, in the lovely Vale of Conwy just off A470, is **Bodnant Garden,** a pilgrimage spot for horticulturists from around the world. Laid out in 1875, the 87 acres are particularly famed for their rhododendrons, camellias, and azaleas. But its reputation as the finest garden in Wales does not rest solely on those; this National Trust garden also has terraces, rock and rose gardens, and a pinetum, while the mountains of Snowdonia form a magnificent backdrop. ✉ *Tal-y-Cafn,* ☎ *01492/650460.* 🎫 *£4.20.* ⏲ *Mid-Mar.–Oct., daily 10–5.*

Llandudno

12 *3 mi north of Conwy, 50 mi northwest of Chester.*

This charmingly old-fashioned North Wales seaside resort has a wealth of well-preserved Victorian architecture and an ornate pier. Unlike other resorts in Wales—and Britain as a whole—Llandudno preserves the genteel look of a bygone age. There is a wide promenade, lined with a huge selection of attractively painted hotels (Llandudno has the largest choice of places to stay in Wales). The shopping streets behind also look the part, thanks to their original canopied walkways.

Llandudno has little in the way of the garish amusement arcades and funfairs that are nowadays such a feature of seaside resorts. Instead, it prefers to stick to its faithful cablecar that climbs San Francisco-style to the summit of the Great Orme headland above the resort. There is also an alpine-style cabinlift to the top, and a large dry ski slope and toboggan run.

Lovers of literature will delight in knowing that Llandudno was the summer home of the family of Dr. Liddell, the Oxford don and father of the immortal Alice, and it was to this resort town that Lewis Carroll was called to entertain the Liddell family (as was his wont). Scholars—who argue persuasively about the "Welshness" of *Alice in Wonderland*—have picked up many aspects of the town in Carroll's beloved book. For instance, the Liddells and Carroll used to drive to nearby Rhos-on-Sea for picnics. This site was known as a favorite haunt of the walrus, and perhaps this is where the author found his inspiration for the Walrus and the Carpenter (some historians are quick to note there was also a lot of construction activity in the town during this time!). The resort's links with Lewis Carroll's *Alice in Wonderland* are reflected in the **Alice in Wonderland Centre,** where Alice's adventures are colorfully brought to life in enchanting displays of the best-known scenes from the book. ✉ *3–4 Trinity Sq., Llandudno,* ☎ *01492/860082.* 🎫 *£2.65.* ⏲ *Daily 10–5, closed Sun. Nov.–Easter.*

Dining and Lodging

££££ ★ ✕🏨 **Bodysgallen Hall.** Set inside wide, walled gardens 2 miles out of town, the Hall is part 17th-, part 18th-century, full of antiques, comfortable chairs by cheery fires, pictures, and polished wood. The bedrooms (a few suites are available) combine elegance and practicality, and from some of them you'll see the mountains. The restaurant serves fine traditional meals, with an emphasis on such local fare as lamb and smoked salmon; its prices are relatively low for the standard it offers. ✉ *LL30 1RS,* ☎ *01492/584466,* FAX *01492/582519. 34 rooms with bath. Restaurant, indoor pool, sauna, tennis court, croquet, exercise room. AE, DC, MC, V.*

£££ ✕🏨 **St. Tudno Hotel.** Set on the seafront in Llandudno, this is one of Britain's top seaside hotels. From the outside, it blends unobtrusively with its neighbors, but inside it's a different story, with richly decorated and opulently furnished rooms. The service is first-class, the cuisine accomplished. ✉ *Promenade, LL30 2LP,* ☎ *01492/860407. 21 rooms with bath. Indoor pool. AE, DC, MC, V.*

££ 🏨 **Bryn Derwen Hotel.** British seaside resort hotels do not enjoy the best reputation; many hoteliers have not moved with the times to upgrade their accommodations and food. If only they were all like Stuart and Val Langfield, whose immaculate Victorian hotel exemplifies how it should be done. Fresh flowers and attractive furnishings set the tone, and the food, prepared by Stuart, an award-winning chef, lives up to the surroundings. Truly excellent value. ✉ *Abbey Rd., LL30 2EE,* ☎ *01492/876804. 9 rooms with bath. MC, V.*

En Route Inland from Rhyl is **Bodelwyddan Castle,** off A55, between Abergele and St. Asaph, a restored Victorian castle in spacious formal gardens, surrounded by lovely countryside. As an offshoot of the National Portrait Gallery in London, it exhibits Regency and Victorian portraits by the likes of Sargent, Lawrence, G. F. Watts, and Landseer. ☎ *01745/584060.* 🎫 *£4; grounds only £2.* ⏲ *Apr.–June and Sept.–Oct., Sat.–Thurs.; July–Aug., daily; Nov.–Mar., Tues.–Thurs. and weekends. Hrs: 10:30–5 (summer), 11–4 (winter).*

Denbigh

⓭ *25 mi southeast of Llandudno.*

This market town was much admired by Dr. Samuel Johnson, who stayed on Pentrefoelas Road at Gwaenynog Hall, where he designed two rooms. A walk along the riverbank at nearby Lawnt, a spot he loved, brings you to a monumental urn placed in his honor. Not that it pleased him: "It looks like an intention to bury me alive," thundered the great lexicographer. **Denbigh Castle** is known as "the hollow crown" because it is not much more than a shell set on high ground, dominating the town. A tiny museum inside is devoted to Denbigh native son H. M. Stanley, the 19th-century journalist and explorer who found Dr. Livingstone in Africa. Market day is Wednesday. ☎ *01745/813979.* 🎫 *£1.70.* ⏲ *May–Sept., daily 10–5.*

Ruthin

⓮ *8 mi southeast of Denbigh, 23 mi west of Chester.*

Ruthin is the capital of "Glyndwr Country," where the 15th-century Welsh hero Owain Glyndwr lived and ruled. Its well-preserved buildings date from the 16th to the 19th centuries. Ruthin also has elegant shops, good inns, and an interesting crafts complex that displays the work of different craftspeople. Since the 11th century, they have been ringing the curfew here each evening at 8.

Lodging

£ ★ **Eyarth Old Railway Station.** This Victorian railway station near Ruthin was closed for 17 years before being converted in 1981 to an award-winning bed-and-breakfast. The bedrooms are spacious, with large windows looking out onto breathtaking rural scenery. ✉ *Llanfair Dyffryn Clwyd, near Ruthin, LL15 2EE,* ☎ *01824/703643,* FAX *01824/707464. 6 rooms with bath. Pool. MC, V.*

Nightlife and the Arts

Theatr Clwyd in Mold, 10 miles northeast of Ruthin, has two theaters within the same arts complex. It has its own professional company, with an international reputation. ☎ *01352/755114.*

MID-WALES: THE HISTORIC HEARTLAND

If your idea of heaven is traditional market towns and country villages, small seaside resorts, quiet, off-the-beaten-track roads, and rolling landscapes filled with hillside sheep farms, forests, and lakes, then heaven exists for you in mid-Wales, the green and rural heart of the country.

As this is Wales's quietest holiday region, accommodations are scattered thinly across the landscape. Apart from one or two largish centers—Aberystwyth and Llandrindod Wells—the accommodations mainly tend toward country inns, small hotels, and farmhouses. This region also has some splendid country-house hotels, set within their own grounds in glorious locations. Although green is the predominant color here, you will notice distinct changes in the landscape as you travel through the region. The borderlands are gentle and undulating, rising to the west into high, wild mountains. Farther north, around Dolgellau, mountainous scenery becomes even more pronounced as you enter the southern section of the Snowdonia National Park. Mountains meet the sea along Cardigan Bay, a long coastline of headlands, peaceful sandy beaches, and beautiful estuaries. A region of peace and tranquility, it has long been a shelter from the madding crowd. Even 100 years ago, Tennyson, Darwin, Shelley, and Ruskin all came here to work and relax—today, thousands more come to delight in the numerous antiquarian bookstores of Hay-on-Wye, the first stop on this itinerary.

Numbers in the margins correspond to points of interest on the Wales map.

Hay-on-Wye

★ 15 *57 mi north of Cardiff, 25 mi north of Abergavenny.*

This town, on the Wales/England border, is dominated by its mostly ruined castle—and bookshops. Hay is a lively place, especially on Sunday, when the rest of central Wales seems to be closed down. In 1961 Richard Booth established a small secondhand and antiquarian bookshop here; other booksellers soon got in on the act, and bookshops now fill several houses, a movie theater, shops, and a pub. At the last count, there were about 25, all in a small town of only 1,500 inhabitants! The town is now the largest secondhand bookselling center in the world, where priceless 14th-century manuscripts rub spines with "job lots" selling for a few pounds. The town's Festival of Literature, held in early summer, attracts famous writers from all over the world.

Dining and Lodging

£££ ✕🏨 **Three Cocks Hotel.** Standing on the western approach to Hay, a few miles from town, this historic hostelry with its cobbled forecourt has been beautifully restored by Michael and Marie-Jeanne Winstone. The cooking is superb, with a strong Continental influence. Room rates fall almost within the ££ category. ✉ *Three Cocks, LD3 0SL,* ☎ FAX *01497/847215. 7 rooms with bath. MC, V.*

££ ✕🏨 **Old Black Lion.** This 17th-century coaching inn is close to the center of Hay, ideal for lunch while ransacking the bookshops, or for an overnight stay. Room rates fall at around the bottom of this price category. The low-beamed, atmospheric bar serves its own food—with tables outside in summer—and the breakfasts are especially good. Its "sophisticated country cooking with an international twist" has been praised by food guides. ✉ *Lion St., HR3 5AD,* ☎ *01497/820841. 10 rooms with bath. AE, MC, V.*

Builth Wells

16 *20 mi northwest of Hay-on-Wye, 60 mi north of Cardiff.*

Builth Wells, a traditional farming town and former spa on the banks of the river Wye, is the site of Wales's biggest rural gathering, the annual Royal Welsh Agricultural Show (☎ 01982/553683), held in late July. The Royal Welsh is not only Wales's prime gathering of farming folk, but also a colorful countryside jamboree that attracts huge crowds.

The countryside around Builth, and its neighbor, Llandrindod Wells, varies considerably. Some of the land is soft and rich, with rolling green hills and lush valleys. Yet close by are the wildernesses of Mynydd Eppynt and the unexplored foothills of the Cambrian Mountains, the lofty "backbone of Wales."

Dining and Lodging

£££–££££ ★ ✕🏨 **Lake Hotel.** This is the place to go for total Victorian country elegance—and total tranquillity, for it is located at Llangammarch Wells, another peaceful former spa about 8 miles west of Builth. Its 50 acres of sloping lawns and lush rhododendrons contain a trout-filled lake that attracts keen anglers. The Lake Hotel is comfortable and quiet; the service is first class, and the cuisine excellent. The rooms are large and tastefully furnished, and some have four-poster beds. ✉ *Llangammarch Wells LD4 4BS,* ☎ *01591/620202,* FAX *01591/620457. 19 rooms with bath. AE, MC, V. Closed 1st 2 wks in Jan.*

Llandrindod Wells

⓱ *7 mi north of Builth Wells, 67 mi north of Cardiff.*

Llandrindod Wells, known locally as Llandod, is an old spa town that will impress lovers of Victorian architecture, for it preserves its original layout and look. Though not to everyone's tastes, it is architecturally fascinating, with an array of fussy turrets, cupolas, loggias, and balustrades, and greenery everywhere. The climate—it is 700 feet above sea level—is said to be exceptionally healthy, and it is well situated for exploring the region. On a mainline rail route, it also enjoys good bus service. Llandrindod emerged as a spa in 1670 but did not reach its heyday until the second half of the 19th century when the railway came and most of the town was built. The **museum,** in Memorial Gardens, details the development of the spa from Roman times and explains some of the Victorian "cures" in gruesome detail. ☎ *01597/824513.* 🎫 *Free.* ⏲ *Mon.–Tues., Thurs.–Fri., and summer Sun. 10–12:30 and 2–4:30, Sat. 10–12:30.*

Llandrindod is easily explored on foot. Cross over to South Crescent, passing the Glen Usk Hotel with its wrought-iron balustrade and the Victorian bandstand in the gardens opposite, and you soon reach Middleton Street, another Victorian thoroughfare. From there head to Rock Park and the path that leads down through wooded glades to the handsomely restored **Pump Room** where visitors would "take the waters." Today, it only serves tea and refreshments and it plays a part during the town's Victorian Festival (☎ 01597/823441) held in late August when shop assistants, hotel staff, and anyone else who cares to join in wear period costume and enjoy suitable "old-style" entertainment. On the other side of town, the lake with its boathouse, café, and gift shop is in a lovely setting: wooded hills on one side, a broad common on the other, flooded in spring by golden daffodils.

Dining and Lodging

£ ✕🏨 **Brynafon Country House.** This hotel is a converted Victorian workhouse on the southern approach to Rhayader, about 9 miles northwest of Llandrindod (☞ En Route *below*). Though its exterior might be still a bit forbidding, it is up to date. Apart from its attractions as a family-run hotel, it also has a good value restaurant, The Workhouse, once the kitchen, with white-painted stone walls and a flagstone floor. ✉ *South St., Rhayader LD6 5BL,* ☎ *01597/810735,* FAX *01597/810111. 2 rooms with bath, 9 with shower. Restaurant, pool. MC, V.*

£ **Guidfa House.** This comfortable guest house, standing at a crossroads a few miles north of Llandrindod Wells, makes a great base for exploring mid-Wales. It's a stylish Georgian house with well-appointed bedrooms; owners Tony and Anne Millan are welcoming hosts. ✉ *Crossgates, near Llandrindod Wells LD1 6RF,* ☎ *01597/851241,* FAX *01597/851875. 7 rooms, 5 with bath. MC, V.*

En Route From Llandrindod, take A4081/A470 to Rhayader, a good pony trekking center and gateway town for the **Elan Valley,** Wales's "Lake District." This 7-mile chain of lakes, winding between gray-green hills, was created in the 1890s by a system of dams to supply water to the city of Birmingham, 73 miles to the east. The giant dam holding back the Claerwen reservoir to the west was built in 1952 to supplement it. The area is one of Britain's foremost ornithological sites, still home to the red kite, peregrine, merlin, and buzzard. You can see and hear all about it at the Elan Valley Visitor Centre by Caban Coch reservoir. ☎ *01597/810898.* *Free.* *Easter–Oct., daily 10–6.*

From the Elan Valley, follow the spectacular and narrow Cwmystwyth mountain road west to Devil's Bridge (☞ Aberystwyth, *below,* for details), a famous beauty spot, then on to Aberystwyth.

Aberystwyth

18 *41 mi northwest of Llandrindod Wells (via A44, not mountain road described in Llandrindod Wells En Route), 118 mi northwest of Cardiff.*

Aberystwyth makes the best of several worlds because, besides being undeniably a holiday resort, it is the oldest university town in Wales, it houses the magnificent National Library of Wales, and it has a little harbor and quite clearly a life of its own. Beautifully situated on the shores of Cardigan Bay, the seaside resort is a good gateway for exploring mid-Wales: there are few towns in Wales that present such a wide variety of scenery within their immediate neighborhood, here ranging from the extraordinary Devil's Bridge to the beautiful Rheidol Valley. The city came to prominence as a Victorian "watering hole," thanks to its curving beach that edges the bay.

Numbers in the margin correspond to bullets on the Aberystwyth map.

19 The modern **university campus,** on the hill above town, includes the National Library, an arts center with galleries, a theater, and concert hall—all open to visitors. The original university, founded in the 19th century, stands on the seafront. *The Library,* ☎ *01970/623816.* *Free.* *Weekdays 9:30–6, Sat. 9:30–5.*

20 The **castle,** at the southern end of the bay, was built in 1277 and rebuilt in 1282 by Edward I. It was one of several strongholds to fall, in 1404, to the Welsh leader Owain Glyndwr. Recaptured by the English, it became a mint in the 17th century, using silver from the Welsh hills. Today, it is a romantic ruin on a headland separating the north shore from the
21 harbor shore. At the end of the promenade, **Constitution Hill** offers the energetic a zigzag cliff path/nature trail to the view from the top. But it's more fun to travel up by the **Aberystwyth Cliff Railway**, the longest electric cliff railway in Britain. Opened in 1896, to great excitement, it has been refurbished without diminishing its Victorian look. It takes you up 430 feet to the **Great Aberystwyth Camera Obscura**, a modern version of a Victorian amusement: A massive 14-inch lens gives a bird's-eye view of more than 1,000 square miles of sea and scenery, including the whole of Cardigan Bay and 26 Welsh mountain peaks, Snowdon among them.

22 The excellent **Ceredigion Museum** in an old theater on Terrace Road displays coins minted at the castle and many items of folk history. There

Castle, **20**
Ceredigion Museum, **22**
Constitution Hill, **21**
University campus sites (old and new), **19**
Vale of Rheidol Railway, **23**

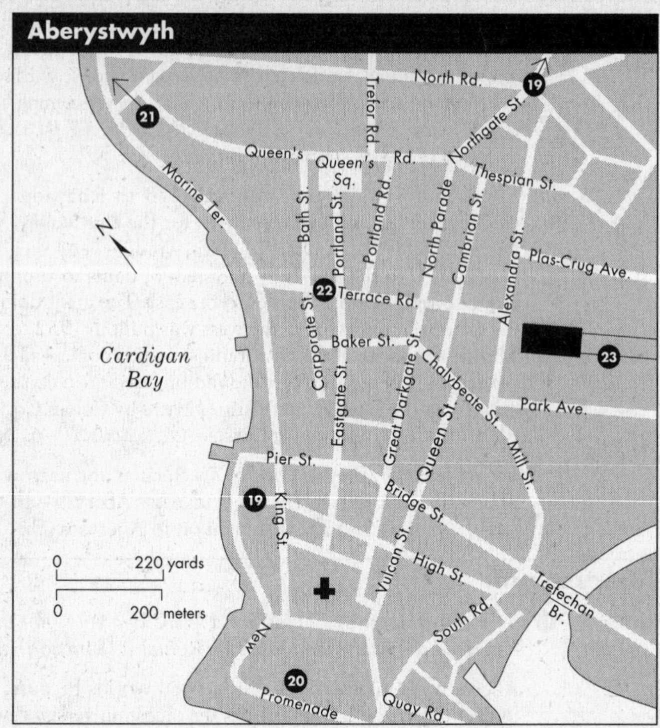

is also a fascinating Aberystwyth Yesterday private collection in the town (housed above the British Rail station), which shows 19th-century fashions, furniture, toys, and photographs. Contact the Tourist Information Center for current information. ✉ *Ceredigion Museum, Terrace Rd.,* ☎ *01970/634212.* 🎫 *Free.* ⏲ *Mon.–Sat. 10–5.*

At Aberystwyth Station you can hop on the narrow-gauge steam-op-
23 erated **Vale of Rheidol Railway** (☎ 01970/625819 or 01970/615993). The terminus, an hour's ride away, is **Devil's Bridge**, where the rivers Rheidol and Mynach meet in a series of spectacular falls. Clamped between two rocky cliffs through which a torrent of water pours unceasingly into a dark pool far below, this bridge well deserves the name it bears—*Pont y Gwr Drwg,* or Bridge of the Evil One, for legend has it that it was the devil himself who built it. There are actually three bridges—the oldest is all of 800 years old—and the walk down to the lowest bridge, "the devil's," is magnificent but strictly for the sure-footed!

OFF THE BEATEN PATH

LLYWERNOG SILVER LEAD MINING MUSEUM – This interesting diversion is 13 miles east of Aberystwyth on A44 at Ponterwyd. Silver and lead were produced in this area from 1740 to 1910; restoration work and an imaginative exhibition, "The California of Wales," have turned the clock back to the mining boom of the 1870s. ☎ *01970/890620.* 🎫 *£4.50, including underground tour.* ⏲ *Daily 10–6; closed Jan.–Feb.*

Dining and Lodging

£–££ ✕ **Gannets.** A simple, good value bistro, Gannets specializes in locally supplied meat, fish, and game, which are transformed into hearty roasts and pies. Organically grown vegetables and a good French house wine are further draws for a university crowd. It is easy to eat enjoyably here in the lowest price category. ✉ *7 St. James's Sq.,* ☎ *01970/617164. MC, V. Closed Sun., Tues.*

£££ ✕🏨 **Conrah Country Hotel.** Part of the appeal of this country-house hotel is its air of seclusion, even though it is only a short drive south from Aberystwyth. The owners have decorated the house with traditional country furnishings and antiques, and fresh flowers fill each room. The restaurant is known for its good food and wines, with imaginative modern and traditional British cuisine making use of local game, fish, and meat. ✉ *Chancery, SY23 4DF,* ☎ *01970/617941,* FAX *01970/624546. 20 rooms with bath. Indoor pool, sauna, croquet. AE, DC, MC, V.*

£££ ✕🏨 **Four Seasons.** In Aberystwyth's town center, this family-run hotel and restaurant has a relaxed atmosphere and friendly staff. The spacious rooms are simply and attractively decorated, while the restaurant serves excellent meals at reasonable prices. ✉ *50–54 Portland St., SY23 2DX,* ☎ *01970/612120,* FAX *01970/627458. 14 rooms with bath. MC, V.*

Machynlleth

24 *18 mi northeast of Aberystwyth.*

Machynlleth, at the head of the beautiful Dovey Estuary, does not look like a typical Welsh country town. Its long and wide main street, lined with a mixed style of buildings—everything from sober gray stone to well-proportioned Georgian—creates an a typical sense of openness and space. Machynlleth's busiest day is on Wednesday, when the street is filled with the stalls of market traders. At one end of the street is the Owain Glyndwr Centre, where a small exhibition celebrates Wales's last native leader who established a Welsh parliament at Machynlleth in the early 15th century. Welsh history of an earlier time is the main theme at **Celtica**, an imaginative new exhibition center in the large parkland behind the shops and pubs, where various interpretive displays take you back to Wales's Celtic past. ☎ *01654/702702.* 🎫 *£4.65.* ⏲ *Daily 10–6 (last entry to main exhibition 4:30).*

OFF THE BEATEN PATH

THE TALYLLYN RAILWAY – This narrow-gauge railway runs on a scenic route into the mountains from Tywyn on the coast. You can stop off on the way and walk through the magnificent foothills of Cader Idris, the bulky mountain that dominates the southern corner of Snowdonia National Park. ☎ *01654/710472.* 🎫 *£7.50.* ⏲ *Apr.–Oct., daily (Sun. service mid-Feb.–Mar.).*

Dining and Lodging

££££ ★ ✕🏨 **Ynyshir Hall.** This supremely comfortable country-house hotel is in a beautiful Georgian house in idyllic private grounds, near a wildlife reserve just off A487, southwest of Machynlleth. The artistic talents of its owners, Joan and Rob Reen, are evident in the bounty of Rob's paintings (he's an established artist) and in the taste of the decoration and furnishings. Personal service is paramount here, and the hotel is noted for its food. ✉ *Eglwysfach, near Machynlleth, SY20 8TA,* ☎ *01654/781209 or 800/777–6536,* FAX *01654/781366. 8 rooms with bath. Restaurant. AE, MC, V.*

££–£££ ✕🏨 **Penhelig Arms.** Along the coast road running west from Machynlleth, the delightful little sailing center of Aberdovey is perched at the mouth of the Dovey Estuary. Here you will find the waterfront Penhelig Arms, a hotel and restaurant run by Robert and Sally Hughes that has always received favorable press (room rates fall into the lower end of the quoted price category). This immaculate, friendly inn is on the water's edge, overlooking the harbor, and most of the rooms have wonderful sea views. You can meet the locals in the wood-paneled Fisherman's Bar, and dine in style at the Penhelig Arms' fine restaurant. ✉

Aberdovey LL35 0LT, ☎ 01654/767215, FAX 01654/767690. 10 rooms with bath. Restaurant, bar. MC, V.

En Route Take A487 north through the woods of the Dyfi Forest and you will soon come to signs for the **Centre for Alternative Technology.** Founded in the 1970s long before energy conservation and proper use of the earth's resources became fashionable in Britain, this "village of the future" has gradually built up an international reputation. Visitors can ride up to the center on an ingenious water-balanced cliff railway (running Easter–Oct.) and follow a self-guided trail that includes a "mole hole," depicting life in the soil. *☎ 01654/702400. £4.95. Daily 10–5.*

Dolgellau

25 *16 mi north of Machynlleth, 34 mi north of Aberystwyth.*

Dolgellau (pronounced "Dolgethlee") is a solidly Welsh town with attractive dark buildings and handsome old coaching inns. It was the center of the Welsh gold trade in the 19th century, when high quality gold was discovered locally; you can still try your luck and pan for gold in the Mawddach. A nugget of Dolgellau gold is still used to make royal wedding rings. From Dolgellau, you can visit an authentic gold mine hidden deep in the forests to the north. The round-trip takes three hours and includes a guided underground tour of the Gwynfynydd Gold Mine. *☎ 01341/423332. Tour £9.50. Courtesy bus leaves from Welsh Gold Visitor Centre in Dolgellau Apr.–Oct., daily 9:30–4 (call ahead to confirm availability).*

The Dolgellau area has strong links with the Quaker movement and the Quakers' emigration to America. To commemorate these historic associations, a **Museum of the Quakers** has been opened in the town square. *☎ 01341/422341. Free. Easter–Oct., daily 10–6.*

To the south rises the menacing bulk of Cadair Idris (2,927 feet); the name means "the Chair of Idris," though no one is completely sure just who Idris was—probably a warrior bard. It is said that anyone sleeping for a night in a certain part of the mountain will awaken either a poet or a madman.

Barmouth

26 *10 mi west of Dolgellau.*

Barmouth is one of the few places along the Welsh coast—certainly along Cardigan Bay—that can be described as a full-fledged seaside resort. On the northern mouth of the picturesque Mawddach Estuary, it features a 2-mile-long promenade, wide expanses of golden beach, and facilities for sea, river, and mountain lake fishing. Its splendid setting is best appreciated from the footpath beside the railway bridge across the mouth of the estuary. Even 100 years ago Barmouth was a popular holiday resort. Tennyson wrote part of *In Memoriam* here, and was inspired to write *Crossing the Bar* by the spectacle of the Mawddach rushing to meet the sea. Percy Bysshe and Mary Shelley stayed here in 1812; Darwin worked on *The Origin of Species* and *The Descent of Man* in a house by the shore. Essayist and art critic John Ruskin was a constant visitor and was trustee of the St. George's cottages built there by the Guild of St. George in 1871.

Lodging

££ ★ **Llwyndu Farmhouse.** It's worth driving a mile or so north from Barmouth for these comfortable accommodations. Don't expect an ordinary Welsh farm—this cozy 17th-century farmhouse has been immaculately and imaginatively restored by Paula and Peter Thompson, retaining lots of original features such as huge open fireplaces and old timbers. Accommodations are within the house itself or in the adjoining converted barn. Llwyndu is located just off A496 north of Barmouth on a hillside overlooking the sea. ✉ *Llanaber, near Barmouth, LL42 1RR,* ☎ *01341 280144,* FAX *01341/281236. 7 rooms with bath. MC, V.*

Welshpool

27 *48 mi east of Barmouth, 19 mi west of Shrewsbury.*

The border town of Welshpool, "Trallwng" in Welsh, is famous as the ★ home of **Powis Castle,** one of mid-Wales's greatest treasures. In continuous occupation since the 13th century, and now a National Trust property, Powis is one of the most opulent residential castles in Britain. Its battlements rearing high on a hilltop, the castle is surrounded by splendid grounds and terraced gardens, bounded by gigantic yew hedges, which fall steeply down to wide lawns and neat Elizabethan gardens. It contains many treasures: Greek vases; magnificent paintings by Gainsborough, Reynolds, and Romney, among others; superb furniture, including a 16th-century Italian table inlaid with marble; and, since 1987, the **Clive of India Museum,** with a fine collection of Indian art. The tearoom here is excellent. ☎ *01938/554336.* *£5.80; gardens only £3.80.* ⏲ *Apr.–June and Sept.–Oct., Wed.–Sun.; July–Aug., Tues.–Sun. Hrs: castle and museum noon–5, gardens 11–6; last admission ½ hr before closing.*

SOUTH WALES: FROM CARDIFF TO CARDIGAN

The south is the most diverse of Wales's three regions. It covers not only the immediate region around Cardiff and the Wales/England border, but also the southwest as far as the rugged coastline of Pembrokeshire. South Wales's scenic variety is reflected in the very different nature of its two national parks. The Brecon Beacons park, a short drive north of Cardiff, is an area of high, grassy mountains, lakes, and craggy limestone gorges. In contrast, the Pembrokeshire Coast National Park is recognized as one of Europe's finest stretches of coastal natural beauty, with mile after mile of spectacular sea-cliffs, beaches, headlands and coves. Other pieces of the complicated south Wales jigsaw include traditional farmlands, cosmopolitan urban areas, rolling border country, wooded vales, and the former industrial valleys where coal was mined in huge quantities during the 19th and early 20th centuries.

Numbers in the margin correspond to points of interest on the Wales map.

Cardiff

28 *23 mi west of the Severn Bridge on the Wales/England border.*

Financially, industrially, and commercially Cardiff is the most important city in Wales, but those things are not exactly exciting touristically. Neither is there much point in seeing the once-important docks, which are just the same as docks the world over. Even the evil reputation of Tiger Bay has been diluted if not washed away. But what Cardiff has to offer is a Civic Centre of extreme distinction, magnificent parklands, and a fascinating city-center castle. There still persists an idea that Cardiff, because it was once a coal town, is dirty. Nothing could be further from the truth. The Civic Centre is, in fact, constructed of dazzling white Portland stone. Buildings of great architectural style are set on wide, tree-lined avenues. The great wealth generated in the docklands was used to good effect to create an imposing Victorian and Edwardian city.

True to the Welsh tradition of vocal excellence, Cardiff is home of Britain's most adventurous opera company, the Welsh National Opera, housed in the New Theater, all red velvet and chandeliers. Cardiff is also the sporting center of Wales, and this means, above all, the Welsh capital of rugby football. To hear the crowds singing their support for the Welsh team is a stirring and unforgettable experience.

★ Any exploration of Cardiff should begin at Cardiff's **castle,** in Bute Park—one section of Cardiff's hundreds of acres of parkland. The castle, which stands just on the edge of the shopping center, is an unusual "three-in-one" historic site, with Roman, Norman, and especially Victorian associations. Parts of the walls are Roman, the solid keep is Norman, and the whole complex was restored—and transformed into an utter Victorian ego flight—a hundred years ago by the 3rd Marquess of Bute. He employed William Burges (1827–81), an architect obsessed by the Gothic period, and Burges transformed the castle inside and out into an extravaganza of medieval color and detailed craftsmanship. It is the perfect expression of the anything-goes Victorian spirit—not to mention the vast fortune made by the marquess in Cardiff's booming docklands. ✉ *Bute Park,* ☎ *01222/822083.* 🎫 *Guided tour of castle £3.70; grounds only £2.30.* 🕐 *May–Sept., daily 10–6, Mar.–Apr. and Oct., daily 10–5; Nov.–Feb., daily 10–4:30; call for tour times.*

Two blocks east of Cardiff Castle is the **Civic Centre**, a well-designed complex of tree-lined avenues and civic buildings with Portland stone facades. The domed City Hall, Neoclassical Law Courts, the Welsh Office (seat of government), and the University campus are all here. The main source of interest, however, is the **National Museum and Gallery** next to the City Hall. Give yourself at least half a day at this splendid museum, which tells the story of Wales through its plants, rocks, archaeology, art, and industry. It also has a fine collection of modern European art, especially Postimpressionist works—don't miss *La Parisienne* by Renoir. ✉ *Main Building, Cathays Park,* ☎ *01222/397951.* 🎫 *£3.* 🕐 *Tues.–Sun. 10–5.*

South of the Civic Centre are the shopping and business areas of Cardiff. Here in a large, modern shopping mall is **St. David's Hall**, one of Europe's best new concert halls, with outstanding acoustics, where people come for classical music, jazz, rock, ballet—even snooker championships. This hall has recently been joined by the **Cardiff International Arena**, a £23 million multipurpose center for exhibitions, concerts, and conferences.

NEED A BREAK? At the bottom of Queen's Street is the **Capitol shopping mall,** with a number of fast-food outlets, ranging from salad bars to Continental food bars—an ideal spot for morning coffee or a light lunch.

The **Welsh Industrial and Maritime Museum** (☎ 01222/481919) is in the old dockland 2 miles south of the city center, now in the process of revitalization as part of the ambitious Cardiff Bay redevelopment. There is also an interesting "hands-on" science and technology center here, known as Techniquest (☎ 01222/460211).

Cross the river Taff and follow Cathedral Road for about 2 miles, to reach **Llandaff,** a suburb of Cardiff that retains its village atmosphere, and **Llandaff Cathedral**, which was completely renovated after serious bomb damage in World War II. Inside you will immediately be drawn to the overwhelming statue by Jacob Epstein (1880–1959) of *Christ in Majesty.*

★ Four miles west of Llandaff is the open-air **Museum of Welsh Life** at St. Fagans. On 100 acres of parkland and gardens lie farmhouses, cottages, and terraced houses that show the evolution of Welsh building styles. There are craft workshops, a saddler, cooper, blacksmith, and woodturner. Special events highlight ancient rural festivals—May Day, Harvest, and Christmas among them. ☎ *01222/569441.* 🎫 *£5.* ⏲ *July–Sept., daily 10–6; Oct.–June, daily 10–5.*

North of Cardiff, 4 miles via A470, beside the village of Tongwynlais,
★ is **Castell Coch,** the Red Castle—a structure so like a romantic, fairy-tale castle that one can only enjoy it. It was built (on the site of a medieval castle) in the 1870s about the time that Ludwig II of Bavaria was creating his fantastic dream castles, and it might almost be one of them. Instead, the castle was another collaboration of the 3rd Marquess of Bute and William Burges, whose work you will already have seen in Cardiff Castle. Here Burges re-created everything—architecture, furnishings, carvings, murals—in a remarkable exercise in Victorian-Gothic whimsy. ☎ *01222/810101.* 🎫 *£2.20.* ⏲ *Late Mar.–late Oct., daily 9:30–6:30; late Oct.–late Mar., Mon.–Sat. 9:30–4, Sun. 11–4.*

Dining and Lodging

££ ✕ **Armless Dragon.** A window-front full of plants enlivens this bright, friendly restaurant out beyond the Cathays stadium, which is popular with the university crowd. Seafood dishes are always a good bet here; much of the fish comes from local waters. For even more uniquely Welsh flavor, try the laverballs, made out of seaweed. ✉ *97 Wyeverne Rd., Cathays,* ☎ *01222/382357. AE, DC, MC, V. No lunch Sat. Closed Sun.–Mon.*

££ ✕ **Le Cassoulet.** This is a genuinely French restaurant, decorated with touches of red and black, in the maze of Victorian streets west of Cathedral Road. Try the namesake dish for a filling meal. The *patron*-chef also creates a very tasty fish soup. ✉ *5 Romilly Crescent,* ☎ *01222/221905. AE, MC, V. No lunch Sat. Closed Sun.–Mon.*

£–££ ✕ **Quayles.** Formerly Gibson's, this neighborhood brasserie is close to Sophia Gardens. The modern Mediterranean-style cuisine is reasonably priced, with a more elaborate Sunday lunch and brunch. A good-value, inexpensive fixed-price menu is available before 8 PM. ✉ *6 Romilly Crescent, Canton,* ☎ *01222/341264. AE, MC, V.*

£££ 🏨 **Cardiff Marriott.** The high-rise Marriott (formerly the Holiday Inn) is a fair representative of Cardiff's new breed of hotels. It is central—close to St. David's Hall and the shopping center—practical, and has plenty of facilities. ✉ *Mill La., CF1 1EZ,* ☎ *01222/399944,* FAX *01222/395578. 182 rooms with bath. Restaurant, coffee shop, indoor pool, sauna, squash. AE, DC, MC, V.*

£ 🏨 **Town House.** A gregarious American couple, Bart and Iris Zuzik,
★ run this immaculate guest house, the best B&B in Cardiff, along Cathedral Road and near the city center. You stay in a tall Victorian building that has been tastefully converted. The bedrooms are neat and well equipped, and guests can enjoy traditional British or American breakfasts in the beautifully appointed dining room. No evening meals are served. ✉ *70 Cathedral Rd., CF1 9LL,* ☎ *01222/239399,* FAX *01222/223214. 6 rooms with bath. No credit cards.*

Nightlife and the Arts

Wales, as might be expected in a country where singing is a way of life, has one of Britain's four major opera companies, the **Welsh National**

Its home base is at the New Theatre in Cardiff, but it spends most of its time touring Wales and England. Its performances, even in a small Welsh town, are of an international standard, and its productions often among the most exciting in Britain. For details of performances contact the Welsh National Opera, John St., Cardiff CF1 4SP, ☎ 01222/464666. As you would expect of Wales's main city, there is a lively night-time scene in Cardiff's clubs and pubs. The big theaters feature a full program of entertainment, from drama to comedy, pop to the classics.

Shopping

Arcade shopping is a distinctive feature of Cardiff's city center. Canopied Victorian and Edwardian arcades, lined with small specialty shops, weave in and out of the city's modern covered shopping complexes. Cardiff's traditional side can also be see in its covered market, which sells a tempting variety of fresh foods.

Abergavenny

29 *28 mi northeast of Cardiff.*

The market town of Abergavenny has a **castle** founded early in the 11th century. At Christmas in 1176 the Norman knight William de Braose invited the neighboring Welsh chieftains to a feast—and, in a crude attempt to gain control of the area, had them all slaughtered as they sat, unarmed, at dinner. Afterward, the Welsh attacked and virtually demolished the castle. Little remains of the building now, but you can visit the **museum**, with exhibits ranging from the Iron Age to the early part of this century. The Welsh Kitchen is particularly appealing, with its old utensils, pans, and butter molds. There is also a delightful **Museum of Childhood and Home** (☎ 01873/856014) in the town. ✉ *Castle Museum, Castle St.,* ☎ *01873/854282.* 🎫 *£1.* ⏲ *Mar.–Oct., Mon.–Sat. 11–1 and 2–5, Sun. 2–5; Nov.–Feb., Mon.–Sat. 11–1 and 2–4.*

30 Taking A40 northwest out of Abergavenny, you pass the Sugar Loaf mountain and **Crickhowell,** a pretty town on the banks of the river Usk with attractive little shops, an ancient bridge, and ruined castle. Two miles farther (by A479) is **Tretower Court,** a splendid example of a fortified medieval manor house. Nearby, and part of the same site, is a ruined Norman castle. ☎ *01874/730279.* 🎫 *£2.20.* ⏲ *Late Mar.–late Oct., daily 9:30–6:30; late Oct.–late Mar., Mon.–Sat. 9:30–4, Sun. 2–4.*

31 East of Swansea, lie the valleys—the Rhondda is the most famous—so well described by Richard Llewellyn in *How Green Was My Valley.* But things have changed, because the slag heaps are green again, thanks to land reclamation schemes. However, to catch a glimpse of what it was once like, head to the **Big Pit Mining Museum,** in Blaenavon, southwest of Abergavenny. Here, ex-miners take you underground on a tour of an authentic coal mine for a look at the life of the South Wales miner. You will also see the pithead baths and workshops. ☎ *01495/790311.* 🎫 *Surface £1.75, combined tour £5.50.* ⏲ *Mar.–Nov., daily 9:30–5 (underground tours 10–3:30).*

Dining and Lodging

£££ ✕🏨 **Bear Hotel.** This old coaching inn, about 5 miles northwest of Abergavenny in the middle of the pretty little town of Crickhowell, is full of character. The bar, decorated with memorabilia from the days when stagecoaches from London used to stop here, is popular with locals and visitors alike; a blazing log fire in winter adds to the atmosphere. Rooms are within the hotel itself or in the attractively converted stableyard under the arch. The Bear is also noted for its food—both the excellent value bar food and more formal restaurant menus. ✉ *Crickhowell NP8 1BW,* ☎ *01873/810408,* FAX *01873/811696. 28 rooms with bath. AE, MC, V.*

Brecon

32 *19 mi northwest of Abergavenny, 41 mi north of Cardiff.*

Brecon is a historic market town of narrow passageways, handsome Georgian buildings, and pleasant riverside walks. There are a number of sights worth seeing here, including the cavernous **cathedral** with its heritage center on the hill above the middle of town, and two good museums—the **Brecknock Museum** (☎ 01874/624121), with its superb collection of carved love spoons, and the **South Wales Borderers' Museum** (☎ 01874/623111), a military museum whose exhibits span centuries of conflict. For the best atmosphere, time your visit to Brecon to coincide with market day (Tuesday and Friday). Don't forget to purchase a hand-carved wooden Welsh love spoon similar to those on display in the museum.

As you travel south of Brecon, the skyline fills with mountains, and wild, windswept uplands stretch to the horizon. Follow the signs for the **Brecon Beacons Mountain Centre,** on Mynydd Illtyd, a high, grassy stretch of upland west of A470 near Libanus. The center, run by the Brecon Beacons National Park, is an excellent source of information for attractions and activities within this 519-square-mile park of rolling hills and open moorlands, and gives wonderful panoramic views across to Pen-y-fan, at 2,906 feet the highest peak in South Wales. Walkers who want to explore Wales's high country should always be well equipped, for mist and rain can quickly descend, and the Beacons' summits can become very exposed to high winds. ✉ *Brecon Beacons Mountain Centre, near Libanus, Brecon LD3 8ER,* ☎ *01874/623366.* *Free, but parking fee.* *Daily 9:30–5 (until 4:30 in winter).*

Dining and Lodging

££££ ★ **Llangoed Hall.** This hotel, the brainchild of Sir Bernard Ashley, widower of Laura Ashley, opened in May 1990 and has established itself as one of the best places to stay in Wales. An early guest was Arthur Miller. The Hall is set in the spectacular valley of the Wye, about 8 miles northeast of Brecon on A470 to Builth Wells, with views over the Black Mountains. Inside there are Laura Ashley fabrics everywhere, of course, complementing the antiques and paintings. The restaurant serves a five-course, set-price menu using mostly local produce. ✉ *Llyswen, near Brecon, LD3 OYP,* ☎ *01874/754525,* FAX *01874/754545. 23 rooms with bath. Restaurant, tennis court, helipad. AE, DC, MC, V.*

££ **Griffin Inn.** In the village of Llyswen close to Llangoed Hall on the same A470 road to Builth, the Griffin is one of the oldest inns in the upper Wye Valley (said to date from 1467). There is easy access to river and lake fishing, shooting, walking, and pony trekking in the Brecon Beacons. A former winner of Britain's "Pub of the Year," the Griffin's hearty and traditional cuisine takes advantage of local produce, such as salmon and beef. The bedrooms are comfortably furnished, and the exposed stonework and old beams contribute to the historic character of the building. ✉ *Llyswen, near Brecon, LD3 0UR,* ☎ *01874/754241,* FAX *01874/754592. 8 rooms with bath. AE, DC, MC, V.*

Shopping

Crickhowell Adventure Gear, on the corner of Ship Street in Brecon (with smaller shops in Crickhowell itself and Abergavenny), sells a good range of outdoor gear—clothes and climbing equipment—for those who want to seriously explore the park.

Swansea

33 *36 mi southwest of Brecon, 40 mi west of Cardiff.*

Swansea is Wales's second city and birthplace of poet Dylan Thomas (1914–53). Go first to Swansea's splendid **Maritime Quarter.** The city was extensively bombed during World War II, and its old dockland has been transformed into a modern marina with attractive housing and shops and a seafront that commands wonderful views across the sweep of Swansea Bay. The **Swansea Maritime and Industrial Museum,** beside the marina, tells the story of the city's growth and houses a fully operational woolen mill. ☎ *01792/650351 or 01792/470371.* *Free.* *Tues.–Sun. 10:30–5:30.*

Within a short walk of the marina is Swansea's modern shopping center. Despite the city's typically postwar, rather utilitarian and undistinguished architecture, the **covered market** here is not to be missed. It's the best fresh-foods market in Wales, where you can buy cockles from the Penclawdd beds on the nearby Gower Peninsula and laverbread, that unique Welsh delicacy made from seaweed, which is normally eaten with bacon and eggs. Swansea marks the end of the industrial region of south Wales. And, as if to make amends for the one-time desecration of so much natural beauty—though the industrial scars have disappeared—the 14-mile-long Gower peninsula, on the neck of which Swansea stands, offers magnificent cliff scenery and unspoiled beaches.

OFF THE BEATEN PATH

CARREG CENNEN CASTLE – This spectacularly located stronghold is north of Swansea. Drive along A483 to Ammanford and on to Llandeilo, a pleasant country town set on a ridge above the Towy Valley. The castle stands at Trapp in the hills a few miles southeast, perched on a sheer cliff overlooking the empty expanses of Black Mountain. This gnarled, weather-beaten medieval fortress powerfully evokes the troubled times of old. It's a stiff climb, but worth every step; the views from the ruined ramparts are magnificent, and you can follow a passageway to an underground chamber deep below the castle's foundations. ☎ *01558/822291.* £2.20. *Late Mar.–late Oct., daily 9:30–6 (until 8, June–Aug.); late Oct.–late Mar., daily 9:30–4.*

Dining and Lodging

££ ✕ **Number One.** This excellent regional restaurant serves dishes such as Penclawdd cockles with laverbread and bacon; fresh sea bass, wild salmon, and monkfish are regularly featured. The atmosphere is friendly and seating is limited, so reservations are advised. ✉ *1 Wind St.,* ☎ *01792/456996. AE, MC, V. No dinner Mon., Tues. Closed Sun.*

£££–££££ ✕ **Fairyhill.** Situated on the west of the Gower Peninsula, about 11 miles from Swansea, Fairyhill is an 18th-century country house with a restful atmosphere, luxuriously furnished public rooms, spacious bedrooms, and extensive wooded grounds. The hotel is known in the area for its hospitality, accomplished cuisine and well-chosen wine list. ✉ *Reynoldston, near Swansea, SA3 1BS,* ☎ *01792/390139,* FAX *01792/391358. 8 rooms with bath or shower. AE, MC, V.*

Tenby

34 *53 mi west of Swansea.*

Tenby is a picturesque seaside resort where pastel-colored Georgian houses cluster around a harbor, and below the hotel-lined clifftop stretch two golden sandy beaches. Medieval Tenby's ancient town walls still stand, enclosing narrow streets and passageways full of shops, inns, and places to eat. The ruins of a castle stand on a headland overlooking the sea, close to the excellent **Tenby Museum** (☎ 01834/842809), which recalls the town's maritime history and growth as a fashionable resort. The **Tudor Merchant's House** (☎ 01834/842279), in town, shows how a prosperous trader would have lived in the Tenby of old. From the harbor, you can take a boat trip to Caldey Island and visit the famous monastery, whose monks make perfume.

Lodging

£££ **Penally Abbey Hotel.** Penally Abbey, overlooking the sea close to town, is a convenient and comfortable base for exploring Pembrokeshire. The dignified old house is full of character, and most bedrooms have four-posters. Hosts Steve and Elleen Warren's lack of formality brings to their hotel a relaxed atmosphere with first-class service. Everything is tuned to the guests' needs, even if that means serving breakfast at 11 AM. The hotel is also noted for its fine food. ✉ *Penally, near Tenby, SA70 7PY,* ☎ *01834/843033,* FAX *01834/844714. 12 rooms with bath. Pool. MC, V.*

Pembroke

35 *11 mi west of Tenby, 13 mi southwest of Haverfordwest.*

You are now entering the heart of Pembrokeshire, one of the most curious regions of Wales. You may begin to doubt whether you are still in Wales, for all around are English names like Deeplake, New Hedges, Rudbaxton. Natives more often than not don't seem to even understand Welsh. And if you approach South Pemborkeshire, you'll be entering the district known as "Little England beyond Wales." History is responsible: In the 11th century, this region was conquered by the English with the aid of the Normans, who intermarried and set about building castles. One of the most magnificent is found here in Pembroke, a **castle** dating from 1190. Its walls remain stout, its gatehouse mighty, and the enormous cylindrical keep proved so impregnable to cannon fire in the Civil War that Cromwell's men had to starve out its Royalist defenders. It was the birthplace, in 1457, of Henry VII, the Tudor king who seized the throne of Britain in 1485, and whose son Henry VIII united Wales and England. ☎ *01646/681510.* *£2.50.* *Summer, daily 9:30–6; winter, daily 10–4.*

St. David's

36 *16 mi northwest of Haverfordwest, 16 mi west of Fishguard.*

This is a place that has been described as the "holiest ground in Great Britain," for here, in the midst of a tiny village, is the venerable Cathedral of St. David, and the shrine of the patron saint of Wales, where his bones rest in a casket behind the main altar. Unlike any other cathedral it does not seek to dominate the surrounding countryside with its enormous mass, for it is set, quaintly enough, in an vast hollow, and the visitor must climb down 39 steps (called locally the Thirty-Nine Articles) to enter the cathedral—this also helped protect the church from Viking raiders. The exterior of the cathedral is simple, but inside, treasures include the fragile fan vaulting in Bishop Vaughan's Chapel, the intricate carving on the choir stalls, and the substantial oaken roof over the nave. Across the brook are the ruins of the medieval **Bishop's Palace.**

The entire area around St. David's, steeped in sanctity and history, was a place of pilgrimage for many centuries, two journeys to St. David's equalling one to Rome. The savagely beautiful coastline here—Pembrokeshire at its unspoiled best—also gives St. David's a special atmosphere. You can walk sections of the coastal footpath or take one of the boat trips available locally (some of which go to Ramsey Island).

Dining

££ ✕ **Harbour Lights.** Tucked away on an attractive stretch of coast about 7 miles northeast of St. David's at the tiny harbor of Porthgain, this family-run shore restaurant prides itself on serving everything homemade, right down to the cheese and biscuits. Try the fresh local seafood dishes. The walls are hung with pictures by local artists. ✉ *Porthgain, Croesgoch SA62 5BW,* ☎ *01348/831549. MC, V. Call ahead in winter for hrs.*

Fishguard

37 *16 mi northeast of St David's, 26 mi north of Pembroke.*

Fishguard is a town of three parts. The modern ferry terminal at Goodwick across the sheltered waters of Fishguard Bay sees activity throughout the year as boats sail to Rosslare across the Irish Sea. Fishguard's main town stands on high ground just south of Goodwick, separating the modern port from its picturesque **old harbor** in the lower town, which was the film location for Dylan Thomas's *Under Milk Wood,* starring Richard Burton, Elizabeth Taylor, and Peter O'Toole. At Carreg Wastad Point, near Fishguard, the "last invasion of Britain" by a foreign army took place: a French force, in 1797, commanded by an American, Colonel Tate. Legend holds that the invaders surrendered after being frightened by a group of women in red shawls and tall black hats whom they mistook for Guardsmen.

Lodging

£–£££ **Tregynon Country Farmhouse Hotel.** This 16th-century farmhouse, overlooking the Gwaun Valley, is ideal for a quiet, reasonably priced stay in the country. The cooking concentrates on whole-food dishes and vegetarian fare, though Tregynon easily satisfies all tastes, serving everything from vegetarian pancakes to oak-smoked bacon. ✉ *Pontfaen, Gwaun Valley, near Fishguard SA65 9TU,* ☎ *01239/820531,* FAX *01239/820808. 8 rooms with bath. MC, V.*

Cardigan and the Teifi Valley

38 *18 mi northeast of Fishguard.*

Cardigan is a charming little market town perched astride the Teifi on an ancient bridge, the scene of a never-allowed-to-be-forgotten victory by the Welsh over the Norman army in 1136. The town is near the mouth of the Teifi, a river that runs through a beautiful wooded valley dotted with traditional market towns and villages, as well as reminders of the area's once-flourishing woolen industry. Cardigan itself has an interesting history, for it was here, in the 12th century, that Wales's first *eisteddfod,* or folk festival, was held. The eisteddfod tradition, based on the Welsh language and culture, is still strong in Wales, and events large and small are held here (mainly in the summer months).

There is precious little left of Cardigan's medieval castle. Neighboring
39 **Cilgerran,** a village a few miles south, steals the limelight thanks to the dramatic ruins of 13th-century **Cilgerran Castle**, standing above a deep wooded gorge through which flows the river Teifi. ☎ *01239/615136.* *£1.70.* *Late Mar.–late Oct., daily 9:30–6:30; late Oct.–late Mar., Mon.–Sat. 9:30–4, Sun. 2–4.*

On the western outskirts of Cilgerran, the beautiful 400-acre **Welsh Wildlife Centre,** a seven-habitat nature reserve with both wetlands and woodlands, offers bird-watching hides, walking and craft workshops with demonstrations, coracle demonstrations, and summer boat trips. Among its network of footpaths there's a walk along the second largest reed bed in Wales. The adventurously designed visitor center features an exhibit called "Animal Kingdom." ☎ *01239/621600.* 🎫 *£1.75.* ⏲ *Daily 10–dusk (visitor center closes 5:30).*

East of Cenarth off A484 a few miles past Newcastle Emlyn, in what was once the most important wool-producing area in Wales, is the fas-
40 cinating **Museum of the Welsh Woolen Industry** at Drefach Felindre. It has working exhibits and displays that trace the evolution of the industry, with regular demonstrations. As a bonus there are other craft workshops and a working woolen mill beside the museum site. ☎ *01559/370929.* 🎫 *£2.* ⏲ *Apr.–Sept., Mon.–Sat. 10–5; Oct.–Mar., weekdays 10–5.*

Lodging

£££ **Penbontbren Farm Hotel.** You won't find a more traditionally Welsh hotel than this friendly one in peaceful countryside off A487 east of Cardigan. Welsh-speakers Barrie and Nan Humphreys have created an unusual hotel at a farm that's been in Nan's family for centuries. Barns have been tastefully converted into comfortable bedrooms, a restaurant is just across the courtyard, and the hotel has its own little Countryside Museum. Good value—it's just over the ££ price category. ✉ *Glynarthen, near Cardigan, SA44 6PE,* ☎ *01239/810248,* FAX *01239/811129. 10 rooms with bath. MC, V.*

WALES A TO Z

Arriving and Departing

By Bus

National Express (☎ 0990/808080) serves Wales from London's Victoria Coach Station and also direct from London's Heathrow and Gatwick airports. Average travel times from London are: 3½ hours to Cardiff; four hours to Swansea; 5½ hours to Aberystwyth; and 4½ hours to Llandudno.

By Car

For Cardiff (157 miles), Swansea (196 miles), and South Wales, take M4 from London. Aberystwyth (211 miles) and Llandrindod in mid-Wales are well-served by major roads. The A40 is also an important route through central and south Wales. From London, M1/M6 is the most direct route to north Wales. A55, the coast road from Chester on the English side of the border, goes through Bangor.

By Plane

London's Heathrow and Gatwick airports, with their excellent door-to-door motorway links with Wales, are convenient gateways. Manchester Airport, which offers a wide range of international flights, is an excellent gateway for north Wales with a journey time to the Welsh border via M56 of under an hour. Wales International Airport near Cardiff has a number of direct international flights to European destinations and connecting services worldwide via Amsterdam (☎ 01446/11111).

By Train

From London's Paddington Station (☎ 0171/262–6767) it is about two hours to Cardiff and three hours to Swansea on the fast InterCity rail service. Fast InterCity trains also run between London's Euston Station (☎ 0171/387–7070) and north Wales; average travel times are: from Euston, 3¾ hours to Llandudno in north Wales (some direct trains, otherwise change at Crewe) and about five hours to Aberystwyth in mid-Wales (changing at Birmingham).

Getting Around

By Bus

Although the overall pattern is a little fragmented, most parts of Wales are accessible by bus. The main operators are: **Cardiff Bus** (☏ 01222/396521), **Newport Transport** (☏ 01633/262914), **South Wales Transport** (☏ 01792/580580), and **Red and White** (☏ 01633/266366) for south Wales; **Crosville Wales** (☏ 01492/592111) for mid- and North Wales. Crosville offers unlimited-travel Day Rover and Weekly Rover tickets. It also has long-distance routes: the daily TransCambria cross-country service between Cardiff and Bangor (calling at Swansea, Carmarthen, Aberystwyth, Dolgellau, and Caernarfon) and other routes such as Wrexham to Aberystwyth (calling at Llangollen, Corwen, Bala, Dolgellau, and Machynlleth).

Although primarily a carrier into Wales, **National Express** (☞ Arriving and Departing, *above*) also has routes through Wales (from Cardiff farther west, for example, or along the North Wales coast).

By Car

Distances in miles may not be great in Wales, but getting from place to place takes time because there are few major highways. The mountains mean that there is no single fast route from north to south, although A470 is good—and scenic—and A487 does run along or near most of the coastline. The mountains also mean that many of the smaller roads are winding and difficult to maneuver, but they do reveal magnificent views of the surrounding landscape.

By Train

The **Regional Railways** service (☏ 01222/228000) covers the valleys of south Wales, western Wales, central Wales, the Conwy Valley, and the north Wales coast on many highly scenic routes: the Cambrian Coast Railway, for example, running 70 miles between Aberystwyth and Pwllheli; the Heart of Wales line, linking Swansea and Craven Arms, near Shrewsbury, 95 miles away. You can buy economical unlimited-travel Rail Rover tickets. If you intend using this network, ask about the money-saving unlimited-travel tickets available (such as "Freedom of Wales," "Rail Rover," and "Wanderer"), some of which include the use of bus services.

Wales is undoubtedly the best place in Britain for narrow-gauge steam railways. The *Great Little Trains of Wales*—narrow gauge—operate during the spring, summer, and autumn months through the mountains of Snowdonia and central Wales (there are also a few lines in south Wales). Many of these lines wind through landscapes of extraordinary grandeur; for example, the Ffestiniog Railway, which links two British Rail lines at the old slate town of Blaenau Ffestiniog and Porthmadog, climbs the mountainside around an ascending loop more reminiscent of the Andes than rural Britain. Tiny, copper-knobbed engines, panting fiercely, haul narrow carriages packed with tourists through deep cuttings and along rocky shelves above ancient oak woods through the heart of Snowdonia National Park. Other lines include: the Talyllyn, following a deep valley from the coastal resort of Tywyn; the Vale of Rheidol Railway, from Aberystwyth to Devil's Bridge; the Welshpool and Llanfair Light Railway, between Welshpool and Llanfair Caereinion; the Welsh Highland Railway, from Porthmadog; the Brecon Mountain Railway, from Merthyr Tydfil; and the Llanberis Lake Railway. Wanderer tickets are available for unlimited travel on the "Great

Little Trains of Wales": four days £25, eight days £32, children half-price. Full details, including summary timetables, are available from Great Little Trains of Wales (✉ c/o The Station, Llanfair Caereinion, Powys SY21 0SF, ☎ 01938/810441).

Snowdonia also has Britain's only alpine-style steam rack railway, the Snowdon Mountain Railway, where little sloping boilered engines on rack-and-pinion track push their trains 3,000 feet up from Llanberis to the summit of Snowdon, Wales's highest mountain. Details of services can be obtained from Snowdon Mountain Railway (Llanberis, Caernarfon, Gwynedd, ☎ 01286/870223).

Contacts and Resources

Car Rentals

Cardiff: Avis, ✉ 4–22 Tudor St., ☎ 01222/342111; **Eurodollar,** ✉ 10 Dominions Way Industrial Estate, Newport Rd., ☎ 01222/496256; **Europcar,** ✉ 1–11 Byron St., ☎ 01222/497110; **Hertz,** ✉ 9 Central Sq., ☎ 01222/224548.

Emergencies

Police, fire, ambulance, ☎ 999.

Golf

There is an excellent choice of golf courses in Wales, ranging from championship-standard links courses to friendly nine-holers. Details from **Wales Tourist Board** (☞ Visitor Information, *below*).

Guided Tours

If you are interested in having a personal guide, contact the **Wales Official Tourist Guide Association** through Derek Jones (✉ Y Stabl, 30 Acton Gardens, Wrexham LL12 8DE, ☎ 01978/351212, FAX 01978/363060). WOTGA only uses guides recognized by the Wales Tourist Board. It will put together tailor-made tours for you and, if you wish, have your guide meet you at the airport. You can book either a driver/guide or someone to accompany you as you drive.

Another good way of seeing Wales is by local tour bus; in summer there's a large choice of day and half-day excursions to most parts of the country. In major resorts and cities you should ask at a tourist information center or bus station for details.

Hiking and Walking

This is the most popular outdoor activity in Wales. The following organizations can help: **Brecon Beacons National Park** (Park Office, ✉ 7 Glamorgan St., Brecon LD3 7DP, ☎ 01874/624437), **Offa's Dyke Association** (✉ West St., Knighton LD7 1EN, ☎ 01547/528753), **Ramblers' Association in Wales** (✉ Ty'r Cerddwyr, High St., Gresford, Wrexham LL12 8PT, ☎ 01978/855148), **Snowdonia National Park** (Park Office, ✉ Penrhyndeudraeth LL48 6LS, ☎ 01766/770274).

Historic Sites

If you intend viewing a few Welsh castles, consider purchasing the **Cadw/Welsh Historic Monuments Explorer Pass,** good for unlimited admission to most of Wales's historic sites. The seven-day pass costs £14 (single adult), £20 (two adults), or £25 (family ticket); the three-day pass costs £9, £15, and £20 respectively. Passes are available at any site covered by the Cadw program. ✉ *Cadw/Welsh Historic Monuments, Brunel House, 2 Fitzalan Rd., Cardiff CF2 1UY,* ☎ *01222/500200.*

Horseback Riding

The **Association of British Riding Schools** (✉ Queen Chambers, 38/40 Queen St., Penzance, Cornwall TR18 2BH, ☎ 01736/69440) publishes a riding holidays brochure that features approved centers, many of which offer accommodation as well (it is free, but send an international mailing coupon to cover postage costs if you can).

Travel Agencies

American Express: ✉ 3 Queen St., Cardiff, ☎ 01222/668858. **Thomas Cook:** ✉ 16 Queen St., Cardiff, ☎ 01222/224886; and ✉ 3 Union St., Swansea, ☎ 01792/464311.

Visitor Information

The Wales Bureau: ✉ The British Travel Centre, 12 Lower Regent St., Piccadilly Circus, London SW1Y 4PQ, ☎ 0171/409–0969. The **Wales Tourist Board:** ✉ Brunel House, 12th floor, 2 Fitzalan Rd., Cardiff CF2 1UY, ☎ 01222/499909.

Tourist information centers are normally open Monday through Saturday 10–5:30 and limited hours on Sunday, but varying according to the season.

Aberystwyth: ✉ Terrace Rd., ☎ 01970/612125. **Betws-y-Coed:** ✉ Royal Oak Stables, ☎ 01690/710426. **Caernarfon:** ✉ Oriel Pendeitsh, opposite castle entrance, ☎ 01286/672232. **Cardiff:** ✉ Central Station, ☎ 01222/227281. **Llandrindod Wells:** ✉ Old Town Hall, ☎ 01597/822600. **Llandudno:** ✉ Chapel St., ☎ 01492/876413. **Llanfairpwll:** ✉ Station Site, Isle of Anglesey, ☎ 01248/713177. **Llangollen:** ✉ Town Hall, ☎ 01978/860828. **Machynlleth:** ✉ Owain Glyndwr Centre, ☎ 01654/702401. **Ruthin:** ✉ Craft Centre, ☎ 01824/703992. **Swansea:** ✉ Singleton St., ☎ 01792/468321. **Tenby:** ✉ The Croft, ☎ 01834/842402. **Welshpool:** ✉ Flash Leisure Centre, ☎ 01938/552043.

11 Lancashire and the Peaks

Manchester, Liverpool, Blackpool, and the Peak District

Birthplace of the boom and bravura of the Industrial Revolution, this region still claims bustling cities like Liverpool, Manchester, and Blackpool. Here, fans of Victorian architecture and of John, Paul, George, and Ringo come to enjoy some of England's most interesting sights. Beyond, however, lies the emerald tranquillity of the Peak District and Derbyshire's Wye Valley—home to two of the most regal houses in the land, Haddon Hall and Chatsworth.

Updated by Jules Brown

THE INDUSTRIAL REVOLUTION THRIVED nowhere more strongly than it did in cities like Manchester and Liverpool in this northwest region of England. Yet anyone who expects to find a bleak, semi-urban landscape will be pleasantly surprised traveling through these counties of Lancashire, Greater Manchester, and Derbyshire. Manchester today may be big and bustling, but it's an attractive mix of Victorian preservation, tasteful modern development, and leafy suburbs. Yes, parts of the Merseyside area containing Liverpool live up to its grimy image as an industrial port, but along the Lancashire coast lies a series of vacation resorts that flourished during the first half of this century; Blackpool, the country's largest seaside resort, draws millions each year to its miles of beaches, acres of gardens, and 19th-century architectural charms. And inland, in Derbyshire (pronounced "Darbyshire"), lies the spectacular Peak District, a huge unspoiled national park at the southern end of the Pennines range, which attracts scores of hikers and ramblers.

By the mid-18th century, the Lancashire cotton industry was firmly established in Manchester and enjoyed a special relationship with the port of Liverpool, to the west. Here, at the massive docks, cotton was imported from America and sent to the Lancashire mills; the finished cotton goods were later returned to Liverpool for export to the rest of the world. Both cities suffered a marked decline during this century, though the downtown areas are currently undergoing a remarkable architectural and cultural revitalization. Today, they remain best known the world over for their musical and sporting prowess. Since 1968, Manchester United and Liverpool soccer clubs have won everything worth winning in Britain and Europe, and Manchester has repeatedly figured as an Olympic-site contender; in 2002 the city will host the Commonwealth Games. The Beatles launched the Merseysound of the '60s; contemporary Manchester groups still ride both British and American airwaves. On the classical side of music, Manchester is also home to Britain's oldest leading orchestra, the Hallé (founded in 1857)—just one of the city's legacies of wealthy 19th-century industrialists' investments in culture.

If you imagine England as a small, cozy country of cottages and gently flowing streams, the Peak District might come as a bit of a surprise. For this is a wilder part of England, a region of crags that rear violently out of the plain. The Pennines, a line of hills that begins in the Peak District and runs as far north as Scotland, are sometimes called the "backbone of England," a fitting description. This is a landscape of rocky outcrops and vaulting meadowland, where you'll see nothing for miles but sheep, dry-stone (unmortared) walls, and farms, interrupted only occasionally by villages whose houses are made of the local dark graystone.

Pleasures and Pastimes

Beatlemania

For babyboomers, Liverpool exerts a strange and powerful lure—it is, after all, the birthplace of the Beatles. John, Paul, George, and Pete Best (Ringo arrived a bit later) set up shop at the Cavern in 1961 and the Liverpool Sound conquered the world. Today, Cavern Mecca in Mathew Street is practically a holy shrine, while fans can follow in the footsteps of the Fab Four at the Beatles Story. Unfortunately, many sites linked with John and Paul have been bulldozed. Don't forget to take a ferry "cross the Mersey"!

Dining

Gustatorily speaking, this section of the country is most famous for its Bakewell Pudding (*never* called "Tart" in these regions, as its imitations are in other parts of England). Its recipe was allegedly discovered when a cook accidentally spilled a rich cake mixture over some jam tarts. The cook was working in the Rutland Arms Hotel, where Jane Austen once stayed while writing *Pride and Prejudice*. Served with either custard or cream, the pudding is the joy of Bakewell, the pretty town where pride of place goes to Market Day, every Monday. Of course, Manchester and Liverpool offer a complete selection of restaurants, including modern British and Continental as well as various ethnic cuisines. In particular, Manchester has one of Britain's most vibrant Chinatowns, while locals also set great store in the 20-odd Asian restaurants along Wilmslow Road, in the suburb of Rusholme, a few miles south of the city center. Here you can enjoy wonderful Bangladeshi, Pakistani, and Indian food.

CATEGORY	COST*
££££	over £40
£££	£25–£40
££	£15–£25
£	under £15

**per person, including first course, main course, dessert, and VAT; excluding drinks*

Lodging

If your trip centers on the cities of the Northwest, we recommend that you base yourself in Manchester and make Liverpool a day trip. Manchester offers a much better choice of accommodations and though the larger city-center hotels rely on business guests during the week, they often offer reduced rates on weekends. There are also numerous smaller hotels and guest houses in the nearby suburbs, many just a short bus ride from downtown. The Manchester Visitor Centre (☞ Visitor Information *in* Lancashire and the Peaks A to Z, *below*) operates a room-booking service, but you must stop by in person to use it.

In Blackpool, the problem is not one of too few accommodations, but too many. There are literally hundreds of small hotels and guest houses in the resort, but because they're small, they fill up quickly, and finding a room in July can be one of life's more frustrating experiences. The Blackpool tourist information office (☞ Visitor Information *in* Lancashire and the Peaks A to Z, *below*) can send you an updated list of accommodations, if you want to book in advance. At other times of the year, you can visit Blackpool without advance reservations; the tourist office can usually help you book a room upon arrival.

CATEGORY	COST*
££££	over £110
£££	£60–£110
££	£50–£60
£	under £50

**All prices are for two people sharing a double room, including service, breakfast, and VAT.*

Exploring Lancashire and the Peak District

Manchester lies at the heart of a tangle of motorways in the northwest of England, about half an hour across the Pennines from Yorkshire. The city spreads west to the coast and the mouth of the river Mersey, where Liverpool is still centered on its port. To the north, in Lancashire, the coast flattens out around the resort of Blackpool—undistinguished country for the most part, though it includes miles of sandy beaches. But for the Northwest's most dramatic scenery—indeed, its only real geological feature of interest—you have to travel to the Peak District, a craggy national park less than an hour's drive southeast of Manchester.

Great Itineraries

Greater Manchester and Merseyside form one of the most built-up areas in Britain, but motorway access between the two, and to the north, to Blackpool, means that it's a fairly quick matter to visit all three places. Three days, at a push, would show you the sights of each city and allow time for a quick seaside jaunt.

To discover England at its most grand and ducal, plan a day trip to the Derbyshire valley of the Wye River to visit two of England's most beautiful stately houses: Chatsworth and Haddon Hall. Majestic 18th-century Chatsworth is just about the most visited house in all Britain; however, as hordes arrive on its doorstep, the Duke of Devonshire—its owner—sells off more art treasures, reducing the house to a shadow of its former self. Haddon Hall is already bare inside, but because it's world famous as the incomparable setting from which Dorothy Vernon eloped with John Manners in the 16th century—the Victorian era made this story into a beloved fable known by every British schoolchild—and has an enchanting Tudor and Jacobean structure, it is widely regarded as "the most romantic house in England."

Two additional days would give you enough time to see the main villages of the Peak District; Buxton itself could be visited on a day trip from Manchester if you wanted to base yourself in that city. But the Peaks require more than just a short drive around the principal sights; to do the national park justice you should allow for perhaps three nights on top of any time you choose to spend in Manchester and Liverpool. Of course, keen hikers won't find even this enough—a week's hiking tour of the Peak District could be constructed with no trouble at all.

Numbers in the text refer to numbers in the margin and on the maps.

IF YOU HAVE 3 DAYS

Base yourself in **Manchester** ① for your first night, which will give you a chance to see the central sights on your first day and catch a show or a movie that night. Get to the Granada Studios Tour early the next morning, before the crowds arrive. You'll need to keep your visit short if you wish to escape the crowds and journey to the lush green and peaceful calm of the Derbyshire Wye to visit two of England's most magnificent stately homes, **Haddon Hall** ㉛ and **Chatsworth** ㉜, spending your second night in **Bakewell** ㉚. If you're traveling when these houses are closed for the season, call in at **Liverpool** ⑮ for an overnight stay. Enjoy a lunch on the Albert Dock, then spend the afternoon in the museums and attractions of this dockside entertainment center.

IF YOU HAVE 5 DAYS

Make **Manchester** ① your base for the first two nights. This way you can spend the best part of two days in the city: time you'll need if you're traveling with children, since visits to Castlefield and the Granada Studios Tour will take up one full day. On the third day, take a overnight trip to **Liverpool** ⑮—with the morning spent in the city center seeing the cathedrals, buildings, and museums, and the afternoon at Albert Dock (over three nights, you'll be very unlucky if your visit doesn't coincide with a musical or theatrical performance of interest in either Manchester or Liverpool). Or opt instead to overnight in **Bakewell** ㉚ to visit romantic **Haddon Hall** ㉛ and regal **Chatsworth** ㉜ in the Derbyshire Wye valley. In summer, provided the weather is fine, the fifth day can be spent in the Peak District, with the last overnight in the spa

Your passport around the world.

- Worldwide access
- Operators who speak your language
- Monthly itemized billing

MCI Calling Card
415 555 1234 2244
J.D. SMITH

©MCI Telecommunications Corporation, 1996. All rights reserved.

Use your MCI Card® and these access numbers for an easy way to call when traveling worldwide.

Austria (CC)♦†	022-903-012
Belarus	
From Gomel and Mogilev regions	8-10-800-103
From all other localities	8-800-103
Belgium (CC)♦†	0800-10012
Bulgaria	00800-0001
Croatia (CC)★	99-385-0112
Czech Republic (CC)♦	00-42-000112
Denmark (CC)♦†	8001-0022
Finland (CC)♦†	9800-102-80
France (CC)♦†	0800-99-0019
Germany (CC)†	0130-0012
Greece (CC)♦†	00-800-1211
Hungary (CC)♦	00▼800-01411
Iceland (CC)♦†	800-9002
Ireland (CC)†	1-800-55-1001
Italy (CC)♦†	172-1022
Kazakhstan (CC)	1-800-131-4321
Liechtenstein (CC)♦	155-0222
Luxembourg†	0800-0112
Monaco (CC)♦	800-90-19
Netherlands (CC)♦†	06-022-91-22
Norway (CC)♦†	800-19912
Poland (CC)✣†	00-800-111-21-22
Portugal (CC)✣†	05-017-1234
Romania (CC)✣	01-800-1800
Russia (CC)✣♦	747-3322
For a Russian-speaking operator	747-3320
San Marino (CC)♦	172-1022
Slovak Republic (CC)	00-42-000112
Slovenia	080-8808
Spain (CC)†	900-99-0014
Sweden (CC)♦†	020-795-922
Switzerland (CC)♦†	155-0222
Turkey (CC)♦†	00-8001-1177
Ukraine (CC)✣	8▼10-013
United Kingdom (CC)†	
To call to the U.S. using BT■	0800-89-0222
To call to the U.S. using Mercury■	0500-89-0222
Vatican City (CC)†	172-1022

To sign up for the MCI Card, dial the access number of the country you are in and ask to speak with a customer service representative.

http://www.mci.com

(CC) Country-to-country calling available. May not be available to/from all international locations. (Canada, Puerto Rico, and U.S. Virgin Islands are considered Domestic Access locations.) ♦ Public phones may require deposit of coin or phone card for dial tone. † Automation available from most locations. ★Not available from public pay phones. ▼Wait for second dial tone. ✣ Limited availability. ■ International communications carrier.

It helps to be pushy in airports.

Introducing the revolutionary new TransPorter™ from American Tourister®. It's the first suitcase you can push around without a fight. TransPorter's™ exclusive four-wheel design lets you push it in front of you with almost no effort–the wheels take the weight. Or pull it on two wheels if you choose. You can even stack on other bags and use it like a luggage cart.

Stable 4-wheel design.

TransPorter™ is designed like a dresser, with built-in shelves to organize your belongings. Or collapse the shelves and pack it like a traditional suitcase. Inside, there's a suiter feature to help keep suits and dresses from wrinkling. When push comes to shove, you can't beat a TransPorter™. For more information on how you can be this pushy, call 1-800-542-1300.

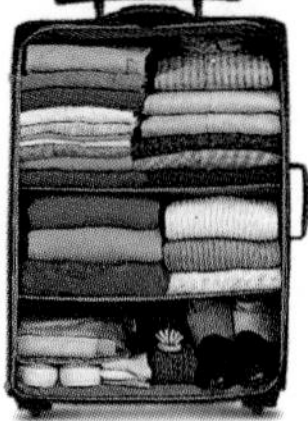

Shelves collapse on command.

Making travel less primitive®.

©1996 American Tourister®

town of 🏨 **Buxton** ㉙, the preferred choice, within easy driving distance of the area's charming villages.

IF YOU HAVE 7 DAYS

It's wisest to split your time between city and national park. Start in **Buxton** ㉙, where there's enough to occupy an afternoon's stroll, before moving on to spend the night in the pretty town of 🏨 **Bakewell** ㉚, from where you can spend the second day journeying to the beautiful Derbyshire Wye valley to visit **Haddon Hall** ㉛ and **Chatsworth** ㉜, both among the top stately houses in all Britain, returning to 🏨 Bakewell for the night. On the morning of the third day, move on to **Matlock** ㉝ and its river, and take a cable-car ride to the Heights of Abraham, before turning back and aiming for **Castleton** ㉞ and its splendid caverns. If you wanted to do any walking around the isolated village of **Edale** ㉟, you should spend the third night back in 🏨 **Buxton** ㉙, making an early start on the day. Having spent some hours walking on the moors, it's just a short drive to 🏨 **Manchester** ①, where one overnight stay will let you see the best of that city, before moving on to enjoy your last two nights and days in 🏨 **Liverpool** ⑮.

When to Tour Lancashire and the Peak District

Manchester has a rather unenviable reputation as one of the wettest cities in Britain, and visiting in summer isn't any guarantee of fine weather. Nevertheless, the nature of many of the sights both here and in Liverpool means that wet or cold weather shouldn't spoil a visit. In addition, the season for the Hallé Orchestra runs from October to May, the Manchester Arts Festival is in October, and winter sees less visitors to the very popular Granada Studios Tour—so a fall or winter visit is a definite option. Blackpool is, obviously, first and foremost a summer destination, though there's a certain poetic attraction to visiting in winter and having the windswept sands and much of the town to yourself; the amusement park will be closed, but the Blackpool Tower stays open all year. Summer is also the optimum time to see the Peak District, especially as early summer sees traditional festivities in many villages; the *only* time to see the great houses of the Derbyshire Wye valley—Chatsworth and Haddon Hall—is from April to September.

MANCHESTER, LIVERPOOL, AND BLACKPOOL

For a taste of the northwest of England, three cities—with interconnected histories and experiences—stand out: Manchester, the port of Liverpool, and the holiday resort of Blackpool. All are relatively new places, at least for a country that measures its age in centuries, but each offers an outstanding wealth of urban and coastal experiences.

The damp northwestern climate was particularly suited to cotton production and by the mid-18th century the Lancashire cotton industry was firmly established, with headquarters in nearby Manchester. During the latter part of the 19th century, both the industrial nouveau-riche and the downtrodden factory worker sought relief in new leisure outlets, with the result that resorts like Blackpool flourished. Later, in the 1970s and 1980s, it, too, suffered a period of decline, as warmer (and often cheaper) European holidays began to look more attractive to Britons. A visit on a busy summer day, however, makes it hard to believe recession ever really set in.

Manchester, with its position at the junction of several motorways and its international airport, is the obvious starting point. From here, it's an easy drive west to Liverpool, and then north and west to the Lancashire coast and Blackpool. Take the train rather than combat local traffic; both Manchester and Liverpool city centers are easy to walk around in.

Numbers in the margin refer to points of interest on the Lancashire and the Peaks map and the Manchester map.

Manchester

1 *43 mi southwest of Leeds, 87 mi north of Birmingham.*

Manchester was known to the Romans, who built a fort here, and to the Vikings, who attempted (but failed) to conquer the town. By the 14th century, the region was home to a flourishing woolen trade. But for these ancient stirrings, the city that stands today is no more nor less than the product of the 18th-century Industrial Revolution—some would say its finest flowering. The mechanization of the cotton industry—the first cotton mill powered by steam opened here in 1783—caused rapid and unprecedented growth; the railway followed in 1830; then, in 1894, the opening of the Manchester Ship Canal turned the world's cotton capital into a major inland port.

These were turbulent times for the city. The factories and industries that procured Manchester's wealth gave rise to an industrial underclass, whose gradual awakening led to social and political unrest. Eleven workers were killed by the local militia at a protest meeting in 1819; the terrible conditions under which factory hands worked were later eloquently recorded by Friedrich Engels (co-author with Karl Marx of the *Communist Manifesto*), who managed a cotton mill in the city. Formal political opposition to the government emerged in the shape of the Chartist movement (which campaigned for universal suffrage) and the Anti-Corn Law League (which opposed trade tariffs), both of which were centered in Manchester.

As with many former English industrial powerhouses, the declining years of the 20th century were not kind to Manchester, which until comparatively recently remained a soot-blackened, forbidding city—unlovely and unloved. But gradually the masterpieces of sturdy Victorian architecture in the city center have been cleaned up and much of the severe damage caused by World War II bombing has been remedied by modern development (not all of it attractive).

More recently still, Manchester has undergone a remarkable transformation, with heavy investment in a new transportation system and in impressive sporting and leisure facilities. In part, this was due to the city's repeated attempts to attract the Olympic Games: Manchester bid unsuccessfully for the 1996 and, most recently, the 2000 games, but was finally rewarded for its persistence by being chosen as the site of the 2002 Commonwealth Games. The result so far has been the development of a fine set of civic and sports amenities that only enhance the city's architectural and cultural heritage.

2 Manchester's exuberant **Town Hall** speaks volumes about the city's 19th-century sense of self-importance—it's a magnificent Victorian Gothic building (1867–76), with extensions added just before World War II. The Great Hall, with its soaring hammerbeam roof, is decorated with murals of the city's proud history, painted between 1852 and 1865 by the Pre-Raphaelite Ford Madox Brown. City guided tours, arranged through the tourist office (housed in the Town Hall Extension), can introduce you to the murals, but it's also a simple matter to present yourself at the front desk and ask to look: Provided the rooms aren't

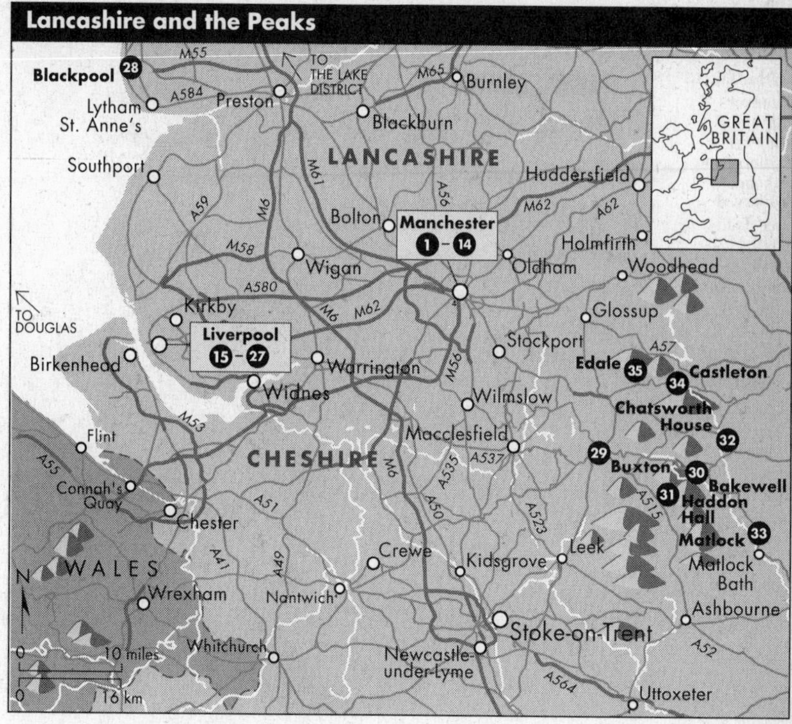

being used for meetings, you'll be allowed to wander in. ✉ *Albert Sq.,* ☎ *0161/234–1900,* ⏲ *Weekdays 8:45–4:30.*

❸ The **Central Library** was erected in 1930 to make an emphatic statement about the city's devotion to local education. The grand reading room is worth seeing; it was, at one time, the biggest municipal library in the world. The Library Theatre (☞ Nightlife and the Arts, *below*) is part of the complex. The library is on the south side of the Town Hall. ✉ *St.Peter's Sq.,* ☎ *0161/234–1900.* ⏲ *Mon.–Thurs. 10–8, Fri. and Sat. 10–5.*

Many industrial barons of the 19th century spent some of their vast wealth on paintings, and their interests are reflected in the displays in

★ ❹ the **City Art Gallery,** a striking, neoclassical building. Apart from a fine collection of work by Pre-Raphaelites (including works by Ford Madox Brown), there are paintings by Gainsborough, Samuel Palmer, Turner, Paul Gaugin, Claude Lorrain, and Bellotto. A re-creation of the living room and studio of L. S. Lowry—the popular Manchester artist who died in 1976—adds a touch of local interest. Stop by the gallery shop and café, too, both of which are a cut above average.

The City Art Gallery also manages several other outlets in Manchester, including the **Atheneum Gallery** next door, a showcase for changing contemporary shows, and the **Gallery of English Costume,** south of the center at Platt Hall in Rusholme. ✉ *City Art Gallery, Mosley St.,* ☎ *0161/236–5244.* 🎫 *Free.* ⏲ *Mon.–Sat. 10–5:45, Sun. 2–5:45. Free guided tours, weekends at 2:30. Details of events and exhibitions at the Atheneum Gallery and Gallery of English Costume available from the City Art Gallery.*

★ ❺ The Italianate **Free Trade Hall** on Peter Street was just one of the buildings in Manchester restored after World War II; only the facade is orig-

Castlefield Visitor Centre, **6**
Cathedral, **13**
Central Library, **3**
City Art Gallery/ Atheneum Gallery, **4**
Free Trade Hall, **5**
Granada Studios Tour, **8**
John Rylands Library, **9**
Museum of Science and Industry, **7**
People's History Museum, **10**
Royal Exchange, **12**
St. Ann's Church, **11**
Town Hall, **2**
Whitworth Art Gallery, **14**

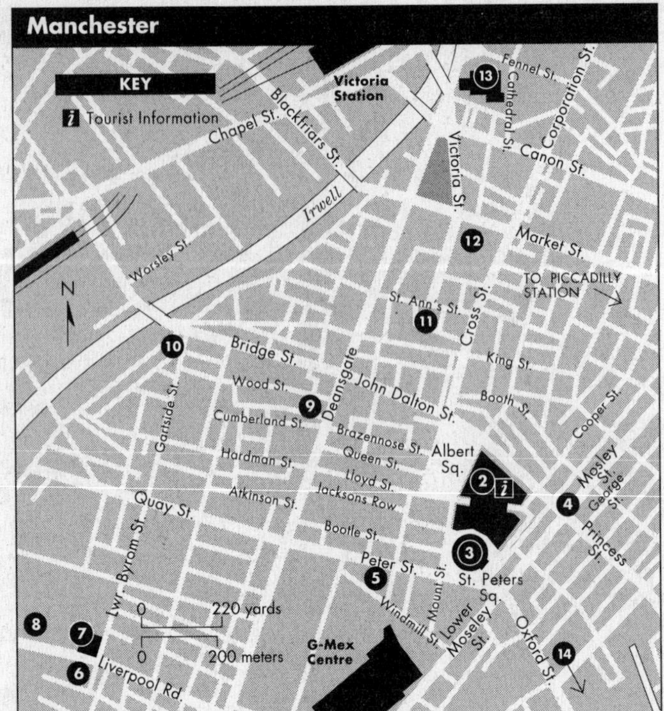

inal. It served as the home of the Hallé Orchestra for more than a century, though the orchestra moved into a custom-built auditorium of its own, Bridgewater Hall, in 1996 (☞ Nightlife and the Arts, *below*). The building is now closed for eventual redevelopment as a hotel—not expected to be open for business for some time, though when it does the facade will be retained. Incidentally, the site on which the Free Trade Hall stands has dark historical associations. In 1819, in what was formerly St. Peter's Field, 60,000 workers attending a meeting on the reform of Parliament were fired upon by the local guard, killing 11 people, an event known widely as the "Peterloo Massacre."

Manchester's commitment to the arts can be seen in several major downtown developments. The **G-Mex Centre** (✉ Lower Mosley St.; ☞ Nightlife and the Arts, *below*), formerly Manchester's central railroad station, now houses the city's biggest and brightest exhibitions and events. In late 1996, the Hallé Orchestra moved into the city's new concert hall, **Bridgewater Hall** (✉ Lower Mosley St., ☞ Nightlife and the Arts, *below*), a scrupulously modern piece of architecture overlooking a new public piazza.

Manchester's origins can be clearly seen in the district of Castlefield, site of an early Roman fort and later the center of Manchester's first canal and railroad developments. The district has since been restored as an urban heritage park—Britain's first—and in addition to the in-
6 formative **Castlefield Visitor Centre,** the 7-acre site contains the reconstructed gate to the Roman fort and the various buildings of the excellent Museum of Science and Industry. ✉ *Visitor Centre, Liverpool Rd.,* ☎ *0161/834–4026.* *Free.* ⏲ *Weekdays 11–4, weekends noon–4.*

★ 7 At the **Museum of Science and Industry,** separate buildings, including the world's oldest surviving passenger railway station, show marvelous collections relating to the city's industrial past and present. You can walk through a reconstructed Victorian sewer and examine a huge collection of working steam mill engines. This section of town is rife with Industrial Revolution landmarks; not far away, on Cooke Street, a certain Henry Royce built his first car in 1904, before he went into partnership with C.S. Rolls. ⊠ *Castlefield, Liverpool Rd.,* ☎ *0161/832–1830.* 🎫 *£4.* ⌚ *Daily 10–5.*

8 In an unlikely city center site, the **Granada Studios Tour** has a lot to offer imaginative children (as well as adults). A British version of the popular Hollywood studio tours, it offers firsthand a behind-the-scenes look at television programs. There are backstage tours (including a walk down Sherlock Holmes's Baker Street and along Downing Street), 3D film shows, and other special events, rides, and entertainments. It's from here that Britain's longest-running TV soap opera, *Coronation Street,* is broadcast, and you can even have a drink in the program's pub, the "Rover's Return." Get there before 11 AM if you want to see everything and experience a full range of rides and tours in one day. ⊠ *Water St.,* ☎ *0161/833–0880.* 🎫 *£12.99.* ⌚ *Mid-Apr.–Sept., daily 9:45–7, last admission at 4; Oct.–mid-Apr., weekdays 9:45–5:30, weekends 9:45–6:30, last admission at 3.*

9 Housed in a lovely mock-Gothic masterpiece, the **John Rylands Library** is named after a rich weaver whose widow spent his money founding the library. It became part of the University of Manchester in 1972. Built in a late-Gothic style in the 1890s, the library houses one of Britain's most important collections—priceless historical documents and charters, Bibles in over 300 languages, manuscripts dating from the dawn of Christianity, and fine bindings. There are always exhibitions from the library's treasures, including one of the possibly accurate likenesses of Shakespeare, the Grafton portrait. ⊠ *150 Deansgate,* ☎ *0161/834–5343.* 🎫 *Free.* ⌚ *Weekdays 10–5:30, Sat. 10–1.*

One of Manchester's more recent museums recounts splendidly the struggles of working people in the city throughout the Industrial Revolu-
10 tion and beyond. The **People's History Museum** not only tells the story of the 1819 Peterloo Massacre, but features an unrivaled collection of trades union banners, tools, toys, utensils, and photographs, which combine to illustrate the working lives and pastimes of the city's people. There's a pleasant café here, too. ⊠ *Bridge St.,* ☎ *0161/228–7212.* 🎫 *£1; free on Fri.* ⌚ *Tues.–Sun. 11–4:30.*

11 **St. Ann's Church,** a handsome 1712 building, comes as a surprise amid resolutely modern surrounding buildings. It contains *The Descent from the Cross,* a painting by Annibale Carracci (1561–1609). Thomas De Quincey was baptized here (having been born in a nearby house, now long since demolished). Guided tours are available if you call in advance, or try and coincide with the organ recitals that usually take place at 12:45 on Tuesday. ⊠ *St. Ann's Sq.,* ☎ *0161/834–0239.*

Throughout its commercial heyday, the city's most important build-
12 ing was the **Royal Exchange,** once the cotton market. The existing structure, built with panache in the early 20th century to accommodate 7,000 traders is the most recent of several buildings to hold the title. Its echoing bulk now houses one of the most imaginative theaters in Britain—a tubular steel-and-glass structure, set down in the middle of the vast space like a space ship delicately parked within a great cathedral. Inside the Royal Exchange, there's also a café, exhibition space, and occasional craft fairs. ⊠ *St. Ann's Sq.,* ☎ *0161/833–9833.*

NEED A BREAK? Close to the Royal Exchange, in the modern Arndale Centre, **Sinclair's Oyster Bar** (✉ Shambles Sq., ☎ 0161/834–0430) is an atmospheric 18th-century pub serving excellent lunches (including, naturally, oysters) and good northern beer. In summer, you can sit outside in the pedestrianized square.

13 Manchester's **Cathedral,** beside the river, was originally the medieval parish church of the city but was elevated in status to a cathedral in 1847. Unusually proportioned, it's very broad for its length; indeed, it's recognized as having the widest medieval-age nave in Britain. Inside is a wealth of attractive items: early 16th-century choir stalls with intriguing misericord seats; paintings of the Beatitudes by Carel Weight (1908–89); a sculpture by Eric Gill (1882–1919), famed for the typeface that he designed and which bears his name; a fine tomb brass of Warden Huntingdon, who died in 1458; and an octagonal chapter house from 1485. ✉ *Deansgate,* ☎ *0161/833–2220.* *Free.* *Daily 8–6.*

One of the most interesting places to visit outside the center of Man-
14 chester is the university-run **Whitworth Art Gallery.** The collections in the gallery are especially strong in British watercolors, old master drawings, and Postimpressionism. And its captivating rooms full of textiles—Coptic and Peruvian fabrics, Spanish and Italian vestments, tribal rugs, and contemporary weaving—are just what you might expect in a city built on textile manufacture. There's a bistro for light meals and a good gift shop. The gallery is southeast of the city center in an area called Moss Side. At the Piccadilly bus terminal ask for a bus to the Manchester Royal Infirmary, which is just across the road from the Whitworth. ✉ *Oxford Rd.,* ☎ *0161/273–4865.* *Free.* *Mon.–Wed., Fri.–Sat. 10–5, Thurs. 10–9.*

OFF THE BEATEN PATH **MINOR MUSEUMS** – Be sure to ask the tourist office about Manchester's lesser-known museums—such as the **Jewish Museum,** the **Chinese Arts Centre,** or the **Charter Street Ragged School**—which deal with thought-provoking aspects of ethnic and urban life that aren't covered in the mainstream city museums.

Dining and Lodging

££ ✕ **Café Primavera.** In a quiet suburb of south Manchester, very near Chorlton Green, this is no mere café, but a very elegant addition to the city's dining scene. Against a background of bright primary colors and jugs full of sunflowers, Mediterranean flavors prevail in a seasonally changing menu that might include mussels with cream and pancetta, roast duck with plum sauce, or fillet steak with green salsa. The tables are a little too close together for comfort, but the service is good-natured. The short wine list has some great surprises, and desserts are memorable. Its sister restaurants, **Alto Café** (✉ 9–11 Wilmslow Rd., Rusholme, ☎ 0161/225–7108) and the **Lime Tree** (✉ 8 Lapwing La., West Didsbury, ☎ 0161/445–1217) are just as enticing, and a little closer to the city center. ✉ *48 Beech Rd., Chorlton,* ☎ *0161/862–9934. MC, V. No lunch.*

££ ★ ✕ **Market Restaurant.** This is an unpretentious, dinner-only spot that is serious about its cooking. Its menu changes monthly, and although there's an emphasis on vegetarian dishes, meat and fish entrées are well thought out and as likely to feature Asian or European as British influences; desserts are always inventive. The proprietor, a beer enthusiast, maintains an excellent selection of international bottled beers, as well as an interesting wine list. ✉ *104 High St.,* ☎ *0161/834–3743. AE, DC, MC, V. Closed 1 wk at Christmas, at Easter, and throughout Aug. No lunch Wed.–Sat.*

££ ✕ **Yang Sing.** One of Manchester's good Chinese restaurants, it's popular with Chinese families, always a good sign, but *so* popular that you must reserve ahead. The cooking is Cantonese, and there's a huge range to choose from. The *dim sum* is always a good bet, and don't forget to ask about the daily specials—they're often only listed in Chinese on the menu. There is also a slightly cheaper offshoot, **Little Yang Sing** (✉ 17 George St., ☎ 0161/228–7722). This was Manchester's original Yang Sing restaurant; it has a rather cramped basement setting but still serves fine Cantonese food. ✉ *34 Princess St.,* ☎ *0161/236–2200. AE, MC, V.*

£–££ ✕ **Café Istanbul.** This popular Turkish place has expanded over the years without losing any of the charm or good service that always characterized it. It's as authentic as you'll find in Britain, which means you can't go wrong ordering the inexpensive *meze—hummus,* stuffed grape leaves, cheese-filled pastries, *taramasalata,* and other treats. Grilled meat and kebab dishes are hugely filling, and to complete the experience there's also a full range of coffee, pastries, and wine—all Turkish, naturally. ✉ *79 Bridge St.,* ☎ *0161/833–9942. MC, V. Closed Sun.*

£–££ ✕ **Sangam.** While most of Rusholme's many Asian eateries pack diners in for quick (though admittedly excellent) meals, this more upscale restaurant—renowned for the quality of its food—allows you more time to linger. There's always a buzz here, though the closely packed tables have something to do with that. The restaurant is a couple of miles south of the city center; take a taxi. ✉ *13–15 Wilmslow Rd.,* ☎ *0161/225–5785. MC, V.*

£ ✕ **Dmitri's.** Set in a covered Victorian arcade, in an old market building, this attractive tapas bar–taverna welcomes a trendy Manchester set. An interesting hybrid menu ranges from Greek and Mediterranean snack dishes to pasta, mixed grills, rice pilafs, and salads. Most meals here cost well under £10. In warm weather, you'll welcome being able to sit outside in the arcade. ✉ *Campfield Arcade, Tonman St., Deansgate,* ☎ *0161/839–3319. No credit cards.*

££££ ★ ✕🏨 **Victoria & Albert Hotel.** Formerly a warehouse, built in 1843, and situated just out of the city center opposite the Granada Studios Tour, this hotel is an object lesson in how to handle renovation without destroying the historic kernel of a building. Exposed brickwork and cast-iron pillars throughout make for highly individualized accommodations—no two rooms are the same. All guest rooms are named after Granada TV programs; four suites have thematic decor (the Sherlock Holmes suite re-creates a slice of Victorian London); and there's a separate "Ladies Wing" designed for solo women travelers, with panic alarms, closed circuit TV, and individual toiletries in the very comfortable bathrooms. Throughout, facilities are first-class. The bar has urban river views from its conservatory, while the highly rated **Sherlock Holmes Restaurant** features special gourmet dinners as well as an à la carte menu of classic English food with a Continental (and occasional Asian) twist. ✉ *Water St., M3 4OQ,* ☎ *0161/832–1188,* FAX *0161/834–2484. 132 rooms with bath. Restaurant (£££; reservations essential, jacket and tie), bar, coffee shop, room service, sauna, exercise room, business services. AE, DC, MC, V.*

££££ 🏨 **Holiday Inn Crowne Plaza Midland.** The name is a real mouthful these days since Holiday Inn took over the management, but the Midland remains the city's finest downtown hotel. The Edwardian splendor of the public rooms—including a grand lobby and bar—evokes turn-of-the-century days when the Midland was Manchester's railroad hotel. Guest rooms are comfortable, though they never quite live up to the standards of the rest of the hotel, but the other facilities are as up-to-the-minute as you'd expect: bar and grill, restaurant, health club, swimming pool, and squash court. And to cap it all, the city's theaters, restaurants, and pubs are all within easy walking distance. Weekend rates here are a particularly good value. Note that during the week, breakfast is not included in the price. ✉ *Peter St., M60 2DS,* ☎ *0161/236–3333,* FAX *0161/228–2241. 303 rooms with bath. 2 restaurants, 2 bars, grill, room service, pool, beauty salon, sauna, exercise room, squash, casino, business services. AE, DC, MC, V.*

£ **Cavendish Hotel.** This suburban guest house 3 miles south of the city center is situated on good bus routes and is also convenient for the little pubs around Chorlton Green. The converted Edwardian house offers comfortable-size rooms with televisions and tea/coffeemaking facilities. ✉ *402 Wilbraham Rd., Chorlton-cum-Hardy, M21 0UH,* ☎ *0161/881–1911. 30 rooms, 15 with showers. MC, V.*

Nightlife and the Arts

For listings of events, festivals, concerts, shows, movies and other entertainment, buy the weekly ***City Life*** magazine from any newsstand.

Manchester's Hallé Orchestra performs at the new **Bridgewater Hall** (✉ Lower Mosley St.), opposite G-Mex. Other classical concerts are held at the **Royal Northern College of Music** (✉ 124 Oxford Rd., ☎ 0161/273–4504). For musical events at **G-Mex** (✉ Lower Mosley St.), call the box office at 0161/832–9000. For rock, reggae, jazz, R&B, and many other kinds of music, the best venue is **Band on the Wall** (✉ 25 Swan St., ☎ 0161/832–6625), which has live music six nights a week.

Manchester has an enviable reputation in the performing arts with productions staged at theaters all over the city. The **Opera House** (✉ Quay St., ☎ 0161/242–2509), hosts touring companies, both British and international, as well as a wide spectrum of entertainment. In the basement of the Central Library, the **Library Theatre** (✉ St. Peter's Sq., ☎ 0161/236–7110), stages mostly classic and serious drama, as well as new writing from local playwrights. The **Royal Exchange Theatre** (✉ St. Ann's Sq., ☎ 0161/833–9833) is an extremely inventive acting space with a sky-high reputation for daring productions. For more offbeat productions, **The Green Room** (✉ 54–56 Whitworth St. W, ☎ 0161/236–1677) puts on a full program of theater, poetry, dance, and performance art.

The **Cornerhouse** (✉ 70 Oxford St., ☎ 0161/228–2463) is a combined visual arts gallery-cinema, with changing exhibitions and arthouse movies. There's also a popular café and bar. The main city-center movie house, for mainstream releases, is the **Odeon** (✉ Oxford St., ☎ 01426/950148).

Manchester hosts an annual **Festival of Arts and Television** in October, when there are theatrical performances, street events, concerts, and shows held at a variety of venues throughout the city. The tourist information center has more information.

The city has, arguably, the best nightlife in the north, with a wide range of pubs and clubs. The **Peveril of the Peak** (✉ Great Bridgewater St., ☎ 0161/236–6364) is a lively, tiled Victorian pub with interesting little nooks and crannies. To sit out by the water, have a drink at **Dukes 92** (✉ Castlefield, ☎ 0161/839–8646), a cavernous but comfortable place converted from old stables, named after the lock number where it's sited on the Rochdale Canal. One of the first new-wave café-bars in the city was **Dry 201** (✉ Oldham St., ☎ 0161/236–5920), now a little faded at the edges, but still full of bright young things. Manchester's most famous club is the **Hacienda** (✉ 11–

13 Whitworth St. W, ☎ 0161/236–5051), which was at the forefront of the 1980s U.K. club revival; it's still going strong.

Manchester also has a burgeoning **gay scene,** based around an area near Princess Street, known as the Gay Village. Here, there are about 20 bars and clubs, as well as restaurants, hotels, shops, and businesses firmly aimed at a gay clientele.

Outdoor Activities and Sports

SOCCER

Matches are played on Saturday (and, increasingly, Sunday and Monday). Admission prices vary, but the cheapest seats start at about £16. The best matches to catch are the local "derby" games between the city's two major teams: Local tourist offices can give you match schedules and directions to the grounds. **Manchester United** plays at Old Trafford (☎ 0161/872–0199). **Manchester City** plays at Maine Road (☎ 0161/226–1191).

WATER SPORTS

Chorlton Water Park in Manchester (✉ Maitland Ave., Barlow Moor Rd., Chorlton, ☎ 0161/881–5639) offers boating, canoeing, windsurfing, and sailing, between Easter and October.

Shopping

The **Royal Exchange Crafts Centre** (✉ St. Ann's Sq., ☎ 0161/833–9833) is an unusual glass structure in the foyer of the Royal Exchange theater specializing in jewelry, ceramics, glassware, and textiles produced throughout the country. The **Royal Exchange Shopping Centre** (✉ St Ann's Sq., ☎ 0161/834–3731) houses the Design Centre, a series of stores featuring the creations of young fashion designers.

The **Manchester Crafts Centre** (✉ 17 Oak St., ☎ 0161/832–4274) is a Victorian building housing 18 workshop-cum-retail outlets, where you can see potters, jewelers, hatters, theatrical costumers, and metal enamelers at work.

The **Whitworth Art Gallery** (✉ Oxford Rd., ☎ 0161/273–4865) has a fine shop that specializes in handmade cards, postcards, and prints. It also sells stationery, art books, jewelry, and ceramics. The **University of Manchester Museum** shop (✉ Oxford Rd., ☎ 0161/275–2000) also sells cards, stationery, and prints, but specializes in books and imaginative toys for children.

For antique clothes, records and tapes, ethnic crafts and jewelry, and bric-a-brac, visit **Aflecks Palace** (✉ 52 Church St., ☎ 0161/834–2039), four floors of retail outlets that attract the city's youth. **Gibb's Bookshop** (✉ 10 Charlotte St., ☎ 0161/236–7179) is a combined secondhand bookshop and classical music store.

Liverpool

⓯ *34 mi southwest of Manchester.*

As part of the 18th-century slave-trade triangle, made up of Africa, America, and Britain, Liverpool quickly grew into the country's largest port, a position it retained even after abolition of the slave trade. The Industrial Revolution placed it firmly at the center of Britain's burgeoning economy, connected to Manchester and the rest of the country by train and to the rest of the world by cargo ships and, later, transatlantic passenger liners.

At the height of its economic power in the late 19th century (when its population was higher than it is today), the city's bustling docks stretched for several miles, alive with goods and traders. As in neighboring Manchester, the wealth generated by this activity was huge, and the city center contains many buildings that reflect those proud days. But Liverpool proved rather less adaptable in the 20th century: As Britain lost its old imperial markets and its cotton industry, and as air transport superseded shipping, the port of Liverpool was left floundering in economic decay. There's been a certain amount of regeneration since the decline following World War II, but in many ways the impression that visitors take away with them is of a city waiting for better times.

Numbers in the margin correspond to points of interest on the Liverpool map.

The best move on arrival in Liverpool—if you wish to understand the
★ 16 city's maritime past—is to head straight for **Albert Dock** on the waterfront. Built in the mid-19th century as part of Liverpool's once mighty stretch of dockside developments, Albert Dock was rescued from neglect in recent times and its fine colonnaded, brick warehouse buildings converted to museums, shops, offices, and restaurants. Now the country's largest heritage attraction, it's a stunning achievement and there's enough here to occupy you for a whole day. And since most of the attractions are indoors, within the old warehouse buildings, it's an obvious choice if your visit coincides with one of the Northwest's rainy spells.

The dock forms part of a venture known as **Liverpool's Historic Waterfront.** The dock itself and some of the attractions are free; others require a separate admission fee or the purchase of a VIP Pass, which gets you into all the museums (Merseyside Maritime Museum, Museum of Liverpool Life, Tate Gallery, Beatles Story) and offers a cruise across the river Mersey. There is free parking at the dock, while a shuttle bus runs here every 30 minutes (Mon.–Sat. only) from Lime Street Station. ⊠ *Liverpool's Historic Waterfront, Albert Dock,* ☎ *0151/708–8574.* 🎫 *General admission free, VIP Pass £7.75.* ⊙ *For opening hrs, see individual attractions.*

17 Part of the Albert Dock complex, the **Merseyside Maritime Museum** is the most relevant museum to the city's history, telling the story of the port of Liverpool by way of models, paintings, and original boats and equipment, spread across five floors. The same admission ticket also grants access into the **Transatlantic Slavery** and **Customs and Excise** exhibitions, the former being especially compelling on the human misery engendered by the slave trade. ⊠ *Albert Dock,* ☎ *0151/207–0001.* 🎫 *£3, including admission to Museum of Liverpool Life.* ⊙ *Daily 10:30–5:30.*

18 The **Tate Gallery**—an offshoot of the London gallery of the same name—exhibits constantly changing displays of challenging modern art. Another attraction of Albert Dock, it has an excellent shop selling prints and posters. ⊠ *The Colonnades, Albert Dock,* ☎ *0151/709–0507.* 🎫 *Free; charge for special exhibitions.* ⊙ *Tues.–Sun. 10–6.*

A more offbeat look at Liverpool's history and culture is available by
19 viewing the exhibits at the **Museum of Liverpool Life,** housed in a former Boat Hall opposite the Albert Dock's Maritime Museum. There are special displays on Merseyside culture: This is the place to discover what it is that makes "Scousers" (as locals are known) tick, and perhaps even what's behind their famed sense of humor. ⊠ *Albert Dock,* ☎ *0151/207–0001.* 🎫 *£3, including admission to Merseyside Maritime Museum.* ⊙ *Daily 10:30–5:30.*

Albert Dock, **16**
Anglican Cathedral, **27**
The Beatles Story, **20**
Lime Street Station, **24**
Merseyside Maritime Museum, **17**
Metropolitan Cathedral, **26**
Museum of Liverpool Life, **19**
Pier Head, **21**
St. George's Hall, **23**
Tate Gallery, **18**
Town Hall, **22**
Walker Art Gallery, **25**

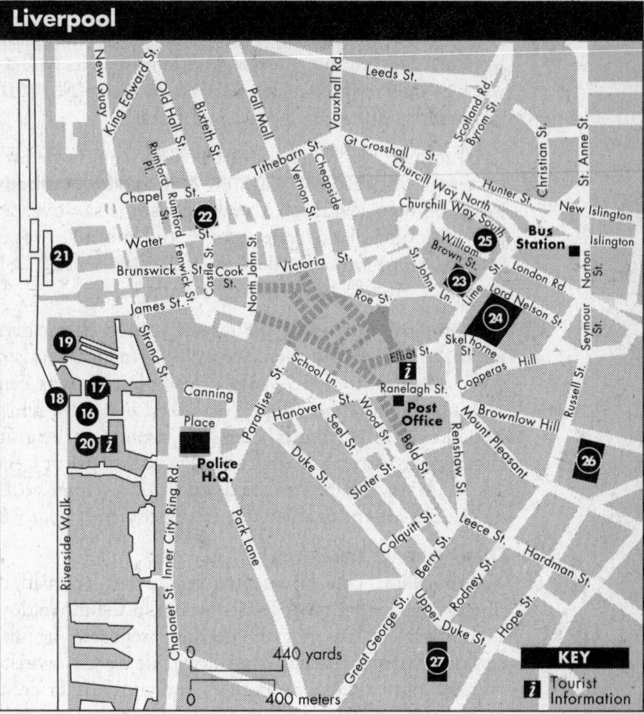

20 Nostalgic visitors can follow in the footsteps of the Fab Four at **The Beatles Story**—one of the more popular attractions of the Albert Dock complex—which features a series of entertaining re-created scenes from their career, as well as a new John Lennon photographic exhibition. ⊠ *Britannia Vaults, Albert Dock,* ☎ *0151/709–1963.* 🎟 *£5.45.* ⏲ *Daily 10–6.*

21 At **Pier Head** you're admirably poised to take a **ferry** across the river Mersey to Birkenhead and back. These leave regularly throughout the day and offer fine views of the city—a journey celebrated in "Ferry 'Cross the Mersey," Gerry and the Pacemakers' 1960s hit song. As you return, you'll look across to see the twin towers of the **Liver Building**—"Lye-ver"—topped by mythical birds, purported to have given the city its name. ⊠ *Pier Head Ferry Terminal, Mersey Ferries,* ☎ *0151/630–1030.* ⏲ *Ferries every 30–60 min, 7:45* AM*–7:15* PM. 🎟 *£1.60 for round-trips 7:45–9:15* AM *and 4:15–7:15* PM*; £2.90 for cruises at other times.*

City center buildings reflect the 19th-century glories of Liverpool. The
22 domed, Georgian **Town Hall** (⊠ Water St., ☎ 0151/707–2391) has
been recently refurbished and its splendidly rich interior is accessible
23 on guided tours in summer, provided you call in advance. **St. George's**
Hall (⊠ Lime St., ☎ 0151/707–2391), built in 1839–47, is considered one of the country's finest Greek Revival buildings; exhibitions and concerts are held inside and the public is allowed in for tours at other selected times in summer. Perhaps the most imposing expres-
24 sion of former industrial might is **Lime Street Station** (☞ Getting Around *in* Lancashire and the Peaks A to Z, *below*), whose cast-iron train shed was the world's largest in the mid-19th century.

★ 25 The **Walker Art Gallery** maintains its position as one of the best art collections outside London with an excellent display of British art (some of the best on show in its refurbished Victorian Gallery) and some superb Italian and Flemish works. In particular, you'll find paintings by Turner, Constable, Stubbs, and Landseer, as well as representative work by the Pre-Raphaelites. ⊠ *William Brown St.,* ☎ *0151/207–0001.* 🎟 *Free.* ⊙ *Mon.–Sat. 10–5, Sun. noon–5.*

A 10-minute walk up Mount Pleasant from Lime Street Station will
26 take you to the Roman Catholic **Metropolitan Cathedral of Christ the King.** Built in 1962, it's a striking—some say overbearing—funnel-like structure of concrete, stone, and mosaic, topped with a glass lantern. ⊠ *Mount Pleasant,* ☎ *0151/709–9222.* 🎟 *Donations welcome.* ⊙ *Mon.–Sat. 8–6, Sun. 8–5.*

27 The **Anglican Cathedral,** the largest church in northern Britain, overlooks the city and the river Mersey. Built of local sandstone, the Gothic-style cathedral took 75 years to complete. It was begun in 1903 by architect Giles Gilbert Scott (who died in 1960), and was finally finished in 1978. Having taken a look around at the grand interior, and climbed the tower, find time to call in at the Visitor Centre; a Refectory (⊙ 10–4) serves light meals and coffee. ⊠ *St. James's Rd.,* ☎ *0151/709–6271.* 🎟 *Donations welcome; £2 for tower.* ⊙ *Daily 8–6.*

Dining and Lodging

££ ✕ **Armadillo.** This downtown restaurant—considered Liverpool's
★ finest—has lost none of its attraction in the move down the street to slightly less spacious, but still relaxing, premises. The fine Mediterranean cooking features classic dishes alongside trendy favorites; starters may include lentil salad or eggplant and mozzarella combinations, and there's always plenty for vegetarians to enjoy. Desserts are a highlight, and the wine list carries some strong French names. Lunches and early suppers (Tues.–Fri. 5–6:45 PM) offer the chance to choose from a less expensive menu of bistro favorites. Service is friendly and informal. ⊠ *31 Matthew St.,* ☎ *0151/236–4123. AE, MC, V. Closed Sun., Mon., and Christmas wk. No lunch Sat.*

£ ✕ **Est Est Est.** This is the top budget choice in the Albert Dock complex, a lively spot for lunch. The restaurant makes good use of the old warehouse brickwork, though tables are a bit cramped. Still, the Italian menu is strong on appetizers—including a feast of antipasto—and includes excellent crisp pizzas. If you're still hungry, the dessert trolley trundles reassuringly round the restaurant. Service is brisk, the atmosphere bubbling, the coffee good. ⊠ *Unit 6, Edward Pavilion, Albert Dock,* ☎ *0151/708–6969. AE, MC, V.*

£££ 🏨 **Liverpool Moat House.** Some may find this uncompromisingly modern hotel unattractive from the outside, but its location and facilities are second to none in Liverpool. It lies right across from Albert Dock, which means that much of what you've come to the city to see is right on your doorstep. Guest rooms are handsome, most featuring two large beds, and about half the rooms are designated as no-smoking. Even if you don't eat in the hotel's restaurants, you can enjoy the afternoon tea service or a drink on the terrace in summer. ⊠ *Paradise St., L1 8JD,* ☎ *0151/471–9988,* FAX *0151/709–2706. 251 rooms with bath. 2 restaurants, bar, coffee shop, no-smoking rooms, room service, pool, sauna, exercise room, business services.*

Nightlife and the Arts

The renowned Royal Liverpool Philharmonic Orchestra plays its concert season at **Philharmonic Hall** (⊠ Hope St., ☎ 0151/709–3789). Major national and international ballet, opera, drama, and musical performances take place at the **Liverpool Empire** (⊠ Lime St., ☎ 0151/709–

1555). For experimental and British productions, check the program at the **Everyman Theatre** (✉ Hope St., ☎ 0151/709–4776).

Liverpool hosts regular pop and rock concerts and stand-up comedy. One of the most appealing venues is the Art Deco-era **Royal Court Theatre** (✉ Roe St., ☎ 0151/709–4321).

Nicest of the city-center pubs is the **Philharmonic** (✉ 36 Hope St., ☎ 0151/709–1163), a Victorian-tiled extravaganza, with comfortable barrooms and over-the-top rest rooms.

Outdoor Activities and Sports

HORSE RACING

Britain's most famous horse race, the **Grand National** steeplechase, has been run at Liverpool's **Aintree Race Course** (✉ Ormskirk Rd., ☎ 0151/523–2600) almost every year since 1839. The race is held every March/April, and even if you don't attend, you'll be able to see the race on every TV in the country. Admission on race days is from £7.

SOCCER

Matches are played on Saturday (and, increasingly, Sunday and Monday). Admission prices vary, but the cheapest seats start at about £15. The best matches to catch are the local "derby" games between major teams: The tourist offices can give you match schedules and directions to the grounds. **Liverpool** plays at Anfield (☎ 0151/260–8680). The city's second major soccer team, **Everton,** plays at Goodison Park (☎ 0151/521–2020).

Shopping

The shop at the **Walker Art Gallery** (✉ William Brown St., ☎ 0151/207–0001) contains a high-quality selection of glassware, ceramics, and jewelry by local designers. The annual Merseycraft exhibition winners are on exclusive display in the shop every December.

For unusual craft items and gifts, visit the **Bluecoat Display Centre** (✉ Bluecoat Chambers, School La., ☎ 0151/709–4014), housed in an 18th-century building.

Numbers in the margin correspond to points of interest on the Lancashire and the Peaks map.

Blackpool

28 *56 mi north of Liverpool, 53 mi northwest of Manchester, 86 mi west of Leeds—the trip is quickest by motorway, but a slower, more scenic route, the A583 and A584, runs along the Fylde coast.*

The largest vacation resort in Europe, Blackpool attracts more than 16 million visitors a year to its 7-mile promenade, sands, piers, parks, and Pleasure Beach—a Coney Island–style amusement park covering more than 40 acres south of the town center. To the British, Blackpool is something of an old joke; the pier and promenade stalls sell sickly Day-Glo candy and plastic hats emblazoned with "Kiss Me Quick" slogans. July and August are the peak months, when accommodations are at a premium and the myriad bars, discos, cafés, and restaurants are stuffed to the gills. The beaches, too, are covered with bodies, though be wary of swimming. The local waters don't qualify for the European Union clean water standard, and you'd do best to amuse children with a donkey ride up and down the sands instead.

Better yet, visit outside the peak summer season, when there's space to explore properly what's left of 19th-century Blackpool. It was one of the earliest British seaside resorts, pulling in workers from the Northwest's industrial cities, and the fixtures and fittings still reflect that era. Trams run up and down the promenade, saving your legs a long walk, and pass the town's three 19th-century piers.

★ The most famous and most prominent landmark is the **Blackpool Tower,** built in 1894 and inspired by the Eiffel Tower. The views from the top of the tower are magnificent, while inside are seven floors of amusements and rides. Take a look, too, at the superbly restored gilt ballroom, the site of daily tea dances. ✉ *Tower World,* ☎ *01253/22242.* *£7.95 (£4.95 in winter).* ⏲ *Apr.–Oct., daily 10 AM–11 PM; Nov.–Mar., Sat. 10–11, Sun. 10–6; daily 10–6 during Christmas wk except Dec. 25.*

NEED A BREAK? **Robert's Oyster Rooms** (✉ 92 North Shore, no phone), close to Blackpool Tower, is an anachronistic survival amid all the fast-food outlets. Stop in at the snug wood-paneled café for fresh oysters on the half shell, accompanied by bread and butter and hot tea, or try one of the other traditional British shellfish snacks: cockles, whelks, winkles, or prawns.

If you are in Blackpool in September or October, you'll coincide with the **Illuminations,** a spectacular light display that runs the length of the promenade. Each year, the switching-on ceremony is performed by a famous personality; one year this duty fell to the horse Red Rum, a British Grand National winner.

Dining and Lodging

£ ✕ **Harry Ramsden's.** Fish-and-chips are the traditional British seaside food, and there's no better place to eat them than at the Blackpool branch of Harry Ramsden's, a famous Yorkshire company. The smart restaurant is competently run, and service is brisk and friendly, though you may have to wait to be seated at lunchtime. Helpings of cod and chips are large and crispy; wine and beer are served, but the best accompaniments are hot tea and bread and butter. ✉ *60–63 The Promenade,* ☎ *01253/294386. MC, V.*

££££ ✕ **The Imperial.** Flushed with Victorian splendor, this Forte Grand hotel sits on the North Promenade, overlooking the sea. It's the favorite choice of Britain's political leaders, who regularly stay during the annual party conferences; the comfortable No. 10 Bar (as in Downing Street) is festooned with mementos and photographs. Guest rooms are furnished in turn-of-the-century style, with long drapes and reproduction period paintings. The celebrated **Palm Court Restaurant** features local specialties, especially fish and shellfish, and has a good carvery, for roast meats. ✉ *North Promenade, FY1 2HB,* ☎ *01253/23971,* FAX *01253/751784. 183 rooms with bath. Restaurant (£££; reservations essential, jacket and tie), 2 bars, pool, sauna, steam room, exercise room. AE, DC, MC, V.*

Outdoor Activities and Sports

HORSEBACK RIDING

Blackpool beach has horseback and donkey riding for adults and children throughout the summer.

SWIMMING

Blackpool's 7 miles of beaches offer safe swimming, but the water quality isn't everything it should be. Instead, it's wiser to rely on one of the town's indoor pools. **Blackpool Sandcastle** (✉ South Promenade, ☎ 01253/343602) is a complete entertainment complex with pools, slides, and chutes, open daily (10–6; £4.50 day-pass) from April to October.

THE PEAK DISTRICT: ON THE ROAD TO CHATSWORTH AND HADDON HALL

Heading southeast, away from the urban congestion of the Northwest, it's not far to the southernmost contortions of the Pennine Hills. Here, sheltered in a great natural bowl, the spa town of Buxton, about an hour from Manchester, has a surprisingly mild climate, considering its altitude: at more than 1,000 feet, it's the second-highest town in England. Buxton makes a convenient base for exploring the 540 square miles of the Peak District, Britain's oldest national park. "Peak" is perhaps misleading; despite being a hilly area, it contains only long, flat-topped rises that don't reach much higher than 2,000 feet. Yet touring around destinations such as Bakewell, Matlock, the stately homes of Chatsworth House and Haddon Hall, Castleton, and, finally, Edale, you'll often have to negotiate fairly perilous country roads, each of which provide enchanting views.

As you might expect, outdoor activities are popular in the Peaks, particularly caving (or "potholing"), which entails underground exploration, and—more realistically for visitors—walking and hiking. Bring all-weather clothing and waterproof shoes. One of the major trails is the **High Peak Trail,** which runs for 17 miles from Cromford (south of Matlock Bath) to Dowlow, following the route of an old railway. For information, guidebooks, guide services, and maps, contact the Peak District National Park Office (☎ 01629/814321).

Buxton

❷❾ *25 mi southeast of Manchester.*

The Romans arrived in AD 79 and named Buxton *Aquae Arnemetiae*—loosely translated as "The Waters of the Goddess of the Grove"—suggesting they considered this Derbyshire hill town to be special. The mineral springs, which emerge from 3,500 to 5,000 feet below ground at a constant 82°F, were believed to cure a variety of ailments, and in the 18th century established the town as a popular spa, a minor rival to Bath. You can still drink water from the ancient St. Anne's Well, and it's also bottled and sold throughout Britain; it's excellent with a good malt whisky.

Buxton's spa days have left a legacy of 18th- and 19th-century buildings, parks, and open spaces that now give the town an air of faded grandeur. A good place to start exploring is **The Crescent** on the northwest side of The Slopes park (the town hall is on the opposite side); almost all out-of-town roads lead toward this central green. The three former hotels that comprise the Georgian-era Crescent, with its arches, Doric colonnades, and 378 windows, were built in 1780 by John Carr for the fifth duke of Devonshire (of nearby Chatsworth House). The splendid ceiling of the former assembly room now looks down on the town's public library, and the thermal baths at the end of The Crescent house look out on a shopping center.

The **Devonshire Royal Hospital,** behind The Crescent, also by John Carr, was originally a stable with room for 110 of the hotel guests' horses; it was converted into a hospital in 1859. The circular area for exercising horses was covered with a massive 156-foot-wide slate-colored dome and incorporated into the hospital.

To discover more about the town and its surroundings, a trip to the **Buxton Museum** is called for. Inside, there's a collection of Blue John stone, a semiprecious mineral found only in the Peak District (☞ Castleton, *below*). The museum also holds local archaeological finds, including a few pieces from Roman times, and there's a small art gallery, too. The museum is on the eastern side of The Slopes. ✉ *Terrace Rd.,* ☎ *01298/24658.* 🎫 *£1.* ⏲ *Tues.–Fri. 9:30–5:30, Sat. 9:30–5, Sun. (summer only) 9:30–5.*

The Octagon, with its ornate iron-and-glass roof, was originally a concert hall and ballroom. Erected in the 1870s, it is still a lively place, with a conservatory, several bars, a restaurant, and a cafeteria, set in 25 acres of well-kept Pavilion Gardens. It's adjacent to The Crescent and The Slopes on the west. ✉ *Pavillion Gardens, no phone.*

Buxton's **Opera House,** built in 1903, is one of the most architecturally exuberant structures in town. Its marble bulk, bedecked with carved cupids, is even more impressive inside—so impressive it may be worth buying a ticket to a concert you might not be eager to hear (☞ Nightlife and the Arts, *below*). ✉ *Water St.,* ☎ *01298/72190.*

Only one church in town stands out amid the elegant buildings, and that's the **Parish Church of St. John the Baptist,** a handsome, Regency-Tuscan–style building dating from 1811, with some extremely fine mosaics and stained glass. ✉ *St. John's Rd.,* ☎ *01298/77856.*

The Peak District's extraordinary geology makes itself felt close to Buxton at **Poole's Cavern,** a large limestone cave far beneath the 100 wooded acres of Buxton Country Park. Named after a legendary 15th-century robber, the cave was inhabited in prehistoric times and contains, in addition to the standard stalactites and stalagmites, the source of the river Wye, which flows through Buxton. Poole's Cavern was also known to the Romans, who built baths nearby; a display of Roman archaeology, a nature trail, and a visitors center are outside. Get there from Buxton by following the Broad Walk through the Pavilion Gardens and continue southwest along Temple Road for about half an hour. ✉ *Green La.,* ☎ *01298/26978.* 🎫 *£3.50, including tour; Country Park and visitor center free.* ⏲ *Easter–Oct., daily 10–5; closed Wed. in Apr., May, and Oct.*

Lodging

£££ **Old Hall.** The building dates from the 16th century, and although everything else has been refurbished, Mary's Bower, in the oldest part of the hotel, still retains its original ceiling moldings; the name recalls Mary, Queen of Scots, who stayed here several times between 1573 and 1582. It's a friendly, centrally located hotel overlooking the Opera House, with a restaurant, wine bar, and in some of the individually styled rooms, four-poster beds. ✉ *The Square, SK17 6BD,* ☎ *01298/22841,* FAX *01298/72437. 37 rooms with bath. Restaurant, bar. AE, MC, V.*

£££ ★ **The Palace.** A hotel on a grand scale from the halcyon days of the spa, it's set on 5 acres overlooking the town center and surrounding hills. The smart rooms are fully equipped with satellite TV, tea- and coffeemaking facilities, hair dryers, and the other usual little comforts, but what makes many of them stand out are the wonderful views. ✉ *Palace Rd., SK17 6AG,* ☎ *01298/22001,* FAX *0298/72131. 122 rooms with bath. Restaurant, bar, lobby lounges, pool, beauty salon, sauna, putting green, croquet, exercise room, library. AE, DC, MC, V.*

£ ★ **Lakenham Guest House.** This large Victorian structure with a sweeping garden has been converted into a comfortable guest house, with some attractive antique furniture and ample parking for guests. Potted plants proliferate, while the tastefully decorated bedrooms all have excellent views; some have small refrigerators. ✉ *11 Burlington Rd., SK17 9AL,* ☎ *01298/79209. 6 rooms, 5 with bath. Dining room. MC, V.*

Nightlife and the Arts

Buxton Opera House (✉ Water St., Buxton, ☎ 01298/72190) presents excellent theater, ballet, and jazz performances all year-round.

Buxton's renowned **Festival of Music and the Arts** (✉ Festival Office, 1 Crescent View, Hall Bank, ☎ 01298/70395), held during the second half of July and early August each year, includes opera, drama, classical concerts, jazz, recitals, and lectures, many of them at the Buxton Opera House on Water Street. The opera house also hosts an amateur drama festival during the summer.

Shopping

You'll find a wide variety of stores in Buxton, especially around Spring Gardens, the main shopping street. Try the **Cavendish Arcade** (✉ The Crescent) built on the site of the old thermal baths, which offers a pleasing range of fashion, cosmetic, and leather stores in stylish surroundings. **Ratcliffe's** (✉ 7 Cavendish Circus, ☎ 01298/23993) specializes in fine silver cutlery. A local **market** is held in Buxton every Tuesday and Saturday.

En Route Heading southeast from Buxton on the A6, you'll pass through the spectacular valleys of Ashwood Dale, Wyedale, and Monsal Dale before reaching Bakewell.

Bakewell

30 *12 mi southeast of Buxton.*

Bakewell, set on the winding river Wye, is extremely appealing, with its narrow streets and houses built out of the local gray-brown stone. A medieval bridge crosses the river in five graceful arches, while the great age of the town is indicated by the 9th-century Saxon cross that still stands outside the local church. For a self-guided stroll around town, pick up a map and town trail from the tourist office; the walk takes just over an hour. The office, readers report, is most helpful and has a museum that explains the terrain of the Peak District, with samples of the limestone and gritstone that comprises the landscape.

Market day (Monday), attended by local farmers, is an event not to be missed, and an interesting agricultural show is held in the first week of August. Bakewell is also the source of the renowned Bakewell Pudding, said to have been created inadvertently when, sometime last century, a cook at the town's Rutland Arms Hotel spilled a rich cake mixture over some jam tarts.

As in other parts of the Peak District, the inhabitants of Bakewell still practice the early-summer custom of "well-dressing," during which certain wells or springs are elaborately decorated or "dressed" with flowers. Although the floral designs usually incorporate biblical themes, they are just a Christian veneer over an ancient pagan celebration of the water's life-giving powers. In Bakewell, the lively ceremony is the focus of several days of festivities in June.

Dining and Lodging

£££–££££ ★ ✕🏨 **Fischer's.** It would be hard to discover a more relaxing and convenient base from which to visit Bakewell and Chatsworth House, either of which are just a few miles drive away by car. The menu at this award-winning establishment, which calls itself a "restaurant with rooms," run by the friendly Fischer family, represents a range of Continental cuisines, with some fine local produce. Fish is a specialty, often served with fresh fragrant pastas and delicately flavored sauces; duck and lamb receive similar care. One of the dining rooms has been converted into a café (closed Sun.), which serves food—including breakfast and afternoon tea—of the same high quality, at slightly lower prices. The six guest rooms are pretty, if rather small, with antique pine furniture. ✉ *Baslow Hall, Calver Rd., Baslow, DE45 1RR,* ☎ *01246/583259,* FAX *01246/583818. Restaurant (££–£££; reservations essential; Sun. dinner closed to non-guests), bar, room service. AE, DC, MC, V.*

Shopping

ELF Gems (✉ King St., ☎ 0169/814944) is, readers have reported, a wonderful source for jewelry and items made out of the rare Blue John stone, which is mined only in the Peak District. (Blue John is amethystine spar; the unusual name is a local corruption of the French *bleu-jaune.*) Edward Fisher has a passion for the stone, and, because Blue John is so brittle, he covers his handcrafted pieces with liquid crystal to protect them.

Haddon Hall

31 *2 mi southeast of Bakewell on A6 Buxton–Matlock.*

Stately-house scholar Hugo Montgomery-Massingberd has called Haddon Hall "the *beau ideal* of the English country house," and once you see this storybook medieval manor set alongside the banks of the river Wye, you may agree with him that it's the most romantic house in all Britain. Famed as the setting—apocryphal or not—for the elopement of Dorothy Vernon with Sir John Manners in the 16th century (a tale popularized in the Victorian era and since known to every English schoolchild), the house conjures up the days "When Knighthood Was in Flower" as no other does. Constructed by generations of the Vernon family during the Middle Ages, Haddon Hall passed into the ownership of the dukes of Rutland. After they moved their county seat to nearby Belvoir Castle, time and history literally passed the house by for centuries; Henry James once commented that "every form of sad desuetude and picturesque decay" had fallen on Haddon. In the early 20th century, however, the 9th duke awoke this sleeping beauty of a castle through a superlative restoration—and a world of visitors once again discovered a magical estate.

The house is virtually unfurnished, but has some treasures, including an impressive selection of tapestries and a famous 1932 painting of the hall and the 9th duke and his son by Rex Whistler. This painting shows the house from a nearby hillside vantage point—a must snapshot for any visitor's Nikon. Bristling with stepped roofs and landscaped with legendary rose gardens, Haddon Hall looks like a medieval miniature come to life. ☎ *0629/812855.* ⏲ *Apr.–Sept., Tues.–Sun. (except Sun. in July, Aug.).*

Chatsworth House

★ 32 *4 mi northeast of Bakewell.*

The approach through glorious parkland tells you all you need to know about Chatsworth House, ancestral home of the dukes of Devonshire and one of England's greatest country houses. A vast expanse of parkland, grazed by deer and sheep, opens before you to set off the Palladian-style elegance of "the Palace of the Peak." Originally an Elizabethan house, altered by various dukes over several generations starting in 1686, Chatsworth was conceived on a grand, even monumental, scale. It is surrounded by woods, elaborate colorful gardens, greenhouses, rock gardens, cascading water, and terraces—all designed by two great landscape artists, Capability Brown and, later, Joseph Paxton, an engineer as well as a brilliant gardener. He was responsible for most of the eye-catching waterworks. Perennially popular with children, there's also a farmyard area with milking demonstrations at 3 PM, and an adventure playground. Plan on at least half a day to explore the grounds properly; avoid going on Sunday, when the place is very crowded. A brass band plays on Sunday afternoons in July and August.

Inside, the 175 rooms are filled with treasures: intricate carvings, Van Dyck portraits, Rembrandt's *Portrait of an Oriental,* sculptures, tapestries, superb furniture, and china. The magnificent condition of much of the furnishings and decorations is largely because the current duchess supervises an ongoing program of in-house repair and restoration. ✉ *Bakewell,* ☎ *01246/582204.* 🎫 *House and gardens £5.75; gardens only £3.50; farmyard and adventure playground £2.20.* ⏲ *House: late Mar.–late Oct., daily 11–4:30. Garden: late Mar.–late Oct., daily 11–5 (opens 10:30 June–Aug.). Farmyard and adventure playground: late Mar.–early Oct., daily 10:30–4:30.*

Matlock

33 *8 mi south of Chatsworth, 8 mi southeast of Bakewell.*

Matlock and its near neighbor Matlock Bath are former spa towns compressed into a narrow gorge on the river Derwent. Some surviving Regency buildings still testify to their former importance, although it's less impressive an ensemble than that presented by Buxton. Nevertheless, the surroundings are particularly beautiful and you may want to stop by, especially if you are able to catch the **Matlock River Illuminations,** a flotilla of beautifully lit boats shimmering after dark along the still waters of the river, which take place on weekends from mid-August through mid-October.

At Matlock Bath, a cable car across the river Derwent takes visitors to the bosky **Heights of Abraham** on the crags above, where there's a visitor center and café. The all-inclusive ticket allows access into the adjacent country park, where there are woodland walks and nature trails, as well as a fascinating descent into an old lead mine. ✉ *Heights of Abraham, Matlock Bath,* ☎ *01629/582365.* 🎫 *£5.50.* ⏲ *Cable car and visitor center Easter–Oct., daily 10–5; also on winter weekends, call for details.*

Dining and Lodging

£££ ★ ✕🏨 **Riber Hall.** This partly Elizabethan, partly Jacobean manor-house hotel is a listed historical building. The half-timber bedrooms have been decorated with antiques, flowers, oak beams, and four-poster beds, in keeping with the inn's origins; some have Jacuzzis. The garden is particularly beautiful and from the quiet terrace it's easy to imagine you've stepped back into a different age. In the restaurant are served imaginative, seasonal dishes with superbly fresh ingredients, many locally produced. There's even a daily vegetarian menu. ✉ *Riber Hall, Matlock, DE4 5JU,* ☎ *01629/582795,* FAX *01629/580475. 11 rooms with bath. Restaurant (reservations essential, jacket and tie), lobby lounge, room service, tennis court. AE, DC, MC, V.*

Castleton

34 *24 mi northwest of Matlock, 9 mi northeast of Buxton.*

The most famous manifestations of the peculiar geology of the Peak District are to be found around the town of Castleton, in the Hope Valley. The limestone caverns bring visitors from far and wide, which means that Castleton evinces a certain commercialization and tends to be crowded in the peak season, but you certainly shouldn't let that put you off: Simply aim for an earlier start to beat the crowds.

The town itself has a main attraction in the shape of the ruins of **Peveril Castle,** built in the 12th century on a crag south of town. There are superb views of the Peak District from here. ☏ *01433/620613.* ▭ *£1.50.* ⏲ *Apr.–Oct., daily 10–6; Nov.–Mar., Wed.–Sun. 10–4.*

Under Peveril Castle in the massive **Peak Cavern**—reputedly Derbyshire's largest natural cave—rope has been made on a great ropewalk for more than 400 years. A prehistoric village has been excavated here as well. ☏ *01433/620285.* ▭ *£3.* ⏲ *Apr.–Oct., daily 10–5; Nov.–Mar., Tues.–Sun. 10–5.*

The Castleton area has a number of caves and mines open to the public, including some former lead mines and Blue John mines. Aim to visit the **Speedwell Cavern,** the only mine in England you can tour by boat, traveling through great illuminated caverns 840 feet below ground to reach the "Bottomless Pit." There is also an exhibition and a store selling Blue John jewelry. It's at the bottom of Winnats Pass, 2 miles west of Castleton. ✉ *Winnats Pass,* ☏ *01433/620512.* ▭ *£5 weekends, bank holidays, and school holidays; £4.50 weekdays at all other times.* ⏲ *Daily 9:30–5 (Nov.–Mar., closes at 4); closed Dec. 25.*

Edale

35 *5 mi north of Castleton.*

At Edale, you're truly in the Peak District wilds. It's a sleepy village in the shadow of Mam Tor and Lose Hill and the moorlands of Kinder Scout (2,088 feet), set among some of the most breathtaking scenery in Derbyshire. Britain can show little wilder than the sight of Kinder Scout, with its ragged edges of gritstone and its seemingly interminable leagues of heather and peat. Late summer brings a covering of reddish-purple as the heather flowers, but the time to really appreciate the somber beauties of Kinder and its neighbors is in late autumn or early winter, when the clouds hang low and every gully seems to accentuate the brooding spirit of the moor.

An extremely popular walking center, Edale is the starting point of the 250-mile **Pennine Way,** which crosses Kinder Scout in its early stages, though if you plan to attempt this take local advice first since bad weather can make the walk treacherous. However, there are several much shorter routes into the Edale valley, like the 8-mile route west to Hayfield, which will give you a taste of the dramatic local scenery.

In the village, the Edale **National Park Information Centre** has maps, guides, and information on all the walks in the area. ☏ *01433/670207.* ⏲ *Daily 9–1 and 2–5:30 (Nov.–Mar., closes at 5).*

LANCASHIRE AND THE PEAKS A TO Z

Arriving and Departing

By Bus

National Express (☏ 0171/730–0202) serves the region from London's Victoria Coach Station. Average travel time to Manchester or Liverpool is four hours. To reach Buxton, you can take a bus from London to Derby and change to the **Trans-Peak** bus service, though you might find it more convenient to travel first to Manchester (☞ Getting Around, *below*).

By Car

To reach Manchester from London, take the M1 north to M6, leaving the M6 at exit 21a and joining the M62 east, which becomes the M602 as it enters Greater Manchester. Liverpool is reached by leaving the M6 at the same junction, exit 21a, and following the M62 west into the city. For Blackpool, continue north on the M6, and take exit 32 for the M55 into town. Travel time to Manchester or Liverpool is about 3–3½ hours. Expect heavy traffic out of London at weekends to all destinations in the Northwest; construction work also often slows progress on M6.

Driving from London to the Peak District, stay on the M1 until you reach exit 29, then head west via the A617/A619/A6 to Buxton. From Manchester, take the A6 southeast via Stockport to Buxton, about an hour's drive.

By Plane

Manchester International Airport (☏ 0161/489–3000) is about 10 miles south of the city. It's northern England's main airport and serves European and other international cities as well as receiving domestic flights from all over Britain. To reach the city center, take the train that runs from the airport direct to Piccadilly Station (24-hour service; departures every 15 minutes, ☏ 0161/832–8353 or 0161/228–7811). Travel time is 20 minutes and the cost is £2.20 (£3.95 in peak hours, before 9:30 AM); for a return ticket, buy either a day return (£4.05) or open return (£4.70). There is also a bus service (No. 44), which leaves every 30 minutes (7 AM–10:30 PM, reduced service after 7 PM) and costs £2; it takes almost an hour to reach Piccadilly Gardens. For more information about this service, call GM Buses South (☞ Getting Around by Bus, *below*).

By Train

British Rail serves the region from London's Euston Station (☏ 0171/387–7070). Direct service to Manchester and Liverpool takes approximately 2½ hours. For Blackpool, take an InterCity train bound for Carlisle, Edinburgh, or Glasgow, and change at Preston. To reach Buxton from London take the Manchester train and switch at Stockport.

Getting Around

By Bus

Manchester's **Chorlton Street Bus Station** (☏ 0161/228–3881) is the departure point for regional and long-distance National Express coaches. For information on Greater Manchester buses, call the **GM Buses** information line (North, ☏ 0161/627–2828; South, ☏ 0161/273–3300); for city center buses, call 0161/228–7811. There's also a tram system—**the Metrolink** (☏ 0161/205–2000)—running through Manchester and its surroundings, with services daily 7:30 AM–11:30 PM (until 10:30 PM Sun.). It's mostly of use to commuters from the outlying suburbs, but you might want to ride the tram from its terminus at Piccadilly Station: either north up High Street, past the Arndale Shopping Centre to Victoria Station; or south, down Mosley Street, past the Crowne Plaza Midland Hotel, to the G-Mex Centre.

In Liverpool, regional and long-distance National Express coaches use the **Norton Street Coach Station** (☏ 0990/808080). Other buses depart from a variety of terminals, some of which are currently under redevelopment. For the latest timetable information for local bus, train, and ferry services in Liverpool, call the **Mersey Travel Line** (☏ 0151/236–7676), or visit one of the information centers located at the

Merseyside Welcome Centre (Clayton Sq.), the Ferries Centre (Pier Head), Williamson Square, or Paradise Street Bus Station.

Bus R1 runs directly to **Buxton** from Manchester's Chorlton Street Bus station every two hours during the day (information, ☎ 0161/228–7811); or you can take local Bus 192 from Piccadilly bus terminal to Stockport Bus Station, where you change to Bus 198 or 199 to Buxton. For local bus information in the Buxton and Peak District area, call Derbyshire Public Transport Unit (☎ 01332/292200) or Trent Buses (☎ 01332/43201).

By Car

Roads within the region are generally very good, although traffic can get bogged down on the M6, especially on holiday weekends. In both Manchester and Liverpool, you're advised to sightsee on foot—leave your car at your hotel to avoid parking problems in the city centers.

By Train

There are trains between **Manchester**'s Piccadilly Station (☎ 0161/832–8353) and **Liverpool** Lime Street (☎ 0151/709–9696) every half-hour during the day; the trip takes approximately 50 minutes. A similar service operates from Manchester Piccadilly to **Blackpool** North (information from Preston, ☎ 01772/259439), taking just over an hour. Local service—one train an hour—from Manchester to **Buxton** (information from Manchester Piccadilly) takes one hour.

Contacts and Resources

Car-Rentals

Manchester: Avis, ✉ 1 Ducie St., ☎ 0161/236–6716, and airport, ☎ 0161/436–2020; **Budget Rent-a-Car,** ✉ 660 Chester Rd., Old Trafford, ☎ 0161/877–5555, and airport, ☎ 0161/499–3042; **Europcar Ltd.,** ✉ York St., Piccadilly Plaza, ☎ 0161/832–4114, and airport, ☎ 0161/436–2200; **Hertz,** ✉ 31 Aytoun St., ☎ 0161/236–2747, and airport, ☎ 0161/437–8208.

Emergencies

For **police, fire brigade,** or **ambulance** services, call ☎ 999.

Guided Tours

Tourist information centers can offer advice about walking trails that take historically-minded visitors through the less-frequented parts of the main cities to see remnants of their fascinating industrial heritage. In addition, tourist offices in Manchester and Liverpool can book visitors on short city coach tours that show you all the main sights.

The **Liverpool Heritage Walk** is a self-guided 7½-mile walk through Liverpool city center, following 75 metal markers that point out sights of historic and cultural interest. An accompanying guidebook (£3.50) is available from either of the Liverpool Tourist Information centers.

Cavern City Tours (✉ Matthew St., Liverpool, ☎ 0151/236–9091) offers a Beatles Magical Mystery Tour of Liverpool, departing from Clayton Square daily at 2:30 PM. The two-hour bus tour, which costs £6.50, runs past John Lennon's childhood home, local schools attended by the Beatles, and other significant mop-top landmarks.

Travel Agencies

American Express: ✉ 54 Lord St., Liverpool, ☎ 0151/708–9202; ✉ 10–12 St. Mary's Gate, Manchester, ☎ 0161/833–0121.

Thomas Cook: ✉ 55 Lord St., Liverpool, ☎ 0151/236–1951; ✉ 23 Market St., Manchester, ☎ 0161/833–1110.

Visitor Information

General information about the region is available from the **North West Tourist Board:** ✉ Swan House, Swan Meadow Rd., Wigan Pier, Wigan WN3 5BB, ☎ 01942/821222. Also contact the **Peak District National Park** (head office, ☎ 01629/814321).

Bakewell: ✉ Old Market Hall, Bridge St., Derbyshire DE4 1DS, ☎ 01629/813227. **Blackpool:** ✉ 1 Clifton St., FY1 1LY, ☎ 01253/21623; ✉ Pleasure Beach, 11 Ocean Blvd., South Promenade, ☎ 01253/403223. **Buxton:** ✉ The Crescent, Derbyshire SK17 6BQ, ☎ 01298/25106. **Liverpool:** ✉ Merseyside Welcome Centre, Clayton Square Shopping Centre, L1 1QR, ☎ 0151/709–3631; ✉ Atlantic Pavilion, Albert Dock, L3 4AE, ☎ 0151/708–8854. **Manchester:** ✉ Town Hall Extension, Lloyd St., M60 2LA, ☎ 0161/234–3157; ✉ International Arrivals Hall, Manchester Airport, ☎ 0161/436–3344. **Matlock:** ✉ The Pavilion, Matlock Bath, DE4 3NR, ☎ 01629/55082.

12 The Lake District

Windermere, Grasmere, Kendal, Keswick

"Let nature be your teacher" . . . Wordsworth's ideal comes true in this fabled region, one of the most charming reservoirs of calm—of green calm—in the British Isles. The Lake District is a vast natural park, a contour map come to life. Some malicious statisticians allot to it about 250 rainy days a year, but when the sun breaks through and the surfaces of the lakes smile benignly, it is a place to remember. Follow in the footsteps of Coleridge, Ruskin, and De Quincey; everywhere you'll find specific locations that inspired great poems.

Updated by
Jules Brown

THE POETS WORDSWORTH AND COLERIDGE can probably be held responsible for the development of the Lake District as a tourist mecca. They, and other English men of letters, found it an inspiring setting for their work—and fashion, and thousands of visitors, have followed ever since. The lakeland district, created in the 1970s as a National Park from parts of the old counties of Cumberland, Westmoreland, and Lancashire, combines so much that is magnificent in mountain, lake, and dales that new and entrancing vistas open out at each corner of the road. Higher mountains there most certainly are in Britain, but none that are finer in outline or that give a greater impression of majesty; deeper and bluer lakes can be found, but none that fit so readily into the surrounding scene.

Perhaps it is only natural that an area so blessed with natural beauties should have become linked with so many prominent figures in English literature. It may have all started on April 15, 1802, when William Wordsworth and his sister Dorothy were walking in the woods of Gowbarrow Park just above Aira Force, and Dorothy happened to remark that she had never seen "daffodils so beautiful." Two years later Wordsworth was inspired by his sister's words to write one of the best-known lyric poems in English, "I Wandered Lonely as a Cloud." In turn, many of the English Romantic poets also came to the region and were inspired by its beauty. In addition to Wordsworth, other literary figures who made their homes in the region include Samuel Taylor Coleridge, Thomas De Quincey, Robert Southey, John Ruskin, Matthew Arnold, and later, Hugh Walpole, and the children's writers Arthur Ransome and Beatrix Potter, who set her beloved stories of Squirrel Nutkin and Mrs. Tiggy-Winkle in the hills and dales of this region.

The Lake District—which lies within the county of Cumbria—measures roughly 35 miles square; it can be crossed by car in about an hour. Its mountains are not high by international standards—Scafell Pike, England's highest peak, is only 3,210 feet above sea level—but they are very tricky and the weather even more so. In the spring, many of the higher summits remain snowcapped long after the weather below has turned mild. The valleys between them cradle famous lakes, more than 100 altogether, ranging in size from tiny mountain pools (called "tarns" in the local dialect) to 11-mile-long Windermere, the largest lake in England.

The Lake District can be one of Britain's most charming reservoirs of calm. Unfortunately, its calm is shattered in high season when the district becomes far too popular for its own good. A little lakeside town, however appealing it may otherwise be, loses its charm when its narrow streets are clogged with tour buses. Similarly, the walks and hiking trails that crisscross the region seem very much less inviting when you find yourself sharing them with a crowd that churns the grass into a muddy quagmire. That is not to say that you should stay away: With a bit of effort you will always be able to escape the crowds, since the Lake District is walking country par excellence. And mass tourism does at least mean that off-season visits here can be a real treat. All those little inns and bed-and-breakfasts that are turning away the crowds in the summer are desperate for business the rest of the year (and their rates drop accordingly).

The district is a sad region under a canopy of rain, but when sunshine breaks through there is in this vast greenhouse a perfect, plant-like peace.

It is not an easy task to avail oneself of a succession of sunny days in the Lake District—some malicious statisticians allot to it about 250 rainy days per year—but when the sun descends upon that vast natural reserve, and the surfaces of the lakes smile benignly, it is truly a place to remember.

Pleasures and Pastimes

Dining

The region of Cumbria, which encompasses the Lake District, is noted for its good country food. Dishes center on the abundant local supply of lamb, beef, game, and fish, especially salmon and river and lake trout hooked from the district's freshwater streams and lakes. Cumberland sausage, a thick, meaty pork sausage, is another regional specialty. Look out, too, for locally baked bread, cake, pastries, gingerbread, and scones. Pubs throughout the region often give the best value at lunchtime, offering appetizing bar lunches at prices beginning at about £4.

CATEGORY	COST*
££££	over £40
£££	£25–£40
££	£15–£25
£	under £15

**per person, including first course, main course, dessert, and VAT; excluding drinks*

Festivals and Folk Sports

The Lake District hosts some of Britain's most unusual country festivals, featuring traditional music, sports, and entertainment. Major festivals are the Cockermouth and Keswick carnivals (June), Ambleside Rushbearing and Sports (July), Grasmere Rushbearing and Sports, and Kendal Folk Festival (August). Folk sports—often the highlights at these local shows—include Cumberland and Westmorland wrestling, a variety of traditional English wrestling in which the opponents must maintain a grip around each other's body. Fell (cross-country) running is also popular in these parts, with the peaks themselves often forming part of the race-route. A calendar of events is available at tourist information centers.

Lodging

If the front hall has a row of muddy boots, you'll know you've made the right choice for a hostelry in the Lake District. The best of these hotels have a marvelous atmosphere in which people eat hugely and loll about in front of roaring fires in the evenings, sharing an almost religious dedication to the mountains. You'll find everything from small country inns to grand lakeside hotels, though the mainstay of the region's accommodations is the local bed-and-breakfast. These come in every shape and size, from the house on Main Street renting out one room to farmhouses with an entire wing to spare. Most country hotels and B&Bs gladly cater to hikers and climbers and can provide you with on-the-spot information and advice. There's also a great camaraderie among walkers in the Lake District's network of youth hostels, which are in fact open to anyone with a membership card from their home country's hostel association. They are extremely inexpensive, but you must book well in advance in summer; local tourist information centers have all the relevant information. Remember that in winter many places close for a month or two, so be sure to confirm plans by phone.

CATEGORY	COST*
££££	over £150
£££	£80–£150
££	£60–£80
£	under £60

**All prices are for two people sharing a double room, including service, breakfast, and VAT.*

Walking

The Lake District is undeniably beautiful, and to see it at its best, it's necessary to get out of the car and walk through at least part of the region. Even if you rarely walk farther than from car to hotel, plan at least for short strolls and meanderings during your stay: The rewards are outstanding. There's enough variation in the area to suit all tastes, from gentle rambles in the vicinity of the most popular towns and villages to full-scale hikes and climbs up some of England's most impressive peaks. Almost every hamlet, village, and town provides scores of walking opportunities—the doyen of Lake District walking, Alfred Wainwright, spent 70 years tramping the hills and valleys. Information boards are posted at car parks throughout the region pointing out the possibilities. For tougher hikes, the famous Old Man of Coniston, the Langdale Pikes, Scafell Pike, and Helvellyn are also all accessible, though for these you'll need a certain amount of walking experience and a great deal of energy. The longest trail, the Cumbria Way (70 miles), crosses the whole of the Lake District, starting at the market town of Ulverston and finishing at Carlisle. Guidebooks to this and other lakeland walks are available in bookstores throughout the region.

For all walks, it's essential that you are dressed correctly and have the right equipment. Good walking shoes or boots are the first requirement, followed by several layers of warm clothing (even in summer, since the weather can be unpredictable), waterproof jacket and trousers, a good map, food, and water. Depending on the route you're tackling, you may also need a compass. Stores throughout the region stock the right equipment, books, and maps; always check on weather conditions before setting out on anything more than just a local stroll, since mist, rain, or worse can roll in without warning.

For short, local walks it's always best to consult the relevant tourist information centers: Those at Ambleside, Cockermouth, Grasmere, Kendal, Keswick, and Windermere can provide maps and experienced advice. The other main sources of information are the various Lake District National Park information centers, whose head office is at Brockhole, near Windermere. If you're sufficiently experienced and want to climb the higher and harder peaks, then you'll probably want to hook up with a specialist climbing organization, of which there are several in the region (☞ Contacts and Resources *in* Lake District A to Z, *below*).

Exploring the Lake District

The Lake District is located in the northwest of England, between the industrial belt of Liverpool, Manchester, and Leeds and the Scottish border. The entire region is contained within the county of Cumbria. The major gateway for those coming from the south is Kendal. Coming from the north, the gateway is Penrith. Both are on the M6 turnpike.

The Lake District National Park breaks into two reasonably distinct sections. The southern lakes and valleys contain the most popular destinations in the entire park, incorporating the largest body of water, Windermere, as well as most of what are considered the quintessential lakeland towns and villages—Kendal, Bowness, Ambleside, Grasmere, Elterwater, Coniston, and Hawkshead. To the north, the landscape opens out across the bleaker fells to reveal challenging (and spectacular) walking country. Here, in the northern lakes, south of Keswick and Cockermouth, you have the best chance to get away from the crowds and soak up the lakeland experience. A third area of interest is the indented southern coast of Cumbria, not a part of the National Park as such, but offering a useful counterpoint to the hills and valleys farther north. Here, too, you are genuinely off the beaten path, at least as far as most Lake District visitors go.

Great Itineraries

You could spend a lifetime tramping the hills, valleys, and fells of the Lake District, but most visitors will have to settle for significantly less time than that. In three days, you could drive through virtually every town, village, and hamlet mentioned in this chapter, but that's no way to see the region. The key is not to try to see or do too much in too short a time. Instead, pick one area—the southern lakes, for example—and spend some time walking in the delightful surroundings, taking a boat out on the water, relaxing in the inns. With five days, you would have the opportunity to stay the night in settlements in both southern and northern lakeland. If you are traveling by public transportation (scarce at the best of times, much reduced in winter), many places will be off-limits entirely.

Numbers in the text refer to numbers in the margin and on the Lake District map.

IF YOU HAVE 3 DAYS

Start in **Kendal** ①, and after you've looked around the market town, move on to **Windermere** ②, where you spend the first night. You'll have time to take a boat trip on the lake that afternoon up to pretty **Ambleside** ⑤. Next day, cross Lake Windermere by ferry, and drive through **Hawkshead** ⑫ and **Coniston** ⑩ to rural **Elterwater** ⑨, where you can have lunch in one of the fine walkers' inns thereabouts. The afternoon is spent in **Grasmere** ⑧, touring the various destinations associated with William Wordsworth—like **Rydal Mount** ⑥ and **Dove Cottage** ⑦. Your second night is in **Keswick** ⑱, and on the third day, you can loop around Derwentwater through the Borrowdale Valley and isolated **Seatoller** ⑲ to **Cockermouth** ⑳, Wordsworth's birthplace. From there it's an easy drive east to the market town of **Penrith** ⑭ and the M6 motorway (or north to Carlisle).

IF YOU HAVE 5 DAYS

Kendal ① again marks the starting point, followed by a drive to **Windermere** ② and a cruise on the lake that afternoon up to **Ambleside** ⑤. The next morning you can mosey around the shops and museums in **Bowness** ③ before venturing on to the National Park Visitor Centre at **Brockhole** ④. In the afternoon, cross Lake Windermere by ferry, stopping in **Hawkshead** ⑫ and **Coniston** ⑩, before ending up at **Elterwater** ⑨. This is a splendid place to spend the night in peaceful rural surroundings, and it gives you the opportunity to take in one of the local walks the next morning. Lunch and that night can be in **Grasmere** ⑧, just a short distance away, giving you plenty of opportunity to explore that lovely village and its environs. From Grasmere, **Keswick** ⑱ is the next obvious overnight stop, allowing you to make a day trip into the gorgeous Borrowdale Valley and perhaps take a boat trip on Derwentwater. On the final day, you can see **Cockermouth** ⑳ and **Penrith** ⑭.

When to Tour the Lake District

June, July, and August hold the best guarantees of fine weather (and host all the major festivals), but you will be sharing the roads, hotels, trails, and lakes with thousands of other visitors. If you come at this time, book accommodation well in advance, turn up early at popular museums and attractions, and expect to have to work to find parking space—or indeed, any space of any kind. April/May and September/October are more clement visiting seasons. Later and earlier in the year than this there will be more space and freedom, but you will find many attractions closed and snow on high ground, precluding any serious walking.

THE SOUTHERN LAKES

Kendal, Windermere, Grasmere, and Coniston Water

The southern lakes form the most popular destination in the region, and with good reason. There's a diverse set of attractions, ranging from the small resort towns ranged around Windermere, England's largest lake, to hideaway valleys, rugged walking centers, and monuments rich in literary associations. What's more, it's the easiest part of the Lake District to reach, with Kendal—the largest town—just a short distance from the M6 motorway. An obvious route from Kendal takes in Windermere—the natural touring center for this whole area—before moving north through Ambleside and Rydal Water to Grasmere. Some of the prettiest of all lakeland scenery is to be found by then turning south, through Elterwater, Hawkshead, and Coniston, from which it's a simple drive south to the coast or east back to Windermere.

Numbers in the margin correspond to points of interest on the Lake District Map.

Kendal

1 *70 mi north of Manchester.*

Approached from the south, the natural gateway to the Lake District is the ancient town of Kendal. One of the most important textile centers in northern England before the Industrial Revolution, it's an attractive place, cut through by a bubbling river and with gray, stone houses framed by the hills behind. So close are these hills that, with the aid of a walking guide picked up from the tourist information center, you can be astride the tops within an hour. Be sure to pack a slab of Kendal Mintcake, the renowned local peppermint candy, which all British walkers and climbers swear by to provide them with energy when the going gets tough. It's on sale in every gift shop in town.

In town, once you're away from the busy main road, you'll discover quiet, narrow, winding streets—known locally as "ginnels"—and charming courtyards, many dating from medieval times. Indeed, there's been a **market** (✉ Market Place, off Stricklandgate) held here since 1189. The old market hall has now been converted into an indoor shopping center, though outdoor stalls still do business here every Wednesday and Saturday.

NEED A BREAK? **Farrers** (✉ 13 Stricklandgate) is a 19th-century building that houses a fine tea and coffee shop, where you can enjoy excellent freshly brewed coffee and specialty teas—and even buy packets of both to take home.

Kendal's finest museums are housed in the 18th-century **Abbott Hall,** which is on the river Kent, adjacent to the parish church. The **Museum of Lakeland Life and Industry,** housed in the former stable block, of-

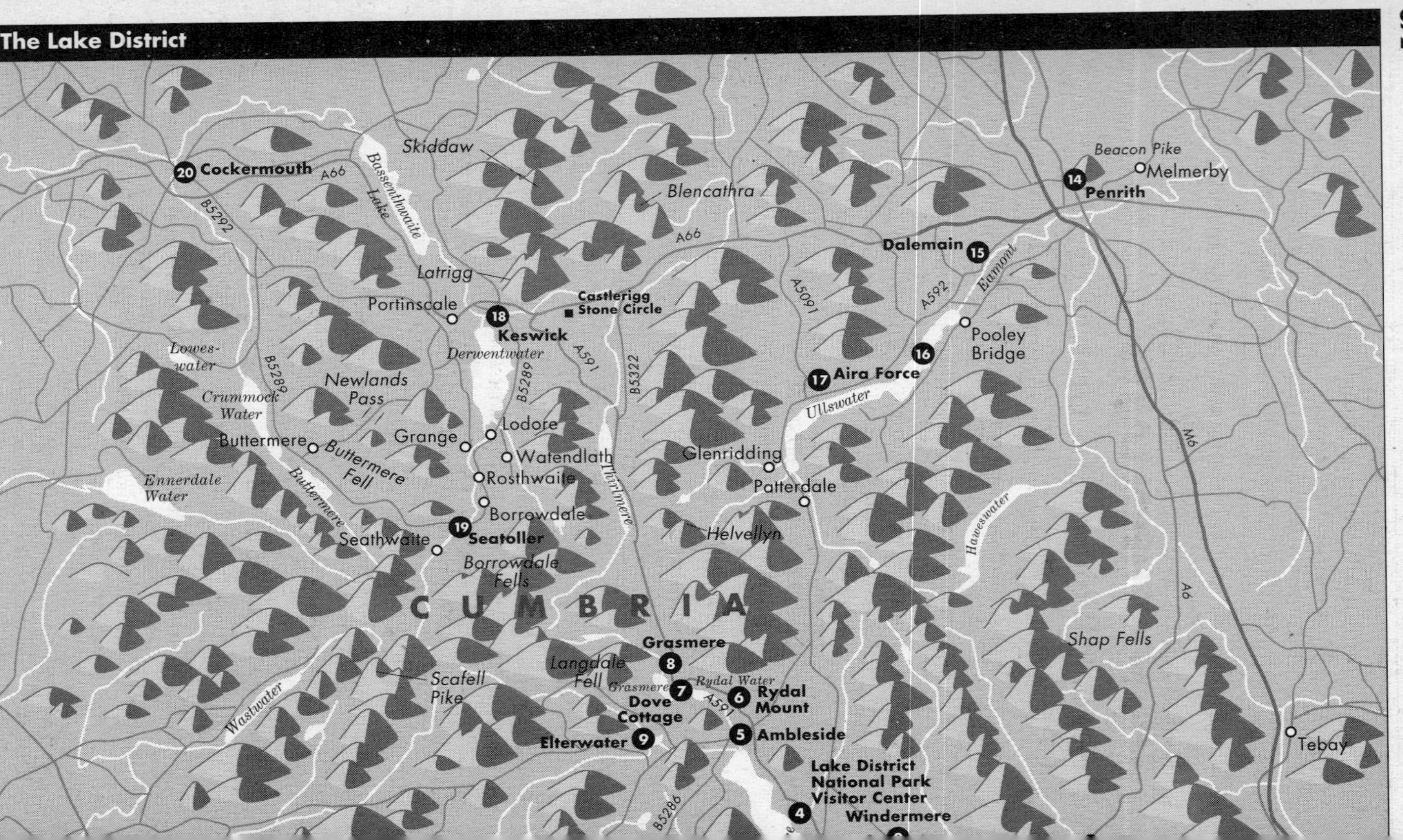
The Lake District
Skiddaw
Beacon Pike
Melmerby
14 Penrith
20 Cockermouth
A66
Bassenthwaite Lake
Blencathra
B5292
A66
Dalemain 15
Eamont
Latrigg
A5091
A592
Portinscale
18 Keswick
Castlerigg Stone Circle
Pooley Bridge
16
Lowes-water
Derwentwater
A591
B5289
B5322
17 Aira Force
Newlands Pass
Crummock Water
B5289
Ullswater
Lodore
Grange
Buttermere
Buttermere Fell
Watendlath
Glenridding
M6
Rosthwaite
Thirlmere
Patterdale
Ennerdale Water
Buttermere
Borrowdale
Haweswater
19 Seatoller
Helvellyn
Seathwaite
Borrowdale Fells
A6
CUMBRIA
Shap Fells
Grasmere
8
Langdale Fell
Grasmere
7
Rydal Water
6 Rydal Mount
Scafell Pike
Dove Cottage
A591
Wastwater
5 Ambleside
Elterwater 9
Tebay
Lake District National Park Visitor Center
B5286
4
Windermere

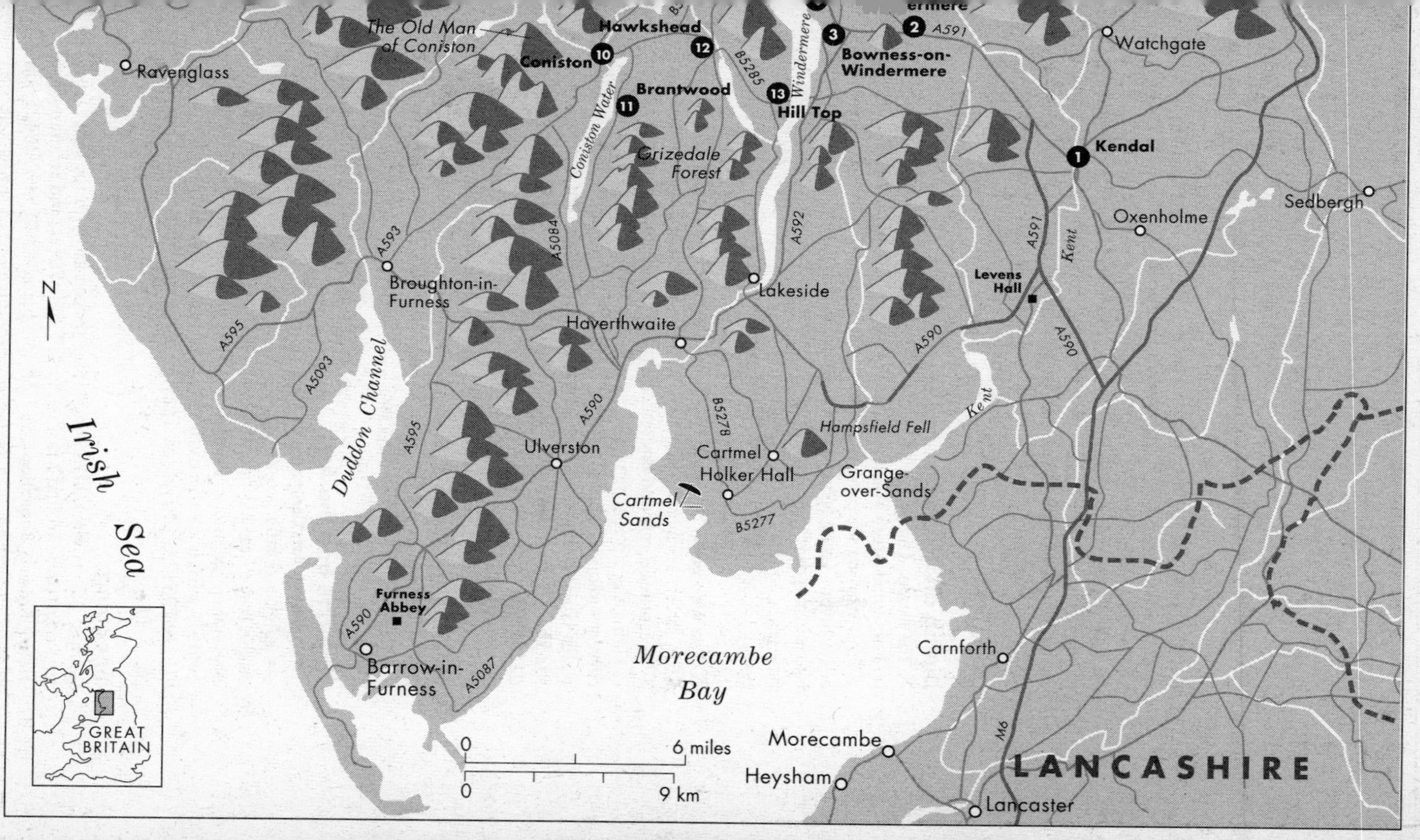

The Old Man of Coniston
Hawkshead
Coniston
Brantwood
Windermere
Bowness-on-Windermere
Hill Top
A591
Watchgate
Ravenglass
Coniston Water
B5285
Grizedale Forest
Kendal
Sedbergh
Oxenholme
A593
A5084
A592
A591
Kent
Levens Hall
Broughton-in-Furness
Lakeside
Haverthwaite
A595
A5093
A590
Duddon Channel
B5278
Hampsfield Fell
Kent
Irish Sea
A595
Ulverston
Cartmel
Holker Hall
Grange-over-Sands
Cartmel Sands
B5277
Furness Abbey
A590
Barrow-in-Furness
A5087
Morecambe Bay
Carnforth
M6
GREAT BRITAIN
0
6 miles
0
9 km
Morecambe
Heysham
LANCASHIRE
Lancaster
N

fers interesting exhibits on blacksmithing, wheelwrighting, farming, weaving, printing, local architecture and interiors, and regional customs. In the main building is the **Art Gallery,** featuring works by Ruskin and 18th-century portrait painter George Romney, who worked (and died) in Kendal. There's a store, too, selling high-quality woven goods, tiles, ceramics, and glass. ✉ *Kirkland,* ☎ *01539/722464.* 🎟 *Museum and gallery £4; one museum £3.* ⏲ *Apr.–Oct., Mon.–Sat. 10:30–5, Sun. 2–5; Nov.–Mar., weekdays 10:30–4, weekends 2–5.*

The Kendal Museum was first founded in 1796, moving into a former wool warehouse in 1913. Its dominant collections are of natural history and archaeology and it details splendidly the flora and fauna of the Lake District, including displays on Alfred Wainwright, the region's most avid chronicler of countryside matters, who died in 1991. His multivolume, hand-written Lake District walking guides are famous the world over; you'll see them in every local book and gift shop. The museum is at the northern end of town, close to the train station. ✉ *Station Rd.,* ☎ *01539/721374.* 🎟 *£2.50.* ⏲ *Mon.–Sat. 10:30–5, Sun. 2–5.*

Dining and Lodging

£–££ ★ ✕ **The Moon.** The Moon has a good local reputation, won with quality homemade dishes on a menu that changes at least monthly. There's always a strong selection of vegetarian dishes, and the cooking can be adventurous, using Mediterranean and Asian flourishes at times. More like a bistro than a restaurant, with cream and burgundy decor, it's a nice place to tarry. ✉ *129 Highgate,* ☎ *01539/729254. MC, V. No lunch. Closed Dec. 25, Jan. 1, and mid-Jan.–mid-Feb.*

££ 🏨 **The Woolpack.** The town's best hotel is ideally placed, right on the main street. Formerly a coaching inn, the building dates back to the 17th century, its ground floor once Kendal's wool auction room, which explains the hotel's name. The public rooms—bar, restaurant, and carvery—retain a whiff of bygone days, with their oak beams and stone walls. Guest rooms are decorated in a modern style, but are no worse for that. ✉ *Stricklandgate, LA9 4ND,* ☎ *01539/723852,* FAX *01539/728608. 54 rooms with bath. Restaurant, 2 bars. AE, MC, V.*

£ 🏨 **Holmfield.** Set on its own grounds in Kendal, a 10 minutes' walk from the center, this fine no-smoking establishment in an Edwardian house treats its guests well; the public rooms have open fireplaces, there's a pool, and advice is freely offered on local walks. ✉ *41 Kendal Green, LA9 5PP,* ☎ FAX *01539/720790. 3 rooms with bath. Pool. No credit cards.*

Nightlife and the Arts

The **Brewery Arts Centre** is a converted brewery that holds an art gallery, a theater, a theater workshop, and a cinema. It also has an excellent coffee bar, a real-ale bar, and a health-food café open for lunch. In November, the annual **Kendal Jazz and Blues Festival** is based at the center, which can provide program details. ✉ *Highgate,* ☎ *01539/725133.* 🎟 *Free, except for special exhibitions.* ⏲ *Mon.–Sat. 9 AM–11 PM.*

Shopping

Kendal has its most interesting stores tucked away in the quiet lanes and courtyards around Market Place, Finkle Street, and Stramongate. **Henry Roberts Bookshop** (✉ 7 Stramongate, ☎ 01539/720425), in Kendal's oldest house (a 16th-century cottage), has a superb selection of Lakeland books. The **Kentdale Rambler** (✉ 34 Market Pl., ☎ 01539/729188) is the best local store for walking boots and equipment, maps, and guides (including Wainwright's illustrated guides). Four miles north of Kendal along the A591, **Peter Hall & Son** (✉ Danes Rd.,

Staveley, ☎ 01539/821633) is a woodcraft workshop selling ornamental bowls and other attractive gifts, all made from local woods.

OFF THE BEATEN PATH **LEVENS HALL** – This 16th-century house, built by James Bellingham, is famous for its rare topiary garden laid out in 1692, with yew and box hedges cut into the most curious and elaborate shapes. The house itself is also notable for its ornate plasterwork, oak paneling, and the leather-covered walls of the dining room. It's just 4 miles south of Kendal, and local buses run here from the town. ✉ *Levens Park, Levens,* ☎ *015395/60321.* *House and gardens £4.20; gardens only £2.50.* *Easter–Sept., Sun.–Thurs. 11–5.*

Windermere

★ 2 *10 mi northwest of Kendal.*

For a natural touring base for the southern half of the Lake District, you don't need to look much farther than Windermere. When the railroad was extended here from Kendal in 1847, local officials named the new station after the lake in order to cash in on Windermere's reputation, already well established thanks to Wordsworth and the Romantic poets. The town flourished, despite being a mile or so from the water, and such was the lake's popularity as a Victorian resort the development eventu-
3 ally spread to envelop the old lakeside village of **Bowness-on-Windermere** as well. Of the two settlements, Bowness is the most attractive, but they are so close it matters little where you stay. Bus W1, leaving hourly from outside Windermere train station, links the two.

The **New Hall Inn,** dating from 1612, is better known as the **Hole in t'Wall** (✉ Fallbarrow Rd., Bowness-on-Windermere), an atmospheric pub, whose most famous landlord was Thomas Longmire, a 19th-century Cumbrian wrestler who won no fewer than 174 championship belts. Charles Dickens stayed at the inn in 1857 and described Longmire as a "quiet-looking giant." Today, you can sample traditional Cumbrian ales and pub lunches in authentic 19th-century surroundings, complete with slate floors and a flagstoned courtyard. There's a spitting log fire in winter.

The **Windermere Steamboat Museum** exhibits a remarkable collection of steam- and motor-powered yachts and launches. ✉ *Rayrigg Rd., Bowness-on-Windermere,* ☎ *015394/45565.* *£2.80.* *Easter–Oct., daily 10–5.*

Children (and not a few adults) might appreciate **The World of Beatrix Potter,** a three-dimensional presentation of some of her most famous characters, alongside videos and films of her stories. There are Beatrix Potter souvenirs here, and a tearoom, though frankly there's more atmosphere (and less commercialism) in Potter's former home at Hill Top, Near Sawrey (☞ Hawkshead, *below*). ✉ *The Old Laundry, Crag Brow, Bowness-on-Windermere,* ☎ *015394/88444.* *£2.85.* *Easter–Sept., daily 10–6:30; Oct.–Easter, daily 10–4.*

There are no sights in Windermere or Bowness to compete with that of **Lake Windermere** itself. At 11 miles long, 1½ miles wide, and 200 feet deep, it fills a rocky gorge between steep, thickly wooded hills. The waters here make for superb fishing, especially for char, a rare kind of reddish lake trout prized by gourmets. During the summer, the lake is alive with all kinds of boats—waterskiing in particular is a favorite pastime here. A boat trip on Windermere, particularly the round-trip from Bowness to Ambleside or down to Lakeside (☞ Getting Around *in* Lake District A to Z, *below*), is a wonderful way of spending a few summer hours.

Although the lake's marinas and piers have some charm, you can bypass the busier stretches of shoreline (and in summer they can be packed solid) by walking beyond the boathouses. Here, from among the pine trees, is a fine view across the lake. The car ferry (which also carries pedestrians) crosses the water at this point to reach Far Sawrey and the road to Hawkshead; the crossing takes just a few minutes. *Cars £1.50, foot passengers 20p. Ferries run every 20 min Mon.–Sat. 6:50 AM–9:50 PM, Sun. 9:10 AM–9:50 PM; winter until 8:50 PM.*

OFF THE BEATEN PATH

ORREST HEAD – For a memorable view of Lake Windermere—at the cost of a rigorous climb—follow signs near the Windermere Hotel (across from the train station) to **Orrest Head.** These will guide you to a rough, uphill track. Eventually you will see a stile on your right; climb over it and continue up the path to a rocky little summit where you can sit on a bench and enjoy a breathtaking panorama of the mountains and lake. The walk back is only a mile but takes most people at least an hour.

Dining and Lodging

££ ★ **Porthole Eating House.** In an intimate 18th-century house in the center of Bowness, the small restaurant has an Italian menu featuring homemade pasta and excellent meat and fish dishes, including stuffed duck, fresh salmon, and (when available) Windermere char. Nice touches include opera recordings played as you eat, good homemade bread, and petits fours served with coffee. In winter, a large open fire adds to the ambience. ✉ *3 Ash St., Bowness-on-Windermere,* ☎ *015394/42793. AE, DC, MC, V. No lunch. Closed Tues. and mid-Dec.–late Feb.*

££ **Roger's.** This is a centrally located restaurant, small and darkly decorated, but lit with candles and boasting a menu that contains the best French food in the region. There's a good selection of cheeses, some very rich desserts, and a short but interesting wine list that covers the New World as well as France. ✉ *4 High St.,* ☎ *015394/44954. AE, DC, MC, V. No lunch. Closed Sun. and 1 wk in Jan.*

££££ ★ **Miller Howe.** This small, white Edwardian hotel with an international reputation for comfort and cuisine is beautifully situated, with views across Windermere to the Langdale Pikes. Every attention has been given to the interior decor, which includes fine antiques and paintings. The lounge has especially comfy chairs, and a conservatory, where afternoon tea is served, overlooks the lake. The bedrooms, too, have exceptional individual style, and fresh and dried flowers are everywhere. The outstanding restaurant serves an imaginative set menu that has been masterminded by John Tovey, renowned for his experimental British cuisine (and for dishes that often utilize alcohol or cream to what might seem, to a curmudgeon, excess). ✉ *Rayrigg Rd., Bowness-on-Windermere LA23 1EY,* ☎ *015394/42536,* FAX *015394/45664. 13 rooms with bath. Room rate includes dinner. Restaurant (reservations essential, jacket and tie). AE, DC, MC, V. Closed Dec.–mid-Mar.*

£££ **Langdale Chase.** This hotel's 5 acres of landscaped gardens overlook Lake Windermere, and it has its own dock. Built in the 19th century and tastefully refurbished, it has an atmosphere of grandeur evoked by the baronial entrance hall and oak-paneled lounge. The hotel is halfway between Windermere and Ambleside, and makes an excellent, relaxed base for local touring. Reasonable dinner, bed, and breakfast rates are available for those who don't wish to drive into Windermere for evening meals. ✉ *Windermere LA23 1LW, just off the A591,* ☎ *015394/32201,* FAX *015394/32604. 35 rooms with bath or shower, 7 in separate lodges. Restaurant, bar, lake, miniature golf, tennis court, boating. AE, DC, MC, V.*

££ **Mortal Man.** This converted 17th-century inn lies in a valley north of Windermere, well away from the bustle of the town; there are magnificent views all around. Fitting the image of a lakeland inn, it has a log fire crackling away in winter. Guest rooms are fairly simple, but pleasantly decorated, and there's a relaxing atmosphere to the place that's hard to beat, helped along by the welcoming staff. Both lunch and dinner are served. ✉ *Troutbeck, 3 mi north of Windermere, LA23 1PL,* ☎ *015394/33193,* FAX *015394/31261. 12 rooms with bath. Restaurant, bar. No credit cards. Closed mid-Nov.–mid-Feb.*

£ **Oakbank Hotel.** Right in the center of Bowness, the very friendly hillside Oakbank provides smart, well-equipped rooms (complete with TV and tea-making facilities), some with fine views over the lake, and all tastefully decorated in pale colors. The breakfast room overlooks town and lake; and you're very near Bowness's restaurants. ✉ *Helm Rd., Bowness-on-Windermere LA23 3BU,* ☎ *015394/43386. 11 rooms with shower. Breakfast room. MC, V.*

Nightlife and the Arts

The Old Laundry provides an intriguing mixture of theater, exhibitions, and events throughout the year. It shares the same premises as the World of Beatrix Potter. ✉ *Crag Brow, Bowness-on-Windermere,* ☎ *015394/88444.* ⏲ *Box office: Easter–Sept., daily 10–6:30; Oct.–Easter, daily 10–4.*

Outdoor Activities and Sports

At **Windermere Lake Holidays Afloat** (✉ Gilly's Landing, Glebe Rd., Bowness-on-Windermere, ☎ 015394/43415) you can rent every kind of boat, from small sailboats to large cabin cruisers.

Shopping

You'll find the best selection of shops at the Bowness end of Windermere, on Lake Road and around Queen's Square: clothing stores, crafts shops, and souvenir stores of all kinds. **Mansion House** (✉ Queen's Sq., ☎ 015394/42568) has an outstanding range of English cut glass and fine bone china. **The Horn Shop** (✉ Crag Brow, ☎ 015394/44519) is one of the last British firms to practice the craft of horn-carving; its craftsmen make a remarkable variety of goods, including jewelry, utensils, mugs, and walking sticks with elaborately carved handles. At **Lakeland Jewellers** (✉ Crag Brow, ☎ 015394/42992), the local experts set semiprecious stones in necklaces and brooches. **The Lakeland Sheepskin Centre** (✉ Lake Rd., ☎ 015394/44466), which also has branches in Ambleside and Keswick, offers moderately priced leather and sheepskin goods.

Lake District National Park Visitor Centre

❹ *At Brockhole, 3 mi northwest of Windermere.*

A magnificent lakeside mansion with terraced gardens sloping down to the water houses the official Lake District National Park Visitor Centre at Brockhole. In addition to tourist information, the center offers a fine range of exhibitions about the Lake District. The gardens are at their best in the spring, when floods of daffodils cover the lawns and the azaleas burst into bloom. Park activities include lectures, guided walks, and demonstrations of fascinating, traditional lakeland crafts like dry-stone-wall building. There's also a bookstore and a café-restaurant. ✉ *Ambleside Rd., near Windermere,* ☎ *015394/46601.* *Free; parking £2 per car.* ⏲ *Easter–late Oct., daily 10–4.*

You can reach the Lake District National Park Visitor Centre by Bus W1 or Bus *555/556* from Windermere train station. It's also accessible by ferry from Ambleside, the service operated by Windermere Lake Cruises (☎ 015394/43360).

Ambleside

❺ *4 mi north of Brockhole.*

When you pull into Ambleside you suddenly feel you have arrived at the very heart of things. Unlike Kendal and Windermere, Kendal seems itself almost part of the hills and fells. It is not difficult to understand why. Its buildings, mainly of local stone and many built in that local traditional style that forgoes the use of mortar in the outer walls, blend perfectly into their setting. The small town sits at the head of Lake Windermere, making it a popular center for Lake District excursions. The town suffers terribly from tourist overcrowding in high season; Wednesdays are particularly busy, when the local market takes place. Nonetheless, there are many fine walks in the vicinity that at least give you a chance of escaping the crowds—popular local routes are north to Rydal Mount or southeast over Wansfell to Troutbeck, either of which will take up to half a day, there and back. Ferries from Bowness-on-Windermere dock down at Ambleside's harbor, called Waterhead, where you can also rent rowboats for an hour or two.

Bridge House, a tiny 17th-century cottage perched on an arched stone bridge, spans Stock Ghyll. The building now houses a National Trust shop and information center. ✉ *Rydal Rd., no phone.* 🎫 *Free.* ⏲ *Easter–Nov., daily 10–5.*

Rydal Mount

❻ *1 mi northwest of Ambleside.*

If there's one poet associated with the Lake District it is William Wordsworth, who made his home at Rydal Mount from 1813 until his death 37 years later. Wordsworth and his family moved to these grand surroundings when he was nearing the height of his career, and his descendants still live here, surrounded by his furniture and portraits. You'll see the study in which he worked, and the 4½-acre garden laid out by the poet himself, which gave him so much pleasure. ✉ *Rydal, Ambleside,* ☎ *015394/33002.* 🎫 *£2.50.* ⏲ *Mar.–Oct., daily 9:30–5; Nov.–Feb., Wed.–Mon. 10–4; closed Jan. 10–Feb. 1.*

Dove Cottage

★ ❼ *1½ mi northwest of Rydal Mount.*

Dove Cottage was William Wordsworth's home from 1799 (he moved here when he was 19) until 1808. First opened to the public in 1891, this tiny house, formerly an inn, still contains much of his furniture and many personal belongings. This was one of the happiest of times for Wordsworth, and when he married, the poet brought his new wife to Dove Cottage. Here, too, he nursed his good friend Coleridge back to health and—Coleridge had drafted his poem "Dejection" during his stay here—good spirits. Dove Cottage is also headquarters of the **Centre for British Romanticism,** which documents the literary contributions made by Wordsworth and the Lake Poets. In front of display cases containing the poets' original manuscripts, headphone sets allow you to hear the poems read aloud. The center holds residential summer study conferences on Wordsworth and the Romantics, as well as winter study schools. There is also a café and restaurant here. ✉ *The Wordsworth Trust, Dove Cottage, Grasmere LA22 9SH,* ☎ *015394/35544.* 🎫 *Dove Cottage £3.90.* ⏲ *Mid-Feb.–mid-Jan., daily 9:30–5.*

Grasmere

8 *1 mi north of Dove Cottage, 4 mi northwest of Ambleside.*

The heart of Wordsworth country, Grasmere is one of the most typical of lakeland villages, sited on a tiny, wood-fringed lake and made up of crooked lanes, whose charming slate-built cottages house little shops, cafés, and galleries. Wordworth lived on the town's outskirts for almost 50 years, walking the local hills with his numerous guests, who included the likes of the authors Ralph Waldo Emerson and Nathaniel Hawthorne.

Wordsworth, his wife Mary, his sister Dorothy, and his daughter Dora are buried in Grasmere churchyard. On the way out of the churchyard, be sure to stop at **The Gingerbread Shop**, housed in a tiny cottage by the gate—once the schoolhouse—where you can buy fine gingerbread made from a 150-year-old recipe (the recipe is kept in a local bank vault).

Dining and Lodging

£££ ★ ✕🏨 **The Swan.** The handsome, flower-decked, 300-year-old Swan, a former coaching inn on the main road just outside the village of Grasmere, was mentioned in Wordsworth's poem "The Waggoner"; Coleridge and Sir Walter Scott were both guests here. Then, as now, the inn's watchword was comfort—a fire in the lounge grate, an oak-beamed restaurant serving lakeland specialties and game, and elegant guest rooms that combine space with fine views of the surrounding fells. Rooms at the rear, overlooking well-kept gardens, are quieter than those at the front. ✉ *Grasmere, on the A591, LA22 9RF,* ☎ *015394/35551,* FAX *015394/35741. 36 rooms with bath. Restaurant (££), bar. AE, DC, MC, V.*

Elterwater

9 *On the B5343, 2½ mi south of Grasmere, 4 mi west of Ambleside.*

The delightful little village of Elterwater, at the eastern end of the Great Langdale Valley, is one of the most popular stops in the Lake District for hikers. It's barely more than a cluster of houses around a village green, but from here a selection of excellent circular walks are possible. Most people have their eyes firmly on the heights of Langdale Fell, to which there are access points from various places along the main road; there are information boards at local parking places. Either stroll up the river valley, or embark on much more energetic hikes to Stickle Tarn or to one of the peaks of the so-called Langdale Pikes.

NEED A BREAK? After a hard walk, there's no more comforting stop than the hiker's bar of the **Old Dungeon Ghyll Hotel** (✉ On the B5343, just west of Elterwater)—one of the most picturesque hostelries of the region. The stone floor and wooden beams echo to the clatter of hikers' boots, while the roaring range rapidly dries out wet walking gear. The homemade soup is just the thing, served with thick slices of bread, or try one of the more substantial main dishes.

Dining and Lodging

££ ★ ✕🏨 **Britannia Inn.** You'll sleep peacefully at the Britannia, a friendly, family-owned inn in the heart of some of the best of the Lake District's walking country. The inn itself has a fine, welcoming atmosphere, with quaint little rooms and outdoor seating, quickly taken up by resting ramblers. The hearty homemade English food served in the bar is excellent—pies are always good—and the local beer the best accompaniment. If you want to eat in the restaurant, rather than the bar, be sure to book in advance—there's a very popular four-course table d'hote dinner served nightly (weekends only from November to mid-March). Guest rooms, modern in style but comfortable, are a little larger than is usual in countryside inns. ✉ *Elterwater, on B5343, 4 mi west of Ambleside, LA22 9HP,* ☎ *015394/37210,* FAX *015394/37311. 13 rooms, 7 with shower. Restaurant, bar. MC, V.*

Coniston

⑩ *5 mi south of Elterwater.*

Formerly a copper-mining village, Coniston is now a small lake resort and boating center at the foot of **The Old Man of Coniston** (2,635 feet). Tracks lead up from the village past an old mine to the peak, which you can reach in about two hours, though many experienced hikers include the peak in an enervating seven-hour circular walk from the village.

★ ⑪ **Brantwood,** on the eastern shore of Coniston Water, was the home of Victorian artist, critic, and social reformer John Ruskin (1819–1900). It's a rambling white 18th-century house (with Victorian alterations) set on a 250-acre estate. Here you'll find a collection of Ruskin's own paintings, drawings, and books, as well as much of the art he collected in his long life, not least a superb group of drawings by Turner. The extensive grounds, complete with woodland walks, were laid out by Ruskin himself. It's an easy drive to Brantwood from Coniston, but it's much more agreeable to travel there by ferry across the lake. Services are with either the Ruskin Ferry (Apr.–Jan., hourly departures from Coniston Pier or Waterhead), or the steam yacht *Gondola* (Apr.–Oct., 4–5 trips daily) from Coniston Pier (☞ Getting Around *in* Lake District A to Z, *below*). ✉ *Brantwood,* ☎ *015394/41396.* *£3.25.* *Mid-Mar.–mid-Nov., daily 11–5:30; mid-Nov.–mid-Mar., Wed.–Sun. 11–4.*

NEED A BREAK? **Brantwood's Jumping Jenny's** (☎ 015394/41715) brasserie and tea-room offers Pre-Raphaelite decor, an open log fire, and mountain views as the setting for morning coffee, lunch, or afternoon tea.

Lodging

£ **Shepherd's Villa Guest House.** This B&B in a stone country house has a prime location on the edge of the village. From here, you can take in wonderful views of the lake and forested hills; packed lunches are available for hikers. The rooms are large and comfortable, and there is a garden for summer relaxing. ✉ *Tilberthwaite Ave., Coniston LA21 8EE,* ☎ *015394/41337. 10 rooms, 5 with bath or shower. MC, V.*

Outdoor Activities and Sports

Coniston Boating Centre (☎ 015394/41366) rents out launches, canoes, or traditional wooden rowboats—and there's a picnic area near the center, too.

Hawkshead

⑫ *3 mi east of Coniston.*

The village of Hawkshead sports the usual lakeland complement of narrow, cobbled streets and little bow-fronted stores. There's rather more to it than most local villages, however. The Hawkshead Courthouse, just outside town, was originally built by the monks of Furness Abbey in the 15th century. Hawkshead lay within the monastic demesne and later derived much wealth from the wool trade, which flourished here in the 17th and 18th centuries. As a thriving market center, it could afford to maintain a school—Hawkshead Grammar School—at which

William Wordsworth was a pupil from 1779 to 1787; he carved his name on a desk inside.

13 **Hill Top** was home of children's author and illustrator Beatrix Potter, most famous for her *Peter Rabbit* stories. Now run by the National Trust, the tiny house is a popular—and often crowded—spot; admission has to be strictly controlled. Try to avoid visiting on summer weekends and during school vacations. It lies 2 miles south of Hawkshead on the B5285, though you can also approach via the car-ferry from Bowness-on-Windermere. ✉ *Near Sawrey, Ambleside,* ☎ *015394/36269.* *£3.30.* ⏲ *Apr.–Oct., Sat.–Wed. 11–4:30.*

PENRITH AND THE NORTHERN LAKES

The scenery of the northern Lakes is considerably more dramatic—some would say bleaker—than much of the landscape to the south. It's a change you'll notice on your way north from Kendal to Penrith, the easiest approach, a 30-mile drive that takes you through the wild and desolate Shap Fells—one of the most notorious moorland crossings in the country—which rise to a height of 1,304 feet. Even in the summer it's a lonely place to be, and in the winter snows, the road can be dangerous. From Penrith, the road leads to Ullswater, possibly the grandest of all the lakes, and then there's a steady route west past Keswick, through the marvelous Borrowdale Valley and to Cockermouth.

Numbers in the margin correspond to points of interest on the Lake District Map.

Penrith

14 *30 mi north of Kendal.*

The red-sandstone town of Penrith was the capital of the semi-independent kingdom of Cumbria in the 9th and 10th centuries. Later, Cumbria was part of the Scottish kingdom of Strathclyde; in the year 1070, it was incorporated into England. Even at this time, Penrith was a thriving market town (an event that still takes place on Tuesday).

The evocative remains of the 14th-century, redbrick **Penrith Castle** are set in its own little park. This was the first line of defense against the invading Scots. The ruins stand across from the town's train station. ✉ *Penrith Castle, no phone.* *Free.* ⏲ *June–Sept., daily 7:30 AM–9 PM; Oct.–May, daily 7:30 AM–4:30 PM.*

To find out more about Penrith's history, stop in at the **Penrith Museum.** Built in the 16th century, the building served as a school from 1670 to the 1970s; it now contains a fascinating exhibit of local historical artifacts as well as the local tourist information center. Ask at the center about the historic "town trail" route, which takes you through narrow byways to the plague stone on King Street, where food was left for the plague-stricken; to a churchyard with 1,000-year-old "hog-back" tombstones (i.e., stones carved as stylized "houses of the dead"); and finally to the castle ruins. ✉ *Robinson's School, Middlegate,* ☎ *01768/64671, ext. 228.* *Free.* ⏲ *Oct.–May, Mon.–Sat. 10–5, Sun. 1–5; June–Sept., Mon.–Sat. 10–7, Sun. 1–6; Nov.–Easter, closed Sun.*

NEED A BREAK? Five miles northeast of Penrith, **The Village Bakery** is well worth a detour—the baking is done in a wood-fired brick oven, and the result is bread, cakes, and sponges that are sensational. The bakery also serves a delicious lunch. ✉ *Melmerby, on the A686,* ☎ *01768/881515. Closed Sun. at Christmas and New Year.*

Dining and Lodging

££ ✕ **Passepartout.** Continental, Italian, and unusually good British specialties are offered here, with the emphasis on local dishes like wild boar and salmon, venison, and lobster. There is also an international wine list. ✉ *51 Castlegate,* ☎ *01768/65852. MC, V. No lunch. Closed Sun., Mon.*

£–££ 🏨 **The George.** This large, rambling coaching inn, right in the center of Penrith, has been hosting guests for more than 300 years. Either stay overnight in one of the modernized rooms, all with private facilities, or just stop in for morning coffee or lunch. The lounges are full of wood paneling, antiques, copper and brass fixtures, old paintings, and comfortable chairs; the attractive restaurant serves extremely good-value set meals. ✉ *Devonshire St., CA11 7SH,* ☎ *01768/62696,* FAX *01768/68223. 30 rooms with bath or shower. Restaurant, bar, lobby lounges. MC, V.*

£ 🏨 **Queen's Head Inn.** The Queen's Head is a very friendly 17th-century inn. Big open fires, plenty of shining copper and brass, pleasant old furniture, and simple, comfortable bedrooms make this a good budget selection. ✉ *Askham, 5 mi south of Penrith, CA10 2PF,* ☎ *01931/712225. 7 rooms, 2 with shower. Restaurant, bar. No credit cards.*

Dalemain

15 *3 mi southwest of Penrith.*

Dalemain, a country house with a 12th-century peel (tower), was built to protect the occupants from raiding Scots. A medieval hall was added, as well as a number of extensions from the 16th to the 18th centuries, culminating in an imposing Georgian facade of local pink sandstone. The result is a delightful hodgepodge of architectural styles. Inside you can see a magnificent oak staircase, furniture dating from the mid-17th century (including Cumbrian "courting" chairs), a Chinese drawing room adorned with hand-painted wallpaper, a 16th-century "fretwork room" with intricate plasterwork, a nursery complete with an elaborate 18th-century dollhouse, and many fine paintings, including masterpieces by Van Dyck. ✉ *Dalemain, just off the A592,* ☎ *017684/86450.* 🎫 *£4.* ⏲ *Easter–Sept., Sun.–Thurs. 11:15–5.*

Ullswater

16 *6 mi southwest of Penrith.*

Hemmed in by towering hills, Ullswater, the region's second-largest lake, has a spectacular setting. Some of the finest views are from the A592 as it sticks to the lake's western shore, through **Glenridding** and **Patterdale** at the southern end. Here, you're at the foot of **Helvellyn** (3,118 feet), which lies to the west. It is an arduous climb to the top and shouldn't be attempted in poor weather or by inexperienced hikers. Paths run from the road between Glenridding and Patterdale and pass by **Red Tarn,** at 2,356 feet the highest Lake District tarn. For those who'd rather see Ullswater from a less exalted level, steamers leave Glenridding's pier for **Pooley Bridge,** offering a pleasant tour along the lake.

★ 17 At **Aira Force,** a spectacular series of waterfalls pound through a wooded ravine to feed into Ullswater. From the parking lot (parking fee charged), it's a 20-minute walk to the falls—bring sturdy shoes in wet weather. Just above Aira Force in the woods of Gowbarrow Park, William Wordsworth and his sister Dorothy were walking on April 15, 1802. Dorothy remarked that she had never seen "daffodils so beautiful. . . they tossed and reeled and danced and seemed as if they verily laughed with the wind that blew upon them." Two years later Wordsworth transformed his sister's words into one of the best-known lyric poems in English, "I Wandered Lonely as a Cloud." Aira Force is 5 miles north of Patterdale, just off the A592.

Dining and Lodging

££££ ★ **Sharrow Bay.** Set between the lush green fields near Pooley Bridge and the increasingly rugged crags around Howtown, the hotel commands a view of exceptional and varied beauty. Its luxurious appointments complement its stunning surroundings; the bedrooms are extremely comfortable, though the rooms in the two annexes are somewhat more simple, especially those in Bank House, about 1½ miles away. The cuisine has been renowned for many years, and it's almost impossible to find fault. Those who can't fit in the Sharrow Bay as an overnight stop should certainly stop by for the splendid afternoon tea, a gargantuan affair that will leave you feeling weak at the knees. ✉ *Howtown Rd., Pooley Bridge, Ullswater CA10 2LZ,* ☎ *017684/86301,* FAX *017684/86349. 28 rooms with bath. Room rates include dinner. Restaurant (reservations essential, jacket and tie). AE, DC, MC, V. Closed Dec.–mid-Feb.*

Keswick

18 *14 mi west of Ullswater.*

The great Lakeland mountains of Skiddaw and Blencathra brood over the gray slate houses of Keswick (pronounced "Kezzick"), on the scenic shores of Derwentwater. Since many of the best hiking routes radiate from here, it is more of a touring base than a tourist destination. People stroll the congested, narrow streets in boots and corduroy hiking trousers, and there are plenty of mountaineering shops in addition to hotels, guest houses, pubs, and restaurants. Walkers may want to leave their cars behind, as parking is difficult in the higher valleys, and both the Derwentwater launches and the Borrowdale bus service between Keswick and Seatoller run frequently.

With a population of only 6,000, Keswick is a compact town, and all the interesting sights lie within easy walking distance of the central streets: Market Place, Main Street, and Lake Road. The town received its market charter in the 13th century, and its Saturday market is still going strong. The handsome 19th-century **Moot Hall** (✉ Market Pl.) has served as both the Keswick town hall and the local prison. Now it houses the main **tourist information center** for the region.

At the **Keswick Museum and Art Gallery** in Fitz Park, exhibits include manuscripts by Wordsworth and other lakeland writers, a diorama of the Lake District, a local geological and natural-history collection, and an assortment of watercolor paintings. ✉ *Station Rd.,* ☎ *017687/73263.* 🎫 *£1.* ⏲ *Easter–Oct., daily 10–4.*

One particular aspect of Keswick's history comes into sharp focus at the **Cumberland Pencil Museum.** Keswick was the first place in the world to manufacture pencils, as graphite (the material from which pencil lead is made) was discovered in neighboring Borrowdale in the 16th century. ✉ *Southey Works, Greta Bridge, Main St.,* ☎ *017687/73626.* 🎫 *£2.50.* ⏲ *Daily 9:30–4.*

★ To understand why **Derwentwater** is considered one of England's finest lakes, take a short walk from Keswick's town center to the lake shore, and follow the Friar's Crag path—about a 15 minutes' level walk from the center. This pine-tree-fringed peninsula is a favorite vantage point, with its view over the lake, the surrounding ring of mountains, and many tiny wooded islands. Ahead you will see the crags that line the **Jaws of Borrowdale** and overhang a dramatic mountain ravine—the perfect setting for a Romantic painting or poem. For the best lake views you should take a wooden-launch **cruise** around Derwentwater. Between late March and November, cruises set off every hour in each direction from a wooden dock at the lake shore. You can also rent a rowboat here. Landing stages around the lake provide access to some spectacular hiking trails in the nearby hills.

Dining and Lodging

££ ✕ **La Primavera.** The river Greta runs below this stylish restaurant, which is somewhat isolated at the north end of town. Here you have a choice of English or Italian dishes—the grilled steaks are particularly good—and a good wine list. The daily specials are always worth inquiring about. ✉ *Greta Bridge, High Hill,* ☎ *017687/74621. MC, V. Closed Mon. and Jan.*

£ ★ ✕ **Four in Hand.** This is a typical Cumbrian pub—once a stagecoach inn on the route between Keswick and Borrowdale—with a 19th-century paneled bar decorated with horse brasses and banknotes. The imaginative touches in its menu include hot asparagus rolled in ham and pâté with red-currant jelly; traditional dishes are steaks, meat pies, and Cumberland sausage. ✉ *Lake Rd.,* ☎ *017687/72069. No credit cards.*

£££ ✕🏨 **Derwentwater Hotel.** Named after the lake it is set on, this handsome hotel west of Keswick has 16 acres of gardens and specializes in activity vacations for those interested in windsurfing, fishing, hiking, mountaineering, and golf. Equipment loans and instruction are offered at the hotel. It's worth paying extra for the deluxe rooms here, which are more spacious and have unrivaled views of the lake. Take your aperitif in the lakeside gardens in good weather—or in the splendid conservatory—and look forward to dinner in the restaurant, where roast meats are a specialty and other dishes include local fish. ✉ *Portinscale, off the A66, CA12 5RE,* ☎ *017687/72538,* FAX *017687/71002. 52 rooms with bath. Restaurant, bar, coffee shop, putting green, tennis court. AE, DC, MC, V.*

£££ ★ ✕🏨 **Keswick Country House Hotel.** The turrets, balconies, and picture windows are the most noticeable architectural characteristics of this Victorian hotel. Built to serve railroad travelers in the 19th century, it has all the grandeur and style of that age, although it has been modernized since to a high standard; all guest rooms have wonderful views. The hotel sits in 4½ acres of private gardens in the center of Keswick; the grounds are overlooked by the elegant Lonsdale Restaurant. Tea or after-dinner coffee is served in a charming conservatory with cane chairs. The room rate includes dinner, as well as breakfast, though you can opt for a stay without dinner if you wish. ✉ *Station Rd., CA12 4NQ,* ☎ *017687/72020,* FAX *017687/71300. 66 rooms with bath. Restaurant, bar, putting green, croquet. AE, DC, MC, V.*

££ 🏨 **Lyzzick Hall Hotel.** On 2 acres on the lower slopes of Skiddaw (2 mi northwest of Keswick on A591), this converted Victorian country house has superb views across Derwentwater. It makes a relaxed base, surrounded by large gardens; two lounges with log fires keep things cozy in winter, while the food in the restaurant is also commendable. There's a special rate for guests taking dinner as well as bed and breakfast, and discounts for longer stays. ✉ *Under Skiddaw, near Keswick, CA12 4PY,* ☎ *017687/72277,* FAX *017687/72278. 24 rooms with bath. Restaurant, bar, pool. AE, DC, MC, V. Closed Feb.*

£–££ 🏨 **Highfield Hotel.** Overlooking the lawns of Hope Park between Keswick and Derwentwater, this small, green slate hotel is comfortable and serves good, home-cooked food. Family run, it's just a few minutes' walk from lake or town and offers super views of the local valley surroundings. ✉ *The Heads, CA12 5ER,* ☎ *017687/72508. 19 rooms, 15 with bath. Restaurant, bar. No credit cards. Closed Nov.–Easter.*

Nightlife and the Arts

The **Keswick Jazz Festival** (☎ 01900/602122 or 017687/73333) is held each May; it consists of four days of music and events and is very popular—bookings are taken before Christmas.

Outdoor Activities and Sports

FISHING

Local permits, for fishing in Derwentwater or Bassenthwaite, are available at **Field & Stream** (✉ 79 Main St., Keswick, ☎ 017687/74396).

HORSEBACK RIDING

Keswick Riding Centre (✉ Swan Hill Stables, ☎ 017687/73804) offers riding lessons, including jumping, as well as trail rides.

WATER SPORTS

Derwentwater Marina (✉ Portinscale, Keswick, ☎ 017687/72912) offers boat rental and instruction in canoeing, sailing, windsurfing, and rowing.

Shopping

Thanks to its size, Keswick is probably the most sophisticated shopping area in the Lake District. You will find a good choice of bookstores, crafts shops, and wool clothing stores. Keswick's **market** is held on Saturday. **George Fisher** (✉ 2 Borrowdale Rd., ☎ 017687/72178) is famous for outdoor clothing: parkas, boots, skiwear, and many other kinds of sportswear. It also sells maps, and daily weather information is posted in the window.

Seatoller

19 *7 mi south of Keswick.*

Seatoller, the southernmost settlement in the Borrowdale valley, is little more than a cluster of buildings and one excellent restaurant. At 1,176 feet, the village is the terminus for buses to and from Keswick as well as the location of a Lake District National Park information center (✉ Dalehead Base, Seatoller Barn, ☎ 017687/77294).

The vaultingly steep **Borrowdale Fells** rise up dramatically behind Seatoller. Get out and walk wherever inspiration strikes, and in the spring, keep an eye open and your camera ready for newborn lambs roaming the hillsides. England's highest mountain, **Scafell** (pronounced "Scarfell") **Pike** (3,210 ft) is visible from Seatoller. The most usual route up the mountain, for experienced walkers, is from the hamlet of Seathwaite, just a mile or so south of Seatoller.

Dining

££ ✕ **Yew Tree Restaurant.** Found at the foot of Honister Pass, the Yee Tree has been converted from two 17th-century cottages. Although the menu is short on inspiration, the low-beamed ceiling, long open fireplace, and excellent bar add to the pleasure of eating here. ✉ *Seatoller, Borrowdale,* ☎ *017687/77634. MC, V. No lunch Fri. Closed Mon. and Jan.–mid-Feb.*

En Route Beyond Seatoller, B5289 turns westward through Honister Pass (1,176 ft) and Buttermere Fell. It's a superb drive along one of the most dramatic of the region's roads, which is lined with huge boulders and at times channels through soaring rock canyons. The road sweeps down from the pass to the appealing lakeland village of **Buttermere,** sandwiched between two lakes—the small, narrow **Buttermere** and the much larger **Crummock Water**—at the foot of high, craggy fells.

Cockermouth

20 *14 mi northwest of Seatoller.*

Cockermouth, an attractive little town at the confluence of the Derwent and Cocker rivers, has a maze of narrow streets that's a delight to wander, and a brisk market-town atmosphere. There's no public access to the ruined 14th-century castle, but the outdoor market, held each Monday, still retains its traditions; an old bell is rung at the start of trading.

Cockermouth was the birthplace of William Wordsworth (and his sister Dorothy), whose childhood home, **Wordsworth House,** is a typical 18th-century North Country gentleman's home, now owned by the National Trust. Some of the poet's furniture and personal items are on display here, and you can explore the garden he played in as a child. Incidentally, Wordsworth's father is buried in the town churchyard, and in the church itself is a stained-glass window in memory of the poet. ✉ *Main St.,* ☎ *01900/824805.* *£2.40.* ⏲ *Apr.–Oct., weekdays 11–5; also Sat. 11–5, July–Aug.*

The **Cumberland Toy and Model Museum** has exhibits of mainly British toys from 1900 to the present. Two buildings contain particularly good model train collections, the re-creation of a 1930s toy shop, and large collections of dolls and dollhouses. There's a play area for younger children, a quiz to take, and special exhibits throughout the year. ✉ *Banks Ct., Market Pl.* ☎ *01900/827606.* *£1.80.* ⏲ *Feb.–Nov., daily 10–5.*

Dining and Lodging

££ ★ ✕ **Kirkstile Inn.** This 16th-century inn stands just 7 miles south of Cockermouth in lovely, quiet surroundings. Low, white, and slate-roofed, this lodging has been welcoming travelers for almost 400 years. There's a cozy pub downstairs, with a roaring fire in winter, and 10 rooms upstairs, arranged along a long, oak-beamed corridor. The rooms are all simple, with rather garish floral carpets, but they're cool in summer, and well-heated in winter, while the beds are supremely comfortable—just the thing after a day's walking. There's perfectly reasonable food available in the bar, but much more adventurous and locally renowned five-course dinners are served in the small, traditionally furnished, restaurant—you must make it clear when you book that you want dinner, since there's very limited room. The inn is quite tricky to find, and you'd do best to phone for directions before setting off. ✉ *Loweswater, CA13 ORU,* ☎ *01900/85219. 10 rooms with bath. Restaurant, bar. MC, V.*

LAKE DISTRICT A TO Z

Arriving and Departing

By Bus

National Express (☎ 0171/730–0202) serves the region from London's Victoria Coach Station. Average travel time to Kendal is just over seven hours; to Windermere, 7½ hours; and to Keswick, 8¼ hours.

By Car

To reach the Lake District from London, take the M1 north to the M6, getting off either at exit 36 and joining the A590/A591 west (around the Kendal bypass to Windermere) or at exit 40, joining the A66 direct to Keswick and the northern lakes region. Travel time to Kendal is about four hours, to Keswick five–six hours. Expect heavy traffic out of London at weekends to all destinations in the Northwest; construction work also often slows progress on the M6.

By Plane

Manchester International Airport (☏ 0161/489–3000; ☞ Chapter 11), is northern England's main airport. The best way to get from there to the Lake District is by car (driving time about 1½ hours) or by bus, from Manchester's Chorlton Street Bus Station.

By Train

British Rail serves the region from London's Euston Station (☏ 0171/387–7070). Take an InterCity train bound for Carlisle, Edinburgh, or Glasgow and change at Oxenholme for the branch line service to Kendal and Windermere. Average travel time to Windermere (including the change) is 4½ hours. If you're heading for Keswick, you can either take the train to Windermere and continue from there by Cumberland bus (Bus 555/556; 70 minutes) or stay on the main London–Carlisle train to Penrith station (four hours), from which Cumberland buses (Bus X5) also run to Keswick (45 minutes).

Getting Around

By Bicycle

Several local operators rent out mountain bikes, an ideal—if energetic—way to see the Lake District countryside. Guided bike tours are often available, too, starting at about £25 per day. Contact local tourist offices for details, or consult one of the following outfits for bike rental:

Keswick Mountain Bikes (✉ Southey Hill, ☏ 017687/75202); **Lakeland Leisure** (✉ Lake Rd., Bowness-on-Windermere, ☏ 015394/44786); **Windermere Cycles** (✉ 12 Main Rd., Windermere, ☏ 015394/47779).

By Boat

Keswick-on-Derwentwater Launch Co. (☏ 017687/72263) conducts cruises on vintage motor launches around Derwentwater, leaving from Keswick.

Steam Yacht Gondola (☏ 015394/41288) runs the National Trust's luxurious Victorian steam yacht *Gondola* between Coniston and Park-a-Moor at the south end of Coniston Water, daily from late March through October.

Ullswater Navigation & Transit Co. (☏ 01539/721626) sends its oil-burning 19th-century steamers the length of Lake Ullswater between Glenridding and Pooley Bridge. Service operates April through October.

Windermere Lake Cruises (☏ 015394/43360) is the umbrella organization for two ferry operators on Lake Windermere: the Bowness Bay Boating Co. runs small vessels between Bowness and Ambleside, and Ambleside and Brockhole National Park Centre. Meanwhile, the Iron Steamboat Co. employs its handsome fleet of vintage cruisers—the largest ships on the lake—in a regular service between Ambleside, Bowness, and Lakeside. Ticket prices vary, though a Freedom of the Lake ticket (£8.50) gives unlimited travel on any of the operators' ferries for 24 hours.

By Bus

Cumberland Motor Services (☏ 01946/63222) operates year-round throughout the Lake District and into north Lancashire. Services between main tourist centers are fairly frequent on weekdays, though service is much reduced on Saturday and especially Sunday and bank holidays. Don't count on being able to reach the more remote parts of the Lakes by bus—for off-the-beaten-track touring, you'll need a car, or strong legs.

In summer, **Mountain Goat** (✉ Victoria St., Windermere, ☎ 015394/45161) runs a local Lake District minibus service linking Keswick, Grasmere, Ambleside, Windermere, and Kendal.

By Car

Roads within the region are generally very good, although many of the Lake District's minor routes and mountain passes can be both steep and narrow. Warning signs are normally posted if snow has made a road impassable; always listen to local weather forecasts in winter before setting out. In July and August and during the long public holiday weekends, expect heavy traffic. The Lake District has plenty of parking lots, which should be used to avoid blocking narrow lanes or gateways.

By Train

Train connections are good around the edges of the Lake District, especially on the Oxenholme–Kendal–Windermere line and the Furness and West Cumbria branch line from Lancaster to Grange-over-Sands, Ulverston, Barrow, and Ravenglass. Note, however, that services on these lines are reduced, or nonexistent, on Sunday. Seven-day regional **North West Rover** tickets (£44) are good for unlimited travel within the area.

The **Lakeside & Haverthwaite Railway Co.** (☎ 015395/31594) runs vintage steam trains between April and October on the 4-mile branch line between Lakeside and Haverthwaite along Lake Windermere's southern tip.

Ravenglass & Eskdale Railway (☎ 01229/717171) offers a steam train service covering the 7 miles of glorious countryside between Ravenglass and Dalegarth. There is daily service from April to October and reduced service in winter.

Contacts and Resources

Car Rentals

Kendal: Avis (✉ Station Rd., ☎ 01539/733582). **Keswick: Keswick Motor Company** (✉ Lake Rd., ☎ 017687/72064).

Guided Tours

The **National Park Authority** (☎ 015394/46601) at Brockhole, near Windermere, has an advisory service that puts you in touch with members of the Blue Badge Guides, who are experts on the area. From Easter until October, they will take you on half-day or full-day walks and introduce you to the history and natural beauties of the Lake District. The Authority has nine information offices throughout the district (☞ Visitor Information, *below*).

English Lakeland Ramblers (☎ 01229/587382) organizes single-base and inn-to-inn tours of the Lake District from May to October. All meals and inn accommodations are included in packages, and guides lead you on informative walks, hikes, and sightseeing around a variety of areas. A lake steamer cruise and a ride on a narrow-gauge steam railroad line are all part of the adventure.

Mountain Goat Holidays (☎ 015394/45161) provides special minibus sightseeing tours with skilled local guides. These are half- and full-day tours, which really get off the beaten track, departing from Bowness, Windermere, Ambleside, and Grasmere.

Tracks North (✉ 1 Railway Terr., Lowgill, Kendal LA8 0BN, ☎ 01539/824666) conducts escorted railroad tours on vintage steam trains. These run mainly on the Settle and Carlisle line but also use other scenic rail routes. The package includes hotel accommodations.

Lakes Supertours (✉ 1 High St., Windermere, ☎ 015394/42751) offers full-day tours by coach and boat, with plenty of opportunities for getting out and strolling around.

Outdoor Activities and Sports

Mountain Adventure Guides (✉ Eel Crag, Melbecks, Braithwaite, west of Keswick, CA12 5TL, ☎ 017687/78517) and **Summitreks** (✉ 14 Yewdale Rd., Coniston LA21 8DU, ☎ 015394/41212) coordinate climbing trips for individuals or groups on a daily or weekly basis, and accommodations are arranged when needed.

Travel Agencies

Thomas Cook: ✉ 49 Stricklandgate, Kendal, ☎ 01539/724258.

Visitor Information

The Cumbria Tourist Board (✉ Ashleigh, Holly Rd., Windermere, Cumbria LA23 2AQ, ☎ 015394/44444) is open Monday–Thursday 9:30–5:30 and Friday 9:30–5.

Ambleside: ✉ The Old Courthouse, Church St., ☎ 015394/32582. **Cockermouth:** ✉ The Town Hall, ☎ 01900/822634. **Coniston:** ✉ Ruskin Ave., ☎ 015394/41533. **Grasmere:** ✉ Redbank Rd., ☎ 015394/35245. **Kendal:** ✉ Town Hall, Highgate, ☎ 01539/725758. **Keswick:** ✉ Moot Hall, Market Sq., ☎ 017687/72645. **Penrith:** ✉ Penrith Museum, Middlegate, ☎ 01768/867466. **Ullswater:** ✉ Main Car Park, Glenridding, ☎ 017684/82414. **Windermere:** ✉ The Gateway Centre, Victoria St., ☎ 015394/46499.

The **Lake District National Park** head office is at **Brockhole,** near Windermere (☎ 015394/46601). There are also helpful regional national park centers. **Bowness:** ☎ 015394/42895. **Coniston:** ☎ 015394/41533. **Grasmere:** ☎ 015394/35245. **Hawkshead:** ☎ 015394/36525. **Keswick:** ☎ 017687/72803. **Pooley Bridge:** ☎ 017684/86530. **Seatoller:** ☎ 017687/77294. **Ullswater:** ☎ 017684/82414. **Waterhead:** ☎ 015394/32729.

13 East Anglia

Cambridge, Bury St. Edmunds, Norwich, Lincoln

A storied, quiet land, with no spectacular mountains or rivers, no mightly cities, East Anglia is still the guardian of all that rural England holds dear. The Vermont of Great Britain, it delights all with its tulip fields, villages adorned with thatched-roof cottages, and, around the valley of the Stour, a Constable landscape to love with passion. Here, too, are the majestic cathedrals of Norwich and Lincoln, the stately houses of Holkham and fit-for-a-Queen Sandringham, and the city of Cambridge—medieval, mesmerizing, and magnificent.

Updated by Caroline Merz

EAST ANGLIA IS ONE OF THOSE BEAUTIFUL English inconsistencies. A storied, quiet land, with no spectacular mountains or rivers, no mighty cities, it is still the guardian of all that rural England holds dear. Occupying an area of southeastern England that juts, knoblike, into the North Sea, its counties of Essex, Norfolk, Suffolk, and Cambridgeshire are a bit cut off from the central routes and pulse of Britain. People from London once called the region "silly Suffolk," and referred to the citizens of Norfolk county as "Norfolk Dumplings." In the troubled times most people now live in, these terms strike an almost complimentary note; America has a parallel in the state of Vermont.

But if this area is England's Vermont, it is also home to some of the greatest thinkers, artists, and poets the country has produced. Milton, Bacon, Newton, Byron, Tennyson, and Thackeray received their education at Cambridge University—one of the world's top centers of learning and arguably the most gorgeous university town on earth. Here, Oliver Cromwell groomed his Roundhead troops, and Tom Paine—the man who wrote "These are the times that try men's souls"—developed his revolutionary ideas. Here, John Constable painted *The Hay Wain* along with luscious landscapes of the Stour valley, and Thomas Gainsborough achieved eminence as England's most elegant portraitist. If East Anglia has remained rural to a large extent, its harvest of legendary minds has been just as impressive as its agricultural crops of wheat.

Today, as for centuries past, East Anglia is still being "discovered" by travelers—*both* English and American. Despite its easy access from London, East Anglia (with the notable exception of Cambridge) remains relatively unfamiliar to tourists. It was a region of major importance in ancient times—as evidenced by the Roman settlements at Colchester and Lincoln—while during the medieval era, trade in wool with the Netherlands saw the East Anglian towns become strong and independent. But with the lack of main thoroughfares and canals, the Industrial Revolution mercifully passed East Anglia by.

The result of being historically a backwater is that the region is enormously rich in the sort of architecture that has been lost in other parts of the country: quiet villages, presided over by ancient churches; tiny settlements in the midst of otherwise deserted fenland; manor houses surrounded by moats. Few parts of Britain can claim so many stately churches and half-timber houses. The towns are more like large villages; even the largest city, Norwich, has a population of only about 130,000.

For many people, the joy of East Anglia is its separateness, its desolate landscapes and isolated beaches. Of these, the fens in Norfolk and Cambridgeshire are the most dramatic (or depressing, depending on your taste); the water in the marshes and dikes reflects the arching sky stretching toward seemingly infinite horizons, a sky deeply blue and with ever-changing cloudscapes. The sunsets here are to be treasured. The fens resemble areas of Holland directly across the North Sea, and, indeed, much of the drainage work here was carried out by Dutch engineers. In both Norfolk and Suffolk, the reed-bordered Broads make a gentler landscape of canals and lakes that are ideal for boating and alive with birds and animals.

If you find such quiet, flat spaces dull, you need travel only a few miles to find the bright lights. Those with a taste for royalty and magnificence will delight in three of England's most splendiferous stately houses—Holkham Hall, Blickling, and Her Majesty's own Sandringham. There are incomparable cathedrals—Durham, Ely, Peterborough, and Norwich—and let's not forget "the finest flower of Gothic in Europe," the King's College Chapel in Cambridge. These are the superlatives of East Anglia. But half the attraction of the region lies in its subtle landscapes, where the beauties of rural England are seen at their enduring best: To rush in search of one or two highlights is to miss the best, which can be enjoyed only by leisurely journeys along the byways.

Pleasures and Pastimes

Biking and Hiking

There is a good reason why Cambridge instantly conjures up the image of the undergraduate, hurtling along the streets on a bicycle with academic gown flowing behind. It's an ideal city to traverse by bike, and everyone seems to do so. The same could be said for the entire region. "Very flat, Norfolk," Noel Coward's remark, is something of an overstatement; nonetheless many of the flat coastal areas of East Anglia are perfect for cycling, though sometimes windswept. East Anglia is also a walker's El Dorado. The long-distance footpath known as the Peddar's Way provides some of the finest walking in England. It follows the line of a pre-Roman road, running from near Thetford through heathland, pine forests and arable fields, and on through rolling chalklands to the Norfolk coast. Another delightfully varied path, the Weaver's Way, passes through medieval weaving villages on its 56-mile route from Cromer to Great Yarmouth.

Dining

The word "Anglia" constantly appears as a prefix to brand names. Hotel menus feature not only specialties of the area, such as duckling, oysters, Norfolk black turkey, hare, or partridge, but also offer more universal foods in a regional fashion. Regional favorites are frequently available. Samphire, sometimes called "poor man's asparagus," is a kind of (delicious) seaweed that grows uniquely in the salt marshes along the North Norfolk and Suffolk coasts. The long coastline also provides a wide selection of fish year-round—Cromer crabs and Yarmouth bloaters (a kind of smoked herring) are notable—and the Essex coast near Colchester has been producing oysters since Roman times. There's an equally venerable East Anglian tradition in wine-making. The Romans first introduced vines to Britain, and they took especially well to this region. Today there are more than 40 vineyards in East Anglia, most of which offer tours and tastings to visitors. If you want to try a bottle (dry whites are best), check wine lists in local restaurants.

Lincoln and Norwich are particularly well served with downtown restaurants. Cambridge, which was once a gastronomic desert, now harbors two of the region's best restaurants.

CATEGORY	COST*
££££	over £40
£££	£25–£40
££	£15–£25
£	under £15

**per person, including first course, main course, dessert, and VAT; excluding drinks*

Water, Water, Everywhere . . .

With its many rivers, lakes, and the sea, East Anglia is ideal for water sports enthusiasts, particularly for yachting and fishing. Boats from small launches to motor cruisers can be hired in several riverside towns, and many boat charter companies are based in London. East Anglia provides plenty of opportunity for fishing, with the season officially running from April to December—the best time for catching pike on the Norfolk Broads is October. Keen British anglers know all about Rutland, Grafham and Pitsford waters, and Ravensthorpe Reservoir, which are trout fisheries of the highest standard. These are the haunts of fishermen in thigh boots who tell fishermen's tales over a noonday pint in the "local."

The Sport of Kings

In Newmarket, the only industry is the turf; inhabitants think, dream, and live horses. Here, at the center of British horse racing, thousands of visitors come to experience "the sport of kings" during the flat-racing season. Two of the country's five classic races are held here—the 1000 Guineas and the 2000 Guineas, usually in early May.

Lodging

The intimate nature of even East Anglia's larger towns has meant that there are few hotels with more than 100 rooms. As a result, even the biggest hostelries have a friendly atmosphere and offer personal service. There's plenty of farmhouse accommodation, while the adventurous can choose to stay in windmills, watermills, or more eccentric locations, such as the Martello Tower at Aldeburgh, built as a lookout post during the Napoleonic Wars. Cambridge has relatively few hotels downtown, and these tend to be rather overpriced: There simply isn't room for hotels among the numerous historic buildings, although there are many guest houses in the suburbs. The town fills up in the summer months, when you may have to look farther afield for accommodations.

CATEGORY	COST*
££££	over £150
£££	£80–£150
££	£60–£80
£	under £60

**All prices are for two people sharing a double room, including service, breakfast, and VAT.*

Exploring East Anglia

Although natives may still dispute the true geographical boundaries of East Anglia, it's easily defined by outsiders as the hump of earth that pushes out into the North Sea, isolated and remote from the north–south routes linking the rest of Britain. For the purposes of exploring, East Anglia can be divided into four main areas: the central area surrounding the ancient university city of Cambridge and including the attractive towns of inland Suffolk; to the east, the region's capital, Norwich, the waterways of Broadland and the beaches and salt marshes of the North Norfolk coast; the southeast, including the ancient Roman town of Colchester, and sweeping upward along the Suffolk Heritage Coast; and finally—the northwest, with Lincoln—landmarked by its tall, fluted cathedral towers, and, in the Lincolnshire Wolds, Boston—from where the Pilgrims made their first, unsuccessful, bid to sail to the New World.

Great Itineraries

East Anglia's reputation for being flat and featureless is undeserved. Admittedly, much of the land is agricultural. But although the fen country in the west may yield more vegetables than it does tourist attractions, visitors will certainly need more than a few days to soak up the medieval atmosphere of Norfolk, Suffolk, and the unspoiled coastal villages—including time to linger over a pint of locally brewed beer in one of the astonishing number of picturesque pubs.

A week or 10 days would enable you to explore some of the variety of East Anglia, allowing yourself to fall in with its slow pace of life and following some of the tiny country lanes to churches and vineyards. If you have five days, you can visit the main historic towns and sample one of the coastal areas, although there won't be much time for lingering en route. In three days, it's better to concentrate on one area, probably Cambridge and its surrounds, rather than trying to cover the large distances separating major sights and towns.

Numbers in the text refer to numbers in the margin and on the maps.

IF YOU HAVE 3 DAYS

Cambridge ① is easy to visit from London—too easy, possibly, to judge from the huge numbers of visitors year-round. It remains a great day trip from London and is also the best base from which to explore the rest of East Anglia in a three-day tour. You'll want to spend at least one full day in the most beautiful city in Britain, exploring some of the ancient university buildings, strolling along the Backs, or punting down the river Cam to Grantchester. The next day, head for **Ely** ⑰, and spend a few hours exploring the medieval town and its majestic cathedral, before moving on via Newmarket to **Bury St. Edmunds** ㉓, an extremely attractive town with graceful Georgian streets. Spend the third day exploring the medieval Suffolk "wool towns" of **Sudbury** ⑳, **Long Melford** ㉑, and **Lavenham** ㉒, before returning to Cambridge.

IF YOU HAVE 5 DAYS

Cambridge ① makes a good starting point. Getting around will certainly be easier if you have a car; if not, skip the coast and stick to the main towns. After staying there for your first night, go south and visit the ancient market town of **Saffron Walden** ⑲ and Gainsborough's House at **Sudbury** ⑳, before continuing on to **Colchester** ㊽, Britain's oldest town. Spend your third day visiting the castle and Roman remains, then head northeast, stopping at **East Bergholt** ㊾, birthplace of the artist John Constable, and on via **Ipswich** ㊿ and **Snape Maltings**—home of Benjamin Britten's world-famous Aldeburgh Festival—to **Aldeburgh** (54) itself. The next day, explore some of the unspoiled coastline, including Dunwich—an ancient city that literally fell into the sea, a victim of coastal erosion—before turning inland to **Norwich** ㉕. Spend part of day five visiting the cathedral and medieval city center before stopping in **Ely** ⑰ on your way back to Cambridge.

IF YOU HAVE 7 DAYS

With a full week's time, you'll be able to linger a little and see more of the sights in and near the main towns. From **Saffron Waldon** ⑲, take the B1052 to Newmarket, where racehorses are always in evidence, and continue eastward to nearby **Bury St. Edmunds** ㉓. Explore the town the next day, making time to visit the charming Manor House Museum, and then head south through Long Melford, Lavenham, and Sudbury to **Colchester** ㊽. The next day, instead of going directly to Aldeburgh, take the B1084 to **Orford** (53), a tiny village with a Norman church and castle and smokehouses, where traditional oak-wood methods of smoking fish are still used. After spending your fourth night in **Aldeburgh** (54), head for **Southwold** (55), a charming seaside town where time seems to have stood still. Take the road via Bungay—notable for its crafts and antiques shops—to **Norwich** ㉕ to visit its cathedral and medieval alleys. The journey northwest from Norwich to **Lincoln** (56)—where you can spend your sixth night—takes you through flat Fenland; en route, visit **King's Lynn** ㊼ or head northward toward to the coast to visit one or two spectacular stately homes—including **Blickling Hall** ㊷, **Holkham Hall** ㊺, and **Sandringham House** ㊻. Lincoln is worthy of a day's exploration: on the way back to Cambridge the next day, make a short detour via **Ely** ⑰.

When to Tour East Anglia

If you want to avoid crowds, stay away from Cambridge and the Norfolk Broads—the region's most popular tourist attractions—in late July and August. The May Bumps, inter-college boat races, are—confusingly—held the first week of June in Cambridge. During the "long vac," of course, Cambridge is empty of its many thousands of students, its life and soul. To see the city in full swing, visit October through June.

The world-famous Aldeburgh Festival of music and the arts, started in 1948 by Benjamin Britten, takes place in June, as does the archaic Dunmow Flitch Ceremony at Great Dunmow in Essex, where a side of bacon is awarded to a married couple who haven't quarreled for a year and a day. King's Lynn and Norwich both have renowned music and arts festivals, in July and October respectively.

Note that many smaller towns and villages still keep to the tradition of an "early closing day," usually on Wednesday or Thursday, when shops and post offices close at 1 PM.

CAMBRIDGE AND THE SUFFOLK WOOL CHURCHES

This central area of towns and villages within easy reach of Cambridge is testament to the amazing changeability of the English landscape. The beautiful towns of Cambridge and Ely are set in a landscape of flat, empty, and apparently endless fenland; only a few miles south and east into Suffolk, however, all this changes to pastoral landscapes of—if not rolling, then gently undulating—hills, clusters of villages and towns with a prettiness easier to appreciate than the eerie romance of the black fens.

Numbers in the margin correspond to points of interest on the East Anglia and Cambridge maps.

Cambridge

❶ *54 mi north of London, 41 mi northwest of Colchester, 63 mi southwest of Norwich.*

With the spires of its university buildings framed by towering trees and expansive meadows, its medieval streets and passages enhanced by gardens and riverbanks, the city of Cambridge is among the loveliest in England. Situated on a bend of the river Cam, it is also one of the most ancient cities in Britain, its foundation lost in the mists of time. That is no cliché, for Cambridge is bedeviled by the mists that rise from the surrounding water meadows. Certainly the city predates the Roman occupation of Britain. There's similar confusion about when the university itself was founded. According to legend it dates from 1234 (a date possibly dreamed up by the Cambridge mathematicians on an off day) when a Spanish prince is said to have established the first college.

Several college buildings survive from the medieval period, and most generations since have added buildings. These were often designed by the best architects of their respective periods and financed by royal or aristocratic foundations, with the result that today the city and university provide an illustrated history of the best of English architecture. Keep in mind there is no recognizable campus here: "Where is the university?" is a question hard to answer—the scattered colleges *are* the university. The town reveals itself only slowly. It is filled with tiny gardens, ancient courtyards, imposing classical buildings, alley-

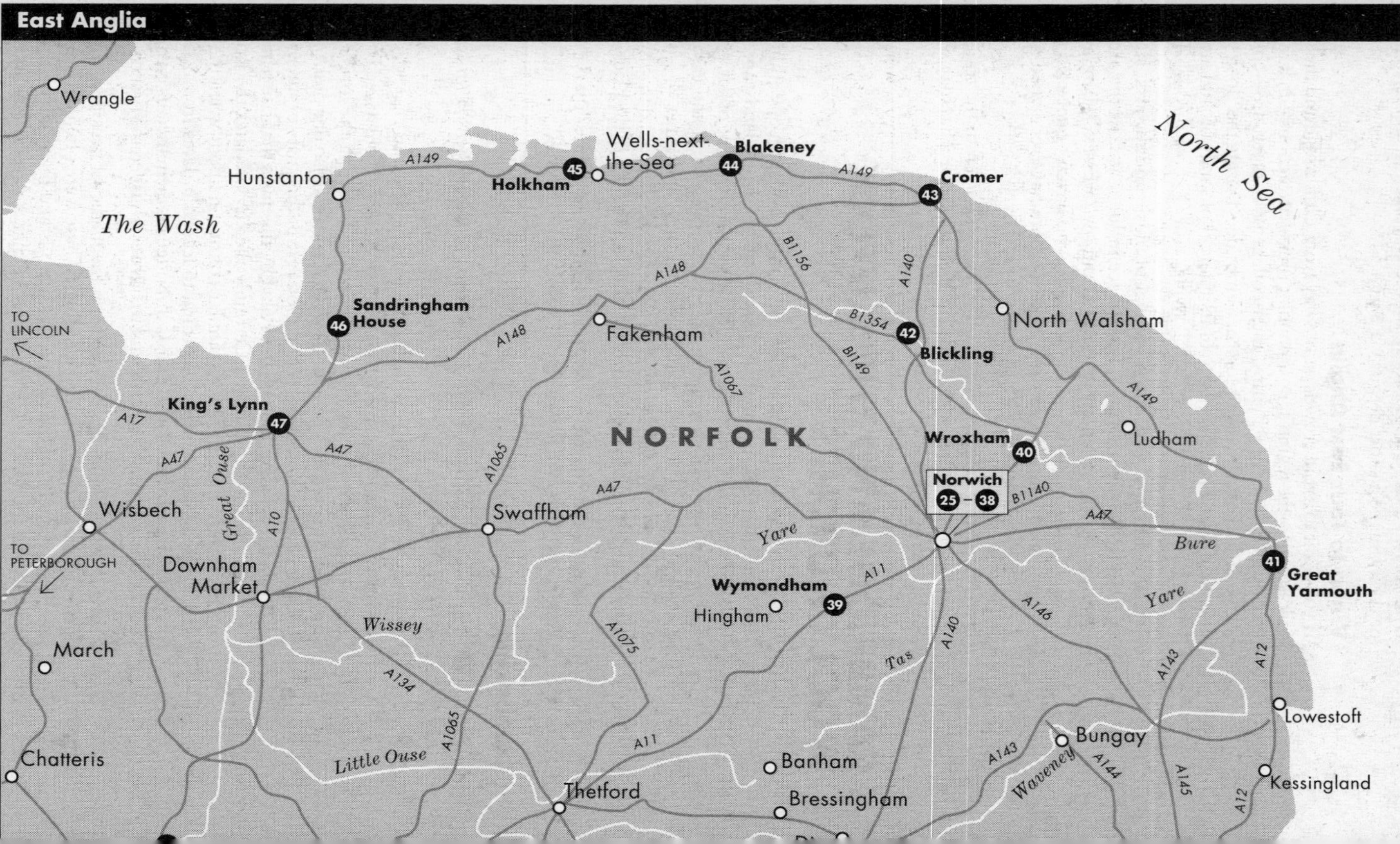
Wrangle
North Sea
Wells-next-the-Sea
Blakeney
44
A149
Cromer
43
Hunstanton
Holkham
45
The Wash
B1156
A140
A148
Sandringham House
46
North Walsham
TO LINCOLN
Fakenham
B1354
42
Blickling
B1149
A1067
A149
Ludham
King's Lynn
47
A17
NORFOLK
Wroxham
40
A47
Great Ouse
A1065
Norwich
25–38
B1140
Wisbech
A10
Swaffham
Yare
Bure
TO PETERBOROUGH
Downham Market
Wymondham
39
A11
41
Great Yarmouth
Hingham
A146
Wissey
A1075
Tas
A143
A12
March
A134
Lowestoft
Bungay
Chatteris
Little Ouse
Banham
A144
A145
Waveney
Kessingland
Thetford
Bressingham

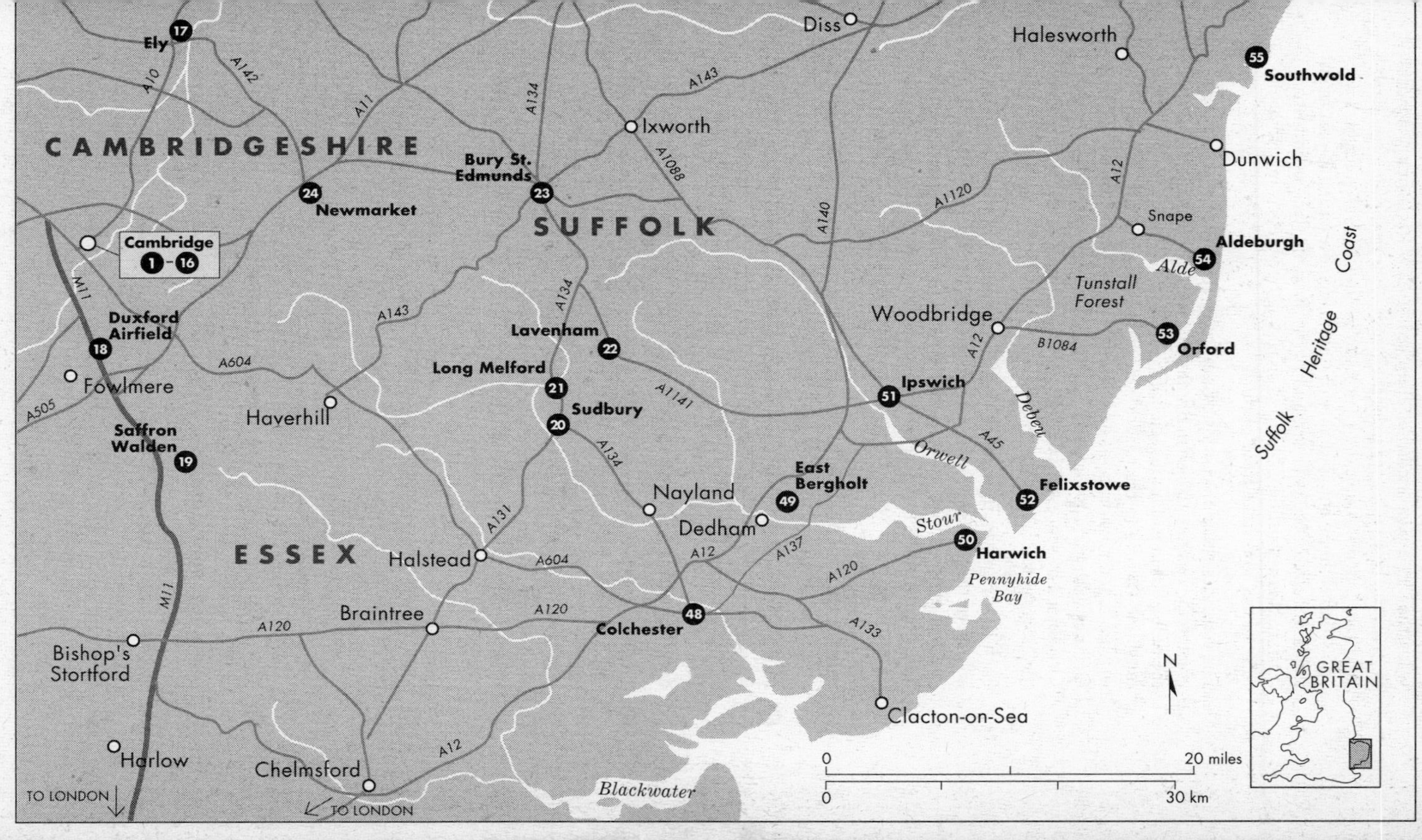

CAMBRIDGESHIRE
SUFFOLK
ESSEX
17 Ely
Diss
Halesworth
55 Southwold
Ixworth
Dunwich
Bury St. Edmunds
23
24 Newmarket
Cambridge 1-16
Snape
54 Aldeburgh
Alde
Tunstall Forest
Woodbridge
53 Orford
Duxford Airfield
18
Fowlmere
Lavenham
22
Long Melford
21
20
Sudbury
51 Ipswich
Haverhill
Saffron Walden
19
East Bergholt
49
Nayland
Dedham
52 Felixstowe
Deben
Orwell
Stour
50 Harwich
Pennyhide Bay
Halstead
Braintree
48
Colchester
Bishop's Stortford
Clacton-on-Sea
Harlow
Chelmsford
Blackwater
TO LONDON
TO LONDON
Suffolk Heritage Coast
A10
A142
A11
A134
A143
A1088
A140
A1120
A12
B1084
A143
A604
A505
M11
A1141
A45
A134
A131
A604
A137
A120
A133
Coast
N
0
20 miles
0
30 km
GREAT BRITAIN

ways that lead past medieval churches, and wisteria-hung facades. Perhaps the best views are from the Backs—the beautiful green parkland that extends along the river Cam behind several colleges. Here you will feel the essential quality of Cambridge. Resulting in part from the larger size of the colleges, and partly from the lack of industrialization, this atmosphere of broad sweeping openness is just what distinguishes Cambridge from Oxford.

For centuries the University of Cambridge has been among the very greatest universities, rivaled in Britain only by Oxford; indeed, ever since the time of its most famous scientific alumnus, Sir Isaac Newton, it has outshone Oxford in the natural sciences. In recent years, the university has taken advantage of its scientific prestige, pooling its research facilities with various high-tech industries. As a result, the city is now surrounded by space-age factories, and a new prosperity has enlivened the city center.

Each of the university's 25 oldest colleges is built around a series of courts, or quadrangles, whose velvety lawns are the envy of many an amateur gardener. As students and fellows (faculty) live and work in these courts, access for tourists is restricted, especially in term time (when the university is in session). Tourists are not normally allowed into college buildings other than chapels and dining halls. The peace of the college courts is quite remarkable, and just to stroll through them gives an immediate sense of more than 700 years of scholastic calm.

2 Cambridge's oldest college is **Peterhouse,** on Trumpington Street, founded in 1281 by the Bishop of Ely. Parts of the dining hall date from 1290; the chapel, in late Gothic style, dates from 1632. On the river side of the buildings is a large and tranquil deer park—without any deer, but with some good apple trees.

3 The first court of **Pembroke College** (1347), has some buildings dating from the 14th century. On the south side Christopher Wren's chapel—his first major commission, completed in 1665—looks like a distinctly modern intrusion. You can walk through the college, around a delightful garden, and past the fellows' bowling green. One of Pembroke's many famous alumni is the British Poet Laureate, Ted Hughes. The college is opposite Peterhouse, on Trumpington Street.

Evident throughout much of Cambridge, the master hand of Christo-
4 pher Wren designed the chapel and colonnade of **Emmanuel College**
(St. Andrew's Street), founded in 1584. Among the portraits of famous
members of the college hanging in Emmanuel Hall is one of John Harvard, founder of Harvard University. Indeed, the college was an early
center of Puritan learning; a number of the Pilgrims were Emmanuel
alumni, and they remembered their alma mater in naming Cambridge,
5 Massachusetts. The gateway of **Christ's College** (1505), also on St. Andrew's Street, bears the enormous coat of arms of its patroness, Lady
Margaret Beaufort, mother of Henry VII, and in the dining hall hang
portraits of John Milton and Charles Darwin, two of the college's
more famous students. Milton is supposed to have planted the mulberry
tree in the Fellows' Garden at the behest of King James I, who was keen
6 to encourage the silk industry. **Sidney Sussex College** (1436), located
where St. Andrew's Street becomes Sidney Street, is a smaller complex
with many 17th- and 18th-century buildings. Oliver Cromwell was a
student here in 1616; the Hall contains his portrait, and his head has
been buried here—in a secret location—since 1960.

7 Unique in Cambridge, the spacious grounds of **Jesus College** incorporate cloisters—a remnant of the nunnery of St. Radegund, which existed on the site before the college was founded in 1496. Parts of the chapel

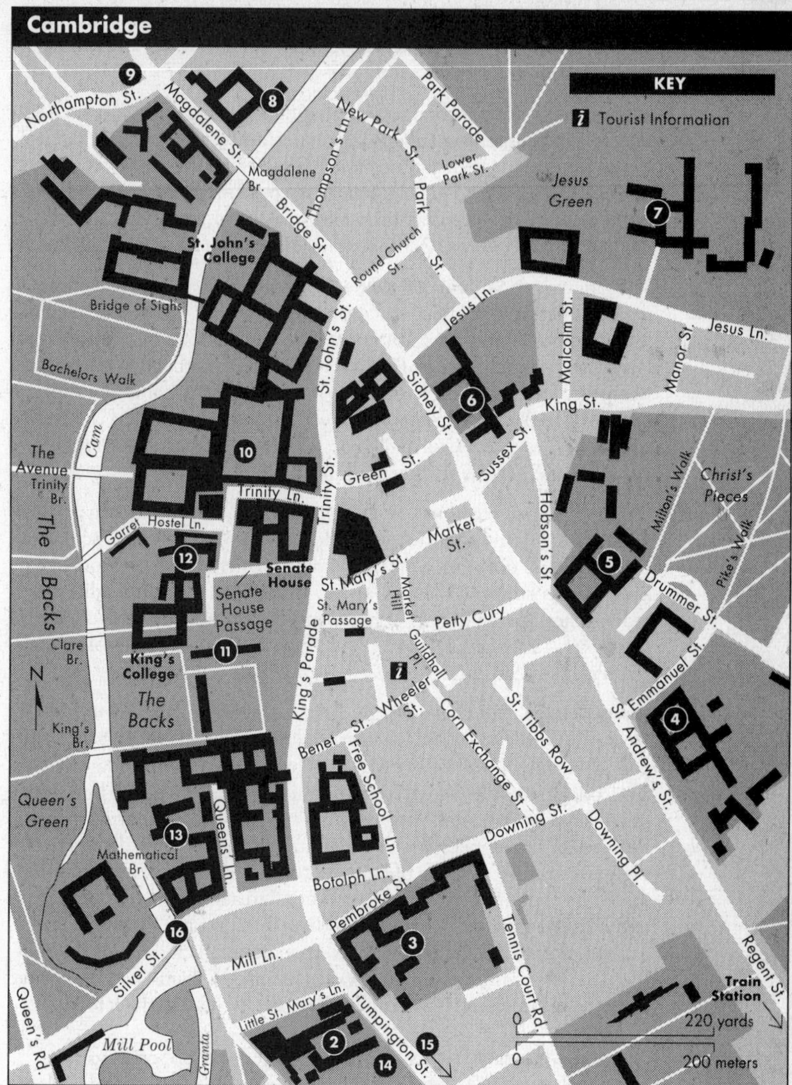

Christ's College, **5**
Emmanuel College, **4**
Fitzwilliam Museum, **14**
Jesus College, **7**
King's College Chapel, **11**
Kettle's Yard, **9**
Magdalene College, **8**
Pembroke College, **3**
Peterhouse, **2**
Queens' College, **13**
Sidney Sussex College, **6**
Silver Street Bridge, **16**
Trinity College, **10**
Trinity Hall, **12**
University Botanic Garden, **15**

here also belonged to the nunnery. Victorian restoration of the building includes some pre-Raphaelite stained-glass windows and ceiling designs by William Morris.

Across Magdalene (pronounced "maudlin") Bridge, a cast-iron 1820
8 structure, is **Magdalene College,** distinguished by pretty redbrick courts. It was a hostel for Benedictine monks for over 100 years before the college was founded in 1542. The college's Pepys Library contains the books and desk of the 17th-century diarist, Samuel Pepys. 🎟 *Free.* ⏲ *Apr.–Sept., daily 11:30–12:30 and 2:30–3:30; Oct.–Mar., daily 2:30–3:30.*

The gateway to **St. John's College** (St. John's Street) is guarded by two mythical beasts holding up its coat of arms: "yales," who have the bodies of antelopes and heads of goats. St. John's is Cambridge's second-largest college, founded in 1511 by Henry VII's mother, Lady Margaret Beaufort. Its structures lie on two sites: from the original buildings, a copy of the Bridge of Sighs in Venice reaches across the Cam to the mock-Gothic New Court (1825), whose white crenellations have earned it the nickname "the wedding cake."

9 Originally a private house owned by a connoisseur of modern art, **Kettle's Yard** is home to a fine collection of 20th-century art, sculpture, furniture, and decorative arts, including works by Henry Moore, Barbara Hepworth, and Henri Gaudier Brzeska. A separate gallery provides space for changing exhibitions of modern art and crafts. ⊠ *Castle St.,* ☎ *01223/352124.* 🎟 *Free.* ⏲ *House Tues.–Sun. 2–4; gallery Tues.–Sat. 12:30–5:30, Sun. 2–5:30.*

10 **Trinity College,** half way down St. John's street, was founded in 1546 by Henry VIII, replacing a 14th-century educational foundation. It's the largest college in either Cambridge or Oxford, with nearly 700 undergraduates. The college straddles the river and can sometimes be reached by a bridge that joins it with neighboring St. John's College. This approach gives a fine view of Christopher Wren's magnificent library, colonnaded and seemingly constructed as much of light as of stone. Many of Trinity's features match its size, not least its 17th-century "great court" and the massive and detailed gatehouse that houses Great Tom, a giant clock that strikes each hour with high and low notes. Past alumni include Sir Isaac Newton; Lords Byron, Tennyson, and Macauley; and William Thackeray; more recently, Prince Charles was an undergraduate here in the late 1960s.

NEED A BREAK?

The **Copper Kettle** is a strategically placed coffee shop, on King's Parade, and a traditional students' hangout, with a view of King's College. If you prefer a pint, head for **The Eagle,** an ancient inn with a cobbled courtyard, on Bene't Street (off King's Parade).

11 **King's College Chapel** is for most people the high point of a visit to Cambridge. It seems almost invidious to single out just one building in Cambridge from the many that are masterpieces, but King's College Chapel is perhaps the supreme architectural work in the city. It was built by Henry VII, the king after whom the college is named, toward the end of the 15th century. It was a crucial moment for the evolution of architecture in Britain, the last period before the classical architecture of the ancient Greeks and Romans, then being rediscovered by the Italians, began to make its influence felt in northern Europe. King's College Chapel is thus the final and, some would say, most glorious flowering of Perpendicular Gothic in Britain.

From the outside, the most prominent features are the expanses of glass, the massive flying buttresses, and the fingerlike spires that line the length of the building. Inside, the most obvious impression is of great space—

the chapel has been described as "the noblest barn in Europe"—and of light flooding in from those huge windows. The brilliantly colored bosses (carved panels at the intersections of the roof ribs) are particularly intense, though hard to see without binoculars. At the far end of the church, behind the altar, is an enormous painting by Peter Paul Rubens of the *Adoration of the Magi.* Every Christmas Eve, a festival of carols sung by the chapel's famous choir is broadcast worldwide from here. Past students of King's College include the novelist E. M. Forster, economist John Maynard Keynes, and the World War I poet Rupert Brooke.

Cambridge's celebrated **"Backs"** are gardens and meadows running down to the river Cam's banks, so named because some colleges back onto
12 them. They are best appreciated from Trinity's neighbor, **Trinity Hall** (1350). Here you can sit on a wall by the river and watch students in punts manipulate their poles under the ancient ornamental bridges of Clare and King's. The **Senate House,** which stands between Clare College and Trinity Hall, is one of the few strictly university buildings (i.e., not part of a particular college). A classical Palladian building of the 1720s, it's still used for graduation ceremonies and other university events.

Great St. Mary's—known as the "university church"—stands opposite the Senate House on King's Parade. Its origins are in the 11th century, though the present building dates from 1478. Celebrated archbishops who have preached here include Cranmer, Ridley, and Latimer. The main reason to visit today is to climb the tower, which—at 113 feet high—offers a superb view over the colleges and the colorful marketplace. ⊠ *Market Hill.* 🎫 *£1.50.* ⊙ *Daily 10–6.*

13 One of the most eye-catching colleges is **Queens' College** (1446), named after the respective consorts of Henry VI and Edward IV. It's tucked away on Queens Lane, next to the wide lawns that lead down from King's to the Backs. The secluded "cloister court" looks untouched since its completion in the 1540s. Queens' boasts a very different kind of masterpiece from King's College Chapel in the **Mathematical Bridge** (best seen from the Silver Street road bridge), an arched wooden structure that was originally held together without fastenings. The present bridge, dating from 1902, is securely bolted.

14 The **Fitzwilliam Museum** is a classical building that houses one of Britain's most outstanding collections of art (including paintings by John Constable, Gainsborough, and the French Impressionists) and antiquities. The opulent interior displays its treasures to marvelous effect, with the Egyptian section in the lower gallery particularly noteworthy. Exhibits here range from inch-high figurines and burial goods to mummies, painted coffins, and stone inscriptions. In addition to its archaeological collections, the Fitzwilliam contains a large display of English Staffordshire and other pottery, as well as a fascinating room full of armor and muskets. The upstairs gallery is devoted to paintings and sculpture. The museum has a coffee bar and restaurant. ⊠ *Trumpington St.,* ☎ *01223/332900.* 🎫 *£2 donation suggested.* ⊙ *Tues.–Sat. 12:30–5:30, Sun. 2:15–5. Guided tours Sun. at 2:30.*

15 The **University Botanic Gardens** were laid out in 1846 and contain, among many rare specimens, a limestone rock garden. The gardens are a five minutes' walk from the Fitzwilliam Museum, past lovely Brookside whose houses overlook a small stream. ⊠ *Cory Lodge, Bateman St.* ☎ *01223/336265.* 🎫 *Free, except weekends Nov.–Mar. (£1.50).* ⊙ *May–Sept., daily 10–6; Feb.–Apr. and Oct., daily 10–5; Nov.–Jan., daily 10–4.*

16 The **Silver Street Bridge** and **Mill Lane** are good places to rent punts on the river. You can either punt along the Backs to Magdalene Bridge and beyond or upstream to Grantchester. For the less energetic, chauffeur punts can be hired from the Spade & Becket Pub on Jesus Green.

OFF THE BEATEN PATH

GRANTCHESTER – This pretty little village 2 miles up the river from the center of Cambridge is a delightful walk or bicycle ride along a path that follows the river through college playing fields and the Grantchester Meadows. The village was immortalized by Rupert Brooke, one of a generation of poets lost in World War I, who lodged here as an undergraduate in the old vicarage. You can also rent a punt to make your way up the river, although it's a long way for an inexperienced punter.

The Arts

The **Cambridge Folk Festival** in late July, spread over two days at Cherry Hinton Hall, attracts major international folk singers and groups. Camping is available on the park grounds—reservations are essential. Details are available from the City Council Amenities and Recreation Department (☏ 01223/358977), or look in the local press.

Cambridge supports its own symphony orchestra, and regular musical events are held in many of the colleges, especially those with large chapels. Evensong at **King's College Chapel** is held Tuesday–Saturday at 5:30 PM, Sunday at 3:30 PM (☏ 01223/350411 for information). Concerts (classical and rock), opera, and ballet are also held in Cambridge's beautifully restored **Corn Exchange** (✉ Wheeler St., ☏ 01223/357851).

The **Cambridge International Film Festival,** one of the best British film festivals outside London, takes place during July at the Arts Cinema in Market Passage (☏ 01223/302929).

The **ADC Theatre** (☏ 01223/359547) on Park Street hosts mainly student and fringe theater productions, including the famous Cambridge Footlights revue, training ground for much comic talent in the last 30 years. The city's main repertory theater, the **Arts Theater,** built by economist John Maynard Keynes in 1936, has been undergoing lengthy and extensive refurbishment. For a progress update, check with the tourist office.

Dining and Lodging

£££ ★ ✕ **Midsummer House.** A classy restaurant set beside the river Cam, across Midsummer Common, the gray-brick Midsummer House is particularly lovely in summer; it has a comfortable conservatory. Set menus for lunch and dinner offer a selection of robust yet sophisticated European and Mediterranean dishes. A typical appetizer might be a shell of foie gras with sweetbreads and scallops, which you could follow with tender noisettes of lamb served on a confit of garlic with artichoke. ✉ *Midsummer Common,* ☏ *01223/369299. Reservations essential. Jacket and tie. AE, DC, MC, V. No lunch Sat., no dinner Sun. Closed Mon.*

££–£££ ✕ **Three Horseshoes.** This is an early 19th-century thatched cottage pub-restaurant with additional dining space in the conservatory. There's a tempting range of beautifully presented dishes, with the emphasis on modern British cuisine—for example pan-fried mallard with rosti potatoes, green cabbage, and wild mushrooms. Desserts tend to be heavy on sugar: Bring your sweet tooth. It can get very busy, and waiting in line may be necessary. ✉ *Madingley (3 mi southwest of Cambridge, 10 min by taxi),* ☏ *01954/210221. AE, DC, MC, V.*

££ ★ ✕ **Twenty-Two.** An intimate dining room in a modest, Victorian house half a mile west of the center of Cambridge, the restaurant offers an extremely good-value fixed-price dinner. Dishes are eclectic, innovative, and drawn from all quarters, including modern British specialties with an emphasis on fish and game, such as baked salmon with herb crust, or roast lamb on a bed of ratatouille. ✉ *22 Chesterton Rd.,* ☎ *01223/351880. AE, MC, V. No lunch. Closed Sun., Mon., and Christmas week.*

£–££ ✕ **Brown's.** This huge, airy, French-American–style brasserie-diner was converted from the outpatient department of the old Addenbrooke's Hospital, directly opposite the Fitzwilliam Museum. Large fans still keep things cool in the pale yellow dining room, while willing staff usher people from bar to table. The bountiful menu ranges from toasted tuna sandwiches, steak-mushroom-and-Guinness pie, house hamburgers, and salads, on up to venison or gigot of lamb; check the daily specials, too—there's usually fresh fish. It's very busy on weekends, when you may have to wait in line. ✉ *23 Trumpington St.,* ☎ *01223/461655. Reservations not accepted. AE, MC, V. Closed Dec. 25–26.*

£ ✕ **Hobbs Pavilion.** Housed in an old cricket pavilion on the western edge of Parker's Piece, this cheery place has wooden walls decorated with memorabilia of Sir Jack Hobbs, a 1920s cricketing equivalent of Babe Ruth. The small terrace makes an ideal spot to watch a few overs of play in spring or early summer. The food is simple but scrupulously prepared; pancakes, both sweet and savory, are the main specialty. Three-course fixed-price menus are a special bargain, with soup or salad before, and dessert after, your pancake. ✉ *Park Terr.,* ☎ *01223/367480. No credit cards. Closed Sun., Mon., and mid.-Aug.–mid-Sept.*

££££ ★ **Garden House Hotel.** Set among the colleges, this luxurious, modern hotel makes the most of its peaceful riverside location. Its gardens, lounge, bar, and conservatories all have river views, as do most of the rooms—if you want one, make it clear when you make your reservation because some of the rooms at the rear of the L-shaped hotel have less desirable views. The recently refurbished guest rooms are comfortable, with minibar and TV and fine bathrooms, and the staff is extremely helpful. A health club, with indoor swimming pool, gym, sauna, and steam room, was being planned at press time. ✉ *Granta Pl., Mill La., CB2 1RT,* ☎ *01223/259988,* FAX *01223/316605. 118 rooms with bath. Restaurant, bar, room service. AE, DC, MC, V.*

£££–££££ **De Vere University Arms Hotel.** An elegant and sympathetically modernized 19th-century hotel, the De Vere is a top choice if you want to be in the city center. Space is at a premium in central Cambridge, and it shows here: The guest rooms are comfortable and well-appointed without being overly large. Many rooms also have views of Parker's Piece, the green backing the hotel. The central lounge provides a comfortable place for afternoon tea, where you can sit by the fire enjoying a pot of Darjeeling and smoked salmon sandwiches. If you don't have a room with a view, then gaze out the windows of Parker's Bar, which also overlooks Parker's Piece. ✉ *Regent St., CB2 1AD,* ☎ *01223/351241,* FAX *01223/315256. 115 rooms with bath. Restaurant, 3 bars, room service. AE, DC, MC, V.*

£–££ **Arundel House Hotel.** This elegantly proportioned Victorian row hotel overlooks the river Cam, with Jesus Green in the background. The bedrooms are all furnished very comfortably with locally made mahogany furniture, and come equipped with TV and tea- and coffeemaking appliances. A novel idea for first-time visitors to Cambridge is a videotaped tour of the city, which can be viewed on the hotel's TV information channel. Ask about the hotel's special weekend rates, which are an excellent value. ✉ *53 Chesterton Rd., CB4 3AN,* ☎ *01223/367701,* FAX *01223/367721. 105 rooms with bath or shower. Restaurant, bar. AE, DC, MC, V. Closed Dec. 25–26.*

Shopping

Cambridge is a main shopping area for a wide region, and it has all the usual chain stores, many situated in the **Grafton Centre** and **Lion's Yard** shopping precincts. More interesting are the small specialty stores found among the colleges in the center of Cambridge, especially in and around Trinity Street, King's Parade, Rose Crescent, and Market Hill.

Bookshops are Cambridge's pride and joy. The **Cambridge University Press** bookshop (✉ 1 Trinity St., ☏ 01223/351688) stands on the oldest bookstore site in Britain, with books sold here since the 16th century. **Heffer's** (✉ 20 Trinity St., ☏ 01223/358351) is one of the world's biggest bookstores, with an enormous stock of books, many rare or imported. The main bookstore is spacious, with a galleried upper floor. There is also a charming children's branch (✉ 30 Trinity St., ☏ 01223/356200). Cambridge is also known for its secondhand bookshops. Antiquarian books can be found at **G. David** (✉ 3 and 16 St. Edward's Passage, ☏ 01223/354619), which is tucked away near the Arts Theater. **The Haunted Bookshop** (✉ 9 St. Edward's Passage, ☏ 01223/312913) offers a great selection of old, illustrated books and British classics. **The Bookshop** (✉ 24 Magdalene St., ☏ 01223/62457) is the best of Cambridge's secondhand bookshops, with a wide variety of books to offer.

Workshop Designs (✉ 31 Magdalene St., ☏ 01223/354326) specializes in leather goods and handcrafted jewelry, much of it made on the premises. **Primavera** (✉ 10 King's Parade, ☏ 01223/357708) is an excellent gallery, where top-class craftspeople exhibit in a small but lively ground floor and basement. Ceramics, glass, paintings, jewelry, and sculpture are all for sale at reasonable prices, often less than £50. The **Benet Gallery** (✉ 19 King's Parade, ☏ 01223/353784) specializes in antique prints and lithographs.

Outdoor Activities and Sports

BICYCLING

Cambridge is the perfect city in which to rent a bike. **Geoff's Bike Hire** (✉ 65 Devonshire Rd., ☏ 01223/65629) is a short walk from the railroad station and charges from £6 per day and £15 per week—or just £4 for up to three hours. Advance reservations are essential in July and August.

Ely

17 *16 mi north of Cambridge.*

Ely is Fenland's "capital," the center of what used to be a separate county called the Isle of Ely (literally "island of eels"). Until the land was drained, Ely was surrounded by treacherous marshland, which inhabitants crossed wearing stilts. It is a small, dense town dominated by its cathedral. The shopping area and little market square lie to the north and lead down to the attractive riverside, while the well-preserved medieval buildings of the cathedral grounds and the King's School (which trains cathedral choristers) spread out to the south and west.

★ **Ely Cathedral,** known affectionately as the Ship of the Fens, can be seen for miles. It stands on one of the few ridges in the whole of the Fens, towering above the flat landscape. The cathedral was begun by the Normans in 1083, on the site of a Benedictine monastery founded by the Anglo-Saxon Queen Etheldreda in the year 673. In the center can be seen a marvel of medieval construction—the octagonal lantern, a sort of stained-glass skylight of colossal proportions, which was built to replace the central tower after it collapsed in 1322. Much of the decorative carving of the 14th-century Lady Chapel was defaced during the Reformation (mostly by knocking off the heads of the statuary), but enough of the delicate tracery-work remains to show its original beauty. The fan-vaulted, carved ceiling remains intact, as it was too high for the iconoclasts to reach.

The diocese of Ely was one of the first to charge admission to a cathedral, not only to help with a major program of restoration but to cover the enormous maintenance costs of a building this size, which run to £1,000 per day. The cathedral's triforium gallery houses a **Stained Glass Museum,** with a wonderful array of exhibits up a flight of 41 steps. ✉ *Chapter Office, The College,* ☎ *01353/667735; Stained Glass Museum* ☎ *01353/778645.* 🎫 *Cathedral £3, free on Sun. (donation requested); museum £1.80.* ⏲ *Cathedral Mon.–Sat. 7–7, Sun. 7:30–5; Stained Glass Museum weekdays 10:30–4, Sat. 10:30–4:30, Sun. noon–5.*

Ely's most famous resident was Oliver Cromwell. The half-timber medieval house that was the home of Cromwell and his family stands in the shadows of the cathedral. During the 10 years he lived here, from 1636, Cromwell was leading the rebellious "Roundheads" in their eventually victorious struggle against King Charles I. **Oliver Cromwell's House** now contains an exhibit on its former occupant and audiovisual presentations both about Cromwell and about the draining of the local fens. The house is also the site of Ely's tourist information center. ✉ *29 St. Mary's St.,* ☎ *01353/662062.* 🎫 *£2.30.* ⏲ *Apr.–Sept., daily 10–6; Oct.–Mar., Mon.–Sat. 10–5:15. Closed Dec. 25–26, Jan. 1.*

OFF THE BEATEN PATH

WICKEN FEN NATURE RESERVE – Nine miles southeast of Ely, this nature reserve is owned by the National Trust and provides the last remaining example of Fenland in its original, undrained state. Reed, sedge, and hay are harvested on the 600 acres of land just as they used to be. You can also visit the restored drainage windpump and fen cottage on the reserve. ✉ *Wicken (A10 from Ely, then A1123),* ☎ *010353/720274.* 🎫 *£2.50.* ⏲ *Daily, dawn–dusk; Fen Cottage Apr.–Oct., Sun. and holidays.*

Dining and Lodging

££ ★ ✕ **Old Fire Engine House.** This restaurant near the cathedral has two dining rooms: The main one, with scrubbed pine tables, opens into the garden; the other, with an open fireplace and a polished wood floor, is also an art gallery. Among the English dishes are traditional Fenland recipes, like pike baked in white wine, as well as eel pie and game in season. Local artists exhibit here, and all their work is for sale. ✉ *25 St. Mary's St.,* ☎ *01353/662582. MC, V. No dinner Sun. Closed 2 wks at Christmas.*

£–££ ✕ **Dominique's.** This delightful little restaurant with stripped pine floors serves brunch, lunch, and dinner in a no-smoking environment. During the day it sees itself as more of a brasserie, while in the evening the specialty is French cuisine with a focus on local game. There are good-value set meals, or choose from the blackboard list of daily specials, which includes vegetarian dishes and a good range of hearty English desserts. There's an outdoor patio in summer. ✉ *8 St. Mary's St.,* ☎ *01353/665011. No credit cards. No dinner Sun. Closed Mon.–Tues.*

£ ★ 🏨 **Black Hostelry.** This bed-and-breakfast has enormous rooms and is right on the cathedral grounds, in one of the finest medieval domestic buildings still in use. It's adjacent to the Chapter House, at the end of Firmary Lane. Extremely comfortable, with antiques and old-fashioned English furnishings, this medieval hostel offers a high degree of privacy. It's so popular that you'll need to reserve a room well in advance. ✉ *Cathedral Close, The College, CB7 4DL,* ☎ *01353/662612.*

2 rooms with bath or shower. Full English breakfast in the Undercroft. No credit cards. Closed Dec. 24–26.

£ **Old Egremont House.** Just a five minutes' walk from the town center, this 17th-century house has beautiful views of the cathedral from its two largest rooms. Inside the oak-beamed house, everything is immaculate—the family still lives here—and there are books and antiques all around. There's a private garden, a delight to sit in during the summer, and the English breakfast includes homemade bread and marmalade. ✉ *31 Egremont St.,* ☎ *01353/663118. 3 rooms, 1 with bath. No credit cards. Closed Christmas wk.*

Shopping

The Old Fire Engine House Restaurant (✉ 25 St. Mary's St., ☎ 01353/662582) has affordable paintings and prints by local Fenland artists. **The Steeplegate Tearooms and Gallery** (✉ Steeplegate St., ☎ 01353/6647310) sells high-quality local crafts, especially wood carvings. **Waterside Antiques** (✉ The Wharf, ☎ 01353/667066) offers a wealth of antiques at very competitive prices, sold in an authentic river warehouse.

Duxford Airfield

18 *9 mi south of Cambridge, 25 mi south of Ely.*

The preserved hangars, control tower, and operations room of this former Royal Air Force base powerfully evoke a World War II air base in action. Duxford was assigned to the U.S. Air Force in the latter years of World War II and is now the Imperial War Museum's aviation branch, set up in the 1970s to house an extensive collection of fighters, bombers, and ancillary equipment. In addition, there are historic examples of civil aircraft, including a prototype Concorde, a high-tech flight simulator, and occasional demonstration flights. ✉ *Duxford, next to junction 10 of M11.* ☎ *01223/835000.* *£6.20.* *Apr.–mid-Oct., daily 10–6; mid-Oct.–Mar., daily 10–4. Closed Dec. 24–26, Jan. 1.*

Lodging

££–£££ **Duxford Lodge Hotel.** This Georgian country house, set on its own grounds in Duxford village, was the operations headquarters for Duxford Airfield during World War II. Extensively renovated, the rooms are comfortably furnished and individually decorated in traditional style. It's worth asking if one of the good-value suites is available: Two of them have four-poster beds. Elsewhere, the hotel is rich in burnished wood, and the garden features an inviting little terrace for relaxing. The restaurant prides itself on serving top-quality English Continental cuisine. ✉ *Ickleton Rd., CB2 4RU,* ☎ *01223/836444,* FAX *01223/832271. 13 rooms with bath, 2 with shower. Restaurant, bar. AE, DC, MC, V. Closed 5 days between Dec. 25 and Jan. 1.*

Saffron Walden

19 *4 mi southeast of Duxford, 14 mi south of Cambridge.*

Best known for its many typically East Anglian timber-frame buildings, the town owes its name to the saffron crocus fields that used to be cultivated in medieval times and processed for their dye. Some of the buildings have elaborate pargeting (decorative plasterwork), especially the walls of the former Sun Inn, which was used by Cromwell during his campaigns. In a similar military vein, the old **Grammar School** here was the World War II headquarters of the U.S. Air Force's 65th Fighter Wing. On the common at the east end of the town, there's a 17th-century circular earth maze, created from space left among the crocus beds.

★ Palatial **Audley End House,** a mile or so west of Saffron Walden, is a famous example of Jacobean (early 17th-century) architecture. It was once owned by Charles II, who bought it as a convenient place to break his journey on the way to Newmarket races. Remodeled in the 18th and 19th centuries, it shows the architectural skill of Sir John Vanbrugh, Robert Adam, and Biagio Rebecca as well as original Jacobean work in the magnificent Great Hall. You can also enjoy a leisurely walk around the park, which was landscaped by Capability Brown in the 18th century. ☎ *01799/522842.* *House and park £5.50, park only £3.30.* *Apr.–Sept., Wed.–Sun. and national holidays; park noon–5, house noon–6.*

Dining and Lodging

£££ **Saffron Hotel.** This conversion of three houses into one has resulted in a comfortable, modern hotel inside a 16th-century building. Three of the bedrooms feature splendid bathrooms and four-poster beds. The light and airy conservatory restaurant has won many local plaudits; the menu is packed with plenty of local specialties. ✉ *10–18 High St., CB10 2AY,* ☎ *01799/522676,* FAX *01799/513979. 24 rooms with bath. Restaurant (reservations essential), bar, lobby lounge. AE, DC, MC, V.*

Sudbury

20 *15 mi east of Saffron Walden, 20 mi south of Bury St. Edmunds, 14 mi northwest of Colchester.*

The prosperity of Sudbury, with its three fine churches and half-timber houses, was founded on the profits of an early silk-weaving industry as well as the wool trade. The town was Charles Dickens's model for "Eatanswill," where Mr. Pickwick stood for Parliament. In real life, Thomas Gainsborough, one of the greatest English portrait and landscape painters, was born here in 1727; a statue of the artist holding his palette stands on Market Hill. His family's home is now a museum, containing paintings by the artist and his contemporaries, as well as an arts center. Although **Gainsborough's House** presents an elegant Georgian facade, with touches of the 18th-century neo-Gothic style, the building is essentially Tudor. In the walled garden behind the house, a mulberry tree planted in 1620 is still growing. ✉ *46 Gainsborough St.,* ☎ *01787/372958.* *£2.50; free in Dec.* *Mid-Apr.–Oct., Tues.–Sat. 10–5, Sun. and national holidays 2–5; Nov.–mid-Apr., Tues.–Sat. 10–4, Sun. 2–5.*

Dining and Lodging

££ ★ **Mabey's Brasserie.** Chef Robert Mabey has created a simple brasserie with a touch of excitement. Dishes are prepared at the front of the house, and the atmosphere benefits accordingly. This isn't pretentious food but excellently prepared local produce, with the specialties always changing depending on the market. This is haute cuisine at middling prices. ✉ *47 Gainsborough St.,* ☎ *01787/374298. AE, MC, V. Closed Sun., Mon.*

£ **Old Bull and Trivets.** This 16th-century inn is furnished with leather chairs and antiques. All the bedrooms have TVs and telephones; some also have beams and galleries, and one even has a four-poster bed. The excellent informal restaurant (dinner only) serves French dishes. It is a 10 minutes' walk from the town center. ✉ *Church St., Ballingdon, CO10 6BL,* ☎ *01787/374120,* FAX *01787/379044. 9 rooms with bath or shower. Restaurant, bar, lobby lounge. AE, DC, MC, V.*

Long Melford

21 *2 mi north of Sudbury, 17 mi south of Bury St. Edmunds.*

It's easy to see how this village got its name, especially if you walk the full length of its 2-mile-long main street, which gradually broadens to include green squares and trees and finally opens out into the large triangular green on the hill. The town's buildings are an attractive mixture—mostly 15th-century half-timber or Georgian—and many house antiques shops. Telegraph poles are banned from both Long Melford and Lavenham, to preserve the towns' ancient look. On the hill, the **Church**—founded by the rich clothiers of Long Melford—is unfortunately obscured by Trinity Hospital, thoughtlessly built there in 1573. But close up, the delicate, flint flush work and huge, 16th-century Perpendicular windows that take up most of the church's walls have great impact, especially as the nave is 150 feet long. Much of the original stained glass remains, notably the Lily Crucifix window. The Lady Chapel has an unusual interior cloister.

Now a National Trust property, **Melford Hall,** distinguished from the outside by its turrets and topiaries, is a mid-16th-century house with a fair number of 18th-century additions. Much of the porcelain and many other fine pieces in the house come from the *Santissima Trinidad,* a ship captured by one of the house's owners in the 18th century, when she was sailing back to Spain full of gifts from the emperor of China. The hall is set in parkland leading down to a walk by Chad Brook. ☎ *01787/880286.* 🎫 *£3.50.* ⏲ *May–Sept., Wed.–Thurs. and weekends 2–5:30 (tours Wed. and Thurs.); Apr. and Oct., weekends 2–5:30.*

Kentwell Hall, half a mile north of Long Melford Green, is a redbrick Tudor manor house with picturesquely shaped chimneys and domes, surrounded by a wide moat. Built between 1520 and 1550, it was heavily restored inside after a fire in the early 19th century. Today, a restoration program is again under way, and the original gardens are being re-created. On many weekends from Easter through September, a reenactment of Tudor life is performed here by costumed "servants" and "farmworkers," with great panache and detail. There's also an organic farm, home to rare-breed farm animals. ☎ *01787/310207.* 🎫 *House, gardens, and farm £4.75; higher fee for special events.* ⏲ *Apr.–June and mid-July–mid-Sept., daily noon–5; also Sun. noon–5 on reenactment weekends.*

Lavenham

22 *4 mi northeast of Long Melford, 15 mi south of Bury St. Edmunds.*

More like a village than a town, Lavenham seems virtually unchanged since the height of its wealth in the 15th and 16th centuries. The weavers' and wool merchants' houses occupy not just one show street but most of the town. These are timber-frame in black oak, the main posts looking as if they could last for another 400 years. The most spectacular building of them all, the **Guildhall of Corpus Christi** (1529), is owned by the National Trust and is open to visitors as a museum of the medieval wool trade. ✉ *Market Pl.,* ☎ *01787/247646.* 🎫 *£2.60.* ⏲ *Apr.–Oct., daily 11–5.*

The **Wool Hall** was torn down in 1913, but it was reassembled immediately at the request of Princess Louise, sister of the then-reigning king, George V. In 1962, it was joined to the neighboring **Swan Hotel** (☞ Dining and Lodging, *below*), a splendid Elizabethan building in its own right. The Swan Hotel had a long history as a coaching inn, and in World War II served as the special pub for the U.S. Air Force's 48th Bomber Group.

NEED A BREAK? Have lunch or tea at **The Priory,** a timber-frame building on Water Street with a garden growing more than 100 varieties of herbs, or at the **Great House** (✉ Market Pl.), where you can dine on fine, French-inspired food in the garden.

Lavenham Church is set apart from the village. It was built with wool money by local cloth merchant Thomas Spring between 1480 and 1520. The height of its tower (141 feet) was meant to surpass those of the neighboring churches. In this it succeeded, though the rest of the church is of perfect proportions, with a spacious design similar to that of Long Melford. A long nave and attractive exterior flush work are its most obvious features, while the southern porch is particularly decorative.

Dining and Lodging

£££–££££ ★ ✕🏨 **Swan Hotel.** This is gloriously atmospheric 14th- to 15th-century lodging, with oak beams, rambling public rooms, and antique furniture. The bedrooms are all individually decorated, and two have four-poster beds; many of them have rich oak cabinets and original wood paneling. The restaurant even retains its minstrel's gallery. ✉ *High St., CO10 9QA,* ☎ *01787/247477,* FAX *01787/248286. 47 rooms with bath, 3 suites. Restaurant, 2 bars, lobby lounges. AE, DC, MC, V.*

Bury St. Edmunds

★ ㉓ *12 mi north of Lavenham, 28 mi east of Cambridge.*

Bury St. Edmunds owes its name—and indeed its existence—to Edmund, the last King of East Anglia, who was hacked to death by marauding Danes in 869. He was subsequently canonized and his shrine attracted pilgrims, settlement, and commerce. In the 11th century the erection of a great Norman abbey confirmed the town's importance as a religious center. Today, only the Norman Gate Tower, the fortified Abbot's Bridge over the river Lark, and a few picturesque ruins remain, for the abbey was one of the many that fell during Henry VIII's dissolution of the monasteries. You can get some idea of the abbey's enormous scale, however, from the surviving gate tower on Angel Hill. The ruins are now the site of the **Abbey Botanical Gardens,** with rare trees, including a Chinese tree of heaven originally planted in the 1830s. The abbey walls enclose separate, specialized gardens. One of these, the yew-hedged **Appleby Rose Garden,** was founded with the royalties from *Suffolk Summer,* a memoir by a U.S. serviceman, John Appleby, who had been stationed at nearby Rougham during World War II.

Originally three churches stood within the abbey walls, which gives some idea of the extent of the grounds, but only two have survived. **St. Mary's,** built in the 15th century, is the finer, with a blue-and-gold embossed "wagon" (i.e., barrel-shaped) roof over the choir. Mary Tudor, Henry VIII's sister and queen of France, is buried here. **St. James's** also dates from the 15th century; the brilliant paintwork of its ceiling and the stained-glass windows gleaming like jewels are the result of restoration in the 19th century by the architect Sir Gilbert Scott. Don't miss the memorial (by the altar) to an event in 1214, when the barons of England gathered here to take a solemn oath to force King John to grant the Magna Carta. The cathedral's original Abbey Gate was destroyed in a riot, and it was rebuilt in the 14th century on clearly defensive lines—you can see the arrow slits. ☎ *01284/757490.* 🎫 *Free.* ⏲ *Weekdays 7:30 AM–½ hr before dusk, weekends 9 AM–dusk.*

A walk along **Angel Hill** is a journey through the history of Bury St. Edmunds. Along one side, the Abbey Gate, cathedral, Norman Gate Tower, and St. Mary's Church make up a continuous display of medieval architecture. On the other side, the elegant Georgian houses include the **Athenaeum,** an 18th-century social and cultural meeting place, which has a fine Adam-style ballroom. The splendid **Angel Hotel** (☞ Dining and Lodging, *below*) was the scene of Sam Weller's meeting with Job Trotter in Dickens's *Pickwick Papers.* Dickens stayed here while he was giving readings at the Athenaeum.

The **Manor House Museum,** a Georgian mansion facing the abbey's grounds, is a delight. It contains excellent art and horological collections: paintings, clocks, watches, furniture, costumes (including regular exhibitions of costumes used in film and TV historical dramas), and ceramics from the 17th to the 20th centuries. The clocks and watches in particular are extraordinarily beautiful, and there's a café and gift shop, too. ⊠ *Honey Hill,* ☎ *01284/757072.* *£2.50.* ⊙ *Mon.–Sat. 10–5, Sun. 2–5.*

NEED A BREAK?

Opposite the Greene King brewery, on Crown Street at the end of Angel Hill, try Greene King draft ale and local sausages in the lofty back room of the **Dog and Partridge,** where the rough brick walls are hung with dray horse mementos. You can also sample the local beer at **The Nutshell** (⊠ Corner of The Traverse and Abbeygate St.), if you can squeeze in—this tiny, ancient pub is said to be England's smallest.

The public buildings within the ancient center of the town (which follows a Norman grid pattern) possess a varied grandeur. The **Guildhall** (⊠ Guildhall St.) dates back to the 15th century but has a 13th-century inner doorway. The **Corn Exchange** (⊠ Corner of Cornhill and The Traverse) is a fine example of Victorian classicism.

The **Art Gallery** is 18th-century classicism as interpreted by Robert Adam. It has no permanent collections; instead there are changing exhibits of paintings, sculpture, and crafts, as well as frequent concerts. ⊠ *Market Cross, Cornhill,* ☎ *01284/762081.* *50p.* ⊙ *Tues.–Sat. 10:30–4:30, Sun. by appointment.*

At the end of Cornhill is the 12th-century **Moyse's Hall,** probably the oldest building in East Anglia, which houses in the original tiny rooms local archaeological collections. It also has a macabre display relating to the Red Barn murder, a case that gained notoriety in an early 19th-century blood-and-thunder theatrical melodrama, *Maria Marten, or the Murder in the Red Barn;* Maria Marten's murderer was executed in Bury St. Edmunds in 1828. ⊠ *Buttermarket,* ☎ *01284/757488.* *£1.25.* ⊙ *Mon.–Sat. 10–5, Sun. 2–5.*

The Arts

Bury St. Edmunds's splendid **Theater Royal,** which offers a wide variety of touring shows, was built in 1819 and is a perfect example of Regency theater design and a delightfully intimate place to watch a performance. It may be closed during parts of the summer, so call ahead. ⊠ *Westgate St.,* ☎ *01284/769505.* ⊙ *Mon.–Sat. 10 AM–8 PM, and for performances; closed Good Fri. and national holiday Mon.*

Dining and Lodging

£££ ★ ✕ **Theobalds.** This is a small, well-established restaurant with a good, varied menu that attracts a regular local clientele. The influences at work are mainly French, though modern British cooking rears its head here, too; hare served with a sauce derived from local berries is a typical entrée. There are excellent desserts, cheeses, and a large wine list with some splendid French names. ⊠ *Ixworth (8 mi northeast of Bury St. Edmunds on A143), 68 High St.,* ☎ *01359/231707. MC, V. No lunch Sat., no dinner Sun. Closed Mon.*

££–£££ ✕ **Mortimer's Seafood Restaurant.** Mortimer's gets its name from the original watercolors by a Victorian artist, Thomas Mortimer, which are displayed on the walls of the dining room. The seafood menu varies with the season's catch, but there are generally grilled fillets of local trout and Scottish salmon as well as mussels and oysters. Cheaper counter lunches are offered in addition to the cheery, full service in the two main dining rooms. ✉ *30 Churchgate St.,* ☎ *01284/760623,* FAX *01284/761611. Weekend reservations (at least wk in advance) essential. AE, DC, MC, V. No lunch Sat. Closed Sun., Dec. 24–Jan. 6, last wk in Aug., 1st wk in Sept.*

£££ ★ ✕🏨 **Angel Hotel.** This is the quintessential ivy-clad, historic, market-town hotel. A former coaching inn, its rooms are spacious and well furnished, with the best ones overlooking the Abbey ruins. Several have four-poster beds, and one, the Charles Dickens Room, is where the man himself stayed. The bed is fairly small, but the rest of the room is in perfect 19th-century English style. Morning coffee and afternoon tea are served in the cozy lobby, complete with open fireplace, while elegant dining is to be found in the Regency Restaurant. Here, overlooking the abbey's main gate, a classic English menu is offered and impeccably served, including dishes like grilled lemon sole, venison sausages, or roast duck with port sauce. ✉ *3 Angel Hill, IP33 1LT,* ☎ *01284/753926,* FAX *01284/750092. 40 rooms with bath. Restaurant (reservations essential), bar. AE, DC, MC, V.*

££–£££ 🏨 **Suffolk Hotel.** This reliable Georgian hotel has nicely proportioned and pleasantly furnished rooms overlooking the busy and historic downtown area. ✉ *38 Buttermarket, IP33 1DL,* ☎ *01284/753995,* FAX *01284/750973. 33 rooms with bath. Restaurant, bar. AE, DC, MC, V.*

££ 🏨 **Ounce House.** This small, friendly, no-smoking bed-and-breakfast is a three minutes' walk from the abbey. The hotel has lots of charm: Guest rooms are attractively and comfortably furnished, and decor is stylish. ✉ *Northgate St., IP33 1HP.* ☎ *01284/761779,* FAX *01284/768315. 3 rooms with bath. MC, V.*

Shopping

The shopping streets of Bury St. Edmunds follow an ancient grid pattern from Abbey Gate to Cornhill, with Abbeygate Street in the center. The **Parsley Pot** (✉ 17 Abbeygate St., ☎ 01284/760289) has a good selection of local crafts, and **Thurlow Champness** (✉ 14 Abbeygate St., ☎ 01284/754747) has above-average silver, jewelry, and Copenhagen porcelain. **Ridley's** grocery store (✉ Abbeygate St. ☎ 01284/754473) is a splendidly old-fashioned establishment with a wonderful display of enormous cheeses in its window.

Outdoor Activities and Sports

There's a good indoor swimming pool at **Bury St. Edmunds Leisure Centre** (✉ Beetons Way, ☎ 01284/753496). The hectic atmosphere of **Rollerbury** (✉ Station Hill, ☎ 01284/701216), England's largest indoor roller-skating arena, won't be to everyone's taste—but it's certainly an experience.

Newmarket

24 *15 mi west of Bury St. Edmunds, 12 mi northeast of Cambridge.*

With its two racecourses on the springy turf of Newmarket Heath, the town has been the center of British horse racing since the 17th century, when it was firmly established under the patronage of Charles II. For information about when race meetings are taking place, call 01638/664151.

In town, the **National Horseracing Museum** traces the history of the sport in entertaining detail and has a fine collection of paintings. The enthusiastic staff also arranges daily full-day tours of all Newmarket's equestrian attractions. ✉ *99 High St.,* ☎ *01638/667333.* 💴 *£3.30; tours £20.* ⏲ *Apr.–Dec., Tues.–Sat. and public holidays 10–5, Sun. noon–4; tours Apr.–Nov., Tues.–Sat. at 9:30* AM.

Britain's **National Stud,** 2 miles southwest of the town, is one of the country's premier institutions for the breeding of champion racehorses. The 75-minute tours offer intimate—sometimes too intimate—views of its glistening pedigree stallions. Breeding mares remain on the property until they have given birth, so in spring and summer you're likely to see foals taking their first faltering steps across the 500 acres of bucolic meadowland. ☎ *01638/663464.* 💴 *£3.50.* ⏲ *Tours Apr.–Sept. (Oct. on race days only) weekdays at 11:15 and 2:30, Sat. at 11:15, Sun. at 2:30. Advance booking essential.*

NORWICH, THE BROADS, AND NORTH NORFOLK

Norwich is a city about which many books have been written, and many more will be written. The cathedral stands in impressive surroundings, and its 15th-century spire dominates the city, the unofficial capital of East Anglia. Norwich is the heart of the eastern and northern part of East Anglia's "bump." Norfolk's continuing isolation from the rest of the country and the fact that so much of its landscape and architecture has been left unspoiled—bypassed by the Industrial Revolution—have proved to be a draw in recent years. Many of the flint-knapped houses in North Norfolk's pretty villages are, nowadays, weekend or holiday homes. Windmills, churches, and waterways are the area's chief defining characteristics. A few miles inland from the Norfolk coast, the Broads begin—a name that caused much comment among GIs during World War II. In fact, these innocent Broads are a network of shallow, reed-bordered lakes, many of them linked by wide rivers. As these are nearly always calm, yachting and fishing are great lures here. The Broads have recently become England's newest National Park.

Numbers in the margin correspond to points of interest on the East Anglia and Norwich maps.

Norwich

25 *63 mi northeast of Cambridge, 110 mi northeast of London.*

It used to be said that Norwich had a pub for each day of the week and a church for each week of the year. Although this is no longer true, both types of institutions are still much in evidence in this "fine city". Established by the Saxons because of its prime trading position on the rivers Yare and Wensum, the town still has its heart in the triangle between the two waterways, dominated by the castle and cathedral. The inner beltway follows the line of the old city wall, much of which is still visible, and it is worth driving around after dark to see the older buildings—thanks to skillful floodlighting—uncluttered by their much newer neighbors.

By the time of the Norman Conquest, Norwich was one of the largest towns in England, though much was destroyed by the Normans to create a new town endowed with grand buildings. Grandest of these is
★ 26 **Norwich Cathedral.** Although its spire, at 315 feet, is visible everywhere, you cannot see the building itself until you pass through St. Ethelbert's Gate. The cathedral was begun in 1096 by Herbert de Losinga, who

had come from Normandy in 1091 to be its first bishop. His splendid tomb is by the high altar. The plain west front and dramatic crossing tower, with its austere, geometrical decoration, are distinctly Norman. The remarkable length of the nave is immediately impressive; unfortunately, the similarly striking height of the vaulted ceiling makes it a strain to study the delightful colored bosses (ornamental knobs at junction points), where Bible stories are illustrated with great vigor and detail—look for the Pharaoh and his cohorts drowning in a vivid Red Sea. Note also the wood carving on the choir-stall misericords (semi-seats), a wonderful revelation of medieval skill and religious beliefs. The stalls were originally intended for the Benedictine monks who ran the cathedral, and the beautifully preserved cloister is part of what remains of their great priory. ✉ *The Close,* ☎ *01603/764385.* 💳 *Free; donation requested.* ⏲ *Mid-May–mid-Sept., daily 7:30–7; mid-Sept.–mid-May, daily 7:30–6; free guided tours June–Sept., weekdays at 11 AM and 2:15 PM, Sat. at 11 AM.*

The Cathedral Close (grounds) is one of the most idyllic places in Norwich. Past the attractive mixture of medieval and Georgian houses, a
27 path leads down to the ancient water gate, **Pulls Ferry.** The grave of Norfolk-born nurse Edith Cavell, the British World War I heroine shot by the Germans in 1915, is at the east end of the cathedral.

28 The decorated stone facing of **Norwich castle,** high on the hill in the center of the city, makes it look like a children's book illustration. In fact, the castle is Norman, but the wooden bailey (wall) on the castle mound was later replaced with a stone keep (tower). The thick walls and other defense works attest to the castle's military function. For most of its history the castle has been a prison, and executions took place here well into the 19th century. There are daily guided tours of the battlements and dungeons. An excellent **museum** here features displays of different facets of Norfolk's history, including a gallery devoted to the Norwich School of painters who, like the Suffolk artist John Constable, devoted their work to the everyday Norfolk landscape and seascape as revealed in the East Anglian light. ✉ *Norwich Castle,* ☎ *01603/223624.* 💳 *£2.20.* ⏲ *Mon.–Sat. 10–5, Sun. 2–5.*

Between the castle and the cathedral is the **marketplace,** the heart of the city for 900 years. Overlooking the market with its blanket of brightly striped awnings, is the imposing—if somewhat severe—early 20th-cen-
29 tury **City Hall,** whose steps are guarded by bronze Norwich lions. Below City Hall and next to the market rises the elaborate church tower
30 of **St. Peter Mancroft.** Narrow lanes and alleys that used to be the main
31 streets of medieval Norwich lead away from the market and end at **Tombland** by the cathedral. Neither a graveyard nor a plague pit, Tombland was the site of the Anglo-Saxon trading place, now a busy thorough-
32 fare. **Elm Hill,** off Tombland, is a cobbled and pleasing mixture of Tudor and Georgian houses, now mostly given over to gift shops and tearooms.

33 **St. Peter Hungate** (at the top end of Elm Hill) is a 15th-century former church that displays church art and furnishings; here you can try your hand at brass rubbing. ✉ *Princes St.,* ☎ *01603/667231.* 💳 *Free; brass rubbing £1.50–£10 (including materials).* ⏲ *Apr.–Oct., Mon.–Sat. 10–5.*

NEED A BREAK? The **Britons Arms Coffee House** (☎ 01603/623367) is an ancient thatched house at the top of Elm Hill, popular with the lunchtime crowd.

34 The past is brought vividly to life at **Strangers' Hall,** a good example of a medieval merchant's house. Built in 1320, it went on growing until

City Hall, **29**
Dragon Hall, **35**
Elm Hill, **32**
Norwich Castle, **28**
Norwich Cathedral, **26**
Pulls Ferry, **27**
Sainsbury Centre for the Visual Arts, **38**
St. Julian's Church, **36**
St. Peter Hungate, **33**
St. Peter Mancroft, **30**
Strangers' Hall, **34**
Tombland, **31**
University of East Anglia, **37**

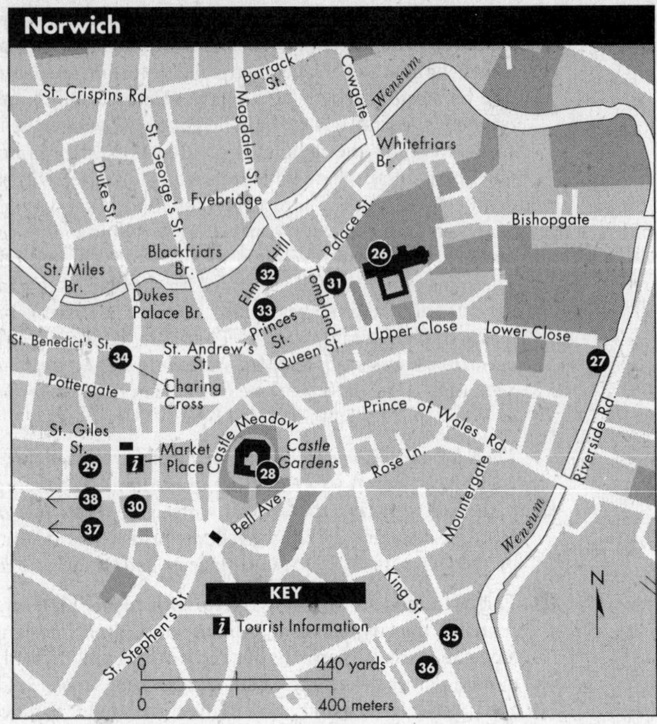

the mid-18th century and is now a museum of domestic life specializing in costumes, clothes (particularly underwear), and dolls. ✉ *Charing Cross,* ☎ *01603/667229.* 🎟 *£1.40.* ⏲ *Tues.–Sat. 10–5, Sun. 2–5.*

The river Yare was once a busy commercial waterway; now most of the traffic is for pleasure. During the summer months, a boat trip starting from Roaches Court at Elm Hill will give you a fresh perspective on Norwich; longer trips are available down the rivers Wensum and Yare to the nearer Broads. A marked riverside walk follows the Wensum from St. George's Bridge to the city wall at Carrow Bridge.

NEED A BREAK?

The Adam and Eve (☎ 01603/667423) is said to be Norwich's oldest pub, dating back to 1249, convenient from both the riverside walk and the cathedral on Bishopgate. The pub's terrace, set up for outdoor dining, and its generous servings of bar food are most pleasant.

If you have time, a visit to King Street, not far from the castle or Tomb-
35 land, is worthwhile; here you will find the **Dragon Hall,** a medieval cloth merchant's hall only recently "discovered" and restored. It gets its name from the intricately painted dragon that adorns the timber-frame Great Hall. ✉ *115–123 King St.,* ☎ *01603/663922.* 🎟 *£1.* ⏲ *Nov.–Mar., weekdays 10–4; Apr.–Oct., Mon.–Sat. 10–4.*

36 Tucked away along a tiny alley is **St. Julian's Church.** In the cell attached to the church Dame Julian of Norwich, one of the most famous mystics of the Middle Ages, lived and wrote her book *Revelations of Divine Love.* Although her hermitage was pulled down during the Reformation, it—along with the church—was repaired after wartime bombing. ✉ *St. Julian's Alley, King St.* ⏲ *May–Sept. daily 8–5:30; Oct.–Apr. daily 6–4.*

37 In complete contrast to Norwich's historical composition is the modern **University of East Anglia** (UEA), built during the great expansion of higher education in the 1960s. Its site on the slopes of the river Yare, 3 miles west of the town center, was used by architect Denys Lasdun to give a dramatic, stepped-pyramid effect. The campus is linked by walkways that open out at different levels and center on a fountain courtyard.

38 The award-winning **Sainsbury Centre for the Visual Arts,** a hangar-like building designed by Norman Foster, is on the UEA campus. It holds the extraordinary private art collection of the Sainsbury family, owners of a huge supermarket chain. The collection includes a remarkable quantity of tribal art and 20th-century works, especially Art Nouveau, and includes pieces by Picasso and Giacometti. There is a coffee bar and restaurant on the premises. Buses 4, 5, 26, and 27 run from Norwich Castle Meadow to UEA, providing access to both the university and the Sainsbury Centre. ⊠ *Earlham Rd.,* ☎ *01603/456060.* *£1.* *Tues.–Sun. noon–5.*

Inspire is a hands-on science center, housed in an old church, where children (and adults) can try simple, entertaining experiments to discover how things work. ⊠ *St. Michael's Church, Coslany St.,* ☎ *01603/612612.* *Tues.–Sun. 10–5:30.*

Norfolk's **Banham Zoo** (⊠ 20 mi southwest of Norwich, off A11 [T], ☎ 01953/887771), houses monkeys, penguins, and seals among some 1,000 species. There are good indoor and outdoor play areas, particularly suitable for young children.

The Arts

The **King of Hearts** (⊠ Fye Bridge St., ☎ 01603/766129) is yet another medieval merchant's house restored and put to good use: It's now a small arts center that holds chamber concerts, recitals, and poetry readings and has an exhibition area for art and sculpture. **Norwich Arts Centre** (⊠ St. Benedict's St., ☎ 01603/660352) has an eclectic program of live music, dance, stand-up comedy and other cultural events, as well as a good café.

The **Maddermarket Theater** (⊠ St. John Maddermarket, ☎ 01603/620917) was patterned after Elizabethan theater design and has been home to the Norwich Players, an amateur repertory company, since 1911. The theater is closed in August. The newly opened **Norwich Playhouse** (⊠ Gun Wharf, St. George's St., ☎ 01603/766466) is a professional repertory theater offering everything from Shakespeare to world premieres of new plays and jazz concerts; it also has a bookshop. Housed in a former church, the **Puppet Theater** (⊠ St. James, Whitefriars, ☎ 01603/629921) isn't just for children: This theater has a national reputation. Norwich's biggest and best-known theater is the **Theater Royal** (⊠ Theater St., ☎ 01603/630000), which plays host to touring companies staging musicals, ballet, and opera as well as plays. Many West End hits are previewed here.

Dining and Lodging

£££ ★ **Adlard's.** This is a very comfortable restaurant, mainly decorated in green, that offers highly accomplished and beautifully presented cooking. The specialties change regularly, but you might find lamb with Jerusalem artichokes or cod baked in a tapenade crust on a coulis of red peppers. The cheese board has lots of English and French cheeses, and the wine list has excellent selections from all over the world. ⊠ *79 Upper St. Giles St.,* ☎ *01603/633522. AE, DC, MC, V. No lunch Sat. Closed Sun.–Mon.*

££–£££ ★ ✕ **Marco's.** The Georgian architecture of this building is complemented inside by paneled walls, open fires, and pictures, all contributing to a warm, friendly, private atmosphere. Specialties of the Italian cuisine include *salmone al cartoccio* (salmon in parchment); game and local crab are served when available. Portions are generous, and there's a good value fixed-price menu at lunchtime. ✉ *17 Pottergate,* ☎ *01603/624044. AE, DC, MC, V. Closed Sun., Mon., and mid-Sept.–mid-Oct.*

££ ✕ **Pinocchio's.** Spacious but still intimate, this Italian restaurant in the fashionable St. Benedict's area has been attractively furnished with scatter rugs and colorful murals. There's a wide choice of inventive pasta specials, such as chicken served with saffron noodles in a red pesto sauce, and regional Italian dishes. The wine list is small, but appealing. Meals are accompanied by live jazz on Monday and Friday evenings. ✉ *11 St. Benedict's St.,* ☎ *01603/613318. AE, DC, MC, V. No dinner Sun.*

££ ✕ **St. Benedict's Grill.** The restaurant is nothing special to look at—homey, and even a little old-fashioned. The food, however, is special. The chef-proprietor, Nigel Raffles, was Roux-trained, and it shows in the cooking: excellent robust English food, such as home-made bangers and mash, fillet of beef with a wild mushroom crust, or roast lamb with sweet and sour red cabbage. ✉ *9 St. Benedict's St.,* ☎ *01603/765377. AE, DC, MC, V. Closed Sun.–Mon.*

££ ✕ **The Last Wine Bar.** Housed in a converted Edwardian shoe factory, the food here is a cut above typical wine-bar fare. You might find breast of pheasant wrapped in bacon with a port and thyme gravy or a wild mushroom stroganoff with herb rice, for example. There are always daily specials, including excellent fish, and a huge but well-chosen selection of wines. In summer, you can eat outside in the leafy courtyard. ✉ *72–76 St. Georges St.,* ☎ *01603/626626. AE, DC, MC, V. Closed Sun.*

£££ **Dunston Hall Hotel & Country Club.** Four miles southwest of the city center, this tudor mansion has undergone extensive renovation and is now a fairly luxurious hotel with good sporting facilities including a golf course. One of its great advantages is its peaceful setting in landscaped gardens and woodland—ideal for relaxing after a day's sightseeing. ✉ *Ipswich Rd., NR14 8PQ,* ☎ *01508/470444,* FAX *01508/471499. 72 rooms with bath. Restaurant, 2 bars, pool, sauna, driving range, golf course, tennis courts, games room. AE, DC, MC, V.*

£££ **Hotel Nelson.** This modern redbrick hotel, beside the river and close to the railway station, is brightly decorated, with good modern furniture especially in the executive wing. Many of the rooms have balconies overlooking the water. They're a little more pricey than the standard rooms, but they're worth it. ✉ *Prince of Wales Rd., NR1 1DX,* ☎ *01603/760260,* FAX *01603/620008. 121 rooms with bath. 2 restaurants, 2 bars, pool, sauna. AE, DC, MC, V.*

££ **The Beeches Hotel.** About a mile west of the city center, this attractive family-run hotel is actually two early Victorian houses, set in an extraordinary garden hidden away from the road, known as the Plantation Gardens. All the rooms are simply but pleasantly furnished, and several have the bonus of looking out over the gardens, which—with their ornate Gothic fountain and Italianate terrace—are gradually being restored to their original, Victorian splendor. ✉ *4–6 Earlham Rd., NR2 3DB,* ☎ *01603/621167,* FAX *01603/ 620151. 27 rooms with bath. Restaurant, bar. AE, DC, MC, V.*

Outdoor Activities and Sports

SWIMMING

If you don't want to risk the—often chilly—waters of the Norfolk coast, your best bet is **Broadland Aquapark** (✉ Drayton High Rd., Hellesdon, Norwich ☎ 01603/788912), about 3 miles north of the city center. With its heated indoor fun pools and water chutes, it's a good place to take children.

Shopping

The medieval lanes of Norwich, around Elm Hill and Tombland, contain the best antiques, book, and crafts stores. **Peter Crowe** (✉ 75 Upper St. Giles St., ☎ 01603/624800) specializes in antiquarian books. The **Black Horse Bookshop** (✉ 8–10 Wensum St., ☎ 01603/626871) sells new books, guides, and maps. Antiques shops abound in Norwich: **James and Ann Tillett** (✉ 12–13 Tombland, ☎ 01603/624914) specializes in antique jewelry and silver. The **Antiques and Collectors Centre** (✉ In Tombland, opposite the cathedral, ☎ 01603/619129) is an old house whose little rooms are crammed full of shops. **St. Michael-at-Plea** (✉ Bank Plain, ☎ 01603/619129) is a church converted into an antiques market. The **Elm Hill Craft Shop** (✉ 12 Elm Hill, ☎ 01603/621076) has interesting stationery and dollhouses. **The Mustard Shop** (✉ Bridewell Alley, ☎ 01603/627889) is both a shop and a museum and delivers what it promises—more kinds of Colman's mustard than you ever imagined existed, together with other mustard memorabilia.

Wymondham

39 *9 mi southwest of Norwich*

Pronounced "Windam," this ancient market town has a market cross at its center and timber-frame houses overhanging the sidewalks. Its magnificent 14th-century **Abbey** seems far too grand not to be a cathedral. The soaring roof has great hammerbeams decorated with flying angels, and the altar screen gleams with golden figures. The remaining structure is only a part of the original building, but it gives a good idea of just how huge Wymondham abbey must have been.

NEED A BREAK? The cozy **Brief Encounter** café (☎ 01572/606433) at Wymondham rail station has a unique atmosphere and style, with seating that comes from an old railway carriage and an open fire, as well as other railway—and movie—memorabilia in honor of the famous British weepie from which the café gets its name.

Wroxham

40 *4 mi northwest of Ranworth, 7 mi northeast of Norwich*

The busy tourist center of Wroxham is Broadland's "capital." Its riverbanks are lined with boatyards, and it's where the majority of boating holidays start from. Touring by car isn't really an option if you want to see something of the Broads, since many are inaccessible by road, but you can take one- to three-hour summer riverbus tours from the bridge at Wroxham along the River Bure; call Broads Tours (☎ 01603/782207) for information. Traditional Norfolk sailing barges, known as wherries, plied their trade all over the area from their main port at Great Yarmouth. In the late 19th and early 20th century, the leisure potential of these fine boats was first realized, and some were built as wherry yachts for luxurious vacations afloat. The *Norada, Olive,* and *Hathor* are historic wherry yachts based at Wroxham. All may be chartered (☎ 01603/782470) for cruises of up to 12 people.

Great Yarmouth

41 *18 mi southeast of Wroxham, 20 mi east of Norwich.*

Once the center of Europe's herring industry, Great Yarmouth is now the busiest seaside resort on the Norfolk coast, with a long (if undistinguished) seafront promenade backed by cafés, guest houses, and amusement arcades. The sands here are usually fairly clean, though the water can be cold and the offshore oil and gas exploration platforms do little to encourage a dip. Dickens stayed at a hotel on the waterfront here in 1848. Unless you book well in advance in summer, you're unlikely to be able to emulate him.

Away from the sea front, some medieval parts of the town remain. The **Tollhouse Museum** (✉ Tollhouse St.) is one of the oldest municipal houses in England and was once the town's courthouse and jail. Near the marketplace—the town's medieval center—the 14th-century **church of St. Nicholas** and the weirdly named **Hospital for Decayed Fishermen,** founded in 1702, are the most interesting buildings.

Pleasurewood Hills Theme Park, 6 miles south of Yarmouth on the road to Lowestoft, is the local answer to Disneyland (on a more modest scale). There are rides suitable for all ages, even very young children. ✉ *Corton Rd, Lowestoft,* ☎ *01502/508200.* ⏲ *Apr.–Oct. Daily 10–6.*

Dining

£££ ✕ **Seafood Restaurant.** A short walk from the center of town, the restaurant features an extensive menu entirely devoted to fresh fish and shellfish. Many dishes are Mediterranean in character and very rich. The food is all very competently cooked, and there's a decent wine list, too. The restaurant is comfortable enough to linger in, and service is attentive. ✉ *85 North Quay,* ☎ *01493/856009. AE, DC, MC, V. No lunch Sat. Closed Sun.*

Outdoor Activities and Sports

WALKING

The 56-mile **Weaver's Way** footpath begins (or ends) at Great Yarmouth, following several lengths of disused railway line, as well as regular footpaths and minor roads, on its way to Cromer. To walk the entire route would take at least three days, and there are overnight facilities (inns, pubs, and B&Bs) in most of the towns and villages en route as well as camping at Manor Farm (☎ 01493/700279), in Tunstall, near Halvergate Marshes, west of Great Yarmouth. For more information, and a walking brochure, contact either Norwich or Great Yarmouth tourist information centers (☞ Contacts and Resources *in* East Anglia A to Z, *below*).

Blickling

★ 42 *15 mi north of Norwich, 27 mi northwest of Great Yarmouth, via North Walsham (turn left onto B1354, then right, down a little lane).*

A first sight of **Blickling Hall** is guaranteed not to disappoint: Cars often come to a screeching halt when they spot the house's famous facade, looming in the far distance behind a wrought-iron gate, looking for all the world like the Taj Mahal of England. A grand vista is created by an imposing allée, formed by two mighty yew hedges: a magnificent frame for the house, a perfectly symmetrical Jacobean masterpiece. The redbrick mansion features towers and chimneys, baroque Dutch gables and—in the center—a three-story timber clocktower. The grounds include a formal flower garden and parkland whose woods conceal a temple, an orangery, a pyramid, and a secret garden. Now a National Trust property, it belonged to a succession of historical figures, including Sir John Fastolf, the model for Shakespeare's Falstaff; Anne Boleyn's family, who owned it until Anne was executed by her husband, Henry VIII; and finally Lord Lothian, an ambassador to the United States. The Long Gallery (127 feet) has an intricate plasterwork ceiling decorated with Jacobean emblems, and the superb 17th-century staircase is also worth examining. Most of the interior is on the austere side, but there is a sumptuous tapestry of Peter the Great, which hangs in its own room. ✉ *Blickling,* ☎ *01263/733084.* 🎫 *House and gardens £5.50; garden only £3.20.* ⏲ *House and gardens Apr.–Oct., Tues.–Wed., Fri.–Sun., and national holidays; house 12:30–4:30, gardens 10:30–5:30.*

NEED A BREAK? The **Buckinghamshire Arms** (☎ 01263/732133), next to the entrance of Blickling Hall, has plenty of atmosphere and a large garden and serves excellent bar meals.

Cromer

43 *10 mi north of Blickling, 38 mi northwest of Great Yarmouth, 24 mi north of Norwich.*

Once a fashionable seaside resort, Cromer has a kind of faded charm that still makes it a memorable place to visit. The town sits high above a fine beach and features an attractive 15th-century church. Plenty of hotels (notably the imposing, Edwardian **Hotel de Paris**) and pubs offer good views of the sea below, while along the back streets you should be able to find locally caught crabs—a delicacy. Don't leave without visiting the pier, at the end of which is the **Lifeboat Museum,** where the town's lifeboat is housed ready for use; there are also exhibits about past deeds of bravery. In summer, the **theater** on Cromer pier hosts "Seaside Special," the last surviving example in the country of what was once a British institution: the end-of-the-pier variety show.

NEED A BREAK? **Mary Jane's** (☎ 01263/511208) restaurant and carry-out on Garden Street, near the sea front serves the best fish and chips on the East coast.

Blakeney

44 *15 mi west of Cromer, 28 mi northwest of Norwich.*

The Norfolk coast begins to feel wild and remote near Blakeney. If you drive along the coast road you'll pass marshes, sandbanks, and coves, as well as a string of villages with harbors used for small fishing boats and yachts—of which Blakeney is one of the most attractive. From the quay here you can take a boat trip past **Blakeney Point,** a National Trust nature reserve, to see the seals on the sandbanks and the birds on the dunes.

NEED A BREAK? You can get a good bar lunch at **The White Horse** (✉ High St., ☎ 01263/740574) hotel in Blakeney or eat in the restaurant. The food is simple, well cooked, and concentrates on local specialties, such as crab, mussels, and whitebait, with nicely stodgy English puddings—like treacle tart—to fill in the gaps.

Holkham

★ 45 *10 mi west of Blakeney, 37 mi northwest of Norwich.*

Holkham Bay is a huge expanse of sandy beaches, dunes, and salt marsh backed by pine woods. The tide goes out for 2 miles here. Opposite the lane leading down to the beach from the coast road (A149) is the entrance to **Holkham Hall.** The estate is the seat of the Coke family, the earls of Leicester. In the late 18th century, Thomas Coke went on the fashionable "grand tour" of the Continent, returning with art treasures and determined to build a house according to the new Italian ideas; the result was this Palladian palace, one of the most splendid in Britain. The magnificence of the Marble Hall pales in comparison to the Great Hall, which is 60 feet high and brilliant with gold and alabaster. Centered by a grand staircase and modeled after the Baths of Diocletian, it may be the most spectacular room in Britain (sadly, the staircase's imperial purple rug has been removed and replaced with an unsightly bannister). Twelve stately rooms follow, each filled with Coke's collection of masterpieces, including paintings by Gainsborough, Van Dyck, Rubens, Raphael, and other old masters. This transplant from neoclassical Italy is set in extensive parkland landscaped by Capability Brown in 1762. ✉ *Near Wells-next-the-Sea,* ☎ *01328/710733.* 🎫 *£3.* ⏲ *Easter weekend and June–Sept., Sun.–Thurs. 1:30–5.*

Sandringham

46 *15 mi southwest of Holkham, 8 mi north of King's Lynn, 43 mi northwest of Norwich.*

Sandringham House, not far from the old-fashioned but still popular seaside resort of Hunstanton, is one of the Queen's country residences—it's where the royal family spends Christmas each year as well as other vacations. This huge, redbrick Victorian mansion was clearly designed for enormous country-house parties, with a ballroom, billiard room, and bowling alley, as well as a shooting lodge on the grounds. The house and gardens are closed when the Queen is in residence, but the woodlands, nature walks, and museum of royal memorabilia (the latter housed in the old stables) remain open, as does the church, medieval but in heavy Victorian disguise. ✉ *Sandringham,* ☎ *01553/772675.* 🎫 *House, gardens, and museum £4; grounds and museum £3.* ⏲ *Mid-Apr.–Sept.; house and museum Mon.–Sat. 11–5, Sun. noon–5, gardens open ½ hr earlier. Closed last 2 wks of July.*

King's Lynn

47 *8 mi south of Sandringham, 40 mi northwest of Norwich.*

The center of King's Lynn was used as the location for old New York in the 1988 movie *Revolution.* It's not difficult to see why: Much of the old port and trading town with its Georgian town houses, guildhalls, and ancient quayside warehouses is still intact, despite some unfortunate "town planning" in the 1950s and '60s. Now an important container port close to the mouth of the Great Ouse on the Wash, King's Lynn gained importance in the 15th century, especially for trade with northern Europe. A Flemish influence is apparent in the church brasses and the style of the town squares—but King's Lynn remains one of the most English of English towns. When the railway deserted it in the 19th century, the grand merchants moved away, leaving it—for all intents and purposes—a British Brigadoon.

Trinity Guildhall (on the north side of the market place), with its striking checkered stone front, is now the Civic Hall of the Borough Council and is not generally open to the public, although you can visit it during the King's Lynn Festival (☞ The Arts, *below*) and on occasional guided tours in the summer; inquire at the tourist information center. It is possible, however, to explore the **Regalia Rooms,** housed in the Guildhall Undercroft, with the aid of a recorded audio tour. The rooms, entered through the Old Gaol (jail) House (now the tourist information center), exhibit charters dating from the time of King John (who reigned 1199–1216), as well as the 14th-century chalice known as King John's Cup. ✉ *Saturday Market Pl.,* ☎ *01553/763044.* 🎫 *£2.* ⏲ *Apr.–Oct., daily 10–5; Nov.–Mar., Fri.–Tues. 10–5.*

Another early 15th-century guildhall, St. George's, forms part of the **King's Lynn Arts Centre,** now a thriving arts and theater complex administered by the National Trust, and the focal point for the annual King's Lynn Festival. There is also an art gallery and a crafts fair every September. The center's coffee bar serves snacks all day. St. George's Guildhall is the largest surviving English medieval guildhall, and it adjoins a Tudor house and a warehouse used during the Middle Ages. ✉ *27 King St.,* ☎ *01553/774725.* 🎫 *Free.* ⏲ *Apr.–Sept., weekdays 10–5, Sat. 10–5; Oct.–Mar., weekdays 11–4, Sat. 11–4. Gallery closed Mon.*

On the quayside, the 15th-century **Hanseatic Warehouse** (✉ St. Margaret's La.) is an impressive brick building with a timber-frame upper story jutting out over the cobbled street below.

The Arts

Much of the **King's Lynn Festival,** which takes place in July, is based at the Arts Centre and encompasses concerts, exhibitions, theater, dance, films, literary events, and children's programs. ✉ *King's Lynn Festival Office, 27 King St., PE30 1HA,* ☎ *01553/773578. Festival program available Apr. or May.*

Dining

££–£££ ★ ✕ **Rococo.** This modern restaurant in an ancient house serves food as stylish as the decor. The cooking is mainly contemporary British, but has other influences. Fish and vegetarian dishes are particularly imaginative—for example, layered vegetable stack and fragrant rice with red onion sauce. Traditional English desserts—such as banana steamed sponge pudding—are a specialty. ✉ *11 Saturday Market Pl.,* ☎ *01553/771483. AE, V. Closed Sun., Mon.*

££ ✕ **Riverside Rooms.** Part of the Arts Centre, the building housing this restaurant reflects the style of the original 15th-century warehouse. There are some tables outside, overlooking the river. The English cuisine emphasizes locally caught fish and Cromer crabs. There is also an inexpensive coffee shop in the historic undercroft that serves homemade snacks and pastries. ✉ *27 King St.,* ☎ *01553/773134. MC, V. Closed Sun.*

Shopping

The Old Granaries antiques center in King's Staithe Lane, off Queen Street, is an Aladdin's cave of china, lamps, silver, jewelry, and other decorative items. There are also well-established open markets in the town center.

Outdoor Activities and Sports

WALKING

The best part of the **Peddar's Way** is the route from Castle Acre, just north of Swaffham, to Holme-next-the-Sea, close to Hunstanton, a distance of about 20 miles. For this route, the best starting point is King's Lynn, whose tourist information center (☞ Contacts and Resources *in* East Anglia A to Z, *below*) can advise about local B&B establishments and hotels. It also sells a comprehensive booklet called *Walking the Peddar's Way,* which gives much more detail about the route.

Peterborough

34 mi southwest of King's Lynn, 36 mi northwest of Cambridge.

This ancient city was an important Roman settlement on the road north from London and has been recently largely developed. But the city's heart is the **cathedral,** whose history traces back to its original 7th-century Anglo-Saxon foundation. Originally a monastery church, the building is basically Norman, but one gets a sense of light inside, partly because the original 12th-century Norman windows were replaced by larger ones in the 13th and 15th centuries and also because Cromwell's troops smashed all the stained glass during the Civil War. The painted wooden nave ceiling, dating from the 13th century, is one of only three surviving in Europe. From the gallery that runs around the inside of the central tower you can see across the fens to Ely. Two queens were buried here. Katherine of Aragon, Henry VIII's first wife, lies under a plain gray stone in the north choir aisle under the 16th-century standards of England and Spain. Mary, Queen of Scots, was buried in the south aisle after her execution in 1587, although her son James I later had her body moved to Westminster Abbey in London. ✉ *Chapter Office, 12 Minster Precincts,* ☎ *01733/343342.* 🎫 *Free.* ⏲ *Weekdays 7–6:30, weekends 7–5:30.*

COLCHESTER AND THE ALDEBURGH COAST

Colchester is the oldest town on record in England, dating back to the Iron Age. One of its Roman founders was the emperor Claudius, and the settlement was soon attacked by Queen Boudicca, queen of the Iceni, noted for having carving knives affixed to her chariot wheels—an early example of dangerous driving. Today the Roman walls still stand, together with a Norman castle, a Victorian town hall, and Dutch-style houses built by refugee weavers from the Low Countries in the late 16th century.

Colchester is the traditional base for exploring Constable Country, that quintessentially English rural landscape on the borders of Suffolk and Essex made famous by the early 19th-century painter, John Constable. This area runs north and west of Colchester along the valley of the river Stour. The Suffolk Heritage coast, which wanders northward from Orford up to Lowestoft, is one of the most unspoiled shorelines in the country.

Colchester

48 *59 mi northeast of London, 51 mi southeast of Cambridge, 68 mi south of Norwich.*

Recent archaeological research indicates a settlement at the head of the Colne estuary at least as early as 1100 BC. At the time of Christ it was the center of the domain of Cunobelin (Shakespeare's Cymbeline), who was king of the Catuvellauni. On Cunobelin's death, the Romans invaded in AD 43. The emperor Claudius—who was supposed to have entered Colchester on an elephant—built his first stronghold here and made it the first Roman colony in Britain, appropriately renaming the town *Colonia Victricensis* ("Colony of Victory"). Colchester had to wait another millennium, however, before it received its royal charter in 1189 from King Richard Lion-Heart.

Evidence of Colchester's four centuries of Roman history is visible everywhere. Although the Romans prudently relocated their administrative center to London after the Celtic queen Boudicca burned the place in AD 60, Colchester was important enough for them to build massive fortifications around the town. The **Roman Walls**—dating largely from the reign of Emperor Vespasian (AD 69–79)—can still be seen, especially along Balkerne Hill (to the west of the town center), with its splendid Balkerne Gate, and along Priory and Vineyard streets, where there is now a Roman drain exposed halfway along. On Maidenburgh Street, near the castle, the remains of a Roman amphitheater have been discovered—the curve of the foundations is outlined in the paving stones of the roadway, and part of the walls and floor have been exposed and preserved in a modern building, where they can be viewed through a window.

Colchester has always had a strategic importance and is still home to a military garrison; a tattoo (military spectacle) is held in even-numbered years. ★ The **castle** was built by William the Conqueror in about 1076, one of the earliest to be built of stone (largely taken from the Roman ruins). All that remains is the keep (main tower), but it is the largest in Europe. The castle was actually built over the foundations of the huge Roman Temple of Claudius, and in the vaults you can descend through 1,000 years of history. A superb museum inside contains an ever-growing collection of prehistoric and Roman remains, mostly from Colchester itself. Spread across two floors of the castle vaults, highly engaging displays chart the original Celtic inhabitation of the region before recording in detail the Roman invasion and subsequent occupation, with recent additions bringing the story through to the Norman Conquest. One of the finest of all Roman Britain's bronze statues—of Mercury, messenger of the gods—stands right by the reception desk, while other exhibits tell of everyday Roman life. Magnifying glasses are available for a closer examination of Roman coins. Children, especially, will appreciate being able to try on a toga, a slave's neck chain, or an actor's mask. To really make your visit come alive, take a guided tour (July–Aug., daily; Apr.–June and Sept., weekends) of the Roman vaults and castle dungeons. If you need a break during your tour, the castle park is an ideal place to rest or stroll awhile. ☎ *01206/282931 or 01206/282932 for information on all Colchester museums.* 🎫 *£2.80.* ⏲ *Mar.–Nov., Mon.–Sat. 10–5, Sun. 2–5; Dec.–Feb., Mon.–Sat. 10–5; closed Christmas wk.*

Hollytrees is an exquisite early 18th-century brick house with a collection of costumes, dolls, and toys that spans three centuries of English design. It's next door to the castle, at the edge of the castle park. ✉ *High St.,* ☎ *01206/712931.* 🎫 *Free.* ⏲ *Tues.–Sat. 10–noon and 1–5.*

The church of **St. Mary-at-the-Wall** on the west side of the town center is now an arts center, offering a varied program throughout the year. Across the way is Colchester's **Mercury Theater** (☞ The Arts, *below*). The town's enormous Victorian redbrick water tower (known locally as "Jumbo") dominates the theater and everything else around it. The massiveness of the Roman **Balkerne Gate** shows how assiduously the Romans fortified the town after Boudicca had razed the previous settlement to the ground in AD 61. Most of its foundations lie beneath the neighboring Hole-in-the-Wall pub.

The broad High Street follows the line of the main Roman road. Halfway down is the splendid Edwardian **Town Hall,** standing on the site of the original Moot (assembly) Hall. On its tower you can see four figures representing Colchester's main industries: fisheries, agriculture, the military, and engineering. The narrow, medieval streets behind the town hall are called the **Dutch Quarter** because weavers—refugees from the Low Countries—settled here in the 16th century, when Colchester was the center of a thriving cloth trade. The medieval Long Wyre Street, Short Wyre Street, and Sir Isaac's Walk, where there are many small antiques stores and crafts and gift shops, are south of High Street and beyond the modern Culver Square pedestrian mall. **Tymperley's Clock Museum,** off Sir Isaac's Walk, on Trinity Street, displays a unique collection of Colchester-made clocks in the surviving wing of an Elizabethan house. ✉ *Trinity St.,* ☎ *01206/712943.* 🎟 *Free.* ⏲ *Apr.–Oct., Tues.–Sat. and national holidays, 10–1 and 2–5.*

Colchester Zoo offers 40 acres of parkland exhibiting more than 150 species of animals, including snow leopards, Siberian tigers, and elephants. Attractions include snake handling and the daily penguin parade, and there's also a miniature railroad. ✉ *Maldon Rd.,* ☎ *01206/330253.* 🎟 *£6.* ⏲ *Apr.–July, daily 9:30–6; Oct.–Apr., daily 9:30–hr before dusk. Closed Dec. 25.*

The **Colne Valley Railway** (☎ 01787/61174) runs steam trains through the Colne Valley, from Castle Hedingham Station (near Halstead on A604). There are dining and buffet cars on the train, and the station itself holds a permanent display of vintage steam and diesel locomotives (⏲ Mid-Mar.–Dec., daily 10–5). "Steam days" take place on most Sundays between Easter and October, as well as at Christmas, and on national holiday weekends.

The Arts

The **Mercury Theater** (✉ Balkerne Gate, ☎ 01206/573948) stages a wide variety of plays, including touring shows, pre–West End runs, and local productions. It's in a modern building not far from the **Colchester Arts Centre** (✉ St. Mary-at-the-Wall, Church St., ☎ 01206/577301), which hosts theater, exhibitions, and workshop events.

Dining and Lodging

££ ✕ **Martha's Vineyard.** Six miles outside Colchester, in the small village of Nayland, this is one of the rising stars of the British restaurant world. Run by a husband-and-wife team (the latter, Larkin Rogers, is the chef), the restaurant is simple and low-key in style, but the food is exceptionally good. A sample menu might include roast tomato soup, braised oxtail, fish stew, and pasta with scallops in cream sauce. All the produce used is local and often organic. ✉ *18 High St., Nayland,* ☎ *01206/262888. MC, V. No dinner Sun.–Wed.; lunch Sun. only.*

££ ✕ **Warehouse Brasserie.** Colchester's most popular eating place has a fairly anonymous exterior and location: It's tucked away in a converted warehouse, down a cul-de-sac off St. John's Street. Inside, though, all is cheerful, with a charming pastel green and rich red split-level dining room, wooden tables, and large wall mirrors. The menu mixes brasserie favorites—fish soup, Caesar salad, and steaks—with classic English dishes like Lancashire hot pot and more daring Asian ones, such as crispy won ton. Service is brisk, if occasionally off-hand, but the large servings more than compensate. There's an above-average selection of wines by the glass as well as a decent range of specialty teas. ✉ *Chapel St. N,* ☎ *01206/765656. MC, V. No dinner Sun.*

£££ 🏨 **Kingsford Park Hotel.** This 18th-century country-house hotel about 2 miles southeast of downtown Colchester boasts individually decorated rooms and antique furniture; some rooms have four-poster beds. ✉ *Layer Rd., CO2 0HS,* ☎ *01206/734301,* FAX *01206/734512. 10 rooms with bath. Restaurant, bar. AE, DC, MC, V.*

££–£££ 🏨 **George Hotel.** In downtown Colchester, this 500-year-old hotel—once a coaching inn—has been renovated to include a modern extension but has lost none of its age-old charm. Many rooms incorporate original oak beams and are comfortably furnished. The George Bar also retains its historic beams, while in the cellar there's a section of Roman pavement and a 16th-century wall painting on display. The Brasserie restaurant has a good à la carte menu that includes local oysters (in season) as well as conventional English meat dishes and lighter alternatives such as salads and pastas. ✉ *116 High St., CO1 1TD,* ☎ *01206/578494,* FAX *01206/761732. 47 rooms with bath. Restaurant, bar, grill. AE, DC, MC, V.*

£ **Gladwins Farm.** This timber farmhouse bed-and-breakfast establishment is in the village of Nayland, 6 miles north of Colchester. It's friendly, quiet, and secluded, with great views of the Stour Valley, Constable's home base. Rooms are pleasantly decorated and full of local character. ✉ *Harpers Hill, Nayland, CO6 4NU.* ☎ *01206/262262,* FAX *01206/263001. 2 rooms with bath. Evening meals by arrangement. Fishing, tennis, horseback riding, children's playground.*

Shopping

Colchester's most interesting stores are in the medieval streets between High Street and St. John's Street, some of which are pedestrianized or have restricted traffic. **Gunton's Food Shop** (✉ 81 Crouch St.) is an old family business, considered a local version of London's Harrods food hall. **Berrimans** (✉ 68 Culver St. E, ☎ 01206/575650) sells china, glass, porcelain, novelties, and collectibles. The **Trinity Antiques Centre** (✉ 7A Trinity St., ☎ 01206/577775) has the town's widest selection of antiques.

Dedham

6 mi north of Colchester, off A12.

Dedham is the heart of Constable Country, that part of Norfolk immortalized by England's greatest landscape painter, John Constable (1776–1837). Here, rolling hills and the cornfields of Dedham Vale, set under the lovely pale skies that are such a notable and delicate feature of the district, inspired the artist to paint some of his most celebrated canvases. He went to school in Dedham village: a tiny, picturebook kind of place that consists of a single street, a church, and a few timber-frame and brick houses. From here you can rent a rowing boat, which (if you're fit enough) is an idyllic way of traveling the 2 miles down the river Stour to **Flatford Mill,** one of the two watermills owned by Constable's father, and the subject of his most famous painting, *The Hay Wain* (1821). Nearby is the 16th-century **Willy Lott's Cottage** also instantly recognizable from *The Hay Wain.* The National Trust now owns Flatford Mill along with the houses around it, including the thatched **Bridge Cottage,** which is open to the public and features a display about the artist's life. ✉ *Near East Bergholt,* ☎ *01206/298260.* *Free.* ⏲ *Apr.–May, Wed.–Sun. 11–5:30; June–Sept., daily 10–5:30; Oct., Wed.–Sun. 11–5:30; Nov., Wed.–Sun. 11–3:30.*

Two miles north of Dedham, off A12, the Constable trail continues in
49 **East Bergholt.** Constable was born here in 1776; only the stables remain of the house that was his birthplace. As well as many other views of the village, he painted the village church, **St. Mary's,** where his parents lie buried. It has one very unusual feature—a free-standing wooden bell house in place of a tower.

NEED A BREAK? The **Marlborough Head** (✉ Mill La.), in Dedham, is an early 18th-century pub opposite Constable's school, serving fine lunches from quiche to steak. It gets very busy during the summer, so get there early to ensure a table.

Dining and Lodging

£££ ✕ **Le Talbooth.** In a Tudor house idyllically situated beside the river Stour, the restaurant has a floodlit terrace where drinks are served in the summer. Inside, original beams, black-lead windows, and a brick fireplace add to the historic atmosphere. A four-course, gourmet fixed-price menu is offered, perhaps including chicken served with various light sauces or fresh fish. After 40 years, the cooking is as accomplished as you would expect. ✉ *Gun Hill,* ☎ *01206/323150. Jacket and tie. AE, MC, V.*

££££ ★ **Maison Talbooth.** This luxury hotel is a peaceful Victorian house, set in the rich meadowlands immortalized by Constable. Each of the rooms is attractively furnished with period antiques, although there's also space for such modern amenities as Jacuzzis. Guests are encouraged to eat in Le Talbooth restaurant, just a short walk down the lane and owned by the same friendly management. ✉ *Stratford Rd., CO7 6HW,* ☎ *01206/322273,* FAX *01206/322752. 10 rooms with bath. Bar. AE, MC, V.*

Harwich

50 *20 mi northeast of Colchester.*

Harwich is a historic port town right on the tip of the peninsula that juts out into the sea east of Colchester. It stands on the estuary of the Stour and Orwell rivers. (The writer George Orwell, who was born Eric Blair, took his pen name from this river in 1932; his parents lived in Southwold, just 35 miles to the north.) Harwich is an important ferry port, providing year-round service to the Netherlands, Germany, Denmark, Sweden, and Norway. If you aren't intending to take a boat, or are just passing through on your way to the Suffolk coast, Harwich is not worth making a special detour. The **Harwich Redoubt** is the one sight worth visiting: It's a circular fort built in 1808 as part of the string of the coastal defenses against Napoleon and now houses a small museum of local history. *£1.* ⏲ *Apr.–Oct., daily 2–5; Sun. 10–noon.*

Ipswich

51 *14 mi north of Colchester, 45 mi south of Norwich.*

One of medieval England's largest towns, home to a prosperous merchant class and, for a time, to Cardinal Wolsey, Ipswich still retains a pleasant center where you could easily spend an afternoon strolling around. It boasts a bevy of medieval parish churches—one now houses the tourist office in an extremely sympathetic conversion—and several buildings dating from its period of greatest prosperity, the 17th and 18th centuries. Most notable is the **Ancient House,** sometimes known as Sparrowe's House, in the Buttermarket. Built in 1670, it is one of the most ornate and baroque examples of pargeting (decorative plasterwork) in England. The tourist office can assist with walking tours.

Dining and Lodging

£££–££££ ★ ✕ **Hintlesham Hall.** This is a luxurious Georgian-style manor house hiding a basically Tudor building; the rear view of redbrick chimneys, overlooking fine gardens, shows visitors the real age of the hall. There are grand public rooms with antique furniture, but the house has been completely renovated and guest rooms are equally impressive—comfortable but not showy and retaining original beams and woodwork in some of the rooms. The restaurant is excellent and features a set weekday lunch that allows you to sample a good cross-section of the talented chef's offerings, including such dishes as ragout of seafood, lamb with rosemary, breast of pheasant, or wild mushroom and spinach ravioli.

The standard room rate includes a simple Continental breakfast, but special rates for stays of two or more nights offer a full English breakfast and dinner. ✉ *Hintlesham IP8 3NS,* ☎ *01473/652334,* FAX *01473/652463. 33 rooms with bath. Restaurant (reservations essential, jacket and tie), pool, sauna, spa, 18-hole golf course, tennis court, croquet, exercise room, fishing, billiards. AE, DC, MC, V. No lunch Sat.*

Felixstowe

52 *10 mi southeast of Ipswich.*

Felixstowe is a fairly attractive seaside resort, across the estuary from Harwich and, like Harwich, it has a ferry service to the Netherlands. **Landguard Fort,** a mile south of town, dates from the 18th century, though built on a site originally fortified by Henry VIII, and remained in use until after World War II. There's a museum inside the fort; try to attend one of the guided tours to make the most of your visit. ☎ *01394/286403.* *Museum £1.50, includes tour.* *June–Sept., Wed. and Sun. 2:30–5; also Thurs. in Aug., 2:30–5. Tours at 2:45 and 4.*

Woodbridge

8 mi northeast of Ipswich, 16 mi north of Felixstowe.

One of the first good ports of call—literally—on the Suffolk Heritage Coast (☞ *below*), Woodbridge is a pleasant little town best known for its many antique shops and for boatbuilding, which has been carried out here since the 16th century—although these days yachts and pleasure craft are being built, not the great ships of the past. Exploring Woodbridge's old quayside is a real delight; the most prominent building is a white clapboard tide mill that dates from the 18th century. Boat trips from the quay (May–Sept., daily 2–5, every 30 min; £2 per person) thread their way deftly through the small craft moored in the harbor and out into the river.

En Route From Felixstowe northward to Kessingland lies the **Suffolk Heritage Coast,** a beautiful 40-mile stretch including many sections designated by an Act of Parliament as "Areas of Special Scientific Interest." You can only reach them on minor roads running east off A12 north of Ipswich.

Orford

53 *10 mi east of Woodbridge along B1084, 35 mi northeast of Colchester.*

This small village is split between the quayside and its ancient center, where small, squat **Orford Castle** surveys the flatlands from atop a green mound pockmarked with picnickers in summer. Its splendid triple-towered keep was built in 1160 as a coastal defense. Climb it for a view over what was once a thriving medieval port (the 6-mile shingle bank of Orford Ness eventually cut off direct access to the sea). ☎ *01394/450472.* *£1.70.* *Apr.–Dec., daily 10–6; Jan.–Mar., Wed.–Sun. 10–4.*

Dining and Lodging

££ ✕ **Butley-Orford Oysterage.** What started as a little café that sold oysters and cups of tea has become a large, bustling, no-nonsense restaurant. It still specializes in oysters and smoked salmon, as well as smoked seafood platters and seasonal fresh fish dishes. The actual smoking takes place in the adjacent smokehouse, and the products are also on sale in a shop around the corner. ✉ *Market Hill,* ☎ *01394/450277. No credit cards. Closed Sun.–Thurs. evenings in winter.*

£££ **Crown and Castle.** Near Orford Castle is this small, well-established hotel in an 18th-century building thought to have had smuggling connections. The tone is set by the timber facade, and inside the rooms are small, cozy, and very quiet. A snug little bar serves lunches and dinners, including fresh fish, but the most attractive aspect is the outdoor terrace, with its grandstand views of the castle. In summer, this is a real suntrap. ✉ *Market Hill, IP12 2LJ,* ☎ *01394/450205,* FAX *01394/450176. 20 rooms with bath. Restaurant, bar, lobby lounge. AE, DC, MC, V.*

Snape

8 mi north of Orford (along B1078 through Tunstall Forest, then B1069), 12 mi northeast of Woodbridge, 37 mi northeast of Colchester.

A small village of the river Alde, Snape is celebrated now as the locale for **Snape Maltings,** an opera house and general arts center hosting the Aldeburgh Festival (☞ Aldeburgh, *below*), founded by the composer Benjamin Britten. Theater goers delight in the auditorium, renovated from a disused Victorian malt works. It's well worth a stop at any time of year to enjoy the Maltings' peaceful riverside setting and perhaps pause for a coffee in the friendly cafeteria. There are also crafts shops and an art gallery at the center. ☎ *01728/688303.* 🎫 *Free.* ⏲ *Daily 10–5.*

Aldeburgh

54 *5 mi east of Snape, 41 mi northeast of Colchester.*

Aldeburgh is now a quiet seaside resort—apart from in June, when the town fills up with festival-goers. Its shingle beach is backed by a long promenade lined with candy-colored dwellings, some no bigger than a doll's house. It was Benjamin Britten's home for some time—though he was actually born in the busy seaside resort of Lowestoft, some 30 miles to the north—and it was here that the composer grew interested in the story of Aldeburgh's native son, the poet George Crabbe, ultimately turning the life story of the poet into the celebrated modern opera, *Peter Grimes*—a piece that perfectly captures the atmosphere of the Suffolk coasts. The sole survivor of more important days in Aldeburgh is the **Elizabethan Moot Hall,** built of flint and timber. When erected, it stood in the center of a thriving 16th-century town; now it's just a few steps from the beach, a mute witness to the erosive powers of the North Sea. ✉ *Market Cross, Sea Front,* ☎ *01728/452871.* 🎫 *45p.* ⏲ *Apr.–May, weekends 2:30–5; June and Sept., daily 2:30–5; July–Aug., daily 10–12:30 and 2:30–5.*

The Arts

The most important arts festival in East Anglia, and one of the best known in Great Britain, is the **Aldeburgh Festival,** held for two weeks in June every year in Snape, at the **Maltings Concert Hall** (☎ 01728/453543). Founded by the composer Benjamin Britten, the festival naturally concentrates on music, but there are also related exhibitions, poetry readings, and even walks. Snape Maltings also offers a year-round program of events, such as the two-day Aldeburgh Folk Festival, held each July to celebrate traditional English folk music, and the Britten Festival in October. *Festival program published (Mar.) by Aldeburgh Foundation,* ✉ *High St., Aldeburgh IP15 5AX,* ☎ *01728/452935,* FAX *01728/ 452715.*

Dining and Lodging

£££ ✕ **The Lighthouse.** A café by day and restaurant by night, this stylish establishment relies exclusively on locally grown—or caught—produce. Seafood, including oysters and Cromer crabs, is a specialty: It comes simply but imaginatively cooked, usually with an interesting sauce. Desserts, like the creamy bread-and-butter pudding, are particularly good. Home-made cakes are also for sale during the daytime. ✉ 77 *High St.,* ☎ *01728/453377. Oct.–Mar., no dinner Sun. and closed Mon.*

£££–£££ ✕🏨 **The Brudenell.** Parts of the very comfortable Brudenell date back to the 16th century, although they're now well hidden beneath a pleasing turn-of-the-century facade. The attractive, spacious guest rooms are furnished in bright colors. Those that face directly across Aldeburgh's shingle beach are available for a small supplementary charge; the remainder look out over the river and marshes. Seven rooms are suitable for guests in wheelchairs. Light meals and beverages are served during the day on a large, sunny, terrace, while on winter evenings a log fire blazes in the elegant lounge bar. Dinner is a real treat; with its sweeping panoramic windows offering uninterrupted vistas of the North Sea, the split-level restaurant has the feel of a luxury cruise ship. Set menus focus on freshly caught local fish, though you can also opt for such traditional English fare as roast pork or lamb cutlets. ✉ *The Parade, IP15 5BU,* ☎ *01728/452071,* FAX *01728/454082. 47 rooms with bath. Restaurant, bar, lobby lounge. AE, DC, MC, V.*

Southwold

55 *4 mi north of Dunwich, 15 mi north of Aldeburgh, 32 mi southeast of Norwich.*

This attractive seaside town is an idyllic place to spend a day. Old-fashioned beach huts painted in bright colors huddle together against the wind on the shingle beach, while up in the town center a pleasing ensemble of old houses lines the main street and surrounds the central green. There aren't many "sights," but since the whole town gives you the sensation of being transported back in time, this doesn't matter very much. George Orwell's parents lived at 36 High Street during the 1930s, though for a house more typical of the town visit the **Southwold Museum,** which is in a Dutch-gabled cottage. ✉ *Victoria St.,* ☎ *01502/723925.* 🎫 *Free.* ⏲ *Mid-Apr.–Sept., daily 2:30–4:30.*

Dining and Lodging

£££ ✕🏨 **Swan Hotel.** This lovely, 17th-century inn near the beach (scenes from the film *David Copperfield* were shot here) features spacious public rooms and decent-size bedrooms decorated in traditional English-country style. Eighteen secluded and quiet garden rooms are set in a superb central position around the old bowling green. In the charming public rooms, you can comfortably sit over tea—or something stronger on a winter's day. The hotel staff prides itself on personal service. The restaurant's bay windows overlook the street; dishes are mainly traditional English, accompanied by a similarly excellent wine list. ✉ *Market Pl., IP18 6EG,* ☎ *01502/722186,* FAX *01502/724800. 45 rooms with bath. Restaurant (reservations essential), bar. AE, DC, MC, V.*

££–£££ ★ ✕🏨 **Crown Hotel.** Like the Swan, the Crown is owned by the old family firm of Adnams's brewery—the major employer in Southwold. In the simple but tastefully decorated yellow-and-gray bar lounge, faultlessly prepared fish dishes—Cromer dressed crab or seafood salad; pan-fried John Dory, cod, brill; or whatever else is fresh—are served at shared wooden trestle tables. You can also dine more formally, with set menus of the same food, in the adjacent restaurant. The Crown has one of the best wine lists in England; you can try a selection by the glass or choose from the enormous stock with the assistance of the friendly, knowledgeable staff. The building itself is 17th century, so though public rooms are spacious enough, you might find some of the guest rooms on the small side. Antique furniture and a pleasing decorative eye by the management more than compensate, however. ✉ *90 High St., IP18 6DP,* ☎ *01502/722275,* FAX *01502/724805. 12 rooms, 9 with bath or shower. Restaurant (reservations essential, closed 2nd wk in Jan.), bar. AE, DC, MC, V.*

Walberswick

8 mi south of Southwold, 15 mi north of Aldeburgh.

This charming little village has been the haunt of artists, writers, and photographers for many years: not for nothing is it sometimes dubbed "Hampstead-on-Sea." The Scottish Art Nouveau architect Charles Rennie Mackintosh lived in Walberswick between 1914 and 1915 and painted many watercolors of plants and flowers here. Walberswick is closer to Southwold on foot than it is by car, separated as it is by the mouth of the river Blyth, over which there's a footbridge (about a mile inland), but no main road bridge. On summer weekends (May–Sept.) you'll find a boatman who ferries foot passengers over the water in a rowboat every few minutes, 9–12:30 and 2–5 (25p). On the far side, you can see the church tower of Southwold piercing the horizon, a half-hour's walk away through the fields.

An unusual wildlife attraction is the **Otter Trust** at Earsham (☎ 01986/893470), just across the Norfolk border from Bungay, Suffolk, where otters can be observed in near-natural conditions; there are also attractive river walks.

BEYOND THE FENS: LINCOLN, BOSTON, AND STAMFORD

The fens of northern Cambridgeshire pass imperceptibly into the three divisions of Lincolnshire. Holland, Kesteven, and Lindsey are all parts of the great county, divided administratively. Holland borders the Isle of Ely and the delightfully named Soke of Peterborough; this marshland spreads far and wide south of the Wash, the names of the district almost reflecting the squelch of mud the inhabitants of pre-drainage times must have encountered daily. The chief attractions are two towns: Lincoln, with its magnificent cathedral, and Stamford, to the southwest.

The countryside around Lincoln, especially the Lincolnshire Wolds (chalk hills) to the northeast, consists of rolling hills and copses, with dry-stone (unmortared) walls dividing well-tended fields. The unspoiled rural area of the Wolds, strikingly evoked in Tennyson's poetry, is particularly worth a visit, while the long coastline with its miles of sandy beaches and its North Sea air offers all the usual, if occasionally tacky, seaside facilities for the family. Tulips are the pride and joy of south Lincolnshire. Perhaps the colorful fields of bloom don't quite match those of the other Holland across the North Sea, but certainly take second place—and draw thousands from all parts of Britain to view the Holland and Kesteven bulb fields during the spring.

Numbers in the margin correspond to points of interest on the Lincolnshire map.

Lincoln

★ 56 *93 mi northwest of Cambridge, 97 mi northwest of Norwich.*

Lincoln's crowning glory is the great **Cathedral of St. Mary.** (Try to see it at night, when it's floodlit.) Commanding views from the top of the steep limestone escarpment above the river Witham reveal the strategic advantages of the city's site from earliest times. Weapons from the pre-Roman, tribal era have been found in the river; later, the Romans (always quick to see the potential of a site) left their usual permanent underpinning; and a wealth of medieval buildings—quite apart from the cathedral and castle—seem to tumble together down the steep hillside lanes leading to the river.

The **cathedral** is the most obvious starting point for any visitor to Lincoln. For hundreds of years, it was the tallest building in Europe, but this magnificent medieval building is now among the least known of the European cathedrals. It was begun in 1072 by the Norman bishop Remigius; the Romanesque church he built was irremediably damaged, first by fire, then by earthquake (in 1185), but you can still see parts of the ancient structure at the west front. The next great phase of building, initiated by Bishop Hugh of Avalon, is mainly 13th century in character. The west front, topped by the two west towers, is a unique structure, giving tremendous breadth to the entrance. It is best seen from the 14th-century Exchequer Gate arch in front of the cathedral, or from the castle battlements beyond.

Inside, a breathtaking impression of space and unity belie the many centuries of building and rebuilding. The stained-glass window at the north end of the transept, known as the Dean's Eye, is one of the earliest (13th-century) traceried windows, while its opposite number at the south end shows a 14th-century sophistication in its tracery (i.e., interlaced designs). St. Hugh's Choir in front of the altar and the Angel Choir at the east end behind it have remarkable vaulted ceilings and intricate carvings. Look for the famous Lincoln Imp upon the pillar nearest to St. Hugh's shrine, and even farther up (binoculars or a telephoto lens will help) to see the 30 angels who are playing musical instruments and who give this part of the cathedral its name.

Among the many chapels is one commemorating Lincolnshire's connections with North America and Australia. Through a side door on the north side lies the chapter house, a 10-sided building that sometimes housed the medieval Parliament of England during the reigns of Edward I and Edward II. The chapter house is connected to the 13th-century cloisters, notable for its grotesquely amusing ceiling bosses. The cathedral library, a restrained building by Christopher Wren, was built onto the north side of the cloisters after the original library collapsed. ☎ *01522/544544.* 🎫 *£2.50 donation requested.* ⏲ *Late May–Aug., Mon.–Sat. 7:15 AM–8 PM, Sun. 7:15–6; Sept.–Apr., Mon.–Sat. 7:15–6, Sun. 7:15–5.*

In the **Minster Yard,** which surrounds the cathedral on three sides, are buildings of various periods, including graceful examples of Georgian architecture. A statue of Alfred, Lord Tennyson, who was born in Lincolnshire, stands on the green near the chapter house exterior, and the medieval **Bishops Old Palace**, on the south side, is open to the public. ☎ *01522/527468.* 🎫 *80p.* ⏲ *Apr.–Sept., daily 10–6.*

NEED A BREAK? The **Pimento** tearoom on Steep Hill (☎ 01522/536361) has a huge selection of leaf teas (served in curious-looking pots), good coffee and home-made cakes.

Lincoln Castle, facing the cathedral across Exchequer Gate, was originally built on two great mounds by William the Conqueror in 1068, incorporating part of the remains of the Roman garrison walls. The castle was a military base until the 17th century, after which it was used primarily as a prison. In the extraordinary prison chapel you can see the cage-like stalls in which Victorian convicts were compelled to listen to sermons. One of the four surviving copies of Magna Carta, signed by King John at Runnymede in 1215, is on display in the same building. ✉ *Castle Hill,* ☎ *01522/511068.* 🎫 *£2.* ⏲ *Apr.–Oct.,*

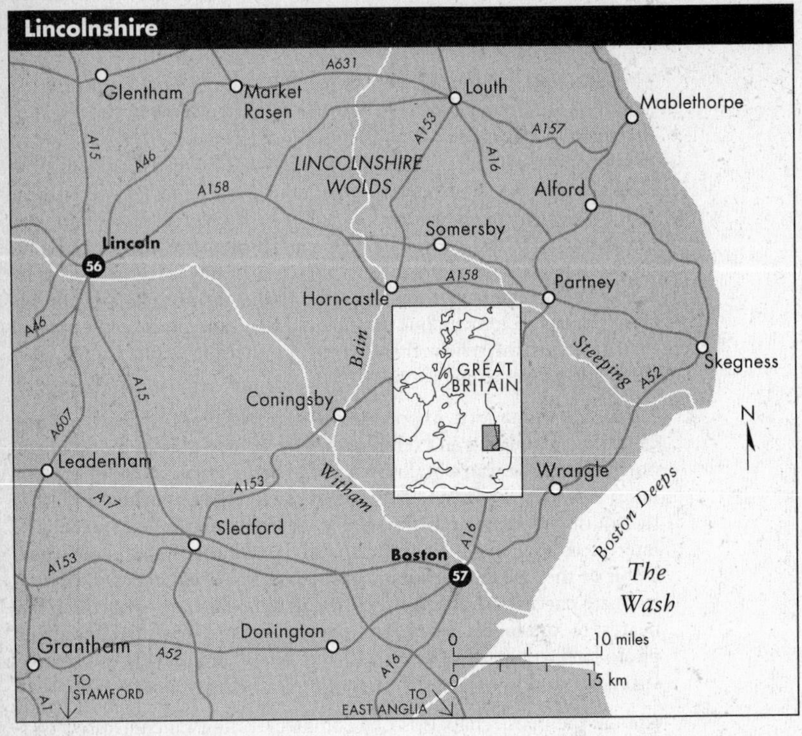

Mon.–Sat. 9:30–5:30, Sun. 11:30–5:30; Nov.–Mar., Mon.–Sat. 9:30–4, Sun. 11–4.

The Roman presence in Lincoln is at its most evident near the cathedral. At the end of Bailgate, traffic still passes under the **Newport Arch,** once the north gate of the Roman city, *Lindum Colonia.* Ermine Street, stretching north from the arch to the river Humber, replaced an important Roman road lying 8 feet below the surface. The foundations of the east gate have been excavated and permanently exposed in the forecourt of the Forte Crest Hotel, and the columns of a 175-foot Roman colonnade are marked along the roadway in Bailgate.

South of the cathedral, narrow medieval streets cling to the hillside, with the aptly named **Steep Hill** at their center. **Jew's House** (✉ The Strait) dating from the early 12th century, is one of several well-preserved domestic buildings in this area. The **Usher Gallery** has an interesting collection of watches and clocks donated by its benefactor, James Ward Usher, a jeweler who invented the legend of the Lincoln Imp. The gallery also contains memorabilia connected with the poet Tennyson, who was born in Lincolnshire. ✉ *Lindum Rd.,* ☎ *01522/527980.* 🎟 *£1.* ⏲ *Mon.–Sat. 10–5:30, Sun. 2:30–5.*

In the city center you can walk under the 15th-century **Stonebow arch** on the site of an old Roman gate. Above it is the **Guildhall,** which houses the city's civic regalia. The river Witham flows unobtrusively under the incongruously named **High Bridge**—a low, vaulted Norman bridge topped by 16th-century, timber-frame houses. West of High Bridge, the river opens out into **Brayford Pool,** still busy with river traffic (and, unfortunately, road traffic, as a large, unsightly, multistory parking lot has been built on one side). Here you can rent various kinds of boats. In addition, from April to September small cruisers tour the river Witham, showing you the city from the water.

Contact Cathedral City Cruises at Brayford Wharf East, ☏ 01522/546853.

The Arts

The **Theater Royal** (✉ Clasketgate, ☏ 01522/525555) is a fine Victorian theater previewing shows before their London runs and offering tour productions. There are also occasionally concerts on Sunday.

Dining and Lodging

££–£££ ★ ✕ **Jew's House.** Situated in one of Lincoln's oldest buildings (12th century), the restaurant has an intimate atmosphere enhanced by antique tables and oil paintings. The cosmopolitan menu, featuring Continental specialties, changes daily, and the restaurant is renowned for its fresh fish and rich desserts, all homemade. *✉ 15 The Strait, ☏ 01522/524851. AE, DC, MC, V. No lunch Mon. Closed Sun. and 2–4 wks in Feb.*

£–££ ✕ **Wig and Mitre.** This interesting downtown pub/café/restaurant stays open all day until 11 PM, offering an extremely wide range of food from breakfast to full evening meals. Produce comes from the local markets, and dishes may include fresh fish, warming seasonal soups, European specialties, or classic English pies and roasts. *✉ 29 Steep Hill, ☏ 01522/535190. AE, DC, MC, V. Closed Dec. 25.*

£££–££££ ★ **White Hart.** Lincoln's most elegant hotel is luxuriously furnished with a wealth of antiques, including some fine clocks and china. The establishment has been a hotel for 600 years, reflecting a volume of experience that makes the service personal and extremely friendly. Each of the bedrooms is individually decorated; many are furnished with antiques, and hardwoods such as walnut and mahogany abound. No-smoking accommodations are available. The hotel abuts the cathedral grounds, although cathedral views are obscured in certain rooms by the surrounding buildings. *✉ Bailgate, LN1 3AR, ☏ 01522/526222, FAX 01522/531798. 35 rooms with bath, 13 suites. Restaurant, bar, coffee shop. AE, DC, MC, V.*

££ **D'Isney Place Hotel.** This charming small hotel is a Georgian and Victorian building near the cathedral. If you like privacy, it's ideal: There's no lounge or other communal space, but breakfast is served, on Minton china, to guests in the beautifully decorated bedrooms. *✉ Eastgate, ☏ 01522/538881, FAX 01522/511321. 17 rooms with bath. AE, DC, MC, V.*

££ **Hillcrest Hotel.** A small, unpretentious hotel, formerly a Victorian rectory, Hillcrest is in a very quiet area about a five minutes' walk north of the cathedral. The interior features simple but pleasing modern furnishings, and service is friendly and relaxed. Rooms at the back look out over the garden and arboretum. *✉ 15 Lindum Terr., LN2 5RT, ☏ FAX 01522/510182. 17 rooms with bath. Restaurant, bar. AE, MC, V. Closed 2 wks at Christmas.*

Shopping

Lincoln's main shopping area, mostly pedestrianized, is at the bottom of the hill below the cathedral, around the Stonebow gateway and Guildhall, and along High Street. However, the best stores are on Bailgate, Steep Hill, and the medieval streets leading directly down from the cathedral and castle. The **Cobb Hall Craft Centre** (✉ St. Paul's La., off Bailgate, ☏ 01522/527317) is a small mall of crafts shops and workshops, selling clocks, candles, and ornaments. Steep Hill has several good bookstores, antiques shops, and crafts and art galleries, such as **Harding House, Steep Hill Galleries,** and **The Long Gallery** (✉ Top of High St.). **David Hansord** (✉ 32 Steep Hill, ☏ 01522/530044) specializes in antiques, especially antique scientific instruments.

Boston

57 *31 mi from Lincoln.*

This town, of course, is of interest to American visitors who like to recall that it was from here that, in 1620, Puritans Isaac Johnson and John Winthrop showed their disapproval of the then-prevailing religious conditions by crossing the Atlantic and helping to found the Massachusetts town of the same name. The Puritans had first tried to set sail for Holland in 1607, but they were arrested, tried, and imprisoned. The town's leading landmark remains the Boston Stump, the lantern tower of the 14th-century **Church of St. Botolph.** With a height of 288 feet, it can be seen for 20 miles from both land and sea and once served to house a light that not only guided ships coming to the old port but also served to direct wayfarers crossing the treacherous marshes; today, it's a directional beacon for aircraft as well. The 15th-century guildhall, now the **Boston Borough Museum,** contains the courtroom where the Pilgrims were tried and the cells where they and their courageous hopes were held. ✉ *St. Mary's Guildhall, South St.,* ☎ *01205/365954.* 🎫 *90p; free on Thurs; admission includes 45-min personal audio tour.* 🕐 *Mon.–Sat. 10–5, Sun. (Apr.–Sept. only) 1:30–5.*

Among several other reminders of Boston's transatlantic links is the early 18th-century **Fydell House,** next to the guildhall, now an adult education center, where a room is set aside for visitors from Boston, Massachusetts. ✉ *South St.,* ☎ *01205/351520.* 🎫 *Free.* 🕐 *Weekdays 9:30–12:30 and 1:30–4:30.*

OFF THE BEATEN PATH

GRANTHAM – This town, 30 miles west of Boston, is worth visiting only if you're curious to see the hometown of former British Prime Minister Margaret Thatcher, whose father was a grocer here. Her birthplace at 2 North Parade is now a restaurant and tearoom.

NEED A BREAK?

The Beehive pub (✉ 10–11 Castlegate, ☎ 01476/67794) in Grantham is famous for its beehive (full of bees) in a tree outside, which has been there since the beginning of the 19th century. Ploughman's lunches—bread, cheese, onions, and pickles—are served, as well as other bar snacks and soups.

Stamford

35 mi southwest of Boston, 14 mi northwest of Peterborough, 47 mi northwest of Cambridge.

One of the prettiest small towns in England, Stamford is set on a hillside overlooking a river and has an extremely well-preserved center, thanks to being designated England's first conservation area in 1967. It's a delightful place to stroll around, admiring the harmonious mixture of Georgian and medieval architecture.

Less than a mile outside Stamford is **Burghley House,** an architectural masterpiece acknowledged as "the largest and grandest house of the first Elizabethan age." The mansion—celebrated for its roofscape bristling with pepperpot chimneys and slat-roof towers—was built in 1587 by William Cecil, first Baron Burghley, when he was Elizabeth I's high treasurer. Set in fine parkland, it has 18 of the most sumptuous staterooms in England, with carvings by Grinling Gibbons and ceiling paintings by Verrio, as well as innumerable paintings and a priceless porcelain collection. A recent chatelain, the sixth Marquess of Exeter, was the famous Olympic runner whose life story inspired the 1980 *Chariots of Fire* film. ☎ *01780/52451.* 🎫 *£5.50.* ⏲ *Apr.–Sept., daily 11–5.*

EAST ANGLIA A TO Z

Arriving and Departing

By Bus

National Express (☎ 0990/808080) serves the region from London's Victoria Coach Station. Average travel times: 2½ hours to Bury St. Edmunds, two hours to Cambridge, two hours to Colchester, four hours to Lincoln, and three hours to Norwich.

By Car

From London, Cambridge (54 miles) is just off M11. At exit 9, M11 connects with A11 to Norwich (114 miles); A14 off A11, goes to Bury St. Edmunds. A12 from London goes through east Suffolk via Colchester, Ipswich, and Great Yarmouth. For Lincoln (131 miles), take A1 via Huntingdon, Peterborough, and Grantham to A46 at Newark-on-Trent. A more scenic alternative is to leave A1 at Grantham and take A607 to Lincoln.

By Plane

Stansted Airport (☎ 01279/680500) in Essex is one of the three major "London" airports. Air UK flies out of **Norwich Airport** (☎ 01603/424244); its service to Amsterdam links with flights to the United States.

By Train

The entire region is served by trains from London's Liverpool Street Station; in addition, there are trains to Cambridge and Lincoln from King's Cross Station, as well as from Liverpool Street. Full information on trains to East Anglia is available from **National Train Enquiries** (☎ 01603/765676 or 01473/693396). Average travel times are 60 minutes to Colchester, 52–90 minutes to Cambridge, one hour 50 minutes to Norwich, and two hours to Lincoln.

Getting Around

By Bus

Eastern Counties (☎ 01603/613613) provides local bus services for Norfolk and parts of the surrounding counties. An **Eastern Counties Explorer ticket** (available on board the bus) gives a day's unlimited travel on the whole network for £4.95; a family pass for two parents and two children costs £9.95. Cambridgeshire's largest bus company is **Cambus** (☎ 01223/317740), which also sells daily and weekly tickets valid for unlimited travel within the city of Cambridge and the county.

By Car

East Anglia has few fast main roads. The principal routes are those covered above (☞ Arriving and Departing by Car, *above*), but once off the A roads, traveling within the region often means taking country lanes with many twists and turns. These are also used by slow-moving farm vehicles, but as the countryside is mainly flat, open land, visibility is excellent.

By Train

You can get a one-day, round-trip ticket for £7 from any station in Norfolk or Suffolk that lets you disembark to explore any of the little towns en route. A Day Ranger ticket from Lincolnshire costs £12 and enables you to explore a wide area, including Cambridge and Ely. A seven-day Regional Rover ticket for unlimited travel in the Anglia Railways region is also available for £49 from major regional train stations. For local travel information, call **National Rail Enquiries** at Cambridge (☎ 0990/468468), Lincoln (☎ 01301/34022), Ipswich (☎ 01473/693396), or Norwich (☎ 01603/765676).

Guided Tours

Qualified guides for walking tours of the major towns, including Bury St. Edmunds, Cambridge, Ely, Colchester, Ipswich, Norwich, and Lincoln can be booked through the respective tourist offices.

Guide Friday (☎ 01223/62444) operates open-top bus tours of Cambridge, taking in the Backs, the colleges, and the American war cemetery (Easter–Sept. every 15 min; Oct.–Easter every 30 min). The tours start from Cambridge train station, but can be picked up at any of Guide Friday's specially marked bus stops throughout the city; tickets can be bought from the driver (£6.50).

Contacts and Resources

Car-Rental Agencies

Cambridge: Avis ✉ 245 Mill Rd., ☎ 01223/212551; **Budget Rent-a-Car,** ✉ 303–305 Newmarket Rd., ☎ 01223/323838; **Hertz,** ✉ Willhire Ltd., Barnwell Rd., ☎ 01223/414600.

Colchester: Avis, ✉ 213 Shrub End Rd., ☎ 01206/41133; **Hertz,** ✉ Willhire Ltd., Union Chapel, Old Ipswich Rd., ☎ 01206/231801.

Lincoln: Avis, ✉ Fina petrol station, Riseholm Rd., ☎ 01522/ 511200; **Eurodollar,** ✉ Newland Rd., ☎ 01522/512233.

Norwich: Avis, ✉ Norwich Airport, Cromer Rd., ☎ 01603/416719; **Budget Rent-a-Car,** ✉ Denmark Opening, Sprowston Rd., ☎ 01603/484004; **Hertz,** ✉ Norwich Airport, Cromer Rd., ☎ 01603/404010.

Fishing

Fishing lodges at Grafham (☎ 01480/810531), Pitsford (☎ 01604/781350), and Rutland (☎ 01780/86770) reservoirs sell day permits and offer boat rental and weekend courses. For other information about the fishing season, angling hotels and licenses, contact the East Anglia Tourist Board (☞ Visitor Information, *below*).

Travel Agencies

American Express: ✉ 25 Sidney St., Cambridge, ☎ 01223/351636.

Thomas Cook: ✉ 18 Market St., Cambridge, ☎ 01223/67724; Grafton Centre, Cambridge, ☎ 01223/322611; ✉ 4 Cornhill Pavement, Lincoln, ☎ 01522/510070; ✉ 15 St. Stephens St., Norwich, ☎ 01603/621547; ✉ 14 London St., ☎ 01603/761876.

Visitor Information

East Anglia Tourist Board, ✉ Toppesfield Hall, Hadleigh, Suffolk IP7 7DN, ☎ 01473/822922, FAX 01473/823063. **Boston:** ✉ Blackfriars Arts Centre, Spain La., ☎ 01205/356656. **Bury St. Edmunds:** ✉ 6 Angel Hill, ☎ 01284/764667. **Cambridge:** ✉ Wheeler St., ☎ 01223/322640. **Colchester:** ✉ 1 Queen St., ☎ 01206/282920. **Ely:** ✉ Oliver Cromwell's House, 29 St. Mary's St., ☎ 01353/662062. **Great Yarmouth:** ✉ Marine Parade, ☎ 01493/842195. **Ipswich:** ✉ St. Stephen's Church, St. Stephen's La., ☎ 01473/258070. **King's Lynn:** ✉ Old Gaol House, Saturday Market Pl., ☎ 01553/763044. **Lincoln:** ✉ 9 Castle Hill, ☎ 01522/529828. **Newmarket:** ✉ 63 The Rookery, ☎ 01638/667200. **Norwich:** ✉ Guildhall, Gaol Hill, ☎ 01603/666071. **Stamford:** ✉ Broad St., ☎ 01780/55611.

14 Yorkshire

Leeds, Bradford, Haworth, York, Scarborough, and Whitby

On a stormy day on the Yorkshire Moors, it's not hard to imagine Emily Brontë's Heathcliff from Wuthering Heights *galloping on horseback over their cloud-swept ridges. Centered around Haworth, Brontë Country remains a pilgrimage for many. Here, too, are the stomping grounds of another author, James Herriot, the celebrated veterinarian who set up shop in Wensleydale. More worldly attractions await: the largest Gothic church in the country at York, picture-perfect villages such as Hutton-le-Hole, and splendidly elegant Castle Howard.*

Updated by Jules Brown

YORKSHIRE IS A COMPLEX SECRET, shared by relatively few. Coming to terms with this region appears altogether too daunting for the majority of casual tourists. They must be truly passionate travelers—passionate enough to endure the blustery moors on a pilgrimage to the haunts of the Brontës, cultured enough to make a special excursion trip to visit isolated Castle Howard, or patient enough to discover gems of Victorian architecture hidden beneath Manchester's much maligned reputation as England's ugliest modern metropolis.

If Yorkshire presents many faces to visitors and locals alike, it remains an intensely rural region. The most rugged of its landscapes are the Yorkshire Moors, a vast area of lonely moorland, inspiration of Emily Brontë's 19th-century novel *Wuthering Heights* (and if ever a work of fiction grew out of the landscape in which its author lived, it was surely this). Brilliant at times with spring flowers and heather, the moors can change dangerously—often within a few minutes—to stormy weather, when you'll be lucky to see as far as the next cloud-swept ridge. Between the bleak areas of moorland and the rocky Pennine hills lie lush, green valleys known as the Yorkshire Dales, where the high rainfall produces luxuriant vegetation, swift rivers, sparkling streams, and waterfalls: The villages here—immortalized through the books of the famous veterinarian, James Herriot—are among the most utterly peaceful in England, though many burst into life as summer walking bases.

But there's also a gritty, urban aspect to Yorkshire, whose towns have changed the very course of British history. Two of Britain's major industrial centers are here: Leeds and Bradford, in the heart of Yorkshire. The white heat of the 19th-century Industrial Revolution was forged, to a great extent, in these cities; today, they are slowly being rescued from modern decline. More pleasing is the northern, walled city of York, dominated by the towers of its great Minster. Settled originally by Romans and Vikings, it was once England's second most important city, and is the best preserved medieval city in the country and home of the largest and, for many, the most noble cathedral in Britain.

There is no county called Yorkshire per se: The region covered in this chapter sprawls over the counties of West Yorkshire, North Yorkshire, and Humberside. As touring bases, we recommend York, Haworth—the center of Brontë Country—or the North Yorkshire seaside resort of Scarborough. Whether you're out to see untamed natural beauty or great medieval art, a journey here will be well worth the effort, and effort it will take: This is not an area for day trips—even the fastest trains take about three hours from London to York.

Pleasures and Pastimes

Dining

Exploring Yorkshire, with its fresh air and exhilarating hilltop walks, positively encourages hearty appetites. Happily, locally produced meat (especially lamb) and vegetables are excellent; roast beef dinners come with Yorkshire pudding, the famous popover-like pastry traditionally cooked under the meat and served with gravy. Fish from the coast is a real treat with freshly fried chips (thick french fries)—cod or haddock is the main local catch. Look for freshly baked bread and homemade cakes, at their best in Yorkshire tearooms. Don't miss out on Wensleydale cheese, which has a subtle, delicate flavor that delivers a slightly honeyed aftertaste. As they are fond of saying, "An apple pie wi'owt tha cheese is like a kiss wi'owt a squeeze."

CATEGORY	COST*
££££	over £40
£££	£25–£40
££	£15–£25
£	under £15

**per person, including first course, main course, dessert, and VAT; excluding drinks*

Hiking and Walking

Some of Britain's finest long-distance footpaths cut through the region and incorporate both coastal and moorland sections. The Dales National Park is criss-crossed with trails and long-distance paths; the North Yorkshire Moors have long, empty swathes of land for tramping; and the dramatic coastline offers a variety of craggy cliff walks. Leading trails include the Cleveland Way (108 miles), from Helmsley to Filey; the hard-going Lyke-Wake Walk (40 miles), from Osmotherley to Ravenscar; and the eastern section of the Coast-to-Coast Walk (190 miles), which starts or finishes in Robin Hood's Bay. In addition, the Dales Way (80 miles) connects Leeds and Bradford with the Lake District; while perhaps the greatest of all English walks, the Pennine Way, which runs from the Peak District to Scotland, has a central section that runs through the Yorkshire Dales.

Lodging

Accommodations to suit all tastes and pocketbooks are available—look for farmhouse bed-and-breakfasts as you're traveling around the countryside, and when you want to be in the center of things, try town inns and hotels, which have more in the way of creature comforts and sophisticated facilities. Combine hotel stays with a couple of nights in countryside bed-and-breakfasts to get a real flavor of northern hospitality and cuisine. In seaside resorts, rooms fill very quickly in July and August; while in winter in the dales and moors, some places close for the season—always call ahead if you're going to remote parts.

CATEGORY	COST*
££££	over £110
£££	£60–£110
££	£50–£60
£	under £50

**All prices are for two people sharing a double room, including service, breakfast, and VAT.*

The Monastic Past

Among the most romantic and picturesque sights that Britain has to offer, the ruined monastic remains of Rievaulx Abbey, Whitby, and Fountains Abbey are must-dos for many travelers in Yorkshire. The monks of medieval Yorkshire were among the richest in Europe by virtue of the wool trade that they conducted from their vast religious estates in the north and they left a wealth of richly decorated and appointed monastic buildings, most in ruins since the 16th-century Dissolution. Thanks to the countless poems written about these ruins by the great Victorian poets, these sites became world-famous for their powerful evocation of life of the Middle Ages.

Exploring Yorkshire

Yorkshire is the largest English region to explore (its fiercely proud inhabitants would say the *only* English region worth exploring). As such, visitors need to plan carefully before launching themselves on a tour, and this chapter carves Yorkshire into separate geographical regions in an attempt to focus attention on the best it has to offer.

The industrial heartland is West Yorkshire, where the cities of Leeds and Bradford were at the forefront of both the late medieval woolen trade and the 19th-century Industrial Revolution. What the tourist office likes to call Brontë Country—basically Haworth, home of the Brontë family—is just to the northwest, while northward spread the hills, valleys, and villages of the Yorkshire Dales, stomping ground of James Herriot, the celebrated veterinarian. In the center of the region, York—for some, the most attractive city in England—deserves special attention, and there's real interest in its environs, too, with day trips to be made to places as diverse as the spa town of Harrogate and the magnificent Fountains Abbey.

Moving east to the coast, Yorkshire reveals itself to be a seaside holiday destination, though never one that will win prizes for summerlike weather. But fine beaches, and a fascinating history await visitors to the resort of Scarborough, the former whaling port of Whitby, Robin Hood's Bay—an erstwhile smuggler's haunt—and the traditional fishing village of Staithes. Finally, every visitor should strike inland to the North Moors National Park, even if it's only to drive back toward York or on to Scotland. Delightful, isolated stone villages, dramatic moorland walks, Rievaulx Abbey, and splendidly elegant Castle Howard are all within easy reach.

Great Itineraries

You could drive across Yorkshire in under a day (as many do, on the way to Scotland), but you would spend little quality time anywhere. Two days would give the opportunity for a night in rural Yorkshire, the Dales or the Moors perhaps, followed by a night in York. However, only with five days does an itinerary begin to take shape: With this amount of time, you could stop longer in York and visit the coast, as well as allow yourself time to get off the beaten track a bit to seek out the abbeys, castles, and old moorland villages. You'll still have to move fast, though, if you want to see every region of Yorkshire—in this case, budget for seven days. This lets you dawdle up the coast or in the Dales, spending an extra night here or there, or perhaps even walking from one village to another.

Numbers in the text correspond to numbers in the margin and on the maps.

IF YOU HAVE 3 DAYS

Start in **York** ⑭, quintessential city of Yorkshire, where—if you arrive early enough in the day—you'll be able to make a short side trip to the coast at **Whitby** ㉞. The next day, make an early start and head for **Fountains Abbey** ㉘, before turning south to the spa town of **Harrogate** ㉖; **Knaresborough** ㉗ and its petrifying well is close enough to make a side trip here, too. The following day you can devote to the Yorkshire Dales, driving to **Skipton** ⑧ and then on to **Grassington** ⑨, and even Wensleydale and Swaledale, before returning to **York.**

IF YOU HAVE 5 DAYS

York ⑭ makes a good starting-point, from where you can head directly to West Yorkshire and **Bradford** ④, taking in the town museums and the model-town of Saltaire before heading on to **Haworth** ⑤, where you overnight. See the Brontë sites in the morning and then head up through the Yorkshire Dales, visiting **Skipton** ⑧ and **Malham** ⑩ before stopping for the night in or around the lovely village of **Grassington** ⑨. The next day head for **Fountains Abbey** ㉘ and **Ripon** ㉙, and then turn south for **Harrogate** ㉖, before finally returning to **York,** where you spend the night (and much of the next day exploring the city). In mid-afternoon, drive across the North York Moors to spend a fourth night on the coast at **Whitby** ㉞, a very scenic fishing town with a fine abbey. Your return to **York** the next day can then be made along the convoluted moor roads leading south in order to take in the delighful villages of **Danby** ㊱ and **Hutton-le-Hole** ㊲ and an afternoon call on spectacular **Castle Howard** ㊵.

IF YOU HAVE 7 DAYS

Starting in **York** ⑭, head for **Bradford** ④ and its museums, and make time for a curry lunch, before spending the afternoon at the nearby model-town of Saltaire. It's then just a short drive to **Haworth** ⑤ for an overnight stop in Brontë Country, though you'll have to wait until next morning to see the sights. After this, you can afford to meander up through the Yorkshire Dales, via **Skipton** ⑧ and **Malham** ⑩ before stopping for the night in **Grassington** ⑨. The next day, soak up more remote scenery as you tour the northern dales, Wensleydale and Swaledale, before hitting the main roads and heading south, via **Fountains Abbey** ㉘, to the spa town of **Harrogate** ㉖. After all this driving, you only have a short journey to **York** the following day, perhaps calling in at **Knaresborough** ㉗ on the way to see the petrifying well. Stay in **York** for two nights, which will give you time to see everything and then early on the morning of departure aim for Helmsley—with a sightseeing stop at either **Rievaulx Abbey** ㊴ or **Castle Howard** ㊵—before driving across the moors to **Danby** ㊱ and on to **Whitby** ㉞ for your overnight stop. The next day, return to **York** along the coast via **Robin Hood's Bay** ㉝ and **Scarborough** ㉜.

When to Tour Yorkshire

Summer is undoubtedly the best time to visit Yorkshire, especially the coastal areas and moors, when there are festivals and regattas, though you can expect resorts and walking centers to be overcrowded, and to have to book accommodation well in advance. York city center will also be packed shoulder-to-shoulder with visitors. Spring and fall bring their own rewards: less crowded attractions and crisp, clear days, though there's also the increased risk of rain and fog. Winter is hard to call: At its best, with glistening snow and bright, clear days, the coast, moors and dales are beautiful—but storms and blizzards set in quickly, moorland roads become impassable, and villages can be cut off from the outside world. During winter, stick to York and the main towns if you can't rely on keeping to a strict timetable.

WEST YORKSHIRE AND BRONTË COUNTRY

Even before the Industrial Revolution, the towns in the hills and river valleys of West Yorkshire were important commercial centers, whose trade in wool made prodigious fortunes for both local merchants and religious foundations. It's still a region synonymous with wool production, and there's a large number of "mill shops" where high-quality knitting wool, sweaters, and woven wool for skirts or suits can be bought at factory prices. Following industrialization, the towns took to new trades—textiles, chemicals, and engineering—which transformed the urban scene, leaving many places today rather unattractive at first sight. However, restoration of once-glorious Victorian architecture and the regeneration of inner-city areas is slowly having a beneficial effect, while relief is always close to hand in the region's striking rural and moorland surroundings.

North of the Calder valley and south of that of the Aire are gaunt hills that is classical ground: This is the district immortalized by the writings of the famous Brontë sisters. Haworth is the Mecca of the Brontë

Yorkshire

Richmond 13
Catterick
Swale
A6108
B6270
Northallerton
A1(T)
11 Askrigg
12 Hawes
Leeming
A684 Aysgarth
Ure
Swale
B6160
A6108
Thirsk
A170
Masham
A61
North Stainley
Grewelthorpe
A6108
Ripon 29
Gouthwaite Res.
28
Studley Royal/ Fountains Abbey
B6265
30 Newby Hall
A61
Ure
9 Grassington
B6265
Pateley Bridge
B6165
10 Malham
Cracoe
WHARFEDALE
Nidd
B6165
B6055
A1(T)
B6265
27 Knaresborough
Blubberhouses
A59
26 Harrogate
A661
A59
Bolton Priory 7
B6265
A59
MARSTON MOOR
8 Skipton
Wharfe
A65
Ilkley 6
Askwith
A61
B1224
AIREDALE
A658
A61
A659
Wetherby
A660
Pool
3 Harewood House
A64
A659
Tadcas
A629(T)
Wharfe
Keighley
A650
Aire
A61
A64
A1
5 Haworth
A629
B6144
A162
4 Bradford
1 Leeds
2 Temple Newsam
M1
A63
Aire
M62
N
TO MANCHESTER
TO SHEFFIELD
TO LONDON

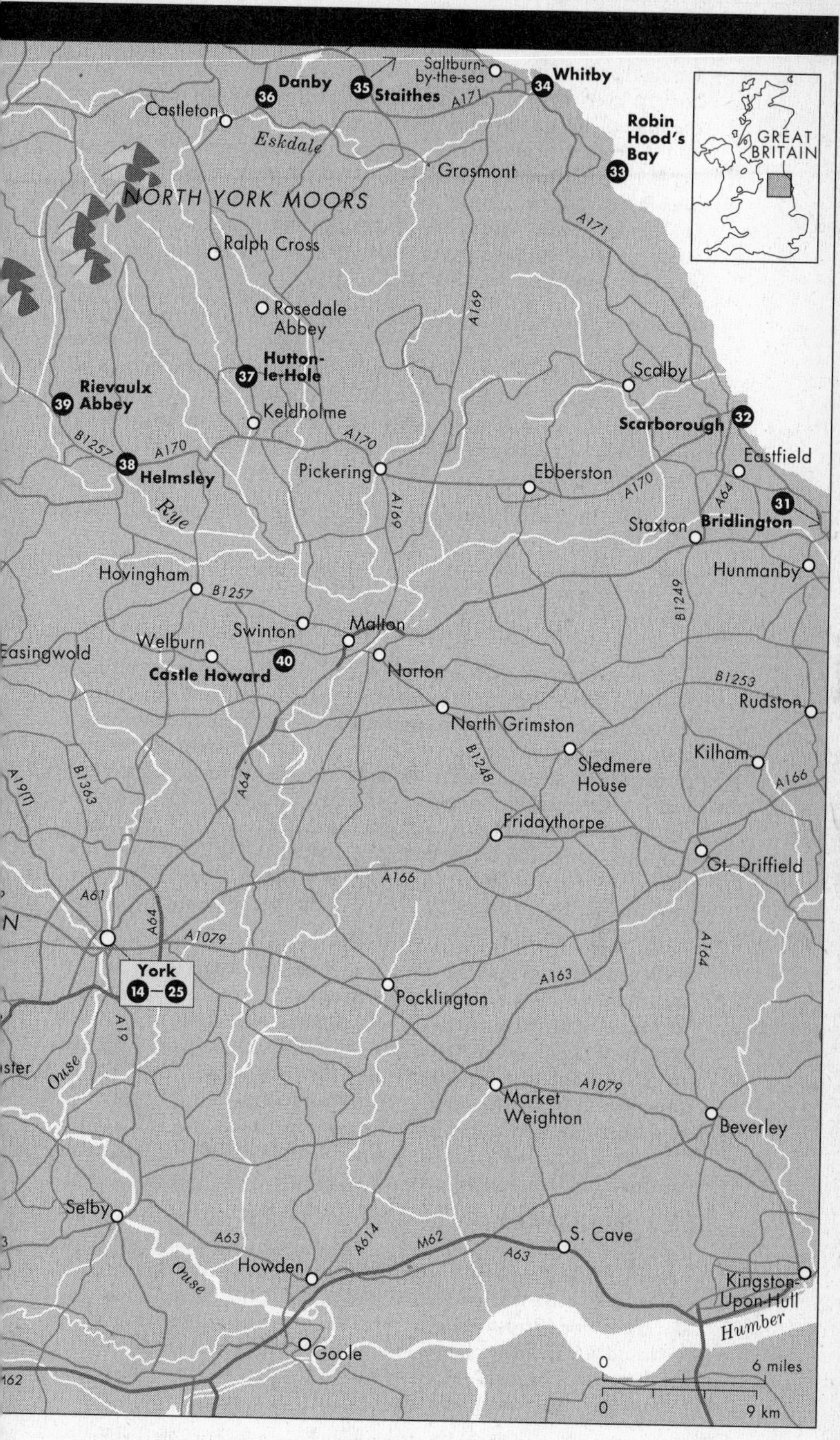

Saltburn-by-the-sea
Danby 36
35 Staithes
34 Whitby
A171
Castleton
Eskdale
Grosmont
Robin Hood's Bay 33
NORTH YORK MOORS
GREAT BRITAIN
A171
Ralph Cross
Rosedale Abbey
A169
Hutton-le-Hole 37
Rievaulx Abbey 39
Scalby
Keldholme
Scarborough 32
B1257
A170
A170
38 Helmsley
Pickering
Ebberston
Eastfield
Rye
A169
A170
A64
31 Bridlington
Staxton
Hunmanby
Hovingham
B1257
B1249
Swinton
Malton
Welburn
Easingwold
Castle Howard 40
Norton
B1253
Rudston
North Grimston
Sledmere House
Kilham
B1248
A19(T)
B1363
A64
A166
Fridaythorpe
Gt. Driffield
A166
A61
A64
A1079
A164
York 14–25
A163
Pocklington
A19
Ouse
A1079
Market Weighton
Beverley
Selby
A63
A614
M62
S. Cave
A63
Howden
Ouse
Kingston-Upon-Hull
Humber
Goole
0 6 miles
0 9 km

enthusiast—a gray West Yorkshire village that certainly might have passed unobserved throughout the years but for the magnetism of the family that lived in the old parsonage, now the museum of the Brontë Society. Every summer, thousands toil up the steep main street to visit the hilltop church and the museum, and then head out to the moors and the ruined farm of High Withens, which everyone calls *Wuthering Heights*. There are people, dwellers in the north of England included, who find the wildness of the moors rather oppressive, but to many there is a beauty of black and white as well as that of oils, and the Brontë scene has been unforgettably etched in the lights and shades that speak of the accomplished artist.

Leeds provides an obvious starting-point, since it's easily reached from the west by the trans-Pennine M62 and from the south by the M1. There are traditional wool towns to the south—like Wakefield, Huddersfield, and Halifax—which each have a modicum of interest, but the main thrust of any visit to West Yorkshire is to the west of Leeds, where Bradford and Brontë Country, around Haworth, really begin to repay investigation.

Numbers in the margin correspond to points of interest on the Yorkshire map.

Leeds

❶ *43 mi northeast of Manchester, 25 mi southwest of York.*

The burgeoning city of Leeds now has a population of more than 400,000 and a reputation as one of the greenest cities in Europe, though its unkempt industrial outskirts and congested traffic make this difficult for first-time visitors to believe. But there has been real progress in the city over the last decade, and what was formerly an industrial city in severe decline has been given a new lease of life. In addition to the parks, long green routes radiate from the city center; there has been major investment in urban heritage projects, and café-bars with outdoor seating are sprouting all over the city. It's not quite the Mediterranean, but there's a tangible vitality in the air these days.

Leeds had a head start on most comparable cities, since its wealthy, 19th-century days had left it a fine architectural bequest. The city is well known for its superb Victorian Arcades, but the Georgian squares and streets of the West End are just as notable. Tucked away among the streets you'll find old pubs and yards that were originally laid out in the 14th century. The **Town Hall,** a classical building of 1853, sits prominently in the city center, one of the finest of all public buildings in Britain. It's of most use to tourists as a landmark, since two of the best attractions—City Art Gallery and City Museum—lie just across the road. ✉ *The Headrow,* ☎ *0113/247–7985.*

The **City Art Gallery** features a fine collection of painting and sculpture, with particularly strong showings of 20th-century British art (including works by Sickert, Lowry, and Spencer, among others). Adjoining the gallery is the **Henry Moore Study Centre.** It's named, of course, for the famous British sculptor, who was a student at Leeds College of Art, and you'll find examples of his work here, as well as sculpture by Barbara Hepworth. ✉ *The Headrow,* ☎ *0113/247–8248.* 🎫 *Free.* ⏲ *Mon.–Tues. and Thurs.–Fri. 10–5, Wed. 10–9, Sat. 10–4.*

It's hard to pigeonhole the **City Museum,** whose collections and exhibits—of geology, natural history, ethnology, and archaeology—run the gamut from stuffed animals and the achievements of prehistoric man, to local life in Roman times. But children are sure to be enthralled, and there's a gift shop, too, with inventive offerings. ✉ *The Headrow,* ☎ *0113/247-8275.* 🎫 *Free.* ⏲ *Tues.–Fri. 9:30–5:30, Sat. 9:30–4.*

Tetley's Brewery Wharf celebrates the history of the English pub through the ages, and since all the main attractions are indoors—including a brewery tour of the Yorkshire company, Tetley's, with free tastings—it's a useful wet-weather standby. If there are blue skies, take advantage of the riverside venue of the outdoor café-bar. ✉ *The Waterfront, River Aire,* ☎ *0113/242–0666.* 🎫 *£4.75.* ⏲ *Apr.–Sept., daily 10–5:30; Oct.–Mar., Wed.–Sun. 10–4:30.*

❷ Just east of the center of Leeds stands **Temple Newsam,** a huge Elizabethan and Jacobean building, which was altered in the 18th century. It was the birthplace in 1545 of Darnley, the doomed husband of Mary, Queen of Scots. Surrounded by one of the largest public parks in Western Europe, the house now belongs to Leeds City Council, which uses it to display its rich collections of furniture, paintings, and ceramics. The vast park, with its walled rose gardens, greenhouses, and miles of woodland walks, was originally laid out by Capability Brown in 1762. The house is 4 miles east of Leeds on the A63. ☎ *0113/264–7321.* 🎫 *£2.20.* ⏲ *Tues.–Sun. 10:30–5:30 (or dusk in winter); last entry 1 hr before closing.*

❸ **Harewood House** (pronounced "Harwood") is home of the earl of Harewood, a cousin of the Queen. This spectacularly impressive neoclassical mansion, built in 1759 by John Carr of York, is known for its Robert Adam interiors, important paintings and ceramics, and Chippendale furniture (Chippendale himself was born in nearby Otley). On the grounds are gardens, woods, a lake, a bird garden, an adventure playground, and a butterfly house. The house is 7 miles north of Leeds, along the A61, though those without cars will be able to visit by bus, which leaves from Leeds's Central Bus Station every 30 minutes. ✉ *Harewood,* ☎ *0113/288–6225.* 🎫 *£5.95.* ⏲ *Apr.–Nov., daily 11–5.*

Dining and Lodging

£££ ✗ **Pool Court.** Right in the center of Leeds, by the river, Pool Court is typical of the new wave of fashionable restaurants becoming popular with northern food fanciers. It's a distinctly elegant, professional place serving modern English food, with Mediterranean influences. Fish is always a good choice, while duck and game are expertly cooked, too, and there are some fine vegetarian dishes. There's a variously priced wine list, with a choice of wines available by the glass. ✉ *42–44 The Calls,* ☎ *0113/244–4242. AE, DC, MC, V. No lunch Sat. Closed Sun.*

££££ 🏨 **42 The Calls.** Taking an old grain mill in the once-dilapidated waterfront area of the city and converting it into a high-tech, high-comfort hotel takes some nerve, but the venture has paid off. Each room shows individual flair, while retaining such original features as exposed beams and brickwork; facilities are up-to-the-minute, with CD players, comfortable bathrooms, and a lobby lounge with eminently cushy armchairs. To eat, look no farther than the adjacent Pool Court restaurant (☞ *above*). ✉ *42 The Calls, LS2 7EW,* ☎ *0113/244–0099,* FAX *0113/234–4100. 41 rooms with bath. Restaurant, bar, breakfast room, lobby lounge, room service. AE, DC, MC, V.*

Nightlife and the Arts

Opera North, England's first major provincial opera company, has its home in Leeds at the **Grand Theatre,** whose opulent, gold-and-plush auditorium is modeled on that of La Scala. ✉ *46 New Briggate,* ☎ *0113/245–9351 or 0113/244–0971.* ⏲ *Box office: Mon.–Sat. 10–9.*

The ultramodern **West Yorkshire Playhouse** was opened in 1990 on the slope of an old quarry and its interior is designed to be completely adaptable to all kinds of staging. ✉ *Playhouse Sq., Quarry Hill,* ☎ *0113/244–2111.* ⏲ *Box office: Mon.–Sat. 9–8.*

The **Town and Country Club** (✉ Cookridge St., ☎ 0113/280–0100) was the first regional offshoot of the famous London live music venue for rock and pop gigs.

Bradford

❹ *9 mi west of Leeds, 12 mi north of Huddersfield, 32 mi northeast of Manchester.*

Bradford was once one of the greatest wool towns in Europe, a trade at which it had excelled since the 16th century. Even as late as the 1960s, wool accounted for a substantial part of its earnings, but as with all the other West Yorkshire textile towns, recession and competition from new markets hit hard. It tries hard to be likeable today, and though much of its grandeur has gone, the center still boasts the odd Victorian building from its period of greatest prosperity: St. George's Hall on Bridge Street (1851) and the Wool Exchange on Market Street (1864) are two fine examples. But not everyone is impressed: American travel writer Bill Bryson, in his *Notes from a Small Island,* claims that "Bradford's role in life is to make every place else in the world look better in comparison, and it does this very well."

Tourists, it must be said, come to Bradford not for the buildings but for the museums, particularly the renowned **National Museum of Photography, Film, and Television,** which opened in 1983. This traces the history of the photographic media. There are plenty of interactive models and machines and related ephemera from early cameras to TV props, though the museum's popularity with children means you're best advised to come early or late in the day if you want to see the displays in peace. Allow time, too, for a screening at the museum's 50-by-60-foot IMAX screen—the biggest in Britain—which shows stomach-churning movies of flights over the Grand Canyon and other remarkable sequences. ✉ *Pictureville, Prince's View,* ☎ *01274/727488.* 🎟 *Museum free; IMAX movie £3.90.* ⏲ *Tues.–Sun. and national holidays 10:30–6.*

Bradford's history as a wool-producing town is outlined at the **Industrial Museum and Horses at Work,** housed in a former spinning mill northeast of the town center. Exhibits include workers' dwellings dating from the 1870s and a mill owner's house from the 19th century. Children love the Shire horses and taking a ride in the horse-drawn tram. ✉ *Moorside Mills, Moorside Rd.,* ☎ *01274/631756.* 🎟 *Free.* ⏲ *Tues.–Sat. 10–5., Sun. noon–5.*

★ Perhaps the most extraordinary attraction in Bradford is the former model factory community of **Saltaire.** Built by textile magnate Sir Titus Salt in the mid-19th century, it's a remarkable example of the enduring trait of philanthropy among certain Victorian industrialists, who erected modern terraced housing for their workers, and furnished them with libraries, parks, hospitals, schools, and educational leisure facilities. Saltaire, fashioned in Italianate style, has been remarkably preserved, its former mills and houses turned into shops, restaurants, and galleries. Even more remarkable is the permanent, retrospective exhibition of 400 works by locally born artist David Hockney in the 1853 Gallery in Salt's Mill (✉ Victoria Rd., ☎ 01274/531163). Saltaire is just 4 miles north of Bradford, and there are regular local bus and train services; drivers should take the A650 and follow the signs.

Dining and Lodging

£££ ✕ **Restaurant Nineteen.** Elegant dining in a suburb of Bradford comes as quite a shock, but the surprises are all pleasant. Set dinner is served every evening in the tranquil dining room, and makes much of modern British techniques and ingredients: menus are seasonal, but there's usually fish and the meat dishes are warm and hearty. ✉ *North Park Rd., Heaton,* ☎ *01274/492559. AE, MC, V. Open Tues.–Sat. No lunch. Closed Sun.–Mon.*

£ ✕ **Kashmir.** Just two minutes from the Museum of Photography, Film, and Television, Morley Street is lined with some of Bradford's finest curry houses. The Kashmir is one of the best, a simple, no-frills place dishing out authentic spicy food at extremely low prices. ✉ *27 Morley St.,* ☎ *01274/726513. No credit cards.*

£££ **Victoria Hotel.** This renovated, former railway hotel in the center of town—built in 1875—makes a comfortable base if you crave an urban Yorkshire stopover. Public areas are smart and stylish, and guest rooms keep up with appearances too: armchairs in checked cloth, plump beds, and crisp, cool decor. The room rate doesn't include breakfast. ✉ *Bridge St., BD1 1JX,* ☎ *01274/728706,* FAX *01274/736358. 63 rooms with bath. Restaurant, bar, sauna, exercise room. AE, DC, MC, V.*

Haworth—Heart of Brontë Country

❺ *10 mi northwest of Bradford, 5 mi southwest of Keighley.*

There's not much, at first glance, that makes the village of Haworth in West Yorkshire special. It's an old, stone-built spot on the edge of the Yorkshire Moors, superficially much like many other craggy Yorkshire settlements. But Haworth has a particular claim to fame; in fact, it's probably the most celebrated literary spot in Britain after Stratford-upon-Avon. It was here, in the middle of the 19th century, that the three Brontë sisters lived, Emily (author of *Wuthering Heights,* 1847), Charlotte (*Jane Eyre,* 1847), and Anne (*The Tenant of Wildfell Hall,* 1848). This unlikely trio, daughters of the local vicar, were responsible for some of the most romantic books ever written.

It is, of course, quite natural to ask whether the Brontës drew their inspiration from the surrounding moors entirely or whether they would have been equally at home had the Reverend Patrick Brontë been incumbent in some other parish. With Emily Brontë, at least, it is impossible to separate the story from its setting. If ever a book emerged from the womb of its creator breathing the same rarefied air that has assailed Emily's lungs for years on end, that book was *Wuthering Heights.* "My sister Emily loved the moors," sister Charlotte once wrote. "Flowers brighter than the rose bloomed in the blackest of the heath for her; out of a sullen hollow in a livid hillside her mind could make an Eden. She found in the bleak solitude many and dear delights; and not the least and best loved was liberty. Liberty was the breath of Emily's nostrils; without it she perished." Today, thousands journey to the straggling stone village of Haworth, which lives a little too readily off its associations: Visitors, in summer, on occasion threaten to overwhelm the place entirely.

Haworth's steep, cobbled **Main Street** has changed little in outward appearance since the early 19th century, but today acts as a funnel for most of the tourists, who crowd into the various points of interest: the **Black Bull** pub, where the reprobate Branwell, the Brontës' only brother, drank himself into an early grave; the **post office** from which Charlotte, Emily, and Anne sent their manuscripts to their London publishers; an **information center** with guides and maps; and the **church,** with its gloomy graveyard (Charlotte and Emily are buried inside the church, Anne in Scarborough; ☞ The North Yorkshire Coast, *below*).

★ The **Brontë Parsonage Museum** is housed in the somber Georgian house in which the sisters grew up and displays original furniture (some bought by Charlotte after the success of *Jane Eyre*), portraits, and books. The museum has some enchanting mementos, including the sisters' spidery, youthful graffiti on the nursery wall, and Charlotte's tiny wedding shoes. ✉ *Main St.,* ☎ *01535/642323.* *£3.80.* *Apr.–Sept., daily 10–5; Oct.–Mar., 11–4:30; closed mid-Jan.–early Feb. and Dec. 25.*

If you know and love the Brontës' works, you'll also probably want to walk (an hour or so along a field path, a lane, and a moorland track) to the **Brontë Waterfall,** described in Emily's and Charlotte's poems and letters. **Top Withins,** 3 miles from Haworth, is the remains of a bleak hilltop farm. Although often taken to be the main inspiration for Heathcliff's gloomy mansion, Wuthering Heights, it probably isn't, as a plaque nearby baldly states. There and back from Haworth is a two-hour walk and you'll need sturdy shoes and protective clothing: If you've read *Wuthering Heights,* you'll have a fairly good idea of what weather can be like on the Yorkshire Moors!

Haworth is one stop on the **Keighley & Worth Valley Railway,** a gorgeous branch line along which steam engines run between Keighley (8 miles north of Haworth) and Oxenhope. Taking the train at least part of the way is exciting enough for everyone, though kids will like it even more on special days when there are family fairs en route, or when Thomas the Tank Engine makes an appearance. ✉ *Railway Station, Keighley,* ☎ *01535/645214 or* ☎ *01535/647777 (24-hr information).* *£4.80 return, £6 day rover ticket, £14 family day rover.* *Trains run weekends year-round, daily June–Aug.; call for schedules and special events.*

Dining and Lodging

£££ ✕ **Weavers.** You'll have to book well in advance, since there are only four rooms available at Weavers, converted from a series of old cottages, but you'll be glad you did. In a fine village location, it's mainly in business as a restaurant, though the pretty, light bedrooms are well turned out, with fine views, and the breakfast is very good. Downstairs, the restaurant (££) serves traditional Yorkshire cuisine, including Yorkshire pudding and local stews. More elaborate dishes include a daily fish special (perhaps in a pie, or baked), and there's a specially priced set dinner for early arrivals; get there before 7 for this. ✉ *15 West La., BD22 8DU,* ☎ *01535/643822. 4 rooms with bath. Restaurant, bar. AE, DC, MC, V.*

THE YORKSHIRE DALES

To the north of the industrial towns of West Yorkshire, the Yorkshire Dales stand in complete and startling contrast. These meandering river valleys fall south and east from the Pennines and, beyond Skipton, present an almost wholly rural aspect. Most, but not all dales take their names from the rivers that run through them and provide a variety of scenery that's quintessentially English: a ruined priory here, there a stone moorland village, a narrow country road, and a bubbling river. Naturally, it's prime walking country, and all the villages covered in this section have access to a fine network of paths and trails, as well as providing a full range of accommodation and hiking services.

Wharfedale, one of the longest of the Yorkshire Dales, is easily accessible from Bradford. A convenient driving route (with only a little early backtracking) would take in Ilkley, the castle at Skipton, and rural Grassington and Malham, before moving farther north to see the glories of Wensleydale and Swaledale and finishing at the attractive market town of Richmond.

Numbers in the margin correspond to points of interest on the Yorkshire map.

Ilkley

6 *10 mi northeast of Haworth, 9 mi southeast of Skipton, 12 mi north of Bradford, 17 mi northwest of Leeds.*

At the former spa town of Ilkley it's easy to stroll up onto **Ilkley Moor,** from where footpaths run right across the top, 6 miles south to Keighley. A famous, and rather grisly, Yorkshire song with dialect words tells the tale of a man who went courting on the moor "baht 'at" (without a hat); he catches cold, dies, and is buried; his body eaten by worms, the worms eaten by ducks, the ducks eaten by people until "we shall all have etten thee." The **White Wells Museum,** about a 20-minute walk from the town center on the northern slopes of the moor, contains an 18th-century natural spring bath, and the tearoom serves tea made with the local spring water. ✉ *Wells Rd., no phone.* 🎫 *Free.* ⏲ *Tues.–Wed., and Fri.–Sun. 10–6.*

Bolton Priory

★ 7 *5 mi northwest of Ilkley.*

Some of the loveliest of the Wharfedale scenery comes into view around Bolton Priory, the ruins of an Augustinian priory, which sits on a grassy embankment inside a great curve of the river Wharfe itself. The priory is just a short walk or drive from the confusingly named village of Bolton Abbey, and once there you can wander through the 13th-century ruins or visit the priory church, which is still the local parish church; it's open daily, with free access in the daytime. Among the famous visitors enchanted by Bolton Priory were William Wordsworth (who described "Bolton's mouldering Priory" in his poem "The White Doe of Rylstone"); J. M. W. Turner, the 19th-century artist, who painted it; and John Ruskin, the Victorian art critic, who rated it most beautiful of all the English ruins he had seen.

Close to Bolton Priory, surrounded by some of the most romantic woodland scenery in England, the river Wharfe plunges between a narrow chasm in the rocks (a dangerous stretch of white water known as "the Strid") before reaching a medieval hunting lodge, **Barden Tower.** Barden Tower is now a ruin and can be visited just as easily as Bolton Priory, on whose grounds it stands.

Dining and Lodging

££££ ★ ✕🏨 **Devonshire Arms.** Originally an 18th-century coaching inn, and still belonging to the dukes of Devonshire, this country house hotel is in a superb setting on the river Wharfe, within easy walking distance of Bolton Priory and the village of Bolton Abbey. Portraits of various dukes hang on the walls, and the individually themed bedrooms in the original building are tastefully decorated by the Duchess of Devonshire; all have four-poster beds and carved furniture. There's even the feminine "Mitford Room" for lady executives traveling alone. The (no-smoking) Burlington restaurant, in the hotel, has a fine, traditional menu, and the good service stands out. ✉ *Bolton Abbey, Skipton, North York-*

shire, BD23 6AJ, ☎ 01756/710441, FAX 01756/710564. 40 rooms with bath. Restaurant (reservations essential; jacket and tie), bar, no-smoking rooms, pool, sauna, tennis court, exercise room, health club, fishing, baby-sitting. AE, DC, MC, V.

Skipton

8 *6 mi west of Bolton Abbey, 9 mi northwest of Ilkley, 12 mi north of Haworth, 22 mi west of Harrogate.*

Skipton in Airedale is a typical Dales market town with as many farmers as tourists milling in the streets (there are markets every day except Tuesday and Sunday), and shops selling local produce much to the fore. **Skipton Castle,** originally built by the Normans in 1090 and unaltered since the Civil War (17th century), is the town's most prominent attraction. It's also one of the best-preserved of all English medieval castles, remarkably complete in appearance—after the Battle of Marston Moor, it remained the only Royalist stronghold in the north of England. In the central courtyard, a yew tree, planted 300 years ago by Lady Anne Clifford, still flourishes. The castle is at the top of the busy High Street. ✉ *Skipton Castle, High St.,* ☎ *01756/792442.* 🎫 *£3.40.* ⏲ *Mar.–Sept., Mon.–Sat. 10–6, Sun. 2–6; Oct.–Feb., Mon.–Sat. 10–4, Sun. 2–4; closed Dec. 25.*

Grassington

★ 9 *10 mi north of Skipton, 14 mi northwest of Ilkley, 25 mi west of Ripon.*

A small, stone village built around an ancient cobbled marketplace, Grassington is well situated for exploring Upper Wharfedale. The Dales Way footpath passes through the village, and there is a surprisingly good range of stores, pubs, and cafés—though this is less of a surprise if you visit during summer, when facilities become positively overwhelmed by day-trippers and walkers. Local walks are easily accomplished, however, and if you're prepared to make a day of it, you'll soon find you leave the crowds behind. The **National Park Centre** has a wide choice of guidebooks, maps, and bus schedules to help you enjoy a day in the Dales. Organized tours depart from the center with qualified guides who explain the botanical and geological features of the area. ✉ *Colvend, Hebdon Rd.,* ☎ *01756/752748.* ⏲ *Apr.–Oct., daily 9:30–5:30; Nov.–Mar., Mon. 10–1, Fri. 1–4:30, weekends 10–12:30 and 1–4:30.*

In the **Upper Wharfedale Folk Museum,** you can trace the history and geology of the region in a series of engaging displays. ✉ *Market Sq., no phone.* 🎫 *50p.* ⏲ *Apr.–Oct., daily 2–4:30; Nov.–Mar., weekends 2–4:30.*

Dining and Lodging

£ ✕ **The Old Hall Inn.** This stone-flagged, rustic country pub with a small garden on the outskirts of Grassington serves an out-of-the-ordinary menu that attracts people from miles around. Main courses might include *nasi goreng* (an Indonesian rice dish with prawns), local sausages with onion confit, or haddock with a tapenade crust. Starters and desserts are just as adventurous. ✉ *Threshfield, 1 mi west of Grassington,* ☎ *01756/752441. No credit cards. No dinner Sun. Closed Mon.*

££ ✕🏨 **Black Horse Hotel.** Set back a little from the main square, the welcoming Black Horse has a good local reputation. The good-value rooms here are just the thing if you've walked in from afar, with comfortable beds, TVs, and tea- and coffeemaking facilities; some have four-posters for a touch of luxury. An extensive bar menu is served, though there's more formal dining in the restaurant where an *à la carte* menu of local and traditional dishes defeats even the heartiest of appetites. In winter, open fires keep things cozy; in summer, sit outside with a drink on the terrace. ✉ *Garrs La., BD23 5AT,* ☎ *01756/752770. 15 rooms with bath. Restaurant, bar. MC, V.*

££ **Ashfield House.** Three converted cottages make room for this amenable, well-run guest house, just off the main street. There's a cheery welcome on arrival, modern but pleasing bedrooms that stay warm right through fall and spring, and a cozy little sitting room. Evening meals are available, too, though there's no shortage of other dining options nearby. ✉ *Ashfield, Grassington, Skipton, BD23 5AE,* ☎ *01756/752584. 7 rooms with bath or shower. Dining room, bar, no-smoking rooms. MC, V. Closed mid-Nov.–mid-Feb.*

Malham

★ ❿ *10 mi west of Grassington; take B6265 south 2 mi through Cracoe, then branch west onto the minor road past Hetton and Calton; also 12 mi northwest of Skipton.*

Malham's surroundings can occupy keen walkers for several days, though the three main destinations—Malham Cove, Gordale Scar, and Malham Tarn—are close enough to see on a circular walk of 8 miles that takes most people four to five hours. **Malham Cove,** a huge natural rock amphitheater, is just a mile north of the village and provides the easiest local walk. At **Gordale Scar,** a deep natural chasm between overhanging limestone cliffs, the white waters of a moorland stream plunge 300 feet; it's 1 mile northeast of Malham. A longer walk, of more than 3 miles, leads north from Malham to **Malham Tarn,** an attractive lake set in windswept isolation. Here, there's a nature reserve on the west bank and an easy-to-follow trail on the east bank.

Maps and displays at Malham's **National Park Centre** will give you some more informed ideas of what there is to do and see locally. ✉ *National Park Centre,* ☎ *01729/830363.* ⏲ *Easter–Oct., daily 9:30–5; Nov.–Easter, weekends 10–4.*

En Route North of Malham, there's a dramatic moorland drive following the minor road that skirts Malham Tarn, to **Arncliffe** in Littondale. Follow the signs southeast for the B6160 and the turn north to through Kettlewell to **Buckden,** the last village in Wharfedale. From here you can go directly through Kidstone Pass (still on the B6160) to **Aysgarth** in Wensleydale, where the river Ure plummets over a series of waterfalls; Askrigg is just 5 miles farther west.

Askrigg

⓫ *25 mi north of Malham.*

Askrigg would be just another typical Wensleydale village, were it not for its association with the James Herriot TV series, which was filmed in and around the village. The tourist board pushes "Herriot Country" hard, but while Askrigg—dubbed "Darrowby" in the program—is a pleasing village, there's not a great deal else to keep you here, apart from walks to a couple of local waterfalls. Before leaving, however, you should visit the **King's Arms Hotel** (✉ Market Pl., ☎ 01969/650258), a wood-paneled, 18th-century coaching inn in the center of the village. Rechristened the Drover's Arms, this figures in many an episode of the program and is a truly atmospheric building, with nook-and-cranny rooms, good local beer, two restaurants, and guest rooms, too.

Hawes

⓬ *5 mi west of Askrigg.*

The best time to visit Hawes—reputedly the highest market town in England—is on Tuesday, when farmers and locals crowd into town for the weekly market. There's a brisk, businesslike atmosphere at other times, too, since Hawes retains some of Wensleydale's more traditional industries, not least its cheese-making. Crumbly, white Wensleydale cheese has been made in the valley for centuries, though only recently has production moved into the town itself. You can buy the cheese at various stores in town, and give yourself time to wander the cobbled side streets, too, some of which sport antiques shops and tearooms.

At the **Wensleydale Creamery Visitor Centre,** on the outskirts of Hawes, a Cheese Museum tells the story of how Wensleydale cheese came to be produced. There's a viewing gallery, to enable you to watch production, and then you can repair to the shop, where tasting of the various cheeses is encouraged before you buy: Quite apart from the regular Wensleydale cheese on offer, try it smoked, or with ginger, or with apple pie, or even with dried fruit. There's a restaurant on the site, too. ✉ *Wensleydale Creamery Visitor Centre,* ☎ *01969/667664.* 🎫 *Museum £1.50.* ⏲ *Daily 9–6; museum by appointment in winter.*

Hawes's National Park Information Centre in the old train station contains the **Dales Countryside Museum,** which helps give a picture of Dales life in past centuries; a traditional rope-making shop here also welcomes visitors. ✉ *National Park Centre, Station Yard,* ☎ *01969/667450.* 🎫 *Museum £1.50.* ⏲ *Centre: Apr.–June and Sept.–Oct., daily 10–4; July–Aug., daily 9:30–4:30. Museum: Apr.–Oct., daily 10–5; some winter weekends, phone for details.*

En Route From Hawes, the most direct route to Swaledale is north by minor road over the **Buttertubs Pass,** a 7-mile run to **Muker,** a lovely village that hosts the annual Swaledale show in September. Many people regard **Swaledale** itself as the finest of all the Yorkshire Dales and it certainly lingers long in the memory. From Muker, the B6270 and A6108 run down the valley to Richmond.

Richmond

⓭ *30 mi northeast of Hawes, 32 mi northwest of Ripon.*

Richmond tucks itself into a curve in the river Swale, with a network of narrow Georgian streets and terraces opening onto the largest cobbled marketplace in the country. It would be a mistake, however, to date the town's provenance to the 18th century, despite appearances. The Normans first swept in during the late 11th century, determined to subdue the local population and establish Norman rule in the north. This they did by building a mighty castle, around which the town grew, and throughout the Middle Ages Richmond was effectively a garrison town. The immense keep of Richmond's Norman **castle** towers above the river Swale and grants excellent views over the surroundings. Dating from the 11th century, it's one of the best-preserved monuments of this era, retaining its curtain wall and chapel, and a great hall that has been partially restored to its medieval splendor; even the 14th-century graffiti has been preserved. ✉ *Castle,* ☎ *01748/822493.* 🎫 *£1.80.* ⏲ *Apr.–Sept., daily 10–6; Oct.–Mar., daily 10–4.*

The tiny **Georgian Theatre Royal** is the oldest theater in England still in use, and unchanged since the days of the 18th-century Shakespearean actor David Garrick; you can watch performances from either smart gallery boxes or old wooden seats. It's an intimate theater, remarkable for its authentic detail (except that it uses electric lights instead of candles). Try to reserve tickets well in advance. Also, outside performance times, the theater has a small museum featuring unique painted scenery dating from 1836. ✉ *Friars Wynd,* ☎ *01748/823710.* 🎫 *Museum £1.* ⏲ *Apr.–Oct., Mon.–Sat. 11–4:45, Sun. 2:30–4:45.*

YORK AND ENVIRONS

It would be unthinkable to visit North Yorkshire without going first to the atmospheric cathedral city of York—and not just because its central location makes it a practical place to start. It would take a fat guidebook to do justice to all the sights in this city. Encircled by a 3-mile ring of massive walls of creamy-colored stone, it is the most completely medieval of all English cities. Named "Eboracum" in Latin, York was the military capital of Roman Britain, and traces of Roman garrison buildings still survive throughout the city. The Vikings also claimed York as their capital and left bountiful evidence of their tenure, while in Norman times were laid the foundations of York Minster, the largest medieval cathedral in England. With so many layers of history, it's not surprising to find that the city center itself is one of the most charming in all Britain—all leaning gables and crooked timbers, such as Stonegate and The Shambles, the latter an incomparable example of a medieval street built between 1350 and 1450—set back from the river Ouse.

There's small incentive, you'd think, ever to leave, though with the North York Moors and coast so close, visitors do eventually move on. But the environs to the northwest are all close enough to see on day trips from the city: the spa town of Harrogate, medieval Knaresborough, the lovely ruins of Fountains Abbey, and the attractive market town of Ripon.

Numbers in the margin correspond to points of interest on the Yorkshire and York maps.

York

★ ⓮ *48 mi southeast of Richmond, 25 mi northeast of Leeds, 82 mi south of Newcastle.*

Following the fall of the Roman Empire in the 5th century, a Saxon town grew up over the ruins of the Roman fort at York. On Christmas Eve, AD 627, the Northumbrian King Edwin introduced Christianity to the area by being baptized in a little wooden church here, and the city grew in importance during the 9th century, after the Viking conquerors of northern and eastern England made York—which they called "Jorvik"—their English capital. You'll notice that many of the city's street names are suffixed with the word "-gate" (Goodramgate, Micklegate, for example)—"gate" was the Viking word for "street." Because of its strategic position on the river Ouse, York developed throughout Norman and Plantagenet times (11th–14th centuries) into an important trade center and inland port, particularly for the export of wool to the Continent. Wealthy guilds of craftsmen and merchants flourished, and it became a favored royal destination. Henry II and Edward II held parliaments here and Richard II gave the city its first Sword of State.

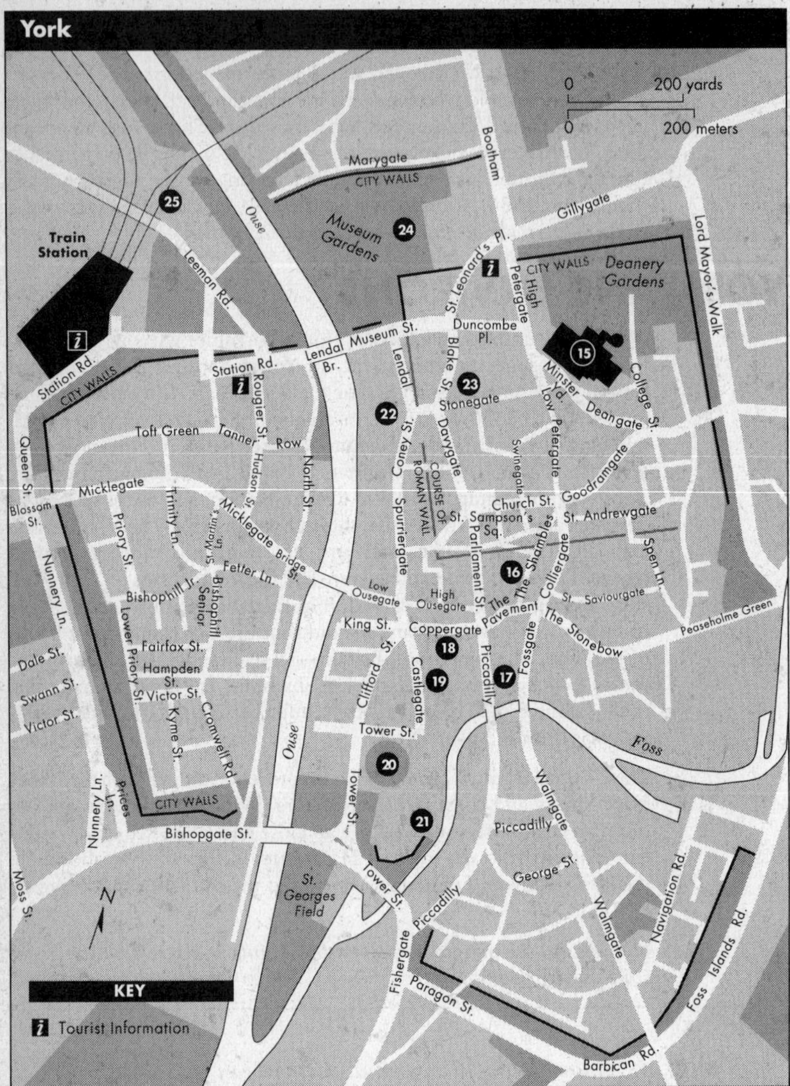

Castle Museum, **21**
Clifford's Tower, **20**
Guildhall, **22**
Jorvik Viking Centre, **18**
Merchant Adventurers' Hall, **17**
National Railway Museum, **25**
St. Mary's/The York Story, **19**
The Shambles, **16**
Stonegate, **23**
York Minster, **15**
Yorkshire Museum, **24**

The old city center of York is a compact, dense web of narrow streets and tiny alleys—"snickleways"—in which congestion is so bad that traffic has been banned around the Minster. It is, conversely, a fine city for walking, provided you have a map, though try to avoid visiting in July and August when crowds choke the narrow streets and cause long lines at the popular museums. April, May, and October are far better; April is also the time to see the embankments beneath the city walls filled with the pale gold ripple of daffodils.

A first, memorable overview of the city can be had by taking a stroll along the **city walls.** Originally earth ramparts erected by York's Viking kings to repel raiders, the present stone structure (probably replacing a stockade) dates from the 14th century and has been extensively restored. A narrow paved walk runs along the top (originally 3 miles in circumference), passing over York's distinctive fortified gates or "bars" and providing delightful views across rooftops and gardens.

15 Focal point of the entire city is **York Minster,** the largest Gothic church in England. This vast cathedral attracts almost as many visitors as London's Westminster Abbey. Inside, the effect created by its soaring pillars, lofty vaulted ceilings, and dazzling stained-glass windows—glowing with deep wine reds and cobalt blues, they are only bested by those of Chartres Cathedral in France—is quite overpowering. The church is 534 feet long, 249 feet across its transepts, and 90 feet from floor to roof; the central towers are 184 feet high. Mere statistics, however, cannot convey the scale and beauty of the building. Its soaring columns; the ornamentation of its 14th-century nave; the great east window, one of the greatest pieces of medieval glazing in the world; the enormous choir screen portraying somewhat whimsical images of every king of England from William the Conqueror (reigned 1066–87) to Henry VI (reigned 1422–61); the imposing tracery of the splendid Rose Window (just one of the minster's 128 stained-glass windows) commemorating the marriage of Henry VII and Elizabeth of York in 1486 (the event that ended the Wars of the Roses and began the Tudor dynasty)—all contribute to its magnificence. Don't miss the exquisite 13th-century **Chapter House** and the **Undercroft Museum and Treasury.** After exploring the interior, you might take the 275 winding steps to the roof of the great **Central Tower** (strictly for those with a head for heights), not only for the close-up view of the cathedral's detailed carving but also for a magnificent panorama of York and the surrounding Yorkshire Moors. ✉ *Duncombe Pl., York Minster Undercroft Museum and Treasury, Chapter House, Crypt, and Central Tower,* ☎ *01904/624426.* 🎟 *Minster free, but £1.50 donation appreciated; foundations (including Treasury) £1.80; Chapter House 70p; Crypt 60p; Central Tower £2.* ⏲ *Minster: summer, daily 7 AM–8:30 PM; winter, daily 7–6. Undercroft, Chapter House, Crypt, and Central Tower: summer Mon.–Sat. 10–5:30, Sun. 1–5:30; winter Mon.–Sat. 10–4:30, Sun. 1–4:30.*

The city center's mixed architectural heritage ranges over many periods, although in some places nondescript modern development has taken
16 its toll. **The Shambles,** however, is a perfectly preserved medieval street with half-timber stores and houses whose overhangs are so massive you could almost reach across the street from one second-floor window to another. It's a little too cute for its own good these days, featuring a line of crafts and souvenir shops—a far cry, certainly, from the days when the Shambles was the city's meat market.

17 The **Merchant Adventurers' Hall,** built (1357–68) and owned by one of the city's richest medieval guilds, is the largest half-timber hall in York, with a pretty garden in the back. ✉ *Fossgate,* ☎ *01904/654818.*

£1.80. *Mid-Mar.–mid-Nov., daily 8:30–5; mid-Nov.–mid-Mar., Mon.–Sat. 8:30–3.*

18 In the **Jorvik Viking Centre,** on an authentic Viking site, archaeologists have re-created a Viking street with astonishing attention to detail. Its "time-cars" whisk visitors through the streets to experience the sights, sounds, and smells of Viking England, while excellent displays show visitors the extraordinary breadth of the Viking culture and social system. *Coppergate, 01904/643211. £4.95. Apr.–Oct., daily 9–7; Nov.–Mar., daily 9–5:30.*

York's 20 or so surviving medieval churches—almost any of which could stand alone as an architectural showpiece—tend to be largely ignored by tourists and are therefore good places to explore without the crowds.
19 **St. Mary's** now houses **The York Story,** an exhibit devoted to the history of the city, through medieval-style embroidered panels, models, original artifacts, and a continuous video show. *Castlegate, 01904/628632. £1.70; joint ticket with Castle Museum (*below*) £5.30. Mon.–Sat. 10–5, Sun. 1–5.*

20 **Clifford's Tower** dates from the early 14th century and stands on the mound originally erected for the keep of York Castle. In 1190 this was the scene of one of the worst outbreaks of antisemitism in medieval Europe, when 150 Jews who had sought sanctuary in the castle were massacred. *Tower St., 01904/646940. £1.60. Apr.–Oct., daily 10–6; Nov.–Mar., daily 10–4. Closed Dec. 25 and Jan. 1.*

21 The **Castle Museum,** a former 18th-century debtor's prison, offers a number of detailed exhibitions and re-creations, including a cobblestone Victorian street complete with crafts shops; a working water mill; domestic and military displays; and, most important, the Coppergate Helmet, a 1,200-year-old Anglo-Saxon helmet discovered during recent excavations of the city. You can also visit the cell where Dick Turpin, the 18th-century highwayman and folk hero, spent the night before his execution. *Clifford St., 01904/653611. £4.20; joint ticket with York Story (*above*) £5.30. Apr.–Oct., Mon.–Sat. 9:30–5:30, Sun. 10–5:30; Nov.–Mar., Mon.–Sat. 9:30–4, Sun. 10–4. Closed Dec. 25 and Jan. 1.*

22 York's mid-15th-century **Guildhall,** right on the river, was once used for pageants and mystery plays. Although damaged by World War II bombing, it has been restored to something approaching its erstwhile glory, although 14 Victorian stained-glass windows were lost forever—now only one, at the west end, remains as a magnificent, bright reminder. The Guildhall is behind the 18th-century Mansion House. *St. Helen's Sq., 01904/613161. Free. Mon.–Thurs. 9–5, Fri. 9–4, Sat. 10–5, Sun. 2–5 (closed weekends Nov.–Apr.).*

23 Pedestrianized **Stonegate,** a narrow street of Tudor and 18th-century storefronts and courtyards, has considerable charm. It has been in daily use for almost 2000 years, since first being paved in Roman times. A passage just off Stonegate, at 52A, leads to a 12th-century Norman stone house, one of the very few to have survived in England. Restored in 1969, only the first-floor hall window remains intact.

NEED A BREAK? At the opposite end of Stonegate from the Minster, **Betty's** (6–8 St. Helen's Sq., 01904/659142), ranged elegantly across two large floors in a beautiful Art Nouveau building, has been a York institution since 1912. Best known for its teas, served with mouth-watering cakes (try the "fat rascal," a plump bun bursting with cherries and nuts), Betty's also offers light meals and a splendid selection of exotic coffees. Get a table on the upper floor if you can, next to the ceiling-to-floor windows.

The gardens and ruins of St. Mary's Abbey, founded in 1089, now house 24 the **Yorkshire Museum.** In these atmospheric gardens, with their crumbling medieval columns and blaze of summer flowers, the city's cycle of mystery plays is performed every four years (☞ Nightlife and the Arts, *below*). The museum itself covers the natural and archaeological history of the whole county, including a great deal of material on the Roman, Anglo-Saxon, and Viking aspects of York. Here you can also see the 15th-century Middleham Jewel, a pendant resplendent with a large sapphire and the best piece of Gothic jewelry found in England this century. It lies just outside the walled city, through Bootham Bar, one of York's old gates. ✉ *Museum Gardens,* ☏ *01904/629745.* 🎫 *£3.* ⏲ *Nov.–Mar., Mon.–Sat. 10–5, Sun. 1–5; Apr.–Oct., daily 10–5.*

25 At the **National Railway Museum** you'll find Britain's national collection of locomotives forming part of the world's largest train museum. Among the exhibits are gleaming giants of the steam era, including *Mallard,* holder of the world speed record for a steam engine (126 mph). You can clamber aboard some of the trains. Passenger cars used by Queen Victoria are also on display, while hands-on changing exhibits explore the future of the railways. ✉ *Leeman Rd.,* ☏ *01904/621261.* 🎫 *£4.20.* ⏲ *Apr.–Oct., Mon.–Sat. 10–6, Sun. 11–6; Nov.–Mar., Mon.–Sat. 10–5, Sun. 11–5.*

Dining and Lodging

£££–£££ ✕ **Melton's.** Just 10 minutes from the Minster, this unpretentious restaurant (once a private house) has local art on the walls and an open kitchen. The seasonal menu proves to be highly imaginative, a legacy of chef Michael Hjort's former stint at the Roux brothers' establishments, and offers modern English, Continental, and fish dishes. ✉ *7 Scarcroft Rd.,* ☏ *01904/634341. MC, V. No dinner Sun., no lunch Mon. Closed 3 wks at Christmas and 1 wk in Sept.*

££–£££ ★ ✕ **19 Grape Lane.** The narrow, slightly cramped restaurant is housed in a typically leaning timbered York building in the heart of town. Hugely popular, it serves modern English food from a blackboard of specials such as medallions of hare with field mushrooms in a red wine sauce, or grilled wild boar sausages. ✉ *19 Grape La.,* ☏ *01904/636366. MC, V. Closed Sun., Mon., 2 wks in Feb., 2 wks in Sept.*

£–££ ✕ **Pierre Victoire.** Saunter in to this airy brasserie at lunchtime and you can feast on three courses of simple French food for just £5, one of the city's best bargains. At dinner, prices increase, but not outrageously so, while the dishes become more elaborate: Choose from roast pheasant on a bed of sweet red cabbage or that old brasserie standby, *moules mariniere* (mussels). ✉ *2 Lendal,* ☏ *01904/655222. MC, V.*

£ ✕ **Pizza Express.** The successful London chain has found another fine building in which to serve its pizzas, this time the River House at Lendal Bridge. You eat in the grand salons of what used to be the York Gentleman's Club; a piano serenades evening diners from the lounge; even the rest rooms are fancy. The pizzas are not always all they could be, but lap up the good house wine and the upscale ambience and all is forgiven. ✉ *River House, 17 Museum St.,* ☏ *01904/672904. MC, V.*

££££ ★ ✕🏨 **Middlethorpe Hall.** This handsome, superbly restored 18th-century mansion is on the edge of the city, about 1½ miles from the center, beside the racetrack. The individually decorated rooms, some in cottage-style accommodations around an 18th-century courtyard, are filled with antiques, paintings, and fresh flowers, and the extensive grounds feature a lake, a 17th-century dovecote, and "ha-ha's"—drops in the garden level that create cunning views. The large garden grows fresh vegetables for the hotel's award-winning wood-paneled Anglo-French restaurant, where you can eat in the original wood-paneled dining room by candlelight. ✉ *Bishopthorpe Rd., YO2 1QB,* ☎ *01904/641241; in the U.S., 800/260–8338;* FAX *01904/620176. 30 rooms with bath. Restaurant (reservations essential; jacket and tie), croquet. AE, DC, MC, V.*

£££ **Dean Court.** This large Victorian house once provided accommodation for the clergy of York Minster, which looms just across the way. It's been refurbished to a high quality and now features comfortably furnished rooms with plump sofas, TVs, and fine views overlooking the Minster. Parking is a few minutes from the hotel, but there is a valet parking service. The restaurant serves good English cuisine, including a hearty Yorkshire breakfast. ✉ *Duncombe Pl., YO1 2EF,* ☎ *01904/625082,* FAX *01904/620305. 40 rooms with bath. Restaurant, bar, coffee shop. AE, DC, MC, V.*

££–£££ **Savages.** Despite its name, this small hotel on a leafy road near the town center is eminently refined, with a reputation for attentive service. Once a Victorian home, it has a stylish and comfortable interior, and there's a bar in which to relax. ✉ *15 St. Peter's Grove, YO3 6AQ,* ☎ *01904/610818,* FAX *01904/627729. 18 rooms with bath or shower. Restaurant, bar. AE, DC, MC, V.*

££ **Grasmead House.** The comfortable bedrooms in this small family-run hotel all have antique four-poster beds. Just beyond the city walls, the lodging is an easy walk from the city center, and the friendly owners are more than willing to share their local knowledge with guests. There are no meals served other than breakfast, but very good restaurants are only a short walk away. ✉ *1 Scarcroft Hill, YO2 1DF,* ☎ FAX *01904/629996. 6 rooms with bath or shower. Bar, no-smoking rooms. MC, V.*

£ **Abbey Guest House.** This pretty, no-smoking, terraced guest house—formerly an artisan's house—is a 10-minute walk from the train station and town center. Although small, it's very clean and friendly, with a peaceful garden right on the river and ducks pottering about outside. Picnic lunches and evening meals can be arranged on request. ✉ *14 Earlsborough Terr., Marygate, YO3 7BQ,* ☎ *01904/627782. 7 rooms, 2 with bath. Breakfast room. AE, MC, V.*

Nightlife and the Arts

FESTIVALS

Playing on its Viking past, York hosts the annual **Viking Festival** in February. The celebrations—including a parade and longship regatta—end with the Jorvik Viking Combat reenactment, when ravaging Northmen confront their Anglo-Saxon enemies. Call for details: ✉ *Jorvik Viking Centre, Coppergate,* ☎ *01904/643211.*

The next quadrennial performance of the medieval **York Mystery Plays** will take place in the summer of 2000. An **Early Music Festival** is held each summer except in Mystery Play years. For details, call the Tourist Information Centre in York (☎ 01904/621756). In York, the annual English **Bonfire Night** celebrations on November 5 have added piquancy, since the notorious 16th-century conspirator Guy Fawkes was a native of the city. They commemorate Fawkes's failure to blow up the Houses of Parliament, and his effigy is burned atop every fire. Ask at the tourist office for the locations of the best fires and fireworks displays.

THEATER

York's **Theatre Royal** is a lively professional theater in a lovely old building, with many other events besides plays: string quartets, choral music, poetry reading, and art exhibitions. ✉ *St. Leonard's Pl.,* ☎ *01904/623568.* ⏲ *Box office Mon.–Sat. 10–8.*

Shopping

The new and secondhand bookstores around Petergate, Stonegate, and the Shambles are excellent. **Blackwell's** (✉ 32 Stonegate, ☎ 01904/624531), has a large stock of new titles and a convenient mail-order service. For secondhand books, old maps, and prints head for the Minster and the **Minster Gate Bookshop** (✉ 8 Minster Gate, ☎ 01904/621812). For something high in quality and typically English, **Mulberry Hall** (✉ Stonegate, ☎ 01904/620736), a large, half-timber house dating from the 15th century, is a sales center for all the famous names in fine bone china and crystal. **Robert Smart Menswear** (✉ Low Petergate, ☎ 01904/652718) is a comfortingly old-fashioned clothes store selling stylish, very English tweeds and woolens. The **York Antiques Centre** (✉ 2 Lendal, no phone) has 34 shops on two floors selling antiques, bric-a-brac, books, and jewelry.

En Route Traveling eastward from Leeds to Harrogate, take the less direct B1224 across **Marston Moor** where, in 1644, Oliver Cromwell won a decisive victory over the Royalists during the Civil War. A few miles beyond, at Wetherby, you can then cut northwest along the A661 to Harrogate.

Harrogate

26 *21 mi west of York, 11 mi south of Ripon, 16 mi north of Leeds.*

During the Regency and early Victorian periods, it became fashionable for the noble and wealthy to retire to a spa for relaxation. Nowhere in Yorkshire reached such grand heights as Harrogate, an elegant town that flourished during the 19th century. When the spas no longer drew crowds, Harrogate shed its old image to become a modern business center and built a huge complex that attracts international conventions. It has been tactfully located so as not to spoil the town's landscape of poised Regency row houses, pleasant walkways, and sweeping green spaces. Of Harrogate's parks, most appealing is the one in the town center, known as **The Stray,** a 200-acre reach of grassland which is a riot of color in the spring. The **Valley Gardens** provide varied attractions, including a boating lake, tennis courts, and a little café.

You can still drink the evil-smelling (and -tasting) spa waters at the **Royal Pump Room Museum,** which charts the story of Harrogate from its 17th-century beginnings. The building dates from 1842, built over the original sulphur well that brought such prosperity to the town. ✉ *Crown Place,* ☎ *01423/503340.* *£1.50.* *Tues.–Sat. 10–5, Sun. 2–5.*

In the **Royal Baths Assembly Rooms** (1897), you may take a Turkish bath or a sauna in its exotic, tiled rooms; allow two hours or so for the full treatment. ✉ *Crescent Rd.,* ☎ *01423/562498.* *£7 per bath and sauna session, massages £10.50–£20.* *Daily; call for men's and women's schedules.*

Dining and Lodging

£££–££££ ✕ **White House.** The White House is an award-winning small hotel, whose facade resembles an Italianate villa. Inside, comfort is all: guest rooms are bright, and reasonably large; flowers, mirrors, paintings, artistic bits and pieces, and even the odd antique abound. In the lounge, sugared almonds await guests who drop by; the library has games and cards. The changing menu in the restaurant (*££–£££*) caters to most tastes with its eclectic mix of Continental and British cuisine. ✉ *10 Park Parade, HG1 5AH,* ☎ *01423/501388,* FAX *01423/527973. 11 rooms with bath or shower. Restaurant, bar, no-smoking rooms. AE, DC, MC, V.*

Nightlife and the Arts

Harrogate's **International Festival**—of ballet, music, contemporary dance, film, comedy, street theater, and more—takes place over two weeks at the end of July and beginning of August each year. ✉ *The Festival Office, Royal Baths, HG1 2RR,* ☎ *01423/562303.*

Knaresborough

27 *3 mi northeast of Harrogate, 17 mi west of York.*

The photogenic old town of Knaresborough is built in a steep, rocky gorge along the river Nidd. Central attractions include its river, lively with pleasure boats, a little marketplace, and a medieval castle—now not much more than a keep—where Richard II was once imprisoned (1399). In a historic park site, amid tree-lined riverside walks, **Mother Shipton's Cave** is said to be the birthplace of the 16th-century prophetess. Events supposedly foretold by her include the Great Fire of London and the earlier defeat of the Spanish Armada. It's just a short walk south of Knaresborough town center. ✉ *Prophesy House, High Bridge,* ☎ *01423/864600.* 🎫 *£4.25.* ⏲ *Easter–Oct., daily 9:30–5:45; Nov.–Easter, daily 10–4:45.*

Studley Royal and Fountains Abbey

★ 28 *9 mi northwest of Knaresborough.*

The 18th-century water garden and deer park, Studley Royal, together with the ruins of Fountains Abbey, blends the glories of English Gothic architecture with a neoclassical vision of an ordered universe. The gardens include lakes, ponds, and even a diverted river, while waterfalls splash around classical temples, statues, and a grotto; the surrounding woods offer long vistas toward the great tower of Ripon Cathedral, some 3 miles north. The majestic ruins of Fountains Abbey, with its own high tower and soaring 13th-century arches, make a striking picture on the banks of the river Skell. Founded in 1132, but not completed until the early 1500s, the abbey still possesses many of its original buildings, and it's one of the best places in England to learn about medieval monastic life. The whole of this complex is now owned by the National Trust. There's a small restaurant (lunch only) and two stores, as well as an exhibition and video display in the 17th-century **Fountains Hall**, one of the earliest neoclassical buildings in northern England. ☎ *01765/601002.* 🎫 *£4.* ⏲ *Jan.–Mar., daily 10–5 (or dusk); Apr.–Sept., daily 10–7; Oct.–Dec., daily 10–5 (or dusk); closed Fri. Nov.–Jan. Guided tours Apr.–Oct., daily at 2:30.*

Ripon

29 *3 mi northeast of Fountains Abbey, 11 mi north of Harrogate, 24 mi northwest of York.*

Ripon was thriving as early as the 9th century as an important market center. Successive churches here were destroyed by the Vikings and the Normans, and the present structure, dating from the 12th and 13th centuries, is particularly noted for its finely carved choir stalls and Saxon crypt. Despite its small size, the church has been designated a cathedral since the mid-19th century, which makes Ripon (only about 15,000 inhabitants) technically a city. Market day here is Thursday, probably the best day to stop by.

30 Make the effort to drive out from Ripon to **Newby Hall,** an early 18th-century house that was redecorated later in the same century by Robert Adam for his patron William Weddell; it contains some of the finest in-

terior decorative art of its period in Western Europe. One room has been designed around a set of priceless Gobelin tapestries, and another was created to show off Roman sculpture. The famous grounds, which extend down to the river Ure, include a collection of old species roses, rare shrubs, and delightful sunken gardens. The children's adventure playground, narrow-gauge steam railroad, river steamers, and garden restaurant make a visit to Newby a full day's outing. It's 5 miles southeast of Ripon. ✉ *Skelton-on-Ure,* ☎ *01423/322583.* 🎫 *£5.40; gardens only £3.80.* ⏲ *Apr.–Sept., Tues.–Sun., grounds 11–5:30, house noon–5.*

Lightwater Valley Theme Park features buggy rides, a miniature Wild West railroad, waterslides, an old-time fair, and pony rides. A factory-store "village," open year-round, should keep the adults occupied. It's 7 miles northwest of Ripon, along the A6108. ✉ *North Stainley, near Ripon,* ☎ *01765/635321.* 🎫 *July–Aug. £9.95; other months £8.95.* ⏲ *Apr.–Oct.; call for opening times.*

THE NORTH YORKSHIRE COAST

Except for during the hottest summers, the North Yorkshire coast isn't the warmest place for a beach vacation. That said, there's plenty to make you glad you came, not least the good sandy beaches, rocky coves, and sea-cliff walks that stretch along the coast, from Bridlington to Saltburn-by-the-Sea. Most coastal towns still support an active fishing industry and every harbor offers fishing and leisure trips throughout the summer. The east coast beaches are usually fine for swimming, though you'll find the water cold. Beaches at Scarborough, Whitby, and Filey have patrolled bathing areas: Swim between the red-and-yellow flags, and don't swim when a red flag is flying. Major towns also have indoor swimming pools.

From York, the coast is about an hour's drive away, and starting at Bridlington, it's a simple matter to follow the main road north to Scarborough (the A165), on to Robin Hood's Bay and Whitby (A171).

Numbers in the margin correspond to points of interest on the Yorkshire map.

Bridlington

31 *41 mi east of York.*

Bridlington, a fishing port with an ancient harbor, makes a fine introduction to the North Yorkshire coast, featuring a wide arc of sand that's typical of the beach resorts in the region. Boat trips through the harbor and up the coast depart very frequently during the summer; or simply join the milling crowds who promenade up and down the seafront, eating fish and chips, browsing at the gift shops and stalls, and frequenting the rides at the small amusement park. At **Flamborough Head** a huge bank of chalk cliffs juts out into the North Sea. A coastal path over the cliff tops ends at **Bempton Cliffs**, one of the finest seabird reserves on the east coast. The reserve is open at all times, though the displays at the neighboring Visitor Centre can help you get more out of the area. ✉ *Visitor Centre, Bempton Cliffs, no phone.* 🎫 *Free, but £1.50 for parking.* ⏲ *Mar.–Oct., daily 10–5.*

Scarborough

32 *18 mi northwest of Bridlington, 34 mi northeast of York.*

A great sweep of cliffs above its sandy bay, a rocky promontory capped by a ruined castle, and a harbor with a lighthouse make Scarborough the classic picture of an English seaside resort. In fact, the city claims to be the earliest one in Britain, dating from the chance discovery in the early 17th century of a mineral spring on the foreshore. Not unexpectedly, this led to the establishment of a spa, whose users were encouraged not merely to soak themselves in seawater but even to drink it. By the late 18th century, when sea bathing was firmly in vogue, no beaches were busier than Scarborough's with "bathing machines," cumbersome wheeled cabins drawn by donkeys or horses into the surf and anchored there. Scarborough's initial prosperity dates from this period, as evidenced in the handsome Regency and early Victorian residences and hotels in the city.

The contrast between the two distinct faces of Scarborough makes the town all the more appealing. Its older, more genteel side in the southern half of town consists of carefully laid out crescents and squares and cliff-top walks and gardens with spectacular views across Cayton Bay. The northern side is a riot of ice-cream stands, cafés, stores selling "rock" (luridly colored, hard candy), crab hawkers, bingo halls, and candyfloss (cotton candy). In addition, enough survives of the tight huddle of streets, alleyways, and red-roofed cottages around the harbor to give an idea of what the city was like before the resort days. One revealing relic is a tall, 15th-century stone house, now a restaurant, which is said to have been owned by Richard III.

Paths link the harbor with the ruins of **Scarborough Castle** on the promontory; dating from Norman times, it is built on the site of a Roman signal station and near a former Viking settlement. From the castle there are spectacular views across the North Bay, the beaches, and the shore gardens. The entrance fee includes a self-guided audio-tape tour. ✉ *Castle Rd.,* ☎ *01723/372451.* 🎫 *£1.80.* ⏲ *Apr.–Sept., daily 10–6; Oct.–Mar., Tues.–Sun. 10–4.*

At Scarborough's little medieval church of **St. Mary** you'll find the grave of Anne, the youngest Brontë sister, who died in 1849; she was taken to Scarborough from Haworth in a final desperate effort to save her life in the sea air. The church is near the castle on the way into town. ✉ *Castle Rd., no phone.*

Wood End was the vacation home of 20th-century writers Edith, Osbert, and Sacheverell Sitwell, and the west wing houses a library of their works as well as portraits and paintings. The rest of the early Victorian house, amid delightful grounds, is taken up by the collections of the **Museum of Natural History.** ✉ *The Crescent,* ☎ *01723/367326.* 🎫 *Free.* ⏲ *May–Sept., Tues.–Sun. 10–5; Oct.–Apr., Fri.–Sun. 11–4.*

Scarborough features one of the first public buildings in the country to be erected as a museum. The **Rotunda Museum,** an extraordinary circular building, was originally constructed in 1829 for William Smith of the Scarborough Philosophical Society to display his geological collection; it now houses important archaeological and local history collections, while the upper gallery displays a schematic section of the local coastline. The museum is just a short walk below Wood End. ✉ *Vernon Rd.,* ☎ *01723/374839.* 🎫 *Free.* ⏲ *May–Sept., Tues.–Sun. 10–5; Oct.–Apr., Fri.–Sun. 11–4.*

Scarborough is full of cheerful attractions that appeal to kids, among them an activity center known as **Kinderland,** designed to keep children (and their parents) entertained whatever the weather. ✉ *Burniston Rd., North Bay,* ☎ *01723/354555.* 🎫 *£3.95.* ⏲ *Easter–Apr., weekends; May–mid-Sept., daily; hrs vary, so call ahead.*

The **Scarborough Sea Life Centre** presents marine life and environmental matters in an entertaining way, with various different marine habitats combined under one roof. ✉ *Scalby Mills, North Bay,* ☎ *01723/376125.* *£4.50.* ⏲ *Fall and spring, daily 10–5; summer, daily 10–9.*

Dining and Lodging

££ ✕ **Lanterna Restaurant.** An intimate atmosphere and a high standard of cuisine make this Italian restaurant a good choice. The classic dishes are all represented, among them tender veal cooked with ham and cheese, but more unusual seasonal specials are worth investigating, too, using fresh vegetables and fish unavailable at other times of the year. The restaurant's also noted for the quality of its service and its wine cellar. ✉ *33 Queen St.,* ☎ *01723/363616. MC, V. No lunch in winter. Closed Sun., Mon.*

£££ **The Crown.** The centerpiece of Scarborough's Regency Esplanade, this period hotel overlooks South Bay and the castle headland. Originally built to accommodate fashionable 19th-century visitors to Scarborough Spa, it has been considerably refurbished and guest accommodations are tasteful and comfortable. The regular room rate doesn't include breakfast, though you might consider the special dinner, bed, and breakfast package. ✉ *The Esplanade, YO11 2AG,* ☎ *01723/373491,* FAX *01723/362271. 78 rooms with bath. Restaurant, bar, beauty salon. AE, DC, MC, V.*

Nightlife and the Arts

Scarborough has an internationally known artistic native son in Alan Ayckbourn, a popular contemporary playwright. The **Stephen Joseph Theatre** (✉ Westborough), which stages many of his plays, moved into spacious new premises in 1996. Call in at the theater for a program or contact the tourist office for box office details.

Outdoor Activities and Sports

FISHING

Sea angling is a busy trade in Scarborough; scheduled fishing trips are much cheaper than individually chartered ones—look for ads in the town or check at the information center. You'll pay from about £10 for a three-hour trip (rods and bait included).

Robin Hood's Bay

★ 33 *13 mi northwest of Scarborough.*

Many visitors' favorite coastal stop is at Robin Hood's Bay, a tiny fishing village squeezed into a narrow ravine near where a stream courses over the cliffs. The name is curious since about the only historical certainty is that there is no connection with the famous English medieval outlaw; the village didn't even come into being until the late 15th century, after which it thrived in a small way as a fishing port and smuggling center. Perilously steep, narrow roads are fringed with tiny, crazily scattered houses and shops, and space is so tight you are not allowed to drive into the village center; use the car parks at the top of the village. The tiny **beach** was once a notorious smugglers' landing; contraband was passed up the streambed beneath the cottages, which were linked to each other by secret passages, often with customs officers in hot pursuit. The tide rushes in very quickly, so take care. Provided the tide is out, you can stroll 20 minutes' south from Robin Hood's Bay, along the exposed stone shore, as far as the curiously named **Boggle Hole**, a steep ravine whose old water mill has been converted into a youth hostel. If the tide comes in during your walk, you can return to Robin Hood's Bay by the cliff-top path (signposted from the hostel).

Several superb, long-distance walks start or finish in, or run through, Robin Hood's Bay. The village marks one end of the 190-mile **Coast-to-Coast walk** (the other is at St. Bees Head on the Irish Sea)—coast-to-coast walkers finish at the Bay Hotel, above the harbor. The coastal **Cleveland Way** runs north (to Whitby) and south (to Scarborough) through the village, while the trans-Moor **Lyke-Wake Walk** finishes just 3 miles away at Ravenscar.

En Route For many, the nicest (and easiest) local walk is the 7-mile coastal section of the Cleveland Way north to Whitby. This takes about 3 hours to complete and hugs the cliffs almost all the way; look for signposts to Whitby (marked CLEVELAND WAY).

Lodging

£££ **Raven Hall Hotel.** This superb Georgian hotel with landscaped grounds features unrivaled coastal views from the headland of Ravenscar, just 3 miles southeast of Robin Hood's Bay. Try your utmost to secure a room with a bay view; if they're occupied, you can console yourself with the same wonderful views from the lounge or restaurant. The Raven Hall Hotel is known for its good sports facilities, though you'll have to be very hardy to use the outdoor pool, despite its enterprising clifftop location. It's worth noting that the bar marks the traditional end of the punishing, long-distance Lyke-Wake Walk, so you may share the comfortable lounge (with fire in winter) with exhausted walkers on occasion. Ask about special winter discounted rates. ✉ *Ravenscar, YO13 0ET* ☎ *01723/870353. 53 rooms with bath. Restaurant, bar, indoor and outdoor pools, 9-hole golf course, 2 tennis courts. AE, DC, MC, V.*

Whitby

★ ㉞ *7 mi northwest of Robin Hood's Bay, 20 mi north of Pickering, 25 mi east of Middlesbrough.*

A small, laid-back resort, at the mouth of the river Esk, Whitby has a longer and more interesting history than most towns on the coast. A religious center as far back as the 7th century, when Whitby Abbey was first founded, it later came to prominence as a whaling port. The first ships sailed from here for Greenland in the mid-18th century, captained by local men like William Scoresby, inventor of the crow's nest, to whom Herman Melville paid tribute in his novel, *Moby Dick*. At much the same time as whaling made Whitby rich, its shipbuilding made it famous: James—later, Captain—Cook (1728–79), explorer and navigator, sailed on his first ship out of the town in 1747 and all four of his subsequent discovery vessels were built in Whitby.

Whitby's glory days are long gone, but there's still much to admire. Fine Georgian houses line some of the central streets on the west side of the river, while across the swing-bridge in the old town, cobbled Church Street is packed shoulder-to-shoulder in summer with visitors exploring the dark alleys, enclosed courtyards, and gift shops.

Climb the 199 steps from the end of Church Street and you are at the rather eccentrically designed Church of **St. Mary,** with its ship's deck roof, triple-decker pulpit, and enclosed galleries. The church dates originally from the 12th century, although almost everything you see today is the (often less-than-happy) result of 19th- and 20th-century renovations. The spooky, weather-beaten churchyard, filled with the crooked old gravestones of ancient mariners, affords superb views of the sea and the town itself. It was here that Bram Stoker's Dracula claimed Lucy as his victim, while if you search around amid the tall grass at the back, you'll find the grave of master mariner William Scoresby. ✉ *Church La., East Cliff, no phone.*

The romantic ruins of **Whitby Abbey,** set high on the East Cliff, are visible from almost everywhere in town. St. Hilda founded the abbey in AD 657, and Caedmon (died circa 670), the first identifiable poet of the English language, was a monk here; an engraved cross, of dubious provenance, which bears his name, stands at the top of the 199 steps near St. Mary's church. ✉ *Abbey La., East Cliff,* ☎ *01947/603568.* 🎫 *£1.60.* ⏲ *Apr.–Sept., daily 10–6; Oct.–Mar., daily 10–4.*

Captain Cook is remembered in various places around town, most notably by his bronze statue on top of the West Cliff, near the pair of arched whalebones. However, the most revealing exhibits relating to the man are to be found in the **Captain Cook Memorial Museum,** tucked into the period rooms of the 18th-century house belonging to shipowner John Walker, where Cook lived as an apprentice from 1746 to 1749. Here, you can see mementos of his epic expeditions, including maps, diaries, and drawings, as well as tracing the privations of his wife and family, left behind to cope with life, loss, and bereavement. ✉ *Grape La.,* ☎ *01947/601900.* 🎫 *£1.80.* ⏲ *Easter–Oct., daily 9:45–5; Mar. and Nov., weekends 11–3.*

Dining and Lodging

£ ✕ **Trencher's.** Whitby is full of fish-and-chip places, but nowhere serves it better than Trencher's, a bright, welcoming diner-style restaurant with a wide menu. Crisply battered, grease-free fillets of fresh haddock or cod come with thick-cut chips; order a large portion, with a side order of mushy peas, and you won't eat again for a week. ✉ *New Quay Rd.,* ☎ *01947/603212. No credit cards. Closed mid-Nov.–mid-Mar.; otherwise daily, but closes at 9 PM.*

£–££ ✕🏨 **The Shepherd's Purse.** In the cobbled old town, this splendid little complex comprises charming boutique-style guest rooms, a vegetarian restaurant, and a health food store. There are two less expensive bedrooms above the store and five more in the galleried courtyard at the back, which just creep into the higher price category. Although small, these are en-suite, with four-poster or brass bedsteads; floors are wooden, the furniture country-style, and the top two even have little balconies. ✉ *95 Church St., YO22 4BH,* ☎ *01947/820228. 7 rooms, 5 with shower or bath. Restaurant. No credit cards.*

£ ★ ✕🏨 **White House and Griffin.** When looking for the perfect inn, you want a characterful old building, a roaring fire in the grate, food to thrill, and an owner eager to please. Step forward the 18th-century White House and Griffin, in which Charles Dickens once slept and railway pioneer George Stephenson lectured. The spruce, renovated rooms are warm and comfortable, while downstairs in the cozy bistro-bar, owner Stewart Perkins presides over a fine, changing menu of locally caught fish and properly hung meat, including game in season. Dinner might be fried Whitby calamari or bouillabaisse, followed by grilled mullet, pan-fried herring, or even a splendid *fruits de mer* assortment of local cooked and cured fish. ✉ *Church St., YO22 4BH,* ☎ *01947/604857. 12 rooms with bath. Restaurant, bar. No credit cards.*

Nightlife and the Arts

The **Whitby Regatta,** held in August every year, is a three-day jamboree of boat races, fun-fair rides, lifeboat rescue displays, parades, and musical events. Music (but also traditional dance and story-telling) is to the fore during **Whitby Folk Week,** usually held one week after Regatta in August, when pubs, pavements, and halls become venues for more than a thousand traditional folk events by performers from all over the country. Make sure you book accommodation well in advance if you come at this time.

Shopping

Whitby is known for its **jet,** a very hard, black form of natural carbon, which has been used locally to make jewelry and ornaments for more than a century, and was particular popular as mourning decoration during the Victorian era. Several shops in the old town along Church Street and parallel Sandgate have fine displays.

Staithes

35 *9 mi northwest of Whitby.*

Like Robin Hood's Bay, which it superficially resembles, the hardy fishing village of Staithes captures imaginations at first sight. Its few houses huddled below the rocky, seagull-studded outcrop of Cowbar Nab, on either side of the beck (stream), have survived storm and flood, and present a hoary, weather-beaten aspect. Not all were so lucky. The Cod and Lobster Inn, at the harbor, is in its third incarnation, while the draper's shop in which James Cook had his first apprenticeship before moving to Whitby fell into the sea entirely in 1745. The house known as Cook's Cottage, near the pub, is supposedly built out of the salvaged remains of the original building.

There's nothing specific to see in Staithes, but there is a powerful atmosphere in the stepped alleys and courtyards. These, and the surrounding coastal cliffs, were captured on canvas by many members of the so-called Staithes School of artists, who were prominent earlier this century. Tourists are a vital part of the local economy these days, with perhaps the most surprising visitors those in wet suits, who know Staithes to have some of the best surfing in the country.

Dining

££ ★ ✕ **The Endeavour.** This rather higgledy-piggledy old house on Staithes's main street, near the harbor, is well-known for its meals of locally caught fish. Menus change seasonally, but you can count on dishes being presented with care and with Mediterranean or Asian flourishes; soups, salmon, and lobster are strong points. Have a drink in the tiny, low-ceiling bar, choose from the blackboard, and don't be afraid to ask for recommendations from the brisk staff. ✉ *1 High St.,* ☎ *01947/840825. No credit cards. No dinner Sun. Closed mid-Jan.–mid-Mar.*

THE NORTH YORK MOORS

The North York Moors is a dramatic swath of high moorland starting 25 miles north of the city of York and stretching east to the coast and west to the Cleveland Hills. Once covered in forest, of which a few pockets survive here and there, the landscape changed with the introduction of sheep in medieval times by monks at the monastic foundations of Rievaulx and Whitby. The evidence is clear for all to see today: rolling, heather-covered hills that, in late summer and early fall, are a rich blaze of crimson and purple, and a series of isolated, medieval, standing stones that once acted as waymarkers on the paths between the abbeys. For more than four decades, the area has been designated a National Park, in order to protect the moors and grassy valleys that shelter brown-stone villages and hamlets. Minor roads and tracks criss-cross the moors in all directions, and there's no one, obvious route through the region. Perhaps the most rewarding approach is southwest from the coast at Whitby, along the

Esk Valley to Danby, which is also accessible on the Esk Valley branch train line between Middlesbrough and Whitby. From Danby, minor roads run south over the high moors reaching Hutton-le-Hole, beyond which main roads lead to interesting towns on the moors' edge, like Helmsley and Malton. Completing the route in this direction leaves you with an easy side trip to Castle Howard before returning to nearby York.

Numbers in the margin correspond to points of interest on the Yorkshire map.

Danby

36 *15 mi west of Whitby; take A171 (to Teesside) and turn south for Danby after 12 mi, after which it's a 3-mi drive over Danby Low Moor to the village. Or take the local train direct from Whitby.*

The straggling, old stone village of Danby nestles in a green valley, just a short walk from the tops of the nearby moors. It's been settled since Viking times—Danby means "village where the Danes lived"—and these days it bumbles along contentedly in a semi-touristed way. There's a pub, and a bakery with tearoom, and if you bring hiking boots with you, within 10 minutes you can be above the village looking down, surrounded by nothing but isolated moorland.

In a converted country house on the eastern outskirts of Danby, the **National Park's Moors Centre** has exhibitions, displays, and a wide range of pamphlets and books about the area. There's a garden out front with picnic tables and superb valley views, and a tearoom, while the summer Moorsbus (☞ Getting Around *in,* Yorkshire A to Z, *below*) operates from the center for the 30-minute journey south to Hutton-le-Hole. ✉ *Danby Lodge,* ☎ *01287/660654.* 🎫 *Free.* ⏲ *Apr.–Oct., daily 10–5; Nov.–Mar., weekends Sun. 11–4.*

En Route From Danby take the road due west for 2 miles to Castleton, and then turn south over the top of the moors toward Hutton-le-Hole. The narrow road offers magnificent views over the national park, especially at the old, stone **Ralph Cross** (5 miles), which marks the highest point. Drive carefully: Sheep-dodging is something of an art in these parts.

Hutton-le-Hole

★ 37 *4 mi south of Rosedale Abbey; follow sign for Rosedale Chimney Bank; also 13 mi south of Danby.*

Even after seeing the varied splendors of villages throughout the national park, it's difficult not to think Hutton-le-Hole the pick of the bunch. It's almost too pastoral to be true: a tiny hamlet, based around a wide village green, with sheep wandering about, and a stream babbling in the background. The surroundings are some of the most attractive in the region, and consequently in summer, the local car parks fill quickly as people arrive to take to the nearby hills for a day's walking. Make sure you visit the 2-acre **Ryedale Folk Museum,** a worthy recent Museum of the Year Award winner, which records life in the Dales from prehistory onward by way of a display of 13 historic buildings: a series of 16th-century cottages, a 19th-century blacksmith's shop, an early photographer's studio, and medieval kiln. ✉ *Hutton-le-Hole,* ☎ *01751/417367.* 🎫 *£3.* ⏲ *Mar.–Oct., daily 10–5:30.*

Helmsley

38 *13 mi west of Pickering, 27 mi north of York.*

For walkers, the pleasant market town of Helmsley, on the southern edge of the Moors, is well known as the starting-point of the long-distance moor-and-coastal footpath, the **Cleveland Way.** Boots are donned at the old cross in the market square, from where it's 50 miles or so across the moors to the coast and then a similar distance south to Filey along the clifftops; all told, 108 miles of walking, which most people aim to complete in nine days. Helmsley itself is attractive enough for a day trip, and features a castle (partly ruined during the Civil War) and a traditional country marketplace surrounded by fine old inns, cafés, and stores. Market day here is Friday. Even inveterate nonwalkers will probably find the very early stages of the Cleveland Way irresistible, since the trail passes close to the ruins of Rievaulx Abbey, just outside the town. A leaflet available from the tourist information center indicates the route.

Lodging

£££–££££ **The Black Swan.** This lovely, ivy-covered property sits right on the edge of the market square and makes a splendid, relaxing base. The building is a hybrid, part 16th-century coaching inn, part Georgian house, but careful restoration and renovation has ensured comfort throughout: Rooms either overlook the square or the fine walled garden at the back, in which, incidentally, there's a croquet lawn for your amusement in summer. A restaurant serves traditional British and local dishes; an open fire keeps things cozy in winter. ✉ *Market Pl., YO6 5BJ,* ☎ *01439/770466,* FAX *01439/770174. 44 rooms with bath. Restaurant, bar. AE, DC, MC, V.*

Rievaulx Abbey

★ 39 *2 mi northwest of Hemlsley.*

One of the most graceful of all medieval English seats of learning, Rievaulx (pronounced "Reevoh") Abbey occupies a dramatic setting on the river Rye. A Cistercian foundation, dating from 1132, its wealth was derived from the wool trade, and the extensive surviving ruins give some indication of the thriving trade with Europe that the medieval monks of North Yorkshire engaged in. The landscaped grounds sport graceful Gothic arches, cloisters, and associated buildings, including the Chapter House, which retains the original shrine of the first abbot, William, by the entrance. The abbey is an hour and a half's walk, northwest, from Helmsley (there's a signposted footpath), or 2 miles by road, taking the B1257. ✉ *Rievaulx Abbey,* ☎ *01439/798228.* 🎫 *£2.50.* ⏲ *Apr.–Sept., daily 10–6; Oct.–Mar., daily 10–4.*

Having wandered among the ruins of Rievaulx Abbey, you might also like to climb (or drive) up to the **Rievaulx Terraces,** a long grassy walkway on the hillside above, terminating in the remains of several Tuscan- and Ionic-style classical temples. The views of the abbey from here are magnificent. ✉ *Rievaulx Terrace,* ☎ *01439/798340.* 🎫 *£2.50.* ⏲ *Apr.–Oct., daily 10:30–6.*

Castle Howard

★ 40 *12 mi southeast of Helmsley, 15 mi northeast of York.*

Standing serene among the Howardian Hills to the west of Malton, Castle Howard is one of the grandest and most opulent stately homes in Britain, an imposing baroque building whose magnificent skyline is punctuated by stone chimneys and a graceful central dome. Many people know it best as Brideshead, the home of the Flyte family in Evelyn Waugh's tale of aristocratic woe, *Brideshead Revisted*; this was where much of the TV series was filmed. The house was designed by Sir John Vanbrugh, who also designed Blenheim Palace for the Howard family (who still live here). Remarkably, this was the first building of any kind that Vanbrugh designed; until then he was best known as a playwright. Do not make the mistake of assuming that this is the work of a man tentatively feeling his way into a new profession. The audacity and confidence of the great Baroque house are startling, proclaiming the wealth and importance of the Howards and the utter self-assurance of its architect. Castle Howard took 60 years to build (1699–1759) and it was worth every year. A magnificent central hallway spanned by a hand-painted (and unfortunately, new) ceiling dwarfs all visitors, while there is no shortage of grandeur elsewhere in the building: vast family portraits, delicate marble fireplaces, immense and fading tapestries, huge pieces of Victorian silver on polished tables, and a great many marble busts. Outside, the stately theme continues in one of the most stunning neoclassical landscapes in England; Horace Walpole, the 18th-century connoisseur, commented that a pheasant at Castle Howard lives better than most dukes elsewhere. Make sure you see the Temple of the Four Winds and the Mausoleum, whose magnificence caused Walpole to comment that all who view it would wish to be buried alive. ✉ *Coneysthorpe,* ☎ *01653/648333.* 🎫 *House and gardens £7; gardens only £4.50.* ⏲ *House mid-Mar.–Oct., daily 11–4:30; grounds daily 10–5.*

YORKSHIRE A TO Z

Arriving and Departing

By Bus

National Express (☎ 0171/730–0202) serves the region from London's Victoria Coach Station. Average travel times are 4½ hours to York, 6½ hours to Scarborough, and 7 hours to Whitby.

By Car

The M1, the principal route north from London, gets you to the region in about two hours, with longer travel times up into north Yorkshire. For York (193 miles) and the Scarborough areas, stay on the M1 to Leeds (189 miles), then take the A64. For the Yorkshire Dales, take the M1 to Leeds, then A660 to A65 north and west to Skipton. For the North York Moors, either take the B1363 north from York to Helmsley, or leave the A64 at Malton and follow the trans-moor A169 that runs to Whitby.

By Train

British Rail serves the region from London's King's Cross (☎ 0171/278–2477) and Euston (☎ 0171/387–7070) stations. Average travel times from King's Cross: 2½ hours to Leeds and two hours to York.

It is possible to reach the North Yorkshire coast by train, though services from London to Scarborough (change at York) and, especially, Whitby (change at Darlington and Middlesbrough) can take anything up to seven hours. It's much less trouble (though not much quicker) to take the direct bus from London.

Getting Around

By Bicycle

Although the countryside is too hilly for bicycle touring, except for the most experienced, you can rent bikes locally in several places. In York, where there are special cycleways, contact **Cycleworks** (✉ 14–16 Lawrence St., ☎ 01904/626664) and pick up a cycling map from the tourist information center. In Robin Hood's Bay contact **Bay Cycles** (✉ Station Rd., ☎ 01947/880488).

By Bus

Each district now has its own bus company, and you may find you need to ring around to discover the full range of services, though local tourist information centers can usually help.

There are local **Metro** buses from Leeds and Bradford (☎ 0113/2457676) into the more remote parts of the Yorkshire Dales. Other companies include: **Harrogate & District** (☎ 01423/566061); **Coastliner** (☎ 01653/692556) for services to Scarborough, Whitby, Malton, Pickering, and Leeds; **United** (☎ 01325/468771) to Ripon; **Tees** (☎ 01642/210131) for Whitby, Scarborough, and Middlesbrough.

In York, the main local bus operator is **Rider York** (✉ 5 Rougier St., ☎ 01904/624161). Many districts have Rover tickets; in York, the **Minster Card** (£8) gives a week's free travel on all Rider York services.

The **Moorsbus** (information from any National Park office) runs every Sunday and bank holiday Monday from late-May to the end of September, and every Tuesday and Wednesday from late-July to the end of August. It connects Danby, Hutton-le-Hole, Helmsley, Rievaulx Abbey, Rosedale Abbey, and Pickering and costs £1 for an all-day ticket.

By Car

The trans-Pennine motorway, the M62, between Liverpool and Hull, crosses the bottom of this region. North of Leeds, the A1 is the major north–south road, though narrow stretches, roadworks, and heavy traffic make this very slow going at times. Some of the steep, narrow roads in the countryside off the main routes are difficult drives and can be particularly perilous (or closed altogether) in winter. Prime candidates for main roads closed annually by snow drifts are the moorland A169 and the coast-and-moor A171. If you're driving in the dales or moors in winter, listen for the weather forecasts.

By Train

There are local services from Leeds to Skipton, from York to Knaresborough and Harrogate and also to Scarborough (which has connections on to the seaside towns of Filey and Bridlington). Whitby can be reached on the minor, and extremely attractive, Esk Valley line from Middlesbrough. England's most scenic railway, the **Settle–Carlisle** line, can be reached from Leeds, where daily trains travel via Shipley, Keighley, and Skipton to the start of the line at Settle. For train times, call Leeds station (☞ *below*).

Two **Regional Rover** tickets for seven days' unlimited travel are available: **North East** and **Coast and Peaks.**

For local travel information, call the following stations: Bradford and Leeds (☎ 0113/2448133), Scarborough (☎ 01723/373486), Whitby (information from Newcastle station, ☎ 0191/2326262), York (☎ 01904/642155).

Contacts and Resources

Car Rentals

BRADFORD

Avis, ✉ Bowling Bridge Service Station, Wakefield Rd., ☎ 01274/626819; **Europcar,** ✉ 172 Thornton Rd., ☎ 01274/733048; **Eurodollar-Rent-a-Car,** ✉ Nelson St., ☎ 01274/722155; **Hertz,** ✉ 20 Laisterdyke, Sticker La., ☎ 01274/666666.

YORK

Budget Rent-a-Car, ✉ Station House, Foss Islands Rd., ☎ 01904/644919, and **Hertz,** ✉ York Rail Station, Station Rd., ☎ 01904/612586.

Emergencies

Call ☎ 999 for the emergency services, **police, fire or ambulance.**

Fishing

For information on licenses and permits, contact the post office in major towns, or the **National Rivers Authority** (✉ Coverdale House, Aviator Court, Amy Johnson Way, Clifton Moor, York YO3 4UZ, ☎ 01904/692296).

Guided Tours

Guide Friday (✉ De Grey Rooms, Exhibition Sq., ☎ 01904/640896) runs frequent city tours of York, including stops at the Minster, the Castle Museum, the Shambles, and the Jorvik Viking Centre, that allow you to get on and off the bus as you please (£6.50). It also conducts tours of the surrounding countryside, including Fountains Abbey and Castle Howard.

The **York Association of Voluntary Guides** (✉ De Grey Rooms, Exhibition Sq., ☎ 01904/640780) arranges short walking tours around the city (free, but a gratuity is appreciated) each morning at 10:15, with additional tours at 2:15 PM from April through October, and one at 7 PM from July through August.

Yorktour (☎ 01904/641737) offers open-top bus, riverboat, and walking tours of the city of York and area attractions.

There are interesting walking tours available in most of Yorkshire's historic towns. Those in Harrogate and Whitby are particularly recommended.

National Parks

For information about local visitor centers, walks, and guided tours, contact: **Yorkshire Dales National Park,** head office, ☎ 01756/752748; and **North York Moors National Park,** head office ☎ 01287/660654).

Travel Agencies

Thomas Cook: ✉ Ivebridge House, 67 Market St., Bradford, ☎ 01274/732411; ✉ 51 Boar La., Leeds, ☎ 0113/2432922; ✉ 47 Westborough, Scarborough, ☎ 01723/364444; and ✉ 4 Nessgate, York, ☎ 01904/653626.

Visitor Information

The Yorkshire and Humberside Tourist Board (✉ 312 Tadcaster Rd., York, North Yorkshire YO2 2HF, ☎ 01904/707961) has information about the entire area.

Bradford: ✉ National Museum of Photography, Film, and TV, Prince's View, West Yorkshire BD5 0TR, ☎ 01274/753678. **Bridlington:** ✉ 25 Prince St., Humberside, YO15 2NP, ☎ 01262/673474. **Harrogate:** ✉ Royal Baths Assembly Rooms, Crescent Rd., North Yorkshire HG1 2RR, ☎ 01423/525666. **Haworth:** ✉ 2–4 West La., West Yorkshire

BD22 8EF, ☎ 01535/642329. **Helmsley:** ✉ The Town Hall, Market Place, North Yorkshire YO6 5BL, ☎ 01439/770173. **Huddersfield:** ✉ Albion St., West Yorkshire HD1 2NW, ☎ 01484/430808. **Knaresborough:** ✉ 35 Market Pl., North Yorkshire HG5 8AL, ☎ 01423/866886. **Leeds:** ✉ Leeds City Station, West Yorkshire LS1 1PL, ☎ 0113/242–5242. **Richmond:** ✉ Friary Gardens, Queen's Rd., North Yorkshire DL10 4AJ, ☎ 01748/850252. **Scarborough:** ✉ St. Nicholas Cliff, North Yorkshire YO11 2EP, ☎ 01723/373333. **Whitby:** ✉ New Quay Rd., North Yorkshire YO21 1YN, ☎ 01947/602674. **York:** ✉ De Grey Rooms, Exhibition Sq., North Yorkshire YO1 2HB, ☎ 01904/621756; ✉ York Railway Station, North Yorkshire YO2 2AY, ☎ 01904/621756; and ✉ 6 Rougier St., North Yorkshire YO1 2HB, ☎ 01904/620557.

15 The Northeast

Durham, Hadrian's Wall, Lindisfarne Island

Ruined castles, holy islands, Roman walls, and the Northumberland Coast—this region embraces history, but refuses to be dwarfed by it. Windswept and wild, this is an area for the intrepid adventurer. Among the numberless monuments of a vigorous and often warlike past, Hadrian's Wall is the most famous. This northern border of the Roman Empire stretches across prehistoric remains and tractless moorland. Other must-sees include Durham Cathedral—more fortress than church—and magical Lindisfarne Island, a landmark of early Christendom.

Updated by Greg Ward

ENGLAND'S NORTHEAST CORNER is relatively unexplored by tourists. Although one of its villages (Allendale Town, southwest of Hexham) lays claim to being the geographical center of the British Isles, a decided air of remoteness pervades much of the region. Consequently, those visitors who do make their way here are often impressed by the wide-open spaces and empty country roads; they also like the value for money in shopping and accommodations, the unspoiled villages and uncrowded beaches, and the warmth and friendliness of the people.

Mainly composed of the two large counties of Durham and Northumberland (in ancient times known as Northumbria), the Northeast includes among its attractions the English side of the Scottish Border area, renowned in ballads and romantic literature for feuds, raids, and battles. Hadrian's Wall, which served to mark the northern limit of the Roman Empire, runs through this region; much of it, remarkably, is still intact. Another Roman wall, the Antonine, was built even farther north about AD 145, but was abandoned as unworkable within about 50 years. Not far north of Hadrian's Wall are Kielder Forest, the largest planted forest in Europe; Kielder Water, the largest man-made lake in northern Europe; and some of the most interesting parts of Northumberland National Park.

On the region's eastern side is a 100-mile line of largely undeveloped coast, including quiet stone-built villages, vast empty beaches with the occasional outcrop of high cliff or offshore rocks, and islands populated by multitudes of seabirds. Several outstanding castles perch on headlands and promontories along here. For 1,000 years, the great cathedral of Durham was the seat of bishops who raised their own armies and ruled the turbulent northern diocese as prince bishops with quasi-royal authority.

In more recent times, industrialization left its mark. Steel, coal, railroads, shipbuilding, and chemicals made prosperous such towns as Newcastle upon Tyne, Darlington, Sunderland, Hartlepool, and Middlesbrough in the 19th and early 20th centuries. Attractions that reflect the area's industrial history are the open-air museum at Beamish (northwest of Durham), voted "Best Museum in Europe"; the Railway Museum at Darlington, on the site of the world's first passenger railroad line; and a tiny cottage at Wylam (west of Newcastle) devoted to George Stephenson, who invented the steam locomotive.

Pleasures and Pastimes

Castles

Fought over for centuries by the Scots and the English, and prey to Viking raiders from across the North Sea, the Northeast is one of the most heavily fortified regions in Britain. Cities such as Durham and Newcastle—where the "new castle" is 900 years old—still boast impressive relics, but exploring the stupendous fortresses along the exposed Northumbrian coastline is among the most memorable experiences the region has to offer. Dunstanburgh Castle near Craster and Bamburgh Castle farther north are especially worth seeing.

Dining

The Northeast is one of the best areas in England for fresh local produce. Keep an eye out for restaurants that serve game from the Kielder Forest, local lamb from the hillsides, and fish both from the streams threading through the wild valleys and from the fishing fleets along the coast. Don't miss out on the simple fresh seafood sandwiches served in many of the region's local pubs. You might also wish to sample Alnwick Vatted Rum, a blend of Guyanese and Jamaican rum, or Lindisfarne mead, a traditional, highly potent spirit produced on Holy Island, and made of honey vatted with grape juice and mineral water.

CATEGORY	COST*
£££	over £25
££	£15–25
£	under £15

**per person, including first course, main course, dessert, and VAT; excluding drinks*

Hiking and Biking

The wide-open Northeast offers superb walking opportunities almost wherever you go, but to combine an awe-inspiring sense of history with stunning scenery nothing can beat a hike—or even just a short stroll—along the route of ancient Hadrian's Wall. The hilltop section near Housesteads Roman Fort—in places you can even walk along the top of the wall itself here—is the best stretch to get a short taste. Otherwise, the russet hills and dales of Northumberland National Park, in the northwest corner of the area, will gladden the heart of any serious walker.

Similarly, cyclists relish the wide vistas, quiet roads, and magnificently fresh air of the region. One ideal spot to rent a mountain bike is Kielder Water, to the north of Hadrian's Wall.

Lodging

The Northeast is not an area where the large hotel chains have much of a presence outside the few large cities. Rather, this is a region where you can expect to find country houses converted into welcoming hotels, old coaching inns that still greet guests after 300 years, and cozy bed-and-breakfasts conveniently located near hiking trails. Visitors are often pleasantly surprised at the low prices of accommodations, even at the very top end of the scale.

CATEGORY	COST*
££££	over £110
£££	£60–£110
££	£50–£60
£	under £50

**All prices are for two people sharing a double room, including service, breakfast, and VAT.*

EXPLORING THE NORTHEAST

The vast majority of visitors travel from the south to arrive at the historic cathedral city of Durham, not far east of the picturesque foothill valleys of the Pennines. Farther north, Newcastle, located on the region's main river, the Tyne, is a major industrial city, but nearby the remarkable Roman fortifications of Hadrian's Wall snake through some superb scenery to the east; farther north lies the wilderness of Northumberland National Park. Starting roughly an hour's drive north of Newcastle, the final 40 miles of England's east coast is absolutely stunning, studded with huge castles and scattered with offshore islands such as Holy Island, also known as Lindisfarne.

Great Itineraries

While it's possible to get a sense of the Northeast through an overnight stop en route to or from Scotland, it's worth setting aside at least three days to explore the region properly. One turn off the A-1—the main north–south highway—and you'll soon learn that driving along the meandering backcountry roads can often be slow business—if only because the spectacular scenery encourages long halts!

Numbers in the text correspond to numbers in the margin and on the maps.

IF YOU HAVE 2 DAYS

Base yourself at either **Durham** ①, with time to inspect the Norman cathedral and the castle to either side of the central Palace Green, or at smaller, quainter **Alnwick** ㉟, with its beautiful riverside castle and cobbled square. Drive inland between the two for at least a brief glimpse of **Hadrian's Wall,** ideally at **Housesteads** ㉗, and wind up at the magical monastic settlement on **Lindisfarne Island** ㊶.

IF YOU HAVE 4 DAYS

Having spent at least half a day exploring **Durham** ①, set aside a full day to follow the course of **Hadrian's Wall.** An overnight stop nearby in **Hexham** ㉔ enables you to see the excellent museums of Roman finds at **Vindolanda** ㉖ and **Housesteads** ㉗. Then drive northeast through the gorgeous countryside to spend the evening in the picturesque little market town of **Alnwick** ㉟. On the next morning, walk from **Craster** ㊲ to the splendidly bleak ruin of **Dunstanburgh Castle** ㊳, then visit one or two of the huge beaches to the north as you head to **Bamburgh** ㊵—overlooking the windswept shore, its famous castle conjures up the days of chivalry as few others do—for the night. Whether you're heading back to Durham from there, or onward to Scotland, visit wind-battered **Lindisfarne Island** ㊶, a short distance north, to soak up the saintly atmosphere.

When to Tour the Northeast

Although Hadrian's Wall and the coastal castles are starkly impressive in a blanket of snow, much the best time to see the Northeast is in summer. Then you can be sure that the museums—and the roads—will be open, and that you'll be able to enjoy the long countryside walks that are one of the region's greatest pleasures. Due to rough seas and inclement weather, there's certainly no question of swimming at any of the magnificent beaches unless you're here in the very height of summer, in July and August. At the end of June, Alnwick plays host to its annual Fair, featuring a costumed reenactment of a medieval fair, processions, a market, and concerts.

DURHAM AND ITS ENVIRONS

Durham is not the southernmost point in the Northeast region, but it's much the most interesting historic city, and it's also the first major northeastern town on the main road up from London. Most of the other cities nearby are brash upstarts that made their fortunes during the Industrial Revolution, and have since subsided into relative decline. Several—such as Darlington, birthplace of the modern railroad—do hold interesting relics of their 19th-century heyday. The land to the west, toward the Pennine Hills, is far more scenic, and a day-long drive leads to natural wonders as well as monuments from all periods of English history.

Numbers in the margin correspond to points of interest on the Northeast and Durham maps.

The Northeast

Durham

1 *400 km (250 mi) north of London; 24 km (15 mi) south of Newcastle.*

The great medieval city of Durham, seat of Durham County, is among the most dramatically sited in Britain. Despite the military advantages offered by the rocky spur on which it stands, Durham was founded surprisingly late, probably in about the year 1000, growing up around a small Saxon church. But it was the Normans, under William the Conqueror, who put Durham on the map, building the castle of the prince-bishops and, in about 1090, beginning work on the cathedral, the main body of which was finished in about 1150. Together, the cathedral and castle stand high on a wooded peninsula almost entirely encircled by the river Wear (rhymes with "beer"). For centuries these two ancient structures have dominated Durham—now a thriving university town, the Northeast's equivalent to Oxford or Cambridge—and the surrounding countryside.

★ 2 Architectural historians come from all over the world to admire and study the Norman masterpiece that is **Durham Cathedral,** on the neat Palace Green in the heart of the city. The cathedral's solidity and strength are a far cry from the airy lightness of later, Gothic cathedrals. Durham is the essence of an almost entirely Norman, or Romanesque, edifice: The roundheaded arches of the nave and the deep zigzag pFatterns carved into them are entirely typical of the heavy, gaunt style of Norman building. Yet if the style looks back rather than forward, the technology of Durham was quite revolutionary at the time. This was the first European cathedral to be given a stone, rather than a wooden, roof, and when you consider the means of construction available to its ambitious builders—the stones that form the ribs of the roof had to be hoisted up by hand and set on a wooded structure, which was then knocked away—their achievement seems little short of staggering.

The origins of the cathedral go back to the 10th century. Monks fleeing a devastating Viking raid in the year 875 on Lindisfarne Abbey brought the body of St. Cuthbert to this site in 995, and soon the wealth attracted by Cuthbert's shrine paid for the construction of a cathedral. The bishop's throne in the cathedral is still the loftiest in all medieval Christendom; his miter is the only one to be encircled by a coronet; and his coat of arms is the only one to be crossed with a sword as well as a crosier.

Upon entering, many visitors take a snapshot of the 12th-century bronze **Sanctuary Knocker**, shaped like the head of a ferocious mythological beast, on the massive northwestern entrance door. By grasping the ring clenched in the animal's mouth, medieval felons could claim sanctuary; cathedral records show that 331 criminals (especially murderers) sought this protection between 1464 and 1524. However, the knocker now in place is, in fact, a replica; the original is kept for security in the cathedral treasury, along with ancient illuminated manuscripts, St. Cuthbert's coffin, and more church treasure. ☎ *0191/386–2367.* 🎟 *Cathedral free but donation welcome; treasury £1.* ⏲ *Cathedral May–Sept., daily 7:15 AM–8 PM; Oct.–Apr. 7:15–6; treasury Mon.–Sat. 10–4:30, Sun. 2–4:30; choral evensong service weekdays at 5:15, Sun. at 3:30.*

3 **Durham Castle,** which faces the Cathedral across Palace Green, commands a strategic position above the river Wear. For more than 750 years the castle was home to successive warlike prince-bishops—from here large tracts of northern England were ruled, and the wild Scots kept at bay. Today it houses University College, one of several colleges

Cathedral, **2**
Durham Castle, **3**
Durham Light Infantry Museum, **6**
Durham University Oriental Museum, **7**
Framwelgate Bridge, **5**
Prebends Footbridge, **4**

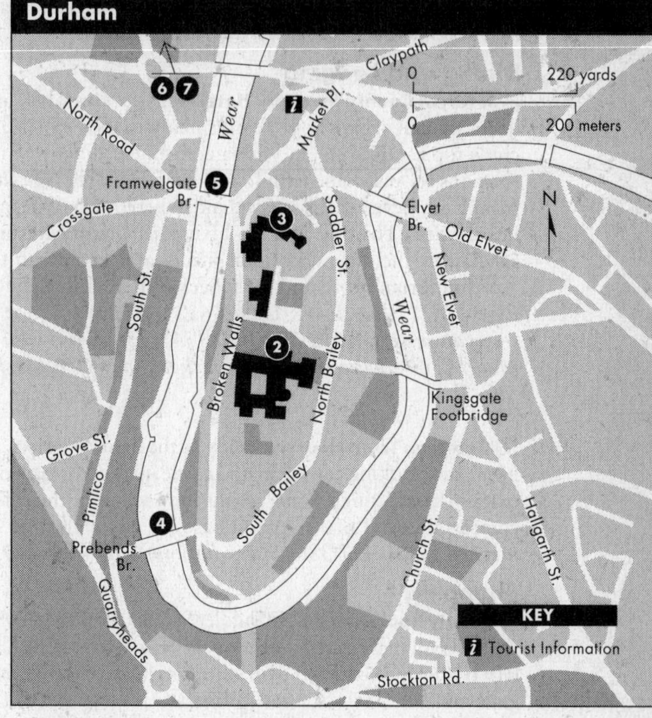

of the University of Durham, the oldest university in England after Oxford and Cambridge. You can tour the castle at certain times, and, during college vacations, tourist accommodations are available. ✉ *Palace Green,* ☎ *0191/374–3800.* 🎫 *£1.50.* ⏲ *July–Sept., daily 10–noon, 2–4:30; Oct.–June (tours only), Mon., Wed., Sat. 2–4:30.*

NEED A BREAK? **Almshouse Café** serves light lunches and afternoon meals in a historic almshouse on Palace Green, between the cathedral and castle.

The river Wear winds through the center of Durham, curving beneath the cathedral and castle, and plays host in mid-June each year to the Durham Regatta, Britain's oldest rowing event. A short stroll along its leafy banks is rewarded by delightful views, especially as you cross
4 **Prebends Footbridge,** reached from the southern end of Palace Green. If you follow the far side of the Wear from here, then recross the river
5 to find **Framwelgate Bridge,** which dates originally from the 12th century. Many of the elegant town houses that line the narrow lanes back up to the cathedral now house departments of the university.

6 The **Durham Light Infantry Museum** at Aykley Heads, ½ mile northwest of Durham city center on A691, is devoted to the history of the county regiment, exhibiting uniforms, weapons, and regalia alongside mementos of British campaigns in India, Iran, the Crimea, and Africa. On the second floor the arts center offers a changing program of events throughout the year. Outdoor events, such as brass-band concerts and military vehicle rallies, take place on the landscaped grounds. ☎ *0191/384–2214.* 🎫 *£1.* ⏲ *Tues.–Sat. 10–5, Sun. 2–5.*

Fine art and craftworks from all parts of Asia are on show at the
7 **Durham University Oriental Museum.** ✉ *Elvet Hill, off South Rd.*

(A1050), ☎ *0191/374–2911.* 🎫 *£1.* ⏲ *Weekdays 9:30–1 and 2–5, weekends 2–5; closed 10 days at Christmas.*

Dining and Lodging

£££ ✕🏨 **Royal County Swallow Hotel.** This comfortable, attractively redecorated Georgian hotel retains many of its historic details. It's the city's top establishment, with a convenient downtown location and spacious rooms, some with four-poster beds. The oak staircase comes from Loch Leven castle in Scotland, where Mary, Queen of Scots, was imprisoned. There is also the luxurious **County Restaurant**, whose specialties include wild boar steaks and such traditional fare as Northumbrian broth and roast beef with Yorkshire pudding. ✉ *Old Elvet, DH1 3JN,* ☎ *0191/386–6821,* FAX *0191/386–0704; toll-free reservations in U.S.,* ☎ *800/444–1545. 150 rooms with bath. Restaurant (££; reservations essential, jacket and tie), coffee shop. AE, DC, MC, V.*

££ 🏨 **Georgian Town House.** Exactly as the name suggests, this well-sited hotel, overlooking cathedral and castle, makes the best of its Georgian exterior and fittings. Some rooms have views of the cathedral; all are comfortable and make a good base for city walks. ✉ *10 Crossgate, DH1 4PS,* ☎ *0191/386–8070. 6 rooms with bath. No credit cards.*

Shopping

University Bookshop (✉ 55 Saddler St., ☎ 0191/384–2095) offers over 25,000 volumes in stock. **Bramwells Jewellers** (✉ 24 Elvet Bridge, ☎ 0191/386–8006) has its own store specialty—a pendant replica of the gold-and-silver cross of St. Cuthbert.

Outdoor Activities and Sports

In Durham, **Brown's Boat House** (✉ Elvet Bridge, ☎ 0191/386–3779) rents rowboats and offers short cruises from April to early November.

Brancepeth

❽ *6 km (4 mi) southwest of Durham.*

The village of Brancepeth was reconstructed early in the 19th century to resemble a traditional Tudor village, and its rows of well-preserved cottages have barely changed since. A flamboyantly restored castle (not open to the public) overlooks the whole ensemble, but the real gem here is the genuine medieval church, complete with an exceptionally ornate rood screen. Tombs in the church hold assorted Nevilles, one of the most powerful northern families in feudal times.

Killhope Lead Mining Centre

❾ *40 km (25 mi) west of Durham.*

At the head of Upper Weardale—a wild, high, remote place—a restored 34-foot-high waterwheel looms over the open-air Killhope Lead Mining Centre. The visitor center uses working models, push-button audiovisual shows, and displays of minerals to portray the story of the local lead mines and the harsh lives of the miners and millworkers. You can pan for lead in the stream and operate the primitive machinery once used to separate valuable ore from gravel, or venture underground into the new but appropriately gloomy Park Level Mine. ✉ *2 mi northwest of Cowshill on A689,* ☎ *01388/537505.* 🎫 *£2.50.* ⏲ *Apr.–Oct., daily 10:30–5; Nov., Sun. 10:30–5.*

Ireshopeburn

⑩ *5 km (3 mi) southeast of Killhope Lead Mining Centre; 45 km (28 mi) west of Durham.*

The **Weardale Folk Museum** occupies a former parsonage in the village of Ireshopeburn, close to a chapel where John Wesley, the founder of Methodism, often preached. One room is set out as an 1870 cottage would have looked, and a collection of crystallized minerals is included in a display on local life and landscape. The caretaker can show you around the adjoining chapel. ☎ *01388/537417.* 🎟 *80p adults.* ⏲ *May–July and Sept., Wed.–Thurs. and Sat. 1–5, Sun. 1–4; Aug., daily 1–5.*

Shopping

Michael and Mary Crompton, Weavers (⊠ Forge Cottage, ☎ 01388/537346) create striking tapestries inspired by the changing seasons of Weardale. Also on sale are smaller spun and handwoven fabrics, including rugs, shawls, bags, belts, and made-to-order items.

Romaldkirk/High Force

⑫ *11 km (7 mi) northwest of Barnard Castle; 40 km (25 mi) southwest of Durham.*

In the pretty village of Romaldkirk, the extravagantly proportioned church is known as "the Cathedral of the Dale," and the stocks for punishing wrongdoers still stand on the village green. Follow B6277 west into the valley of Teesdale, and after just over 7 miles you come
★ ⑪ to England's highest waterfall, the 72-foot **High Force,** just south of B6277. A moorland road north from here provides an exhilarating drive "over the tops."

Barnard Castle/Bowes

⑬ *40 km (25 mi) southwest of Durham.*

The substantial ruins of the fortress that gave its name to the market town of Barnard Castle cling to an aerie on a cliff overlooking the river Tees. Inside, you can see parts of the 14th-century Great Hall and the cylindrical, 13th-century tower, built by the castle's original owners, the Anglo-Scottish Balliol family. ☎ *01833/638212.* 🎟 *£1.80.* ⏲ *Apr.–Sept., daily 10–6; Oct.–Mar., Wed.–Sun. 10–4; call ahead in winter.*

In the town of Barnard Castle, the unusual butter-market hall, surmounted by a fire alarm bell, marks the junction of the streets Thorngate, Newgate, and Market Place, which are lined with stores, pubs, and cafés. In 1838 Charles Dickens stayed at the **King's Head Inn** here while researching his novel *Nicholas Nickleby,* which dealt with the abuse of children in local boarding schools. The local tourist office has a *Dickens Drive* leaflet of the places he visited in the area. The
★ main attraction is the **Bowes Museum,** a vast French-inspired chateau built between 1869 and 1885 to house an art collection that includes paintings by Canaletto and Boucher and one of the greatest collections of 18th-century French furniture in the world. Children may enjoy the collection of 19th-century games, toys, models, and dollhouses, while there's also a splendid 18th-century silver swan that Mark Twain described in *Innocents Abroad.* Once every day an attendant ceremoniously activates the mechanism that enables the swan to gracefully catch and swallow a silver fish to the accompaniment of a haunting tune. ⊠ *Follow signs from Barnard Castle town*

center, ☎ *01833/690606.* 🎫 *£3.* ⏲ *Mon.–Sat. 10–5:30, Sun. 2–5; closed Christmas wk, New Year's.*

14 In the village of **Bowes,** 6½ kilometers (4 miles) southwest of Barnard Castle, the house on which Dickens modeled *Nicholas Nickleby*'s Dotheboys Hall can still be seen, although it's not open to the public. West of the village, look for the main street's last building, which housed a notoriously cruel boarding school in the 19th century. The courtyard pump described in the novel is still there.

Raby Castle

15 *10 km (6 mi) northeast of Barnard Castle; 30 km (19 mi) southwest of Durham.*

Raby Castle, home of the 11th Baron Barnard, stands amid 200 acres of landscaped deer park just outside Staindrop. It displays luxuriously furnished rooms crammed with treasures, in addition to well-preserved medieval kitchens, with original Victorian copperware and other domestic equipment. Stone arcades display five full-length portraits of Raby personages, including Richard III's mother, who died here. ✉ *1 mi north of Staindrop,* ☎ *01833/660202.* 🎫 *£3.50; park, gardens, and carriage collection £1.* ⏲ *Easter–June, Wed., Sun. 1–5 (castle), 11–5:30 (park and gardens); July–Sept., Sun.–Fri. 1–5 (castle), 11–5:30 (park and gardens).*

Bishop Auckland

16 *20 km (13 mi) northeast of Barnard Castle; 19 km (12 mi) southwest of Durham.*

The prince-bishops of Durham had their official residence in **Auckland Castle,** in the town of Bishop Auckland. This grand episcopal palace dates mainly from the 16th century, though the limestone and marble chapel, with its dazzling stained-glass windows, was built in 1665 from the ruins of a 12th-century banqueting hall. The unusual 18th-century "deerhouse" of adjoining Bishops Park testifies to at least one of the bishops' extracurricular interests. The castle itself offers architectural styles ranging from the medieval to the neo-Gothic. ✉ *Off Market Pl.,* ☎ *01388/601627.* 🎫 *£2.* ⏲ *Mid-May–Sept., Tues. 10–12:30, Wed.–Thurs. and Sun. 2–5; also Sat. in Aug. 2–5; chapel only Thurs. 10–noon.*

Darlington

17 *34 km (21 mi) south of Durham.*

Still visibly rooted in its 19th-century industrial past, the town of Darlington "rocketed" to fame in 1825, when George Stephenson established the first steam passenger railroad, from Stockton to Darlington. Although *Stephenson's Rocket* traveled at just 15 mph, it claimed rail travel's first fatality on its very first run by killing a British Member ★ of Parliament. The **Darlington Railway Centre and Museum** is housed in one of the original railroad stations, built in 1842. You can inspect historic engines, including Stephenson's *Locomotion I,* as well as photographs, documents, and models. ✉ *North Road Station,* ☎ *01325/460532.* 🎫 *£1.80.* ⏲ *Daily 9:30–5; closed Dec. 25, Jan. 1.*

Middlesbrough

18 *19 km (12 mi) east of Darlington, 35 km (22 mi) southeast of Durham.*

In 1802, a mere dozen people lived in Middlesborough, near the mouth of the river Tees. With the discovery of iron ore, however, it became a boom town, with steel mills and later, chemical industries. Middlesborough's unusual **Transporter Bridge,** built in 1911, is the largest of its kind in the world, a vast structure like a giant's Erector-set model, whose gantry system still takes 12 cable cars, holding 200 passengers each, across the river every 20 minutes. A special viewing platform stands on the south bank. Upstream you'll find Newport Bridge, the world's largest lift span bridge, another remarkable sight. ☎ *01642/247563. Crossing time 2 min.* 🎫 *25p pedestrians, 70p cars.* ⏲ *Mon.–Sat. 5 AM–11 PM, Sun. 2–11.*

The life and times of Captain Cook, the celebrated 18th-century circumnavigator and explorer are vividly depicted in the **Captain Cook Birthplace Museum,** in the leafy Middlesborough suburb of Marton. Displays cover his remarkable voyages to Australia, New Zealand, Canada, Antarctica, and Hawaii, where he met his death, while a conservatory near the museum houses specimens of the exotic plants Cook discovered during his travels. ✉ *Stewart Park, Marton, off A174, south of city center. Museum* ☎ *01642/311211; conservatory* ☎ *01642/300202.* 🎫 *Museum £1.40; conservatory free.* ⏲ *Museum: Oct.–May, Tues.–Sun. 9–4; June–Sept., Tues.–Sun. 10–5:30. Conservatory: Mar.–Oct., daily 11–6; Nov.–Feb., weekends 11–dusk.*

Washington

⓳ *19 km (12 mi) north of Durham.*

★ Careful navigation through the often bewildering "new town" of Washington will take you to **Washington Old Hall,** the ancestral home of the first U.S. president. George Washington's direct forebears lived here between 1183 and 1288; other members of the family continued to live in the house until 1613, when the present property was rebuilt. Now owned by the National Trust, the mansion retains a decidedly Jacobean (17th-century) appearance. There are special celebrations on the Fourth of July. ✉ *From A1(M), 5 mi west of Sunderland, follow signs to Washington New Town, District 4, and then on to Washington Village.* ☎ *0191/416–6879.* 🎫 *£2.30.* ⏲ *Apr.–Oct., Sun.–Thurs. and Good Fri. 11–5 (last admission 4:30).*

Beamish

⓴ *14 km (9 mi) north of Durham; 5 km (3 mi) west of Chester-le-Street.*

★ Set aside at least half a day to enjoy the 260-acre **Beamish Open-Air Museum,** in the town of Beamish. Historic buildings have been brought here from throughout the region, and a streetcar will take you across a reconstructed 1920s High Street, including a dentist's operating room, a pub, and a grocery. A stableman will talk to you about the Clydesdale workhorses in his care, once used to draw brewery wagons. On the farm you can see such local breeds as Durham Shorthorn cattle and Teeswater sheep. Other attractions include a railroad station, a coal mine, and a transportation collection. The large gift store specializes in period souvenirs and locally made crafts. ✉ *Off A693, between Chester-le-Street and Stanley,* ☎ *01207/231811.* 🎫 *£7, £8, or £3 (depending on season).* ⏲ *Apr.–mid-July and Sept.–Oct., daily 10–5; mid-July–Aug., daily 10–6; Nov.–Mar., Tues.–Thurs. and weekends 10–4; closed 2 wks at Christmas and New Year's.*

Dining and Lodging

££££ ✕🏨 **Lumley Castle Hotel.** This is a real castle, right down to the dungeons, and a hotel experience not to be missed. Located 5 kilometers (3 miles) west of Beamish, Lumley Castle has superb bedrooms in all sizes (some with four-poster beds and/or Jacuzzis) combined with up-to-date facilities. There's plenty of space to wander and an appealing library-bar, with more than 3,000 books and a log fire, for before-dinner drinks. The **Black Knight Restaurant** features English specialties such as *filet de boeuf* (prime roast beef with Stilton cheese, wrapped in bacon) and Landes duck (duck caramelized and served with pâté de foie gras, mango, and piquant ginger sauce). Lumley Castle is also noted for its five-course Elizabethan banquets, held in the original baronial hall two to five nights each week, when guests are plied with mounds of traditional food and drink and entertained by costumed fools. ✉ *1 mi east of Chester-le-Street by B1284, DH3 4NX,* ☎ *0191/389–1111,* FAX *0191/387–1437. 60 rooms with bath. Restaurant. AE, DC, MC, V. Closed Dec. 25, Jan. 1.*

Newcastle upon Tyne

21 *26 km (16 mi) north of Durham.*

The main city of the Northeast, Newcastle upon Tyne—or Newcastle, as it's more commonly known—still manages to impress with its sweeping, central neoclassical streets, despite the decay wrought by economic decline—a common late 20th-century problem in this part of the country. Overlooking the Tyne river, the remains of the **Norman castle** remind visitors of the city's earlier status as a defensive stronghold. This was the "new castle," originally built in 1080, that gave the city its name. ✉ *St. Nicholas St.,* ☎ *0191/232–7938.* 🎫 *£1.* ⏲ *Apr.–Sept., Tues.–Sun. 9:30–5:30; Oct.–Mar., Tues.–Sun. 9:30–4:30.*

Newcastle's university buildings house the city's best museums. Here you'll find a **Museum of Antiquities**, showing finds from Hadrian's Wall, as well as the interesting **Shefton Museum of Greek Art and Archaeology**, containing ancient arms, ceramics, and terra-cotta pieces. ✉ *The University,* ☎ *0191/222–7844 or 0191/222–6000.* 🎫 *Free.* ⏲ *Museum of Antiquities Mon.–Sat. 10–5; Hatton Gallery weekdays 10–5:30; Shefton Museum weekdays 9:30–12:30 and 2–4:30.*

The Arts

Newcastle's **Theatre Royal** (✉ Grey St., ☎ 0191/232–2061) is the region's most established theater, with a variety of high-quality productions.

Dining

££ ✕ **Courtney's.** This converted quayside building offers a changing dinner menu each week. Typical entrées using fresh local produce include roast sea bass with leek and balsamic vinaigrette. It's a relaxed place for inexpensive set lunches. ✉ *5–7 The Side,* ☎ *0191/232–5537. AE, MC, V. No lunch Sat. Closed Sun., 2 wks in May, and 1 wk at Christmas.*

Shopping

In a wonderful medieval friary in the heart of Newcastle's traditional guilds district, **Northumbria Makers** is a cooperative selling local crafts such as textiles and wrought ironwork. ✉ *Friars Green, Stowell St.,* ☎ *0191/261–4307.*

Jarrow

22 *6 km (4 mi) east of Newcastle.*

The name of Jarrow is to British ears forever linked to the "Jarrow Crusade," a protest march to London led by unemployed former workers from the town's steelworks and shipyards in the depths of the 1930s. Travelers are attracted here, however, by much more ancient history. **Bede's World** and **St. Paul's Church** offer substantial monastic ruins, a visitor center-cum-museum, and the church of St. Paul, all reflecting the long tradition of religion and learning that began here in AD 681. Visits are designed to provide an authentic experience of medieval life; in the reconstructed farm buildings erected on the Anglo-Saxon farm landscape, you're encouraged to get close to rare animal breeds such as Dexter cattle and Iron-Age pigs. Still used for regular worship, St. Paul's contains some of the oldest stained glass in Europe and the oldest dedicatory church inscription in Britain (a carved stone inscribed in AD 685). ✉ *Church Bank; from southern exit traffic circle at South Tyne tunnel, take A185 to South Shields, then follow signs to "St. Paul's Church and Jarrow Hall"*; ☎ *0191/489–2106.* 🎫 *£2.50.* ⏲ *Apr.–Oct., Tues.–Sat. 10–5:30, Sun. 2:30–5:30; Nov.–Mar., Tues.–Sat. 11–4:30, Sun. 2:30–5:30.*

Dining

££ ✕ **Marsden Grotto.** Built into a cliff a couple of miles east of Jarrow at South Shields, from which there are spectacular views of the sea and the Marsden Rock Bird Sanctuary, this unusually sited restaurant is entered from the clifftop promenade via an elevator that descends into the rock. Fresh local fish, such as sole, halibut, and plaice, are prepared to your specifications, and steak is another specialty. ✉ *Coast Rd., Marsden,* ☎ *0191/455–2043. AE, MC, V. Closed Mon. in winter.*

Wylam

23 *6 km (4 mi) west of Newcastle.*

George Stephenson's Birthplace is a tiny, red-roofed stone cottage in Wylam, now a wooded suburb of Newcastle upon Tyne. Here, in 1781, the "Father of the Railroads" was born. One room of the house is open to the public—a modest tribute to an engineer whose invention of the steam locomotive touched every corner of the world. You can park your car in the village by the war memorial, a 10 minutes' walk away. ✉ *Wylam, 1½ mi south of A69,* ☎ *01661/853457.* 🎫 *£1.* ⏲ *Apr.–Oct., Thurs., weekends 1–5:30; other times by appointment.*

HADRIAN'S WALL COUNTRY

The formidable line of fortifications that marked the northern border of the Roman Empire—which stretched eastward for 2,500 miles to ★ what is now Iraq—**Hadrian's Wall** was constructed after the Roman emperor Hadrian's visit in AD 122, in response to repeated barbarian invasions from Scotland. It spanned 117½ kilometers (73 miles) from Wallsend ("Wall's End") just north of Newcastle, in the east, to Bowness-on-Solway beyond Carlisle, in the west, and was completed just four year's after the emperor's visit—which gives a pretty good idea of Roman determination and efficiency in that nontechnological era. Its construction bears all the hallmarks of Roman efficiency. It stretches across the narrowest part of the country and is built following as straight a path as possible. There is a fortified tower every 500 yards, and a fortress every mile, the so-called "milecastles."

Today, excavating, documenting, interpreting, repairing, displaying, and generally managing the Roman remains is a Northumbrian growth industry, and anyone sufficiently motivated could spend endless time there. At the forts—notably at Chesters, Housesteads (the best preserved fort), Vindolanda, and at Carvoran Museum near Greenhead—people can browse and get a good introduction to the life led by Roman soldiers on the frontier. It is also possible to walk along the wall, but no one should imagine that it would just entail an afternoon stroll. It is very hard going, and once you are committed to it, it's not possible to get off just anywhere and step back onto the road. The western part is the most scenic. For photographers, one spot above most others produces a memorable souvenir: looking east toward the fort of Housesteads from Cuddy's Crag, the wall can be seen snaking up and down across the wildest, most inhospitable country imaginable. The town of Hexham makes the most convenient base to explore the 10-mile length of the wall still standing today.

Fishing

The rivers and lakes in the Hadrian's Wall region have brown and rainbow trout, salmon, and other game fish. You'll need an NRA rod license (£13.25), which is good from January until December and is available from the Hexham tourist information office. The best fishing spots are **Kielder Water,** with 43½ kilometers (27 miles) of shoreline and boat-fishing available; **Derwent Reservoir** (☎ 01207/55250), 16 kilometers (10 miles) southeast of Hexham; and **Langley Dam** (☎ 01434/688846), 13 kilometers (8 miles) west of Hexham. The fishing season at all these places runs from around March to October, and advance booking is advised.

Walking and Horseback Riding

A long-distance footpath traces the entire course of Hadrian's Wall, but this is rugged country, unsuited to the inexperienced hiker. Most trekkers choose instead to walk short stretches in the vicinity of the various visitor centers. There are also several riding schools in the region, offering hour-long rides to full-day treks on horseback. For a full list, contact the Hexham tourist information office; advance booking in summer is essential.

Hexham

24 *35 km (22 mi) west of Newcastle; 50 km (31 mi) northwest of Durham.*

Best-known as the gateway to Hadrian's Wall country, the historic market town of Hexham, on A69 about 34 kilometers (21 miles) west of Newcastle, is well worth a visit for its own sake.

Hexham's central **Market Place,** ringed with interesting shops and fine old buildings, has been the site since 1239 of a weekly market, held each Tuesday. Crowded stalls set out under the long slate roof of the Shambles; other stalls take their chances with the weather, protected only by their bright awnings.

★ Ancient **Hexham Abbey,** a tranquil place of Christian worship for more than 1,300 years, forms one side of the town's main square. Inside, you can climb the 35 worn stone "night stairs," which once led from the main part of the abbey to the canon's dormitory, to overlook the whole ensemble. Most of the present building dates from the 12th century, and much of the stone was taken from the Roman fort at Corstopitum a few miles northeast. ✉ *Beaumont St.,* ☎ *01434/602031.* 🎫 *Suggested donation £2.* ⏲ *May–Sept., daily 9–7; Oct.–Apr., daily 9–5. No tours during services.*

Queens Hall, accessible along parkland footpaths from Hexham Abbey, was built in the style of a French chateau. It's now home to one of the Northeast's most adventurous arts venues, the Queen's Hall Arts Centre (☎ 01434/606787), which offers drama, dance, and exhibition space for local artists. ✉ *Beaumont St.,* ☎ *01434/607272.* 🎫 *Free.* ⏲ *Galleries Mon.–Sat. 9:30–5:30; hall closed Sun.*

NEED A BREAK? **Mrs. Miggin's Coffee Shop** (✉ St. Mary's Wynd, off Beaumont St.) serves light refreshments and homemade cakes on pine tables or at a sofa where you can read magazines and newspapers.

Dating from 1330, Hexham's original jail—the **Manor Office,** across Market Place from the abbey—houses the town's Information Center as well as the **Border History Museum.** Photographs, models, drawings, a reconstructed blacksmith's shop, a Border house interior, armor, and weapons help tell the story of the "Middle March"—the medieval administrative area governed by a warden and centered on Hexham. ✉ *The Old Gaol, Hallgate,* ☎ *01434/652200, ext. 235.* 🎫 *£1.50.* ⏲ *Easter–Oct., Mon.–Sat. 10–4:30; Feb.–Easter and Nov., Sat.–Tues. 10–4:30.*

Dining and Lodging

£££ ✕ **Black House.** A mile south of central Hexham, this restaurant is housed in converted farm buildings, fitted with lots of old furniture and attractive china. The menu features imaginative modernizations of traditional English dishes. ✉ *Dipton Mill Rd.,* ☎ *01434/604744. MC, V. No lunch Tues.–Sat.*

£ ✕ **Harlequin's Restaurant.** Occupying the ground floor of the Queen's Hall Arts Centre, this light and airy place overlooks the park and abbey. The dining room is decorated with original modern paintings, and the cheerful staff is busy at lunchtime serving neighborhood workers and shoppers. ✉ *Beaumont St.,* ☎ *01434/607230. AE, DC, MC, V. Closed Sun., national holidays.*

£££ ✕🏨 **County Hotel.** This old-fashioned, homey establishment, bedecked with colorful flowers, is known simply as "the County" to local people, who frequent the hotel bar (it's usually crowded with farmers on auction days). High teas (late-afternoon meals, served 5:30–6:30) are a specialty, and homemade meat pies, pastries, and Northumbrian lamb are often featured on the menu, along with international dishes. The guest rooms are small but adequate. ✉ *Priestpopple, NE46 1PS,* ☎ *01434/602030. 9 rooms, 6 with bath. Restaurant, bar, lobby lounge. AE, MC, V.*

£££ ✕🏨 **Langley Castle Hotel.** A genuine 14th-century castle was rescued by its American owner and converted into a luxury hotel and restaurant. Its 7-foot-thick walls are complete with turrets and battlements. All public rooms are grandly furnished, and the bedrooms have luxurious appointments; one has a private sauna, another a four-poster bed, and so on. The restaurant has an unusual atmosphere—although perhaps not for a castle—with exposed beams, wall tapestries, and a welcoming fire. Specialties include a casserole of local pheasant with shallots and sultanas, flavored with Bordeaux and game gravy. ✉ *Langley-on-Tyne (6 mi west of Hexham), NE47 5LU,* ☎ *01434/688888,* FAX *01434/684019. 16 rooms with bath. Restaurant. AE, DC, MC, V.*

£££ ✕🏨 **Lord Crewe Arms Hotel.** A historic hotel that once provided guest accommodations for Blanchland Abbey, this unusual place in the tiny stone village of Blanchland, south of Hexham, has lots of intriguing medieval and Gothic corners, including a priest's hideout and a vault-roofed crypt with its own bar. The bedrooms are solidly furnished with antique wood and exposed oak-beamed ceilings—one is said to be haunted by the ghost of a local girl; the restaurant's decor reinforces an atmosphere of cloistered calm. ✉ *Off B6306, about 8 mi south of Hexham, DH8 9SP,* ☎ *01434/675251,* FAX *01434/675337. 20 rooms with bath. Restaurant, bar. AE, DC, MC, V.*

Shopping

The **Abbey Gift Shop** (✉ Beaumont St., ☎ 01434/603057) provides a good selection of moderately priced gifts, such as commemorative plates and tapes of choir and music recitals. **Abbey Prints** (✉ 22 Hallgate, ☎ 01434/602244) sells a collection of paintings and prints by local artists. It's a good place to look for images of Hadrian's Wall and the surrounding countryside.

Greenhead

25 *29 km (18 mi) west of Hexham; 78 km (49 mi) northwest of Durham.*

The **Roman Army Museum,** at the garrison fort of Carvoran, near the village of Greenhead, makes an excellent introduction to Hadrian's Wall. Full-size models and excavations bring to life this remote outpost of empire; you can even inspect authentic Roman graffiti on the walls of an excavated barracks. The gift store stocks, among other unusual items, Roman rulers (1 foot = 11.6 inches) and Roman cookbooks. Opposite the museum, at Walltown Crags on the Pennine Way (a long-distance hiking route), are 400 yards of the best-preserved section of the wall. ☎ *016977/47485.* *£3.50.* *May–Aug., daily 10–6; Mar.–Apr. and Sept.–Oct., daily 10–5; 2nd ½ Feb. and 1st ½ Nov., daily 10–4.*

Dining and Lodging

£ **Holmhead Guest House.** This former farmhouse is not only built *on* Hadrian's Wall but also *of* it. It has stone arches, exposed beams, and antique furnishings; there's open countryside in front and a ruined castle almost in the backyard. In addition to "the longest breakfast menu in the world," a set dinner is served (for guests only) at the farmhouse table in the stone-arched dining room, and ingredients for all three courses are likely to have been growing in the kitchen garden only hours before. Specialties include homemade soup, steak-and-kidney pie, and roast rack of lamb with fresh herbs, and organic wines are also served. Local guidebooks are on hand, and Mrs. Pauline Staff is a qualified guide who can give talks and slide shows on Hadrian's Wall and the area. ✉ *Off A69, about 18 mi west of Hexham, CA6 7HY,* ☎ *016977/47402. 4 double rooms with shower. No smoking. AE, MC, V. Closed Dec. 25, Jan. 1.*

Vindolanda

26 *16 km (10 mi) west of Hexham; 66 km (41 mi) northwest of Durham.*

The great garrison fort of Vindolanda holds the remains of eight successive Roman forts and civilian settlements. Excavations are always going on here, and a section of the wall has been reconstructed. Recorded information interprets the site, and the museum contains leather, wood, glass, and pottery exhibits. There's even a reconstructed Roman kitchen. ✉ *Near Bardon Mill,* ☎ *01434/344277.* *Grounds only £1.75, grounds and museum £3.25.* *Museum May–Aug., daily 10–6; Apr. and Sept., daily 10–5:30; Mar. and Oct., daily 10–5; Nov.–Feb., daily 10–4; last admission ½ hr before closing.*

Housesteads Roman Fort

★ 27 *11 km (7 mi) west of Hexham; 61 km (38 mi) northwest of Durham.*

If you have time to visit only one Hadrian's Wall site, Housesteads Roman Fort is your best bet. It offers an interpretive center, views of long sections of the wall, the excavated 5-acre fort itself, and a museum. It's a steep, 10-minute walk up from the parking lot by B6318 to the site, but it's worth the effort, especially for the view of the wall disappearing over hills and crags into the distance. The excavations reveal granaries, gateways, barracks, and the commandant's house. There are also altars, inscribed stones, and models. ⊠ *3 mi northeast of Bardon Mill,* ☎ *01434/344363.* 🎟 *£2.30.* ⏲ *Apr.–Sept., daily 10–6; Oct.–Mar., daily 10–4. Closed Dec. 25, Jan. 1.*

Chesters Roman Fort

28 *6 km (4 mi) north of Hexham; 56 km (35 mi) northwest of Durham.*

Chesters Roman Fort—"Cilurnum," in a wooded valley on the banks of the North Tyne River—protected the point where the wall crossed the river. Visitors approach it directly from the parking lot, and, while the site cannot compete with Housesteads in terms of setting, it does hold a fascinating collection of Roman artifacts, including statues of river and water gods, altars, milestones, iron tools, weapons, and handcuffs. The military bathhouse near the river is the best-preserved example in Britain. Drawings and diagrams provide an idea of what the fort looked like originally; its present, mellowed appearance gives little sense of the Romans' brightly painted pillars, walls, and altars. ⊠ *½ mi southwest of Chollerford (on B6318),* ☎ *01434/681379.* 🎟 *£2.20.* ⏲ *Apr.–Sept., daily 10–6; Oct.–Mar., daily 10–4. Closed Dec. 25 and Jan. 1.*

Corbridge

29 *30 km (19 mi) west of Newcastle; 46 km (29 mi) northwest of Durham.*

Corbridge is a small town of honey-colored stone houses and riverside walks, a prosperous-looking place with an abundance of welcoming pubs and attractive shops. In the churchyard of St. Andrew's Church by Market Place is the Vicar's Pele. Nearly 700 years old, this fortified tower was a refuge from Scottish raiders and was built from stones taken from Corstopitum.

The Roman fort of Corstopitum, now preserved to the west of Cor-
30 bridge as the **Corbridge Roman Site,** was occupied longer than any other fort on Hadrian's Wall. In fact, these ruins predate the wall by 40 years. Strategically positioned at the junction of the east-west and north–south Roman routes—Stanegate ran west to Carlisle, Dere Street led north to Scotland and south to London—the fort now contains a museum rich in artifacts. The Corbridge Lion sculpture probably decorated an important tomb at one time; it later graced a fountain. A temple frieze depicts Castor and Pollux, the god Jupiter's twin sons, and there is an altar dedicated to their father as well. ⊠ *On a back road ½ mi northwest of Corbridge,* ☎ *01434/632349.* 🎟 *£2.20.* ⏲ *Apr.–Oct., daily 10–6; Nov.–Mar., Wed.–Sun. 10–4. Closed Dec. 25 and Jan. 1.*

Kielder Water

31 *35 km (22 mi) northwest of Hexham; 85 km (53 mi) northwest of Durham.*

In the rugged hills on the western edge of Northumberland National Park, only about 5 kilometers (3 miles) from the Scottish border, lies Kielder Water, northern Europe's largest man-made lake, surrounded by Europe's largest planted forest. This modern reservoir has become an established attraction since it was completed in 1982, and it actually encourages visitors, offering facilities for such aquatic sports as waterskiing. A cruise service (☎ 01434/240436 or 01434/220423) operates from May to September from Tower Knowe Visitor Centre. Fishing is popular, and the upper part of the lake, designated a conservation area, attracts many bird-watchers.

The **Tower Knowe Visitor Centre** (☎ 01434/240398), at the southeast corner of Kielder Water, is a springboard from which to enjoy and explore not only the lake area but also the vast **Forest of Kielder.** Exhibitions and films illustrate the region's wildlife and natural history, and guided forest walks are offered in the summer.

32 Now a Forestry Commission visitor center, **Kielder Castle,** at the northwest corner of Kielder Water, was once a shooting lodge belonging to the duke of Northumberland. It's also the start of a 12-mile toll road that heads deep into the Forest of Kielder to the north, to meet A68 south of Carter Bar close to the Scottish border.

Outdoor Activities and Sports

Mountain bikes can be rented from **Kielder Bikes** at Kielder Water, with outlets at Hawkhope Car Park (☎ 01434/220392) and at Kielder Castle at the opposite end of the reservoir (☎ 01434/250392). There's also a 10-mile horseback riding trail at **Kielder Water. Northumbria Waters** offers a wide range of water-sports facilities at Kielder Water and 16 other regional reservoirs. *Details from Regent Center, Gosforth,* ☎ *0191/284–3151.*

Wallington House

33 *24 km (15 mi) northeast of Hexham; 30 km (19 mi) northwest of Newcastle.*

Wallington House, a striking 17th-century mansion with Victorian decoration, stands in the midst of an extensive, sparsely populated agricultural region at the village of Cambo. In addition to the house, with its fine plasterwork, furniture, porcelain, and dollhouse collection, the walled, terraced garden is a major attraction. During the summer, open-air events are held in the gardens and grounds (there are 100 acres of woodlands and lakes), including recitals, productions of Shakespeare, and concerts. ☎ *01670/774283.* 🎟 *£4.60.* ⏲ *House Apr.–Oct., Wed.–Mon. 1–5:30; walled garden Apr.–Sept., daily 10:30–7; Oct., daily 10–6; Nov.–Mar., daily 10:30–4.*

Rothbury

34 *40 km (25 mi) northeast of Hexham; 14 km (9 mi) southwest of Alnwick.*

A mile north of the beautifully situated village of Rothbury, the extraordinary Victorian mansion of **Cragside** was built between 1864 and 1895 by the first Lord Armstrong, an early electrical engineer. It is a must-see for anyone interested in the glorious age of the Victorian country house. Picturesquely nestled into a forested mountainside, this was the first house to be lit by hydroelectricity, generated by the ingenious lord's system of artificial lakes and underground piping. In the library you can see antique vases adapted for use as electric lamps; staircase banisters are topped with specially designed lights. An energy center, with restored mid-Victorian machinery, including a hydraulic pump and a water turbine, is being established on the grounds; this project has won a Ford European Conservation Award. In June, rhododendrons bloom in the 660-acre park surrounding the mansion; 30 rooms of the house, some with pre-Raphaelite paintings, are open to the public. ☎ *01669/620333.* 🎟 *£6; country park £3.75.* ⏲ *House Apr.–Oct., Tues.–Sun. 1–5:30; country park and energy center Easter–Oct., daily 10:30–7 or dusk; Nov.–Dec., Tues. and weekends 10:30–4.*

Dining and Lodging

£££ ✕🏨 **Embleton Hall.** The 5 acres of beautiful grounds are reason enough to stay in this stone country mansion, parts of which date back to 1730; its individually furnished rooms are decorated with lovely antiques and original paintings. Another reason to visit is the restaurant—its chintz draperies and cut-glass chandeliers are perfect accompaniments to the traditional English dishes served here, such as roast Northumbrian pheasant. ✉ *Near Longframlington, on A697, 10 mi southwest of Alnwick, NE65 8DT,* ☎ *01665/570249,* FAX *01665/570056. 10 rooms with bath. Restaurant. AE, DC, MC, V.*

££ ✕🏨 **Granby Inn.** This is a regular pub, with excellent bar food and a restaurant serving great fresh fish dishes and homemade soups. It was a stopping place for 17th-century coaches along Weardale. All the rooms are comfortably furnished and have TV and tea-coffeemaking appliances. ✉ *High St., Longframlington NE65 8DP,* ☎ *01665/570228. 6 rooms, 5 with bath. Restaurant, bar. MC, V.*

£ ✕🏨 **Queen's Head Hotel.** This cheery inn in the heart of Rothbury offers pleasant, straightforward rooms with an old-fashioned touch. The first-floor dining room serves traditional English dishes, with an emphasis on seafood and a number of vegetarian options. ✉ *Rothbury, Morpeth NE65 7SR,* ☎ *01669/620470,* FAX *01830/520530. 9 rooms, 3 with bath or shower. Restaurant, bar. MC, V.*

THE FAR NORTHEAST COAST

Before England gives way to Scotland, the final 64 kilometers (40 miles) of the Northeast coast—lined with extraordinarily medieval fortresses and monasteries—is counted by many the best stretch anywhere on the North Sea. Northumbria can claim to have been one of the few enclaves where the flame of learning was kept alive during Europe's "Dark Ages," most notably at Lindisfarne, the "Holy Island of saints and scholars." Castles abound, including the spectacularly sited one at Bamburgh, which legend declares to have been the Joyous Garde of Sir Lancelot du Lac, the fabled knight of King Arthur. The region also has some magnificent broad beaches. Only on rare summer days is swimming at all advisable, but the opportunities for walking are tremendous. The 3-mile walk from Bamburgh to Seahouses gives splendid views over to the Farne Islands, while the 2-mile hike from Craster to Dunstanburgh Castle is unforgettable.

Alnwick

35 *48 km (30 mi) north of Newcastle; 74 km (46 mi) north of Durham.*

Alnwick (pronounced "Ann-ick") is the best base from which to explore the dramatic coast and countryside of northern Northumberland. Once a county seat, the town is dominated by its vast castle, but there is plenty more to see. A weekly open-air market (every Saturday) has been held in Alnwick's cobbled **Market Place** for more than 800 years. Note the market cross, built on the base of an older cross; the town crier once made his proclamations from here. Starting on the last Sunday in June, this site is host to the annual week-long Alnwick Fair, a festival noteworthy for the enthusiastic participation of a local populace colorfully decked-out in medieval costume (✉ Alnwick Fair, Box 2, Alnwick NE66 1AA, ☎ 01665/605004 or 01665/602234).

The grimy bottles in the window of **Olde Cross Inn,** on Narrowgate Street toward the southern end of Alnwick, have been left untouched for more than 150 years. Why? A 19th-century proprietor fell down dead while arranging the window display, and all subsequent proprietors have refused to touch the bottles, believing them to carry a curse. Not surprisingly, the pub has been nicknamed "The Dirty Bottles."

★ **Alnwick Castle,** on the edge of the town center just above the junction of Narrowgate and Bailiffgate, is still the home of the dukes of Northumberland, whose family (the Percys) dominated the Northeast for centuries. Everything about this castle is on a grand scale, earning it the well-justified epithet "the Windsor of the North." In contrast with the cold, formidable exterior, the inside of the building has all the opulence of the palatial home it still is: Although you are only permitted to see six of more than 150 rooms, among the treasures on show are a galleried library, Meissen dinner services, ebony cabinets mounted on gilded wood, tables inlaid with intricate patterns, niches with larger-than-life-size marble statues, and Venetian-mosaic floors. ☎ *01665/510777.* *£4.50.* *Easter–mid-Oct. daily 11–5.*

Dining and Lodging

££ ✕ **John Blackmore's.** A stone town house, close to the castle, is the place to try some imaginative modern British cooking by owner and chef John Blackmore. Mousses are a house specialty—vegetarians like the fennel mousse with mushrooms and Stilton sauce—while fresh fish and seafood are always popular. ✉ *1 Dorothy Foster Ct., Narrowgate,* ☎ *01665/604465. AE, DC, MC, V. No lunch Tues.–Sat. Closed Sun.–Mon. and Jan.*

££ ✕ **White Swan Hotel.** Standing on the site of the Old Swan Inn on the stagecoach route between Newcastle and Edinburgh, this building was restored by a Victorian architect, Salvin, who also worked on Alnwick Castle. The main lounge, reconstructed from the paneling and furnishings of the *Olympic*—sister ship of the ill-fated *Titanic*—is memorable. One of the hotel's assets is its refurbished restaurant. The modern but romantic blue-and-pink decor is a relaxing background for a menu largely drawn from classic Northumbrian cooking. Specialties include Kielder game pie, cooked in rich Guinness sauce, and cranachan, a thick cream dessert made with Alnwick rum, raspberries, and oatmeal. ✉ *Bondgate Within, NE66 1TD,* ☎ *01665/602109,* FAX *01665/510400. 50 rooms with bath. Restaurant. AE, MC, V.*

£ ✕ **Bondgate House Hotel.** This is a small, family-run hotel, close to the medieval town gateway. Housed in a 250-year-old building, it's a reasonably priced base for touring the area, and it has parking space for eight cars. ✉ *20 Bondgate Without, NE66 1PN,* ☎ *01665/602025. 8 rooms, 5 with bath. Restaurant. MC, V.*

Shopping

Northumbria (✉ 35 Fenkle St., no phone) is chock-full of collectors' items on three floors, including paintings, pottery, ceramics, and figurines. **Narrowgate Pottery** (✉ 22 Back Narrowgate, ☎ 01665/604744) is a small workshop specializing in domestic stoneware pottery, including the distinctive Alnwick "pierced ware." The **House of Hardy** (☎ 01665/602771), just outside Alnwick (from downtown, take A1 south to just beyond traffic circle on left, clearly marked), is one of Britain's finest stores for country sports, especially fishing. It has a worldwide reputation for handcrafted tackle.

Chillingham Park

36 *25 km (16 mi) northwest of Alnwick; 16 km (10 mi) southwest of Bamburgh.*

Ruled by a bull "king," the famous wild cattle of Chillingham Park are thought to be descendants of the extinct European bison. A herd may have been enclosed when the 600-acre Chillingham estate was walled in over 700 years ago. These creamy-white cattle with curved, black-tipped horns can be dangerous; approach them only under the supervision of an experienced guide, as they can charge without warning. On one occasion, they did so: Thomas Bewick, the 18th-century artist and wood engraver found this out for himself—he finished his sketch of a Chillingham bull up a tree. ✉ *Estate House*, ☎ *01668/215250.* 🎫 *£2.50.* ⊙ *Apr.–Oct., Mon. and Wed.–Sat. 10–noon and 2–5, Sun. 2–5.*

Craster

37 *10 km (6 mi) northeast of Alnwick.*

The harbor smokehouses of the tiny fishing village of Craster are known for that great English breakfast delicacy, kippers: herring salted and smoked over smoldering oak shavings. You can visit the tar-blackened smokehouses, eat your fill of fresh and traditionally smoked fish, and even have smoked salmon mailed home to your friends.

NEED A BREAK? Opposite the smokehouse near the harbor, you can savor Craster kippers for lunch or afternoon tea at **Craster Fish Restaurant** (⊙ Easter–Sept.). Or stop in at the **Jolly Fisherman** pub, opposite, where you can feast on its famous fresh crab sandwiches while enjoying the views of crashing waves from the pub's splendid picture window.

38 Perched romantically on a cliff 100 feet above the shore, the ruins of **Dunstanburgh Castle** can be reached along a bracingly windy, mile-long coastal footpath from Craster. Built in 1316 by the earl of Lancaster as a defense against the Scots, and later enlarged by John of Gaunt (the powerful duke of Lancaster who virtually ruled England in the late 14th century), the castle is known to many from the popular paintings by 19th-century artist J.M.W. Turner, and more recently from scenes in the 1990 film version of *Hamlet* with Mel Gibson. Several picturesque sandy bays indent the coastline immediately to the north. ☎ *01665/576231.* 🎫 *£1.40.* ⊙ *Apr.–Sept., daily 10–6; Oct.–Mar., Tues.–Sun. 10–4; closed Dec. 25.*

The Farne Islands

39 *11 km (7 mi) north of Craster; 21 km (13 mi) northeast of Alnwick.*

Regular boat trips (2½ hours) from the village of Seahouses enable visitors to land on two of the Farne Islands (owned by the National Trust), which host impressive colonies of seabirds and gray seals. Inner Farne, where St. Cuthbert, the great abbot of Lindisfarne, died in AD 687, features a tiny chapel dedicated to his memory. ☎ *01665/720308; Seahouses Tourist Information Centre (Easter–Oct.) 01665/720884.* 🎫 *£5; landing fees vary and are payable to the wardens.* ⊙ *Apr.–Sept., daily (weather permitting); access restricted during seal breeding season (May 15–July 15).*

Bamburgh

40 *23 km (14 mi) north of Alnwick.*

Especially stunning when floodlit at night, Bamburgh Castle dominates the coastal view for miles, set atop a great crag to the north of Seahouses and overlooking a magnificent sweep of sand backed by high dunes. Once regarded as the legendary Joyous Garde of Sir Lancelot du Lac, one of King Arthur's fabled nights, it's one of the most picturesque castles in Britain. Its ramparts offer sweeping views of Lindisfarne (Holy Island), the Farne Islands, the stormy coastline, and the Cheviot hills inland. Much of the castle has been restored—although the great Norman keep (central tower) remains intact—and the present Lady Armstrong lives there now. Exhibits include collections of armor, porcelain, jade, furniture, and paintings. There are apartments for rent inside the castle, one of the most romantic addresses in the world for those who can afford it. ✉ *Bamburgh, 3 mi north of Seahouses,* ☎ *01668/214208.* £2.75. ⊙ *Apr.–Oct., daily 11–5.*

In the village of Bamburgh, the **Grace Darling Museum** commemorates a local heroine as well as the Royal National Lifeboat Institute, an organization of unpaid volunteers who keep watch at the rescue stations on Britain's coasts. Grace Darling became a folk heroine in 1838, when she and her father rowed out to save the lives of nine shipwrecked sailors from the SS *Forfarshire.* ✉ *Radcliffe Rd., opposite church near village center.* £1. ⊙ *Apr.–mid-Oct., Mon.–Sat. 11–7, Sun. 2–6.*

Dining and Lodging

££££ ✕ **Waren House Hotel.** Set on 6 acres of woodland off the road on a quiet bay between Bamburgh and Holy Island, this Georgian hotel has tastefully decorated bedrooms each with different styles of decor, from Victorian to Oriental. There are romantic views of Holy Island from the restaurant, which serves fresh local produce—the fish is highly recommended, and there are good vegetarian choices. ✉ *Waren Mill, Belford NE70 7EE,* 01668/214581, FAX 01668/214484. 8 rooms with bath, 2 suites. Restaurant, bar, library. AE, DC, MC, V.

£–££ ✕ **Lord Crewe Arms.** This is a cozy stone-walled inn with oak beams and open fires, in the heart of the village close to Bamburgh Castle, an ideal spot to have lunch while touring the area and its wild coast. The bedrooms are fairly simple, but the food, especially the local seafood, is excellent. ✉ *Front St., NE69 7BL,* ☎ *01668/214243. 25 rooms, 21 with bath. Restaurant. MC, V. Closed late Oct.–Mar.*

Lindisfarne Island

★ 41 *35 km (22 mi) north of Alnwick; 12 km (8 mi) southeast of Berwick-upon-Tweed.*

Cradle of northern England's Christianity and home of St. Cuthbert, Lindisfarne Island (or Holy Island) is reached from the mainland by a long drive along a causeway. The causeway is flooded at high tide, so you *must* check locally to find out when crossing is safe. The times, which change every day, are displayed at the causeway, and printed in local newspapers. As traffic can be heavy, allow at least a half hour for your return trip. The religious history of the island dates from the very origins of Christianity in England, for St. Aidan established a monastery here in AD 635. Under its greatest abbot, the sainted Cuthbert, Lindisfarne became one of the foremost centers of learning in Christendom. But in the year 875, Vikings destroyed the Lindisfarne community; only a few monks managed to escape, carrying with them Cuthbert's bones, which they finally reburied in Durham. It was reestablished in the 11th century by monks from Durham, and today the Norman ruins of the **Lindisfarne Priory** remain both impressive and beautiful. ☎ *01289/89200.* £2.50. ⊙ *Apr.–Sept., daily 10–6; Oct.–Mar., Tues.–Sun. 10–4; closed Dec. 25, Jan. 1.*

Seen from a distance, **Lindisfarne Castle,** reached by a pretty walk around the curving rocky coast of Holy Island, appears to grow out of the rocky pinnacle on which it was built 400 years ago—looking for all the world like a fairy-tale illustration. In 1903, architect Sir Edwin Lutyens sensitively converted the castle into a private home that retains the original's ancient features. Across several fields from the castle is a walled garden, surprisingly sheltered from the storms and winds; its 16th-century plan was discovered in, of all places, California, and the garden has since been replanted, providing again a colorful summer display. ✉ *Holy Island, 6 mi east of A1, north of Bamburgh,* ☎ *01289/89244.* 🎟 *£3.60.* ⏲ *Apr.–Oct., Sat.–Thurs. 1–5:30.*

Berwick-upon-Tweed

42 *48 km (30 mi) north of Alnwick; 123 km (77 mi) north of Durham.*

Although Berwick-upon-Tweed now lies just inside the border of England, historians estimate that it has changed hands between the Scots and the English 14 times. The market on Wednesday and Saturday draws plenty of customers from both sides of the border. The town's 16th-century walls are among the best-preserved in Europe (a path follows the ramparts). The parish church, Holy Trinity, was built during Cromwell's Puritan Commonwealth with stone from the castle.

NEED A BREAK? The **Town House** (✉ Marygate) serves a delicious variety of fresh quiches, pastries, and other snacks. It's a bit tricky to find: Cross Buttermarket under the Guildhall and go through the old jail. The café's proprietors say, "Please persevere to find your way in—it's easy when you know how!"

In Berwick's **Military Barracks,** built between 1717 and 1721, three accommodation wings surround a square, with the decorated gatehouse forming the fourth side. An exhibition called "By Beat of Drum" depicts the life of the common soldier from the 1660s to the 1880s. ✉ *The Parade, off Church St. in town center,* ☎ *01289/304493.* 🎟 *£2.20.* ⏲ *Apr.–Sept., daily 10–6; Oct.–Mar., Wed.–Sun. 10–4; closed Dec. 25, Jan. 1.*

Dining and Lodging

£££ ✕🏨 **Coach House.** Sixteen kilometers (10 miles) southwest of Berwick-upon-Tweed and less than that from the Scottish border, this friendly guest house is part of a cluster of attractive, well-converted farm buildings, including Northumberland's oldest unfortified house. The spacious bedrooms, some of which feature exposed wooden beams, share an appealing, homespun atmosphere; guests can enjoy three pleasant acres of gardens, with miles of stunning scenery on the doorstep. ✉ *3 mi north of Milfield on A697.* ☎ *01890/820293. 10 rooms, 7 with bath. Restaurant, bar. MC, V.*

£–££ ✕🏨 **Funnywayt'Mekalivin.** This has become famous as an idiosyncratic eatery, and with a name like that who could resist? Set in a 17th-century building in the heart of town, crammed with eccentric oddments and a mere 20 yards from the Elizabethan walls, it's very much a one-woman show. In the seven-table dining room, chef-owner Elizabeth Middlemiss produces her own much-acclaimed variations on local specialties such as venison casserole, seafood crumble, or carrot and apple soup. Lunch buffets provide a chance to sample her cooking at bargain prices. Three basic guest rooms are available upstairs. ✉ *41 Bridge St., TD15 1ES,* ☎ *01289/308827. 3 rooms, without bath. Restaurant. MC, V. No dinner Mon., Tues. Closed Sun.*

NORTHEAST A TO Z

Arriving and Departing

By Bus

National Express (☎ 0171/730–0202) serves the region from London's Victoria Coach Station. Average travel times are 4¾ hours to Durham, 5¼ hours to Newcastle, and 8¼ hours to Berwick-upon-Tweed. Connecting services to other parts of the region leave from Newcastle.

By Car

The most direct north–south route is A1, linking London and Edinburgh via Newcastle (274 mi from London; 5–6 hrs) and Berwick-upon-Tweed (338 mi from London; 2 hrs past Newcastle). A697, which branches west off A1 north of Morpeth, is a more attractive road, leading past the 16th-century battlefield of Flodden. A696/A68 northwest out of Newcastle is also more appealing than A1, but it is an increasingly busy road.

By Train

British Rail (☎ 0171/278–2477) serves the region from London's King's Cross Station, en route to Scotland. Average travel times are 2¾ hours to Darlington, three hours to Durham, 3¼ hours to Newcastle, and 3¾ hours to Berwick-upon-Tweed.

Getting Around

By Bus

The United Bus Company (☎ 01325/465252) in Darlington and **Northumbria Motor Services** (☎ 0191/232–4211) in Newcastle offer reasonable one-day "Explorer" tickets for unlimited local travel. For information on the area's fairly limited bus service, pick up a Northumberland public transport guide (£1) from a local tourist office.

By Car

A66 and A69 run east–west, providing cross-country access. Many traffic-free country roads provide quiet and scenic, if slower, alternatives to the main routes. Part of the Cheviot hills, which run along the Northumbrian side of the Scottish border, is now a military firing range. Don't drive here when the warning flags are flying. The military, though, has restored the Roman road, Dere Street, which crosses this region. Try also B6318, which is a well-maintained road that runs alongside Hadrian's Wall on the south side.

By Train

From Newcastle, there is local service north to Alnmouth (for Alnwick) and to Corbridge and Hexham on the east–west line to Carlisle. "Northeast Regional Rover" tickets, allowing unlimited travel in the area—including on the scenic Carlisle–Settle line—cost £59 for seven consecutive days, or £49 for four days of travel within an eight-day period. For information, call ☎ 01289/306771.

Contacts and Resources

Car-Rental Agencies

Durham: Ford Rent-a-Car, ✉ Durham City Ford, A1(M) Carrville, ☎ 0191/386–1155. **Hexham: Mint Hire Ltd,** ✉ County Buildings, ☎ 01434/601263; **Tyne Mills Motor Company,** ✉ Tyne Mills Industrial Estate, ☎ 01434/607091. **Newcastle upon Tyne: Avis,** ✉ 1 George St., ☎ 0191/232–5283; **Hertz,** ✉ Central Station, Neville St., ☎ 0191/261–1052.

Guided Tours

The Northumbria Tourist Board (☎ 0191/384–6905) has a register of professional guides. **Escorted Tours Ltd.** (☎ 0191/536–3493) runs day and half-day tours of Northumbria by luxury minibus; itineraries vary. Based near Sunderland, the company picks you up at your hotel in Durham or Newcastle. **Further Afield** (☎ 016977/47358) offers group walking tours of Northumbria. **Holiday with a Knight** (☎ 01287/632510) is run by Shirley Knight, a guide specializing in general tours of northern England, as well as theme tours based on history, literature, and ghosts and legends. **Northumbria Experience** (☎ 0191/374–3454) has specialized in Northeast tours for 25 years.

Travel Agencies

Thomas Cook: ✉ 24–25 Market Pl., Durham, ☎ 0191/384–8569; ✉ 6 Northumberland St., Newcastle, ☎ 0191/261–2163.

Visitor Information

Northumbria Regional Tourist Board, ✉ Aykley Heads, Durham DH1 5UX, ☎ 0191/384–6905. ⏲ Mon.–Thurs. 8:30–5, Fri. 8:30–4:30.

Tourist information centers, normally open Mon.–Sat. 9:30–5:30, but varying according to the season, include:

Alnwick: ✉ The Shambles, Northumberland NE66 1TN, ☎ 01665/510665. **Berwick-upon-Tweed:** ✉ Castlegate Car Park, Northumberland TD15 1JS, ☎ 01289/330733. **Durham:** ✉ Market Pl., Co. Durham DH1 3NJ, ☎ 0191/384–3720. **Hexham:** ✉ Manor Office, Hallgate, Northumberland NE46 1XD, ☎ 01434/605225. **Newcastle upon Tyne:** ✉ Central Library, Princess Sq., Tyne and Wear NE99 1DX, ☎ 0191/261–0691, and an office in the train station (open during the summer), ☎ 0191/230–0030.

16 Scotland: Edinburgh and the Borders

One of the world's stateliest cities and proudest capitals, Edinburgh—built on seven hills like Rome—is the perfect setting for the ancient pageant of history. Gaze down the ruler-straight magnificence of Princes Street: If you do not thrill at the vista of its great castle, you will be a stolid visitor indeed. Explore the New Town, the Royal Mile, and discover the fascinating museums of the Athens of the North. Then head south to the Borders, whose splendid heather-clad hills were immortalized by Sir Walter Scott.

SCOTLAND IS A SMALL COUNTRY, no bigger than the state of Maine, and contains barely a 10th of the United Kingdom's population. Yet the idea of Scotland is world-embracing. She has produced some of the world's stormiest history, most romantic heroes and heroines, most admired literature, and most important inventions. Her local products, customs, music, and traditional dress—whiskey, haggis, tartan, tweed, bagpipes—travel all over the globe. Scots throughout history, especially those who emigrated to the United States, Canada, Australia, and New Zealand, have been superb propagandists for the land of their ancestors, the land they love. Recently—thanks to Mel Gibson's *Braveheart* and Liam Neeson's *Rob Roy*—Scotland came to the big screen in all its Hollywoodian splendor to enchant and intrigue a new generation.

Someone once described Scotland as a sandwich: great chunks of dry bread (the Highlands and Southern Uplands) on either side of a tasty piece of meat (the Lowlands). There really are two Scotlands: the Lowlands (not low at all, but chains of hills along river valleys), where populous cities such as Edinburgh and Glasgow are found; and the Highlands, which contain the highest mountains in the British Isles, the wildest lochs (lakes), and most of the islands. It is often assumed that as you travel north you proceed from lowlands to highlands. In fact, it is more of an east-west divide. Most travelers start out with Scotland's greatest city, Edinburgh. After a while, however, all feet march in the direction of mythical Brigadoon—toward those splendid heather-clad mountain slopes and the shimmering lochs, the fast-flowing streams where salmon leap and the great castles of baronial pride standing hard among the hills.

Edinburgh—pronounced, by the way, Edin"-boro," not Edin"-burg"—seems to have been designed as a tourist attraction. A variety of factors make this city appealing: its outstanding geography—like Rome, it is built on seven hills—the Old Town district, with all the evidence of its colorful history, and the New Town with its large number of elegant, classical buildings conceived in the surge of artistic creativity of the second half of the 18th century.

The Borders area comprises the great rolling hills, moors, wooded river valleys, and farmland that stretch south from Lothian, the region crowned by Edinburgh, to England. All the distinctive features of Scotland—paper currency, architecture, opening hours of pubs and stores, food and drink, and accent—start right at the border; you won't find the Borders a diluted version of England. Northeast of Edinburgh, on the windswept east coast, the ancient town of St. Andrews makes another excellent excursion from the capital—filled with historic sights and known the world over as the home of golf. Many a traveler hopes to return home with the tale of a Road Hole birdie on the Old Course.

Pleasures and Pastimes

Arts

There is no escaping a literal sense of theater if you visit Edinburgh from August to early September. As the host for the annual International Edinburgh Festival, the city is quite literally filled with cultural events during this period—in every art form from classic theater and big-name classical concerts to jazz and the most experimental forms of dance and theater. Even more obvious to the casual stroller during this time is the Edinburgh Festival Fringe, the refreshingly irreverent, ever-growing, unruly child of the official festival. A few well-known names in the theater got their start at the Edinburgh Fringe in past years; a Fringe performance—seats are cheap and surroundings are makeshift—is always an experience. During the same time period, that stirring Scottish extravaganza—the Edinburgh Military Tattoo—is also performed.

Dining

It's not a bad idea to remind yourself from time to time that it's history, not food, that brought you to Edinburgh. Nevertheless, it's now easier than ever for the traveler in Scotland to sample a genuine Scottish cuisine—whether grand meals in baronial hotel-restaurants, balance-on-your-knee pub lunches, or even the "carry oot" (to go) meal. Look out for the "Taste of Scotland" sign in restaurant windows indicating the use of the best of Scottish products including marvelous salmon and venison. Culinary delights await—including nouvelle variations on Partan Bree (crab with rice and cream), Loch Fyne herring, and haggis (an acquired taste and almost impossible to describe). Like all cosmopolitan centers, Edinburgh also has an enormous range of ethnic cooking, from Chinese to Indian. Make reservations well in advance, especially at festival time.

CATEGORY	COST*
££££	over £40
£££	£25–£40
££	£15–£25
£	under £15

**per person, including first course, main course, dessert, and VAT; excluding drinks*

Golfing

In the "East Neuk," one of the prettiest scenic areas of Scotland, the quiet town of St. Andrews beckons with its indelibly monastic and academic air, its clean gray stone, and the many fragments of distant history. While you will want to take in the colleges of the university (Scotland's first), the ruined castle and cathedral above the sandy shore, its hoary "pends" and "wynds," the main lure is, of course, its famous golf course, where the Royal & Ancient, the ruling body of the game worldwide, has its headquarters. But even if St. Andrews is not your headquarters, Scotland remains a golfer's paradise. Golf aficionados head for the courses first— then realize most of them "have charming old towns close by them."

Hiking and Walking

Walks in the Edinburgh area range from city walkways—along the banks of the Water of Leith, for example—to fairly demanding excursions on Scotland's only east–west official footpath, the Southern Upland Way. This is a signposted 212-mile route, from Cockburnspath on the east coast to Portpatrick in the far southwest of Galloway; the terrain along the way ranges from windswept moorland and hilltops to lush river valleys and woodland. One place of recreation for the locals is the Pentland Hills, with their breezy but not over-demanding slopes especially popular on weekends; there's easy access to the Hills at Hillend, by the artificial ski slope, or in Bonaly Country Park. Alternatively, there is also good East Lothian coastal walking at many points from Aberlady, eastward.

As the Borders are essentially rural and hilly, there are a number of walking options, of which Loch Skeen above the Grey Mare's Tail Waterfall, northwest of Moffat, is just one example; the walk here is not too demanding, but strong footwear is advised. Peebles, within easy reach of Edinburgh, offers excellent level walking along the banks of the river Tweed, while a visit to Melrose, with its abbey, can be further enjoyed by a climb to the top of the Eildon Hills with wonderful views, though you should allow a couple of hours. Again, strong shoes or boots (and lungs!) are advised.

Lodging

From grand hotel suites done up in tartan fabrics and prints of old Edinburgh to personal-touch bed-and-breakfasts, Edinburgh is splendidly served by a wide variety of guest accommodations. Some of the best are in lovely traditional Georgian properties—some even in the New Town, a few minutes from downtown. Upscale hotels are based mainly in downtown, and each has an international flavor.

CATEGORY	COST*
££££	over £110
£££	£80–£110
££	£50–£80
£	under £50

**All prices are for two people sharing a double room, including service, breakfast, and VAT.*

Exploring Edinburgh and the Borders

We have divided our coverage of Edinburgh into two sections—the Old and New Towns—but only the Old Town and Royal Mile area easily lend themselves to being organized routes. The New Town, north of Edinburgh Castle, is ideal for unstructured wandering, drinking in the classical elegance of the squares and terraced houses, exploring the antiques shops, and dropping into pubs or wine bars. The Borders surveys Sir Walter Scott territory south of Edinburgh among ruined abbeys. This area can be explored in one long day, or better still, taken in two bites, returning to Edinburgh overnight.

Great Itineraries

Ideally, to include excursions to the Borders, visitors to the Edinburgh area would need nearly a week to take in the diversity of sights and scenery. If you have a shorter period of time, and wish to remain in Edinburgh, the main attractions could be seen in two or three days. Four or five days might also allow for a day trip to St. Andrews. A little longer, and the larger area of the Borders could be explored.

Numbers in the text correspond to numbers in the margin and on the maps.

IF YOU HAVE 2–3 DAYS

Probably all visitors to **Edinburgh** ① are drawn to **Edinburgh Castle** ②. It is worth spending a few hours at the castle because of the range of displays, museums, architecture, and city views. Also on the **Royal Mile** ③, other important sights are **Gladstone's Land** ⑥, **St. Giles Cathedral** ⑬, and the **Palace of Holyroodhouse** ⑲. Among the more impressive museums to take in during a short visit are the **Royal Museum of Scotland** ⑪, the **National Gallery of Scotland** ㉑, and the **Royal Scottish Academy** ㉒. Break up your three day visit with an overnight excursion to the Borders, visiting **Galashiels** to take a look at Sir Walter Scott's delightful **Abbotsford House** ㉜ while enjoying a rural change of pace from Edinburgh—or for a one day trip, check out the golfers' heaven of **St. Andrews** ㊸.

IF YOU HAVE 6 DAYS

At least two days and nights should be spent in **Edinburgh** ① to allow for visits to all of the most important Old and New Town sights. In the Old Town, the main sights on and off the **Royal Mile** ③, **Edinburgh Castle** ②, **Gladstone's Land** ⑥, the **Grassmarket** ⑧, **Greyfriars Kirk** ⑩,

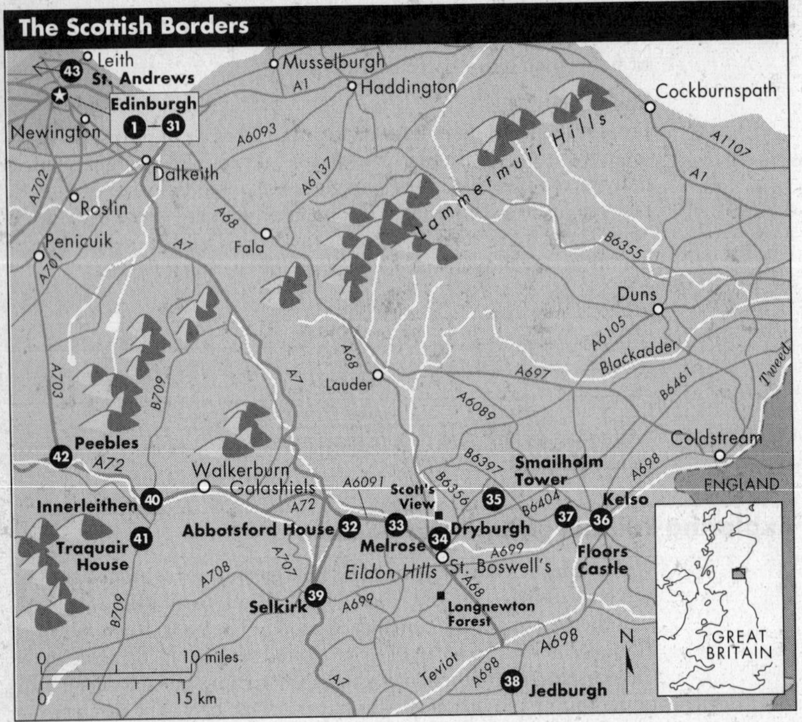

The Scottish Borders

the **Royal Museum of Scotland** ⑪, **St. Giles Cathedral** ⑬, **John Knox House** ⑯, and the **Palace of Holyroodhouse** ⑲, are all good destinations around which to explore the closes off the High Street and Cannongate. The New Town, from the splendid architecture of Charlotte Square and the residential **Moray Place** ㉙ to the panoramic views from **Calton Hill** ㉕ are all well within the scope of an enjoyable walk, as are the main New Town thoroughfares of George Street and Princes Street. To drink in some stately houses and magnificent estate gardens, three places just outside the city beckon: the **Royal Botanic Garden** ㉛ and two Neoclassical mansions designed by the great Robert Adam, **Hopeton House** or **Paxton House**; the former is noted for its grounds, the latter for its paintings. For your third night and fourth nights, head south for the Borders to explore Sir Walter Scott Country. Start out (and return to overnight) in 🏨 Galashiels, paying a call on **Abbotsford House** ㉜, the 19th-century home of the Borders' most famous literary resident. Take in the best of the outdoor sights, such as Scott's View at **Dryburgh** ㉞ as well as of the sights slightly farther afield, for instance the abbey at **Jedburgh** ㊳. For those interested in grand Scottish residences of the past, a visit to **Floors Castle** ㊳ will be a must. After enjoying the glories of the Scottish countryside on an afternoon walk, spend your last overnight in 🏨 **Kelso** ㊱ before heading back to the capital.

When to Tour Edinburgh and the Borders

August is far and away the most exciting time to visit Edinburgh, largely because of the International Festival (☞ Nightlife and the Arts, *below,* for 1997 dates). The sheer amount of theater and music going on make the city buzz with cultural activity. However, this is also inevitably the busiest time, and anyone wishing to visit Edinburgh during August and the beginning of September will have to plan and book months in advance. The winters can be cold and wet, but the long summer evenings—with sunsets as late as 10:30 PM—from June to September are magical. The Borders are also busiest during festival time with visitors taking a break from city life, but its landscape can be fully appreciated in March and April as well.

EDINBURGH

In a skyline of sheer drama, Edinburgh Castle watches over the city, frowning down on Princes Street as if disapproving of its modern razzmatazz. Its ramparts still echo with gunfire when the one o'clock gun booms out each day, startling unwary tourists. The top of Calton Hill, to the east, is cluttered with sturdy neoclassical monuments—like an abandoned set for a Greek drama. Also conspicuous from Princes Street is Arthur's Seat, a mountain of bright green and yellow furze rearing up behind the spires of the Old Town. This child-size mountain jutting 800 feet above its surroundings has steep slopes and little crags, like a miniature Highlands set down in the middle of the busy city. These theatrical elements give a unique identity to downtown, but turn a corner, say, off George Street (parallel to Princes Street), and you will see, not an endless cityscape, but blue sea and a patchwork of fields. This is the county of Fife, beyond the inlet of the North Sea called the Firth of Forth; a reminder, like the northwest Highlands glimpsed from Edinburgh's highest points, that the rest of Scotland lies within easy reach.

The Old Town

❶ The dark, brooding presence of the castle, the very essence of Scotland's martial past, dominates **Edinburgh.** The castle is built on a crag of hard, black volcanic rock formed during the Ice Age when an eastbound glacier scoured around this resistant core, creating steep cliffs on three sides. On the fourth side, a "tail" of rock was left, forming a ramp from the top that gradually runs away eastward. This became the street known as the Royal Mile, the backbone of the Old Town, leading from the castle down to the Palace of Holyroodhouse, which later became the seat of the Royal Stuarts. "The Mile" is actually made up of one thoroughfare that bears, in consecutive sequence, different names—the Esplanade, Castle Hill, Lawnmarket, Parliament Square, High Street, and Canongate.

These streets and passages winding into their tenements or "lands" are crammed onto the ridgeback of "the Mile." This really *was* Edinburgh until the 18th century saw expansions to the south and north. Everybody lived here, the richer folk on the lower floors, with less well-to-do families on the upper floors—the higher up, the poorer. There are guided walking tours of the Royal Mile that emphasize its historical—and sinister—aspects. For besides being the haunt of kings, its dark alleys hid bodysnatchers, witches, and warlocks. Time and redevelopment have swept away some of the narrow closes (alleyways) and tall tenements of the Old Town, but enough survive for you to be able to imagine the original profile of Scotland's capital. Sir Walter Scott, Robert Louis Stevenson, David Hume, James Boswell, and the painter Allan Ramsay—these and many other well-known names are associated with the Old Town. But perhaps three are more famous than any others—John Knox; Mary, Queen of Scots; and Prince Charles Edward Stuart.

A Good Walk

Numbers in the text correspond to numbers in the margin and on the Edinburgh map.

A perfect place to begin a tour of the Old Town is **Edinburgh Castle** ②. Having absorbed the many attractions within the castle and taken in the marvelous city views, you can begin to stroll down the grand promenade that is the **Royal Mile** ③. To the left of Castlehill, the Outlook Tower offers armchair views of the city with its **Camera Obscura** ④. Opposite, the **Scotch Whisky Heritage Centre** ⑤ offers an unusual chance to discover Scotland's liquid gold—stop off for a sample. The six-story tenement known as **Gladstone's Land** ⑥, a survivor of 16th century domestic life, is on the left walking down. Close by Gladstone's Land, down yet another close, is **The Writers' Museum** ⑦, housed in a good example of 17th-century urban architecture known as Lady Stair's House. Built in 1622, it evokes Scotland's literary past with exhibits on Sir Walter Scott, Robert Louis Stevenson, and Robert Burns.

Farther down on the left, the **Tolbooth Kirk** ("kirk" means church) boasts the tallest spire in the city—240 feet. From Lawnmarket you can start your discovery of the **Old Town closes,** the alleyways that spread like ribs from the Royal Mile backbone. For a worthwhile shopping diversion, turn right down George IV Bridge, then to the right down Victoria Street, a 19th-century improvement—or intrusion—on the shape of the Old Town. Its shops offer antiques, old prints, clothing, and quality giftware. Down in the **Grassmarket** ⑧, which for centuries was, as its name suggests, an agricultural market, the shopping continues.

Walk from the Grassmarket back up Victoria Street to George IV Bridge, where you'll see the **National Library of Scotland** ⑨. Farther down George IV Bridge, to the right, is the **Greyfriars Kirk** ⑩. Why not stop for a cup of coffee or tea and some elephant-shape shortbread or a light lunch—while taking in superb views of the castle—at the Elephant Cafe, just across the road from the National Library.

Before returning to Lawnmarket, you might detour down Chambers Street, which leads off from George IV Bridge. Here, in a lavish Victorian building, the **Royal Museum of Scotland** ⑪ displays a wide-ranging collection. Return to High Street and, near Parliament Square, look for **Parliament House** ⑫, partially hidden by the bulk of **St. Giles's Cathedral** ⑬, another crucial sight in any tour of the Old Town. Just east of St. Giles is another Old Town landmark, the **Mercat Cross** ⑭, which is still the site of royal proclamations.

At the North Bridge and South Bridge junction, you will find the **Tron Kirk.** Although this is no longer in use as a church and is closed to the public as such, it houses the useful **Old Town Information Center** in the summer months. On the High Street, a short walk from the North Bridge-South Bridge junction, is the **Museum of Childhood** ⑮. In contrast, across the street lies **John Knox House** ⑯, reputed to have been the residence of Scotland's severe 16th-century religious reformer.

Beyond this point, you would once have passed beyond the safety provided by the town walls. A plaque outside the **Netherbow Arts Centre** depicts the **Netherbow Port** (gate), which once stood here. Below is the Canongate area, now the site of Holyroodhouse, named for the Canons who once ran the abbey at Holyrood. Here you will find the handsome **Canongate Tolbooth** ⑰, and, almost next door, the graveyard of **Canongate Kirk,** and **Huntly House** ⑱, a museum of local history. Facing you at the end of Canongate are the elaborate wrought-iron gates of the **Palace of Holyroodhouse** ⑲, official residence of the Queen when she is in Scotland, and a fittingly regal end to your walk down the Royal Mile.

Sights to See

Numbers in the margin correspond to points of interest on the Edinburgh map.

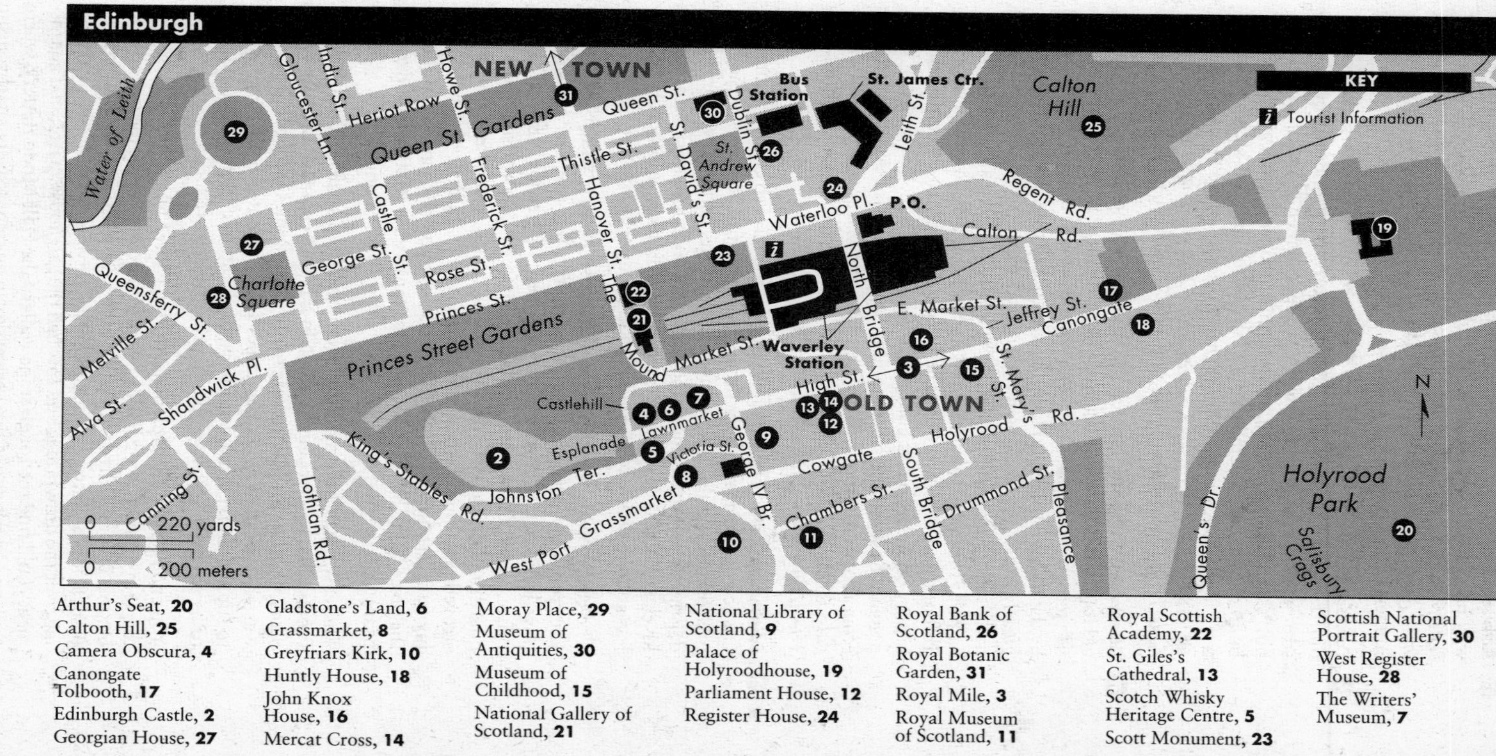

Arthur's Seat, **20**
Calton Hill, **25**
Camera Obscura, **4**
Canongate Tolbooth, **17**
Edinburgh Castle, **2**
Georgian House, **27**
Gladstone's Land, **6**
Grassmarket, **8**
Greyfriars Kirk, **10**
Huntly House, **18**
John Knox House, **16**
Mercat Cross, **14**
Moray Place, **29**
Museum of Antiquities, **30**
Museum of Childhood, **15**
National Gallery of Scotland, **21**
National Library of Scotland, **9**
Palace of Holyroodhouse, **19**
Parliament House, **12**
Register House, **24**
Royal Bank of Scotland, **26**
Royal Botanic Garden, **31**
Royal Mile, **3**
Royal Museum of Scotland, **11**
Royal Scottish Academy, **22**
St. Giles's Cathedral, **13**
Scotch Whisky Heritage Centre, **5**
Scott Monument, **23**
Scottish National Portrait Gallery, **30**
West Register House, **28**
The Writers' Museum, **7**

20 **Arthur's Seat.** For a grand bird's-eye view of Edinburgh, make your way up the 800 feet of the city's only mini-mountain, Arthur's Seat, set in the park behind the ☞ **Palace of Holyroodhouse.** It is a steep walk, but well worth it for the views from here and its neighboring eminence, Salisbury Crags.

4 **Camera Obscura.** Want to view Edinburgh as Victorian travelers once did? Head for the Outlook Tower, where you'll find this optical instrument—a sort of projecting telescope—which offers armchair and bird's-eye views of the whole city illuminated onto a concave table. The building was constructed in the 17th century, but was significantly altered in the 1840s and 1850s for the installation of the "magic lantern." ☎ *0131/226–3709.* *£2.90.* ⏲ *Apr.–Oct., weekdays 9:30–6, weekends 10–6; Nov.–Mar., weekdays 10–5, weekends 10–3:30.*

17 **Canongate Tolbooth.** Named for the canons who once ran the abbey at Holyrood, Canongate originally was an independent "burgh," a Scottish term meaning, essentially, a community with trading rights granted by the monarch. This explains the presence of the Canongate Tolbooth. Nearly every city and town in Scotland once had a tolbooth—originally signifying a customs house where tolls were gathered, the name came to mean the town hall and later a prison. Today, the Canongate Tolbooth is the setting for "The People's Story," an exhibition on the history of the people of Edinburgh. Next door is the graveyard of Cannongate Kirk, where some notable Scots, including Adam Smith, the economist and author of *The Wealth of Nations,* are buried. ✉ *Canongate,* ☎ *0131/200–2000, ext. 4057.* *Free.* ⏲ *June–Sept., Mon.–Sat. 10–6, Sun. during festival 2–5; Oct.–May, Mon.–Sat. 10–5.*

★ 2 **Edinburgh Castle.** The crowning glory of the Scottish capital, Edinburgh Castle is popular not only because of its symbolic value as the heart of Scotland but also due to the views from its battlements: On a clear day the vistas—stretching to the "kingdom" of Fife—are of breathtaking loveliness. Clear days are frequent now; Edinburgh is officially smokeless and the nickname "Auld Reekie" no longer applies.

The castle opens the chronicle of Scottish history, which will engulf you from now until you leave the country. You will hear the story of how Randolph, Earl of Moray, nephew of freedom-fighter Robert Bruce, scaled the heights one dark night in 1313, surprised the English guard, and recaptured the castle for the Scots. At the same time he destroyed every one of its buildings except for St. Margaret's Chapel, dating from around 1076, so that successive Stuart kings had to rebuild the place bit by bit. This accounts for the castle's relatively modern appearance.

The castle has been held by Scots and Englishmen, Catholics and Protestants, soldiers and royalty. In the 16th century Mary, Queen of Scots, chose to give birth there to the future James VI of Scotland, who was also to rule England as James I. In 1573, it was the last fortress to support Mary's claim as the rightful Catholic queen of Britain, only to be virtually destroyed by English artillery fire.

You enter across the **Esplanade,** the huge forecourt, which was built in the 18th century as a parade ground and now serves as the castle parking lot. It comes alive with color each year when it is used during the Festival for the Tattoo, a magnificent military display and pageant. Heading over the drawbridge and through the gatehouse, past kilted guardsmen, you'll find the rough stone walls of the **Half Moon Battery,** where the one o'clock gun is fired every day in an impressively anachronistic ceremony. Climb up through a second gateway and you come to the oldest surviving building in the complex, the tiny 11th-century **St. Mar-**

garet's **Chapel.** Head up farther still to enter the heart of the mighty complex, the dark and still-gruesome medieval fortress. Here, along the dimly lit, echoing corridors you'll find the **Crown Room,** containing the "Honors of Scotland"—the crown, scepter, and sword that once graced the Scottish monarch; the Great Hall, under whose 16th-century hammer-beam roof official banquets are still held; and **Queen Mary's apartments,** where she gave birth to James. ☎ *0131/244–3101.* 🎫 *£5.50.* ⏲ *Apr.–Sept., daily 9:30–5:15; Oct.–Mar., daily 9:30–4:15.*

6 **Gladstone's Land.** A standout for those in search of the authentic atmosphere of old Edinburgh, this is a six-story tenement just beside the Assembly Hall that dates from the 17th century. Its theatrical setting includes an arcaded ground floor and a second-story entrance; the entire edifice is furnished in the style of a 17th-century merchant's house. ☎ *0131/226–5856.* 🎫 *£2.60.* ⏲ *Apr.–Oct., Mon.–Sat. 10–5, Sun. 2–5; last admission 4:30.*

8 **Grassmarket.** As its name suggests, this was for centuries an agricultural market. Today, the shopping continues, but the goods have changed—antiques, old prints, clothing, and quality giftware. More boutiques can be found nearby along Victoria Street, one of the most popular shopping centers of the city.

10 **Greyfriars Kirk.** Here, on the site of a medieval monastery, the National Covenant was signed in 1638, declaring the Presbyterian Church in Scotland independent of government control, this triggering decades of civil war. Be sure to search out the graveyard—one of the most evocative in Europe. ✉ *Greyfriars Pl.,* ☎ *0131/225–1900.* 🎫 *Free.* ⏲ *Easter–Sept., weekdays 10:30–4:30, Sat. 10:30–2; Oct.–Easter, Thurs. 1:30–3:30.*

18 **Huntly House.** This attractive timber-front building houses a fascinating museum of local history, a must for those interested in the details of Old Town life. ✉ *142 Canongate,* ☎ *0131/225–2424, ext. 4143.* 🎫 *Free.* ⏲ *June–Sept., 10–6, Sun. during festival 2–5; Oct.–May, Mon.–Sat. 10–5.*

Then there's the little chamber in which, in 1566, David Rizzio, secretary to Mary, Queen of Scots, met an unhappy end. Partly because Rizzio was hated at court for his social climbing ways, Mary's second husband, Lord Darnley, burst into the queen's rooms with his henchmen, dragged Rizzio into an antechamber, and stabbed him more than 50 times (a bronze plaque marks the spot). Darnley himself was murdered in Edinburgh the next year, to make way for the queen's marriage to her lover, Bothwell. When Charles II assumed the British throne in 1660, he ordered Holyrood rebuilt in the architectural style of France's "Sun King," Louis XIV, and that is the palace that visitors see today. When the royal family is not in residence, visitors are free to walk around the palace and go inside for a conducted tour. Behind the palace lie the open grounds of Holyrood Park, which enclose Edinburgh's own mini-mountain, ☞ **Arthur's Seat.** ☎ *0131/556–7371 or 0131/556–1096 (recorded information).* 🎫 *£5.* ⏲ *Apr.–Oct., Mon.–Sat. 9:30–5:15, Sun. 10:30–4:30; Nov.–Mar., Mon.–Sat. 9:30–3:45; closed during royal and state visits.*

16 **John Knox House.** A typical 16th-century dwelling, this was certainly not the home of Knox, Scotland's fiery religious reformer (1514–72), but is full of mementos of his life. ✉ *45 High St.,* ☎ *0131/556–2647.* 🎫 *£1.75.* ⏲ *Mon.–Sat. 10–4:30.*

14 **Mercat Cross.** A great landmark of Old Town life, the Mercat Cross ("mercat" means "market") can be seen just east of St. Giles's Cathe-

dral (☞ *below*). As its name suggests, it was a mercantile center, and, in early days, it also saw executions and was the spot where royal proclamations were—and are still—read. The present cross is comparatively modern, dating from the time of Gladstone, the great Victorian prime minister and rival of Disraeli.

15 **Museum of Childhood.** An excellent diversion, this collection is a celebration of toys that even adults will enjoy. ✉ *42 High St.,* ☎ *0131/225–2424.* *Free.* ⊙ *June–Sept., Mon.–Sat. 10–6, Sun. during festival 2–5; Oct.–May, Mon.–Sat. 10–5.*

9 **National Library of Scotland.** Situated on George IV Bridge, this research library is a special magnet for genealogists investigating family trees. Even amateur family sleuths will find the staff helpful in their research. *Free.* ⊙ *Mon.–Tues. and Thurs.–Fri. 9:30–8:30, Wed. 10–8:30, Sat. 9:30–1.*

★ 19 **Palace of Holyroodhouse.** Haunt of Mary, Queen of Scots, and the setting for high drama—including at least one notorious murder, a spectacular funeral, several major fires, and centuries of the colorful lifestyles of larger-than-life, power-hungry personalities—this is now the Queen's official residence in Scotland. A doughty and impressive palace standing at the foot of the Royal Mile in a hilly public park, it is built around a graceful, lawned central court. Many monarchs, including Charles II, Queen Victoria, and George V have left their mark on its rooms. Highlights include the **Great Picture Gallery**, 150 feet long and hung with the portraits of 111 Scottish monarchs. These were commissioned by Charles II, eager to demonstrate his Scottish ancestry; in the absence of reliable likenesses to copy, the artist gave most of them Charles's features.

12 **Parliament House.** The seat of government until 1707, when the crowns of Scotland and England were united, is partially hidden by the bulk of St. Giles's Cathedral. ✉ *Parliament Sq.,* ☎ *0131/225–2595.* *Free.* ⊙ *Weekdays 9:30–4:30.*

3 **Royal Mile.** The most famous thoroughfare of Edinburgh begins immediately below the Esplanade. It runs roughly west to east, from the castle to the Palace of Holyroodhouse and progressively changes its name from Castlehill to Lawnmarket, High Street, and Canongate. Strolling downhill from the castle, it is easy to imagine and re-create the former life of the city, though you will need sharp eyes to spot the numerous historic plaques and details of ornamentation.

★ 11 **Royal Museum of Scotland.** Housed in a lavish Victorian-era building, this museum displays a wide-ranging collection drawn from natural history, archaeology, the scientific and industrial past, and the history of mankind and civilization. The great Main Hall, a fine example with its soaring roof of Victorian municipal building, is architecturally interesting in its own right. ✉ *Chambers St.,* ☎ *0131/225–7534.* *Free.* ⊙ *Mon.–Sat. 10–5, Sun. noon–5.*

13 **St. Giles's Cathedral.** Not really a cathedral but a "high kirk," St. Giles's is about one-third of the way along the Royal Mile from Edinburgh Castle. This is the city's principal church, but anyone expecting a rival to Notre Dame or London's Westminster Abbey will be disappointed: St. Giles's is more like a large parish church than a great European cathedral. Outside, the building is dominated by a stone crown, towering 161 feet above the ground; inside, the atmosphere is dark and forbidding. At the far end you'll find a life-size bronze statue of the Scot whose spirit still dominates the place, the great religious reformer and preacher John Knox, before whose zeal all Scotland once trembled. The most

elaborate feature inside the church is the **Chapel of the Order of the Thistle,** which refers to Scotland's highest order of chivalry and is the counterpart to England's Order of the Garter. It's rather alarming to imagine all 18 of these worthy knights crammed into this dark, little room, resplendent in their attire of dark green robes and plumed hats, under the Queen's commands—as they must whenever a new knight is installed. ✉ *High St.,* ☎ *0131/225–4363.* 🎫 *Free; Thistle Chapel 50p.* ⏲ *Mon.–Sat. 9–5 (until 7 in summer), Sun. 2–5 (services at 8 AM, 10 AM, 11:30 AM, 8 PM).*

❺ **Scotch Whisky Heritage Centre.** If you've ever been interested in learning about the mysterious process that turns malted barley and spring water into one of Scotland's most important exports, this is the place. ✉ *358 Castlehill,* ☎ *0131/220–0441.* 🎫 *£3.80.* ⏲ *Daily 10–5 (extended hrs in summer).*

The **Tolbooth Kirk.** Built in 1842–44 for the General Assembly of the Church of Scotland, this structure features the tallest spire in the city—240 feet. It is not open to the public.

❼ **The Writers' Museum.** Close by Gladstone's Land, down yet another close, is The Writers' Museum, housed in a good example of 17th-century urban architecture known as Lady Stair's House. Built in 1622, it evokes Scotland's literary past with exhibits on Sir Walter Scott, Robert Louis Stevenson, and Robert Burns. ✉ *Off Lawnmarket,* ☎ *0131/225–2424, ext. 4901.* 🎫 *Free.* ⏲ *June–Sept., Mon.–Sat. 10–6, Sun. during festival 2–5; Oct.–May, Mon.–Sat. 10–5.*

The New Town and Beyond

It was not until the Scottish Enlightenment, a civilizing time of expansion in the 1700s, that the city fathers decided to break away from the Royal Mile's rocky slope and build another Edinburgh below the castle, a little to the north. This is the New Town, with elegant squares, classical facades, wide streets, and harmonious proportions. The main street, Princes Street, was conceived as an exclusive residential address with an open vista toward the castle. It has since been completely altered by the demands of business and shopping.

In 1767, a civic competition to design a new district for Edinburgh was won by an unknown young architect, James Craig. His plan was for a grid of three main east–west streets, balanced at either end by two grand squares. These streets survive today, though some of the buildings that line them were altered by later development. Princes Street is the southernmost, with Queen Street to the north and George Street as the axis, punctuated by St. Andrew and Charlotte squares. A look at the map will show you its geometric symmetry, unusual in Britain. Even Princes Street Gardens are balanced by Queen Street Gardens to the north.

A Good Walk

Start your walk on **The Mound,** the sloping street that joins Old and New Towns. Two museums tucked immediately east of this great linking ramp are both the work of W. H. Playfair (1789–1857), an architect whose neoclassical buildings contributed greatly to Edinburgh's earning the title, the "Athens of the North." **The National Gallery of Scotland** ㉑ has a wide-ranging selection of paintings, from the Renaissance to Postimpressionism, and one of the most impressive collections of Scottish art. The other gallery, **The Royal Scottish Academy** ㉒, with its imposing columned facade overlooking Princes Street, holds an annual exhibition of students' work.

Princes Street is the humming center of 20th-century Edinburgh—a ceaseless promenade of natives and visitors alike patter along its mile or so of shops. Citizens lament the disappearance of the dignified old shops that once lined this street; now one long sequence of chain stores has replaced them all. Luckily, the well-kept gardens on the other side of the street act as a wide green moat to the castle on its rock; the street is still a grand viewpoint for the dramatic grouping of the castle on its rocky outcrop and the long tail of Royal Mile tenements descending from it. Walk east until you reach the soaring Gothic spire of the 200-foot-high **Scott Monument** ㉓, built in 1844 in honor of Scotland's most famous author, Sir Walter Scott (1771–1832), author of *Ivanhoe, Waverley,* and many other novels and poems.

Register House ㉔, on the left, marks the end of Princes Street. One of the jewels of neoclassical architecture in Scotland, it was designed by Robert Adam. The statue in front is of the duke of Wellington. Immediately west of Register House is the **Café Royal** (⊠ 17 W. Register St.), one of the city's most interesting pubs. It has good beer and lots of character, with ornate tiles and stained glass contributing to the atmosphere.

The monuments on **Calton Hill** ㉕, growing ever more noticeable ahead as you walk east along Princes Street, can be reached by continuing along Waterloo Place, and either climbing steps to the hilltop or taking the road farther on that loops up at a more leisurely pace. The incomplete Parthenon look-alike is known as Edinburgh's Disgrace—it was intended as a National War Memorial in 1822, but contributions fell short. On the opposite side of the road, in the Calton Old Burying Ground, is a monument to Abraham Lincoln and the Scottish-American dead of the Civil War.

Make your way to St. Andrew Square by cutting through the **St. James Centre** shopping mall and the bus station. On St. Andrew Square, next to the bus station, is the headquarters of the **Royal Bank of Scotland** ㉖; take a look inside at the lavish decor of the central banking hall. In the distance, at the other end of George Street, on Charlotte Square, you can see the copper dome of the former St. George's Church. Walk west along George Street, with its variety of shops, to Charlotte Square. Note particularly the palatial facade of the square's north side, designed by Robert Adam—it's considered one of Britain's finest pieces of civic architecture. Here you will find the **Georgian House** ㉗, which the National Trust for Scotland has furnished in period style to show the elegant domestic arrangements of an affluent family of the late 18th century. Also in the square, the former St. George's Church now fulfills a different role as **West Register House** ㉘, an extension of the original Register House.

To explore further in the New Town, choose your own route northward, down the wide and elegant streets centering on **Moray Place** ㉙, a fine example of an 1820s development, with imposing porticoes and a central, secluded garden. A neo-Gothic building on Queen Street houses the **Scottish National Portrait Gallery** ㉚ and the **Museum of Antiquities,** two unusual and diverting museums, with fine portraits and curious and beautiful Scottish artifacts. Another attraction within reach of the New Town is the 70-acre **Royal Botanic Garden** ㉛. Walk down Dundas Street, the continuation of Hanover Street, and turn left and across the bridge over the Water of Leith, Edinburgh's small-scale river. You will reach the gardens, one of the most cherished spots for many residents as well as an important center for scientific research.

Sights to See

★ ㉕ **Calton Hill.** A marvelous vantage point from which to gain panoramic views, Calton Hill is also address to numerous historic monuments, including the incomplete Parthenon, the National War Memorial of 1822, the Calton Old Burying Ground, a monument to Abraham Lincoln and the Scottish-American dead of the Civil War, and the **Nelson Monument,** completed in 1816. ☎ *0131/556-2716.* 🎫 *£1.* ⏲ *Apr.–Sept., Mon. 1–6, Tues.–Sat. 10–6; Oct.–Mar., Mon.–Sat. 10–3.*

Edinburgh Brass Rubbing Centre. A delightfully hands-on way to explore the past, brass-rubbing attracts more and more serious tourists every year. Here, they will find a fascinating selection of replica brasses and inscribed stones, with full instructions and materials supplied. ✉ *Trinity Apse, Chalmers Close, Royal Mile,* ☎ *0131/556–4364.* 🎫 *Free; 40p–£10.50 for each rubbing.* ⏲ *June–Sept., Mon.–Sat. 10–6, Sun. during festival 2–5; Oct.–May, Mon.–Sat. 10–5.*

Edinburgh Butterfly and Insect World. A warm and humid indoor experience of breathtaking color, this educational center offers butterflies in profusion, along with other insect life. ✉ *Melville Nurseries, near Dalkeith,* ☎ *0131/663–4932.* 🎫 *£3.35.* ⏲ *Mar.–Dec., daily 10–5:30 (last entry at 5).*

Edinburgh Zoo. This zoo now offers areas for children to approach or handle animals. Noted for its penguins, the zoo puts them on a delightful parade every day during the summer. Check out the new Darwin Evolutionary Maze. ✉ *Corstorphine Rd.,* ☎ *0131/334–9171.* 🎫 *£5.50.* ⏲ *Apr.–Sept., Mon.–Sat. 9–6, Sun. 9:30–6; Oct.–Mar., Mon.–Sat. 9–4:30, Sun. 9:30–4:30.*

27 **Georgian House.** Thanks to the National Trust for Scotland, this house has preserved, as if in amber, the domestic lifestyle of an affluent late 18th-century family. ✉ *7 Charlotte Sq.,* ☎ *0131/225–2160.* 🎫 *£3.* ⏲ *Apr.–Oct., Mon.–Sat. 10–5, Sun. 2–5; last admission 4:30.*

29 **Moray Place.** With imposing porticoes and a central, secluded garden, this is an especially fine example of an 1820s development. The area remains primarily residential, in contrast to the area around Princes Street. The Moray Place gardens are still for residents only.

★ 21 **The National Gallery of Scotland.** The honey-colored neoclassical building that is Scotland's National Gallery, midway between the Old and the New Towns, contains just about the best collection of Old Masters in Britain outside the great London museums. Moreover, the gallery has the advantage of being relatively small, so you can easily tour the whole collection in no more than an hour. There are superb works by Velásquez, El Greco, Rembrandt, Turner, Degas, Monet, and van Gogh, among many others. Scottish painters are also well to the fore, chief among them the 18th-century portrait painter Henry Raeburn. Among recent headline-making acquisitions is Canova's famous 19th-century statue, *The Three Graces,* which Scotland managed to snag despite the hopes (and millions) of the United State's Getty Art Museum. ✉ *The Mound.* ☎ *0131/556–8921.* 🎫 *Free.* ⏲ *Mon.–Sat. 10–5 (extended during festival), Sun. 2–5; print room, weekdays 10–noon and 2–4, by appointment.*

24 **Register House.** Marking the end of Princes Street, Scotland's first custom-built archives depository was partly funded by the sale of estates, then forfeited by Jacobites after their last rebellion in Britain (1745–46). Work on the building, designed by Robert Adam, Scotland's most famous neoclassical architect, started in 1774. ☎ *0131/556–6585.* 🎫 *Free.* ⏲ *Legal collection weekdays 9:30–4:30; historical collection weekdays 9–4:30.*

Rosslyn Chapel. A 15th-century chapel houses some of Scotland's finest examples of stone carving, including the ornate **Prentice Pillar.**

☎ 0131/440–2159. 🎟 £2. ⏲ Apr.–Oct., Mon.–Sat. 10–5, Sun. noon–4:45.

26 **Royal Bank of Scotland.** On St. Andrew Square, next to the bus station, is the headquarters of the national bank; take a look inside at the lavish decor of the central banking hall. This was originally the town house of Sir Lawrence Dundas, a wealthy and influential baronet who somehow managed to talk the city fathers out of building a church on this site (which would have matched St. George's Church nearby and been a grand city setpiece of the New Town).

31 **Royal Botanic Garden.** Just north of the city center, a 15-minute bus ride from Princes Street, the Royal Botanic Garden is second only to Kew Gardens in London for the variety of the plants it contains, and for the charm of its setting. The 70-acre site presents an immense display of specimens, from tropical to Nordic. Perhaps the best displays are the enormous rhododendrons, which bloom with huge flowers in the spring. The entire complex is free, making this one of the city's best-value bets. There is also a convenient café, as well as an art gallery with temporary exhibitions. *⊠ Inverleith Row, ☎ 0131/552–7171. 🎟 Free; voluntary donation for greenhouses. ⏲ Mar.–Apr. and Sept.–Oct., daily 10–6; May–Aug., daily 10–8; Nov.–Feb., daily 10–4. Café, shop, and exhibition areas Mar.–Oct., daily 10–5; Nov.–Feb. daily 10–3:30.*

22 **The Royal Scottish Academy.** A fine neoclassical temple complete with grand columns, this academy holds temporary exhibitions of various kinds, including an annual students' exhibition. *⊠ Princes St., ☎ 0131/225–6671. Admission charges vary, depending on exhibition. ⏲ Late Apr.–July, Mon.–Sat. 10–5, Sun. 2–5.*

30 **Scottish National Portrait Gallery** and the **Museum of Antiquities.** The gallery contains a magnificent Gainsborough and portraits by the Scottish artists Ramsay and Raeburn. In the museum, don't miss the 16th-century Celtic harps and the Lewis chessmen—mysterious, grim-faced chess pieces carved from walrus ivory in the Middle Ages. *☎ 0131/225–7534. 🎟 Both free. ⏲ Both Mon.–Sat. 10–5, Sun. 2–5.*

23 **Sir Walter Scott Monument.** Of all the multitude of statues and monuments in Edinburgh, none is so striking as that honoring Sir Walter Scott (1771–1832). The author's great poems and novels (such as *Ivanhoe* and *Waverley*) created a world frenzy for Scotland; the Scots were duly grateful and put up this great Gothic memorial to him in 1846. Under its graceful spire sits Scott himself, his dog, Maida, at his feet. Its prime location on Princes Street makes the monument impossible to miss. Behind the monument is one of the prettiest city parks in Britain, the **Princes Street Gardens.** In the open-air theater, amid the park's trim flower beds, stately trees, and carefully tended lawns, brass bands and Scottish country dances occasionally perform in the summer. But you needn't pay to go in; watch and listen for free from the slopes around the theater. *⊠ Princes St., ☎ 0131/549—4143. 🎟 £1. ⏲ Apr.–Sept., Mon.–Sat. 9–6 (last admission 5:45); Oct.–Mar., Mon.–Sat. 9–3.*

28 **West Register House.** As an extension of the original Register House, this research facility has records open for public examination. *☎ 0131/556–6585. 🎟 Free. ⏲ Exhibitions weekdays 10–4, research room weekdays 9–4:45.*

OFF THE BEATEN PATH

Hopetoun House – Ten miles west of Edinburgh and designed by the great Robert Adam, this is the largest and finest stately home in the area (⊠ South Queensferry, off A904, ☎ 0131/331-2451). Its grounds include a grand approach, beautiful gardens, a deer park, and a nature trail. Inside, you'll find the usual stately home panoply of fine furniture, paintings, tapestries, and carpets.

Paxton House – Another stately home designed by Robert Adam, Paxton House (✉ Berwick-upon-Tweed, ☎ 01289/386291) is now used by the National Gallery as a kind of distant annex, with rooms filled with an impressive array of masters. The house's riverside grounds include extensive woodlands by the river Tweed.

Dining and Lodging

Edinburgh is a diverse, sophisticated city, which its cuisine reflects with an interesting mix of traditional and exotic food, from Scottish dishes to infinite ethnic variety. Today, in the best establishments, old Scottish classics are getting a new, updated twist, including nouvelle variations on Partan Bree (crab with rice and cream), Loch Fyne herring, and haggis (an acquired taste and almost impossible to describe). The fact that a menu is written in mock antique Scots, however, does not guarantee that it is adventurous ("tassie o' bean bree"—"tassie" being an uncommon word for "cup," and "bree" usually meaning "soup" or "brine"—translates as a cup of coffee).

Book hotels, of course, months in advance for the festival. **Dial-a-Bed,** a new free central reservations service (toll-free in the U.K., ☎ 0800/616947; from the U.S., ☎ 131/556–3955, FAX 131/557–4365) can book rooms in more than 70 Edinburgh hotels and guest houses.

££££ ✕ **Le Pompadour.** The decor here, with its elegant plasterwork and rich murals, is inspired by the France of Louis XV, as may be expected in a restaurant named after the king's mistress, Madame de Pompadour. The cuisine is also classic French, with top-quality Scottish produce, such as sea bass, lobster, and venison, featured on the menu. The well-chosen wine list is extensive. Lunchtime here tends to be more relaxed and informal. ✉ *Caledonian Hotel, Princes St.,* ☎ *0131/459–9988. Reservations essential. Jacket and tie. AE, DC, MC, V.*

£££ ✕ **L'Auberge.** A number of Edinburgh restaurants take the best Scottish food and prepare it French style, but the long established L'Auberge is actually French through and through. The menu changes frequently, but you may be able to choose a seafood terrine, guinea fowl with mushrooms and claret sauce, or a hearty ragoût à la paysanne for lunch or a superbly delicate salmon in cream and celery sauce for dinner. The impressive and constantly enlarged wine list includes excellent dessert wines. ✉ *56–58 St. Mary's St.,* ☎ *0131/556–5888. AE, DC, MC, V.*

£££ ✕ **Indian Cavalry Club.** The menu of this cool and sophisticated restaurant reflects a confident, up-to-date approach—with its steamed specialties it's almost an Indian *nouvelle cuisine.* The **Club Tent** in the basement serves light meals (££). ✉ *3 Atholl Pl.,* ☎ *0131/228–3282,* FAX *0131/225–1911. AE, DC, MC, V.*

£££ ✕ **Jackson's.** Intimate and candlelit in a historic Old Town close, Jackson's offers good Scots fare. Aberdeen Angus steaks and Border lamb are excellent, but you might also try adventurous dishes like langoustini baked in white port. The decor is rustic, with lots of greenery, stone walls, pine farmhouse-style tables and chairs, and fresh flowers. The wine list includes 60 malt whiskeys and some Scottish country wines to complete the Scottish experience. ✉ *2 Jackson Close, 209–213 High St., Royal Mile,* ☎ *0131/225–7793. AE, MC, V. No lunch Sat. Closed Sun.*

£££ ★ ✕ **Martins.** Don't be put off by the look of this restaurant on the outside. It's tucked away in a little back street, and has a typically forbidding northern facade. All's well inside, though, and the food is tops. The specialties are all light and extremely tasty, with fish and game in the lead. Try the halibut with leeks and carrot and basil coulis, or the breasts of mallard and pigeon with red cabbage and raisins, plus gorgeous homemade sorbets. ✉ *70 Rose St. (between Castle and Frederick Sts.),* ☎ *0131/225–3106. AE, DC, MC, V. No lunch Sat. Closed Sun., Mon.*

££ ✕ **Howie's.** Here's a simple neighborhood bistro with a lively clientele; it's unlicensed, so you have to bring your own bottle. The steaks are tender Aberdeen beef, the Loch Fyne herring are sweet-cured to Howie's own recipe. ✉ *75 St. Leonard's St.,* ☎ *0131/668–2917;* ✉ *63 Dalry Rd.,* ☎ *0131/313–3334. MC, V. No lunch Mon.*

££ ✕ **Kweilin.** This excellent, very popular Chinese restaurant specializes in Cantonese cuisine made from very fresh ingredients. The water-chestnut pudding is recommended. Service is particularly speedy and efficient. ✉ *19–21 Dundas St.,* ☎ *0131/557–1875. AE, MC, V.*

£ ✕ **Henderson's.** This long-established haven for fans of fine vegetarian cuisine, complete with its own shop and bakery, offers dishes as adventurous as vegetarian haggis! ✉ *94 Hanover St.,* ☎ *0131/225–2131. AE, MC, V. Closed Sun. except during festival.*

£ ★ ✕ **Kalpna.** This eatery has a reputation for outstanding value, especially its lunchtime buffet. Indian art adorns the walls, enhancing your enjoyment of the exotic specialties like *shahi sabzi* (spinach and nuts in cream sauce), and mushroom curry. All dishes are vegetarian and are skillfully and deliciously prepared. ✉ *2–3 St. Patrick's Sq.,* ☎ *0131/667–9890. MC, V. Closed Sun.*

£ ✕ **Pierre Victoire.** An Edinburgh success story with five in-town branches and franchises as far as London and Bristol, this bistro chain serves tasty unpretentious French cuisine in excellent set menus, especially good value at lunch. Try the monkfish in butter and lemon sauce. ✉ *38 Grassmarket,* ☎ *0131/226–2442;* ✉ *10 Victoria St.,* ☎ *0131/225–1721, closed Sun.;* ✉ *8 Union St.,* ☎ *0131/557–8451, closed Mon.;* ✉ *17 Queensferry St., Edinburgh,* ☎ *0131/225–1890; and* ✉ *5 Dock Pl., Leith,* ☎ *0131/556–6178, closed Sun. MC, V.*

££££ ★ ✕🏨 **Balmoral Hotel.** The attention to detail in the elegant rooms and the sheer élan that has re-created the Edwardian splendor of this former grand railroad hotel make staying at the Balmoral a very special way to see Edinburgh. Here, below the impressive clocktower marking the east end of Princes Street, you get a strong sense of being at the center of Edinburgh life. The main restaurant is the plush and stylish Grill Room (jacket and tie), serving delicacies such as beef carpaccio with warm mushroom salad and grilled salmon steak with hollandaise sauce. ✉ *Princes St. EH2 2EQ,* ☎ *0131/556–2414,* FAX *0131/557–8740. 167 bedrooms, 22 suites. 2 restaurants, bar, patisserie, health club. AE, DC, MC, V.*

££££ ★ ✕🏨 **The Caledonian Hotel.** "The Caley" recalls the days of the great railroad hotels, although its nearby station has long gone. Modernized at vast expense, its imposing Victorian decor has been faithfully preserved and has lost none of its original dignity and elegance, the fifth floor rooms being the most recent to be refurbished. In addition to the Le Pompadour (☞ *above*), the less formal Carriages restaurant supplies traditional Scottish roasts, fish, and game. ✉ *Princes St., EH1 2AB,* ☎ *0131/459–9988,* FAX *0131/225–6622. 239 rooms with bath. 2 restaurants. AE, DC, MC, V.*

££££ ★ 🏨 **George Intercontinental Hotel.** This imposing and extensively refurbished 18th-century building in the heart of the New Town retains some elegant Georgian features in its public areas, while the bedrooms are up-to-date and moderately luxurious. Although busy keeping this large hotel running smoothly, the courteous staff will always take the time to be helpful. ✉ *19 George St., EH2 2PB,* ☎ *131/225–1251,* FAX

0131/226–5644. 195 rooms with bath. 2 restaurants, bar. AE, DC, MC, V.

£££ 🏨 **Albany.** Three fine Georgian houses with many of their original features have been carefully converted into a comfortable city-center hotel. There's a good restaurant in the basement, and a friendly bar with piano. ✉ *39 Albany St., EH1 3Q4,* ☎ *0131/556–0397,* FAX *0131/557–6633. 20 rooms with bath. MC, V.*

£££ 🏨 **Channings.** Five Edwardian terraced houses have become an elegant hotel in an upscale neighborhood minutes from Princes Street. Restrained colors, antiques, quiet rooms, and great views toward Fife (from the north-facing rooms) set the tone. The Brasserie offers excellent value, especially at lunchtime; try the crab cakes with crayfish bisque. ✉ *South Learmonth Gardens, EH4 1EZ,* ☎ *0131/315–2226,* FAX *0131/332–9631. 48 rooms with bath. Restaurant. AE, DC, MC, V.*

£££ 🏨 **Mount Royal Hotel.** The front bedrooms at this modern hotel have views of Edinburgh Castle and Princes Street Gardens. With a friendly staff, the Mount Royal is conveniently located near major sights and shopping. ✉ *53 Princes St., EH2 2DQ,* ☎ *0131/225–7161,* FAX *0131/220–4671. 156 rooms with bath. Restaurant. AE, DC, MC, V.*

££ 🏨 **Dorstan Private Hotel.** A villa dating from the Victorian era, this hotel, in a quiet neighborhood a fair way from the city center, has been lately refurbished providing smart, cottage-style bedrooms. ✉ *7 Priestfield Rd., EH16 5HJ,* ☎ *0131/667–6721,* FAX *0131/668–4644. 14 rooms, 9 with bath or shower. MC, V. Closed Dec. 24–Jan. 2.*

£ ★ 🏨 **Salisbury Guest House.** This guest house in a Georgian building is in a peaceful conservation area. It is also convenient for city touring, and offers excellent value for the money. ✉ *45 Salisbury Rd., EH16 5AA,* ☎ FAX *0131/667–1264. 12 rooms, 9 with bath or shower. No credit cards. Closed Dec. 25, Jan. 1.*

Nightlife and the Arts

CASINOS

Berkeley Casino Club (✉ 2 Rutland Pl., ☎ 0131/228–4446) is a private club that offers free membership on 48 hours' notice, as do **Casino Martell** (✉ 7 Newington Rd., ☎ 0131/667–7763) and **Stanleys** (✉ 5B York Pl., ☎ 0131/556–1055). **Stakis Regency Casino** (✉ 14 Picardy Pl., ☎ 0131/557–3585) also makes membership available after a 48-hour waiting period. Its restaurant is highly rated.

COCKTAIL BARS

Harry's Bar is an Americana-decorated basement bar with disco music that is hugely popular with locals. ✉ *7B Randolph Pl.,* ☎ *0131/539–8100.* ⏲ *Daily noon–1 AM.*

L'Attache is another basement bar with live folk/rock music nightly. ✉ *Beneath the Rutland Hotel, 1 Rutland Pl.,* ☎ *0131/229–3402.* ⏲ *Sun.–Thurs. 8 PM–1:30 AM, Fri.–Sat. 8 PM–2 AM.*

Madogs was one of Edinburgh's first all-American cocktail bar/restaurants; it remains popular with professionals after work, with live music most weeknights. ✉ *38A George St.,* ☎ *0131/225–4308.* ⏲ *Sun. 6:30 PM–2 AM, Mon.–Wed. noon–2 AM, Thurs.–Sat. noon–3 AM. No sneakers.*

CONCERT HALLS

Usher Hall (✉ Lothian Rd., ☎ 0131/228–1155) is Edinburgh's grandest, and the venue for the Royal Scottish Orchestra in season; the **Queen's Hall** (✉ Clerk St., ☎ 0131/668–3456) is more intimate in scale and hosts smaller recitals. The **Playhouse** (✉ Greenside Pl., ☎ 0131/557–2692) leans toward popular artists.

DISCOS/NIGHTCLUBS

Buster Browns offers mainstream sounds. ✉ *25–27 Market St.,* ☎ *0131/226–4224.* ⏲ *Fri.–Sun. 10:30 PM–2 AM.*

The Cavendish has a variety of different clubs and types of music. ✉ *W. Tollcross,* ☎ *0131/228–3252.* ⏲ *Thurs.–Sat. 9 PM–3 AM.*

The Lanes is a basement bar with a dance floor, popular with the 20s–30s crowd. ✉ *South Charlotte La.,* ☎ *0131/226–6828.* ⏲ *Mon.–Thurs. 9 PM–3 AM, Fri. 5 PM–3 AM, weekends 7 PM–3 AM.*

Minus One has live music and a DJ on Friday and Saturday, DJ only on Thursday, playing mainstream sounds; the place is not for teeny boppers or old fogies. ✉ *Carlton Highland Hotel, North Bridge,* ☎ *0131/556–7277.* ⏲ *Thurs.–Sat. 10 PM–3 AM.*

Red Hot Pepper Club plays mainstream music. ✉ *3 Semple St.,* ☎ *0131/229–7733.* ⏲ *Fri.–Sat. 10 PM–4 AM.*

FESTIVALS

The flagship of arts events in the city is the **Edinburgh International Festival** (1997 dates are Aug. 10–30), which for 45 years has attracted performing artists of international caliber in a great celebration of music, dance, and drama. *Advance information, programs, tickets, and reservations during the festival:* ✉ *Edinburgh Festival Office, 21 Market St., Edinburgh EH1 1BW,* ☎ *0131/226–4001.*

The **Edinburgh Festival Fringe** offers a huge range of theatrical and musical events, some by amateur groups (you have been warned), and is much more of a grab bag than the official festival. The fringe offers a vast choice (a condition of Edinburgh's artistic life found only during the three- or four-week festival season). During festival time, it's possible to arrange your own entertainment program from morning to midnight and beyond. *Information, programs, and tickets:* ✉ *Edinburgh Festival Fringe, 180 High St., Edinburgh EH1 1QS,* ☎ *0131/226–5257 or 0131/226–5259.*

The **Edinburgh Film Festival,** held in August, is yet another aspect of this summer festival logjam. *Advance information, tickets, and programs:* ✉ *The Filmhouse, 88 Lothian Rd., Edinburgh EH3 9BZ,* ☎ *0131/228–4051.*

The **Edinburgh Military Tattoo** might not be art, but it is certainly entertainment. It is sometimes confused with the festival itself, partly because the dates overlap (1997 dates: Aug. 2–24). This great celebration of martial music and skills is set on the castle esplanade, and the dramatic backdrop augments the spectacle. Dress warmly for the late-evening performances. Even if it rains, the show most definitely goes on. *Tickets and information:* ✉ *Edinburgh Military Tattoo, 22 Market St.,* ☎ *0131/225–1188.*

Away from the August–September festival overkill, the **Edinburgh Folk Festival** usually takes place around Easter each year. The 10-day event presents performances by Scottish and international folk artists of the very highest caliber.

FOLK MUSIC CLUBS

Various pubs throughout the city regularly feature folk performers. At the **Edinburgh Folk Club** (✉ Cafe Royal, 17 W. Register St., ☎ 0131/339–4083) there's folk music every Wednesday at 8 PM.

SCOTTISH ENTERTAINMENTS AND CEILIDHS

Several hotels present traditional Scottish music evenings in the summer season, including the **Carlton Highland Hotel** (✉ North Bridge, ☎

0131/556–7277) and **George Hotel** (✉ George St., ☎ 0131/225–1251).

Another well-established Scottish entertainment venue is **Jamie's Scottish Evening** (✉ King James Hotel, Leith St., ☎ 0131/556–0111).

The **Scottish Experience and Living Craft Centre** (✉ 12 High St., ☎ 0131/557–9350) puts on Scottish evenings, offering traditional food, song, and dance.

THEATER

Edinburgh's main theaters are the **Royal Lyceum** (✉ Grindlay St., ☎ 0131/229–9697), which offers contemporary and traditional drama; the **King's** (✉ Leven St., ☎ 0131/229–1201), for such "heavyweight" material as ballet, and light entertainment, like Christmas pantomime; the **Traverse** (✉ Cambridge St., ☎ 0131/228–1404), housed in specially designed flexible space that's ideal for its avant-garde plays; and the new **Edinburgh Festival Theatre** (✉ Nicolson St., ☎ 0131/529–6000), which stages operas, plays, and musicals and excellent, occasional tours (check with box office for details.

Outdoor Activities and Sports

GOLF

Edinburgh is well endowed with golf courses, with 20 or so near downtown (even before the nearby East Lothian courses are considered). **Braids United** course, south of the city center, welcomes visitors (☎ 0131/447–6666); **Bruntsfield Links** (☎ 0131/336–1479) and **Duddingston** (☎ 0131/661–7688) permit visitors to play on weekdays by appointment; all have 18 holes. Here are three courses in the Borders, to go with the abbeys we list—**Jedburgh** (☎ 01835/863587) and **Melrose** (☎ 01896/822855), with nine holes, and **St. Boswells** (☎ 01835/822359), with 18 holes.

A quite exceptional destination is **Gullane** (☎ 01620/842255), about 20 miles east of Edinburgh on A198, with three courses, all 18-hole, and several others nearby, among them **Luffness New** (☎ 01620/843336, FAX 01620/842933). A round on a Scottish municipal course costs very little, and most Scottish clubs, apart from a few pretentious places modeled on the English fashion, demand only comparatively modest entrance fees.

JOGGING

The most convenient spot downtown for joggers is **West Princes Street Gardens,** which is separated from traffic by a 30-foot embankment, with a half-mile loop on asphalt paths. In **Holyrood Park,** stick to the road around the volcanic mountain for a 2¼-mile trip. For a real challenge, charge up to the summit of Arthur's Seat, or to the halfway point, the Cat's Nick.

Shopping

In Scotland, many visitors go for Shetland and Fair Isle woolens, tartan rugs and materials, Edinburgh crystal, Caithness glass, Celtic silver, and pebble jewelry. Hand-made chocolates, often with whiskey or Drambuie filings, and the traditional "petticoat tail" shortbread in tin boxes are popular. At a more mundane level, try some of the boiled sweets in jars from particular localities—Berwick cockles, Jethart snails, Edinburgh rock, and other delights. Other edibles that visitors take home include Dundee cake and marmalades and heather honeys.

Edinburgh features a cross-section of Scottish specialties, such as tartans and tweeds. If you are interested in learning the background of your tartan purchases, try **Scotland's Clan Tartan Centre** (✉ James Pringle

Ltd., Bangor Rd., Leith), where extensive displays on various aspects of tartanry will keep you informed.

For some ideas on exactly what Scotland has to offer in the way of crafts, visit the **Royal Mile Living Craft Centre** (✉ 12 High St.), where you can chat with and buy from craftspeople as they work. Also along the Royal Mile, you will find several shops selling high-quality tartans and woolen goods. **Judith Glue** (✉ 64 High St.) carries brilliantly patterned Orkney knitwear and a wide selection of crafts, cards, wrapping paper, jewelry, toiletries, and candles.

A popular gift selection comes from **Edinburgh Crystal,** just a few miles from the city, in Penicuik (✉ Eastfield, ☎ 01968/75128).

The antiques business is suffering from the economic recession and shops open and close with great rapidity, so it's smart to concentrate on areas with a number of stores close together, for instance, **Bruntsfield Place, Causewayside,** or **St. Stephen Street.**

PRINCES STREET

Jenners (✉ Princes St., across from the Scott Monument), is Edinburgh's last independent department store, specializing in upscale tweeds and tartans. The **Edinburgh Woollen Mill** (✉ 62 Princes St.), popular with overseas visitors, also sells top-quality items. **Gleneagles of Scotland** (✉ Near Princes St. in Waverley Market), is a mid-range department store.

GEORGE STREET

George Street features a few London names, such as **Laura Ashley** and **Liberty. Waterston's** (✉ 35 George St.) carries stationery and a range of Scottish gifts. Farther along, there is a good selection of Scottish titles in the **Edinburgh Bookshop** (✉ 57 George St.).

VICTORIA STREET/WEST BOW/GRASSMARKET

Where these three streets run together, there's a number of specialty stores in a small area. **Ampersand** (✉ 18 Victoria St.) is an interior designer's that also stocks a large selection of small collectibles and unusual fabrics by the yard. **Robert Cresser's** brush store (✉ 40 Victoria St.) features, not surprisingly, brushes of all kinds, each one handmade. **Pine & Old Lace** (✉ 46 Victoria St.) has a carefully chosen selection of antique textiles and small pieces of furniture. **Iain Mellis Cheesemonger** (✉ 30A Victoria St.) has about 30 varieties of British cheese; the shop's brochure is an education in itself. **Kinnells House Tea and Coffee Emporium** (✉ 36–38 Victoria St.) serves morning coffee, lunches, and teas, and sells nearly 100 different types of freshly roasted coffees and specialty teas to take out and try at home. **Le Magasin** (✉ 14 Victoria St.) stocks every imaginable edible item from France for homesick Francophiles: groceries, cheese, charcuterie, wine.

At **Mr. Wood's Fossils** (✉ Grassmarket), an unusual item, such as a small shark encased in rock, may solve your gift-buying problems. **Bill Baber** (✉ 68 Grassmarket) is another long-established, enterprising, and original Scottish knitwear designer.

STOCKBRIDGE

This northern suburb is an oddball shopping area of some charm, particularly on St. Stephen Street. Look for **Hand in Hand** (✉ 3 NW Circus Pl.) for beautiful antique textiles. There are also several antiques shops and yet more knitwear.

WILLIAM STREET/STAFFORD STREET

This is a small, upscale shopping area in a Georgian setting. **Sprogs** (✉ 45 William St.) sells end-of-season children's designer clothes in modern, not traditional styles, at 50%–70% off. **Something Simple** (✉

10 William St.) offers a pleasing selection of women's classic clothing. **Studio One** (✉ 10–14 Stafford St.) is well established and wide-ranging in its inventory of gift articles.

THE BORDERS: SIR WALTER SCOTT COUNTRY

The Borders region is the heartland of minstrelsy, ballad, and folklore, much of it arisen from murky deeds of the past. It is the homeland of the tweed suit and cashmere sweater, of medieval abbeys and hints of Elfland, of the lordly Tweed and its salmon and of the descendants of the raiders and reivers (cattle thieves) who harried England. It is also the native soil of Sir Walter Scott, the early 19th-century poet, novelist, and creator of *Ivanhoe* who singlehandedly transformed Scotland's image from that of a land of brutal savages to one of romantic and stirring deeds and magnificent landscapes. One of the best ways to approach this district is to take as the theme of your tour the life and works of Scott. The novels of Scott are not read much nowadays—in fact, frankly, some of them are difficult to wade through—but the mystique that he created, the aura of historical romance, has outlasted his books and is much in evidence in the ruined abbeys, historical houses, and grand vistas of the Borders.

Numbers in the margin correspond to points of interest on the Scottish Borders map.

Abbotsford House

★ 32 *Route A7, to Galashiels, 27 mi southeast of Edinburgh, then 1 mi farther on A6091, through the Moorfoot Hills.*

The most visited of Scottish literary landmarks, **Abbotsford House,** is the modestly sized mansion that Sir Walter Scott made his home in the 1820's. A damp farmhouse called Clartyhole when Scott bought it in 1811, it was soon transformed into what John Ruskin called "the most incongruous pile that gentlemanly modernism ever devised." A pseudo-baronial, pseudo-monastic castle chocablock with Scottish curios, Ramsay portraits, and mounted deer heads, it is an appropriate domicile for a man of such an extraordinarily romantic imagination. To Abbotsford came most of the famous poets and thinkers of Scott's day, including Wordsworth and Washington Irving. Abbotsford is still owned by Scott's descendants. ✉ *Galashiels, B6360,* ☎ *01896/752043.* *£3.* *Late Mar.–Oct., Mon.–Sat. 10–5, Sun. 2–5.*

Dining and Lodging

££££ ✕ **Woodlands House Hotel.** This Gothic Revival–style hotel with chintz-hung and traditionally furnished interiors has stunning views over Tweeddale. The main restaurant specializes in fresh seafood and hearty Scottish cuisine, while Sanderson's Steakhouse is named after a former owner of the house, whose portrait gazes down on diners. There is also a lounge bar serving light meals ✉ *Windyknowe Rd., TD1 1RG,* ☎ FAX *01896/754722. 8 rooms with bath. 3 restaurants, golf privileges, horseback riding, fishing. MC, V.*

Melrose

33 *3 mi east on A6091.*

In the peaceful little town of Melrose, 3 miles east on A6091, you'll find the ruins of a Cistercian abbey that was the most famous of the great Borders abbeys. All the abbeys were burned in the 1540s in a calculated act of destruction by English invaders acting on the orders of Henry ★ VIII; Scott himself supervised the partial reconstruction of **Melrose Abbey,** one of the most beautiful ruins in Britain. "If thou would'st view fair Melrose aright/Go visit it in the pale moonlight," says Scott in his "The Lay of the Last Minstrel," and so many of his fans took the advice literally that a sleepless custodian begged him to rewrite the lines. ✉ *Main Sq.,* ☎ *01896/822562.* *£2.50.* *Apr.–Sept., Mon.–Sat. 9:30–6, Sun. 2–6; Oct.–Mar., Mon.–Sat. 9:30–4, Sun. 2–4.*

At the Ormiston Institute in the Square at Melrose is the **Trimontium Trust,** exhibits of Roman artifacts reclaimed from excavations at the Roman fort at Newstead. Tools and weapons, a replica Roman horse saddle, blacksmith's shop, pottery, and scale models of the fort are included in the display. ✉ *The Square, Melrose,* ☎ *01896/822463.* *£1.* *Apr.–Oct., daily 10:30–4:30.*

Scotland's teddy bear museum, **Teddy Melrose,** tells the story of British teddy bears from the early 1900s onward. There is—inevitably—a collector's bear shop. ✉ *High St.,* ☎ *01896/822464.* *£1.50.* *Mon.–Sat. 10–5, Sun. 11–5.*

At the **Melrose Motor Museum,** you can view early products of Scottish manufacture, including a 1909 Albion and a 1926 Arrol Johnston. ✉ *Annay Rd.,* ☎ *01896/822624 or 01835/822356.* *£2.* *May–Oct., daily 10:30–5:30.*

Dining and Lodging

££ ★ ✕ **Marmion's Brasserie.** Outstanding country-style cuisine is the attraction at this cozy restaurant; it's a great place to stop for lunch after visiting Abbotsford. ✉ *Buccleuch St.,* ☎ *01896/822245. MC, V. Closed Sun.*

£££ ✕ **Burts Hotel.** This distinctive black-and-white traditional town hostelry dating from the early 18th century offers up-to-date comfort in refurbished rooms. The elegant dining room features dishes such as pheasant terrine, and venison with a whiskey-and-cranberry sauce. Bar food is also on offer. ✉ *Market Sq., TD6 9PN,* ☎ *01896/822285,* FAX *01896/822870. 21 rooms, 14 with bath, 7 with shower. Restaurant (reservations essential). AE, DC, MC, V.*

Dryburgh

34 *5 mi southeast of Melrose, still on A6091.*

At Dryburgh, another of the ruined Borders abbeys, you'll find Scott's burial place, set in a bend of the Tweed among strikingly shaped trees. Combine a visit here with a stop at **Scott's View,** 3 miles north on B6356, which provides a magnificent panoramic view of the Tweed valley and the Eildon Hills—quintessential Borders countryside. It is said that the horses pulling Scott's hearse paused automatically at Scott's View, because their master had so often halted them there. ✉ *Dryburgh, near St. Boswells,* ☎ *01896/820835.* *£2.* *Apr.–Sept., Mon.–Sat. 9:30–6, Sun. 2–6; Oct.–Mar., Mon.–Sat. 9:30–4, Sun. 2–4.*

Smailholm

5 mi east of St. Boswells, off B6404.

35 Another famous Borders lookout point is **Smailholm Tower.** Beloved by Scott as a child, the 16th-century watchtower now houses a museum displaying costumed figures and tapestries relating to Scott's Borders folk ballads. Scott spent his childhood on a nearby farm, where he imbibed his love of Borders traditions and romances. ✉ *Smailholm,* ☎ *01573/460332.* *£1.50.* *Apr.–Sept., Mon.–Sat. 9:30–6, Sun. 2–6.*

Dining and Lodging

£££ ✕🏨 **Dryburgh Abbey Hotel.** Right next to the abbey ruins, this civilized hotel is surrounded by beautiful scenery and features a restaurant specializing in Scottish fare. (Bar snacks are also available.) Extensively renovated in 1992, the restrained decor in shades of cream, peach, terra-cotta, green, and gray creates a peaceful atmosphere in keeping with its setting. ✉ *St. Boswells TD6 ORQ,* ☎ *01835/822261,* FAX *01835/823945. 26 rooms with bath. Restaurant (reservations essential, jacket and tie), golf privileges. AE, MC, V.*

Kelso

36 *From Smailholm, take B6397 and then eastward on A6089.*

The Tweedside roads through Kelso and Coldstream sweep with a river through parkland and game preserve and past romantic redstone gorges. In Kelso, Scott attended grammar school. The town has an unusual Continental air, with fine Georgian and early Victorian buildings surrounding a spacious, cobbled marketplace. Only a fragment remains of its once magnificent abbey. Just across the road from the abbey ruins is **Kelso Museum and the Turret Gallery,** one of the town's oldest buildings, in which you can see some excellent re-creations of 19th-century town life, including a Victorian schoolroom, 19th-century marketplace, a reconstructed skinner's workshop, and an interpretation of Kelso Abbey, as well as an art and crafts gallery. ✉ *Abbey Ct.,* ☎ *01573/225470.* 🎫 *80p.* ⏲ *Easter–late Oct., Mon.–Sat. 10–noon, 1–5, Sun. 2–5.*

37 Rennie's Bridge on the edge of town provides good views of **Floors Castle,** yet another example and an early one of Scotland's greatest neoclassicist, Robert Adam. The largest inhabited house in Scotland, Floors is an architectural extravagance bristling with peppermill-mill turrets and towers that stand on the "floors" or flat terraces of the Tweed bank opposite the barely visible ruins of Roxburghe Castle. Seat of the Dukes of Roxburghe, it was conceived in 1718 by Sir John Vanbrugh, arch exponent of massive Baroque architecture, and afterward given mock-Tudor touches in the 19th century. A holly tree in the magnificent deer park marks the place where King James II was killed in 1460 by a cannon that "brak in the shooting." ✉ *A6089,* ☎ *01573/223333.* 🎫 *£3.80; £1.80 grounds only.* ⏲ *Easter–Oct., daily 10:30–5:30. Check locally for variations.*

NEED A BREAK? Try the 18th-century coaching inn, the **Queen's Head** (✉ Bridge St., Kelso), for ample helpings of home-cooked food and a selection of cool draft ales.

Lodging

£££ ★ 🏨 **Ednam House Hotel.** This large, attractive hotel is right on the banks of the river Tweed, close to Kelso's grand abbey and the old Market Square. Ninety percent of the guests are return visitors, and the open fire in the hall, sporting paintings, and cozy armchairs give the place a homey feel. ✉ *Bridge St., TD5 7HT,* ☎ *01573/224168,* FAX *01573/226319. 32 rooms with bath or shower. Restaurant, golf privileges, fishing. MC, V. Closed Dec. 25–early Jan.*

Jedburgh

38 *12 mi southwest on A698.*

To round out your tour of the Borders abbeys, head for Jedburgh, a little town just 13 miles north of the border, which lay in the path of marauding armies for centuries. **Jedburgh Abbey,** although in ruins like so many Borders abbeys, is relatively intact and is a superb example of abbey architecture. It has an informative visitor center that explains the role of the abbeys in the life of the Borders until their destruction around 1545. ✉ *High St.,* ☎ *01835/863925.* 🎫 *£2.50.* ⏲ *Apr.–Sept., Mon.–Sat. 9:30–6, Sun. 2–6; Oct.–Mar., Mon.–Sat. 9:30–4, Sun. 2–4.*

Also in the town, **Mary, Queen of Scots's House** is a fortified house highly characteristic of the 16th century, some say contemporaneous with Mary herself. Though historians disagree on whether or not she actually visited here, the house exhibits many displays commemorating this legendary figure. ✉ *Queen St.,* ☎ *01835/863331.* 🎫 *£1.20.* ⏲ *Mar.–mid-Nov., daily 10–5.*

Lodging

££ **Spinney Guest House.** Made up of unpretentiously converted and modernized farm cottages, this is a bed-and-breakfast offering the very highest standards for the price. ✉ *Langlee, TD8 6PB,* ☎ FAX *01835/863525. 1 room with bath, 2 with shower. No credit cards. Closed Dec.–Feb.*

Selkirk

39 *From Jedburgh, take A68 7 mi north to the A699 junction, turn left, and follow A699 7 mi.*

After traveling through miles of attractive river-valley scenery, you'll reach the ancient hilltop town of Selkirk. Scott was sheriff (county judge) of Selkirkshire from 1800 until his death in 1832, and his statue stands in Market Place, outside the courthouse where he presided. A display within the courtroom examines Scott's life, his writings, and his time as sheriff. ✉ *Sir Walter Scott's Courtroom,* ☎ *01750/20096.* 🎫 *Free.* ⏲ *Apr.–Oct., weekdays 10–12:30 and 1:30–4, Sat. 10–2, Sun. 2–4.*

Tucked off the main square in Selkirk, **Halliwell's House Museum** is set in what was once an ironmonger's shop, which has been re-created downstairs; the upstairs exhibit tells the story of the town. ✉ *Market St.,* ☎ *01750/20096.* 🎫 *Free.* ⏲ *Late Mar.–Oct., Mon.–Sat. 10–5, Sun. 2–4; July–Aug., daily 10 until 6; Nov.–mid-Dec., daily 2–4.*

Lodging

£££ ★ **Philipburn House Hotel.** This many-gabled country house stands on 4 acres of gardens and woodland. The decor throughout features pine paneling and furnishings, plain walls, and crisp floral or checked fabrics, which give an Austrian feel to the hotel. A wide range of room options makes it especially good for families: There are even poolside suites or a pine lodge available, and a number of rooms have been recently upgraded. The restaurant features the excellent Scottish beef, lamb, game, and salmon you might expect, but also European influences such as Swiss rosti potatoes or grilled langoustine. ✉ *Linglie Rd., TD7 5LS,* ☎ *01750/20747,* FAX *01750/21690. 16 rooms with bath or shower. Restaurant, pool. DC, MC, V.*

En Route Take A707 north from Selkirk and turn west onto A72 to reach Walkerburn, where you'll find the **Scottish Museum of Woollen Textiles,** with the entrance through a tempting tweeds and woolens store. ☎ *01896/870619.* 🎫 *Free.* ⏲ *May–Oct., Mon.–Sat. 9–5:30, Sun. 11–5; Nov.–Apr., weekdays 10–5, Sun. noon–4.*

Innerleithen

40 *3 mi west of Walkerburn on A72.*

Once famous as the setting of Scott's novel *St. Ronan's Well* and as an spa, Innerleithen is home to **Robert Smail's Printing Works,** a fully restored Victorian print shop with its original machinery in working order and a printer in residence. ✉ *7 High St.,* ☎ *01896/830206.* 🎫 *£2.* ⏲ *Easter–Oct., Mon.–Sat. 10–1 and 2–5, Sun. 2–5; last admission 45 min before closing, morning and afternoon.*

★ 41 Turn south on B709 to reach **Traquair House,** the oldest continually occupied house in Scotland and, many would add, the friendliest and most cheerful of the Borders' grand houses; ale is still brewed in the 18th-century brewhouse here, and is recommended!

Lodging

££ 🏨 **Traquair Arms.** Near Innerleithen, famous for its medicinal springs and for Traquair House, this family-run hotel is a fine traditional inn offering a warm welcome, simple, clean rooms, and very good food. ✉ *Traquair Rd., EH44 6PD,* ☎ *01896/830229,* FAX *01896/830260. 8 rooms with shower, 2 with bath. 2 restaurants, bar, fishing. AE, DC, MC, V.*

Peebles

42 *From Traquair, return to A72 and continue west 7 mi*

Set in a lush and green countryside, with rolling hills deep cleft by gorges and waterfalls, Peebles is a pleasant town on the banks of the Tweed. Walk for 15 minutes upstream until **Neidpath Castle** comes into view through the tall trees, perched artistically above a bend in the river. The castle is a medieval structure remodeled in the 17th century, with dungeons hewn from solid rock. You can return on the opposite riverbank after crossing an old, finely skewed railroad viaduct. ✉ *Near Peebles,* ☎ *01721/720333.* 🎫 *£2.* ⏲ *Easter–Sept., Mon.–Sat. 11–5, Sun. 1–5.*

Dining and Lodging

£££ ✕🏨 **Cringletie House Hotel.** A Scottish baronial mansion set amid 28 acres of gardens and woodland, Cringletie is run by a family that believes in spoiling guests with friendly, personalized service. They make you feel as if you're their houseguest. The first-floor drawing room, decorated in shades of cream, white, and turquoise, with views extending up the valley, is particularly restful. Much of the fruit and vegetables served in the restaurant comes from the hotel's own garden. Afternoon tea served in the conservatory is especially recommended. ✉ *Peebles, EH45 8PL,* ☎ *01721/730233,* FAX *01721/730244. 13 rooms with bath. Restaurant (reservations essential), putting green, tennis court, croquet. AE, MC, V.*

ST. ANDREWS: THE GOLFER'S HEAVEN

It may have a ruined cathedral and a grand university—the oldest in
43 Scotland—but the modern fame of **St. Andrews** is mainly as the home of golf. Forget that Scottish kings were crowned here, or that John Knox preached, or Reformation reformers were burned at the stake. Thousands come to St. Andrews to play at the Old Course, home of the Royal & Ancient Club, and follow in the footsteps of Hagen, Sarazen, Jones, and Hogan, who have all contributed to the saga of the Road Hole and the other perils of the championship course. To enter the golfer's Valhalla, drive west from Edinburgh 9 miles to the Forth Road Bridge, where you'll cross over the Firth of Forth. Continue north 6 miles on M90 to junction 3, where you can turn east to follow A92, then A91, 38 miles to the quiet town of St. Andrews. An alternate route branches off the A92 at Largo onto the A915, then A917—a slightly longer route that takes in several attractive coastal villages.

On the Royal & Ancient's course, golf was originally played with a piece of driftwood, a shore pebble, and a convenient rabbit hole on the sandy, coastal turf. It has been argued that golf came to Scotland from Holland, but the historical evidence points to Scotland being the cradle, if not the birthplace, of the game. Citizens of St. Andrews were playing golf on the town links (public land) as far back as the 15th century. Rich golfers, instead of gathering on the common links, formed themselves into clubs by the 18th century. Arguably, the world's first golf club was the Honourable Company of Edinburgh golfers (founded in Leith in 1744), which is now at Muirfield in East Lothian. The Society of St. Andrews Golfers, founded in 1754, became the Royal & Ancient Gold Club of St. Andrews in 1834.

The **St. Andrews Links** (☎ 01334/473393) has six seaside courses, which all welcome visitors; five have 18 holes—the Old Course, New Course, Jubilee, Eden, and Strathtyrum—while the Balgrove Course has nine holes. For information, write to the Secretary, Pilmour Cottage, St. Andrews, Fife KY16 9SF.

St. Andrews offers a wide range of attractions for nongolfers. The **cathedral,** its ancient university (founded in 1411), and **castle** are poignant reminders that the town was once the ecclesiastical capital of Scotland. The now largely ruined cathedral was one of the largest churches ever built in Scotland. The castle is now approached via a visitor center with audiovisual presentation. ☎ *0131/244–3101.* *Cathedral museum and St. Rule's Tower £1.50, castle £2, combined ticket £3.* *Cathedral museum, castle visitor center, and tower Apr.–Sept., Mon.–Sat. 9:30–6, Sun. 2–6; Oct.–Mar., Mon.–Sat. 9:30–4, Sun. 2–4.*

NEED A BREAK? **Ma Brown's** (✉ 24 North St., ☎ 1334/473997), close to the castle, is a traditional tearoom with Victorian-inspired decor, serving coffee, light lunches, and teas in premises that used to be a grocer's and wine store.

The **Sea-Life Centre** at St. Andrews offers a fascinating display of marine life. ✉ *The Scores, St. Andrews,* ☎ *01334/474786.* *£4.25.* *Oct.–Mar., daily 10–6, Apr.–Sept. daily 10–7.*

Dining and Lodging

£–£££ **Grange Inn.** This old farmhouse-type building houses a simple, traditional restaurant where excellent bar lunches are individually prepared. Dinner is a candlelit affair, with fine food—try the gravlax with sweet dill mustard—and a good selection of malt whiskeys. For overnight stays, there are two comfortable twin bedrooms. ✉ *Grange Rd.,* ☎ *01334/472670,* FAX *01334/478703. 1 room with bath, 1 with shower. Restaurant (reservations essential). AE, DC, MC, V.*

££££ **Greywalls.** Gullane, on the Firth of Forth, is 19 miles northeast of Edinburgh by A198 and totally surrounded by golf links. It is, in fact, the ideal hotel to choose for a golfing vacation, comfortably furnished with stylish fabrics from the likes of Nina Campbell, Colefax and Fowler, and Osborne and Little, predominantly in shades of restful green. Service is attentive, and the food is award-winning modern British cuisine using local produce. The house itself is an architectural treasure. Edward VII used to stay here, as have Nicklaus, Trevino, Palmer, and a host of other golfing greats. ✉ *Muirfield, Gullane EH31 2EG,* ☎ *01620/842144,* FAX *01620/842241. 22 rooms with bath. Restaurant, golf privileges, tennis court, croquet. AE, DC, MC, V. Closed Dec.–Mar.*

££££ **Rusack's Hotel.** Right beside the Old Course, this is clearly a hotel for the well-heeled golfer. It has plenty of opulent Victorian elements in the decor, all freshly refurbished. Some of the bedrooms have stunning views. Dinner is included. ✉ *Pilmour Links KY16 9JQ,* ☎ *01334/474321,* FAX *01334/477896. 48 rooms with bath, 2 suites. Restaurant, sauna, solarium. AE, DC, MC, V.*

EDINBURGH AND THE BORDERS A TO Z

Arriving and Departing

By Bus

Several companies provide bus service to and from London, including **Scottish Citylink Coaches** (✉ Bus Station, St. Andrew Sq., ☎ 0131/556–8464, recorded timetable ☎ 0131/556–8414). Edinburgh is approximately eight hours by bus from London.

By Car

Downtown Edinburgh usually means Princes Street, which runs east–west. Entering from the east coast, drivers will come in on A1, Meadowbank Stadium serving as a good landmark. The highway bypasses the suburbs of Musselburgh and Tranent; therefore, any bottlenecks will occur close to downtown. From the Borders, the approach to Princes Street is by A7/A68 through Newington, an area offering a wide choice of budget accommodations. Approaching from the southwest, drivers will join the west end of Princes Street, via A701 and A702, while those coming east from Glasgow or Stirling will meet Princes Street from A8 on the approach via M90/A90. From Forth Road Bridge, Perth, and the east coast, the key road for getting downtown is Queensferry Road.

By Plane

Edinburgh Airport has air links with all the major airports in Britain and many in Europe. The **Airport Information Centre** (☎ 0131/333–1000) answers questions regarding schedules, tickets, and reservations.

BETWEEN THE AIRPORT AND DOWNTOWN

Buses run at 15-minute intervals during peak times from the Edinburgh Airport main terminal building to Waverley Bridge downtown; they are less frequent after rush hours and on weekends. The roughly 25-minute trip costs £3 one-way; the 20-minute trip by taxi costs roughly £12. By car, the airport is about 7 miles west of Princes Street downtown, and is clearly marked from A8. The usual route to downtown is via Corstorphine.

By Train

Edinburgh's main train station, Waverley, is downtown, below Waverley Bridge. The station has recorded summaries of services to King's Cross Station in London (☎ 0171/278–2477)—telephone for weekday information (☎ 0131/557–3000), Saturday service (☎ 0131/557–2737), and Sunday service (☎ 0131/557–1616). For information on all other destinations, or other inquiries, telephone 0131/556–2451. Travel time from Edinburgh to London by train is as little as four hours.

Getting Around

By Bus

Lothian Region Transport (☎ 0131/555–6363), operating dark red-and-white buses, is the main operator within Edinburgh. **S.M.T.** (☎ 131/313–1515), operating green buses, provides much of the service into Edinburgh, and also offers day tours around and beyond the city. **Lowland Scottish Omnibuses** (☎ 01896/752237) serve the Borders.

The Edinburgh Silver Freedom ticket, allowing unlimited one-day travel on the city's buses, can be purchased in advance. More expensive is the Tourist Card, available in units of from two to 13 days, which gives unlimited access to buses (except Airlink) and includes vouchers for savings on tours. Two travel passes are available for one or seven days unlimited travel: the Reiver Rover for services within the Borders area, and the Waverley Wanderer for services within the Borders and to Edinburgh and Carlisle.

By Car

Edinburgh can be explored easily on foot, so a car is hardly needed.

Guided Tours

Bus Tours

Lothian Region Transport and **S.M.T.** both offer tours in and around the city (☞ Getting Around, *above*).

Chauffeured Tours

Ghillie Personal Travel (✉ 64 Silverknowes Rd. E, ☎ 0131/336–3120) and **Little's Chauffeur Drive** (✉ 33 Corstorphine High St., ☎ 0131/334–2177) both offer flexible, customized tours in all sizes of cars and buses, especially suitable for groups.

Walking Tours

The Cadies and Witchery Tours (☎ 0131/225–6745) organizes historic Old Town walks, Ghost Hunt, pub, and Murder and Mystery tours of Edinburgh throughout the year.

Contacts and Resources

Car-Rental Agencies

Edinburgh: Avis, ✉ 100 Dalry Rd., ☎ 0131/337–6363, also at the airport; **Budget Rent-a-Car,** ✉ Royal Scot Hotel, 111 Glasgow Rd., ☎ 0131/334–7739; **Europcar,** ✉ 24 E. London St., ☎ 0131/661–1252, also at the airport; **Hertz U.K. Ltd.,** ✉ 10 Picardy Pl., ☎ 0131/556–8311, also at the airport and Edinburgh Waverley railway station.

Travel Agencies

American Express: ✉ 139 Princes St., Edinburgh EH2 4BR, ☎ 0131/225–7881. **Thomas Cook:** ✉ 79A Princes St., Edinburgh EH2 2ER, ☎ 0131/220–4039.

Visitor Information

The **Edinburgh and Scotland Information Centre** is adjacent to Edinburgh Waverley railway station, above Waverley Market. Here, visitors arriving in Edinburgh can get expert advice on what to see and do in the city and throughout Scotland; other services include accommodation reservations, route-planning, coach tour tickets, theater reservations, a Scottish bookshop, and currency exchange. Visitors can also buy National Trust, Historic Scotland, and Great Britain Heritage passes. ✉ *3 Princes St.,* ☎ *0131/557–1700; 24-hr Talking Tourist Guide,* ☎ *01891/775700 (36p/minute cheap rate, 48p at all other times).* ⏲ *May–June and Sept., Mon.–Sat. 9–7, Sun. 11–7; July–Aug., Mon.–Sat. 9–8, Sun. 11–8; Nov.–Mar., Mon.–Sat. 9–6; Oct. and Apr., Mon.–Sat. 9–6, Sun. 11–6.*

Within Scotland, an integrated network of 170 tourist information centers is run by a variety of area tourist boards, offering comprehensive information and on-the-spot accommodation bookings. The area tourist board for the Borders region is in **Jedburgh** (✉ Murrays Green, Borders TD8 6BE, ☎ 01835/863435). The **St. Andrews Tourist Center** is at ✉ 78 South St., St Andrews KY16 9JX, ☎ 01334/472021.

17 Scotland: Royal Deeside to Inverness

Fling a tartan scarf around your neck and get ready to discover the Scotland of the travel posters—shimmering lochs, fast-flowing streams where salmon leap, and great castles of baronial pride standing hard among the hills. Royal Deeside—fabled realm of Queen Victoria—and the Inverness area are both made of the stuff of tourism. Explore the picturesque wonders of Castle Country, then head north to Loch Ness, home to "Nessie," mythical monster and charter member of the local Chamber of Commerce.

Updated by Brandy Whittingham

BEYOND THE BORDERS, the pleasures and treasures of Northeast Scotland and the Highlands await. Here, some of the country's most famous icons beckon—including Loch Ness (with its monster on its doorstep) and the Victorian splendor of Royal Deeside, seat of Balmoral, the Scottish abode of Her Majesty. A map of Scotland gives a hint of the grandeur and beauty to be found here: fingers of inland lochs (lakes), craggy and steep-sided mountains, ragged promontories, and deep inlets. But the map does not give an inkling of the brilliant purple and emerald moorland, the forests, and the astonishingly varied wildlife: mountain hares, red deer, golden eagles, and all sorts of birds and fish. Nor does it prepare you for the swift changes that sunshine, clouds, and rainbows bring to landscapes and seascapes; nor for the courtesy of the softly spoken inhabitants; nor for the depth of ancestral memory and clan mythology.

To some, this is a paradise of salmon-fishing and castle hopping. Highland tourism was once the prerogative of the sporting nobility and gentry, and a few château-style hotels and great houses maintain the values of that era. Alongside these palaces, however, you can find some of the most inexpensive accommodations—little farmhouses, cottages, and camp sites—in the British Isles, in part due to the simplicity of the Highland lifestyle.

A car is essential if you want to explore the wildest and most beautiful districts. Roads are always well surfaced (remember, McAdam was a Scot) though narrow in places. The area is not large, but road distances make it so: Bremar to Aviemore, for example, is 21 miles as the eagle flies, but it's 98 miles by the shortest road! If you have time on your hands, local buses can be rewarding, not least for the conversation. But the network is sketchy and schedules are poor (but improving).

For the short-term visitor, a bus excursion from Edinburgh or Aberdeen can possibly give the best value. Whatever mode of transport, try to spend a couple of days in a small Highland bed-and-breakfast, grand estate hotel, or fishing inn. Only then you'll discover the spell of the Highlands, that insidious magic that brings people back year after year. Keep in mind this is not a district for winter touring: Braemar often records Britain's lowest temperatures and minor roads are frequently snowbound. And if you head north of Aberdeen and Inverness, travel can be limited on Sunday. This is the region of strict Presbyterianism—with many still practicing the Scots Sabbath.

Pleasures and Pastimes

Dining

Welcome to the land of Arbroath "smokies" (smoked haddock), Cullen Skink (fish soup), Aberdeen-Angus steak, and the spicy haggis—a succulent mixture of chopped offal (heart, liver, lungs, etc.) and oatmeal cooked in a sheep's stomach—usually served with "neaps and tatties" (mashed turnip and potato). Today, in the best establishments, these old classics are getting a new, updated twist. Remember that Scotland is traditionally the "Land o'Cakes" so be sure to enjoy some of those delicious buns, pancakes, scones, and biscuits.

Never assume that because a restaurant is off the beaten track its cuisine lacks sophistication. In the Highlands, the reverse is often true. Local game and seafood are often presented with great flair, while oatmeal, local cheeses, and even malt whiskey (turning up in any course) amplify the Scottish dimension. Whiskey goes with everything—try the "single malts," the pale, unblended spirits, now growing fashionable and expensive. Purists drink their "malts" neat, though water, ice, and even mineral water may be added to blended whiskeys.

As for fish, many restaurants deal directly with local boats, so freshness is guaranteed. The quality and range of fish is such that local residents in the east-coast fishing towns in particular can afford curious prejudices; mackerel, for instance, no matter how tasty, is considered second-class fare. With rich pastures supporting the famous Aberdeen-Angus beef cattle, good meat is also guaranteed.

CATEGORY	COST*
££££	over £40
£££	£25–£40
££	£15–£25
£	under £15

**per person, including first course, main course, dessert, and VAT; excluding drinks*

Golf

Everyone wants to play just the big names in the British Open—St. Andrews, Turnberry, Troon, and so on. This is a pity. There are more golf courses in Scotland per head of population than anywhere else in the world. Out of the 400 or so, there are plenty of gems, from challenging coastal links courses such as Cruden Bay or Royal Dornoch in the north to pinewoody parkland delights such as Boat of Garten, near Inverness.

Highland Games

Caber-tossing (the "caber" is a long, heavy pole) and other traditional events figure in the Highland Games, staged throughout the Highlands during summer. All Scottish tourist information centers have full details. It is said that these games, a unique combination of music, dancing, and athletic prowess, grew out of the contests held by clan chiefs to find the strongest men for bodyguards, the fastest runners for messengers, and the best musicians and dancers to entertain guests and increase the chief's prestige.

Hiking and Walking

Well below the "Highland line," the Galloway Forest Park offers a good range of not overly demanding woodland trails, as well as some excursions into the higher hills. However, it is the north that makes real walking demands. The Scots themselves invented the term "the Munros"—a Munro is any Scottish hill over 3,000 feet—and there are 279 of them, though this figure varies a little, depending on the map. With many Scots active outdoor enthusiasts, these hills are a passion. Some tracks are well used (some might say loved to death) and moderately demanding in places. Local tourist information centers carry details of Ranger Services that conduct guided walks of varying lengths. Look out, too, for signposted trails on property controlled by the Forestry Commission (the government forest agency) as well as Highland beauty spots such as the Hermitage, near Dunkeld, or the Bruar Falls above Blair Atholl. Both make pleasant interludes to driving the main A9 to Inverness.

Lodging

Since the removal of much of its indigenous population by forced emigration, many parts of the Highlands became playgrounds for estate owners or Lowland industrialists, who built for themselves shooting lodges, grand mansions, and country estates. Many of these are now fine hotels. Do not, however, expect your hosts always to be Scots—many experienced hoteliers from the wealthy south of England fulfill their ambitions by opening a Highland hotel, where real estate is cheaper, the scenery beautiful, and the pace of life relaxed.

CATEGORY	COST*
££££	over £110
£££	£80–£110
££	£50–£80
£	under £50

**All prices are for two people sharing a double room, including service, breakfast, and VAT.*

Shopping

In this region you will find excellent woolens and tweeds and edibles such as the ubiquitous shortbread and Scottish preserves. Keep an eye out for unusual designs in Scottish jewelry, especially when they incorporate local stones. Scotland has always been a very bookish country, priding itself on a high rate of literacy, and you will often find a surprisingly well-stocked secondhand bookshop in a fairly remote town.

Exploring Royal Deeside, Castle Country, and the Inverness Area

Queen Victoria loved to make "Great Expeditions" to explore the Scottish countryside around her royal burg of Balmoral. Through this verdant countryside, the river Dee proceeds in a succession of rapids, pools, and sweeping bends through valleys of rich forest and lush pasture, past prosperous towns and villages and romantic castles. This section of Scotland is, unsurprisingly, known as Royal Deeside. The closer you get to Aberdeen, the less royal and more industrial the countryside becomes. Slightly to the north of the Deeside river valley, you enter uplands lapped by a tide of farms and dotted with some of Scotland's most beautiful abodes—this is known as Castle Country.

Inverness is the capital of the Highlands and is the only sizeable town in northern Scotland (though it is quite small, nonetheless). It is a clean and compact place, built on both banks of the river Ness, just below Loch Ness. The loch itself is 24 miles long and very deep, and the drive around it leads you through scenery that is the match of any in Scotland. Loch Ness is the supposed home of "Nessie," world-famous monster and founding member of the local chamber of commerce.

Great Itineraries

Getting to know Scotland is about appreciating the contrasts of this relatively small country—try to make time to take in both the soft, mild, and often wet west, as well as the more vigorous and go-ahead east with its whiskey distilling, castles, picturesque fishing villages, and often rugged coastline. We start off with a three-day tour of Royal Deeside, then head north to Loch Ness, Inverness, and the northeast coast.

Numbers in the text correspond to numbers in the margin and on the maps.

IF YOU HAVE 3 DAYS

Starting from Scotland's third largest city, **Aberdeen** ①, follow in the footsteps of Queen Victoria and take a trip among the castles and glens of the Royal Deeside. You may agree with Her Majesty that ". . . the scenery all around is the finest almost I have seen anywhere . . . we are certainly in the finest part of the Highlands. . . .You can walk forever . . . and the wildness, the solitariness of everything is so delightful, so refreshing, the people so good and so simple . . ." Set out for

Banchory ②, with its largely unchanged Victorian High Street, to arrive for lunch—or stock up here on provisions for a picnic at the grand gardens of nearby **Crathes Castle** ③. After lunch, follow the river upstream to Aboyne, turning due north for 6 miles for a panorama (signposted on the B9119) known as The Queen's View, a bit north of Dinnet—this is one of the most spectacular vistas in northeast Scotland and was greatly loved by Victoria. The view stretches across the Howe of Cromar to Lochnagar. Then continue on the B9119 dropping gently downhill through the birchwoods at Dinnet to reach **Ballater** ④ to the west. Here, stop for your first overnight stay. Enjoy the many little granite shops displaying their BY APPOINTMENT signs. The next morning, set off for Her Majesty's own **Balmoral** ⑥, take in the royal ballroom and beautiful grounds, do a country walk or a pony trek—but note that Balmoral is only open for three months every year. Nearby is Glen Muick, a nature reserve managed by Balmoral Estates with the famous climb of Lochnagar, so beloved by Victoria. Before setting off, Royal-watchers will want to take in Crathie Kirk, the small, and rather dull, parish church built by Victoria and still used by the Windsors. Head for unostentatious **Braemar** ⑤ for your second overnight stay. The next morning set off for Castle Country and some serious castle-hopping—**Corgarff** ⑦, **Kildrummy** ⑧, **Craigievar** ⑨, and **Fraser** ⑩—then return to Aberdeen.

IF YOU HAVE 7 DAYS

If, after our three-day tour of Royal Deeside, you wish to continue exploring the Highlands, turn due north, after visiting one or two houses in Castle Country, at **Castle Fraser** ⑩. Take the A944 from CF west, enjoying the valley of the River Don as far as Corgarff on the A939. Lunch somewhere by the river—Strathdon is a fine spot. Then the road climbs into the brown hills to Tomintoul, highest village in the Highlands. From there, continue west, drop into Speyside to pick up the main A9 at Carrbridge to arrive by evening at **Inverness** ⑪ for your third and fourth nights. Spend the next day relaxing and exploring the city. Set out the following morning to pay a call on Nessie at Drumnadrochit on the banks of **Loch Ness** ⑫. Return to Inverness, then follow signposts to **Culloden Moor** ⑬ and famed **Cawdor Castle** ⑮. Continue on to either **Nairn** ⑭ or **Elgin** ⑯ for your sixth overnight.

When to Tour Northeast Scotland

Spring in the Highlands can be glorious, when there is still snow on the highest peaks. Those exuberant Highland Gatherings—featuring caber-tossing, hammer-throwing and all the rest—are held during June (Aberdeen), August (Aboyne), and September (Braemar), the latter gathering often held in the presence of members of the royal family. If you wish to drop in on Balmoral, the royal residence on the Dee River, keep in mind it's only open during several weeks in the summer. If the royals are in residence, even the grounds are closed to visitors, so be sure to call in advance. Autumn in Royal Deeside is very colorful.

ABERDEEN AND ROYAL DEESIDE

Aberdeen—Scotland's third-largest city—is the gateway to a rural hinterland with a wealth of castles and an unspoiled and, in places, spectacular coastline. Deeside, the valley running west from Aberdeen along which the river Dee flows, earned its "Royal" appellation when Queen Victoria and her consort, Albert, built their exquisite Scottish fantasy house, Balmoral, here. To this day, where royalty goes, lesser aristocracy and fastbuck millionaires from around the globe follow. Their yearning to possess an estate here is understandable, since piney hill slope, purple moor, and blue river intermingle most tastefully, as you will see from the main road.

Numbers in the margin correspond to points of interest on the Royal Deeside map.

Aberdeen

1 *131 mi north of Edinburgh.*

In the 18th century, local granite quarrying produced a durable silver stone that would be used to build the Aberdonian structures of the Victorian era. Thus granite was used boldly—in glittering blocks, spires, columns, and parapets—to build the downtown Aberdeen seen today, which remains one of the United Kingdom's most distinctive urban environments, although some would say it depends on the weather and the brightness of the day. The mica chips embedded in the rock are a million mirrors in sunshine; in rain and heavy clouds, however, their sparkle is snuffed out.

The North Sea has always been an important feature of Aberdeen: In the 1850s, the city was famed for its fast clippers, sleek sailing ships that raced to India for cargoes of tea. In the late-1960s, the course of Aberdeen's history was unequivocally altered when oil and gas were discovered in the North Sea. Aberdeen at first seemed destined to become an oil-rich boomtown, and throughout the 1970s the city was overcome by new shops, new office blocks, new hotels, new industries, and new attitudes. Fortunately, some innate local caution has helped the city to retain a sense of perspective and prevented it from selling out entirely.

What Princes Street is to Edinburgh, **Union Street** is to Aberdeen: the central pivot of the city plan and the product of a wave of enthusiasm to rebuild the city in a contemporary style in the early 19th century. Some hints of an older Aberdeen have survived and add to the city's charm. Conversely, today's plans are also changing the face of Aberdeen, but it is still a city of handsome granite buildings that give it a silvery complexion.

★ **Marischal College,** dominating Broad Street, was founded in 1593 by the Earl Marischal as a Protestant alternative to the Catholic King's College in Old Aberdeen, though the two combined to form Aberdeen University in 1860. (The earls Marischal held hereditary office as keepers of the king's mares.) The original university buildings on this site have undergone extensive renovations. What you see in front of you is a facade built in 1891. The spectacularly ornate work is set off by the gilded flags, and this turn-of-the-century creation is still the second-largest granite building in the world. Only the Escorial in Madrid is larger. ✉ *Broad St.,* ☎ *01224/632727.* 🎫 *Free.* ⏲ *Museum weekdays 10–5, Sun. 2–5.*

A survivor from an earlier Aberdeen can be found beyond the concrete supports of St. Nicholas House (of which the tourist information center is a part): **Provost Skene's House** (*provost* is Scottish for mayor) was once part of a closely packed area of town houses. Steeply gabled and rubble-built, it survives in part from 1545. It was originally a domestic dwelling house and is now a museum portraying civic life, with restored furnished period rooms and a painted chapel. ✉ *Guestrow, off Broad St.,* ☎ *01224/641086.* 🎫 *Free.* ⏲ *Mon.–Sat. 10–5.*

In **Upperkirkgate,** at the lowest point, are two modern shopping malls—the **St. Nicholas Centre** on the left, the **Bon-Accord Centre** on the right.

At the top of Schoolhill, as the slope eases off, there is a complex of silver-toned buildings, in front of which stands a **statue of General Charles Gordon,** the military hero of Khartoum (1885).

Aberdeen Art Gallery plays an active role in Aberdeen's cultural life and is a popular rendezvous for locals. It houses a wide-ranging collection—from the 18th century to contemporary work. The sculpture court is certainly worth seeing, with its gallery supported by columns of different shades of polished granite. ✉ *Schoolhill,* ☎ *01224/646333.* 🎫 *Free.* 🕗 *Mon.–Sat. 10–5, Thurs. 10–8, Sun. 2–5.*

A library, church, and nearby theater on **Rosemount Viaduct** are collectively known by all Aberdonians as Education, Salvation, and Damnation! Silvery and handsome, the **Central Library** and **St. Mark's Church** date from the last decade of the 19th century, while **His Majesty's Theatre** (1904–08) has been restored inside to its full Edwardian splendor. If you carry a camera, you can choose an angle that includes the statue of Scotland's first freedom fighter, Sir William Wallace, in the foreground, pointing majestically to Damnation.

On **Union Terrace,** a statue of **Robert Burns** stands, addressing a daisy. Behind Burns are the **Union Terrace Gardens,** faintly echoing Edinburgh's Princes Street Gardens in that they separate the older part of the city to the east. Most of the buildings on Union Terrace around the grand-looking Caledonian Hotel are late-Victorian, when exuberance and confidence in style was at its height.

A colonnaded facade of 1829 screens the churchyard of **St. Nicholas Kirk** from the shopping hustle and bustle of Union Street. Its earliest features are the pillars—supporting a tower built much later—and its clerestory windows: Both date from the original 12th-century structure. St. Nicholas was divided into east and west kirks at the Reformation, followed by a substantial amount of renovation from 1741 on. Some early memorials and other works have survived. ✉ *Union St.* 🕗 *Weekdays 10–1, Sun. services.*

At the east end of Union Street, within the original old town, is the **Castlegate.** The actual castle once stood somewhere behind the **Salvation Army Citadel** of 1896, an imposing baronial granite tower whose design was inspired by Balmoral Castle. The impressive **Mercat Cross** (built in 1686 and restored in 1820), always the symbolic center of a Scottish medieval burgh, stands just beyond King Street. Along its parapet are 12 portrait panels of the Stewart monarchs.

★ **Provost Ross's House,** of 1593 date, now houses **Aberdeen's Maritime Museum,** telling the story of the city's involvement with the sea, from early inshore fisheries by way of tea clippers to the North Sea oil boom. It is a fascinating place for grade-schoolers, with its ship models, paintings, and equipment associated with the fishing, local shipbuilding, and North Sea oil and gas industries. ✉ *Provost Ross's House, Ship Row,* ☎ *01224/585788.* 🎫 *Free.* 🕗 *Mon.–Sat. 10–5.*

Below Ship Row is the **harbor,** which contains some fine architecture from the 18th and 19th centuries. Explore it if time permits and if you don't mind the background traffic.

Dining and Lodging

££–£££ ★ ✕ **The Silver Darling.** Situated right on the quayside, the Silver Darling is one of Aberdeen's most acclaimed restaurants. It specializes, as its name suggests, in fish. The style is French provincial, with an indoor barbecue guaranteeing flavorful grilled fish and shellfish. ✉ *Pocra Quay, Footdee,* ☎ *01224/576229. AE, DC, MC, V. No lunch weekends, no dinner Sun. Closed 2 wks at Christmas.*

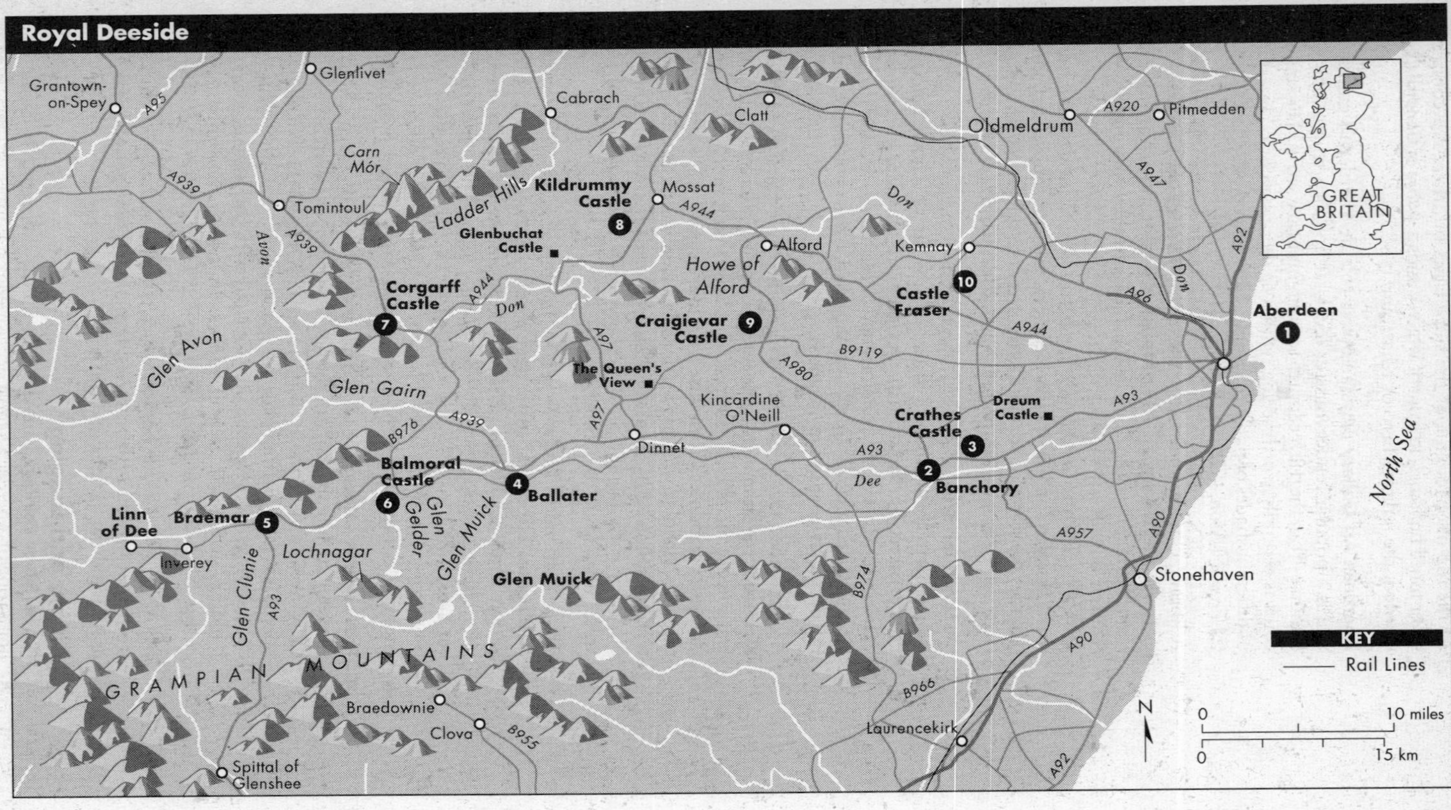
Royal Deeside
Grantown-on-Spey
Glenlivet
Cabrach
Clatt
Oldmeldrum
Pitmedden
GREAT BRITAIN
Carn Mór
Ladder Hills
Kildrummy Castle
Mossat
Tomintoul
Glenbuchat Castle
Alford
Kemnay
Howe of Alford
Castle Fraser
Aberdeen
Corgarff Castle
Craigievar Castle
Glen Avon
Glen Gairn
The Queen's View
Kincardine O'Neill
Crathes Castle
Dreum Castle
Dinnet
Balmoral Castle
Ballater
Banchory
North Sea
Linn of Dee
Braemar
Inverey
Lochnagar
Glen Gelder
Glen Muick
Glen Muick
Glen Clunie
Stonehaven
GRAMPIAN MOUNTAINS
Braedownie
Clova
Spittal of Glenshee
Laurencekirk
KEY
Rail Lines
N
0
10 miles
0
15 km
Avon
Don
Dee
A95
A939
A944
A97
A980
B9119
A96
A92
A947
A920
A93
B976
A957
A90
B974
B966
B955

£–£££ ✕ **Brasserie Gerard's.** Set on a side street moments away from the West End, Gerard's is a long-established stop on the Aberdeen dining scene. Classic French cuisine meets hearty Scottish appetites, ably supported by local produce, fish, and red meat in particular: Your Angus fillet steak, for example, is stuffed with pâté, ham, mushrooms, and more, then wrapped in bacon and served in a red wine sauce. Nouvelle cuisine this is not, but it's satisfying, and the fixed-price lunch is especially good value. The relaxed, softly lit setting includes a flagstone-floor garden room with greenery and tile or marble tables. ✉ *50 Chapel St., ☎ 01224/639500, FAX 01224/630688. AE, DC, MC, V.*

££–£££ ★ ✕ **Atholl Hotel.** One of Aberdeen's many splendid silver-granite properties, the Atholl Hotel is turreted and gabled and set within a leafy residential area to the west of the city. Rooms are done in rich, dark colors; the larger rooms are on the first floor. The restaurant prepares traditional dishes such as lamb cutlets and roast rib of beef. ✉ *54 Kings Gate, Aberdeen AB9 2YN, ☎ 01224/323505, FAX 01224/321555. 35 rooms with bath or shower. Restaurant. MC, V.*

££–£££ ✕ **Craighaar Hotel.** Don't be fooled by the modern exterior—this is a hotel with some character, a refreshing change from the faceless business-type hotel of which Aberdeen has so many. Although it is business-oriented during the week—it is very convenient to the airport—what makes this establishment stand out is the personal service. The comfortable restaurant serves cuisine with a Scottish slant, such as Orkney oysters, smoked trout, crab claws, gourmet scampi, and chargrilled steaks. Cheerful bedrooms have bright floral prints on bed linens and other fittings; the split-level gallery suites are outstanding. ✉ *Waterton Rd., Bucksburn, AB2 9HS, ☎ 01224/712275, FAX 01224/716362. 15 rooms with bath, 40 with shower. Restaurant, bar. AE, DC, MC, V.*

The Arts

His Majesty's Theatre (✉ Rosemount Viaduct, ☎ 01224/641122) has been restored inside to its full Edwardian splendor. The Central Library and St. Mark's Church alongside, together with the theater, are collectively known by all Aberdonians as Education, Salvation, and Damnation! Live shows are presented throughout the year, many of them in advance of their official opening in London's West End.

Shopping

Aberdeen is a market town—droves of Scots come to do their major shopping here, lured by big, modern chain stores. However, there are still delightful specialty shops to be found. **Colin Wood** (✉ 25 Rose St., ☎ 01224/643019) is the place to go for antiques, maps, and prints. **Elizabeth Watt** (✉ 69 Thistle St., ☎ 01224/647232) is the place to look for smaller antiques, especially china and glassware. At the **Aberdeen Family History Shop** (✉ 164 King St., ☎ 01224/646323) you can browse through a huge range of publications related to local history and genealogical research.

Banchory

❷ *19 mi west of Aberdeen on A93.*

Banchory is an immaculate place with a pinkish tinge to its granite. It is usually bustling with ice cream–licking city strollers, out on a day trip from Aberdeen. If you visit in autumn and have time to spare, drive out to the **Brig o'Feuch** ("Bridge of," then pronounce it "Fyooch" with "ch" as in loch). Here, salmon leap in season, and the fall colors and foaming waters make for an attractive scene.

3 Three miles east of Banchory is **Crathes Castle,** once home of the Burnett family. Keepers of the Forest of Drum for generations, the family acquired lands here by marriage and later built a new castle, completed in 1596. Crathes is in the care of the National Trust for Scotland; the Trust also looks after the grand gardens, with their calculated symmetry and clipped yew hedges. ✉ *Off the A93,* ☎ *01330/844525.* *Grounds only £1.60; castle only £1.60; castle, garden, and grounds £4.10.* *Castle Apr.–Oct., daily 11–5:30, garden and grounds year-round, daily 9:30–sunset.*

NEED A BREAK? Sample the excellent National Trust for Scotland's home baking in Crathes Castle's **tearoom** (☎ 01330/844525).

Dining and Lodging

£££–££££ ✕ **Raemoir Hotel.** The core of this large mansion dates from the 18th century, though a number of additions have been built over the years. Central heating has been added as well, so there is no need to fear chilly, windy rooms. All the guest rooms are comfortable and well appointed; many are hung with beautiful tapestries. The hotel is set on spacious grounds and overshadowed by the 1,500-foot-high Hill of Fare. ✉ *Raemoir, Kincardineshire AB3 4ED,* ☎ *01330/824884,* FAX *01330/822171. 28 rooms with bath. Restaurant, sauna, 9-hole golf course, tennis court, fishing, baby-sitting, helipad. AE, DC, MC, V.*

Ballater

4 *25 mi west of Banchory, 43 mi west of Aberdeen.*

The quaint holiday resort of Ballater, once noted for the curative properties of its local well, has profited from the proximity of the royals nearby at Balmoral. Visitors are amused by the array of BY ROYAL APPOINTMENT signs proudly hanging from many of its shops (even monarchs need bakers and butchers). If you get a chance, take time to stroll around this neat community—well laid out in silver-gray masses. Note that the railway station now houses the tourist information center as well as a display on the former glories of this Great North of Scotland branch line, closed in the 1960s along with many others in this country.

Dining and Lodging

££££ ✕ **Craigendarroch.** This magnificent country-house hotel, just outside Ballater on a hillside overlooking the river Dee, really does manage to keep everyone happy. Hotel guests are cosseted in luxurious surroundings and can also use the nearby leisure facilities. An even better value are the pine lodges set among the trees around the hotel. These self-catering cottages are geared to family groups and fitted with every kind of labor-saving appliance. There is also a solid choice of on-site restaurants, including the top-quality Oaks for à la carte dinners, and The Clubhouse poolside brasserie. ✉ *Ballater, AB35 5XA,* ☎ *013397/55858,* FAX *013397/55447. 44 rooms with bath, including 7 suites. 2 restaurants, 2 indoor pools, wading pool, beauty salon, hot tub, sauna, tennis court, exercise room, squash. AE, DC, MC, V.*

££–£££ ✕ **Darroch Learg Hotel.** Amid tall trees on a hillside, the Darroch Learg is everything a Scottish country-house hotel should be, with the added bonus that the charming town of Ballater is only moments away. Built in the 1880s as a country residence, the hotel exudes charm. Most bedrooms enjoy a stunning panoramic view south across Royal Deeside. The food served in the conservatory restaurant is sophisticated—delicately flavored terrines and soups. ✉ *Braemar Rd., Ballater, Aberdeenshire AB35 5UX,* ☎ *013397/55443,* FAX *013397/55252. 20 rooms with bath. Restaurant. AE, DC, MC, V.*

Braemar

5 *17 mi west of Ballater, 51 mi north of Perth via A93.*

The village of Braemar is dominated by **Braemar Castle,** dating from the 17th century, with defensive walls later built in the outline of a pointed star. At Braemar (the braes or slopes of the district of Mar), the standard, or rebel flag, was first raised at the start of the spectacularly unsuccessful Jacobite rebellion of 1715. Thirty years later, during the last rebellion, Braemar Castle was strengthened and garrisoned by Hanoverian (government) troops. ✉ *Braemar,* ☎ *013397/41219, off-season* ☎ *013397/41224.* *£2.* *Easter–Oct., Sat.–Thurs. 10–6.*

Braemar is associated with the **Braemar Highland Gathering** held every September. Although it's one of many such events celebrated throughout Scotland, Braemar's gathering is distinguished by the presence of the royal family, due to the proximity of their summer residence at Balmoral.

6 As you approach the headwaters of the Dee, in increasingly delightful scenery, you will come upon **Balmoral Castle,** the royal family's Scottish summer residence. Balmoral is a Victorian fantasy, designed, in fact, by Prince Albert himself in 1855. "It seems like a dream to be here in our dear Highland Home again," Queen Victoria wrote. "Every year my heart becomes more fixed in this dear Paradise." Balmoral's visiting hours depend on whether the royals are in residence. In truth, there are more interesting and historic buildings to explore, as the only part of the castle on view is the ballroom, with an exhibition of royal artifacts. From its exterior, however, Balmoral appears to be everyone's dream of a Scottish castle. In fact, the queen loved Balmoral more for its countryside than its house. The grounds offer delightful opportunities for hiking in unspoiled countryside. As Victoria observed, "I seldom walk less than four hours a day and when I come in I feel as if I want to go out again." While hiking to the nearby beauty spots—Cairn O'Mount, Cambus O'May, the Cairngorms from the Linn of Dee—try to spot two animals immortalized by the queen's favorite painter, Sir Edwin Landseer, the red deer and the red grouse. ✉ *On the A93,* ☎ *013397/42334.* *£2.50.* *May–July, Mon.–Sat. 10–5.*

A little way north of Braemar is the **Linn of Dee.** *Linn* is a Scots word meaning rocky narrows, and the river's rocky gash here is deep and roaring. Park beyond the bridge and walk back to admire the sylvan setting of the river and woodland, replete with bending larch bows and deep, tranquil pools with salmon glinting in them.

Dining and Lodging

£££ ✕ **Invercauld Arms Thistle.** This handsome stone-built Victorian hotel in the center of Braemar makes a good base for exploring Royal Deeside. Interiors are traditional in style and have been recently refurbished, with a multitude of interesting prints decorating the walls. The restaurant, with magnificent views overlooking Braemar Castle, serves an international cuisine with Scottish overtones, not least in the use of local fish, game, lamb, and beef. ✉ *AB35 5YR,* ☎ *01339/741605,* FAX *01339/741428. 68 rooms with bath. Restaurant (reservations essential), bar. AE, DC, MC, V.*

Outdoor Activities and Sports

Braemar has a tricky golf course laden with foaming waters. Erratic duffers take note: The compassionate course managers have installed, near the water, poles with little nets on the end for those occasional shots that go awry.

Corgarff Castle

❼ *23 mi northeast of Braemar, 14 mi northwest of Ballater.*

Eighteenth-century soldiers paved a military highway, now the A939, north from Ballater to Corgarff Castle, a lonely tower house with another star-shaped defensive wall—a curious replica of Braemar Castle. Corgarff was built as a hunting seat for the earls of Mar in the 16th century. After an eventful history that included the wife of a later laird being burned alive in a family dispute, the castle ended its career as a garrison for Hanoverian troops. ✉ *Signposted off A939,* ☎ *0131/668–8600.* 🎟 *£2.* ⏲ *Apr.–Sept., Mon.–Sat. 9:30–6, Sun. 2–6; Oct.–Mar., Sat. 9:30–4, Sun. 2–4.*

En Route If you return east from Corgarff Castle to the A939/A944 junction and then make a left onto the A944, the excellent castle signposting will tell you that you are on the **Castle Trail.** The A944 meanders along the River Don to the village of Strathdon, where a great mound by the roadside—on the left—turns out to be a *motte,* or the base of a wooden castle, built in the late 12th century. The A944 then joins the A97 (go left) and just a few minutes later a sign points to Glenbuchat Castle, a plain Z-plan tower house.

Kildrummy

18 mi northeast of Corgarff, 23 mi north of Ballater, 22 mi north of Aboyne.

★ ❽ **Kildrummy Castle** is significant because of its age (13th century) and because it has ties to the mainstream medieval traditions of European castle building. It shares features with Harlech and Caernarfon in Wales, as well as with continental sites, such as Château de Coucy near Laon, France. Kildrummy had undergone several expansions at the hands of English King Edward I when, in 1306, back in Scottish hands, the castle was besieged by King Edward I's son. The defenders were betrayed by a certain Osbarn the Smith, who had been promised a large amount of gold by the English besieging forces. They gave it to him after the castle fell, pouring it molten down his throat, or so the ghoulish story goes. ☎ *0131/668–8600.* 🎟 *£1.50.* ⏲ *Apr.–Sept., Mon.–Sat. 9:30–6, Sun. 2–6.*

NEED A BREAK? The **Mossat Shop,** 4 miles north of Kildrummy, at the junction of the A97 and the A944, is a possible pit stop for tea or some light shopping. If you have more time, visit the **village hall** in the tiny rural community of Clatt (7 miles northeast just off the A97). It has a savory reputation for its home baking; local ladies bake the delicious breads and cakes at this cooperatively run establishment (summer weekends only). People come from miles around to sample the results. There is also a produce and crafts shop.

Dining and Lodging

££££ ✕🏨 **Kildrummy Castle Hotel.** A grand, late-Victorian country house, this hotel offers an attractive blend of a peaceful setting, attentive service, and sporting opportunities. Oak paneling, beautiful plasterwork, and gentle color schemes create a serene environment, enhanced by the views of Kildrummy Castle Gardens next door. The award-winning cuisine features local game and seafood. ✉ *Kildrummy (by Alford), Aberdeenshire AB33 8RA,* ☎ *019755/71288,* FAX *019755/71345. 16 rooms with bath or shower. Restaurant, golf privileges, fishing. AE, MC, V.*

Alford

9 mi east of Kildrummy, 28 mi west of Aberdeen.

★ 9 Two of the finest castles on the Castle Trail are near Alford. **Craigievar**'s historic structure represents one of the finest traditions of local castle building. It also has the advantage of having survived intact, much as the stonemasons left it in 1626, with its pepper-pot turrets and towers, the whole slender shape covered in a pink-cream pastel. It was built in relatively peaceful times by William Forbes, a successful merchant. Centuries of care and wise stewardship have ensured that the experience proffered today's visitor is as authentic as possible. The castle is located about 5 miles to the south of Alford on the A980. ☎ *013398/83635.* *£5.20; grounds only £1 (honesty box).* *May–Sept., daily 1:30–5:30 (last admission 4:45); grounds year-round, daily 9:30–sunset.*

10 The massive **Castle Fraser** is the largest of the castles of Mar. While this building shows a variety of styles reflecting the taste of previous owners from the 15th to the 19th centuries, its design is typical of the castles that exist here in the Northeast. It has the further advantages of a walled garden, a picnic area, and a tearoom. ✉ *8 mi east of Alford off the A944,* ☎ *01330/833463.* *£3.60.* *Easter, May, June, and Sept., daily 1:30–5:30; July–Aug., daily 11–5:30; Oct., weekends 1:30–5:30 (last admission 4:45); gardens year-round, daily 9:30–6 or sunset; grounds daily 9:30–sunset.*

INVERNESS, LOCH NESS, AND THE NORTHEAST COAST

Inverness is home to one of the world's most famous myths: the Loch Ness monster. In 1933, during a quiet news week for the local paper, the editor decided to run a story about a strange sighting of something splashing about in Loch Ness. More than 60 years later the story lives on, and the dubious Loch Ness phenomenon continues to keep cameras trained on the deep waters, which have an ominous tendency to create mirages in still conditions. The area sees plenty of tourist traffic, drawn by the well-marketed hokum of the Loch Ness monster. But there is much, much more to see.

The northern Highlands are often described as one of Europe's last wilderness areas. For some, the landscapes of the northwest have no equal anywhere else in Britain. This stark, uncompromising landscape, glittering with lochans (small lakes), will either cast a lifetime spell on you or make you long for the safety of the pastoral regions to the south.

Numbers in the margin correspond to points of interest on the Inverness and the Northeast map.

Inverness

11 *69 mi north of Fort William, 102 mi northwest of Aberdeen.*

Inverness is a logical touring base, with excellent roads radiating out from it to serve an extensive area. Although popularly called the Capital of the Highlands, Inverness is far from Highland in flavor. Part of its hinterland includes the farmlands of the Moray Firth coastal strip, as well as of the Black Isle. It is open to the sea winds off the Moray Firth, while the high hills, although close at hand, are mainly hidden. Few of Inverness's buildings are of great antiquity—thanks to the Highland clans' careless habit of burning towns to the ground. Even

Inverness and the Northeast

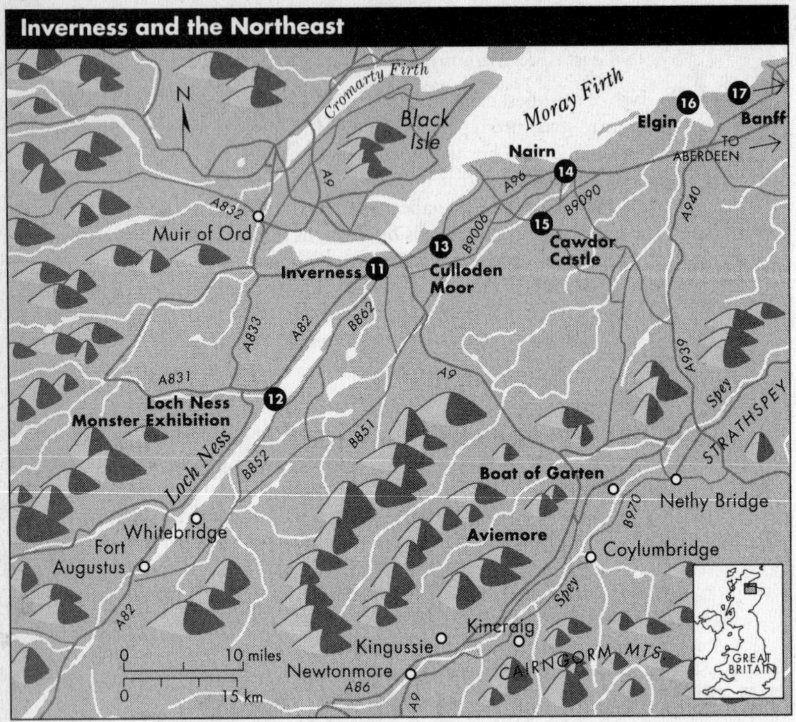

its castle is a Victorian-era replacement on the site of a fort blown up by Bonnie Prince Charlie. Now bypassed by A9, the town still does not simply bustle in summer, it positively roars. Be careful in its one-way traffic system, whether walking or driving.

Dining and Lodging

££££ ★ **Dunain Park Hotel.** Guests receive individual attention in a "private house" atmosphere in this 18th-century mansion 2½ miles southwest on A82. A log fire awaits you in the living room, where you can sip a drink and browse through books and magazines. Antiques and traditional decor make the bedrooms cozy and attractive. You can enjoy French-influenced Scottish dishes in the restaurant, where service is on bone china with crystal glasses. Saddle of venison in port sauce and boned quail stuffed with pistachios are two of the specialties. ✉ *Dunain IV3 6JN,* ☎ *01463/230512,* FAX *01463/224532. 14 rooms with bath. Restaurant, indoor pool, sauna. AE, DC, MC, V.*

££ **Ballifeary House Hotel.** A redecorated and well-maintained Victorian property, this one serves good home cooking and offers especially high standards of comfort and service. The hotel is within easy reach of downtown Inverness. ✉ *10 Ballifeary Rd., IV3 5PJ,* ☎ *01463/235572,* FAX *01463/717583. 8 rooms with bath. MC, V. No smoking in hotel. Closed Nov.–Apr.*

£ **Atholdene House.** This family-run, late 19th-century stone villa offers a friendly welcome and modernized accommodations. Evening meals can be provided, on request. The bus and railway stations are a short walk away. ✉ *20 Southside Rd., IV2 3BG,* ☎ *01463/233565. 9 rooms, 7 with shower. No credit cards.*

£ ★ **Daviot Mains Farm.** A 19th-century farmhouse 5 miles south of Inverness on A9 provides the perfect setting for home comforts and, for resident guests only, traditional Scottish cooking; lucky guests may find wild salmon on the menu. ✉ *Daviot Mains,* ☎ *01463/772215. 3 rooms, 1 with bath, 1 with shower. MC, V.*

The Arts

Inverness's theater, the **Eden Court** (☎ 01463/221718), is a reminder that just because a town is in northern Scotland, it need not be an artistic wasteland. This multipurpose 800-seat theater and its art gallery offer a varied program year-round.

Shopping

As you would expect, Inverness features a number of shops with a distinct Highland flavor. **James Pringle Weavers** (✉ Holm Woollen Mill, Dores Rd., ☎ 01463/223311) offers self-guided mill tours and a restaurant; a fine shop also on the premises sells lovely tweeds, tartans, and, of course, wool clothing. **Hector Russell Kiltmakers** (✉ 4–9 Huntly St., ☎ 01463/222781, FAX 01463/713414)) has a huge selection of kilts, or will run one up for you made to measure. It can supply by mail order overseas. **Duncan Chisholm & Sons** (✉ 49 Castle St., ☎ 01463/234599, FAX 01463/223009) is another fine shop specializing in Highland tartans, woolens, and crafts. Mail-order and made-to-measure services are available.

Loch Ness

★ ⓬ *9 mi southwest of Inverness.*

Inverness is the northern gateway to the Great Glen, the result of an ancient earth movement that dislocated the entire top half of Scotland. The fault line is filled by three lochs; the most well known, Loch Ness, can be seen from the main A82 road south, though leisurely drivers may prefer the east bank road, B862 and B852, to Fort Augustus, at the lake's southern end (32 miles). If you're in search of the infamous loch beast, Nessie, it's best to continue northward along the coast on the A82. At Drumnadrochit you will find the "official" **Loch Ness Monster Exhibition,** midway on the west bank. Loch Ness's huge volume of water has a warming effect on the local weather, making the lake conducive to mirages in still, warm conditions. These are often the circumstances in which the "monster" appears, and you may draw your own conclusions. ✉ *Drumnadrochit,* ☎ *01456/450573 and 01456/450218,* FAX *01456/450770.* 🎫 *£4.* ⏲ *July–Aug., daily 9–8:30; June and Sept., daily 9:30–6:30; Easter–May, 9:30–5:30; Oct.–Mar. 10–4; last admission 1 hr before closing.*

Lodging

£££–££££ 🏨 **Knockie Lodge Hotel.** Part 18th-century hunting lodge, with traditional and antique furniture, this hotel offers very peaceful surroundings, though with easy access to Inverness, 20 miles northeast. The dining room seats 18; nonguests are welcome if there's space. ✉ *Whitebridge, IV1 2UP, off B862 south of Loch Ness,* ☎ *01456/486276,* FAX *01456/486389. 10 rooms with bath. Dining room, fishing. AE, DC, MC, V. Closed Nov.–Apr.*

Culloden Moor

⓭ *5 mi east of Inverness on B9006.*

Culloden Moor was the scene of the last battle fought on British soil. Here, on a cold April day in 1746, the outnumbered Jacobite forces of Bonnie Prince Charlie were decimated by the superior firepower of George II's army. The victorious commander, the duke of Cumberland (George II's son), earned the name of "Butcher" Cumberland for the bloody reprisals carried out by his men on Highland families, Jacobite or not, caught in the vicinity. The National Trust for Scotland has, slightly eerily, re-created the battlefield as it looked in 1746. The uneasy silence of the open moor almost drowns out the merry clatter from the visitor center's coffee shop and the tinkle of cash registers. ☏ *01463/790607.* *Visitor center and audiovisual display £2.60.* *Apr.–Oct., daily 9–6; Feb.–Mar. and Nov.–Dec., daily 10–4 (closed Dec. 25–26).*

Nairn

14 *17 mi east of Inverness, 92 mi northwest of Aberdeen.*

Once an unusual mixture of prosperous fishing port and farming community, Nairn still has a harmonious blend of old buildings in its busy shopping streets. The town's history has been preserved in the **Nairn Fishertown Museum,** a hall crammed with artifacts, photographs, and model boats. This is an informal museum in the best sense, where the volunteer staff is full of information and eager to talk. ✉ *Laing Hall, King St.,* ☏ *01667/456798.* *30p.* *June–Sept,, Mon.–Sat. 2:30–4:30, also Mon., Wed., and Fri. 6:30 PM–8:30 PM.*

15 **Cawdor Castle,** just south of Nairn, is a cheerfully idiosyncratic, mellow and mossy family seat with a 15th-century central tower. Shakespeare's Macbeth was the Thane (or clan chief) of Cawdor, but the sense of history that exists within these turreted walls is more than fictional. Cawdor is a lived-in castle, not an abandoned structure preserved in aspic. The rooms contain family portraits, tapestries, and fine furniture reflecting 600 years of history. ☏ *01667/404615.* *£4.70; garden and grounds only £2.50.* *May–mid-Oct., daily 10–5.*

Dining and Lodging

£££ ★ **Clifton House.** This very attractive, creeper-clad Victorian villa, full of antiques, flower arrangements and open fires, offers great views over the Moray Firth. You may want to drop by for a meal while touring eastward; there are two excellent dining rooms to choose from and the seafood is especially good. Most unusually, this hotel is also licensed as a theater, and in March and November each year, you can enjoy live performances—both theatrical and musical—of an excellent standard. ✉ *Viewfield St., IV12 4HW,* ☏ *01667/453119,* FAX *01667/452836. 15 rooms with bath, 1 with shower. 2 restaurants. AE, DC, MC, V. Closed Dec.–Jan.*

Outdoor Activities and Sports

Cawdor Castle Nature Trails provides a choice of four hikes through some of the most beautiful and varied woodlands in Britain. You will pass ancient oaks and beeches, magnificent waterfalls, and deep river gorges. ✉ *Cawdor Castle (Tourism) Ltd., Cawdor Castle, Nairn, near Inverness,* ☏ *01667/404615.* *May–mid-Oct.*

En Route If you continue eastward along the Moray Firth from Nairn, you'll pass miles of inviting sandy beaches and a string of fishing communities. From Nairn to Fraserburgh at the extreme eastern end of the coast is about 70 miles.

Elgin

16 *24 mi east of Nairn, 41 mi east of Inverness.*

At the center of the fertile Laigh (low-lying lands) of Moray, Elgin has been of local importance for centuries. Like Aberdeen, it is self-supporting and previously remote, sheltered by great hills to the south and lying between two major rivers, the Spey and the Findhorn. Beginning in the 13th century, Elgin became an important religious center, a cathedral city with a walled town growing up around the cathedral and adjacent to the original settlement. Left in peace for at least some of its history, Elgin prospered and became, by the early 18th century, a mini-Edinburgh of the north and a place where country gentlemen came to spend the winter. It even echoed Edinburgh in the large-scale reconstruction of the early 19th century: Much of the old town was swept away in a wave of rebuilding, giving Elgin the fine Neoclassical buildings that survive today. Visitors can also recall Elgin's past by observing the arcaded shop fronts—some of which date from the late 17th century—that give the main shopping street its gruffy, aged appeal.

The most conspicuous, positively unavoidable building is **St. Giles Church,** which divides High Street. The grand foursquare building built in 1828 exhibits the style known as Greek Revival. Farther east, past the arcaded shops, you can see the **Little Cross** (17th century), which marked the boundary between the town and the cathedral grounds.

Cooper Park, a short distance to the southeast across the modern bypass road, is home to a magnificent ruin, the **cathedral,** consecrated in 1224. The cathedral's eventful story included devastation by a 1390 fire set in retaliation by Alexander Stewart, the Wolf of Badenoch; the illegitimate son-turned-bandit of King David II had sought revenge for his being excommunicated by the bishop of Moray. The cathedral was rebuilt but finally fell into disuse after the Reformation in 1560.

Dining and Lodging

££££ ✕🏨 **Mansion House Hotel.** This Scots-baronial mansion complete with tower is set on the river Lossie. The rooms are individually decorated; all provide comfort and pleasant surroundings. Head chef John Alexander produces flavorful dishes such as halibut with spinach sauce, or loin of venison with redcurrant sauce. ✉ *The Haugh, IV30 1AW,* ☎ *01343/548811,* FAX *01343/547916. 23 rooms with bath. Restaurant (reservations essential), bar, indoor pool, beauty salon, sauna, exercise room. AE, DC, MC, V.*

Shopping

Elgin has, in addition to the usual range of High Street stores, **Gordon and MacPhail** (✉ South St., ☎ 01343/545111), an outstanding delicatessen and wine merchant that, in addition to wine, stocks a breathtaking range of otherwise scarce malt whiskeys. This is a good place to shop for gifts for the foodies in your circle.

Banff

⑰ *36 mi east of Elgin, 47 mi north of Aberdeen.*

Midway along the northeast coast is the interesting little town of Banff—interesting because it is about a million miles from the usual tartan-clad image of Scotland. Instead, it is a typical small east-coast salty town with a tiny harbor and some fine Georgian domestic architecture. It is also within easy reach of plenty of unspoiled coastline—cliff and rock to the east at Gardenstown and Pennan, or beautiful little sandy beaches westward toward Sandend or Cullen.

However, the jewel in Banff's crown is the grand mansion of **Duff House,** a splendid William Adam–designed Baroque mansion that has been completely restored as an outstation of the National Galleries of Scotland. Many fine paintings are displayed in rooms furnished to reflect the days when the house was occupied by the dukes of Fife. ☎ *01261/818181.* 🎫 *£2.50.* ⏲ *Apr.–Sept., Wed.–Mon. 10–5; Oct.–Mar., Thurs.–Sun. 10–5.*

Dining and Lodging

££ ★ ✕ **Old Monastery.** Sitting high on a hillside, with fabulous views, this restaurant is in a building that was formerly a priory. It has pine ceilings and walls stenciled by monks 100 years ago. The chef's imaginative recipes make use of very fresh seafood and local game. ✉ *Drybridge, near Buckie (west of Banff off A98),* ☎ *01542/832660. AE, MC, V. Closed Sun., Mon., 2 wks in Nov., 3 wks in Jan.*

££ **Eden House.** Surrounded by woodland, this Georgian mansion house set high above the river Deveron has magnificent views and makes an elegant but comfortable base from which to explore the northeast coast east of Inverness. Since it is also home to the proprietors, you are likely to feel like a house guest rather than a room number. Tennis, billiards, and fishing can all be arranged, while numerous golf courses are within easy reach. Relax in the evening surrounded by carefully chosen antiques. Dinner (resident guests only) might include local seafood, Deveron salmon, game, or Scottish beef. ✉ *AB45 3NT,* ☎ *01261/821282,* FAX *01261/821283. 5 rooms, 2 with bath, 1 with shower. No credit cards. Closed Dec. 25, Jan. 1.*

£ ★ **Academy House.** This top-of-the-range bed-and-breakfast offers accommodation in what was once the headmaster's house for the local secondary school. Traditional decor and some well-chosen antique furniture enhance the spacious, well-proportioned rooms. Evening meals are served upon request. ✉ *School Rd., Fordyce AB45 2SJ,* ☎ *01261/842743. 3 rooms (share bath). No credit cards.*

£ **Broom Farm.** Set on a hilltop overlooking Sandend Bay with its beautiful, deserted sandy beach, seals basking on the rocks, and dolphins cruising the Moray Firth, this working farm offers bed-and-breakfast accommodations in a private wing of the main house. Guests have their own bathroom, a bunkroom for children, bedroom, and dressing room, all with traditional pine furniture and pastel color schemes. ✉ *Broom Farm, Sandend, Portsoy, Banffshire AB45 2UD,* ☎ FAX *01542/840401. 1 suite. No credit cards.*

ROYAL DEESIDE/INVERNESS AREA A TO Z

Arriving and Departing

By Bus

Long-distance coach service operates to and from most parts of Scotland, England, and Wales. Main operators include **Scottish Citylink** (Aberdeen bus station, ☎ 01224/212307) and **National Express** (☎ 01738/33481).

By Car

It is now possible to travel from Edinburgh to Aberdeen on a continuous stretch of the A90/M90, a fairly scenic route that runs up Strathmore. The coastal route, the A92, is a more leisurely alternative. The most scenic route, however, is probably the A93 from Perth, north to Blairgowrie and into Glen Shee. The A93 then goes over the Cairnwell Pass, the highest main road in Scotland (not recommended in winter, however).

By Plane

Aberdeen Airport (☎ 01224/722331) serves both international and domestic flights and is located in Dyce, 7 miles west of the city center on the A96 (Inverness). It is served by British Airways, Air UK, Business-Air, Knight Air, EasyJet, SAS, Brymon, and Gill Air.

Inverness Airport (☎ 01463/232471) is central for a wide range of internal flights covering the Highlands and islands region; there are also flights from London and Manchester. All flights are operated by British Airways.

By Train

Intercity West Coast and **ScotRail** service the area from London's Euston Station (☎ 0171/387–7070). Travelers can reach Aberdeen directly from Edinburgh (3 hours), and Inverness (2 hours). See ScotRail timetable for full details. There are sleeper connections from London to Inverness, as well as reliable links from Edinburgh. There are also London-Aberdeen routes that go through Edinburgh and the east-coast main line. For those interested in train service to Aberdeen's airport, Dyce is on Scotrail's Inverness–Aberdeen route.

Getting Around

By Bus

The **Scottish Citylink** office in Glasgow (✉ Buchanan Street Bus Station, ☎ 0990/505050) sells a Tourist Trail Pass providing from three to 30 days of unlimited travel on the entire British National Express/Scottish Citylink network. Inverness is well served from the central belt of Scotland (✉ Inverness coach station, ☎ 01463/238924). Getting around the Inverness area and Royal Deeside are best done by car, but there are a number of post-bus services that can help get you to the remote areas.

By Car

Great improvements have been made on Highland roads in recent years. The A9 now has some stretches of divided highway, and A835 puts the northwest touring base of Ullapool little more than an hour beyond Inverness. Ballachulish Bridge, on the Oban–Fort William road, and Kylesku Bridge, north of Lochinver, have replaced ferries and reduced crossing times. If you are coming from eastern Scotland, allow a comfortable 3½ hours from Edinburgh to such Highland destinations as Inverness, and two hours to Aberdeen via the A90.

By Train

Trains depart Edinburgh for Aberdeen, Inverness, and other towns in the north (local train information, ☎ 0141/204–2844). ScotRail "Rover" tickets cover almost the entire ScotRail network, and "West Highland" and "North Highland" local Rovers are also available (☎ 0345/212282 for details).

Freedom of Scotland Travelpass

The comprehensive "Freedom of Scotland Travelpass" covers nearly all train and ferry transport and gives discounts on buses in the Highlands and islands for 8 or 15 consecutive days, or 8 days out of 15 consecutive days. It is available at any main train station in Scotland.

Contacts and Resources

B&B Reservations

It is perfectly acceptable to contact individual establishments directly. **Tourist information centers** all offer a same-night local booking service, usually free of charge although there may occasionally be a small fee. They also operate the national **Book-A-Bed Ahead (BABA)** service, arranging for accommodation in another locality in Scotland (personal callers only, small booking fee and 10% deposit payable). The **Scottish Tourist Board's London office** (✉ 19 Cockspur St., ☎ 0171/930–

8661) will book accommodation, although its main office in Edinburgh cannot do so.

Car-Rental Agencies

Aberdeen: Avis (✉ 16 Broomhill Rd., ☎ 01224/574252, airport 01224/722282); **Europcar** (✉ 121 Causewayend, ☎ 01224/631199, airport 01224/770770); **Hertz** (✉ Railway Station, ☎ 01224/210748, airport 01224/722373).

Inverness: Europcar Ltd. (✉ The Highlander Service Station, Millburn Rd., ☎ 01463/235337); **Hertz** (✉ Dalcross Airport, ☎ 01667/462652).

Discount Admission Tickets

The **Historic Scotland Explorer Ticket,** available from any staffed Historic Scotland property, and many tourist information centers, allow visits to HS properties over a 7- or 14-day period. The **Touring Ticket** issued by the National Trust for Scotland (☎ 0131/226–5922) is also available for 7 or 14 days and allows access to all NTS properties. It is available from the NTS or main tourist information centers.

Emergencies

Dial **999** from any telephone (no coins are needed for emergency calls from public telephones), to obtain assistance from the police, ambulance, fire brigade, mountain rescue, or coastguard.

Guided Tours

The following Glasgow companies run regular **bus tours** around the region: Scott Guide Coaches (☎ 0141/204–0444), Southern Coaches (☎ 0141/876–1147), and Weirs Tours Ltd. (☎ 0141/941–2843). **The Scottish Tourist Guides Association** (☎ FAX 0141/776–1052) can recommend fully qualified guides who will arrange walking or driving excursions of varying lengths to suit your interests. **Little's Chauffeur Drive** (Glasgow, ☎ 0141/883–2111) also offers car-and-driver tours tailored to your personal interests and needs.

Visitor Information

The **Scottish Tourist Board Central Information Department** (✉ Box 705, Edinburgh EH4 3EU, ☎ 0131/332–2433, FAX 0131/315–4545), for telephone and written inquiries only, will answer any question on any aspect of your Scottish holiday and can supply literature by post. It cannot, however, make accommodation bookings.

The **Scottish Tourist Board in London** (✉ 19 Cockspur St., near Trafalgar Sq., London SW1Y 5BL, ☎ 0171/930–8661), open weekdays year-round and Saturday mid-June–mid-September, can supply information and also has an accommodation and travel booking agency.

Within Scotland, an integrated network of 170 **tourist information centers** is run by a variety of area tourist boards, offering comprehensive information and on-the-spot accommodation bookings. **Aberdeen:** ✉ St. Nicholas House, Broad St., Aberdeen AB9 1DE, ☎ 01224/632727. **Ballater:** ✉ Station Sq., ☎ 013397/55306. **Inverness:** ✉ Castle Wynd, Inverness IV1 1EZ, ☎ 01463/234353. **Kincardine and Deeside Tourist Board:** ✉ Bridge St., Banchory, ☎ 01330/822066.

18 Portraits of Great Britain

Great Britain at a Glance: A Chronology

Kings and Queens and All That

Splendid Stones: An Introduction to British Architecture

Books and Videos

GREAT BRITAIN AT A GLANCE: A CHRONOLOGY

2800 BC First building of Stonehenge (later building 2100–1900)

54 BC Julius Caesar's exploratory invasion of England

AD 43 Romans conquer England, led by Emperor Claudius

60 Boudicca, a native British queen, razes the first Roman London (Londinium) to the ground

122–27 Emperor Hadrian completes the Roman conquest and builds a wall across the north to keep back the Scottish Picts

145 The Antonine Wall built, north of Hadrian's, running from the Firth of Forth to the Firth of Clyde

300–50 Height of Roman colonization, administered from such towns as Verulamium (St. Albans), Colchester, Lincoln, and York

383–410 Romans begin to withdraw from Britain; waves of Germanic invaders—Jutes, Angles, and Saxons

circa 490 Possible period for the legendary King Arthur, who may have led resistance to Anglo-Saxon invaders; in 500 the Battle of Badon is fought

563 St. Columba, an Irish monk, founds monastery on the Scottish island of Iona; begins to convert Picts and Scots to Christianity

597 St. Augustine arrives in Canterbury to Christianize Britain

550–700 Seven Anglo-Saxon kingdoms emerge—Essex, Wessex, Sussex, Kent, Anglia, Mercia, and Northumbria—to become the core of English social and political organization for centuries

731 Bede completes the *Ecclesiastical History*

800s Danish Viking raids solidify into widespread colonization

871–99 Alfred the Great, king of Wessex, unifies the English against Viking invaders, who are then confined to the northeast

919–54 Short-lived Norse kingdom of York

1040 Edward the Confessor moves his court to Westminster and founds Westminster Abbey

1066 William, duke of Normandy, invades; defeats Harold at the Battle of Hastings; is crowned at Westminster in December

1086 Domesday Book completed, a survey of all taxpayers in England, drawn up to assist administration of the new realm

1167 Oxford University founded

1170 Thomas à Becket murdered in Canterbury; his shrine becomes center for international pilgrimage

1189 Richard the Lionhearted embarks on the Third Crusade

1209 Cambridge University founded

1215 King John forced to sign Magna Carta at Runnymede; it promulgates basic principles of English law: no taxation except through Parliament, trial by jury, and property guarantees

1272–1307 Edward I, a great legislator; in 1282–83 he conquers Wales and reinforces his rule with a chain of massive castles

1295 The Model Parliament sets future parliamentary pattern, with membership of knights from the shires, lower clergy, and civic representatives

1296 Edward I invades Scotland

1314 Robert the Bruce routs the English at Bannockburn

1337–1453 Edward III claims the French throne, starting the Hundred Years War. In spite of dramatic English victories—1346 at Crécy, 1356 at Poitiers, 1415 at Agincourt—the long war of attrition ends with the French driving the English out from all but Calais, which finally fell in 1558

1348–49 The Black Death (bubonic plague) reduces the population of Britain to around 2½ million; decades of social unrest follow

1381 The Peasants Revolt is defused by the 14-year-old Richard II

1399 Henry Bolingbroke (Henry IV) deposes and murders his cousin Richard II; beginning of the rivalry between houses of York and Lancaster

1402–10 The Welsh, led by Owain Glendwr, rebel against English rule

1455–85 The Wars of the Roses—the York/Lancaster struggle erupts in civil war

1477 William Caxton prints first book in England

1485 Henry Tudor (Henry VII) defeats Richard III at the Battle of Bosworth, and founds the Tudor dynasty; he suppresses private armies, develops administrative efficiency and royal absolutism

1530s Under Henry VIII the Reformation takes hold; he dissolves the monasteries, finally demolishes medieval England and replaces it with a new society

Henry's marital history—in 1534 he divorces Katherine of Aragon after 25 years of marriage; in 1536 Anne Boleyn (mother of Elizabeth I) is executed in the Tower of London; in 1537 Jane Seymour dies giving birth to Edward VI; in 1540 Henry marries Anne of Cleves (divorced same year); in 1542 Katherine Howard is executed in the Tower; in 1542 he marries Katherine Parr, who outlives him

1554 Mary I marries Philip II of Spain; tries to restore Catholicism to England

1555 Protestant Bishops Ridley and Latimer are burned in Oxford; in 1556 Archbishop Cranmer is burned

1558–1603 Reign of Elizabeth I—Protestantism re-established; Drake, Raleigh, and other freebooters establish English claims in the West Indies and North America

1568 Mary, Queen of Scots, flees to England; in 1587 she is executed

1588 Spanish Armada fails to invade England

1603 James VI of Scotland becomes James I of England

1605 Guy Fawkes and friends in Catholic plot to blow up Parliament

1611 King James Authorized Version of the Bible published

1620 Pilgrims sail from Plymouth on the *Mayflower* and settle in New England

1629 Charles I dissolves Parliament, decides to rule alone

1642–49 Civil War between the Royalists and Parliamentarians (Cavaliers and Roundheads); the Parliamentarians win

1649 Charles I executed; England is a republic

1653 Cromwell becomes Lord Protector, England's only dictatorship

1660 Charles II restored to the throne; accepts limits to royal power

1666 The Great Fire of London, accession of William III (of Orange) and his wife, Mary II, as joint monarchs; royal power limited still further

1694 Bank of England founded

1706–09 Marlborough's victories over the French under Louis XIV

1707 The Act of Union: England, Scotland, and Wales join in the United Kingdom of Great Britain (as against the countries being united in the person of the king)

1714 The German Hanoverians succeed to the throne; George I's lack of English leads to a council of ministers, the beginning of the Cabinet system of government

1700s Under the first four Georges, the Industrial Revolution develops and with it Britain's domination of world trade

1715/1745 Two Jacobite rebellions fail to restore the House of Stuart to the throne; in 1746 final defeat takes place at Culloden Moor

1756–63 Seven Years War; Britain wins colonial supremacy from the French in Canada and India

1775–83 Britain loses its American colonies

1795–1815 Britain and its allies defeat French in the Napoleonic Wars; in 1805 Nelson is killed at Trafalgar; in 1815 Battle of Waterloo is fought

1801 Union with Ireland

1811–20 Prince Regent rules during his father's (George III) madness—the Regency period

1825 The Stockton to Darlington railway, the world's first passenger line with regular service, is established

1832 The Reform Bill extends the franchise, limiting the power of the great landowners

1834 Parliament outlaws slavery

1837–1901 The long reign of Victoria—Britain becomes the world's richest country, and the British Empire reaches its height; railways, canals, and telegraph lines draw Britain into one vast manufacturing net

1851 The Great Exhibition, Prince Albert's brainchild, is held in Crystal Palace, Hyde Park

1861 Prince Albert dies

1887 Victoria celebrates her Golden Jubilee; in 1901 she dies, marking the end of an era

1911–12 Rail, mining, and coal strikes

1914–18 World War I: Fighting against Germany, Britain loses a whole generation, with 750,000 men killed in trench warfare alone;

enormous debts and inept diplomacy in the postwar years undermine Britain's position as a world power

1919 Ireland declares independence from England; bloody Black-and-Tan struggle results

1926 General Strike in sympathy with striking coal miners

1936 Edward VIII abdicates to marry American divorcée, Mrs. Wallis Simpson

1939–45 World War II—Britain faces Hitler alone until Pearl Harbor; London badly damaged during the Blitz, September '40–May '41; Britain's economy shattered by the war

1945 Labour wins a landslide victory; stays in power for six years, transforming Britain into a welfare state

1952 Queen Elizabeth accedes to the throne

1969 Serious violence breaks out in Northern Ireland

1972 National miners' strike

1973 Britain joins the European Economic Community after referendum

1975 Britain begins to pump North Sea oil

1981 Marriage of Prince Charles and Lady Diana Spencer

1982 Falklands regained

1987 Conservatives under Margaret Thatcher win a third term in office

1990 Glasgow is European Cultural Capital for the year

1990 John Major takes over as prime minister, ending Margaret Thatcher's illustrious, if controversial, career in office

1991 The Persian Gulf War

1992 Great Britain and the European countries join to form one European Community (EC), whose name was officially changed to European Union in 1993.

1994 Official opening of the Channel Tunnel by Queen Elizabeth II and President Mitterand

1997 Official opening of the reconstruction of Shakespeare's Globe Theatre in London

KINGS AND QUEENS AND ALL THAT: A MINI-HISTORY

THE BRITISH HAVE MONARCHS the way other people have mice. It is impossible to visit the country, to tour historic houses, even to walk down the street, without coming face to face with more than a thousand years of kings and queens. In order to help you sort them out and place them in their right order, here is a brief rundown of those who have sat on the throne (before 1603, the throne of England; after that, the joint throne of England, Scotland, and Wales). Even if a monarch was not very important as a ruler, he or she may have given the name to an age—Queen Anne, for example—so, putting them all in perspective can be very helpful.

1042–66	Edward the Confessor
1066	Harold

House of Normandy

1066–87	William I—The Conqueror
1087–1100	William II—Rufus (murdered)
1100–35	Henry I
1135–54	Stephen

House of Plantagenet

1154–89	Henry II
1189–99	Richard I—Lionheart (killed in battle)
1199–1216	John
1216–72	Henry III
1272–1307	Edward I
1307–27	Edward II (murdered)
1327–77	Edward III
1377–99	Richard II (deposed, then murdered)
1399–1413	Henry IV
1413–22	Henry V
1422–61	Henry VI (deposed)

House of York

1461–83	Edward IV
1483	Edward V (probably murdered)
1483–85	Richard III (killed in battle)

House of Tudor

1485–1509	Henry VII
1509–47	Henry VIII
1547–53	Edward VI
1553	Jane (beheaded)
1553–58	Mary I
1558–1603	Elizabeth I

House of Stuart

1603–25	James I (VI of Scotland)
1625–49	Charles I (beheaded)

Commonwealth

1653–58	Oliver Cromwell (Protector)
1658–59	Richard Cromwell

House of Stuart (Restored)

1660–85	Charles II
1685–88	James II (deposed and exiled)
1689–95	William III and Mary II (joint monarchs)
1695–1702	William III (reigned alone)
1702–14	Anne
House of Hanover	
1714–27	George I
1727–60	George II
1760–1820	George III
1820–30	George IV (Regent from 1811)
1830–37	William IV

House of Saxe-Coburg

1837–1901	Victoria
1901–10	Edward VII

House of Windsor

1910–36	George V
1936	Edward VIII (abdicated)
1936–52	George VI
1952–	Elizabeth II

SPLENDID STONES: AN INTRODUCTION TO BRITISH ARCHITECTURE

IN BRITAIN, YOU CAN SEE structures that go back to the dawn of history, in the hauntingly mysterious circles of monoliths at Stonehenge or Avebury, for example; or the resurrected remains of Roman empire builders preserved in towns such as St. Albans or Cirencester. On the other hand, you can startle your eyes with the very current, very controversial designs of contemporary architects in new developments, including London's Docklands area. Appreciating the wealth of Britain's architectural heritage does not require a degree in art history, but knowing a few hallmarks of various styles can enhance your enjoyment of what you see. Here, then, is a primer of nearly a millennium of various architectural styles.

Norman

The solid Norman style, ideal for castle building, arrived in England slightly before the Conquest, with the building of Westminster Abbey in 1040. From 1066 to around 1200, it was clearly the style of choice for buildings of any importance. Norman towers tended to be hefty and square, arches always round-topped, and the vaulting barrel-shaped. Decoration was mostly geometrical, but within those limits, ornate. *Best seen in the Tower of London, St. Bartholomew's and Temple Churches, London; and in the cathedrals of St. Albans, Ely, Gloucester, Durham, and Norwich, and at Tewkesbury Abbey.*

Gothic Early English

From 1130–1300, pointed arches began to supplant the rounded ones, buttresses became heavier than the Norman variety, and the windows lost their rounded tops to become "lancet" shaped. Buildings climbed skyward, less squat and heavy, with the soaring effect accentuated by steep roofs and spires. *Best seen in the cathedrals of York, Salisbury, Ely, Worcester, Canterbury (east end), and Westminster Abbey's chapter house.*

DECORATED

From the late 1100s until around 1400, elegance and ornament became fully integrated into architectural design, rather than applied onto the surface of a solid basic form. Windows filled more of the walls and were divided into sections by carved mullions. Vaulting grew increasingly complex, with ribs and ornamented bosses proliferating; spires became even pointier; arches took on the "ogee" shape, with its unique double curve. This style was one of England's greatest gifts to world architecture. *Best seen at the cathedrals of Wells, Lincoln, Durham (east transept), and Ely (Lady Chapel and Octagon).*

PERPENDICULAR

In later Gothic architecture, the emphasis on the vertical grew even more pronounced, featuring slender pillars, huge expanses of glass, and superb fan vaulting resembling the formalized branches of frozen trees. Walls were divided by panels. One of the chief areas in which to see Perpendicular architecture is East Anglia, where the rich wool towns built magnificent churches in the new style. Houses, too, began to reflect prevailing taste. Perpendicular Gothic lasted for well over two centuries from its advent around 1330. *Best seen at St. George's Chapel, Windsor; the cathedrals of Gloucester (cloister), and Hereford (chapter house); Henry VII's Chapel, Westminster Abbey; and King's College Chapel, Cambridge.*

Tudor

With the great period of cathedral building over, from 1500 to 1560 the nation's attention turned to the construction of spacious homes, characterized by this new architectural style. The rapidly expanding *nouveau riche* class—created by the first two Tudor Henrys (VII and VIII) to challenge the power of the aristocracy—built spacious manor houses, often on the foundations of pillaged monasteries, thus beginning the era of the great stately homes. Brick replaced stone as the most popular medium, with plasterwork and carved wood to carry the elaborate motifs of the age. Another way the new rich could make their mark—and ensure their place in the next world—was by building churches. This was the age of the splendid parish churches built on fortunes made in the wool trade. Some of the most magnificent are in Suffolk, Norfolk, and the Cotswolds. *Domestic architecture is best seen at Hampton Court and St. James's Palace, London; for wool churches, Lavenham, and Long Melford, though its tower is much later, both in Suffolk.*

Renaissance Elizabethan

For a short period under Elizabeth I, 1560–1600, this development of Tudor flourished as Italian influences began to seep into England, seen especially in symmetrical facades. The most notable example was Hardwick Hall in Derbyshire, built in the 1590s by Bess of Hardwick—the jingle that describes it goes "Hardwick Hall, more glass than wall." But, however grand the houses were, they were still on a human scale, warm and livable, built of a mellow amalgam of brick and stone. *Other great Elizabethan houses are Montacute, Somerset; Longleat, Wiltshire; and Burghley House, Cambridgeshire.*

Jacobean

For the first 15 years of the reign of James I (the name Jacobean is taken from the Latin word for James, Jacobus) there was little noticeable change. Windows were still large in proportion to the wall surfaces. Gables, in the style of the Netherlands, were popular. Carved decoration in wood and plaster (especially the geometrical patterning called "strapwork," like intertwined leather belts, also of Dutch origin) was still exuberant, now even more so. But a change was on the way. Inigo Jones (1573–1652), the first great modern British architect, was attempting to synthesize the architectural heritage of England with the current Italian theories. Two of his finest remaining buildings—the Banqueting Hall, Whitehall, and the Queen's House at Greenwich—epitomize his genius, which was to introduce the Palladian style that dominated British architecture for centuries. It uses the classical Greek orders—Doric, Ionic, and Corinthian. This was grandeur. But the classical style that was so monumentally effective under a hot Mediterranean sun was somehow transformed in Britain, domesticated and tamed. Columns and pediments were used to decorate the façades, and huge frescoes provided acres of color to interior walls and ceilings, all in the Italian manner. But these architectural elements had not yet been totally naturalized. There were in fact two quite distinct styles running concurrently, the comfortably domestic and the purer classical in public buildings. They were finally fused together by the talent of Christopher Wren (1632–1723). *Jacobean is best seen at the Bodleian Library, Oxford; Hatfield House, Herefordshire; Audley End, Essex; and Clare College, Cambridge.*

Wren

Sir Christopher Wren's work constituted an era all by itself. Not only was he naturally one of the world's greatest architects, but he was also given an unparalleled opportunity when the disastrous Great Fire of London in 1666 wiped out the center of the capital, destroying no fewer than 89 churches and 13,200 houses. Although Wren's great scheme for a totally new city center was rejected, he did build 51 churches, the greatest of which was St. Paul's, completed in just 35 years. The range of Wren's designs is extremely wide, from simple classical shapes to the extravagantly dramatic baroque. He was also at home with domestic architecture, where his combinations of brick and stone produced a warm, homey effect. *Wren's ecclesiastical architecture is best seen at St. Paul's Cathedral and the other remaining city churches, his domestic style at Hampton Court Palace, Kensington Palace, and the Royal Hospital in Chelsea.*

Palladian

This style is often referred to as Georgian, so-called from the Hanoverian kings George I through IV, although it was introduced as early as Inigo Jones's time. Classical inspiration has now been thoroughly acclimatized. Though they were completely at home among the hills, lakes, and trees of the British countryside, Palladian buildings were derived from the designs of the Italian architectural theorist Palladio, with pillared porticoes, triangular pediments, and strictly balanced windows. In domestic architecture, this large-scale classicism was usually modified to quiet simplicity, preserving mathematical proportions of windows, doors, and the exactly calculated volume of room space, to create a feeling of balance and harmony. There were some outrageous departures from the classical manner at this time, most notably with the Brighton Pavilion, built for the Prince Regent (later George IV). The Regency style comes under the Palladian heading, though strictly speaking it lasted only for the few years of the actual Regency. In Britain, the Palladian style was handled with more freedom than elsewhere in Europe, and America took its cue from the British architects. *Among the best Palladian examples are Regent's Park Terraces (London); the library at Kenwood (London); Royal Crescent and other streets in Bath; Holkham Hall, Blenheim Palace, and Castle Howard.*

Victorian

Elements of imaginative fantasy, already seen in the Palladian era, came to the fore during the long reign of Victoria. The country's vast profits made from the Industrial Revolution were spent lavishly. Civic building accelerated in all the major cities with town halls modeled after medieval castles or French châteaus. The Victorians plundered the past for styles, with Gothic—about which the scholarly Victorians were very knowledgeable—leading the field. The supreme example here is the Houses of Parliament in London. (To distinguish between the Victorian variety and an earlier version, which flourished in the late 1700s, the earlier one is commonly spelled "Gothick.") But there were many other styles in the running, including the attractively named—and self-explanatory—"Wrenaissance." *Among the most striking examples are Truro Cathedral, the Albert Memorial (London), Manchester Town Hall, the Foreign Office (London), Ironbridge, and Cragside (Northumberland).*

Edwardian

Toward the end of the Victorian era, in the late 1800s, architecture calmed down considerably, with a return to a solid sort of classicism, and to even a muted baroque. The Arts and Crafts movement, especially the work and inspiration of William Morris, produced simpler designs, returning often to medieval models. *Best seen in Buckingham Palace and the Admiralty Arch in London.*

Modern

A furious public debate has raged in Britain for many years between traditionalists and the adherents of modernistic architecture. Britons are strongly conservative when it comes to their environment. These arguments have been highlighted and made even more bitter by the intervention of such notable figures as Prince Charles, who derides excessive modernism, and said, for instance, that an advanced design for the new wing of the National Gallery in Trafalgar Square would be like "a carbuncle on a much-loved face." One reason for the strength of the British attitude is that the country suffered from far too much ill-conceived building development after World War II, when large areas of city centers had to be rebuilt after the devastation of German bombs, and there was a pressing need for housing. Town planners and architects at this time encumbered the country with endless badly built and worse-designed tower blocks and shopping areas.

The situation that was thus created in the '50s and '60s is gradually being reversed. High-rise apartment blocks are being blown up and replaced by more user-friendly housing. Large-scale commercial areas, such as the Bull Ring in Birmingham, are being rethought and slowly rebuilt, although so much ill-considered building went on in the past that Britain can never be completely free of it. The emphasis is gradually, far too gradually, moving to a type of planning, designing, and construction that pays more attention to the needs of the inhabitants of buildings. At last, the lessons of crime statistics and the sheer human misery caused by unacceptable living conditions are being learned. There is, too, a healthier attitude now to the conservation of old buildings. As part of the post-war building splurge, houses that should have been treasured for posterity were torn down wholesale. Happily many of those that survived the wreckers' ball are now being restored and put back to use.

The architecture styles employed nowadays are very eclectic. A predominant one, favored incidentally by Prince Charles, draws largely on the past, with nostalgic echoes of the country cottage, and leans heavily on variegated brickwork and on close attention to decorative detail. Supermarkets are going up in every town designed on a debased form of this style. Stark modernism does crop up every now and again. The Lloyd's Tower in the City of London, by Sir Richard Rogers, designer of the Pompidou Center in Paris, is perhaps the leading, and most flamboyantly extreme, example. Another, gentler one is the Queen's Stand at the Epsom Racecourse. This elegant building by Richard Horden is rather like an elegant, white ocean liner, berthed beside the racetrack, with sweeping, curved staircases inside, and viewing balconies outside. But England generally is still light years behind the States in experimentation with design. The skyscrapers of the City of London are the exception in Britain rather than the rule.

However, public buildings are being built on a smaller scale; schools and libraries, designed in a muted modernism, use traditional, natural materials, such as wood, stone, and brick. A slightly special case, though representative of what can be achieved, is the new Visitors' Centre at the National Trust's most popular venue, Fountains Abbey in Yorkshire. Designed by Edward Cullinan, it is a fusion of dry stone walls, lead and wooden-shingle roofs outside, white-painted steel pillars and flowing ceilings inside. It is perfectly conceived for the needs of such a historically important site. Unfortunately, the recession has stopped most commercial building dead in its tracks, so the architectural debate will be largely a theoretical one for years to come. *Among the new buildings to see are the Lloyd's Tower, some of the Docklands development, Richmond House (79 Whitehall), and the Clore Building at the Tate Gallery (all in London); the campus of Sussex University (outside Brighton), the Royal Regatta Building (Henley), the Sainsbury Centre (Norwich), the Burrell Collection (Glasgow); the Queen's Stand at Epsom, Surrey; The Visitors' Centre, Fountains Abbey, Yorkshire.*

BOOKS AND VIDEOS

Books

Many writers' names have become inextricably linked with the regions in which they set their books or plays. Hardy's Wessex, Daphne Du Maurier's Cornwall, Wordsworth's Lake District, Shakespeare's Arden, and Brontë Country are now evocative catch phrases, treasured by local tourist boards. But however hackneyed the tags may now be, you *can* still get a heightened insight to an area through the eyes of authors of genius, even though they may have written a century or more ago. Here are just a few works that may provide you with an understanding of their authors' loved territory.

Thomas Hardy's *Mayor of Casterbridge, Tess of the D'Urbervilles, Far from the Madding Crowd,* and indeed almost everything he wrote is solidly based on his Wessex (Dorset) homeland. Daphne Du Maurier had a deep love of Cornwall from her childhood; *Frenchman's Creek, Jamaica Inn,* and *The King's General* all capture the county's Celtic atmosphere. The Brontë sisters' *Wuthering Heights, The Tennant of Wildfell Hall,* and *Jane Eyre* all breathe the sharp air of the high Fells around their Haworth home. William Wordsworth, who was born at Cockermouth in the Lake District, depicts the area's rugged beauty in many of his poems, especially the *Lyrical Ballads.*

Virginia Woolf's visits to Vita Sackville-West at her ancestral home of Knole, in Sevenoaks, resulted in the novel *Orlando.* The stately home is now a National Trust property. The country around Batemans, near Burwash in East Sussex, the home where Rudyard Kipling lived for more than 30 years, was the inspiration for *Puck of Pook's Hill* and *Rewards and Fairies.* Lamb House in Rye, also in East Sussex, was home to the American writer, Henry James, and after him E. F. Benson, whose delicious Lucia books are set in a thinly disguised version of the town. Both Batemans and Lamb House are National Trust buildings.

A highly irreverent—and very funny—version of academic life, *Porterhouse Blue,* by Tom Sharpe, will guarantee that you look at Oxford and Cambridge with a totally different eye. John Fowles's *The French Lieutenant's Woman,* largely set in Lyme Regis, is full of local color for visitors to Dorset.

James Herriot's successfully televised veterinary surgeon books, among them *All Creatures Great and Small,* give evocative accounts of life in the Yorkshire dales.

Mysteries are almost a way of life in Britain, partly because many of the best English mystery writers set their plots in their home territory. Modern whodunits by P. D. James and Ruth Rendell can be relied on to convey a fine sense of place, while Ellis Peters's Brother Cadfael stories re-create life in medieval Shrewsbury with a wealth of telling detail. There are always, of course, the villages, vicarages, and scandals of Agatha Christie's "Miss Marple" books.

For the many fans of the Arthurian legends, there are some excellent, imaginative novels, which not only tell the stories, but give fine descriptions of the British countryside. Among them are *Sword at Sunset,* by Rosemary Sutcliffe; *The Once and Future King,* by T. H. White; and the four Merlin novels by Mary Stewart, *The Crystal Cave, The Hollow Hills, The Last Enchantment,* and *The Wicked Day.*

An animal's close-to-the-earth viewpoint can reveal all kinds of countryside insights about Britain. *Watership Down,* by Richard Adam, was a runaway best seller about rabbits in the early '70s, and *Wind in the Willows,* by Kenneth Grahame, gives a vivid impression of the Thames Valley 80 years ago which still holds largely true today.

Anyone interested in writers and the surroundings that may have influenced their works should get *The Oxford Literary Guide to the British Isles,* edited by Dorothy Eagle and Hilary Carnell, and *Literary Britain,* by Frank Morley.

Two good background books on England are *The English World,* edited by Robert Blake, and Godfrey Smith's *The English Companion. The London Encyclopaedia,* by Ben Weinreb and Christopher Hibbert, is invaluable as a source of information on the capital.

The Buildings of England and *The Buildings of Scotland,* originally by Nicholas Pevsner, but much updated since his death, are a multivolume series, organized by county, which sets out to chronicle every building of any importance. The series contains an astonishing amount of information. For a grand introduction to one of England's leading 18th-century portraitists, read *Gainsborough* by Sir Ellis Waterhouse.

Videos

From *Wuthering Heights* to *Jane Eyre,* many great classics of British literature have been rendered into great classics of film. It's surprising to learn, however, how many of them were creations of Hollywood and not the British film industry (which had its heyday in the 1940s to 1960s). From Laurence Olivier to today's Kenneth Brannagh, noted directors/actors have long cross-pollinated the two centers of cinema. Any survey of British film, of course, begins with the dramas of Shakespeare: Olivier's *Othello* and *Hamlet,* Orson Welles's *Macbeth,* and Brannagh's *Much Ado About Nothing* are just some of the superlative film renditions. Charles Dickens also provided the foundation for many a film favorite: David Lean's immortal *Great Expectations,* George Cukor's *David Copperfield,* and Sir Carol Reed's Oscar-winning musical, *Oliver!,* top this list.

Another, more recent, author has provided fodder for many beloved flicks: Agatha Christie. Of the many film versions of her books, one is especially treasured: *Murder, She Said,* which starred the inimitable Margaret Rutherford: With its setting of quaint English village, harpsichord film score, and the dotty Miss Marple of La Rutherford, this must be the most English of all the Christie films.

For lovers of opulence, spectacle, and history, there are many selections to look for. In particular, Robert Bolt's version of Sir Thomas More's life and death, *A Man for All Seasons,* and his *Lady Caroline Lamb*—surely the most beautiful historical film ever made. Richard Harris made a stirring Lord Protector in *Cromwell,* while the mini-series on Queen Elizabeth I, starring Glenda Jackson, is a great BBC addition to videos.

Quintessentially British are some comedies of the 1950s and 1960s: Alec Guinness's *Kind Hearts and Coronets,* Peter Sellers's *The Mouse That Roared,* and Tony Richardson's Oscar-winner, *Tom Jones,* starring Albert Finney, are some best bets. Today, everyone's visions of turn-of-the-century England have been captured by the Merchant and Ivory films, notably their recent *Howard's End,* which won innumerable awards. The most moving British film of all time? Well, some people regard Bryan Forbes's little known *Whistle Down the Wind* as the contender for this title. Alan Bates portrays a drunken bum who is mistaken as Jesus Christ by a villageful of children. Unlikely as it may seem, this film is now in preparation to be a musical by Andrew Lloyd Webber.

INDEX

C

M

N

S

T

U

V

W

Y

Z

NOTES

NOTES

NOTES

NOTES

NOTES

Fodor's Travel Publications

Available at bookstores everywhere, or call 1-800-533-6478, 24 hours a day.

Gold Guides

U.S.

Alaska
Arizona
Boston
California
Cape Cod, Martha's Vineyard, Nantucket
The Carolinas & the Georgia Coast
Chicago
Colorado
Florida
Hawai'i
Las Vegas, Reno, Tahoe
Los Angeles
Maine, Vermont, New Hampshire
Maui & Lāna'i
Miami & the Keys
New England
New Orleans
New York City
Pacific North Coast
Philadelphia & the Pennsylvania Dutch Country
The Rockies
San Diego
San Francisco
Santa Fe, Taos, Albuquerque
Seattle & Vancouver
The South
U.S. & British Virgin Islands
USA
Virginia & Maryland
Washington, D.C.

Foreign

Australia
Austria
The Bahamas
Belize & Guatemala
Bermuda
Canada
Cancún, Cozumel, Yucatán Peninsula
Caribbean
China
Costa Rica
Cuba
The Czech Republic & Slovakia
Eastern & Central Europe
Europe
Florence, Tuscany & Umbria
France
Germany
Great Britain
Greece
Hong Kong
India
Ireland
Israel
Italy
Japan
London
Madrid & Barcelona
Mexico
Montréal & Québec City
Moscow, St. Petersburg, Kiev
The Netherlands, Belgium & Luxembourg
New Zealand
Norway
Nova Scotia, New Brunswick, Prince Edward Island
Paris
Portugal
Provence & the Riviera
Scandinavia
Scotland
Singapore
South Africa
South America
Southeast Asia
Spain
Sweden
Switzerland
Thailand
Tokyo
Toronto
Turkey
Vienna & the Danube

Fodor's Special-Interest Guides

Caribbean Ports of Call
The Complete Guide to America's National Parks
Family Adventures
Gay Guide to the USA
Halliday's New England Food Explorer
Halliday's New Orleans Food Explorer
Healthy Escapes
Kodak Guide to Shooting Great Travel Pictures
Net Travel
Nights to Imagine
Rock & Roll Traveler USA
Sunday in New York
Sunday in San Francisco
Walt Disney World, Universal Studios and Orlando
Walt Disney World for Adults
Where Should We Take the Kids? California
Where Should We Take the Kids? Northeast
Worldwide Cruises and Ports of Call

Fodor's

Special Series

Affordables

Caribbean

Europe

Florida

France

Germany

Great Britain

Italy

London

Paris

Fodor's Bed & Breakfasts and Country Inns

America

California

The Mid-Atlantic

New England

The Pacific Northwest

The South

The Southwest

The Upper Great Lakes

The Berkeley Guides

California

Central America

Eastern Europe

Europe

France

Germany & Austria

Great Britain & Ireland

Italy

London

Mexico

New York City

Pacific Northwest & Alaska

Paris

San Francisco

Compass American Guides

Arizona

Canada

Chicago

Colorado

Hawaii

Idaho

Hollywood

Las Vegas

Maine

Manhattan

Montana

New Mexico

New Orleans

Oregon

San Francisco

Santa Fe

South Carolina

South Dakota

Southwest

Texas

Utah

Virginia

Washington

Wine Country

Wisconsin

Wyoming

Fodor's Citypacks

Atlanta

Hong Kong

London

New York City

Paris

Rome

San Francisco

Washington, D.C.

Fodor's Español

California

Caribe Occidental

Caribe Oriental

Gran Bretaña

Londres

Mexico

Nueva York

Paris

Fodor's Exploring Guides

Australia

Boston & New England

Britain

California

Caribbean

China

Egypt

Florence & Tuscany

Florida

France

Germany

Ireland

Israel

Italy

Japan

London

Mexico

Moscow & St. Petersburg

New York City

Paris

Prague

Provence

Rome

San Francisco

Scotland

Singapore & Malaysia

Spain

Thailand

Turkey

Venice

Fodor's Flashmaps

Boston

New York

San Francisco

Washington, D.C.

Fodor's Pocket Guides

Acapulco

Atlanta

Barbados

Jamaica

London

New York City

Paris

Prague

Puerto Rico

Rome

San Francisco

Washington, D.C.

Mobil Travel Guides

America's Best Hotels & Restaurants

California & the West

Frequent Traveler's Guide to Major Cities

Great Lakes

Mid-Atlantic

Northeast

Northwest & Great Plains

Southeast

Southwest & South Central

Rivages Guides

Bed and Breakfasts of Character and Charm in France

Hotels and Country Inns of Character and Charm in France

Hotels and Country Inns of Character and Charm in Italy

Hotels and Country Inns of Character and Charm in Paris

Hotels and Country Inns of Character and Charm in Portugal

Hotels and Country Inns of Character and Charm in Spain

Short Escapes

Britain

France

New England

Near New York City

Fodor's Sports

Golf Digest's Best Places to Play

Skiing USA

USA Today The Complete Four Sport Stadium Guide

Fodor's Vacation Planners

Great American Learning Vacations

Great American Sports & Adventure Vacations

Great American Vacations

Great American Vacations for Travelers with Disabilities

National Parks and Seashores of the East

National Parks of the West

Escape to ancient cities and exotic

islands with CNN Travel Guide, a wealth of valuable advice. Host Valerie Voss will take you

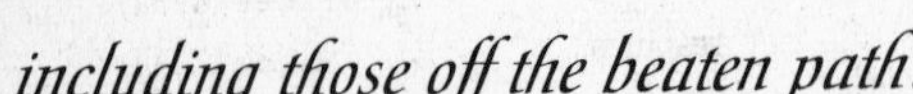

to all of your favorite destinations,

including those off the beaten path.

Tune into your passport to the world.

CNN TRAVEL GUIDE

SATURDAY 12:30 PM ET SUNDAY 4:30 PM ET

CNN Airport Network

Your Window To The World While You're On The Road

Keep in touch when you're traveling. Before you take off, tune in to CNN Airport Network. Now available in major airports across America, CNN Airport Network provides nonstop news, sports, business, weather and lifestyle programming. Both domestic and international. All piloted by the top-flight global resources of CNN. All up-to-the minute reporting. And just for travelers, CNN Airport Network features two daily Fodor's specials. "Travel Fact" provides enlightening, useful travel trivia, while "What's Happening" covers upcoming events in major cities worldwide. So why be bored waiting to board? **TIME FLIES WHEN YOU'RE WATCHING THE WORLD THROUGH THE WINDOW OF CNN AIRPORT NETWORK!**

WHEREVER YOU TRAVEL, HELP IS NEVER FAR AWAY.

From planning your trip to providing travel assistance along the way, American Express® Travel Service Offices are always there to help.

Great Britain

American Express Travel Service
82 North Street
Brighton
1273/321-242

American Express Travel Service
78 Brompton Road
Knightsbridge, London
171/584-6182

American Express Travel Service
6 Haymarket
London
171/930-4411

American Express Travel Service
4 Queen Street
Oxford
1865/792-033

American Express Travel Service
139 Armada Way
Plymouth
1752/228-708

Travellers World (R)
34 Catherine Street
Salisbury
1722/411-200

Eton Travel Agency (R)
104/105 High Street
Eton, Windsor
1753/671-747

American Express Travel Service
6 Stonegate
York
1904/670-030

Travel

http://www.americanexpress.com/travel

American Express Travel Service Offices are found in central locations throughout the United Kingdom.

Listings are valid as of May 1996. (R) = Representative Office. Not all services available at all locations. © 1996 American Express Travel Related Services Company, Inc.